Adams Family

John Adams
(1735–1826)

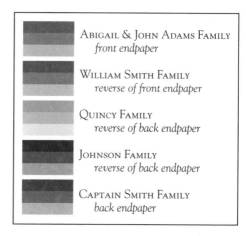

	Abigail & John Adams Family *front endpaper*
	William Smith Family *reverse of front endpaper*
	Quincy Family *reverse of back endpaper*
	Johnson Family *reverse of back endpaper*
	Captain Smith Family *back endpaper*

Caroline Amelia Smith
(1795–1852)
m. 1814

John Peter De Windt
(1787–1870)

therine Adams 2nd
811–1812)

ter Adams 1812)	Isaac Hull Adams (1813–1900) m. 1856?	John Quincy Adams (1815–1854)	Joseph Harrod Adams (1817–1843)

Mary Francis Griffis
(c. 1815–1857)

D1384913

WILLIAM SMITH FAMILY

Reverend William Smith (1707–1783)	m. 1740	**Elizabeth Quincy** (1722–1775)	

Mary Smith (1741–1811)	m. 1762	**Richard Cranch** (1726–1811)	

- **Elizabeth Cranch** (1763–1811) — m. 1789 — **Reverend Jacob Norton** (1764–1858)
- **Lucy Cranch** (1767–1846) — m. 1795 — **John Greenleaf** (1763–1848)
- **William Cranch** (1769–1855) — m. 1795 — **Anna "Nancy" Greenleaf** (1772–1843)

Abigail Smith (See Adams Family)

William Smith Jr. (1746–1787)	m. 1771	**Catharine "Kitty" Louisa Salmon** (1749–1824)	

- **Elizabeth "Betsy" Smith** (1771–1854) — m. 1798 — **James Hiller Foster** (1773–1862)
- **Louisa Catherine Smith** (1773–1857)
- **William "Billy" Smith** (1774–1801) — m. 1799 — **Sarah Jane Mallet** (1782–1801)
- **Mary Smith** (1776–1797)
- **Charles Salmon Smith** (1779–1797)
- **Isaac Smith** (1781–post 1796)

Elizabeth "Betsy" Smith (1750–1815)	m. 1. 1777	**Reverend John Shaw** (1748–1794)	
	m. 2. 1795	**Reverend Stephen Peabody** (1741–1819)	

- **William "Billy" Smith Shaw** (1778–1826)
- **Elizabeth "Betsy" Quincy Shaw** (1780–1798)
- **Abigail Adams Shaw** (1790–1859) — m. 1816 — **Joseph Barlow Felt** (1789–1869)

Library of America, a nonprofit organization,
champions our nation's cultural heritage
by publishing America's greatest writing in
authoritative new editions and providing resources
for readers to explore this rich, living legacy.

ABIGAIL ADAMS

ABIGAIL ADAMS

LETTERS

Edith Gelles, *editor*

THE LIBRARY OF AMERICA

Visit our website at www.loa.org.

This paper meets the requirements of
ANSI/NISO Z39.48–1992 (Permanence of Paper).

Distributed to the trade in the United States
by Penguin Random House Inc.
and in Canada by Penguin Random House Canada Ltd.

Library of Congress Control Number: 2015935694
ISBN 978–1–59853–465–8

———

First Printing
The Library of America—275

Manufactured in the United States of America

Abigail Adams: Letters
is published in memory of

STUART UPCHURCH BUICE
(1942–2015)

with support from

The Acriel Foundation

Abigail Adams: Letters
is kept in print in honor of

PHYLLIS LEE LEVIN

by a gift from

Emme & Jonathan Deland,
Kate Levin & Mark di Suvero,
Anna & Peter Levin,
and Candace Wainwright

to the Guardians of American Letters Fund,
established by The Library of America
to ensure that every volume in the series
will be permanently available.

Contents

REVOLUTION, 1773–1777

COURTSHIP AND MARRIAGE
1763–1773

To Isaac Smith Jr.

Dear Cousin   Weymouth March 16 1763

Tis no small pleasure to me, to hear of the great proficioncy you have made in the French tongue, A Tongue Sweet, and harmonious, a Tongue, useful to Merchants, to Statesmen; to Divines, and especially to Lawyers and Travellers; who by the help of it, may traverse the whole Globe; for in this respect, the French language is pretty much now, what I have heard the Latin formerly was, a universal tongue.

By the favor of my Father I have had the pleasure of seeing your Copy of Mrs. Wheelwrights Letter, to her Nephew, and having some small acquaintance with the French tongue, have attempted a translation; of it, which I here send, for your perusal and correction.

I am sensible that I am but ill qualified for such an undertaking, it being a maxim with me that no one can translate an author well, who cannot write like the original, and I find by Experience that tis more difficult to translate well, than to write well.

You will see that I have endeavourd to translate the letter as literally as I could, without treading on the heels of my Lady abbess, Esteeming literal translations to be the best as well as truest. Should be glad if you would favor me with your translation, for you, being taught the French language by one of the greatest masters, I make no doubt but that your performance shines in all the beauty and perfection of Language.

That you may daily grow in virtue and useful Learning, and be a bright Orniment in Church or State is the sincere wish of Dear Cousin Your affectionat Friend,   Nabby Smith

N B. How the Lady abbess came to subscribe herself Serviteur, which you know is of the masculine Gender I cannot devise unless like all other Ladies in a convent, she chose to make use of the Masculine Gender, rather than the Feminine.

Excuse the writing for tis late at night.

"A TYE MORE BINDING"

To John Adams

My Friend   Weymouth August th 11 1763

If I was sure your absence to day was occasioned, by what it generally is, either to wait upon Company, or promote some good work, I freely confess my Mind would be much more at ease than at present it is. Yet this uneasiness does not arise from any apprehension of Slight or neglect, but a fear least you are indisposed, for that you said should be your only hindrance.

Humanity obliges us to be affected with the distresses and Miserys of our fellow creatures. Friendship is a band yet stronger, which causes us to feel with greater tenderness the afflictions of our Friends.

And there is a tye more binding than Humanity, and stronger than Friendship, which makes us anxious for the happiness and welfare of those to whom it binds us. It makes their Misfortunes, Sorrows and afflictions, our own. Unite these, and there is a threefold cord—by this cord I am not ashamed to own myself bound, nor do I believe that you are wholly free from it. Judge you then for your Diana has she not this day had sufficient cause for pain and anxiety of mind?

She bids me tell you that Seneca, for the sake of his Paulina was careful and tender of his health. The health and happiness of Seneca she says was not dearer to his Paulina, than that of Lysander to his Diana.

The Fabrick often wants repairing and if we neglect it the Deity will not long inhabit it, yet after all our care and solisitude to preserve it, it is a tottering Building, and often reminds us that it will finally fall.

Adieu may this find you in better health than I fear it will, and happy as your Diana wishes you.

Accept this hasty Scrawl warm from the Heart of Your Sincere   Diana

"CAST IN THE SAME MOULD"

To John Adams

Weymouth Sepbr. th 12 1763

You was pleas'd to say that the receipt of a letter from your Diana always gave you pleasure. Whether this was designed for a complement, (a commodity I acknowledg that you very seldom deal in) or as a real truth, you best know. Yet if I was to judge of a certain persons Heart, by what upon the like occasion passess through a cabinet of my own, I should be apt to suspect it as a truth. And why may I not? when I have often been tempted to believe; that they were both cast in the same mould, only with this difference, that yours was made, with a harder mettle, and therefore is less liable to an impression. Whether they have both an eaquil quantity of Steel, I have not yet been able to discover, but do not imagine they are either of them deficient. Supposing only this difference, I do not see, why the same cause may not produce the same Effect in both, tho perhaps not eaquil in degree.

But after all, notwithstanding we are told that the giver is more blessed than the receiver I must confess that I am not of so generous a disposition, in this case, as to give without wishing for a return.

Have you heard the News? that two Apparitions were seen one evening this week hovering about this house, which very much resembled you and a Cousin of yours. How it should ever enter into the head of an Apparition to assume a form like yours, I cannot devise. When I was told of it I could scarcly believe it, yet I could not declare the contrary, for I did not see it, and therefore had not that demonstration which generally convinces me, that you are not a Ghost.

The original design of this letter was to tell you, that I would next week be your fellow traveler provided I shall not be any encumberance to you, for I have too much pride to be a clog to any body. You are to determine that point. For your—

A. Smith

P S Pappa says he should be very much obliged to Your

Cousin if he would preach for him tomorrow and if not to morrow next Sunday. Please to present my complements to him and tell him by complying with this request he will oblige many others besides my pappa, and especially his Humble Servant,   A. Smith

SMALLPOX INOCULATION

To Cotton Tufts

Dear Unkle   Weymouth April th 2. 1764

I should not have been unmindful of you, even tho you had not call'd upon me to exert myself. I should be the most ungrateful of Mortals, if I did not always with Gratitude remember so kind a Benefactor, as you have been to me both in Sickness, and in Health.

How often has your kind hand supported me when I was more helpless than an Infant. How often have you revived me by your Vital Heat? And for how many Nights lodging am I indebted to you? Fain would I repay you, tho not in kind now. I fancy you are by this time too infectious for a Being of purity, to wish for any Communication with you. How do you feel? I think you are in good Spirits, at which I rejoice.

Our friend thinks you dieted too low. Says you look'd as if a puff of wind would have blown you off your Horse, and that He could see through you, (which by the way is more than every one can) wants to hear how you fare, before he begins Lent. We have almost brought him over to the faith, tho' he still continues some what doubtful. Says if he was to follow his own judgment, he should not go into the method prescribed, but since his Friends advise other ways he will *Submit*. This looks like a pretty hopeful Speach, I wonder if one may not improve upon such a Heart? I expect nothing more from you, than saying, it is a good example Child, and if you value your own happiness you will in many cases follow it. Aye it may be so, but we wont dispute that point now.

Inclosed you will find two very curious Letters. I have had some doubt whether it would be best to send one of them, for indeed tis a very Saucy one, but tis in Character I believe—and Nature I suppose you will say.

I shall send them by Mr. Eyers that you may have opportunity to see Dr. Perkins and more leisure for writing, than you would have if I waited till thursday when Tom will be down.

I see the Good Man has given you some account of himself. He will have it that he is temperate in all things, but I know Doctor you understand his constitution better than to believe him, tho you need not mention this, for perhaps Mercury will be no benifit to him upon that account.

As for News, we have neither Foreign nor Domestick, Civil nor Ecclesiastical nor so much as one word of Scandle Stiring, that I hear of.

I have been a very good Girl since your absence, and visited your Lady almost every day. She would have impowerd me to have written to you in her Name, but I told her I had no inclination at present to have any communication with any Man in the character of a wife, besides I who never own'd a Husband did not know how to address one. I think she Supports your absence like a Heroine. She complaind a Day or two ago of a Tooth ake, which She Suspected to be the forerunner of some great event, Suppose you best understand what. Your Son Seems to be finely recoverd, has got his Neck at liberty again, and is as great a Rogue as ever. Our pale Face desires to be rememberd to you, keeps at the old notch, and according to Pope—("Not to go back, is something to advance") may be say'd to be a little better.—Thus haveing run my rig, think it time to draw towards a close. By Tom hope to receive a token of remembrance, and to hear that you are as Speckled as you desire to be. I am not affraid of your Virmin if you roast them well, otherways fear they will be too hard for my Digestion. I leave that to your care, and Conclude assureing you that no person wishes you more Health and Happiness than Your affectionate Niece,   Abll. Smith

Please to remember me to my Brother and tell him he should write to me, for he has little else to do.

To John Adams

Sir   Weymouth April 7. 1764

How do you now? For my part, I feel much easier than I did an hour ago, My Unkle haveing given me a more particuliar, and favorable account of the Small pox, or rather the operation of the preparation, than I have had before. He speaks greatly in favor of Dr. Perkins who has not, as he has heard lost one patient. He has had since he has been in Town frequent opportunities of visiting in the families where the Doctor practises, and he is full in the persuasion that he understands the Distemper, full as well if not better than any physician in Town, and knows better what to do in case of any dificulty. He allows his patients greater liberty with regard to their Diet, than several other physicians. Some of them (Dr. Lord for one) forbid their patients a mouthful of Bread. My unkle says they are all agreed that tis best to abstain from Butter, and Salt—And most of them from meat.

I hope you will have reason to be well satisfied with the Dr., and advise you to follow his prescriptions as nigh as you find your Health will permit. I send by my unkle some balm. Let me know certainly what Day you design to go to Town, Pappa Says Tom shall go that Day and bring your Horse back.

Keep your Spirits up, and I make no doubt you will do well eno'. Shall I come and see you before you go. No I wont, for I want not again, to experience what I this morning felt, when you left Your   A. Smith

To John Adams

My Friend   Weymouth April th 16 1764

I think I write to you every Day. Shall not I make my Letters very cheep; don't you light your pipe with them? I care not if you do, tis a pleasure to me to write, yet I wonder I write to you with so little restraint, for as a critick I fear you more than any other person on Earth, and tis the only character, in which I ever did, or ever will fear you. What say you? Do you approve of that Speach? Dont you think me a Courageous Being? Courage is a laudable, a Glorious Virtue in your Sex, why not in mine? (For my part, I think you ought to applaud me for mine.)—Exit Rattle.

Solus your Diana.

And now pray tell me how you do, do you feel any venom working in your veins, did you ever before experience such a feeling?—This Letter will be made up with questions I fancy—not set in order before you neither.—How do you employ yourself? Do you go abroad yet? Is it not cruel to bestow those favours upon others which I should rejoice to receive, yet must be deprived of?

I have lately been thinking whether my Mamma—when I write again I will tell you Something. Did not you receive a Letter to Day by Hones?

This is a right Girls Letter, but I will turn to the other side and be sober, if I can—but what is bred in the bone will never be out of the flesh, (as Lord M would have said).

As I have a good opportunity to send some Milk, I have not waited for your *orders*; least if I should miss this, I should not catch such an other. If you want more balm, I can supply you.

Adieu, evermore remember me with the tenderest affection, which is also borne unto you by Your——   A Smith

"THOU HAST THE CURIOSITY OF A GIRL"

To John Adams

Thursday Eve.—Weymouth April th 19 1764

Why my good Man, thou hast the curiosity of a Girl. Who could have believed that only a slight hint would have set thy imagination a gig in such a manner. And a fine encouragement I have to unravel the Mistery as thou callest it. Nothing less truly than to be told Something to my disadvantage. What an excellent reward that will be? In what Court of justice did'st thou learn that equity? I thank thee Friend such knowledg as that is easy eno' to be obtained without paying for it. As to the insinuation, it doth not give me any uneasiness, for if it is any thing very bad, I know thou dost not believe it. I am not conscious of any harm that I have done, or wished to any Mortal. I bear no Malice to any Being. To my Enimies, (if any I have) I am willing to afford assistance; therefore towards Man, I maintain a Conscience void of offence.

Yet by this I mean not that I am faultless, but tell me what is the Reason that persons had rather acknowledg themselves guilty, than be accused by others. Is it because they are more tender of themselves, or because they meet with more favor from others, when they ingenuously confess. Let that be as it will there is something which makes it more agreeable to condemn ourselves than to be condemned by others.

But altho it is vastly disagreeable to be accused of faults, yet no person ought to be offended when such accusations are deliverd in the Spirit of Friendship.—I now call upon you to fullfill your promise, and tell me all my faults, both of omission and commission, and all the Evil you either know, or think of me, be to me a second conscience, nor put me off to a more convenient Season. There can be no time more proper than the present, it will be harder to erase them when habit has strengthned and confirmd them.

Do not think I triffle. These are really meant as words of Truth and Soberness—for the present good Night.

Fryday Morning April th 20

What does it signify, why may not I visit you a Days as well as Nights? I no sooner close my Eyes than some invisible Being, swift as the Alborack of Mahomet, bears me to you. I see you, but cannot make my self visible to you. That tortures me, but it is still worse when I do not come for I am then haunted by half a dozen ugly Sprights. One will catch me and leep into the Sea, an other will carry me up a precipice (like that which Edgar describes to Lear,) then toss me down, and were I not then light as the Gosemore I should shiver into atoms—an other will be pouring down my throat stuff worse than the witches Broth in Macbeth.—Where I shall be carried next I know not, but I had rather have the small pox by inoculation half a dozen times, than be sprighted about as I am. What say you can you give me any encouragement to come? By the time you receive this hope from experience you will be able to say that the distemper is but a triffle. Think you I would not endure a triffle for the pleasure of seeing Lysander, yes were it ten times that triffle I would.—But my own inclinations must not be followed—to Duty I sacrifice them. Yet O my Mamma forgive me if I say, you have forgot, or never knew—but hush.—And do you Lysander excuse me that something I promis'd you, since it was a Speach more undutifull than that which I Just now stop'd my self in—for the present good by.

Fryday Evening

I hope you smoke your Letters well, before you deliver them. Mamma is so fearful least I should catch the distemper, that she hardly ever thinks the Letters are sufficently purified. Did you never rob a Birds nest? Do you remember how the poor Bird would fly round and round, fearful to come nigh, yet not know how to leave the place—just so they say I hover round Tom whilst he is smokeing my Letters.

But heigh day Mr. whats your Name?—who taught you to threaten so vehemently "a Character besides that of critick, in which if I never did, I always hereafter shall fear you."

Thou canst not prove a villan, imposible. I therefore still insist upon it, that I neither do, nor can fear thee. For my part I know not that there is any pleasure in being feard, but if there is, I hope you will be so generous as to fear your Diana that she may at least be made sensible of the pleasure.

Mr. Ayers will bring you this Letter, and the *Bag*. Do not repine—it is fill'd with Balm.

Here is Love, respects, regards, good wishes—a whole waggon load of them sent you from all the good folks in the Neighbourhood.

To morrow makes the 14th Day. How many more are to come? I dare not trust my self with the thought. Adieu. Let me hear from you by Mr. Ayers, and excuse this very bad writing, if you had mended my pen it would have been better, once more adieu. Gold and Silver have I none, but such as I have, give I unto thee—which is the affectionate Regard of Your

A Smith

To John Adams

Weymouth May. th 9 1764

Welcome, Welcome thrice welcome is Lysander to Braintree, but ten times more so would he be at Weymouth, whither you are affraid to come.—Once it was not so. May not I come and see you, at least look thro a window at you? Should you not be glad to see your Diana? I flatter myself you would.

Your Brother brought your Letter, tho he did not let me see him, deliverd it the Doctor from whom received it safe. I thank you for your Catalogue, but must confess I was so hardned as to read over most of my Faults with as much pleasure, as an other person would have read their perfections. And Lysander must excuse me if I still persist in some of them, at least till I am convinced that an alteration would contribute to his happiness. Especially may I avoid that Freedom of Behaviour which according to the plan given, consists in Voilations of Decency, and which would render me unfit to Herd even with the Brutes. And permit me to tell you Sir, nor disdain to be a learner, that there is such a thing as Modesty without either Hypocricy or Formality.

As to a neglect of Singing, that I acknowledg to be a Fault which if posible shall not be complaind of a second time, nor should you have had occasion for it now, if I had not a voice harsh as the screech of a peacock.

The Capotal fault shall be rectified, tho not with any hopes of being lookd upon as a Beauty, to appear agreeable in the Eyes of Lysander, has been for Years past, and still is the height of my ambition.

The 5th fault, will endeavour to amend of it, but you know I think that a gentleman has no business to concern himself about the Leggs of a Lady, for my part I do not apprehend any bad effects from the practise, yet since you desire it, and that you may not for the future trouble Yourself so much about it, will reform.

The sixth and last can be cured only by a Dancing School.

But I must not write more. I borrow a hint from you, therefore will not add to my faults that of a tedious Letter—a fault I never yet had reason to complain of in you, for however long, they never were otherways than agreeable to your own

A Smith

"YOU MAY TAKE ME"

To John Adams

Sir   Boston Octobr. 4. 1764

I am much obliged to you for the care you have taken about help. I am very willing to submit to some inconveniences in order to lessen your expences, which I am sensible have run very high for these 12 months past and tho you know I have no particuliar fancy for Judah yet considering all things, and that your Mamma and you seem to think it would be best to take her, I shall not at present look out any further.

The cart you mentiond came yesterday, by which I sent as many things as the horse would draw the rest of my things will be ready the Monday after you return from Taunton. And—then Sir if you please you may take me. I hope by that time, that you will have recoverd your Health, together with your formour tranquility of mind. Think you that the phylosopher who laught at the follies of mankind did not pass thro' life with more ease and pleasure, than he who weept at them, and perhaps did as much towards a reformation. Tis true that I have had a good deal of fatigue in my own affair since I have been in town, but when I compare that with many other things that might have fallen to my Lot I am left without any Shadow of complaint. A few things, indeed I have meet with that have really discomposed me, one was haveing a corosive applied when a Lenitive would have answerd the same good purpose. But I hope I have drawn a lesson from that which will be useful to me in futurity, viz. never to say a severe thing because to a feeling heart they wound to deeply to be easily cured.—Pardon me this is not said for to recriminate, and I have only mentiond it, that when ever there is occasion a different method may be taken.

I do not think of any thing further to add, nor any thing new to tell you, for tis an old Story tho I hope as pleasing as it is true, to tell you that I am unfeignedly Your   Diana

"YOUR DIANA BECOME A MAMMA"

To Hannah Storer Green

My Good old Friend

How many months have passed away since I have either written or received a line from my Dear Caliope? What various Scenes have I passed thro? Your Diana become a Mamma—can you credit it? Indeed it is a sober truth. Bless'd with a charming Girl whose pretty Smiles already delight my Heart, who is the Dear Image of her still Dearer Pappa. You my Friend are well acquainted with all the tender feelings of a parent, therefore I need not apologize for the present overflow. I have many things to say to you. Gratitude demands an acknowledgment for your kind present to my Daughter. She I hope will live to make you some return for your unmerited goodness to her.

post July 14, 1765

DOMESTICITY

To Mary Smith Cranch

My Dear Sister   Braintree Jan'ry. 31 1767

I have just returnd from Weymouth, where I have been for a week past. It seems lonesome here, for My Good Man is at Boston; after haveing been in a large family, for a week, to come and set down alone is very solitary; tho we have seven in our family, yet four of them being domestick when my partner is absent and my Babe a sleep, I am still left alone. It gives one a pleasing Sensation my Dear Sister, after haveing been absent a little while to see one's self gladly received upon a return, even by one's Servants. I do not know that I was ever more sensibly affected with it than I was to Day; I could behold joy sparkle in the Eyes of every one of them as I enterd the House, whilst they unaffectedly express'd it some to me and some to my Babe.—One runs to the Door, O Mam, I am glad to see you come home again, how do you do? Whilst an other catches the child, and says Dear creature I was affraid she would forget me, and a third hovers round and crys Nab, do you know Polly, and will you come to her?—These little instances shew their regard, and they endear them to us.

Thus far I wrote last fryday. But my good Man arriving with the News papers, put an end to writing any further at that time. However I have now reassumed my pen, tho I am something tierd, haveing dined Nine Gentlemen to Day. When I set down with such a friendly circle, I always look round and wish that the company was not incompleat by the absence of two Dear Friend's. Here now sets our Sister Elizabeth, and we both of us haveing been talking and wishing for you. She will leave me to morrow, tho She came but to Day, and has not been here since She came from Salem, before now. Father, the Doctor and Mr. Wibird (who made three of the company to Day) tell me that they all of them design for Salem to morrow. I know how rejoiced you will be to see them. I feel glad for you, but methinks so many good Friends ought not to go together—if they went but one at a time I should chance to hear three times from you which would as Sarah Cotton used to say make me three times glad.—I sent your Camblet to Unkle Smiths last week, and hope it has reach'd you before now. The coulour I know you will not like. I do not think Dawson used me well, tis a discourageing thing, when one has tried to have a thing look well and done their part towards it, then to have it ruined in the dying or weaveing, is very provoking, but if Mr. Cranch dislikes it, I would not have you think your-selves under any oblagation to take it, for I shall not be any ways troubled if you send it back again.—I have a couple of Books, which when I have read thro I design to send to you, for your perusal—they are called Sermons to young women. I cannot say how much I admire them, and should I attempt to say how justly worthy they are of admiration I fear I should not do justice to this most Excellent performance.— My Letter will be a mess medly in Spite of any efforts to the contarary—for from Sermons I must desend to Cards and tell you I should be glad, Mr. Cranch would send me a pair. Nabby sends her Love to her cousin Betsy and would be very glad of her company, to tend Miss Doll, who is a very great favorite of theirs.—I send you a little yarn for a pair of Stockings and a little flax for some thread—because I know you seek wool and flax, and work willingly with your hands. Accept of them with my sincere regards to you and yours From your affectionate Sister,   Abigail Adams

P.S. You must burn this for it is most dismal writing.

"COME PAPPA COME HOME"

To John Adams

Sunday Eveng. Weymouth

My Dearest Friend   Sepbr. 14 1767
The Doctor talks of Setting out tomorrow for New Braintree. I did not know but that he might chance to see you, in his way there. I know from the tender affection you bear me, and our little one's that you will rejoice to hear that we are well, our Son is much better than when you left home, and our Daughter rock's him to Sleep, with the Song of "Come pappa come home to Brother Johnny." Sunday seems a more Lonesome Day to me than any other when you are absent, For tho I may be compared to those climates which are deprived of the Sun half the Year, yet upon a Sunday you commonly afforded us your benign influence. I am now at Weymouth. My Father brought me here last night. To morrow I return home, where I hope soon to receive the Dearest of Friends and the tenderest of Husbands, with that unabated affection which has for Years

past, and will whilst the vital Spark lasts, burn in the Bosom of
your affectionate   A Adams

PS Poor Mr. Gridly died a thursday very suddenly, we hear
and was yesterday buried.

September 13, 1767

"WOMEN . . . INHERIT AN EAQUEL SHARE OF CURIOSITY"

To Isaac Smith Jr.

Dear Sir   Braintree April the 20 1771
    I write you, not from the Noisy Buisy Town, but from my
humble Cottage in Braintree, where I arrived last Saturday and
here again am to take up my abode.

> "Where Contemplation plumes her rufled Wings
> And the free Soul look's down to pitty Kings."

Suffer me to snatch you a few moments from all the Hurry and
tumult of London and in immagination place you by me that I
may ask you ten thousand Questions, and bear with me Sir, tis
the only recompence you can make for the loss of your
Company.
    From my Infancy I have always felt a great inclination to
visit the Mother Country as tis call'd and had nature formed
me of the other Sex, I should certainly have been a rover.
And altho this desire has greatly diminished owing partly I
believe to maturer years, but more to the unnatural treatment
which this our poor America has received from her, I yet retain a curiosity to know what ever is valuable in her. I thank
you Sir for the particular account you have already favourd
me with, but you always took pleasure in being communica-
tively good.
    Women you know Sir are considerd as Domestick Beings,
and altho they inherit an Eaquel Share of curiosity with the
other Sex, yet but few are hardy eno' to venture abroad, and
explore the amaizing variety of distant Lands. The Natural

tenderness and Delicacy of our Constitutions, added to the many Dangers we are subject too from your Sex, renders it almost imposible for a Single Lady to travel without injury to her character. And those who have a protecter in an Husband, have generally speaking obstacles sufficent to prevent their Roving, and instead of visiting other Countries; are obliged to content themselves with seeing but a very small part of their own. To your Sex we are most of us indebted for all the knowledg we acquire of Distant lands. As to a Knowledg of Humane Nature, I believe it may as easily be obtained in this Country, as in England, France or Spain. Education alone I conceive Constitutes the difference in Manners. Tis natural I believe for every person to have a partiality for their own Country. Dont you think this little Spot of ours better calculated for happiness than any other you have yet seen or read of. Would you exchange it for England, France, Spain or Ittally? Are not the people here more upon an Eaquality in point of knowledg and of circumstances—there being none so immensly rich as to Lord it over us, neither any so abjectly poor as to suffer for the necessaries of life provided they will use the means. It has heretofore been our boasted priviledg that we could sit under our own vine and Apple trees in peace enjoying the fruits of *our own labour*—but alass! the much dreaded change Heaven avert. Shall we ever wish to change Countries; to change conditions with the Affricans and the Laplanders for sure it were better never to have known the blessings of Liberty than to have enjoyed it, and then to have it ravished from us.

But where do I ramble? I only ask your ear a few moments longer. The Americans have been called a very religious people, would to Heaven they were so in earnest, but whatever they may have been I am affraid tis now only a negitive virtue, and that they are only a less vicious people. However I can quote Mr. Whitefield as an authority that what has been said of us is not without foundation. The last Sermon I heard him preach, he told us that he had been a very great traveller, yet he had never seen so much of the real appearence of Religion in any Country, as in America, and from your discription I immagine you join with him in Sentiment. I think Dr. Sherbear in his remarks upon the english Nation has some such observation as this. In London Religion seems to be periodical, like an ague which only returns once in Seven Days, and then attacks the inhabitants with the cold fit only, the burning never succeeds in this Country. Since which it seems they have found means to rid themselves intirely of the ague.—As to news I have none to tell you, nor any thing remarkable to entertain you with. But you Sir have every day new Scenes opening to you, and you will greatly oblige me by a recital of whatever you find worthy notice. I have a great desire to be made acquainted with Mrs. Maccaulays own history. One of my own Sex so eminent in a tract so uncommon naturally raises my curiosity and all I could ever learn relative to her, is this that she is a widdow Lady and Sister to Mr. Sawbridge. I have a curiosity to know her Education, and what first prompted her to engage in a Study never before Exibited to the publick by one of her own Sex and Country, tho now to the honour of both so admirably performed by her. As you are now upon the Spot, and have been entroduced to her acquaintance, you will I hope be able to satisfie me with some account, in doing which you will confer an oblagation upon your assured Friend,

Abigail Adams

P.S. I thank you Sir for the West Indian, tis really a prety performance and afforded me an hours or two of very agreable entertainment.

"REQUESTING A CORRESPONDENCE"

To Mercy Otis Warren

Madam   Boston July 16 1773

The kind reception I met with at your House, and the Hospitality with which you entertained me, demands my gratefull acknowledgment. By requesting a correspondence you have kindly given me an opportunity to thank you for the happy Hours I enjoyed whilst at your House. Thus imbolden'd I venture to stretch my pinions, and tho like the timorous Bird I fail in the attempt and tumble to the ground yet sure the Effort is laudable, nor will I suffer my pride, (which is greatly increased since my more intimate acquaintance with you) to debar me the pleasure, and improvement I promise myself from this correspondence tho I suffer by the comparison.

I Had a very Hot and unplesent ride the afternoon I left your House. I arrived at my own habitation on Monday, and found my family well. Since my return we have had several fine showers which have, I hope extended, as far as Eel river, and watered with their blessings every sod and plant belonging to my much valued Friends. Air, Sun, and Water, the common blessings of Heaven; we receive as our just due, and too seldom acknowledg our obligations to the Father of the rain; and the Gracious dispencer of every good and perfect gift, yet if but for a very little while these blessings are withheld, or spairingly dealt out to us, we then soon discover how weak, how little and how blind, we are.

When I was at Plymouth Madam you may remember I mentiond Mrs. Seymore upon Education, and upon your expressing a desire to see it, I promised to send it you. I now take the earlyest opportunity to comply with your request. Not from an opinion that you stand in need of such an assistant, but that you may give me your Sentiments upon this Book, and tell me whether it corresponds with the plan you have prescribed to yourself and in which you have so happily succeeded. I am sensible I have an important trust committed to me; and tho I feel my-self very uneaquel to it, tis still incumbent upon me to discharge it in the best manner I am capable of. I was really so well pleased with your little offspring, that I must beg the favour of you to communicate to me the happy Art of "rearing the tender thought, teaching the young Idea how to shoot, and pouring fresh instruction o'er the Mind." May the Natural Benevolence of your Heart, prompt you to assist a young and almost inexperienced Mother in this Arduous Buisness, that the tender twigs alloted to my care, may be so cultivated as to do honour to their parents and prove blessings to the riseing generation. When I saw the happy fruits of your attention in your well ordered family, I felt a Sort of Emulation glowing in my Bosom, to imitate the

"Parent who vast pleasure find's
In forming of her childrens minds
In midst of whom with vast delight
She passes many a winters Night
Mingles in every play to find
What Bias Nature gave the mind
Resolving thence to take her aim
To guide them to the realms of fame
And wisely make those realms the way
To those of everlasting day.

Each Boisterous passion to controul
And early Humanize the Soul
In simple tales beside the fire,
The noblest Notions to inspire.
Her offspring conscious of her care
Transported hang around her chair."

I must beg your pardon for thus detaining you. I have so long neglected my pen that I am conscious I shall make but a poor figure. To your Friendship and candour I commit this, and would only add my regards to Coll. Warren from his and your obliged Friend & Humble Servant,   Abigail Adams

REVOLUTION
1773–1777

To Mercy Otis Warren

My Dear Mrs. Warren   Boston December 5. 1773
     Do not my Worthy Friend tax me with either Breach of
promise; or neglect towards you, the only reason why I did not
write to you immediately upon your leaving Town, was my
being seized with a Fever which has confined me almost ever
since, I have not for these many years known so severe a fit of
Sickness.

     I am now thro' the favour of Heaven so far restored as to be
able to leave my chamber some part of the Day. I will not
make any other apology for my past neglect being fully sensible
that I alone have been the Sufferer. My pen which I once
Loved and delighted in; has for a long time been out of credit
with me. Could I borrow the powers and faculties of my much
valued Friend, I should then hope to use it with advantage to
my-self and delight to others.

     Incorrect and unpolished as it is I will not suffer a mistaken
pride so far to lead me astray as to omit the present opportunity of improvement, and should I prove a tractable Scholer,
you will not find me tardy.

     You Madam are so sincere a Lover of your Country, and so
Hearty a mourner in all her misfortunes that it will greatly ag-
gravate your anxiety to hear how much she is now oppressed
and insulted. To you, who have so throughly look'd thro the
Deeds of Men, and Develloped the Dark designs of a Rapatio's
Soul, No action however base or sordid, no measure however
Cruel and Villanous, will be matter of any Surprize.

     The Tea that bainfull weed is arrived. Great and I hope Ef-
fectual opposition has been made to the landing of it. To the
publick papers I must refer you for perticuliars. You will there
find that the proceedings of our Citizens have been United,
Spirited and firm. The flame is kindled and like Lightning it
catches from Soul to Soul. Great will be the devastation if not
timely quenched or allayed by some more Lenient Measures.

     Altho the mind is shocked at the Thought of sheding Hu-
mane Blood, more Especially the Blood of our Countrymen,

25

and a civil War is of all Wars, the most dreadfull Such is the present Spirit that prevails, that if once they are made desperate Many, very Many of our Heroes will spend their lives in the cause, With the Speach of Cato in their Mouths, "What a pitty it is, that we can dye but once to save our Country."

"Tender plants must bend but when a Goverment is grown to Strength like some old oak rough with its armed bark, it yealds not to the tug, but only Nods and turns to sullen State."

Such is the present Situation of affairs that I tremble when I think what may be the direfull concequences—and in this Town must the Scene of action lay. My Heart beats at every Whistle I hear, and I dare not openly express half my fears.— Eternal Reproach and Ignominy be the portion of all those who have been instrumental in bringing these fears upon me. There was a Report prevaild that to morrow there will be an attempt to Land this weed of Slavery. I will then write further till then my worthy Friend adieu.

December 11

Since I wrote the above a whole week has Elapsed and nothing new occurred concerning the tea. Having met with no opportunity of sending this I shall trespass further upon your patience. I send with this the 1 volume of Moliere, and should be glad of your oppinion of them. I cannot be brought to like them, there seems to me to be a general Want of Spirit, at the close of every one I have felt dissapointed. There are no characters but what appear unfinished and he seems to have ridiculed Vice without engageing us to Virtue, and tho he sometimes makes us Laugh, yet tis a Smile of indignation. There is one negative Virtue of which he is possess'd I mean that of Decency. His Cit. turnd Gentleman among many others has met with approbation—tho I can readily acknowledg that the cit. by acting so contrary to his real character has displayed a stupid vanity justly deserving ridicule, yet the Fine Gentleman who defrauds and tricks him, is as much the baser character as his advantages are superior to the others. Moliere is said to have been an Honest Man, but sure he has not coppied from his own Heart—tho he has drawn many pictures of real Life, yet all pictures of life are not fit to be exibited upon the Stage. I fear I shall incur the charge of vanity by thus criticising upon an Author who has met with so much applause. You Madam I hope will forgive me. I should not have done it, if we had not conversd about it before. Your judgment will have great weight with Your Sincere Friend,

Abigail Adams

"HOW MANY SNOW BANKS DEVIDE THEE AND ME"

To John Adams

Weymouth December 30 1773

Alass! How many snow banks devide thee and me and my warmest wishes to see thee will not melt one of them. I have not heard one Word from thee, or our Little ones since I left home. I did not take any cold comeing down, and find my self in better Health than I was. I wish to hear the same account from you. The Time I proposed to tarry has Elapsed. I shall soon be home sick. The Roads at present are impassible with any carriage. I shall not know how to content myself longer than the begining of Next week. I never left so large a flock of little ones before. You must write me how they all do. Tis now so near the Court that I have no expectation of seeing you here. My daily thoughts and Nightly Slumbers visit thee, and thine. I feel gratified with the immagination at the close of the Day in seeing the little flock round you inquiring when Mamma will come home—as they often do for thee in thy absence.

If you have any news in Town which the papers do not communicate, pray be so good as to Write it. We have not heard one Word respecting the Tea at the Cape or else where.

I have deliverd John the Bearer of this the key of your linnen. I hope you have been able to come at some by taking the Draw above it out. I should be obliged if you would send me that Book of Mr. Pembertons upon the Classicks and the progress of Dulness which is at Mr. Cranchs.

You will not fail in remembering me to our little ones and telling Johnny that his Grand mama has sent him a pair of mittins, and Charlly that I shall bring his when I come home.

Our little Tommy you must kiss for Mamma, and bid Nabby write to me. Dont dissapoint me and let John return without a few lines to comfort the heart of Your affectionate

Abigail Adams

"SO MANY TERRORS"

To Mercy Otis Warren

Your agreable favour of January 19 demands from me more than I am able to pay. My coin will have more alloy tho it bears the same Stamp of Friendship with your own.

I was not sensible till I received yours that my last Letter to you abounded with so many terrors. I am not Naturally of a gloomy temper nor disposed to view objects upon the dark Side only. I rejoice that all my fears on that account were so soon drowned in an ocean of water instead of being verified by the sheding of Blood. Nor would I again alarm you with apprehensions of tumult and disorder the ensuing week by a dethroned chief Justice attempting to take his Seat upon the bench, who if he should meet with opposition would say with the fallen Angels

What tho the place be lost? All is not lost,
The unconquerable Will And Study of revenge,
Immortal hate And courage never to submit or yield,
And what is else not to be overcome;
That Glory never shall their Wrath or might
Extort from me.

What a pitty it is that so much of that same Spirit which prompted Satan to a revolt in heaven should possess the Sons of men and eradicate every principal of Humanity and Benevolence. How unbounded is ambition and what ravages has it made among the human Species. It was that which led Alaxander to weep for more Worlds to conquer, and Caesar to say he had rather be the first man in a village than the second in Rome and the arch Fiend Himself to declare he had rather Reign in Hell than serve in Heaven. But that Ambition which would establish itself by crimes and agrandize its possessor by the ruin of the State and by the oppression of its Subjects, will most certainly defeat itself. When Alexander Weep't he degraded himself. He would certainly have acquired much greater Glory by a wise and prudent goverment of those kingdoms he had conquerd, than by childishly blubering after new Worlds. This passion of Ambition when it centers in an honest mind possess'd of great Abilities may and often has done imminent Service to the World. There are but few minds if any wholy destitute of it and tho in itself it is Laudible yet there is nothing in Nature so amiable but the passions and intrest of Men will pervert to very base purposes. When I consider the Spirit which at present prevails throughout this continent I really detest that restless ambition of those artfull and designing men which has thus broken this people into factions—and I every day see more and more cause to deprecate the growing Evil. This party Spirit ruins good Neighbourhood, eradicates all the Seeds of good nature and humanity—it sours the temper and has a fatal tendancy upon the Morals and understanding and is contrary to that precept of christianity thou shallt Love thy Neighbour as thy self. I have some where met with an observation of this kind that Zeal for a publick cause will breed passions in the hearts of virtuous persons to which the Regard of their own private interest would never have betrayed them.— You Madam encourage me to hope that these discords and divisions will e'er long cease and ancient fraud shall fail; returning justice lift aloft her Scale. We shall not then see the Worst of Men possessd of every place of eminence in order to serve a party nor the best disregarded because they will not stoop to those methods which would gratify their faction, "and barter Liberty for gold." I wish to rejoice with you in the happy completion of your prophysy.

I congratulate you Madam upon the return of the very worthy bearer of this Letter. I have had a Sympathy for you in his absence being often Subject to the same Misfortune. We have had but little of his company he has been so much engaged in the affairs of the State.—By this opportunity I send you the 3 part of the progress of Dulness, the production of a young Gentleman who is now studiing Law with Mr. Adams and who is look'd upon as a real Genious.—I wish you would confide so much in your Friend as to favour her now and then with some of your poetical productions—they would be a great gratification to your assured Friend,   Abigail Adams

c. February 25, 1774

ROLLIN'S ANCIENT HISTORY

To John Adams

Braintree August 19 1774

The great distance between us, makes the time appear very long to me. It seems already a month since you left me. The great anxiety I feel for my Country, for you and for our family renders the day tedious, and the night unpleasent. The Rocks and quick Sands appear upon every Side. What course you can or will take is all wrapt in the Bosom of futurity. Uncertainty and expectation leave the mind great Scope. Did ever any Kingdom or State regain their Liberty, when once it was invaded without Blood shed? I cannot think of it without horror.

Yet we are told that all the Misfortunes of Sparta were occasiond by their too great Sollicitude for present tranquility, and by an excessive love of peace they neglected the means of making it sure and lasting. They ought to have reflected says Polibius that as there is nothing more desirable, or advantages than peace, when founded in justice and honour, so there is nothing more shameful and at the same time more pernicious when attained by bad measures, and purchased at the price of liberty.

I have received a most charming Letter from our Friend Mrs. Warren. She desires me to tell you that her best wishes attend you thro your journey both as a Friend and patriot—hopes you will have no uncommon difficulties to surmount or Hostile Movements to impede you—but if the Locrians should interrupt you, she hopes you will beware that no future Annals may say you chose an ambitious Philip for your Leader, who subverted the noble order of the American Amphyctions, and built up a Monarchy on the Ruins of the happy institution.

I have taken a very great fondness for reading Rollin's ancient History since you left me. I am determined to go thro with it if posible in these my days of solitude. I find great pleasure and entertainment from it, and I have perswaided Johnny to read me a page or two every day, and hope he will from his desire to oblige me entertain a fondness for it.—We have had a charming rain which lasted 12 hours and has greatly revived the dying fruits of the earth.

I want much to hear from you. I long impatiently to have you upon the Stage of action. The first of September or the month of September, perhaps may be of as much importance to Great Britan as the Ides of March were to Ceaser. I wish you every Publick as well, as private blessing, and that wisdom which is profitable both for instruction and edification to conduct you in this difficult day.—The little flock remember Pappa, and kindly wish to see him. So does your most affectionate   Abigail Adams

"A LITTLE CLASHING OF PARTIES"

To John Adams

Dearest Friend   Braintree Sepbr. 14 1774
Five Weeks have past and not one line have I received. I had rather give a dollar for a letter by the post, tho the consequence should be that I Eat but one meal a day for these 3 weeks to come. Every one I see is inquiring after you and when did I hear. All my intelligence is collected from the news paper and I can only reply that I saw by that, that you arrived such a day. I know your fondness for writing and your inclination to let me hear from you by the first safe conveyance which makes me suspect that some Letter or other has miscaried, but I hope now you have arrived at Philidelphia you will find means to convey me some inteligance.

We are all well here. I think I enjoy better Health than I have done these 2 years. I have not been to Town since I parted with you there. The Govenor is making all kinds of warlike preperations such as mounting cannon upon Beacon

Hill, diging entrenchments upon the Neck, placeing cannon
there, encamping a regiment there, throwing up Brest Works
&c. &c. The people are much allarmed, and the Selectmen
have waited upon him in concequence of it. The county congress have also sent a committee—all which proceedings you
will have a more particuliar account of than I am able to give
you from the publick papers. But as to the Movements of this
Town perhaps you may not hear them from any other person.
In consequence of the powders being taken from Charlstown,
a general alarm spread thro many Towns and was caught pretty
soon here. The report took here a fryday, and a Sunday a Soldier was seen lurking about the common. Supposed to be a
Spy, but most likely a Deserter. However inteligence of it was
communicated to the other parishes, and about 8 o clock a
Sunday Evening there passed by here about 200 Men, preceeded by a horse cart, and marched down to the powder
house from whence they took the powder and carried it into
the other parish and there secreeted it. I opened the window
upon there return. They pass'd without any Noise, not a word
among them till they came against this house, when some of
them perceiveing me, askd me if I wanted any powder. I replied not since it was in so good hands. The reason they gave
for taking it, was that we had so many Tories here they dare
not trust us with it. They had taken Vinton in their Train, and
upon their return they stoped between Cleverlys and Etters,
and calld upon him to deliver two Warrents. Upon his producing them, they put it to vote whether they should burn them
and it pass'd in the affirmitive. They then made a circle and
burnt them, they then call'd a vote whether they should huzza,
but it being Sunday evening it passd in the negative. They
call'd upon Vinton to swear that he would never be instrumental in carrying into execution any of these new atcts. They
were not satisfied with his answers however they let him rest. A
few Days after upon his making some foolish speaches, they
assembled to the amount of 2 and [   ] hundred, swore
vengance upon him unless he took a solemn oath. Accordingly,
they chose a committee and sent them with him to Major
Miller to see that he complied, and they waited his return,
which proving satisfactory they disperced. This Town appear

as high as you can well immagine, and if necessary would soon be in arms. Not a Tory but hides his head. The church parson thought they were comeing after him, and run up garret they say, an other jumpt out of his window and hid among the corn whilst a third crept under his bord fence, and told his Beads.

September 16 1774

I Dined to Day at Coll. Quincys. They were so kind as to send me, and Nabby and Betsy an invitation to spend the Day with them, and as I had not been to see them since I removed to Braintree, I accepted the invitation. After I got there, came Mr. Samll. Quincys wife and Mr. Sumner, Mr. Josiah and Wife. A little clashing of parties you may be sure. Mr. Sam's Wife said she thought it high time for her Husband to turn about, he had not done half so clever since he left her advice. Said they both greatly admired the most excellent and much admired Speach of the Bishop of St. Asaph which suppose you have seen. It meets, and most certainly merrits the greatest encomiums.

Upon my return at night Mr. Thaxter met me at the door with your Letter dated from Prince town New Jersy. It really gave me such a flow of Spirits that I was not composed eno to sleep till one oclock. You make no mention of one I wrote you previous to that you received by Mr. Breck and sent by Mr. Cunningham. I am rejoiced to hear you are well; I want to know many more perticuliars than you wrote me, and hope soon to hear from you again. I dare not trust myself with the thought of how long you may perhaps be absent. I only count the weeks already past, and they amount to 5. I am not so lonely as I should have been, without my two Neighbours. We make a table full at meal times, all the rest of their time they spend in the office. Never were two persons who gave a family less trouble than they do. It is at last determined that Mr. Rice keep the School here. Indeed he has kept ever since he has been here, but not with any expectation that He should be continued, but the people finding no small difference between him and his predecessor chose he should be continued. I have not sent Johnny. He goes very steadily to Mr. Thaxter who I believe takes very good care of him, and as they seem to have a liking to each other believe it will be best to continue him with him. However when you return we can then consult what will be best. I am certain that if he does not get so much good, he gets less harm, and I have always thought it of very great importance that children should in the early part of life be unaccustomed to such examples as would tend to corrupt the purity of their words and actions that they may chill with horrour at the sound of an oath, and blush with indignation at an obscene expression. These first principals which grow with their growth and strengthen with their strength neither time nor custom can totally eradicate.—You will perhaps be tired. No let it serve by way of relaxation from the more important concerns of the Day, and be such an amusement as your little hermitage used to afford you here. You have before you to express myself in the words of the Bishop the greatest National concerns that ever came before any people, and if the prayers and petitions assend unto Heaven which are daily offerd for you, wisdom will flow down as a streem and Rithousness as the mighty waters, and your deliberations will make glad the cities of our God.

I was very sorry I did not know of Mr. Cary's going. It would have been so good an opportunity to have sent this as I lament the loss of. You have heard no doubt of the peoples preventing the court from setting in various counties, and last week in Taunton, Anger urged the courts opening, and calling out the action, but could not effect it.

I saw a Letter from Miss Eunice wherein she gives an account of it, and says there were 2000 men assembled round the court house and by a committee of nine presented a petition requesting that they would not set, and with the uttmost order waited 2 hours for there answer, when they disperced.

Your family all desire to be remember'd to you, as well as unkle Quincy who often visits me, to have an hour of sweet communion upon politicks with me. Coll. Quincy desires his complements to you. Dr. Tufts sends his Love and your Mother and Brothers also. I have lived a very recluse life since your absence, seldom going any where except to my Fathers who with My Mother and Sister desire to be rememberd to you. My Mother has been exceeding low, but is a little better. —How warm your climate may be I know not, but I have had my bed warmed these two nights.—I must request you to procure me some watermellon seads and Muskmellon, as I determine to be well stocked with them an other year. We have had some fine rains, but as soon as the corn is gatherd you must release me of my promise. The Drought has renderd cutting a second crop impracticable, feeding a little cannot hurt it. However I hope you will be at home to be convinced of the utility of the measure.—You will burn all these Letters least they should fall from your pocket and thus expose your most affectionate Friend,   Abigail Adams

"IF THE SWORD BE DRAWN"

To John Adams

My Much Loved Friend   Braintree october 16 1774
     I dare not express to you at 300 hundred miles distance how ardently I long for your return. I have some very miserly Wishes; and cannot consent to your spending one hour in Town till at least I have had you 12. The Idea plays about my Heart, unnerves my hand whilst I write, awakens all the tender sentiments that years have encreased and matured, and which when with me were every day dispensing to you. The whole collected stock of ten weeks absence knows not how to brook any longer restraint, but will break forth and flow thro my pen. May the like sensations enter thy breast, and (in spite of all the weighty cares of State) Mingle themselves with those I wish to communicate, for in giving them utterance I have felt more sincere pleasure than I have known since the 10 of August.— Many have been the anxious hours I have spent since that day—the threatning aspect of our publick affairs, the complicated distress of this province, the Arduous and perplexed Buisness in which you are engaged, have all conspired to agitate my bosom, with fears and apprehensions to which I have heretofore been a stranger, and far from thinking the Scene closed, it looks as tho the curtain was but just drawn and only the first Scene of the infernal plot disclosed and whether the

end will be tragical Heaven alone knows. You cannot be, I know, nor do I wish to see you an inactive Spectator, but if the Sword be drawn I bid adieu to all domestick felicity, and look forward to that Country where there is neither wars nor rumors of War in a firm belief that thro the mercy of its King we shall both rejoice there together.

I greatly fear that the arm of treachery and voilence is lifted over us as a Scourge and heavy punishment from heaven for our numerous offences, and for the misimprovement of our great advantages. If we expect to inherit the blessings of our Fathers, we should return a little more to their primitive Simplicity of Manners, and not sink into inglorious ease. We have too many high sounding words, and too few actions that correspond with them. I have spent one Sabbeth in Town since you left me. I saw no difference in respect to ornaments, &c. &c. but in the Country you must look for that virtue, of which you find but small Glimerings in the Metropolis. Indeed they have not the advantages, nor the resolution to encourage our own Manufactories which people in the country have. To the Mercantile part, tis considerd as throwing away their own Bread; but they must retrench their expenses and be content with a small share of gain for they will find but few who will wear their Livery. As for me I will seek wool and flax and work willingly with my Hands, and indeed their is occasion for all our industry and economy.

You mention the removal of our Books &c. from Boston. I believe they are safe there, and it would incommode the Gentlemen to remove them, as they would not then have a place to repair to for study. I suppose they would not chuse to be at the expence of bording out. Mr. Williams I believe keeps pretty much with his mother. Mr. Hills father had some thoughts of removing up to Braintree provided he could be accommodated with a house, which he finds very difficult.

Mr. Cranch's last determination was to tarry in Town unless any thing new takes place. His Friends in Town oppose his Removal so much that he is determind to stay. The opinion you have entertaind of General Gage is I believe just, indeed he professes to act only upon the Defensive. The People in the Country begin to be very anxious for the congress to rise. They have no Idea of the Weighty Buisness you have to transact, and their Blood boils with indignation at the Hostile prepairations they are constant Witnesses of. Mr. Quincys so secret departure is Matter of various Specculation—some say he is deputed by the congress, others that he is gone to Holland, and the Tories says he is gone to be hanged.

I rejoice at the favourable account you give me of your Health; May it be continued to you. My Health is much better than it was last fall. Some folks say I grow very fat.—I venture to write most any thing in this Letter, because I know the care of the Bearer. He will be most sadly dissapointed if you should be broke up before he arrives, as he is very desirous of being introduced by you to a Number of Gentlemen of respectable characters. I almost envy him, that he should see you, before I can.

Mr. Thaxter and Rice present their Regards to you. Unkle Quincy too sends his Love to you, he is very good to call and see me, and so have many other of my Friends been. Coll. Warren and Lady were here a monday, and send their Love to you. The Coll. promiss'd to write. Mrs. Warren will spend a Day or two on her return with me. I told Betsy to write to you. She says she would if you were her *Husband*.

Your Mother sends her Love to you, and all your family too numerous to name desire to be rememberd. You will receive Letters from two, who are as earnest to write to Pappa as if the welfare of a kingdom depended upon it. If you can give any guess within a month let me know when you think of returning to Your most Affectionate   Abigail Adams

"THE CAUSE OF AMERICA"

To Catharine Sawbridge Macaulay

Madam

In the last Letter which Mr. Adams had the honour to receive from you, you express a Desire to become acquainted with our American Ladies. To them Mrs. Macaulay is sufficiently distinguished by her superior abilities, and altho she who is now ventureing to address her cannot lay claim to eaquil accomplishments with the Lady before introduced, yet she flatters herself she is no ways deficient in her esteem for a Lady who so warmly interests herself in the cause of America—a Cause madam which is now become so serious to every American that we consider it as a struggle from which we shall obtain a release from our present bondage by an ample redress of our Grieveances—or a redress by the Sword. The only alternative which every american thinks of is Liberty or Death.

"Tender plants must bend, but when a Goverment is grown to strength like some old oak rough with its armed bark it yealds not to the tug, but only nods and turns to sullen state."

Should I attempt to discribe to you the complicated misiries and distresses brought upon us by the late inhumane acts of the British parliment my pen would faill me. Suffice it to say, that we are invaded with fleets and Armies, our commerce not only obstructed, but totally ruined, the courts of Justice shut, many driven out from the Metropolis, thousands reduced to want, or dependant upon the charity of their neighbours for a daily supply of food, all the Horrours of a civil war threatning us on one hand, and the chains of Slavery ready forged for us on the other. We Blush when we recollect from whence these woes arise, and must forever execrate the infamous memory of those Men whether they are Americans or Brittons, whose contagious Ambition first opened the pandoraen Box, and wantonly and cruelly scatterd the fatal ingrediants—first taught us filled with grief and anxiety to inquire

> Are these thy deeds o Britton? this the praise
> That points the growing Lusture of thy Name
> These glorious works that in thy latter Days
> fild the bright period of thine early fame
> To rise in ravage and with arm prophane
> From freedoms shrine each sacred Gift to rend
> and mark the closing annals of thy reign
> With every foe subdued, and every Friend.

You will think Madam perhaps from the account I have given you, that we are in great confusion and disorder—but it is far otherways. Tho there are but few who are unfealing or insensible to the general calimity, by far the greater part support it with that firmness, that fortitude, that undaunted resolution which ever attends those who are conscious that they are the injured not the *injurer*, and that they are engaged in a righteous cause in which they fear not to "bare their bold Breasts and pour their generous Blood." Altho by the obstruction of publick justice, each individual is left at a loose, to do that which is right in his own Eyes, yet each one strives to shew his neighbour that the restraints of Honour and of conscience are more powerful motives, than the judiciary proceedings of the Law. Notwithstanding the inveterate Malice of our Enimies who are continually representing us, as in a state of anarchy and confusion, torn up with intestine broils, and guilty of continual riots and outrage, yet this people never saw a time of greater peace and harmony among themselves, every one uniting in the common cause, and strengthning each other with inconceivable constancy and sumpathetick ardor.

I mean always to Except those whose venal Souls barter freedom for Gold, and would sell their Country, nay gladly see an innocent land deluged with Blood, if they could riot upon its Spoils, which heaven Avert!—Tis with anxious Hearts and eager expectations that we are now waiting for the result of the united Supplications of America. Yet having so often experienced their Enefficacy we have little reason to hope. We think we have more to expect from the firm and religious observance of the association which accompanied them—for tho it was formerly the pride and ambition of Americans to indulge in the fashions and Manufactures of Great Brittain now she threatens us with her chains we will scorn to wear her livery, and shall think ourselves more decently attired in the coarse and plain vestures of our own Manufactury than in all the gaudy trapings that adorn the slave.—Yet connected as we are by Blood, by commerce, by one common language, by one common religion as protestants, and as good and loyal subjects of the same king, we earnestly wish that the three fold cord of Duty, interest and filial affection may not be snapped assunder. Tis like the Gordean knot. It never can be untied, but the sword may cut it, and America if she falls to use the words of the revered and ever honourd Mr. Pitt, will fall like a strong Man, will embrace the pillars of State and pull down the constitution along with her.

I must intreat your pardon Madam for Detaining you so
long from the important Services in which you are engaged,
but having taken up my pen I could not refrain giving utterance to some of those Emotions which have agitated my
Bosom and are the cause of many anxious hours to her who
begs leave to subscribe herself Dear Madam your great admirer
& humble Servant,   Abigail Adams

November–December 1774

"THE DIE IS CAST"

To Mercy Otis Warren

My Dear Mrs. Warren

The die is cast. Yesterday brought us such a Speach from the
Throne as will stain with everlasting infamy the reign of George
the 3 determined to carry into Execution "the acts passd by
the late parliment, and to Mantain the authority of the Legislature over all his dominions." The reply of the house of commons and the house of Lords shew us the most wicked and
hostile measures will be persued against us—even without
giving us an opportunity to be heard in our defence. Infatuated Brittain! poor distressed America. Heaven only knows
what is next to take place but it seems to me the Sword is now
our only, yet dreadful alternative, and the fate of Rome will be
renued in Brittain. She who has been the envy of nations will
now become an object of their Scorn and abhorance, and as it
was said of Rome that she governd other people by her will
but her own by Law, they now behold her governd herself by
will, by the Arbitary Will of the worst of her own citizens, and
arrived at that period which has been foretold when the people
co-operateing with the Enimies of the constitution by Electing
those to represent them who are hired to betray them, or by
submitting tamely when the mask is taken of or falls of, and
the attempt to bring beggary and Slavery is avoued or can be
no longer concealed. When this happens the Friends of Liberty, should any such remain will have one option still left, and

will rather chuse no doubt to die the last British freemen, than bear to live the first of British Slaves, and this now seems to be all that is left to americans with unfeigned and penitant suplications to that Being who delights in the welfare of his creatures, and who we humbly hope will engage on our side, and who if we must go forth in defence of our injured and oppressed Country will we hope deliver us from the hands of our enimies and those that persecute us. Tho an hoste should encamp against us our hearts will not fear. Tho war should rise against us, in this will we be confident, that the Lord reigneth. Let thy Mercy o Lord be upon us according as we hope in thee.

Mr. Adams is in Boston. I have not seen him since the royal mandate arrived. Nor have I been able to learn any further news. I wait for his return with anxiety even tho I expect to be confirmed in all my apprehensions. Those who have most to loose have most to fear. The Natural timidity of our sex always seeks for a releif in the encouragement and protection of the other.

Thus far I wrote with a Heart tremblingly anxious, and was prevented from persuing my Subject by companys comeing in. Upon Mr. Adams'es return I experienced the truth of your observation. He laughed at my fears and in some Measure dispelld them—made me see that we were not called either rebels or Trators, told me that there was no other news by this Ship and he still thought that their fears might have weight with them. I would not have my Friend immagine that with all my fears and apprehension, I would give up one Iota of our rights and privilages. I think upon the Maturest deliberation I can say, dreadful as the day would be I had rather see the Sword drawn. Let these truths says the admired Farmer be indelibly impressed on our Minds that we cannot be happy without being free, that we cannot be free without being secure in our property, that we cannot be secure in our property if without our consent others may as by right take it away.—We know too well the blessings of freedom, to tamely resign it— and there really seems to be a ray of light breaking thro the palpable darkness which has for so long a time darkened our hemisphere and threatned to overwhelm us in one common ruin and I cannot but hope with you for more favorable Scenes, and brighter Days. Lord North has luckely thought of a new explanation of his Neroisim. What ever may be their secret motives to a change of Measures is uncertain, but from their formour conduct we shall have little reason to think that justice or Humanity were the motives, and must ever mantain a jealous Eye over those who have acted so repugnant to all Laws both Humane and Divine. May justice and Liberty finally prevail and the Friends of freedom enjoy that Satisfaction and tranquility which ever attends upright intentions and is the sure recompence of virtue.

But if adverse Days are still alloted us, which neither wisdom or prudence can prevent, it must be a continual Source of Satisfaction that every method consistant with reason and religion have been adopted to avert the calimities. But if Innocence must be exposed to Caluminy and virtue become the object of percecution and the upright individual fall a sacrifice to his own virtue, still we must not arraign the divine justice which acts not by partial but by general Laws and may have very important and extensive concequences to answer for the general good of Society.

My Friend assures me that she will comply with my request and gratify my curiosity, but at the same time holds me to conditions which if I comply with it will be only to obtain the greater good for the less. Very selfish motives you will say, tho but few I believe would withstand the temptation.

I observe my Friend is labouring under apprehensions least the Severity with which a certain Group was drawn was incompatable with that Benevolence which ought always to be predominant in a female character. "Tho an Eagles talon asks an Eagles Eye" and Satire in the hands of some is a very dangerous weapon yet when it is so happily blended with benevolence, and is awakend only by the Love of virtue, and abhorance of vice, when Truth is invoilably preserved, and ridiculous and vicious actions are alone the Subject, it is so far from blameable, that it is certainly meritorious; and to suppress it would be hideing a talent like the slothful Servant in a napkin.

"Who combats virtues foe is virtue's friend"

and a keen Satire well applied, has some times found its way when persuasions, admonitions, and Lectures of morality have failed—such is the abhorance of humane nature when it diviates from the path of rectitude, to be represented in its true coulours.

> "Well may they Dread the Muses fatal skill
>   Well may they tremble when she draws the quill
>   Her Magick quill that like Ithuriels Spear
>   Reveals the cloven hoof, or lengthen'd Ear,
>   Bids vice and folly take their Nat'ral Shapes
>   Turns Counsellors to knaves and Beaux to apes
>   Drags the vile whisp'rer from his dark abode
>   Till all the Deamon starts up from the toad."

You will say perhaps that our Sex is partial to each other. That objection if it carries any weight may be made against the person you appeald to. But give me leave to Quote a poet upon the Subject.

> "When Virtue sinks beneath unnumberd Woes
>   And passions born her Friends, revoult her foes
>   Tis Satire's power tis her corrective part
>   To calm the wild disorders of the heart
>   She points the arduous height where glory lies
>   And teaches mad ambition to be wise
>   In the Dark Bosome wakes the fair desire
>   Draws good from Ill, a Brighter flame from fire
>   Strips black oppression of her gay disguise
>   And bids the hag, in native horrour rise
>   Strikes tow'ring pride and Lawless rapine Dead
>   And plants the Wreath on Virtues awful head."

I must intreat a compliance with my other request. I shall esteem it an obligation conferd upon Your much obliged Friend,   Abigail Adams

c. February 3, 1775

"WE HAVE HAD SEVERAL ALLARMS"

To Mercy Otis Warren

My dear Mrs. Warren   Braintree May 2 1775

What a scene has opened upon us since I had the favour of your last! Such a scene as we never before Experienced, and could scarcely form an Idea of. If we look back we are amazed at what is past, if we look forward we must shudder at the view. Our only comfort lies in the justice of our cause; and in the mercy of that being who never said, "Seek ye me in vain." These are consolations which the unbeliever knows not of, and which are a comfortable support, under all we feel, and all we fear. All our worldly comforts are now at stake—our nearest and dearest connections are hazarding their lives and properties. —God give them wisdom and integrity sufficent to the great cause in which they are engaged.—I long most earnestly for the society of my much valued Mrs. Warren—it would be a cordial to my spirits. I must entreat you to write to me every opportunity. I feel the absence of my better half, in this Day of Distress. We have had several allarms from apprehensions of men of wars barges.—Colln. Quincys family have several Times been obliged to flee from their house and scatter themselves about. I cannot say that I am at present under any apprehensions of them here; I have determined to stay as long as it will be safe for any person to tarry upon the sea coast. I am much distressed for our poor Boston Friends. What course they can take I know not, I believe they are kept in for security to the troops. They have involved the Country in great difficulties by their obstinately persevereing to tarry in Town. I fear their distresses will drive them to such compliances as will be inconsistant with their honour.—I hear you have thoughts of going to Taunton, but I hope you will not be obliged to quit your own habitation.—O Britain Britain how is thy glory vanished —how are thy Annals stained with the Blood of thy children.

Adieu my Dear Friend & believe me at all times most affectionately yours,   Abigail Adams

To John Adams

24 May Braintree 1775

Suppose you have had a formidable account of the alarm we had last Sunday morning. When I rose about six oclock I was told that the Drums had been some time beating and that 3 allarm Guns were fired, that Weymouth Bell had been ringing, and Mr. Welds was then ringing. I immediatly sent of an express to know the occasion, and found the whole Town in confusion. 3 Sloops and one cutter had come out, and droped anchor just below Great Hill. It was difficult to tell their design, some supposed they were comeing to Germantown others to Weymouth. People women children from the Iron Works flocking down this Way—every woman and child above or from below my Fathers. My Fathers family flying, the Drs. in great distress, as you may well immagine for my Aunt had her Bed thrown into a cart, into which she got herself, and orderd the boy to drive her of to Bridgwater which he did. The report was to them, that 300 hundred had landed, and were upon their march into Town. The allarm flew like lightning, and men from all parts came flocking down till 2000 were collected—but it seems their expidition was to Grape Island for *Levet's* hay. There it was impossible to reach them for want of Boats, but the sight of so many persons, and the fireing at them prevented their getting more than 3 ton of Hay, tho they had carted much more down to the water. At last they musterd a Lighter, and a Sloop from Hingham which had six port holes. Our men eagerly jumpt on board, and put of for the Island. As soon as they perceived it, they decamped. Our people landed upon the Island, and in an instant set fire to the Hay which with the Barn was soon consumed, about 80 ton tis said. We expect soon to be in continual alarms, till something decisive takes place. We wait with longing Expectation in hopes to hear the best accounts from you with regard to union and harmony &c. We rejoice greatly on the Arival of Doctor Franklin, as he must certainly be able to inform you very perticuliarly of the situation of affairs in England. I wish you would write if you can get time; be as perticuliar as you *may*, when you write—every one here abouts comes to me to hear what accounts I have. I was so unlucky as not to get the Letter you wrote at New York. Capn. Beals forgot it, and left it behind. We have a flying report here with regard to New York, but cannot give any credit to, as yet, that they had been engaged with the Ships which Gage sent there and taken them with great looss upon both sides.

Yesterday we have an account of 3 Ships comeing in to Boston. I believe it is true, as there was a Salute from the other Ships, tho I have not been able to learn from whence they come. Suppose you have had an account of the fire which did much damage to the Warehouses, and added greatly to the distresses of the inhabitants whilst it continued. The bad conduct of General Gage was the means of its doing so much damage.

Tis a fine growing Season having lately had a charming rain, which was much wanted as we had none before for a fortnight. Your meadow is almost fit to mow. Isaac talks of leaving you, and going into the Army. I believe he will. Mr. Rice has a prospect of an *adjutant* place in the Army. I believe he will not be a very hardy Soldier. He has been sick of a fever above this week, and has not been out of his chamber. He is upon the recovery now.

Our House has been upon this alarm in the same Scene of confusion that it was upon the first—Soldiers comeing in for lodging, for Breakfast, for Supper, for Drink &c. &c. Sometimes refugees from Boston tierd and fatigued, seek an assilum for a Day or Night, a week—you can hardly imagine how we live.

> "Yet to the Houseless child of want
> our doors are open still.
> And tho our portions are but scant
> We give them with good will."

I want to know how you do? How are your Eyes? Is not the weather very hot where you are? The children are well and send Duty to Pappa. This day Month you set of. I have never once inquired when you think it posible to return; as I think you could not give me any satisfactory answer. I have according to your direction wrote to Mr. Dilly, and given it to the care of Capn. Beals who will deliver it with his own hand; I got Mr. Thaxter to take a coppy for me, as I had not time amidst our confusions; I send it to you for your approbation. You will be careful of it as I have no other coppy. My best wishes attend you both for your Health and happiness, and that you may be directed into the wisest and best measures for our Safety, and the Security of our posterity. I wish you was nearer to us. We know not what a day will bring forth, nor what distress one hour may throw us into. Heitherto I have been able to mantain a calmness and presence of Mind, and hope I shall, let the Exigency of the time be what they will.

Mrs. Warren desires to be rememberd to you with her sincere regards. Mr. Cranch and family send their Love. He poor man has a fit of his old disorder. I have not heard one Syllable from Providence since I wrote you last. I wait to hear from you, then shall act accordingly. I dare not discharge any debts with what I have except to Isaac, least you should be dissapointed of the remainder. Adieu Breakfast calls your affectionate   Portia

Sister Betsy is with me, and desires her kindest Wishes, and most affectionate Regards may be presented to you.

THE BATTLE OF BUNKER HILL

To John Adams

Dearest Friend   Sunday June 18 1775
    The Day; perhaps the decisive Day is come on which the fate of America depends. My bursting Heart must find vent at my pen. I have just heard that our dear Friend Dr. Warren is no more but fell gloriously fighting for his Country—saying better to die honourably in the field than ignominiously hang upon the Gallows. Great is our Loss. He has distinguished himself in every engagement, by his courage and fortitude, by animating the Soldiers and leading them on by his own example. A particuliar account of these dreadful, but I hope

Glorious Days will be transmitted you, no doubt in the exactest manner.

The race is not to the swift, nor the battle to the strong, but the God of Israel is he that giveth strength and power unto his people. Trust in him at all times, ye people pour out your hearts before him. God is a refuge for us.—Charlstown is laid in ashes. The Battle began upon our intrenchments upon Bunkers Hill, a Saturday morning about 3 o clock and has not ceased yet and tis now 3 o'clock Sabbeth afternoon.

Tis expected they will come out over the Neck to night, and a dreadful Battle must ensue. Almighty God cover the heads of our Country men, and be a shield to our Dear Friends. How many have fallen we know not—the constant roar of the cannon is so distressing that we can not Eat, Drink or Sleep. May we be supported and sustaind in the dreadful conflict. I shall tarry here till tis thought unsafe by my Friends, and then I have secured myself a retreat at your Brothers who has kindly offerd me part of his house. I cannot compose myself to write any further at present. I will add more as I hear further.

Tuesday afternoon

I have been so much agitated that I have not been able to write since Sabbeth day. When I say that ten thousand reports are passing vague and uncertain as the wind I believe I speak the Truth. I am not able to give you any authentick account of last Saturday, but you will not be destitute of inteligence. Coll. Palmer has just sent me word that he has an opportunity of conveyance. Incorrect as this scrawl will be, it shall go. I wrote you last Saturday morning. In the afternoon I received your kind favour of the 2 june, and that you sent me by Captn. Beals at the same time.—I ardently pray that you may be supported thro the arduous task you have before you. I wish I could contradict the report of the Doctors Death, but tis a lamentable Truth, and the tears of multitudes pay tribute to his memory. Those favorite lines of Collin continually sound in my Ears

> How sleep the Brave who sink to rest,
> By all their Countrys wishes blest?
> When Spring with dew'ey fingers cold
> Returns to deck their Hallowed mould

She their shall dress a sweeter Sod
Than fancys feet has ever trod.
By fairy hands their knell is rung
By forms unseen their Dirge is sung
Their Honour comes a pilgrim grey
To Bless the turf that wraps their Clay
And freedom shall a while repair
To Dwell a weeping Hermit there.

I rejoice in the prospect of the plenty you inform me of, but cannot say we have the same agreable veiw here. The drought is very severe, and things look but poorly.

Mr. Rice and Thaxter, unkle Quincy, Col. Quincy, Mr. Wibert all desire to be rememberd, so do all our family. Nabby will write by the next conveyance.

I must close, as the Deacon waits. I have not pretended to be perticuliar with regard to what I have heard, because I know you will collect better intelligence. The Spirits of the people are very good. The loss of Charlstown affects them no more than a Drop in the Bucket.—I am Most sincerely yours,   Portia

"CONTINUAL EXPECTATION OF HOSTILITIES"

To John Adams

Dearest Friend   June 25 1775 Braintree
My Father has been more affected with the distruction of Charlstown, than with any thing which has heretofore taken place. Why should not his countanance be sad when the city, the place of his Fathers Sepulchers lieth waste, and the gates thereof are consumed with fire, scarcly one stone remaineth upon an other. But in the midst of sorrow we have abundant cause of thankfulness that so few of our Breathren are numberd with the slain, whilst our enimies were cut down like the Grass before the Sythe. But one officer of all the Welch fuzelers remains to tell his story. Many poor wretches dye for want of proper assistance and care of their wounds.

Every account agrees in 14 and 15 hundred slain and wounded

upon their side nor can I learn that they dissemble the number themselves. We had some Heroes that day who fought with amazing intrepidity, and courage—

> "Extremity is the trier of Spirits—
> Common chances common men will bear;
> And when the Sea is calm all boats alike
> Shew mastership in floating, but fortunes blows
> When most struck home, being bravely warded, crave
> A noble cunning."   *Shakespear.*

I hear that General *How* should say the Battle upon the plains of Abram was but a Bauble to this. When we consider all the circumstances attending this action we stand astonished that our people were not all cut of. They had but one hundred foot intrenched, the number who were engaged, did not exceed 800, and they had not half amunition enough. The reinforcements not able to get to them seasonably, the tide was up and high, so that their floating batteries came upon each side of the causway and their row gallies keeping a continual fire. Added to this the fire from fort hill and from the Ship, the Town in flames all round them and the heat from the flames so intence as scarcely to be borne; the day one of the hottest we have had this season and the wind blowing the smoke in their faces— only figure to yourself all these circumstances, and then consider that we do not count 60 Men lost. My Heart overflows at the recollection.

We live in continual Expectation of Hostilities. Scarcely a day that does not produce some, but like Good Nehemiah having made our prayer with God, and set the people with their Swords, their Spears and their bows we will say unto them, Be not affraid of them. Remember the Lord who is great and terible, and fight for your Breathren, your sons and your daughters, your wives and your houses.

I have just received yours of the 17 of june in 7 days only. Every line from that far Country is precious. You do not tell me how you do, but I will hope better. Alass you little thought what distress we were in the day you wrote. They delight in molesting us upon the Sabbeth. Two Sabbeths we have been in such Alarms that we have had no meeting. This day we have set under our own vine in quietness, have heard Mr. Taft, from psalms. The Lord is good to all and his tender mercies are over all his works. The good man was earnest and pathetick. I could forgive his weakness for the sake of his sincerity—but I long for a *Cooper* and an *Elliot*. I want a person who has feeling and sensibility who can take one up with him

> "And in his Duty prompt at every call
> Can watch, and weep, and pray, and feel for all."

Mr. Rice joins General Heaths regiment to morrow as adjutant. Your Brother is very desirous of being in the army, but your good Mother is really voilent against it. I cannot persuaid nor reason her into a consent. Neither he nor I dare let her know that he is trying for a place. My Brother has a Captains commission, and is stationd at Cambridge. I thought you had the best of inteligence or I should have taken pains to have been more perticuliar. As to Boston, there are many persons yet there who would be glad to get out if they could. Mr. Boylstone and Mr. Gill the printer with his family are held upon the black list tis said. Tis certain they watch them so narrowly that they cannot escape, nor your Brother Swift and family. Mr. Mather got out a day or two before Charlstown was distroyed, and had lodged his papers and what else he got out at Mr. Carys, but they were all consumed. So were many other peoples, who thought they might trust their little there; till teams could be procured to remove them. The people from the Alms house and work house were sent to the lines last week, to make room for their wounded they say. Medford people are all removed. Every sea port seems in motion.—O North! may the Groans and cryes of the injured and oppressed Harrow up thy Soul. We have a prodigious Army, but we lack many accomadations which we need. I hope the apointment of these new Generals will give satisfaction. They must be proof against calumny. In a contest like this continual reports are circulated by our Enimies, and they catch with the unwary and the gaping croud who are ready to listen to the marvellous, without considering of consequences even tho there best Friends are injured.—I have not venturd to inquire one word of you about your return. I do not know whether I ought to wish for it—it seems as if your sitting together was absolutely necessary whilst every day is big with Events.

Mr. Bowdoin called a fryday and took his leave of me desiring I would present his affectionate regards to you. I have hopes that he will recover—he has mended a good deal. He wished he could have staid in Braintree, but his Lady was fearful.

I have often heard that fear makes people loving. I never was so much noticed *by some people* as I have been since you went out of Town, or rather since the 19 of April. Mr. Winslows family are determined to be sociable. Mr. A——n are quite Friendly.—Nabby Johny Charly Tommy all send duty. Tom says I wish I could see *par*. You would laugh to see them all run upon the sight of a Letter—like chickens for a crum, when the Hen clucks. Charls says *mar* What is it any good news? and who is for us and who against us, is the continual inquiry.— Brother and Sister Cranch send their Love. He has been very well since he removed, for him, and has full employ in his Buisness. Unkel Quincy calls to hear most every day, and as for the Parson, he determines I shall not make the same complaint I did last time, for he comes every other day.

Tis exceeding dry weather. We have not had any rain for a long time. Bracket has mowed the medow and over the way, but it will not be a last years crop.—Pray let me hear from you by every opportunity till I have the joy of once more meeting you. Yours ever more, Portia

P.S. Tell Bass his father and family are well.

"DANGER THEY SAY MAKES PEOPLE VALIENT"

To John Adams

Braintre July 5 1775

I have received a good deal of paper from you; I wish it had been more coverd; the writing is very scant but I must not grumble. I know your time is not yours, nor mine. Your Labours must be great, and your mouth closed, but all you may communicate I beg you would. There is a pleasure I know not whence it arises nor can I stop now to find it out, but I say there is a degree of pleasure in being able to tell new's—especially any which so nearly concerns us as all your proceedings do.

I should have been more particuliar but I thought you knew every thing that pass'd here. The present state of the inhabitants of Boston is that of the most abject slaves under the most cruel and despotick of Tyrants. Among many instances I could mention let me relate one. Upon the 17 of june printed hand Bills were pasted up at the corner of streets and upon houses forbideing any inhabitant to go upon their houses or upon any eminence upon pain of death. The inhabitants dared not to look out of their houses nor bee heard or seen to ask a Question. Our prisoners were brought over to the long wharff and there laid all night without any care of their wounds or any resting place but the pavements till the next day, when they exchanged it for the jail, since which we hear they are civily treated. Their living cannot be good, as they can have no fresh provisions. Their Beaf we hear is all gone, and their own wounded men die very fast, so that they have raisd a report that the Bullets were poisond. Fish they cannot have—they have renderd it so difficult to procure it, and the Admiral is such a villan as to oblige every fishing schooner to pay a Dollor every time they go out. The money that has been paid for passes is incredible. Some have given ten twenty 30 and forty Dollors, to get out with a small proportion of their things. Tis reported and believed that they have taken up a number of persons and committed them to jail—we know not for what in perticuliar. Master Lovel is confined to the Dungeon, a Son of Mr. Edes is in jail. One Mr. Wendle who married a Hunt, and one Wiburt a ship carpenter is now upon trial for his life. God alone knows to what lengths these wretches will go, and will I hope restrain their malice.

I would not have you be distressd about me. Danger they say makes people valient. Heitherto I have been distress'd, but not dismayed. I have felt for my Country and her Sons, I have bled with them, and for them. Not all the havock and devastation they have made, has wounded me like the death of Warren. We wanted him in the Senate, we want him in his profession, we want him in the field. We mourn for the citizen, the senator, the physician and the Warriour. May we have others raised up in his room.

I have had a very kind and friendly visit from our dear Friends Col. Warren, Lady and Son. Mrs. Warren spent a week almost with me, and he came and met her here and kept Sabbeth with me. Suppose she will write to you, tho she says you are in her debt.

You scarcely make mention of Dr. Franklin. Surely he must be a valuable member. Pray what is become of your Judas. I see he is not with you upon the list of Delegates? I wish I could come and see you. I never suffer myself to think you are about returning soon. Can it, will it bee? May I ask? May I wish for it? When once I expect you the time will crawl till I see you—but hush—do you know tis eleven o clock at Night?

We have had some very fine rains, since I wrote you last. I hope we shall not now have famine added to war. Grain Grain is what we want here—meat we may have enough and to spair. Pray dont let Bass forget my pins. Hardwick has applied to me for Mr. Bass to get him a 100 of needles no. 6 to carry on his stocking weaving. He says they in Phyladelphia will know the proper needle. We shall very soon have no coffee nor sugar nor pepper here—but huckle berrys and milk we are not obliged to commerce for.

All the good folks here send their regards. Unkle Quincy is just gone from here, sends his love. You dont say in the two last Letters I received how you do. I hope I have not felt unwell by sympathy, but I have been very unwell for this week tho better now. I saw a Letter of yours to Col. Palmer by General Washington. I hope I have one too.

Good Night with thoughts of thee do I close my Eyes; Angels gaurd and protect thee, and may a safe return ere long bless thy   Portia

THE HAYDEN AFFAIR

To John Adams

Dearest Friend   Braintree July 12. 1775

I have met with some abuse and very Ill treatment. I want you for my protector and justifier.

In this Day of distress for our Boston Friends when every one does what in them lyes to serve them, your Friend Gorge Trott and family moved up to Braintree, went in with her two Brothers and families with her Father, but they not thinking themselves so secure as further in the Country moved away. After they were gone Mr. Church took the house and took a number of borders. Mr. Trott had engaged a house near his Friends but being prevented going quite so soon as he designd, and the great distress people were in for houses, the owner had taken in a family and dissapointed Mr. Trott, nor could he procure a house any where, for the more remote from the sea coast you go the thicker you find the Boston people. After this dissapointment, he had his Goods without unloading brought back to Braintree, and he with all his family were obliged to shelter themselves in your Brothers house till he could seek further. You know, from the situation of my Brothers family it was impossible for them to tarry there, Mrs. Trots circumstances requiring more rooms than one. In this extremity he applied to me to see if I would not accommodate him with the next house, every other spot in Town being full. I sent for Mr. Hayden and handsomely asked him, he said he would try, but he took no pains to procure himself a place. There were several in the other parish which were to be let, but my Gentleman did not chuse to go there. Mr. Trot upon account of his Buisness which is in considerable demand wanted to be here. Mr. Trott, finding there was no hopes of his going out said he would go in with him, provided I would let him have the chamber I improved for a Dairy room and the lower room and chamber over it which Hayden has. I then sent and asked Mr. Hayden to be so kind as to remove his things into the other part of the house and told him he might improve the kitchen and back chamber, the bed room and the Dairy room in which he already had a bed. He would not tell me whether he would or not, but said I was turning him out of Door to oblige Boston folks, and he could not be stired up, and if you was at home you would not once ask him to go out, but was more of a Gentleman. (You must know that both his Sons are in the army, not but one Days Work has been done by any of them this Spring.) I as mildly as I could represented the distress of Mr. Trot and the difficulties to which he had been put—that I looked upon it my Duty to do all in my power to Oblige him—and that he Hayden would be much better accommodated than hundreds who were turnd out of Town—and I finally said that Mr. Trott should go in. In this State, Sister Adams got to bed and then there was not a Spot in Brothers house for them to lie down in. I removed my dairy things, and once more requested the old Man to move into the other part of the house, but he positively tells me he will not and all the art of Man shall not stir him, even dares me to put any article out of one room into an other. Says Mr. Trot shall not come in—he has got possession and he will keep it. What not have a place to entertain his children in when they come to see him. I now write you an account of the matter, and desire you to write to him and give me orders what course I shall take. I must take Mr. Trott in with me and all his family for the present, till he can look out further or have that house. It would make your heart ake to see what difficulties and distresses the poor Boston people are driven to. Belcher has two families with him. There are 3 in Veses house, 2 in Etters, 2 in Mr. Savils, 2 in Jonathan Bass'es and yet that obstinate Wretch will not remove his few things into the other part of that house, but live there paying no rent upon the distresses of others.

It would be needless to enumerate all his impudence. Let it suffice to say it moved me so much that I had hard Work to suppress my temper. I want to know whether his things may be removed into the other part of the house, whether he consents or not? Mr. Trott would rejoice to take the whole, but would put up with any thing rather than be a burden to his Friends. I told the old Man I believed I was doing nothing but what I should be justified in. He says well tis a time of war get him out if I can, but cannon Ball shall not move him. If you think you are able to find 3 houses, for 3 such tenents as you have they must abide where they are, tho I own I shall be much mortified if you do not support me.

I feel too angry to make this any thing further than a Letter of Buisness. I am most sincerely yours,   Abigail Adams

MEETING GENERAL WASHINGTON

To John Adams

Dearest Friend   Braintree July 16 1775
I have this afternoon had the pleasure of receiving your
Letter by your Friends Mr. Collins and Kaighn and an English
Gentle man his Name I do not remember. It was next to seeing
my dearest Friend. Mr. Collins could tell me more perticuliarly
about you and your Health than I have been able to hear since
you left me. I rejoice in his account of your better Health, and
of your spirits, tho he says I must not expect to see you till next
spring. I hope he does not speak the truth. I know (I think I
do, for am not I your Bosome Friend?) your feelings, your
anxieties, your exertions, &c. more than those before whom
you are obliged to wear the face of chearfulness.

I have seen your Letters to Col. Palmer and Warren. I pity
your Embaresments. How difficult the task to quench out the
fire and the pride of private ambition, and to sacrifice ourselfs
and all our hopes and expectations to the publick weal. How
few have souls capable of so noble an undertaking—how often
are the lawrels worn by those who have had no share in earning
them, but there is a future recompence of reward to which the
upright man looks, and which he will most assuredly obtain
provided he perseveres unto the end.—The appointment of
the Generals Washington and Lee, gives universal satisfaction.
The people have the highest opinion of Lees abilities, but you
know the continuation of the popular Breath, depends much
upon favorable events.

I had the pleasure of seeing both the Generals and their Aid
de camps soon after their arrival and of being personally made
known to them. They very politely express their regard for
you. Major Miflin said he had orders from you to visit me at
Braintree. I told him I should be very happy to see him there,
and accordingly sent Mr. Thaxter to Cambridge with a card to
him and Mr. Read to dine with me. Mrs. Warren and her Son
were to be with me. They very politely received the Message
and lamented that they were not able to upon account of Expresses which they were that day to get in readiness to send of.

I was struck with General Washington. You had prepaired me to entertain a favorable opinion of him, but I thought the one half was not told me. Dignity with ease, and complacency, the Gentleman and Soldier look agreably blended in him. Modesty marks every line and feture of his face. Those lines of Dryden instantly occurd to me

> "Mark his Majestick fabrick! he's a temple
> Sacred by birth, and built by hands divine
> His Souls the Deity that lodges there.
> Nor is the pile unworthy of the God."

General Lee looks like a careless hardy Veteran and from his appearence brought to my mind his namesake Charls the 12, king of Sweeden. The Elegance of his pen far exceeds that of his person. I was much pleased with your Friend Collins. I persuaded them to stay coffe with me, and he was as unreserved and social as if we had been old acquaintances, and said he was very loth to leave the house. I would have detaind them till morning, but they were very desirous of reaching Cambridge.

You have made often and frequent complaints that your Friends do not write to you. I have stired up some of them. Dr. Tufts, Col. Quincy, Mr. Tudor, Mr. Thaxter all have wrote you now, and a Lady whom I am willing you should value preferable to all others save one. May not I in my turn make complaints? All the Letters I receive from you seem to be wrote in so much haste, that they scarcely leave room for a social feeling. They let me know that you exist, but some of them contain scarcely six lines. I want some sentimental Effusions of the Heart. I am sure you are not destitute of them or are they all absorbed in the great publick. Much is due to that I know, but being part of the whole I lay claim to a Larger Share than I have had. You used to be more communicative a Sundays. I always loved a Sabeth days letter, for then you had a greater command of your time—but hush to all complaints.

I am much surprized that you have not been more accurately informd of what passes in the camps. As to intelegance from Boston, tis but very seldom we are able to collect any thing that may be relied upon, and to report the vague flying

rumours would be endless. I heard yesterday by one Mr. Role-
stone a Goldsmith who got out in a fishing Schooner, that
there distress encreased upon them fast, their Beaf is all spent,
their Malt and Sider all gone, all the fresh provisions they can
procure they are obliged to give to the sick and wounded. 19
of our Men who were in Jail and were wounded at the Battle
of Charlstown were Dead. No Man dared now to be seen
talking to his Friend in the Street, they were obliged to be
within every evening at ten o clock according to Martial Law,
nor could any inhabitant walk any Street in Town after that
time without a pass from Gage. He has orderd all the melasses
to be stilld up into rum for the Soldiers, taken away all Li-
cences, and given out others obligeing to a forfeiture of ten
pounds L M if any rum is sold without written orders from the
General. He give much the same account of the kill'd and
wounded we have had from others. The Spirit he says which
prevails among the Soldiers is a Spirit of Malice and revenge,
there is no true courage and bravery to be observed among
them, their Duty is hard allways mounting guard with their
packs at their back ready for an alarm which they live in continual hazard of. Doctor Eliot is not on bord a man of war, as has
been reported, but perhaps was left in Town as the comfort
and support of those who cannot escape, he was constantly
with our prisoners. Mr. Lovel and Leach with others are certainly in Jail. A poor Milch cow was last week kill'd in Town
and sold for a shilling stearling per pound. The transports arrived last week from York, but every additional Man adds to
their distress.—There has been a little Expidition this week to
Long Island. There has been before several attempts to go on
but 3 men of war lay near, and cutters all round the Island that
they could not succeed. A number of whale boats lay at Germantown; 300 volenters commanded by one Capt. Tupper
came on monday evening and took the boats, went on and
brought of 70 odd Sheep, 15 head of cattle, and 16 prisoners 13
of whom were sent by Simple Sapling to mow the Hay which
they had very badly executed. They were all a sleep in the
house and barn when they were taken. There were 3 women
with them. Our Heroes came of in triumph not being observed
by their Enimies. This spiritted up others. They could not endure the thought that the House and barn should afford them

any shelter. They did not distroy them the night before for fear
of being discoverd. Capt. Wild of this Town with about 25 of
his company, Capt. Gold of Weymouth with as many of his,
and some other volenters to the amount of an 100, obtain
leave to go on and distroy the Hay together with the House
and barn and in open day in full view of the men of war they
set of from the Moon so call'd coverd by a number of men
who were placed there, went on, set fire to the Buildings and
Hay. A number of armed cutters immediately Surrounded the
Island, fired upon our Men. They came of with a hot and
continued fire upon them, the Bullets flying in every direction
and the Men of Wars boats plying them with small arms. Many
in this Town who were spectators expected every moment our
Men would all be sacrificed, for sometimes they were so near
as to be calld to and damnd by their Enimies and orderd to
surrender yet they all returnd in safty, not one Man even
wounded. Upon the Moon we lost one Man from the cannon
on board the Man of War. On the Evening of the same day a
Man of War came and anchord near Great Hill, and two cutters came to Pig Rocks. It occasiond an alarm in this Town and
we were up all Night. They remain there yet, but have not
ventured to land any men.

This Town have chosen their Representative. Col. Palmer is
the Man. There was a considerable musture upon Thayers
side, and Vintons company marched up in order to assist, but
got sadly dissapointed. Newcomb insisted upon it that no man
should vote who was in the army—he had no notion of being
under the Military power—said we might be so situated as to
have the greater part of the people engaged in the Military,
and then all power would be wrested out of the hands of the
civil Majestrate. He insisted upon its being put to vote, and
carried his point immediately. It brought Thayer to his Speach
who said all he could against it.—As to the Situation of the
camps, our Men are in general Healthy, much more so at
Roxbury than Cambridge, and the Camp in vastly better
order. General Thomas has the character of an Excelent officer. His Merit has certainly been overlook'd, as modest merit
generally is. I hear General Washington is much pleased with
his conduct.

Every article here in the West india way is very scarce and dear. In six weeks we shall not be able to purchase any article of the kind. I wish you would let Bass get me one pound of peper, and 2 yd. of black caliminco for Shooes. I cannot wear leather if I go bare foot the reason I need not mention. Bass may make a fine profit if he layes in a stock for himself. You can hardly immagine how much we want many common small articles which are not manufactured amongst ourselves, but we will have them in time. Not one pin is to be purchased for love nor money. I wish you could convey me a thousand by any Friend travelling this way. Tis very provoking to have such a plenty so near us, but tantulus like not able to touch. I should have been glad to have laid in a small stock of the West India articles, but I cannot get one copper. No person thinks of paying any thing, and I do not chuse to run in debt. I endeavour to live in the most frugal manner posible, but I am many times distressed.—Mr. Trot I have accommodated by removeing the office into my own chamber, and after being very angry and sometimes persuaideding I obtain the mighty concession of the Bed room, but I am now so crouded as not to have a Lodging for a Friend that calls to see me. I must beg you would give them warning to seek a place before Winter. Had that house been empty I could have had an 100 a year for it. Many persons had applied before Mr. Trot, but I wanted some part of it my self, and the other part it seems I have no command of.—We have since I wrote you had many fine showers, and altho the crops of grass have been cut short, we have a fine prospect of Indian corn and English grain. Be not afraid, ye beasts of the field, for the pastures of the Wilderness do spring, the Tree beareth her fruit, the vine and the olive yeald their increase.

We have not yet been much distressed for grain. Every thing at present looks blooming. O that peace would once more extend her olive Branch.

> "This Day be Bread and peace my lot
> All Else beneath the Sun
> Thou knowst if best bestowed or not
> And let thy will be done."

But is the Almighty ever bound to please
Ruild by my wish or studious of my ease.
Shall I determine where his frowns shall fall
And fence my Grotto from the Lot of all?
Prostrate his Sovereign Wisdom I adore
Intreat his Mercy, but I dare no more.

Our little ones send Duty to pappa. You would smile to see
them all gather round mamma upon the reception of a letter
to hear from pappa, and Charls with open mouth, What does
par say—did not he write no more. And little Tom says I wish
I could see par. Upon Mr. Rice's going into the army he asked
Charls if he should get him a place, he catchd at it with great
eagerness and insisted upon going. We could not put him of,
he cryed and beged, no obstical we could raise was suffcient to
satisfy him, till I told him he must first obtain your consent.
Then he insisted that I must write about it, and has been every
day these 3 weeks insisting upon my asking your consent. At
last I have promised to write to you, and am obliged to be as
good as my word.—I have now wrote you all I can collect
from every quarter. Tis fit for no eye but yours, because you
can make all necessary allowances. I cannot coppy.

There are yet in Town 4 of the Selectmen and some thou-
sands of inhabitants tis said.—I hope to hear from you soon.
Do let me know if there is any prospect of seeing you? Next
Wednesday is 13 weeks since you went away.

I must bid you adieu. You have many Friends tho they have
not noticed you by writing. I am sorry they have been so neglegent. I hope no share of that blame lays upon your most affectionate   Portia

Mr. Cranch has in his possession a Barrel of Mrs. Wilkings
Beer which belonged to the late Dr. Warren. He does not
know what to do with it. Suppose you should take it and give
credit for it, as there will be neither wine, lemmons or any
thing else to be had but what we make ourselves. Write me
your pleasure about it.

DEATH OF JOHN'S BROTHER

To John Adams

Dearest Friend   Braintree August 10 1775
     Tis with a sad Heart I take my pen to write to you because I
must be the bearer of what will greatly afflict and distress you.
Yet I wish you to be prepaired for the Event. Your Brother
Elihu lies very dangerously sick with a Dysentery. He has been
very bad for more than a week, his life is despaired of. Er'e I
close this Letter I fear I shall write you that he is no more.
     We are all in great distress. Your Mother is with him in great
anguish. I hear this morning that he is sensible of his Danger,
and calmly resigned to the will of Heaven; which is a great
Satisfaction to his mourning Friend's. I cannot write more at
present than to assure you of the Health of your own family.
Mr. Elisha Niles lies very bad with the same disorder.—Adieu.

                                                    August 11
     I have this morning occasion to sing of Mercies and judg-
ments. May I properly notice each—a mixture of joy and grief
agitate my Bosom. The return of thee my dear partner after a
four months absence is a pleasure I cannot express, but the joy
is overclouded, and the Day is darkened by the mixture of
Grief and the Sympathy I feel for the looss of your Brother, cut
of in the pride of life and the bloom of Manhood! in the midst
of his usefulness; Heaven sanctify this affliction to us, and make
me properly thankful that it is not my sad lot to mourn the loss
of a Husband in the room of a Brother.
     May thy life be spaired and thy Health confirmed for the
benefit of thy Country and the happiness of thy family is the
constant supplication of thy Friend.

To John Adams

Dearest Friend   Braintree Sepbr. 8 1775

Since you left me I have passed thro great distress both of Body and mind; and whether greater is to be my portion Heaven only knows. You may remember Isaac was unwell when you went from home. His Disorder increasd till a voilent Dysentery was the consequence of his complaints, there was no resting place in the House for his terible Groans. He continued in this state near a week when his Disorder abated, and we have now hopes of his recovery. Two days after he was sick, I was seaz'd with the same disorder in a voilent manner. Had I known you was at Watertown I should have sent Bracket for you. I sufferd greatly betwen my inclination to have you return, and my fear of sending least you should be a partaker of the common calamity. After 3 days an abatement of my disease relieved me from that anxiety. The next person in the same week was Susy. She we carried home, hope she will not be very bad. Our Little Tommy was the next, and he lies very ill now—there is no abatement at present of his disorder. I hope he is not dangerous. Yesterday Patty was seazd and took a puke. Our House is an hospital in every part, and what with my own weakness and distress of mind for my family I have been unhappy enough.

And such is the distress of the neighbourhood that I can scarcly find a well person to assist me in looking after the sick. Mrs. Randle has one child that is not expected to live out the night, Mrs. Belcher has an other, Joseph Bracket an other, Deacon Adams has lost one, but is upon the recovery himself, and so are the rest of his family. Mr. Wibird lies bad. Major Miller is dangerous. Revd. Mr. Gay is not expected to live.

So sickly and so Mortal a time the oldest Man does not remember. I am anxious for you. Pray let me hear from you soon. I thought you would have left me a Letter at Watertown as you staid so long there. I was disapointed that you did not.—As to politicks I know nothing about them. The distresses of my own family are so great that I have not thought about them. I have wrote as much as I am able to, being very week. I hope to add a more pleasing account er'er I close. Adieu.

Sunday Sepbr. 10.

Tis now two days since I wrote. As to my own Health I mend but very slowly—have been fearful of a return of my disorder to day but feel rather better now. Hope it is only oweing to my having been fatigued with looking after Tommy as he is unwilling any body but Mamma should do for him, and if he was I could not find any body that is worth having but what are taken up already with the sick. Tommy I hope is mending, his fever has abated, his Bowels are better, but was you to look in upon him you would not know him, from a hearty hale corn fed Boy, he is become pale lean and wan. Isaac is getting better, but very slowly. Patty is very bad. We cannot keep any thing down that she takes, her situation is very dangerous. Mr. Trot and one of his children are taken with the disorder.

I shall write every day if I am able. Pray let me hear from you often. Heaven preserve both your life and health and all my sufferings will be but small. By the first safe conveyance be kind eno to send me 1 oz. of turkey Rhubub, the root, and to procure me 1 quarter lb. of nutmegs for which here I used to give 2.8 Lawful, 1 oz. cloves, 2 of cinnamon. You may send me only a few of the nutmegs till Bass returns. I should be glad of 1 oz. of Indian root. So much sickness has occasiond a scarcity of Medicine.

Distroy this. Such a doleful tale it contains can give no pleasure to any one. Our other children are well and send Duty to pappa. Bracket has been complaining but has got better. The small pox in the natural way was never more mortal than this Distemper has proved in this and many neighbouring Towns. 18 have been buried since you left us in Mr. Welds parish. 4, 3 and 2 funerals in a day for many days. Heitherto our family has been greatly favourd. Heaven still preserve us. Tis a melancholy time with us. I hope you will not think me in the dismals, but publick and private judgments ought to be noticed by every one. I am most affectionately Yours,   Portia

To John Adams

Braintree Sepbr. 16 Sunday 1775

I set myself down to write with a Heart depressed with the Melancholy Scenes arround me. My Letter will be only a Bill of Mortality, tho thanks be to that Being who restraineth the pestilence, that it has not yet proved mortal to any of our family, tho we live in daily Expectation that Patty will not continue many hours. A general putrefaction seems to have taken place, and we can not bear the House only as we are constantly clensing it with hot vinegar. I had no Idea of the Distemper producing such a state as hers till now. Yet we take all posible care by shifting her bed every day. Two of the children John and Charlss I have sent out of the house, finding it difficult to keep them out of the chamber. Nabby continues well. Tommy is better, but intirely striped of the hardy robust countanance as well as of all the flesh he had, save what remains for to keep his bones together. Jonathan is the only one who remains in the family but what has had a turn of the disorder. Mrs. Randle has lost her daughter, Mrs. Bracket hers, Mr. Thomas Thayer his wife. 2 persons belonging to Boston have died this week in this parish. I know of eight this week who have been buried in this Town.

In Weymouth it is very sickly, but not Mortal. Dr. Tufts tells me he has betwen 60 and 70 patients now sick with this disorder. Mr. Thaxter has been obliged to go home as it was not posible for me to accommodate him. Mr. Mason came this week, but if he had been inclined I could not have taken him now. But the general Sickness in the Towns determined him to return home for the present. The dread upon the minds of people of catching the distemper is almost as great as if it was the small pox. I have been distress'd more than ever I was in my life to procure watchers and to get assistance.

I hear Mr. Tudor has been dangerously sick, but is now upon the recovery. Mr. Wibird is very low indeed, scarcly able to walk a step. We have been 4 Sabbeths without any meeting. Thus does pestilence travel in the rear of War to remind us of our intire dependance upon that Being who not only directeth the arrow by day, but has also at his command the pestilence which walketh in Darkness. So uncertain and so transotory are all the enjoyments of Life that were it not for the tender connections which bind us here, would it not be folly to wish for a continuance here? I think I shall never be wedded to the World, and were I to loose about a Dozen of my dearest Connections I should have no further realish for Life.

But perhaps I deceive my self, and know but little of my own Heart;

"To Bear and Suffer is our portion here."

And unto him who mounts the Whirlwind and directs the Storm I will chearfully leave the ordering of my Lot, and whether adverse or prosperous Days should be my future portion I will trust in his right Hand to lead me safely thro, and after a short rotation of Events fix me in a state immutable and happy.

You will think me melancholy. Tis true I am much affected with the distress'd Scenes around me but I have some Anxietyes upon my mind which I do not think it prudent to mention at present to any one. Perhaps when I hear from you, I may in my next Letter tell you. In the mean time I wish you would tell me whether the intercepted Letters have reachd Phyladelphia and what affect they have there. There is a most infamous versification of them I hear sent out. I have not been able to get it. As to politicks there seems to be a dead calm upon all sides. Some of the Tories have been sending out their children. Col. Chandler has sent out his children, and Mr. Winslow has sent out his daughter. People appear to be gratified with the remonstrance, address and petition, and most earnestly long for further intelegance.

God helps them that help themselves as King Richard said and if we can obtain the divine aid by our own virtue, fortitude and perseverance we may be sure of releaf.

Tomorrow will be 3 weeks since you left home in all which time I have not heard one word from you. Patience is a Lesson I have not to learn so can wait your own time, but hope it will not be long er'e my anxious heart is releaved. Adieu. I need not say how sincerely I am your affectionate   Portia

September 17, 1775

"A HEAVY HEART"

To John Adams

Dearest Friend   Braintree Sepbr. 25 1775

I set down with a heavy Heart to write to you. I have had no other since you left me. Woe follows Woe and one affliction treads upon the heal of an other. My distress for my own family having in some measure abated; tis excited anew upon the distress of my dear Mother. Her kindness brought her to see me every day when I was ill and our little Tommy. She has taken the disorder and lies so bad that we have little hopes of her Recovery. She is possess'd with the Idea that she shall not recover, and I fear it will prove but too true.

In this Town the distemper seems to have abated. We have none now so bad as Patty. She has lain 21 days, each day we had reason to think would be her last, but a good Constitution, and youth for ought I know will finally conquer the distemper. She is not able to get out of Bed, nor can she help herself any more than a new born infant. Yet their are symptoms which now appear in her favour.

The desolation of War is not so distressing as the Havock made by the pestilence. Some poor parents are mourning the loss of 3, 4 and 5 children, and some families are wholy striped of every Member.

Wherefore is it that we are thus contended with? How much reason have I for thankfulness that all my family are spaired whilst so many others are striped of their parents, their children, their husbands.

O kind Heaven spair my parents, spair my Dearest Friend and grant him Health. Continue the lives and health of our dear children. Sister Elihu Adams lost her youngest child last night with this disorder. I can add no more than Supplications for your welfare, and an ardent desire to hear from you by every opportunity. It will alleviate every trouble thro which it may be my Lot to pass. I am most affectionately your distress'd

Portia

DEATH OF ABIGAIL'S MOTHER

To John Adams

Weymouth october. 1 1775

Have pitty upon me, have pitty upon me o! thou my beloved for the Hand of God presseth me soar.

Yet will I be dumb and silent and not open my mouth becaus thou o Lord hast done it.

How can I tell you (o my bursting Heart) that my Dear Mother has Left me, this day about 5 oclock she left this world for an infinitely better.

After sustaining 16 days severe conflict nature fainted and she fell asleep. Blessed Spirit where art thou? At times I almost am ready to faint under this severe and heavy Stroke, seperated from *thee* who used to be a comfortar towards me in affliction, but blessed be God, his Ear is not heavy that he cannot hear, but he has bid us call upon him in time of Trouble.

I know you are a sincere and hearty mourner with me and will pray for me in my affliction. My poor father like a firm Believer and a Good christian sets before his children the best of Examples of patience and submission. My sisters send their Love to you and are greatly afflicted. You often Express'd your anxiety for me when you left me before, surrounded with Terrors, but my trouble then was as the small dust in the balance compaird to what I have since endured. I hope to be properly mindful of the correcting hand, that I may not be rebuked in anger.—You will pardon and forgive all my wanderings of mind. I cannot be correct.

Tis a dreadful time with this whole province. Sickness and death are in almost every family. I have no more shocking and terible Idea of any Distemper except the Plague than this.

Almighty God restrain the pestilence which walketh in darkness and wasteth at noon day and which has laid in the dust one of the dearest of parents. May the Life of the other be lengthend out to his afflicted children and Your distressd

Portia

"THE KEEN EDG OF SORROW"

To John Adams

Braintree october 9 1775

I have not been composed enough to write you since Last Sabbeth when in the bitterness of my soul, I wrote a few confused lines, since which time it has pleased the great disposer of all Events to add Breach to Breach—

> "Rare are solitary woes, they Love a Train
> And tread each others heal."

The day week that I was call'd to attend a dying parents Bed I was again call'd to mourn the loss of one of my own Family. I have just returnd from attending Patty to the Grave. No doubt long before this will reach you, you have received a melancholy train of Letters in some of which I mention her as dangerously sick. She has lain 5 weeks wanting a few days so bad as that we had little hopes of her Recovery; the latter part of the Time she was the most shocking object my Eyes ever beheld, and so loathsome that it was with the utmost dificulty we could bear the House. A mortification took place a week before she dyed, and renderd her a most pityable object. We have great sickness yet in the Town; she made the fourth Corpse that was this day committed to the Ground. We have many others now so bad as to dispair of their lives. But Blessed be the Father of Mercies all our family are now well, tho I have my apprehensions least the malignincy of the air in the House may have infected some of them, we have fevers of various kinds, the Throat Distemper as well as the Dysentery prevailing in this and the Neighbouring Towns.

How long o Lord shall the whole land say I am sick? O shew us wherefore it is that thou art thus contending with us? In a very perticuliar manner I have occasion to make this inquiry who have had Breach upon Breach, nor has one wound been permitted to be healed e'er it is made to Blead affresh, in six weeks I count 5 of my near connections laid in the grave. Your Aunt Simpson died at Milton about ten days ago with the Dysentery.

But the heavy stroke which most of all distresses me is my dear Mother. I cannot overcome my too selfish sorrow, all her tenderness towards me, her care and anxiety for my welfare at all times, her watchfulness over my infant years, her advice and instruction in maturer age; all, all indear her memory to me, and highten my sorrow for her loss. At the same time I know a patient submission is my duty. I will strive to obtain it! But the lenient hand of time alone can blunt the keen Edg of Sorrow. He who deignd to weep over a departed Friend, will surely forgive a sorrow which at all times desires to be bounded and restrained, by a firm Belief that a Being of infinite wisdom and unbounded Goodness, will carve out my portion in tender mercy towards me! Yea tho he slay me I will trust in him said holy Job. What tho his corrective Hand hath been streatched against me; I will not murmer. Tho earthly comforts are taken away I will not repine, he who gave them has surely a right to limit their duration, and has continued them to me much longer than I deserved. I might have been striped of my children as many others have been. I might o! forbid it Heaven, I might have been left a solitary widow.

Still I have many blessings left, many comforts to be thankfull for, and rejoice in. I am not left to mourn as one without hope.

My dear parent knew in whom she had Believed, and from the first attack of the distemper she was perswaded it would prove fatal to her. A solemnity possess'd her soul, nor could you force a smile from her till she dyed. The voilence of her disease soon weakened her so that she was unable to converse, but whenever she could speak, she testified her willingness to leave the world and an intire resignation to the Divine Will. She retaind her senses to the last moment of her Existance, and departed the World with an easy tranquility, trusting in the merits of a Redeamer. Her passage to immortality was marked with a placid smile upon her countanance, nor was there to be seen scarcly a vestage of the king of Terrors.

> "The sweet remembrance of the just
> Shall flourish when they sleep in Dust."

Tis by soothing Grief that it can be healed.

"Give Sorrow words.
The Grief that cannot speak
Whispers the o'er fraught heart and bids it Break."

Forgive me then, for thus dwelling upon a subject sweet to me, but I fear painfull to you. O how I have long'd for your Bosom to pour forth my sorrows there, and find a healing Balm, but perhaps that has been denied me that I might be led to a higher and a more permamant consolater who has bid us call upon him in the day of trouble.

As this is the first day since your absence that I could write you that we were all well, I desire to mark it with perticuliar gratitude, and humbly hope that all my warnings and corrections are not in vain.

I most thankfully received your kind favour of the 26 yesterday. It gives me much pleasure to hear of your Health. I pray Heaven for the continuance of it. I hope for the future to be able to give you more intelegance with regard to what passes out of my own little circle, but such has been my distress that I knew nothing of the political world.

You have doubtless heard of the viliny of one who has professd himself a patriot, but let not that man be trusted who can voilate private faith, and cancel solem covanants, who can leap over moral law, and laugh at christianity. How is he to be bound whom neither honour nor conscience holds?—We have here a Rumor that Rhodiland has shared the fate of Charlstown —is this the Day we read of when Satan was to be loosed?

I do not hear of any inhabitants getting out of Town. Tis said Gage is superceeded and How in his place, and that How released the prisoners from Gaoil. Tis also said tho not much credited that Burgoine is gone to Philadelphia.

I hope to hear from you soon. Adieu. Tis almost twelve o clock at Night. I have had so little Sleep that I must bid you good Night. With hearty wishes for your return I am most sincerely Your   Portia

"THE SICKNESS HAS ABATED"

To John Adams

Braintree October 21 1775

Tis ten Days since I have wrote you a line; I have received one Letter since dated 27 of Sepbr. You do not mention having heard from me altho I have wrote six Letters. I thought I should have heard oftner from you in this absence than I had ever done before, but it has been quite otherways. I never found the communication so difficult, and tis only in my Night visions that I know any thing about you.

I have now the pleasure to tell you that we are all well. Charlly has had an ill turn since I wrote, but soon got better. Mr. Thaxter and Mr. Mason are returnd to me, and my family begins again to appear as it used to. Hayden does not stir. Says he will not go out of the parish unless he is carried out—and here nobody will let him come in. I have offerd him part of the House that Field is in if he will but go out, but no where suits, and it is not to be wonderd at as he has wood at free cost and has plunderd pretty well from the family they live with many articles. I have a great mind to send a sheriff and put him out.

The sickness has abated here and in the Neighbouring Towns. In Boston I am told it is very sickly among the inhabitants and the soldiry. By a Man one Haskings who came out the day befor yesterday I learn; that there are but about 25 hundred Soldiers in Town. How many there are at Charlstown he could not tell. He had been in Irons 3 weeks, some malicious fellow having said that he saw him at the Battle of Lexinton, but he proved that he was not out of Boston that day, upon which he was releazd, and went with two other men out in a small boat under their Eye to fish. They play'd about near the shore a while catching small fish, till they thought they could possibly reach Dorchester Neck; no sooner were they perceived attempting to escape than they had 20 cannon dischargd at them, but they all happily reachd the shore. He says no Language can paint the distress of the inhabitants, most of them destitute of wood and of provisions of every kind. The Bakers say unless they have a new supply of wood they cannot bake above one fortnight longer—their Bisquit are not above one half the former size. The Soldiers are obliged to do very hard duty, and are uneasy to a great degree, many of them declareing they will not continue much longer in such a state but at all hazards will escape; the inhabitants are desperate, and contriveing means of escape. A floating Battery of ours went out two nights ago, and row'd near the Town, and then discharged their Guns. Some of the Ball went into the Work house, some through the Tents in the common, and one through the Sign of the Lamb Tavern; he says it drove them all out of the common, Men, women and children screaming, and throe'd them into the utmost distress. But very unhappily for us in the discharge of one of the cannon, the Ball not being properly ramed down one of them split and killd 2 men and wounded 7 more, upon which they were obliged to return. He also says that the Tories are much distressd about the fate of Dr. Church, and very anxious to obtain him, and would exchange Lovel for him. This Man is so exasperated at the ill usage he has received from them that he is determined to inlist immediately. They almost starved him whilst he was in Irons, he says he hopes it will be in his power to send some of them to Heaven for mercy.

They are building a fort by the Hay market and rending down houses for timber to do it with. In the course of the last week several persons have found means to escape. One of them says tis talked in Town that How will issue a proclamation giving Liberty to all who will not take up arms to depart the Town, and make it death to have any intercourse with the Country afterwards.

At present it looks as if there was no likelihoods of peace. The Ministry are determind to proceed at all events. The people are already slaves, and have neither virtue or spirit to help themselves or us. The time is hastning when Gorge like Richard may cry a kingdom a kingdom for a horse, and want even *that* wealth to make the purchase.

I hope by degrees we shall be innured to hardships and become a virtuous valient people, forgetting our formour Luxery and each one apply with industery and frugality to Manufactory and husbandery till we rival all other Nations by our Virtues.

I thank you for your amuseing account of the Quakers. Their great stress with regard to coulours in their dress &c. is not the only ridiculous part of their Sentiments with regard to Religious Matters.

> There's not a day, but, to the Man of thought,
> Betrays some secret, that throws new reproach
> on life, and makes him sick of seeing more.

What are your thoughts with regard to Dr. Church? Had you much knowledg of him? I think you had no intimate acquaintance with him.

> "A foe to God was ne'er true Friend to man
> Some sinister intent taints all he does."

It is a matter of great Speculation what will be his punishment. The people are much enraged against him. If he is set at liberty, even after he has received a severe punishment I do not think he will be safe. He will be dispised and detested by every one, and many suspisions will remain in the minds of people with regard to our rulers; they are for supposing this person is not sincere and *that* they have jealousy of.

Have you any prospect of returning. I hoped to have heard from you by the Gentlemen who came as a committe here, but they have been here a week, and I have not any Letters.

My Father and Sister Betsy desire to be rememberd to you. He is very disconsolate. It makes my heart ake to see him and I know not how to go to the House; he said to me the other day child I see your Mother, go to what part of the house I will. I think he has lost almost as much flesh as if he had been sick, and Betsy poor Girl looks broke and worne with Grief. These near connextions how they twist and cling about the Heart and when torn of draw the best Blood from it—

> "Each Friend snatchd from us is a plume
> pluck'd from the wing of Humane vanity."

Be so good as to present my Regards to Mrs. Hancoke. I hope she is very happy. Mrs. Warren call'd upon me on her Way to Watertown. I wish I could as easily come to you, as she can go to Watertown but tis my Lot. In the 12 years we have been married I believe we have not lived together more than six.

If you could with any conveniancy procure me the articles I wrote for I should be very glad, more especially the needles and cloth. They are in such demand that we are really distressd for want of them.

We have had abundance of rain since you left us. I hope the Sickness with which we have been excersised has not reach'd Philadelphia. Mr. Wibird has not been able to preach since you left us, and is in a very low state.

Our little ones are well. Tommy is so fat he can scarcly see out of his Eyes, but is still excersiced with them fits. Dr. Tufts son is sick with a slow fever. Adieu. I think of nothing further to add but that I am With the tenderest Regard your

Portia

PS Since I wrote the above I have received a Letter by Mr. Bayard for which I thank you. It gives me pleasure to find you in so good health. I have heard this Evening that a Man of War has been sent to Falmouth to make a demand of wood, upon which an express was sent of to our camp, and the express says a few hours after he set out, he heard a smart cannonade. The truth has not yet reachd us. We are anxious to hear from Canady.—If you can procure me some Carolina pink root from any of the Apothecarys I wish you would for Tommy. We think knots of worms is the occasion of his fits. I have tried worm Seed, but it has no Effect.—Write if you can to my Father and Sister. Send the news papers they are very acceptable.

BENJAMIN FRANKLIN

To John Adams

November 5 1775

I have been prevented writing you for more than a Week past by a Whitlow upon the fore finger of my right Hand. Tis now so tender that I can manage a pen but poorly.

I hope you have received several Letters from me in this fortnight past. I wrote by Mr. Linch, and by Dr. Frankling the latter of whom I had the pleasure of dining with, and of admiring him whose character from my Infancy I had been taught to venerate. I found him social, but not talkative, and when he spoke something usefull droped from his Tongue; he was grave, yet pleasant, and affable.—You know I make some pretensions to physiognomy and I thought I could read in his countanance the Virtues of his Heart, among which patriotism shined in its full Lusture—and with that is blended every virtue of a christian, for a true patriot must be a religious Man. I have been led to think from a late Defection that he who neglects his duty to his Maker, may well be expected to be deficient and insincere in his duty towards the public. Even suppose Him to possess a large share of what is called honour and publick Spirit yet do not these Men by their bad Example, by a loose immoral conduct corrupt the Minds of youth, and vitiate the Morrals of the age, and thus injure the publick more than they can compensate by intrepidity, Generosity and Honour?

Let revenge or ambition, pride, lust or profit tempt these Men to a base and vile action, you may as well hope to bind up a hungry tiger with a cobweb as to hold such debauched patriots in the visionary chains of Decency or to charm them with the intellectual Beauty of Truth and reason.

But where am I running. I mean to thank you for all your obliging favours lately received and tho some of them are very Laconick, yet were they to contain only two lines to tell me that you were well, they would be acceptable to me. I think however you are more apprehensive than you need to be. The Gentleman to whose care they have always been directed has been very kind in his conveyances and very careful. I hope however that it will not now be long before we shall have nearer interviews. You must tell me that you will return next Month. A late appointment will make it inconveniant (provided you accept) for you to go again to Congress.

The little flock in receiving pappas Letters have been more gratified than they could have been by any other present. They are very proud of being thus noticed. I am much obliged by the Sermons lately received. The Dedication of Dr. Zublys is both spirited and zealous. I was greatly pleased with it, but suppose it will be casting of pearl before Swine.

It seems Humane Nature is the same in all ages and Countrys. Ambition and avarice reign every where and where they predominate their will be bickerings after places of Honour and profit. There is an old adage kissing goes by favour that is daily verified.

I enclose to you the paper you sent for. Your Buisness in collecting facts will be very difficult, and the Sufferings of this people cannot be circumscribed with pen, ink and paper. Besides these Ministers of Satan are rendring it every day more and more difficult by their ravages and devastation, to tell a tale which will freeze the young Blood of succeeding Generations as well as harrow up the Souls of the present.

Nothing new has transpired since I wrote you last. I have not heard of one persons escaping out of Town, nor of any Manuover of any kind.

Master John is very anxious to write, but has been confined for several days with a severe cold which has given him soar Eyes, but he begs me to make his Excuse and say that he has wrote twice before, but it did not please him well enough to send it. Nabby has been with her Aunt Betsy ever since her Grandmammas Death. Charlly and Tommy beg mamma to thank pappa for their Letters, and wish they could write to tell him so. Brother and Sister Cranch send their Love. Mrs. Cranch's disorder left her soon, the Sickness has greatly abated all round us. Your Mother speaks pathetically of you, and always sends her Love to you. I will only ask you to Measure by your own the affectionate regard of Your Nearest Friend.

A NEW FORM OF GOVERNMENT

To John Adams

November 27 1775

Tis a fortnight to Night since I wrote you a line during which, I have been confined with the Jaundice, Rhumatism and a most voilent cold; I yesterday took a puke which has releived me, and I feel much better to day. Many, very many people who have had the dysentery, are now afflicted both with the Jaundice and Rhumatisim, some it has left in Hecticks, some in dropsies.

The great and incessant rains we have had this fall, (the like cannot be recollected) may have occasiond some of the present disorders. The Jaundice is very prevelant in the Camp. We have lately had a week of very cold weather, as cold as January, and a flight of snow, which I hope will purify the air of some of the noxious vapours. It has spoild many hundreds of Bushels of Apples, which were designd for cider, and which the great rains had prevented people from making up. Suppose we have lost 5 Barrels by it.

Col. Warren returnd last week to Plymouth, so that I shall not hear any thing from you till he goes back again which will not be till the last of this month.

He Damp'd my Spirits greatly by telling me that the Court had prolonged your Stay an other month. I was pleasing myself with the thoughts that you would soon be upon your return. Tis in vain to repine. I hope the publick will reap what I sacrifice.

I wish I knew what mighty things were fabricating. If a form of Goverment is to be established here what one will be assumed? Will it be left to our assemblies to chuse one? and will not many men have many minds? and shall we not run into Dissentions among ourselves?

I am more and more convinced that Man is a dangerous creature, and that power whether vested in many or a few is ever grasping, and like the grave cries give, give. The great fish swallow up the small, and he who is most strenuous for the Rights of the people, when vested with power, is as eager after the perogatives of Goverment. You tell me of degrees of perfection to which Humane Nature is capable of arriving, and I believe it, but at the same time lament that our admiration should arise from the scarcity of the instances.

The Building up a Great Empire, which was only hinted at by my correspondent may now I suppose be realized even by the unbelievers. Yet will not ten thousand Difficulties arise in the formation of it? The Reigns of Goverment have been so long slakned, that I fear the people will not quietly submit to those restraints which are necessary for the peace, and security, of the community; if we seperate from Brittain, what Code of Laws will be established. How shall we be governd so as to retain our Liberties? Can any goverment be free which is not adminstred by general stated Laws? Who shall frame these Laws? Who will give them force and energy? Tis true your Resolutions as a Body have heithertoo had the force of Laws. But will they continue to have?

When I consider these things and the prejudices of people in favour of Ancient customs and Regulations, I feel anxious for the fate of our Monarchy or Democracy or what ever is to take place. I soon get lost in a Labyrinth of perplexities, but whatever occurs, may justice and righteousness be the Stability of our times, and order arise out of confusion. Great difficulties may be surmounted, by patience and perseverance.

I believe I have tired you with politicks. As to news we have not any at all. I shudder at the approach of winter when I think I am to remain desolate. Suppose your weather is warm yet. Mr. Mason and Thaxter live with me, and render some part of my time less disconsolate. Mr. Mason is a youth who will please you, he has Spirit, taste and Sense. His application to his Studies is constant and I am much mistaken if he does not make a very good figure in his profession.

I have with me now, the only Daughter of your Brother; I feel a tenderer affection for her as she has lost a kind parent. Though too young to be sensible of her own loss, I can pitty her. She appears to be a child of a very good Disposition—only wants to be a little used to company.

Our Little ones send Duty to pappa and want much to see him. Tom says he wont come home till the Battle is over— some strange notion he has got into his head. He has got a political cread to say to him when he returns.

I must bid you good night. Tis late for one who am much of an invalide. I was dissapointed last week in receiving a packet by the post, and upon unsealing it found only four news papers. I think you are more cautious than you need be. All Letters I believe have come safe to hand. I have Sixteen from you, and wish I had as many more. Adieu. Yours.

"A MOST PAINFULL SEPERATION"

To Mercy Otis Warren

My Dear Marcia

Our Country is as it were a Secondary God, and the first and greatest parent. It is to be perferred to parents, to wives, children, Friends and all things the Gods only excepted.

These are the considerations which prevail with me to consent to a most painfull Seperation.

I have not known how to take my pen to write to you. I have been happy and unhappy. I have had many contending passions dividing my Heart, and no sooner did I find it at my own option whether my Friend should go or tarry and resign; than I found his honour and reputation much dearer to me, than my own present pleasure and happiness, and I could by no means consent to his resigning at present, as I was fully convinced he must suffer if he quitted. The Eyes of every one are more perticuliarly upon that assembly, and every motion of every member is inspected, so that he can neither be droped nor resign without creating a thousand Jealousies in the minds of the people, nor even obtain leave for a few weeks absence to visit his family, without a thousand malicious Suggestions and Suspicions—first I suppose broached by the tories and from them catchd by the Gaping multitude. All those who act in publick life have very unthankful offices and

> "will often sigh to find the unwilling Gratitude
> of base Mankind."

I believe you will think me petulant, but believe me I could fill this paper with Stories of Expulsion from Congress, loss of influence, affronts from Dickinson, deserting the cause, affraid of being hung &c. &c.

All of which are not worth regarding only as they serve to shew Humane Nature, popular favour and the Gratitude of ones Country, whilst a person is giving up to distruction all their own private concerns, depriving themselves of all the pleasures and comforts of domestick life, and exerting all the powers both of Body and Mind, and spending their lives in the Service of their Country. Thus does it reward them whilst it will hug a canting hypocrate who has been drawing out its vitals. The post of honour is a private Station. Tis certainly the most comfortable Station. Yet in these days of peril whilst the vessel is in a storm, it would be guilt in an able passenger not to lend his assistance.

Thus having run a rig and given a losse to my pen I would ask my Friend how she does? and why she does not let me hear oftner from her.

Since I wrote you last all my Little ones have had a setled fever. Johnnys was a plurisy, and he was very dangerous. I have been confined myself for more than a week; but have Recruited again. I hope you and yours are well.

You make a request, I dare not comply with. I am so apprehensive least my Letters should miscarry that unless I knew the hand by which I sent them I am affraid to write any thing which ought not to come to the publick Eye. I have many reasons to be careful of what I write as the fates if I may so express myself seem to delight in bringing into publick view private correspondencyes, and making a malicious use of very trifling circumstances. I have reason for saying this which I may one day or other explain to you.

We have not any thing new at present, tis conjectured that a Storm will e'er long succeed to the present calm. I pray heaven it may be an Efectual one. Let me hear from you soon which will much oblige your Friend,   Portia

January 1776

FORTIFICATION OF DORCHESTER HEIGHTS

To John Adams

Saturday Evening March 2
I was greatly rejoiced at the return of your servant to find you had safely arrived, and that you were well. I had never heard a word from you after you left New york, and a most ridiciolous story had been industerously propagated in this

and the neighbouring Towns to injure the cause and blast your Reputation, viz. that you and your President had gone on board a Man of War from N–y and saild for England. I should not mention so idle a report, but that it had given uneasiness to some of your Friends, not that they in the least credited the report, but because the Gaping vulgar swallowed the story. One man had deserted them and proved a traitor, an other might &c. I assure you such high Disputes took place in the publick house of this parish, that some men were collerd and draged out of the shop, with great Threats for reporting such scandelous lies, and an unkle of ours offerd his life as a forfeit for you if the report proved true.

However it has been a nine days marvel and will now cease. I heartily wish every Tory was Extirpated from America, they are continually by secret means undermineing and injuring our cause.

I am charmed with the Sentiments of Common Sense; and wonder how an honest Heart, one who wishes the welfare of their country, and the happiness of posterity can hesitate one moment at adopting them; I want to know how those Sentiments are received in Congress? I dare say their would be no difficulty in procuring a vote and instructions from all the Assemblies in New England for independancy. I most sincerely wish that now in the Lucky Minuet it might be done.

I have been kept in a continual state of anxiety and expectation ever since you left me. It has been said to morrow and to morrow for this month, but when the dreadfull to morrow will be I know not—but hark! the House this instant shakes with the roar of Cannon.—I have been to the door and find tis a cannonade from our Army, orders I find are come for all the remaining Militia to repair to the Lines a monday night by twelve o clock. No Sleep for me to Night; and if I cannot who have no guilt upon my Soul with regard to this Cause, how shall the misirible wretches who have been the procurers of this Dreadfull Scene and those who are to be the actors, lie down with the load of Guilt upon their Souls.

Sunday Eve March 3

I went to Bed after 12 but got no rest, the Cannon continued firing and my Heart Beat pace with them all night. We

have had a pretty quiet day, but what to morrow will bring
forth God only knows.

Monday Evening

Tolerable quiet to day. The Militia have all musterd with 3 days
provision and are all march'd by 8 o clock this afternoon tho their
notice was no longer than 8 o clock Saturday, and now we have
scarcly a Man but our regular guards either in Weymouth, Hingham or Braintree or Milton and the Militia from the more remote
towns are call'd in as Sea coast Guards. Can you form to yourself
an Idea of our Sensations. Palmer is chief Colonel, Bass is Leit.
Colonel and Soper Major and Hall Captain.

I have just returnd from Penn's Hill where I have been sitting to hear the amazing roar of cannon and from whence I
could see every shell which was thrown. The sound I think is
one of the Grandest in Nature and is of the true Speicies of the
Sublime. Tis now an incessant Roar. But O the fatal Ideas
which are connected with the sound. How many of our dear
country men must fall?

Twesday morning

I went to bed about 12 and rose again a little after one. I
could no more sleep than if I had been in the ingagement. The
ratling of the windows, the jar of the house and the continual
roar of 24 pounders, the Bursting of shells give us such Ideas,
and realize a scene to us of which we could scarcly form any
conception. About Six this morning, there was quiet; I rejoiced
in a few hours calm. I hear we got possession of Dorchester
Hill Last Night. 4000 thousand men upon it to day—lost but
one Man. The Ships are all drawn round the Town. To night
we shall realize a more terible scene still. I sometimes think I
cannot stand it—I wish myself with you, out of hearing as I
cannot assist them. I hope to give you joy of Boston, even if it
is in ruins before I send this away.—I am too much agitated to
write as I ought, and languid for want of rest.

Thursday Fast day

All my anxiety, and distress, is at present at an End. I feel
dissapointed. This day our Militia are all returning, without
effecting any thing more than taking possession of Dorchester

Hill. I hope it is wise and just, but from all the Muster and Stir I hoped and expected more important and decisive Scenes; I would not have sufferd all I have for two such Hills. Ever since the taking of that we have had a perfect calm nor can I learn yet what Effect it has had in Boston. I do not hear of one persons escapeing since.

I was very much pleased with your choise of a committe for Canada. All those to whom I have venturd to shew that part of your Letter approve the Scheme of the Priest as a master stroke of policy. I feel sorry that General Lee has left us, but his presence at New York was no doubt of great importance as we have reason to think it prevented Clinton from landing and gathering together such a nest of virmin as would at least have distressd us greatly. But how can you spair him from there? Can you make his place good—can you supply it with a man eaquelly qualified to save us? How do the Virginians realish the Troops said to be destined for them? Are they putting themselves into a State of Defence? I inclose to you a Coppy of a Letter sent by Capt. Furnance who is in Mr. Ned Churchs imploy and who came into the Cape about 10 days ago. You will learn the Sentiments of our Cousin by it, some of which may be true, but I hope he is a much better divine than politician.

I hear in one of his Letters he mentions certain intercepted Letters which he says have made much Noise in England, and Laments that you ever wrote them.

What will he and others say to Common Sense? I cannot Bear to think of your continuing in a State of Supineness this winter.

> "There is a tide in the affairs of Men
> Which taken, at the flood leads on to fortune;
> omitted, all the voyage of their life
> is bound in shallows and in miseries.
> On such a full sea are we now afloat;
> And we must take the current when it serves,
> or lose our ventures."
>
> Shakespear

Sunday Eve March 10

I had scarcly finished these lines when my Ears were again assaulted with the roar of Cannon. I could not write any further. My Hand and heart will tremble, at this domestick fury, and firce civil Strife, which cumber all our parts. Tho,

> Blood and destruction are so much in use
> And Dreadfull objects so familiar,

Yet is not pitty chok'd, nor my Heart grown Callous. I feel for the unhappy wretches who know not where to fly for safety. I feel still more for my Bleading Country men who are hazarding their lives and their Limbs.—A most Terible and incessant Cannonade from half after 8 till Six this morning. I hear we lost four men kill'd and some wounded in attempting to take the Hill nearest the Town call'd Nook Hill. We did some work, but the fire from the ships Beat off our Men so that they did not secure it but retired to the fort upon the other Hill.

I have not got all the perticuliars I wish I had but, as I have an opportunity of sending this I shall endeavour to be more perticuliar in my next.

All our Little ones send duty. Tommy has been very sick with what is call'd the Scarlet or purple fever, but has got about again.

If we have no Reinforcements here, I believe we shall be driven from the sea coast, but in what so ever state I am I will endeavour to be therewith content.

> Man wants but Little here below
> Nor wants that Little long.

You will escuse this very incorrect Letter. You see in what purtubation it has been written and how many times I have left of. Adieu pray write me every opportunity. Yours.

Tooks Grammer is the one you mention.

March 1776

END OF THE SIEGE OF BOSTON

To John Adams

Braintree March 16 1776
I last Evening Received yours of March 8. I must confess my

self in fault that I did not write sooner to you, but I was in continual Expectation that some important event would take place and give me a subject worth writing upon. Before this reaches you I immagine you will have Received two Letters from me; the last I closed this Day week; since that time there has been some movements amongst the Ministerial Troops as if they meant to evacuate the Town of Boston. Between 70 and 80 vessels of various sizes are gone down and lay in a row in fair sight of this place, all of which appear to be loaded and by what can be collected from our own observations and from deserters they have been plundering the Town. I have been very faithless with regard to their quitting Boston, and know not how to account for it, nor am I yet satisfied that they will leave it—tho it seems to be the prevailing opinion of most people; we are obliged to place the Militia upon Gaurd every Night upon the shoars thro fear of an invasion. There has been no firing since Last tweseday, till about 12 o clock last Night, when I was waked out of my sleep with a smart Cannonade which continued till nine o clock this morning, and prevented any further repose for me; the occasion I have not yet heard, but before I close this Letter I may be able to give you some account of it.

By the accounts in the publick papers the plot thickens; and some very important Crisis seems near at hand. Perhaps providence see's it necessary in order to answer important ends and designs that the Seat of War should be changed from this to the Southeren colonies that each may have a proper sympathy for the other, and unite in a seperation. The Refuge of the Believer amidst all the afflictive dispensations of providence, is that the Lord Reigneth, and that he can restrain the Arm of Man.

Orders are given to our Army to hold themselves in readiness to March at a moments warning. I'll meet you at Philippi said the Ghost of Caesar to Brutus.

Sunday Noon

Being quite sick with a voilent cold I have tarried at Home to day; I find the fireing was occasiond by our peoples taking possession of Nook Hill, which they kept in spite of the Cannonade, and which has really obliged our Enemy to decamp this morning on board the Transports; as I hear by a mesenger just come from Head Quarters. Some of the Select Men have been to the lines and inform that they have carried of every thing they could possibly take, and what they could not they have burnt, broke, or hove into the water. This is I believe fact, many articles of good Household furniture having in the course of the week come on shore at Great Hill, both upon this and Weymouth Side, Lids of Desks, mahogona chairs, tables &c. Our People I hear will have Liberty to enter Boston, those who have had the small pox. The Enemy have not yet come under sail. I cannot help suspecting some design which we do not yet comprehend; to what quarter of the World they are bound is wholy unknown, but tis generally Thought to New york. Many people are elated with their quitting Boston. I confess I do not feel so, tis only lifting the burden from one shoulder to the other which perhaps is less able or less willing to support it.—To what a contemptable situation are the Troops of Britain reduced! I feel glad however that Boston is not distroyed. I hope it will be so secured and guarded as to baffel all future attempts against it.—I hear that General How said upon going upon some Eminence in Town to view our Troops who had taken Dorchester Hill unperceived by them till sun rise, "My God these fellows have done more work in one night than I could make my Army do in three months" and he might well say so for in one night two forts and long Breast Works were sprung up besides several Barracks. 300 & 70 teems were imployed most of which went 3 load in the night, beside 4000 men who worked with good Hearts.

From Pens Hill we have a view of the largest Fleet ever seen in America. You may count upwards of 100 & 70 Sail. They look like a Forrest. It was very lucky for us that we got possession of Nook Hill. They had placed their cannon so as to fire upon the Top of the Hill where they had observed our people marking out the Ground, but it was only to elude them for they began lower upon the Hill and nearer the Town. It was a very foggy dark evening and they had possession of the Hill six hours before a gun was fired, and when they did fire they over shot our people so that they were coverd before morning and not one man lost, which the enemy no sooner discoverd than Bunker Hill was abandoned and every Man decamp'd as soon

as he could for they found they should not be able to get away
if we once got our cannon mounted. Our General may say
with Ceasar veni vidi et vici.

What Effect does the Expectation of commisioners have with
you? Are they held in disdain as they are here. It is come to that
pass now that the longest sword must deside the contest—and
the sword is less dreaded here than the commisioners.

You mention Threats upon Braintree. I know of none, nor
ever heard of any till you mentiond them. The Tories look a
little crest fallen; as for Cleverly he looks like the knight of the
woful countanance. I hear all the Mongrel Breed are left in
Boston—and our people who were prisoners are put into Irons
and carried of.

As to all your own private affairs I generally avoid mentioning them to you; I take the best care I am capable of them. I
have found some difficulty attending the only Man I have
upon the place, being so often taking of. John and Jonathan
have taken all the care in his absence, and performed very well.
Bass got home very well. My Fathers horse came home in fine
order and much to his satisfaction. Your own very poor.—
Cannot you hire a Servant where you are. I am sorry you are
put to so much difficulty for want of one.—I suppose you do
not think one word about comeing home, and how you will
get home I know not.

I made a mistake in the Name of the Grammer—tis Tandons, instead of Took. I wish you could purchase Lord Chesterfields Letters—I have lately heard them very highly spoken
of. I smiled at your couplet of Lattin, your Daughter may be
able in time to conster it as she has already made some considerable proficiency in her accidents, but her Mamma was obliged
to get it translated.

Pray write Lord Sterlings character. I want to know whether
you live in any harmony with ———— and how you setled
matters. I think he seems in better humour.

I think I do not admire the Speach from the Rostrum, tis a
heavy unelegant, verbose performance and did not strike my
fancy at all. I am very sausy suppose you will say. Tis a Liberty
I take with you; indulgance is apt to spoil one. Adieu—Yours
most Sincerely.

PS Pray convey me a little paper. I have but enough for one Letter more.

Monday morning
A fine quiet night—no allarms no Cannon. The more I think of our Enemies quitting Boston, the more amaz'd I am, that they should leave such a harbour, such fortifications, such intrenchments, and that we should be in peaceable possession of a Town which we expected would cost us a river of Blood without one Drop shed. Shurely it is the Lords doings and it is Marvelous in our Eyes. Every foot of Ground which they obtain now they must fight for, and may they purchase it at a Bunker Hill price.

"REMEMBER THE LADIES"

To John Adams

Braintree March 31 1776
I wish you would ever write me a Letter half as long as I write you; and tell me if you may where your Fleet are gone? What sort of Defence Virginia can make against our common Enemy? Whether it is so situated as to make an able Defence? Are not the Gentery Lords and the common people vassals, are they not like the uncivilized Natives Brittain represents us to be? I hope their Riffel Men who have shewen themselves very savage and even Blood thirsty; are not a specimen of the Generality of the people.

I am willing to allow the Colony great merit for having produced a Washington but they have been shamefully duped by a Dunmore.

I have sometimes been ready to think that the passion for Liberty cannot be Eaquelly Strong in the Breasts of those who have been accustomed to deprive their fellow Creatures of theirs. Of this I am certain that it is not founded upon that generous and christian principal of doing to others as we would that others should do unto us.

Do not you want to see Boston; I am fearfull of the small

pox, or I should have been in before this time. I got Mr. Crane to go to our House and see what state it was in. I find it has been occupied by one of the Doctors of a Regiment, very dirty, but no other damage has been done to it. The few things which were left in it are all gone. Crane has the key which he never deliverd up. I have wrote to him for it and am determined to get it cleand as soon as possible and shut it up. I look upon it a new acquisition of property, a property which one month ago I did not value at a single Shilling, and could with pleasure have seen it in flames.

The Town in General is left in a better state than we expected, more oweing to a percipitate flight than any Regard to the inhabitants, tho some individuals discoverd a sense of honour and justice and have left the rent of the Houses in which they were, for the owners and the furniture unhurt, or if damaged sufficent to make it good.

Others have committed abominable Ravages. The Mansion House of your President is safe and the furniture unhurt whilst both the House and Furniture of the Solisiter General have fallen a prey to their own merciless party. Surely the very Fiends feel a Reverential awe for Virtue and patriotism, whilst they Detest the paricide and traitor.

I feel very differently at the approach of spring to what I did a month ago. We knew not then whether we could plant or sow with safety, whether when we had toild we could reap the fruits of our own industery, whether we could rest in our own Cottages, or whether we should not be driven from the sea coasts to seek shelter in the wilderness, but now we feel as if we might sit under our own vine and eat the good of the land.

I feel a gaieti de Coar to which before I was a stranger. I think the Sun looks brighter, the Birds sing more melodiously, and Nature puts on a more chearfull countanance. We feel a temporary peace, and the poor fugitives are returning to their deserted habitations.

Tho we felicitate ourselves, we sympathize with those who are trembling least the Lot of Boston should be theirs. But they cannot be in similar circumstances unless pusilanimity and cowardise should take possession of them. They have time and warning given them to see the Evil and shun it.—I long to hear that you have declared an independancy—and by the way in the new Code of Laws which I suppose it will be necessary for you to make I desire you would Remember the Ladies, and be more generous and favourable to them than your ancestors. Do not put such unlimited power into the hands of the Husbands. Remember all Men would be tyrants if they could. If perticuliar care and attention is not paid to the Laidies we are determined to foment a Rebelion, and will not hold ourselves bound by any Laws in which we have no voice, or Representation.

That your Sex are Naturally Tyrannical is a Truth so thoroughly established as to admit of no dispute, but such of you as wish to be happy willingly give up the harsh title of Master for the more tender and endearing one of Friend. Why then, not put it out of the power of the vicious and the Lawless to use us with cruelty and indignity with impunity. Men of Sense in all Ages abhor those customs which treat us only as the vassals of your Sex. Regard us then as Beings placed by providence under your protection and in immitation of the Supreem Being make use of that power only for our happiness.

April 5

Not having an opportunity of sending this I shall add a few lines more; tho not with a heart so gay. I have been attending the sick chamber of our Neighbour Trot whose affliction I most sensibly feel but cannot discribe, striped of two lovely children in one week. Gorge the Eldest died on wedensday and Billy the youngest on fryday, with the Canker fever, a terible disorder so much like the throat distemper, that it differs but little from it. Betsy Cranch has been very bad, but upon the recovery. Becky Peck they do not expect will live out the day. Many grown persons are now sick with it, in this [   ] 5. It rages much in other Towns. The Mumps too are very frequent. Isaac is now confined with it. Our own little flock are yet well. My Heart trembles with anxiety for them. God preserve them.

I want to hear much oftener from you than I do. March 8 was the last date of any that I have yet had.—You inquire of whether I am making Salt peter. I have not yet attempted it, but after Soap making believe I shall make the experiment. I find as much as I can do to manufacture cloathing for my family which would else be Naked. I know of but one person in this part of the Town who has made any, that is Mr. Tertias Bass as he is calld who has got very near an hundred weight which has been found to be very good. I have heard of some others in the other parishes. Mr. Reed of Weymouth has been applied to, to go to Andover to the mills which are now at work, and has gone. I have lately seen a small Manuscrip describing the proportions for the various sorts of powder, fit for cannon, small arms and pistols. If it would be of any Service your way I will get it transcribed and send it to you.—Every one of your Friends send their Regards, and all the little ones. Your Brothers youngest child lies bad with convulsion fitts. Adieu. I need not say how much I am Your ever faithfull Friend.

"A LIST OF FEMALE GRIEVANCES"

To Mercy Otis Warren

Braintree April 27 1776

I set myself down to comply with my Friends request, who I think seem's rather low spiritted.

I did write last week, but not meeting with an early conveyance I thought the Letter of But little importance and tos'd it away. I acknowledg my Thanks due to my Friend for the entertainment she so kindly afforded me in the Characters drawn in her Last Letter, and if coveting my Neighbours Goods was not prohibited by the Sacred Law, I should be most certainly tempted to envy her the happy talant she possesses above the rest of her Sex, by adorning with her pen even trivial occurances, as well as dignifying the most important. Cannot you communicate some of those Graces to your Friend and suffer her to pass them upon the World for her own that she may feel a little more upon an Eaquality with you?—Tis true I often receive large packages from Philadelphia. They contain as I said before more News papers than Letters, tho they are not forgotton. It would be hard indeed if absence had not some alleviations.

I dare say he writes to no one unless to Portia oftner than to your Friend, because I know there is no one besides in whom he has an eaquel confidence. His Letters to me have been generally short, but he pleads in Excuse the critical state of affairs and the Multiplicity of avocations and says further that he has been very Busy, and writ near ten Sheets of paper, about some affairs which he does not chuse to Mention for fear of accident.

He is very sausy to me in return for a List of Female Grievances which I transmitted to him. I think I will get you to join me in a petition to Congress. I thought it was very probable our wise Statesmen would erect a New Goverment and form a new code of Laws. I ventured to speak a word in behalf of our Sex, who are rather hardly dealt with by the Laws of England which gives such unlimitted power to the Husband to use his wife Ill.

I requested that our Legislators would consider our case and as all Men of Delicacy and Sentiment are averse to Excercising the power they possess, yet as there is a natural propensity in Humane Nature to domination, I thought the most generous plan was to put it out of the power of the Arbitary and tyranick to injure us with impunity by Establishing some Laws in our favour upon just and Liberal principals.

I believe I even threatned fomenting a Rebellion in case we were not considerd, and assured him we would not hold ourselves bound by any Laws in which we had neither a voice, nor representation.

In return he tells me he cannot but Laugh at My Extrodonary Code of Laws. That he had heard their Struggle had loosned the bands of Goverment, that children and apprentices were dissabedient, that Schools and Colledges were grown turbulant, that Indians slighted their Guardians, and Negroes grew insolent to their Masters. But my Letter was the first intimation that another Tribe more numerous and powerfull than all the rest were grown discontented. This is rather too coarse a complement, he adds, but that I am so sausy he wont blot it out.

So I have help'd the Sex abundantly, but I will tell him I have only been making trial of the Disintresstedness of his Virtue, and when weigh'd in the balance have found it wanting.

It would be bad policy to grant us greater power say they since under all the disadvantages we Labour we have the assendancy over their Hearts

And charm by accepting, by submitting sway.

I wonder Apollo and the Muses could not have indulged me with a poetical Genious. I have always been a votary to her charms but never could assend Parnassus myself.

I am very sorry to hear of the indisposition of your Friend. I am affraid it will hasten his return, and I do not think he can be spaired.

> "Though certain pains attend the cares of State
> A Good Man owes his Country to be great
> Should act abroad the high distinguishd part
> or shew at least the purpose of his heart."

Good Night my Friend. You will be so good as to remember me to our worthy Friend Mrs. W————e when you see her and write soon to your   Portia

VISIT TO A WARSHIP

To John Adams

Plimouth June 17 a remarkable Day

I this day Received by the Hands of our Worthy Friend a large packet, which has refreshed and comforted me. Your own sensations have ever been similar to mine. I need not then tell you how gratified I am at the frequent tokens of remembrance with which you favour me, nor how they rouse every tender sensation of my Soul, which sometimes find vent at my Eyes nor dare I discribe how earnestly I long to fold to my fluttering Heart the dear object of my warmest affections. The Idea sooths me, I feast upon it with a pleasure known only to those whose Hearts and hopes are one.

The approbation you give to my conduct in the Management of our private affairs is very gratefull to me and sufficently compensates, for all my anxieties, and endeavours to discharge the many duties devolved upon me in consequence of the absence of my dearest Friend. Were they discharged eaquel to my wishes I should merrit the praises you bestow.

You see I date from Plimouth. Here I came upon a visit to our amiable Friends accompanied by My Sister Betsy a day or two ago, and is the first night I have been absent since you left me. Having determined upon this visit for some time, I put my Family in order and prepaird for it, thinking I might leave it with safety. Yet the day I set out I was under many apprehensions by the comeing in of ten Transports who were seen to have many Soldiers on board, and the determination of the people to go and fortify upon Long Island, Peticks Island, Nantasket and Great Hill. It was apprehended they would attempt to land some where, but the next morning I had the pleasure to hear they were all driven out, Commodore and all. Not a Transport, a Ship or a tender to be seen. This shews what might have been long ago done. Had this been done in season the ten Transports with many others in all probability would have fallen into our Hands, but the progress of wisdom is slow.

Since I arrived here, I have really had a scene quite novel to me. The Brig Defence from Connecticut put in here for Balist. The officers who are all from thence and who were intimately acquainted at Dr. Lorthropes, invited his Lady to come on board and bring with her as many of her Friends as she could collect. She sent an invitation to our Friend Mrs. Warren and to us. The brig lay about a mile and half from the Town, the officers sent their Barge and we went, every mark of Respect and attention which was in their power, they shewd us. She is a fine Brigg, Mounts 16 Guns, 12 Swivells and carries 100 & 20 men. 100 & seventeen were on board; and no private family ever appeard under better Regulation than the Crew. It was as still as tho there had been only half a dozen, not a prophane word among any of them. The Captain himself is an exemplary Man, Harden his name, has been in nine Sea engagements, says if he gets a Man who swears and finds he cannot reform him he turns him on shoar, Yet is free to confess that it was the sin of his youth. He has one lieutenant a very fine fellow, Smelden by name. We spent a very agreable afternoon and drank tea on board, they shew'd us their Arms which were sent

by Queen Ann, and every thing on board was a curiosity to
me. They gave us a mock engagement with an Enemy, and the
manner of taking a ship. The young folks went upon Quarter
deck and danced. Some of their Jacks played very well upon
the voilene and German flute. The Brig bears the continental
Colours and was fitted out by the Colony of Connecticut. As
we set of from the Brig they fired their Guns in honour to us,
a ceremony I would have very readily dispenced with.

I pitty you and feel for you under all the difficulties you have
to encounter. My daily petitions to Heaven for you, are, that
you may have Health, Wisdom and fortitude sufficent to carry
you thro the great, and arduous Buisness in which you are engaged; and that your endeavours may be crownd with success.
—Canady seems a dangerous and ill fated place. It is reported
here that General Thomas is no more, that he took the small
pox and died with it. Every day some circumstance arises and
shews me the importance of having that distemper in youth.
Dr. Bulfinch has petitiond the General Court for leave to
open a Hospital some where, and it will be granted him. I shall
with all the children be one of the first class you may depend
upon it.

I have just this moment heard that the Brig on which I was
on board a Saturday and which saild yesterday morning from
this place fell in with two Transports having each of them a
100 & 50 Men on board and took them and has brought them
into Nantasket road, under cover of the Guns which are
mounted there. Will add further perticuliars as soon as I am
informd.

I am now better informd and can give you the Truth. The
Brig Defence, accompanied by a smaller privateer saild in concert a Sunday morning. About 12 o clock they discoverd two
Transports, and made for them. Two privateers who were
small had been in chase of them, but finding the enemy were
of much larger force; had run under Cohasat Rocks. The Defence gave a Signal Gun to bring them out. Capt. Burk who
accompanied the Defence being a prime Sailor came up first
and pourd a Broad Side on board a 16 Gun Brig. The Defence
soon attack'd her upon her Bows, an obstinate engagement
ensued, their was a continual Blaze upon all sides for many
Hours and it was near mid Night before they struck. In the

engagement the Defence lost one Man and 5 wounded. On board Burk not one Man received any damage. On board the enemy 14 killd among whom was a Major and 60 wounded. They are part of the Hiland Soldiers. The other Transport mounted 6 Guns. When the Fleet saild out of this Harbour last week they blew up the light House. They met 6 Transports comeing in which they carried of with them. Hope we shall soon be in such a posture of defence as to bid them defiance.

I feel no great anxiety at the large armyment designd against us. The remarkable interpositions of Heaven in our favour cannot be too gratefully acknowledged. He who fed the Isralites in the wilderness, who cloaths the lilies of the Field and feeds the young Ravens when they cry, will not forsake a people engaged in so righteous cause if we remember his Loving kindness.

We wanted powder, we have a Supply. We wanted guns, we have been favour in that respect. We wanted hard money, 22000 Dollors and an Eaquel value of plate are deliverd into our Hands.

You mention your peas, your cherries, your strawberries &c. Ours are but just in Blosome. We have had the coldest Spring I ever knew, things are 3 weeks back of what they generally used to be. The corn looks poor, the season now is rather dry.—Our Friend has Refused his appointment. I am very sorry. I said every thing I could think to persuaid him, but his Lady was against it. I need say no more.—I believe I did not understand you when in a former Letter you say, "I want to resign my office for a thousand reasons." If you meant that of judge I know not what to say. I know it will be a dificult and arduous station but divesting my self of private intrest which would lead me to be against your holding that office, I know of no person who is so well calculated to discharge the Trust, or who I think would act a more consciencious part.

My paper is full. I have only room to thank you for it.

June 17, 1776

THE DECLARATION OF INDEPENDENCE

To John Adams

Boston July 13 1776

I must begin with apoligising to you for not writing since the 17 of June. I have really had so many cares upon my Hands and Mind, with a bad inflamation in my Eyes that I have not been able to write. I now date from Boston where I yesterday arrived and was with all 4 of our Little ones innoculated for the small pox. My unkle and Aunt were so kind as to send me an invitation with my family. Mr. Cranch and wife and family, My Sister Betsy and her Little Neice, Cotton Tufts and Mr. Thaxter, a maid who has had the Distemper and my old Nurse compose our family. A Boy too I should have added. 17 in all. My unkles maid with his Little daughter and a Negro Man are here. We had our Bedding &c. to bring. A Cow we have driven down from Braintree and some Hay I have had put into the Stable, wood &c. and we have really commenced housekeepers here. The House was furnished with almost every article (except Beds) which we have free use of, and think ourselves much obliged by the fine accommodations and kind offer of our Friends. All our necessary Stores we purchase jointly. Our Little ones stood the opperation Manfully. Dr. Bulfinch is our Physician. Such a Spirit of innoculation never before took place; the Town and every House in it, are as full as they can hold. I believe there are not less than 30 persons from Braintree. Mrs. Quincy, Mrs. Lincoln, Miss Betsy and Nancy are our near Neighbours. God Grant that we may all go comfortably thro the Distemper, the phisick part is bad enough I know. I knew your mind so perfectly upon the subject that I thought nothing, but our recovery would give you eaquel pleasure, and as to safety there was none. The Soldiers innoculated privately, so did many of the inhabitants and the paper curency spread it everywhere. I immediately determined to set myself about it, and get ready with my children. I wish it was so you could have been with us, but I submit.

I received some Letters from you last Saturday Night 26 of June. You mention a Letter of the 16 which I have never received, and I suppose must relate something to private affairs which I wrote about in May and sent by Harry.

As to News we have taken several fine prizes since I wrote you as you will see by the news papers. The present Report is of Lord Hows comeing with unlimited powers. However suppose it is so, I believe he little thinks of treating with us as independant States. How can any person yet dreem of a settlement, accommodations &c. They have neither the spirit nor feeling of Men, yet I see some who never were call'd Tories, gratified with the Idea of Lord Hows being upon his passage with such powers.

Sunday july 14

By yesterdays post I received two Letters dated 3 and 4 of July and tho your Letters never fail to give me pleasure, be the subject what it will, yet it was greatly heightned by the prospect of the future happiness and glory of our Country; nor am I a little Gratified when I reflect that a person so nearly connected with me has had the Honour of being a principal actor, in laying a foundation for its future Greatness. May the foundation of our new constitution, be justice, Truth and Righteousness. Like the wise Mans house may it be founded upon those Rocks and then neither storms or temptests will overthrow it.

I cannot but feel sorry that some of the most Manly Sentiments in the Declaration are Expunged from the printed coppy. Perhaps wise reasons induced it.

Poor Canady I lament Canady but we ought to be in some measure sufferers for the past folly of our conduct. The fatal effects of the small pox there, has led almost every person to consent to Hospitals in every Town. In many Towns, already arround Boston the Selectmen have granted Liberty for innoculation. I hope the necessity is now fully seen.

I had many dissagreable Sensations at the Thoughts of comeing myself, but to see my children thro it I thought my duty, and all those feelings vanished as soon as I was innoculated and I trust a kind providence will carry me safely thro. Our Friends from Plymouth came into Town yesterday. We have enough upon our hands in the morning. The Little folks are very sick then and puke every morning but after that they

are comfortable. I shall write you now very often. Pray inform
me constantly of every important transaction. Every expression
of tenderness is a cordial to my Heart. Unimportant as they
are to the rest of the world, to me they are *every Thing*.

We have had during all the month of June a most severe
Drougth which cut of all our promising hopes of english Grain
and the first crop of Grass, but since july came in we have had
a plenty of rain and now every thing looks well. There is one
Misfortune in our family which I have never mentiond in
hopes it would have been in my power to have remedied it,
but all hopes of that kind are at an end. It is the loss of your
Grey Horse. About 2 months ago, I had occasion to send
Jonathan of an errant to my unkle Quincys (the other Horse
being a plowing). Upon his return a little below the church
she trod upon a rolling stone and lamed herself to that degree
that it was with great difficulty that she could be got home. I
immediately sent for Tirrel and every thing was done for her
by Baths, ointments, politiceing, Bleeding &c. that could be
done. Still she continued extreem lame tho not so bad as at
first. I then got her carried to Domet but he pronounces her
incurable, as a callous is grown upon her footlock joint. You
can hardly tell, not even by your own feelings how much I
lament her. She was not with foal, as you immagined, but I
hope she is now as care has been taken in that Respect.

I suppose you have heard of a fleet which came up pretty
near the Light and kept us all with our mouths open ready to
catch them, but after staying near a week and makeing what
observations they could set sail and went of to our great mortification who were [   ] for them in every respect. If our
Ship of 32 Guns which was Built at Portsmouth and waiting
only for Guns and an other of [   ] at Plimouth in the same
state, had been in readiness we should in all probability been
Masters of them. Where the blame lies in that respect I know
not, tis laid upon Congress, and Congress is also blamed for
not appointing us a General.—But Rome was not Built in a
day.

I hope the Multiplicity of cares and avocations which invel-
lope you will not be too powerfull for you. I have many anxietyes upon that account. Nabby and Johnny send duty and
desire Mamma to say that an inflamation in their Eyes which

has been as much of a distemper as the small pox, has prevented their writing, but they hope soon to be able to acquaint Pappa of their happy recovery from the Distemper.—Mr. Cranch and wife, Sister Betsy and all our Friends desire to be rememberd to you and foremost in that Number stands your

Portia

PS   A little India herb would have been mighty agreable now.

THE DECLARATION READ IN BOSTON

To John Adams

July 21 1776 Boston

I have no doubt but that my dearest Friend is anxious to know how his Portia does, and his little flock of children under the opperation of a disease once so formidable.

I have the pleasure to tell him that they are all comfortable tho some of them complaining. Nabby has been very ill, but the Eruption begins to make its appeerence upon her, and upon Johnny. Tommy is so well that the Dr. innoculated him again to day fearing it had not taken. Charlly has no complaints yet, tho his arm has been very soar.

I have been out to meeting this forenoon, but have so many dissagreable Sensations this afternoon that I thought it prudent to tarry at home. The Dr. says they are very good feelings. Mr. Cranch has passed thro the preparation and the Eruption is comeing out cleverly upon him without any Sickness at all. Mrs. Cranch is cleverly and so are all her children. Those who are broke out are pretty full for the new method as tis call'd, the Suttonian they profess to practice upon. I hope to give you a good account when I write next, but our Eyes are very weak and the Dr. is not fond of either writing or reading for his patients. But I must transgress a little.

I received a Letter from you by wedensday Post 7 of July and tho I think it a choise one in the Litterary Way, containing many usefull hints and judicious observations which will greatly assist me in the future instruction of our Little ones, yet it Lacked some essential engrediants to make it compleat. Not one word respecting yourself, your Health or your present Situation. My anxiety for your welfare will never leave me but with my parting Breath, tis of more importance to me than all this World contains besides. The cruel Seperation to which I am necessatated cuts of half the enjoyments of life, the other half are comprised in the hope I have that what I do and what I suffer may be serviceable to you, to our Little ones and our Country; I must beseach you therefore for the future never to omit what is so essential to my happiness.

Last Thursday after hearing a very Good Sermon I went with the Multitude into Kings Street to hear the proclamation for independance read and proclamed. Some Field peices with the Train were brought there, the troops appeard under Arms and all the inhabitants assembled there (the small pox prevented many thousand from the Country). When Col. Crafts read from the Belcona of the State House the Proclamation, great attention was given to every word. As soon as he ended, the cry from the Belcona, was God Save our American States and then 3 cheers which rended the air, the Bells rang, the privateers fired, the forts and Batteries, the cannon were discharged, the platoons followed and every face appeard joyfull. Mr. Bowdoin then gave a Sentiment, Stability and perpetuity to American independance. After dinner the kings arms were taken down from the State House and every vestage of him from every place in which it appeard and burnt in King Street. Thus ends royall Authority in this State, and all the people shall say Amen.

I have been a little surprized that we collect no better accounts with regard to the horrid conspiricy at New York, and that so little mention has been made of it here. It made a talk for a few days but now seems all hushed in Silence. The Tories say that it was not a conspiricy but an association, and pretend that there was no plot to assasinate the General. Even their hardned Hearts feel ———— the discovery. We have in Gorge a match for a Borgia and a Catiline, a Wretch Callous to every Humane feeling. Our worthy preacher told us that he believed

one of our Great Sins for which a righteous God has come out
in judgment against us, was our Biggoted attachment to so
wicked a Man. May our repentance be sincere.

Monday morg. july 22

I omitted many things yesterday in order to be better informed. I have got Mr. Cranch to inquire and write you, concerning a French Schooner from Martineco which came in
yesterday and a prize from Ireland. My own infirmities prevents
my writing. A most Excruciating pain in my head and every
Limb and joint I hope portends a speedy Eruption and prevents my saying more than that I am forever Yours.

The children are not yet broke out. Tis the Eleventh Day
with us.

"GOD BLESS THE UNITED STATES OF AMERICA"

To John Adams

Boston August 14 1776

Mr. Smith call'd upon me to day and told me he should set
out tomorrow for Philadelphia, desired I would write by him.
I have shewn him all the civility in my power since he has been
here, tho not all I have wished too. Our Situation and numerous family as well as sick family prevented our asking him to
dine. He drank tea with us once and Breakfasted once with us.
I was much pleasd with the account he gave us of the universal
joy of his province upon the Establishment of their New Government, and of the Harmony subsisting between every branch
of it. This State seems to be behind hand of their Neighbours.
We want some Master workmen here. Those who are capable
seem backward in this work and some who are so tenacious of
their own perticuliar plan as to be loth to give it up. Some who
are for abolishing both House and Counsel, affirming Buisness
was never so well done as in provincial Congress, and they
perhaps never so important.

Last Sunday after Service the Declaration of Independance
was read from the pulpit by order of Counsel. The Dr. con-

cluded with asking a Blessing upon the united States of America even untill the final restitution of all things. Dr. Chancys address pleasd me. The Good Man after having read it, lifted his Eyes and hands to Heaven—God Bless the united States of America, and Let all the People say Amen. One of His Audiance told me it universally struck them.

I have no News to write you, I am sure it will be none to tell you that I am ever yours,   Portia

SAFELY INOCULATED FOR SMALLPOX

To John Adams

My Dearest Friend   August 31 1776
You know not How dissapointed I was to Night when the Post came in and I received no Letter from You. Tis the first Saturdays post which has come in since I have been in Town without a Letter from you. It has given me more pain to Night than it would any other time, because of some Falce and foolish reports I hope.

I will not, more than I can help, give way to rumours which I have no reason to believe true. Yet at such a time as this when all the Malice of Satan has possessd our foes, when they have recourse to secret poison, assassanation and every wicked art that Hell can Musture, I own my self allarmd and my fears sometimes overpower me.

But I commit you to the great Gaurdian and protecter of the just, and trust in him that we shall meet and rejoice together, in spight of all the Malice of Earth and Hell.

I hope before this time that Bass has arrived with your Horses, and that you are prepairing to return to your own State. How anxiously do I expect you. On Monday I return to my own habitation with our Little Charles who is weak and feeble, and who wants the air and excercise of the Country to restore him. The Little flock have all left me but Him. Mrs. Cranch came into Town yesterday and carried out Nabby and Tommy, the Dr. would not consent to Charles going till Monday. His are but just cleverly turnd. Your

Worthy Parent mett them, Mrs. Cranch writes me, upon their return and weept for joy to see them again. I have often pittied her anxiety which I know has been great upon this occasion. My own dear Mother is saved all she would have felt. My Unkle Quincy has been a parent to us, with us every week, anxious to the greatest Degree about you, solisitious about your return, declared he would sit of for you himself if Bass would not come immediately.

Mr. A did not get here till the 27 of the month, not till I had engaged your Horses and they were ready to come away.

In the Letter by Him you say you wonder whether the General Court have thought of doing any thing for you, at which I was a Little surprizd.

When I was at Plymouth Coll. Warren mentiond some accounts which were left with Him upon which a committe was orderd but he never got them to do any thing. Said Cushing had got all His setled and he reminded them of that, but nothing had been done. He further said that a Member from Road Island wrote to Him to know what was given to the Delegates here and he asked C———g who told him that they were allowd 12s. pr. day and their expences. 18 was allowd at Road Island to theirs. I replied that it must be something which had been lately done for I knew nothing of it. He said no he understood C———g that it had been allowed from the first, that is from last April twelve month. I however believed that you had never Received any thing more than your expences tho I could not absolutely say.

This I know they will be very willing you should Labour for them as long as your Health and Strength will last, and when they are intirely exausted you may provide for yourself and family as you can.

September 2. 1776

This is a Beautifull Morning. I see it with joy, and I hope thankfullness. I came here with all my treasure of children, have passd thro one of the most terible Diseases to which humane Nature is subject, and not one of us is wanting. I should go home with a much lighter Heart if I had heard from you. I wish you would not miss a Post whilst you tarry tho you write no more than that you are well.

In the Course of the week past we have had many reports of Battles at New York, none of which gain credit. An other peice of Trechery is come to light and as it is in the Military way I hope an Example will be made of the Wretch. What Blindness, what infatuation to suffer the Mayor of the city after having proved himself such a rascel and villan to go at large. To err upon the Leniant Hand is best no doubt, but to suffer such crimes to go unpunished is offensive in the sight of Heaven I doubt not.

Little Charles stands by and sends Duty to Pappa, says Mamma did you get any Letters a Saturday? No. Then why do you write Mamma.

Adieu. Ever ever Yours.

"DOMESTICK AFFAIRS REQUIRE YOUR PRESENCE"

To John Adams

Braintree Sepbr. 20 1777

I sit down this Evening to write you, but I hardly know what to think about your going to N.Y.—The Story has been told so many times, and with circumstances so perticuliar that I with others have given some heed to it tho my not hearing any thing of it from you leaves me at a loss.

Yours of Sepbr. 4 came to hand last Night, our Worthy unkle is a constant attendant upon the Post office for me and brought it me.

Yours of Sepbr. 5 came to Night to Braintree and was left as directed with the Cannister. Am sorry you gave yourself so much trouble about them. I got about half you sent me by Mr. Gerry. Am much obliged to you, and hope to have the pleasure of making the greater part of it for you. Your Letter damp't my Spirits; when I had no expectation of your return till December, I endeavourd to bring my mind to acquiess in the too painfull Situation, but I have now been in a state of Hopefull expectation. I have recond the days since Bass went away a hundred times over, and every Letter expected to find the day set for your return.

But now I fear it is far distant. I have frequently been told that the communication would be cut of and that you would not be ever able to return. Sometimes I have been told so by those who really wish'd it might be so, with Malicious pleasure. Sometimes your timid folks have apprehended that it would be so. I wish any thing would bring you nearer. If there is really any danger I should think you would remove. Tis a plan your Enemies would rejoice to see accomplished, and will Effect if it lies in their power.

I am not apt to be intimidated you know. I have given as little heed to that and a thousand other Bug Bear reports as posible. I have slept as soundly since my return not withstanding all the Ghosts and hobgoblings, as ever I did in my life. Tis true I never close my Eyes at night till I have been to Philadelphia, and my first visit in the morning is there.

How unfealing are the world! They tell me they Heard you was dead with as little sensibility as a stock or a stone, and I have now got to be provoked at it, and can hardly help snubing the person who tells me so.

The Story of your being upon this conference at New york came in a Letter as I am told from R. T. Paine to his Brother in Law Greenleafe. Many very many have been the conjectures of the Multitude upon it. Some have supposed the War concluded, the Nation setled, others an exchange of prisoners, others a reconsiliation with Brittain &c. &c.

I cannot consent to your tarrying much longer. I know your Health must greatly suffer from so constant application to Buisness and so little excercise. Besides I shall send you word by and by as Regulus'es steward did, that whilst you are engaged in the Senate your own domestick affairs require your presence at Home, and that your wife and children are in Danger of wanting Bread. If the Senate of America will take care of us, as the Senate of Rome did of the family of Regulus, you may serve them again, but unless you return what little property you possess will be lost. In the first place the House at Boston is going to ruin. When I was there I hired a Girl to clean it, it had a cart load of Dirt in it. I speak within Bounds. One of the chambers was used to keep poultry in, an other sea coal, and an other salt. You may conceive How it look'd. The House is so exceeding damp being shut up, that the floors are mildewd, the sealing falling down, and the paper mouldy and falling from the walls. I took care to have it often opened and aird whilst I tarried in Town. I put it into the best state I could.

In the next place, the Lighter of which you are or should be part owner is lying rotting at the wharf. One year more without any care and she is worth nothing. You have no Bill of Sale, no right to convey any part of her should any person appear to purchase her. The Pew I let, after having paid a tax for the repairs of the meeting House.

As to what is here under my more immediate inspection I do the best I can with it, but it will not at the high price Labour is, pay its way.

I know the weight of publick cares lye so heavey upon you that I have been loth to mention your own private ones.

The Best accounts we can collect from New York assure us that our Men fought valiantly. We are no ways dispiritted here, we possess a Spirit that will not be conquerd. If our Men are all drawn of and we should be attacked, you would find a Race of Amazons in America.

But I trust we shall yet tread down our Enemies.

I must intreat you to remember me often. I never think your Letters half long enough. I do not complain. I have no reason to, no one can boast of more Letters than Your   Portia

September 20, 1776

"MY PEN IS MY ONLY PLEASURE"

To John Adams

Sepbr. 23 1776

There are perticuliar times when I feel such an uneasiness, such a restlessness, as neither company, Books, family Cares or any other thing will remove, my Pen is my only pleasure, and writing to you the composure of my mind.

I feel that agitation this Evening, a degree of Melancholy has seazd my mind, owing to the anxiety I feel for the fate of our Arms at New York, and the apprehensions I have for your Health and Safety.

We Have so many rumours and reports that tis imposible to

know what to Credit. We are this Evening assurd that there has
been a field Battle between a detachment of our Army commanded by General Miflin and a Detachment of British Troops
in which the Latter were defeated. An other report says that we
have been obliged to Evacuate the city and leave our cannon,
Baggage &c. &c. This we cannot credit, we will not Believe it.

Tis a most critical day with us. Heaven Crown our arms with
Success.

Did you ever expect that we should hold Long Island? And
if that could not be held, the city of New York must lie at their
mercy. If they command New York can they cut of the communication between the Colonies?

Tho I sufferd much last winter yet I had rather be in a situation where I can collect the Truth, than at a distance where I
am distressd by a thousand vague reports—

> War is our Buisness, but to whom is Give'n
> To die, or triumph, that determine Heav'n!

I write you an abundance, do you read it all? Your last Letters have been very short. Have you buried, stifled or exausted
all the—I wont ask the question you must find out my meaning if you can.

I cannot help smileing at your caution in never subscribeing
a Letter, yet frank it upon the outside where you are obliged to
write your name.

I hope I have a Letter by Saturdays Post. You say you are
sometimes dissapointed, you can tell then How I feel. I endeavour to write once a week.

Poor Barrel I see by the paper is dead. So is our Neighbour
Feild.

GENERALS LEE AND WASHINGTON

To Mercy Otis Warren

Dear Marcia

Tis so long since I took a pen up to write a line that I fear
you have thought me unmindfull of you; I should not have

neglected writing to you immediately upon the receipt of your obliging favour especially as you was then under great anxiety. My Eyes ever since the small pox have been great Sufferers. Writing puts them to great pain.—I now congratulate my Friend upon the Recovery of her amiable family from so Malignant a disease and Mr. Winslow in perticuliar who I heard was under some concern and apprehension from it.

You my Friend then experienced in some measure what I passd through in the Summer past only with this difference that your Friend was within a days ride of you mine hundreds of miles Distant.—O Marcia how many hundred miles this moment seperate us—my heart Bleads at the recollection. Many circumstances conspire to make this Seperation more greivious to me than any which has before taken place. The distance, the difficulty of communication, and the many hazards which my immagination represents as real (if they are not so) from Brittains, Hessians and Tories, render me at times very unhappy. I had it in my Heart to disswade him from going and I know I could have prevaild, but our publick affairs at that time wore so gloomy an aspect that I thought if ever his assistance was wanted, it must be at such a time. I therefore resignd my self to suffer much anxiety and many Melancholy hours for this year to come. I know you have a sympathetick feeling Heart or I should not dare indulge myself in relateing my Griefs.

Many unfortunate as well as prosperious Events have taken place in our publick affairs since I had the pleasure of seeing or writing to you. Lee poor Lee—the loss at forts Washington and Lee together did not affect me eaquelly with the loss of that Brave and Experienced General. He has an unconquerable Spirit, imprisonment must be greivious indeed to him.

I am apt to think that our late misfortunes have called out the hidden Excellencies of our Commander in chief—"affliction is the good mans shining time." The critical state of our affairs has shown him to great advantage. Heaven grant that his Successes may be continued to him, tis Natural to estimate the military abilities of a man according to his Successes.

Can you, do you? credit the report that is circulating with regard to the Farmer. We may well adopt the words of the Psalmist—

Lord what is Man?

I was mortified the other day when I heard the Colonel passd this House without calling. I hope he will not forget me when he returns. My Regards to Mrs. Lothrope and all the little folks. Pray write to me soon, I will endeavour to be better for the future. Yours,   Portia

January 1777

PREGNANCY

To John Adams

Braintree March 8 1777

We have had very severe weather almost ever since you left us. About the middle of Febry. came a snow of a foot and half deep upon a Level which made it fine going for about 10 day's when a snow storm succeeded with a High wind and banks 5 and 6 feet high. I do not remember to have seen the Roads so obstructed since my remembrance; there has been no passing since except for a Horse.

I Have wrote you 3 Letters since your absence but whether you have ever received one of them I know not. The Post office has been in such a Situation that there has been no confiding in it, but I hear Hazard is come to put it upon a better footing.

We know not what is passing with you nor with the Army, any more than if we lived with the Antipodes. I want a Bird of passage. It has given me great pleasure to find by your Letters which I have received that your Spirits are so Good, and that your Health has not sufferd by your tedious journey. Posterity who are to reap the Blessings, will scarly be able to conceive the Hardships and Sufferings of their Ancesstors.—"But tis a day of suffering says the Author of the Crisis, and we ought to expect it. What we contend for is worthy the affliction we may go through. If we get but Bread to eat and any kind of rayment to put on, we ought not only to be contented, but thankfull. What are the inconveniencies of a few Months or years to the

Tributary bondage of ages?" These are Sentiments which do Honour to Humane Nature.

We have the Debates of Parliment by which it appears there are Many who apprehend a War inevitable and foresee the precipice upon which they stand. We have a report Here that Letters are come to Congress from administration, and proposals of a treaty, and some other Stories fit to amuse children, but Experienced Birds are not to be caught with chaff. What is said of the english nation by Hume in the Reign of Harry the 8th may very aptly be applied to them now, that they are so thoroughly subdued that like Eastern Slaves they are inclined to admire even those acts of tyranny and violence which are exercised over themselves at their own expence.

Thus far I wrote when I received a Letter dated Febry. 10, favour by —— but it was a mistake it was not favour by any body, and not being frank'd cost me a Dollor. The Man who deliverd it to my unkle brought him a Letter at the same time for which he paid the same price. If it had containd half as much as I wanted to know I would not have grumbld, but you do not tell me How you do, nor what accommodations you have, which is of more consequence to me than all the discriptions of cities, states and kingdoms in the world. I wish the Men of War better imployd than in taking flower vessels since it creates a Temporary famine Here, if I would give a Guiney for a pound of flower I dont think I could purchase it. There is such a Cry for Bread in the Town of Boston as I suppose was never before Heard, and the Bakers deal out but a loaf a day to the largest families. There is such a demand for Indian and Rye, that a Scarcity will soon take place in the Country. Tis now next to imposible to purchase a Bushel of Rye. In short since the late act there is very little selling. The meat that is carried to market is miserabley poor, and so little of it that many people say they were as well supplied in the Seige.

I am asshamed of my Country men. The Merchant and farmer are both alike. Some there are who have virtue enough to adhere to it, but more who evade it.

March 9

I have this day Received a most agreable packet favour by Mr. Hall, for which I return you my most hearty thanks, and which contains much amusement, and gave me much pleasure. Rejoice with you in your agreable situation, tho I cannot help wishing you nearer. Shall I tell you how near? You have not given me any politicks tho, have you so much of them that you are sick of them?

I have some thoughts of opening a political correspondence with your namesake. He is much more communicative than you are, but I must agree with him to consider me as part of one of the Members of Congress. You must know that since your absence a Letter designd for you from him fell into my Hands.

You make some inquiries which tenderly affect me. I think upon the whole I have enjoyed as much Health as I ever did in the like situation—a situation I do not repine at, tis a constant remembrancer of an absent Friend, and excites sensations of tenderness which are better felt than expressd.

Our Little ones are well and often talk and wish for ———. Master T. desires I would write a Letter for him which I have promised to do. Your Mamma tenderly inquires after you. I cannot do your Message to Betsy since the mortification I endure at the mention of it is so great that I have never changd a word with her upon the subject, altho preparations are making for house keeping. The ordination is the 12th of this month. I would not make an exchange with her for the mountains of Mexico and Peru. She has forfeited all her character with me and the world for taste &c. All her acquaintance stand amazd. —An Idea of 30 years and unmarried is sufficent to make people do very unacountable things. Thank Heaven my Heart was early fix'd and never deviated. The early impression has for succeeding years been gathering strength, and will out last the Brittle frame that contains it—tis a spark of Celestial fire and will burn with Eternal vigor.

Heaven preserve and return in safety the dearest of Friends to His   Portia

                                                              March 10
I have just now heard that one of my unkle's flower vessels arrived safe yesterday, at which there is great joy. You can scarcly conceive the distress there has been for Bread, it is but a mouthfull. Flower is sold at 4.16 per Barrell not withstanding

what has been done. Indeed the risk and the high price it bears with you, no person can send for it without sinking half the Cargo.

I see by the news papers you sent me that Spado is lost. I mourn for him. If you know any thing of His Master pray Let me hear, what treatment he meets with, where he is confined &c.

A considerable number of our 3 Months Militia have re-turnd, deserted, some belonging both to this Town and Wey-mouth, and they say others from other Towns. The Story they tell is this, that a great number of the standing Army were under inoculation for the small pox, and they were obliged to do duty where they were constantly exposed to it, that they would have been innoculated but as they had so short a time to tarry were not allowd to, that they applied to their Col. for leave to come of but could not obtain it, that those who had it in the natural way 4 out of 5 died with it, and that it was death for any of the Militia to be innoculated. This does not seem to be likely but is told by all of them. What will be the conse-quence I know not. I hear of but a few in this Town who are inlisted for the standing Army. Suppose they will be drawn soon.

"MAR, I NEVER SAW ANY BODY GROW SO FAT"

To John Adams

April 17. 1777

Your obliging favours of March 14, 16 and 22, have received, and most sincerely thank you for them. I know not How I should support an absence already tedious, and many times attended with melancholy reflections, if it was not for so fre-quently hearing from you. That is a consolation to me, tho a cold comfort in a winters Night.

As the Summer advances I have many anxieties, some of which I should not feel or at least should find them greatly alle-viated if you could be with me. But as that is a Satisfaction I know I must not look for, (tho I have a good mind to hold You to your promise since some perticuliar circumstances were really upon that condition) I must summon all the Phylosophy I am mistress of since what cannot be help'd must be endured.

Mrs. Howard a Lady for whom I know you had a great respect died yesterday to the inexpressible Grief of her Friends. She was deliverd of a Son or Daughter I know not which yesterday week, a mortification in her Bowels occasiond her death. Every thing of this kind naturally shocks a person in similar circumstances. How great the mind that can overcome the fear of Death! How anxious the Heart of a parent who looks round upon a family of young and helpless children and thinks of leaving them to a World full of snares and temptations which they have neither discretion to foresee, nor prudence to avoid.

But I will quit the Subject least it should excite painfull Sensations in a Heart that I would not willingly wound.

You give me an account in one of your Letters of the removal of your Lodgings. The extravagance of Board is greater there than here tho here every thing is at such prices as was not ever before known. Many articles are not to be had tho at ever so great a price. Sugar, Molasses, Rum, cotton wool, Coffe, chocolate, cannot all be consumed. Yet there are none, or next to none to be sold, perhaps you may procure a pound at a time, but no more. I have sometimes stoped 15 or 20 Butchers in a day with plenty of meat but not a mouthfull to be had unless I would give 4 pence per pound and 2 pence per pound for bringing. I have never yet indulged them and am determined I will not whilst I have a mouthfull of salt meat, to Eat, but the act is no more regarded now than if it had never been made and has only this Effect I think, that it makes people worse than they would have been without it. As to cloathing of any sort for myself or family I think no more of purchaseing any than if they were to live like Adam and Eve in innocence.

I seek wool and flax and can work willingly with my Hands, and tho my Household are not cloathed with fine linnen nor scarlet, they are cloathed with what is perhaps full as Honorary, the plain and decent manufactory of my own family, and tho I do not abound, I am not in want. I have neither poverty nor Riches but food which is conveniant for me and a Heart to be thankfull and content that in such perilous times so large a share of the comforts of life are allotted to me.

I have a large Share of Health to be thankfull for, not only for myself but for my family.

I have enjoyed as much Health since the small pox, as I have known in any year not with standing a paleness which has very near resembled a whited wall, but which for about 3 weeks past I have got the Better of. Coulour and a clumsy figure make their appearence in so much that Master John says, Mar, I never saw any body grow so fat as you do.

I really think this Letter would make a curious figure if it should fall into the Hands of any person but yourself—and pray if it comes safe to you, burn it.

But ever remember with the tenderest Sentiments her who knows no earthly happiness eaquel to that of being tenderly beloved by her dearest Friend.

COUNTERFEIT MONEY

To John Adams

May 6 1777

Tis ten days I believe since I wrote you a Line, yet not ten minuts passes without thinking of you. Tis four Months wanting 3 days since we parted, every day of the time I have mournd the absence of my Friend, and felt a vacancy in my Heart which nothing, nothing can supply. In vain the Spring Blooms or the Birds sing, their Musick has not its formour melody, nor the Spring its usual pleasures. I look round with a melancholy delight and sigh for my absent partner. I fancy I see you worn down with Cares, fatigued with Buisness, and solitary amidst a multitude.

And I think it probabal before this reaches you that you may be driven from the city by our Barbarous and Hostile foes, and the City shareing the fate of Charlestown and Falmouth, Norfolk and Daunbury. So vague and uncertain are the accounts with regard to the Latter that I shall not pretend to mention them. Tis more than a week since the Event, yet we have no accounts which can be depended upon. I wish it may serve the valuable purpose of arousing our degenerated Country Men

from that state of security and torpitude into which they seem
to be sunk.

May 9

I have been prevented writing for several days by company
from Town. Since I wrote you I have received several Letters,
2 of the 13 of April, one of the 19 and one of the 22. Tho some
of them were very short, I will not complain. I rejoice to hear
from you tho you write but a line. Since the above we have
some accounts of the affair at Daunbury and of the loss of
General Wocester. That they had no more assistance tis said
was owing to six expresses being stoped by the Tories. We shall
never prosper till we fall upon some method to extirpate that
Blood thirsty set of men. Too much Lenity will prove our ruin.
We have rumours too of an action at Brunswick much to our
advantage but little credit is yet given to the report. I wish we
may be able to meet them in the Feald, to encounter and
Conquer so vile an Enemy.

The two Continental frigates lie wind bound with 3 brigs of
20 Guns and some others who are all going out in company.
We have had a very long season of cold rainy weather, and the
trees are not yet out in Blossome, the wind has been a long
time at East, and prevented the vessels from going out.—I was
mistaken in my Brothers going with MacNeal. He is going in
the Tarter a vessel which mounts 24 Guns, is private property
but sails with the Fleat.

I cannot write you half so much as I would. I have left company because I would not loose an opportunity of sending this.

The children are well. I cannot say that I am so well as I have
been. The disorder I had in my Eyes has in some measure left
them but communicated itself all over me and turnd to the salt
rhume which worries me exceedingly, and is very hurtfull in
my present situation. However I am doing what I dare to to
carry it of.—Believe me at all times most affectionately yours.

I must add a little more. A most Horrid plot has been discoverd of a Band of villans counterfeiting the Hampshire currency to a Great amount, no person scarcly but what has more
or less of these Bills. I am unlucky enough to have about 5
pounds LM of it, but this is not the worst of it. One Col.

Farington who has been concernd in the plot, was taken sick, and has confessd not only the Counterfeiting, but says they had engaged and inlisted near 2 thousand Men who upon the Troops comeing to Boston were to fall upon the people and make a General Havock. How much more mercifull God than man, in thus providentially bringing to light these Horrid plots and Schemes. I doubt not Heaven will still continue to favour us, unless our iniquities prevent. The Hampshire people have been stupid enough to let one of the principal plotters Col. Holland out upon Baill and he has made his excape.

ENCLOSURE

1700 Barrells Pork
  50 Do: Beef
 700 Basketts Wheat
   7 Hhds. Rum
   6 Do: Bread
  11 Tierces Claret
   3 Quarter Cask Wine
  12 or 1700 Wheat—Rye & Corn
  12 Coile Rope
  10 Waggons
1600 Tents mostly old

The above is a true State of our Loss, in the affair at Danbury. 20 Men killed. 5 Missing. 17 Houses burnt. A Party that went out to bury the Dead have returned, and Report, that they have buried 62 Regulars.

FEARING AN ATTACK ON BOSTON

To John Adams

This is the 15 of June. Tomorrow our new Edition of the Regulating act takes place, and will I fear add wrath to Bitterness. No arguments which were urgd could prevail upon the court to repeal it. A committee in this Town is chosen to see it inforced, and I suppose in other Towns. I am surprizd that when the ill Effects of it are so visible, and the spirit of opposition to it so general and voilent that there should be a determination to enforce it.

There is a very evil spirit opperating and an encreasing Bitterness between the Town and Country. The Town of Boston has lost its leaders, and the respectable figure it once made is exchanged for party squables, for Avarice, venality, Animosity, contention, pride, weakness and dissapation. I wish I could say this spirit was confined to the Capital, but indeed too much of it prevails in the cottage.

Really we are a most ungratefull people, favourd as we have been with peculiar Blessings and favours to make so poor returns. With the best opportunities for becomeing a happy people, and all the materials in our power, yet we have neither skill nor wisdom to put them together.

The House and Counsel have come to a determination to form a Goverment, and to send it out to the people for their inspection. I expect there will be great difficulty as ninety two Towns I am told have sent no representitives, and the Countys of Worcester and Berkshire make up more than a third of the House. Some have instructed their rep's to form a Goverment, others have directly forbid them.

There has been a list of Tories belonging to this Town made out, and Deliverd in to the Town 13 in number. I will enclose the list. Some of them I believe had as goods have been omitted. It will put them to some expence but the practice is to employ one or two gentlemen of the Bar, who generally make out to get them acquitted. Then I expect they will be returnd to us, more Rancorous than before.

There is a movement of Hows, whether he designs for Boston or Road Island or where is as yet unknown—I hope for neither. I think I could not tarry here with safety should he make an attack upon either, and the thought of being driven from my own Habitation at this time is more distressing than ever. If I had only myself to look after it would be less anxiety to me; if you hear of our being invaded this way, I think you must return. I used to have courage, but you cannot wonder at my apprehensions when you consider my circumstances. I can but poorly walk about House; However I am not of an over anxious make; I will trust in providence that I shall be provided for. I think we shall know in a week whether he designs this way, and you I suppose will know as soon as we. I wish you would advise me what I had best do if we should be attacked this way.—We have not a Man either upon the Castle or at Nantasket. I believe our Enimies know it.

Two continental vessels have arrived with Salt from Bilbo in the last week, and four prizes sent in by the Fleet. As they came in a Saturday have not learnt with what they are loaded.

Have received two letters since I wrote last, one of May 24 and one of May 27. As to your injuntions with regard to my taking any money but this States and continental, I have strictly adhered to them. I know of whom I received the Hampshire money, and returnd it again. I took it of Sister Adams as part of the pay for the Lighter, and she of Vose of Milton. She returnd it the same week to Him, which she took it but He refused to receive it, and tho she has twice sent it to Him, and he does not pretend to say He did not pay it to her, Yet he will not take it again. What can be done? I had several other Bills, but knowing of whom I received them, I found no difficulty in returning them again.—There will no money pass in this State after next month but continental and this States.

How is your cold? Are you better than you was? I feel anxious for your Health. Let me know every time you write How you do. A certain Gentleman was ask'd when he expected to go to Philadelphia. O he did not know. That depended upon some of the others returning. He supposed they would be running Home again in a month or two, as they always were. For his part he had tarried so many months.—A great merrit to tarry from Home when a man loves any place better than home. I am for having them all stay now, to keep him at home as a punishment. Tis of no great importance where he is.

Adieu most sincerely yours.

June 15, 1777

FEARS FOR A STILLBIRTH

To John Adams

July 9 1777

I sit down to write you this post, and from my present feelings tis the last I shall be able to write for some time if I should do well. I have been very unwell for this week past, with some complaints that have been new to me, tho I hope not dangerous.

I was last night taken with a shaking fit, and am very apprehensive that a life was lost. As I have no reason to day to think otherways; what may be the consequences to me, Heaven only knows. I know not of any injury to myself, nor any thing which could occasion what I fear.

I would not Have you too much allarmd. I keep up some Spirits yet, tho I would have you prepaird for any Event that may happen.

I can add no more than that I am in every Situation unfeignedly Yours, Yours.

BEGINNING OF LABOR

To John Adams

July 10 9 o clock Evening

About an Hour ago I received a Letter from my Friend dated June 21: begining in this manner "my dearest Friend." It gave me a most agreable Sensation, it was a cordial to my Heart. That one single expression dwelt upon my mind and playd about my Heart, and was more valuable to me than any part of the Letter, except the close of it. It was because my Heart was softned and my mind enervated by my sufferings, and I wanted the personal and tender soothings of my dearest Friend, that renderd it so valuable to me at this time. I have no doubt of the tenderest affection or sincerest regard of my absent Friend, yet an expression of that kind will sooth my Heart to rest amidst a thousand anxietyes.

Tis now 48 Hours since I can say I really enjoyed any Ease, nor am I ill enough to summons any attendance unless my sisters. Slow, lingering and troublesome is the present situation. The Dr. encourages me to Hope that my apprehensions are groundless respecting what I wrote you yesterday, tho I cannot say I have had any reason to allter my mind. My spirits However are better than they were yesterday, and I almost wish I had not let that Letter go. If there should be agreable News to tell you, you shall know it as soon as the post can convey it. I pray Heaven that it may be soon or it seems to me I shall be worn out. I must lay my pen down this moment, to bear what I cannot fly from—and now I have endured it I re-assume my pen and will lay by all my own feelings and thank you for your obligeing Letters.—A prize arrived this week at Marble Head with 400 Hogsheads of rum a board sent in by Manly.—Every article and necessary of life rises here daily. Sugar has got to [   ] per hundred, Lamb to 1 shilling per pound and all other things in proportion.—We have the finest Season here that I have known for many years. The fruit was injured by the cold East winds and falls of, the Corn looks well, Hay will be plenty, but your Farm wants manure. I shall endeavour to have Sea weed carted every Leasure moment that can be had. That will not be many. Help is so scarce and so expensive I can not Hire a days mowing under 6 shillings.

How has done himself no honour by his late retreat. We fear most now for Tyconderoga. Tis reported to day that tis taken. We have a vast many men who look like officers continually riding about. I wonder what they can be after, why they do not repair to the army.

We wonder too what Congress are a doing? We have not heard of late.

How do you do? Are you glad you are out of the way of sour faces. I could look pleasent upon you in the midst of sufferings—allmighty God carry me safely through them. There I would hope I have a Friend ever nigh and ready to assist me, unto whom I commit myself.

This is Thursday Evening. It cannot go till monday, and then I hope will be accompanied with more agreable inteligance.

Most sincerely Yours.

July 11

I got more rest last night than I expected, this morning am rather more ill than I was yesterday. This day ten years ago master John came into this world. May I have reason again to recollect it with peculiar gratitude. Adieu.

July 1777

"NUMBERD WITH ITS ANCESTORS"

To John Adams

July 16 1777

Join with me my dearest Friend in Gratitude to Heaven, that a life I know you value, has been spaired and carried thro Distress and danger altho the dear Infant is numberd with its ancestors.

My apprehensions with regard to it were well founded. Tho my Friends would have fain perswaded me that the Spleen or the Vapours had taken hold of me I was as perfectly sensible of its discease as I ever before was of its existance. I was also aware of the danger which awaited me; and which tho my sufferings were great thanks be to Heaven I have been supported through, and would silently submit to its dispensations in the loss of a sweet daughter; it appeard to be a very fine Babe, and as it never opened its Eyes in this world it lookd as tho they were only closed for sleep. The circumstance which put an end to its existence, was evident upon its birth, but at this distance and in a Letter which may possibly fall into the Hands of some unfealing Ruffian I must omit particuliars. Suffice it to say that it was not oweing to any injury which I had sustaind, nor could any care of mine have prevented it.

My Heart was much set upon a Daughter. I had had a strong perswasion that my desire would be granted me. It was—but to shew me the uncertanty of all sublinary enjoyments cut of e'er I could call it mine. No one was so much affected with the loss of it as its Sister who mournd in tears for Hours. I have so much cause for thankfullness amidst my sorrow, that I would not entertain a repineing thought. So short sighted and so little a way can we look into futurity that we ought patiently to submit to the dispensation of Heaven.

I am so comfortable that I am amaizd at myself, after what I have sufferd I did not expect to rise from my Bed for many days. This is but the 5th day and I have set up some Hours.

I However feel myself weakend by this exertion, yet I could

not refrain from the temptation of writing with my own Hand to you.

Adieu dearest of Friends adieu—Yours most affectionately.

To Mercy Otis Warren

August 14. 1777. Braintree

This is the memorable fourteenth of August. This day 12 years the Stamp office was distroyd. Since that time what have we endured? What have we suffer'd? Many very many memorable Events which ought to be handed down to posterity will be buried in oblivion merely for want of a proper Hand to record them, whilst upon the opposite side many venal pens will be imployd to misrepresent facts and to render all our actions odious in the Eyes of future Generations. I have always been sorry that a certain person who once put their Hand to the pen, should be discouraged, and give up so important a service. Many things would have been recorded by the penetrateing Genious of that person which thro the multiplicity of Events and the avocations of the times will wholly escape the notice of any future Historian.

The History and the Events of the present day must fill every Humane Breast with Horrour. Every week produces some Horrid Scene perpetrated by our Barbarous foes, not content with a uniform Series of cruelties practised by their own Hands, but they must let loose the infernal Savages "those dogs of War" and cry Havock to them. Cruelty, impiety and an utter oblivion of the natural Sentiments of probity and Honour with the voilation of all Laws Humane and Divine rise at one veiw and characterise a George, a How and a Burgoine.

O my dear Friend when I bring Home to my own Dwelling these tragical Scenes which are every week presented in the publick papers to us, and only in Idea realize them, my whole Soul is distress'd. Were I a man I must be in the Feild. I could not live to endure the Thought of my Habitation desolated, my children Butcherd, and I an inactive Spectator.

August 15

I enclose to you a Coppy of Mr. Lees Letter. It came to me with some restrictions to be shewn only to those whom I could confide in. I think by that our affairs abroad look'd as favorable as we could expect, but we have a great many hardships to endure yet I fear e'er we shall receive any assistance from others.

Letters from my Friend to the 20 of july mention the loss of Ticondoroga with much regreat, but says tis an Event which he has feard would take place for some time. People that way were much disposed to censure, but that they had not received any perticuliar accounts by which a true judgment could be formd.

August 16

We are bless'd my Friend with a fine Season. I hope the charming rains this afternoon have reachd Plimouth and re-freshd the Feilds of Eal river.

You mention some French cotton. I am much obliged to you but I have since I saw you been accommodated in that way. The Russel I should be very glad of either one or two yards just as you can spair it, and Shooe binding, if it is to be had. Garlick thread I am in great want of, if you should know of any be so good as to let me know.

I am really asshamed to tell my Friend that I have not yet been able to get Home the cloth. All that was in my power to do to it, has been done 3 months ago and I have been sending and going almost every week since. I saw the Man yesterday and he has promised me that I shall have it next week, but if his word prove no better than it has done I cannot say you may depend upon it. All I can say is that my endeavours have not been wanting. As soon as I can get it it shall be forwarded by your affectionate Friend,   Portia

BRITISH SURRENDER AT SARATOGA

To John Adams

Boston October 25 1777 Saturday Evening
The joyfull News of the Surrender of General Burgoin and
all his Army to our Victorious Troops prompted me to take a
ride this afternoon with my daughter to Town to join to morrow with my Friends in thanksgiving and praise to the Supreem
Being who hath so remarkably deliverd our Enimies into our
Hands.

And hearing that an express is to go of tomorrow morning,
I have retired to write you a few line's. I have received no letters from you since you left Philadelphia by the post, and but
one by any private Hand. I have wrote you once before this.
Do not fail writing by the return of this express and direct your
Letters to the care of my unkle who has been a kind and faithfull hand to me through the whole Season and a constant attendant upon the post office.

Burgoine is expected in by the middle of the week. I have
read many Articles of Capitulation, but none which ever containd so generous Terms before. Many people find fault with
them but perhaps do not consider sufficently the circumstances
of General Gates, who by delaying and exacting more might
have lost all. This must be said of him that he has followed the
golden rule and done as he would wish himself in like circumstances to be dealt with.—Must not the vapouring Burgoine
who tis said possesses great Sensibility, be humbled to the
dust. He may now write the Blocade of Saratago. I have heard
it proposed that he should take up his quarters in the old
South, but believe he will not be permitted to come to this
Town.—Heaven grant us success at the Southard. That saying
of king Richard often occurs to my mind "God helps those
who help themselves" but if Men turn their backs and run
from an Enemy they cannot surely expect to conquer them.

This day dearest of Friends compleats 13 years since we were
solemly united in wedlock; 3 years of the time we have been
cruelly seperated. I have patiently as I could endured it with
the Belief that you were serving your Country, and rendering

your fellow creatures essential Benefits. May future Generations rise up and call you Blessed, and the present behave
worthy of the blessings you are Labouring to secure to them,
and I shall have less reason to regreat the deprivation of my
own perticuliar felicity.

Adieu dearest of Friends adieu.

ADDENDUM BY WILLIAM SMITH

Please to enquire of Mr. Reese Meredeth if he has received a
Letter from my father enclosing a Bill upon Philadelphia.—
Yrs., WS

COMMISSIONER TO FRANCE

To James Lovell

Dear Sir

Your Letters arrived in the absence of Mr. Adams who is
gone as far as Portsmouth, little thinking of your plot against
him.

O Sir you who are possessd of Sensibility, and a tender
Heart, how could you contrive to rob me of all my happiness?

I can forgive Mr. Geary because he is a Stranger to domestick felicity and knows no tenderer attachment than that which
he feels for his Country, tho I think the Stoickism which every
Batchelor discovers ought to be attributed to him as a fault.

He may retort upon me and ask if in such an Instance as this
he is not the happier Man of the two, for tho destitute of the
highest felicity in life he is not exposed to the keen pangs
which attend a Seperation from our dear connexions. This is
reasoning like a Batchelor still.

Desire him from me to make trial of a different Situation
and then tell me his Sentiments.

But you Sir I can hardly be reconciled to you, you who so
lately experienced what it was to be restored to your family
after a painfull absence from it, and then in a few weeks torn
from it by a call from your Country. You disinterestedly obeyed
the Summons. But how could you so soon forget your suffer-

ings and place your Friend in a more painfull situation considering the Risk and hazard of a foreign voyage. I pittied the conflict I saw in your mind, and tho a Stranger to your worthy partner sympathized with her and thought it cruel in your Friends to insist upon such a Sacrifice.

I know Sir by this appointment you mean the publick good, or you would not thus call upon me to sacrifice my tranquility and happiness.

The deputing my Friend upon so important an Embassy is a gratefull proof to me of the esteem of his Country. Tho I would not wish him to be less deserving I am sometimes almost selfish enough to wish his abilities confind to private life, and the more so for that wish is according with his own inclinations.

I have often experienced the want of his aid and assistance in the last 3 years of his absence and that Demand increases as our little ones grow up 3 of whom are sons and at this time of life stand most in need of the joint force of his example and precepts.

And can I Sir consent to be seperated from him whom my Heart esteems above all earthly things, and for an unlimited time? My life will be one continued scene of anxiety and apprehension, and must I cheerfully comply with the Demand of my Country?

I know you think I ought, or you would not have been accessary to the Call.

I have improved this absence to bring my mind to bear the Event with fortitude and resignation, tho I own it has been at the expence both of food and rest.

I beg your Excuse Sir for writing thus freely, it has been a relief to my mind to drop some of my sorrows through my pen, which had your Friend been present would have been poured only into his bosome.

Accept my sincere wishes for your welfare and happiness and Rank among the Number of your Friends, Your Humble Servant,   AA

c. December 15, 1777

THE YEARS ABROAD
1778–1788

To Hannah Quincy Lincoln Storer

My dear Mrs. Storers obliging favour was handed me to day. It found me with an additional Weight of anxiety upon my mind. I had been just able by the force of philosophy and I would fain hope by nobler Motives, to acquire a sufficent Stock of fortitude to support me under the most painfull Seperation I have yet been call'd to endure, when last Mondays paper gave me a Shock that I was not armd against.

Against an open and avowed Enemy we may find some guard, but the Secret Murderer and the dark assassin none but that Being without whose Notice not a Sparrow falls to the ground, can protect or secure us. My own solicitude will not avail. When I was call'd to this trial, I asked not my Heart what it could, but what it ought to do, and being convinced that my Friend might be more extensively usefull in this department at this perticuliar time than in any other, hard as the Struggle was I consented to the Seperation. Most willingly would I have hazarded the danger of the Sea to have accompanied him, but the dangers from Enemies was so great that I could not obtain his consent.

You have a sympathetick Heart, and have often I dare say compasionated your Friend who feels as if she was left alone in the world, unsupported and defenceless, with the important weight of Education upon her hands at a time of life when the young charge stand most in need of the joint Efforts and assistance of both parents. I have sacrificed my own personal happiness and must look for my Satisfaction in the consciousness of having discharged my duty to the publick. Indulge me my Friend when I say few people have so valuable a treasure to resign, none know the Struggle it has cost me. Tender as Maternal affection is, it was swallowed up in what I found a much stronger, nor had it, its full opperation till after the departure of my Son when I found a larger portion of my Heart gone than I was aware of.

I was in hopes that a few Months would releave me from a Large Share of anxiety by the happy tidings of the safe arrival of my Friend, but a new Source of Distress has opened to my view. I was not aware of the assasinating knife of a Ravelick. Join with me my Friend in Suplications to Heaven for the safety of my Friend, and for the success and faithfull discharge of the important trust committed to him.

I rejoice in the happiness of my Friend, tho my own felicity is over cast. I little thought so much time would have elapsed before I had the pleasure of seeing her in her own habitation. She has left a vacancy here which cannot be supplied, but I will not regret it since she has contributed to the happiness of a worthy Man, and a deserving family—to whom as a peculiar Blessing of Heaven may she long be continued which will contribute much to the happiness of her affectionate

Portia

c. March 1, 1778

"I HAVE TRAVELLED WITH YOU"

To John Adams

March 8 1778

Tis a little more than 3 weeks since the dearest of Friends and tenderest of Husbands left his solitary partner, and quitted all the fond endearments of domestick felicity for the dangers of the Sea, exposed perhaps to the attack of a Hostile foe, and o good Heaven can I add to the dark assassin, to the secret Murderer and the Bloody Emissary of as cruel a Tyrant as God in his Riteous judgments ever sufferd to Discrace the Throne of Brittain.

I have travelled with you over the wide Atlantick, and could have landed you safe with humble confidence at your desired Haven, and then have set myself down to have enjoyed a negative kind of happiness, in the painfull part which it has pleased Heaven to allot me, but this intelligence with Regard to that great Philosopher, able Statesman and unshaken Friend of his Country, has planted a Dagger in my Breast and I feel with a double Edge the weapon that pierced the Bosom of a Franklin—

> "For Nought avails the Virtues of the Heart
> Nor tow'ring Genious claims its due Reward
> From Britains fury, as from Deaths keen dart
> No worth can save us and no Fame can guard."

The more distinguished the person the greater the inveteracy of these foes of Humane Nature. The Arguments of my Friends to alleviate my anxiety by perswading me that this shocking attempt will put you more upon your Gaurd and render your person more secure than if it had never taken place, is kind in them and has some weight, but my greatest comfort and consolation arrisses from the Belief of a Superintending providence to whom I can with confidence commit you since not a Sparrow falls to the ground without his Notice. Were it not for this I should be misirable and overwhelmed by my fears and apprehensions.

Freedom of sentiment the life and soul of Friendship is in a great measure cut of by the Danger of Miscarrages, and the apprehension of Letters falling into the hands of our Enemies. Should this meet with that fate may they Blush for their connextion with a Nation who have renderd themselves infamous and abhorred by a long list of crimes which not their high atchivements nor the Lusture of former Deeds, nor the tender appellation of parent nor the fond connextion which once subsisted, can ever blot from our remembrance or wipe out those indellible stains cruelty and baseness. They have engraven them with a pen of Iron and Led in a Rock forever.

To my dear Son Remember me in the most affectionate terms. I would have wrote to him but my notice is so short that I have not time. Injoin it upon him Never to Disgrace his Mother, and to behave worthy of his Father. Tender as Maternal affection is, it was swallowed up in what I found a stronger, or so intermingld that I felt it not in its full force till after he had left me. I console myself with the hopes of his reaping advantages under the carefull Eye of a tender parent which it was not in my power to bestow upon him.

There is nothing material taken place in the politicall world since you left us. This Letter will go by a vessel for Bilboa from whence you may perhaps get better opportunities of

conveyance than from any other place. The Letter you deliverd
to the pilot came safe to hand. All the little folks are anxious
for the Safety of their Pappa and Brother to whom they desire
to be rememberd—to which is added the tenderest Sentiments
of affection and the fervent prayers for your happiness and
Safty of Your   Portia

"DIFFICULT AS THE DAY IS"

To John Adams

May 18 1778

I have waited with great patience, restraining as much as
posible every anxious Idea for 3 Months. But now every Vessel
which arrives sits my expectation upon the wing, and I pray my
Gaurdian Genious to waft me the happy tidings of your Safety
and Welfare. Heitherto my wandering Ideas Rove like the Son
of Ulissis from Sea to Sea, and from Shore to Shore, not knowing where to find you. Sometimes I fancy'd you upon the
Mighty Waters, sometimes at your desired Haven; sometimes
upon the ungratefull and Hostile Shore of Britain, but at all
times and in all places under the protecting care and Guardian-
ship of that Being who not only cloathes the lilies of the Feild
and hears the young Ravens when they cry, but hath said of
how much more worth are ye than many Sparrows, and this
confidence which the world cannot deprive me of, is my food
by day and my Rest by Night, and was all my consolation
under the Horrid Ideas of assassination, the only Event of
which I had not thought, and in some measure prepaird my
mind.

When my Imagination sits you down upon the Gallick
Shore, a Land to which Americans are now bound to transfer
their affections, and to eradicate all those national prejudices
which the Proud and Haughty Nations whom we once revered, craftily instilld into us whom they once stiled their children; I anticipate the pleasure you must feel, and tho so many
leagus distant share in the joy of finding the great Interest of
our Country so generously espoused, and nobly aided by so

powerfull a Monarck. Your prospects must be much brightned, for when you left your Native Land they were rather Gloomy. If an unwearied Zeal and persevering attachment to the cause of truth and justice, regardless of the allurements of ambition on the one Hand or the threats of calamity on the other, can intitle any one to the Reward of peace, Liberty and Safety, a large portion of those Blessings are reserved for my Friend, in His Native Land.

> O Would'st thou keep thy Country's loud Applause
> Lov'd as her Father, as her God ado'rd
> Be still the bold assertor of her cause
> Her Voice, in Council; (in the Fight her Sword)
> In peace, in War persue thy Countrys Good
> For her, bare thy bold Breast, and pour thy Gen'rous
>   Blood.

Difficult as the Day is, cruel as this War has been, seperated as I am on account of it from the dearest connexion in life, I would not exchange my Country for the Wealth of the Indies, or be any other than an American tho I might be Queen or Empress of any Nation upon the Globe. My Soul is unambitious of pomp or power. Beneath my Humble roof, Bless'd with the Society and tenderest affection of my dear partner, I have enjoyed as much felicity, and as exquisite happiness as falls to the share of mortals; and tho I have been calld to sacrifice to my Country, I can glory in my Sacrifice, and derive pleasure from my intimate connexion with one who is esteemed worthy of the important trust devolved upon him.

Britain as usual has added insult to injustice and cruelty, by what she calls a conciliary plan. From my Soul I dispice her meaness, but she has long ago lost that treasure which a great authority tells us exalteth a Nation, and is receiving the reproaches due to her crimes.

I have been much gratified with the perusal of the Duke of Richmonds Speach. Were there ten such Men to be found, I should still have some hopes that a revolution would take place in favour of the virtuous few; "and the Laws, the Rights, the Generous plan of power deliverd down, From age to age by our renown'd forefathers" be again restored to that unhappy Island.

I hope by the close of this month to receive from you a large packet. I have wrote twice before this, some opportunities I may miss of, by my distance from the Capital. I have enjoyed a good share of Health since you left me. I have not mentiond my dear son tho I have often thought of him since I began this Letter, becaus I propose writing to him by this opportunity. I omit many domestick matters becaus I will not risk their comeing to the publick Eye. I shall have a small Bill to draw upon you in the month of june. I think to send it to Mr. MacCrery who by a Letter received since you went away I find is Setled in Bordeaux in the mercantile way, and I dare say will procure for me any thing I may have occasion for. I wish you would be so good as to write him a line requesting the favour of him to procure me such things as I may have occasion for, and in addition to the Bills which may be drawn Let him add ten pounds Sterling at a time, if I desire it. The Bills will be at 3 different times in a year. If they should arrive safe they would render me essential service. Our Publick finnances are upon no better footing than they were when you left us. 500 Dollors is now offerd by this Town per Man for 9 Months to recruit the Army, 12 pounds a Month for Farming Labour is the price, and not to be procured under. Our Friends are all well and desire to be rememberd to you. So many tender sentiments rush upon my mind when about to close this Letter to you, that I can only ask you to measure them by those which you find in your own Bosome for your affectionate   Portia

FIRST LETTER TO HER SON

To John Quincy Adams

My Dear Son   June [   ] 1778

Tis almost four Months since you left your Native land and Embarked upon the Mighty waters in quest of a Foreign Country. Altho I have not perticuliarly wrote to you since yet you may be assured you have constantly been upon my Heart and mind.

It is a very dificult task my dear son for a tender parent to bring their mind to part with a child of your years into a distant

Land, nor could I have acquiesced in such a seperation under any other care than that of the most Excellent parent and Guardian who accompanied you. You have arrived at years capable of improving under the advantages you will be like to have if you do but properly attend to them. They are talents put into your Hands of which an account will be required of you hereafter, and being possessd of one, two, or four, see to it that you double your numbers.

The most amiable and most usefull disposition in a young mind is diffidence of itself, and this should lead you to seek advise and instruction from him who is your natural Guardian, and will always counsel and direct you in the best manner both for your present and future happiness. You are in possession of a natural good understanding and of spirits unbroken by adversity, and untamed with care. Improve your understanding by acquiring usefull knowledge and virtue, such as will render you an ornament to society, an Honour to your Country, and a Blessing to your parents. Great Learning and superior abilities, should you ever possess them, will be of little value and small Estimation, unless Virtue, Honour, Truth and integrety are added to them. Adhere to those religious Sentiments and principals which were early instilled into your mind and remember that you are accountable to your Maker for all your words and actions. Let me injoin it upon you to attend constantly and steadfastly to the precepts and instructions of your Father as you value the happiness of your Mother and your own welfare. His care and attention to you render many things unnecessary for me to write which I might otherways do, but the inadvertency and Heedlessness of youth, requires line upon line and precept upon precept, and when inforced by the joint efforts of both parents will I hope have a due influence upon your Conduct, for dear as you are to me, I had much rather you should have found your Grave in the ocean you have crossd, or any untimely death crop you in your Infant years, rather than see you an immoral profligate or a Graceless child.

You have enterd early in life upon the great Theater of the world which is full of temptations and vice of every kind. You are not wholy unacquainted with History, in which you have read of crimes which your unexperienced mind could scarcely believe credible. You have been taught to think of them with Horrour and to view vice as

> a Monster of so frightfull Mein
> That to be hated, needs but to be seen.

Yet you must keep a strict guard upon yourself, or the odious monster will soon loose its terror, by becomeing familiar to you. The Modern History of our own times furnishes as Black a list of crimes as can be paralleld in ancient time, even if we go back to Nero, Caligula or Ceasar Borgia. Young as you are, the cruel war into which we have been compelld by the Haughty Tyrant of Britain and the Bloody Emissarys of his vengance may stamp upon your mind this certain Truth, that the welfare and prosperity of all countries, communities and I may add individuals depend upon their Morals. That Nation to which we were once united as it has departed from justice, eluded and subverted the wise Laws which formerly governd it, sufferd the worst of crimes to go unpunished, has lost its valour, wisdom and Humanity, and from being the dread and terror of Europe, has sunk into derision and infamy.

But to quit political subjects, I have been greatly anxious for your safety having never heard of the Frigate since she saild, till about a week ago, a New York paper inform'd that she was taken and carried into Plimouth. I did not fully credit this report, tho it gave me much uneasiness. I yesterday heard that a French vessel was arrived at Portsmouth which brought News of the safe arrival of the Boston, but this wants confirmation. I hope it will not be long before I shall be assertaind of your safety. You must write me an account of your voyage, of your situation and of every thing entertaining you can recollect. Your Sister and Brothers are well. The last desire I would write for them, but I have not time by this opportunity. Your Sister I chide for her neglegence in this way. I have wrote several times to your papa, hope the Letters will not Miscarry. Let Stevens know his Mother and Friends are well.

Be assurd I am most affectionately yours.

Mr. Hardwick desires if such a thing as stocking weavers needles are to be had that Stevens or you would procure 2 thousand No. 6 and convey with any thing your pappa may have to send to me.

June 10, 1778

FEAR THAT JOHN WAS CAPTURED

To James Lovell

Dear Sir

Will you forgive my so often troubling you with my fears and anxieties; Groundless as some of them have been they were real to me for a time, and had all the force of truth upon me. I most sincerely wish my present uneasiness may arise from as ficticious a cause as the former proved to be but from many circumstances I fear it will not. Tis near four months since the Boston saild, in all which time we have not received the least inteligance from her, a vessel arrived from France in a passage of 32 days and did not leave France till after the Boston had been out 7 weeks, but neither saw or heard any thing of her. Last week there was I am told a paragraph in the Newport paper taken from the New york Gazzet that the Boston was taken and carried into Portsmouth with the Name of the Ship which took her, but what date I know not. There was no mention of Mr. Adams'es being on board which is the only reason I have to think that posibly she might be taken after landing him.

Tis full time if he was safe to hear from him. My anxiety daily increases, and I write to you Sir who have been acquainted with sorrow and affliction in various shapes, enduring with unshaken fortitude the Horrours of Capitivity and chains, in hopes that you will communicate to me some share of that hidden strength, which Throws out into practice

> Virtues which shun the day, and lie conceal'd
> In the smooth Seasons, and the calms of life

that I may endure this misfortune with becomeing fortitude, and to request of you to inform me what Steps congress will take in consequence of it. Will they endeavour an exchange immediately, or is it possibal that his most christian Majesty will demand him as an Ambassador from the united States of America.

June 12, 1778

RENTING OUT THE FARM

To John Adams

Dearest of Friends

By Mr. Tailor, who has promised me to deliver this with his own hand to you, or distroy it if necessary, I take the liberty of writing rather more freely than I should otherways venture to do. I cannot think but with pain of being debared this privilidge, the only one left me for my consolation in the many solitary and I may add melancholy hours which pass. I promissed myself a negative kind of happiness whenever I could hear of your safe arrival but alass I find a craving void left akeing in my Breast, and I find myself some days especially more unhappy than I would even wish an Enemy to be. In vain do I strive to divert my attention, my Heart, like a poor bird hunted from her nest, is still returning to the place of its affections, and fastens upon the object where all its cares and tenderness are centered. I must not expect, I ought not indeed for the sake of your repose to wish to be thus frequently, and thus fondly the subject of your meditation, but may I not believe that you employ a few moments every day from the Buisness and pleasures which surround you in thinking of her who wishes not her existance to survive your affection, who never recollects the cruel hour of seperation but with tears. From whence shall I gather firmness of mind bereft of the amicable prop upon which it used to rest and acquire fortitude? The subject is too tender to persue. I see it touches your Heart. I will quit it at the midnight hour, and rise in the morning suppressing these too tender sensibilities.

Tis 5 month since the Boston sailed during all which time I have only received two very short Letters. That you have wrote more I know tho you do not mention them. Cautious as tis necessary you should be, methinks you need not be so parsi-monious. Friendship and affection will suggest a thousand things to say to an intimate Friend which if ridiculed by an Enemy will only be an other proof among the thousands we already have of a savage barbarity. A variety of new scenes must arise the discription of which would afford ample amusement to your domestick Friend.

I had the pleasure of drinking tea a few days ago with Sir James Jay and Mr. Diggs. It was a pleasure to hear so directly from you and my dear Jack. The Gentlemen were very social and communicative. I found they had throughly enterd into the character of my Friend, who they represented as rather re-lucttantly entering into the modes and customs of ——— and rather conforming from necessity than inclination. They di-verted me with an account of the Freedoms and fondness of the . . . . . . for the venerable Doctor. At the same time I could not refrain figuring to myself a grave American republi-can starting at the sight unaccustomed to such freedoms even from the partner of his youth. After 13 years intimate connex-ion, who can recollect the time when had she laid her hand upon his—a universal Blush would have coverd her.—Much however must be allowed for Forms and Customs which ren-der even dissagreable practise'es familiar. I can even consent that they should practise their *Forms* upon your Lordship considering your natural fondness for the practise whilst I hold possession of what I think they cannot rob me of. Tis mine by a free gift, mine by exchange, mine by a long possession, mine by merrit and mine by every law humane and divine.

If I was sure this would reach you I should say many things which I dare not venture to. I stand corrected if I have said any thing already which I ought not to. I feel myself embaresse'd whilst my Heart overflows, and longs to give utterance to my pen. Many domestick affairs I wish to consult upon. I have studied for a method of defraying the necessary expences of my family. In no one Instance is a hundred pound L M better than thirteen pounds Six and Eight pence used to be, in for-eign Articles no ways eaquel, in taxes but a fourth part as good. Day Labour at 24 shillings per day. What then can you think my situation must be? I will tell you after much embaresment in endeavouring to procure faithfull hands I concluded to put out the Farm and reduce my family as much as posible. I sit about removeing the Tenants from the House, which with much difficulty I effected, but not till I had paid a Quarters Rent in an other House for them. I then with the kind assistance of Dr. Tufts procured two young Men Brothers newly married and placed them as Tenants to the halves retaining in my own Hands only one Horse and two Cows with pasturage for my Horse in summer, and Quincy medow for fodder in winter. At present I have no reason to repent of my situation, my family consists at present of only myself, two children and two Domesticks. Our daughter is at School in Boston, and I wait only to know how I shall be able to discharge my schooling for Master Charles to place him at Haverhill. Debts are my abhorrance. I never will borrow if any other method can be devised. I have thought of this which I wish you to assent to, to order some saleable articles which I will mention to be sent to the care of my unkle Smith a small trunk at a time, containing ten or 15 pounds Sterling, from which I may supply my family with such things as I need, and the rest place in the hands of Dr. Tufts Son who has lately come into Trade, and would sell them for me, by which means if I must pay extravagant prices I shall be more upon an eaquel footing with my Neighbours.

I have been obliged to make fence this year to the amount of 100 & 50 Dollors. I have occasion for only a pair of cart wheels for which I must give 60 pounds Lawfull money. I mention these few articles to serve as a specimen of the rest. I inquired the price of a new carrage the other day and found it to be no *more* than 300 pounds Lawfull money—at this rate I never will ask for a supply of this *light commodity* from any Body let my situation be what it will. The Season has been fine for grass but for about 3 weeks past we have had a sharp and severe Drouth which has greatly injured our grain and a blast upon english grain with a scarcity for flower so that a loaf which once sold for 4 pence is 4 shillings. Tis rumourd that the French fleet to the amount of 18ten have arrived of Chesepeak. The Enemy have left Philidelphia, but for politicks I refer you to the publick Letters which will accompany this.—Mr. Tailor promises to bring Letters from you whenever he returns. I am in daily expectation of hearing from you. I lament that you lay so far from the sea ports that you must omit some opportunities of writing. I will not suppose that with more leisure you have less inclination to write to your affectionate and Lonely Friend   Portia

c. July 15, 1778

"I HEAR THE ALARM GUNS FIRED"

To John Thaxter Jr.

Dear Sir   Sepbr. 2. 1778
I was much surprized to Night upon receiving a Letter from you, in which you say you have not heard from Home since june; I have wrote many Letters to you since that time and have sent 4 or 5 from your Friends all under cover to Mr. Lovell to you. What can have become of them I know not, unless some of them being directed to York Town travelled that way and have been lost. Do not think unkindly of us, for I assure you many Letters have been sent since that time. I saw your Mamma last week. She is very anxious for your Health. I deliverd with my own hand the Letter to your sister. You mention comeing home in october. Your Mamma and Sister are very desirous of seeing you, but say they would not have you return, unless you mean to quit your place. You know your own situation best, and whether it is worth your while to tarry longer. You may be assured of a Hearty welcome from your correspondent, tho I shall regreat the loss of my intelligencer.

You will hear no doubt before this reaches you of our unhappy Failure in the Rhode Island expedition, and yet no one to be blamed that I know of either for want of courage or conduct, but the Hand of providence was against us. The Terible Storm I mentiond to you in my last so impaired and shatterd the Counts Fleet that he was under a necessity of comeing into Boston to refit, in consequence of which the Enemy took the advantage of it, and attacked our Army. A pretty smart engagement ensued, in which we lost tis said a hundred Men killd and a 100 & 80 wounded, but did not loose ground, drove the Enemy back to their entrenchments, their loss have not heard. By orders since from General Washington the Island is quitted and every thing brought of without molestation. The reason for leaving it, is that How had sent his Fleet that course, and now finding the Island evacuated they are hovering about this coast 20 Sail of them. Poor Boston is again distress'd, and I own my Spirits not a little agitated. Tis now past Eleven o clock, and as I sit writing to you I hear the alarm Guns fired; the Count has this day orderd his Men to entrench upon Georges Island. Guns are carrying to Nantasket, what ships he has fit for an engagement are drawn up in order of Battle, but his own is disabled more than any other. The seat of war appears to be drawing into this quarter again. Should they attempt landing here, which I can scarcly believe, they will I hope meet with distruction, but they come upon us rather unexpectedly, and would greatly distress us. More Guns—I believe I shall not sleep very soundly to Night.

You inquire after my Dearest Friend. O Sir, I know not how to curb my impatience, only twice have I heard and those Letters dated in April. I wish a thousand times I had gone with him. We have not had a vessel from France since july when I heard by Sir James Jay. I think it very strange indeed and apprehend they must have been taken.

I would be more perticuliar but the News paper will tell you all the New's. We are very dry here, our crops are very much cut of, and this Fleet raises the price of every article which before exceeded in Lawfull money what they used to be in old tenor. I cannot say I shall come to the Town for a support, for I think I ought to come to the Continent. Some where or other I must find it, what signifies what one was once possessd of, when a hundred pounds Lawfull Money is reduced to thirteen pounds, six & 8 pence. I cannot name you an article save House Rent but what exceeds and eaquels that difference.

Tis very late, but I will not seal to Night. I will add a few lines in the morning if I am not captivated before that time.

Thursday morg. 3

I heard nothing further last Night. What tremours they had in Town I know not, but am inclined to think they were pretty great, as the Night before the Bells rung and the Militia were paraded at Eleven o clock at Night.

I must hasten and close or loosse this conveyance. Excuse all inaccuracies from your Friend   Portia

"WRITE ME A LETTER EN FRANCOIS"

To John Quincy Adams

My Dear Son   Sepber. 29 1778
Writing is not A la mode de Paris, I fancy or sure I should have heard from my son; or have you wrote and have I been so unfortunate as to lose all the Letters which have been written to me for this five months.

I have sufferd great anxiety in not hearing from your pappa, or you. I hope you have not been so unlucky in those Letters sent to you.

I want to know your situation, what proficiency you make in the Language. I expect you will write me a Letter en Francois á vous dire le vray, un si long silence commençoit déja á me donner de l'inquietude.

We have here a large portion of the French Navy. I never wanted to speak the language half so much before, it is difficult holding any intercourse with them. Many of the officers appear to be Gentleman of Education.

I wrote you one very long Letter, hope you received it. You must be very perticuliar when you write. I think it very hard when a vessel arrives without a Letter for me. You know the pleasure I always took in hearing from your pappa in his frequent absence from me. You must think now both he and you are at such a distance from me that Letters are more acceptable than ever.

Your Friends here are all well. The next opportunity you have for writing you must not forget your Grandmamma. Mr. Thaxter is at Philadelphia yet, tho he talks of returning this month.

Does the climate of France suit your constitution. You used to be unwell in the spring and fall. It is very sickly here with the dysentery.

We have heard of the engagement between the French and English Fleets, and are much gratified with the good conduct of our Allies.

After the faileure of the late Expedition against Rhoad Island, we were in great apprehension of an attack upon Boston, as the Fleet lay in that harbour, but haveing looked in upon them Lord How thought it best to retire to New York after plundering 9000 Sheep from Martha Vinyard.

Your Brothers send their Love to you, and thank you for their Letters, will write to you as soon as they are capable of it. Charlly got his pen to day and attempted it but could not please himself. I believe I must not write an other Letter to Paris till I hear from thence. Be dutifull my dear Son, be thoughtfull, be serious, do not gather the Thorns and the Thistles, but collect Such a Garland of flowers as will flourish in your native climate, and Bloom upon your Brows with an unfading verdure.

This will rejoice the Heart and compensate for the continual anxiety of your affectionate   xxxxxxx xxxxx

"THE FREEDOM I TAKE IN SCRIBLING"

To James Lovell

Your favour of Jan'ry 19 never reachd me till the 26 of this Month. The only reason why I did not mention the recept of your Letter November 27 and acknowledge with thanks Mr. Lovell's kind care and attention to the Box which arrived safe was oweing to my not receiving the least intimation of it, till after my Letter was sent to the post office.

In reply to a certain congratulation, can only say that the Idea of suffering for those who are dear to us beyond the power of words to express, raise sensibilities in the Heart which are blendid with a delicate pleasing Melancholy, and serve to mitigate the curse entailed upon us.

Since I wrote last I have been relieved from a great degree of anxiety by the arrival of the Miflin in which came a large packet of Letters of various dates, and one so late as December 2d. In reply to some pathetick complants, my Friend assures me that he has wrote 3 Letters where he has received one, and that he has full as much reason to complain of his Friends as they have of him. From Mr. Adams he writes he has received only one short card, from Mr. Gerry not a Syllable, from Mr. Lovell only 2 or 3 very short, tho he candidly allows for them supposing that they must have wrote oftner but attributes to the score of misfortune that so few have reachd him. I mention this that you may be assured he has not been unmindfull of his Friends. The occasion of my inquiry in a former Letter was oweing to my receiving inteligance that alterations had taken place and that my Friend was removed. He had received some such inteligance when he wrote in December. Why may I not wish that the removal might be to America. I reclined my Head upon my Hand, my pen in the other whilst I revolvd that wish in my mind.—Lie still thou flutterer. How pleasing were the Ideas that rushd upon my Soul whilst I was wholy absorbed in Self. But a superiour claim silenced the voice of pleading nature and I revoked the ardent wish—whilst I will endeavour to keep in view those patriotick sons of freedom and imitate their virtuous examples who whilst they long for private life and pant for Domestick felicity with painfull patience, incessant care and mixt anxiety are sacrificeing the vigor of their days to secure Independance and peace to the rising age.

But my Heart recoils with Indignation when I see their generous plans of Freedom sapped and undermined by guilefull Arts and Machinations of Self Love, Ambition and Avarice. Whether the late indiscreet appeal to the publick may be considerd in this light time will determine, but an open and Avowed Enemy to America could not have fixed upon a more successfull method of rasing Jealousys among the people or of sowing the seeds of discord in their minds, and such have been the Effects of it here that it produced a very extrodinary motion in a late assembly of which I dare say you have heard.

> Virtue! without thee,
> There is no ruling Eye, no Nerve in States;
> War has no vigour and no safety peace;
> Even justice warps to party, laws oppress.

> For, lost this social cement of Mankind,
> The greatest empires, by scarce felt degrees,
> Will moulder soft away—till tottering loose
> They prone at last to total ruin rush.

Since I first took up my pen a fortnight has slid a way without any thing material taking place unless the News paper altercation upon the important Subject of Balls and assemblies may come under the head of *Material*.—More than 2 years I think has elapsed since you was even a visitor in your Native Town. If you absent yourself much longer you will be under the same necessity which it is said Timon was in Athens of lighting a candle to find a *Man*. Monkies, Maccoronies and pate Ma'ters have multiplied like Egypt Locusts. Luxery, Luxery with her enticeing charms has unbraced their Nerves and extinguished that Noble Ardor, that Zeal for Liberty, "that Manly Soul of Toil," that impatient Scorn of base Subjection which once distinguished the inhabitants of your Native Town and led them first and foremost in the present glorious strugle.

Alass how changed! but I will quit a subject that I know must give you pain and ask if you are at Liberty to tell me the important News which is said to have arrived from Spain, which is good, very good and so good that nobody must know it. Various are the conjectures concerning it.

Mr. Thaxter acknowledges your reproof just and kissis the rod, makes his excuses I suppose in the enclosed Letter.

I will seek one in the benevolent Friendship of Mr. Lovell for the Freedom I take in Scribling to him. I love every one who Manifests a regard or Shews an Attachment to my Absent Friend, and will indulgently allow for the overflowings of a Heart softned by absence, pained by a seperation from what it holds most dear upon Earth. A similarity of circumstances will always lead to Sympathy and is a further inducement to subscribe myself your Friend & Servant,   Portia

February–March 1779

To Abigail Adams 2nd

My Dear Daughter   Braintree, February, 1779
    It is with inexpressible pleasure that I enclose to you a letter
from your brother, and that I can tell you, that I last night received four letters of various dates from your papa, and one so
late as the 6th of November. I would send forward the letters,
but know not how to part with them. Your papa writes that he
has enjoyed uncommon health for him, since his arrival in
France; that your brother is well, and, what is still more grateful to a parent's ears, that he conducts with a becoming prudence and discretion; that he assiduously applies himself to his
books. And your papa is pleased to say, "that the lessons of
his mamma are a constant law to him, and that they are so to
his sister and brothers, is a never failing consolation to him, at
times when he feels more tenderness for them than words can
express." Let this pathetic expression of your papa's, my dear,
have a due influence upon your mind.
    Upon politics, your papa writes thus: "Whatever syren songs
of peace may be sung in your ears, you may depend upon it,
from me, (who unhappily have been seldom mistaken in my
guesses of the intention of the British government for fourteen
years,) that every malevolent passion, and every insidious art,
will predominate in the British cabinet against us. Their threats
of Prussians and of great reinforcements, are false and impracticable, and they know them to be so; but their threats of
doing mischief with the forces they have, will be verified as far
as their power."
    This we see, in their descent upon Georgia, verified this very
hour.
    Almost all Europe, the Dutch especially, are at this day
talking of Great Britain in the style of American sons of liberty.
He hopes the unfortunate event at Rhode Island will not produce any heart-burnings between Americans and the Count
D'Estaing, who is allowed by all Europe to be a great and
worthy officer, and by all that know him to be a zealous friend
of America.

After speaking of some embarrassments in his public business, from half anglified Americans, he adds, "But from this court, this city and nation, I have experienced nothing but uninterrupted politeness."

I have a letter from a French lady, Madam la Grand, in French—a polite letter, and wrote in consequence of your papa's saying that, in some cases, it was the duty of a good citizen to sacrifice his all for the good of his country. She tells him that the sentiment is worthy of a Roman and a member of Congress, but cannot believe he would sacrifice his wife and children. In reply, he tells her that I possessed the same sentiment. She questions the truth of his assertion; and says nature would operate more powerfully than the love of one's country, and whatever other sacrifices he might make, it would be impossible for him to resign those very dear connections, especially as he had so often given her the warmest assurances of his attachment to them; and she will not be satisfied till she has related the conversation, and appealed to me for my sentiments upon the subject. She is an elderly lady, and wife to the banker, expresses great regard for your brother, of whom she is very fond, says he inherits the spirit of his father, and bids fair to be a Roman like him.

When I have fully translated the letter I will send it forward. I would have written to Mrs. Warren, but have much writing to do, and you may communicate this letter to her, if she can read it; but 'tis badly written, and I have not time to copy.

Let me hear from you soon, who am, at all times, your affectionate mamma,   A. A.

c. February 11, 1779

CONDITIONS AT HOME

To John Adams

My Dearest Friend   June 8th 79

Six Months have already elapsed since I heard a syllable from you or my dear Son, and five since I have had one single opportunity of conveying a line to you. Letters of various dates have lain months at the Navy Board, and a packet and Frigate both ready to sail at an hours warning have been months waiting the orders of Congress. They no doubt have their reasons, or ought to have for detaining them. I must patiently wait their Motions however painfull it is—and that it is so your own feelings will testify. Yet I know not but you are less a sufferer than you would be to hear from us, to know our distresses and yet be unable to relieve them. The universal cry for Bread to a Humane Heart is painfull beyond Discription, and the great price demanded and given for it, verifies that pathetick passage of sacred writ, all that a Man hath will he give for his life. Yet he who Miraculously fed a Multitude with 2 loaves and 5 fishes has graciously interposed in our favour and deliverd many of the Enimies supplies into our hands so that our distresses have been Mitigated. I have been able as yet to supply my own family spairingly but at a price that would astonish you. Corn is sold at 4 dollors hard money per Bushel which is eaquel to 80 at the rate of exchange.

Labour is at 8 dollors per Day and in 3 weeks at 12 tis probable, or it will be more stable than any thing else. Goods of all kinds are at such a price that I hardly dare mention it—Linnins at 20 dollors per yard the most ordinary sort calicow at 30 and 40, Broad cloths sold at 40 pounds per yard—West India goods full as high, Molasses at 20 dollors per Gallon, sugar 4 dollors per pound, Bohea Tea at 40 dollors and our own produce in proportion, Butchers meat at 6 and 7 and 8 shillings per pound, Board at 50 and 60 dollors per week. Rates high, that I suppose you will rejoice at, so would I, did it remedy the Evil. I pay 5 hundred Dollors, and a New continental rate has just appeard, my proportion of which will be 2 hundred more. I have come to this determination to sell no more Bills unless I can procure hard money for them altho I shall be obliged to allow a discount. If I sell for paper I through away more than half, so rapid is the depreciation, nor do I know that it will be received long. I sold a Bill to Blodget at 5 for one which was lookd upon as high at that time. The week after I received it, two Emissions were taken out of circulation and the greater part of what I had proved to be of that sort, so that those to whom I was indebted are obliged to wait and before it becomes due or is exchanged, it will be good for—as much as it will fetch, which will be nothing if it goes on as it has done for this 3 Months past, but I will not tire your patience any longer. I have not drawn any further upon you, I mean to wait the return of the Alliance which with longing Eyes I wait for. God grant it may bring me comfortable tidings from my dear dear Friend whose welfare is so essential to my happiness that it is entwined round my Heart, and cannot be impared or seper-ated from it without rending it assunder.

In contemplation of my situation I am sometimes thrown into an agony of distress. Distance, dangers—and O! I cannot name all the fears which sometimes oppress me and harrow up my soul. Yet must the common Lot of Man one day take place whether we dwell in our own Native Land, or are far distant from it. That we rest under the shadow of the Almighty is the consolation to which I resort, and find that comfort which the World cannot give. If he sees best to give me back my Friend, or to preserve my life to him, it will be so.

Our worthy Friend Dr. Winthrope is numberd with the great congregation to the inexpressible loss of Harvard College.

> Let no weak drop
> be shed for him. The Virgin in her bloom
> cut off, the joyous youth, and darling child
> These are the Tombs, that claim the tender Tear
> And Elegiac Song. But Winthrope calls
> For other Notes of Gratulation high
> That now he wanders through those endless worlds
> He here so well discried, and wandering talks,
> And Hymns their Author with his glad compeers.

The Testimony he gave with his dyeing Breath in favour of revealed Religion, does honour to his memory and will endear it to every Lover of Virtue.

I know not who will be found worthy to succeed him.

Our Brother Cranch is immersd in publick Buisness—and so cumbered with it that he fears He shall not be able to write you a line.

Congress have not yet made any appointment of you to any other court. There appears a dilatoryness, an indisicion in their proceedings. I have in Mr. Lovell an attentive Friend who kindly informs me of every thing which passes relative to you and your situation, gives me extracts of your Letters both to himself and others. I know you will be unhappy whenever it is not in your power to serve your country—and wish yourself at home where at least you might serve your family.—I cannot say that I think our affairs go very well here. Our currency seems to be the source of all our Evils. We cannot fill up our continental Army by means of it, no bounty will prevail with them. What can be done with it, it will sink in less than a year. The advantages the Enemy daily gain over us is oweing to this. Most truly did you prophesy when you said that they would do all the mischief in their power with the forces they had here.

Many Letters lay in Boston for you which have been wrote Months. My good unkle Smith yesterday let me know that a Letter of Mark bound for Nants would sail in a day or two. I eagerly seaze the opportunity and beg you to give my blessing to my son to whom I have not time now to write. I dare not trust myself with the Idea nor can express how ardently I long to see both the parent and son. Our whole family have enjoyed great Health since your absence. Daughter and sons who dayly delight themselves with talking of Pappa and Brother present their Duty and Love. Your Worthy Mamma who is now here requests me to add her tenderest affection to you, who next to the writer is anxious to hear from you. Your Brother requests me to desire you to procure for him 2 peices of Linnin to the amount of 24 dollors which he will pay to me, and to send them whenever you have an opportunity of sending to me. I shall not write for any thing till the Alliance returns and I find what success she has had.

My tenderest regards ever attend you in all places and situations know me to be ever ever yours.

"I AM NOT IN A VERY GOOD HUMOUR"

To James Lovell

Do you love the Natural sentiments of the Heart? Take them then as they flow from the pen of Portia. Having been to take a ride this afternoon upon my return stopt at my Brother Cranchs when one of the family came to the chaise and told me a Gentleman from Boston had left a large packet for me in the House. My Heart bounded for joy—I besought him to deliver them Instantly to me. The Bulk of the packet insured them a pressure to my Bosom. My spirits danced. It was dark, I could not see the hand writing but was in no doubt from whence they came. The Space between my Brothers and my own house was a *dozen mile* and it seemd like an age to get to it. I sprang from the chaise, calld for a light before I got into the house, but when I came to the light it was Mr. Lovell's hand writing. O the Letters had arrived at Philadelphia, and he ever attentive to the calls of Friendship had coverd them to me. I broke the Seal and the dear delusion vanished like the "baseless fabrick of a vision." An involuntary tear (it could not be helpd) found its way and for the first time I did not feel that pleasure which always before accompanied a Letter from Mr. Lovell. Six Months and not one line. Expectations so raised and so damped must plead my excuse for so unpolite a reception to my much valued correspondent, to whom for the future I shall *give leave* to make use of what ever expressions he pleases in order to prove that my Benevolence is eaquel to *my power*, having from a further acquaintance with him discoverd that the talent for which I formerly censured him is natural to him and that far from being a slothfull servant he has improved it tenfold. Nor would I rob him of the pleasure he takes in thus indulgeing the *too pleasing art*, since it must be acknowledged that he is an accomplished proficient in it.

I will not disclaim the Epethet of amiable since it is a character which if I do not already possess it I would wish to obtain even to the value of her whose price was far above rubies.

Your dissertation upon Letter peaping diverted me. I am glad however that you had no curiosity to gratify, or held yourself otherways restrained from inspecting the Letters of Portia. For having flatterd me with a place in your Esteem I should have been loth to have forfeited it, since I have no right to expect nor a wish to obtain from any other than the person to whom they were addressd that which an Antient Sage has told us covereth a multitude of faults. The Manuscript you mention did not come by the hand which brought the Letters.

I am happy sir if any of the contents of the Trunk were service-able to you and you will oblige both my absent Friend for whom I know I can answer as well as the present writer in re-taining both the Jacket and Stockings and in never mentioning them again.

I stand indebted to you sir for a Letter dated March 9th. as well as June 5th in the former of which you say there is a strange delay and some thing of Mystery in the propositions which have been lately made here respecting our foreign af-fairs, but be assured that I have not yet perceived any thing which will probably affect Mr. A in a dissagreable Manner.

I wish you had explain'd yourself more fully or was it out of tenderness to me that you would not tell me that I might have reason to daily expect his return, knowing the anxiety I must suffer in the interval.

If he has not been recall'd I know not how to account for a passage in a Letter which has come to hand since I took my pen to you. It is from Dr. Winship belonging to the Alliance, to his wife and dated Brest harbour 7 of April. "It is now de-termined that we return to Boston as soon as may be, and what convinces me that we shall make *all possible speed* is that Mr. Adams is to return in the ship." 97 prisoners had been sent from England with which the ship would be well man'd. I have since heard some resolves of congress which I think makes it probable that he would return either with *or without* leave, since if he was not in a situation to serve his country, he would be unhappy absent from his family. God grant him a safe re-turn, and that in future he may retire from publick life.

There has been 3 several appointments here of gentlemen for members of congress, all of whom have declined. This state will find it something difficult to supply the places of the pres-ent *indefatagable Labourers* there. It begins to be consider'd as rather burdensome and no loaves and fishes to be caught.— But if virtue says my absent Friend on a similar occasion, was to be rewarded with wealth it would not be virtue, if virtue was to be rewarded with fame it would not be virtue of the sublimist kind. Who would not rather be Fabricus than Ceasar, who would not rather be Aristedes than even William the 3d. Who? Nobody would be of this mind but Aristedes and Fabricius.

I fancy I had better close this Letter without any further addition least you should discover that I am not in a very good humour, possibly from wrong information. I will therefore endeavour to suppress every dissagreable Idea of publick Slight and indignity till assertained of the Truth or falcity by Mr. S. Adams whose daily arrival is expected, and in the mean time I shall anxiously wait for the return of the Alliance, perplexd with a thousand fears and apprehension *which I do not owe the publick* and for which—but hush, did I not say I would close but not till I have assured you that I am with sentiments of Esteem your Friend & humble Servant,   Portia

June 18–26, 1779

JOHN LEAVES FOR FRANCE AGAIN

To John Adams

Dearest of Friends   November 14 1779

My habitation, how disconsolate it looks! My table I set down to it but cannot swallow my food. O Why was I born with so much Sensibility and why possessing it have I so often been call'd to struggle with it? I wish to see you again, was I sure you would not be gone, I could not withstand the temptation of comeing to town, tho my Heart would suffer over again the cruel torture of Seperation.

What a cordial to my dejected Spirits were the few lines last night received. And does your Heart forebode that we shall again be happy. My hopes and fears rise alternately. I cannot resign more than I do, unless life itself was called for.—My dear sons I can not think of them without a tear, little do they know the feelings of a Mothers Heart! May they be good and usefull as their Father then will they in some measure reward the anxiety of a Mother. My tenderest Love to them. Remember me also to Mr. Thaxter whose civilities and kindness I shall miss.

God almighty bless and protect my dearest Friend and in his own time restore him to the affectionate Bosom of

                                                        Portia

"WHY WAS I BORN WITH SO MUCH SENSIBILITY"

To James Lovell

Sir   Braintree November 18 1779
   In a Letter from my Dear absent Friend the day before he saild dated on Board the Frigate he informd me that the Evening before he received a Letter from his much Esteemed Friend Mr. Lovell in which he complained that "Portia did not write to him." Could *Portia* have given a greater proof of the high value she placed upon his Friendship and correspondence she would not have withheld her hand. But can Mr. L——l so soon forget that he had prohibited her from writing by prescribing conditions to her that *he knew she could not practise.*
   He must have divested himself of that sensibility which vibrates with every sentiment of his mind and every motion of his Heart to suppose that she could

> "Give sorrow vent. The Grief that cannot speak
> Whispers the o'er fraught heart and bids it Break."

   Cannot you believe me sir when I tell you that there is but one more conflict in life harder to be endured than that which I have pass't through. Why was I born with so much sensibility, why possessing it have I so often been call'd to struggle with it?
   A few more such trials would distroy a tabernacle already impaired by them. Could I find pleasure and happiness in a thousand sources from whence many others would derive them, I should feel less keenly the wound, but to me the world and all its enjoyments are hazarded at once.

> Fame, wealth and honour, what are ye to Love?

   Do not expose me sir, the world think differently I know. You should not call for my pen unless determined to pardon my weakness. Two sons have accompanied their Father, the Eldest but 12 years of age. Mr. Thaxter too, who has lived in the Family near 6 years and was like a Brother in kindness and Friendship, makes one of the absent Family, whilst one daughter and Little son, are my solitary companions.
   Your former kindness and attention leads me to rely upon

your future Friendship which notwithstanding former prohibitions I hope is not forfeited by the present sentiments of

Portia

"ANY IMPORTANT AND INTERESTING MATTERS"

To James Lovell

Enclosed I return according to your direction a duplicate Number of the journals. Number 29 is missing. I do not fully understand you when you say that I must not keep any of the pages 78. Do you mean that I must return them to you or forward them to Mr. Adams. I have no journals left but part of 75 and 76. All that Mr. Adams could find or procure of a later date he took with him; I read the journals and the news papers which you are so kind as to forward, but I still find myself a looser. I have not the pleasure of the intelligence which used to be communicated to my Friend with the perusal of which he always indulged me. I dare venture to say this only to you, since a hint of this kind would restrain many Gentlemens pens possessd of less liberal sentiments.

I have ever made it a rule in life never to seek for a Secret which concernd the honour of a person to withhold, and have been too proud to divulge one when once confided in, and on this account probably I have met with more indulgence. I am not seeking Sir for communications improper to be made to a Lady—only wish to know from time to time any important and interesting matters which may take place. I find that congress are Drawing Bills at 25 for one upon Mr. Lawrens and Jay to the amount of 100,000 Sterling. Have they any prospect that their draughts will be answerd, or do they depend upon the exertions of those Gentlemen to procure it after their arrival. Why may I ask do they demand only 25 when 30 has been currently given here, and if I have not been misinformd 40 at Philadelphia.

You may always give me the go by, when I ask an improper Question and I shall take no umbrage but it will not be one I suppose to inquire after Mr. Adamse's accounts and vouchers and to ask what has ever been done with them? as he never heard a syllable about them since they were sent to the board of treasury and left in charge that I should inquire after them.

I have the pleasure to inform you that I received a Letter from my friend 5 days after he sailed dated 200 leigues distant by way of a privateer which they brought too, and which soon after arrived here. They had met with one Storm which did them but little damage. They had not seen any Enemy and were all well except Mr. Dana who was very Sea Sick. Have nothing new this way but what the papers will inform you of. A Great hugh and cry raised by John Paul Jones the former valient commander of the Ranger. I have a curiosity to know more of this mans history, he first drew my attention by his Knight Errant expedition to St. Marys Ile and his Letter to Lady Selkirk which I have no doubt you have seen. Unhappy for us that we had not such a commander at the Penobscot expedition. We should not have been groaning under disgrace, dissapointment and the heavyest debt incurred by this State since the commencement of the war.

Have wrote you several times lately, but have not yet received a line in reply. Possibly you may have removed as I have heard it was in contemplation. Be so good as to let Mr. Nurse know that I received the Letter for Mr. Thaxter which shall be safely conveyed to him by an opportunity which will offer within a few days, when I shall send forward the papers and journals entrusted to my care.

December 13, 1779

"MY WANTS ARE CIRCUMSCRIBED"

To John Lowell

Sir   Braintree December 27

Your very polite reply to my Letter demands my acknowledgment. If I should find myself embarressed at any time I shall not fail making use of your kindly offerd Friendship and assistance. If Sir it will be of any service to you to receive the Hard Money giving me the current exchange it is at your

Service if you will please to signify it, tho it will be but small sums that I shall exchange at a time and that as seldom as possible.

Mr. Adams has a small Farm upon which I live, and by Letting it to the Halves it supplies me with many necessaries. My family is not numerous, and my wants are circumscribed in a small compass

> "Having learnt the virtue and the Art
> To live on little with a cheerful Heart."

For ever since Mr. Adams engaged in publick Buisness I relinquished the prospect of any thing more than a competent support. His motives you know Sir were not mercenary and he has too much honour and Integrity to serve himself or his family at the expence of his country. I frankly own that I derive more pleasure from this reflection than wealth could bestow.

Excuse Sir this freedom and permit me to assure you that at this cottage I shall welcome Mr. and Mrs. Lowell whenever her Health will afford that pleasure To your obliged Friend & Humble Servant, A Adams

December 27, 1779

"TIMES IN WHICH A GENIOUS WOULD WISH TO LIVE"

To John Quincy Adams

My dear Son Janry. 19 1780

I hope you have had no occasion either from Enemies or the Dangers of the Sea to repent your second voyage to France. If I had thought your reluctance arose from proper deliberation, or that you was capable of judgeing what was most for your own benifit, I should not have urged you to have accompanied your Father and Brother when you appeared so averse to the voyage.

You however readily submitted to my advice, and I hope will never have occasion yourself, nor give me reason to Lament it. Your knowledge of the Language must give you greater advantages now, than you could possibly have reaped whilst Ignorant of it, and as you increase in years you will find your understanding opening and daily improveing.

Some Author that I have met with compares a judicious traveller, to a river that increases its stream the farther it flows from its source, or to certain springs which running through rich veins of minerals improve their qualities as they pass along. It will be expected of you my son that as you are favour'd with superiour advantages under the instructive Eye of a tender parent, that your improvements should bear some proportion to your advantages. Nothing is wanting with you, but attention, dilligence and steady application, Nature has not been deficient.

These are times in which a Genious would wish to live. It is not in the still calm of life, or the repose of a pacific station, that great characters are formed. Would Cicero have shone so distinguished an orater, if he had not been roused, kindled and enflamed by the Tyranny of Catiline, Millo, Verres and Mark Anthony. The Habits of a vigorous mind are formed in contending with difficulties. All History will convince you of this, and that wisdom and penetration are the fruits of experience, not the Lessons of retirement and leisure.

Great necessities call out great virtues. When a mind is raised, and animated by scenes that engage the Heart, then those qualities which would otherways lay dormant, wake into Life, and form the Character of the Hero and the Statesman.

War, Tyrany and Desolation are the Scourges of the Almighty, and ought no doubt to be deprecated. Yet it is your Lot my Son to be an Eye witness of these Calimities in your own Native land, and at the same time to owe your existance among a people who have made a glorious defence of their invaded Liberties, and who, aided by a generous and powerfull Ally, with the blessing of heaven will transmit this inheritance to ages yet unborn.

Nor ought it to be one of the least of your excitements towards exerting every power and faculty of your mind, that you have a parent who has taken so large and active a share in this contest, and discharged the trust reposed in him with so much satisfaction as to be honour'd with the important Embassy, which at present calls him abroad.

I cannot fulfill the whole of my duty towards you, if I close this Letter, without reminding you of a failing which calls for a strict attention and watchfull care to correct. You must do it for yourself. You must curb that impetuosity of temper, for which I have frequently chid you, but which properly directed may be productive of great good. I know you capable of these exertions, with pleasure I observed my advice was not lost upon you. If you indulge yourself in the practise of any foible or vice in youth, it will gain strength with your years and become your conquerer.

The strict and invoilable regard you have ever paid to truth, gives me pleasing hopes that you will not swerve from her dictates, but add justice, fortitude, and every Manly Virtue which can adorn a good citizen, do Honour to your Country, and render your parents supreemly happy, particuliarly your ever affectionate Mother,   AA

"MAKE YOURSELF MASTER OF WHAT YOU UNDERTAKE"

To Charles Adams

My dear Charles   Janry. 19 1780

How does my son after the fatigues of a voyage. A young adventurer indeed, how many times did you wish yourself by mammas fireside. But pappa wrote me that you made as good a sailor as your Brother, flatterd you a little I suppose, But I was very glad to hear you did so well.

I hope before this time that you are safe landed possibly arrived at Paris and placed at school, where I hope you will strive to obtain the Love and good will of every Body by a modest obliging Behaviour. You was a favorite in the Neighbourhood at home, all of whom wonder how Mamma could part with you. Mamma found it hard enough tis true, but she consulted your good more than her own feelings, and hopes you will not dissapoint her hopes and expectations by contracting vices and follies, instead of improveing in virtue and knowledge which can only make you usefull to society and happy to yourself.

You have an opportunity very early in life of seeing a foreign Country and of Learning a Language which if you live may be very serviceable to you, and even at this early period of your life you may form Friendships, if you behave worthy of your country, which will do honour to you in future, but in order to [   ] this you must be very attentive to your Books, and to every Branch of knowledge and improvement with which your pappa is pleasd to indulge you.

Let your ambition lead you to make yourself Master of what you undertake, do not be content to lag behind others, but strive to excell.

I hope soon to hear of your welfare and happiness which are always near the heart of your ever affectionate Mother.

LORD CHESTERFIELD'S LETTERS TO HIS SON

To Mercy Otis Warren

Febry. 28 1780

How does my Dear Mrs. Warren through a long and tedious Winter? in which I have never been honourd with a single line from her hand. Possibly she may think me underserving of her favours; I will not presume to lay claim to them upon the score of merit, but surely she should have charitably considered my lonely State, and Brightned the Gloomy hour with the Benign Rays of her Friendship dispenced through her elegant pen.

A Succession of tormenting whitlows has prevented me from inquiring after the Health of my much valued Friend. Those difficulties being now removed I have the pleasure of making that inquiry? and of communicating to her the agreable intelligance I received last week, by a vessel arrived at Newburyport from Corruna in Spain, of the safe arrival of Mr. Adams at that Port, in Eighteen days after he left Boston. I have not as yet, received any Letters, nor any certain account why they made that port, it is rumourd that the vessel sprung a leak.

I suppose he will proceed by land to France tho a journey of 700 miles, from whence I hope soon to be favourd with the certainty of his arrival.

By Capt. Sampson there came two Letters, one from Mr.

Lee and one from a Mr. Gellee, to Mr. Adams. By Mr. Lee's I find that affairs go on in the old course at Passy. "The Counsel there is composed of the same Honorable Members, says Mr. Lee, as when you left it, with the reinforcement of Samll. Wharton, Samll. Petrie and the Alexanders, a match is concluded between one of the daughters and Jonathan Williams this *August* and natural family compact will I hope promote the publick as well as private Interests."

There is a party in France of worthless ambitious intrigueing Americans, who are disposed to ruin the reputation of every Man whose Views do not coinside with their selfish Schemes. Of this you will be satisfied when I tell you that Mr. Gellee writes thus,

"After your departure reports were circulated here that you were gone to England and that during your Station here, you had entertaind an Illicit correspondence with the British Ministry. It was even published here that Mr. Samll. Adams had headed a conspiration and contrived to surrender Boston to the English. In vain did I endeavour to shew them the absurdity of the former opinion, by your embarking in the same ship with the Chevalier, but you know the people in this country are in general very Ignorant of American affairs which give designing Men an opportunity to shew their Malignity."

How happy my dear Madam would America have been, had it been her Lot, to have contended only with foreign Enemies, but the rancour of her internal foes have renderd the task of the patriot peculiarly difficult and Dangerous.

I sometimes contemplate the situation of my absent Friend, honourd as he is at present with the confidence of his Country, as the most critical and hazardous Embassy to his reputation, his honour, and I know not but I may add life, that could possibly have been entrusted to him. I view him beset with the machinations of envy, the Snares of Treachery, the malice of Dissimulation and the Clandestine Stabs of Calumny.

Can the Innocence of the dove or the wisdom of a more subtle animal screne him from all these foes? Can the strictest integrity and the most unwearied exertions for the benefit and happiness of Mankind secure to him more, than the approbation of his own Heart.

All other applause without that would be of small Estima-

tion, yet one would wish not to be considerd as a selfish, designing, Banefull foe, when they have worn out their lives in
the service of their country.

Those who Envy him, his situation see not with my Eyes,
nor feel with my Heart. Perhaps I feel and fear too much.

I have heard this winter of a Letter from a Lady to her son
containing Strictures upon Lord Chesterfields Letters. I have
not been favour'd with a sight of it, tho I have wished for it. A
collection of his Lordships Letters came into my Hands this
winter which I read, and tho they contain only a part of what
he has written, I found enough to satisfy me, that his Lordship
with all his Elegance and graces, was a Hypocritical, polished
Libertine, a mere Lovelace, but with this difference, that Lovelace was the most generous Man of the two, since he had justice sufficient to acknowledge the merrit he was distroying,
and died penitently warning others, whilst his Lordship not
content himself with practiseing, but is in an advanced age,
inculcateing the most immoral, pernicious and Libertine principals into the mind of a youth whose natural Guardian he was,
and at the same time calling upon him to wear the outward
Garb of virtue knowing that if that was cast aside, he would
not be so well able to succeed in his persuits.

I could prove to his Lordship were he living that there was
one woman in the world who could act consequentially more
than 24 hours, since I shall dispise to the end of my days that
part of his character. Yet I am not so blinded by his abuse upon
our sex, as not to allow his Lordship the merrit of an Elegant
pen, a knowledge of *Mankind* and a compiler of many Excellent maxims and rules for the conduct of youth, but they are
so poisoned with a mixture of Libertinism that I believe they
will do much more injury than benifit to Mankind. I wish my
dear Madam you would favor me with a coppy of the Letter
said to be in your power.

How does that patient sufferer Mrs. Lothrope? She is one of
those who is to be made perfect through sufferings, nor will
the prediction be unaccomplished in her, my affectionate regard to her, and a tender commiseration for her sufferings.

I spent a most agreable Evening with you not long since in
immagination. I hope to realize it in the approaching Spring.

My respectfull regards to Generall Warren, complements to my young Friends from their and your affectionate Friend,

Portia

My Daughter presents her duty and reflects with pleasure upon the winter she so agreably spent with you. She remembers Master George with affection, the other young Gentlemen with complacency.

"NOT WITHOUT HONOUR SAVE IN HIS OWN COUNTRY"

To Elbridge Gerry

Sir   March 13th 1780

Altho this is the first time I ever took up my pen to address you, I do it in perfect confidence that you will not expose me, having been long ago convinced that you are the sincere and constant Friend of one deservedly Dear to me, whose honour and character it is my Duty at all times to support.

I observed in a late Philadelphia paper of Janry. 27, that the Philosophical Society had chosen a Number of Members, among whom they were pleased to place The Honorable John Adams Esqr. *late Member of Congress*, no doubt with an intention of confering an Honour upon him. Before him is placed—His *Excellency* John Jay Esqr. *Minister of the united States* at *the court of Madrid*.

May I ask you Sir, why this distinction? Tho I do not know that you are any ways connected with the Society, I presume no person will say that the commission with which Mr. A——s is invested, is of less importance than that of Mr. J—ys. I suppose they both bear the same title of Minister plenipotentary. Mr. A——s had acted under a commission from Congress near two years before Mr. J—ys appointment, which if I am not mistaken, both in the Army and Navy gives a pre'eminence of Rank.

It may be considerd as pride and vanity in me Sir, for ought I know, to take notice of such a circumstance, nor should I have done it, if I had not before observed similar Instances with regard to Mr. A——s.

In a publick Society where they mean to Confer an Honorary Distinction, such things as these ought to be attended to, especially as they have a much greater influence abroad where Rank is considerd of more importance than in our Young Country.

I do not Imagine Sir that this distinction was aim'd so much at the person, as the State. You have not been so long conversant with the Southern Department as to be inattentive to the jealousy that there is of the Massachusets, and of every Man of any Eminence in it.

Is it not therefore particuliarly incumbent upon the Members of this State carefully to gaurd the Honor of it, and of those who represent it, which never can be done if such Little Stigmas are sufferd to be fixed upon them.

The journals of Congress will sufficently shew the various Departments in which Mr. A——s acted whilst a Member of it. Those who sat with him, are the best judges of the Integrity of his conduct, an ample testimony of which has been given him by the unsolicited honor conferd upon him, in the important Embassy with which he is at present charged. Yet there is envy and jealousy sufficient in the world to seek to lessen a character however benificial to the Country or useful to the State.

Nor are these passions Local. They are the Low, Mean and Sordid inhabitants of all countries and climates, an Instance of which I can give you, with regard to Mr. A——s. When he first arrived in France, he found great pains had been taken to convince all Ranks that the person sent them in a publick character was not the *famous* Adams. Who then could it be? Why some one of no importance, of whom the World never heard before, tho he however was not under the necessity of borrowing a reputation, nor had he any reason to complain of the French court or nation, from whom he received every mark of respect and attention.

A prophet is not without honour save in his own country. By that, he was left in a situation which I need not discribe to you sir who felt it for him, but which I am now satisfied, arose

more from the Embarrassment in which foreign affairs were
involved, than from any designed slight or neglect of Mr.
A——s. Yet the light in which it was viewd abroad gave designing malicious persons an opportunity to shew their malignity, and they improved it to that purpose, for imediately upon
Mr. A——s quitting France a report was circulated, (as I have
learnt from a Letter lately received from a correspondent of
Mr. A——s directed to him) that during his station there, he
had entertaind an illicit correspondence with the British Min-
istery, and that he was gone to England. "In vain says the
writer did I endeavour to shew them the absurdity of such an
opinion, by your embarking in the same ship with the Chevalier, but the people in this country are very Ignorant of American affairs, and eagerly swallow any thing."

If Sir America means to be respected abroad, she must chuse
out such characters to represent her as will disinterestedly persue her Interest and happiness, in whom she can place an approved confidence, and whenever she is in possession of such
characters, she must support them with honour and delicacy,
nor hearken to the Machinations of envy, jealousy, vanity or
pride. For if those who have stood foremost in her cause, supported her through all her perils and dangers, borne a large
share in some of the most hazardous of them, do not find
themselves and their characters defended and protected by
her, will it be any wonder if she should finally be forsaken by
every Man of Merrits withdrawing from her Service.

I can answer for my absent Friend that he never regarded
the appendages of Rank and precedence any other ways than
they affected the publick; more Espicially this State, and that
he would think himself happier in a private Station, beneath
this Humble cottage in the cultivation of his farm, and the
Society of his family, than in his envyed Embassy at foreign
courts, where tho he possesst the Innocence of the dove, and
the wisdom of a more subtle animal, they would be found in-
sufficient to screne him against the Clandestine Stabs of
calumny.

I have presumed to write thus freely to you sir, upon a subject which will not bear noticeing to any but a confidential
Friend. In that light my dear Mr. A——s has always considerd
you, and from the intimate union which constitutes us one,

permit me through him, to consider you in the same character and to Subscribe myself your Friend and Humble Servant,

Portia

"THE SUBJECT OF SELF-KNOWLEDGE"

To John Quincy Adams

My dear son   March 20 1780
   Your Letter last evening received from Bilboa relieved me from much anxiety, for having a day or two before received Letters from your Pappa, Mr. Thaxter and Brother in which packet I found none from you, nor any mention made of you, my mind ever fruitfull in conjectures was instantly allarmed. I feard you was sick, unable to write, and your Pappa unwilling to give me uneasiness had concealed it from me and this apprehension was confirmed by every persons omitting to say how long they should continue in Bilboa.

   Your Pappas Letters came in Capt. Lovett to Salem, yours by Capt. Babson to Newburry Port, and soon gave ease to my anxiety, at the same time that it excited gratitude and thankfullness to Heaven for the preservation you all experienced in the imminent Dangers which threatned you. You Express in both your Letters a degree of thankfulness. I hope it amounts to more than words, and that you will never be insensible to the particular preservation you have experienced in both your Voyages.

   You have seen how inadequate the aid of Man would have been, if the winds and the seas had not been under the particular goverment of that Being who streached out the Heavens as a span, who holdeth the ocean in the hollow of his hand, and rideth upon the wings of the wind.

   If you have a due sense of your preservation, your next consideration will be, for what purpose you are continued in Life?—It is not to rove from clime to clime, to gratify an Idle curiosity, but every new Mercy you receive is a New Debt upon you, a new obligation to a diligent discharge of the various relations in which you stand connected; in the first place to your Great Preserver, in the next to Society in General, in particular to your Country, to your parents and to yourself.

The only sure and permanant foundation of virtue is Religion. Let this important truth be engraven upon your Heart, and that the foundation of Religion is the Belief of the one only God, and a just sense of his attributes as a Being infinately wise, just, and good, to whom you owe the highest reverence, Gratitude and Adoration, who superintends and Governs all Nature, even to Cloathing the lilies of the Field and hearing the young Ravens when they cry, but more particularly regards Man whom he created after his own Image and Breathed into him an immortal Spirit capable of a happiness beyond the Grave, to the attainment of which he is bound to the performance of certain duties which all tend to the happiness and welfare of Society and are comprised in one short sentence expressive of universal Benevolence, "Thou shalt Love thy Neighbour as thyself" and is elegantly defined by Mr. Pope in his Essay on Man

> "Remember, Man, the universal cause
> Acts not by partial, but by general laws
> And makes what happiness we justly call
> Subsist not in the good of one but all
> Theres not a Blessing individuals find
> But some way leans and hearkens to the kind."

Thus has the Supreme Being made the good will of Man towards his fellow creatures an Evidence of his regard to him, and to this purpose has constituted him a Dependant Being, and made his happiness to consist in Society. Man early discoverd this propensity of his Nature and found

> "Eden was tasteless till an Eve was there."

Justice, humanity and Benevolence are the duties you owe to society in general. To your Country the same duties are incumbent upon you with the additional obligation of sacrificeing ease, pleasure, wealth and life itself for its defence and security.

To your parents you owe Love, reverence and obedience to all just and Equitable commands. To yourself—here indeed is a wide Field to expatiate upon. To become what you ought to be and, what a fond Mother wishes to see you, attend to some precepts and instructions from the pen of one who can have no motive but your welfare and happiness, and who wishes in this way to supply to you, the personal watchfulness, and care which a seperation from you, deprives you of at a period of Life when habits are easiest acquired, and fixed, and tho the advise may not be new, yet suffer it to obtain a place in your memory, for occasions may offer and perhaps some concuring circumstances give it weight and force.

Suffer me to recommend to you one of the most usefull Lessons of Life, the knowledge and study of yourself. There you run the greatest hazard of being deceived. Self Love and partiality cast a mist before the Eyes, and there is no knowledge so hard to be acquired, nor of more benifit when once throughly understood. Ungoverned passions have aptly been compaired to the Boisterous ocean which is known to produce the most terible Effects. "Passions are the Elements of life" but Elements which are subject to the controul of Reason. Who ever will candidly examine themselves will find some degree of passion, peevishness or obstinancy in their Natural tempers. You will seldom find these dissagreable ingredients all united in one, but the uncontroulable indulgence of either is sufficient to render the possessor unhappy in himself and dissagreable to all who are so unhappy as to be wittnesses of it, or suffer from its Effects.

You my dear son are formed with a constitution feelingly alive, your passions are strong and impetuous and tho I have sometimes seen them hurry you into excesses, yet with pleasure I have observed a frankness and Generosity accompany your Efforts to govern and subdue them. Few persons are so subject to passion but that they can command themselves when they have a motive sufficiently strong, and those who are most apt to transgress will restrain themselves through respect and Reverence to Superiours, and even where they wish to recommend themselves to their equals. The due Government of the passions has been considered in all ages as a most valuable acquisition, hence an inspired writer observes, He that is slow to anger is better than the Mighty, and he that ruleth his Spirit than he that taketh a city. This passion unrestrained by reason cooperating with power has produced the Subversion of cities, the desolation of countries, the Massacre of Nations, and filled the world with injustice and oppression.—Behold your own Country, your Native Land suffering from the Effects of Lawless power and Malignant passions, and learn betimes from your own observation and experience to govern and controul yourself. Having once obtained this self goverment you will find a foundation laid for happiness to yourself and usefullness to Mankind. "Virtue alone is happiness below," and consists in cultivating and improveing every good inclination and in checking and subduing every propensity to Evil. I have been particular upon the passion of Anger, as it is generally the most predominant passion at your age, the soonest excited, and the least pains taken to subdue it.

"What composes Man, can Man destroy."

I do not mean however to have you insensible to real injuries. He who will not turn when he is trodden upon is deficient in point of spirit, yet if you can preserve good Breeding and decency of Manners you will have an advantage over the agressor and will maintain a dignity of character which will always insure you respect even from the offender.

I will not over burden your mind at this time. I mean to persue the Subject of Self-knowledge in some future Letter, and give you my Sentiments upon your future conduct in life when I feel disposed to reassume my pen. In the mean time be assured no one is more sincerely Interested in your happiness than your ever affectionate Mother,   A A

May 8th

This Letter has lain ever since March waiting for a passage. Since it was written I have had the pleasure of receiving Letters from your Pappa by the Marquiss Fayette, your Sister and Brother Letters from you. Your Sister replies to you, your Brother wishes to. If I have time I shall write for him. It gives me great pleasure to hear that you and your Brother are setled in a regular way. Roving is not benificial to study at your age, Learning is not attained by chance, it must be sought for with ardour and attended to with diligence. I hope you have received Letters from me long e'er now, I have written to you often. My dear Charles I hope is a good Boy. Remember my

Dear your example will have great weight with him. Your Pappa commends your Steadiness. If you could once feel how gratefull to the Heart of a parent the good conduct of a child is, you would never be the occasion of exciteing any other Sensations in the Bosom of your ever affectionate Mother,

A A

Do not expose my Letters. I would coppy but hate it. Enclosed are two patterns which I wish you to deliver to your Pappa.

IMPORTATION BUSINESS

To John Adams

My dearest Friend   April 15 1780
By Mr. Guile who is bound to Amsterdam and from thence to France, I embrace this opportunity of writing to you; and inquiring after your welfare. Mr. Guile was the Bearer from Mrs. Dana who received them, of the first Letters I received from you. I wish he may be the safe conveyer of mine to you.

I have written to you various times since your absence, but have never had one direct conveyance to France, and I am apprehensive I shall hear but very seldom from you, unless you convey your Letters by way of Spain and Holland. Be sure not more than once a year, which is a situation I deprecate. Experience has however taught me more patience, tho it has not lessend my anxiety, or my affection. I wish to know your situation, and to hear of your welfare and happiness, I have philosophized so long upon my own that I have brought my mind to a patient acquiescence in it. The social and tender affections have been sacrificed to it, yet the agitation of my mind and spirits, has debilitated my faculties and impaired my Health but I find myself at the same time less attached to the world and the enjoyments of it, whether I am better fitted for an other is a matter I am not resolved in.

I have been very fortunate in receiving all your Letters from Spain. I have traced and followed you upon the Maps through all your peregrinations. It has been a pilgrimage indeed, and the care of the children must have added greatly to your anxiety. I cannot wish to have shared with you as it would have been an additional Burden to you.

I have received by Capt. Babson the articles you orderd for me. Mr. Guardoqui has given in his commissions and Mr. Tracy & Co. the freight, which I esteem very kind in them as I find 15 per cent freight was paid out of articles imported in the same vessel by others.

All the articles you were so kind as to send me were very acceptable. The tumblers came safe. They were all of one size. I should have rather had a part in wine Glasses, but nothing comes amiss. The Linnens tho rather coars were an article I stood in great need of, and they are in great demand here. The Tea proves of the best kind, the Hankerchiefs will turn to good account sold for hard Money, the only currency that can be delt in without immense loss. I do not wish to tell you the state of our currency, you may learn it by word of mouth from others.

I am about purchaseing an article which you directed me to, and for which you gave me Liberty to draw upon you for payment. I shall only do it in part. The remittance lately made me in hankerchiefs only would make the purchase, but as the person would gladly take Bills for the whole, I thought I would give one for a part as the risk would be his, and pay the remainder here.

I would not have drawn even for that, but I have some prospect of making a purchase of the House and land, belonging formerly to Natell. Belcher who died this winter. I have been trying to agree with the Heir, he asked the moderate price of 20 thousand Dollors when exchange was at 30, it is now 60 and he doubles his demand. There are several persons very eager to purchase it, which has determined the owner to put it up to vendue, if he does shall endeavour to buy it. People here tell me that it was formerly valued at a hundred pounds Lawfull money. It is not so good now as then, yet I should have ventured to have exceeded that price as it would accommodate this place so well, if I could have done any thing with him, but he was more distracted in his hard money price than in his paper. If he puts it up to vendue, believe that will be the best chance for obtaining it.

Mr. C. Tufts has left with me a list of a Number of articles which I enclose, which he wants for his own use, and 7 Louis D'ors, but asked it as a favour that I would keep the money and let his risk be but once. I ventured to do it, as I enclose a set of Bills of a much larger amount from which I knew you could deduct the sum if you pleased. I should be obliged if you will order me 12 Ells of Led coulourd Lutestring and 12 of black and white changeable with half a peice of black ribbon and a peice of Narrow about 4 sols per yard with 3 yards of plain black Gauze and 3 of figured.

If you should think proper not to deduct the 7 Louis from the Bills you will please to order the remainder remitted in common Calico and hankerchiefs which are the most saleable articles here. I request at the same time that you would not straiten yourself for supplies to me, especially whatever you may esteem a superfluity.

Your Brother I fear will very soon become a widower. It appears to me and to others that his wife is far gone in a consumption. Your Mother is in tolerable Health tho much broken I think with the Severity of the winter which has been very unfavourable to people in years. The old gentleman is almost helpless.

All the rest of our Friends are well. Publick News you will learn from the papers.

Some vessel or other will sail for France soon by which I shall again write. The Spring is advanceing fast, which after the rigour of a Canadian Winter is more particuliarly agreable to those who do not feel that Lassitude from it; which anxiety of mind, confinement, and want of exercise produce in your ever affectionate   Portia

DEATH OF SISTER-IN-LAW

To John Adams

My dearest Friend   June 13 1780
    The Palles which I thought had saild a fortnight ago, still lies at Newbury Port, and gives me the opportunity of

acquainting you with the death of a Sister in Law, who I followed to the grave a week ago, leaving behind a Babe about 5
days old, and a distressd family of children, by which loss your
Brother is bereved of an Excellent wife and his children a most
kind and affectionate Mother. I have had one of the little Girls
with me, and shall keep her till he can supply his family with
better assistance.

We are greatly anxious for the fate of Charlestown, no
Fleet arrived, yet no Alliance—am tired a looking for them.—
Constitution will pass, will be accepted, we shall have a constitution of good goverment soon.—Mr. Lovell writes me your
accompts are pass't. There is a balance in your favour for which
the treasurer will draw Bills of exchange. Shall I send them to
you, or sell them here for hard Money which I can easily do?
Shall wait your determination when ever I receive them. Enclosed is a pattern of which should be glad of 4 yards.—Friends
all well—impatiently waiting to hear from you. Most affectionately Yours.

Love to the children. But a moments warning to write this.

"COULD YOU BRING THE OLIVE BRANCH"

To John Adams

My Dearest Friend   October 8 1780
My unkle who is very attentive to acquaint me with every
opportunity of conveyance, last Evening let me know of a
vessel going to Spain, and tho my Letters cost you much more
than they are worth; I am bound as well by inclination, as your
repeated injunctions to omit no opportunity of writeing.

My last to you was by way of Bilboa. A vessel will soon sail
for Amsterdam, by which I shall write largely to you, to my
dear Boys, and to my agreable correspondent.

I am not without some prospect that the Letters may find
you at that very port. I not long ago learnt that a commission
for Holland was forwarded to you.

I was much surprized to find that you had not heard from
Congress by the date of your last, the 17 of June. The commu-

nication from that Quarter is worse than it is from here, bad
enough from both, for an anxious wife and an affectionate
Mother.

I know not how to enter into a detail of our publick affairs—
they are not what I wish them to be. The successes of the
Enemy at Charlestown are mortifying. General Gates misfortune will be anounced to you before this reaches you, and the
enclosed Gazet will give you all the information of the treachery of Arnold which has yet come to hand.

How ineffectual is the tye of Honour to bind the Humane
Mind, unless accompanied by more permanent and Efficacious
principals? Will he who laughs at a future state of Retribution,
and holds himself accountable only to his fellow Mortals disdain
the venal Bribe, or spurn the Ignoble hand that proffers it.

Yet such is the unhappy lot of our native land, too, too many
of our chief Actors *have been and are unprincipled wretches*, or
we could not have sufferd as we have done. It is Righteousness,
not Iniquity, that exalteth a Nation. There are so many and so
loud complaints against some persons in office that I am apt to
think neither *age* nor *Fame* will screen them. All hopes that I
had entertained of a vigorous campaign, have been obstructed
by a superiour British naval force, and the daily Rumours of a
reinforcement from France, rise and vanish with the day. The
season is now so far advanced, that little or no benifit would
accrue from their arrival, yet with all the force of Graves and
Rodny nothing has yet been attempted, they content themselves with the conquests of Clinton, and give out that the
Northern States are not worth possessing.

Peace, Peace my beloved object is farther and farther from
my Embraces I fear, yet I have never asked you a Question
which from the Nature of your Embassy I knew you could not
determine. It is however an object so near my Heart, that it
lies down and rises with me. Yet could you bring the olive
Branch, even at the expiration of an *other year*, my present
sacrifices should be my future triumph, and I would then try if
the Honour, as I am sometimes told, could then compensate
for the substantial Blessings I resign. But my dear Friend well
knows that the Honour does not consist so much in the Trust
reposed, as in the able, the Honest, the upright and faithfull
discharge of it. From these sources I can derive a pleasure,

which neither accumulated Honours, wealth, or power, could bestow without them.

But whether does my pen lead me? I meant only to write you a short Letter, if writing to you I could do so. Some months ago I wrote you an account of the death of sister Adams and of her leaving a poor Babe, only 3 days old. The death of Mr. Hall, who full of years, was last week gatherd to the great congregation, will be no matter of surprize to you. Your Mother is gone to your Brother, till a change in his condition may render her services unnecessary, which with a young family of 5 children, is not likely to be very soon. Whatever she calls upon me for shall endeavour to supply her with. She would have been more comfortable with me, but her compassion lead her to him. She desires me to remember, ever her tenderest affection to you. I always make her a sharer with me in whatever I receive from you, but some small present from your own Hand to her, would I know be particularly gratefull to her, half a dozen yards of dark chints, if you are at a loss to know what, or any thing—it is not the value but the notice which would be pleasing. Excuse my mentioning it, I know you burden with matters of more importance, yet these attentions are the more gratefull on that very account.

Pray make my Respectfull complements to Mr. Dana and tell him that his Lady made me a Friendly visit last week, and we talked as much as we pleased of our dear *Absents*, compared Notes, Sympathized, Responded to each other, and mingled with our sacrifices some *little pride* that no Country could boast two worthyer Hearts than *we* had *permitted* to go abroad—and then they were such honest souls too, and so intirely satisfied with their American dames, that we had not an apprehension of their roveing. We mean not however to defy the Charmes of the Parissian Ladies, but to admire the constancy and fidelity with which they are resisted—but enough of Romance.

Be so good as to let Mr. Thaxter know that his Friends are all well, and will write by the Amsterdam vessel. This will be so expensive a conveyance that I send only a single Letter.

I have been very sick for a month past with a slow fever, but hope it is leaving me. For many years I have not escaped a sickness in the Fall.—I hope you enjoy Health, Dr. Lee says you grow very fat. My poor unfortunate trunk has not yet reachd America, that was forced to share the Fate of party and caballs, was detaind by Dr. Windship. I wish it in other Hands, do not let it go for Philadelphia if you can prevent it. Mr. Lovell has sent me a set of Bills, which I enclose, but is much short of the balance reported in your favour. I take the remainder to be included with the other gentlemens accounts. After having stated the balance they say thus—"we beg leave to remark, that the examination of the coppy of an account marked A, which they received with Mr. A's other accounts and is for joint expences of himself Doctr. Franklin and Mr. Deane, cannot be gone into at present, the monies credited therein having been received, and the vouchers to said account remaining with them."

Our dear daughter is in Boston but would send her duty and Love by all opportunities tho I cannot prevail with her to write so often as I wish.

Little Tom sends his Duty, learns fast now he has got a school master. My tenderest regard to my two dear Sons. The account of their good conduct is a gratefull Balm to the Heart of their & your ever affectionate   A A

PS   Stevens Friends are all well. You will hear a strange story about the Alliance—the officers of the Ship ran away with her to Boston. Barre has got the command of her now. Pray write me by way of Bilboa. Holland is a fine place for Buisness—there is much trade from here there, many vessels go and come from thence, as well as to Spain. I am quite impatient to hear from you again, 4 months since the last date.

MINISTER TO THE DUTCH REPUBLIC

To John Adams

My dearest Friend   November 13th 1780
   How long is the space since I heard from my dear absent Friends? Most feelingly do I experience that sentiment of Rousseaus' "that one of the greatest evils of absence, and the

only one which reason cannot alleviate, is the inquietude we are under concerning the actual state of those we love, their health, their life, their repose, their affections. Nothing escapes the apprehension of those who have every thing to lose." Nor are we more certain of the present condition than of the future. How tormenting is absence! How fatally capricious is that Situation in which we can only enjoy the past Moment, for the present is not yet arrived. Stern Winter is making hasty Strides towards me, and chills the warm fountain of my Blood by the Gloomy prospect of passing it *alone*, for what is the rest of the World to me?

"Its pomp, its pleasures and its nonesence all?"

The fond endearments of social and domestick life, is the happiness I sigh for, of that I am in a great measure deprived by a seperation from my dear partner and children, at the only season in life when it is probable we might have enjoyed them all together. In a year or two, the sons will be so far advanced in life, as to make it necessary for their Benifit, to place them at the Seats of Learning and Science, indeed the period has already arrived, and whilst I still fondle over one, it is no small relief to my anxious mind, that those, who are seperated from me, are under your care and inspection. They have arrived at an age, when a Mothers care becomes less necessary and a Fathers more important. I long to embrace them. The Tears my dear Charles shed at parting, have melted my Heart a thousand times. Why does the mind Love to turn to those painfull scenes and to recollect them with pleasure?

I last week only received a Letter written last March, and sent by Monseiur John Baptiste Petry. Where he is I know not. After nameing a Number of persons of whom I might apply for conveyance of Letters, you were pleased to add, they were your great delight when they did not censure, or complain, when they did they were your greatest punishment.

I am wholy unconscious of giving you pain in this way since your late absence. If any thing of the kind formerly escaped my pen, had I not ample retaliation, and did we not Balance accounts tho the sum was rather in your favour even after having distroyed some of the proof. In the most Intimate of Friendships, there must not be any recrimination. If I complaind, it was from the ardour of affection which could not endure the least apprehension of neglect, and you who was conscious that I had no cause would not endure the supposition. We however wanted no mediating power to adjust the difference, we no sooner understood each other properly, but as the poet says, "The falling out of Lovers is the renewal of Love."

> Be to my faults a little Blind
> Be to my virtues ever kind

and you are sure of a Heart all your own, which no other Earthly object ever possessd. Sure I am that not a syllable of complaint has ever stained my paper, in any Letter I have ever written since you left me. I should have been ungratefull indeed, when I have not had the shadow of a cause; but on the contrary, continual proofs of your attention to me. You well know I never doubted your Honour. Virtue and principal confirm the indissoluable Bond which affection first began and my security depends not upon your passion, which other objects might more easily excite, but upon the sober and setled dictates of Religion and Honour. It is these that cement, at the same time that they ensure the affections.

> "Here Love his golden shafts employs; here lights
> His *constant* Lamp, and waves his purple wings."

November 24.

I had written thus far when Capt. Davis arrived. The News of your being in Amsterdam soon reachd me, but judge of my dissapointment when I learnt that he had thrown over all his Letters, being chased by an American privateer, who foolishly kept up British coulours till she came along side of him. One only was saved by some accident and reachd me after hearing that the whole were lost. This tho short was a cordial to my Heart, not having received a line of a later date than 17 of June. This was the fourth of Sepbr., and just informd me of your Health and that you had been in Amsterdam a few weeks. My dear sons were not mentiond, and it was only by a *very* polite Letter from Mr. de Neufville that I learnt they were with you, and well. He is pleased to speak in high terms of them, I hope they deserve it.

A week after a Brig arrived at Providence and brought me

your favour of Sepbr. 15 and Mr. Thaxters of August and Sepbr. from Paris. You do not mention in either of your Letters which were saved, how long you expect to reside in Holland. I fancy longer than you then Imagined, as Capt. Davis informs that you had not heard of the Capture of Mr. Lawrence. This event will make your stay there necessary. I fear for your Health in a Country so damp, abounding in stagnant water, the air of which is said to be very unfriendly to Foreigners. Otherways if I was to consult my own feelings I should wish your continuance there, as I could hear more frequently from you. If it is not really nearer, its being a sea port, gives me that Idea, and I fancy the pains of absence increase in proportion to distance, as the power of attraction encreases as the distance diminishes. Magnets are said to have the same motion tho in different places. Why may not we have the same sensations tho the wide Atlantick roll between us? I recollect your story to Madam Le Texel upon the Nature and power of Attraction and think it much more probable to unite Souls than Bodies.

You write me in yours of Sepbr. 15 that you sent my things in the Alliance. This I was sorry to see, as I hoped Mr. Moylan had informd you before that time, that Dr. Winship to whom he deliverd them neither came in the vessel or sent the things. I am not without fears that they will be embezzled. I have taken every opportunity to let you know of it, but whether you have got my Letters is uncertain. The cabals on Board the Ship threw the officers into parties, and Winship chose to involve my trunk in them. He certainly sent goods by the same vessel to other persons. General Warren, my unkle and others examined and went on Board, but could find no Trunk for me. The Articles sent by private hands I believe I have got, except you sent more than one packet by Col. Flury who arrived at Newport and sent forward a package containing a few yards of Black Silk. A month afterwards, received a Letter from him desireing to know if I received two packages and some Letters which he brought. I received no Letter, and but one package by him. I have been endeavouring to find out the mistery, but have not yet develloped it.—The Articles you sent me from Bilboa have been of vast service to me, and greatly assisted me in dischargeing the load of Taxes which it would have otherways been impossible for me to have paid; I will enclose you a list of what I have paid, and yet remains due from july to this day. The Season has been so unfortunate in this state, that our produce is greatly diminished. There never was known so severe and so long a drought, the crops of corn and grass were cut of. Each Town in this State is called upon to furnish a suffering Army with provision. This Towns supply is 40 thousand weight of Beaf or money to purchase it. This has already been collected. Our next tax is for Grain to pay our six months and our 3 Months militia, to whom we wisely voted half a Bushel per day, the state pay, and a Bounty of a Thousand dollors each or money Equivalent to purchase the Grain. This is now collecting and our Town tax only is four times larger than our continential. You hear no such sound now, as that money is good for nothing. Hard money from 70 to 75 is made the standard, that or exchange is the way of dealing, everything is high, but more steady than for two years before. My Tenants say they must leave the Farm, that they cannot live. I am sure I cannot pay more than my proportion yet I am loth they should quit. They say two Cows would formerly pay the taxes upon this place, and that it would now take ten. They are not alone in their complaints. The burden is greater I fear than the people will bear—and whilst the New England states are crushed by this weight, others are lagging behind, without any exertions, which has produced a convention from the New England States. A motion has been made, but which I sincerely hope will not be adopted by our Goverment, I mean to vest General Washington with the power of marching his Army into the state that refuses supplies and exacting it by Martial Law. Is not this a most dangerous step, fraught with Evils of many kinds. I tremble at the Idea. I hope Congress will never adopt such a measure, tho our delegates should receive such Instructions.

Our publick affairs wear a more pleasing aspect, as you will see by the inclosed Gazet yet are we very far from extirpating the British force. If we are not to look for peace till that event takes place, I fear it is very far distant. Small as our Navy is, it has captured near all the Quebeck Fleet, 19 have arrived safe in port, and fill'd Salem and Cape Ann with Goods of all kinds. Besides not a week passes but gives us a prize from some Quarter.

As to the affairs of our common wealth, you will see who is Govenour. Two good Men have been chosen as Leiut. Governour, both of whom have refused. The late judge of probate is now Elected, and tis thought will accept. Last week his Excellency gave a very Grand Ball, to introduce our Republican form of Goverment properly upon the Stage.

It was a maxim of Edward king of Portugal, that what ever was amiss in the manners of a people, either proceeds from the bad example of the Great, or may be cured by the Good. He is the patriot who when his Country is overwhelmed by Luxery, by his example stems the Torrent and delivers it from that which threatens its ruin. A writer observes with Regard to the Romans, that there must have been a considerable falling off, when Sylla won that popular favour by a shew of Lions, which in better times he could only have obtained by substantial services.

I have twice before enclosed a set of Bills, received from Mr. Lovell for you. I ventured to detain one hopeing for an opportunity to send to Holland. I enclose it now together with a list of the Articles if you think you can afford them to me. If not I shall be better satisfied in a refusal than in a compliance. The Articles you were so kind as to send me were not all to my mind. The Led coulourd Silk was clay coulour, not proper for the use I wanted it for, it was good however. A large Quantity of ordinary black ribbon, which may possibly sell for double what it cost, if it had been coulourd there would have been no difficulty with it. The tape is of the coarsest kind, I shall not lose by it, but as I wanted it for family use, it was not the thing. The Tea was Excellent, the very best I ever had and not so high priced as from other places. All the rest of the articles were agreable.—I have written to Mr. de Neufville encloseing a duplicate Bill, and a list of the same articles, but directed him to take your orders and govern himself by them. When ever you send me any thing for sale, Linnens especially Irish, are always saleable. Common calico, that comes cheep from Holland, any thing of the wollen kind such as Tamies, Durants or caliminco with ordinary linnen hankerchiefs answer well.

I have written a very long letter. To what port it will go first I know not; it is too late for any vessel to go to Holland this winter from hence.—Our Friends all well. Your Brother has lost his youngest daughter. I will write to my dear John and Charles and hope [   ] Letters will not meet the fate of theirs.

Ever & at all time yours,   Portia

ENCLOSURE

26 yards of Dutch bed tick
2 Gray muffs and tippets
2 Bundles of english pins
2 sets of House Brushes
1 doz. of blew and white china tea cups and sausers
half a doz. pint china Bowls
half a doz. diaper table cloths   2, 5 Ells wide   2 four   2 three.
one Scotch carpet 4 yards square or 6 Ells.
half a doz. white gauze handerchifs the same size that the black
    were
NB   an Ell in Holland is but 3 quarters of our yard.

You will be so good as to find out where that young gentleman is and forward the Letter.

"THE INFAMOUS ARNOLD"

To John Adams

My dearest Friend   Janry. 15 1781
    Capt. Caznew is now just about to sail. I wrote large packets to go by him a month ago, but hearing Capt. Trash was going from Newbury to Bilboa I sent them by him. It was thought that Caznew would not sail till Febry.
    But all of a suden I am calld upon unprepaird having but an hours warning—he shall not however go without a line or two. Your last which I have received was by way of Philadelphia dated in Sepbr. 15.
    I see by last weeks paper that a Capt. Updike is arrived at Providence. I fear he has no Letters for me, as he brings word that the Fame saild the day before him, but has not yet been heard of. We are Fearfull that she is lost, or taken.—I have

written to you twice since Davis arrived, and told you that he threw over all his dispatches, being chased, to my great sorrow and mortification. The things however which you were so kind as to order for me, came safe to hand. I shall be obliged for ought I know to part with them, to pay taxes, which are beyond account. 20 thousand dollors are already assessed upon this place for the last year.

I have written to the House of de Neufville for a few articles, which I wrote to you about by way of Bilboa. I have inclosed them a Bill, and at the same time directed them to take your orders with regard to them.

Neither Jones or Sampson have yet reachd America. We have had a moderate winter and a general Health throughout the State. We are making *every* Effort to fill up the continental Army, and hope to succeed. Our paper Credit has kept a steady value for more than 3 months. 75 for one is the rate of exchange. Our hard Money tax is punctually paid for the redemption of it. I cannot say that the Money appreciates yet, but it certainly must from the great taxes which are daily collecting. We now see where our errors lay, but a people must feel to be convinced.

I enclose to you a Letter and resolve of Congress forwarded to me by Mr. Lovell. It contains an approbation of more value to you, than a Lucrative reward and it communicates pleasure to me, in proportion as it is valuable to you, and as it is a testimony, that your assiduity and attention to the publick Interest is gratefully noticed by your Country. To Merrit and receive it, is the only compensation I can receive for the loss I sustain of your society.

The Letter containing remarks upon Lord Gorge Germains Speach, was first published in Philadelphia and sent me by Mr. L——l. I had it republished here—it is much approved of. The Enemy lose ground every day in Carolina. The infamous Arnold is gone with a Number of Troops to Virgina—he was too knowing to come out, as was first talkd of against New england who to a Man would have risen to have crushd the monster. Whilst Andry has been lamented by a Generous Enemy Arnold has been execrated by all ranks.

My Love to my dear Sons, there Letters by Davis I mourn the loss of. I designd to have written to them by this vessel but fear I shall not have time. I wrote by Trash to Mr. Thaxter. Our Friends are all well—excuse haste, from your ever affectionate   Portia

To John Quincy Adams

My dear Son   Braintree Janry. 21 1781
    Tis a long time since I had the pleasure of a Letter from you. If you wrote to me by Capt. Davis as I suppose you did, your Letters were all thrown over Board.

If you have since written by a Brig call'd the *Fame*, I fear it will never reach me. She is still missing and must be taken or lost. The *Mars* from France we daily expect. The last Letters which I received from you came by the Alliance, and were dated in April so that tis Nine Months since a single line from your own hand reachd me.

I expect your observations upon your New Situation, an account of Holland, and what you find there, worthy of remark, what improvements you have made in the languages, in the Sciences, and the fine Arts.

You are now become resident in a Country famous for its industery and frugality, and which has given Birth to many Learned and great Men. Erasmus, Grotius and Boerhaave, so well known in the Literary world, stand foremost in the List of Fame.

You must not be a superficial observer, but study Men and Manners that you may be Skilfull in both. Tis said of Socrates, that the oracle pronounced him the wisest of all Men living because he judiciously made choice of Humane Nature for the object of his Thoughts. Youth is the proper season for observation and attention—a mind unincumberd with cares may seek instruction and draw improvement from all the objects which surround it. The earlier in life you accustome yourself to consider objects with attention, the easier will your progress be, and more sure and successfull your enterprizes. What a Harvest of true knowledge and learning may you gather from the numberless varied Scenes through which you pass if you are not wanting in your own assiduity and endeavours. Let your ambition be engaged to become eminent, but above all things support a virtuous character, and remember that "an Honest Man is the Noblest work of God."

I hope you will not let any opportunity slip or any vessel sail, which is bound for America without Letters from you. Your Friends here all desire to be rememberd to you. Your cousin Billy has written to you several times, and is quite impatient to hear from you. Your sister—not a word in excuse will I say for her. She ought to write to you and I call upon her too, but she is very neglegent.

I am my dear Son with sincere wishes for your Health and happiness affectionately yours,   A A

"HAVE YOU LEARNED TO SKATE FINELY?"

To John Quincy Adams and Charles Adams

My dear sons   Febry. 8 1781

I fear you will think Mamma is unmindfull of you if she does not write you a few lines by so good an opportunity. I wrote to both of you by Mr. Beals of this Town about a week ago, and my notice by this vessel is very short. I can only find time to tell you that tis a very long time since I heard from your Pappa, and much longer since I had a Letter from either of you. I think Dr. Lee brought the last.

I hope you are both well and very good children which is the best News I can possibly hear from you. I cannot prevail with your Sister to write—I believe she is affraid you will shew her Letters and she is so proud that she thinks she cannot write well enough. I do not like it that she is not more socible with her Brothers. Thommy would write if he could. He sends Love, is a very good Boy, and wants to know if you cannot send him some present from Holland.

Is my Charles grown as fat as his Brother? Can he talk French, Dutch, &c.

Ask Mr. Thaxter to write me word whether he bought Mr.

Trottes and Mrs. Welchs things. I know nothing about them. Tell Pappa I am like to have a fine Neighbour. General Warren has bought the Farm at Milton, that formerly belonged to Governor Hutchinson and moves in April.

We have had a fine pleasent winter, as mild as the last was severe. How has it been in Holland, have you learned to skate finely?

Master Samll's Pappa is a going to France. I send this Letter by him. Col. Lawrence has got some for Pappa and Mr. Thaxter.—Your Grandpappa sends his Love to you, talks about you with much pleasure, so does your Grandmamma, who is so very infirm I fear you will never see her again. I do not see any prospect of your speedy return. It wants but a few days of 15 months since you left home. Do you not want to see the rugged rocks of Braintree again?

Some day or other, I wish it may not be far distant when I shall embrace my dear Sons in their Native land. Till that period arrives I would have them ever mindfull of writeing to their affectionate Mother,   A A

"OUR OWN AMERICAN AFFAIRS"

To John Adams

My Dearest Friend   April 23 1781
        You will wonder I suppose to what part of the world all the Letters you have written since the 25 of Sepbr. are gone, that not a line of a later date has reachd me, even up to this 23 day of April. My Heart sickens at the recollection, and I most sensibly feel the sacrifice of my happiness from the Malignant Union of Mars with Belona. My two dear Boys cannot immagine how ardently I long to fold them to my Bosom, or the still dearer parent conceive the flood of tenderness which Breaks the prescribed Bounds and overflows the Heart, when reflection upon the past, and anticipation upon the future unite in the mind of Portia. Unaccustomed to tread the stage of dissipation, I cannot shake of my anxiety for my Country and my dearest connextions, in the *Beau Mond*, whilst the one is

Bleading, and the others seperated far, far from me, but in a frugal and republican stile; I pass the lonely Hour, with few enviers and fewer Imitators.

Your predictions with regard to peace and war are verified and the united Provinces are at last obliged to declare themselves. Happy for them if they had sooner attended to the voice of their Friends, they would then I dare venture to affirm been sooner upon their gaurd against the Hostile depredations of Britain, but if the old Batavian Spirit still exists among them, Britain will Rue the Day that in Breach of the Laws of Nations, she fell upon their defenceless dominions, and drew upon her, as it is thought she must, the combined force of all the Neutral powers. If these people do not possess an ambition for conquest, yet they have heretofore exhibited a spirit superior to domination, that Spirit which prompted them to repel the Tyranny of Philip administerd by the cruel Alva, will excite them under superior advantages to Retaliate the Hostilities of the British Alva, that Spirit which prompted from Prince William that Heroick reply, "that he would die in the last Ditch, e'er he would see his Countrys ruin," will cement an indissoluble bond of union between the united States of America and the united Provinces who from a similarity of circumstances have each arrived at Independance disdaining the Bondage and oppression of a Philip and a Gorge.

Our own American affairs wear a more pleasing aspect. Maryland has acceeded to the confederation at the very time when Britain is deludeing herself with the Idea that we are crumbling to peices. New York has given up her claims to Vermont, and a 14tenth State will soon lift her Head under the auspices of Congress. Our Leavies are generally raised for 3 years and on their March to join the main Army. The Spring is advanceing and our Soldiers will have less occasion for cloathing—patience, perseverance and intrepidity have been their Armour and their cloathing through an inclemnant Winter. Who is answerable for the shamefull conduct which deprived them of their outward cloathing which they had reason to expect and justice demanded. I presume not to say, but if the omission has arisen from fraud, negligence or cabal, may the inhumane wretches be exposed to view and meet the infamy they justly merit.

You will see by the paper inclosed that the Seat of war is chiefly in the Southern States, and there our Enemies by victories and defeats are wasteing daily, whilst they are training to Arms, and inureing to dicipline and hardships those states as they have before our Northern ones, to persue them to Inevitable distruction, and to prove to all Europe the falsity of their assertions, when not a single State submits to their haughty userpations, in all their Boasted conquered dominions.

Our Finnances have been upon a much more respectable footing for some time. Goods of all kinds fell in their prices, and exchange kept at 75 for one for five months. The Capture of Eustatia and the War between Holland and england has raised Goods again Tea in a particular manner to double what it ever has been before, it was down to a hard dollor per pound or 75 it is now at 15 Shillings.

I have thought that a small chest of about one hundred weight of Bohea Tea, would turn to as good an account as any thing you could send me. This Letter is to go by a vessel of Mr. Tracys. If you think it expedient you may order it by her, as it will come freight free if consigned to him, as the other articles were from Bilboa.

The best Green Tea I have ever had was that sent by Davis. If you send again, let it be Suchong, it is not so dear and answers better here. The Bandano hankerchiefs from Holland were the best article for sale I have ever received. The chints you were so kind as to order me by Sampson arrived—safe I cannot say. They were put up with some things which came to Mr. Austins Brother and were so unfortunate as to be wet, and half of them damaged, mildewed and in a manner spoilt. I parted with them in the best manner I could, the damaged for rather more than the sterling cost and the others very well. They were all good as well as handsome which renderd it more unfortunate to have them wet, but the cargo was so in general.—As to my long expected trunk, it has at last arrived in Philadelphia. I am loth to discribe the state of it, because I am loth to make you angry, yet you ought to know it, least the person who put them up should again be imployed by you. I have neither Letter or invoice, which is the first time an omission of this kind has taken place. I cannot determine the price of a single article or know what were really put up, or what omitted.

From your Letters alone in which you have repeated that all was orderd which was requested, and the loss of all Dr. Tufts things; leads me to think that the many others which are missing were stolen out. My Muslin hankerchiefs, Aprons, Nabbys plumes, Mr. Tufts Buckles, Brothers velvet, the linings and trimmings for the Gentlemens cloaths are among the missing articles. According to Mr. Lovell's invoice for I have not yet seen them. When I found they would be like to go to Philadelphia I requested Mr. L——l to receive them for me when ever they arrived, and it was well he did or what remaind would have been intirely lost. They were put in a Box without any wraper, through the cracks of which you might see the things; they were liable not only to be wet but plunderd, both of which they sufferd. Dr. Winship whom I have seen, says that when Mr. Moylan requested him to take them; he refused them, unless he would repack them, and purchase a hair Trunk for them; he replied that he had no money in his hands, that he had sent the account to you, and you had paid it, and that if he would not take it, he would deliver it to Capt. Jones, which he accordingly did; when Mr. L——l received them together with a Box for Mr. Gerry, they were in a smoaking state. He examined his, found them rotton upon which Mr. L——l unpacked mine and found them so wet as to oblige him to dry every thing by the fire. The linnings, the diaper all damaged, Mrs. Cranchs cambrick mildewed, happily the wollen cloths were only wet, the leather Gloves quite rotton. I could wish you to repeat that article by the first opportunity and order a peice of wollen between every pair as they are the most liable to damage by wet. The Box of china was deliverd safe to Mr. L——l. If this should reach you before the *Alliance* leaves France be so kind as to order me one half a dozen tombour worked Muslin hankerchiefs, 4 Ells Book Muslin, one pound of white threads, 12 Ells of light crimson caliminco with a peice of coarse cambrick and any light wollen stuff that will answer for winter gowns, half a dozen coulourd plumes and a small Box of flowers for Miss Nabby at her request to her pappa. My chints came just in time to enable me to purchase the 3 part of a Man which fell to my share in the class to which I belonged at the head of which I had the *Honour* to stand. We gave 300 hard Dollors for 3 years, and a third part fell to my share, a third part is paid in hand, the remainder annually. The Town was divided into classes, and in about a months time the men were all raised. 38 fell to the share of this Town.

Poor Mrs. Dana says she is taxed to death and she shall be ruined if he stays any longer. What shall I say—why that I have paid 21 hundred pounds since last july, Lawfull money, and have a thousand pound still to pay, and that you have enabled me to do it—but I do not increase in wealth, nor yet diminish the capital.—I have ventured to make some improvements in Husbandry and have a desire to become a purchaser in the State of Vermont. I may possibly run you in debt a hundred dollors for that purpose. Many people are removeing from this Town, and others. Land is sold at a low price, what do you think of a few thousand acres there? I know you would like it, so shall venture the first opportunity a hundred and 20 or 30 dollors will Buy a thousand acres.

I have written very often to you by way of Spain and Bilboa, which places I wish you would try. If you sent me any thing by the Fame, let me know. She is lost or taken—and Mr. Guile we fear in her. Adieu my dear Friend my Love *must* suffice my dear Lads now. I have not time to write to them or Mr. Thaxter.

Yours ever yours,   Portia

STOLEN LETTERS

To James Lovell

Upon opening your favour of April 17 my Heart Beat a double stroke when I found that the Letter which I supposed had reachd you was the one captured in the room of that you received which was what I had supposed lost, but I should have been secure from the knowledge of the writer if Mr. Cranchs Letter and one I wrote at the same time had not accompanied it. The Letter which I would not have chosen should have come to any hand but yours, was in reply to two of yours and contain some Stricktures upon the conduct of a Friend. Least you should imagine it freer than it really was I enclose the coppy. I risk no more should it be captured than what the Enemy already have.—The Letter which occasiond some of the remarks I have not yet seen, tho I find it was published in the Halifax paper as well as Riveingtons. If what I have heard with regard to its contents is true, I cannot open my lips in defence of a Friend whose character I would wish to justify, nor will I secret from him that it suffers exceedingly even in the Eyes of his Friends from his so long absenting himself from his family. How well he may satisfy her who is nearest concernd I presume not to say, but if she possesses that regard for her partner which I presume she does, she must be exceedingly hurt even by the Speach of the world, if she is otherways sufficiently convinced of the attachment and affections of her partner. I write from a Sense of the feelings which under similar circumstances would harrow up my Soul, and wound with a Bearded Arrow. I have but a very small personal acquaintance with the Lady whom I esteem and commisirate, those who have speak highly of her. I have as little personal acquaintance with the Gentleman connected with her; but it has so happened that I have stood in need of his services, and he has exhibited an assiduity and Friendship in the discharge of them that has bound me to him in the bond of Friendship. Add to this he is the particular Friend and correspondent of him who is dearest to me and for whose sake alone I should Esteem him, but it would mortify me not a little to find I had mistaken a character and in the room of a philosopher, a *man* of the *world* appeard. If I could credit the report [   ]

May 10, 1781

"YOU WILL BE SPOILT"

To Charles Adams

My dear Charles   May 26 1781
    I am sometimes affraid my dear Boy that you will be spoilt by being a favorite. Praise is a Dangerous Sweet unless properly tempered. If it does not make you arrogant, assuming and self

sufficient, but on the contrary fires your Breast with Emulation to become still more worthy and engageing, it may not opperate to your Disadvantage. But if ever you feel your Little Bosom swell with pride and begin to think yourself better than others; you will then become less worthy, and loose those Qualities which now make you valuable. Worthy and amiable as I hope you are, there are still imperfections enough in every Humane Being to excite Humility, rather than pride.

If you have made some small attainments in knowledge, yet when you look forward to the immense sum; of which you are still Ignorant, you will find your own, but as a grain of sand, a drop, to the ocean.

If you look into your own Heart, and mind, you will find those amiable Qualities, for which you are beloved and esteemed, to result rather from habit and constitution, than from any solid, and setled principal. But it remains with you to Establish, and confirm that by choise and principal which has hitherto been a natural impulse.

Be modest, be diffident, be circumspect, kind and obligeing. These are Qualities which render youth engageing, and will flourish like a natural plant; in every clime.

I long to receive Letters from you. To hear of your Health and that of your dear pappas, would give me a pleasure that I have not experienced for 8 months.

O My dear children, when shall I fold you to my Bosom again? God only knows and in his own time will I hope return you safe to the Arms of your ever affectionate Mother,

A Adams

ON STUDYING HISTORY

To John Quincy Adams

My dear John   May 26 1781
    I hope this Letter will be more fortunate than yours have been of late. I know you must have written many times since I had the pleasure of receiving a line from you, for this month completes a year since the date of your last Letter.

Not a line from you or my dear Charles since you arrived in Holland, where I suppose you still are.

I never was more anxious to hear yet not a single vessel arrives from that port, tho several are looked for.

I hope my dear Boy that the universal neatness and Cleanliness, of the people where you reside, will cure you of all your slovenly tricks, and that you will learn from them industery, oconomy and frugality.

I would recommend it to you to become acquainted with the History of their Country; in many respects it is similar to the Revolution of your own. Tyranny and oppresion were the original causes of the revoult of both Countries. It is from a wide and extensive view of mankind that a just and true Estimate can be formed of the powers of Humane Nature. She appears enobled or deformed, as Religion, Goverment, Laws and custom Guide or direct her.

Firce, rude, and savage in the uncultivated desert, Gloomy, Bigoted and Superstitious where Truth is veiled in obscurity and mistery. Ductile, pliant, Elegant and refined—you have seen her in that dress, as well as the active, Bold, hardy and intrepid Garb of your own Country.

Inquire of the Historick page and let your own observations second the inquiry, whence arrises this difference? And when compared, learn to cultivate those dispositions and to practise those Virtues which tend most to the Benifit and happiness of Mankind.

The Great Author of our Religion frequently inculcates universal Benevolence and taught us both by precept and example when he promulgated peace and good will to Man, a doctrine very different from that which actuates the Hostile invaders, and the cruel ravagers of mighty kingdoms and Nations.

I hope you will be very particular when you write, and let me know how you have past your time in the course of the year past.

Your favourable account of your Brother gave me great pleasure—not only as it convinced me that he continues to cultivate that agreable disposition of mind and heart, which so greatly endeared him to his Friends here, but as it was a proof of the Brotherly Love and affection of a son, not less dear to his Parents.

Your Brother Tommy has been very sick with the Rhuma-tism, taken by going too early into water, by which means he lost the use of his Limbs and a fever ensued. He has however happily recoverd, and learnt wisdom I hope by his sufferings. He hopes soon to write you a Letter. He has a good school and is attentive to his Books. I shall write to your Brother, so shall only add the sincere wishes for your improvement and happiness of your ever affectionate Mother,   A A

DR. THOMAS WELSH

To John Adams

My dearest Friend   May 27 1781

I have written so largely to you by Mr. Storer who goes in the same vessel, that I should not have taken up my pen again, but in compliance with the request of a Friend whose partner is going abroad, and desires a Letter to you as an introduction. Of Mr. Dexter the Bearer I know nothing but his Name. I have inclosed the Letter which I received from his partner who you know is a valuable Gentleman, and Eminent in his profession.

As Election is not passed I have nothing New to add. My wishes for your Health and happiness and my anxiety to hear from you are an old Story. Should I tender you my warmest affections, they are of a date, almost with my first knowledge of you, and near coeval with my existance, yet not the less valu-able I hope to a Heart that knows not a change, but is unalter-ably the treasure of its ever affectionate   Portia

"WE WILL BEGIN A NEW SCORE"

To James Lovell

My dear Sir   July   th 1781

Your favour by General Ward was not deliverd me till this day or I should have replied to it by the last post; the Generous acknowledgement of having transgressed forbids any further recrimination even tho I had more than the Right of a Friend. The serious part of your Letter drew a tear from the Eye of Portia. She wished for ability she wished for power to make happy the Man who so richly deserved far better treatment than he had ever yet met with. The pittance you mention, is meaner than my Immagination could possibly form tho I have had sufficient Specimins of it here to fore but it must and shall be enlarged if the Friends to whom Portia is determined to apply have any influence in a Body who too often strain at a knat while they gulph down a camel with great facility.

I am gratified however to have from your own Hand arguments to rectify the Ideas of some who I really believe your Friends, but who not knowing or fully attending to the circumstances you mention, have been left to wonder at a conduct they could not account for. The affectionate regard you profess for a Lady who I believe every way deserving of it, intirely banishes from my mind the insinuations of Cornelia, and I could wish that Letter might not be submitted as you tell me others have been, least it should unnecessaryly give pain to a Lady I must more and more Esteem—and with whom I am determined to cultivate a more particular acquaintance. Possibly I may be able to render her some small services. I cannot be so particular as I wish because this must take its chance by the post. I will not thank you for your comments upon my Letter of March 17th. They are not generous. However as I have never spaired my correspondent when I thought him wrong, I will suppose that he really believed Portia deserving the censure he has bestowed.—"Dutch Idea" abominable. You know I meant by the Word property, only an exclusive right, a possession held in ones own right. Will you please to consult Johnson upon the term?—Still more Sophistical is your comment upon the fine tuned Instrument. If I did not know you I should suppose you a practiseing Attorney. There is one thing however that sticks a little hardly by me—"I am very unwilling that it should be submitted to the Eye of one so *very much* my Friend as *you profess yourself to be.*" This looks like such a distrust of my sincerity as wounds me. There are some other strokes to which I am not callous, but can forgive them considering the freedom I have exercised in my own remarks.

Will you balance accounts? and we will begin a New Score upon the old Stock of Friendship. I do not pretend to exculpate from censure what I really thought deserving of it, but only the doubtfull right I had to use it as it did not at that time particularly affect me.

You have not fulfilled one part of your promise which was to transmit to me some Annecdotes respecting my Friend abroad and as a preparitive I was to see Mr. ———. I have & *received my preparitive.* In the Name of Indignation can there be any thing more diabolical than what is put into my Hands? False insinuating disembling wretch—is it for this your Grey Head is spaired—is this the language of courts?—is this the reward of an Independant Spirit, and patriotick virtue? Shall the Zealous and Strenuous asserter of his countrys rights be sacrificed to a court Sycophant? This finished Courtier has first practised his Arts upon the Minister till he has instilled into his mind the most ungenerous prejudices, played over the same Game he practised against Dr. Lee by reporting Speaches I dare say that were never made, or taking them seperately from what might be connected with them and therby rendering offensive what in an other view might be quite harmless—and having gained his point there, is now in the most specious manner crocodile like whining over the prey he means to devour, to your Body who if they mean peace and good will to their country will immediately accept a resignation which it is said he has tendered but for Heavens sake do not join him in commission with my Friend, they cannot act in concert, after such a proof of jealousy, envy and malice can you suppose it?

Join to him an upright honest Man of real abilities and he will thank you for an assistant should a negotiation commence, but do not *Saddle* him with a Man who looks no further than the present state of existance for a retribution of his virtues or his vices, but who considering this world as the summum bonum of Man might I think have a little more regard to the happiness of his fellow Mortals in the present state, and not quite so willing to relinquish their Natural Rights. One will speak a bold and firm language becomeing a free sovereign and Independant Nation, the other will be indesisive yealding fauning flattering. Are these consistant qualities? Very justly does he observe that they do not always hold the same

language and the one may erase the impressions of the other.—
If after all the Efforts of the Friends of Liberty Congress should
join them you may be assured my Friend will resign his commission. I shall intreat him to, but he will not want persuasion.
He shall not share if I can prevent it in the disgrace which will
most assuredly fall upon these States. Humiliating thought,
that so much Blood and treasure should be sacrificed to state
intrigues and our negotiation disgraced by a Man—but I will
believe a more virtuous Majority exists among you. I ask not
the support of my Friend because he is my Friend—I ask it no
further than as you find he persues the best Good of his country, than as you find he acts a disinterested part.

July 14, 1781

A FRIEND IN CONGRESS

To Elbridge Gerry

Sir   Braintree july 20. 1781
    When I looked for your Name among those who form the
Representative Body of the people this year I could not find it.
I sought for it with the Senate, but was still more dissapointed.
I however had the pleasure of finding it amongst the delegates
of this Commonwealth to Congress, where I flatter myself you
will still do us Honour which posterity will gratefully acknowledge; and the virtuous few now confess. But as you are no
worshiper of the rising Sun, or Adulator at the shrine of power,
you must expect with others, who possess an Independant
Spirit, to be viewed in the shade, to be eyed askance, to be
malign'ed and to have your Good evil spoken of. But let not
this Sir discourage you in the arduous Buisness. I hope America has not yet arrived at so great a pitch of degeneracy as to be
given up by those alone who can save her; I mean the disinterested patriot—who possessing an unconfined Benevolence will
persevere in the path of his duty. Tho the Ingratitude of his
constituents and the Malevolence of his Enemies should conspire against him, he will feel within himself the best Intima-
tions of his duty, and he will look for no external Motive.

History informs us that the single virtue of Cato, upheld the Roman Empire for a time, and a Righteous few might have saved from the impending Wrath of an offended deity the Ancient cities of Sodom and Gomorah. Why then my dear Sir, may I ask you, do you wish to withdraw yourself from publick Life?

You have supported the cause of America with zeal with ardour and fidelity, but you have not met even with the gratitude of your fellow citizens—in that you do not stand alone.

You have a mind too Liberal to consider yourself only as an Individual, and not to regard both your Country and posterity—and in that view I know you must be anxiously concerned when you consider the undue Influence excercised in her Supreme Counsels. You can be no stranger I dare say Sir, to matters of the Highest importance to the future welfare of America as a Nation; being now before her Representitives—and that she stands in need of the collected wisdom of the United States, and the Integrity of her most virtuous members.

I will not deny Sir, that personally I feel myself much Interested in your attendance there. I fear there is a spirit prevailing, too powerfull for those who wish our prosperity; and would seek our best Interests. Mr. L——ll and Mr. A——s have informed you I suppose of the Intrigues and malicious aspersions of my absent Friends character, if they have not, I will forward to you a coppy of a Letter which will not want any comment of mine.

The plan which appears to be adopted both at Home and abroad, is a servile adulation and complasance to the Court of our Allies, even to the giving up some of our most valuable privileges. The Independant Spirit of your Friend, abroad, does not coinside with the selfish views and inordinate ambition of your Minister, who in consequence of it, is determined upon his distruction. Stung with envy at a merit he cannot emulate, he is allarmed with the apprehension of losing the Honour of some Brilliant action; and is useing his endeavours that every enterprize shall miscarry, in which he has not the command. To Effect this purpose he has insinuated into the minds of those in power the falsest prejudices against your Friend, and they have so far influenced the united Counsels of these States, as to induce them to join this unprincipled Man, in Commission with him for future Negotiations. If Congress had thought proper to have joined any Gentleman of real abilities and integrity with our Friend, who could have acted in concert with him; he would have gratefully received his assistance—but to clog him with a Man, who has shewn himself so Enimical to him, who has discovered the marks of a little and narrow Spirit by his malicious aspersions, and ungenerous insinuations, and whose measures for a long time they have had no reason to be gratified with, is such a proof to me of what my absent Friend has reason to expect, and what you know Sir, I very early feared; that I can see nothing but dishonour, and disgrace attending his most faithfull, and zealous exertions for the welfare of his Country.

These Ideas fill me with the deepest concern. Will you suffer Female influence so far to operate upon you; as to step forth and lend your aid to rescue your Country and your Friend, without inquiring

> "What can Cato do
> Against a World, a base degenerate World
> which courts a yoke and bows its Neck to Bondage."

There is a very serious Light in which this matter is to be viewed; the serious light in which a late distinguished Modern writer expresses it—"that we are all embarked on the same Bottom, and if our Country sinks, we must Sink with it."

Your acknowledged Friendship and former politeness has led me to the freedom of this address, and prevents my asking an excuse which I should otherways think necessary for her who has the Honour to subscribe herself your Friend and Humble Servant,   Portia

PS   The communication of the minister at Versails being joined with my Friend was made in confidence—I wish it may not be mentiond at present.

"FALSEHOOD AND FRAUD"

To John Adams

August 1 1781

O that I could realize the agreable reverie of the last Night when my dear Friend presented himself and two Sons safely returnd to the Arms of the affectionate wife and Mother. Cruel that I should wake only to experience a renual of my daily solicitude. The next month will compleat a whole year since a single Line from your Hand has reachd the longing Eyes of Portia. No vessels have arrived here since the declaration of war from Holland. Congress have no dispatches later than october from you. I hope and hope till hope is swallowed up in the victory of Dispair. I then consider all my anxiety as vain since I cannot benifit any one by it, or alter the established order of things. I cannot relieve your mind from the burden of publick cares, or at this distance alleviate the anxiety of your Heart, tho ever so much distressed for the welfare of your Native land or protect you from the Slanderous arrow that flieth in Secret, a Specimin of which you will find inclosed in a Letter from Mr. Cranch but which you must I think have received before as many coppies have been sent. My Indignation is too big for utterance.

> Falsehood and fraud shoot up in ev'ry soil
> The product of all climes—Rome had its Ceasar.

I will not comment upon this low this dirty this Infamous this diabolical peice of envy and malice as I have already done it where I thought I might be of service—to your two Friends Lovell and Gerry.

> True consious Honour is to know no Sin—

and the firm patriot whose views extend to the welfare of Mankind tho obstructed by faction and vice, tho crossed by fortune, tho wounded by calumny and reproach, shall find in the end that his generous Labour is not lost—even tho he meets with no other reward than that self approveing hour, which the poet tells us out weighs whole years of stupid starers and of loud Huzzas.

When ever any opportunity occurs write, and write me a volume to amuse, to comfort and inform me. I turn to the loved pages of former days and read them with delight. They are all my comfort, all my consolation in the long long interval of time that I have not received a line. Should I name my dear Boys a tear will flow with the Ink—not a line have I received from them for more than a Year. May they be their Fathers comfort and their Mothers delight.

No very important military events have taken place since I wrote you last which was by Capt. Young to Bilboa. Green is driving Cornwallis acting with much Spirit and viggour. We are here looking upon each other in a mere maze. Our old currency died suddenly, the carkases remain in the hands of individuals, no Burial having been yet provided for it. The New was in Good repute for a time, but all of a Sudden and in one day followed its Elder Brother—so that with old and New in my hand, I can not purchase a single Sixpence worth of any thing yet taxes must be paid, men must be raised for Road Island and West Point and paid too, yet the profits of what each one has sold for paper avails them not. This was a stroke of our Enemies by employing Emissaries to depreciate it who were detected and put into jail. Barter and hard money is now the only trade. The strugle will be to supply our army. How after having sold our commodities for paper we can raise hard money to pay the next demand which must be speedy, I know not. I had collected a sufficient Sum of paper to pay a very large tax which the last Session of the court levied. It now will avail me not a groat. I mentioned in a former Letter that I wished you to send me a chest of Bohea tea by any vessel of Mr. Tracys or Smiths. It would turn into money quicker [   ]

"NECESSARY TO KEEP A WATCHFULL EYE OVER YOU"

To James Lovell

20 Sepbr.

In truth Friend thou art a Queer Being—laugh where I must, be candid where I can.—Your pictures are Hogarths. I shall find you out by and by—I will not Build upon other peoples judgements. My *philosopher* (I like the Name exceedingly) used to say I was a physiognomist. I have tried not unsuccessfully to find out the Heart of many a one by the countanance. I do not recollect that I ever had that opportunity with my correspondent, twice only in my life do I remember to have seen him, and then my harp was so hung upon the willows that I cared not whose face was sweet or sour. Yet do I remember the traits of Friendship and Benevolence were so conspicuous that they demanded a return in kind, and something like compassion, pitty, commisiration, call it by what Name you please I remember to have felt for the unjust sufferings of a worthy Man. But I did not study the Eye that best Index to the mind to find out how much of Rogury there was in the Heart, so here I have been these four years obtaining by peacemeal what I could have learnt in half an hour.

You may easily suppose that I have before me your Letters of August 4th and 23 and Sepbr. 10th but where the inteligence is which you say you told me from Mason I know not. Possibly Rivington may give it to me. I suspect it was with the captured post. I perceive you are up in alt with your Superlatives. So am I. Rejoice with me, for I have got a Letter at last. My Dear Friend well—that is a cordial to my Heart. Longs to come home to his American dame—for all the French Spanish Dutch Madams. That is flattering to my vanity—but he does not say so. I only find it out by his saying if he once gets back he will never leave me again. If I ever live to see that *once* I will hold him to his word. My dear Charles, sweet Boy, been sick of a Fever, and no Mother at hand to nurse and administer to the dear fondling. How does this inteligence soften every fibre and improve the Mothers sad Capacity of pain.

Thus do I run on because I know you take an Interest in my

happiness and because I know I can make you feel. I hate an unfealing mortal. The passions are common to us all, but the lively sweet affections are the portion only of a chosen few. I rejoice to find you have recoverd your Health and Spirits. Maria too tells me she has been sick, by Sympathy I suppose— that she will come and see me as soon as she can ride. The embargo is taken off I find. If she comes suppose I should make an exchange, give her my Letters for hers. No I wont, I will keep them for—for—there would be too much honey for me who have no right to it.—Laugh and Satirize as much as you please. I Laugh with you to see what a figure your inventive Genious makes in picking up terms—tis necessary to keep a Watchfull Eye over you.

Now to be a little serious, I think my good Gentleman is not very well pleased with the slow movements of the Mynheres— they do not accord with his feelings. He has no doubt forwarded his memorial with his Letters. The date of mine is the 22 of May. If any thing of a later date is sent to Congress, I wish you to transmit it by a private hand, I fear the post. We are in great hopes and high expectations of good News from the South. May it be better than our deserts or our hopes will again be Blasted. This vessel brings us News of a Naval engagement between Sir Peter Parker and some dutch Ships. You will have it in the papers. Many thanks for your attention to my and others things. If I had known of your Intention of again opening them I should have requested you to have kept out the white cloth and blew Sasnet to have forwarded provided an opportunity had offered. The rest may take their chance when they can.

I did not misapply Cornelia for Portia. I new it to be no fiction. There realy existed the Dialogue I related and nearly in the same words as I could recollect.

c. September 26, 1781

JOHN QUINCY AND CHARLES LEAVE THEIR FATHER

To John Adams

My dearest Friend   Sepbr. 29 1781
  Three days only did it want of a year from the date of your
last Letter, when I received by Capt. Newman in the Brig
Gates your welcome favour of May 22d.

By various ways I had collected some little intelligence of
you, but for six months past my Heart had known but little
ease—not a line had reachd me from you, not a syllable from
my children—and whether living or dead I could not hear.
That you have written many times, I doubted not, but such is
the chance of War; and such the misfortune attending a communication between absent Friends.

I learn by Mr. Brush, that Mr. Dana is gone to Petersburgh,
and with him Master John. For this I am not sorry. Mr. Danas
care and attention to him, I shall be well satisfied in—and
Russia is an Empire I should be very fond of his visiting. My
dear Charles I hear is comeing home with Gillion.

I know not your motives for sending him but dare say you
have weighty reasons. That of his Health is alone sufficient, if
the low countries are as prejudicial to him, as I fear they are—
and will be to his Father too. Why did you not write me about
it? At first I learnt it, only by hearing of a list of passengers who
were to come in the Indian, amongst which was a son of Mr.
A—s. This made me very uneasy—I had a thousand fears and
apprehensions. Nor shall I be much at ease, you may well
suppose, untill I hear of her arrival. I fear she will be an object,
for the British to persue. The Event I must commit to the Supreme Ruler of the universe.—Our Friends here are all well,
your Mother has recoverd beyond my expectation, my Father
too is in good Health for his years. Both our parents remember
you with affection.

General Green, is making the Requisition you require, and
setling the preliminarys for a Peace, by extirpating the British
force from Carolina. We are from the present prospect of affairs in daily expectation that Cornwallis will meet the Fate of
Burgoine. God Grant it—and that this winter may produce to

America an *honorable Peace*. But my fears are well grounded
when I add, that some of your Colleagues are unfit for the
Buisness and I really am in suspence whether you will hold
your Garbled commission, for reasons to which you will be no
stranger before this reaches you. But if you resign, I am not
the only person by hundreds who dread the consequences, as
it is probable you will find, from instructions which I hear are
to be sent, from several States to their delegates in Congress.
You have a delicate part to act. You will do what you esteem to
be your duty, I doubt not; fearless of consequences, and futurity will discriminate the Honest Man from the knave tho the
present Generation seem little disposed to.

I cannot write so freely as I wish. Your Memorial is in high
estimation here.

So you have set down at Amsterdam in the House keeping
way. What if I should take a trip across the Atlantick? I tell
Mrs. Dana we should pass very well for Natives.—I have received a very polite Letter from Mr. DeNeufvilla. How did this
Man discover, that extolling my Husband was the sweetest
Musick in my ears? He has certainly touched the key which
vibrates Harmony to me!

I think I have requested you to send me a chest of Bohea Tea,
by any vessel of Mr. Tracys. Do not think me extravagant—I
economize with the utmost Frugality I am capable of, but our
Taxes are so high, and so numerous, that I know not which
way to turn. I paied 60 hard dollars this week for a State and
county Rate. I have 30 more to pay immediately for hireing a
Man for 6 months in the Service, and a very large town tax,
now comeing out. Hard Money is our only currency. I have a
sum of old and new paper which lies by me useless at present.
Goods of the West India kind are low as ever they were—Bills
Sell greatly below par. Hard money is very scarce, but I hope
never to see an other paper Medium. Difficult as the times are,
and dull as Buisness is, we are in a better situation than we
were before.

Where is my Friend Mr. Thaxter? that not a line has reachd
me from him? His Friends are all well, but longing and impatient to hear from him. We see by the paper that he was well
enough to celebrate independence on the fourth of july.—The
Robinhood had Letters to all my Friends which I hope you

have received. I send many to Bilboa, do you get any from thence, pray write to me by way of France and Bilboa.

This is to go by a Brig to France which I heard of but yesterday. You have I suppose received a commission for forming a Quadrupple alliance—such an one is made out.

O my dear Friend, how far distant is the day when I may expect to receive you in your Native Land?

Haughty Britain sheath your sword in pitty to yourselves. Let not an other village be added to the long list of your depredations. The Nations around you shudder at your crimes. Unhappy New London Named after your capital—may she close the devastation.

How many tender Sentiments rise to mind when about to bid you adieu. Shall I express them or comprise them all in the assurence of being ever Ever Yours,   Portia

"MY LIST OF GRIEVENCES"

To John Adams

My Dearest Friend   December 9 1781

I hear the Alliance is again going to France with the Marquis Fayett and the Count de Noiales. I will not envy the Marquis the pleasure of Annually visiting his family, considering the risk he runs in doing it. Besides he deserves the good wishes of every American and a large portion of the Honours and applause of his own Country.

He returns with the additional Merrit of Laurels won at York Town by the Capture of a whole British Army. America may boast that she has accomplished what no power before her ever did, contending with Britain—Captured two of their celebrated Generals and each with an Army of thousands of veteran Troops to support them. This Event whilst it must fill Britain with despondency, will draw the union already formed still closer and give us additional Allies; if properly improved must render a negotiation easier and more advantageous to America.

But I cannot reflect much upon publick affairs; untill I have unburthend the load of my own Heart. Where shall I begin my list of Grievances? Not by accusations, but lamentations. My first is that I do not hear from you. A few lines only dated in April and May, have come to hand for 15 Months. You do not mention receiving any from me, except by Capt. Caznew, tho I wrote by Col. Laurence, by Capt. Brown, by Mr. Storer, Dexter and many others. By Babson to Bilboa by Trash, and several times by way of France. You will refer me to Gillion I suppose. Gillion has acted a base part, of which no doubt you are long e'er now apprized. You had great reason to suppose that he would reach America, as soon or sooner than the Merchant vessels and placed much confidence in him, by the treasure you permited to go on Board of him. Ah! how great has my anxiety been, what have I not sufferd since I heard my dear Charles was on Board and no intelligence to be procured of the vessel for 4 months after she saild. Most people concluded that she was founderd at Sea, as she sailed before a voilent Storm. Only 3 weeks ago did I hear the contrary. My unkle dispatchd a Messenger the Moment a vessel from Bilboa arrived with the happy tidings that She was safe at Corruna, that the passengers had all left the Ship in consequence of Gillions conduct, and were arrived at Bilboa. The vessel saild the day that the passengers arrived at Bilboa so that no Letters came by Capt. Lovett but a Dr. Sands reports that he saw a child whom they told him was yours and that he was well. This was a cordil to my dejected Spirits. I know not what to wish for. Should he attempt to come at this Season upon this coast, it has more Horrours than I have fortitude. I am still distresst. I must resign him to the kind protecting Hand of that Being who hath heitherto preserved him, and submit to what ever dispensation is alloted me.

What is the matter with Mr. Thaxter, has he forgotten all his American Friends, that out of four vessels which have arrived, not a line is to be found on Board of one of them from him?

I could Quarrell with the climate, but surely if it is subject to the Ague, there is a fever fit as well as the cold one. Mr. Guile tells me he was charged with Letters, but left them with his other things on Board the frigate, She gave him the Slip, he stept on Board Capt. Brown and happily arrived safe. From him I have learnt many things respecting my dear connexions, but still I long for that free communication which I see but little prospect of obtaining. Let me again intreat you to write by way of Guardoca, Bilboa is as safe a conveyance as any I know of.—Ah my dear John, where are you—in so remote a part of the Globe that I fear I shall not hear a Syllable from you.—Pray write me all the intelligence you get from him, send me his Letters to you. Do you know I have not a line from him for a year and half.—Alass my dear I am much afflicted with a disorder call'd the *Heartach*, nor can any remedy be found in America, it must be collected from Holland, Petersburgh and Bilboa.—And now having recited my Greifs and complaints, the next in place are those of my Neighbours. I have been applied to by the parents of several Braintree youth to write to you in their behalf, requesting your aid and assistance if it is in your power to afford it. Capt. Cathcart in the privateer Essex from Salem, went out on a cruise last April into the Channel of England, and was on the 10 of June So unfortunate as to be taken and carried into Ireland, the officers were confined there, but the Sailors were sent prisoners to Plimouth jail 12 of whom are from this Town, a list of whom I inclose. The Friends of these people have received Intelligence by way of an officer who belonged to the *Protector*, and who escaped from the jail; that in August last they were all alive, several of them very destitute of cloathing, having taken but a few with them, and those for the Summer, particularly Ned Savils and Jobe Feild. There request is that if you can, you would render them some assistance, if not by procuring an exchange, that you would get them supplied with necessary cloathing.

I have told them that you would do all in your power for them, but what that would be I could not say. Their Friends here are all well, many of them greatly distresst for their Children, and in a particular manner the Mother of Jeriah Bass.

I wish you to be very particular in letting me know by various opportunities and ways, after the recept of this, whether you have been able to do any thing for them, that I may relieve the minds of these distresst parents. The Capt. got home about 3 months ago, by escapeing to France, but could give no account of his Men after they were taken.

Two years my dearest Friend have passd away since you left your Native land. Will you not return e'er the close of an other year? I will purchase you a retreat in the woods of Virmont and retire with you from the vexations, toils and hazards of publick Life. Do you not sometimes sigh for such a Seclusion—publick peace and domestick happiness,

> "an elegant Sufficency, content
> Retirement, Rural quiet, Friendship, Books
> Ease and alternate Labour, usefull Life
> progressive Virtue and approveing Heaven."

May the time, the happy time soon arrive when we may realize these blessings so elegantly discribed by Thomson, for tho many of your country Men talk in a different Stile with regard to their intentions, and express their wishes to see you in a conspicuous point of view in your own State, I feel no ambition for a share of it. I know the voice of Fame to be a mere weathercock, unstable as Water and fleeting as a Shadow. Yet I have pride, I know I have a large portion of it.

I very fortunately received by the Apollo, by the Juno and by the Minerva the things you sent me, all in good order.

They will enable me to do I hope without drawing upon you, provided I can part with them, but Money is so scarce and taxes so high, that few purchasers are found. Goods will not double, yet they are better than drawing Bills, as they cannot be sold but with a large discount. I could not get more than 90 for a hundred Dollers, should I attempt it.

I shall inclose an invoice to the House of Ingraham Bromfild, and one to de Neufvilla. There is nothing from Bilboa that can be imported with advantage, hankerchiefs are sold here at 7 dollers & half per dozen. There are some articles which would be advantageous from Holland, but Goods there run high, and the retailing vendues which are tolerated here ruin the Shopkeepers. The articles put up, by the American House were better in Quality, for the price than those by the House of de Neufvilla. Small articles have the best profit, Gauze, ribbons, feathers and flowers to make the Ladies Gay, have the best advance. There are some articles which come from India I should suppose would be lower priced than many others—bengalls, Nankeens, persian Silk and Bandano hankerchiefs, but the House of Bromfeild & Co. know best what articles will suit here.

I have been fortunate and unfortunate. The things which came in Jones remain at Philadelphia yet.

Our Friends here are all well. Your Mother is rather in better Health, and my Father is yet sprightly. Believe me with more affection than Words can express ever Ever Yours,

Portia

P.S. I have inclosed a memorandom of some articles. I have not written to any one about them. You will give it to whom you think best and send it when you can. I shall in some future Letter mention a list of articles which I wish you to bring home with you whenever the happy time comes, but which I do not want without you. Adieu.

"SHALL . . . SLANDER IMPEACH AND ABUSE"

To James Lovell

Yes I have been Sick confined to my chamber with a slow fever. I have been unhappy through anxiety for my dear Boy, and still am apprehensive of our terrible coast should he come upon it, besides the tormenting cruizers infest our Bay with impuinity and take every thing. You have heard I suppose that the passengers all left the Ship and went to Bilboa upon Gillions abusive treatment of them. My Son was arrived there the day the vessel which brought the News sailed, since which time have heard nothing from thence. The sympathetick part you took in my suposed loss, bespeaks a feeling Heart. I thank Heaven I have not yet been called to taste the bitter cup.

Your kind endeavours have at last happily succeeded and the Boxes have arrived in safety, all the articles in much better Situation than I expected. The contents agree with your former invoice tho not with Mr. A—s memorandom—the china came all safe, one plate and Glass excepted, which for such a journey is trifling indeed. I shall acknowledge General Lincolns kind attention by a few lines to him.

You Query why Portia has not written to you as usual. The real reason was that she was perplexed. The character which she supposed she had in former times corresponded with, was that of a Man of Honour in publick and in private Life, sincere in his professions a Strickt observer of his *vows*, faithfull to his promises—in one word a Moral and a Religious Man. Shall the cruel tongue of Slander impeach and abuse this character by reporting that the most sacred of vows is voilated, that a House of bad fame is the residence, and a Mistress the *Bosom associate*. *Truth* is the one thing wanting to forever withhold a pen.

An infamous falsehood I would believe it. My reason for inquiring a character was founded upon the report. Sure I am I sought it not. Since the recept of your last, I have endeavourd to come at the report in such a manner as should give you Satisfaction, this is the reason why I have delayed writing but as I did not chuse to inquire but in a transient manner, I have not been able to obtain it. I observed to you in my last that Massachusets air was necessary for you. I still think so, as it would be the most effectual way to silence the abuse which for near a year has circulated. I know your former reasons will recur and perhaps with more force than ever. Indeed I pitty you. If cruelly used, my Heart Bleads for your troubles, and *for your real and substantial misfortunes*. I suppose I know your meaning.

Post conveyances are so doubtfull and have been so dangerous that I cannot write freely neither upon publick or private affairs.

You had as good be in Europe as Pensilvana for all the intelligence we have from Congress. No journals, no news papers and very few Letters pass. Deans is taking great Latitudes, one would think him a pensioned hireling by his Letters. Would to Heaven that the whole of his Letters could be proved as false as the greater part of them, but are there not some Sorrowfull Truths?

Sir   Janry 8. 1782

Whilst I acknowledge your kind attention to a couple of Boxes in which I was interested and which you was kind enough to forward with Safety by your waggon to Boston, I would not omit congratulating you upon your late honorable appointment which gives universal Satisfaction in your native State at the same time that it demonstrates the Sense which your Country entertain of your meritorious Services. It gives a pleasing prospect to those who wish her prosperity to see those advanced to office whos virtue and independant Spirit have uniformly shone from the begining of this unhappy contest.

CHARLES ARRIVES SAFELY

To Elizabeth Smith Shaw

My dear sister

I yesterday received a congratulatory Letter from you, upon the safe arrival of my dear Charles, an event which has relieved me from many anxieties and filld my Heart with gratitude to that gracious Being who protected him from the perils of the deep, and from the hostile foe, who raised him from Sickness and has restored him to his Native Land, undepraved in his mind and morals, by the facinating allurements of vice, decked in Foreign garbs—and this I assure you I esteem not among the least favours with which his absence has been distinguished.

The fond Mother would tell you that you may find in him the same solid sober discreet Qualities that he carried abroad with a modesty bordering upon diffidence, no ways inclined to relate his adventures but as you question him concerning them—perfectly attached to the modest republican Stile of Life, as tho he had never experienced any other. As to any alteration in his person, I perceive none but growth which has not been rapid. If no unforeseen disaster prevents I hope to bring him to visit you in the course of the Spring. He desires his duty to you, and love to his unknown cousins.

I wrote you a long Letter a months ago, but thought to coppy it as it was very carelessly written. I was that Night calld to attend the Sick and I greatly feared dying Bed of our worthy Brother Cranch. For ten days I beheld him in this critical state. Encompassed with my own anxiety, and the anguish of his whole family, I was greatly distresst. Gracious Heaven has restored the good Man to his family and Friends who were trembling least he should cease to be and the faithfull faill from among the children of Men. Whilst I attended round his Bed, I could not avoid often looking abroad and in imagination beholding my dearest Friend laid upon his sick Bed unattended by the wife, the sister or daughter, whose constant and solicitous care and attention might mitigate the riggour of the fever, and alleviate the pain—but with strangers and in a foreign Land my dear Friend has experienced a most severe sickness. In November he wrote to Charles in Bilboa that he was recovering from a fever which had left him very weak and lame, and this is the latest intelligence I have received.

You may well suppose me anxious. My Heart sometimes misgives me. I long yet fear to hear. I have one only confidence to repair to. Shall not the judge of all the earth do right and have I not experienced signal favours—shall I distrust his providentiall care?

I am sorry to hear you complain as the Spring approaches. You have but a slender constitution. I would advise you to a free use of the Bark and a journey. I hope you are not in the increasing way, as I think your Health ill able to bear it. We have none of us nursing constitutions—twice my life was nearly sacrificed to it.

Is our intelligence true that you are like to have cousin B——y for a Neighbour. I hope it will prove for her happiness and then I shall most sincerely rejoice in it. Mrs. Gray is like soon to confirm the observation that there scarce was ever any such thing under the Sun as an inconsolable widow. Grief is no incurable disease; but time, patience and a little philosophy with the help of humane fraility and address will do the Buisness. She is however like to be joined to one of the most amiable of Men, which is too great a temptation to be over balanced by the Sum total of 5 children.

Let me hear from you oftner my Sister. I really am conscience smitten at my neglect. A Good example will awaken my future attention and produce the consequent reformation of your ever affectionate Sister,   A A

February–March 1782

JOHN SICK IN HOLLAND

To John Adams

My dearest Friend   April 10th. 1782
   How great was my joy to see the well known Signature of
my Friend after a Melancholy Solicitude of many months in
which my hopes and fears alternately preponderated.
   It was January when Charles arrived. By him I expected
Letters, but found not a line; instead of which the heavy tidings of your illness reachd me. I then found my Friends had
been no strangers of what they carefully conceald from me.
Your Letter to Charles dated in November was the only consolation I had; by that I found that the most dangerous period of
your illness was pass'd, and that you considerd yourself as recovering tho feeble. My anxiety and apprehensions from that
day untill your Letters arrived, which was near 3 months, conspired to render me unhappy. Capt. Trowbridge in the Fire
Brand arrived with your favours of October and December
and in some measure dispeld the Gloom which hung heavy at
my heart. How did it leap for joy to find I was not the misirable
Being I sometimes feared I was. I felt that Gratitude to Heaven
which great deliverences both demand and inspire. I will not
distrust the providential Care of the supreem disposer of
events, from whose Hand I have so frequently received distinguished favours. Such I call the preservation of my dear Friend
and children from the uncertain Element upon which they
have frequently embarked; their preservation from the hands
of their enimies I have reason to consider in the same view,
especially when I reflect upon the cruel and inhumane treatment experienced by a Gentleman of Mr. Laurences age and
respectable character.
   The restoration of my dearest Friend from so dangerous a
Sickness, demands all my gratitude, whilst I fail not to suppli-
cate Heaven for the continuance of a Life upon which my
temporal happiness rests, and deprived of which my own existance would become a burden. Often has the Question which
you say staggerd your philosophy occured to me, nor have I
felt so misirable upon account of my own personal Situation,

when I considerd that according to the common course of
Nature, more than half my days were allready passt, as for
those in whom our days are renewed. Their hopes and prospects
would vanish, their best prospects, those of Education, would
be greatly diminished—but I will not anticipate those miseries
which I would shun. Hope is my best Friend and kindest comforter; she assures me that the pure unabated affection, which
neither time or absence can allay or abate, shall e'er long be
crowned with the completion of its fondest wishes, in the safe
return of the beloved object; the age of romance has long ago
past, but the affection of almost Infant years has matured and
strengthend untill it has become a vital principle, nor has the
world any thing to bestow which could in the smallest degree
compensate for the loss. Desire and Sorrow were denounced
upon our Sex; as a punishment for the transgression of Eve. I
have sometimes thought that we are formed to experience more
exquisite Sensations than is the Lot of your Sex. More tender
and susceptable by Nature of those impressions which create
happiness or misiry, we Suffer and enjoy in a higher degree. I
never wonderd at the philosopher who thanked the Gods that
he was created a Man rather than a Woman.

I cannot say, but that I was dissapointed when I found that
your return to your native land was a still distant Idea. I think
your Situation cannot be so dissagreable as I feared it was, yet
that dreadfull climate is my terror.—You mortify me indeed
when you talk of sending Charles to Colledge, who it is not
probable will be fit under three or four years. Surely my dear
Friend fleeting as time is I cannot reconcile myself to the Idea of
living in this cruel State of Seperation for [   ] or even three
years to come. Eight years have already past, since you could call
yourself an Inhabitant of this State. I shall assume the Signature
of Penelope, for my dear Ulysses has already been a wanderer
from me near half the term of years that, that Hero was encountering Neptune, Calipso, the Circes and Syrens. In the poetical
Language of Penelope I shall address you

> "Oh! haste to me! A Little longer Stay
> Will ev'ry grace, each fancy'd charm decay:
> Increasing cares, and times resistless rage
> Will waste my bloom, and wither it to age."

You will ask me I suppose what is become of my patriotick virtue? It is that which most ardently calls for your return. I greatly fear that the climate in which you now reside will prove fatal to your Life, whilst your Life and usefullness might be many years of Service to your Country in a more Healthy climate. If the Essentials of her political system are safe, as I would fain hope they are, yet the impositions and injuries, to which she is hourly liable, and daily suffering, call for the exertions of her wisest and ablest citizens. You know by many years experience what it is to struggle with difficulties—with wickedness in high places—from thence you are led to covet a private Station as the post of Honour, but should such an Idea generally prevail, who would be left to stem the torrent?

Should we at this day possess those invaluable Blessings transmitted us by our venerable Ancestors, if they had not inforced by their example, what they taught by their precepts?

"While pride, oppression and injustice reign
the World will still demand her Catos presence."

Why should I indulge an Idea, that whilst the active powers of my Friend remain, they will not be devoted to the Service of his country?

Can I believe that the Man who fears neither poverty or dangers, who sees not charms sufficient either in Riches, power or places to tempt him in the least to swerve from the purest Sentiments of Honour and Delicacy; will retire, unnoticed, Fameless to a Rustick cottage there by dint of Labour to earn his Bread. I need not much examination of my Heart to say I would not willingly consent to it.

Have not Cincinnatus and Regulus been handed down to posterity, with immortal honour?

Without fortune it is more than probable we shall end our days, but let the well earned Fame of having Sacrificed those prospects, from a principal of universal Benevolence and good will to Man, descend as an inheritance to our ofspring. The Luxery of Foreign Nations may possibly infect them but they have not before them an example of it, so far as respects their domestick life. They are not Bred up with an Idea of possessing Hereditary Riches or Grandeur. Retired from the Capital, they see little of the extravagance or dissipation, which prevails there, and at the close of day, in lieu of the Card table, some usefull Book employs their leisure hours. These habits early fixed, and daily inculcated, will I hope render them usefull and ornamental Members of Society.—But we cannot see into futurity.—With Regard to politicks, it is rather a dull season for them, we are recruiting for the Army.

The Enemy make sad Havock with our Navigation. Mr. Lovell is appointed continential Receiver of taxes and is on his way to this State.

It is difficult to get Gentlemen of abilities and Integrity to serve in congress, few very few are willing to Sacrifice their Interest as others have done before them.

Your favour of december 18th came by way of Philadelphia, but all those Letters sent by Capt. Reeler were lost, thrown over Board. Our Friends are well and desire to be rememberd to you. Charles will write if he is able to, before the vessel sails, but he is sick at present, threatned I fear with a fever. I received one Letter from my young Russian to whom I shall write—and 2 from Mr. Thaxter. If the vessel gives me time I shall write. We wait impatiently for the result of your demand. These slow slugish wheels move not in unison with our feelings.

Adieu my dear Friend. How gladly would I visit you and partake of your Labours and cares, sooth you to rest, and alleviate your anxieties were it given me to visit you even by moon Light, as the faries are fabled to do.

I cheer my Heart with the distant prospect. All that I can hope for at present, is to hear of your welfare which of all things lies nearest the Heart of Your ever affectionate

Portia

"REDUCED MY PURSE PRETTY LOW"

To John Adams

My dearest Friend   July 17 1782

I have delayed writing till the vessel is near ready to Sail, that my Letters may not lay 3 weeks or a month after they are written, as is commonly the case. Mr. Rogers and Lady are going

passengers in this vessel; and tho I have only a slight knowledge
of them I shall commit my Letters to their care. I have not
heard from you since the arrival of Capt. Deshon. Your last
Letters were dated in March. I replied to them by the last vessel which saild for France dated about a month ago tho she
has not sailed more than a fortnight. I again grow impatient
for intelligence. From the last accounts which reachd us by
way of Nantys we learn that the Dutch are acquiring a firmness of conduct, that they have acknowledged the independance of America, and are determined to turn a deaf Ear to
that prostituted Island of Britain. If this is true, and I sincerely
hope it is, I congratulate you upon the Success of your negotiations, and hope your Situation is more eligible than for the
time past. If I know you are happy, it will tend to alleiviate the
pains of absence.

The Count de Grasse misfortune in the West Indias, we
sensibly feel. The British will feed upon it for ages, but it will
not save their Nation from the destruction which awaits them.

The Season has advanced thus far without any military Ex-
ploit on either Side. We want the one thing necessary for persueing the War with Vigor. Were we less Luxurious we should
be better able to support our Independance with becomeing
dignity, but having habituated ourselves to the delicacies of
Life, we consider them as necessary, and are unwilling to tread
back the path of Simplicity, or reflect that

> "Man wants but little here below
> Nor wants that little long."

By the Enterprize I gave you a particular account of the
dangerous Situation our dear Brother Cranch is in. He still
continues, but we have little to build our hopes upon of his
long continuance with us. Heaven be better to us than our
fears. The rest of our Friends are well. Charles has been to
see a publick Commencement; and has returned to night
much gratified with the exhibitions. He has followed his
Studies with attention, since his return, under the care of a
Mr. Thomas of Bridgwater; who appears well calculated for
the instruction of youth; and is said by good judges, to be
an admirable proficient in the Languages. But with him we
are obliged to part immediately, as he is going into Buisness.

I know not what to do with my Children. We have no Grammer School in the Town, nor have we had for 5 years. I give this Gentleman 2s. 6 pr week a peice, for my two. I must (could I find a School abroad to my mind) Board them at 18 Shillings pr week which is the lowest. In Boston 6 and 8 dollers is given by Gentlemen there for Board, formerly a Gentleman Boarded as well for 12 Shillings, but such is the difference. I know not how to think of their leaving Home. I could not live in the House were it so deserted. If they are gone only for a day, it is as silent as a Tomb.

What think you of your daughters comeing to keep House for you? She proposes it. Could you make a Bridge she would certainly present herself to you, nor would she make an ungracefull appearence at the Head of your table. She is rather too silent. She would please you the better. She frequently mourns the long absence of her Father, but she knows not all she suffers in consequence of it. He would prudently introduce her to the world, which her Mamma thinks proper in a great measure to seclude herself from, and the daughter is too attentive to the happiness of her Mamma to leave her much alone, nor could repeated invitations nor the solicitation of Friends joined to the consent of her Mamma, prevail with her to appear at commencement this year. But much rather would the Mamma and daughter embrace the Husband and Father in his Native Land than think of visiting foreign climes. Will the cottage be sweet? Will Retirement be desirable? Does your Heart pant for domestick tranquility, and for that reciprocation of happiness you was once no stranger to. Is there ought in Courts, in Theaters or Assemblies that can fill the void? Will Ambition, will Fame, will honour do it. Will you not reply— all, all are inadequate, but whether am I led? I cannot assume an other Subject—the Heart is softned. Good night.

July 18th

Sol rises this morning with great splendor. I had much rather have seen his face overspread with clouds dispenseing their fruitfull drops to the thirsty earth. It is very dry. Our Corn suffers. Should we be cut of or shortned in our crops we should more sensibly feel it, as our celebrated Siberian wheat is universally blasted, and much of the Rye. Our Success with a little last year led my Tennant to sow 3 acres this year, which we were obliged to mow for foder. Col. Quincy succeeded last year, and raised a hundred and sixty Bushels of as fine wheat as I ever saw, but his Has shared the same fate, and it is so where ever I hear of it. My favorite Virmont is a delightfull Grain Country. I cannot tell why, but I feel a great fondness for the prosperity of that State. I wrote you in my last that I had laid aside the thoughts of being an adventurer there for the present—but soon after Col. Davis of Woster to whom the township was granted, with his associates, brought me the Charter, and the proceedings of Congress with Regard to Virmont by which it appears that Virmont had complied with the requisitions of Congress and the committe to whom, the Matter was committed, report that having complied they consider Congress as obliged to set them of and ratify their independance. This Gentleman has taken pains to have every propriater persons of character and property and that they should all belong to this State. He says it is one of the best situated townships in the State, and will rise in value daily. Salem is the Name it bears. As he had got the deeds all drawn and executed I recollected the old adage Nothing venture nothing have; and I took all the Lots 5 in number 4 of which I paid him for, and the other obligated myself to discharge in a few months. You are named in the Charter as original propriater, so no deed was necessary. Each lot is to contain 300 and 30 acres at about 11 pounds a Lot. This payment has reduced my purse pretty low; having a little before paid Charles passage and repaird Buildings to the amount of a hundred dollers. My taxes I might mention as a heavy load, but as every Body complains, I will be silent, tho I might with as much reason; my continental tax which I am calld upon to pay next week, and is only a half year tax, amounts to 50 dollers. 19 pounds 15 & 10 pence I paid about a Month ago for a State tax and 7 pounds 10 & 2 pence for a town tax and 6 pound some shillings for a ministerial tax, to make up paper money deficiencies, besides 9 pounds 13 & six pence for Class number 7 towards hireing a Man for 3 years. All this I have discharged since April, as will appear by my Receits.

I have not drawn any Bills and will not if I can possibly help it. I shall have no occasion to, if I can get black and white

Gauze and Gauze hankerchiefs. It may not be to the Credit of my country but it is a certain fact, that no articles are so vendible or yeald a greater profit. It was with difficulty I could keep a little for my own use of what I last received. I inclosed a list of articles by the Enterprize which I wish you to direct Ingraham and Bromfield to forward, and should they meet with the same Success my former adventures have, and arrive safe, they will be much more benificial than drawing Bills upon which I must discount. I shall inclose a duplicate of the articles with an addition of 5 yard of scarlet Broad cloth of the best kind and 3 yard of Sattin of the same coulour which I want for my own use leaving it at all times to you to determine the Quantity which you think proper to remitt.

You have heard I suppose that Gillion arrived at Philadelphia in june. Only two Letters have come to hand. Dr. Waterhouse left him at the Havanah but was unfortunately taken upon his passage home and carried to New York, by which means the rest of the Letters perished.—I wrote you by the Alliance respecting the Braintree prisoners, but have not received a line in which you make mention of them. That you took measures to relieve them several have testified to their Friends, but it would be more satisfactory if you had mentiond them yourself. There is in Boston a Mr. Marstins' who belonged on Board Gillion who paid yesterday to Charles in Boston a Jo which he said you lent him. I mention this to his Honour and justice. Of all the money due to you, upon Book or note, I have not received a copper since your absence and must have been distresst but for the remittances you have made me.

I long to receive Letters from all my dear Friends. I wish you would write by way of France and send your Letters to Mr. Warren. He would be particuliarly carefull of them. Two vessels have just arrived in 30 days passage from Nants. Your Friends here make great complaint, that you do not write to them. Uncle Smith says he will not write you any more, yet believe he does not keep his word, for he writes by every vessel. Genrll. Warren says you have forgotton him and Dr. Tufts complains. You see how important a line from you is considerd.

I say all I can for you, but wish you would find leisure to notice those Friends who write to you. Uncle Quincy desires his regards to you. Your aged Mamma wishes to see you, but fears she never shall. My Father injoys as Good State of Health as his years will admit. My most affectionate regards to my Dear John from whom I have received but one Letter since his visit to Petersburg.

Adieu my dearest Friend, and Believe me your Most affectionate   Portia

Black and white Gauze
Spotted and striped Gauze hankerchiefs
tapes Quality bindings low priced ⅞ths linnen
Black caliminco   red tamies   fine thread   low
priced dark grounded calicos   Ribbons—10 yd of
blew and white dark striped cotton

Nabby has just been giving me a Letter for you. I read it, and really beleive the child thinks herself serious; but you can give her better advice. Mr. Foster has just sent me word that he designs to wait upon me to morrow for Letters so that I shall give them to Him as he is kind enough to come out to see me. You will not fail to take notice of him.

ENCLOSURE

6 lb. best Hyson Tea
2 China Cooffee Pots
1 doz: handled Cups & Saucers—China
2 doz Soup Plates & a Tureen
  doz: flat do.
  doz small long dishes
2 pr Pudding do.
3 or 4 house Brushs

Mrs. Warren has left this memorandum with a request that she may have these articles and she will pay the money to me or send to her Son for any thing I may want from France, but at present I know of nothing, so that I should be glad if they are sent they may not be put with any thing which belongs to me, but invoiced and put up by them selves.

To John Adams

My dearest Friend   Sepbr. 5 1782
    Your kind favours of May 14th and June 16th came to Hand last Evening; and tho I have only just time to acknowledge them, I would not omit a few lines; I have written before by this vessel; which is Bound to France. Mr. Allen your old fellow traveller is a passenger on Board, and promises to be attentive to the Letters. In my other Letter I mention a serious proposal made in a former; but do not inform you of the Nature of it, fearing a rejection of my proposal and it is of so tender a Nature I could scarcly bear a refusal; yet should a refusal take place, I know it will be upon the best grounds and reasons. But your mention in your two kind favours, your wishes with more seariousness than you have ever before exprest them, leads me again to repeat my request; it is that I may come to you, with our daughter, in the Spring, provided You are like to continue abroad. In my other Letter I have stated to you an arrangement of my affairs, and the person with whom I would chuse to come; I have slightly mentiond it to him; and he says he should like it exceedingly and I believe would adjust his affairs and come with me. Mr. Smith is the person I mean, I mention him least my other Letter should fail.
    I am the more desirious to come now I learn Mr. Thaxter is comeing home. I am sure you must feel a still greater want of my attention to you. I will endeavour to find out the disposition of Congress, but I have lost my intelligence from that Quarter by Mr. Lovels return to this State. I have very little acquaintance with any Gentleman there. Mr. Jackson and Mr. Osgood are the only two Members there from this State. Mr. Lovell has lately returnd. I will see him and make some inquiry; as to peace you have my opinion in the Letter referd to by this vessel.
    The acknowledgment of our Independance by the United provinces is considerd here as a most important Event, but the Newspapers do not anounce it to the world with that Eclat, which would have been rung from all Quarters had this Event

been accomplished by a certain character. Indeed we have never received an official account of it untill now. Let me ask you Dear Friend, have you not been rather neglegent in writing to your Friends? Many difficulties you have had to encounter might have been laid open to them, and your character might have had justice done it. But Modest Merrit must be its own Reward. Bolingbrook in his political tracts observes, rather Ironically (but it is a certain fact,) that Ministers stand in as much need of publick writers, as they do of him. He adds, "in their prosperity they can no more subsist without daily praise, than the writers without daily Bread, and the further the Minister extends his views the more necessary are they to his Support. Let him speak as contemptuously of them as he pleases, yet it will fare with his ambition, as with a lofty Tree, which cannot shoot its Branches into the Clouds unless its Root work into the dirt."

You make no mention of receiving Letters from me, you certainly must have had some by a vessel which arrived in France some time before the Fire Brand reachd Holland. She too had Letters for you.

Accept my acknowledgement for the articles sent. As the other arrived safe, I could have wished my little memorandom by the Fire Brand had reachd you before this vessel saild; but no Matter, I can dispose of them. My Luck is great I think. I know not that I have lost any adventure you have ever sent me. Nabby requests in one of her Letters a pair of paste Buckles. When your hand is in you may send a pair for me if you please.

Adieu my dearest Friend. Remember that to render your situation more agreable I fear neither the Enemy or old Neptune, but then you must give me full assureance of your intire approbation of my request. I cannot accept a half way invitation. To say I am happy here, I cannot, but it is not an idle curiosity that make me wish to hazard the Watery Element. I much more sincerely wish your return. Could I hope for that during an other year I would endeavour to wait patiently the Event.

Once more adieu. The Messenger waits and hurrys me.— Ever Ever yours,   Portia

To John Adams

My dearest Friend   october 8th 1782

Your favour of August 17th is just put into my hands with
word that Capt. Grinnel is to sail tomorrow, all of a sudden
without having been to see me, or warning me of his going. I
made a little excursion to Haverhill with our daughter and son
Charles which prevented my getting my Letters ready. However I am determined not to close my eyes to Night untill I
have written to you, and will send Charles of tomorrow morning by sun rise. Mr. Guile is come safe and sends me word he
will see me tomorrow or next day. I shall be impatient untill he
comes. I want to know all about my dear Friend—O! that I
could add Companion. Permit me my Dearest Friend to renew
that Companionship. My Heart sighs for it. I cannot O! I
cannot be reconcild to living as I have done for 3 years past. I
am searious. I could be importunate with you. May I? Will you
let me try to soften, if I cannot wholy releave you, from your
Burden of Cares and perplexities? Shall others for their pleasure hazard, what I cannot have courage to incounter from an
affection pure as ever burned in a vestal Heart—Warm and
permanant as that which glows in your own dear Bosom. I
Hardly think of Enemies of terrors and storms. But I resolve
with myself, to do as you wish. If I can add to your Happiness,
is it not my duty? If I can soften your Cares, is it not my duty?
If I can by a tender attention and assiduity prolong your most
valuable Life, is it not my duty? And shall I from Female apprehensions of storms of winds, forego all these Calls? Sacrifice
them to my personal ease? Alass I have not even that, for
wakeing or sleeping I am ever with you. Yet if you do not
consent so much is my Heart intent upon it, that your refusal
must be couched in very soft terms, and must pledge yourself
to return speedily to me.

Yet my dear sir when I can conquer the too soft sensibility of
my Heart; I feel loth you should quit your station untill an
Honorable peace is Established, and you have added that to

your other Labours. Tis no small satisfaction to me that my country is like to profit so largely by my sacrifices.

I doubt not of your Numerous avocations. Yet when you can get time to write to your Friends here, it is of vast service to you. It sets tongues and pens at work. It informs the people of your attention to their Interests, and our negotiations are extolled and our Services are held up to view. I am unfortunate in not having in my possession a News paper to inclose, in which some person, has done justice to your patience, to your perseverance, and held up as far as was prudent the difficulties you have had to encounter.

I hope you are releaved by my last Letters in some measure from your anxiety about our dear Friend and Brother Cranch. He is recoverd far beyond our expectations; he is for the first time this week attending Court. I am of opinion that his Lungs are affected, and am in terrors for him least he should have a relapse. He owes his Life the doctors say under providence, to the incessant, unwearied, indefatigable watchfull care of his wife; who has almost sacrificed her own, to save his Life.—O! my dear Friend, how often is my Heart torn with the Idea, that I have it not in my power, let sickness or misfortune assail you thus to watch round your Bed and soften your repose.

To the Care of a gracious providence I commit you.

Your good Mother went from here this afternoon, and desires her kind Regards to you. Uncle Quincy send his Love, is always attentive to hear from you. He applied to me a little while ago, to send for 2 yards of green velvet proper for a pulpit cushing with fring and tassels for it or half a pound of green sewing silk. He would have sent the Money, but I refused it, because I knew it would give you pleasure to make this little present to our Church. You will be so good as to order it put up by the next conveyance. The Fire Brand is not yet arrived. We are under apprehension for her. We have a large French Fleet in our Harbour, yet are daily insulted by British cruizers. There are several officers who belong to the Fleet who hire rooms in the Town, some of them Men of learning and Character. Several of them have got introduced to me. I treat them with civility, but rather avoid a large acquaintance. I have been on Board one 84 gun ship by the particular invitation of the

Captain. Col. Quincy and family accompanied me. This afternoon a Sweed, in the French Service made me a second visit.
He speaks english, is a Man of learning and is second in command of the America; which is given by Congress in lieu of the
ship which was lost in comeing into the Harbour. These Gentry take a good deal of pains to get an introduction here;
seem to consider an acquaintance of much more importance
to them, than the people who call themselves geenteel, and
who compose our Beau Mond, but who have chiefly risen
into Notice since you left the Country. As I have not sought
their acquaintance, nor ever appeard in publick since your
absence, I have not the *Honour* to be known to many of
them—concequently am forgotten or unnoticed by them in
all their publick entertainments. Our Allies however recollect
that the only Gentleman who is employed abroad in publick
Service from this state May probably have a Lady and a daughter, and it may be proper to notice them out of Regard to the
Gentlemans publick Character; and accordingly Send out their
invitations which I decline and send the daughter. This has
been repeatedly the case. I care not a stiver as it respects my
own country. Mrs. Dana is treated in the same Manner, but
people who are accustomed to politeness and good Manners
notice it. The Manners of our Country are so intirely changed
from what they were in those days of simplicity when you
knew it, that it has nothing of a Republick but the Name.
Unless you can keep a publick table and Equipage you are but
of very small consideration.

What would You have thought 15 years ago, for young
practicioners at the Bar to be setting up their Chariots, to be
purchaseing—not paying for—their country seats. P. M——n,
B——n H——n, riding in their Chariots who were clerks in
offices when we removed from Town. Hogarth may exhibit his
world topsa turva. I am sure I have seen it realized.

Your daughter has been writing to you. Indeed my dear sir
you would be proud of her. Not that she is like her *Mamma*.
She has a Statliness in her manners which some misconstrue
into pride and haughtyness, but which rather results from a
too great reserve; she wants more affability, but she has prudence and discretion beyond her years. She is in her person tall
large and Majestick, mammas partialiaty allows her to be a

good figure. Her sensibility is not yet sufficiently a wakend to give her Manners that pleasing softness which attracts whilst it is attracted. Her Manners rather forbid all kinds of Intimacy; and awe whilst they command.

Indeed she is not like her Mamma. Had not her Mamma at her age too much sensibility, to be *very prudent.* It however won a Heart of as much sensibility—but how my pen runs. I never can write you a short Letter. My Charles and Tommy, are fine Boys. My absent one is not forgotten. How does he, I do not hear from him.

Adieu my dear Friend. How much happier should I be to fold you to my Bosom, than to bid you this Languid adieu, with a whole ocean between us. Yet whilst I recall to your mind tender scenes of happier days, I would add a supplication that the day May not be far distant, that shall again renew them to your Ever Ever affectionate   Portia

1 peice of white blond Lace 2 pr Moroco Shoes for Nabby 4 yd Book Muslin thread for working Muslin 6 pr Black Worsted Breaches patterns.

This is written in so much haste that I cannot revise. I took Miss Nabbys Letter to inclose and found I was mistaken. That it is to Mr. Thaxter instead of papa. So I will recall some of my observations about sensibility.

AN ANNIVERSARY LETTER

To John Adams

My Dearest Friend   *October* 25 1782

The family are all retired to rest, the Busy scenes of the day are over, a day which I wished to have devoted in a particular manner to my dearest Friend, but company falling in prevented nor could I claim a moment untill this silent watch of the Night.

Look—(is there a dearer Name than Friend; think of it for me;) Look to the date of this Letter—and tell me, what are the thoughts which arise in your mind? Do you not recollect that

Eighteen years have run their anual Circuit, since we pledged our mutual Faith to each other, and the Hymeneal torch was Lighted at the Alter of Love. Yet, yet it Burns with unabating fervour, old ocean has not Quenched it, nor old Time smooth-erd it, in the Bosom of Portia. It cheers her in the Lonely Hour, it comforts her even in the gloom which sometimes possessess her mind.

It is my Friend from the Remembrance of the joys I have lost that the arrow of affliction is pointed. I recollect the untitled Man to whom I gave my Heart, and in the agony of recollection when time and distance present themselves together, wish he had never been any other. Who shall give me back Time? Who shall compensate to me those *years* I cannot recall? How dearly have I paid for a titled Husband; should I wish you less wise, that I might enjoy more happiness? I cannot find that in my Heart. Yet providence has wisely placed the real Blessings of Life within the reach of moderate abilities, and he who is wiser than his Neighbour sees so much more to pitty and Lament, that I doubt whether the balance of happiness is in his Scale.

I feel a disposition to Quarrel with a race of Beings who have cut me of, in the midst of my days from the only Society I delighted in. Yet No Man liveth for himself, says an authority I will not dispute. Let me draw satisfaction from this Source and instead of murmuring and repineing at my Lot consider it in a more pleasing view. Let me suppose that the same Gra-cious Being who first smiled upon our union and Blessed us in each other, endowed my Friend with powers and talents for the Benifit of Mankind and gave him a willing mind, to im-prove them for the service of his Country.

You have obtain honour and Reputation at Home and abroad. O may not an inglorious Peace wither the Laurels you have won.

I wrote you per Capt. Grinnel. The Fire Brand is in great haste to return, and I fear will not give me time to say half I wish. I want you to say many more things to me than you do, but you write so wise so like a minister of state. I know your Embarassments. Thus again I pay for titles. Life takes its com-plexion from inferiour things; it is little attentions and assidu-ities that sweeten the Bitter draught and smooth the Rugged Road.

I have repeatedly expresst my desire to make a part of your Family. "But will you come and see me" cannot be taken in that serious Light I should chuse to consider an invitation from those I Love. I do not doubt but that you would be glad to see me; but I know you are apprehensive of dangers and fatigues. I know your Situation may be unsetled—and it may be more permanant than I wish it. Only think how the word 3 and 4 and 5 years absence sounds!! It sinks into my Heart with a Weight I cannot express. Do you look like the Minature you sent? I cannot think so. But you have a better likeness I am told. Is that designd for me? Gracious Heaven restore to me the original and I care not who has the shadow.

We are hoping for the fall of Gibralter, because we imagine that will facilitate a peace—and who is not weary of the war? The appointment of Dr. F. to the Sweedish Court is considerd as a curious step, especially at his own Instance. Tis probable others will write you more particularly (the French Fleet still remain with us, and the British cruizers insult them, more American vessels have been captured since they have lain here than for a year before). The Generall Green is taken and carried into Halifax, by which I suppose I have lost some Small Bundles or packages. Beals told me that you gave him 7 small packages which he deliverd Capt. Bacon for me. The prisoners have all arrived except Savil who is yet in France. I mentiond to you before; that some of them had been with me, and offerd to repay the money with which you supplied them. I could only tell them that I had never received a line from you concerning the Matter, that I chose first to hear from you: I would not receive a farthing unless I had your express direction and your Hand writing to prove that what you had done was from your private purse—which I was confident was the case; or you would have been as ready to have relieved others if you had any publick fund for that purpose as those which belonged to this Town. I found a story prevailing that what you had done, was at the publick expence; this took its rise either from Ignorance or ingratitude—but it fully determined me to receive your direction. The persons who have been with me are the two Clarks, the two Bealses and Jobe Feild. I have a cousin in England for whom his good Mother is greatly distresst, she wishes me to write to you concerning him, if you should find by way of C. Storer that he is needy and should supply him with 5, 6 or 10 Guineys, they will be repaid to me upon your noticeing it. I have been Virmont Mad I suppose you will say. I own I have straitned myself in concequence of it—but I expect they will be fine Farms for my children or Grand children or great Grand children. If you send me any thing per the return of the Fire Brand, pray Let an attest come that every thing is unBritish. I believe I will inclose a small invoice of proper articles.

Adieu my dear Friend. Ever Ever Yours   Portia

"YOU HAVE BEEN A GREAT TRAVELLER"

To John Quincy Adams

November 13th 1782

How is it my dear son? You who used to be so punctual in your returns to your Friends that I your affectionate Mother have received but one Letter from You since you left Amsterdam.

Has the cold Nothern Regions frozen up that Quick and Lively immagination which used to give pleasure to your Friends? Has it chilled your affections, or obliterated the Remembrance of her who gave you Birth?

To what Cause shall I attribute your Silence? The further you are removed from me, and the more difficult it is to hear from you; the greater my anxiety. It is too, too, hard, to be totally deprived of the company and Society of your Father, as I have been for three years past and to be forgotton by my Son.

Neither Time or distance have in the Least diminished that Maternal Regard, and affection which I bear you. You are ever upon my heart and Mind, both of which take no Small interest in your advancement in Life. Consider my dear Son; what your Situation is. Your Fathers Station abroad, holds you up to view, in a different Light from that of a Common Traveller. And his virtues will render your faults; should you be guilty of any, more conspicuous. But should you as I would fondly hope Religiously adhere to the precepts you have received from him, and to the advise and instruction of your Friend and patron, then shall I see you become a usefull Member of Society, a Friend to your Country and a Guardian of her Laws and Liberties—for such is the example you have before you.

This day 3 years ago, you quitted your Native Land. You have been a great traveller for your years, and must have made many observations Worthy a place in your memory.

The Empire where you now reside, must afford ample Scope for a Genious to descant upon. But you are confined to your studies you will tell me, and have little opportunity for observation. But you cannot reside amongst a people, without learning Something of their Laws customs and Manners. Nor can you if you are capable of the Reflection which I think you are, omit compareing them with those of your own Country, and others which you have travelled through. It will be of advantage to you to compare the Monarchical goverments with the Republican to reflect upon the advantages, and disadvantages arising from each, and to commit your thoughts to writing, to watch with attention the judgment and opinions of Learned Men whom you may hear conversing upon Subjects of this Nature. Attend to the Historians you read, and carefully observe the Springs and causes that have produced the rise and fall of Empires. And give me your own reflections in your own Language. I do not expect the Elegance of a Voltair nor the Eloquence and precisian of a Robinson, yet they will have a preferable value to me, because they will shew me what you have gained by attention and observation. Mr. Dana will I doubt not; be ever ready to assist you with his advice and counsel. Endeavour by an obligeing Respectfull attentive Behaviour to secure his Friendship, he will not advise you but for your good, he will not chide you, but for your amendment. Attend to him as your guardian, patron, and Friend.

Your sister desires to be rememberd to you. She has written to you twice since your residence in Petersburgh but has not received a line from you. Your Brothers live at home under the tuition of a Mr. Robins. They make good proficiancy in their studies. Tommy has written you a Letter which I shall inclose. Your Worthy Grandparents are still Living and desire to be rememberd to you. Your uncle Cranch has had a long and dangerous sickness, but is in a great measure recoverd.

I most sincerely wish the contending Nations at peace, for

after all the great and mighty victories of conquering Nations, this war upon our own species is a savage Buisness, unworthy a Rational and immortal Being whose study ought to be the happiness and not the destruction of Mankind.

Make my most Respectfull Regards to Mr. Dana and tell him I feel myself indebted to him for his care and kindness to you. Tell him his worthy Lady was well this week, and that I expect to pass a few days with her soon. Believe me my dear Child with the tenderest wishes for your Health and happiness your ever affectionate Mother   Abigail Adams

ROYALL TYLER

To John Adams

My dearest Friend   December 23. 1782

I have omited writing by the last opportunity to Holland; because I had but small Faith in the designs of the owners or passengers. The vessel sails from Nantucket, Dr. Winship is a passenger, a Mr. Gray and some others—and I had just written you so largely by a vessel bound to France, the General Galvaye, that I had nothing New to say. There are few occurences in this Northen climate at this Season of the year to divert or entertain you—and in the domestick way should I draw you the picture of my Heart, it would be what I hope you still would Love; tho it containd nothing New; the early possession you obtained there; and the absolute power you have ever mantaind over it; leaves not the smallest space unoccupied. I look back to the early days of our acquaintance; and Friendship, as to the days of Love and Innocence; and with an undiscribable pleasure I have seen near a score of years roll over our Heads, with an affection heightned and improved by time— nor have the dreary years of absence in the smallest degree effaced from my mind the Image of the dear untittled man to whom I gave my Heart. I cannot sometimes refrain considering the Honours with which he is invested as badges of my unhappiness. The unbounded confidence I have in your attachment to me, and the dear pledges of our affection, has soothed the solitary hour, and renderd your absence more supportable; for had I have loved you with the same affection, it must have been misiry to have doubted. Yet a cruel world too often injures my feelings, by wondering how a person possesst of domestick attachments can sacrifice them by absenting himself *for years.*

If you had known said a person to me the other day; that Mr. Adams would have remained so long abroad; would you have consented that he should have gone? I recollected myself a moment, and then spoke the real dictates of my Heart. If I had known Sir that Mr. A. could have affected what he has done; I would not only have submitted to the absence I have endured; painfull as it has been; but I would not have opposed it, even tho 3 years more should be added to the Number, which Heaven avert! I feel a pleasure in being able to sacrifice my selfish passions to the general good, and in imitating the example which has taught me to consider myself and family, but as the small dust of the balance when compaired with the great community.

Your daughter most sincerely regreets your absence, she sees me support it, yet thinks she could not imitate either parent in the disinterested motives which actuate them. She has had a strong desire to encounter the dangers of the sea to visit you. I however am not without a suspicion that she may loose her realish for a voyage by spring. The tranquility of mine and my dear sisters family is in a great measure restored to us, since the recovery of our worthy Friend and Brother. We had a most melancholy summer. The young folks of the two families together with those of Col. Quincys and General Warren preserve a great Intimacy, and as they wish for but few connections in the Beau Mond, it is not to be wonderd at that they are fond of each others company. We have an agreable young Gentleman by the Name of Robbins who keeps our little school, son to the Revd. Mr. Robbins of Plimouth. And we have in the little circle an other gentleman who has opend an office in Town, for about nine months past, and boarded in Mr. Cranch's family. His Father you knew. His Name is Tyler, he studied Law upon his comeing out of colledge with Mr. Dana, but when Mr. Dana went to congress he finished his studies with Mr. Anger. Loosing his Father young and having a very pretty patrimony left him, possessing a sprightly fancy a warm imagination and an agreable person, he was rather negligent in persueing his buisness in the way of his profession; and dissipated two or 3 years of his Life and too much of his fortune for to reflect upon with pleasure; all of which he now laments but cannot recall. At 23 the time when he took the resolution of comeing to Boston and withdrawing from a too numerous acquaintance; he resolved to persue his studies; and his Buisness; and save his remaining fortune which sufferd much more from the paper currency than any other cause; so that out of 17 thousand pounds which fell to his share; he cannot now realize more than half that sum; as he told me a few days past. His Mamma is in possession of a large Estate and he is a very favorite child. When he proposed comeing to settle here he met with but little encouragement, but he was determined upon the trial. He has succeeded beyond expectation, he has popular talants, and as his behaviour has been unexceptionable since his residence in Town; in concequence of which his Buisness daily increases—he cannot fail making a distinguished figure in his profession if he steadily persues it. I am not acquainted with any young Gentleman whose attainments in literature are equal to his, who judges with greater accuracy or discovers a more delicate and refined taste. I have frequently looked upon him with the Idea that You would have taken much pleasure in such a pupil. I wish I was as well assured that you would be equally pleased with him in an other character, for such I apprehend are his distant hopes. I early saw that he was possest with powerfull attractions, and as he obtaind and deserved, I believe the character of a gay; tho not a criminal youth, I thought it prudent to keep as great a reserve as possible. In this I was seconded by the discreet conduct of a daughter, who is happy in not possessing all her Mothers sensibility. Yet I see a growing attachment in him stimulated by that very reserve. I feel the want of your presence and advise. I think I know your sentiments so well that the merit of a gentleman will be your first consideration, and I have made every inquiry which I could with decency; and without discloseing my motives. Even in his most dissipated state he always applied his mornings to study; by which means he has stored his mind with a fund of usefull knowledge. I know not a young fellow upon the stage whose language is so pure—or whose natural disposition is more agreable. His days are devoted to his office, his Evenings of late to my fire side. His attachment is too obvious to escape notice. I do not think the Lady wholy indifferent; yet her reserve and apparent coldness is such that I know he is in misirable doubt. Some conversation one Evening of late took place which led me to write him a Billet and tell him, that at least it admitted a possibility that I might quit this country in the Spring; that I never would go abroad without my daughter, and if I did go, I wished to carry her with a mind unattached, besides I could have but one voice; and for that I held myself accountable to you; that he was not yet Established in Buisness sufficient to think of a connection with any one;—to which I received this answer—

Madam

    I have made an exertion to answer your Billet. I can only say that the second impulse in my Breast is my Love and respect for you; and it is the foible of my nature to be the machine of those I Love and venerate. Do with me as seemeth good unto thee. I can safely trust my dearest fondest wishes and persuits in the hands of a Friend that can feel, that knows my situation and her designs. If reason pleads against me, you will do well to hestitate. If Friendship and reason unite I shall be happy— only say I shall be happy when *I deserve*; and it shall be my every exertion to augment my merit, and this you may be assured of, whether I am blessed in my wishes or not, I will endeavour to be a character that you shall not Blush once to have entertaind an Esteem for. Yours respectfully &c.

    What ought I to say? I feel too powerful a pleader within my own heart and too well recollect the Love I bore to the object of my early affections to forbid him to hope. I feel a regard for him upon an account you will smile at, I fancy I see in him Sentiments opinions and actions which endeared to me the best of Friends. Suffer me to draw you from the depths of politicks to endearing family scenes. I know you cannot fail being peculiarly interested in the present. I inclose you a little paper which tho trifling in itself, may serve to shew you the truth of my observations. The other day the gentleman I have been speaking of; had a difficult writ to draw. He requested the favour of looking into your Book of forms, which I readily granted; in the Evening when he returned me the key he put in to my hands a paper which I could not tell what to make of; untill he exclaimed "O! Madam Madam, I have new hopes that I shall one day become worthy your regard. What a picture have I caught of my own Heart, my resolutions, my designs! I could not refrain breaking out into a Rhapsody. I found this coppy of a Letter in a pamphlet with observations upon the study of the Law and many excellent remarks; you will I hope forgive the theft, when I deliver the paper to you; and you find how much benifit I shall derive from it."

I daily see that he will win the affections of a fine Majestick Girl who has as much dignity as a princess. She is handsome, but not Beautifull. No air of levity ever accompanies either her words or actions. Should she be caught by a tender passion, sufficient to remove a little of her natural reserve and soften her form and manners, she will be a still more pleasing character. Her mind is daily improveing, and she gathers new taste for literature perhaps for its appearing in a more pleasing form to her. If I can procure a little ode which accompanied an ice Heart I will inclose it to you.

It is now my dear Friend a long long time since I had a line from you. The Fate of Gibralter leads me to fear that a peace is far distant, and that I shall not see you—God only knows when; I shall say little about my former request, not that my desire is less, but before this can reach you tis probable I may receive your opinion. If in favour of my comeing to you; I shall have no occasion to urge it further, if against it, I would not embarrass you; by again requesting it. I will endeavour to set down and consider it as the portion alloted me. My dear sons are well their application and improvements go hand in hand. Our Friends all desire to be rememberd. The Fleet of our allies expect to sail daily but where destined we know not; a great harmony has subsisted between them and the Americans ever since their residence here. I wish to write to Mr. Thaxter but fear I shall not have time. Mrs. Dana and children are well. The judge has been very sick of a fever but I believe is better. This Letter is to go by the Iris which sails with the Fleet. I hope it will reach you in safety. If it should fall into the hands of an Enemy, I hope they will be kind enough to distroy it; as I would not wish to see such a family picture in print; adieu my dear Friend. Why is it that I hear so seldom from my dear John; but one Letter have I ever received from him since he arrived in Petersburgh? I wrote him by the last oppertunity. Ever remember me as I do you; with all the tenderness which it is possible for one object to feel for an other; which no time can obliterate no distance alter, but which is always the same in the Bosom of   Portia

"THEY SUBMIT TO MY PROHIBITION"

To John Adams

My dearest Friend   April 7 1783
    Tis a long a very long time since I had an opportunity of conveying a single line to you. I have upon many accounts been impatient to do it. I now most sincerely rejoice in the great and important event which sheaths the Hostile Sword and, gives a pleasing presage that our spears may become prunning hooks; that the Lust of Man is restrained, or the powers and revenues of kingdoms become inadequate to the purposes of distruction.
    I have had the good fortune to receive several Letters from you of late; I thank you for them; they are always too short, but I do not complain knowing the thousand avocations you must have upon your mind and Hands. Yours of December 4th, gave me the highest pleasure.

"And shall I see his face again
And shall I hear him speak"

are Ideas that have taken full possession of my Heart and mind. I had much rather see you in America, than Europe. I well know that real true and substantial happiness depend not upon titles Rank and fortune; the Gay coach, the Brilliant attire; the pomp and Etiquet of Courts; rob, the mind of that placid harmony, that social intercourse which is an Enemy to cere-mony. My Ambition, my happiness centers in him; who sighs

for domestick enjoyments, amidst all the world calls happiness—
who partakes not in the jovial Feast; or joins the Luxurious
table, without turning his mind to the plain unadulterated
food which covers his own frugal Board, and sighs for the
Feast of reason and the flow of soul.

Your Letter of Janry. 29 created perturbations, yet allayed
anxiety. "Your "Image your "Superscription, Your Emelia would
tell you, if she would venture to write to you upon the subject;
that it was not the superficial accomplishments of danceing,
singing, and playing; that led her to a favorable opinion of
Selim; since she knew him not, when those were his favorite
amusements—nor has he ever been in the practise of either,
since his residence in this Town; even the former Beau, has been
converted into the plain dressing Man; and the Gay volatile
Youth, appears to become the studious Lawyer. Yet certain reasons which I do not chuse to enumerate here, have led me to
put a present period, as far as advise and desires would go, to the
Idea of a connection, to extirpate it from the Hearts and minds
of either is not I apprehend in my power, voilent opposition
never yet served a cause of this nature. Whilst they believe me
their best Friend, and see that their Interest is near my Heart,
and that my opposition is founded upon rational principals, they
submit to my prohibition, earnestly wishing for your return, and
more prosperous days; as without your approbation, they never
can conceive themselves happy.

I will be more particular by the first direct conveyance. Mr.
Guile who kept Sabbeth with me, tells me he has a vessel which
will sail tomorrow for Virgina; and from thence to Europe, yet
he knows not for certain to what part, but as this is the only
opportunity since December; I would not let it slip. We are all
well, our two Sons go on Monday with Billy Cranch to Haverhill; there to be under the care and tuition of Mr. Shaw who
has one in his family which he offers for colledge in july. I have
done the best I could with them. They have been without a
school ever since janry. I tried Mr. Shutes but could not get
them in, he having seven in his family; and four more engaged
to him. Andover was full and so is every other private School.
They do not like the thoughts of mammas going a broad, and
my little Neice who has lived 5 years with me prays that her
uncle may return, and hopes he will not send her away when

he comes. This day has been our meeting for the choise of a
Governour. The vote in this Town was for Genll. Lincoln.
There were proposals of chuseing an absent Man, but I dis-
couraged it wherever I heard it mentiond.

Be kind enough to let the young Gentlemen who reside
with you know, that their Friends are well and that I will do
myself the pleasure of answering their Letters by the first vessel
which sails from this port.

Adieu and believe me most affectionately and tenderly yours

Portia

Mr. Smith is to be my Gaurdian and protector if I cross the
Atlantick. He comes whether I do or not. Emelia has spent the
winter in Boston, during that time it has been currently reported that *preliminary articles* were setled between this gentleman and her. She took no pains to discountanance this
report—but alass her Heart is drawn an other way—and Mr. S.
never entertaind an Idea of the kind.

"HINTS . . . WHICH MIGHT SERVE YOUR INTEREST"

To Royall Tyler

june 14th 1783

I had thoughts of writing to you before I received my last
Letters from abroad, because you have frequently flatterd me
with an assurance that my advise is not unacceptable to you. I
thought I had some hints to drop to you which might Serve
your interest. I feel an additional motive to take my pen, and
communicate to you a passage from my Last Letter.

"My dear daughters happiness employs my Thoughts Night
and day. Do not let her form any connection with any one who
is not devoted intirely to Study and to Buisness—To honour
and to virtue. If there is a Trait of Frivolity and dissapation left
I pray that She may renounce it forever; I ask not Fortune nor
favour for mine, But prudence Talents and Labour—She may
go with my consent whereever She can find enough of these."

You have before you sentiments and principals which your

Reason must assent to, and your judgment approve, as the only solid foundation upon which a youth can Build: who is entering into Life, with satisfaction to his own mind, or a prospect of happiness for his connections. Talants are not wanting, shall they lack Labour for improvement, or industery for cultivation?

Honour and virtue, are they not inmates and companions? Is their a Trait of Frivolity and dissapation left? Examine your own Heart with candour, let it not deceive you. These are the Rocks and quick Sands. Dissapation enervates the Man, dissolves every good purpose and resolution, it excuses a thousand ways his deviations from the path of Rectitude, and in the end becomes his distroyer. It puts on like a mere Proteous a thousand different forms, and too frequently calls itself Relaxation. The one is necessary the other ruinous. To draw the line requires both skill and judgment; perhaps there is no more certain cure for dissapation, than method, and order, and were I to advise any one liable to this infirmity, it would be to portion out the Day, and appropriate a certain Number of Hours to Study, or to Buisness. With a determined Resolution to be inflexable against every temptation which might allure them from their purpose; untill fixed habits were formed which could not be easily shaken.

Perhaps more industery and application, are necessary, in the profession of the Law, in order to become Eminent; than in either phisick, or divinity; if it is, as I realy believe, in the power of my young Friend, to become so; it is also a duty incumbent upon him. Doubling the Talant of him, who possesst but one, would have obtain him the Eulogy of a Faithfull Servant, but if he to whom ten was committed had gained only one, how neglegent and Sothfull would he have been deemed?

Have you not Ambition, let it warm you to Emulation, let it fire you to rise to a Superiour height; to be well accomplished in your profession, I have heard a Friend of mine observe that it was indispensably necessary to have a perfect knowledge of the Theory of Goverment, and foundations of society, to study Humane Nature not to disguise, but to present Truth in her Native Loveliness. Shall I not See you become an honour to

your profession in the excersise of a generous candour; an inflexable integrity; strict punctuality, and exact decision, virtues which are by no means incompatable with your profession, notwithstanding the Sarcastick reflexions it is daily liable to. If you can find within your own breast any additional motives, let them serve to enforce my Recommendations. I have so far interested myself in your advancement in Life, as to feel a peculiar satisfaction in your increasing Buisness. I shall rejoice in your success, and in the consistancy of your Character. Much depends upon a uniformity of conduct. There is a strenght of mind, a firmness and intrepidity which we look for in a masculine character—an April countanance, now Sunshine and then cloudy, can only be excused in a Baby faced girl—in your sex, it has not the appearence of Nature, who is our best guide.——
Be assured you have my best wishes that you may merit and obtain whatever may conduce to your happiness, for I am most Sincerely a Friend to Your Fame; and a Lover of your Virtues. Adieu—

"I DO NOT WISH YOU TO ACCEPT AN EMBASSY"

To John Adams

My Dearest Friend   Braintree June 20th 1783
    If I was certain I should welcome you to your native Land in the course of the summer, I should not regret Mr. Smiths going abroad without me. Should it be otherways, should you still be detained abroad—I must submit, satisfied that you judge best, and that you would not subject me to so heavy a dissapointment, or yourself to so severe a mortification as I flatter myself it would be, but for the general good: a European life would, you say, be the ruin of our Children. If so, I should be as loth as you, to hazard their embibeing sentiments and opinions which might make them unhappy in a sphere of Life which tis probable they must fill, not by indulging in luxuries for which tis more than possible they might contract a taste and inclination, but in studious and labourious persuits.

You have before this day, received the joint commission for forming a commercial treaty with Britain. I am at a loss to determine whether you will consider yourself so bound by it, as to tarry longer abroad. Perhaps there has been no juncture in the publick affairs of our country; not even in the hour, of our deepest distress, when able statesmen and wise Counsellors were more wanted than at the present day. Peace abroad leaves us at leisure to look into our own domestick affairs. Altho upon an Estimate of our National debt, it appears but as the Small Dust of the balance, when compared to the object we have obtained, and the benifits we have secured, yet the Restless spirit of man will not be restrained; and we have reason to fear that Domestick Jars and confusions, will take place, of foreign contentions and devastations. Congress have commuted with the Army by engageing to them 5 years pay, in lieu of half pay for Life. With Security for this they will disband contented. But our wise Legislators are about disputing the power of Congress to do either; without considering their hands in the mouth of the Lion, and if the just and necessary food is not supplied, the outragious animal may become so ferocious as to spread horrour, and devastation, or an other Theseus may arise who by his reputation, and exploits of valour, whose personal character and universal popularity, may distroy our Amphictinik system and subjugate our infant republicks to Monarchical domination.

Our House of Representitives is this Year composed of more than a hundred New Members, some of whom no doubt are good Men. Near all the able and skillfull Members who composed the last House have lost their Seats, by voting for the return of Mr. Brattle; notwithstanding the strongest evidence in his favour, and the many proofs which were produced of his Friendly conduct towards America. For this crime, our worthy Friend Mr. Cranch was droped by this Town. The Senate is a loser this year by the resignation of some excellent Members. We have in this state an impost of 5 per cent, and an excise act, whilst the Neighbouring states have neither. Foreigners finding this the case, cary their Cargoes to other states. At this the Merchant grumbles, the Farmer groans with his taxes, and the Mechanick for want of employ. Heaven Avert that like the Greek Republicks we should by civil discension weaken

our power, and crush our rising greatness; that the Blood of our
citizens, should be shed in vain: and the labour, and toil, of
our statesmen; be finally bafled; through niggardly parsimony;
Lavish prodigality; or Ignorance of our real Interest. We want
a Soloman in wisdom, to guide and conduct this great people:
at this critical ære, when the counsels which are taken, and the
measures which are persued; will mark our future Character
either with honour, and Fame, or disgrace, and infamy; in adversity, we have conducted with prudence and magninimity.
Heaven forbid, that we should grow giddy with prosperity, or
the height to which we have soared, render a fall conspicuously
fatal.

Thus far I had written when your welcome favour of March
28th reached me; I was not dissapointed in finding you uncertain with regard to the Time of your return; should the appointment which I fear; and you have hinted at; take place, it
would indeed be a dull day to me. I have not a wish to join in
a scene of Life so different from that in which I have been educated; and in which my early and I must suppose, happier
days, have been Spent; curiosity satisfied and I should sigh for
tranquil Scenes,

> "And wish that Heaven had left me still
> The whisp'ring Zephyr, and the purling rill?"

Well orderd home is my chief delight, and the affectionate domestick wife with the Relative duties which accompany that
character my highest ambition. It was the disinterested wish of
sacrificeing my personal feelings to the publick utility, which first
led me to think of unprotectedly hazarding a voyage. I say unprotectedly for so I consider every lady who is not accompanied
by her Husband. This objection could only be surmounted by
the earnest wish I had to soften those toils which were not to be
dispenced with, and if the publick welfare required your Labours
and exertions abroad, I flatterd myself, that if I could be with
you, it might be in my power to contribute to your happiness
and pleasure, but the day is now arrived, when with honour and
well earned Fame, you may return to your native land—when I
cannot any longer consider it as my duty to submit to a further
Seperation, and when it appears necessary that those abilities

which have crownd you with Laurels abroad, should be exerted at home for the publick Safety.

I do not wish you to accept an Embassy to England, should you be appointed. This little Cottage has more Heart felt Satisfaction for you than the most Brilliant Court can afford, the pure and undiminished tenderness of weded Love, the filial affection of a daughter who will never act contrary to the advise of a Father, or give pain to the Maternal Heart. Be assured that she will never make a choice without your approbation which I know she considers as Essential to her happiness. That she has a partiality I know, and believe, but that she has submitted her opinion to the advise of her Friends, and relinquished the Idea of a connection upon principals of prudence and duty, I can with equal truth assure you. Yet nothing unbecomeing the Character which I first entertaind has ever appeard in this young Gentleman since his residence in this Town, and he now visits in this family with the freedom of an acquaintance, tho not with the intimacy of a nearer connection. It was the request of Emelia who has conducted with the greatest prudence, that she might be permitted to see and treat this Gentleman as an acquaintance whom she valued. "Why said she should I treat a Gentleman who has done nothing to forfeit my Esteem, with neglect or contempt, merely because the world have said, that he entertained a preferable regard for me? If his foibles are to be treated with more severity than the vices of others, and I submit my judgment and opinion to the disapprobation of others in a point which so nearly concerns me, I wish to be left at liberty to act in other respects with becomeing decency." And she does and has conducted so as to meet with the approbation of all her Friends. She has conquerd herself. An extract from a little poetick peice which Some months ago fell into my Hands may give you some Idea of the Situation of this Matter. You will tell me you do not want a poet, but if there is a mind otherways well furnished, you would have no objection to its being a mere amusement. You ask me if this Gentleman is a speaker at the Bar. He attends Plimouth Court and has spoke there. He is not yet sworn in to the Superiour Court, but is proposed to be sworn in the Next court, with his cotemporaries. I cannot say what he will make, but those who most intimately know him, say he has talants to make what he pleases, and fluency to become a good Speaker.

His buisness encreases here, and I know nothing but what he is well esteemed. His temper and disposition appear to be good. The family in which he boards find no fault with his conduct. He is Regular in his liveing, keeps no company with Gay companions, seeks no amusement but in the society of two or 3 families in Town, never goes to Boston but when Buisness calls him there. If he has been the Gay thoughtless young fellow which he is said to have been and which I believe he was, he has at least practised one year of reformation. Many more will be necessary to Establish him in the world, whether he will make the man of worth and steadiness time must determine.

Our two sons are placed under the care, and in the family of Mr. Shaw. They have been near 3 months absent from me. This week with my daughter and Mr. Smith to accompany us I go to see them. My dear John, where is he? I long to see him. I have been very anxious about him. Such a winter journey. I hope he is with you. I want to receive a Letter from him. If you should continue abroad untill fall I should be glad you would make me a small remittance, goods will not answer. We are glutted with them. I do not wish for any thing more, than I want for my family use. In this way a few peices of Irish linnen and a peice of Russia sheeting together with 2 green silk umbrellas I should be glad of as soon as convenient. If you should have an opportunity from France to send me 3 Marsels cotton and silk quilts I should be very glad; they are like the Jacket patterns you sent me by Charles. I want a white, a Blew and a pink. Mr. Dana sent 3 to Mrs. Dana; I think she said Mr. Bonfeild procured them. I mentiond in a former Letter a few other articles. I am going to marry one of my family to a young fellow whom you liberated from jail, a son of Capt. Newcombs, to the Jane Glover who has lived 7 years with me and as she never would receive any wages from me I think myself obligated to find her necessaries for house keeping. I have been buying land, and my last adventure came to so poor a market, that I am quite broke. My letter is an unreasonable long one, yet I may take an other sheet of paper—not to night however. I will bid you good by. I seal this least Mr. Smith should sail before I return. Mean to write more. Have a Letter for Mr. Thaxter.

DEATH OF ABIGAIL'S FATHER, WILLIAM SMITH

To John Adams

My dearest Friend   Braintree Sepbr 20 1783

Dearer if possible than ever; for all the parental props which once sustaind and supported me are fallen! My Father, my Father, where is he? With Humble confidence I can say; he is with the spirits of just Men made perfect, become an inhabitant of that Country, from whose Bourn no traveller returns.

In my last Letter to you, I recollect to have particularly mentiond both our dear and venerable parents. My Father then appeard to sustain his age, with fewer of the infirmities of it, than most aged persons are subject to, his Health, his spirits, and his activity were remarkable. He sat out upon a visit to my sister at Haverhill, and with an intention of carrying our son Charles, who had just recoverd from the Measles: he reachd here for the Night, and tho he complaind of having felt rather unwell for a few days, he spent as pleasent and cheerfull an evening as I had known him for many Years. About midnight, I waked with his calling a servant, and desireing him to rise, upon which I rose, and went into his Chamber, I found him in great distress with the strangery; I made every application which I could think of untill morning, but his pain increasing he could neither lie nor set, he insisted upon being carried home. It was with great difficulty to himself, that he reachd his own House, where for 15 days he lived in most exquisite distress, during which time no medicine or outward application procured him relief. He supported himself through his distressing pain, and exemplified that Christian patience and fortitude, which he had, through his whole Life taught to others.

> "Here real and, apparent, were the same
> We saw the Man, We saw his hold on heaven
> A lecture silent, but of sov'reign power!
> to vice confusion, but to virtue peace."

Not a complaint fell from his Lips during his sickness, his reason was clear to the last moment of his Life; every hour of which, he exerted himself, to admonish and warn the youth, who attended round his Bed, intreating them to devote themselves early to their Maker. To them and to others, he was with a most Cheerfull resignation, manifesting the joy and comfort, derived from unfeigned piety; and a Life well Spent; he had a well grounded hope; and his last end was peace.

His affection towards his children and his grandchildren seemed heightned by the Idea, of parting with them.

O my children, said he, you are so kind and tender, I fear you will make me loth to leave you. Through his sickness he was but once heard to say, that he wished it had pleased God to have spaired his Life longer, and that was, to have seen the return of my dearest Friend; but tell him says he, I hope to meet him in a better world.

> "The Sweet remembrance of the just,
>   Shall flourish when they sleep in dust."

Sweet indeed, is the remembrance of this my dear parent; and his death bed Scene the greatest consolation for his loss. Painfull as it was, I would not have exchanged it, for the triumph of the Greatest Monarch.

> "The Chamber where the good Man meets his Fate
> is privileg'd beyond the common walk
> of virtuous Life, quite in the verge of Heaven
> whatever farce the Boastfull Hero plays,
> virtue alone has Majesty in death."

How trifling, and of how little importance does such a scene, make all the wealth, power and greatness of the world appear. I have; Said my dear parent, made two things the principal Study of my Life, let me injoin the Same upon my Children. I have endeavourd to do all the good I could with the talants committed to me, and to honour God with my substance. Well may his Children rise up; and call him blessed—gratefully acknowledging the hand which bestowed upon them such a parent, doubling their diligence to walk in his Steps. Like good old Jacob, our parent blessed all his ofspring, may our children never forget the Solemn Scene.

> "We gaze'd we wept, mixt tears of greif and joy."

I know my dear Friend, you will most sensibly feel this

bereavement. You have lost one of your firmest Friends, no man could be more delighted, with your successes, or entertaind a higher sense of them, than my dear parent, he knew your Worth, and he honourd it at all times. No man was happier in the sons his daughters had given him, two of whom attended him in his last moments, administering to him, those kind offices, which his afflicted daughters could not perform.

> "His God sustaind him in his final hour!
> his final hour brought Glory to his God
> Mans Glory Heaven vouchsafes to call her own."

In the midst of my affliction several of your kind Letters were brought me. My Heart I hope was not unthankfull to Heaven for the blessing, but my Mind is not sufficiently calm to reply to them. I shall close this and wait a more tranquil hour; how much do I feel the want of the Soothing kindness of the Friend of my Heart. The Idea is too painfull—adieu. Your   *Portia*

"NO COURTSHIP SUBSISTS"

To John Adams

My dearest Friend   October 19 1783
     My last Letter to you was written in Sepbr. I closed it, because I knew not how to think upon any other subject than the solemn one I had just past through; since that date I have received a Number of Letters from you, written in April, May, june and 2 in july.
     To hear from you is a satisfaction, but the whole tenor of your Letters rather added to my melancholy, than mitigated it. The state of your Health gives me great anxiety; and the delay of your return increases it. The Season is now so far advanced, that if you embark I shall have a thousand terrors for you; if you tarry abroad; I fear for your Health.
     If Congress should think proper to make you an other appointment, I beg you not to accept it. Call me not to any further trials of the kind! Reflect upon your long absence from

your family, and upon the necessity there is, of your returning in order to recover that Health which you have unhappily impaired and lost abroad.

Your Children have a demand upon You, they want your care, your advice and instruction; I mean at all times to consult and promote their interest and happiness, but I may be mistaken in it; I cannot feel so safe or so satisfied as I should if Your approbation was added to it.

There was a time when I had brought my mind to be willing to cross the Seas to be with you, but tho one strong tie which held me here, is dissolved, the train of my Ideas for six months past has run wholy upon your return; that I now think nothing short of an assurance from you, that your happiness depended upon it, would induce me to alter my oppinion. The Scenes of anxiety through which you have past, are enough to rack the firmest constitution, and debilitate the strongest faculties. Conscious Rectitude is a grand support, but it will not ward of the attacks of envy, or secure from the assaults of jealousy. Both ancient and modern history furnish us with repeated proofs, that virtue must look beyond this shifting theatre for its reward; *but* the Love of praise is a passion deeply rooted in the mind and in this we resemble the Supreem Being who is most Gratified with thanksgiving and praise. Those who are most affected with it, partake most of that particle of divinity which distinguishes mankind from the inferiour Creation; no one who deserves commendation can dispise it, but we too frequently see it refused where it is due, and bestowed upon very undeserving characters. "Treachery venality and villainy must be the Effects of dissipation voluptuousness and impiety, says the Great Dr. Price and adds, these vices sap the foundation of virtue, they render Men necessitous and Supple, ready at any time to sacrifice their consciences. Let us remember these Truths in judging of Men. Let us consider that true goodness is uniform and consistant; and learn never to place any great confidence in those pretenders to publick Spirit, who are not men of virtuous Characters. They may boast of their attachment to a publick cause, but they want the living root of virtue, and should not be depended upon."

You call upon me to write you upon a subject which greatly embarrasses me, yet I ought to tell you what I conceive to be the real Truth. The Gentleman whom I formerly mentiond to you, resides here Still, and boards in the same family. I wrote you the Truth when I informd you that the connection was broken of—and nothing particular has since past. Yet it is evident to me, as well as to the family where he lives, that his attachment is not lessned. He conducts prudently, and tho nothing is said upon the subject I do not immagine that he has given up the Hope, that in some future Day he may be able to obtain your approbation. Your daughter so highly values your esteem and approbation, that She has frequently said she never could be happy without it. That she will not act contrary to the opinion of her Friends, I am fully satisfied, but her sentiments with regard to this Gentleman she says are not to be changed but upon a conviction of his demerrit. I wish most sincerely wish you was at Home to judge for yourself. I shall never feel safe or happy untill you are. I had rather you should inquire into his conduct and behaviour, his success in Buisness and his attention to it, from the family where he lives, than Say any thing upon the subject myself. I can say with real Truth that no Courtship subsists between them, and that I believe it is in your power to put a final period to every Idea of the kind, if upon your return you think best. There is a young Gentleman, who formerly kept our school, by the Name of Perkings, who is now studying Law with Mr. Tyler. He has been in Virgina for a twelve month past and designs to return there again.

I was very unhappy to find by your Letters that you was so long without any intelligence from America, but I hope you have been amply compensated before this time. Your Letters which were dated in April May and june did not reach me untill Sep'br. I must request you in future to calculate those you send to Philadelphia for the post office. Every line of yours is invaluable to me, yet blank paper is not so, and the double covers pay as large postage, as if they were wholy written. I have disputed the matter some time with the postmaster, and now he will not deliver a Letter untill the postage is pay'd. I payd 3 dollors the other day for what one sheet of paper would have containd. I do not yet believe that congress mean to make their foreign ministers subject to postage, and I design to write to Mr. Gerry upon the Subject.

I hear of a vessel bound to France. I will forward this and

write to Mr. Thaxter by way of England. I hear he is there, and that Mr. Smith arrived after a short passage. At this I rejoice tho I was not his companion. Our two sons are gone to Haverhill. I hope to hear frequently from you if I do not see you, which I now almost dispair of, this winter. Adieu my dearest Friend ever yours   Portia

"AFTER TWO YEARS SILENCE"

To John Quincy Adams

Braintree November 20. 1783

This evening as I was Setting, with only your sister by my side, who was scribling at the table to some of her correspondents, my Neighbour Feild enterd, with "I have a letter for you Madam"; my immagination was wandering to Paris, ruminating upon the long, long absence of my dear son, and his parent; that I was rather inattentive to what he said, untill he repeated; I have Letters for you from abroad. The word abroad, roused my attention, and I eagerly seazied the Letters, the hand writing and Seal of which gave me hopes that I was once more like to hear from my Young Wanderer; nor was I dissapointed.

After two years silence; and a journey of which I can scarcly form an Idea; to find you safely returnd, to your parent, to hear of your Health, and to see your improvements!

You cannot know, should I discribe to you; the feelings of a parent. Through your pappa, I sometimes heard from you, but one Letter only, ever reach'd me after you arrived in Russia. Your excuses however, have weight; and are accepted; but you must give them further energy by a ready attention to your pen in future. Four years have already past away since you left your native land, and this rural Cottage—Humble indeed, when compared to the Palaces you have visited, and the pomp you have been witness too. But I dare say you have not been so inattentive an observer, as to suppose that Sweet peace, and contentment, cannot inhabit the lowly roof, and bless the tranquil inhabitants, equally guarded and protected, in person and property, in this happy Country, as those who reside in the most elegant and costly dwellings.

If you live to return, I can form to myself, an Idea of the pleasure you will take, in treading over the ground, and visiting every place your early years were accustomed wantonly to gambol in—even the rocky common and lowly whortleberry Bush will not be without its Beauties.

My anxieties have been, and still are great least the Numerous temptations and Snares of vice, should vitiate your early habits of virtue, and distroy those principals, which you are now capable of reasoning upon; and discerning the Beauty, and utility, of, as the only rational Source of happiness here, or foundation of felicity here after, placed as we are, in a transitory Scene of probation, drawing nigher and still nigher, day after day to that important Crisis, which must introduce us into a New System of things. It ought certainly to be our principal concern to become qualified for our expected dignity.

What is it that affectionate parents require of their Children; for all their care anxiety and toil on their accounts? Only that they would be wise and virtuous, Benevolent and kind.

Ever keep in mind my son, that your parents are your disinterested Friends, and if at any time their advise militates with your own opinion, or the advise of others, you ought always to be, diffident of your own judgment, because you may rest assured that their opinion is founded in experience, and long observation, and that they would not direct you; but to promote your happiness.

Be thankfull to a kind providence who has hitherto preserved the lives of your parents, the natural guardians of your youthfull years. With Gratitude I look up to heaven blessing the Hand, which continued to me my dear and honoured parents untill I was setled in Life, and tho I now regreet the loss of them, and daily feel the want of their advise and assistance, I cannot suffer as I should have done, if I had been early deprived of them.

You will doubtless have heard of the Death of your worthy Grandpappa, before this reaches you. He left you a Legacy, more valuable than Gold or silver—he left you his blessing and his prayers, that you might return to your Country and Friends improved in knowledge, and matured in virtue, that you might become a usefull citizen, a Guardian of the Laws Liberty and Religion of your Country, as your Father, (he was pleased to Say) had already been. Lay this bequest up in your memory, and practise upon it, believe me, you will find it a treasure that neither Moth, or Rust can devour.

I received Letters from your Pappa last evening dated in Paris the 10 of sepbr. informing me of the necessity of his continuance abroad this winter. The Season is so far advanced that I readily sacrifice the desire of seeing him, to his safety. A voyage upon this coast at this Season, is fraught with dangers. He has made me a request, that I dare not comply with at present; No Husband, no Son, to accompany me upon the Boisterous ocean, to animate my courage, and dispell my fears, I dare not engage with so formidable a combatant.

If I should find your Pappa fixed in the Spring; and determined to continue abroad a year or two longer, the earnest desire I have to meet him, and my dear son, might overcome the reluctance I feel, at the Idea of engaging in a New Scene of Life and the love I have for domestick attachments—and the still calm of Life. But it would be much more agreeable to me, to enjoy all my Friends together in my own Native land. From those who have visited foreign climes I could listen with pleasure; at the narative of their adventures, and derive satisfaction from the learned detail, content myself that the "little Learning I have gaine'd is all from Simple Nature divind."

I have a desire that you might finish Your Education at our university, and I see no chance for it, unless You return in the course of a year. Your cousin Billy Cranch expects to enter next july. He would be happy to have you his associate.

I hope your Pappa will indulge you with a visit to England this winter, it is a country I should be fond of your Seeing. Christianity which teaches us to forgive our enemies, prevents me from enjoining upon you a similar vow, to that which Hamilcar obtained from his son Hanible, but I know not how to think of loveing those haughty Islanders.

Your Brothers will write to you soon. Your sister I see is prepairing a Letter; Your Friends send you their affectionate regards. And I enjoin it upon you to write often to Your ever affectionate Mother.   A *Adams*

To John Adams

My Dearest Friend   Braintree December 15 1783

I returned last Evening from Boston, where I went at the kind invitation of my uncle and Aunt, to celebrate our Anual festival. Doctor Cooper being dangerously Sick, I went to hear Mr. Clark; who is Setled with Dr. Chauncey; this Gentleman gave us an animated elegant and sensible discourse, from Isaah 55 chapter and 12th verse—"For ye shall go out with joy, and be led forth with Peace; the Mountains and the Hill Shall break forth before you into singing, and all the Trees of the Field shall clap their Hands."

Whilst he asscribed Glory and praise unto the most high, he considerd the Worthy disinterested, and undaunted Patriots as the instruments in the hand of providence for accomplishing what was marvelous in our Eyes; he recapitulated the dangers they had past through, and the hazards they had run; the firmness which had in a particular manner distinguished Some Characters, not only early to engage in so dangerous a contest, but in spight of our gloomy prospects they persevered even unto the end; untill they had obtained a Peace Safe and Honorable; large as our designs, Capacious as our wishes, and much beyond our expectations.

How did my heart dilate with pleasure when as each event was particularized; I could trace my Friend as a Principal in them; could say, it was he, who was one of the first in joinning the Band of Patriots; who formed our first National Counsel. It was he; who tho happy in his domestick attachments; left his wife, his Children; then but Infants; even surrounded with the Horrours of war; terified and distresst, the Week after the memorable 17th. of April, Left them, to the protection of that providence which has never forsaken them, and joined himself undismayed, to that Respectable Body, of which he was a member. Trace his conduct through every period, you will find him the same undaunted Character: encountering the dangers of the ocean; risking Captivity, and a dungeon; contending with wickedness in high places; jeoparding his Life, endangerd by the intrigues, revenge, and malice, of a potent; tho defeated Nation.

These are not the mere eulogiums of conjugal affection; but certain facts, and solid truths. My anxieties, my distresses, at every period; bear witness to them; tho now by a series of prosperous events; the recollection, is more sweet than painfull.

Whilst I was in Town, Mr. Dana arrived very unexpectedly, for I had not received your Letter by Mr. Thaxter. My uncle fortunately discoverd him, as he come up into State Street, and instantly engaged him to dine with him, acquainting him that I was in Town, and at his House. The news soon reached my Ears. Mr. Dana arrived, Mr. Dana arrived—from every person you saw, but how was I affected? The Tears involuntary flowed from my eyes, tho God is my witness, I envyed not the felicity of others. Yet my Heart swelled with Grief, and the Idea that I, I only, was left alone, recall'd all the tender Scenes of seperation, and overcame all my fortitude. I retired and reasoned myself into composure sufficient; to see him without a childish emotion.

He tarried but a short time, anxious as you may well imagine, to reach Cambridge. He promised me a visit with his Lady, in a few days, to which I look forward with pleasure.

I reach'd home last evening, having left Nabby in Town, to make her winter visit. I found Mr. Thaxter just arrived before me. It was a joyfull meeting to both of us, tho I could not prevail with him only for half an hour; his solicitude to see his Parents was great, and tho I wished his continuance with me, yet I checked not the fillial flow of affection. Happy youth! who had parents still alive to visit, Parents who can rejoice in a Son returned to them after a long absence; untainted in his morals, improved in his understanding; with a Character fair and unblemished.

But O my dearest Friend what shall I say to You in reply to your pressing invitation; I have already written to you in answer to your Letters which were dated Sepbr. 10th and reachd me a month before those by Mr. Thaxter. I related to you all my fears respecting a winters voyage. My Friends are all against it, and Mr. Gerry as you will see, by the Coppy of his Letter inclosed, has given his opinion upon well grounded reasons. If I should leave my affairs in the Hands of my

Friends, there would be much to think of, and much to do, to place them in that method and order I would wish to leave them in.

Theory and practise are two very different things; and the object magnifies, as I approach nearer to it. I think if you were abroad in a private Character, and necessitated to continue there; I should not hesitate so much at comeing to you. But a mere American as I am, unacquainted with the Etiquette of courts, taught to say the thing I mean, and to wear my Heart in my countantance, I am sure I should make an awkward figure. And then it would mortify my pride if I should be thought to disgrace you. Yet strip Royalty of its pomp, and power, and what are its votaries more than their fellow worms? I have so little of the Ape about me; that I have refused every publick invitation to figure in the Gay World, and sequestered myself in this Humble cottage, content with rural Life and my domestick employments in the midst of which; I have sometimes Smiled, upon recollecting that I had the Honour of being allied to an Ambassador. Yet I have for an example the chaste Lucretia who was found spinning in the midst of her maidens, when the Brutal Tarquin plotted her distruction.

I am not acquainted with the particular circumstances attending the renewal of your commission; if it is modeled so as to give you satisfaction I am content; and hope you will be able to discharge it, so as to receive the approbation of your Sovereign.

A Friend of yours in Congress some months ago, sent me an extract of a Letter, requesting me to conceal his Name, as he would not chuse to have it known by what means he procured the Coppy. From all your Letters I discoverd that the treatment you had received, and the suspence You was in, was sufficiently irritating without any thing further to add to Your vexation. I therefore surpresst the extract; as I knew the author was fully known to you: but seeing a letter from Gen. Warren to you, in which this extract is alluded to; and finding by your late Letters, that your situation is less embarrassing, I inclose it; least you should think it much worse than it really is: at the same time I cannot help adding an observation which appears pertinant to me; that there is an ingredient necessary in a Mans composition towards happiness, which people of feeling would do well to acquire—a certain respect for the follies of Mankind. For there are so many fools whom the opinion of the world entittles to regard; whom accident has placed in heights of which they are unworthy, that he who cannot restrain, his contempt or indignation at the sight, will be too, often Quarrelling with the disposal of things to realish that Share, which is allotted to himself." And here my paper obliges me to close the subject—without room to say adieu.

OBSERVATIONS ON GOVERNMENTS

To John Quincy Adams

My Dear Son   Braintree December 26. 1783
    Your Letters by Mr. Thaxter I received; and was not a little pleased with them; if you do not write with the precision of a Robertson, nor the Elegance of a Voltaire, it is evident you have profited by the perusal of them.

    The account of your northern journey and your observation upon the Russian Goverment; would do credit to an older pen.

    The early age at which you went abroad; gave you not an opportunity of becomeing acquainted with your own Country. Yet the Revolution in which we were engaged, held it up in So striking and important a Light, that you could not avoid being in some measure irradiated with the view. The Characters with which you were connected, and the conversation you continually heard; must have impressed your mind with a Sense of the Laws, the Liberties, and the Glorious privileges, which distinguish the Free sovereign independant States of America.

    Compare them with the vassallage of the Russian Goverment you have discribed, and Say, were this highly favourd land Barren as the mountains of Swisserland, and coverd ten months in the Year with Snow; would she not have the advantage, even of Italy, "with her orange Groves, her Breathing Statues, and her melting Strains of Musick" or of Spain with her treasures from Mexico and Peru; not one of which can Boast that first of Blessings, the Glory of Humane Nature; the inestimable privelege of setting down under their vines; and fig trees, enjoying in peace and security what ever Heaven has lent them; having none to make them affraid.

Let your observations and comparisons produce in your mind, an abhorrence, of Domination and power, the Parent of Slavery Ignorance, and barbarism, which places Man upon a level with his fellow tennants of the woods.

> "A day, an hour of virtuous Liberty,
>   is worth a whole eternity of Bondage."

You have seen Power in its various forms—a Benign Deity, when exercised in the surpression of fraud, injustice, and tyranny, but a Demon when united with unbounded, ambition: a wide wasting fury, which has distroyed her thousands: not an age of the World, but has produced Characters, to which whole humane Hecatombs have been sacrificed.

What is the History of mighty kingdoms and Nations but a detail, of the Ravages, and cruelties, of the powerfull over the weak? Yet it is instructive to trace the various causes, which produced the strength of one Nation, and the decline and weakness of an other; to learn by what arts one Man has been able to Subjugate millions of his fellow creatures; the motives which have put him upon action, and the causes of his Success— Sometimes driven by ambition and a lust of power; at other times, swallowed up by Religious enthusiasm, blind Bigotry, and Ignorant Zeal, Sometimes enervated with Luxury, debauched by pleasure, untill the most powerfull Nations have become a prey, and been subdued by these Syrens; when neither the Number of their Enemies, nor the prowess, of their Arms, could conquer them.

History informs us that the Assyrian empire sunk under the Arms of Cyrus with his poor, but hardy Persians. The extensive, and opulent empire of Persia, fell an easy prey to Alexander, and a handfull of Macedonians, and the Macedonian empire when enervated by the Luxury of Asia, was compelld to receive the yoke of the victorious Romans. Yet even this mistress of the World, as she is proudly stiled, in her turn, defaced her glory, tarnished her victories, and became a prey to Luxury, ambition, faction, pride, Revenge, and avarice, so that Jugurthy after having purchased an acquittance for the blackest of crimes, breaks out into an exclamation, "O city, ready for Sale, if a Buyer rich enough can be found!"

The History of your own country, and the late Revolution, are striking and recent Instances of the mighty things achived by a Brave inlightned and hardy people, determined to be free, the very yeomanry of which, in many instances, have shewn themselves superiour to corruption, as Britain well knows, on more occasions than the loss of her Andry.

Glory my son in a Country which has given birth, to Characters, both in the civil and military Departments, which may vie with the wisdom and valour of antiquity. As an immediate descendent of one of those characters, may you be led to an imitation of that disinterested patriotism and that Noble Love of your country, which will teach you to dispise wealth, tittles, pomp and equipage, as mere external advantages, which cannot add to the internal excellence of your mind or compensate for the want of Integrity and virtue.

May your mind be throughly impressed with the absolute necessity of universal virtue and goodness as the only sure road to happiness, and may you walk therein with undeviating steps—is the Sincere and most affectionate wish of your Mother   Abigail Adams

PREPARATIONS TO SAIL

To John Adams

My dearest Friend   Sunday Janry 3. 1784
    I have already written you 3 Letters, which have been waiting a long time for a passage; they will now all go in one ship, provided I can get this to Town to morrow; tho She was ordered for sailing to day, yet I trust to the delay which vessels usually have.

    Last evening I received a packet of Letters from Nabby who has been in Town a month; inclosing Your Letters by Mr. Robbins, who arrived in a passage of 33 days only. By him, I was happy to hear you were well when he left you, but alass! you know not the anxiety I suffer upon account of your Health, or how often my Heart is overwhelmed, with the Idea that I never shall see you more.

I cannot without terrour, think of your going to reside at the Hague, indeed you cannot live in that country, and you have repeatedly told me so. Why then will you risk a Life invaluably dear to me; and for the comfort and enjoyment of which, there is no earthly pleasure, I would not willingly relinquish; and it is the apprehension which I have for your precarious Health, and the hope that by a watchfull attention I may be able to preserve it, that leads me seriously to think of quitting all my Friends and my dear Boys, to cross the ocean, coward as I am; without Husband or son to protect or support me; it is one thing to encounter dangers or difficulties with you; and an other without you.

Why with a Heart Susceptable of every tender impression, and feelingly alive, have I So often been called to Stand alone and support myself through Scenes which have almost torn it assunder, not I fear, because I have more resolution or fortitude than others, for my resolution often fails me; and my fortitude wavers.

As my own judgment, and the advice of my Friends, will prevent my comeing out this winter, I shall by spring know the determinations of congress with respect to your situation, and in some measure be governed by them.

Your Daughter writes me thus, "this mor'g I was agreeably Surprized by the sight of Mr. Robbins, who came with Letters from Pappa and my Brother. You will see that I have taken the liberty to open them, which I hope your own feelings will lead you to excuse. I find my dear Pappa has again been sick with a severe fever. O Mamma what have we not to fear from his continuance abroad in climates so enemical to his Health? I shudder at the thought, and wish he could be prevailed upon to consider his danger."

"I know perfectly well how I should act with regard to Pappas requests, were I exatly in your situation, tho I own, I now dread the result. Yet my duty, and my fears for the critical state of his Health, operate so powerfully upon my mind being never absent from my thoughts, that I would rather influence than dissuade you from going."

In concequence of your last Letters I shall immediately set about putting all our affairs in such a train as that I may be able to leave them in the spring; you have written to me with Regard to Mr. Alleynes Farm, during the war he talked of selling; but I have heard nothing of it of late. I will have him sounded, and if he should sell, leave it in charge with some Friend to purchase if you can; the land you mention belonging to Col. Quincy I know he wants to sell. Mr. Tyler applied to him for it tho not very pressingly, before he purchased Mrs. Borelands Farm, but the Col. had got such wild notions of foreigners of fortune comeing over to settle here, and the high value of Land, that there was no reason in him; but after he heard that Mrs. Boreland had sold her Farm, of which he had then no Idea, he was shagreen'd that he did not sell it, and has since offerd it to him, but he asked 26 pound pr acre. I will take the opinion of your Brother and one or two others, of the real value of it; and make him an offer, through some Friend, for if he should suspect that you wanted it, he would immediately suppose that it was because you knew of gentlemen of fortunes comeing over, and supposed land would run very high near Boston.

There is a method of laying out money to more advantage than by the purchase of land's, which a Friend of mine advised me to, for it is now become a regular merchandize. Dr. Tufts has sold a Farm with a design of vesting it in this manner, viz in State Notes. Provision is now made for the anual payment of Interest, and the Notes have all been consolidated. Foreigners and monied Men have, and are purchaseing them at 7 shillings upon the pound, 6 and 8 pence they have been sold at. I have mentiond to you that I have a hundred pounds sterling in the hands of a Friend, I was thinking of adding the 50 you sent me, and purchaseing 600 pounds L M in state Notes provided I can get them at 7 shillings or 6 and 8 pence. This would yeald me an anual interest of 36 pounds subject to no taxes: and be some thing to leave in the hand of a Friend for the support of our Sons.

If I should do this I shall have occasion to draw upon you, tho not for any large sum. I wish you would put me in a way to have my Bills answerd in London, as those will sell above par.

If I come out in the Spring I hope to prevail with Dr. Tufts to take under his patronage our little cottage and Farm. The care of our two sons I will leave in charge with my two Sisters, but as they reside at Haverhill, it will chiefly devolve upon Mrs. Shaw. To Mr. Shaw I shall leave the trust of the Medford estate which was left jointly between my sister and me. It will be his interest to take the best care of it, and to make such arrangements from time to time as he may find necessary. I shall direct him to receive my part of the Rent, as part pay for the schooling of the children. Forgive me if I sometimes use the singular instead of the plural, alass I have been too much necessitated to it. Mr. Pratt our old tenant still lives upon the Farm. If he continues here it will be necessary to come into new conditions with him.

Your account Books I put six months ago; into the hands of Mr. Tyler, that the whole might not be lost, by insolvent debtors and Refugee Tories as a great part already is. He is in a way to get them adjusted; some little money he has received, many of the accounts he has got into Notes of Hand, which if sued will not admit of dispute as accounts do. Many persons very barefacedly deny their accounts. This is not so much to be wonderd at, when they can totally forget Notes of Hand. The Sloans Bond I sued, and got some land under mortgage which I put upon record. I have some thoughts of selling at vendue part of the house furniture, as I suppose I could purchase new for what this would fetch. With regard to cloathing, there will be no occasion of my taking more than a change. I could wish to receive any particular directions which you may think proper to give before I embark.

To my uncle Smith I shall apply to look me out a proper vessel captain &c.

My Neice I must send to her Mother. She mourns sadly at the thoughts of my going. I must seem nearer to her than her own Parent, as she has lived 6 years with me, and has little remembrance of any thing before she came to me. She has been as earnest to know the result of every letter from you as if her life depended upon it. I have promised with your consent; that if I live to return she shall come again to me; but I fear that I can no more live in Holland than you; tis a climate no way suited to Rheumatick complaints, of which I have had a larger share than I have for many winters before, and I am so subject to a nervious pain in my head that I think my own Health in a precarious situation. Adieu, ever, ever Yours   AA

Love to my son. I have written him by this vessel.

"YOU CALL ME TO FOLLOW YOU"

To John Adams

Febry. 11th. 1784

Two days only are wanting to campleat six years since my dearest Friend first crost the Atlantick. But three months of the Six Years have been Spent in America. The airy delusive phantom Hope, how has she eluded my prospects. And my expectations of your return from month to month, have vanished "like the baseless Fabrick of a vision."

You invite me to you, you call me to follow you, the most earnest wish of my soul is to be with you—but you can scarcly form an Idea of the conflict of my mind. It appears to me such an enterprize, the ocean so formidable, the quitting my habitation and my Country, leaving my Children, my Friends, with the Idea that prehaps I may never see them again, without my Husband to console and comfort me under these apprehensions—indeed my dear Friend there are hours when I feel unequal to the trial. But on the other hand I console myself with the Idea of being joyfully and tenderly received by the best of Husbands and Friends, and of meeting a dear and long absent Son. But the difference is; my fears, and anxieties, are present; my hopes, and expectations, distant.

But avaunt ye Idle Specters, the desires and requests of my Friend are a Law to me. I will sacrifice my present feelings and hope for a blessing in persuit of my duty.

I have already arranged all my family affairs in such a way that I hope nothing will suffer by my absence. I have determined to put into this House Pheby, to whom my Father gave freedom, by his Will, and the income of a hundred a year during her Life. The Children furnished her to house keeping, and she has ever since lived by herself, untill a fortnight ago, she took unto her self a Husband in the person of Mr. Abdee whom you know. As there was no setled minister in Weymouth I gave them the liberty of celebrating their nuptials here, which they did much to their satisfaction.

I proposed to her taking care of this House and furniture in my absence. The trust is very flattering to her, and both her

Husband and She Seem pleased with it. I have no doubt of their care and faithfullness, and prefer them to any other family. The Farm I continue to let to our old tennant, as no one thinks I shall supply myself better.

I am lucky too in being able to supply myself with an honest faithfull Man Servant. I do not know but you may recollect him, John Brisler, who was brought up in the family of Genll. Palmer, has since lived with Col. Quincy and is recommended by both families as a virtuous Steady frugal fellow, with a mind much above the vulgar, very handy and attentive. For a maid servant I hope to have a Sister of his, who formerly lived with Mrs. Trott, who gives her a good character. It gave me some pain to refuse the offerd service of an old servant who had lived 7 years with me, and who was married from here, as I wrote you some time ago. Both she and her Husband solicited to go, but I could not think it convenient as Babies might be very inconvenient at Sea, tho they offerd to leave it at Nurse if I would consent to their going, but tho I felt gratified at their regard for me I could not think it would answer. On many accounts a Brother and sister are to be prefered. This far have I proceeded but I know not yet what Ship, or what month or what port I shall embark for, I rather think for England.

I wrote you largely by Capt. Love, who saild for England 3 weeks ago. By him I mentiond a set of Bills which I expected to draw in favour of Uncle Smith for 200 dollors. He did not send me the Bills untill yesterday. Instead of 60 pounds Lawfull, he requested me to sign a Bill for 60 Sterling, as that was just the sum he wanted, and that it would oblige him. I have accordingly drawn for that; as I supposed it would not make any great odds with you; whether I drew now; or a month hence, as I suppose I shall have occasion before I embark. You will be so kind as to honour the Bill.

I have not heard from you since Mr. Robbins arrived. I long to hear how your Health is. Heaven preserve and perfect it. Col. Quincy lies very dangerously ill of the same disorder which proved fatal to my dear and honourd parent. The dr is apprehensive that it will put a period to his life in a few days.

Your Honourd Mother is as well as usual. The thoughts of my going away is a great Grief to her, but I shall leave her with

a particular request to my sister Cranch, to pay the same attention to her during her Life, which I have done, and to supply
my place to her in sickness and Health.

However kind sons may be disposed to be, they cannot be
daughters to a Mother. I hope I shall not leave any thing
undone which I ought to do. I would endeavour in the discharge of my duty towards her, to merit from her the same
testimony which my own parent gave me, that I was a good
kind considerate child as ever a parent had. However undeserving I may have been of this testimony, it is a dear and
valuable Legacy to me and will I hope pruve a stimulous to
me, to endeavour after those virtues which the affection and
partiality of a parent asscribed to me.

Our sons are well. I hope your young companion is so too.
If I should not now be able to write to him, please to tell him
I am not unmindfull of him.

I have been to day to spend a few Hours with our good
Uncle Quincy, who keeps much confined a winters and says he
misses my two Boys almost as much as I do; for they were very
fond of visiting him, and used to go as often as once a week
when they lived at home.

There is nothing stiring in the political world. The Cincinati
makes a Bustle, and will I think be crushed in its Birth.—Adieu
my dearest Friend. Yours most affectionately   A.A

"I . . . HAVE ENGAGED MY PASSAGE"

To John Adams

My dearest Friend   Boston May 25 1784
    I came to Town yesterday and have engaged My passage on
Board the ship Active Capt. Lyde, agreable to the advise of my
Friends: she will sail in about a fortnight or 3 Weeks and is the
only good vessel now going. Mrs. Jones with whom I hoped
to have been a passenger is still in so poor Health that there is
no prospect of her going very soon and my Uncle Smith upon
whose judgment and care I place much dependance advises me

by no means to delay my passage. It gives me some pain that I can only hear of you by second hand; and that not since the last of Janry. I find Congress have commissiond the Gentlemen now abroad to transact and form all their commercial Treaties, and Mr. Gerry wishes me to give you the earliest notice; and requests that Mr. Jay may be prevented from returning. There was a trial to add Mr. Jefferson to you, but I cannot learn that it is done.

And now my dear Friend let me request you to go to London some time in july that if it please God to conduct me thither in safety I may have the happiness to meet you there. I am embarking on Board a vessel without any Male Friend connection or acquaintance, my servant excepted, a stranger to the capt. and every person on Board, a situation which I once thought nothing would tempt me to undertake. But let no person say what they would or would not do, since we are not judges for ourselves untill circumstances call us to act. I am assured that I shall have a state room to myself and every accommodation and attention that I can wish for. It is said to be a good vessel copper Bottom and an able Captain. Should I arrive I know not where to apply for accommodations. I shall carry with me a Number of Letters and rely upon the Captains care of me. The United States, Capt. Scot, is not yet arrived tho we are in hourly expectation of it. I hope to hear from you by her. Tis six months since a single line reachd me from you. All communication seems to be shut out between Amsterdam and America. I think after the arrival of the Letters by Capt. Love, that you would write as you would not then look for me untill july. I have given you my reasons for not going with Capt. Callihan. I could get no satisfaction from Mr. Gerry with regard to the movements of Congress untill this month.

Our children are all well. Charles and Tommy are both at home now but will return to Haverhill next week. The expence attending my voyage will be great I find. The Captns. have got into a method of finding every thing and have from 20 to 25 guineys a person. I shall draw Bills upon you for this purpose but in whose favour I do not yet know. I shall embark with a much lighter Heart if I can receive Letters from you. I dare not trust my self with anticipating the happiness of meeting you;

least I should unhappily meet with a bitter alloy. I have to combat my own feelings in leaving my Friends. And I have to combat encourage and Sooth the mind of my young companion whose passions militate with acknowledged duty and judgment. I pray Heaven conduct me in safety and give me a joyful and happy meeting with my long long seperated best Friend and ever dear companion and long absent son to whom my affectionate Regards. I hope to be benefitted by the voyage as my Health has been very infirm and I have just recoverd from a slow fever. I have one anxiety on account of the Maid who attends me. She has never had the small pox. The one I expected to have come with me undertook to get married and dissapointed me. The one I have is a daughter of our Neighbour Feilds and has lived with me ever since Jinny was married. I shall be very happy in two excellent servants.—Adieu my dear Friend. Heaven preserve us to each other. Yours with the tenderest affection   A Adams

SHIP DIARY

To Mary Smith Cranch

Latitude 44 Long 24
on Board the Ship Active
twesday July 6 1784
My dear Sister   *from the ocean*

I have been 16 days at sea, and have not attempted to write a single Letter; tis true I have kept a journal when ever I was able, but that must be close locked up; unless I was sure to hand it you with safety.

Tis said of Cato the Roman censor, that one of the 3 things which he regreted during his Life, was going once by sea when he might have made his journey by land; I fancy the philosopher was not proof against that most disheartning, disspiriting malady, Sea sickness. Of this I am very sure, that no Lady would ever wish; or a second time try the Sea; were the objects of her pursuit within the reach of a land journey; I have had frequent occasion since I came on Board, to recollect an observation of my best Friends, "that no Being in Nature was so dissagreable as a Lady at Sea," and this recollection has in a great measure reconciled me to the thought of being at sea without him; for one would not wish my dear sister; to be thought of, in that Light: by those to whom we would wish to appear in our best array; the decency and decorum of the most delicate female must in some measure yeald to the necessitys of Nature; and if you have no female, capable of rendering you the least assistance; you will feel gratefull to any one who will feel for you and relieve, or compassionate your sufferings.

And this was truly the case of your poor sister, and all her female companions, when not one of us could make our own Beds; put on, or take of our shoes, or even lift a finger. As to our other cloathing we wore the greater part of it, untill we were able to help ourselves; added to this misfortune Brisler my Man servant was as bad as any of us; but for Jobe, I know not what we should have done; kind, attentive quick, neat, he was our Nurse for two days and Nights, and from handling the sails at the top gallant masthead, to the more femenine employment of making wine cordial, he has not his equal on Board; in short he is the favorite of the whole ship.

Our sickness continued for ten days; with some intermissions. We crawled upon deck when ever we were able, but it was so cold and damp that we could not remain long upon it, and the confinement of the Air below, the constant rolling of the vessel and the Nausea of the Ship which was much too tight, contributed to keep up our disease. The vessel is very deep loaded with oil and potash, the oil leaks the potash smoaks and ferments, all adds to the *flavour*. When you add to all this the horrid dirtiness of the ship, the slovenness of the steward, and the unavoidable sloping spilling occasiond by the tossing of the Ship, I am Sure you will be thankfull that the pen is not in the hands of Swift, or Smollet, and still more so that you are far removed from the Scene. No sooner was I able to move; than I found it necessary to make a Bustle amongst the waiters, and demand a Cleaner abode; by this time Brisler was upon his feet; and as I found I might reign mistress on Board without any offence I soon exerted my Authority with scrapers mops Brushes, infusions of viniger; &c. and in a few hours you would have thought yourself in a different Ship. Since which our abode is much more tolerable and the Gentlemen all thank me for my care; our Captain is an admirable Seaman—always attentive to his Sails, and his rigging, keeps the deck all night, carefull of every body on Board; watchfull that they run no risks, kind and humane to his Men; who are all as still and quiet as any private family, nothing cross or Dictatorial in his Manners, a much more agreable Man than I expected to find him; he cannot be called a polished gentleman; but he is so far as I have Seen; a very clever Man.

We have for passengers a Col. Norten, who is a grave sedate Man, of a Good Natural understanding, improved by Buisness, and converse with Mankind; his litterary accomplishments not very great. A Mr. Green, a scotch Man I am persuaded, high perogative Man plumes himself upon his country; haughty and imperious, but endeavours to hide this with the appearence of politeness; which however he is too apt to transgress upon any occasion; whenever any subject arises, which does not intirely agree with his sentiments. He calls himself an english Man, has been in the British Service during the war as a secretary on Board some of the British Admirals; he is a Man of sense and of reading, the most so of any we have on Board. Next to him is Dr. Clark to whom we are under obligations for every kindness, and every attention that it is in the power of a Gentleman and a physician to shew. Humane Benevolent tender and attentive, not only to the Ladies, but to every one on Board, to the servant, as well as the master, he has renderd our voyage much more agreeable and pleasent than it possibly could have been without him, his advice we have stood in need of, and his care we have felt the Benifit of, a Brother could not have been kinder, nor a parent tenderer, and it was all in the pleasent easy cheerfull way, without any thing studied Labourd, or fullsome, the natural result of a good Heart, possesst with a power of making others happy.

Tis not a little attention that we Ladies stand in need of at sea, for it is not once in the 24 hours that we can even Cross the cabbin; without being held, or assisted. Nor can we go upon deck without the assistance of 2 Gentlemen; and when there, we are allways bound into our Chairs: whilst you I imagine are scorching under the mid summer heat; we can comfortably bear our double calico Gowns; our Baize ones upon them; and a cloth cloak in addition to all these.

Mr. Foster is an other passenger on Board, a Merchant; a Gentleman soft in his manners; very polite and kind, Loves domestick Life, and thinks justly of it. I respect him on this account. Mr. Spear brings up the Rear, a single Gentleman; with a great deal of good humour, some wit; and much drollery, easy and happy blow high or blow low, can sleep and laugh at all seasons. These are our Male companions. I hardly thought a Leiut. Mellicot worth mentioning who is I believe a mere pot companion, tho he keeps not with us, except at meal times, when he does not behave amiss. My Name sake you know, she is a modest pretty woman; and behaves very well. I have accustomed myself to writing a little every Day when I was able; so that a small motion of the Ship does not render it more unintelligible *than usual.*

But there is no time since I have been at sea; when the Ship is what we call still; that its motion is not equal to the moderate rocking of a cradle. As to wind and weather since we came out; they have been very fortunate for us in general, we have had 3 Calm days, and 2 days contrary wind with a storm, I call'd it, but the Sailors say it was only a Breeze. This was upon the Banks of Newfoundland, the Wind at East. Through the day we could not set in our Chairs, only as some Gentleman set by us, with his Arm fastned into ours; and his feet braced against a table or chair that was lashed down with Ropes, Bottles, Mugs, plates crasshing to peices, first on one side; and then on the other. The Sea running mountain high, and knocking against the sides of the vessel as tho it would burst the sides. When I became so fatigued with the incessant motion; as not to be able to set any longer; I was assisted into my Cabbin, where I was obliged to hold myself in; with all my might the remainder of the Night: no person who is a Stranger to the sea; can form an adequate Idea, of the debility occassiond by sea Sickness. The hard rocking of a Ship in a storm, the want of sleep for many Nights, alltogether reduce one to such a lassitude, that you care little for your fate. The old Sea men thought nothing of all this, nor once entertain an Idea of danger, compared to what they have sufferd; I do suppose it was trifling, but to me it was allarming and I most heartily prayed: if this was only a Breeze; to be deliverd from a storm.

Our accommodations on Board are not what I could wish, or hoped for. We cannot be alone, only when the Gentlemen are thoughtfull enough to retire upon deck, which they do for about an hour in the course of the day; our *state* rooms are about half as large as Cousin Betsys little Chamber, with two Cabbins in each. Mine had 3, but I could not live so; upon which Mrs. Adams'es Brother gave up his to Nabby, and we are now stowed, two and two. This place has a small grated window, which opens into the Companion, and is the only air admitted. The door opens into the Cabbin where the Gentlemen all Sleep; and where we sit dine &c. We can only live with our door Shut, whilst we dress and undress. Necessity has no law, but what should I have thought on shore; to have layed myself down to sleep, in common with half a dozen Gentlemen? We have curtains it is true, and we only in part undress, about as much as the Yankee Bundlers, but we have the satisfaction of falling in, with a set of well behaved, decent Gentlemen, whose whole deportment is agreeable to the strickest delicacy both in words and action.

If the wind and weather continues as favorable as it has hietherto been; we expect to make our passage in 30 days, which is going a hundred miles a day. Tis a vast tract of ocean which we have to traverse; I have contemplated it with its various appearences; it is indeed a secret world of wonders, and one of the Sublimist objects in Nature.

> "Thou makest the foaming Billows roar
> Thou makest the roaring Billows sleep."

They proclaim the deity, and are objects too vast for the controul of feble Man, that Being alone, who maketh the Clouds his Chariots and rideth upon the wings of the wind; is equal to the Goverment of this Stupendous part of Creation.

And now my dear sister after this minute account of my *important self*, which judgeing by myself, you take an affectionate interest in, I call upon you to inquire after your welfare, my much Esteemed Brothers, and my dear Neices? Not a day, or Night, but I visit your calm retreat, look at my own deserted Habitation, and recollect past endearments, with a melancholy composure. And realy am so vain, as to commisirate you, on account of the vacuity I fancy my absence occasions.

We are so formed, says an injenious writer, as to be always pleased with some what in prospect, however distant or however trivial; thus do I gratify myself with the Idea of returning to my Native land, tho the prospect is distant. Pleasures, says Pope are ever in our hands or Eyes. I have lost part of the other line, but the Idea is, that if We are not in the present possession of them, they rise to us in prospect. I will now tell you, where I am sitting, at a square table in the Great Cabin, at one corner of which is Col. Norten and Mr. Foster engaged in playing back Gammon, at the other, Mr. Green writing, and at the fourth, Dr. Clark eating ham. Behind Col. Norten, Mr. Spear reading Tompsons Seasons with his Hat on, young Lawrence behind me reading Ansons Voyages, Ester kniting, the Steward and Boys Bustling about after wine and porter, and last of all as the least importantly employ'd Mrs. Adams, and Nabby in their Cabbin a sleep and this at 12 oclock in the day. O Shame! The Captain comes down and finds me writing, kindly tenders me some large paper to write upon. I believe he thinks I shall have occasion for it. This man has a kindness in his disposition which his countanance does not promise.

Mr. Green comes down from deck and reports that the Mate says we are 16 hundred miles on our Way. This is good hearing. I can scarcly realize myself upon the ocean, or that I am within 14 hundred miles of the British coast. I rejoice with trembling. Painfull and fearfull Ideas, will arise and intermix, with the pleasureable hopes of a joyfull meeting of my long absent Friend. I frequently recollect some lines of Miss Mores, in her Sir Eldred of the Bower. Discribing a mixture of hope and anxiety, she says

> "Twas such a sober sense of joy
> As Angles well might keep
> A joy Chastis'd by piety
> A Joy prepair'd to weep."

I shall write whilst I am on Board when ever I can catch a quiet time, it is an amusement to me, reading tires me, work I do sometimes, but when there is no writing there is less pleasure in working; I shall keep the Letter open untill I arrive and put it on Board the first vessel I find comeing to America. Tis impossible for me to find any variety at Sea to entertain my Friends with, so that this Letter with all its inaccuracies must be submitted to them. Do not however expose me, especially where I have a little credit; you know very well that affection and intimacy will cover a multitude of faults.

July 7th
    If I did not write every day, I should lose the days of the month, and of the week, confined all day on account of the weather; which is foggy, misty, and wet. You can hardly judge how urksome this confinement is; when the whole ship is at our Service; it is little better than a prison; we Suppose ourselves near the western Islands. O dear variety! how pleasing to the humane mind is Change; I cannot find such a fund of entertainment within myself as not to require outward objects for my amusement. Nature abounds with variety, and the mind unless fixed down by habit, delights in contemplating new objects, and the variety of Scenes which present themselves to the Senses, were certainly designd to prevent our attention from being too long fixed upon any one object; and this says a late celebrated medical writer; greatly conduces to the Health of the animal frame. Your studious people and your deep thinkers, he observes, seldom enjoy either health or spirits. This writer I recommend to your perusal; and will tell you that you may borrow it of our Friend Mrs. Warren, tis Buchans domestick Medicine. I have read him since I came to Sea with much pleasure.

    I have been in much trouble, upon looking over my Letters since I came on Board, to find those given me, by my Friend Mrs. Warren; missing; I cannot account for it, in any other way; than that I must have put them into the pocket of the Chaise, when I received them; which I recollect; and I did not think to take them out; you remember the day, with all its circumstances, and will accordingly apoligize to our Friend, whose goodness, I know will pardon the omission; nor add to my mortification, by charging it to inattention.

July 8th
    An other wet drisly day, but we must not complain, for we have a fair wind; our sails all square and go at 7 knots an hour.

I have made a great acquisition, I have learnt the Names and places of all the masts and sails; and the Captain compliments me by telling me that he is sure I know well enough how to *steer* to take a trick at Helm; I may do pretty well in fair weather, but tis your masculine Spirits that are made for Storms. I love the tranquil scenes of Life; nor can I look forward to those in which tis probable I shall soon be engaged, with those pleasureable Ideas; which a retrospect of the past presents to my mind.

I went last evening upon deck, at the invitation of Mr. Foster to view that phenomenon of Nature; a blaizing ocean. A light flame Spreads over the ocean in appearence; with thousands of thousands Sparkling Gems, resembling our fire flies in a dark Night. It has a most Beautifull appearence. I never view the ocean without being filled with Ideas of the Sublime, and am ready to break forth with the psalmist, "Great and Marvellous are thy Works, Lord God Almighty; in Wisdom hast thou made them all."

Saturday 10th

Yesterday was a very pleasent day, very little wind; but a fine sun and smooth sea. I spent the most of the day upon deck reading; it was not however so warm; but a Baize gown was very comfortable; the ship has gradually become less urksome to me. If our cook was but tolerably clean, I could realish my victuals, but he is a great dirty lazy Negro; with no more knowledge of cookery than a savage; nor any kind of order in the distribution of his dishes, but *hickel tapickelta*, on they come with a leg of pork all Brisly, a Quarter of an hour after a pudding, or perhaps a pair of roast fowls first of all, and then will follow one by one a peice of Beaf and when dinner is nearly compleated a plate of potatoes. Such a fellow is a real imposition upon the passengers—but Gentlemen know but little about the matter, and if they can get enough to eat five times a day all goes well. We Ladies have not eat upon our whole passage, more than just enough to satisfy nature; or to keep body and soul together.

thursday 15 of july

A Sunday I wrote part of a Letter to Sister Shaw; since which

I have not used my pen, even in my journal. Monday we had a fair wind but too much to be able to write, as it was right aft, and we pitch'd exceedingly, which is a motion more dissagreeable to me than the rocking's tho less fatigueing; a twesday a Calm. Should you not suppose that in a Calm we at least had the Satisfaction of lyeing still? Alass it is far otherways; as my flesh, and bones, witness. A Calm generally succeeds a storm or a fresh Breeze; the Sea has a great swell after the wind is silent, so that the Ship lies intirely at the mercy of the waves, and is knocked from side to side with a force you can form no Idea of without experience; I have been more wearied and worn out with the motion and exercise of a calm, than in rideing 50 miles in a day. We have had 3 days in succession nearly calm. The first is the most troublesome, as the motion of the Sea Subsides in a degree. It is however a great trial of ones patience, to think yourself within a few days of your desired port, to look at it, as the promised land; and yet to be held fast.

"Ye too ye winds, I raise my voice to you
    In what far distant region of the Sky
    Hush'd in deep Silence, Sleep you when tis Calm?"

I begin to think that a Calm is not desireable in any situation in life, every object is most Beautifull in motion, a ship under sail trees Gently agitated with the wind, and a fine women danceing, are 3 instances in point; Man was made for action, and for Bustle too I believe. I am quite out of conceit with calms. I have more reason for it too, than many others, for the dampness of the ship has for several day threatned me with the Rheumatisim, and yesterday morning I was seazed with it in good earnest; I could not raise my Head, nor get out of bed without assistance, I had a good deal of a fever and was very sick; I was fearfull of this before I came to sea and had medicine put up proper, which the doctor administerd. What with that, good Nursing and rubbing, flannel, &c. I am able to day to set up in my Bed, and write as you see. To day we have a small wind, but tis night a Head. This is still mortifying, but what we had reason to expect. Patience, patience, patience is the first second and third virtues of a seaman, or rather as necessary to them, as to a statesman. 3 days good wind would give us land.

fryday

We have an other wet misty day; the Cabbin so damp that I
dare not set in it; am therefore obliged confined as it is to keep
in my own little room; and upon my bed. I long for the day
which will give us land. Ester makes but a poor hand at sea;
scarcly a day but what she is sick some part of it, I hope she will
be the better for it when she gets on shore. We have but one
passenger which we should have been willing to have been
without; I have no particular reason to dislike him, as he is
studiously complasant to me; but I know his politeness to me,
is not personally upon my own account; but because of my
connection which gives me importance sufficient to intitle me
to his *notice*. Nabby says he is exactly Such a Character as Mr.
Anger; I realy think there is a stricking resemblance; he is always inquiring who was such a General? What was his origin
and rank in Life? I have felt a Disposition to quarrel with him
several times; but have restraind myself; and only observed to
him mildly, that merit; not tittles, gave a man preeminence in
our Country, that I did not doubt it was a mortifying circumstance to the British nobility, to find themselves so often conquerd by mecanicks and mere husband men—but that we
esteemed it our Glory to draw such characters not only into
the field, but into the Senate; and I believed no one would
deny but what they had shone in both. All our passengers enjoyed this conversation, and the *Gentleman* was civil enough
to drop the Subject, but the venom Spits out very often; yet
the creature is sensible and entertaining when upon indifferent
Subjects: he is a haughty Scotchman. He hates the French, and
upon all occasions ridicules them and their Country. I fancy
from his haughty airs, that his own rank in Life has not been
superiour to those whom he affects to despise. He is not a man
of liberal Sentiments, and is less beloved than any passenger we
have on Board. A mans humour contributes much to the
making him agreable, or other ways, dark and sour humours,
especially those which have a spice of malevolence in them are
vastly dissagreable. Such men have no musick in their Souls. I
believe he would hardly be so complasant if he knew how
meanly I thought of him; but he deserves it all, his whole
countanance shews his Heart.

Saturday 17 of july

Give me joy my dear sister, we have sounded to day and found bottom 55 fathom. We have seen through the course of the day 20 different Sail, Spoke with a small Boat, upon a smuggling expedition, which assured us we were within the Channel.

july 18

This day four weeks we came on Board, are you not all cal-culating to day that we are near the land? Happily you are not wrong in your conjectures, I do not dispair of seeing it yet before night, tho our wind is very Small and light. The Captain has just been down to advise us as the vessel is so quiet, to get what things we wish to carry on shore into our small trunks. He hopes to land us at Portsmouth 70 miles distant from London tomorrow or next, day. From thence we are to pro-ceed in post chaises to London. The ship may be a week in the channel before she will be able to get up.

Be so good as to let Mrs. Feild know that Ester has stood her voyage as well as I expected. She has been very sick Some-times, but not a day since a few of the first, but what she has been able to go upon deck when it was proper weather. She says she is not home sick, nor has ever repented her comeing. I have sometimes thought she had reason too, and have won-derd how she could help it when she has sufferd so much, and no greater temptation to carry her out, than just comeing with me; she has not wanted for any kind of care, as the doctor has been very good, Jobe and Brisler very attentive. The doctor thinks she will enjoy her Health much better than ever.

Deal july 20

Heaven be praised I have Safely landed upon the British coast. How flattering how smooth the ocean how delightfull was Sunday the 18 of July. We flatterd ourselves with the pros-pect of a gentle Breeze to carry us on shore at Portsmouth where we agreed to land, as going up the channel always proves tedious, but on sunday Night the wind shifted to the south-west, which upon this coast, is the same with our north East winds: it blew a gale on sunday night on monday and monday night equal to an Equinoctial. We were obliged to carry double reef top sails only, and what added to our misfortune was; that, tho we had made land the day before it was so thick that we could not certainly determine what land it was; it is now tuesday and I have slept only four hours since Saturday night, such was the tossing and tumbling in Board our ship. The Captain never left the deck the whole time either to eat or sleep, tho they told me there was no danger, nor do I suppose that there realy was any; as we had sea room enough. Yet the great number of vessels constantly comeing out of the channel and the apprehension of being run down, or being nearer the land than we imagined kept me constantly agitated. Added to this I had a voilent sick head ack. O! what would I have given to have been quiet upon the land. You will hardly wonder then at the joy we felt this day in seeing the cliffs of Dover: Dover castle and town. The wind was in Some measure subsided. It raind, however; and was as squaly as the month of March, the sea ran very high. A pilot boat came on Board at about ten oclock this morning; the Captain came to anchor with his ship in the downs and the little town of Deal lay before us. Some of the Gentlemen talkd of going on shore with the pilot Boat, and sending for us if the wind subsided. The boat was about as large as a Charlstown ferry boat and the distance from the Ship about twice as far as from Boston, to Charlstown. A Shore as bald as Nantasket Beach, no wharf, but you must be run right on shore by a wave where a number of Men stand to catch hold of the Boat and draw it up. The surf ran six foot high.

But this we did not know untill driven on by a wave, for the pilots eager to get money assured the gentlemen they could land us safe without our being wet, and we saw no prospect of its being better through the day. We accordingly agre'd to go. We were wraped up and lowerd from the ship into the boat; the whole ships crew eager to assist us, the gentlemen attentive and kind as tho we were all Brothers and sisters! We have Spent a month together, and were as happy as the sea would permit us to be. We set of from the vessel now mounting upon the top of a wave high as a steeple, and then so low that the boat was not to be seen. I could keep myself up no other way than as one of the Gentlemen stood braced up against the Boat, fast hold of me and I with both my Arms round him. The other ladies were held, in the same manner whilst every wave gave us a Broad side, and finally a Wave landed us with the utmost force upon the Beach; the Broad Side of the Boat right against the shore, which was oweing to the bad management of the men, and the high Sea.

(Thus far I had proceeded in my account when a summons to tea prevended my adding more; Since which I have not been able to take my pen; tho now at my Lodgings in London I will take up the thread where I left it, untill the whole Ball is unwound; every particular will be interesting to my Friends I presume, and to no others expose this incorrect Scral.)

We concequently all pressd upon the side next the Shore to get out as quick as possible, which we need not have done, if we had known what I afterwards found to be the Case, that it was the only way in which we could be landed, and not as I at first supposed oweing to the bad management of the Boatmen; we should have set still for a succession of waves to have carried us up higher, but the roar of them terrified us all, and we expected the next would fill our Boat; so out we sprang as fast as possible sinking every step into the sand, and looking like a parcel of Naiades just rising from the sea. A publick house was fortunately just at hand, into which we thankfully enterd, changed our cloathing, dried ourselves and not being able to procure carriages that Day we engaged them for Six oclock the next morning, and took lodgings there, all of us; ten in Number. Mr. Green set of immediately for London—no body mourn'd.

We were all glad to retire early to rest. For myself I was so faint and fatigued that I could get but little; we rose by 5 and our post Chaise being all at the door we set of in the following order. Mr. Foster myself and Ester in one, Dr. Clark and Nabby in the second, Col. Norten Mrs. Adams and Brother in the 3 and Mr. Spear and Lieut. Millicot brought up the rear. Our first Stage was 18 miles from Deal, to Canteburry where we Breakfasted, the roads are fine, and a stone a Novelty. I do not recollect to have seen one, except the pavements of Canteburry, and other Towns; from Deal to London which is 72 miles; vast Feilds of wheat, oats, english Beans, and the horse Bean, with hops: are the produce of the country through

which we past; which is cultivated like a Garden down to the
very edges of the road, and what surprized me was, that very
little was inclosed within fences. Hedg fence, are almost the
only kind you see, no Cattle at large without a herdsman, the
oxen are small, but the Cows and Sheep very large, such as I
never saw before. When we arrived at the end of our Stage; we
discharge the first carriages, call for New ones which will be
ready in a few moments after you issue your orders. Call for
Breakfast. You have it perhaps in ten moments for ten people,
with the best of attendance and at a reasonable price.

Canteburry is a larger town than Boston, it contains a Number of old Gothick Cathedrals, which are all of stone very
heavy, with but few windows which are grated with large Bars
of Iron, and look more like jails for criminals, than places
designd for the worship of the deity. One would Suppose from
the manner in which they are Gaurded, that they apprehended
devotion would be stolen. They have a most gloomy appearence and realy made me shudder. The Houses too have a
heavy look being chiefly thatched roofs or coverd with crooked
brick tile. Now and then you would see upon the road a large
woods looking like a Forest, for a whole mile inclosed with a
high Brick Wall or cemented stone, an enormous Iron gate
would give one a peep as we passt of a large pile of Building,
which lookd like the castles of some of the ancient Barons; but
as we were strangers in the Country, we could only conjecture
what they were, and what they might have been.

We proceeded from Canterburry to Rochester about 15
miles, an other pretty town, not so large as the former, from
thence to Chatam where we stoped at a very Elegant Inn to
dine. As soon as you drive into the yard you have at these
places as many footmen round you as you have Carriages, who
with their politest airs take down the step of your Carriage assist you out, inquire if you want fresh horses or carriages; will
supply you directly, Sir, is the answer. A well dresst hostess
steps forward, making a Lady like appearence and wishes your
commands. If you desire a chamber, the Chamber maid attends; you request dinner, say in half an hour, the Bill of Fare
is directly brought, you mark what you wish to have, and suppose it to be a variety of fish, fowl, meat, all of which we had,
up to 8 different dishes; besides vegetables. The moment the

time you stated, is out, you will have your dinner upon table in as Elegant a stile, as at any Gentleman's table, with your powdered waiters, and the master or Mistress always brings the first Dish upon table themselves. But you must know that travelling in a post Chaise, is what intitles you to all this respect.

From Chatham we proceeded, on our way as fast as possible wishing to pass Black Heath before dark. Upon this road, a Gentleman alone in a chaise past us, and very soon a coach before us stoped, and there was a hue and cry, a Robbery a Robbery. The Man in the chaise was the person robbed and this in open day with carriages constantly passing. We were not a little allarmed and every one were concealing their money. Every place we past, and every post chaise we met were crying out a Robbery. Where the thing is so common I was Surprized to see such an allarm. The Robber was pursued and taken in about two miles, and we saw the poor wretch gastly and horible, brought along on foot, his horse rode by a person who took him; who also had his pistol. He looked like a youth of 20 only, attempted to lift his hat, and looked Dispair. You can form some Idea of my feelings when they told him aya, you have but a short time, the assise set next Month, and then my Lad you Swing. Tho every robber may deserve Death yet to exult over the wretched is what *our* Country is not accustomed to. Long may it be free of such villianies and long may it preserve a commisiration for the wretched.

We proceeded untill about 8 oclock. I was set down at Lows Hotel in Covent Gardens, the Court end of the Town. These Lodgings I only took for one night untill others more private could be procured as I found Mr. Adams was not here, I did not wish such expensive appartments. It was the Hotel at which he kept when he resided here. Mr. Spear set out in quest of Mr. Smith, but he had received intelligence of my comeing out with Capt. Lyde and had been in quest of me but half an hour before at this very place; Mr. Spear was obliged to go first to the custom house, and as good fortune would have it, Mr. Smith and Mr. Storer, were near it and saw him allight from the coach, upon which he informd them of my arrival. Tho a mile distant, they set out upon a full run (they say) and very soon to our mutual satisfaction we met in the Hotel. How do you and how do ye? We rejoice to see you here, and a thousand such kind of inquiries as take place between Friends who have not seen each other for a long time naturally occured.

My first inquiry was for Mr. Adams. I found that my son had been a month waiting for my arrival in London, expecting me in Callighan, but that upon getting Letters by him, he returnd to the Hague. Mr. Smith had received a Letter from his Father acquainting him that I had taken passage in Capt. Lyde. This intelligence he forwarded three days before I came, so that I hourly expect either Mr. Adams or Master John. I should have mentiond that Mr. Smith had engaged lodgings for me; to which Mr. Storer and he accompanied me this morning after paying a Guiney and half for tea last evening and Lodging and Breakfast, a coach included; not however to carry me a further distance than from your House to our own; the Gentlemen all took less expensive lodgings than mine, excepting Dr. Clark who tarried with us, said he would not quit us untill we were fixed in our present Hotel, the direction to which is Osbornes new family Hotel, Adelphi at Mrs. Sheffields No. 6. Here we have a handsome drawing room Genteely furnished, and a large Lodging room. We are furnished with a cook, chamber maid waiter &c. for 3 Guineys per week—but in this is not included a mouthfull of vituals or drink all of which is to be paid seperately for.

fryday july 23

I have little time for writing now, I have so many visitors. I hardly know how to think myself out of my own Country I see so many Americans about me; the first persons who calld to see me after my arrival here, were Mr. Jackson Mr. Winslow Warren Mr. Rogers Mr. Ward Boylstone, Mrs. Atkingson, and yesterday mor'g before I had Breakfasted, (for the fashonable hours of the city had taken hold of me, not out of choice but necessity Miss Adams having a hair dresser, I had directed Breakfast at 9 oclock—it was ten however, but those were early visiting hours for this fine city). Yet whilst I was Breakfasting who should be anounced to me; but *Parson Walter* and Mrs. Hollowell. Both appeard very glad to see me, Mrs. Hollowell treated me with her old affibily and engaged me to dine with her to day. Not says she to a feast, for we make none, but to an unceremonious family dinner. Luxery says she is the mode, but we know too, how to practise frugality and oconomey.

I am not a Little surprized to find dress unless upon publick occasions, so little regarded here. The Gentlemen are very plainly dresst and the Ladies much less so than with us. Tis true you must put a hoop on and have your hair dresst, but a common straw hat, no Cap, with only a ribbon upon the crown, is thought dress sufficient to go into company. Muslins are much in taste, no silks but Lutestrings worn but send not to London for any article you want, you may purchase any thing you can Name much lower in Boston. I went yesterday into Cheepside to purchase a few articles, but found every thing higher than in Boston. Silks are in a particular manner so. They say when they are exported there is a draw back upon them which makes them lower with us.

Our Country, alass our Country they are extravagant to astonishment in entertainments compared with what Mr. Smith and Mr. Storer tell me of this. You will not find at a Gentlemans table more than two dishes of meat tho invited several days before hand. Mrs. Atkinson went out with me yesterday and Mrs. Hay to the shops. I returnd and dined with Mrs. Atkinson by her invitation the Evening before, in company with Mr. Smith Mrs. Hay Mr. Appleton. We had a turbot; a Soup and a roast leg of Lamb, with a cherry pye. I was more gratified by the social friendly stile in which I was treated than if a sumptuous feast had been set before me. Mr. Goreham, Dr. Parker, Mr. Bromfeild, a Mr. Murray from the Hague came to see me yesterday morning, and when I returnd last evening I found cards left by a Number of Gentlemen, Some of whom I knew others I did not. But knowing Mr. Adams and being Americans they calld to make their compliments. Prentice Cushing I met with yesterday at Mr. Atkinson's. I am going to day to see Mr. Copeleys pictures. I am told he has an Excellent likeness of Mr. Adams. Mr. Murray informd me that he left Mr. Adams last fryday, excessively anxious for my arrival; he had removed Mr. Dumas and family in expectation of my comeing: says John with whom he went to the Hague, was melancholy when Callihan arrived without me, and Mr. Adams more so; I have sent to day by the post to acquaint him with my being here, but hope every hour to see him or Master John. The wind has prevented the arrival of the post.

The city of London is pleasenter than I expected, the Buildings more regular the streets much wider and more Sun shine than I thought to have found, but this they tell me is the pleasentest season to be in the city. At my lodgings I am as quiet as any place in Boston, nor do I feel as if it could be any other place than Boston. Dr. Clark visits us every day, says he cannot feel at home any where else, declares he has not seen a handsome woman since he came into the city, that every old woman looks like Mrs. Haley and every young one like, like the d—l. They paint here, near as much as in France, but with more art, the head dress disfigures them in the Eye of an American. I have seen many Ladies; but not one Elegant one since I came; there is not to me that neatness in their appearence which you see in our Ladies.

The American Ladies are much admired here by the Gentlemen, I am told, and in truth I wonder not at it. O my Country; my Country; preserve; preserve the little purity and simplicity of manners you yet possess. Believe me, they are jewells of inestimable value.

The softness peculiarly characteristick of our sex and which is so pleasing to the Gentlemen, is Wholy laid asside here; for the Masculine attire and Manners of Amazonians.

This moment a very polite card is deliverd me from Mrs. Hallowell desireing me to remove my lodging to her House whilst I continue in London—to which I have replied with thanks excuseing myself, that I am very well accommodated and in hourly expectation of my son, not the less obliged however by her politeness. Mr. Ellworthy I have not yet seen, tho I have had Several Messages from him. This is not oweing to inattention in him, but to being informd that every thing was done for me before my arrival which I stood in need of. Our ship is not yet got up the Channel. What a time we should have had of it, if we had not landed.

Mr. Smith expects to sail on Monday or twesday, I shall keep open this Letter untill he goes. Let Sister Shaw see it, and read such parts as you think proper to the rest of our Friends, but do not let it go out of your hands. I shall not have time to write to the rest of my Friends, they must not think hardly of me. I could only repeat what I have here written, and I think it is best to have the whole Bugget together. Besides Nabby writes to all her acquaintance which must answer for me. Remember me to them all, first to my dear and aged parent, to whom present my duty—to Dr. Tufts to my Aunt to Uncle Quincy to Mr. Wibird, to all my Friends and Neighbours. Tell Mrs. Feild that Ester is very well that She sleeps in the Same Chamber with me; and keeps in it constantly, Which I chuse rather than that She Should mix below with Dick Tom and Harry whom I know nothing of. My drawing room and Chamber are up one pair of stairs. Into a closet by my chamber, water is conveyd by pipes, and as there is not half an inch of Ground unoccupied we have no occasion to go out of our rooms, from one week to an other, for by ringing the bed chamber bell, the Chamber Maid comes; and the drawing room Bell brings up the other waiters; who when you go out attend you from the Stairs to the Carriage, the Land Lady waiting at the foot to recive you, and so again upon your return. This is the stile of the Hotels.

Sunday morg july 25

I went yesterday accompanied by Mr. Storer and Smith to Mr. Copelys to see Mr. Adams picture. This I am told was taken at the request of Mr. Copely and belongs to him. It is a full Length picture very large; and a very good likeness. Before him stands the Globe: in his hand a Map of Europe, at a small distance 2 female figures representing peace and Innocence. It is a most Beautifull painting. From thence we went to what is calld Mr. Copelys exhibition. Here is the celebrated picture, representing the death of Lord Chatham in the House of Commons, his 3 Sons round him, each with strong expressions of Grief and agitation in their countanances. Every Member is crouding round him with a mixture of surprize and distress. I saw in this picture, what I have every day noticed since I came here, a Strong likeness of some American, or other, and I can scarcly persuade myself, but what I have seen this person, that and the other before, there countanances appear so familiar to me, and so strongly mark our own Decent.

There was an other painting which struck me more than this. It is the death of Major Peirson the particulars account of which I inclose to you; I never saw painting more expressive than this. I lookt upon it untill I was faint, you can scarcly believe but you hear the groans of the sergant who is wounded and holding the hankerchief to his side, whilst the Blood Streams over his hand. Grief dispair and terror, are Strongly marked, whilst he grows pale and faint with loss of Blood. The officers are holding Major Peirson in their Arms, who is Mortally wounded, and the black servant has leveld his peice at the officer who killd him. The distress in the countanance of the women who are flying, one of whom has a Baby in her Arms, is Beautifully represented. But my discriptions, of these things give you but a faint resemblance of what in reality they are.

From thence I went to see the celebrated Mrs. Wright, Mr. Storer, and Smith, accompanying us. Upon my entrance (my Name being sent up) she ran to the Door, caught me by the Hand, "Why is it realy and in truth Mrs. Adams, and that your daughter? Why you dear Soul you, how young you look! Well I am glad to See you, all of you Americans! Well I must kiss you all." Having passt the ceremony upon me and Nabby, she runs to the Gentleman. "I make no distinction," says she, and gave them a hearty Buss, from which we had all rather have been excused; for her appeerence is quite the slattern. "I love every body that comes from America," says she, "here," running to her desk, "is a card I had from Mr. Adams. I am quite proud of it, he came to see and made me a noble present, dear creature I design to have his Head." "There," says she pointing to an old Man and women who were sitting in one corner of the room, "is my old Father and Mother. Dont be ashamed of them because they look so. They were good folks," (these were there figures in wax work), "they turnd quakers and never would let their children eat meat, and that is the reason we were all so injenious; you had heard of the ingenious Mrs. Wright in America I suppose." In this manner She ran on for half an hour. Her person and countanance resemble an old maiden in your Neighbourhood Nelly Penniman, except that one is neat, the other the Queen of sluts, and her tongue runs like, Unity Badlams. There was an old Clergyman sitting reading a paper in the middle of the room, and tho I went prepaird to See strong representations of real Life, I was effectually deceived in this figure for 10 minuts, and was finally told that it was only Wax.

From Mrs. Wrights I returnd to my Hotel, dresst and at 4 went to dine with Mrs. Hollowel; he had in the morning been to see me and Mr. Thomas Boylstone, both of whom urged me to take up my Lodgings with Mrs. Hollowell. I chose to decline, but went and dined with them, here I found Parson Walter. We had a handsome dinner of salt fish pea soup Boild fowl and tongue roast and fry'd Lamb, with a pudding and fruit. This was a little in the Boston stile. Mr. Smith and Storer dined with us. Mr. Hollowell lives handsomely, but not in that Splendour which he did in Boston. On Sunday I engaged to take a Coach for the day which is *only* 12 and 6 pence sterling, and go to church to the foundling Hospital, Mrs. Atkingson Smith and Storer with me.

Monday morg

Well my dear sister if you are not tired with following me I will carry you to the Foundling Hospital where I attended divine service yesterday morning. Realy glad I was, that I could after so long an absence, again tread the Courts of the most high and I hope I felt not unthankfull for the mercies I had received.

This Hospital is a large Elegant Building situated in a Spot as airy, and much more Beautifull than Boston Common. The chapel which is upon the second floor is as large as what is called the Old South with us. There is one row of Galleries: upon the floor of this Chapel there are rows of seats; like a concert hall; and the pulpit is a small ornamented Box near the center. There were about 2000 person, as near as I could guess, who attended. In the Gallery, opposite to where I set, was the organ loft, upon each side an allcove; with Seats, which run up like a piramid. Here the foundlings sat, upon one side the Boys; upon the other the Girls, all in uniform, none appeard under 5 nor any older than 12, about 300 attended the service. The uniform of the Boys was a brown cloth with a red coller and a red stripe upon the shoulder. The Girls were in brown with a red Girdle round the Waist, a checked stomacher and apron sleeves turnd up and white cloth caps with a Narrow

lace, clean and neat as wax. Their governessess attended with
them. They performd the vocal Musick, one Man, and Woman,
upon each side the organ; who sang an Anthem; both blind,
and educated at this foundling hospital. When we came down
we went into the dining rooms which were upon each side the
assent into the Chaple; here the tables were all arranged, and
the little creatures curtssying and smiling; some as sweet children as ever you saw. There is an inscription over the door in
gold Letters—Can a Mother forget her Sucking child &c. In a
hall are placed the pictures of many noted Benefactors and
founders of this institution (I should have mentiond that the
chaple windows are painted Glass, the Arms, and Names of the
most distinguishd Benefactors are in the Different Squares of
the Glass). We were Shewn into their bed Chambers which are
long airy chambers with 10 or 15 windows in each; and about
50 or 60 beds placed in rows upon each side; coverd with blew
and white furniture check. At the head of the Chamber is a
bed for the Governess. When you have seen one of them you
have a specimin of the whole.

I dined with Mr. and Mrs. Atkinson in company with Mr.
Jackson, Smith &c. Mr. Atkinson is a very modest worthy Man
and Mrs. Atkinson a most amiable woman, you see no parade
no ceremony. I am treated with all the kindness of a sister, in as
easy a way as I could wish. As I took the Carriage for the day;
after forenoon service, we rode out to see Mrs. Atkinsons
twins, who are at Nurse at Islington; about 2 miles from the
city. It is a fine ride. We went through a Number of the great
Squares. Portland Square is one of the finest. In short the
representations which you and I, amused ourselves with looking at, not long ago, are very near the Life. When we returnd
we dined, and at six oclock went to the Magdeline Hospital,
which is 3 miles from where I dined, for this is a *Monstrous*
great city. We were admitted with a ticket, this assembly was
very full and crouded. Yet no Children or Servants are admitted. In Short I begin to hope that this people are more Serious
and religious than I feard they were. Their is great decorum
and decency observed, here are only two small Galleries which
hold the unhappy beings who are the Subjects of this Mercifull
institution. Those who attend the Service, are placed upon
seats below like a concert Hall. The Building is about as large

again as Braintree Church, in a most delightfull Situation surrounded by weeping Willows. All the Publick Buildings here
have large open spaces arround them, except those churches
which are in the Heart of the city. I observed upon going in; a
Gallery before me railed very high and coverd with Green
canvas. Here set these unhappy women screened from publick
view. You can discern them through the canvas, but not
enough to distinguish countenances. I admired the delicacy of
this thought. The Singing was all performd by these females
accompanied with the organ. The Melancholy melody of their
voices, the Solemn Sound of the organ, the serious and affecting discourse of the preacher together with the Humiliating
objects before me, drew tears from my Eyes. The Chapel to
these appartments is always in the Heart of the building, the
dinning working and lodging appartments surround them.

Returnd about 8 oclock, found many cards left for me, some
from Virginians some from Marylanders some from Conneticut. Col. Trumble has call'd twice upon me but I was so unfortunate as not to be at home. Amongst the Americans who calld
yesterday to see me during my absence was Mr. Joy. He left his
Name and direction with a polite Billet, inviteing me to dine
with him a tuesday if I was not engaged, and if I was the first
day I was disengaged. I have replied to him that I will wait
upon him on wednesday. Invited by Mr. Jackson and by Mr.
Murray to the play this evening, declined going in hopes my
best Friend will be here to attend me very soon. Besides have
no cloaths yet which will do. No Mail from Holland yet arrived. The wind has been so contrary that two are now due.
Dr. Clark our constant and daily visitor is just come in to drink
tea with me; Mr. Smith and Storer are here great part of the
day. Captain Lyde did not get up the Channel untill Sunday;
so that I have no occasion to repent landing when I did. Contrary winds and bad weather prevented his comeing up only
with the tide; his vissel too like to have been sunk by a Collier
running foul of him, they did him a good deal of damage.
These are vessels that take pleasure in injureing others. He told
me many dismall stories about comeing up the Channel, which
made me determine to Land at any rate.

On Saturday Mr. Elworthy calld upon me, and tenderd me
any service I could wish for; I thanked him, but Mr. Smith

Storer and Dr. Clark render any other assistance necessary, as either and all of them are ready and willing to oblige me. On Sunday morning Mr. and Mrs. Elworthy, came to see me. She is a very agreeable Women, *and looks like one of us*, that she had more of our American neatness about her than any Lady I have seen, for I am yet so unpolite as not to be reconciled to the jaunty appearence, and the Elegant Stoop. There is a rage of fashion which prevails here with dispotick Sway, the coulour and kind of silk must be attended to; and the day for putting it on and of, no fancy to be exercised, *but it is* the *fashion* and that is argument sufficient to put one in, or out of countanance. I am comeing on half way; I Breakfast at 9 and dine at 3 when at home, but I rise by six. I am not obliged to conform in that, but the other hours I am forced to submit to upon account of company. This morning Dr. Clark and Col. Trumble are to Breakfast with me. I long for the hour when I shall set of, for the Hague or see Mr. Adams here; I meet with so many acquaintance; that I shall feel loth to quit the city, upon that account. There are no Americans in Holland and the language will prevent any Sociability but what I find in my own family. But having a house, Garden, and Servants, at command, feeling at home will in some measure compensate for the rest. I have a journey of 80 miles to make to Margate before I can embark, and as soon as Mr. Jefferson arrives suppose we must go to France. I have not executed your orders with regard to Sattin because upon inquiry I find you can Buy cheeper with you; I have not found any thing except shoes that are lower. Such a sattin as my black you must give as much sterling for a yard as I gave lawfull Money. No silk but Lutestring and those which are thinner are worn at this Season; mode cloaks Muslin and Safnet, Gauze Hats Bonnets and ribbons—every thing as light and thin as possible, different gowns and skirts. Muslin Skirts flounced; chintz with Borders, white, with a trimming that looks like Gartering. The Silk which is most in taste is what is calld new mown Hay, the pattern I inclose and this part of the Letter is for the tastety folks of my acquaintance. Mr. Smith brings home a Specimin of the Newest fashion hats.

tweesday morning
Determined to Tarry at home to day and see company. Mr.

Joy came in and Spent an hour. He is the Same pleasing Man
you formerly knew him, that Bashfull difidence is supplied by a
manly confidence, and acquaintance with the world has given
ease and politeness to his Manners; he realy is quite the accomplished Gentleman, bears a very good Character, has made a
great deal of Money, and married a Yorkshire Lady of a handsome fortune about [   ] months since. He again repeated
his invitation to me, to dine with him accompanied by Mr.
Smith. Tomorrow I go. Many Gentleman have called upon me
this forenoon so that I have only time to dress before dinner,
which I order at an earlier hour than the London fashion; at 3
is my hour and Breakfast at 9. I cannot dine earlier because
from nine till 3 I am subject to company. From the hours of 3
till 5 and 6 I am generally alone, or only Mr. Smith or Storer
here to whom I am never denied. The servant will frequently
come and ask me if I am at home!

Wednesday

I have walked out to day for the first time, and a jaunt Mr.
Storer has led me. I shall not get the better of it for a week.
The walking is very easy here, the sides of the street being
wholy of flat stones, and the London Ladies walk a great deal,
and very fast. My walk out, and in was only four miles, judge
you then what an Effect it had upon me. I was engaged to dine
out. I got home at one but was obliged to lie upon the bed an
hour, and have not recoverd it yet.

At four I was obliged to go out. Mr. Joy lives 3 miles from
where I lodge, the house in which he lives is very Elegant;
not large but, an air of taste and neatness is seen in every
appartment.

We were shewn into the drawing room where he waited us
at the door, and introduced us to his Lady and her sister.

She is quite young, delicate as a lily, modest and diffident,
not a London Lady by any means. After we had dinned, which
was in company with 5 American Gentlemen, we retired to the
drawing room, and there I talked off the Ladies reserve, and
she appeard agreeable. Her dress pleased me and answerd to
the universal neatness of the appartments furniture and entertainment. It was a delicate blew and white copper plate calico
with a blew Lutestring skirt flounced, a Muslin Apron and a

hankerchief, which are much more worn than Gauze; her hair
a fine black, drest without powder; with a fashionabl cap, and
Straw ribbons, upon her head and Breast, with a Green Moroco Sliper. Our dinner consisted of fryed fish of a small kind;
a boiled ham a fillet of veal a pair of roast ducks an almond
pudding; current and goose berries, which in this country are
very fine. Painted Muslin is much worn here, a straw hat, with
a deep Crown lined, and a white Green, or any coulourd ribbon you chuse. I returnd and found a Number of Cards left
from Gentleman who had called during my absence. To morrow I am invited to dine again with Mr. Atkingson and Lady. I
feel almost ashamed to go again, but not being otherways engaged they insist upon it. It is a thanksgiving day, for the
Peace. I design to hear Mr. Duchee who officiates at the Assylum or orphan house.

thursday

I found myself so unwell that I could not venture to day
into a crouded assembly. My walk Yesterday gave me a pain in
my head, and stiffned me so that I can scarcly move. Nabby
too has the London cold, which they say every body experiences who comes here. But Mr. and Mrs. Atkinson would not
excuse my dinning with them and Charly Storer came for us.
We went and found the same friendly hospitable attention,
nothing more on account of the day, a neat pretty dinner
consisting of two dishes and vegatables. After dinner returnd
the visit of Mr. and Mrs. Elworthy who were very glad to see
me. Mr. Elworthy carried us to Drapers Hall. This is a magnificent Building belonging to a company of that people, to
which is attached a most Beautifull Garden, to walk. In some
of these places; you would think yourself in a land of enchantment. It would just Suit my dear Betsys romantick fancy. Tell
her I design very soon to write to her; it shall be a discription
of some pretty Scene at the Hague, and Lucy shall have a Parissian Letter. But writing to one, I think I am writing to you
all.

fryday

To day my dear Sister I have determined upon tarrying at
home in hopes of seeing my Son; or his Pappa; but from a hint

dropt by Mr. Murray I rather think it will be my Son, as political reasons will prevent Mr. Adams'es journey here. Whilst I
am writing a servant in the family runs puffing in, as if he was
realy interested in the matter. "Young Mr. Adams is come."
"Where where is he," we all cried out? "In the other house
Madam, he stoped to get his Hair dresst." Impatient enough I
was, yet when he enterd, (we have so many Strangers), that I
drew back not realy believing my Eyes—till he cried out, "Oh
my Mamma! and my dear Sister." Nothing but the Eyes at first
Sight appeard what he once was. His appearence is that of a
Man, and in his countanance the most perfect good humour.
His conversation by no means denies his Stature. I think you
do not approve the word *feelings*, but I know not what to
Substitute in lieu, or even to discribe mine. His sister he says
he should have known in any part of the World. He inquired if
his Cousin Betsy had received a long letter of Several pages
which he wrote her in April.

Mr. Adams chuses I should come to the Hague, and travell
with him from thence. Says it is the first journey he ever lookd
forward to with pleasure since he came abroad; I wish to set
out on fryday, but as we are obliged to purchase a Carriage
and many other matters to do, Master John thinks we cannot
go untill the twesday after. In the mean time I shall visit the
curiositys of the city, not feeling 20 years younger, as my best
Friend says he does, but feeling myself exceedingly Matronly
with a grown up Son on one hand, and Daughter upon the
other, and were I not their Mother, I would Say a likelier pair
you will seldom see in a summers day.

You must supply words where you find them wanting and
imagine what I have left unfinished, for my letter is swelled to
such a Bulk, that I have not even time to peruse it. Mr. Smith
goes to morrow morning, and I must now close requesting
you to make the distribution of the little matters I send as directed. Tell Dr. Tufts my dear and valued uncle, and Friend,
that I design to write to him by the next vessel.

Particularly remember me to Uncle Quincy to Mrs. Quincy
and Nancy to all my dear Boston Friends. Tell Mr. Storer, that
Charly is very good to me; and that walking with Nabby the
other day; she was taken for his wife. Ask him if he consents?
Mr. and Mrs. Atkinson treat me like a sister, I cannot find

myself in a strange land. I shall experience this when I get to a country the language of which I cannot speak. I sincerely wish the treaty might have been concerted here. I have a partiality for this Country—but where my treasure is there shall my heart go. I know not when to close. You must write often to me and get Uncle Smith to cover to Mr. Atkinson, then where ever I am the letters will come safe. Adieu once more my dear sister and believe me most affectionately yours

A Adams

LANDED IN ENGLAND

To John Adams

London july 23. 1784. Osbornes
new family Hotel, Adelphi at
Mrs. Sheffields No. 6

My dearest Friend

At length Heaven be praised I am with our daughter safely landed upon the British Shore after a passage of 30 days from Boston to the Downs. We landed at Deal the 20 instant, rejoiced at any rate to set our feet again upon the land. What is past, and what we sufferd by sickness and fatigue, I will think no more of. It is all done away in the joyfull hope of soon holding to my Bosom the dearest best of Friends.

We had 11 passengers. We travelled from Deal to London all in company, and tho thrown together by chance, we had a most agreeable Set, 7 Gentlemen all except one, American, and marri'd men, every one of whom strove to render the passage agreeable and pleasent to us. In a more particular manner I feel myself obliged to Mr. Foster who is a part owner of the Ship, a modest kind obliging Man, who paid me every Service in his power, and to a Dr. Clark who Served his time with Dr. Loyd and is now in partnership with him. He took a kind charge of Nabby in a most Friendly and Brotherly way, shewed us every attention both as a Gentleman physician and sometimes Nurss, for we all stood in great want of both. My Maid was unfortunately sick the whole passage, my Man servant was so sometimes, in short for 2 or 3 days the Captain and

Dr. who had frequently been to sea before, were the only persons who were not sea sick. Capt. Lyde is a Son of Neptune, rather rough in his Manners, but a most excellent Sea man, never leaving his deck through the passage for one Night. He was very obligeing to me. As I had no particular direction to any Hotel when I first arrived a Gentleman passenger who had formerly been in London advised me to Lows Hotel in Covent Garden, where we stoped. My first inquiry was to find out Mr. Smith, who I presumed could inform me with respect to you. Mr. Spear a passenger undertook this inquiry for me, and in less than half an hour, both he and Mr. Storer, were with me. They had kindly provided lodgings for me to which I removed in the morning, after paying a Guiney and half for tea after I arrived and lodging and Breakfast a coach included to carry me to my lodgings. I am now at lodgings at 34 and 6 pence per week for myself daughter and two servants, my Man servant I left on Board the Ship to come up with it, but it has not yet got up. I drew upon you before I left America one Bill in favour of Dr. Tufts of an hundred pound Lawfull Money, 98 of which I paid for our passages. This Bill is to be paid to Mr. Elworthy. I drew for two hundred more in favour of Natll. Austin to be paid in Holland. One hundred and 80 pounds of this money I Shall bring with me to the Hague as I cannot use it here without loss, it being partly Dollors partly french crowns and French Guineys. Mr. Smith has advised me to this and tells me that what money I have occasion for he can procure me here. My expences in landing travelling and my first Nights entertainment have amounted to 8 Guineys. I had a few english Guineys with me. I shall wish to shelter myself under your wing immediately for the expences frighten me. We shall be dear to you in more senses than one. Mr. Jefferson I left in Boston going to Portsmouth where he designd spending a week and then to return to Newyork to take passage from thence to France. He urged me to wait his return and go with him to New York, but my passage was paid on Board Capt. Lyde, the Season of the Year was the best I could wish for, and I had no desire to take Such a journey in the Heat of summer. I thanked him for his politeness, but having taken my measures, I was determined to abide by them. He said Col. Humphries the Secretary to the commercial commission had

sailed before he left Philadelphia, and that he did not doubt I
Should find you in France. I have a Letter from him which I
inclose and Several other Letters from your Friends. Mr. Smith
thinks Master John will be here to Night from the intelligence
he forwarded to you before I arrived. I do not wish to tarry a
day here without you, so that if he comes I shall immediately
set out, provided I have not to wait for the Ship to come up.
How often did I reflect during my voyage upon what I once
heard you say, that no object in Nature was more dissagreeable
than a Lady at sea. It realy reconciled me to the thought of
being without you, for heaven be my witness, in no situation
would I be willing to appear thus to you. I will add an observation of my own, that I think no inducement less than that of
comeing to the tenderest of Friends could ever prevail with me
to cross the ocean, nor do I ever wish to try it but once more.
I was otherways very Sick, beside Sea Sickness, but you must
not expect to see me pined, for nothing less than death will
carry away my flesh, tho I do not think I eat more the whole
passage than would have sufficed for one week. My fatigue is
in some measure gone of and every hour I am impatient to be
with you.

Heaven give us a happy meeting prays your ever affectionate
A Adams

LONDON

To Elizabeth Smith Shaw

My dear sister   London july 28. 1784
I think when I finishd the last page I was rubbing myself
up on Board Ship. But this was not the only rubbing I had to
go through, for here is the stay maker, the Mantua maker,
the hoop maker, the shoe maker, the miliner and hair dresser
all of whom are necessary to transform me into the fashionable Lady. I could not help recollecting Molieres fine Gentleman with his danceing master his musick Master &c. nor
dispiseing the tyranny of fashion which obliges a reasonable
creature to submit to Such outrages. You inquire of me how I

like London. For particulars I refer you to sister Cranches
Letter, but I charge you as you expect to hear again from me,
not to expose it, or let any body see it, except Brother Shaw,
who is one and the same with yourself. My Lads may read it if
they please. I assure you my dear sister I am better pleased
with this city than I expected. It is a large magnificent, and
Beautifull city, most of the Streets 40 feet wide built strait, the
houses all uniform, no [   ] small tennaments, many fine
open Squares where the nobility reside, and where most of the
publick Buildings are Erected. I have been only to two or 3,
the foundling Hospital where I attended divine service on
sunday morning and to the Magdeline in the afternoon, of
which you will find an account in the Letter to which I refer
you. You will also learn from that all the particulars of my
voyage and journey. Mr. Adams is not yet come from the
Hague. I wrote him by the first opportunity, but the wind has
been contrary ever since I arrived. He had removed the family
which was in the House, out more than a month ago, and sent
Master John to wait for my Arrival in Calihan where he expected I had taken passage. He tarried here a month and upon
Callihans comeing went back, very low Spirited, and made his
Father more so, I am told by a Gentleman who accompanied
my son back, a Mr. Murray whom you will find mentiond in
my Letter to sister Cranch. Americans from all Quarters are
daily calling upon me, some of whom I know, and others whom
I never saw; out of Respect I presume to Mr. Adams, or curiosity
to see the wife and daughter. Amongst those of my American
acquaintance who have calld upon me, is a Mr. Joy of whom *you
once* had some knowledge. Nay Blush not my sister, he is still a
Character that you need not blush at having an Esteem for. I
was unfortunately not at home. He left his card with his Name,
and direction and a polite Billet requesting me to dine with him
to day if I was not engaged, and if I was, the first day I was
disengaged. He married a Yorkshire Lady and is in high esteem
here. So tomorrow I dine with him, being the first day I have.
I have received great politeness and attention from some of my
(Tory) acquaintanc. Mr. and Mrs. Hollowell came to see me
upon my arrival, invited me to dine with them, and then sent
an invitation to me to take up my Lodgings with them whilst I
resided in the city, then sent and presst me to accept the offer,

but I excused myself not chuseing on many accounts to encumber a private family, and having a large leavie, to Speak in
Stile. I however accepted their invitation to Dinner, and was
treated with a great deal of hospitality and kindness. Mrs. Atkinson [   ] and I have dined twice with her. Mrs. Hay I
have dined with once. She lives a mile or two from the city. I
was invited last Night to the play; but declined going for several reasons. Parson Walter amongst others has made me a
visit.

Tis Nine oclock and I have not Breakfasted, for we dine at
four and I am half dead. Dr. Clark one of my fellow passengers
whom I mentiond before and Col. Trumble are to Breakfast
with me, and here they are.

Two oclock.

From nine till 2 I have not had a moment. Mr. Appleton,
Mr. Joy Mr. Cushing Mr. Murray Mr. Storer and Smith have
all been to make their morning visits. Morning in this country
signifies from Nine oclock till 3 and from that hour till four,
you are left to yourself to dress for dinner. I do not conform
wholy, when I dine at my Lodgings, I have dinner at 3, but an
earlier hour would Subject me to company. The buisness of
this city is all done before dinner. I have never Supped abroad,
Suppers are little practised here, unless upon publick invitations. Mr. Smith received a Letter from Mr. Adams last evening
in replie to one he wrote him informing him that I had taken
passage in Captain Lyde. He tells him that it is the most agreeable News Next to that of my certain arrival, gives some directions with regard to me, expects to be obliged to set out for
France as soon as I reach the Hague. Before this; he has from
my own hand, received an account of my arrival. This is
wednesday; on fryday, I expect either Mr. Adams, or Master
John, and this day week, I shall set of for the Hague. I design
to see this week, Westminster Abbey, and the British Museum,
together with Mr. Wests paintings. I have been to see a very
Elegant picture of Mr. Adams which belongs to Mr. Copely,
and was taken by him, it is a larg full length picture. He is
drawn with a Globe before him: the Map of Europe in his
hand and at a distance 2 female figures representing Innocence,
and Peace. It is said to be an admirable likeness. I went from

Mr. Copelys to the Hay Market, to what is called Mr. Copelys exhibitions. These are open only for a certain Season: there are two or 3 most [   ] paintings here, the death of Lord Chatham in the house of Lords [   ] likenesses of every Member, and an other picture more Strikeing [   ] than that. This was a picture of Major Peirson and the defeat of the [   ] Troops in the Island of Jersey. Mrs. Cranch will send you the account of this which I have inclosed to her. One is ready upon viewing these pictures to apply those Lines of Popes upon Kneller.

> "Copely! by heavn and not a Master taught
> Whose Art was Nature, and whose pictures thought;"

Here is Mr. Storer come to Breakfast with me and then I am going out to *Cheep Side*; if to be found, but it is not this Side Boston I assure you; I am astonished to find that you can purchase no article here by retail but what comes much dearer than in Boston. I had heard these Stories; but never believed them before. I shall dine with Mr. Joy to day and when I return I will tell you all about our entertainment.

thursday morning

I went out yesterday as I told you I should; I had never been out before but in a Coach. Mr. Storer advised me to walk as it was a fine morning and the sides of the streets here are laid with flat stone as large as tile. The London Ladies walk a vast deal and very fast. I accordinly agreed to go out with him, and he led me a jaunt of full four miles. I never was more fatigued in my life, and to day am unable to walk across the room; having been on Board ship for some time, and never being used to walking: it was two miles too far for my first excursion; but if I was to live here I would practise Walking every day when the weather was pleasent. I went out at Nine and did not return untill one, when I was obliged to lye upon the bed an hour before I could dress me. In the mean time Mrs. Copely called upon me; and the Servant came up and asked me if *I was at Home*? The replie ought to have been no, but Ester not being yet accustomed to London Stile, replied yes. Fortunately Nabby was near dresst, so we past off Miss Adams, for Mrs. Adams, one being at home, the other not. You must know, having brought a concience from America with me, I could not reconcile this to it, but I am told not [   ] home; means no more, than that you are not at home to company. [   ] London visitors call, leave a card, without even an intention, or desire [   ] company; I went to see a Lady; the Gentleman inquired of the servant if his Mistress was at home, the servant replied "no sir," upon which he questiond the servant again, (this Gentleman was Husband to the Lady), upon which he stept out and return'd, "*realy* Mrs. Adams" Says he "She is gone out, and I am very sorry for it."

Well say you, but have you been yet to dine as you told me, with my old Friend? Yes I have: and was much pleased. This Gentleman retains all that pleasing softness of manners which he formerly possesst, in addition to these, he has all the politeness and ease of address which distinguish the Gentleman. He has been Married to a Yorkshire Lady about 3 Months, a Lady of fortune I am told. She has been Educated in the Country, and has none of the London airs about her. She is small, delicate as a Lily and Blushing as a rose, diffident as the sensitive plant which shrinks at the touch, their looks declare a unison of Hearts; Mr. Joy has made a great deal of money during the war and lives Elegantly, the dinning room and morning room were the most elegant of any I have Seen, the furniture all New, and had an air of neatness which pleased me; I am in Love with what I have seen of the London Stile of entertaining company. There were 4 American gentlemen who dinned with us. I would mention that fish and poultry of all kinds are extravagantly high here; we had a table neatly set, fish of a small kind, at the head; a ham in the middle, and a roast fillet of veal at the foot, peas and collyflower, an almond pudding and a pair of roast ducks were brought on, when the fish was removed, cherries and coosburries. One servant only to attend, but he a thorough master of his Buisness. This I am told was a much higher entertainment than you will commonly meet with at a Gentlemans table who has an income of 10 thousand a year. I have dined out Six times by invitation and have never met with so much as or so great a variety as yesterday at Mr. Joys table. This is a day set apart for publick thanksgiving for the peace. The Shops are all shut and there is more the appearence of Solemnity than on the Sabbeth, yet that is kept with more decency and decorum than I expected to find it.

The Churches which I attended last Sunday were large, yet were they crouded. I was to have attended divine Service to day at the Assylum or orphan House where Mr. Duchee formerly of Philadelphia, and chaplin to Congress, officiates, but my walk yesterday and a bad head ack prevents me; for in this country they keep the doors and windows shut; this in a crouded assembly is not only prejudicial to Health, but I soon grow faint; Nabby has taken a Sad cold by comeing out last Sunday from the Magdelin, tho we were in a coach; but tis the fashion they Say for all Stranger to have colds and coughs. I wonder not at it if they attend publick assemblies. It has not been warm enough, since I came into the city, to Set with the windows open, and for two Nights past I have had my bed warmed. Mr. and Mrs. Atkinson would not excuse us from dinning with them to day. Charles Storer calld for us about 3 oclock. This is a fine young fellow, uncorrupted amidst all the licentiousness of the age, he seems like a child to me; is as attentive and obligeing as possible. There is not a day when I do not have 10 to a dozen Americans to see me, many of the refugees amongst them. Mr. Leanard of Taunton made me a visit to day, assured me Mrs. Leanard would call upon me. Col. Norton Mr. Foster Mr. Spear Mr. Appleton Mr. Mason Mr. Parker have been our morning visitors. Dr. Clark comes 2 miles twice a day to see us, and is like one of our family. When say you do you write? Why I rise early in the morning and devote that part of the day to my pen. I have not attempted writing to many of my Friends, the Bugget is pretty much together. I have no leisure to coppy or correct, on that account beg I may not be exposed, for you know if one has a little credit and reputation we hate to part with it, and nothing but the interest which my Friends take in my welfare can possibly excuse Such a Scrible.

In the afternoon I called and drank tea with Mr. and Mrs. Elworthy to whom I had letters, and who very early called upon me. Mrs. Elworthy is a Neice of Brother Cranchs. They are Buisness folk, worthy good people, make no pretentions to fine living, but are of the obligeing Hospitable kind. He lives near a publick Building call'd Drapers Hall. The tradesmen of this Country are all formed into companys, and have publick Buildings belonging to them. This is a magnificent Eddifice at the end of which is a most Beautifull Garden surrounded by a very high wall, with four alcoves and rows of trees placed upon each side the walks: in the middle of the Garden is a fountain of circular form, in the midst of which is a large Swan; out of whose mouth the water pours; and is convey'd there by means of pipes under ground. Flowers of Various Sorts ornament this Beautifull Spot: when you get into these appartments and others which I have Seen similar; you are ready to fancy yourself in Fairy land, and the representations which you have seen of these places through Glasses, is very little hightned.

Whilst we were at dinner to day a Letter was brought to Nabby from her cousin Betsy. You can form an Idea how pleasing it was to hear from home only 25 days since. Dear Romantick Girl, her little narative of her visit to the deserted cottage made me weep; my affection for which is not lessned by all the Magnificent Scenes of the city, tho vastly beyond what our country can boast. Mr. Jefferson had a very quick passage, and tho he saild a fortnight after me, arrived here only Six days after me. He landed at Portsmouth and is gone on for France; this I imagine will make an alteration in my excursion to the Hague, as my Friends here advise me not to go on, untill Mr. Adams is acquainted with Mr. Jeffersons arrival. I know he must go to Paris, and by going directly there much time fatigue and expence will be Saved.

Either Master John or his Pappa will be here to day, unless detained by the wind. Mr. Smith sets of tomorrow in order to embark for America, so that my Letter must Soon come to a close. I send a Book for my little Nephew, and as I am going to France, I think to purchase your lace there where it can be bought upon better terms than here. Remember me to Mr. Thaxter. Tell him he must write to me, and he will find me punctual in return.

My dear Boys I will write them if I can possibly. My Love to them. Remember me to Mr. Whites family and to Judge Sergants, to good Mrs. Marsh and all others who inquire after Your ever affectionate Sister   A Adams

To John Adams

My dearest Friend

I was this day made very happy by the arrival of a son in whom I can trace the strongest likeness of a parent every way dear to me. I had thought before I saw him, that I could not be mistaken in him, but I might have set with him for some time without knowing him.

I am at a loss to know what you would wish me to do, as Mr. Jefferson arrived last week at Portsmouth, immediately from Boston, altho he saild a fortnight after me, and went on to Paris.

Some of my Friends suppose that you would rather I should proceed from hence; and agree upon meeting at Brussels than make the journey first to the Hague. If I was to follow my own inclinations I should set off next tuesday, but our son thinks I cannot come with convenience untill fryday. We have concluded upon this, to wait your replie to these Letters untill this day week, and come to the Hague or set of for Paris as you think best, or meet you at any place you may appoint. As to the article of cloathing I am full as much at a loss as you can possibly be. I have bought a Lutestring for myself and Nabby which I have had made, and Nabby is equipt with a rideing dress, but I thought the fewer I purchased here the better, as I was so soon to go to Paris, where I suppose it will be necessary to conform to the fashion. If by comeing on first to the Hague, I could relieve you from any trouble, or render you any assistance, I will most cheerfully perform the journey, but Mr. Storer thinks it will be attended with less trouble and expence; which is a matter worth considering, to proceed with my family to Paris. The sooner we meet the more agreeable it will be to me, for I cannot patiently bear any circumstance which detains me from the most desirable object in my estimation that hope has in store for me. I hardly dared flatter myself with the prospect of your comeing for me yourself, and was the less dissapointed when Master John arrived. I shall feel myself perfectly safe under his care. There are many Americans in this city, most of whom I believe have called upon me, some of whom were quite strangers to me. I have not been to any publick entertainment or even seen the curiositys of the city. I chose to wait yours or my Sons comeing. I have not sent on the Letters which I have for you as they contain no particular intelligence, are mere Letters of Friendship.

Nabby has had Letters from Boston, from Dr. Welch and her Cousin Betsy written only 25 days since. Mr. Tracy came out with Mr. Jefferson.

Adieu and believe me most affectionately, most tenderly yours and only yours and wholly yours.   A Adams

I have two excellent servants tho they are not used to the manners and customs of the country, one of whom the maid I am anxious for, never having had the small pox. Dr. Clark would have innoculated her upon her first comeing but I knew not whether we should stay here till she got through it.

July 30, 1784

AUTEUIL

To Elizabeth Cranch

My dear Betsy   Auteuil Sepbr. 5 1784

I am situated at a small desk in an appartment about 2 thirds as large as your own little Chamber; this appartment opens into my lodging Chamber which is handsome and commodious, and is upon a range with 6 or 7 others all of which look into the Garden. My Chamber is hung with a rich India patch, the bed, Chairs and window curtains of the same, which is very fashionable in this Country, two handsome Beaureaus, with marble tops make up the furniture, which wants only the addition of a carpet to give it all, the air of Elegance, but in lieu of this is a tile floor, in the shape of Mrs. Quincys carpet, with the red much worn of and defaced, the dust of which you may suppose not very favourable to a long train. But since I came we have been at the expence of having several of the floors new painted. This is done with Spanish brown and [   ] afterward with melted wax, and then rubbed with a hard Brush; upon which a Man sets his foot and with his Arms a kimbow striped to his Shirt, goes driveing round your room. This Man is called a Frotteurer, and is a Servant kept on purpose for the Buisness. There are some floors of wood which resemble our black walnut, these are made of small strips of wood about six inches wide, and placed on Squares; which are rubbed with wax, and Brushes in the same manner I have before discribed: water is an article spairingly used. I procured a woman when I first came, (for the house was excessive dirty), to assist Ester in cleaning. I desired her to wash up the dinning room floor, which is stone made in the same shape of the tile, so she turnd a pail of water down and took a house Brush and swept it out. You would think yourself poisoned, untill time reconciled you to it.

I have however got this place to look more like neatness than any thing I have yet seen. What a contrast this to the Hague? The Garden Betsy! let me take a look at it. It is delightfull, such a Beautifull collection of flowers all in Bloom, so sweetly arranged with rows of orange Trees, and china vases of flowers. Why you would be in raptures. It is square and contains about 5 acres of land, about a 3d. of the Garden is laid out in oblongs, octagons, circles &c. filled with flowers; upon each side are spacious walks with rows of orange trees and pots of flowers, then a small walk, and a wall coverd with grape vines; in the middle of the Garden a fountain of water in a circle walled; about 2 foot, and a thin circle of fence painted Green, in the midst of which are two little images carved in Stone. Upon each Side, and at a proper distance, are two small alcoves filled with curious plants exoticks; and round these are placed pots of flowers which have a most agreable appearence, then a small open chineess fence coverd with grape vines, and wall fruit incloses 2 Spots upon each side, which contains vegetables surrounded by orange trees; which prevents your view of them untill you walk to them: at the bottom of the Garden are a number of Trees, the Branches of which unite and form Beautifull Arbours, the tops of the Trees cut all even enough to walk upon them, and look as I set now at the window like one continued tree through the whole range. There is a little summer house coverd by this thicket, Beautifull in ruins, 2 large alcoves in which are two statues terminate the view; the windows to all the apartments in the house are rather Glass doors, reaching from the Top to the bottom, and opening in the middle; give one a full and extensive view of the Garden. This is a Beautifull climate, soft and serene and temperate, but *Paris* you must not ask me how I like it—because I am going to tell you of the pretty little appartment next to this in which I am writing; why my dear you cannot turn yourself in it without being multiplied 20 times. Now that I do not like; for being rather clumsy and by no means an elegant figure, I hate to have it so often repeated to me. This room is about ten or 12 foot large, is 8 cornerd and panneld with looking Glasses, a red and white india patch with pretty borders encompasses it: low back stuft chairs with Garlands of flowers incircleing them adorn this little chamber, festoons of flowers are round all the Glasses, a Lusture hangs from the cealing adornd with flowers, a Beautifull Soffa is placed in a kind of alcove with pillows and cushings in abundance the use of which I have not yet investigated. In the top of this alcove over the Soffa in the cealing is an other Glass, here is a Beautifull chimny peice with an elegant painting of Rural Life in a country farm house, lads and lasses jovial and happy. This little apartment opens in to your cousins bed Chamber. It has a most pleasing view of the Garden, and it is that view which always brings my dear Betsy to my mind, and makes me long for her to enjoy the delights of it with me; in this appartment I sit and sew, whilst your uncle is engaged at Passy where the present negotiations are carried on, and your cousin John in his appartment translating lattin, your cousin Nabby in her chamber writing, in which she employs most of her time: she has been twice at the opera with her Brother, of which I suppose she will write you an account. The present owner of this House and the Builder of it, is a M. le Comte de Rouhaut. He married young to a widow worth 1,800,000 Livres per annum, 80,000 £ Sterling, which in the course of a few years they so Effectually dissipated, that they had not 100,000 £ Sterling remaining. They have been since that seperated. By some inheritances and legacies the count is now worth about a 100,000 livres a year and the Countess 75,000. They have a Theatre in this house now gone to decay, where for 8 years together they play'd Comedies and tragedies twice a week, and gave entertainments at the same time which cost them 200 £ Sterling every time, they entertaind between 4 and 5 hundred persons at a time. The looking Glasses in this house I have been informd cost 300 thousand liveres. Under this Chamber which I have discribed to you is a room of the same bigness in which is an elegant Bathing convenience let into the floor and the room is encompassed with more Glass than the Chamber, the ceiling being intirely glass. Here too is a Soffa surrounded with curtains.

Luxury and folly are strong and characteristick traits of the Builder. There are appartments of every kind in this House, many of which I have never yet enterd.

Those for which I have a use are calculated for the ordinary purposes of Life, and further I seek not to know.

Write to me my dear Girl and tell me every thing about my dear Friends and country. Remember me to your Brother, to your sister I will write, to Mr. Tyler I hope to be able to send at least a few lines. Tis very expensive sending letters by the post, I must look for private opportunities to London. Adieu I hear the carriage; your uncle is come. I go to hasten tea of which he is still fond: yours sincerely   AA

PARIS

To Lucy Cranch

My dear Lucy   Auteuil Sepbr 5 1784

I promised to write to you from the Hague, but your uncles unexpected arrival at London prevented me. Your uncle purchased an Excellent travelling Coach in London, and hired a post chaise for our servants. In this manner We travelled from London to Dover, accommodated through England with the best of Horses postilions, and good carriages, clean neat appartments, genteel entertainment, and prompt attendance, but no sooner do you cross from Dover to Caliss than every thing is reversed, and yet the distance is very small between them.

The cultivation is by no means equal to that of England, the villages look poor and mean the houses all thatchd and rarely a Glass window in them. Their Horses instead of being hand-somely harnessed as those in England are, have the appearence of so many old cart horses. Along you go with 7 Horses tied up with roaps and chains rattleing like trucks, 2 ragged postil-ions mounted with enormous jack Boots, add to the comick Scene. And this is the Stile in which a Duke or a count travel through this kingdom. You inquire of me how I like Paris? Why they tell me I am no judge, for that I have not seen it yet. One thing I know, and that is, that I have smelt it. If I was agreeably dissapointed in London, I am as much dissapointed in Paris. It is the very dirtyest place I ever saw. There are some Buildings and some Squares which are tolerable, but in general the streets are narrow, the shops, the houses inelegant, and dirty, the Streets full of Lumber and Stone with which they Build. Boston cannot Boast so elegant publick Buildings, but in every other respect, it as much Superiour in my Eyes to Paris, as London is to Boston. To have had Paris tolerable to me; I should not have gone to London. As to the people here, they are more given to Hospitality than in England, it is said.

I have been in company with but one French Lady since I arrived, for strangers here make the first visit and nobody will know you untill you have waited upon them in form.

This Lady I dined with at Dr. Franklings. She enterd the Room with a careless jaunty air. Upon seeing Ladies who were strangers to her, she bawled out ah Mon dieu! where is Frank-ling, why did you not tell me there were Ladies here? You must suppose her speaking all this in French. How said she I look? takeing hold of a dressing chimise made of tiffanny which She had on over a blew Lutestring, and which looked as much upon the decay as her Beauty, for she was once a handsome woman. Her Hair was fangled, over it she had a small straw hat with a dirty half gauze hankerchief round it, and a bit of dirtyer gauze than ever my maids wore was sewed on behind. She had a black gauze Skarf thrown over her shoulders. She ran out of the room. When she returnd, the Dr. enterd at one door she at the other, upon which she ran forward to him, caught him by the hand, helas Frankling, then gave him a double kiss one upon each cheek and an other upon his forehead. When we went into the room to dine she was placed between the Dr.

and Mr. Adams. She carried on the chief of the conversation at dinner, frequently locking her hand into the Drs. and sometimes spreading her Arms upon the Backs of both the Gentlemans Chairs, then throwing her Arm carelessly upon the Drs. Neck.

I should have been greatly astonished at this conduct, if the good Doctor had not told me that in this Lady I should see a genuine French Woman, wholy free from affectation or stifness of behaviour and one of the best women in the world. For this I must take the Drs. word, but I should have set her down for a very bad one altho Sixty years of age and a widow. I own I was highly disgusted and never wish for an acquaintance with any Ladies of this cast. After dinner she threw herself upon a settee where she shew more than her feet. She had a little Lap Dog who was next to the Dr. her favorite. This She kisst and when he wet the floor she wiped it up with her chimise. This is one of the Drs. most intimate Friends, with whom he dines once every week and She with him. She is rich and is my near Neighbour, but I have not yet visited her. Thus my dear you see that Manners differ exceedingly in different Countries. I hope however to find amongst the French Ladies manners more consistant with my Ideas of decency, or I shall be a mere recluse.

You must write to me and let me know all about you. Marriages Births and preferments—every thing you can think of. Give my respects to the Germantown family. I shall begin to get Letters for them by the next vessel.

Good Night. Believe me your most affectionate Aunt

Abigail Adams

HOUSEKEEPING IN FRANCE

To Mary Smith Cranch

My dear Sister   Autuel distant from Paris 4 miles

It is now the 5th of September, and I have been at this place more than a fortnight, but I have had so many Matters to arrange, and so much to attend to, since I left London, that I have scarcly touchd a pen. I am now vastly behind hand in many things which I could have wished to have written down and transmitted to my American Friends, some of which would have amused them: and others diverted them. But such a rapid succession of events, or rather occurrences have been crouded into the last two Months of my Life, that I can scarcly recollect them, much less recount them by detail. There are so many of my Friends who have demands upon me, and who I fear will think me neglegent that I know not which to address first.

Nabby has had less of care upon her, and therefore has been very attentive to her pen, and I hope will supply my difficiences.

Auteuel is a Village 4 miles distant from Paris, and one from Passy. The House we have taken is large, commodious, and agreeably situated, near the woods of Bolign which belong to the King, and which Mr. Adams calls his park, for he walks an hour or two every day in them. The House is much larger than we have need of, upon occasion 40 beds may be made in it. I fancy it must be very cold in Winter. There are few houses with the privilege, which this enjoys, that of having the saloon as it is called the Appartment where we receive company upon the first floor. This room is very elegant and about a 3d larger than General Warrens Hall. The dinning room is upon the right hand, and the saloon; upon the left of an entry, which has large Glass doors opposite to each other, one opening into the Court as they call it, the other into a large and beautifull Garden. Out of the dinning room you pass through an entry into the kitchen which is rather small for so large a House. In this entry are stairs which you assend, at the Top of which; is a long Gallery fronting the street with 6 windows and opposite each window, you open into the Chambers, which all look into the garden.

But with an expence of 30,000 liveres in looking Glasses there is no table in the house better than an oak Board, nor a carpet belonging to the House. The floors I abhor, made of red tile in the shape of Mrs. Quincys floor cloth tile. These floors will by no means bear water, so that the method of cleaning them is to have them wax't and then a Man Servant with foot Brushes drives round Your room dancing here, and there, like a merry Andrew. This is calculated to take from your foot every atom of dirt, and leave the room in a few moments as he found it. The house must be exceeding cold in winter. The dinning rooms; of which you make no other use, are laid in small stone like the red tile, for shape and size. The Servants appartments are generally upon the first floor; and the Stairs which you commonly have to assend to get into the family appartments; are so dirty that I have been obliged to hold up my Cloaths as tho I was passing through a cow yard. I have been but little abroad; it is customary in this country for strangers to make the first visit. As I cannot speak the language, I think I should make rather an awkward figure; I have dined abroad several times; with Mr. Adams'es particular Friends the Abbes, who are very polite and civil, 3 Sensible worthy Men. The Abbe Mabble has lately published a Book which he has dedicated to Mr. A. This Gentleman is near 80 years old the Abbe Charnon 75 and Arnou about 50, a fine sprightly Man, who takes great pleasure in obligeing his Friends, their appartments were really nice. I have dinned once at Dr. Franklings, and once at Mr. Barcleys our Consuls, who has a very agreeable woman for his wife, and where I feel like being with a Friend. Mrs. Barcley has assisted me in my purchases, gone with me to different shops &c. Tomorrow I am to dine at Monsieur Grands. But I have really felt so happy within doors, and am so pleasingly situated that I have had little inclination to change the Scene. I have not been to one publick Amusement as yet, not even the opera tho we have one very near us. You may easily suppose I have been fully employed beginning house keeping anew, and Arrangeing my family, to our no small expence and trouble, for I have had bed linnen table linnen to purchase and make, spoons and forks to get made of silver 3 dozen of each, besides tea furniture, china for the table, servants to procure &c. The expence of living abroad I always supposed to be high, but my Ideas were no ways adequate to the thing. I could have furnished myself in the Town of Boston with every thing I have, 20 and 30 per cent cheaper than I have been able to do it here. Every thing which will bear the name of Elegant, is imported from England, and if you will have it, you must pay for it, duties and all. I cannot get a dozen handsome wine Glasses under 3 guineys, nor a pair of small decanters, for less than 1 and half. The only gauze fit to wear is english at a crown per yard, so that realy a guiney goes no

further than a Copper with us. For this House Garden Stables
&c we give 200 Guineys per year. Wood is 2 Guineys and half
per Cord. Coal 6 livers per Basket about 2 Bushel. This article
of fireing we calculate at a 100 Guineys per Year. The difference
of comeing upon this negotiation to France, and that of remaining at the Hague where the House was already furnisht at
the expence of a thousand pounds Sterling, will increase the
expence here to 600 Guineys or 700, at a time too, when
congress have Cut of 500 Guineys from what they have heretofore given. For our coachman and horses alone, (Mr. Adams
purchased a coach in England) we give 15 Guineys per month.
It is the policy of this country to oblige you to a certain number of servants, and one will not touch what belongs to the
buisness of an other, tho he or she has time enough to perform
the whole. In the first place there is a Coachman who does not
an individual thing but attend to the Carriages and horses.
Then the Gardner who has buisness enough. Then comes the
cook, the Maiter de Hotle, his Buisness is to purchase articles
into the family and oversee that no body cheats but himself, a
valet de Chamber John serves in this capacity, a femme de
Chambre Ester serves in this line, and is worth a dozen others,
a Coëffeire de Chambre, for this place I have a french Girl
about 19 whom I have been upon the point of turning away
because Madam will not brush a Chamber. It is not de fashion,
it is not her buisness. I would not have kept her a day longer,
but found upon inquiry that I could not better myself. Hair
dressing here is very expensive unless you keep such a Madam
in the house. She Sews tolerably well so I make her as usefull as
I can, she is more particularly devoted to Madamosel. Ester
diverted me yesterday evening by telling me that she heard her
go muttering by her chamber door after she had been assisting
Nabby in dressing. Ha mon dieu, tis provokeing, tis provokeing. She talks a little english. Why whats the matter Paulin,
what is provokeing? Why Mademosel look so pretty I so
Mauvai.

There is an other indispensable Servant who is called a
Frotteurer. His buisness is to rub the floors, and to do a still
dirtier peice of Buisness, for it is the fashion of the country,
and against that neither reason convenience or any thing else
can stand, or prevail, tho there is plenty of land and places

sufficiently convenient for Buildings, no such thing is known out of your own House, to every appartment of which, you have accommadations. But I hate them as a part of their poison.

We have a servant who acts as Maiter de Hottle, whom I like at present, and who is so very gracious as to act as footman too, to save the expence of an other servant; upon condition that we give him a Gentlemans suit of cloath in lieu of a Livery. Thus with 7 servants and hireing a chore woman upon occasion of company, we may possibly make out to keep house; with less we should be hooted at as ridiculous and could not entertain any company. To tell this in our own Country would be considerd as extravagance, but would they send a person here in a publick Character to be a publick jeast. At Lodgings in Paris last year, during Mr. Adams negotiations for a peace, it was as expensive to him as it is now at house keeping without half the accommodations.

Washing is an other expensive article. The servants are all allowed theirs; besides their wages, our own cost us a Guiney a week; I have become Steward and Book keeper determining to know with accuracy what our expences are, and to prevail with Mr. Adams to return to America if he finds himself straigtned as I think he must be. Mr. Jay went home because he could not support his family here, with the whole Sallery. What then can be done, curtailled as it now is with the additional expence. Mr. Adams is determined to keep as little company as he possibly can, but some entertainments we must make and it is no unusual thing for them to amount from 50 to 60 Guineys at a time. More is to be performed by way of negotiation many times at one of these entertainments, than at 20 serious conversations, but the policy of our country has been, and still is, to be a penney wise, and a pound foolish. We stand in sufficient need of oconomy, and in the curtailment of other salleries I suppose they thought it absolutely necessary to cut of their foreign ministers, but my own interest apart, the system is bad, for that Nation which degrades their own ministers by obligeing them to live in narrow circumstances cannot expect to be held in high estimation themselves. We spend no evening abroad, make no suppers attend very few publick entertainments or spectacles as they are called, and avoid every expence which is not held indispensable. Yet I cannot but think it hard, that a Gentleman who has devoted So great a part of his Life to the publick service, who has been the means in a great measure, of procureing such extensive territories to his country, who saved their fisheries, and who is still Labouring to procure them further advantages; should find it necessary so cautiously to Calculate his pence for fear of over running them. I will add one more expence. There is now a court mourning and every foreign minister with his family must go into mourning, for a prince of eight years old whose Father is an ally to the King of France, this mourning orderd by the Court and to be worn Eleven days only: poor Mr. Jefferson had to hie away for a Tailor to get a whole black silk suit made up in two days, and at the end of Eleven days should an other death happen, he will be obliged to have a new Suit of mourning of Cloth, because that is the Season when Silk must be cast of. We may groan and scold but these are expences which cannot be avoided. For Fashion is the Deity every one worships in this country and from the highest to the lowest you must submit. Even poor John and Ester had no comfort amongst the servants, being constantly the Subjects of their ridicule, untill we were obliged to direct them to have their Hair drest. Ester had several Crying Spells upon the occasion that she should be forced to be so much of a fool: but there was no way to keep them from being trampled upon but this; and now they are a la mode de Paris, they are much respected. To be out of fashion is more criminal than to be seen in a state of Nature to which the Parissians are not averse. What my dear Sister can you conceive of the Manners of a Country, one city of which has 52 thousand licenced unmarried women, Who, are so lost to a sense of shame, and virtue, as publickly to enter their Names at the police, for abandoned purposes. This I heard from the mouth of one of the Abbee's who is a man of virtue, and unblemished Character.

Sunday here bears the nearest resemblance to our commencement and Elections days. Every thing is jolity and mirth and recreation.

But to quit these subjects, pray tell me how you all do. I long to hear from you. House and Garden with all its decorations, are not so dear to me as my own little Cottage connected with the Society I used there to enjoy, for out of my own family I have no attachments in Europe, nor do I think I ever shall have. As to the language I speak it a little, bad grammer, and all, but I have So many French Servants that I am under a necessity of trying.

Could you my sister and my dear cousins come and see me, as you used to do, walk in the Garden and delight ourselves in the alcoves and Arbours, I should enjoy myself much better. When Mr. Adams is absent, I set in my little writing room, or the chamber I have discribed to Betsy, and read, or sew. Nabby is for ever at her pen, writing or learning French. Sometimes company and sometimes abroad we are fully employed.

Who do you think dined with us the other day. A Mr. Mather and his Lady son of Dr. Mather and Mrs. Hay who have come to spend the winter in France; I regret that they are going to some of the provinces. To day Mr. Tracy Mr. Williams Mr. Jefferson and Humphries are to dine with us, and one day last week we had a company of 27 persons. Dr. Frankeling Mr. Hartly and his Secretary &c. &c. But my paper warns me to close. Do not let any body complain of me. I am going on writing to one after an other as fast as possible. If this vessel does not carry them the next will. Give my Love to one of the best Men in the world. Affectionately Yours.   A A

September 5, 1784

OFFICIAL DINNERS AND HAIRDRESSING

To Elizabeth Cranch

No. 3

My dear Betsy   December 3. 1784

I had my dear Girl such an obligeing visit from you last Night, and such sweet communion with you that it has really overcome the reluctance which I have for my pen, and induced me to take it up, to tell you that my Night was more to my taste than the day, altho that was spent in the company of Ambassadors Barons &c. and was one of the most agreeable parties we have yet entertaind.

I do not recollect that I once mentiond to you during all
your visit, the company of the day, nor any thing respecting
the Customs and habits of the Country where I reside. I was
wholly wrapt up in inquiries after those Friends who are much
dearer to me, and who are bound faster to my Heart, I think
for being seperated from them. And now my dear girl I have
told you a truth respecting the pleasure your company afforded
me, and the pleasing account you gave me of our own dear
Friends and Country. I suppose your curiosity is a little raised
with respect to the Company I mentiond. I could write you an
account every week, of what I dare say would amuse you, but
I fear to take my pen least I should give it a Scope that would
be very improper for the publick Character with which I am
connected, and the Country where I reside.

It is necessary in this Country for a Gentleman in a publick
Character to entertain Company once a week, and to have a
Feast in the Stile of the Country. As your uncle had been invited to dine at the Tables of many of the foreign ministers
who reside here, it became necessary to return the civility, by
at least giving them as good dinners, tho it could take 2 years
of an American ministers Sallery to furnish the equipage of
plate which you will find upon the tables of all the Foreign
ministers here; Monsieur D'Ambassodor de Sweed was invited
together with Mr. d'Asp the Secratary of Legation, the Baron
de Geer and the Baron de Walterstorff, two very agreeable
young Noble Men who Speak english. The Sweedish Ambassodor is a well made genteel Man very polite and affable, about
30 years old. Mr. Jefferson and Dr. Franklin were both invited
but were too sick to come out. Col. Humphries Secratary to
the American Embassy and Mr. Short private Secratary to Mr.
Jefferson, Mr. Jackson and Mr. Tracy Mr. and Mrs. Bingham
Dr. Bancroft and Chevalier Jones made up the company.

Col. Humphries is from Connetticut a dark complextion
Stout well made Warlike looking gentleman of about 30 years
old, you may read in his face industery probity and good
Sense. Mr. Short is a younger Man, he is but just arrived from
Virginna, appears to be modest and Soft in his Manners. Mr.
Jackson and Tracy you know. Dr. Bancroft is a Native of
America. He may be 35 or 40 years old. His first appearence is
not agreeable, but he has a smile which is of vast advantage to

his features enlightening them and dispelling the Scowl which appears upon his Brow. He is pleasent and entertaining in conversation, a Man of literature and good Sense. You know he is said to be the Author of Charles Wentworth. Chevalier Jones you have heard much of. He is a most uncommon Character. I dare Say you would be as much dissapointed in him as I was. From the intrepid Character he justly Supported in the American Navy, I expected to have seen a Rough Stout warlike Roman. Instead of that, I should sooner think of wraping him up in cotton wool and putting him into my pocket, than sending him to contend with Cannon Ball.

He is small of stature, well proportioned, soft in his Speach easy in his address polite in his manners, vastly civil, understands all the Etiquette of a Ladys Toilite as perfectly as he does the Masts Sails and rigging of a Ship. Under all this appearence of softness he is Bold enterprizing ambitious and active.

He has been here often, and dined with us several times. He is said to be a Man of Gallantry and a favorite amongst the French Ladies: whom he is frequently commending for the neatness of their persons their easy manners and their taste in dress. He knows how often the Ladies use the Baths, what coulour best suits a Ladys complextion, what Cosmecticks are most favourable to the skin. We do not often See the Warriour and the *Abigail* thus united. Mr. and Mrs. Bingham bring up the rear, both of whom are natives of America. He is about 25 and she 20. He is said to be rich and to have an income of four thousand a year. He married this Lady at Sixteen, She is a daughter of Mr. Willing of Philadelphia. They have two little Girls now with them, and have been travelling into England Holland and France. Here they mean to pass the winter in the gaietys and amusements of Paris. Tis Said he wishes for an appointment here as foreign Minister, he lives at a much greater expence than any American minister can afford to. Mrs. Bingham is a fine figure and a Beautifull person, her manners are easy and affible but she was too young to come abroad without a pilot, gives too much into the follies of this Country, has money enough and knows how to lavish it with an unspairing hand. Less money and more Years may make her wiser, but She is so handsome she must be pardoned. Mr. and Mrs. Church are here too, alias Cartar. Mrs. Church is a delicate little woman. As to him, his character is enough known in America.

December 13

Since writing the above I have had the pleasure of receiving your obliging Letter of September 26. I believe I wrote you a Letter of nearly the Same date in which I think I must have satisfied some of your particular inquiries respecting House Gardens and appartments, and if it will be any Satisfaction to you to know where this Letter is written, I will tell you; in your Cousin Jacks Chamber. He is writing at his desk and I at a table by the fire. It is customary in this Country to live upon the second floor. There are a Row of Chambers the length of the House which all look into the Garden, into the first which makes one corner of the House I am now writing. It is [   ] in the Same manner as if it was paper, with a [   ] white chinzt, the bed, curtains, window curtain, and Chairs, of the Same. A Marble mantletree over which is a looking Glass in the fashion of the Country, which are all fixed into the walls, it is about four foot wide and 5 long. Then their is between the windows a handsome Bureau with a Marble Top, the draws gilded like trimming them with a broad gold Lace, and another looking Glass like that I have just mentiond; there is a little appartment belonging to this Chamber about as larg as your Library; which has a Soffa of red and white copper plate and 6 chairs of the Same. This too looks into the Garden and is a pritty summer appartment. Between this Chamber and the Next is the stair case upon the other side of which is the Chamber in which we all associate together when we are not in our seperate rooms. This is properly Your uncles Room, because there he writes and receives his forenoon company. This Chamber has two large glasses and furnished much in the same stile with the one I have discribed, the furniture being red and white. Next to that is a Chamber calld an antichamber paperd with a blew and white paper one glass only and one window. [   ] this going into my lodging Chamber which is large and furnishd in the same stile with the others only that the figures are all chinese, [   ] horrid looking creatures. Out of my chamber all in the same row is a little Room for a dressing room and one of the same kind next to it, which is in warm weather my writing room, having 2 little Book cases and a small Escriture. Next to that is the *Delicious* little appartment which I formerly told you of: and then your Cousins Nabbys appartment which makes the other corner of the house. There are very Clever apartments up the second pair of stairs over these chambers, but they are out of repair. Their are two wings in which there are a number of Chambers, one of which Ester and Paulina keep in, allways having a fire to themselves. Who say you is Paulina? Why she is Your cousins Chamber Maid and our Hair Dresser. Every Lady here must have a female Hair dresser, so these Girls serve an apprentiship to the buisness like any other trade, and give from 5 to 8 Guineys for their lerning. Then they are qualified to dress a Lady, make her bed, and sew a very little. I have however got this to lay asside some of her airs and to be a very clever girl. Whilst Ester was sick she was as kind to her and as carefull, as if she was her sister, watching with her night after night. The Cook too, upon this occasion was very kind. And Paulina has under taken to learn Ester to dress Hair, which will be a vast advantage to me if as I fear, I should be obliged to go away this winter. It is very unpleasent to break up a house, to part with ones servants and to set all affloat, not knowing where your next residence will be.

What a Letter this? I hope it is sufficiently particular to sat- isfy all your curiosity, but do not shew it as a specimin of Aunt A's abilities. Enter Miss Paulina, Madam vous alléz faire mettre des papillottes a vos Cheveux aujourd'hui? Il est midi. Oui. Je viens, so you see my pen must be laid asside for this important buisness. I commonly take a play of Voltaire or some other French Book to read, or I should have no patience. The buis- ness being compleated I, have a little advice to give you re- specting the French [   ] You had begun to learn it before I left America. Your good pappa many years ago gave me what is called a little smattering of it, but Indolence and the apprehen- sion that I could not read it without a preceptor made me ne- glect it. But since I came here, I found I must read french or nothing. Your uncle to interest me in it, procured for me Ra- cine, Voltaire Corneille and Cribillons plays, all of which are at times acted upon the French Theater. I took my dictionary and applied myself to reading a play a day, by which mean I have made considerable progress, making it a rule to write down every word which I was obliged to look. Translating a few lines every day into english would be an other considerable help and as your pappa so well understands the language he would assist in inspecting Your translation. By this means and with the assistance of the Books which You may find in the office you will be able to read it well in a little while. Do you look in the office for Racines plays and Voltaires and engage in them I will answer for your improvement, especially that volum of Voltaire which contains his Zaire, and Alzire, the latter is one of the best plays I ever read; there is a commedy of his called Nanine which I saw acted. I wish my dear I could transport you in a Baloon and carry you to the Stages here: you would be charmed and enchanted with the Scenerary the Musick the dresses and the action.

An other time I will discribe to you all these Theaters. At present I am shortned for time. Mr. Jackson and Mr. Tracy talk of going on thursday, and Say our Letters must be ready. They will be out here tomorrow morning, and I have not written to more than half the Friends I designd to. Give my Love to cousin Lucy and tell her she is indebted to me a Letter. How is Aunt Tufts. You did not say a word about her. My duty to her, I will give her some account of some pretty place that it is probable I shall visit before long. Who is [   ] at Weymouth? And are they like to settle any body? How does Mr. and Mrs. Weld. I had a visit from Mrs. Hay since I have been here. She is in France at a place called Beaugenci about a 100 miles from Paris. I have had several Letters from her. She was well about 10 days ago.

Let Mrs. Feild know that Ester is very happy and contented, that I have not been able in France to procure for her the small pox as I expected; she has not been exposed living out of Paris and in Paris it is not permitted to innoculate. I made inquiries about it of a physician. If I should go to London again I shall there endeavour that she has it. She and my other Chamber Maid keep in a chamber by themselves. One of them makes the Beds and the other sweeps the Chambers which is all they have to do in the [   ] way from monday morning, till Saturday night. When Ester was well, she undertook with Palina to wash and do up my muslin and lawn, because they batterd it to death here. She is cleverly now, tho she had a severe turn for a week. John has not had very good Health, he was sick soon after he came here; but is pretty smart now, and an honest good servant. John always waits upon me when I dine abroad and tends behind my chair as the fashion of this Country is always to carry your servants with you. He looks very smart with his Livery, his Bag and his ruffels and his Lace hat. If possible I will write to Germantown, but I neglect writing when I ought, and when I feel roused I have so much of it to do; that Some one has cause to be offended at my neglect; and then I never know when I once begin how to come to that part which bids you adieu, tho beginning and end I can always assure you of the affectionate Regard of Your Aunt

Abigail Adams

"PARIS IS A HORRID DIRTY CITY"

To Elizabeth Smith Shaw

My dear Sister   Auteuil December 14th 1784

I know your good will to have written to me if you had been able. It gives me pain to hear that you were not. Hearing of your indisposition was the only alloy to the pleasure I experienced when my last pacquet arrived. I fear you are not sufficiently carefull of your Health. Let me beg of you, and if you will not hear, Let me desire Mr. Shaw to assert the authority of a *Husband* and forbid your ever touching *wet* Cloaths, or Ironing, which is but a slow poison for you in Your state of Health. You know my sister that you were not the production of sound Health, but that the infirmities of the Parent have been visited upon the Child, and that your constitution is heriditarily feeble. Let me read you a medical lesson from a favorite Author, Buckhan, who says more consumptive patients date the beginning of their disorders from wet feet; damp Beds, Night air, wet Cloaths or catching cold; than to any other especially after the body has been overheated. As to the Regimin for people of weak lungs; he advices to Milk light food fruits &c and to riding even long journeys to a voyage at sea, but for the latter I imagine you will have no inclination.

From the interest you take in every thing which concerns your Friends, I hear you inquiring how I do? How I live, whom I see? Where I visit, who visits me? I know not whether Your curiosity extends So far as the coulour of the House which is white stone, and to the furniture of the Chamber where I sleep. If it does you must apply to Betsy Cranch for information whose fancy has imployd itself so Busily as to seek for intelligence even in the minutias; and altho they look trifling upon paper, yet if our Friends take an interest in them that renders them important, and I am the rather tempted to a compliance from the recollection, that when I have received a sentimental Letter from an absent Friend, I have passt over the sentiment at the first reading, and hunted for that part which more particuliarly related to themselves.

This Village where we reside is four miles from Paris, and is famous for nothing that I know of, but the learned Men who have inhabitted it. Such was Boileau, Mollire, d'Aguesseau and Helvitius. The first and last lived near this Hotel, and Boileaus garden is preserved as a Choice relict. As to my own Health it is much as usual. I suffer through want of excersise, and grow too fat. I cannot persuade my self to walk an hour in the day in a long entry which we have merely for exercise, and as to the Streets they are continually a Quagmire; no walking there without Boots or Wooden Shoes, neither of which are my feet calculated for. Mr. Adams makes it his constant practise to walk several miles every day without which he would not be able to preserve his Health; which at best is but infirm. He professes himself so much happier for having his family with him, that I feel amply gratified in having ventured across the ocean. He is determined that nothing but the enevitable Stroke of Death shall in future seperate him; at least from one part of it, So that I know not what climates I may yet have to visit. More I fear than will be agreeable to either of us. Master John, who is a Man in most respects: all I may say but age; wishes to return to his own Country, and to become a while a resident in your family; that he may acquire what ever knowledge is necessary, for spending one year at Harvard Colledge. I know not how I shall part with him, for he is companion; assistant interpreter &c. Yet he lives a recluse life for a young fellow of his age, he has no companions of his own, and never stirs out unless to accompany his Mamma or Sister. The consideration alone of his advantage will prevail with us, but we shall make a great Sacrifice in doing it. My other dear Lads are well I hope and good and dutifull. I have got their profiles stuck up which I look at every morning with pleasure and sometimes speak to; as I pass, telling Charles to hold up his Head. My little Cousins too, I hope are well. Can they say Aunt Adams yet?

If you want to know the manners and customs of this Country, I answer you that pleasure is the buisness of Life, more especially upon a Sunday. We have no days with us, or rather with you, by which I can give you any Idea of them, except commencment and Elections. We have a pretty woods within a few rods of this house which is called the Bois Boulogne. This is cut into many Regular Walks, and during the Summer Months upon Sundays, it looked like Boston and Cambridge Common upon the publick Days I have mentiond. Paris is a Horrid dirty City, and I know not whether the inhabitants could exist, if they did not come out one day in the week to Breath a Fresh air. I have set at my window of a Sunday and seen whole cart loads of them at a time. I speak literally, for those who neither own a Coach, nor are able to hire one, procure a cart, which in this country are always drawn by Horses. Sometimes they have a peice of canvase over it. Their are benches placed in them, and in this vehicle you will see as many well drest women and children as can possibly pile in, led out by a Man or drove just at the entrance of the wood they descend. The day is spent in musick danceing and every kind of play. It is a very rare thing to see a Man with a Hat any where, but under his Arm, or a Women with a Bonet upon her Head. This would brush of the powder, and Spoil the elegant *tupee*. They have a fashion of wearing a hood or veil either of Gauze or silk. If you send for a Tailor in this Country, your servant will very soon introduce to you a Gentleman full drest in Black, with his Head as white as a Snow Bank, and which a Hat never rumpled. If you send to a Mantua Maker she will visit you in the same stile, with her silk gown and peticoat, her hood in ample order, tho prehaps she lives up five pair of Stairs and eats nothing but Bread and water, as two thirds of these people do. We have a Servant in our family who dresses more than his young Master, and would not be *guilty of tending table* unfriz'd upon any consideration. He dresses the Hair of his young Master, but has his own drest by a Hair Dresser. By the way I was guilty of a sad mistake in London. I desired the Servant to procure me a Barber; the fellow staird, was loth to ask for what purpose I wanted him. At last he said you mean a Hair Dresser Mam, I believe. Aya says I, I Want my Hair drest. Why Barbars Madam in this country do nothing but Shave. When I first came to this Country I was loth to submit to Such an unnecessary number of Domesticks as it appeard to me. But I soon found that they would not let me do without them, because every one having a fixed and settled Department; they would not lift a pin out of it: all tho two thirds of their time they had no employment. We are however thankfull that we are able to make 8 do for us, tho we meet with some difficulties for want of the ninth.

Do not Suppose from this that we live remarkably nice. I never put up in America with what I do here. I often think of Swifts High Dutch Bride who had So much Nastiness and So much pride.

With regard to Cloathing for the Children, the distance I am at from a sea port makes it very difficult to send any thing to them. Their Brother has written to the Hague to have a trunk of Cloaths sent home which he has out grown. If they arrive some will answer for one and some for the other, and what ever else they want You will be kind enough to provide for them drawing upon Dr. Tufts for the money. Mr. Tracy and Jackson assure me they shall set of for London a thursday, and that they will be here tomorrow to take leave. Remember me to Mr. Thaxter. How does he, I think he ought to tell me himself. Alass poor Mrs. White. I am grieved for her, to every body remember me. Your best Friend be sure. My paper is too short, but I dare not take an other sheet. I must find room to say your   A A

FRENCH MANNERS

To Royall Tyler

My Dear sir

Half the pleasure of a Letter consist in its being written to the moment and it always gave me pleasure to know when and Where Friends received my Letter. Know then sir that this fourth of Janry 1785 of which I give you joy, I was sitting by my fire side at one end of a table and at the other my best Friend studying his favorite Author Plato. I was a reading a French comedy called the, procurerer which I saw acted a few evenings ago and was at that part in which Aristes who is the Attorney says,

> D'ailleurs, j'ai voulu voir Si, Sous ce vêtement,
> Un homme ne pouvoit aller droit un moment,
> Si cette Robe etoit d'essence corruptible
> Si l'honneur avec etoit incompatible

when John Brisler entered with two large packets in his hand, upon which I cried from America I know from America and seizd my sizer to cut them open. Emelia and her Brother went to Paris this afternoon and have run away to some play I fancy by their not being yet returnd, so that we had the reading of our Letter wholy to ourselves. Hers I have tuckd away with an intention of teazing her a little. This packet is dated November 6th. and is the second received from you since my arrival. I wrote to my Friends about 10 days since, but only a few line to you as I wished to set down and write you a long Letter, but the receipt of this 2d Letter has determined me to Seaize my pen this very moment and thank you for both your excellent Letters. To discribe to you the pleasure that a packet from America gives me, I must take a theatrical Stile and Say it is painted upon my face it Sparkles in my Eyes and plays round my Heart. News that is not what I want, politicks well enough by the by. I Love to hear every domestick occurrence then I live with you tho absent from you, and your paper of occurrences I approve much. It is not my fault that Cap. Lyde did not take my Letters, I sent them to London with orders to be put on board of him, but Mr. Tracy gave them to some other Captain. London is the best and only way of safety by which you may convey Letters or to Amsterdam. I write by no other way than London; direct there to Mr. Cranchs Friend Mr. Elworthy.

You and the rest of my Friends seem to think me engaged in a round of pleasures and amusements. I have pleasures and I have entertainments but they are not what the Beau Mond would esteem such. I never was more domestick or studious in my Life. I will tell You how, and give you a journal not in the stile of Swift, but of my own. We rise in the morning, not quite so early as I used to when I provided the turkies and Geese we used to Feast upon, but as soon as my fire is made and my room cleaned I then repair to Emelias Chamber and rouse her, from thence knock at my sons door, who always opens it with his Book in his hand: by that time we are all assembled to Breakfast, after which Mr. A sets down either to writing or reading, I to prepareing work for my Chamber Maids or sewing myself, for I still darn stockings, my son retires to his Chamber to his studies and translations of Horace and Tacitus, Emelia to her room to translating Telemack. In this manner we proceed till near 12 oclock when Mr. A takes his cain and hat for his forenoon walk which is commonly 4 miles, this he compleats by two. The Ladies at 12 repair to the toilite where some Author employs their dressing hour. At 2 we all meet together and dine, in the afternoon we go from one room to an other sometimes chat with my son or make him read to me. Emelia in the same manner works reads or plays with her Brother which they can do together in a game of Romps very well. The afternoon here are very short and tea very soon summons us all together. As soon as that is removed the table is coverd with mathamatical instruments and Books and you hear nothing till nine oclock but of Theorem and problems besecting and desecting tangents and [   ] which Mr. A is teaching to his son; after which we are often called upon to relieve their brains by a game of whist. At 10 we all retire to rest, and this is the common method in which we spend our time varying sometimes by receiving and sometimes by going into company. Ten oclock and these young folks not returnd, a dark stormy night too, but then there are Lamps from Paris here which enlightens the road. This is a very pretty ride in agreeable weather, for upon your right hand you have the River Sein; Ceasar barks and the gate bell rings which announces the return of the Carriage. Now for a little pleasure of which you shall have the whole History. Enter Miss A, "What are you cold?" Enter Mr. JQA with a set of Mathamatical instruments, "Pray what Spectacle have you been at to Night?" "A Variety, into the palais Royal. I have seen du palais du bon goüt l'Intendant comedien malgre lui; le Mensonge excusable, et le nouveau parvenu." Now what had I best do, give her these letters to night which will keep her up till 12 or give them for her Breakfast to morrow morning? "Hem, come take of your Cloak and I will give you an etrennes"; which in plain english signifies a new Years Gift. Off went the Cloak in an instant, then I delt out the letters one by one, at every one Miss calling out for more, more untill I had exhausted the bugget; but so secret and so affraid that one can hardly get a peep at a single line. I believe you will think by my thus trifling that I am tinctured with the frivolity of the Nation. Manners are very catching I assure you, and dissagreeable as I found many customs when I first came here, 5 months habitude have made them less so. For instanc when I dine abroad I am not so grosely offend at seeing a Gentleman take a partridge by the leg and put it to his Nose to see if it is in a condition to offer to the Ladies, because I have learnt that this is politeness instead of incivility. Nor do I look with so much amazement when I see a Lady wrapturously put her Arms round a Gentleman and Salute him first upon one cheeck and then upon the other, I consider it as a thing of mere course. I can even see that the Rouge gives an additional splendour to the Eyes: I believe however there are some practices which neither time nor Custom will ever make me a convert to. If I thought they would, I would fly the Country and its inhabitants as a pestilence that walketh in darkness and a plague that waisteth at noon day. I believe you need be under no apprehension respecting a young Lady of your acquaintance, who has never yet found her self so happy in Europe as America, and who I dare say will ever find in herself a preference to the manners of her Native Country. She has had an ernest desire to spend half a Year in a celebrated Convent in Paris for the purpose of acquiring the Language perfectly, but her Father entertained not so favourable an opinion of those abodes as some who have placed their Children there, and thought that the advantages arising from speaking the Language perfectly would never compensate for one less strickt Idea either of Modesty or Manners. I pretended not to judge in this Case. There is a certain saying not the less true for being often repeated, that habit is second nature. The Phythagorian doctrine of Reverenceing thyself is little practised among the Females of this Nation; for in this Idea if I comprehend it aright is included an incorruptable virtue joined to the strickest modesty. There is so little Regard paid here to the conjugal union that it naturally introduces every kind of licentiousness. The distinction of families is the corrupt Source from whence the pestilential Streems issue. The affections of the Heart are never traced. The Boy of 14 or 15 is married to the miss of 10 or 11, he is sent upon his travels and she confined in a convent. At 20 or 21 he returns and receives his wife; each of them perhaps cursing their shackels. Dispositions and inclinations varying, he seeks a mistress more pleasing, and she a Gallant more affectionate and complasant. Or if it is thought necessary to perpetuate the family titles and estate perhaps a year or twos fidelity is necessary upon the Ladys part, and it is esteemed a sad misfortune when more than two or 3 children fall to the share of a family. The young Ladies of a family are gaurded like the Hesperian fruit and never sufferd to be in company without some watchfull dragon. They have no Idea of that sure and only method of teaching them to reverence themselves which Prior so beautifully discribes—

> Be to her faults a little blind,
> Be to her virtues ever kind
> Let all her ways be unconfine'd
> And clap the padlock on her mind.

Yet dissolute as the manners of this people are said to be they Respect virtue in the Female Character almost to Idolating and speak of a Lady whose Character is unblemished and some such there are even here, as the Phoenix of the age. A Gentleman carries his Galantry to such a pitch here that altho he knows that his Lady has her Lover, yet if any person dares to insinuate the least reflextion upon her honour, nothing but blood can wash it out. I have had a Rouncounter related to me which happend last year at the opera where they frequently have Mask Balls. The Count D Artois the kings youngest Brother taking a fancy to a Lady in a Mask and supposeing her a Lady of pleasure used some familiarity with the Lady which she resented. Feeling his Rank he gave her a Box on the ear, upon which he was instantly seizd and his Mask torn of. The Lady proved to be the sister of the Duke de Bourbon. This being an offence for which even the kings Brother could not attone by asking pardon, he was challenged by the Duke they fought and the Count was wounded. Are not these things lessons to our Country to avoid family titles and every distinction but those which arise from Superiour Merit and Virtue: to cut of the Hydra headed Cincinnati and every appendage which pertains to it. The Heraditary Monster is already routd, but who sees not others which in time may grow to be equally distructive? The most fatal poison is that Secreet kind which distroys without discovery.

I can offer you no advise, at this distance but such as you already have upon paper and if as you are pleased to say you feel disposed at all times to attend to it, I flatter myself it has ever been of that kind which will promote both your honour and Reputation, for which you may be assured I am not less solicitious when I view you with more confidence as the person to whose care and protection I shall one day resign a beloved and only daughter. Industery integrity frugality and honour are the Characteristick Virtues which will recommend and ensure to you parental Regard and Fraternal affection and which will continue to you the Friendship the Esteem and the Maternal Regard of   A Adams

January 4, 1785

VISIT TO AN ORPHANAGE

To Elizabeth Smith Shaw

My Dear Sister   Auteuil January 11 1785
   I was doubly rejoiced to receive a Letter from you not only on account of the pleasure which I usually enjoy from your

pen: but because it informd me of your recovery from a dangerous illness. In a Letter which I wrote you the latter part of December, I have given you a long lesson respecting your Health: which altho it might savor something of the Quack, and a little of the Authority of Eldership, Spoke not my Heart, if it manifested not the tender solicitude of a Sister anxious for the Health of one deservedly Dear to her. I must therefore repeat to you; not to encumber your family beyond your Strength. A life of ease, and gentle excercise, is absolutly requisite for you: a tranquil State of mind, which has much to hope and nothing to fear. A different Situation would remove you, much sooner than Your Friends wish, to a state greatly Superiour to that which you now possess. I own myself so selfish that tho I doubt not of your qualifications for it, I hope to see you remain many years subject to the incident infirmities of Mortality, and like your fellow Mortals grow Grey and wrinkled here, before you Bloom afresh in the regions of immortality. I am not a little rejoiced that my Letters proved so benificial to you as you describe, and that I was capable of serving you, tho so far removed from you. A sudden exhilaration of the spirits, has proved of vast service in many disorders. I have experienced the benifit myself. Your family narrative afforded me pleasure because it related those calamities which were happily past, and displayd a more pleasing picture.

I am rejoiced to find that my Sons have been bless'd with so large a share of health since my absence, if they are wise they will improve the rigor of their early Days, and the Bloom of their Health in acquiring such a fund of learning, and knowledge, as may render them usefull to themselves, and benificial to Society, the great purpose for which they were sent into the World. That knowledge which is obtain in early Life becomes every day more usefull, as it is commonly that which is best retaind. To be Good, and do Good, is the whole Duty of Man, comprized in a few words; but what a capacious Field does it open to our view? And how many Characters may grow from this root, whose usefull branches may shade the oppressd; May comfort the dejected: may heal the wounded: may cure the sick, may defend the invaded; may enrich the poor. In short those who possess the disposition will never want employment.

How justly did you describe my Ideas; when you said "a parents thoughts flew quick." Mine, I own, had outstriped that passage; I would not, that a son of mine, should form any sentiments with respect to any female, but those of due decorum, and a general complasance, which every Youth acquainted with good manners, and civility will practise towards them, untill years have matured their judgment, and learning has made them wise. I would; that they should have no passion but for Science, and no mistress but Literature: "so shall discretion preserve them and understanding keep them. If they incline their ears to wisdom and apply their Hearts to understanding."

The age of the Young Lady relieved me from some anxiety, especially as I have since heard that she has much older admirers. Charles's disposition, and sensibility will render him more liable to female attachments, than the Young Hercules who sits beside me, and who like many other Youths pretends to brave the danger which has never assaild him; but who in time, like that Hero, may find an Omphalia to bring him to the distaff, but who, at present is much better occupied with his Horace and Tacitus.

I thank you for all your kind Maternal care towards my sons. I hope they will be both sensible of it; and gratefull for it, and that both their uncles and your advice to them will not fail to have a due influence upon their conduct.

I suppose every Letter I write; you will expect that I should give you some account of the amusements I have; and the curiosities I see; there are enough of each in Paris to employ my pen. But of the amusements, the theaters are those only which have yet occupied me; the description of which I must reserve for my Young correspondents. As there are a variety of cuorisities I shall endeavour to adapt the account of them to the different tastes of my Friends; I am going this afternoon to visit the Enfans trouvés, which at my return I will recount to you because I know your Benevolence will lead you to rejoice in an institution calculated to save from Death and wretchedness, those helpless Indigent Beings brought into existance by criminality; and owned by no one.

I have returned from my visit to the Hopital des enfans-Trouves, and truly it is a painfull pleasing sight. This House

was built in the Reign of Louis 14th. in the year 1747. It was
built by a decree of the king and is under the direction of Eight
administrators, and is Superintended by Nuns, or charity sisters
as they are call'd. We were shewn into a Room Large and airy
which contain about a hundred cribs, cradles they call them,
but they are more properly cribs, as they are fixd all round the
room and are not moveable. Through the middle of the appartment are two more rows the length of the Room, which
was I am almost tempted to say the cleanest I have seen in
France. Every bed was white linnen, and every child in them
appeard neat, and with cloathing that lookd comfortable. I
observed too; the large quantitys of necessary linnen which
hung at fires in the different rooms, which like every thing else
which I saw here; was very white and clean. The rooms too
were sweet, which was an other proof of the attention of the
Nurses. There were numbers in the Arms; great numbers a
sleep; and several crying, which you will easily credit, when I
tell you; that this is but the Eleventh day of the Month, and
the Charity sister who appeard an intellegent well bred woman
informd us; that two hundred had been brought in since the
year commenced. Whilst I stood talking with her there was
one brought in which appeard to be 3 months old. They generally receive at this House Six thousand a year, (there is an
other House of the same kind.) Last year she told us that five
thousand five hundred were lodged there, and that House had
sent into the provinces 15 thousand which were now at nurse:
they keep them out untill they are 5 years old. Children are
received here at any hour of the Day, or Night, in the day they
are brought in at the door, and in the Night the Nuns watch
to receive them. There are certain parts of Paris which are appropriated to this purpose, and small Boxes which may be
drawn out from under a cover; in which the child is deposited,
and the person who finds it Carries it to this House; where
they are received without any further form or declaration from
the Commissary of the quarter than naming the place the Day
and Hour when the child was found. The person is not obliged
to relate any other circumstance. They have always four wet
nurses in each appartment for the youngest and weakest of the
children: but as fast as they can provide accommodations for
them in the Country, they are sent there: where the Air is purer

and better than in Paris. The Governess told us that about a third of them died, notwithstanding all their care and attention, that they were sometimes so chill'd with the cold; and so poorly clad that they could not bring them to any warmth, or even make them swallow.

> "Where can they hope for pity, peace or rest
> Who move no softness in a parents Breast."

The Hôpital de la pitié which joins upon this is the place where they are received when they return from the Country. There they are taught to read and write, the Boys to knit, and the Girls to sew and make lace. When they have made their first communion which is from 10 to 12 years of age they are put to trades. They have a church which belongs to the Hospitals, but I had not time to see it. Whilst we approve the Charatable disposition, and applaud the wise institution which alleviates the fate of helpless innocence; can we draw a veil over the Guilty Cause, or refrain from comparing a Country grown old in Debauchery and lewdeness with the wise Laws and institutions of one wherein Mariage is considerd as holy and honourable, wherein industry and sobriety; enables parents to rear a numerous ofspring, and where the Laws provide a resource for illegitimecy by obliging the parents to a maintenance; and if not to be obtaind there, they become the charge of the town or parish where they are born: but how few the instances of their being totally abandoned by their parents? Whereas I have been credibly informd that one half the Children anually born in that immense City of Paris, are enfans trouvés.

Present my Regards to Mr. Shaw, to whom I will write if I have time. Pray has Mr. Allen carried home his Lady yet?!

I believe Mr. Thaxter has forgotton that I was formerly a correspondent of his, but I design soon to remind him of it. I hear of his success with pleasure; you will not fail to remember me to your Venerable Neighbour at the foot of the Hill, and all her Worthy family. I feel for the sore calimity of Mrs. White: by how many instances are we taught, not to place our affections too firmly upon earthly objects. How doatingly fond was this good Lady of her children, and she had reason to be fond, for they were both amiable and good. To Judge Sergant and family present my Regards. Honest, Modest Mr. Flint shall not be forgotten by me. The air of Haverhill Hill is too keen for him, he should live below it. Mr. Adams by me, presents his affectionate Regards to Mr. Shaw and my worthy Sister, to whom I tender the compliments of the New Year. May this and many succeeding ones find her happy is the ardent wish of her affectionate Sister   Abigail Adams

Will my sister accept a peice of sattin for a peticoat, which if I can smuggle into England in the form of a large Letter; will I hope go safe to her hand. There is a trunk of Cloaths sent from the Hague for the Children which you will be so good as to let me know when they arrive. Whatever is out grown you will dispose of as you think best and if there is any thing which will serve Mrs. West, who prehaps may be more needy than some others, you will be so good as to give them to her but dont mention my name, as they are all at your disposal.

COMMISSION TO LONDON

To Cotton Tufts

Dear Sir   Auteuil May 2d. 1785
    It was not untill the 21 of April that your Letter of December 1st. reach'd me, tho forwarded by Mr. Elworthy the 2 of Feb'ry. Where it has lain ever since I cannot divine, as many letters from all quarters come to us weekly. The contents of yours were not so political as to have made it necessary to have detaind them so long, four hundred and fifty thousand livres anual Salary to the intendant of posts for decyphering and Copying Letters one would think a sufficient Sum to render them expert at the buisness.
    This Letter I trust will be deliverd you by my son whose departure from hence will be Soon. You will easily believe that we make a Sacrifice of our present enjoyment in consenting to his return without us. Indeed he has been so usefull that I know not what his Father will do without him, as close application to writing is become so injurious to him that he never

applies himself a few hours together to his pen without Suffering for it, and there is So much Copying to do for a person in publick Life, that I think he cannot do without a secretary. But neither Mr. Adams or I are willing that our Sons should be brought up without a regular Education and some profession or Buisness by which they may honestly earn their Bread. For this purpose we have thought it best, that he should return to America and pass a Year or more at Colledge, and by obtaining a degree there be able to rank amongst his fellow citizens. Altho so long in Europe I think I may with confidence Say, that he will carry Home neither the vices or Fopperies of it. Tho he has been a Witness to the pomp and Splendour of Courts, he is I hope Republican enough to leave these Ideas in their native Soils, and to exhibit an example of prudence and frugality which he knows to be very necessary for him in order to the compleation of his and his Brothers Education. I recommend him Sir to your Friendship your care and patronage, as well as his Brother who I Suppose will enter Colledge this Year. Mr. Adams has written you upon this Subject and requested you to take the charge upon you of Supplying their expences and drawing upon him for the discharge of them. I am sensible it is an important Charge, because merely paying their Bills is not all we ask of you. We beg you to counsel and advise them as Children of your own, and we hope and trust that they will not give you any unnecessary trouble. I know that your Family is not calculated to receive them at the vacancies. I have therefore requested Mr. and Mrs. Cranch to let them make their House their Home, and Mrs. Cranch will be kind enough to take care of their linen and cloathing, for I would not over burthen one Friend. It is uncertain whether my son JQA, will be admitted to Colledge this year. The Gentlemen who examine him will judge of his qualifications and advise him with regard to his Studies, which we think if he does not enter colledge at present, he had better persue at Haverhill under the care of his uncle. You will find by conversing with him, that in many branches of knowledg he has few superiours of his age, and he has a habit of Study and application which I hope will not quit him by a Change of climate.

With regard to our family affairs Mr. Adams has written you upon them, he has however directed me to enlarge to you upon the subject of Bills, and to request you to invest 3 or four hundred pounds sterling in them, and in that kind which you shall judge most for his advantage. I should think it might not be amiss to invest one hundred pounds in the Army certificates which tho not so valuable at present, will become so in time. But all this we leave to your judgment. I see by the publick papers that there had been some frauds practised in alterations of figures. You will not let that matter escape you I dare say. And you will be so good as to inform Mr. Adams whether it would be best to make larger purchases if he should find himself able. But of that I despair unless Congress should see fit to place the Salaries upon the former footing, nor then neither if as I have reason to apprehend Mr. Adams should be sent to England, where it is Still more expensive liveing than here. If we had a private fortune which we could afford to add, to what Congress allow, we might then be in Some measure upon a footing with the publick ministers of other powers, but it would then be, as it is now, a dissagreable Life to me. My happiness has ever been in a domestick State, in the Society of my Friends, rather than the World. In these European Countries you must either engage in a Life of dissipation and amusement, company and play continually, or you must live a retired one without any intimates, and See company only in a ceremonious Way. There are very few Foreign Ministers here who do not expend their Salarys their private fortunes and run deep into debt besides, unless like the Count d'Aranda the Spanish minister, they have the income of a prince. Judg you Sir whether Seperate from the Idea of serveing ones Country, any satisfaction or pleasure is to be derived to persons feeling, and thinking as we do. Few Ministers it is true have ever met with more Success than has Crownd Mr. Adams's endeavours for the publick Service, but I wonder now, much more than I did before I came abroad; how he has lived through the perplexing Scenes he has had to encounter: twice it has very nearly cost him his Life, and if he should be as I fear he will appointed to England he will not have a less thorny road to tread than those which he has already past. There are many difficulties and perplexities to adjust in order to bring England and America yet together even in a commercial intercourse. The passions of both Nations instead of being cooler, appear more irritable every day: Greivious words Stir up Wrath, and perhaps our Countrymen are not sufficently aware that it is the wish of some other nations to keep us still at varience, or that the *Friendship* of *Nations* is only an other Word for interest. Mr. Adams has been so long abroad, and so largly engaged in the Field of politicks, so accustomed to "look quite through the deeds of Men," and haveing himself no other views or desires, but those of promoteing the welfare of his Country, and laying a foundation for its permanant Glory and happiness that I think he would be more likely to succeed in England than a New Hand. I cannot therefore oppose it should he be appointed, but at the same time I must solicit to return to America next Spring unless some important unfinishd negotiation Should oblige us to a longer Stay. I think from the conversation which Mr. Adams had yesterday with Mr. Hales the British Charge des affairs that if he was in England he would be like to Succeed in obtaining the Frontier Posts, and bringing matters upon a more amicable footing. Here neitheir England or Spain will treat, and no great object can be accomplishd. If he does not Succeed in England, America will know better than now; what course to take. Mr. Adams met Mr. Hales at dinner at Count Sarsfields and fell designedly into conversation with him upon the Subject of the Frontier Posts. He ask'd him what could be the reason of the delay to surrender them. Mr. Hales replied that he could not pretend to say precisely, but he had no doubt it was the private interest of some individual officer or Trader which had heitherto studied pretences, and excuses for delay, but that he might depend upon it, there were no thought at Court, or in the Nation, of holding these posts; he said Mr. Pit was a man of the most perfect Moral Character, and of the highest Sense of publick and private honour, and would abhor every Idea of voilating the National Faith. He askd Mr. Adams if he did not think Mr. Pit a wonderfull young Man? He replied that he did, and that he had often seen with Surprize his firmness and coolness and his perfect command of himself, qualities in which he had shewn him self superiour to all his Rivals, that he seem'd to be the Man for the Salvation of the Nation if it was yet in a Salvable State, but that he did not appear to be sufficiently sensible how large a share America must have in assisting him to Save it, that he would finally miss his object, and fail in all the great projects if he did not place the intercourse with America upon a proper footing. Mr. Hales laughd and said it was very true; and as soon says he as we have Settled with Ireland, we will take you in Hand, and settle with you, upon honest and generous terms, but it is dangerous attempting too many things at once. This Mr. Hales appears to be a well informd sensible Man, he supports a good Character here. His Grace the Duke of Dorset I have not yet seen, but expect that honour soon, as he is to dine here this week, together with Mr. Hales and other company. Mr. Adams has dined with the Duke several times who has always been very civil and gracious to him. He lives very magnificiently here, the British court allow him a salary of nine thousand some say ten a year, but tis said he spends that, and his private fortune too. He keeps a publick table twice a week, and tho a sensible Man is a lover of pleasure, and some say, of Play too.

April 26, 1785

Company comeing in I broke of my writing, last evening. Mr. Jefferson came in from Paris and informd us that the March packet had arrived and that he had received some Letters, one of which from Mr. Gerry acquainted him that Congress had appointed Mr. Adams Minister to London. This is an event tho not unexpected, from the late Letters which have been received, yet an event which will load with cares and anxieties the Head and Heart of my Friend, subject him I suppose to many censures, and no small share of ill nature. I hope each State will do all in their power to render the burden as light as they can, by stricktly adhereing to the National Faith and honour pledged by the Treaty, that they will suffer no undue warmth to prevail, or the intrigues of any Nation to blind their eyes to the prejudice of their own.

The Spring is opening now in great Beauty, and Auteuil begins to look Charming. The exchange of climate must be for the worse. I shall regreet that, and the loss of Mr. Jeffersons Society. In some respects I shall find myself happier in England. I expect that we shall necessarily be subject to much more company, and concequently more expence, but I will not be over anxious. Our Country will not forget their best Friends, and our Children I hope will be qualified to earn their Bread.

What ever you find necessary to be done in our private affairs, you will do, tho you have not immediate opportunity to inform us of it. With Regard to Mr. Pratt, you will do what you think just and reasonable. And be so good as to add to the list of the poor the wife of John Hayden, the old Man who lives by the meeting house. 2 dollors to her, but at different seasons of the Year. I wish it was in my power to enlarge the sums, and increase the number. I reflect upon this trifle with more pleasure than all the Sums I am necessatated to spend here.

My most affectionate Regards to my Aunt and cousins. Pray sir continue to write to me. Writing to my Friends and Receiveing Letters from them; is one of the highest pleasures I enjoy here. I know not when we shall be obliged to leave this Country, as no official account has yet reachd us, nor any commission, but I suppose Congress see so fully the necessity of adjusting their affairs in England, that they will not delay the Matter. Your next Letters you will address to London and to Mr. Adams as Minister there. Nabby sends her duty to you and my Aunt. She is well, and a Good child. I hope she will ever be a happy one, and to this purpose sir I wish you to give advise to a Young Friend of hers, when ever you see it necessary. I was not without anxiety, as every thoughtfull young person must be, when they are going to connect themselves for Life, when I changed a Single for a Married State. I need not say to you Sir that my own union has been of the happiest kind, but I am not the less desirious that my daughters should prove so too, tho I have had more fears and more anxieties for her than ever I felt for myself. This Sir is between ourselves. I will leave my Letter open untill my Son goes and possibly I may fill my paper.

May 10th

Mr. Adams has received his commission and we must hasten to arrange our affairs as soon as possible. We talk of going the 20th. I hope however not quite so soon, tho the nature of the Buisness is such as requires an immediate attention, and we shall make no unnecessary delay. Mr. Adams is full of anxiety. If he does not succeed it will not be oweing to any want of application or endeavours for the publick service. The Duke of

Dorset has been so polite as to tell him, that either in a publick or private capacity he should be happy to serve him. Mr. Smith the Secretary of Legation has not yet arrived. Dr. Franklin has received leave to return and talks of going out in july, but with his disorder I cannot conceive how he will bear a voyage.

By my son I have sent you 50 pounds Lawfull Money, part of which is money which I brought with me, but not passing neither here or in England I thought it best to return it, to America. With this money which I call mine I wish you to purchase the most advantageous Bills and keep them by themselves. If hereafter I should be able to add to it, I may establish a little fund for my pensioners.

My Son will give you all the politicks of the Day. Yours

A A

PS. As there is a communication between the Medical Society of Paris and Boston I thought it might not be amiss for the improvement of one of its members to communicate the inclosed, as a Specimen for his future practise. It is usual for Physicians when they attend any person of character to write daily as you see, and very particularly the Symptoms of their paitients. A Lady who is my Neighbour being very sick, I sent frequently to inquire after her and have a collection of such kind of Billets in replie.

"WHO SHOULD I HAVE TO LOVE ME THEN?"

To Mary Smith Cranch

My Dear Sister   Auteuil May 8th 1785

Can my dear sister realize that tis near eleven Months since I left her. To me it seems incredible, more like a dream than a reality. Yet it ought to appear the longest ten Months of my Life if I was to measure the time by the variety of objects which have occupied my attention. But amidst them all my Heart returns like the Dove of Noah and rest only in my native land. I never thought myself so selfish a being as since I have become a traveller, for altho I see Nature arround me in a much higher

State of cultivation than our own Country can boast, and elegance of taste and manners in a thousand forms, I cannot feel intrested in them. It is in vain for me, that here

> "Kind Nature wakes her genial power
> Suckles each herb, & nurtures every flower"

Tis true the garden yeilds a rich profusision, but they are neither plants of my hand, or children of my care. I have bought a little Bird lately, and I realy think I feel more attached to that, than to any object out of my own family animate, or inanimate. Yet I do not consider myself in the predicament of a poor fellow who not having a house, in which to put his Head, took up his abode in the stable of a Gentleman; but tho so very poor he kept a Dog, with whom he daily divided the small portion of food which he earnd. Upon being ask'd why when he found it so difficult to live himself, he still kept a Dog, What Says the poor fellow part with my Dog! Why who should I have to Love me then? You can never feel the force of this replie unless you were to go into a foreign Country without being able to Speak the language of it. I could not have believed if I had not experienced it, how strong the Love of Country is in the humane mind. Strangers from all parts of America who visit us, feel more nearly allied than the most intimate acquaintance I have in Europe. Before this will reach you, you will have learnt our destination to England. Whether it will prove a more agreeable situation than the present, will depend much upon the state of politicks. We must first go to Holland to arrange our affairs there and to take leave of that Court. I shall wish to be moveing as soon as my family lessens, it will be so lonesome. We have as much company in a formal way as our Revenues will admit, and Mr. Jefferson with one or two Americans visits us in the Social friendly way. I shall realy regreet to leave Mr. Jefferson, he is one of the choice ones of the Earth. On Thursday I dine with him at his house, on Sunday he is to dine here, on Monday, we all dine with the Marquis, and on Thursday we dine with the Swedish Ambassador, one of the most agreeable Men and the politest Gentleman I have met with, he lives like a prince. I know you Love to know all my movements which make me so particular to you.

I wrote to you by the last pacquet which sailed for New York in which letter I requested you to take upon you the care of Charles, after he shall have enterd Colledge, and let him make your House his Home in vacancies &c. Will you also give your Elder Nephew that leave too? At the same time we mean to pay their Board, and every other expence which they may occasion to you. I know however there are many for which you will not be pay'd only by the pleasure you take in doing good, and in sisterly kindness and affection. I hope Charles will be placed with a good Chamber mate, as much depends upon that. I do not desire that you should attend to having their washing done in your family, only be so good as to see that they have a good place at Cambridge for it, provided they should both be in colledge at the same time, which I scarcely expect will take place this year.

I have many affairs upon me at present, what with my sons going away, my own adjustments for a final leave of this Country, many things must pass through my hands. But I am the less anxious to write as your Nephew will tell you all about us. You will think I ought to have written you more now, but I am almost sick of my pen, and I know you will see what I write to others. I will not however close untill the day before he quits this House.

ante May 5, 1785

May 10th.

Tomorrow morning, My son takes his departure for America, and we go next week to England. I have nothing further to add than my Regards to Mr. Cranch and a desire that you would let me hear from you by every opportunity. I shall lose part and the greatest part of American intelligence by quitting France, for no person is so well informd from all the states as the Marquis de la Fayette. He has Established a correspondence in all the states and has the News Papers from every quarter.

Adieu my dear sister and be assured I am most affectionately yours,   A Adams

My Regards to Madam Quincy and daughter to Mr. Wibird to Mr. Alleynes family, and my duty to unkle Quincy.

LAFAYETTE

To Mercy Otis Warren

Dear Madam   May 10 1785

I cannot let my son return to America without a few lines to you, nor will I doubt their being acceptable altho it is nine months since I left Home during all which time neither Mr. Adams or I have had the honour of receiving a line either from the General or your Ladyship, altho we have repeatedly written to you. Your Son who is resident in Lisbon and mine who has inhabited France have regularly corresponded by which means I have had the pleasure of knowing that there was one Branch of the Family yet on this side the land of forgetfullness. I left America not a little anxious for the Health of my two young Friends Mr. Charles and Henery, and tho I have heard from them by way of my Braintree Friends, it would have been more agreeable to me to have received the account from the Hand of their Mama. My son has made a wise choice I think in prefering to return to his own country and compleat his education at Harvered that he may become acquainted with the Youth of his own Standing and form connextions in early life amongst those with whom he is to pass his days. An acquaintance and intimacy in your family will be an object with him, and as you and I Love to praise our children and why when deserving should we not? I think you will find him as intelligent as most young Men of his age, and as little tincturd with the vices and follies of Europe. He loves his Studies too well to be much addicted to any thing else. Having spent ten years abroad uncorrupted, I hope he will not be less cautious in his own country where there is little less danger than in Europe. But as he is yet young the advice and Friendship of the ancient Friends of his Parents will ever be usefull to him.

You will hear before this reaches you of the completion of an ancient prophecy of yours, but I do not recollect whether you auguerd good or evil from it. At present there are so many Clouds to peirce, some of them armd with thunder and lightning that I query whether the Electrical Phylosopher himself could devise means to secure a person from the burning flashes. I think too it has been said that when clouds meet from opposite directions the severest tempest ensues. What then can a person expect who stands unshelterd beneath so inclemnant a hemisphere?

But to quit Allegory we are destined to England. An embassy I dare say in which your penetration discovers many difficulties, some arising from one side of the Atlantick and Some on the other. I never could find either sufficient honour or profit to balance the anxiety which I have both seen and felt in the various employments to which my friend has been call'd. His Success and the benifit derived to our Country from that, has given me great pleasure. Whether his usual good fortune in negotiation will follow him in this embassy time must unfold, but it has brought a weight of care and a load of anxiety upon him. I shall feel some Regreets at quitting so agreeable a climate and the delightfull Garden which is just unfolding all its Beauties. My acquaintance with French Ladies is rather small and none that I value much save Madam da la Fayette, who is a Lady with whom you would be much pleased. Her high Rank and family have not made her like most others forget eitheir the Maternal or Domestick Character. She said to me in conversation one day that she dissaproved very much the Manner in which the conjugal connection was formed in this Country. I was married said she before I was capable of Love. It was very happy for me that my friends made so wise a choice. I made it the Study of my Life to perform my duty and I have always been so happy as to find my pleasures result from the performance of my duty. I am happier says she and I have more reason to be so than many others of my sex and country. They seek their pleasures in dissapation and amusement, they become insipid to them; and they have no resource in Domestick Life. She is passionately fond of America and she has reason to be so, for America has shewn itself passionately fond of her family. The Marquis you know. He is dangerously amiable, sensible, polite, affible insinuating pleasing hospitable indefatiguable and ambitious. Let our Country Gaurd let them watch let them fear his virtues and remember that the summit of perfection is the point of declension. This Gentleman has had the offer of going to America in the quality of minister Plenipotentiary, but he would not accept it because it would forfeit him the right of citizenship. The Apotheose of the ancient Romans is not yet introduced into our Country, but it may follow the Knights of Cincinnatus, as regularly as Statues &c., and these are honours which are paid only to Military Characters, that the people may look to them, and them only as the preservers of their Country and the supporters of their freedom. That they have deserved well of their Country no one will dispute. But no Man or body of Men can Merit the sacrifice of the Liberties of a people for the agrandizement of them or their families. It is not a little mortifying that both the Secretarys of Legation are knights of the order. Col. Humphries is a sensible worthy Man, and I believe abhors the Idea which those who have more maturely traced concequences fear from these family distinctions, but tis dissagreeable laying aside a Badge of Merit, which he sees and feels give him weight and distinction here. Col. Smith is a perfect stranger to us. Col. Humphries gives him a good Character and so does the Marquiss of whose family he has been.

We are told here that Governour Hancok has resignd the Chair!!!—and are much at a loss for his Successor out of the many candidates which will no doubt be upon the list. I hope our state will not get so divided as to fall into unhappy parties. I hear Mrs. Macauly says that she does not find so much Republicanism as she expected. She went there ten years too late. Yet let her serch whatever part of the Globe she pleases, it is not probable that she will find a larger Proportion of it else where. Pray make my Respectfull compliments to her, and remember me to all my Friends of your family. Be assured Dear Madam that frequent communication with you will give real pleasure to your Friend and Humble Servant   A Adams

ENGLISH NEWSPAPERS

To Thomas Jefferson

Dear Sir   London Bath Hotel Westminster June 6. 1785
    Mr. Adams has already written you that we arrived in London upon the 27 of May. We journey'd slowly and sometimes

silently. I think I have somewhere met with the observation that nobody ever leaves Paris but with a degree of tristeness. I own I was loth to leave my Garden because I did not expect to find its place supplied. I was still more Loth on account of the increasing pleasure, and intimacy which a longer acquaintance with a respected Friend promised, to leave behind me the only person with whom my Companion could associate; with perfect freedom, and unreserve: and whose place he had no reason to expect supplied in the Land to which he is destinied.

At leaving Auteuil our domesticks surrounded our Carriage and in tears took leave of us, which gave us that painfull kind of pleasure, which arises from a consciousness, that the good will of our dependants is not misplaced.

My little Bird I was obliged, after taking it into the Carriage to resign to my Parissian Chamber Maid, or the poor thing would have flutterd itself to death. I mourn'd its loss, but its place was happily supplied by a present of two others which were given me on Board the Dover pacquet, by a young Gentleman whom we had received on Board with us, and who being excessively sick I admitted into the Cabin, in gratitude for which he insisted upon my accepting a pair of his Birds. As they had been used to travelling, I brought them here in safety, for which they hourly repay me by their melodious Notes. When we arrived we went to our old Lodgings at the Adelphia, but could not be received as it was full, and almost every other hotel in the city. From thence we came to the Bath hotel where we at present are, and where Mr. Storer had partly engaged Lodgings for us, tho he thought we should have objections upon account of the Noise, and the Constant assemblage of Carriages round it, but it was no time for choice, as the sitting of parliament, the Birth Day of the King, and the celebration of Handles Musick had drawn together such a Number of people as allready to increase the price of Lodgings near double. We did not however hesitate at keeping them tho the four rooms which we occupy costs a third more than our House and Garden Stables &c. did at Auteuil. I had lived so quietly in that Calm retreat, that the Noise and bustle of this proud city almost turnd my Brain for the first two or three Days. The figure which this city makes in respect to Equipages is vastly superiour to Paris, and gives one the Idea of superiour wealth and grandeur. I have seen few carriages in Paris and no horses superiour to what are used here for Hackneys. My time has been much taken up since my arrival in looking out for a House. I could find many which would suit in all respects but the price, but none realy fit to occupy under 240 £. 250, besides the taxes, which are serious matters here. At last I found one in Grovenor Square which we have engaged.

Mr. Adams has written you an account of his reception at Court, which has been as gracious and as agreeable as the reception given to the Ministers of any other foreign powers. Tomorrow he is to be presented to the Queen.

Mr. Smith appears to be a Modest worthy Man, if I may judge from so short an acquaintance. I think we shall have much pleasure in our connection with him. All the Foreign Ministers and the Secrataries of Embassies have made their visits here, as well as some English Earls and Lords. Nothing as yet has discoverd any acrimony. Whilst the Coals are coverd the blaize will not burst, but the first wind which blows them into action will I expect envelop all in flames. If the actors pass the ordeal without being burnt they may be considerd in future of the Asbestos kind. Whilst I am writing the papers of this day are handed me. From the publick Advertiser I extract the following. "Yesterday morning a Messenger was sent from Mr. Pitt to Mr. Adams the American plenipotentiary with notice to suspend for the present their intended interview." (absolutely false.) From the same paper.

"An Ambassador from America! Good heavens what a sound! The Gazette surely never announced anything so extraordinary before, nor once on a day so little expected. This will be such a phænomenon in the Corps Diplomatique that tis hard to say which can excite indignation most, the insolence of those who appoint the Character, or the meanness of those who receive it. Such a thing could never have happened in any former Administration, not even that of Lord North. It was reserved like some other Humiliating circumstances to take place

> Sub Iove, sed Iove nondum
> Barbato——"

From the morning post and daily advertiser it is said that

"Mr. Adams the Minister plenipotentiary from America is extremly desirious of visiting Lord North whom he Regards as one of the best Friends the Americans ever had." Thus you see sir the begining Squibs.

I went last week to hear the Musick in Westminster Abbey. The Messiah was performd, it was Sublime beyond description. I most sincerely wisht for your presence as your favorite passion would have received the highest gratification. I should have sometimes fancied myself amongst a higher order of Beings; if it had not been for a very troublesome female, who was unfortunately seated behind me; and whose volubility not all the powers of Musick could still.

I thank you sir for the information respecting my son from whom we received Letters. He desires to be remembered to you to Col. Humphries and to Mr. Williamos. My Daughter also joins in the same request. We present our Love to Miss Jefferson and compliments to Mr. Short. I suppose Madam de la Fayettee is gone from Paris. If she is not be so good sir as to present my Respects to her. I design writing her very soon. I have to apoligize for thus freely scribling to you. I will not deny that there may be a little vanity in the hope of being honourd with a line from you. Having heard you upon some occasions express a desire to hear from your Friends, even the Minutia respecting their Situation, I have ventured to class myself in that number, and to Subscribe myself, Sir Your Friend and Humble Servant   A Adams

ENCLOSURE

The publick Advertiser—

Yesterday Lord Gerge Gordon had the Honour of a long conference with his Excellency John Adams (honest John Adams) the Ambassador of America, at the hotel of Mons. de Lynden Envoye extraodinaire de Leurs Hautes Puissances.

This is true, and I suppose inserted by his Lordship who is as wild and as enthusiastic as when he headed the Mob. His Lordship came here but not finding Mr. Adams at home was determind to see him, and accordingly follow'd him to the Dutch Ministers. The conversation was curious, and pretty much in the Stile of Mrs. Wright with whom his Lordship has frequent conferences.

An other paragraph from the same paper—"Amongst the various personages who drew the attention of the drawing-room on Saturday last, Mr. Adams, minister plenipotentiary from the States of America was not the least noticed. From this Gentleman the Eye of Majesty and the Court glanced on Lord——; to whose united Labours this Country stands indebted for the loss of a large territory and a divided and interrupted Commerce."

PRESENTATION AT COURT

To Mary Smith Cranch

june 24. 1785
My dear sister   London Bath hotel westminster

Captain Lyde is arrived and I have 3 Letters by him, one from Doctor Tufts one from Dr. Welch and one from Mrs. Storer. I will not accuse my dear sister because I know she must have written to me tho I have not yet received it. I know so well how many accidents may prevent for a long time the reception of Letters, that whilst I ask candour for myself, I am willing to extend it to others.

I have been here a month without writing a single line to my American Friends. About the 28th. of May we reachd London and expected to have gone into our old quiet Lodgings at the Adelphia, but we found every hotel full, the Sitting of parliament, the Birth day of the King, and the famous Celebration of the Musick of Handle at Westminster Abbey, had drawn together such a concourse of people, that we were glad to get into Lodgings at the moderate price of a Guiney per day, for two Rooms and two Chambers, at the Bath hotel Westminster Picadily, where we yet are. This being the Court end of the city, it is the resort of a vast concourse of carriages, it is too publick and noisy for pleasure, but necessity is without Law. The Ceremony of presentation, upon one week, to the King and the Next to the Queen was to take place, after which I was to prepare for mine. It is customary upon presentation to receive visits from all the Foreign ministers, so that we could not exchange our Lodgings for more private ones, as we might and should; had we been only in a private character. The Foreign ministers and several english Lords and Earls have paid their compliments here and all heitherto is civil and polite. I was a fortnight all the time I could get looking of different Houses, but could not find any one fit to inhabit under 200. besides the taxes which mount up to 50 & 60 pounds. At last my good Genious carried me to one in Grovenor Square, which was not let because the person who had the care of it, could let it only for the remaining lease which was one Year and 3 quarters. The price which is not quite 200, the Situation and all together induced us to close the Bargain and I have prevaild upon the person who lets it; to paint two rooms which will put it into decent order so that as soon as our furniture comes I shall again commence house keeping. Living at a hotel is I think more expensive than house keeping in proportion to what one has for their money. We have never had more than two dishes at a time upon our table, and have not pretended to ask any company and yet we live at a greater expence than 25 Guineys per week. The Wages of servants horse hire house meat and provision are much dearer here than in France. Servants of various sorts and for different departments are to be procured, their Characters to be inquird into, and this I take upon me even to the Coachman; you can hardly form an Idea how much I miss my son on this as well as many other accounts. But I cannot bear to trouble Mr. Adams with any thing of a domestick kind, who from morning untill Evening has sufficient to occupy all his time. You can have no Idea of the petitions Letters and private applications for a pittance which crowd our doors. Every person represents his case as dismal, some may really be objects of compassion, and some we assist, but one must have an inexhaustable purse to supply them all. Besides there are so many gross impositions practised as we have found in more instances than one, that it would take the whole of a persons time to trace all their stories. Many pretend to have been American soldiers, some to have served as officers. A most glaring instance of falshood however Col. Smith detected in a man of these pretentions, who sent to Mr. Adams from the Kings bench prison and modestly desired 5 Guineys, a qualified cheet but evidently a man of Letters and abilities.

But if it is to continue in this way a Galley Slave would have an easier task.

The Tory venom has begun to spit itself forth in the publick papers as I expected, bursting with envy that an American Minister should be received here with the same marks of attention politeness and civility which is shewn to the Ministers of any other power. When a minister delivers his credentials to the king, it is always in his private closet attended only by the minister for Foreign affairs, which is called a private audience, and the Minister presented makes some little address to his Majesty, and the same ceremony to the Queen, whose replie was in these Words, "Sir I thank you for your civility to me and my family, and I am glad to see you in this Country," then very politely inquired whether he had got a house yet? The answer of his Majesty was much longer, but I am not at liberty to say more respecting it; than that it was civil and polite, and that his Majesty said he was glad the Choice of his Country had fallen upon him. The News Liars know nothing of the Matter, they represent it just to answer their purpose. Last thursday Col. Smith was presented at Court, and tomorrow at the Queens circle my Ladyship and your Neice make our compliments. There is no other presentation in Europe in which I should feel so much as in this. Your own reflections will easily [   ] the reasons. I have received a very friendly and polite visit from the Countess of Effingham. She calld and not finding me at Home left a Card. I returnd her visit, but was obliged to do it by leaving my Card too: as she was gone out of Town. But when her Ladyship returnd she sent her compliments, and word that if agreeable she would take a Dish of tea with me; and named her Day. She accordingly came, and appeard a very polite sensible woman. She is about 40, a good person, tho a little masculine, elegant in her appearence, very easy and social. The Earl of Effingham is too well rememberd by America to need any particular recital of his Character. His Mother is first Lady to the Queen. When Her Ladyship took leave, she desired I would let her know the day that I would favour her with a visit, as she should be loth to be absent. She resides in summer a little distance from town. The Earl is a Member of Parliament which obliges him now to be in town and she usually comes with him and resides at a hotel a little distance from

this. I find a good many Ladies belonging to the Southern
states here, many of whom have visited me. I have exchanged
visits with several, yet neither of us have met. The Custom is
however here, much more agreeable than in France, for it is as
with us, the Stranger is first visited. The ceremony of presentation here is considerd as indispensable. Their are four minister
plenipotentiarys Ladies here, but one Ambassador and he has
no Lady. In France the Ladys of Ambassadors only are presented there. One is obliged here to attend the circles of the
Queen which are held in Summer one a fortnight, but once a
week the rest of the year, and what renders it exceedingly expensive is, that you cannot go twice the same Season in the
same dress, and a Court dress you cannot make use any where
else. I directed my Mantua Maker to let my dress be elegant
but plain as I could possibly appear with Decency, accordingly
it is white Lutestring coverd and full trimd with white Crape
festoond with lilick ribbon and mock point lace, over a hoop
of enormus extent. There is only a narrow train of about 3 yard
length to the gown waist, which is put into a ribbon upon the
left side, the Queen only having her train borne, ruffel cuffs for
married Ladies thrible lace ruffels a very dress cap with long
lace lappets two white plumes and a blond lace handkerchief,
this is my rigging. I should have mentiond two pearl pins in
my hair earings and necklace of the same kind.

thursday morning

My Head is drest for St. James and in my opinion looks very
tasty. Whilst Emelias is undergoing the same operation, I set
myself down composedly to write you a few lines. Well
methinks I hear Betsy and Lucy say, what is cousins dress,
white my Dear Girls like your Aunts, only differently trimd,
and ornamented, her train being wholy of white crape and
trimd with white ribbon, the peticoat which is the most showy
part of the dress coverd and drawn up in what is calld festoons,
with light wreaths of Beautifull flowers. The Sleaves white
crape drawn over the silk with a row of lace round the Sleave
near the shoulder an other half way down the arm and a 3d.
upon the top of the ruffel little flowers stuck between. A kind
of hat Cap with 3 large feathers and a bunch of flowers a wreath
of flowers upon the hair. Thus equipd we go in our own

Carriage and Mr. A and Col. Smith in his. But I must quit my
pen to put myself in order for the ceremony which begins at 2
oclock. When I return I will relate to you my reception, but do
not let it circulate as there may be persons eager to Catch at
every thing, and as much given to misrepresentation as here. I
would gladly be excused the Ceremony.

fryday morning
Congratulate me my dear sister it is over. I was too much
fatigued to write a line last evening. At two a clock we went to
the circle which is in the drawing room of the Queen. We past
through several appartments lined as usual with Spectatirs
upon these occasions. Upon entering the antiChamber, the
Baron de Linden the Dutch Minister who has been often here
came and spoke with me. A Count Sarsfield a French nobleman with whom I was acquainted paid his compliments. As I
passt into the drawing room Lord Carmathan and Sir Clement
Cotterel Dormer were presented to me. Tho they had been
several times here I had never seen them before. The sweedish
the polish ministers made their compliments and several other
Gentleman, but not a single Lady did I know, untill the
Countess of Effingham came who was very civil. There were 3
young Ladies daughters of the Marquiss of Lothan who were
to be presented at the same time and two Brides. We were
placed in a circle round the drawing room which was very full,
I believe 200 person present. Only think of the task the Royal
family have, to go round to every person, and find small talk
enough to speak to all of them. Tho they very prudently speak
in a whisper, so that only the person who stands next you can
hear what is said. The King enters the room and goes round to
the right, the Queen and princesses to the left. The Lord in
waiting presents you to the King and the Lady in waiting does
the same to her Majesty. The King is a personable Man, but
my dear sister he has a certain Countenance which you and I
have often remarked, a red face and white eye brows, the
Queen has a similar countanance and the numerous Royal
family confirm the observation. Persons are not placed according to their rank in the drawing room, but tranciently, and
when the King comes in he takes persons as they stand. When
he came to me, Lord Onslow said, Mrs. Adams, upon which I

drew of my right hand Glove, and his Majesty saluted my left
cheek, then asked me if I had taken a walk to day. I could have
told his Majesty that I had been all the morning prepareing to
wait upon him, but I replied, no Sire. Why dont you love
walking says he? I answerd that I was rather indolent in that
respect. He then Bow'd and past on. It was more than two
hours after this before it came to my turn to be presented to
the Queen. The circle was so large that the company were four
hours standing. The Queen was evidently embarrased when I
was presented to her. I had dissagreeable feelings too. She
however said Mrs. Adams have you got into your house, pray
how do you like the Situation of it? Whilst the princess Royal
looked compasionate, and asked me if I was not much fatigued,
and observed that it was a very full drawing room. Her sister
who came next princess Augusta, after having asked your neice
if she was ever in England before, and her answering yes, inquird of me how long ago, and supposed it was when she was
very young. And all this is said with much affability, and the
ease and freedom of old acquaintance. The manner in which
they make their tour round the room, is first the Queen, the
Lady in waiting behind her holding up her train, next to her
the princess royal after her princess Augusta and their Lady in
waiting behind them. They are pretty rather than Beautifull,
well shaped with fair complexions and a tincture of the kings
countanance. The two sisters look much alike. They were both
drest in lilack and silver silk with a silver netting upon the coat,
and their heads full of diamond pins. The Queen was in purple
and silver. She is not well shaped or handsome. As to the Ladies of the Court, Rank and title may compensate for want of
personal Charms, but they are in general very plain ill shaped
and ugly, but dont you tell any body that I say so. If one wants
to see Beauty they must go to Ranaleigh, there it is collected in
one bright constellation. There were two Ladies very elegant at
court Lady Salsbury and Lady Talbot, but the observation did
not in general hold good that fine feathers make fine Birds. I
saw many who were vastly richer drest than your Friends, but I
will venture to say that I saw none neater or more elegant,
which praise I ascribe to the taste of Mrs. Temple and my
Mantua Maker, for after having declared that I would not have
any foil or tincel about me, they fixd upon the dress I have

described. Mrs. Temple is my near Neighbour and has been very friendly to me. Mr. Temple you know is deaf so that I cannot hold much conversation with him.

The Tories are very free with their compliments. Scarcly a paper excapes without some scurrility. We bear it with silent Contempt, having met a polite reception from the Court. It bites them Like a serpent and stings them like an adder. As to the success the negotiations may meet with time alone can disclose the result, but if this nation does not suffer itself to be again duped by the artifice of some and the malice of others, it will unite itself with America upon the most liberal principals and sentiments.

Captain Dashood came why I have not half done. I have not told your Aunt yet that whilst I was writing I received her thrice welcome Letters, and from my dear cousins too, Aunt Shaw and all, nor how some times I laught and sometimes I cry'd, yet there was nothing sorrowfull in the Letters, only they were too tender for me. What not time to say I will write to all of them as soon as possible. Why I know they will all think I ought to write, but how is it possible? Let them think what I have to do, and what I have yet to accomplish as my furniture is come and will be landed tomorrow. Eat the sweet meats divide them amongst you, and the choisest sweet meat of all I shall have in thinking that you enjoy them.

I hope you have got all my Letters by my son from whom I shall be anxious to hear.

Adieu adieu.

Esther is well, John poorly. Do not any of you think hard of me for not writing more, my pen is good for nothing. I went last Evening to Raneleigh, but I must reserve that story for the young folks. You see I am in haste, believe me most tenderly yours   A Adams

june 28

Make the corrections, I have not time; Mr. Storer was well this morning when he left us, he was of the party last evening.

"POLITE CIRCLES ARE MUCH ALIKE"

To Elizabeth Smith Shaw

My dear sister

I have been situated here for near six weeks. It is one of the finest squares in London. The air is as pure as it can be so near a Great city. It is but a small distance from Hide Park, round which I sometimes walk, but oftner ride. It resembles Boston Common, much larger and more beautified with Trees. On one side of it is a fine river. St. James Park and Kensington Gardens are two other fashonable walks which I am very sensible I ought to improve oftner than I do. One wants society in these places. Mrs. Temple is the only person near me with whom I can use the freedom of calling upon to ride or walk with me, and she to my no small regret I am going to lose. Mrs. Rogers is an American and one of the most Benevolent women in the world: but is 3 miles distant from me. A sister of hers is like to be setled near you I hear. Visit her my sister, she is the counterpart of the amiable Mrs. Rogers. I have some acquaintance with her, she is the Friend and correspondent of your Neice. Mrs. Rogers and she too, have too much of "the tremblingly alive all over" to be calculated for the rough Scenes of Life. Mrs. Hay resides out at Hamstead about 4 miles from London. We visit, but they have such a paltry custom of dinning here at night, that it ruins that true American Sociability which *only* I delight in. Polite circles are much alike throughout Europe. Swift's journal of a modern fine Lady tho written 60 years ago is perfectly applicable to the present day, and tho noted as the changeable sex; in this Scene of dissapation they have been steady.

I shall never have much society with these kind of people, for they would not like me, any more than I do them. They think much more of their titles here than in France. It is not unusual to find people of the highest rank there, the best bred and the politest people. If they have an equal share of pride, they know better how to hide it. Until I came here, I had no idea what a National and illiberal inveteracy the English have against their better behaved Neighbours, and I feel a much greater partiality for them than I did whilst I resided amongst them. I would recommend to this Nation a little more liberality and discernment. Their contracted sentiments leads them to despise all other Nations: perhaps I should be chargable with the same narrow sentiments if I give America the preference over these old European Nations. In the cultivation of the arts and improvement in manufactories they greatly excell us, but we have native Genious capacity and ingenuity equal to all their improvements, and much more general knowledge diffused amongst us. You can scarcly form an Idea how much superiour our common people as they are termd, are to those of the same rank in this country. Neither have we that servility of Manners which the distinction between nobility and citizens gives to the people of this Country. We tremble not, neither at the sight or Name of Majesty. I own that I never felt myself in a more contemptable situation than when I stood four hours together for a gracious smile from Majesty. Witness to the anxious solicitude of those around me for the same mighty *Boon*. I however had a more dignified honour as his Majesty *deigned to salute me.*

I have not been since to the drawing room, but propose going to the next. As the company are chiefly out of Town the ceremony will not be so tedious.

As to politicks, the English continue to publish the most abusive bare faced falshoods against America that you can conceive of. Yet glaring as they are, they gain credit here, and shut their Eyes against a friendly and liberal intercourse. Yet their very existance depends upon a friendly union with us. How the pulse of the Ministry beat, time will unfold, but I do not promise or wish to myself a long continuance here. Such is the temper of the two Nations towards each other, that if we have not peace we must have war. We cannot resign the intercourse and quit each other. I hope however that it will not come to that alternative.

Captain Callihan arrived last week from Boston which place he left 4 of July. I was not a little mortified in not receiving a single Letter by him. I sought for them in every place where I thought it probable they might be. I am not without hope that the Captain himself may yet have some in his private care as the letters in the bag generally are landed at Dover and sent by land several days before the ship gets up, but as Captain Lyde sails directly I must finish my Letters and send them this afternoon.

I am not a little anxious for my son, as we have the News papers from New York up to july 6th and he was not then arrived. He sailed the 21 of May, and must have a very tedious passage. I shall wait very impatiently for the next packet. I had hoped that he was in Boston by that time.

How did Charles succeed, I want very much to know? And how Tommy comes on. I have sent him a Book and one to each of my neices and Nephews. I wish it was in my power to do more for my Friends, but thus it is. We did not bring the last year about upon our anual allowence, and very far were we from being extravagent.

Remember me kindly to Mr. Shaw, Mr. Thaxter and all our Friends and believe me most affectionately   Your sister

c. August 15, 1785

SAMUEL RICHARDSON

To Lucy Cranch

London, (Grosvenor Square,)
My dear Lucy   27 August, 1785

I have not yet noticed your obliging favor of April 26th, which reached me by Captain Lyde, whilst I was at the Bath Hotel. I had then so much upon my hands, that I did not get time to write but to your mamma and cousin, who I hope is with you before now. By him I wrote many letters, and amongst the number of my friends, my dear Lucy was not omitted.

If I did not believe my friends were partial to all I write, I should sometimes feel discouraged when I take my pen; for, amongst so large a number of correspondents, I feel at a loss how to supply them all.

It is usual at a large entertainment, to bring the solid food in the first course. The second consists of lighter diet, kickshaws, trifles, whip syllabub, &c.; the third is the dessert, consisting of the fruits of the season, and sometimes foreign sweetmeats. If it would not be paying my letters too great a compliment to compare any of them to solid food, I should feel no reluctance at keeping up the metaphor with respect to the rest. Yet it is not the studied sentence, nor the elaborate period, which pleases, but the genuine sentiments of the heart expressed with simplicity. All the specimens, which have been handed down to us as models for letter-writing, teach us that natural ease is the greatest beauty of it. It is that native simplicity too, which gives to the Scotch songs a merit superior to all others. My favorite Scotch song, "There's na luck about the house," will naturally occur to your mind.

I believe Richardson has done more towards embellishing the present age, and teaching them the talent of letter-writing, than any other modern I can name. You know I am passionately fond of all his works, even to his "Pamela." In the simplicity of our manners, we judge that many of his descriptions and some of his characters are beyond real life; but those, who have been conversant in these old corrupted countries, will be soon convinced that Richardson painted only the truth in his abandoned characters; and nothing beyond what human nature is capable of attaining, and frequently has risen to, in his amiable portraits. Richardson was master of the human heart; he studied and copied nature; he has shown the odiousness of vice, and the fatal consequences which result from the practice of it; he has painted virtue in all her amiable attitudes; he never loses sight of religion, but points his characters to a future state of restitution as the sure ground of safety to the virtuous, and excludes not hope from the wretched penitent. The oftener I have read his books, and the more I reflect upon his great variety of characters, perfectly well supported, the more I am led to love and admire the author. He must have an abandoned, wicked, and depraved heart, who can be tempted to vice by the perusal of Richardson's works. Indeed, I know not how a person can read them without being made better by them, as they dispose the mind to receive and relish every good and benevolent principle. He may have faults, but they are so few, that they ought not to be named in the brilliant clusters of beauties which ornament his works. The human mind is an active principle, always in search of some gratification; and those writings which tend to elevate it to the contemplation of truth and virtue, and to teach it that it is capable of rising to higher degrees of excellence than the mere gratification of sensual appetites and passions, contribute to promote its mental pleasures, and to advance the dignity of our natures. Sir Joshua Reynolds's observations with respect to painting may be applied to all those works which tend to refine the taste, "which, if it does not lead directly to purity of manners, obviates, at least, their greatest depravation, by disentangling the mind from appetite, and conducting the thoughts through successive stages of excellence, till that contemplation of universal rectitude and harmony, which began by taste, may, as it is exalted and refined, conclude in virtue."

Why may we not suppose, that, the higher our attainments in knowledge and virtue are here on earth, the more nearly we assimilate ourselves to that order of beings who now rank above us in the world of spirits? We are told in scripture, that there are different kinds of glory, and that one star differeth from another. Why should not those who have distinguished themselves by superior excellence over their fellow-mortals continue to preserve their rank when admitted to the kingdom of the just? Though the estimation of worth may be very different in the view of the righteous Judge of the world from that which vain man esteems such on earth, yet we may rest assured that justice will be strictly administered to us.

But whither has my imagination wandered? Very distant from my thoughts when I first took my pen.

We have a large company to dine with us to-day, and I have some few arrangements to make before dinner, which obliges me to hasten to a conclusion; among the persons invited, is a gentleman who married the only daughter of Richardson. She died about six months ago. This gentleman has in his possession the only portrait of her father which was ever taken. He has several times invited me to go to his house and see it. I design it, though I have not yet accepted his invitation.

Write to me, my dear Lucy, and be assured I speak the words of truth and soberness when I tell you that your letters give real pleasure to Your affectionate aunt,   A.A.

"I WAS ONE CONTINUED SHUDDER"

To Elizabeth Cranch

No 8   London Sepbr 2 1785
My dear Betsy   Grosvenor Square
   At the Bath hotel I received my dear Neices Letter of April.
I have told your Sister and other Friends why I did not write
then, but I should have no excuse to give if I omitted so good
an opportunity as now offers by Mr. Storer.
   This day two months ago we removed here, where I should
be much delighted if I could have my Sisters my Cousins and
connections round me, but for want of them every Country I
reside in, lacks a principal ingredient in the composition of my
happiness.
   London in the Summer season is a mere desert, no body of
concequence resides in it, unless necessitated too, by their
Buisness. I think the Gentry quite [   ] in every view to retire to their Country seats, residing upon them is generally a
great benefit to the propriater. Many noble Men expend vast
sums anually in improveing and Beautifying their estates. I am
told that one must visit some of these Manors and Lordships
to form a just estimate of British Grandeur and Magnificence.
   All the Villages which I have seen round London are mere
Gardens, and shew what may be effected by Culture, but we
must not expect for many Years to see America thus improved.
Our numbers are few in comparison with our acres, and property is more equally distributed which is one great reason of
our happiness; Industery there, is sure to meet with its recompence and to preserve the Labourer from famine from Nakedness and from want. The Liberal reward which Labour meets
with in America is an other Source of our National prosperity,
population and increasing wealth result from it. The condition
of our Labouring poor is preferable to that of any other Country, comparatively speaking. We have no poor except those
who are publickly supported. America is in her early vigor, in
that progressive state, which in reality is the Cheerful and
flourishing state to all the different orders of Society. It is so to
the humane constitution, for when once it has reachd the

meridian it declines towards the Setting Sun. But America has much to do e'er she arrives at her Zenith. She possesses every requisite to render her the happiest Country upon the Globe. She has the knowledge and experience of past ages before her. She was not planted like most other Countries with a Lawless Banditti, or an Ignorant savage Race who cannot even trace their origon, but by an enlightned a Religious and polished people. The Numerous improvement which they have made during a Century and half, in what was then but a howling Wilderness, proves their state of civilisation. Let me recommend to you my dear Girl to make yourself perfect mistress of the History of your own Country if you are not so allready; no one can be sufficiently thankfull for the Blessings they enjoy, unless they know the value of them.

Were you to be a witness to the Spectacles of wretchedness and misiry which these old Countries exhibit, crouded with inhabitants; loaded with taxes, you would shuder at the sight. I never set my foot out, without encountering many objects whose tatterd party coulourd garments, hide not half their Nakedness, and speak as Otway expresses it "Variety of Wretchedness," coverd with disease and starving with hunger; they beg with horrour in their countanances; besides these, what can be said of the wretched victims who are weekly Sacrificed upon the Gallows, in numbers Sufficient to astonish a civilized people? I have been credibly informd that hundreds of Children from 4 years and upwards, sleep under the trees fences and Bushes of Hide Park nightly, having no where else to lay their heads, and subsist by day; upon the Charity of the passenger. Yet has this Country as many publick institutions for charitable support of the infirm, as any country can Boast. But there must be some essential defect in the Government and Morals of a people when punishments lose their efficacy and crimes abound.

But I shall make you sick with my picture of wretchedness. Let it excite us to thankfulness my Dear Girl that our lives have fallen to us in a happier Land, a Land of Liberty and virtue, comparatively speaking. And let every one so far as there Sphere of action extends, and none so contracted as to be without Some influence, Let every one consider it as a duty which they owe to themselves to their Country and to posterity to practise virtue, to cultivate knowledge and to Revere the deity as the only means, by which not only individuals, but a people or a Nation can be prosperous and happy. You will think I have turnd preacher. I know I am not writing to a thoughtless, but to a reflecting Solid young Lady, and that shall be my excuse.

How have you advanced in your musick. The practise of Musick to those who have a taste and ear for it, must be one of the most agreeable of Amusements. It tends to soften and harmonize the passions, to elevate the mind, to raise it from earth to Heaven. The most powerfull effects of Musick which I ever experienced, was at Westminister Abbey. The place itself is well calculated to excite solemnity, not only from its ancient and venerable appearence, but from the dignified Dust, Marble and Monuments it contains. Last year it was fitted up with seats and an organ loft sufficienly large to contain six hundred Musicians, which were collected from this and other Countries. This Year the Musick was repeated. It is call'd the celebration of Handles Musick. The sums collected are deposited, and the income is appropriated to the support of decayed Musicians. There were 5 days set apart for the different performances. I was at the peice call'd the Messiah, and tho a Guinea a ticket, I am sure I never spent one with more satisfaction. It is impossible to describe to you the Solemnity and dignity of the Scene. When it came to that part, the Hallelujah, the whole assembly rose and all the Musicians, every person uncoverd. Only conceive six hundred voices and instruments perfectly chording in one word and one sound! I could scarcly believe myself an inhabitant of Earth. I was one continued shudder from the begining to the end of the performance. Nine thousand pounds was collected, by which you may judge of the rage which prevaild for the entertainment.

How do all my good Friends and old Neighbours. Let me hear as often as possible from you. Never conceive that your Letters are trifling, nothing which relates to those I Love appears so to me. This Letter is to go by Mr. Storer, as I told you in the begining; a smart youth for some of you; and what is better a virtuous and good Young Man. We are sorry to part with him, for he is quite Domesticated with us, but we hope he will be benifited by the exchange. It is time for him to be

some way fixed in a profession for Life. He thinks of Divinity,
and now I am talking of Divinity I will inquire after my Friend
Mr. Wibird and chide you all for never mentioning him—for I
have seen him twenty times Since my absence come up your
yard, and enter the house, and inquire (after having thrown
aside his cloak) "Well, have you heard from your Aunt? What
does She say, and how do they all?"

I hope you have seen your cousin before this time and in
your next you must tell me how you like him. You must cure
him of some foibles which he has. He will take it kindly of you,
for he is a good youth only a little too possitive. My paper only
allows me to say that I am Yours   AA

ACROBATICS

To Lucy Quincy Tufts

My Dear Aunt   London Sepbr 3d. 1785
    And why my dear Madam have you not written a few lines,
and tuckt into a corner of my good uncles Letters when he has
favourd me with one? Perhaps you think I ought first to have
adrest you. I knew I was writing to both, whenever I scribled
to my honourd Friend, and that my sisters and Neices would
communicate to you their Letters whenever there was any
thing worthy your notice.

    I know Madam that you Live a Life so retired and are now
so frequently seperated from your worthy companion that I
flatter myself a few lines from me will not be unacceptable to
you: tho I were to amuse you with what is the Ton of London,
The learned pig, dancing dogs, and the little Hare that Beats
the Drum. It is incredible what sums of Money are nightly
lavishd upon these kinds of Amusements, many of them fit
only to please children. The Tumbling and rope Dancing is
worth seeing once or twice, because it gives you an Idea of
what skill agility and dexterity the Humane frame is capable of,
and of which no person can form an Idea without having seen
it. The House where these wonderfull feats are exhibited is
calld Sadlers Wells and is accomodated with Boxes and a Stage

in the manner of a play House. Upon the Stage two machines are fixed upon which a rope is extended about 15 foot from the floor. Upon this the Dancers mount drest very neat with a Jocky and feathers and a silk Jacket and Breaches, the Jacket very tight to the waist and a sash tied round the Jacket. He bows to the company; upon which a person who stands near him gives him a long pole made thick at each end. With this pole which serves to Balance him, he commences his dance to the Musick which he keeps time with. He will run backwards and forwards poise himself upon one foot, kneel jump across the rope, spring upon it again, and finally throws down the pole and jumps 6 foot into the air repeatedly, every time returning upon the rope with the same steadiness as if it was the floor, and with so much ease, that the spectator is ready to believe he can perform, the same himself. There is one man who is stilled the little devil, who dances with wooden shoes, and I have seen him stand upon his head with his feet perpendicular in the air. All this is wonderfull for a Man, but what will you say, when I assure you I have seen a most Beautifull Girl perform the same feats! Both in Paris and England. Why say you what could she do with her peticoats? It is true that she had a short silk skirt, but she was well clad under that, with draws, and so are all the female Dancers upon the stage, and there is even a law in France that no woman Shall dance upon the stage without them; But I can never look upon a woman in such situations, without conceiving all that adorns and Beautifies the female Character, delicacy modesty and diffidence, as wholy laid asside, and nothing of the woman but the Sex left.

In Europe all the lower class of women perform the most servile Labour, and work as hard with out door as the Men. In France you see them making hay, reaping sowing plowing and driveing their carts alone. It would astonish you to see how Labourious they are, and that all their gain is coars Bread and a little ordinary wine, not half so good as our cider. The Land is all owned by Marquisses Counts and Dukes, for whom these poor wretches toil and sweat. Their houses through all the villages of France consist of thatched roof Huts, without one single pane of glass. When they have any buisness which requires light, they set out of Door, and this they usually do through the whole season, for Heaven has blesst them with an admirable Climate, and a soil productive of every necessary and delicacy that Luxery can pant for. But there Religion and Government Mar all heavens Bounty. In Spain I have been told that it is much worse. I believe in England the common people live more comfortably, but there is wretchedness and oppression enough here, to make a wise Man mad.

If I was not attached to America by a Naturel regard, as my native Country, when I compare the condition of its inhabitants, with that of the Europeans, I am bound to it by every feeling of phylanthropy, and pray that the Blessings of civil and Religious Liberty, knowledge and virtue may increase and shine upon us, in proportion as they are clouded and obstructed in the rest of the Globe, and that we may possess wisdom enough to estimate aright our peculiar felicity.

I will not close untill I have inquired after your Health and that of your Son and Neice to whom present my Love. Mr. Adams and your Neice also tender you their regards. As I esteem a good domestick I would not forget them in the number of your family, or any of my Towns folks who may think it worth while to inqure after Your affectionate Friend and Neice

Abigail Adams

"THERE ARE SO MANY BONES OF CONTENTION"

To John Quincy Adams

No 4.   London Sepbr 6. 1785
My Dear Son   Grosvenor Square
    Yesterday being Sunday I went with your papa to the Foundling Church, Dr. Price whom we usually attend being absent a few weeks in the Country. When I returnd from Church I went into my closet and took up my pen with an intention of writing to you; but I really felt so *trist* at not having heard of your arrival that I could not compose myself sufficently to write to you, so I scribled to your Brothers. By the time I had finishd my Letters, I was call'd to tea. Mr. Brown the painter came in and spent part of the Evening. I read a

sermon in Barrow upon the Government of the Tongue, and went to Bed with one of my old impressions that Letters were near at Hand. This Morning went below to Breakfast, the Urn was brought up Boiling, the Chocolate ready upon the table, Enter Mr. Spiller the Butler, who by the way is a very spruce Body, and after very respectfully bowing with his Hands full "Mr. Churchs compliments to you Sir, and has brought you this pacquet, but could not wait upon you to day as he was obliged to go out of Town." Up we all jumpt, your Sister seized hold of a Letter, and cry'd my Brother, my Brother. We were not long opening and perusing, and I am so glad, and I am so glad, was repeated from one to an other. Mamma did not fail remarking her old impression. The Chocolate grew cold, the top of the tea pot was forgotton, and the Bread and Butter went down uneaten, yet nobody felt the loss of Breakfast, so near akin is joy and grief that the effect is often similar.

Your Pappa had a prodigious quantity of writing to do before, and his packets from Congress just received has increased it much. I know not what he would have done if Mr. Storer had not lent him a hand, and copied his Letters for him. Yet it is a little hard upon him, as he is very buisy in preparing for his voyage. The Prussian Review which was to commence upon the 20th of last Month, was drawing together all the great Military Characters in Europe. It was like to prove an object of vast importance as it was to consist not only of the best troops, but of the greatest number, and to be reviewd by the most celebrated military Sovereign now living. Col. Smith considerd it as an object which merited his attention, and requested leave of absence for a few weeks. Your Pappa readily granted his request, as at that time there was little prospect of Buisness, but it has so happend that from Holland from France, America and here, there has been much to do, and much yet remains undone. Dispatches must be got ready for Mr. Storer who is to sail in a few days. The Col. has been gone a month, we have received two Letters from him and may I think look for his return daily. He does not live with us, he has appartments in Leiscester Fields, he always dines with us. I like him much, but I do not rely wholy upon my own opinion. I will quote your pappas words writing of him to the President of Congress. "Col. Smith has been very active and attentive to Buisness, and is much respected. He has as much honour and spirit as any Man I ever knew. His principals are those of his Country, and his abilities are worthy of them. He has not the poetical Genius of Humphries, but he has much superiour talants, and a more independant temper as a politician. In short you could not have given me a Man more to my taste." I may further add that he is sedate, not too much given to amusement, and a mind above every little mean thought or action. He appears formed for a Military Life, and will figure at the Head of an Army should we have occasion for him. I assure you I am not without apprehensions that such an event is not so far distant as I once hoped: the temper and disposition of this People is as hostile towards us, as it was in the midst of the War. Pride envy and Revenge rankles in their Hearts and they study every method in their power to injure us, in the Eyes of all Europe by representing us as Lawless, divided amongst ourselves, as Bankrupts. Every hireling Scribler is set to work to vilify us in the most reproachfull terms, and they refuse to publish any thing of a contrary tenor unless you will bribe them to. Much of this bilingsgate is circulated in order to prevent Emigrations from Ireland. If your Pappa had attended to the Letters he has received, and would have given any encouragement, he might have settled whole States, but he has always refused to do any thing upon the Subject. There is scarcly a day passes without applications.

Our Countrymen have most essentially injured themselves by running here in Shoals after the Peace, and obtaining a credit which they cannot Support. They have so shackld and hamperd themselves that they cannot now extricate themselves; merchants who have given credit, are now Suffering, and that naturally creates ill will, and hard words. His Majesty and the Ministry shew every personal respect and civility which we have any right to expect. "The Marquiss de la Fayette, writes that he had always heard his Majesty was a great dissembler but he never was so throughly convinced of it, as by the reception given to the American Minister." I wish there conduct with regard to our Country was of a Peice with that which they have shewn to its representitive. The Marquis of Carmathan and Mr. Pitt, appear to possess the most liberal Ideas with respect to us, of any part of the Ministry. With regard to the Negroes they are full and clear that they ought to be payd for, but as to the posts; they say, the relinquishment of them, must depend upon certain other matters, which you know they were not at liberty to explain in private conversation. But it is no doubt they mean to keep them, as a security for the payment of the Debts, and as a rod over our Heads. They think we are as little able to go to war, as they are. The Bugget has not yet been offically opend. A Generous Treaty has been tenderd them, upon which they are now pondering and brewing. The fate of the Irish propositions has thrown weight into the American Scale, but there are so many Bones of contention between us, that snarling spirits will foment into rage, and cool ones kindle by repeated Irritation. It is astonishing that this Nation Catch at every straw which swims, and delude themselves with the Buble that we are weary of our independance, and wish to return under their Government again. They are more actuated by these Ideas in their whole System towards us, than any generous plans which would become them as able statesmen and a Great Nation. They think to Effect their plans by prohibitary acts and heavy duties. A late act has past prohibiting the exportation of any tools of any kind. They say they can injure us; much more than we can them, and they seem determined to try the experiment. Those who look beyond the present moment foresee the concequences, that this Nation will never leave us untill they drive us into Power, and Greatness that will finally shake this kingdom. We must struggle hard first, and find many difficulties to encounter, but we may be a Great and a powerfull Nation if we will; industery and frugality, wisdom, and virtue must make us so. I think America is taking Steps towards a reform, and I know her Capable of whatever she undertakes. I hope you will never lose sight of her interests, but make her welfare your study, and spend those hours which others devote to Cards and folly in investigating the Great principals by which nations have risen to Glory and eminence, for your Country will one day call for your services, either in the Cabinet or Feild. Qualify yourself to do honour to her.

You will probably hear before this reaches you of the extrodanary affair respecting the Cardinal Rohan. It is said that his confinement is in concequence of his making use of the

Queens name to get a diamond Neclace of immence value into his Hands. Others say it is in concequence of some reflections cast upon the Character of the Queen. Others suppose that the real fact is not known. I send you one Newspaper account of the matter, and have not room to add more than that I am your affectionate   A A

Please to remember I have not a single Line from you.

PURCHASING TABLECLOTHS

To Thomas Jefferson

Dear sir   London October 7th. 1785
   Your very polite favour was handed me by Col. Franks. I am much obliged to you for the execution of the several commissions I troubled you with. Be assured sir that I felt myself Honourd by your commands, tho I have only in part executed them, for I could not find at any store table Cloths of the dimensions you directed. The width is as you wisht, but they assure me that four yds and three quarters are the largest size ever used here, which will cover a table for 18 persons. To these Cloths there are only 18 Napkins, and to the smaller size only twelve. I was the more ready to credit what they said, knowing that I had been obliged to have a set of tables made on purpose for me, in order to dine 16 or 18 persons. These rooms in general are not calculated to hold more and it is only upon extraordinary occasions that you meet with that number at the tables here. The Marquis of Carmarthan who occasionally dines the Foreign Ministers, and has a House found him by his Majesty, cannot entertain more than 15 at once, and upon their Majesties Birth days, he is obliged to dine his company at his Fathers the Duke of Leeds. The person where I bought the Cloth offerd to have any size made, that I wisht for, and agreed to take eight pounds ten shillings for 20 Napkins and a cloth 5 yds long. I gave seven for this which I send, and shall wait your further directions. I took the precaution of having them made and marked to secure them against the custom House,

and hope they will meet your approbation. I think them finer than the pattern, but it is difficult judging by so small a scrap. I have also bought you two pair of Nut crackers for which I gave four shillings, we [   ] convenient that I thought they would be equally so to you. There is the article of Irish linen which is much superiour here to any that is to be had in France, and cheeper I think. If you have occasion for any you will be so good as to let me know. It cannot easily pass without being made, but that could be easily done, only by sending a measure. At the rate of 3 shilling & six pence pr yd by the peice, the best is to be had. As we are still in your debt, the remainder of the money shall be remitted you or expended here as you direct. Mr. Adams supposed there might be something of a balance due to him in the settlement of a private account with Mr. Barclay, which he has orderd paid to you. He will also pay the money here for the insurence of Mr. Hudons Life, by which means what ever remains due to you can be easily settled.

Haveing finishd the article of Buisness, I am totally foild at that of Compliment. Sure the air of France, conspired with the Native politeness and Complasance of the writer to usher into the World such an assemblage of fine things. I shall value the warrior Deity the more for having been your choise, and he cannot fail being in taste in a Nation which has given us such proofs of their Hostility; forgiveness of injuries is no part of their Character, and scarcly a day passes without a Boxing match; even in this square which is calld the polite and Court end of the city. My feeling have been repeatedly shock'd to see Lads not more than ten years old striped and fighting untill the Blood flow'd from every part, enclosed by a circle who were claping and applauding the conquerer, stimulating them to continue the fight, and forceing every person from the circle who attempted to prevent it. Bred up with such tempers and principals, who can wonder at the licentiousness of their Manners, and the abuse of their pens. Their arrows do not wound, they rebound and fall harmless [   ]. But amidst their boasted freedom of the press, one must bribe [   ] to get a paragraph inserted in favour of America, or her Friends. Our Country has no money to spair for such purposes; and must rest upon her own virtue and magninimity. [   ] may too late convince this Nation that the treasure which they knew not how to value, has irrecoverably past into the possesion of those who were possesst of more policy and wisdom.

I wish I might flatter myself with the hope of seeing you here this winter. You would find a most cordial welcome from your American Friends, as well as from some very distinguished literary Characters of this Nation.

My best regards to Miss Jefferson to Col. Humphries to Mr. Short, or any other Friends or acquaintance who may inquire after Your Friend and humble servant   A Adams

My daughter presents her respectfull regards to you and compliments to the rest of the Gentleman.

ON STUDYING AMERICAN HISTORY

To Charles Adams

Dear Charles

Your Letters of october 23 and your last by capt Lyde gave me great pleasure, and the account your uncle Aunt and other Friends give me of your conduct and behaviour makes me very happy. A perceverence in the same steady course will continue to you the regard and Esteem of every worthy character and what is of infinate more importance your own peace of mind and the Approbation of your Maker. I am very glad you have engaged in the reading of History. You recollect I dare Say how often I have recommended to you an acquaintance with the most important events both of ancient and modern times. You have begun properly by attending to that of your own Country first. It would not be amiss if you was to read Hubbards history of the Indian Wars and Neals history of Massa. Those with Hutchinsons will give you a just Idea of the first Settlement of America and the dangers perils and hardships which our Ancestors encounterd in order to establish civil and Religious Liberty. As there was no settlement on any part of the continent Northward of Maryland except in Massachusets for more than fifty years after the landing of our ancesters at

Plimouth. That state may be considerd as the parent of all the other new England states, altho the first setlers fled to obtain liberty of conscience. They appear to have carried with them much superstition and bigotary, which may be attributed in some measure to the Spirit of the times in which they lived and the percecution they had sufferd, which always tends to narrow the mind and to make it more tenacious of its principals. At the same time they possessd that zeal for religion and that Strickt Piety together with the principals of civil Liberty which enabled them to brave every hardship and to build them up as a people, and laid the foundation for that Noble Structure which the present generation have founded, and which Ranks us as an Nation and which if we depart not from the first principals of our ancestors will in a course of years render us the admiration of future ages. Tho as individuals each may think himself too unimportant to effect so desirable an event, yet every one is accountable for his conduct and none so insignificient as not to have some influence. Ever keep in mind my Dear Son that virtue is the dignity of Humane nature. As you peruse history, remark the characters their views persuits, and the concequence of thir actions. See what an influence justice honour integrity and Reverence for the deity had upon the Nations and kingdoms when ever they predominated either in the Rulars or the people. Behold the Havock and devastation of Rapine cruelty Luxery avarice and ambition; there is an other course of reading which I would recommend to your attention. I mean moral Philosophy. There are a number of valuable Books upon this subject, Grove Butler Smith. Dr Watts upon the improvement of the Mind is particularly calculated to assist a Young Studient. This Book I advise you to an immediate attention to. I think you must find them all in the library.

By the time this reaches you your Brother will also become a student at Colledge. He will advise you with judgment. I hope you will preserve the Strickest Friendship for each other. If you can get time to pay Some attention to your handwriting it will be an advantage to you. This part of Your Education has been too much neglected oweing to Your commencing traveller too Young.

I am very happy to find that you have a studious youth for

your companion. The enlargment of knowledge should be the constant view and design of every student, reflection and observation must form the judgment. We must compare past event with the present in order to form a just estimate of Truth never taking any thing merely from the opinion of others, but weigh and judge for ourselves.

Your sister will write to you I suppose. She is well and so is your Pappa. Your uncles and Aunts are so kind to you that they releive me from any apprehension of Your being any ways neglected. I have sent a peice of Linnen which your Aunt will apply to those of you who stand most in need of it, and I have seald you a Small present in the corner of the Letter. Remember me to Mrs Dana and family and to your cousin Cranch and believe me your most affectionate Mother   A A

c. February 16, 1786

WILLIAM STEPHENS SMITH

To John Quincy Adams

My Dear Son   London Febry 16 1786

Captain Lyde is arrived to our no small joy and brought us a charming parcel of Letters, amongst which I found one from each of my Dear Sons. You know how happy a circumstance of this kind always makes me. Two days before we had heard of his arrival in the River, and waited every hour with impatience for the Letters, for those by Young have not yet come to hand, he is still at Plimouth repairing his Ship.

Yesterday we went to dine with a mr and mrs Blake, who came formerly from Carolina, but who have many years been setled in this Country. Mr Blake is said to be the richest citizen belonging to the Southern State of carolina. I am loth to mention that he owns 15 hundred Negroes upon one plantation; as I cannot avoid considering it disgracefull to Humanity. His anual income is said to amount to 15 hundred sterling, which is very handsome for any Country. He lives in a stile of great elegance. Soon after my arrival in this Country his Lady visited me at the Bath hotel, he was then in carolina. Upon his return, he immediately paid his respects, after which we invited him and his Lady to dine; he came but the Lady decline'd, knowing that the compliment ought first to pass from them to us. A short time after: we received the invitation of yesterday. They appear a very amiable family. It is not the fashion in this Country to dine large parties, few rooms are calculated for it. There were no Ladies present except myself, your sister, mrs Blake, and daughter mr Bridgen whom you know; two young Carolinians, who have lately arrived and dinned with us some time before; your Pappa and col. Smith made the company. We past our time very agreably but still the Letters kept running in my Head. About nine oclock we returnd home, and John Brisler who you know is never so happy as when he has any good News for me, opend the Carriage Door with a smiling countanance, and an "O Mam"! There are a thousand Letters come. This quickned my pace you may be sure. Well says your Pappa as he was getting out, now I shall see your Eyes Glisten, nobody ever enjoy'd a Letter more than you. During this discourse Miss was fled, and had mounted the stairs before I could get into the House, nor could the col. keep pace with the nimble footed Daphne. From that moment untill half past twelve we were all employd in reading our Letters. Even the Watchmans Cry, of "half past ten oclock" which upon other nights puts your pappa in motion for bed, past unheeded by.

Mr S. amused himself, or tried too, with reading the News papers, yet I saw he watchd my countanance at every Letter. A little before 12 the servant informed him that his carriage was at the Door, he rose and comeing to me placed himself in a pensive attitude, then askd me if I would write by a vessel going this week to Newyork? I replied yes I will to my son. Will you said he, with an expression which I easily read from his Heart, will you remember me . . . to him—I promised him I would. Know then my dear Son that this Gentleman is like to become your Brother. I dare say you frequently heard honorable mention of him whilst you was in Newyork. His Character is not only fair and unblemishd, but in high reputation wherever he is known. At the early age of 21 he commanded a regiment and through the whole war conducted with prudence Bravery and intrepidity, when armd against the foe, but when Conquerer, he never forgot the Man in the Soldier. True Courage is always humane and from many accounts, which his Friend col Humphries has given me, with justice may be applied to him those lines of Douglas in the Tragidy—

> "His Eyes were like the Eagle's yet sometimes
> Liker the Dove's, and as he pleasd he won
> All hearts with Softness, or with Spirit aw'd."

Delicacy of sentiment and honour are the striking traits of his Character. Perhaps col Humphries might be a little poetic, when speaking of him, he said "it would take more proofs and arguments to convince him that col S. could be guilty of a dishonorable action, than any other Man he ever knew in his Life." What a contrast some will say? but comparisons are odious—let the memory of former attachments, since the recollection of them can only be attended with pain, sleep in oblivion. As they proved not to be founded upon a durable superstructure, they have properly vanishd like the baseless fabrick of a vision, nor do I think even a wreck is left behind—you will say, is not this Sudden?

Rouchfoucault says, and shakspear makes the same observation that a Heart agitated with the remains of a former passion is most susceptible of a new one. But sitting this aside, you know the pensive sedateness which had long hung upon the brow of your Sister. This was not mitigated amidst all the hurry and bustle of the scenes which surrounded us when we first came to this Country. Loth very loth was she to believe and still more so to confess it, but at last fully convincd from the neglect with which she was treated, (and the account of some Friend I know not whom) of the unsteadiness and dissipation of a certain Gentleman, that he was unworthy her regard. She wrote him a letter very soon after we arrived here, expressive of her mind, tho she did not at that time make it known to her Friends. But she afterward produced a copy of the Letter as a full proof that her conduct was the result of proper conviction and mature deliberation. The final dismission and the last Letter she ever wrote him was in concequence of my expressing a doubt of his strickt honour. It was then as I think I before related to you, that she disclosed her mind fully upon the subject, and askt advise of your pappa, upon which he told her if she had sufficient reason to doubt both his honour and veracity, he had rather follow her to the Grave than see her united with him.

I will not disguise to you that we had not been long removed to this House, before I saw that the Gentleman who made a part of the family was happier in sitting down and reading to the Ladies, in walking riding or attending us to the Theaters, than of any other company or amusement. I began to feel very anxious because I knew he was a stranger to your sisters Situation. Yet nothing could be said, as I really believe he was not him self conscious of his Situation, till I thought it my duty to hint to him carelessly her being under engagements in America. This led him to know himself, and to request an explanation from her; Which She gave him with the utmost frankness. Upon which he immediately ask'd leave of absence, and went to the Prussian Review determined never more to think upon the Subject, for upon his return, he took an early opportunity to assure me that nothing should ever pass from him, inconsistant with the strickest Honour, and the laws of hospitality, that his attentions in future should only be general, and askt my excuse if upon some occasions he should even appear neglegent. I commended his resolutions, and approved his plan, without the most distant hint to him, of the connections being dissolved. Accordingly he did not make one at any of our Parties, he dined with us and then immediately retired. Thus we went on for several weeks at a perfect distance, and you will easily judge of my reasons for wishing to keep from him a real state of facts. But the Little Deity tho represented blind, has a wonderfull nack at making discoveries. Perhaps it was assureances similar to those made to me, which might draw from her an explanation. This is a matter that I shall not be very likely to learn, but I perceived all at once upon a Day, a Dejection dispell'd, a Brightness of countanance, and a lightness of Heart and in the Evening the Gentleman ask'd permission to attend us to the Theatre where we were going with col Humphries; when we returned it was late, and Pappa was gone to bed: as the Gentleman was going: he ask'd a moments audience of me' upon which he put into my Hand with much emotion a Bundle of papers and a letter, which he requested me to read, and communicate to your Pappa; the Papers were votes of congress and commissions, with the amplest testimonies from the Generals under whom he had served of his Brave and good conduct. The letter informd me, "that as the connection which appear'd an insurmountable obstacle to the accomplishment of the wishes nearest his Heart, existed no longer—and from the opinion he had of the Lady, he was persuaded that nothing dishonourable on her part could have occasiond its dissolution. He hoped that Mrs Adams would not be surprised at his early anxiety to gain the confidence of her Daughter, and to lay a proper foundation for a future Connection, provided it should meet with the approbation of her Parents and Friends." There were many other matters in the Letter which were: mention of his family situation &c. I according to request communicated to your Pappa the Papers and Letters. As it appeard to him that this Gentleman possesst all those qualifications necessary to make a faithfull and agreeable companion, he left it wholy to your Sister to determine for herself. I begd her to satisfy herself that She had no prepossession left in her mind and Heart, and she assured me She never could be more determind. I think she must feel a calmness and serenity in her present connextion; which she never before experienced. I am sure it has releived my mind from a Weight which has hung heavy upon it, for more than two years; I rejoice that her conduct meets the approbation of her Friends. I doubt not but her present choise will do so equally. I think she will herself communicate the matter to you.

Coll Humphries has made us a visit of two Months. He has publishd an other Poem much longer than the former, its poetick merit is fully equal to the first. By the first vessel which sails for your port, I will send you one. A more intimate acquaintance; discovers him to be a Man possesst of much more learning, judgment and genuine wit, than I had any Idea of. His visit has raisd him greatly in all our estimations, and we parted with him last monday with much regret.

Your sister I suppose has acquainted you with the Death of poor Williamos. He tarried in paris untill he could not leave it, for debt; and he had borrowd of every American there; untill he could get no further credit. His Death was perhaps fortunate both for him self and others. During his Sickness he must have sufferd, but for the kindness of mr Jefferson, who tho he had found it necessary to check mr W. and had urged him so much to go out to America that he had quitted mr J——n, he supplied him with necessaries during all his sickness. Thus ended the Days of this curious adventurer, who possesst Benevolence, without conduct, and learning without Sense.

Mr and Mrs Bingham arrived here about 3 weeks ago with a full determination to go out to America in March, but having as usual Spaired no pains to get introduced to the families of my Lord Landsdown and my Lady Lucans, they are so *supreemly blest*, that poor America looks like a bugbear to them. "O! now I know mr Bingham you wont go out this Spring. Give me but ten Years, and take all the rest of my Life." Who can withstand flattery and admiration? What female mind young beautifull rich—must she not be more than woman if vanity was not the predominate passion? I accompanied her last thursday to Court and presented her both to the King and Queen, and I own I felt not a little proud of her. St James's did not, and could not produce an other so fine woman. Yet it was the most crouded drawing Room I ever attended, except the late Birth Day. You know this Ladies taste in dress is truly elegant. She had prepaird herself in France for this occasion, and being more fleshy than I have seen her before, she is concequently handsomer than ever.

"She Shone a Goddess, and She moved a Queen."

The various whispers which I heard round me, and the pressing of the Ladies to get a sight of her, was really curious, and must have added an *attom* to the old *score*, for she could not but see how attractive She was. Is she an American, is she an American, I heard frequently repeated? And even the *Ladies* were *obliged to confess* that she was truly an elegant woman. You have, said an English Lord to me, but whose name I knew not, one of the finest Ladies to present, that I ever saw. The Emperers Ambassador Whisperd your Pappa, sir your Country produces exceeding fine women. Aya replied your Pappa bowing and Men too, presenting to him at the same time a mr Chew of Philadelphia, a very likely Youth who with several others have been lately presented by your Pappa to their Majesties. There is a Young Lady here a Miss Hamilton one of the lovelyest Girls in the World, whom I expect next to present.

She has a finer face than Mrs Bingham, her person well pro-
portiond. She does not equal Mrs Bingham in stature, but
person and mind!! I have thought it was fortunate for you that
you went to America, for she is a good deal intimate with your
Sister, and it is impossible not to be charmd with her sweet
modest affible deportment, animated with the Sparkling Eye
of sensibility. Her uncle is doatingly fond of her, never said he,
to me one day did Girl possess more discretion. I could always
leave her to direct herself, and I never had occasion to say, Ann
why do you so? He is wisely going to carry her to America this
summer. She is not yet 18. She is the adopted heir of this rich
uncle.

The Royal family appeard much out of spirits yesterday, the
prince of Wales like Benidict the married Man. The Nation are
all in a ferment, tho they hardly dare speak loud. It seems this
amourus Prince has been for two years voilently in Love, with
a widow Lady near 40 years of age. As she is said to be a Lady
of a virtuous Character she avoided him, but he percecuted
her so that she was obliged to flee to Paris. After having resided
there for a year and half, she returnd in hopes that absence and
other objects had banishd her from his remembrance. He
however renew'd his attacks, and finding that he could not
bring her to his terms, he swore that as he never expected to
be king of England for his Father would out live him, he would
please himself. And it is said and universally believed that he
has married the Lady, Setled 6 thousand pr An upon her, for
which the Duke of Queensburry is responsible, and she now
appears with him at the opera, rides in his carriage with her
servants behind it. He is 3 times a day at her House. The Clergyman who married them is absconded, as it is Death to him.
In the Eye of Heaven the marriage may be valid, but the law of
the land annuls it. She can never be Queen, or the children
ligitimate. Such a step in the British heir Apparant you may
well suppose, gives an allarm. They say his toast is, fat fair and
forty, what a taste. This is the Ladies 3 marriage.

Having given you so many Domestick occurrences, I shall
not write you a word of politicks. Your Friend Murry has been
very sick, looks almost like a Ghost.

I shall write you again by captain Lyde. If there is any thing
in particular which you want let me know. Would that my

ability was equal to my inclination, but here we stand at the old Standerd, tho our expences are a Quarter part more. You go beyond the mark methinks I hear you say. We do, but let C—ss Blush that they continue to degrade themselves in the Eyes of Europe as well as England. This time twelve months, and unless different measures are persued, from what there is now any prospect of, I quit this kingdom for my native Land. I quit it without one regreet, but with a firm belief that it is Devoted to destruction. Like the Swine, they know not the value of the Jewel, once placed in the Bourben scale, poor old England will kick the Beam.

Begone politicks I hate you, did not I say I would not speak of you.

I do not know how to consent that you should give up your diary, it is the kind of Letters which I love best of any. Your sister has been very closely writing ever since she received your Letters. I am rejoiced to find that you are no ways dissapointed in the reception I promisd you from your Friends. Your sister Eliza as you justly term her is very dear to me, as you well know, and that my own children only, are dearer to me than those of my sisters. Never was there a stronger affection than that which binds in a threefold cord your Mamma and her dear sisters. Heaven preserve us to each other for many Years to come.

Your Pappa has a vast deal of writing to do, and he sometimes groans and says but little comes of it. Yet do I know much essential service results from it, and much more might, were our Country wise as they ought to be.

I presume it will not be long before I hear from you at Cambridge. Watch over your Brother, gain his confidence be his Friend as well as Brother. Reverence yourself, and you will not go asstray. Your Friends give me most flattering accounts of you and I give a ready credit to their word, may your honour your integrity and virtue always prove your safe gaurd.

I fear mr King will think I intrude upon him by requesting him to frank this bulky Letter. By captain Lyde I shall write to all my Friends. Let your Aunt know I have received her kind Letters. O but I must mention to you a Gentleman who designs to visit Cambridge in the course of the summer, whom you will notice tho he has no Letter to you, a mr Anstey who

is appointed to go to America by this Government to assertain
the claims of the Loyallists. Lord Carmarthan introduced him
to your Pappa, and askd Letters from him to the different
Governours which your Pappa gave him. He dinned with us
and appears a sensible modest Gentleman, he saild in the last
packet.

Remember me to all my Haverhill Friends and cross the
River present my congratulations. Love to my Thommy and
be assured you are all equally dear to your ever affectionate
Mother   A A

ROYALL TYLER'S CONDUCT

To Mary Smith Cranch

My dear sister   London March 21 1786
    I have just returnd from a visit to Moor Place Moor feilds,
Where I have been to take leave of my much esteemed Friends,
mr and Mrs Rogers, who set out on wedsday for France, and
from thence are to sail in the April Packet for Newyork. Mr
Rogers thinks it most for his benifit, and those connected with
him, to quit England, and endeavour to adjust his affairs himself in America. She communicated their design to me some
time ago in confidence, only our own family and Mr Copleys
are acquainted with their intention. I hope he will be able to
settle his buisness to his own advantage, for he is a worthy
Man, and she one of the best and most amiable of women.
There is not an other family who could have left London that
I should have so much mist, go and See her my sister when she
arrives. You will find her one of those gentle Spirits in whom
very little alteration is necessary to fit for the world of Spirits,
and her Husband seems to be made on purpose for her.

    Only two days ago did your Letter by captain Young reach
me. The contents of it more and more convince me of the
propriety of your Neices conduct, and give me reason to rejoice that I crost the atlantick with her. But what Shall I do
with my Young soldier, who is much too zealous to be married,

and will hardly give me time to tell my Friends that such an event is like to take place. I have no Idea of such a hurry, and so I tell him. He presses the matter to me, but cannot get me to communicate it, because I know very well, that mr A. would have so much compassion for the Young folks, that he would consent directly. He remembers what a dance he led. Now tho I have no objection to the Gentleman, yet I think marriage ought not to be his immediate object. The Services he has renderd his Country, joined to the abilities he possessess will always ensure to him a distinguished Rank in her service. His Character is universally amiable, and I have the prospect of seeing my daughter united to a Man of Strict honour and probity. But I wish he would not be quite so much in a Hurry. I believe not one of our American acquaintance Suspect the Matter. Mrs Rogers excepted to whom I told it.

Mr T. I Suppose has received my Letter by way of Newyork, after which I presume he will not be very solicitious for a voyage. Your Neice has never noticed a line from him, since She closed the correspondence by way of Dr Tufts. She received two very long Letters from him, both of which I have seen, they were perfectly Characteristic of the Man.

In one of them he reflected very severely upon you, and threw out insinuations respecting many other of her correspondents, who I know had never mentiond his Name. But I know he must be mortified, so I can pardon him, wish him well and forgive him, nay thank him for no longer wearing a disguise. The Creature has many good qualities, but that first of virtues Sincerity. How small a portion has fallen to his share! I have written to you by mrs Hay and sent the Lutestring &c by her. Captain Lyde deliverd me the Chocolate safe, but Young, *half seas over*, let the customhouse Seize his, which could not have happend if he had put it into his Trunk. It would do you good if you was to see how Mr Adams rejoices over his Breakfast, for the stuff we get here is half bullocks Blood. Mr Rogers will be a good hand to Send any little matter, he knows how to manage. I will write to My Dear Neices by Lyde. It mortifies me that the length of my purse is so curtaild that I cannot notice them as I wish. What letters are not ready for Cushing expect in Lyde. Do not fail of writing by way of Newyork, only do not send any News papers or very large packets that way, because every vessel stops at some out-port and sends her Letters up by Land.

Remember me affectionately to all my dear Friends, particularly to my honourd Mother to whom I have sent by mrs Hay Lutestring for a Gown. Mrs Quincys silk will send by Lyde.

It is 3 oclock, and I am not drest for dinner tho Esther warnd me that it was past dressing hour some time ago, but I would finish my Letter. A double rap at the door signifies a visit. Adieu I must run, affectionately Yours,   Abigail Adams

"LADIES ROUTE"

To Elizabeth Cranch

My dear Neice   London April 2. 1786

I think my dear Betsy that some Letter of yours must have faild, as I have none of a later date, than that which you sent me from Haverhill by mr Wilson, by which I find that you are studying Musick with Miss White. This is an accomplishment much in vogue in this Country, and I know of no other civilized Country which stands in so much need of harmonizing as this. That ancient Hospitality for which it was once so celebrated, seems to have degenerated into mere ceremony. They have exchanged their Humanity for ferocity and their civility, for, for; fill up the blank, you can not give it too rough a name.

I believe I once promised to give you an account of that Kind of visiting call'd "Ladies Route." There are two kinds, one where a Lady sets apart a particular day in the week to see Company, these are held only 5 months in the Year it being quite out of fashion to be seen in London during the summer. When a Lady returns from the Country she goes round and leaves a Card with all her acquaintance, and then sends them an invitation to attend her Routes during the season. The other kind are where a Lady sends to you for certain Evenings and their Cards are always addrest in their own names both to Gentlemen and Ladies. Their Rooms are all set open and card tables set in each Room. The Lady of the House receives her company at the door of the drawing Room, where a set number of Curtizes are given; and received, with as much order, as is necessary for a soldier who goes through the different Evolutions of his excercise. The visotor then proceeds into the Room without appearing to notice any other person and takes her Seat at the Card table.

> "Nor can the Muse her aid impart
> unskild in all the terms of art
> Nor in harmonious Numbers put
> the deal the shuffle and the cut
> Go Tom and light the Ladies up
> It must be one before we Sup."

At these Parties it is usual for each Lady to play a rubber as it is termd, where you must lose or win a few Guineas; to give each a fair Chance, the Lady then rises and gives her seat to an other set. It is no unusual thing to have your Rooms so crouded that not more than half the company can sit at once, Yet this is calld *Society and Polite Life*. They treat their company with Coffe tea Lemonade orgee and cake. I know of but one agreeable circumstance attending these parties which is that you may go away when you please without disturbing any body. I was early in the winter invited to Madam de Pintos the Portegeeze Ministers. I went accordingly, there were about 200 persons present. I knew not a single Lady but by sight, having met them at Court, and it is an establishd rule tho you was to meet as often as 3 Nights in the Week, never to speak together or know each other unless particularly introduced. I was however at no loss for conversation, Madam de Pinto being very polite, and the foreign ministers being the most of them present, who had dinned with us and to whom I had been early introduced. It being *Sunday* evening I declined playing at Cards. Indeed I always get excused when I can.

> "Heaven forbid, I should catch the manners living as
> they rise"

Yet I must Submit to a Party or two of this kind. Having attended Several, I must return the compliment in the same way.

Yesterday we dinned at mr Paridices. I refer you to mr Storer for an account of this family. Mr Jefferson, col. Smith, the

Prussian and Venitian Ministers were of the company, and several other persons who were strangers. At 8 oclock we returnd home in order to dress ourselves for the Ball, at the French Ambassadors to which we had received an invitation a fortnight before. He has been absent ever since our arrival here till 3 weeks ago. He has a levee every Sunday evening at which there are usually several hundred persons. The Hotel de France, is Beautifully situated, fronting St James park, one end of the House standing upon Hyde park. It is a most superb Building. About half past nine we went, and found some Company collected. Many very Brilliant Ladies of the first distinction were present. The Dancing commenced about 10, and the rooms soon filld. The Room which he had built for this purpose, is large enough for 5 or 6 hundred persons. It is most elegantly decorated, hung with a Gold tissue ornamented with 12 Brilliant cut Lustures, each containing 24 candles. At one end there are two large Arches, these were adornd with wreaths and bunches of Artificial flowers upon the walls; in the Alcoves were Cornicup loaded with oranges sweet meats &c coffe tea Lemonade orgee &c were taken here by every person who chose to go for it. There were coverd seats all round the room for those who did not chuse to dance. In the other Rooms card tables and a large Pharo table were Set. This is a New kind of game which is much practised here. Many of the company who did not dance retired here to amuse themselves. The whole Stile of the House and furniture is such as becomes the Ambassador from one of the first Monarchs in Europe. He had 20 thousand Guineas allowd him, in the first instance to furnish his House and an anual sallery of 10 thousand more. He has agreeably blended the magnificence and splendour of France with the neatness and elegance of England. Your cousin had unfortunately taken a cold a few days before and was very unfit to go out. She appeard so unwell that about *one* we retird without staying Supper, the sight of which only I regreeted, as it was in a stile no doubt superiour to any thing I have seen. The Prince of Wales came about eleven oclock. Mrs Fitzherbet was also present, but I could not distinguish her. But who is this Lady methinks I hear you say? She is a Lady to whom against the Laws of the Realm the Prince of Wales is privately married, as is universally believed. She appears with him in all publick parties, and he avows his marriage where ever he dares. They have been the topick of conversation in all companies for a long time, and it is now said that a young Gorge may be expected in the Course of the Summer. She was a widow of about 32 years of age whom he a long time perceecuted in order to get her upon his own terms, but finding he could not succeed, he quieted her conscience by Matrimony, which however valid in the Eye of Heaven, is set asside by the Law of the Land which forbids a Prince of the Blood to marry a subject.

As to dresses I believe I must leave them to describe to your sister. I am sorry I have nothing better to send you than a sash and a vandike ribbon, the narrow is to put round the Edge of a hat, or you may trim what ever you please with it. I have inclosed for you a Poem of col Humphriess. Some parts you will find perhaps, too high season. If I had observed it before publication, I know he would have alterd it.

When you write again tell me whether my fruit trees in the Garden bear fruit, and whether you raisd any flowers from the seed I sent you. O I long to be with you again, but my dear Girl, Your cousin, must I leave her behind me? Yes, it must be so, but then I leave her in Honorable Hands.

Adieu I have only room to Say Your affectionate

Aunt A A

TRIBUTE FOR BARBARY PIRATES

To Isaac Smith Sr.

Dear sir   London April 8th. 1786
The Barrel of Cramberries you was so kind as to send me in the fall never reachd me till this week, oweing to Captain Youngs long passage and being obliged to put into port to repair the ship, he did not get up to London till about a Week ago. The Cramberries I believe were very fine by the Appearance of the few which remain; and would have proved a most acceptable present if they had arrived in season. We are not however less obliged to you for them, but I would just mention to those who wish to send presents of this kind to their

Friends, that Casks about as large as raison casks, made water tight, with just water sufficient to cover the cramberry, preserves them best. This I found by a cask of that kind which col Smiths Friends sent him, and which were as fine as if they had just been gatherd. Captain Lyde has a cask of Split peas on Board addrest to you. If you will be so good as to send Mrs Cranch a peck of them, and accept the remainder, you will do me a favour.

I wish Sir I could give you a pleasing account of affairs here, as they respect America but the reluctance which the States Shew to give Congress powers to regulate commerce, is to this nation a most agreeable event. They hold it up as a proof that a union of counsels is not to be expected, and treat with contempt the Authority and measures of the different States. There have been however some motions lately, within a few days past, and mr Pitt has requested that an other project of a Treaty might be offerd. It was agreed to, and is now before the Cabinet, but whether any thing is meant to be done, time only can unfold. You will see by the publick papers that mr Pitt's Surpluss, is much doubted, and it is Said that the Mountain is in Labour, whilst the people are trembling through fear of new burdens.

Letters have been received from Mr Randle at Madrid. He and his principal expected to arrive in Algiers some time in March. From mr Barclay, no intelligence has yet come. The embassy of these Gentleman may serve this good purpose, the terms of each Barbery State may be learnt. Congress may then compare them, With those transmitted to them from hence. But the Sum required is so much beyond the Idea of our Countrymen that I fear they hazard a War rather than agree to pay it. They will I hope count the cost of a war first, and consider that afterwards they must pay them a larger Subsidy. Portugal is treating with them and they will soon be at Peace with all other powers and at Liberty to prey upon us. The Tropoline minister who is here, and with whom mr Adams has had several conferences, appears a Benevolent sedate Man. He declares his own abhorrence of the cruel custom of making Slaves of their prisoners. But he says, it is the law of their great Prophet that all christian Nations shall acknowledge their power, and as he cannot alter their Law, he wishes by a perpetual Peace with the Americans to prevent the opperation of it. He swore by his Beard that nothing was nearer his Heart, than a speedy settlement with America, which he considerd as a great Nation, and a people who had been much oppresst and that the terms which he had mentiond were by one half the lowest which had ever been tenderd to any nation. He could answer for Tunis also, and he believed for the other powers with whom the Tripolines had great interests. He said that Spain could not get a Peace with Algiers, untill, tripoli interposed, and he was willing and ready to do every thing in his power to promote a Peace. Every circumstance has been transmitted to Congress, and they must determine.

You will however Sir mention this only to particular Friends, as the Tropoline has been cautious to keep all his transactions from this People, would never have the english interpretor which is allowd by this Court, present.

Be so good as to present my Duty to my Aunt from whom I received a kind letter, and to whom I design soon to write. Regards to the two mr Smiths. Love to cousin Betsy mrs Otis Mrs Welch, and all other Friends. I am dear Sir affectionately Yours   A Adams

My daughter thanks you for your kind mention of her in your Letter and presents her duty to you and her Aunt.

ABIGAIL 2ND IS MARRIED

To Mary Smith Cranch

four oclock morg
My Dear Sister   Grosvenour Square London june 13. 1786

Any agitation of mind, either painfull or pleasureable always drives slumber from my Eyes. Such was my Situation last Night; when I gave my only daughter, and your Neice to *the man* of *her choice*, a Gentleman esteemed by all who know him, and equally beloved by his Friends and acquaintance. A Man of strict honour, unblemish'd reputation and Morals, Brave modest and delicate, and whose study through life will be I doubt not, to make her whom he has chosen for his companion happy. Yet Satisfied as I am with the person, the event is too Solemn and important not to feel an agitation upon the occasion, equal to what I experienced for myself, when my own lot was cast. God bless them, and make them as happy through Life as their Parents have heitherto been.

When I wrote you last I informd you that the marriage would be in the course of a Month or two, but it was hastned on account of the Bishop of St Asaph going into the Country, and the ceremony can be performd but in two ways in this Country, either by regular publication, or a licence Speicial from the arch Bishop of Canteburry. A Licence from him dispences with going to Church, but they are only granted to Members of Parliament, and the Nobility. When col Smith applied, the arch Bishop said it was a new case, (for you know we are considerd as foreigners) and he wisht to ask advice upon it. The next Day he wrote a very polite Letter and said that considering mr Adams's Station, he had thought proper to grant the Licence, and mentiond in a friendly stile the forms which it was necessary for col Smith to go through previous to it. And as the Lady was not 21 a Notary publick must wait upon mr Adams for an attestation of his consent. All forms being compleated, the Bishop of Saint Asaph, and the Clerk of St Gorges Parish in which we live; yesterday afternoon being sunday, performd the ceremony in presence of mr, mrs and Miss Copley, mr Parker of Watertown whom you know, and Col Forest, two intimate Friends of col Smiths. It was the wish and desire of both mr Smith and your Neice, to have as few persons present as with any decency could be. I really felt for her because upon this occasion, however affectionate a Parent may feel a companion of their own Sex and age must be preferable. Miss Hamilton the only Young Lady with Whom she was intimate, was gone to America, and next to her the amiable Mrs Rogers, but both were gone. Mr and Mrs Copley were the next persons with whom we were intimate, each of them of delicate manners, and worthy good people. The ceremony has some things which would be better left out; and the Bishop was so liberal as to omit the grosest, for which we thankd him in our Hearts.

In what a World do we live, and how Strange are the

visisitudes? Who that had told your Neice two years ago, that an English Bishop should marry her, and that to a Gentleman whom she had then never seen; who of us would have credited it? Had Such an Idea been Started, she would never have consented to have come abroad, but the Book of futurity is wisely closed from our Eyes. When the ceremony was over, the good Bishop came to me and told me that he had never married a couple with more pleasure in his life, for he was pleas'd to add, that from the knowledge he had of the Parties, he never saw a better prospect of happiness. Heaven grant that his words may be prophetick. Think of Dr Bartlets Character, and you will know the Bishops. He is a fine portly looking Man, mild in his manners and Speach, with a Grace and dignity becomeing his Character. The arch Bishop is a still finer looking Man.

I feel a pleasure in thinking that the person who has now become one of our family, is one whom all my Friends will receive a Satisfaction in owning and being acquainted with. Tell my cousins Betsy and Lucy, that they would Love him for that manly tenderness, that *real* and *unaffected* delicacy both of Mind and Manners which his every sentiment and action discovers.

On Saturday night Some evil Spright sent mr T. to visit me in a dreem. I have felt for him I own, and if he *really had any regard* for the person whom he *profest* so *much*, he must be chagrined. Sure I am that his conduct in neglecting to write to her as he did for months and Months together, was no evidence of regard or attachment. Yet I have repeatedly heard her tell him, that she would erase from her Heart and mind every sentiment of affection how Strong so ever, if she was conscious that it was not returnd and that She was incapable of loveing the Man, who did not Love her. And Such has been the conduct of mr T. Since her absence, that I hope every step she has taken with respect to him, will justify her conduct both in the Sight of God and Man.

Much and many Months did she suffer before She brought herself to renounce him for ever, but having finally done it, she has never put pen to paper since. When she received a Letter from him this last fall, it was before she had given any incouragement to col S. and during his absence, she laid the Letter before her Father and beggd him to advise her, if upon perusing it he considerd it as a satisfactory justification, she would receive it as such. May he never know or feel, half the Misiry She sufferd for many days. Upon perusing the Letter mr A. was much affected. I read it—but I knew the Hyena too well, I knew his *cant* and *grimace*, I had been too often the dupe of it myself. I then thought it my duty to lay before mr A. Some letters from you, which he had never seen and he returnd the Letter of mr T's to your Neice and told her the Man was unworthy of her, and advised her not to write him a line. At the same time he thought it proper that I should write to him. I did so by the same conveyance which carried some letters and News papers in December. Since which not a line has come from him, and I hope never will again.

I wish I Could send a Balloon for one of my Neices. I shall want a female companion Sadly. My desires will daily increase to return to Braintree. We shall take a journey soon and then the young folks go to Housekeeping in wimpole Street. I have made them agree to Dine every day with us, so that only occasionally will they be obliged to keep a table by themselves. Adieu my dear Sister there are parts of this Letter which you will keep to yourself. There is one ceremony which they have got to go through at Court, which is a presentation to their Majesties upon their marriage. This is always practised.

Mr and Mrs Smith present their regards to all their Friends and mine. We hope for an arrival from Boston daily, this Letter col Smith Sends for me by way of Newyork. I hope all the vessels which have saild from hence have arrived safe, if So you will find that I have not been unmindfull of you. Ever yours

A A

"HE HAS TAKEN MY DAUGHTER FROM ME"

To Thomas Jefferson

Dear Sir   London july 23. 1786

Mr Trumble will have the honour of delivering this to you, the knowledge you have of him, and his own merit will ensure him a favourable reception. He has requested a Letter from me, and I would not refuse him, as it gives me an opportunity of paying my respects to a Gentleman for whom I entertain the highest esteem, and whose Portrait dignifies a part of this room, tho it is but a poor substitue for those pleasures which we enjoy'd some months past.

We console ourselves however by the reflection which tends to mollify our Grief for our departed Friends; that they are gone to a better Country, and to a Society more congenial to the benevolence of their minds.

I supposed sir that Col Smith was your constant correspondent, and that his attention, left me nothing to inform you of. This Country produced nothing agreeable and our own appears to be taking a Nap, as severals vessels have lately arrived without a Scrip, from any creature. By one of the papers we learn that col Humphries was safely arrived.

Perhaps neither of the Gentleman may think to acquaint you, that the Lords of the admiralty have orderd home Captain Stanhopes ship, and calld upon him for a justification of his conduct to Govenour Bowdoin. That having received what he offerd as such, they voted it not only unsatisfactory, but his conduct highly reprehensible. As such they have represented it to his Majesty, and Captain Stanhope will not be permitted to return to that station again. Thus far we must give them credit.

I suppose you must have heard the report respecting col Smith—that he has taken my daughter from me, a contrivance between him and the Bishop of St Asaph. It is true he tenderd me a Son as an equivilent and it was no bad offer, but I had three Sons before, and but one Daughter. Now I have been thinking of an exchange with you sir, suppose you give me Miss Jefferson, and in some future day take a Son in lieu of her. I am for Strengthening [   ] federal Union.

Will you be so good as to let Petite apply to my shoe maker for 4 pr of silk Shoes for me. I would have them made with Straps, 3 pr of summer-Silk and one pr blew Sattin. Col Trumble will deliver you a Guiney for them. Whenever I can be of service to you here, pray do not hessitate to commission me, be assured you confer a favour upon your Humble Servant

A Adams

HOLLAND

To Mary Smith Cranch

My Dear Sister   London Sepbr 12th 1786
     I am again safe arrived in this city after an absence of five
weeks. By the last vessels I wrote Some of my Friends that I
was going to visit Holland. That I had a desire to see that
Country you will not wonder at, as one of those Theatres
upon which my Partner and fellow traveller had exhibited
some of his most important actions, and renderd to his country lasting Blessing. It has been the policy of some of our Allies,
to keep as much as possible those events out of Sight and of
some of our Countrymen to lessen their value in the Eyes of
mankind. I have seen two Histories of the American War written in French, and one lately publishd in English by a mr Andrews. In one of them no notice is taken, or mention made of
our Alliance with Holland, and the two others mention it, as
slightly as possible, and our own Countrymen set them the
example. France be sure was the first to acknowledge our independance, and to aid us with Men and money, and ought always to be first-rank'd amongst our Friends. But Holland
surely ought not to be totally neglected. From whence have
we drawn our supplies for this five years past, even to pay to
France the interest upon her loan, and where else could we
now look in case of a pressing emergincy? Yet have I observed
in Sermons upon publick occasions in orations &c France is
always mentiond with great esteem. Holland totally neglected.
This is neither policy or justice. I have been led to a more
particular reflection upon this subject from my late visit to that
Country. The respect, attention civility and politeness which
we received from that people, where ever we went, was a striking proof not only of their personal esteem, but of the Ideas
they entertain with respect to the Revolution which gave birth
to their connection with us, and laid as they say, the foundation
for their Restoration to priviledges which had been wrested
from them and which they are now exerting themselves to recover. The Spirit of Liberty appears, to be all alive in them, but

whether they will be able to accomplish their views, without a scene of Blood and carnage, is very doubtfull.

As to the Country, I do not wonder that Swift gave it the name of Nick Frog, tho I do not carry the Idea so far as some, who insist that the people resemble the frog in the shape of their faces and form of their Bodies. They appear to be a well fed, well Cloathed contented happy people, very few objects of wretchedness present themselves to your view, even amidst the immence Concourse of people in the city of Amsterdam. They have many publick institutions which do honour to Humanity and to the particular directors of them. The Money allotted to benevolent purposes, is applied Solely to the benifit of the Charities, instead of being wasted and expended in publick dinners to the Gaurdians of them which is said to be the case too much in this Country. The civil government or police of that Country must be well Regulated, since rapine Murder nor Robery are but very seldom found amongst them.

The exchange of Amsterdam is a great curiosity, as such they carried me to see it. I was with mr van Staphorst, and tho the croud of people was immence, I met with no difficulty in passing through, every person opening a passage for me. The exchange is a large Square surrounded with piazza. Here from 12 till two oclock, all and every person who has buisness of any kind to transact meet here, sure of finding the person he wants, and it is not unusal to see ten thousand persons collected at once. I was in a Chamber above the exchange, the Buz from below was like the Swarming of Bees.

The most important places which I visited were Roterdam, Delpt the Hague Leyden Harlem Amsterdam and utrech. I was through many other villages and Towns, the Names I do not recollect. I was 8 days at the Hague and visited every village round it, amongst which is Scaven, a place famous for the Embarkation of king Charles. From Utrech I visited Zest, a small Town belonging wholy to the Moravians, who mantain the same doctrines with the Moravians at Bethelem in Pensilvana, but which are not the best calculated for fulling the great command of replenishing the earth. I visited Gouda and saw the most celebrated paintings upon Glass which are to be found. These were immence window reaching from the Top to the bottom of a very high Church and containd Scripture History. Neither the faces or attitudes, had any thing striking, but the coulours which had stood for near two hundred years were beautiful beyond imagination. From Amsterdam we made a party one day to Sardam a few hours Sail only, it was their anual Fair, and I had an opportunity of seeing the people in their Holly day Suits. This place is famous for being the abode of the Czar Peter whose ship Carpenter shop they Still Shew. At every place of Note, I visited the Cabinets of paintings Natural History and all the publick buildings of distinction, as well as the Seats of several private gentlemen, and the Princ of oranges House at the Hague where he holds his Court during the Summer Months, but the difference which subsists between him and the States, occasiond his retreat to Loo, concequently I had no opportunity of being presented to that Court. We were invited to dine one Day at Sir James Harris's the British Minister at that Court, who appears a very sensible agreeable Man. Lady Harris who is about 24 years old may be ranked with the first of English Beauties. She was married at seventeen and has four fine Children, but tho very pretty, her Ladyship has no dignity in her manners or solidity in her deportment. She rather Seems of the good humourd gigling class, a mere trifler, at least I saw nothing to the contrary. I supped at the Marquiss de Verac the French Ambassadors with about 50 gentlemen and Ladies. His own Lady is dead, he has a Daughter in Law who usually lives with him, but was now absent in France. Upon the whole I was much gratified with my excursion to a Country which cannot Shew its like again. The whole appearence of it is that of a Medow, what are calld the dykes, are the roads which being raised, Seperate the canals, upon these you ride, through Rows of Willow Trees upon each side, not a Hill to bee seen. It is all a continued plain, so that Trees medows and canals, Canals trees and medows are the unvaried Scene. The Houses are all Brick and their streets are paved with Brick. It is very unusual to see a Single Square of glass broken; or a brick out of place even in the meanest House. They paint every peice of wood within, and without their houses, and what I thought not so wholsome, their milk pails are painted within and without, and So are their Horse carts, but it is upon a principal of economy. The Country is exceeding fruitfull and every house has a Garden Spot, plentifully stored with vegetables. The dress of all the Country people is precisely the same that it was two Hundred years ago, and has been handed down from generation to Generation unimpaird. You recollect the Short peticoats and long short Gowns, round [   ] caps with Strait borders and large Straw Hats which the german woman wore when they first Setled at Germantown. Such is now the dress of all the lower class of people who do not even attempt to imitate the Gentry. I was pleas'd with the trig neatness of the women, many of them wear black tammy Aprons, thick quilted coats or russel Skirts, and Small hoops, but only figure to yourself a child of 3 or four drest in the Same way. They cut a figure I assure you. Gold earrings are universally worn by them and Bracelets upon Holly days. The dress of the Men is full as old fashiond, but the Court and Geenteel people dress part English and part French. They generally Speak both the languages, but French most. Since their intercourse with America, the English Language is considerd as an essential part of education. I would not omit to mention that I visited the Church at Leyden in which our forefathers worshipd when they fled from hierarchical tyranny and percecution. I felt a respect and veneration upon entering the Doors, like what the ancients paid to their Druids.

Upon my return home I found that Captain Cushing had arrived in my absence, and a noble packet was handed me by your Neice soon after I arrived, but as we had not seen each other for 5 weeks, we had much to say. And in addition to that I had not closed my Eyes for two days and nights, having had a Stormy Boisterous passage of 3 days attended with no small danger, and as I had rode seventy five miles that day, they all voted against my opening my Letters that Night. Mortifying as it was I submitted, being almost light headed with want of rest, and fatigue. But I rose early the Next morning, and read them all before Breakfast. And here let me thank my dear sister for the entertainment hers afforded me, but like most of the Scenes of Life, the pleasure was mixed with pain. The account of the Death of our Dear and Worthy Aunt, reach'd me in a Letter from Cousin W. Smith the week before I went my journey. Altho I took a final leave of her when I quitted America, yet I have been willing to flatter myself with the hope that I might be mistaken, and that her Life would be prolonged beyond my expectations. How often has her Image appeard to me in the Same Form that she addrest me when I left her House. You know how susceptable her Heart was to every tender impression. She saw how much I was distresst, and strove herself for a magninimity that gave to her whole appearence a placid Solemnity which spoke more forcibly than words. There was a Something undecribable, but which to me seemd Angelick in her whole manner and appearence that most powerfully impressd my mind; and I could not refrain when I arrived here mentioning it, to mr Smith who I dare say will recollect it. Like the Angle she then appeard, she now really is, fitted by a Life of piety and benevolence to join her kindred Spirits, she has left us her example and the Memory of her Many virtues to Comfort our afflicted Hearts—Beloved, Regreated and Lamented! She was like a Parent to me, and my full Heart has paid the tributary Tears to her Memory.

Cut of in early Life, and under circumstances peculiarly distressing is the young Branch of a family who never before experienced an affliction of this kind. The Tree fell whilst the Branch survived to keep alive the source from whence their Sorrows Spring. When you see the family, remember me affectionately to them. My Heart feels for all their sorrows. Nor am I without a Share of Sympathy for the family distresses of a Gentleman who not withstanding his follies I cannot but feel for. I know there is in his disposition a strange mixture, there is benevolence and kindness without judgment, good Sense without prudence and learning without conduct. Early in Life that man might have been moulded into a valuable vessel, in the hands of a steady and Skilfull Master. Let all remembrance of his connection with this family cease, by a total Silence upon the Subject. I would not, add to his mortification, or be the means of giving him a moments further pain. My Friends will do me a kindness by strcktly adhering to this request. I wish him well and happy.

Adieu my dear Sister I Shall write you soon, more fully upon the subjects of your Letters. Remember me affectionately to my dear and aged Parent for whom I have purchased a tabinet.

It is more costly than a silk, but I thought more suteable for her years. I shall send it by the first opportunity. Should any offer sooner than Cushing I shall forward this Letter.

I know not to whom we are indebted for the Chocolate, by captain cushings prudence in taking it out and getting it on shore a few pounds at a time we Saved it, tho he poor Man has had his vessel seaizd and been put to much difficulty and trouble. The Chocolate came very opportunely. Mr Adams was just mourning over his last pound. You see I have only room to add Yours   A A

SHAYS'S REBELLION

To John Quincy Adams

My dear Son   November 28 1786
    Since I wrote you, the packet from N york has arrived after a passage of 43 days, and by that your Letter of August 30th came safe to hand, and upon reading it I was glad to find that your sentiments so nearly agreed with mine. You will inquire into mr Parsons' Terms and with the advise of Dr Tufts look out for Board. But I will get your Father to write you I had rather you should have his opinion directly than at Second hand.

I hope you will not apply so constantly to your Studies as to injure your Health: exersise is very necessary for you, but from the accounts from my Friends I fear you do not pay attention enough to it.

By captain Callihan you received your Books and Letters I presume. I am quite impatient to get Letters from my Friends, tho I know they will be such as to give me pain. The Newspapers and Letters from Newyork are filld with accounts of the most allarming Nature, and I could not refrain shedding tears over them, to behold my Countrymen who had so nobly fought and bled for freedom, tarnishing their glory, loosing the bands of society, introducing anarchy confusion and despotisim, forging domestick Chains for Posterity. For the experience of ages, and the Historick page teach us, that a popular

Tyrranny never fails to be followed by the arbitrary government of a Single person. Who can refrain from anxiety, who can feel at Peace or set Idle, and see whole Bodies of Men giving into those very practices which are sure to work their destruction, breaking a constitution by the very same errors that so many have been broken before?

Common sense and plain reason will ever have some general influence upon a free people, and I will Still hope and believe that a Majority of our CountryMen will bear their testimony against such lawless proceedings, and that by wisdom and firmness they will be able to restore order and harmony without the dreadfull necessity of Shedding Blood. Rome had her Cæsars and her Pompeys, nor will America be less productive; civil dissensions never fail to spirit up the ambition of private Men; the Same Spirit which prompted Honestus to attack the order of the Lawyers, as he terms them, has diffused itself throughout Massachusets, His publications were calculated to sow the seeds of discontent, and dissention amongst the populace and to pull down the pillars of the State. Would to Heaven that none but such as himself, might be crushed by the fall.

I had flatterd myself with the hope that my Children would reap the benifits of an equitable and peaceable Government, after the many Perils and difficulties which their Father had pass'd through to obtain one. But if this is not like to be the case, I would enjoin it upon each of them to turn their attention and their Studies to the Great Subject of Government, and the Rights of Mankind, that they may be qualified to defend them, in the senate, and in the Feild if necessary. You have an Elder Brother whose Heroic Soul and independant Spirit, Breaths the ardour of a Hero and a Freeman, and I have reason to bless the hand of Providence which saved a beloved child from impending ruin, and gave her a Protector, in a Man of Honour and integrity. We are as happy, as the distance from our Friends, and the dissagreeable state of our Country will permit us to be.

I am glad to find by your Letter your Brother Tommy is admitted colledge. I hope you will watch over him with the care of a parent, and the affection of a Brother. I fear their will be no passenger by this packet to whom we can commit our

Letters, and if so I am wholy at a loss for a conveyance as Cushing is not like to get out till Spring.

December 3. 1786

I have a Letter or two for some other of my Friends but they must wait. I heard yesterday that Captain Sayer was arrived. I received one Letter only and that from Mrs Rogers dated 16 of october, which came up by the post. I trust the captain is orderd to deliver his Letters himself. As the Wind is against his comeing up, it may yet be Several days before we get our Letters which you know is very mortifying to Your affectionate Mother   A. A.

"I THINK VERY OFTEN OF YOUR BEING ALONE"

To John Adams

Abbe Green, Bath decem 23 1786

We arrived here about four oclock a fryday afternoon, after a very pleasent journey. The weather was somewhat cold, but a clear Sky and a fine Sun Shine was ample compensation. We found convenient apartments, Good Beaf Mutton and excellent fish for dinner; it was fortunate that we engaged Lodgings before we came, as every House is full. To day being rainy and fogy we have not made any excursion, or looked about us. We wanted a little remit after rising 3 mornings by candle light and riding through the cold. I hope an additional quantity of bed Cloaths will make you comfortable; we had the city Musick this morning to wait upon us, and welcome us to Bath. I Suppose we Shall have some more compliments of the Same kind. I think the Bath road has more of an American appearence than any I have traveld in this Country. The Stone Walls and the Hills and the Towns bearing the Same Names, Reading Malborough newburry all reminded me of New England. I think you would have been better pleasd if you had come with us, than you was when you traveld this road formerly, in summer it must be delightfull. I think very often of your being alone, but whilst the Book lasts you will not want employment, tho you may amusement. Be so good as to let me hear from you, tell me how you do, and direct under cover to col Smith at mr   abbe Green. But why it is calld so I know not, as it is a small paved square and nothing Green to be seen about it.—A Good Nights repose to you tho more than a hundred miles distant my thoughts are very often in Grosveneur Square, and we drink your Health every Day. Mr and Mrs Smith present their Duty. Yours ever   A A

"BE ATTENTIVE TO EXCERCISE"

To John Quincy Adams

My dear Son   London Janry 17 1787
  I wrote you so largly by the Newyork December packet, that a few lines must now suffice. I cannot let a vessel sail without some token from me, and tho I do not insist upon Letter for Letter, you should recollect how dissapointed you used to be when your Friends omitted writing.
  Your Aunt Cranch wrote me in the fall, that you had been unwell with a swiming in your Head. I know by experience how dissagreeable that complaint is for I was Seaizd with it on my return from Holland, to an allarming degree untill I was Bled which relieved me. As you and I both are inclined to corpulence we should be attentive to excercise. Without this a Sedantary Life will infallibly destroy your Health, and then it will be of little avail that you have trim'd the midnight Lamp. In the cultivation of the mind care should be taken, not to neglect or injure the body upon which the vigor of the mind greatly depends. Youth are seldom wise, but by experience, and unhappily few are so attentive in the first portion of Life as to remark with accuracy the causes of indisposition occasiond by excesses, either of food animal or Mental. A great Student ought to be particularly carefull in the regulation of his diet, and avoid that bane of Health late suppers.
  I would advise you upon the approach of Spring to lose some Blood, the Headacks and flushing in your face with which you used to be troubled was occasiond by too great a

Quantity of Blood in your Head. I know you will smile at these precautions, but if you do not heed them; repentance may come too late. Your Brothers Charles and Tommy will I hope be equally attentive, particularly the latter of Night damps and dews. Your sister I have had with me for these ten days suffering under a severe cold taken at Bath. I have not known her so sick since we left America. She is however getting better. With the *Beau mond*, we have made a Tour to Bath for a fortnight. We made up a party of ten or a Dozen Americans, Mr and Mrs Rucker and Miss Ramsey whom you know, were a part of the company. Your Pappa insisted upon my going, tho he could not, as the printers would have waited for him, not then having compleated his Book. I returnd to London quite surfeited with Balls concerts &c.

The seditions in Massachusetts induced your Pappa to give to the World a Book which at first he designed only for a few Friends. He thought it was a critical moment and that it might prove usefull to his Countryman and tend to convince them that salutary restraint is the vital principal of Liberty, and that those who from a turbulent restless disposition endeavour to throw of every species of coercion, are the real Enemies of freedom, and forge chains for themselves and posterity.

I send you by Captain Cushing half a dozen shirts. I shall have another half dozen ready for you by Barnard. Let me know if they fit.

To day we have a Clerical party to dine with us, amongst whom are the two American Bishops dr Price dr Kippis dr disney Dr Rees and several other Clergymen. Adieu my dear son, and accept my best wishes this and every succeeding year of your Life, for Health of body and peace of mind, "for peace o virtue!, peace is all thy own." Affectionatly yours,   A A

Inclosed is a little poetick peice written at the Hyde and the particular description I gave You of the owner and the place, will explain the peice to you.

Accept the little coin inclosed if this and an other which I sent some time ago comes safe to your Hand, make a mark in your next letter thus .

BATH

To Mary Smith Cranch

My dear sister   London Janry 20th 1787

Since the Sailing of captain Folger by whom I wrote you, I have received Letters from you of the following dates, Sepbr 24 and 28th 8th 9 and 22 of october and November 18th. I cannot sufficiently thank you for the entertainment afforded me in them. Some accounts you give me respecting a certain family Shocked me. I should suppose that the peace and happiness of the family was totally destroy'd in a Country like ours, where conjugal infidelity is held in the utmost abhorrence, and brands with eternal infamy the wretch who destroys it. Had the Parties lived in France or Viena where the perplexing word reputation has quite an other meaning than what we have been accustomed to, the Husband might have lookd upon the Gallant as Men do upon their deputies, who take the troublesome part of the buisness off their Hands. But in a Country where the absolution of the Priest is not considerd a compensation for crimes, and Marriage is esteemed holy and honorable, the seducer should be considerd as the worst of assassins. But in this case it may be difficult to determine which was the Seducer, and I feel more inclined to fix it upon the female than the paramour. At any rate she is more Guilty, in proportion as her obligations to her Husband her children her family and the Religion of which she is a professer are all scandilized by her and she has sacrificed her Honour her tranquility and her virtue. Well might Mrs Guile say that she had not ink black enough to describe the vile story, and my Gentle Friend Mrs Rogers writes me, "I think my young Friend will ever have reason to bless the period when prior prospects terminated as they did." The Letter you mention is proof that the *confident was the Author* of the distresses complaind of. But I quit a subject so painfull to reflect upon to give you some account of my late Tour to Bath, that Seat of fashionable Resort, where like the rest of the World I spent a fortnight in Amusement and dissipation, but returnd I assure you, with double pleasure to my own fire side, where only thank heaven, my substantial happiness subsists. Here I find these satisfaction which neither Satiate by enjoyment nor pall upon reflection, for tho I like Some times to mix in the Gay World, and view the manners as they rise, I have much reason to be gratefull to my Parents that my early Education gave me not an habitual taste for what is termd fashionable Life. The Eastern Monarch after having partaken of every gratification and Sensual pleasure which power Wealth and dignity could bestow, pronounced it all Vanity and vexation of spirit, and I have too great a respect for his wisdom to doubt his Authority. I however past through the Routine, and attended 3 Balls 2 concerts, one Play and two private parties besides dinning and Breakfasting abroad. We made up a Party of Americans, Mr and Mrs Smith mr and Mrs Rucker and Miss Ramsey, mr Shippen mr Harrison mr Murry mr Paridice mr Bridgen and a Count Zenobia a venition Nobleman. These with our domesticks made a considerable train, and when we went to the Rooms we at least had a party to speak to. As I had but one acquaintance at Bath, and did not seek for Letters of introduction. I had no reason to expect half the civility I experienced. I was however very politely treated by mr Fairfax and Lady who had been in America and own an estate in Virginia, and by a sister of mr Hartleys, who tho herself a criple, was every way attentive and polite to us. Mr John Boylstone whom I dare say you recollect, was the acquaintance I mentiond. He visited us immediatly upon our arrival, and during our stay made it his whole study to shew us every civility in his power. We Breakfasted with him, and he dinned with us. He has very handsome apartments tho he lives at Lodgings. We drank tea and spent an Evening with him in a stile of great elegance, for he is one of the nicest Batchelors in the World, and bears his age wonderfully retaining the vivacity and sprightliness of Youth. He has a peculiarity in his Manners which is natural to him but is a Man of great reading and knowledge. He is a firm friend and well wisher to America, as he amply testified during the War by his kindness to the American Prisoners. And now you will naturally expect that I Should give you some account of Bath, the antiquity of it, and the fame of its waters having been So greatly celebrated. The story which is related of its first discovery is not the least curious part of it. A Certain King Bladud said to be a descendent from

Hercules, was banishd his Fathers court on account of his
having the Leporissa. Thus disgraced he wanderd in disguise
into this part of the Country, and let himself to a swineherd, to
whom he communicated the Disease as well as to the Hogs. In
driving his Hogs one day at some distance from his home, they
wanderd away to these Streams, of which they were so fond
that he could not get them out: untill he inticed them with
Acorns. After their wallowing in them for several Successive
days he observed that their Scales fell of, and that his herd
were perfectly cured, upon which he determined to try the
experiment upon himself, and after a few Bathings he was
made whole. And Bladuds figure in stone is placed in the Baths
known by the Name of the kings Bath with an incription relating his discovery of these Baths 863 years before Christ.

Bath lies in a great vally surrounded with Hills. It is handsomely built, chiefly with free Stone, which is its own growth
and is dug from the Sides of its Hills. The streets are as narrow
and inconvenient for Carriages as those of Paris, so that Chairs
are chiefly used particularly in the old Town. Bath was formerly
walld in and was a very small place, but of late years it is much
extended, and the New buildings are erected upon Hills. Since
it has become a place of such fashionable resort it has been
embellished with a circus and a Cressent. The parades are
magnificient piles of buildings. The square is a noble one and
the Circus is said to be a beautifull peice of architecture, but
what I think the beauty of Bath; is the Cressent. The front
consists of a range of Ionic Colums on a rustick basement. The
Ground falls gradually before it, down to the River Avon about
half a miles distance, and the rising Country on the other side
of the River holds up to it a most delightfull prospect. The
Cressent takes its name from the form in which the houses
Stand; all of which join. There is a parade and street before
them a hundred foot wide and nothing in front to obstruct
this Beautifull prospect. In this situation are the New assembly
Rooms which are said to exceed any thing of the kind in the
Kingdom both as to size, and decoration, but large as they
were they were compleatly crouded the Evenings that I at-
tended. There is a constant emulation subsisting between the
New and old Rooms, similar to the North and South end of
Boston. It was said whilst I was there that there were fourteen

thousand persons more than the inhabitants of Bath. By this you may judge what a place of resort it is, not only for the infirm, but for the Gay the indolent the curious the Gambler the fortune hunter and even for those who go as the thoughtless Girl from the Country told Beau Nash (as he was stiled,) that She came *out of wanteness.* It is one constant scene of dissipation and Gambling from Monday morning till saturday Night, and the Ladies set down to cards in the publick rooms as they would at a private party. And not to spend a fortnight or Month at Bath at this season, of the year, is as unfashionable as it would be to reside in London during the summer Season. Yet Bath is a place I should never visit a second time for pleasure. To derive a proper improvement from company it ought to be select, and to consist of persons respectable both for their Morals, and their understandings. But such is the prevailing taste, that provided you can be in a crowd, with here and there a Glittering Star, it is considerd of little importance what the Character of the person is, who wears it. Few consider that the foundation stone and the pillar on which they Nest the fabrick of their felicity must be in their own Hearts, otherways the winds of dissipation will shake it and the floods of pleasure overwhelm it in ruins. What is the Chief end of Man? is a Subject well Worth the investigation of every rational Being. What indeed is Life or its enjoyments without settled principal, laudable purposes, Mental exertions and internal comfort, that sun shine of the soul, and how are these to be acquired in the hurry and tumult of the World; my visit to Bath and the scenes which I mixed in, instead of exciting a gayety of disposition, led me to a train of moral reflections which I could not refrain detailing to you in my account of it.

Upon my return I had a new scene of folly to go through which was prepairing for the Birth day, but as the fashionable Magizine will detail this matter I shall omit any account of Birth day dresses and decorations only that I most sincerely wish myself rid of it. It is a prodigious expence from which I derive neither pleasure or satisfaction. Mrs Smith did not go this year, for reasons you can Guess I suppose. We have advised col Smith to give up his House and return here again, as it will be vastly inconvenient to me to have her out of the family, no sister no cousin no Aunt who could be at all with her. So that in March they will remove here again, and in April tis probable your Sister may be a Grandmama. New Relatives create new anxieties.

And now for a few domestick Matters. You will find that before I received your Letters I was uneasy and had written to you and Dr Tufts both upon the subject of Board; there can be no reason that you should be at any expence on their account and it would give me pain to know you were. It will be cruel indeed if our Country will not allow us enough to educate our children in the frugal manner we wish for, when for 12 years mr Adams has devoted himself and all his talants to their service, and if they have not reaped all the benifit they might from him, it is there own fault. He has not been laying up a fortune nor has he been squandering one away—nor is there an other Minister either in France England or Holland whose allowence is not splendid to his. But I will not reflect upon our Situation. I will only say that my children Shall not whilst we remain here, live upon my friends or be chargeable to them. Whilst he resided in Holland and his allowence was better he was able to save a little but the publick have no right to expect that she should expend that, any more then that he should run out the little estate he has in America.

I hope captain Folger arrived safe as well as my Trunk. I have sent you by captain Cushing a Hamper of 4 doz porter a double gloucester cheese for commencment, and a cask of Split peas. Be so kind as to Send Sister Shaw half a dozen quarts. I got mr Elworthy to procure them for me, and I dare say he has done his best. If the porter is agreeable it May save you some wine and make a variety. It mortifies me that I cannot do all I wish but take the will for the deed.

The Roits and dissentions in our state have been matter of very serious concern to me. No one will suppose that our situation here is renderd more Eligible in concequence of it, but I hope it will lead the wise and sensible part of the community in our state as well as the whole union to reflect seriously upon their Situation, and having wise Laws execute them with vigor justice and punctuality. I have been gratified with perusing many late publications in our Boston papers, particularly the Speach of the Chief justice which does him great honour. Mr Adams you will see by the Books which captain cushing has

carried out, has been employed in strengthning and supporting our Governments, and has spaired no pains to collect examples for them and shew them in one short comprehensive
statement the dangerous concequences of unbalanced power.
We have the means of being the freest and the happiest people
upon the Globe.

Captain Scot I hear is just arrived, but it may be a week,
perhaps ten days before he will get up himself, so that whatever
Letters he may have I shall not be able to get them before
captain Cushing Sails. This is rather unfortunate as there may
be something I might wish to replie to. As to India handkerchief I give 2 Guineys a peice here for them so that they are
lower with you as well as all other India goods. I give more for
an oz of spice than I used to for a quarter of a pound in America. Only think too of 5 shillings Sterling for every pound of
coffe we use. O pray by the next oppertunity Send me a peck
of Tuscorora Rice. Let it be sifted, I want it only to Scour my
hands with. Tuscorora rice say you, why I suppose She means
Indian meal. Very true my dear sister, but I will tell you a good
story about this said rice. An Ancestor of a family who now
hold their Heads very high is said to have made a fortune by it.
The old granddame went out to America when its productions
were not much known here and returnd rather in Indigent
circumstances. After some time knowing the taste in all ages
for cosmeticks, made out a pompus advertizement of a costly
secreet which she possesst for purifying and beautifying the
complexion, nothing less than Tuscorora Rice at a Guiney an
oz. The project took like the olympian dew at this Day, and
Barrel after Barrel was disposd of at the moderate price before
mentiond, till one fatal day, a sailor whose wife had procured
one Quarter of an oz was caught in the very act of useing it.
The sailor very roughly threw away this darling powder upon
which his wife exclamed that he had ruined her, as She could
procure no more there being an unusual Scarcity at that time.
The fellow examined the paper and swore it was nothing but
Indian meal and that he would bring her two Barrels for a
Guiney the next voyage he went. Upon this the imposture was
discoverd and the good woman obliged to decamp. Now tho I
do not esteem it so highly as the sailors wife I pronounce it the
best antidote to sea coal cracks that can be found. One Friend

and an other has supplied me ever since I have been here, but now I am quite destitute. It is an article in so small quantity that will not be an object for the custom house, so that it may come safely. Remember me most affectionately to all my Friends. I cannot write to half of them. My Neices shall hear from me by Bairnard—in the mean time be assured my dear Sister of the warmest affection of your Sister   A Adams

"THE TUMULTS IN MY NATIVE STATE"

To Thomas Jefferson

My dear sir   London Janry 29th 1787
    I received by Col Franks Your obliging favour and am very sorry to find your wrist Still continues lame. I have known very Salutary effects produced by the use of British oil upon a spraind joint. I have Sent a Servant to See if I can procure some. You may rest assured that if it does no good: it will not do any injury.
    With regard to the Tumults in my Native state which you inquire about, I wish I could say that report had exagerated them. It is too true Sir that they have been carried to so allarming a Height as to stop the Courts of Justice in several Counties. Ignorant, wrestless desperadoes, without conscience or principals, have led a deluded multitude to follow their standard, under pretence of grievences which have no existance but in their immaginations. Some of them were crying out for a paper currency, some for an equal distribution of property, some were for annihilating all debts, others complaning that the Senate was a useless Branch of Government, that the Court of common Pleas was unnecessary, and that the Sitting of the General Court in Boston was a grieveince. By this list you will see, the materials which compose this Rebellion, and the necessity there is of the wisest and most vigorous measures to quell and suppress it. Instead of that laudible Spirit which you approve, which makes a people watchfull over their Liberties and alert in the defence of them, these Mobish insurgents are for sapping the foundation, and distroying the whole fabrick at

once. But as these people make only a small part of the State, when compared to the more Sensible and judicious, and altho they create a just allarm, and give much trouble and uneasiness, I cannot help flattering myself that they will prove Sallutary to the state at large, by leading to an investigation of the causes which have produced these commotions. Luxury and extravagance both in furniture and dress had pervaded all orders of our Countrymen and women, and was hastning fast to Sap their independance by involving every class of citizens in distress, and accumulating debts upon them which they were unable to discharge. Vanity was becoming a more powerfull principal than Patriotism. The lower order of the community were prest for taxes, and tho possest of landed property they were unable to answer the Demand. Whilst those who possesst Money were fearfull of lending, least the mad cry of the Mob should force the Legislature upon a measure very different from the touch of Midas.

By the papers I send you, you will see the benificial effects already produced, an act of the Legislature laying duties of 15 pr cent upon many articles of British manufacture and totally prohibiting others. A Number of Vollunteers Lawyers Physicians and Merchants from Boston made up a party of Light horse commanded by col Hitchbourn Leit col Jackson and Higgonson, and went out in persuit of the insurgents and were fortunate enough to take 3 of their Principal Leaders, Shattucks Parker and Page. Shattucks defended himself and was wounded in his knee with a broadsword. He is in Jail in Boston and will no doubt be made an example of.

Your request my dear sir with respect to your daughter shall be punctually attended to, and you may be assured of every attention in my power towards her.

You will be so kind as to present my Love to Miss Jefferson, compliments to the Marquiss and his Lady. I am really conscience Smitten that I have never written to that amiable Lady, whose politeness and attention to me deserved my acknowledgment.

The little balance which you Stated in a former Letter in my favour, when an opportunity offers I should like to have in Black Lace at about 8 or 9 Livres pr Ell. Tho late in the Month, I hope it will not be thought out of season to offer my best wishes for the Health Long Life and prosperity of yourself and family, or to assure you of the Sincere Esteem and Friendship with which I am Yours &c &c   A Adams

"JOIN THE MILITARY COMPANY"

To Thomas Boylston Adams

Dear Tommy   London March 15th 1787
     I would not omit writing you, because you seem to think you have been agrieved. I do not recollect what I wrote you, but I have Some Idea, that it was an enumeration of the vari-ous accidents you had met with, and advising you to more care and attention in future. I had no occasion to chide you for want of application to your studies, because your uncles your Aunts & your Brothers had been witnesses for you, and all of them had Spoken well of you. it has indeed been a great and an abundant pleasure both to your Father & to me to hear the repeated & constant testimony of all our Friends with regard to the conduct of all our Sons, and I flatter myself that what ever else may be our lot & portion in Life, that of undutifull and vicious children will not be added to it.— Not only youth but maturer age is too often influenced by bad exampls, and it requires much reason much experience firmness & resolution to stem the torrent of fashion & to preserve the integrity which will bear the Scrutiny of our own Hearts. virtue like the stone of Sysiphus has a continual tendency to roll down Hill & requires to be forced up again by the never ceasing Efforts of succeeding moralists. if humane nature is thus infirm & liable to err as daily experience proves let every effort be made to acquire strength. nature has implanted in the humane mind nice sensibilities of moral rectitude and a natural love of excel-lence & given to it powers capable of infinate improvement and the state of things is so constituded that Labour well be-stowed & properly directed always produces valuable Effects. the resolution you have taken of persueing such a conduct as shall redound to your own honour & that of your family is truly commendable. it is an old & just observation, that by

aiming at perfection we may approach it much more nearly than if we sat down inactive through despair—

you will do well to join the military company as soon as you are qualified. every citizen should learn the use of arms & by being thus qualified he will be less likely to be calld to the use of them. War cannot be ranked amongsts the liberal arts, and must ever be considerd as a scourge & a calamity, & should Humiliate the pride of man that he is thus capable of destroying his fellow creatures— I am glad to find you mending in your hand writing, during the vacancies you & your Brother Charles would do well to attend to that. it is of more importance than perhaps you are aware of, more for a Man than a Woman, but I have always to lament my own inattention in this matter. inclosed you will find a little matter which you will make a good use of. your sister sends her Love and will write you soon. I am my dear Son most affectionately Yours

A A

"I AM A GRANDMAMMA!"

To Lucy Cranch

my dear Neice   London April 26 1787—

I write you a few lines my dear Lucy to thank you for your kind Letter, and to inform you that I am a *Grandmamma*! my Grandson be sure is a fine Boy, & I already feel as fond of him as if he was my own son, nay I can hardly persuade myself that he is not, especially as I have been sick for six weeks, I cannot however Nurse him so well as his mamma, who is already so fond of him, that I sometimes quote mrs Storer to her. who could have thought it?

He was Christened last thursday by dr Price and called William after his pappa. in this Country Children are not carried to church, so we had the Christning in the House and about a dozen of our Friends together upon the occasion. we supped & drank the young Heroes Health, & that of our Country and Friends. Mrs Smith dinned below with us, the day 3 weeks frum her confinement, and I have carried little master to ride 3 or four times already. he is very quiet and good, but his pappa is already obliged to leave him, & yesterday morning very reluctantly set of on a journey to portugal, in his way to which he takes France & Spain, & will be absent we expect near four Months, but thus it must be with those who are in publick office. at the same time mr Adams set of for portsmouth in order to hear the examination of a set of villians who have been counterfeiting the paper money of the American States, and mr Cutting accompanied him, so that we are quite alone. as soon as mrs Smith is able we shall make a little excursion into the Country, which I hope will reestablish my Health. My disorder has been long accumulating, & arises from a Billious state of my Blood. it has afflicted me spring & fall for several years, and has at last produced a slow intemitting fever. some days I am able to go out, others not, but it has wholy prevented my attendance upon Routes dinners theatres &c and o Lamentable, I have not been able to go to saint James for more than two months. all this I could have borne with tolerable patience, but what has been really matter of regret to me, is that I have been dissapointed of Seven Lectures out of 12 to which I Subsribed, and which I fear I shall never have the opportunity of attending. they would have afforded me much matter for future recollection & amusement from a retrospect of the Beauties of Nature, and her various opperations manifested in the Works of creation, an assemblage of Ideas entirely new, is presented to the mind. the five Lectures which I attended were experiments in Electricity, Magnetism Hydrostatics optics pemematicks, all of which are connected with, and are subservient to the accommodation of common Life. it was like going into a Beautifull Country, which I never saw before, a Country which our American Females are not permitted to visit or inspect, untill dr Moyes visited America, all experimental Phylosophy was confined within the walls of our Colledges— The Study of Household Good, as milton terms it, is no doubt the peculiar province of the Female Character. Yet surely as rational Beings, our reason might with propriety receive the highest possible cultivation. knowledge would teach our Sex candour, and those who aim at the attainment of it, in order to render themselves more amiable & usefull in the world would derive a double advantage from it, for in proportion as the mind is informed, the countanance would be improved & the face ennobled as the Heart is elevated, for wisdom says Soloman maketh the face to shine. even the Luxurious Eastern Sage thought not of rouge or the milk of roses—but that the virtuous wife should open her mouth with wisdom & the law of kindness dwell upon her Tongue, nor did he think this inconsistant with looking well to the ways of her household, or suppose that she would be less inclined to superintend the domestick oeconomy of her family, for having gone beyond the limits of her dressing room & her kitchen I quote Soloman on this occasion, as we may naturally suppose the picture drawn of a virtuous wife to be the result of his experience & his wisdom, after ranging at large amongst the Eastern Beauties: he pronounces the price of a virtuous woman to be far above rubies & the only character on which the Heart of a Husband may safely rest— the present mode of fashionable education is not calculated to form the rising generation upon the system of soloman. futile accomplishments are substituded in stead of rational improvements settled principals of Truth integrity & Honour are little attended to, Laudible motives of action & incentives to virtue, give place to the form of the Body, the Grace of motion, and a conscious air of superiority which knows neither the Blush of modesty, or diffidence. a Boarding school miss, that should discover either would be thought quite a novice—

But whither has my subject led me? I must return to the Female sphere & talk to you of fashions— the Sandals which I send, I fear will prove too large, but the shoe maker says they are according to the measure. the Novelty of taste has brought the immitation of the Scotch plad into vogue, Waistcoats Bonets & ribbons are all plad, sashes &c I send you a specimin of their Beauty and must quit my Pen to pay my devotions to the kind goddess of Health; whom I am to seek in the Park, or if warm enough in kensington gardens. Flora & Virtumnus will meet me there. adieu my dear girl. may the best of Heavens blessings rest upon you

Your ever affectionate   Aunt A Adams

May 6th

from the Character of the reviewers I bought Louissa a novel the story of which is very interesting I send it you for your amusement

A DEFENCE OF THE CONSTITUTIONS

To Elizabeth Smith Shaw

my dear sister   May 2d 1787 London
    mr Blodget is going passenger in Captain Callihan and has
offerd to take a Letter to you, who are his great favorite. he
will be able to tell you that he has seen my little Grandson who
was, not the first, but the 2d of April Born. we had him
brought down on purpose that mr Blodget might report to
you, that he is a fine Boy. His Mamma is as well as persons
usually are she dinned below the day 3 weeks from her confinement, rather for the pleasure of dinning with mr Smith, who
was to set of for portugal the next day, than because she was
more than usually robust, for I think that she is so good a
Nurse, that it keeps her rather feeble than otherways. She
sends her duty to you, and little master would send his to his
great Aunt if he knew her. you may put up with the term, since
your sister is obliged to; with that of *Gandmamma* I have
spirits my dear sister, but my Health is very feeble. I have been
labouring with Billious disorders, and a slow intermitting fever
near two months. I hope however that it is leaving me
    your kind Letter of Febry 8th came safe to hand. As to our
publick affairs, they make me sick, having weatherd the storms
of War, I had hoped peace would have confirmed to us the
Blessings we had dearly Earned, but this rather proves the wish
of Benevolence, than an investigation into the Character of
Humane Nature—an unprincipald mob is the worst of all
Tyrannies. Wisdom to our Rulers and uninimity to our patriots, and virtue to all our fellow citizens, will remedy the present
Tumults, and to their Honour, no small share of these qualities
have already shewn themselves most sincerely can I join in the
prayer of the Churchmen. Give us peace in our day good Lord.
I shall form my judgment of the sentiments of the people by
their Elections. one of the best symptoms will be the Reelection of the Governour, and such senators, and members as
have taken the most open and decided part in favour of government, and the quelling that spirit of sedition against the

Bar & Bench, which first fomented, and Countananced this Rebellion. Shays has not been a greater incendary than Honestus. Shame to our citizens that they should wish to curtail the sallery of their Governour. do they want to make him a man of straw? it is impossible whilst humane Nature is such as we find it that the people should venerate a man unless he is supported according to his Rank and station. they are the first to despise & laugh at him and to contemn his power and Authority—

You will see by the Defence of the American Constitutions, what the Sentiments of my Friend are. the Book has met with a favourable reception here, and the critical Reviewers of last month, who are mostly Scotchmen, and concequently unfriendly to America, have treated it with great civility, nay they have said as many Handsome things of it, as could have been expected.

it was really the work of 3 months only. the subject is still persueing with more leisure in a 2d volm

I am very glad to find my Friend Mrs Allen like to increase her family. I have kept my word & send the Christning suit by mr Blodget to your care, pray deliver it with my Love to her and best wishes for her safety. the suit cost one pound sixteen & six pence sterling. I mention this only to you that in case any Bodys curiosity should be excited, they might be satisfied and not to enhance the value of my present. in the same Box you will find a sash for my little Neice, sent not for the Beauty of it in my Eye, but to shew you how various a dame Fashion is, wastcoats Bonnets ribbons, all in the plad figure & coulours. I expect we shall have silks & calicoes in the same manner.

I hope my Neice received the Books I sent her & my dear sister the silk. it is a great pleasure to me to find Tommy so well situated. it would be strange indeed if a visit to your House, was not like going Home. can there be a more agreeable sensation than that of being joyfully received by Friends who Love us? a pleasure of which I have been deprived for near 3 years, but which in the course of an other, I hope to experience. adieu my dear sister. The sun breaks out, and I must go and ride in quest of Health. present me affectionately to mr Shaw mr Thaxter & all inquiring Friends and believe me your ever affectionate Sister   A Adams

May 6th

PS—mrs Smith has had a large Boil gather upon one of her Breast which tho not so bad as a broken Breast, has made her very sick & brought her quite low it broke to day, & she is much better—accept my dear sister a bit of muslin for a slip for my Neice I think if you make the skirt a yd long & wealt it, there will be enough for 2 waists—

POLLY JEFFERSON

To Thomas Jefferson

my dear sir   London june 26 1787

I have to congratulate you upon the safe arrival of your Little daughter, whom I have only a few moments ago received. She is in fine Health and a Lovely little girl I am sure from her countanance, but at present every thing is strange to her, & She was very loth to try New Friends for old. She was so much attachd to the Captain & he to her, that it was with no Small regreet that I Seperated her from him, but I dare say I shall reconcile her in a day or two. I tell her that I did not see her sister cry once. she replies that her sister was older & ought to do better, besides she had her pappa with her. I Shew her your picture. She says she cannot know it, how should she when she should not know you. a few hours acquaintance and we shall be quite Friends I dare say. I hope we may expect the pleasure of an other visit from you now I have so strong an inducement to tempt you. if you could bring miss Jefferson with you, it would reconcile her little Sister to the thoughts of taking a journey. it would be proper that some person should be accustomed to her. the old Nurse whom you expected to have attended her, was sick & unable to come She has a Girl of about 15 or 16 with her, the sister of the servant you have with you— as I presume you have but just returnd from your late excursion, you will not put yourself to any inconvenience or Hurry in comeing or Sending for her: you may rely upon every attention towards her & every care in my power. I have just endeavourd to amuse her by telling her that I would carry her to sadlers wells, after describing the amusement to her with an honest simplicity. I had rather Says She See captain Ramsey one moment, than all the fun in the world.

I have only time before the post goes, to present my compliments to mr Short. mr Adams & Mrs Smith desire to be rememberd to you. Captain Ramsey has brought a Number of Letters. as they may be of importance to you to receive them we have forwarded them by the post— miss Polly sends her duty to you & Love to her Sister & says she will try to be good & not cry. so she has wiped her Eyes & layd down to sleep—

believe me dear sir affectionately yours &c &c

A Adams

SALLY HEMINGS

To Thomas Jefferson

dear sir   London june 27 1787

I had the Honour of addressing you yesterday and informing you of the safe arrival of your daughter. She was but just come when I sent of my Letter by the post, & the poor little Girl was very unhappy being wholy left to strangers this however lasted only a few Hours, & miss is as contented to day as she was misirable yesterday. She is indeed a fine child. I have taken her out to day and purchased her a few articles which she could not well do without & I hope they will meet your approbation. The Girl who is with her is quite a child, and captain Ramsey is of opinion will be of so little service that he had better carry her back with him, but of this you will be a judge. she seems fond of the child and appears good Naturd.

I sent by yesterdays post a Number of Letters which captain Ramsey brought with him not knowing of any private hand, but mr Trumble has just calld to let me know that a Gentleman sets off for Paris tomorrow morning. I have deliverd him two Letters this afternoon received, and requested him to wait that I might inform you how successfull a Rival I have been to captain Ramsey, & you will find it I imagine as difficult to Seperate miss Polly from me as I did to get her from the Captain. She stands by me while I write & asks if I write every day to her pappa? but as I have never had so interesting a subject to him to write upon [   ] hope he will excuse the hasty scrips for the [   ] intelligence they contain, and be assured dear Sir that I am with Sentiments of sincere esteem your Humble Servant   A Adams

PURCHASING PEACEFIELD

To Cotton Tufts

My dear Sir   July 4 1787 London

In replie to your Letters by Captain Scot Mr. Adams and I wrote You on the first of the Month. We intended the Letters for the New York packet, but hearing that very day of a vessel, British bottom ready to Sail for Boston, Captain Collins I think, we sent the Letter to his Bag, but being very desirious You should hear from us as soon as possible I write this for the packet. The purport of the other Letters were to request you to purchase Mr. Borlands place immediately upon the best terms You can for ready money, and to draw for the Sum. If Mr. Borland wishes to pay it here to Mr. Vassel Mr. Adams will do it at ten days sight of the Bills, Mr. Borland allowing the same for the Bills that others will give. You know Sir that Mr. Tyler sold two peices of the land one to Mr. Webb and one to Deacon Bass. What little he could give I know not, but still if the land has been paid for, it will be disagreeable to get into a Squable about it. You will be so good as to see how that matter stands. Mr. Tyler set up a frame. Has that been coverd and what other repairs has he made? Can the materials for repairs be purchased at a reasonable rate? What is necessary to be done? And if you purchase as I hope You will without delay, will You be so good as to send me the bigness of the rooms and the height. The Number of acres belonging to the place and the Tenant who now occupies we should like to know. Mr. Adams has also written to You to request you to Buy

FT. Veseys but between You and I dont be in a hurry about that. If we Buy Mr. Borlands, I think that peice which Col. Quincys gave his Grandsons will be an object more worth our persuit. Mr. Veseys I know Mr. Adams will have if he lives to return and can possibly accomplish it. You will continue to procure Notes as You find opoortunity till You invest the 200 pounds in them which I wrote You about some time ago, What do You think Sir of selling our House in Boston and investing the money in those Notes? Shoud You advise to it, would it sell well at this time? The Letter of advise in favour of Mr. Hill is come to hand, but no Bills have yet been offerd. Have my Friends all forgotten me, or is any disaster befallen them that they keep from me, that you alone are the only person from whom I have received a line either by Barnard Davis or Scot. I hope however Captain Scot has Letters. He is not yet come up. Yours came by the post. If I should not find any Letters, I shall be very uneasy through apprehension, for you do not as usual speak of my children or Friends. That was needless if they have written. If they have not, it will be a subject of anxiety untill I hear. My own Health is very indifferent, and has been so for these Six Months. I want to return home but I would that my Country was quiet. I have lived through turbulant Scenes enough, and wish for peace the remainder of my days. My Love to all Friends. I shall not write by the packet to them, but by Barnard who expects to sail the last of the month. Yours affectionately   A A

POLLY JEFFERSON'S TRAVEL PLANS

To Thomas Jefferson

my dear sir   London july 6 1787
    If I had thought you would so soon have Sent for your dear little Girl, I should have been tempted to have kept her arrival here, from you a secret. I am really loth to part with her, and she last evening upon petit's arrival, was thrown into all her former distresses, and bursting into Tears, told me it would be as hard to leave me, as it was her Aunt Epps. She has been so

often deceived that she will not quit me a moment least She should be carried away, nor can I scarcely prevail upon her to see petit. Tho she says she does not remember you, yet she has been taught to consider you with affection and fondness, and depended upon your comeing for her. she told me this morning, that as she had left all her Friends in virgina to come over the ocean to see you, she did think you would have taken the pains to have come here for her, & not have sent a man whom she cannot understand. I express her own words. I expostulated with her upon the long journey you had been; & the difficulty you had to come and upon the care kindness & attention of petit, whom I so well knew, but she cannot yet hear me. she is a child of the quickest Sensibility, and the maturest understanding, that I have ever met with for her Years. she had been 5 weeks at sea, and with men only, so that on the first day of her arrival, She was as rough as a little Sailor, and then she been decoyed from the Ship, which made her very angry, and no one having any Authority over her; I was apprehensive I should meet with some trouble, but where there are such materials to work upon as I have found in her, there is no danger. she listened to my admonitions, and attended to me advice, and in two days, was restored to the amiable lovely Child which her Aunt had formed her. in short she is the favorite of every Creature in the House, and I cannot but feel Sir, how many pleasures you must lose; by committing her to a convent, yet situated as you are, you cannot keep her with you. The Girl she has with her, wants more care than the child, and is wholy incapable of looking properly after her, without Some Superiour to direct her.

As both miss Jefferson & the maid had cloaths only proper for the Sea, I have purchased & made up for them; Such things as I should have done had they been my own; to the amount of about Eleven or 12 Guineys. the particulars I will send by petit.

Captain Ramsey has Said that he would accompany your daughter to paris provided she would not go without him, but this would be putting you to an expence that may perhaps be avoided by petits staying a few days longer. the greatest difficulty in familiarizing her to him, is on account of the language. I have not the Heart to force her into a Carriage against her

Will and send her from me, almost in a Frenzy; as I know will be the case, unless I can reconcile her to the thoughts of going and I have given her my word that petit shall stay untill I can hear again from you. Books are her delight, and I have furnishd her out a little library, and She reads to me by the hour with great distinctness, & comments on what she reads with much propriety.

mrs Smith desires to be rememberd to you, and the little Boy his Grandmamma thinks is as fine a Boy as any in the Kingdom— I am my dear sir with Sentiments of Esteem Your Friend and Humble Servant A Adams

"NEITHER BE AN IDLE OR A USELESS SPECTATOR"

To Mary Smith Cranch

my dear sister   London july 16 1787
    If as the poet says, expectation makes the blessing sweet, your last Letter was peculiarly so, as you conjectured I was not a little anxious that neither Captain Barnard or Davis brought me a line. I was apprehensive that Something was the matter some imminent danger threatning some Friend, of which my Friends chose not to inform me untill thir fate was decided. I sent on board the Ship, the Solitary Box of meal was searchd throughout. What not one line, from my dear sister Cranch, she who has never before faild me, can it be possible, uncle Smith did not as usual say in his Letter that all Friends were well. Dr Tufts for the first time omitted mentioning my children, that might be because they thought that they had written, thus was my mind agitated untill Captain Scotts arrival who brought me your kind Letter of May the 20th, but none from either of my Neices or Children those dear Lads do not write so often as I wish them to, because they have nothing more to say than that they are well, not considering how important that intelligence is to an affectionate parent. mr J Cranch wrote me soon after Barnards arrival and sent me an extract of a Letter from miss B Palmer with a particular

account of the performances in April at Cambridge, in which
your son & mine bore a part. These Young Gentlemen are
much indebted to her for her partiality, and the very flattering
manner in which she describes them. I hope they will continue
to deserve the esteem of all good judges and do honour to
themselves and their Country. the account you give me of the
Health of JQA, is no more than I expected to hear. I warnd
him frequently before he left me, and have been writing him
ever since. I hope he will take warning before it is too late. it
gives me great satisfaction to learn that he has past through the
university with so much reputation, and that his fellow Students are attached to him. I have never once regreeted the
resolution he took of quitting Europe, and placing himself
upon the Theatre of his own Country, where if his Life is
spaired, I presume he will neither be an Idle or a useless Spectator. Heaven grant that he may not have more distressing
scenes before him, and a Gloomier stage to tread than those
on which his Father has acted for 12 years past, but the curtain
rises before him, and instead of peace waving her olive branch,
or Liberty seated in a triumphal car or commerce Agriculture
and plenty pouring forth their Stores, Sedition hisses Treason
roars, Rebellion Nashes his Teeth. Mercy Suspends the justly
merited blow, but justice Striks the Guilty victim. here may the
Scene close and brighter prospects open before us in future. I
hope the political machine will move with more safety and security this year than the last, and that the New Head may be
endowed with wisdom sufficient to direct it. there are Some
good Spokes in the Wheels, tho the Master workmen have
been unskilfull in discarding some of the best, and chusing
others not sufficiently Seasond, but the crooked & cross graind
will soon break to peices, tho this may do much mischief in the
midst of a jouney, and shatter the vehicle, yet an other year
may repair the Damages, but to quit Allegory, or you will think
I have been reading Johnny Bunyan. The conduct of a certain
Gentleman is rather curious. I really think him an honest Man,
but ambition is a very wild passion, and there are some Characters that never can be pleasd unless they have the intire direction
of all publick affairs, and when they are unemployd, they are
continually blaming those in office, and accusing them of Ignorance or incapacity, and Spreading allarms that the Country is

ruined and undone, but put them into office, and it is more than probable they will persue the same conduct, which they had before condemned, but no Man is fit to be trusted who is not diffident of himself Such is the frailty of humane Nature, & so great a flatterer is Self Love, that it presents false appearences, & deceives it votaries.

The comedy writer has been drawing his own Character and an other Gentlemans I fancy. strange Man, would he act as well as he can write, he might have been an ornament to Society, but what signifies a Head, without a Heart, what is knowledge but an extensive power to do evil, without principal to direct and govern it? "unstable as water, thou shalt not excell" I have often quoted to him. I look upon him as a lost Man. I pity his folly, and am sorry he is making himself so conspicuous. I think Sir John Temple was the writer of the Letter from Newyork giving an account of the Play, Birds of a Feather— The House at Braintree which you mention I would not fail of having, & am sorry the dr did not bargan for it without waiting to hear from us. We have written him twice upon the subject, as to building we shall never be able to do that, if the dr should purchase it. I wish you would look it over and let us know what repairs are necessary. I shall not be able to write much by Captain Barnard, as we are prepairing for a long jouney. I have been so very unwell through the Spring and winter that the dr Says a journey and change of air is absolutly necessary for me our intention is to visit Devenshire & to go as far as plimouth which is about 200 & 30 miles. as we take the Baby and a Nursery maid, Esther a footman & coachman we shall make a large calvacade and be absent a month or 5 weeks. Col Smith we do not expect back till September. we hear from him by every post. I am distrest for Sister Shaw & her children the disorder is of the most infectious Nature, and a House, linen, & every thing & person requires as much cleansing as with the Small pox, of which I fear people are not sufficently aware. When Mr Copley about a year & half ago lost two fine children with it, the doctors advised to these precautions, & gave large doses of the bark to the attendance. I think Sister Shaw would have done well to have sent both her children out of Haverhill. I pray Heaven preserve them— I did not get a line from her by either of the vessels. I have had with me for a fortnight a little daughter of mr Jeffersons, who arrived here with a young Negro Girl her Servant from Virginia. mr Jefferson wrote me some months ago that he expected them & desired me to receive them. I did so and was amply repaid for my trouble a finer child of her age I never saw, so mature an understanding, so womanly a behaviour and so much sensibility united is rarely to be met with. I grew so fond of her, & she was so attached to me, that when mr Jefferson sent for her, they were obliged to force the little creature away. She is but 8 years old. She would Set some times and discribe to me the parting with her Aunt who brought her up, the obligations she was under to her & the Love she had for her little cousins, till the Tears would stream down her cheeks, and now I had been her Friend and she loved me, her pappa would break her Heart by making her go again. she clung round me so that I could not help sheding a tear at parting with her. she was the favorite of every one in the House. I regreet that Such fine spirits must be spent in the walls of a convent. She is a beautifull Girl too, my little Boy grows finely and is as playfull as a Lamb, is the Healthest child I ever saw, and pretty enough. his Mamma I think looks the better for being a Nurse. he is very content with being twice a day supplied by her, feeds the rest, and never misses being twice a day carried out to walk in the air when it is fair weather You see what a mere Grandmama I am that can fill up half a page in writing of the child. this I presume is commencment week. I dare say the young folks feel anxious. I dont know whether I should venture to be a hearer if I was in America I should have as many pertubations as the Speakers. I hope they will acquit themselves with honour. mr Adams desires me to tell cousin Cranch that any of his Books are at his service I believe we must send some of these Young Men to settle at Vermont. can they get their Bread in Massachussets? but the World is all before them, may providence be their Guide.

I send my dear sisters each a tea urn, which must prove comfortable in a hot summers day I have orderd them put up in a Box together and addrest to uncle Smith. the Heater, & the Iron which you put it in with, is to be packed in the Box by the Side of them. whilst your water is boiling, you heat the Iron & put it in to the little tin inclosure always minding that the water is first put in. this keeps it hot as long as you want to use it.— how are English Goods now? cheeper I suppose than I can buy them here, and India much lower, in the article of Spice could you credit it if I was to tell you that I give 2 pound Eleaven Shillings sterling pr pound for Nutmegs—and other Spice in proportion yet tis really so— I cannot write my Neices now, but hope my journey will furnish materials—my Love to them. who owns Germantown now, is mr Palmers family in any way of Buisness? how is miss payne, & where is she?— Mrs Parkers arrival will be an acquisitions to our American acquaintance. she appears an agreeable woman we have a General Stuart & Lady here Philadelphians, lately from Ireland. I knew him when I first came here. he went to Ireland and has been there with her two years, they spend the winter here. Mrs Gardner has never visited me untill yesterday, tho she has been here a Year conceequently I have never Seen her, for it is an invariable rule with me to receive the first visit. I have formed a very agreeable acquaintance with a Sir George Stanton & Lady. I know not a warmer American. he cultivats their acquaintance, and is a very sensible learned Man. Lady Staunton is an amiable woman and we visit upon very social and Friendly terms. I must however add that Sir George is an Irishman by birth & I have invariably found in every Irish Gentleman, a Friend to America. it is an old observation that mutual Sufferings begets Friendships. Lady Effingham is just returnd to Town after an absence of a 12 Month. her Ladyship drank tea with me on Sunday, & I Supd & spent the Evening with her the week after. She has traveld much in Russia Sweeden Denmark Holland France Ireland, and has a most Sprightly lively fancy: joind to a volubility of Tongue which united with good sense & a knowledge of the World renders her a pleasing companion, but She like all the rest of the English Ladies, with whom I have any acquaintance is destitute of that Softness & those feminine graces which appear so lovely in the females of America. I attribute this in a great measure to their constant intercourse at publick places. I will see how they are in the Country. I have been gratified however in finding that all Foreigners who have any acquaintance with American Ladies give the preference to them, but john Bull thinks nothing equal to himself and his Country; you would be Surprizd to see & hear the uncivil things Said against France, and all its productions I have never found so much illiberality in any Nation as this, but there are many Worthy & amiable Characters here whom I shall ever respect, and for whose Sakes this Country is preserved from total Ruin & destruction. but I am running on at a Strange rate. adieu my dear sister, remember me to my Worthy Mother Brothers & all my Nephews Neices & Neighbours, and believe me at all times your affectionate Sister   Abigail Adams.

PS having sent you a Lamp I now Send you something to Light it with the directions are with it. I have given these into the care of a mrs Wentworth who came here last Spring in persuit of an estate which I have no doubt belongs to her, but for want of Money She cannot come at it. She is a virtuous well behaved deserving woman. she has been I believe as much as a month at different times in my family, and can tell you more about us than perhaps 20 Letters. Dr Bulfinch recommended her to us, when she came. I tried to get her some employ but could not succeed, and she is now obliged to return much poorer than when she came, and without any prospect of Success. when you go to Town, if you send for her to uncle Smiths, She will come and see you as I have desired her.— Inclosed you find a Louis d'or

"STERLING METAL IN THE POLITICAL CRUSIBLE"

To Thomas Jefferson

Dear sir   London Sep^br 10th
    your obliging favours of july and August came safe to Hand. the first was brought during my absence on an excursion into the Country. I was very happy to find by it, that you had received your daughter safe, and that the dear Girl was contented. I never felt so attached to a child in my Life on so short an acquaintance, tis rare to find one possessd of so strong & lively a sensibility. I hope she will not lose her fine spirits within the

walls of a convent, to which I own I have many, perhaps false prejudices.

Mr Appleton delivererd my Lace & gloves Safe. be so good as to let Petit know that I am perfectly satisfied with them. Col smith has paid me the balance which you say was due to me, and I take your word for it, but I do not know how. the Bill which was accepted, by mr Adams in the absence of col Smith, I knew would become due, in our absence, and before we could receive your orders. the money was left with Brisler our Servant, who paid it when it was presented. on our return we found the Bill which you had drawn on mr Tessier, but upon presenting it he refused to pay it, as he had not received any letter of advise tho it was then more than a month from its date, but he wrote immediatly to mr Grand, and by return of the next post, paid it.

with regard to your Harpsicord, Col Smith who is now re-turnd, will take measures to have it Sent to you. I went once to mr Kirkmans to inquire if it was ready. his replie was, that it should be ready in a few days, but [   ] no orders further than to report when it was [   ] to write you, but he seemd to think that he had done all that was required of him. The Canister addrest to mr Drayton deliverd to mr Hayward with Special directions, and he assured me he would not fail to de-liver it.

The ferment and commotions in Massachusetts has brought upon the Surface abundance of Rubbish; but Still there is Some sterling metal in the political crusible. the vote which was carried against an emission of paper money by a large ma-jority in the House, shews that they have a sense of justice: which I hope will prevail in every department of the State. I send a few of our News papers, some of which contain Sensible speculations.

To what do all the political motions tend which are agitating France Holland and Germany? will Liberty finally gain the as-sendency, or arbitrary power Strike her dead.

Is the report true that is circulated here, that mr Littlepage has a commission from the King of Poland to his most Chris-tian Majesty?!

we have not any thing from mr Jay later than 4th of july.

there was not any congress then, or expected to be any; untill the convention rises at Philadelphia

Col Smith I presume will write you all the politiks of the Courts he has visited—and I will not detain you longer than to assure you that I am at all times your Friend and Humble Servant   A A

September 10, 1787

SOUTH WEST ENGLAND

To Mary Smith Cranch

my dear sister   Sepbr 15th Grosvenour Square

When I wrote you last, I was just going to Set out on a journey to the West of England. I promised you to visit mr Cranchs Friends and Relatives, this we did as I shall relate to you we were absent a month, and made a Tour of about six hundred Miles. the first place we made any stay at, was Winchester. There was formerly an Earl of Winchester, by the Name of Saar de Quincy. he was created Earl of Winchester by King john in 12.24. and Signed Magna Charta, which I have seen, the original being now in the British Museum with his Hand writing to it.

it is said that the year 1321 the Title became extinct, through failure of male Heirs, but I rather think through the poverty of some branch unable to contend for it. the family originally came from Normandy in the Time of William the Conquerer. they bear the same Arms with those of our Ancesters except that ours Substituded an animal for the crest in lieu, of an Earls coronet. I have a perfect remembrance of a parchment in our Grandmothers possession, which when quite a child I used to amuse myself with. this was a Geneological Table which gave the descent of the family from the Time of William the conquerer this parchment mr Edmund Quincy borrowed on some occasion, & I have often heard our Grandmother Say with some anger, that she could never recover it. as the old Gentleman is still living, I wish mr Cranch would question him about it, & know what Hands it went into, & whether there is a probability of its ever being recoverd, and be so good as to ask uncle Quincy how our Grandfather came by it, & from whence our Great Granfather came? where he first Settled? & take down in writing all you can learn from him, & mr Edmund Quincy respecting the family. you will Smile at my Zeal, perhaps on this occasion, but can it be wonderd at, that I should wish to Trace an Ancesstor amongst the Signers of Magna Carta, amongst those who voted against receiving an explanatory Charter in the Massachusetts, Stands the Name of our venerable Grandfather, accompanied only with one other. this the journals of the House will shew to his immortal honour. I do not expect either titles or estate from the Recovery of the Geneoligical Table, were there any probability of obtaining it, yet if I was in possession of it, money should not purchase it from me.

But to return to winchester, it is a very ancient place, and was formerly the residence of the Saxon and Norman Kings. there still remains a very famous Cathedral church, in the true Gothic Architecture, being partly built in the year 1079. I attended divine service there, but was much more entertaind with the Venerable and Majestic appearence of the Ancient pile, than with the Modern flimsy discourse of the preacher, a meaner performance I do not recollect to have heard, but in a Church which would hold several thousands it might truly be said, two or three, were met together, and those appeard to be the lower order of the people. from Winchester we proceeded to Southhampton, which is a very pretty sea port Town and much frequented during the summer months as a Bathing place, and here for the first time in my Life I tried the experiment. it would be delightfull in our warm weather as well as very salubrious if such conveniencys were Erected in Boston, Braintree, Weymouth, which they might be with little expence. the places are under cover, you have a woman for a Guide, a small dressing room to yourself an oil cloth cap, a flannel Gown and socks for the feet; we tarried only two days at Southhampton, and went ten miles out of our way in order to visit Weymouth merely for its Name. this like my Native Town is a Hilly country a small sea port, with very little buisness, & wholy supported by the resort of company during the Summer Months, for those persons who have not Country Houses of their own, resort to the Watering places as they are call'd, during the summer months, it being too vulgar and unfashionable to remain in London, but where the object of one is Health, that of 50 is pleasure, however far they fall short of the object. this whole Town is the property of a widow Lady. Houses are built by the Tenants & taken at Life Rents, which upon the discease of the Leasors revert back again to the owner of the Soil; thus is the landed property of this Country vested in Lordships, and in the Hands of the Rich altogether. the pesantry are but slaves to the Lord, notwithstanding the mighty boast they make of Liberty, 6 pence & 7 pence pr day is the usual wages given to Labourers, who are to feed themselves out of the pittance. in travelling through a Country fertile as the Garden of Eden, loaded with a Golden harvest, plenty Smiling on every side, one would imagine the voice of poverty was rarely heard, and that she was seldom seen, but in the abodes of indolence and vice, but it is far otheways. the Money earned by the sweat of the Brow must go to feed the pamperd Lord & fatten the Greedy Bishop, whilst the misierble shatterd thatched roof cottage crumbles to the dust for the want of repair. to hundreds & hundreds of these abodes have I been a witness in my late journey. the cheering Rays of the Sun are totally excluded, unless they find admittance through the decayed roof equally exposed to cold & the inclemnant season, a few Rags for a Bed, a joint Stool, comprise the chief of their furniture, whilst their own appearence is more wretched, than one can well conceive. during the season of Hay and Harvest, Men women & children are to be seen labouring in the Fields, but as this is a very small part of the year, the little they acquire then is soon expended, and how they keep soul and Body together the remainder of the year; is very hard to tell. it must be oweing to this very unequal distribution of property that the poor rate, is become such an intollerable burden. the inhabitants are very thinly scatterd through the Country, though large Towns are well peopled. to reside in & near London, and to judge of the Country from what one sees here, would be forming a very eronious opinion. How little cause of complaint have the inhabitants of the united States, when they compare their Situation, not with despotic monarchies, but with this Land of Freedom? the ease with which honest industry may acquire property in America the equal distribution of justice, to the poor as well as the rich, and the personal Liberty they enjoy, all call upon them to support their Governments and Laws, to respect their Rulers, and gratefully acknowledge their Superiour Blessings, least Heaven in wrath Should Send them a. . . .

From Weymouth our next excursion was to Axmister the first Town in the County of Devonshire. it is a small place, but has two manufactures of Note, one of Carpets & one of Tapes—both of which we visited; the manufactory of the carpets is wholy performed by women and children. you would have been suprized to see, in how ordinary a Building this rich manufactory was carried on, a few glass windows in some of our Barns would be equal to it. they have but two prices for their carpets wove here, the one is Eighteen shilling, and the other 24, a square yard. they are wove of any dimensions you please, and without a seam, the coulours are most beautifull, and the carpets very durable here we found mr J Cranch, he dined with us, and we drank Tea with him; this is a curious Genious, he is a middle sizd man of a delicate countanance, but quite awkerd in his manners. he seldom looks one in the Face, and seems as if he had been crampd and cow'd in his youth; in company one is pained for him, yet is he a man of Reading and an accurate taste in the fine Arts, poetry, painting, musick, sculpture, Architecture; all of them have engaged his attention. his profession does not seem to be the object of his affections, and he has given up the practise, with an intention of persueing some other employment; he appears to me to be a man whose soul wants a wider expansion than his situation & circumstances allow. dejected spirits he is very liable to, I do not think him a happy man, his sentiments are by no means narrow or contracted; yet he is one by himself— he accompanied us in our journey to Exeter Plimouth and Kings-Bridge. at Exeter we tarried from Saturday till monday afternoon mr Bowering came to visit us. you know him by character, he appears a Friendly honest worthy man, active in buisness a warm and Zealous Friend to America, ready to serve his Friends, and never happier than when they will give him an opportunity of doing it his wife and daughter were on a visit to their Friends at Kings Bridge, so that we did not see them. he requested however that we would drink tea with him after meeting, and as our intention was to see mr Cranchs Brother Andrew, he engaged to get him to his House. the old Gentleman came, with some difficulty, for he is very lame and infirm; he seemd glad to see us, and asked many questions, respecting his Brother & sister in America. I think he must have had a paralityc stroke as his Speach is thick. he has not been able to do any buisness for a Number of years, and I believe is chiefly supported by his son, who is in the Clothiers buisness with mr Bowering. Mrs Cranch, tho near as old as her Husband, is a little smart, sprightly active woman, and is wilted just enough to last to perpetuity. She told me that her Husband took it very hard that his Brother had not written to him for a long time. I promised her that he should hear from him before long; and I know he will not let me be surety for him; without fulfilling my engagement. mr Cranchs daughter married mr Bowerings Brother, they have three sons. she is a sprightly woman like her Mother, and mr Bowerings daughter married a son of mr Natll Cranchs, so that the family is doubly linked together, and what is more; they all seem united, by the strongest ties of family harmony and Love. from Exeter we went to plimouth there we tarried Several days, and visited the fortifications, plimouth dock, & crossd over the water to mount Edgcume; a seat belonging to Lord Edgcume.

the Natural advantages of this place are superiour to any I have before seen, commanding a wide and extensive view of the ocean, the whole Town of plimouth, and the adjacent Country with the Mountain of cornwall— I have not much to Say with respect to the improvements of art, there is a large park well stockd with Deer, and some shady walks, but there are no Grottos Statuary Sculpture or Temples.—

at Plimouth we were visited by a mr & mrs Sawry; with whom we drank Tea one afternoon; mr Sawry is well known to many Americans, who were prisoners in plimouth jail during the late war. the money which was raised for their relief, past through his Hands and he was very kind to them, assisting many in their escape.— from plimouth we made an enterprize one day to Horsham and as we attempted it in a coach & four, we made a curious peice of work, taking by mistake a wrong road, but this part of my story I must reserve for my dear eliza.

our next Movement was a Kings Bridge, but before I relate

this, I ought to inform you, that we made a stop at a place call Ivey Bridge where we dined, and mr Adams accompanied mr Cranch to Brook about 3 miles distant, to visit his uncle mr William Cranch, who has been for several years quite lost to himself and Friends. there is some little property in the hands of the family who take charge of him, sufficient to Support a person who has no more wants than he has. he appeard clean & comfortable, but took no notice either of the conversation, or persons. the only thing which in the least roused him, was the mention of his wife, he appeard to be wrestless when that Subject was touchd. The Character of this Man, as given by all his Friends and acquaintance, leads one to regreet in a particular manner the loss of his intellects, possesst of a Genious superiour to his station, a thirst for knowledge which his circumstances in Life permitted him not to persue, most amiable and engageing in his manners, formed to have adornd a superiour Rank in Life, fondly attachd to an amiable wife, whom he very soon lost, he fell a sacrifice to a too great Sensibility, unable to support the shock, he grew melancholy and was totally lost.— But to return to Kings Bridge, the Chief resort of the Cranch family. we arrived at the Inn, about Six oclock a saturday Evening, about 8 we were saluted with a ringing of Bells—a circumstance we little expected. very soon we were visited by the various Branches of the Cranch family both male & female amounting to 15 persons, but as they made a strange jumble in my Head, I persuaded my fellow Traveller to make me out a Genealogical Table, which I send you. mr & mrs Burnell mr & mrs Trathan, both offerd us beds and accommodations at their houses, but we were too numerous to accept their Kind invitation, tho we engaged ourselves to dine with mr Burnell, & to drink Tea with mr Trathan the next day. Mrs Burnell has a strong resemblance to mrs palmer she is a Geenteel woman, and easy & polite. we dinned at a very pretty dinner, and after meeting drank Tea at the other House mr Trathans. their Houses are very small, but every thing neat and comfortable, mr Burnel is a shoe maker worth 5000 pounds and mr Trathan a Grocier in good circumstances. the rest of the families joind us at the two houses. they are all serious industerius good people amongst whom the greatest family harmony appears to Subsist. the people of this County appear more like our Newengland people than any I have met with in this Country before, but the distinction between Tradesmen & Gentry as they are termd is widely different from those distinctions in our Country. with us in point of Education and manners the Learned professions and many merchants Farmers & Tradesmen, are upon an equality with the Gentry of this Country. it would be degrading to compare them with many of the Nobility here. as to the Ladies of this Country their manners appear to be totally depraved, it is in the middle ranks of society, that virtue & morality are yet to be found. nothing does more injury to the Female Character, than frequenting publick places, and the rage which prevails now for the Watering places and the increased Number of them, is become a National evil as it promotes and encourages dissapation, mixes all characters promiscuously, is the resort of the most unprincipald female characters who are not ashamed to shew their faces wherever men dare to go modesty and diffidence, are calld ill Breeding, and Ignorance of the world. an impudent stare, is substituted in lieu of that modest deportment and that retireing Grace which aws, whilst it enchants. I have never seen a female Modle here, of such unaffected modest, & sweetly amiable manners, as mrs Guile mrs Russel, & many other American females exhibit.—

Having filld 8 pages I think it is near time to hasten to a close. Cushing and Folger are both arrived, by each I have received Letters from you. a new sheet of paper must contain a replie to them, this little Space Shall assure you of what is not confined to Time or place the ardent affection of your sister

A Adams.

September 15, 1787

REPAIRS TO PEACEFIELD

To Cotton Tufts

Dear Sir   London Nov^br 6th 1787—

Last week Captains Folger & Callihan arrived by whom we received all your Letters & Bills. the Bills were imediatly accepted, & will be paid when due. I feel under great obligations to you my dear sir, for all your kind care, & attention to our affairs. I am glad to find the buisness closed with mr Borland, and at a price which I think must be reasonable judging by what was formerly given for it, for I do not recollect how many acres of Land there are belonging to it. I know there is a wood lot containing 25 acres, & an other Lot of four, besides the Six which were sold to deacon Webb.— with regard to the repairs painting both without & within I should be glad to have compleated as soon as possible in the Spring, as the Smell is always pernicious to me. the east lower room to be painted what is calld a French Grey and as the furniture is red, a paper conformable, will look best. the Chamber over it will have Green furniture, and may be in the same manner, made uniform by a paper Green & white. the mahogany room, I know not what to say about it, making the two windows into the Garden will dispell much of the Gloom, & if it is not much abused & injured, had it not better remain as it is? can there be a Closset contrived in the Room when the windows are made, I could wish to have one, to make a uniform appearence, must there not be windows in the Chamber above, in the east Room. I think there are two clossets by the side of the Chimney. what would be the expence of taking them away & making arches in the Room of them? Iron Backs to the Chimneys & Brass Locks upon the Doors of the two best rooms & Chambers are all the particular directions I think of at present with regard to the other part of the House I shall leave it wholy to your judgment to make such repairs as you deem necessary and consistant with œconomy. as to any aditional building we cannot at present afford any. in some future day perhaps we may think of making the House Square by adding a Library, which mr A will really want, but at present, some chamber must be a substitute. The Frame set up by mr T. you do not mention. it is best to let it remain in its present state untill we return. in the painting you will be so good as to employ a person who properly understands the Buisness. I mention this, because I once Sufferd & was obliged to have a room 3 times painted when one would have answerd—

Mr Adams has written to you respecting our Farm, & mr Pratt. it has become so poor & misirable, that we must take some measures for making it better that we may be able to get our Bread from it. indeed I think I should enjoy better Health, to come Home & make butter & Cheese, raise poultry & look after my Garden, than by the inactive Life I am compelld to lead here. it will require my strickest attention to oconomy to be able to live & compleat the Education of our children, but this does not terify me. I can conform to Whatever is necessary, with regard to the pocket expences of Charles & Tommy—you know sir, that on the one hand, we would not wish to have them too Spairingly Supplied, nor on the other permit them so much, as to lead them into Idleness & dissapation. if any thing of the kind appears you will check your Hand. Mrs Cranch knows what her son expended, and I do not see why mine Should require more. I shall write to them both, & exort them to prudence in their expences. I would venture Sir one hundred pounds more in the purchase of paper. I am fully of your mind with respect to Land and whatever purchases we may make in future, I could wish it might be better than what we already own—

it is mr A's intention to retire to Braintree as a private man, nor need any one fear that he will become a competitor with them for offices. he has always dealt too openly & candedly with his Countrymen to be popular, & whatever they may assert with regard to his principals, he says they may be assured that he will never conceal a Sentiment of his Heart, however unpopular it may be, which he considers for the interest of His Countrymen to know & consider, altho he should forfeit by it the highest offices in the united states. he was never yet the partizan of any Country, nor will he ever become a Tool to any party, if fourteen years unremitted attention to the Service of his Country has not convinced them that he is their unshaken Friend, it would be in vain to attempt a conviction at this day. The English Review which you mention & which I see several of the states have carefully reprinted, was written by that Honour to his Country Silas Dean, who lives here as his appearence indicates, in real want & Horrour, and is Said to be a half crown Gazzet writer. I have only room to add that the Form of Government by the late Convention is esteemed here as a sublime work. they add that it is so good that they are perswaided the Americans will not accept it, it may admitt of some amendments but it is certainly a great Federal Structure. I shall write to all my Friends by Folger. my little Boy has got well through the small pox. adieu yours &c &c   A A—

"MRS A EXCEPTS GREEN"

To Thomas Jefferson

London Grosvenour square December 5ᵗʰ 1787—
Mrs Adams presents her respectfull compliments to Mr Jefferson and asks the favour of him to permit petit to purchase for her ten Ells of double Florence of any fashionable coulour, orange excepted which is in high vogue here. Mrs A excepts green also of which she has enough. Mr Rucker if in Paris will be so kind as to take Charge of it, & mrs Adams will send the money by mr Trumble who will be in Paris some time next week—

By Letters this day received from Boston, it appears that a convention was agreed too, by both Houses, & that it is to meet, the second wednesday in Janᵃʳʸ

Mr King writes that mr Jeffersons commission, is renewed at the court of France, and mr Adams's resignation accepted, so that we shall quit this country as soon in the Spring as we can go with Safety.

Love to the Young Ladies & thank my dear Polly for her pretty Letter—

DEATH OF BROTHER WILLIAM SMITH

To Mary Smith Cranch

London Febʳʸ 10ᵗʰ 1788
Since I have had any opportunity of conveyence to my dear Sister, I have received from her Letters of the following dates August 19 Sepᵇʳ 23. & 30th october 21 & Novᵇʳ 14ᵗʰ· the contents of which have variously affected me— The Scripture tells

us that it is better to go to the House of mourning than the House of Feasting. to that I think I have oftener been calld through the progress of your several Letters, and I may say with dr young

"my dyeing Friend's come o'er me like a cloud"

our Second parents House is become desolate, disconsolate & mourns, but the dear inhabitants have exchanged it for a more permanant inheritance, yet we have reason to bewail their loss, for they were ornaments to Society, and their exemplary Lives adornd the Religion they profess'd. very few persons have closed the last Scenes of Life with So pure and unblemishd Characters as the worthy pair whose memory's deserve these tributary Tears. long may their virtues Survive in our memories and be transplanted into the lives of all their connections. They do Survive them we see in their amiable Children the Fruits of seeds sown by their parents, Nursd with uncommon care, and matured by long & undeviating Labour. I rejoice most sincerely that mr Smith so happily connected himself during the Life of his worthy Father, as it must have afforded him consolation in the close of Life to leave a Friend and companion to his orphan Daughter— my dear Friend mrs otis, I have often thought of her with the tenderest Sympathy. how many Severe trials has She been calld to encounter in the Space of a few years? "God suits the wind to the shorne Lamb, Says yorick" and she is blessd with a happy equinimity of temper Supported by those Sentiments of Religion which teach a patient Submission to the dispensations of providence

"Why should we grieve, when grieving we must bear?
And take with Guilt, what Guiltless we might share"

When I reflect upon the Death of an other Relative, I can only say, the judge of all will do right. I cannot however upon a Retrospect of His Education refrain from thinking that some very capital mistakes were very undesignedly made. the experience which you and I have since had with regard to the different dispositions & tempers of children would lead us to a very different conduct. I say this to you who will not consider it, as any reflection upon the memory of our dear parents, but only as a proof how much the best & worthyest may err, & as some mitigation for the conduct of our deceast Relative.

And now my dear sister the period is very near when I am to quit this country. I wrote Dr Tufts that we had taken our passage in Captain Callihans Ship, and that he would sail the latter end of march, or begining of April, so that I hope God willing, to see you & the rest of my dear Friends in May. I have much to do as you will naturally suppose by way of arrangment, and my Health, not what I wish it was. There is a natural tendency in our family to one particular Disorder, Father Aunts & uncle have more or less shared it, and I am not without Similar complants, which like the centinal at the door of King philip, warn me of what frail materials I am compose'd. that was a part of my complant last year and has afflicted me still more greviously this. at present I am relieved & hope that I shall have no return of it through the fatigue which I have to pass through in packing & getting ready for my voyage. I almost wish I had nothing to remove but myself & Baggage, but to part with our furniture would be such a loss, & to take it is such a trouble that I am almost like the *Animal* between the two Bundles *of* Hay

I want to write to you all, yet feel as if I had not a moments time. mr & mrs Smith take private Lodgings next week. in the course of which we have to go to Court & take Leave, to visit all the Foreign ministers & their Ladies & to take leave of all our acquaintance, pack all our Furniture Give up our House discharge all our Bills and make all other arrangments for our departure.

added to all this, I have the greatest anxiety upon Esthers account, if I bring her Home alive I bring her Home a marri'd woman & perhaps a Mother which I fear will take place at sea. this as yet is known only to myself & mrs Smith. Brisler as good a servant as ever Bore the Name, and for whom I have the greatest regard is married to her, but Sitting asside her Situation, which I did not know untill a few days ago, her general state of Health is very bad. I have not made it worse, I hope by what has been done for her, but her Life has been put in Jeopardy, as many others have before her, ignorantly done, for however foolish it may appear to us, I must believe that she had no Idea of being with child, untill the day before she came in the utmost distress to beg me to forgive her, and tho I knew that it was their intention to marry when they should return to America Yet so totally blinded was I, & my physician too, that we never once suspected her any more than she did herself, but this was oweing to her former ill state of Health.

I have related this to you in confidence that you may send for her Mother & let her know her situation. as in a former Letter to dr Tufts, I expressd my apprehensions with regard to her, & tho the chief difficulty is now accounted for I look upon her situation as a very dangerous one. I have engaged an Elderly woman to go out with me, who formerly belonged to Boston, and I hear there is an other woman going as a stearige passenger, and I shall hurry Callihan to get away as soon as possible, for I think I dread a norester on Board ship, more than an Equinox we have but about ten days longer before we shall leave London—and in addition to every thing else, I have to prepare for her what is necessary for her situation, but tis in vain to complain, & then poor Brisler looks so humble and is so attentive, so faithfull & so trust worthy, that I am willing to do all I can for them. do not let any thing of what I have written be known to any body but her mother. I hope captain Folger arrived Safe with my Letters. adieu my dear sister, do not let my Friends think unkindly of me if I do not write to them. I would had I time my Love to them all from your ever affectionate sister   A A

TAKING LEAVE

To Thomas Jefferson

My dear sir   London Feb^ry. 21 1788.

in the midst of the Bustle and fatigue of packing, The parade & ceremony of taking leave at Court, and else where, I am informd that mr Appleton and mrs Parker, are to set out for Paris tomorrow morning. I Cannot permit them to go without a few lines to my much Esteemed Friend, to thank him for all his kindness and Friendship towards myself and Family, from the commencment of our acquaintance, and to assure him that the offer he has made of his correspondence, is much too flattering, not to be gratefully accepted.

The florence and stockings were prefectly to my mind, and I am greatly obliged to you sir, for your care and attention about them. I have sent by Mrs Parker the balance due to you, agreeable to your statement, which I believe quite right

Be so good as to present my Regards to the marquiss de la Fayett, and his Lady, and to the Abbés—assure them that I entertain a gratefull rememberance of all their civilities and politeness during my residence in Paris. To mr Short and the young Ladies your Daughters Say every thing that is affectionate for me, and be assured my dear Sir, that I am with the Greatest Respect Esteem & Regard Your Friend and Humble Servant   Abigail Adams

THE CONSTITUTION IS RATIFIED

To John Adams

my dearest Friend   Bath Hotell March 23 1788
    I received yours of the 14th and ever Since thursday have been in Hourly expectation of seeing you I hope it is oweing to all the packets being detaind upon this Side, as is reported, and not to any indisposition that your return is delayed, that unpleasing detention is sufficiently mortifying particularly as we wish to proceed to Falmouth as soon as possible, tho I shall fear to go from hence untill the ship is gone, for from the best information I can get callihan has as yet scarcly any thing but our Bagage &c on Board, and even that has been several days delay'd by him. I came last monday Evening to this Hotell, that the Beds & remaining furniture might be sent on Board and the House given up. this will be wholy accomplish'd on the morrow if the weather permits, & has been oweing to that, for several days that all has not been accomplished

The packet arrived this week from Newyork and brings an account that seven states had accepted the Constitution. the

Massachusetts convention consisted of 300 & 40 members. it was carried by a Majority of Nineteen Georgia & South Carolina are the two other states of which we had not before any certain accounts. New Hamshire was sitting. Newyork are becomeing more National and mr Duer writes mr Smith, that he may consider the constitution as accepted, & begining to operate at the Commencment of an other Year. Newyork had agreed to call a convention—thus my dear Friend I think we shall return to our Country at a very important period and with more pleasing prospects opening before her than the turbulent Scenes which massachusetts not long since presented. May wisdom Govern her counsels and justice direct her opperations.

mr & Mrs Smith set off this week for Falmouth. she is now confined with a Soar throat, similar to the complaint which afficted me ten days ago. I write in hopes the Baron de Lynden will meet you on your return.

I shall be exceedingly anxious if I do not see, or hear from you soon

adieu & believe me ever yours   A Adams

Diary of Her Return Voyage to America, March 30–May 1, 1788

Sunday London March 30. We took our departure from the Bath Hotell where I had been a Fortnight, and sat out for Portsmouth, which we reachd on Monday Evening. We put up at the Fountain Inn. Here we continued a week waiting for the Ship which was detain'd by contrary winds in the River. The wind changing we past over to the Isle of Wight and landed at a place call'd Ryed, where we took post Chaises and proceeded to Newport to dine. From thence to Cows where our Ship was to call for us. Here Mr. Adams, myself and two Servants took up our abode at the Fountain Inn kept by a widow woman whose Name is Symes. Our Lodging room very small, and the drawing room Confin'd and unpleasent. I found myself on the first Night much disposed to be uneasy and discontented. On the next day I requested the Land Lady to let me have a very large Room from whence we had a fine view of the Harbour, vessels, east Cowes and surrounding Hills. I found my Spirits much relieved. Never before experienced how much pleasure was to be derived from a prospect, but I had been long used to a large House, a large Family and many and various cares. I had now got into an unpleasent place without any occupation for mind or Body. Haveing staid at Portsmouth untill I had read all our Books and done all the Work I had left out, I never before experienced to such a degree what the French term enui. Monday took a walk to the Castle and upon a Hill behind it which commanded a pleasent view of the Harbour and Town which is a small villiage subsisting chiefly by fishing and piloting Vessels. Cowes is a safe and commodious Harbour. Here many Boats ply to take up the oyster which is always found in an Infant State. Small Vessels calld Smacks receive them and carry them to Colchester where they throw them again into water where the Sea only flows up by tides, and there they fatten and are again taken up and carried to the London market. The Isle of Wight is taken all together a very fertile agreable place 24 miles Long and 12 Broad. Produces great plenty of Grain, Sheep and Cattle, is a hilly country and a very Healthy Situation. On tuesday we went to Newport in order to visit Carisbrook Castle. This is a very ancient Ruins. The first account of it in English History is in the year 1513. This is the castle where Charles the first was kept a prisoner and they shew you the window from whence he attempted to escape. In this castle is a well of such a depth that the water is drawn from it by an ass walking in a wheel like a turn spit dog. The woman who shew it to us told us it was 300 feet deep. It is Beautifully stoned and in as good order as if finishd but yesterday. She lighted paper and threw it down to shew us its depth and dropping in a pin, it resounded as tho a large stone had been thrown in. We went to the Top of the citidal which commands a most extensive prospect. We returnd to Newport to dine. After dinner a Gentleman introduced himself to us by the Name of Sharp. Professed himself a warm and zealous Friend to America. After some little conversation in which it was easy to discover that he was a curious Character he requested that we would do him the Honour to go to his House and drink Tea. We endeavourd to excuse ourselves, but he would insist upon it, and we accordingly accepted. He carried us home and introduced to us an aged Father of 90 Years, a very surprizing old Gentleman who tho deaf appeard to retain his understanding perfectly. Mrs. Sharp his Lady appeard to be an amiable woman tho not greatly accustomed to company. The two young Ladies soon made their appeerence, the Youngest about 17 very Beautifull. The eldest might have been thought Handsome, if she had not quite spoild herself by affectation. By aiming at politeness she overshot her mark, and faild in that Symplicity of manners which is the principal ornament of a Female Character.

This Family were very civil, polite and Friendly to us during our stay at Cowes. We drank Tea with them on the Sunday following and by their most pressing invitation we dined with them the tuesday following. Mr. Sharp is a poet, a man of reading and appears to possess a good mind and Heart and is enthusiastick in favor of America. He collected a number of his Friends to dine with us all of whom were equally well disposed to our Country and had always Reprobated the war against us. During our stay at Cowes we made one excursion to Yarmouth about 15 miles distant from Cowes, but the road being Bad it scarcly repaid us for the trouble as we did not meet with any thing curious. After spending a whole fortnight at Cowes the Ship came round and on Sunday the 20 of April we embarked on Board the ship Lucretia Captain Callihan with three Gentlemen passengers viz. Mr. Murry a Clergyman, Mr. Stewart a grandson of old Captain Erwin of Boston who is going out to Bermudas collector of the Customs in that Island, His parents being British subjects, Mr. Boyd of Portsmouth a young Gentleman who received His Education in this Country.

The wind with which we saild scarcly lasted us 5 hours, but we continued our course untill Monday Evening when it blew such a gale that we were driven back and very glad to get into Portland Harbour. Here we have lain ever since, now 8 days, a Situation not to be desired, yet better far than we should have been either at Sea or in the downs. Whenever I am disposed to be uneasy I reflect a moment upon my preferable Situation to the poor Girl my maid, who is very near her Time, in poor Health and distressingly Sea sick, and I am then silent. I Hush every murmer, and tho much of my anxiety is on her account, I think that God will suit the wind to the shorn Lamb, that we may be carried through our difficulties better than my apprehensions. Trust in the Lord, and do good. I will endeavour to practise this precept. My own Health is better than it has been. We fortunately have a Doctor on Board, and I have taken an old woman out of kindness and given her a passage who seems kind, active and cleaver, is not Sea sick and I hope will be usefull to me. I am much better accommodated than when I came and have not sufferd so much by Sea Sickness. Want of Sleep is the greatest inconvenience I have yet sufferd but I shall not escape so. This day 3 weeks Mr. and Mrs. Smith saild and my dear Grandson just one Year old for New York in the Thyne packet. I fear they will have a bad time as the Westerly Winds have been so strong. God protect them and give us all a happy meeting in our Native Land. We Lie Here near the Town of Weymouth, and our Gentlemen go on shore almost every day which is an amusement to them and really some to me, as they collect something or other to bring Back with them either Mental or Bodily food. This is Sunday 27 April. Mr. Murry preachd us a Sermon. The Sailors made them-selves clean and were admitted into the Cabbin, attended with great decency to His discourse from these words, "Thou shalt not take the Name of the Lord thy God in vain, for the Lord will not hold him Guiltless that taketh His Name in vain." He preachd without Notes and in the same Stile which all the Clergymen I ever heard make use of who practise this method, a sort of familiar talking without any kind of dignity yet perhaps better calculated to do good to such an audience, than a more polishd or elegant Stile, but in general I cannot approve of this method. I like to hear a discourse that would read well. If I live to return to America, how much shall I regreet the loss of good Dr. Prices Sermons. They were always a delightfull entertainment to me. I revered the Character and Loved the Man. Tho far from being an orator, his words came from the Heart and reached the Heart. So Humble, so diffident, so liberal and Benevolent a Character does honour to that Religion which he both professes and practises.

On Sunday Eve the wind changed in our favour, so much as to induce the Captain to come to sail. This is Thursday the first of May, but we have made very small progress, the winds have been so light; yesterday we past Sylla and are now out of sight of Land. The weather is very fine and we only want fresher winds. The confinement of a Ship is tedious and I am fully of the mind I was when I came over that I will never again try the Sea. I provided then for my return in the Resolution I took, but now it is absolute. Indeed I have seen enough of the world, small as [   ] has been, and shall be content to learn what is further to be known from the page of History. I do not think the four years I have past abroad the pleasentest part of my Life. Tis Domestick happiness and Rural felicity in the Bosom of my Native Land, that has charms for me. Yet I do not re-greet that I made this excursion since it has only more attached me to America.

VICE PRESIDENT'S LADY
1788–1796

To Abigail Adams Smith

My Dear Child: Braintree, July 7th, 1788.
It has been no small mortification to me since my arrival
here, that I have not been able to hold a pen, or use my hand
in writing, until this day. I came on shore with three whitloes
upon the thumb and two fingers of my right, and two upon
the left hand, so that I could not do the least thing for myself.
I begged my friends to write, and let you know of our arrival,
after a very tedious passage of eight weeks and two days. My
first inquiry was of Mr. Knox, who came on board as soon as
we made the light-house, after my dear son and daughter; and
by him I had the happiness to learn of your safe arrival. When
I came up to town, I received your kind letter with the greatest
pleasure; it afforded me much entertainment. I wrote you one
letter at sea, which contained a statement of occurrences until
a fortnight before our arrival, when my fingers began to torment me.

The newspapers have no doubt informed you of our gracious reception, and of our residence at the Governor's; from
whom, and his lady, we received the most pointed civility and
attention, as well as from the ladies and gentlemen of Boston.
The Governor was for escorting us to Braintree in his coach
and four, attended by his light horse; and even Braintree was
for coming out to Milton bridge to meet us, but this we could
by no means assent to. Accordingly we quitted town privately;
your papa one day, and I the next. We went to our worthy
brother's, where we remained until the next week, when our
furniture came up. But we have come into a house not half
repaired, and I own myself most sadly disappointed. In height
and breadth, it feels like a wren's house. Ever since I came, we
have had such a swarm of carpenters, masons, farmers, as have
almost distracted me—every thing all at once, with miserable
assistance. In short, I have been ready to wish I had left all my
furniture behind. The length of the voyage and heat of the
ship greatly injured it; some we cannot get up, and the

shocking state of the house has obliged me to open it in the garret. But I will not tire you with a recital of all my troubles.

I hope soon to embrace you, my dear children, in Braintree; but be sure you wear no feathers, and let Col. Smith come without heels to his shoes, or he will not be able to walk upright. But we shall be more arranged by that time, and, I hope, the chief of our business done. We have for my comfort, six cows, without a single convenience for a dairy. But you know there is no saying nay.

Sweetly do the birds sing. I will not tell you your brother is here, because he has not written to you. But I must leave off, or you will think me as bad as Esther; indeed, I feel almost bewildered.

Affectionately yours,   A. Adams.

BIRTH OF JOHN ADAMS SMITH

To John Adams

my dearest Friend   Jamaica December 3ᵈ 1788—

This day three weeks I left Home, since which I have not heard a word from thence. I wrote you from Hartford and once from this place since my arrival. I cannot give you any account eitheir of Newyork or Jamaica as I got into the first at seven in the Evening & left it at Nine the next morning, and in this place my only excursion has been in the garden. the weather has been bad cloudy & rainy ever since I came untill within these two days, and now it is very cold & Blustering. when I think of the distance I am from Home, the Idea of winter & Snow has double terrors for me. I think every Seperation more painfull as I increase in Years. I hope you have found in the Learned & venerable Company you proposed keeping, an ample compensation for my absence. I imagine however if these cold Nights last a little vital Heat must be wanting. I would recommend to you the Green Baize Gown, and if that will not answer, you recollect the Bear skin. I hope you will gaurd with all possible precaution against the Riggors of winter. I wish to hear how mr John Q A stands this cold. I hope he rest well, and duly excercises. I learn nothing further in politicks for except when col Smith goes to Town which is but seldom, we hear no News & see nobody but the Family. Mrs Smith remains very well for the Time and young master grows, but he and William should change Names, as William bears not the least likness to His Father or Family & the Young one is very like. for myself I am tolerably a little Homeish, however, the more so perhaps through the fear of not being able to reach it, just when I wish. if our out of Door Family should increase in my absence, I hope proper attention will be paid to the preservation of the Young family. if it should be numerous it will be rather expensive, and I would offer to your consideration whether two of the young Females had not better be put in a condition for disposal, viz fatted. The Beaf I Suppose is by this time in the cellar. I wish you would mention to Brisler & to Esther, a constant attention to every thing about House to Gaurd against the incroachment of Rats & mice. the cider should be drawn off, and my pears and Apples picked over & repack'd. if I should not reach Home by christmass—would it not be best to purchase a pork for winter, & to secure a few legs of pork to Bacon? I wish amongst other things you would frequently caution them about the fires a Nights. I should be loth to trust any one in this Matter but Brisler.—

pray write me by the next post and tell me how you all do.

mr & mrs Smith present their duty pray do not forget to present mine to our venerable parent little William says Grandpa ha ha. I should certainly bring him home if it was not winter and such a distance

Love to mrs Cranch & my Neices:—

Yours most tenderly   A Adams

my Trunk has not yet arrived so that I could not go abroad if I would— Barnard was to sail the Sunday after I left Town

"ALL OUR VOTES . . . FOR VICE PRESIDENT"

To John Adams

My dearest Friend   Jamaica december 15th 1788

   It was not untill yesterday that I received your Letter & mrs
Cranchs. mr mccomick came up & brought them both to my
no small satisfaction, and this was the first that I had heard
from Home since I left it, except by the News papers which I
have engaged George Storer to forward to me. I have written
to you every week since I left you, and Subjected you to more
postage than my Letters are worth, which I did not know untill
Saturday when mr Jay offerd to Frank my Letters & requested
me to have mine sent to him. Members of congress it seems
have not that privilege but when they are upon duty. mr Jay
came out on Saturday to visit me. he had been waiting some
Time for mrs Jay, but the children were sick with the measles
and prevented her. Col smith was gone to Town, so we had all
the Talk to ourselves, and very social we were, just as if we had
been acquainted Seven years. He expresst a great desire to see
you, and thought you might have come on without subjecting
yourself to any observations, tho he knew your Reasons were
those of Delicacy. I replied to him that your wish to see him
was mutual that a visit from him to you would have made you
very happy, but that you was become quite a Farmer and had
such a fondness for old Professions that you talk'd of returning
to the Bar again. he replied with some warmth, that if your
Countrymen permitted it, they would deserve to be brought
to the Bar—that you must not think of retireing from publick
Life. you had received your portion of the bitter things in
politicks it was time you should have some of the sweets. I askt
him where he thought the sweets in the new Government
were to grow. he smild and said that he hoped for good things
under it. I askd him whether the oppositition in virginia was
not likely to become troublesome, particularly when joind by
this state. he said it was his opinion that they might be quieted,
by the New Governments assureing them that a convention
should be called to consider of amendments at a certain period. Col Smith dinned at club on Saturday. col Hammilton

shew him a Letter from madison in which he "Says, we consider your Reasons conclusive. the Gentleman you have named
will certainly have all our votes & interest for vice President,"
but there is interest making amongst the antifeds for Clinton
both in Newyork and virginia, and if the Electers should be of
that class tis Said General washington will not have the vote of his
own State for Pressident. Col Wadsworth says he is sure of
connecticut with respect to a vice president— I am rather at a
loss to know how to act. I find there is much inquiry made for
me in Newyork. one Lady is sending to know when I am comeing to Town & an other where I shall keep and Tickets for the
assembly have been sent up to me. mr Jay requested me to
make his House my Home, but I have no maid with me and
should experience many difficulties in concequence of it if I
went where I should be exposed to so much company and I
was previously engaged to mrs Atkinson, but my Trunk with
all my Cloaths is not yet arrived, & I am Sadly of, even here
having only one gown with me. and I must be obliged to return home without even Seeing Newyork should Barnard be
driven off to the west Indies, if a good snow comes I shall not
wait. the Ladies must stay their curiosity till my Leve day, and
if that never comes, they will have no further curiosity about
seeing A A—who it seems was of so much concequence or
somebody connected with her, that at every Inn upon the
Road it was made known that I was comeing. I find the peice
called a Tribute justly paid &c is in the Nyork & conneticut
papers— I see several political maneuvers in our Boston papers
particularly the Letter which places a certain Gentleman in the
chair dividing the state into two parties one for the Late & the
other for the present Governour, & supposing they mean both
to unite in mr A. an other peice dated at Braintree, which I am
persuaded was never written there I dare say I shall tell you
News out of your own papers

Mrs Smith desires me to present her duty to you. she is very
weak yet, but otherways well. mr Jay upon seeing william cry'd
out well here is Grandpappa over again. he is a fine red cheekd
chubby Boy, as good temperd as I ever saw a child. Mrs Cranch
says you are very solitary and that she cannot get you to see
her. they tell me here that the Great Folks in Newyork are
never solitary, if the wife is absent why they supply her place,

now rather than my Husband should do so, I would stick to him, cleave I believe is the proper word all the days of my Life. I hope the Lads are all well and that Esther takes good care of them & of their things. Mrs Smith says I am in better spirits since I got my Letters. I believe it is true I know I was near home sick before. I think of a thousand things which I ought to be doing, and here I am near 300 miles distant. my duty to your good mother, I hope she has recoverd from her Fall & is able to visit you sometimes. pray write me all about the Family and cover your Letters to mr Jay— adieu most affectionately yours—   A Adams

INAUGURATION

To John Adams

my dearest Friend   Braintree May 1. 1789

I received your kind favours of the 19 & 22 of April. the printers were very obliging in taking particular care to supply me daily with the paper's by which I learnt the arrival and Reception of the President, & vice Pressident. if I thought I could compliment in so courtly and masterly a stile, I would say that the address to the Senate was exactly what it ought to be, neither giving too little, or too much, it has been much admired, yet every one do not see the force of the first part of it; when I read the debates of the House, I could not but be surprized at their permitting them to be open, and thought it would have been a happy circustance if they could have found a dr Johnson for the Editor of them. I think there is much of the old leaven in the New Loaf "I dare not lay a duty upon salt, the people will not bear it, I dread the concequences to the people" is a language to teach the people to rise up in opposition to Government, the people would bear a 5 pr ct duty upon every article imported, & expect as much, but will grumble perhaps at the duty upon molasses. be sure it is a little hard for *us Yankees* who Love it so well & make such liberal use of it, it has already raised the price of it here. I hope the Senate will never consent to draw backs. it will be a constant source of knavery, will not small duties operate best, be most productive and least atroxious? Johnson, whom you know I have lately been reading with great attention, and have become his great admirer, more fully convinc'd than ever, that he was a very accurate observer of Human Life & manners. Johnson in one of his papers proves that there is no such thing as domestick Greatness— such is the constitution of the world that much of Life must be spent in the same manner by the wise & the Ignorant the exalted and the low. Men However distinguish'd by external accidents or intrinsick qualities, have all the same wants, the same pains, and as far as the senses are consulted the same pleasures. the petty cares and petty duties are the same in every station to every understanding, and every hour brings us some occasion on which we all sink to the Common level. we are all naked till we are dressed, and hungry till we are fed. the Generals Triumph and Sage's disputation, end like the Humble Labours of the smith or plowman in a dinner or a sleep— Let this plead my excuse when I frequently call of your attention from weighty National objects to the petty concerns of domestick Life. I have been trying to dispose of the stock on Hand, but no purchaser appears—immediate profit is what all seek, or credit, where little is to be given. the weather is cold the spring backward, and the stock expensive. you will not wonder that I am puzzeld what to do, because I am in a situation which I never was before. yours I presume cannot be much better the Bill is setled with 48$^{£.}$ 18^s damages— vacancy is up and the children have returnd to Cambridge.

my best Respects attend mr Jay and his Lady whose health I hope is mended. you do not mention mrs Smith or the little Boys—nor have I heard from them since mr Bourn came. by the way I heard a Report yesterday that Marble Head & Salem had voted you an anual present of ten Quintals of fish.— how well founded the Report is I can not presume to say, time must determine it. I want to hear how you do & how you can bear the application & confinement of your office. I say nothing about comeing. you will know when it will be proper & give me timely notice. the Children desired me to present their duty. I am my dearest Friend with the tenderest affection ever yours—   Abigail Adams

Esther is very impatient to hear from her Husband the child is better & she comfortable put your Frank upon your Letters if you please

JOINING JOHN IN NEW YORK

To John Adams

my dearest Friend   Sunday May 31. 1789

I received yesterday your Letter of May the 24th and shall begin tomorrow to get such things in readiness as will enable us to keep House. I feel a reluctance at striping this wholy at present, because I am well persuaded that we shall in some future period if our lives are prolonged return to it, and even supposing a summer recess, we might wish to come & spend a few months here. an other reason is, that I do not wish to bring all our own furniture, because congress are not, or do not possess sufficient stability to be sure of continuing long in any one state,— I am fully satisfied with the House you have taken & glad that it is a little removed from the city. the advantages will overbalance the inconvenience I doubt not. I suppose Barnard has arrived before this. would it not be best to let him know that he will have a full freight ready, returns as soon as he will, and that I must look out for some other vessel if he delay's, tho I have not the least prospect of getting one, for mr Tufts's is yet at Newyork Barnard's is calculated for the Buisness, & I could get a small vessel to come here to mr Blacks & take in my things & carry them along side of Barnard, which will be less expence, & damage than carting them to Boston. in the mean time I will get the Dr to look out, & see if any other vessel can be hired for the purpose provided Barnard should delay at Newyork. this you can advise me of by the next post. with the greatest expedition I do not think I can get them ready under a week— I must leave Brisler to come by water with them, if you think it best for me to come before my furniture is ship'd, but I do not see what advantage I can be of, to you situated as you are. an additional incunberence to mr Jays family would be still more indelicet than imposing the vice Pressident upon him for several months, and rendering his situation so delicate that he could neither leave him with decency, or stay with decorum, and to be at Jamaica I could do no more than if I was at Braintree to assist in any thing the Trunks which I sent contain Bed & table Linnen some Cloths & the cases contain carpets. I will however be directed wholy by your wishes & come next week if you think it best, and you have any place to put me. you must be sensible from the tenor of Your Letters that I have not known hitherto what to do, any more than you have from your situation, What to direct. you will be as patient as possible & rest assured that I will do my utmost with the means I have, to expidite every thing. as to insurence there will be no occasion for it by Barnard who is so well acquainted with the coast, & at this season of the Year

The Pressident & Lady dinned with me yesterday. he has got permission for Charles's absence— Polly Tailor would cry a week if I did not bring her, for a House maid I know not where I could get her equal. Elijahs mother thinks it is too far for her son to go, but if they consent mr Brisler can take him on Board Barnard when he comes, but I shall not press it. Poor daniel has been sick with a soar which gatherd in his Throat & which nearly proved fatal to him. he expected from you some gratuity for himself, oweing to the multiplicity of cares which on all sides surrounded you, at that time, it was omitted. as it was Customary & daniels expectations were dissapointed, he mentiond it to one or two persons, amongst whom woodard was one, who having just returnd from Newyork, clapt his hands into his pocket & taking out two crowns, gave them to him, telling him that you was so much engaged at the time, that it had slipt your mind but that he saw you at Newyork & that he had brought them for him. this came to my knowledge by the way of mr Wibird who insisted upon letting me know it. I immediatly repaid mr woodard & thank'd him for his kindness—

your Brother I believe will take care of the place when I leave it. the leave for Breaking up the Hill came too late for this season, the weather is remarkably cold & Backward, the pastures bare & vegetation very slow there is a fine blow upon the place, & if the frost last week which killd Beans, has not injured the Blossom, we shall have a large crop of fruit. I had yesterday a fine plate of fair Russets upon the table, sound as when they were taken from the Trees my Garden looks charmingly, but it wants warmth— I have got some Large asparagrass Beds made, & my little grass plots before the door, pay well for the manure which I had put on in short I regreet leaving it. your Mother is well as usual. her Eyes are very troublesome to her. you will let me hear from you by the next post. I hope to be able to relieve you soon from [   ] domestick, cares & anxieties. at least my best endeavours shall not be wanting. I know you want your own Bed & pillows, your Hot coffe & your full portion of kian where habit has become Natural. how many of these little matters, make up a large portion of our happiness & content, and the more of publick cares & perplexities that you are surrounded with, the more necessary these alleviations our blessings are sometimes enhanced to us, by feeling the want of them. as one of that Number it is my highest ambition to be estimated, & shall be my constant endeavour to prove in all situations & circumstances affectionatly yours   A Adams

JOURNEY TO NEW YORK

To Mary Smith Cranch

My dear sister   Richmond Hill june 28th 1789

I wrote you from Providence some account of my polite reception there & closed my Letter just as I had accepted an invitation to dine with mr Brown & Lady. the forenoon was pass't in receiving visits from all the principal gentlemen and Ladies of the Town, who seemed to vie with each other, to convince me that tho they were inhabitants of an Antifederal state. they were themselves totally against the measures persued by it, and that they entertaind the highest Regard and Respect for the Character with which I was so intimately connected, altho to their great mortification they had been prevented the Honour of having any share in placing him in his respected station

Mr Brown sent his Carriage & Son to conduct me his House

which is one of the Grandest I have seen in this Country. every thing in and about it, wore the marks of magnificence & taste. mrs Brown met me at the door & with the most obliging Smile accosted me with—"Friend I am glad to see thee here" the simplicity of her manners & dress with the openness of her countanance & the friendlyness of her behaviour charmed me beyond all the studied politeness of European manners— they had colleted between 22 persons to dine with me tho the notice was so short, & gave an Elegant entertainment upon a service of Plate. towards Evening I made a Tour round the Town, & drank Tea & spent the Evening with mr & Mrs Francis whom I mentiond to you before. here the company was much enlarged, & many persons introduced to me who had no opportunity before of visiting me, amongst those Ladies, with whom I was most pleased was the Lady & two sisters of Governour Bowen. about Eleven I returnd To my lodgings and the next morning went on Board the Handcock packet we had contrary wind all Day, by which means we did not reach Newport untill Seven oclock. I had been only a few moments arrived when mr Merchant came on Board and insisted that I with my whole Family should go on shore & Lodge at his House. he would take no refusal. he sent his daughter down to receive & accompany my Neice, & came himself in a few moments with a carriage to attend me. at his House I was kindly & Hospitably Treated by his Lady & daughters. we slept there & the next morning were early summond on Board the packet. Captain Brown had very civily taken his wife to attend upon me, & accomodate me during my passage I found her a very well Bred Geenteel woman, but neither civility attention or politeness could remedy the sea sickness or give me a fair wind or dispell the Thunder Gusts which attended us both night & day. in short I resolved upon what I have frequently before, that I would never again embark upon the water, but this resolution I presume will be kept as my former ones have been. we were five days upon the water. Heat want of rest, sea sickness & terror for I had my share of that, all contributed to fatigue me and I felt upon my arrival quite tame & spiritless Louissa was very sick, but behaved like a Heroine Matilda had her share but when she was a little recoverd she was the life of us all Polly was half dead all the Passage &

sufferd more from sea sickness than any of us. Charls eat &
slept without any inconvenience. when we came to the wharff,
I desired the Captain to go to our Friend mr MacCormick and
inform him of my arrival, if he was not to be found to go to
the Senate Chamber & inform mr A. who from the hour of
the day I knew must be there. mr otis the secretary came to me
with a Carriage & I reach'd Richmond Hill on Thursday one
oclock to my no small joy I found mr Adams in better Health
than I feard mr & mrs Smith quite well & every thing so well
arranged that Beds & a few other articles seem only necessary
towards keeping House with comfort, and I begin to think,
that my furniture will be troublesome to me, some part of it I
mean whilst mrs Smith remains with me. master John was
grown out of my knowledge, william is still at Jamaica. our
House has been a mere Levee ever since I arrived morning &
Evening. I took the earliest opportunity (the morning after my
arrival) to go & pay my respects to mrs Washington mrs Smith
accompanied me. She received me with great ease & politeness, she is plain in her dress, but that plainness is the best of
every article. she is in mourning, her Hair is white, her Teeth
Beautifull, her person rather short than otherways, hardly so
large as my Ladyship, and if I was to speak sincerly, I think she
is a much better figure, her manners are modest and unassuming, dignified and femenine, not the Tincture of ha'ture about
her. *his majesty* was ill & confined to his Room. I had not the
pleasure of a presentation to him, but the satisfaction of hearing that he regreeted it equally with myself. col Humphries
who had paid his compliments to me in the morning & Breakfasted with me, attended mrs washington & mr Lear the Private
Secretary, was the introducter— thus you have an account of my
first appearence— the Principal Ladies who have visited me are
the Lady & daughter of the Governour Lady Temple the Countess de Brehim, Mrs Knox & 25 other Ladies many of the Senators,
all their Ladies all the Foreign ministers & some of the Reps.

We are most delightfully situated, the prospect all around is
Beautifull in the highest degree, it is a mixture of the sublime
& Beautifull— amidst it all I sigh for many of my dear Friends
and connections. I can make no domestick arrangment till
Brisler arrives— remember me affectionatly to all my Friends

particularly my aged parent, to my children to whom I cannot write as yet to my dear Lucy & worthy dr Tufts in short to all whom I love yours most tenderly   A Adams

PATRONAGE

To Mary Smith Cranch

my dear sister   Richmond Hill july 12ᵗʰ 1789
    I received your kind Letter by mr Brisler who reachd here on the 4th of july, Since which you will easily suppose I have been very buisily engaged in arraneging my Family affairs. this added to the intence heat of the season Some company (tho for three days I was *fashionably* not at Home,) and some visiting which was indispensable, having more than fifty upon my list, my Time has been so wholy occupied that I have not taken a pen, yet my Thoughts have not been so occupied, but that they have frequently visited you, and my other Friends in the Neighbourhood, and tho I have here, as to situation one of the most delightfull spots I have seen in this Country, yet I find the want of some of my particular connection's but an all wise Providence has seen fit to curtail our wishes and to limit our enjoyments, that we may not be unmindfull of our dependance or forget the Hand from whence they flow. I have a favour to request of all my near and intimate Friend's it is to desire them to watch over my conduct and if at any time they perceive any alteration in me with respect to them, arising as they may suppose from my situation in Life, I beg they would with the utmost freedom acquaint me with it. I do not feel within myself the least disposition of the kind, but I know Mankind are prone to deceive themselves, and Some are disposed to misconstrue the conduct of those whom they conceive placed above them.
    our August Pressident is a singular example of modesty and diffidence. he has a dignity which forbids Familiarity mixed with an easy affibility which creates Love and Reverence. the Fever which he had terminated in an absess, so that he cannot

sit up. upon my second visit to mrs Washington he sent for me
into his Chamber. he was laying upon a settee and half raising
himself up, beggd me to excuse his receiving me in that posture, congratulated me upon my arrival in New york and askd
me how I could realish the simple manners of America after
having been accustomed to those of Europe. I replied to him
that where I fund simple manners I esteemed them, but that I
thought we approachd much nearer to the Luxery and manners of Europe according to our ability, than most persons
were sensible of, and that we had our full share of taste and
fondness for them. The Pressident has a Bed put into his Carriage and rides out in that way, allways with six Horses in his
Carriage & four attendants mrs Washington accompanies him.
I requested him to make Richmond Hill his resting place, and
the next day he did so, but he found walking up stairs so difficult, that he has done it but once. Mrs Washington is one of
those unassuming Characters which Creat Love & Esteem, a
most becomeing plasentness sits upon her countanance, & an
unaffected deportment which renders her the object of veneration and Respect, with all these feelings and Sensations I
found myself much more deeply impressd than I ever did before their Majesties of Britain.

You ask me concerning politicks, upon my word I hear less
of them here, than I did in Massa'ts the two Houses are very
buisy upon very important Bill's the judiciary, and the Collecting Bills. the Senate is composed of many men of great abilities,
who appear to be liberal in their sentiments and candid towards
each other. the House is composed of some men of equal talants, others—the debates will give you the best Idea of them,
but there is not a member whose sentiment clash more with
my Ideas of things than mr. G——y he certainly does not
comprehend the Great National System which must render us
Respectable abroad & energetick at Home and will assuredly
find himself lost amidst Rocks & Sands—

My dear sister some parts of your Letter made me melancholy. are you in any difficulties unknown to me I know very
well that a small Farm must afford you a scanty support and
that you are a sufferer from being obliged to receive pay in
paper but I know your Prudence & oeconomy has carried you
along, tho not in affluence, yet with decency & comfort, and I

hope you will still be able to live so. you have one daughter comfortably situated, your son will from his merit & abilities soon get into some buisness your other daughter, you have every reason to be satisfied with do not look upon the gloomy side only. how easily might your situation be changed for the worse. even if you were in possession of Riches yet there is a competancy which is so desirable that one cannot avoid an anxiety for it. I have a request to make you, desire mr Cranch to make out his account which he has against mr A. I gave cousin Lucy a memmorandum—let the balance be drawn and inclose to me, and I will send you a Receit in full This I consider myself at full liberty to do, because the little sum Lent you was my own pocket money. put the Letter under cover to mrs Smith, it will then fall into no hands but my own but cover the whole for a frank to mr A.— do not talk of oblagations. reverse the matter & then ask yourself, if you would not do as much for me?

I wish it was in mr A's power to help mr Cranch to some office at Home which would assist him. mr A exprest the same wish to me, but at present he does not see any, tho a certain Lady in the full assurance of hope, wrote him that he now had it in his power to establish his own Family & Successfully help his Friends and that she is sure of his Patronage—for certain purposes—to which mr A. replied, "that he has no patronage but if he had, neither her children or his own could be sure of it beyond his own clear conviction of the publick good, that he should bely the whole course of his publick and private conduct, and all the maxims of his Life, if he should ever consider publick Authority entrusted to him, to be made subservient to his private views, or those of his Family and Friends." you cannot mistake who the Lady was, I know no other equally ambitious, but I presume her pretentions & those of her Family will fail, as I think they ought to if one Quarter part is true which has been reported of them. I fancy a constant correspondence is kept up between mr W——n & mr G——y and like enough with several other jealous Partizans, but I hope they will never have sufficient interest to disturb the Government. I really believe mr G——y to be an honest man. the other has been grosely misled, and I do soberly think by the unbridled ambition of one She told me upon her last visit, that she did not perceive any alteration in *mr A's* conduct towards them. I am sure she must have told what was not true if she had said there was none in mine, for I feel it, and I cannot deceive. with regard to mr A he has dealt by them like a sincere Friend, and an honest Man and their own Hearts must approve his conduct, however grateing to their feelings. I am most sincerely sorry for the cause. they were my old and dear Friend's for whom I once entertaind the highest respect

Col mrs Smith Charles & little Jack are gone this week to Jamaica to get out of the Bustle at home and are not yet returnd. C. will not go into any company but such as his Father or col Smith introduces him to. he appears steady and sedate & I hope will continue so—Time and example will prevail over youthfull folly I trust. my Love to mrs Norten, how does she do? Louissa appears very happy, but I am obliged to keep her a mere prisoner on account of the small Pox of which there is always danger in N York as soon as the weather will permit shall have her innoculated. I find as many servants necessary here as in England, but not half as well calculated for their buisness. the distance from Town requires one or two extra as they are obliged to go & come always four, & frequently six times a day. we have to send constantly to market in addition, but not withstanding all this I would not change this situation for any I know of in Town. Richmond Hill is situated upon the North River which communicates with Albany. Pauls hook as it is calld is in full sight, & the Jersy shore. vessels are constantly passing up & down. the House is situated upon a high Hill which commands a most extensive prospect, on one side we have a view of the city & of Long Island, the River in Front, Jersy and the adjasant Country on the other side, you Turn a litle from the Road and enter a Gate a winding Road with trees in clumps leads you to the House, and all round the House, it looks wild and Rural as uncultivated Nature. the House is convenient for one family, but much too small for more, you enter under a Piazza into a Hall & turning to the right Hand assend a stair case which lands you in an other of equal dimensions of which I make a drawing Room. it has a Glass door which opens into a gallery the whole Front of the house which is exceeding pleasant. the Chambers are on each side. the House is not in good repair, wants much done to it, and if we continue here I hope it will be done. there is upon the back of the House a Garden of much greater extent than our Braintree Garden, but it is wholy for a walk & flowers. it has a Hawthorn hedge & Rows of Trees with a Broad Gravel Walk.

how happy would it make me to see here my dears Brothers Sister Nephew Neices, and to delight them with the prospect. mr Guile & dr Craigy dinned with us yesterday. I find I have local attachments, and am more rejoiced to see a citizen of my own state than any other. Remember me affectionatly to my worthy Mother & Family to mrs Palmer & family who I hope are comfortably situated, to mrs Brisler too. I hope she will be able to come this way before long

my Letter is written in haste the weather very hot and I too laizy to Coppy

most affectionatly yours   A Adams

Tell Lucy she must write to me

PRESIDENT WASHINGTON

To Mary Smith Cranch

my dear sister   Richmond Hill August 9th 1789

If I should ask why I have not heard from my sister or Friends, for several weeks past, would she not answer me by retorting the question? in replie I could only say that I had designd writing every day for a long time, but we have had such a lassitude of weather, and such a long continuence of it, that I have really felt unfit for every thing which I was not necessitated to perform, & for many of those which I have been obligated to, from my situation, such as dressing receiving & paying visits, giving dinners &c I have never before been in a situation in which morning noon & afternoon I have been half as much exposed to company. I have laid down one rule which is, not to make any morning visits myself, and in an afternoon after six oclock I can return 15 or 20 & very seldom find any Lady to receive me, but at Richmond Hill, it is expected that I am at Home both to Gentlemen & Ladies when ever they come out, which is almost every day since I have been here, besides it is a sweet morning ride to Breakfast I propose to fix a Levey day soon. I have waited for mrs washington to begin and she has fix'd on every fryday 8 oclock. I attended upon the last, mrs smith & charles. I found it quite a crowded Room. the form of Reception is this, the servants announce—& col Humphries or mr Lear—receives every Lady at the door, & Hands her up to mrs washington to whom she makes a most Respectfull curtzey and then is seated without noticeing any of the rest of the company. the Pressident then comes up and speaks to the Lady, which he does with a grace dignity & ease, that leaves Royal George far behind him. the company are entertaind with Ice creems & Lemonade, and retire at their pleasure performing the same ceremony when they quit the Room. I cannot help smiling when I read the Boston puffs, that the Pressident is unmoved amidst all the dissipations of the city of New york. now I am wholy at a loss to determine the meaning of the writer. not a Single publick amusement is their in the whole city, no not even a publick walk, and as to Dinners, I believe their are six made in Boston to one here, unless it is for some particular person to whom a Number of families wish to pay attention. there are Six Senators who have their Ladies and families with them, but they are in Lodgings the chief of them, & not in a situation to give dinners— as to the mode of visiting, less time is expended in this way, than in sending word to each person & passing an afternoon with them, tho I own on the score of pleasure that would be to me the most agreeable. I have returnd more than Sixty visits all of them in 3 or 4 afternoons & excepting at the Pressidents, have drank tea only at two other places and dined but once out, since I arrived

Indeed I have been fully employd in entertaining company, in the first place all the Senators who had Ladies & families, then the remaining Senators, and this week we have begun with the House, and tho we have a room in which we dine 24 persons at a Time, I shall not get through them all, together with the publick Ministers for a month to come the help I find here is so very indifferent to what I had in England, the weather so warm that we can give only one dinner a week. I cannot find a cook in the whole city but what will get drunk, and as to the Negroes—I am most sincerely sick of them, and I can no more do without mr Brisler, than a coach could go without wheels or Horses to draw it. I can get Hands, but what are hands without a Head, and their chief object is to be as expensive as possible. this week I shall not be able to see any company unless it is to Tea—for my Family are all sick mrs smiths two Children with the Hooping cough Charles with the dysentary, Louissa & Polly with a complaint Similar. To Charles I gave a puke last night & his complaints have abated. Louissa & Polly are to take one to night. if we had not been so fortunate in our situation I do not know how we could have lived. it is very sickly in the City.

As to politicks, I presume many of the dissapointed Candidates will complain. some will quarrel with men & some with measures. I believe the Presideent Strove to get the best information he could, but there are some men who will get much said in their favour when they do not merit it.— the News papers will give you the Debates of the house to the President their system is as liberal as I could expect I leave the world to judge how it is with respect to their vice President from whom they expect more entertainment the House was New furnishd for the President & cost ten thousand Dollors as the Board of Treasury say. the use & improvement of this they have granted him, which is but just & right. He never rides out without six Horses to his Carriage, four Servants, & two Gentlemen before him, this is no more state than is perfectly consistant with his station, but then I do not Love to see the News writers fib so. He is Perfectly averse to all marks of distinction say they, yet on the 4th of july when the cincinnati committee waited upon him he received them in a Regimental uniform with the Eagal most richly set with diamonds at his Button, yet the News writers will fib—to answer particular purposes— I think he ought to have still more state, & time will convince our Country of the necessity, of it. here I say not any thing upon the subject. it would be asscribed to a cause I dispise if I should speak my mind. I hear that the vote which mr A gave in the Senate, respecting the Removal of officers by the President independant of the senate, has been by some of his own state construed, as voting power into his own Hands—or having that in view, but his Rule through life has been to vote and act, independant of Party agreeable to the dictates of his conscience and tho on that occasion he could have wisht on account of the delicacy of his situation not to have been obliged to have determind the Question, yet falling to him, he shrunk not, not a word did any of our state say when his vote reduced the duty upon molasses, all was silence then they could not possibly ascribe it to any Sinister motive but uneasy wrestless Spirits are to be found in all quarters of the world.

And now my dear sister I wish to know how you do. mrs Norten Lucy not a line from either, nor a word from sister shaw.

Mr Bond will tell you that he saw us all, he was out two or three times. I wish you could come with our dear Brother Cranch & spend the Evening with us. We do not have company on Sundays. we go to meeting, but alass I do not find a dr Price. I hope I shall visit Braintree next summer. I wonder sister Smith has never written a word to Louissa. I am glad to find Tommy has got a good Chum. I hope he will continue steady. Charles studies with mr Hamilton goes to the office when his Father goes to senate & returns with him at 4 oclock. he has not discoverd the least inclination for getting into company and has no acquaintance but George Storer—pray make my best Regards to all my Friends, to my Mother present my duty. Remember me to mrs Palmer & family. the Beautifull prospect here from every quarter makes me regreet less than I otherways should do the spot I quitted. the rooms are lofty and was the House in good repair I should find it, very convenient for my own Family. at present we are crowded for want of Chamber Room. my family consists of 18— How does the place look. I must get my Butter all put up & sent me from Braintree. I have Breakfasted constantly upon milk, I cannot eat the Butter here— I must write the dr upon several subjects by twesdays post. I shall not get ready by this.

pray let me hear from you. the season is plentifull. Let us rejoice & be glad Cheer up my good sister, a merry Heart does good like a medicine— we all send abundance of Love— I must go to look after my invalids

ever yours   A Adams

"ALL DISTINCTION YOU KNOW IS UNPOPULAR"

To Mary Smith Cranch

my dear sister   Jan^ry 5th 1790

I begin my Letter with the congratulations of the season, to you and all my other Friends & for many happy returns in Succeeding years. the New years day in this State, & particularly in this city is celebrated with every mark of pleasure and satisfaction. the shops and publick offices are Shut, there is not any market upon this day, but every person laying aside Buisness devote the day to the Social purpose of visiting & receiving visits. the churches are open & divine Service performed begining the year in a very proper manner by giving Thanks to the great Governour of the universe for past mercies, & imploring his future Benidictions there is a kind of cake in fashion upon this day call'd New years cooky. this & cherry Bounce as it is calld is the old Dutch custom of treating their Friends upon the return of every New Year. the common people who are very ready to abuse Liberty, on this day are apt to take rather too freely of the good things of this Life, and finding two of my servants not alltogether qualified for Buisness, I remonstrated to them, but they excused it saying it was new year, & every body was joyous then. the V P. visited the President & then returnd home to receive His Friends. in the Evening I attended the drawing Room, it being mrs W——s publick day. it was as much crowded as a Birth Night at St James, and with company as Briliantly drest, diamonds & great hoops excepted my station is always at the right hand of Mrs W. through want of knowing what is right, I find it some times occupied, but on such an occasion the President never fails of Seeing that it is relinquishd for me, and having removed Ladies Several times, they have now learnt to rise & give it me, but this between our selves, as *all distinction* you know is unpopular. Yet this same P. has so happy a faculty of appearing to accommodate & yet carrying his point, that if he was not really one of the best intentiond Men in the world he might be a very dangerous one. he is polite with dignity, affable without familiarity, distant without Haughtyness, Grave without

Austerity, Modest, Wise, & Good these are traits in his Character which peculiarly fit him for the exalted station he holds—and God Grant that he may Hold it with the same applause & universal Satisfaction for many many years—as it is my firm opinion that no other man could rule over this great peopl & consolidate them into one mighty Empire but He who is Set over us.

I thank you my dear sister for several kind Letters, the reason why I have not written to you has been that the post office would not permit Franks even to the V. P. and I did not think my Letters worth paying for— I wrote you a long Letter a little before mr Adams's return, but being under cover to him, I had the mortification to receive it back again. I am perfectly satisfied with what you did for son Thomas, and thank you for all your kind care of him it has saved me much trouble, but I do not think his Health good, he is very thin pale & sallow. I have given him a puke, & think he is the better for it. Charls is quite fat. he is very steady and studious. there is no fault to be found with his conduct, he has no company or companions but known & approved ones, nor does he appear to wish for any other. I some times think his application too intence, but better so, than too remis.

I was really surprizd to learn that Sister Shaw was likly to increase her Family. I wish her comfortably through, but shall feel anxious for her feeble constitution as to my Neice mrs Norten I doubt not she will find her Health mended by becomeing a mother, and you will soon be as fond of your Grandchildren as ever you was of your own. I hope however she will not follow her cousins example, and be like always to have one, before the other is weaned. John does not go alone yet. William becomes every day more & more interesting he is a very pleasant temperd Boy, but the other will require the whole house to manage him. with Regard to the cellar I know if very cold weather should come we shall lose our red wine & Porter, but as to the key, tis a point I do not chuse to meddle with tho all the Liquors shoud suffer by it. I did not leave it where it is, nor do I hold myself answerable for the concequences of neglect. the fruit which came here was like refuse, rotton & Bruised, a specimin of what I expected but you know there are cases where silence is prudence, and I think without flattering myself I have attaind to some share of that virtue. we live in a world where having Eyes, we must not see, and Ears we must not hear

10 Jan^ry

I designd to have written much more to you and some other Friends, but publick days, dinning parties &c have occupied me so much for this fort night, that I must close my Letter now or lose the conveyance.

remember me affectionatly to all Friends. living two miles from meeting obliges me to hasten or lose the afternoon Service. adieu yours   A Adams—

"GREAT ANXIETY FOR THE PRESSIDENT"

To Cotton Tufts

dear sir   N york 30 May 1790.

I received your kind Letter of May   last week I was very sorry to hear that you and your Family had not escaped the prevailing sickness. the disorder has universally prevaild here. not a single one of our Family, except mr Adams has escaped, and Polly, it was very near proving fatal too. We Have been in very great anxiety for the President. during the state of Suspence, it was thought prudent to say very little upon the Subject as a general allarm might have proved injurious to the present state of the Government. he has been very unwell through all the Spring, labouring with a Billious disorder but thought, contrary to the advise of his Friends that he should exercise it away without medical assistance; he made a Tour upon Long Island of 8 or ten days which was a temporary Relief, but soon after his return he was Seazd with a voilent Plurisy Fever attended with every bad Symptom, and just at the Crisis was seazd with Hicups & rattling in the Throat, so that mrs washington left his Room thinking him dying the Physicians apprehended him in a most dangerous state. James powders had been administerd, and they produced a happy Effect by a profuse perspiration which reliefd his cough &

Breathing, and he is now happily so far recoverd as to ride out daily. I do not wish to feel again Such a state of anxiety as I experienced for several days I had never before entertaind any Idea of being calld to fill a Place that I have not the least ambition to attain to, the age of the two gentlemen being so near alike that the Life of one was as Probable as that of the other, but such a Train of fearfull apprehensions allarm'd me upon the threatning prospect, that I Shudderd at the view. the weight of Empire, particularly circumstanced as ours is, without firmness without age and experienced without, a Revenue setled, & establishd, loaded with a debt, about which there is little prospect of an agreement, would bow down any man who is not supported by a whole Nation & carry him perhaps to an early Grave with misiry & disgrace. I saw a Hydra Head before me, envy Jealousy Ambition, and all the Banefull passions in League. do you wonder that I felt distrest at the view? yet I could not refrain from thinking that even a Washington might esteem himself happy to close his days before any unhappy division or disasterous event had tarnishd the Lusture of his Reign

For the Assumption of the debts you will see in the papers a wise and judicious Speach of Father Sherman as he is call'd, and a very able & Lengthy one of mr Ames's. all has been Said upon the subject that reason justice, good policy could dictate. I hope it will yet take place, but mr M—— leads the Virginians like a flock of sheep. if congress should rise without assuming, I perdict that the Next year will not be so tranquil as the last, let who will hold the Reigns

With Regard to our own private affairs mr A says the Money for mr Parsons shall be ready at the Time when our sons time is up and that he approves of your proposal that John Should pay it himself to mr Parsons. as to the House, he thinks that, if a credible person or Family could be found to take the rest of the House at a Rent, equal to the present after deducting what must be given for an office, it would be advisable to let mr J—— have it, but if not an office had better be procured else where, and he would request you to use your own judgment about it. if you are in want of 30 pounds before commencment you will draw for it. I am fully of your mind that the place which Pratt lives upon had better be let at a certain sum under restrictions. as to the other, it would be better for us if the whole sum had been laid out in paper securities, then one might have had a *chance* of some benifit from it. Pratt has such an Army to mantain, & tho an honest Man I believe, he must be embarressd with such a Numerous Family. I believe G Thayer a much better Farmer.

As to commencment I do not know what Thomas wishes. if I could have been at Home to have taken the trouble upon myself I should have been willing that he should have made a similar entertainment to his Brothers, and am willing that it should be so now, but know not how to trouble our Friends with it. it has given both mr A & me great satisfaction to learn that he acquited himself so much to his Honour & the pleasure of his Friends at the exhibition

The Hams arrived safe and appear to be very fine. I shall pay Barnard the money for them.

Present me kindly to all inquiring Friends and believe me Sincerely Yours   A Adams

you will be so good as to write me Soon

BIRTHDAY LETTER

To John Quincy Adams

my dear son   N York July 11th 1790

I believe this is your Birth day, may you have many returns of this Period, encreasing in wisdom knowledge wealth and happiness at every Aniversary. it is a long time since I wrote to you, yet I have not been unmindfull of you I am anxious for your welfare, and Solicitious for your success in Buisness. you must expect however to advance slowly at first and must call to your aid Patience and perseverence, keeping in mind the observation of that great Master of Life and manners who has said, "that there is a tide in the affairs of Men" it must be some dire misfortune or calamity, if I judge not amiss, that will ever place you in the shallows, but you must expect to contend with envy Jealousy and other malignant passions, because they exist in Humane Nature. as the poet observes "envy will merrit as its shade persue" but a steady adherence to principals of Honour and integrity, will Baffel even those foes. "make not haste to be rich" is a maxim of Sound policy tho contrary to the Sentiments of Mankind, yet I have ever observed that wealth suddenly acquired is seldom balanced with discretion, but is as suddenly dissipated, and as happiness is by no means in proportion to Wealth, it ought to make us content even tho we do not attain to any great degree of it but to quit moralizing, col Hamilton has agreed to write to Gen[ll] Lincoln to furnish 5 Hundred dollars one hundred pounds of which you are to receive and the remainder is to be subject to dr Tufts order. I would advise you to keep your Horse at Braintree. you can easily get him when you want him—

you will see by the publick papers that we are destined to Philadelphia, a Grievious affair to me I assure you, but so it is ordained— when I shall see you and the rest of my Friends I know not, but if I can hear that you are doing well it will be a great satisfaction to me. Your sister and the children are here to day and send their Love to you. adieu it shall not be so long again before I write to you. Let me hear from you

Yours most affectionatly   A Adams

BIRTH OF THOMAS HOLLIS SMITH

To Mary Smith Cranch

my dear sister   Newyork 8 August 1790

I have the pleasure to inform you that last Night mrs Smith got to Bed with an other fine Boy. We could have all wisht it had been a Girl, but rest satisfied with the sex as it is a very fine large handsome Boy and both mother and child are well. She spent the day with me on fryday, and I urged her as I had Several times before, to accept a Room here, and lie in here, as the house in which she is is Small and Hot. she told me she would come out, and the next day intended to get her things ready for the purpose, but found herself so un well on Saturday, yesterday that she could not effect it. I have been very un well myself for a fortnight, so that she did not let me know she was ill, untill I had the agreeable intelligence of her being safe abed. I shall get her here as soon as possible I have both the children with me. I have not heard a word from you since commencment, and I expect all my intelligence from you. Congress rise on twesday I wish and long to come to Braintree, but fear I shall not effect it. how does mrs Norten stand the Hot weather? your Grandson grows a fine Boy I dare say I should be quite charmd to see him & my dear cousin Lucy when is she to be married to that said Gentleman? pray give my Love to her and tell her she need not have been so sly about it. I had a few lines from Thomas just before he set out for Haverhill I expect him on here daily, and think he had best send his things Round by Barnard. I have nothing new to entertain you with unless it is my Neighbours the Creeck Savages who visit us daily. they are lodgd at an Inn at a little distance from us. they are very fond of visiting us as we entertain them kindly, and they behave with much civility. yesterday they signd the Treaty, and last Night they had a great Bond fire dancing round it like so many spirits hooping, singing, yelling, and expressing their pleasure and Satisfaction in the true Savage Stile. these are the first savages I ever saw. mico maco, one of their kings dinned here yesterday and after dinner he confered a Name upon me the meaning of which I do not know, Mammea he took me by the Hand, bowd his Head and bent his knee, calling me Mammea, Mammea. they are very fine looking Men placid contanances & fine shape. mr Trumble says, they are many of them perfect Models. MacGillvery, dresses in our own fashion speaks English like a Native, & I should never suspect him to be of that Nation, as he is not very dark he is grave and solid, intelligent and much of a Gentleman, but in very bad Health. they return in a few days.

adieu my dear sister Remember me affectionatly to all Friends I see miss Nancy Quincy is married, I wish her much happiness

Yours   A Adams

ADVICE ON MARRYING

To John Quincy Adams

Dear Son　　　　　　　　Richmond Hill 20 August 1790

I congratulate you upon your having setled yourself thus far, and am pleasd to find you so well accommodated. you have a good office, a Good Library, and an agreable Family to reside in. be patient and persevering. you will get Buisness in time, and when you feel disposed to find fault with your stars, bethink yourself how preferable your situation to that of many others, and tho a state of dependance must ever be urksome to a generous mind, when that dependance is not the effect of Idleness or dissapation, there is no kind parent but what would freely contribute to the Support and assistance of a child in proportion to their ability. I have been daily in expectation of seeing your Brother Thomas here. he must be expeditious in his movements or he will be calld to an account for *visiting* a most heinious offence you know in the view of those, who think there is more merrit in staying at Home. Your Father talks of taking a Tour to the eastward. it would be peculiarly agreeable to me to accompany him, but there are reasons, not of state, but of purse which must prevent it; and yet I think I could plan the matter so as that it would be no great object, to pass a couple of Months with our Friend's. Lady Temple & mrs Atkinson will set out tomorrow by way of RhoadIsland. they have offerd to take Letters to my Friends, but I have been rather neglegent in writing the weather has been so extreeme Hot. I have the two Boys with me Billy & John, and it is employment enough to look after them. your sister has a third Son. heaven grant that she may add no more to the stock untill her prospects brighten. a Marshells office will poorly feed a Family and I see no prospect of any other at present. I will give you one peice of advise, never form connextions untill you see a prospect of supporting a Family, never take a woman from an Eligible situation and place her below it. remember that as some one says in a play "Marriage is chargeable" and as you never wish to owe a fortune to a wife, never let her owe Poverty to you. Misfortunes may Surround even the fairest prospects. if so Humbly kiss the Rod in silence, but rush not upon distress and anxiety with your Eyes open— I approve your spirit. I should be ashamed to own him for a son who could be so devoted to avarice as to marry a woman for her fortune. Pride and insolence too often accompany wealth and very little happiness is to be expected from sordid souls of earthy mould. I always loved Nancy Quincy from a native good humour and honesty of heart which she appeard to possess—but I never was in earnest in ralying you about it. (if you should perceive that the spelling of this Letter is different from what you have been accustomed too, you must Set it down for Websters New) plan. I write in haste, as I must dress for the *drawing Room* this Evening, and take my Letter to Town—

We have had our Friends the Creeks very near us for a Month and very constant visiters to us some of them have been— I have been amused with them and their manners. tho they could not converse but by signs they appeard Friendly, manly, generous gratefull and Honest. I was at Federal Hall when the Ceremony of Ratifying the Treaty took place it was truly a curious scene, but my pen is so very bad that however inclined I might be to describe it to you, I cannot write with pleasure. I inclose you some papers that I believe were mislaid before

Remember me to the dr and mrs Welch and all other Friends— you must go to mr Thatchers meeting and get a seat in the old pew—

yours   A A

"REMOVAL TO PHILADELPHIA"

To Mary Smith Cranch

my Dear sister   Sunday eve Nyork August 29 1790

I last Night received your Letter which I have long expected, dated 9ᵗʰ of August, and thank you for your account of commencment, as well as your care. I have written to you a number of times and wonderd much at not hearing from you. by dr Jeffries I wrote you an account of mrs Smiths getting well to

Bed. She is very cleverly and has been once out to see me tho only three weeks last Night since she got to Bed, but the weather being so warm she has got the Air very soon or rather never Shut it out. She was going to dine below stairs to day, and said if she was not asshamed she would go with me to take leave of mrs washington who sets out tomorrow for Mount Vernon. I am going into Town for that purpose, and shall part with her, tho I hope, only for a short time, with much Regreet. no Lady can be more deservedly beloved & esteemed than she is, and we have lived in habits of intimacy and Friendship. in short the Removal of the principal connections I have here serves to render the place delightfull as it, is much less pleasent than it has been.

I have been almost upon the point of visiting Braintree. I even made several arrangments for that purpose in my own mind, but had it all overthrown by an arrangment for a Removal to Philadelphia this fall mr Adams talks now of going there, to look out a House, as he begins to think he shall be very misirable at Lodgings, but I will hope that I may come next summer, and be a Border with you for some months if we should let our House if the people you mention are responsible and worthy people I should have no objection to letting it to them with the furniture the best carpet & china & Glass tho not much excepted.— I know more injury may be done to furniture in one year than a House can easily sustain in several. a Hundred dollars goes but a little way in good furniture. perhaps they may run away with a fancy that as the house is unoccupied we would readily let it for trifle. the House I should rather let at a low Rent than it should stand empty, but not the furniture 200 dollors a year or not much less I should expect to have for it including the Garden stables &c there are three Beds two very good and three carpets besides the best; at Philadelphia we must give four hundred for an empty house and that out of the City, but I shall have opportunity to write you more fully if they should have any fancy for taking it and I would consult the dr about it.

we are anxious to get Thomas here and wonder that he does not come on pray hasten him as mr Adams is very desirious to have him here— my dear Sister I never take the ten guineys so pray say no more about them I am under obligations to you for the care and attention to my children which nothing pecuniary can repay & it hurts me that I have it not in my power to do as I wish— I hope our young folks will get into Buisness I am glad mr Cranch will be like to get something for his hard Labour— I hope the remaining part of the debt will be provided for in less than ten years— our publick affairs look very auspicious not withstanding the grumbling I have many more things to Say to you but am obliged to close to go into Town, but will write to you soon again— we are all well. you may write by the post they have not Chargd us postage yet and I presume will not as the New act if it had past excepts the Pressident and vice Pressident, and as it is known to be the intention of congress, I suppose they will not tax us with postage under the present act.

Love to all Friends ever yours   A Adams

RENTING PEACEFIELD

To Cotton Tufts

dear sir   New york Sep^{br} 6 1790

Mr Adams received your Letter dated August 31. he sat of that morning after for Philadlphia and desired me to let you know that he would transmit to you an order from the treasury for the Sum you received of Generall Lincoln upon his return. where is Thomas we have been daily expecting him for near a Month, and mr Adams delay^d going his journey a week expecting him here. he wrote me that he could not come on imediatly after commencment as you had not sufficient in your hands for that purpose. I accordingly sent on by dr Jeffries 35 dollors— directed to you, which I presume you received. I have written to his Brother & last week to him advising him to come by the Way of RhoadIsland, but have not heard a single word where he is, nor why he does not come if he is sick, or met with any accident we should be glad to know it. Mrs Cranch wrote me that a Gentleman and Lady from Demerara wanted to take a ready furnishd House, and inquired if we would Let ours. I could wish that a place which cost us so much Money might be made a little profitable to us. I have desired mrs Cranch that you might be consulted about it, and if any terms should be offerd that you think would compensate for the use of House garden and furniture, you will be so good as to inform us— things are not conducted there according to my mind, because we do not know how they are managed. mr Adams had thoughts of going to Braintree, but his journey to Philadelphia will prevent it as I suppose if he can get a House there, we must remove next month. he wishes you to inform him, the Sum you have of paper, and the different kind's

the wine which mr Codman has in his care we will thank you to Send round by Barnard as we can remove it with our other things. I do not expect to see my Friends untill an other year, when I hope to spend the summer with them.

How will Elections go? are they Still in a rage for Rotations in Massachusetts? or does the Clamour rise from a few wrestless spirits who have no other importance. if they change mr Gerry for a mr any body else, they will lose one of the firmest men they have as independant a man, and as honest a one. in the first Session, his mind was irritated & he was hurt, his speaches were misrepresentd, and his conduct misconstrued, but through the whole of this last session no man has exerted himself more for the honour and Reputation of the Nation, nor more firmly gaurded the constitution against innovation. I most sincerely hope he will be reelected.

I hope my dear sir that all your Family are well and that you enjoy good Health yourself. I am very sorry to hear that we are like to lose Governour Bowdoin, from the accounts we hear, I fear there is little hope of his recovery—

All Letters addrest to the V President are frankd in the post office, so that you may write by that conveyance when you please.

will you be so good as to tell mr Codman that as the President and Secretary of State are both absent, there cannot any application be made at present in favour of his Brother, that on a former occasion when mr A Named a Gentleman to the Pressident as proper for consul, he replied that he had no other objection than that a much greater Number had been appointed from N England than from any other of the States, and that his object had been to distribute offices as equally as possible. mr A will however communicate to mr Lear the contents of the Letter.

I am dear sir your affectionate   A Adams

"COMMON FAME REPORTS THAT YOU ARE ATTACHD"

To John Quincy Adams

my dear son   Newyork Nov^br 7th 1790
    perhaps a few lines from my own Hand may serve to put you more at your ease than an account of my Health from any other person. I have indeed had a very severe sickness in which both Body and mind sufferd, and the care which devolved upon me in consequence of my being in the midst of Removal I found too much for me. the least buisness put me into such a Tremour as would prevent my getting any sleep for a whole Night. tis a Month to day since I was first taken sick—as yet I have daily returns of fever tho much lessned—and I have gained strength for this week past so much that I hope to be able to begin my journey tomorrow. the vessel saild on thursday last and I have been in Town with your sister ever Since. she thinks a little hard of you that you have not written to her She has been in great trouble for her Baby which she came very near loosing with the small Pox, but which is now happily recoverd

    I received a Letter from you during my Sickness which did not add to my spirits. I was unable to answer it at the Time, or I should have chid you for your impatience, and depression of Spirits tho I know it is your Sensibility which occasions it. that received by your Brother Charls last Evening has induced me to write you this Letter. there is some Money in the hands of mr Cranch which he received for mr Brisler this money I will request him to pay to you and I will repay it to Brisler as soon as the amount of the Sum is forwarded to me. the Rent of the House where you are tho a small sum you should receive and I will write to the dr to call upon Pratt who must have money in his Hands as we have concluded to take neither his Butter or cheese as we shall be so far distant. your Father wrote you to get your uncle to supply you with Hay and with wood from our own place and I would have you apply to him for it. if you have any difficulties on that account or any other write to me freely about them. I wish any method could be fallen upon to make Pratts place more productive to us— when I have more strengh I will write to you upon a subject that gives me some anxiety. common Fame reports that you are attachd to a young Lady. I am sorry such a report should prevail, because whether there is or is not cause for such a Roumour, the report may do an injury to the future prospects of the Lady as your own are not such as can warrent you in entering into any engagements, and an entanglement of this kind will only tend to depress your spirits should you be any time before you get into Buisness and believe me my dear son a too early marriage will involve you in troubles that may render you & yours unhappy the remainder of Your Life. you will say that you have no Idea of connecting yourself at present. I believe you, but why gain the affections of a woman, or why give her cause to think you attachd to her. do you not know that the most cruel of situations to a young Lady is to feel herself attachd to a Gentleman when he can testify it in no other way than by his actions; I mean when his Situation will not permit him to speak

I did not design to have said so much at this time, but my anxiety for you has led me on; perhaps I ought not to have delayd being explicit so long— my strengh will not permit me to say more than that I am ever your Affe M.   A A

"ALL MY TROUBLES"

To Mary Smith Cranch

my dear sister   Philadelphia dec^br 12 1790

I have received your two kind Letters one dated in october the 30 day I think & the 14 of Nov^br as the last came by a private Hand it did not reach me till last Evening. you will suppose that I might have written to you long e'er this, but as my letters would only have been a detail of grivences and troubles I was reluctant at taking my pen, and put it of from day to day. I reachd this city after 5 days journey. I was so weak as to be able to travel only 20 miles a day, but I gaind strength daily and was much better when I got here than when I set out; my Furniture arrived the day before me. I came up to the House expecting to have found every thing in readiness to put up the furniture agreable to promise but how was I dissapointed to find the painters with their Brushes and some of the most necessary matters untouch'd the House had not been inhabited for four years & being Brick you may judge of the state of it. we had fires made in every part, the furniture must come in, and we must inhabit it unfit as it was for to go with 14 or 16, for Brislers family were all with me, to Lodings was much beyond my Revenue's I expected to suffer. We got in on fryday— on the Monday following Louissa was taken sick I gave her a puke & set her up again, but on the thursday following Polly Tailor was taken sick with a voilent Plurisy fever confined to her Bed bled 3 times puked & Blisterd; and tho it is a month she has got no further down stairs than to my chamber for after the fever left her the old Ague took her in her Head and face. She is however upon the mending order, but this is not the worst of all my troubles. Thomas has been 18 days totally deprived of the use of his Limbs by the acute Rhumatism, attended with great inflamation and fever. the fever has abated after having been 3 times Bled puked and many other applications he is yet unable to help himself. he is carried from his Bed to the Settee & fed like an infant. I have not left his Chamber excepting a nights and meal times for the whole time. the disorder seazd his Breast as well as his Limbs and produced all the complaints of Gravel by affecting his kidneys. I never knew him half so sick in my Life. I will not lay either of the disorders to this place tho I believe they were hastned & renderd worse by the dampness of the House. Polly has had 2 Fevers of the same kind since she has been with me, & Thomas Rhumatism has been comeing on for some time, yet they were peculiarly unfortunate to attack them at the time of Removal. dr Rush has attended them and I have found him a kind Friend as well as Physician. I will not detail to you that in the midst of all this, the Gentlemen and Ladies solicitious to manifest their respect were visiting us every day from 12 to 3 oclock in the midst of Rooms heepd up with Boxes trunks cases &c. thanks to a kind Providence I have got through the worst I hope of my difficulties and am in tolerable Health tho much fallen away in flesh I have a source of anxiety added to my portion on my dear daughters account, col smith having saild last week for England his going was sudden and unexpected to us, but some private family Debts which were due in England to his Fathers estate was one motive, and some prospects of assisting his Family by his voyage was a still further motive. I do not know what has really been the cause why he has been so poorly provided for in the distribution of offices. the P—— has always said that he was sensible to his merrit & meant to Provide for him, but has not yet seen the way open to do it; She poor Girl is calld to quite a different trial from any she has before experienced, for tho the col was once before absent, she was in her Fathers House. now she writes that she feels as if unprotected, as if alone in the wide world one of his Brothers & sisters remain with her during the cols absence. I have Johnny here with me, and would gladly send for her, to pass the winter with me, but a young Baby and some other obstacles prevent. pray my dear sister write to her and comfort her. no station in Life was ever designd by providence to be free from trouble and anxiety. the portion I believe is much more equally distributed than we imagine. Guilt of conscience is the work of our own Hands and not to be classed with the inevitable evils of Humane Life.—

Dec^{br} 14

I wrote thus far on sunday. Thomas is very little better. Charles got here on saturday and is a great assistance to me. I want my dear sisters & cousins. notwithstanding I have been such a Mover. I feel in every New place more & more the want of my own near & dear connexions. I hope to see you all next spring. pray let my son J Q A know that his Brother is sick, that we should be glad to have him come here in Jan^{ry} or this Month if more convenient to him, but that I cannot write to him till the Next post— adieu I have only time to say yours as the Post is going   A Adams

COLONEL SMITH'S ABSENCE

To Abigail Adams Smith

My Dear Child, Philadelphia, 25 January, 1791.

You must not flatter yourself with the expectation of hearing from Colonel Smith until the February packet arrives. It is as soon as you ought to think of it. You see by the papers, that a minister is in nomination from England, and Mrs. C——— writes, will come out soon. Mrs. P———, from whom I received a letter, writes me by the last packet, that Mr. Friere is certainly appointed from Portugal, and that he only waits for the arrival of Count ———, his successor, in England, before he sails for America. Mrs. P——— likewise communicates the agreeable intelligence of Mr. P———'s having forsaken the bottle, and that the Countess B——— had another child, and was vastly happy, beloved by her dear Count, &c.; all in the true style of Mrs. P———. She desires to be kindly remembered to you and the Colonel.

Present me kindly to all my New York friends. That I was attached to that place is most true, and I shall always remember with pleasure the fifteen months passed there; but, if I had you and your family, I could be very well pleased here, for there is an agreeable society and friendliness kept up with all the principal families, who appear to live in great harmony, and we meet at all the parties nearly the same company. To-morrow the President dines with us, the Governor, the Ministers of State, and some Senators. Of all the ladies I have seen and conversed with here, Mrs. Powell is the best informed. She is a friendly, affable, good woman, sprightly, full of conversation. There is a Mrs. Allen, who is as well bred a woman as I have seen in any country, and has three daughters, who may be styled the three Graces.

My best respects to your good mamma and family. Tell Mrs. C——— I hope she makes a very obedient wife. I am sure she will be a good one. I think I shall see you in April. Why do you say that you feel alone in the world? I used to think that I felt so too; but, when I lost my mother, and afterwards my father, *that* "alone" appeared to me in a much more formidable light.

It was like cutting away the main pillars of a building; and, though no friend can supply the absence of a good husband, yet, whilst our parents live, we cannot feel unprotected. To them we can apply for advice and direction, sure that it will be given with affection and tenderness. We know not what we can do or bear, till called to the trial. I have passed through many painful ones, yet have enjoyed as much happiness through life as usually falls to the lot of mortals; and, when my enjoyments have been damped, curtailed, or molested, it has not been owing to vice, that great disturber of human happiness, but sometimes to folly, in myself or others, or the hand of Providence, which has seen fit to afflict me. I feel grateful for the blessings which surround me, and murmur not at those which are withheld.— But my pen runs on, and my lads, at whose table I write, wonder what mamma can find to write about.

Adieu. My love to the children. From your ever affectionate

A Adams.

SUMMER AT BRAINTREE

To Cotton Tufts

Dear sir   Philadelphia March 11. 1791

I received your kind Letter of the 23 Feb[ry] and was happy to learn that our Friends were all well. my son Set of on his return to Boston last week, in company with mr Gerry & Ames. he was desirious of going then that he might have the pleasure of good company. this tho a very agreeable circumstance on a long journey, will I believe scarcly compensate for the badness of the Roads at this season; provided they should be eaqually so, to the Eastward as they are here. March is not a favourable Month for Congress to break up. this Session sir has been marked with great dispatch of Buisness, much good humour & tho varying in sentiment upon some very important subjects those subjects have been ably discussd, and much light thrown upon them, and finally carried by large majorities. the Bank is one, which Bill as past I inclose to you and the supplement it is thought here by those who are esteemed the best judges that it will not have any of those concequences which some of its opponents have imagined. as it will be the interest of those individuals who are incorporated and subscribers, to watch carefully over its interest, and to gaurd it with Argus Eyes you will see by the Bill that you may purchase a share with four hundred dollers one fourth of which must be specie the Accession of the state of vermont during this Session to the union, and the uninimnity with which they were received is a most happy and important event in our Annals and will add weight to the Northen Scale. Kentucky is also agreed to be received but her Government is not yet organizd. thus sir one pillar rises after an other, and add strength I hope to the union. the people here in this state feel the Benificial effects of their own state Governments having three Branches in lieu of one assembly, and tho the old squabling spirit is not intirely extinct, it appears to be near its dissolution. they have placed their Governour upon a respectable sallery of 5 thousand dollors pr Annum, the Governour of the state upon the same footing with the V.P of the united states, whom they have obliged to remove twice at his own expence in the course of two years— and to a city where the expence of living is a third dearer than at N york. I hope to spend 5 Months of the present year at Braintree and to be there by the first of May. the Roads will not permit us to try them sooner. as my Family will consist of 8 persons I must request some little provision to be made previous to our comeing, such as wood, (Hay I presume we have in our Barn) 50 Bushels of oats. these articles I think mr Adams ought to write to his Brother to look to, and if he was not his Brother I would do it, but now I have said I will not, therefore I think it not unlikly that we may be Destitute of some of them. I have engaged to write to you for those things which may be imediatly necessary upon our arrival viz a Box of candles part mould & part dipt a Barrel of soap a Barrel of super fine flower a Loaf of sugar 14 Brown 1 pd suchong Tea half dozen pd coffe ditto chocolat. Grain Rye & Indian are easily procured suppose I need not be anxious about that. Beaf and Hams you have already secured cider is an other article of which we shall want half a dozen Barrels in Articles of furniture I want mr Pratt or any one Else to make me 2 kichin tables one a common seize one of 6 foot long 4 wide a Bread peal a roling pin, kitchin Tongues & slice I have none a spit, I must request Miers to have them ready for me. some other articles may have escaped my memory but I have no design to get a superfluous article. a couple of wash Tubs I shall find necessary to have made. the Garden I should like to have manured and dug mrs Cranch wrote me respecting a Negro Man who lived with Pheby. if you think proper you will be so good as to employ him about it. I am sorry sir to be so troublesome to you, but your many kind offices, and long habit of doing good, has always made me consider you in the different characters, of Friend, Gaurdian & Parent, and as such the whole Family look to you for advice & assistance. if you have not any cash in your Hands belonging to us, I suppose I may get credited for a month or two.

Before your Letter arrived here sir the Supervisors were all appointed for the different states. I own I was surprized to see the Name of G——m instead of Jackson who I supposed would have had it. mr A after your Letter came went and talkd with the secretary of the Treasury knowing that there would be inspectors of districts, but he was told that the intention was to multiply officers as little as possible and to divide the state of Massachusetts only into two, and mr Jackson was determind upon for that part of the country the President has Appointed col smith supervisor for the state of Nyork; it will be an arduous office but one for which I believe he is very well calculated, and if he can perform the whole duty of supervisor & inspector that state will not be divided, and the compensation will be something handsome this will be much more agreeable to me & to his Family than sending him abroad. we have not yet heard from him, but the packet in which he saild the Prince William Henry is upon Loyds list of arrivals the 2 of Jan[ry] which gives him a passage of 28 days my best respects to your good Lady whom I hope e'er long to embrace and the rest of my Friends. be assured dear sir that I am with sincere Regard your affectionate Neice   A. Adams

APPOINTMENT AS SUPERVISOR OF REVENUE

To William Stephens Smith

Dear Sir: Bush Hill, March 16th, 1791.
 Although we have reason to expect, and hope for your speedy return, yet I would not let so good an opportunity as this, by the Portland packet, pass without writing you a few lines, partly to inform you, that your son is in perfect health, and has been so through the winter; that he is full of mirth and glee, and as fine a boy as you can wish him: and partly to congratulate you upon your appointment to the office of Supervisor for the State of New-York, under the new Revenue Bill, which I am so anxious to forward to you, that I have determined to put you to the expense of it by the packet. I have sent the bill to Mrs. Smith, that she may forward one to you by some private vessel. You will see by the bill the necessity there is of your returning with all possible despatch. The Secretary of the Treasury told Mr. Adams that he would write to you, and it is probable that he will by this opportunity. He informed Mr. Adams, that it was the President's intention to unite the office of Supervisor and Inspector for the State of New-York, and not to divide the state, as he will be obliged to do, in some states where there are many ports of entry, consequently the salary will be something handsome, and well worth your acceptance, though the duties of the office will be proportionably arduous. I thought it would be of importance to you to get sight of the bill as soon as possible.
 Congress closed their session on the fourth of March, and met again the fourth Monday in October. No session has been marked with so many important events, or has been conducted with so much harmony; great despatch of important business, a most surprising rise of public credit, an increasing confidence in the national government, are some of the fruits. The accession of Vermont and Kentucky are two additional pillars to the noble building; every circumstance has conspired to add dignity and glory to our rising empire; an expiring murmur from the old dominion has been lost amidst the general peace and harmony which pervades all the states: though its noxious

breath reached North Carolina and contaminated a few members, the northern climate soon dispersed the southern vapour. Rhode Island is become one of the most federal states in the union, and the antis now declare, they would willingly make any submission for their past conduct. Poor France! what a state of confusion and anarchy is it rushing into? I have read Mr. Burke's letter, and though I think he paints high, yet strip it of all its ornament and colouring, it will remain an awful picture of liberty abused, authority despised, property plundered, government annihilated, religion banished, murder, rapine and desolation scourging the land. I am sorry that my worthy and venerable divine should expose himself, at this late period of his life, to so severe a censure. I love and venerate his character, but think his zeal a mistaken one, and that he is a much more shining character as a divine, than politician. To Mr. Hollis, and the rest of our friends, give my regards; I have a love for that same country, and an affection for many of its valuable inhabitants.

The President of the United States, is just setting out upon a tour to his southern dominions; he means to visit Georgia and Carolina; he will be absent three months. Mr. Lewis is gone home to Virginia to be married; Mr. Jackson is the only aid now remaining. We propose setting out for the eastward by the last of April, and passing the summer at Braintree. I heard this day from Mrs. Smith; she was well, and your boys—she had just received your letter, dated Falmouth, informing her of your safe arrival.

I am, dear sir, with sincere regard and affection, Yours, &c.

A. Adams.

"THANK YOU . . . FOR YOUR FRIENDLY LETTER"

To Martha Washington

my dear Madam   Braintree june 25 1791

I was honourd with your much esteemed favour on the 15 of this month. the state of my Health, Body and mind suffering most Severely with repeated attacks of an intermitting fever will plead my apoligy for omitting to thank you at an earlyer date for your Friendly Letter. I have been so weakned & debilitated as to be unable to walk alone, and my Nerves so affected as to oblige me to seclude myself from all company except my most intimate connextions. I hastned Home with great ardour in hopes the Northern Air and the quiet country Breize might restore me, but my disorder was of too obstinate a Nature to quit me so easily. I hope I have now got the better of it, as it is more than a week since the Ague left me we have had more very Hot weather than is usual at this season. I fear you have sufferd by it in Philadelphia. I hope Heat there is not attended with a Sharp drought, as it is here. the Feilds which a few week ago wore a most pleasing aspect, are now Robd of their verdure and our vegatables droop & dye. I was most sincerly grieved at reading in a late Philadelphia paper an account of the death of Dr Jones. the more I had the pleasure of knowing him, the greater esteem I had for him, as an amiable Sensible and Benevolent Man. You Madam must more particularly feel his loss as he was your Family Physician.

I am happy to learn by your Letter as well as by the publick accounts that the President has enjoyd his Health during his Arduous Southern Tour. I presume er'e this Time I may congratulate you upon his return to Philadelphia I must beg you Madam to present to him my most respectfull Regards and my congratulation upon his safe return. I hope you will have as agreable a journey to mount vernon as I should have had to massachussets but for that vile Ague which Tormented me. the whole Country through which we past was in full Bloom, and every spot wore the face of Peace & contentment. the people instead of murmers & complaints, expresst themselves happy and satisfied under the administration of their Government. there are however two inhabitants envy and Jealousy who are not perfectly content, but as they are characters for whom I have an utter aversion I can only pitty their folly and avoid them. Mr Adams desires me to present his best Respects to the President & to you Madam, and an affectionat remembrance to master Washington & miss Custos Compliments to mr and mrs Lear I hope the little Boy is finely recoverd from the small pox. shall I be an intruder if I ask again to hear from my dear mrs washington whose Health and happiness Shall ever be the

Ardent & Sincere wish of her who has the Honour to subscribe herself her affectionat Friend and Humble servant

A Adams

To a Heart less benevolent I should apologize for relating my Grief, but I know that you Madam can sympathize with those who mourn as well as rejoice in their felicity

June 29, 1791

"THE BUSTLE OF REMOVAL"

To Mary Smith Cranch

my dear Sister   Philadelphia october 30th 1791

I wrote to you upon my journey whilst I was at Brookfield the sunday after I left you and was sorry to find by your Letter, that you had not received it. I wrote to you from N york but have been so engaged in moveing, & so embarressd with company in the midst of it, tho only a complimentary call, that I have had scarcly a moment that I could call my own. it was kind in you to let mr Cranch to superscribe your Letter. I thank you for the precaution, because I open every Letter from you with trembling and fear. I rejoice most Sincerely with you in your prospect of a recovering Limb. if the Life of our dear Friend is Spaired, we cannot be sufficiently thankfull to a kind Providence, even tho the recovery should be long and Tedious. my Heart bled to leave you in such distress

we Have nearly got through the Bustle of Removal, but my House is no way to my mind. the Rooms so small and not able to lay two together, renders it very troublesome to see so much company as we must be obliged to. the weather is very pleasent and my Health better than for some months past Thomas is less threatned with Rhumaticks than he was on our journey. Louissa as well as usual. mr Adams is much recoverd to what he was, has been able to attend his duty in Senate, tho Sometimes a good deal exhausted.

you mention in your Letter getting the House blockd up. I forgot to inform you that there was cider and potatoes to be put into the cellar and that Brother had engaged to see the cellar Bank'd up, but if it should not be done I would wish to have it secured before the Frost. for the Reasons above mentiond I directed Polly to leave the keys of the House with them, the Keys of the cellar to bring to you. I wonder mrs Jeffry has not sent for Polly. she appeard so solicitious to get her. I hope no one has done her an injury. Polly had qualifications peculiarly fitted for my Family, and might still have been in it, but for a little unruly member. I like katy very well and beleive I could not have been better suited. mrs Brisler is with me, feeble & sick tho better than she was. I do not see but she must remain with me, unless Lucy returns to take care of her and her children.

my things have not yet arrived from Boston, I fear I shall lose my Pears.

I am anxious for Billy Shaw least he should be a criple all his day's

Let me hear from you often for I am still anxious. Remember me kindly to all inquiring Friends.

Yours affectionatly   A Adams.

THE SMITHS MOVE TO ENGLAND

To John Quincy Adams

my dear son   Philadelphia Fe^{bry} 5 1792—

Tis a very long time since I wrote to you, or heard from you I have been more engaged in company than is my choice but living in Town has necessarily devolved more of it upon us than heretofore, and tho we have not seen more than in reality we ought to considering our publick Character, yet it is much of an Egyptian task, and fall some times much heavier upon me than my state of health will bear. we have regularly dined from 16 to 18 and sometimes 20 person every wednesday in the week Since I removed into Town, and on Mondays I see company. the rest of the week is or might be altogether taken up in Parties abroad, many of which I have been obliged to decline on account of my Health. Your sister has been with me these 5 weeks and william, the col & Charles part of the time.

they will leave me in a week or 10 days, and when we are to meet again, is in the Bosom of futurity The col & Family embark for England in the March Packet, not in a Publick capacity, but under such advantageous private contracts that tho it is with the utmost regreet I can consent to the seperation yet I think I ought not to say any thing to discourage them. tis probable two years will be the least time they will be absent. the matter has been only a few days in agitation, and the determiniation of going in the March packet will hasten them from hence Sooner than I am willing to part with them. I am glad to see one of the Family in a prosperous situation, as from the col account I have reason to believe he is. I wish your Father would propose Thomass going with him. I think it would be advantageous to his Health and would give him a good opportunity of seeing Something more of the world he could be in the col's Family and of service to him in his transactions but I dare not venture upon the proposition, and as the cols going was communicated to him but yesterday I believe the thought has not yet occurd to him. Congress proceed so slowly in Buisness that I fear I shall be detaind here till May to my great regreet Post office Bill Representation & Indian War are great subjects of debate, the latter a melancholy one indeed— the secretary at War and of the Treasury are attackd and handled pretty Roughly in the News papers. your transactions for me in the Buisness way met my approbation. Cheeseman however did not act the Man of Honour and shall not be employd by me again. if I found Cealia, as I did, he was to have only 8 dollors which he was to call upon me for here. I never gave him any Authority to apply to you. When you receive the Rent of the House, Buy a Peice of Linnen and cambrick for them & get cousin Lucy Cranch to make your shirts and pay her for doing it out of the Rent. I know you must want a peice.

we are all in pretty good Health, the old intermitting still torments us at times tho it does not amount to the Ague yet—

inclosed is a Ticket: see if it is worth any thing and let me know the cider you bought should be drawd of this month or the begining of March.

Let me hear from you soon and be assured that I am Your affectionate Mother   A Adams

we send you Espinasse printed here judge Lowel is so good
as to take it

"A DEVISION OF THE . . . STATES"

To Mary Smith Cranch

My dear sister   Philadelphia April 20th 1792
    I have just received your kind Letter as I was about to write
to you to inform you that we proposed Sitting out on our
journey on monday or twesday next. the weather has been so
rainy that I have not been able to ride So often as I wishd in
order to prepare myself for my journey, and how I shall stand
it, I know not. this everlasting fever still hangs about me &
prevents my intire recovery. a critical period of Life Augments
my complaints I am far from Health, tho much better than
when I wrote you last. I see not any company but those who
visit me in my chamber nor have I once been out of my carriage, but to see my Friend mrs dalton who was sick before I
got well, tho not till I was so much better as to do without her
kind care. cousin Betsy smith has been with me for the greatest
part of the Time the last Month, and a good child She is, tender and affectionate as her good Mother was. I thank you for
your care about my things. we have sent last week to Boston
by the Brigg Isabella a number of Boxes & Barrels. they are
addrest to the care of J Q A. but I wish you to ask the dr to be
so kind as to see that a carefull Team brings them to Braintree,
& that Hay or straw is put into the cart, or the things will get
Broken. the Bill of laiding was inclosed to mr Adams. I shall
send by the Brig Maria my Trunk of cloaths &c she is now
here. I am glad to hear that Spring is forward as I hope to find
the Roads good in concequence of it, but I always fear for the
fruit. if the things you mention could be accomplishd before
we arrive, it would be a great relief to me— I am grieved for my
dear sister shaw, tho I have not been able to write and tell her
so, for I was seazd with an inflamation in one of my Eyes when
I was first taken sick which has not yet left me. I could not bear

a light in the Room, nor even the fire to Blaize. it is much better—but writing reading or sewing are all painfull to me mr Adams has not had any return of his Ague but lives in continual apprehension. Thomas is thin & pale but does not complain. we must leave him on account of his studies yet it will be with apprehensions that I shall hear of his being sick— I do not particuliarly recollect any thing I want, you know as well as I & better for you provided for me before. if you go to Boston I should like to have a pr of Brass Andirons at about 8 dollors price, Tongues & shovel proper for my best Room but you need take no extra trouble for them. you will be So good as to have the Beds aird &c if Bety is in Braintree She may be engaged for to stay if you think best till Cealia gets Home I shall send her by the vessel now here. I am not so perfectly easy on account of travelling Home as I should have been with Robert when he was sober, but he really got to such a pass that I have been obliged to part with him & have taken one who has not driven me more than once or twice, but I hope we shall reach Home safe— Terrible is the distress in Nyork, from the failure of many of the richest people there, and from the Spirit of Speculation which has prevaild & brought to Ruin many industerous Families who lent their Money in hopes of gain— I was mortified to See our worthy Friend stand so low on the list of senators who I had been accustomed to see stand foremost, but such is the Instability of the people. popular Leaders catch their ear and they are credulous to their own injury— in the House of Representatives of the U. states matters are not going better. the Southern Members are determined if possible to Ruin the Secretary of the Treasury, distroy all his well built systems, if possible and give a Fatal stab to the funding system. in senate they have harmonized well, no unbecomeing heats or animosity. the Members are however weary & long for a recess one after an other are droping off, which gives weight to the opposite side. Many of the southern Members have written long speaches & had them printed, which has had more influence than our Nothern Friends are aware of who depending upon the goodness of their cause, have been inattentive to such methods to influence the populace. the V President, they have permitted to sleep in peace this winter, whilst the minister at war, & the Secretary of the Treasury have been their Game the Secretary of state & even the President has not escaped. I firmly believe if I live Ten years longer, I shall see a devision of the Southern & Northern states, unless more candour & less intrigue, of which I have no hopes, should prevail Should a War or any dire calamity assail us, then they would Hugg us, but politicks avaunt— my dear mrs smith has been a Month gone. it pains me to the Heart, but who of us can say, that we have not our troubles? our portion of happiness is no doubt equal to our deserts—

adieu my dear sister I hope to see you in a few weeks Remember me affectionatly to all our Friends and believe me as ever yours   A Adams

SECOND PRESIDENTIAL ELECTION

To John Adams

my dearest Friend   Quincy Dec^br 4th 1792

I was very happy to receive on thanksgiving day the 29 of Nov^br. your Letter dated Hartford. I feard that you had not reachd so far the weather was so dissagreable, but if the Roads have mended as much with you as they have this way, you have reachd Philadelphia by this time. I shall with impatience wait to hear of your arrival there. the snow remaind with us but one week Since which we have had pleasent weather. there has not anything occurd material that I know of since you left us— if you get Russels paper you will see a little deserved Burlisque upon the Govenours speach respecting the expressions made us of by Congress which gave him such umbrage. Tomorrow is a very important day to the united states, much more important to them, than it can possibly be to you or to me for think of it as they please tomorrow will determine whether their Government shall stand four years longer or Not. mr Clinton Seems to be the only competitor held up. I fancy he will receive no aid from N England. I hope you will order Fenno to continue his paper to me. We have had a Gang of Thieves infesting this Town since you left it. the thursday after you went away Shaw & James went into the woods & in the day time the best saddle was stolen out of the Barn closset. the same Night mr Cary had his best Horse stolen and mr smith who lives on mrs Rows place had his taken the same night and last Sunday morning James came Running in to inform me that his Stables had been attempted, & his Lock broken, but being doubly secured the villan could not effect his purpose. he tried the Coach house door & split of a peice of the door, but could not get the Bar out. he went on to mr Adams's at Milton & stole his Horse a Traveller lodged at Marshes Tavern on saturday night, who got up in the Night Rob'd the House of various articles of wearing Apparal and made of. we Suppose that he was the person who attempted our stables and that he belongs to a Gang. they are in persuit of him

your Mother was well this day she spent it with me. She and your Brother & family all dinned with me on thanksgiving day as well as our Son. tis the first thanksgiving day that I have been at Home to commemerate for Nine years. Scatterd and dispersed as our Family is, God only knows whether we shall ever all meet together again much of the pleasure and happiness resulting from these N England Annual feltivals is the family circles & connections which are brought together at these times, but whether seperate or together I am sensible that every year has been productive of many Blessings, and that I have great cause of thankfulness for preserving mercies both to myself & Family.

I inclose a Letter for Brisler I wish him to inquire the price of Rye that I may know whether it would quit cost to send me a dozen Bushel tis five & six pence pr Bushel here. Superfine flower I want to know the price of, it has taken a rise here

my Love to Thomas tell him to write me often I hope the House of Reps will be in a little better humour after all Elections are over. I trust they will not follow the French example & Lop of Heads, even of departments. they appear to have a great terror of them I see a Lucius & a Marcus, I should like to know who they are. [   ] many compliments & respects to all my good Friends in Philadelphia. I flatter myself I have some there, and be assured of the affectionate Regard of your

A Adams

REQUEST TO MOVE NEARER

To Abigail Adams Smith

My dear Mrs Smith.   Quincy February 28. 1793.
I wrote to you by your brother making a proposal to you
which you might not consider me in earnest about— Since
then I have two additional motives to request the Col^s consideration and your's of the subject. If setting aside family connexions it is with respect to business a matter of indifference
which city you reside in I certainly could wish it might be
Philadelphia for four years to come. The late vote respecting
salary will certainly prevent our becoming Housekeepers there
in public life. We have suffered too much already by being involved in debt at the close of the four years and obliged to give
up our house, dispose of one pair of horses and in other respects retrench our expenses. The five thousand dollars at this
period is not in the purchase of any article of life more than
half equal to what it was at the time it was first granted—
Knowing as I do what the expense of living there as well as
here is I cannot think of seeing your father again subjected to
the like inconvenience—yet to live half the year separated of
the few years which I have reason to think are remaining to me
is a sacrifice that I do not consider at this day my duty— I shall
not make any observation upon past services or my own estimation of things— I will conform to what is and should be
glad to enjoy the Society of my family as much as I can. My
furniture is stored in Philadelphia. If the Colonel and you
think it inconsistent with your arrangements and prejudicial to
his affairs to reside in Philadelphia I shall think it best after
consulting your Father to order the furniture home, though I
know not what to do with the greater part of it. I should be
tempted to sell what I have not room for if I did not know that
it must be at a great loss. If you think proper to go there I will
endeavor to have it stored till such time as you might incline to
take a house there— If we take lodgings with you, 'tis probable
that our family will not exceed five persons, and we could I
presume make such arrangements as would render each of us
happy— I will not again take charge of a family and sacrifice

my health in that city as I have done— Though a small family we are and always have been a scattered flock, my infirm state of health leads me to wish for those pleasures which domestic life affords. I love society, but 'tis the rational not the dissipated which can give true delight.

I fear the roads will be so bad as to prevent your coming to see me so soon as I wish but in April the passage by way of Rhode Island will be both pleasant and safe and as you are an old and experienced sailor you will find that way much pleasanter than by land and much less fatiguing.

Let me, my dear daughter, hear from you as often as possible remember me affectionately to all friends

Your's most tenderly   A. Adams.

YELLOW FEVER EPIDEMIC

To John Adams

my dearest Friend   Quincy Nov^br 28 1793
My early rising still continues, and I am writing by candle light. it is a week this day since you left me. I have rejoiced in the fine weather for your Sake. it has sometimes been cold and Blustering, but the Air has been pure and bracing. on saturday Night we had a plentifull Rain Succeeded by a fine day. I presume you reachd N York yesterday. I hope you found all our Friends well tho I have not heard from mrs Smith for a long time. I could wish if you must go to Philadelphia that you could have gone immediatly to your old Lodgings Brisler could make Breakfast & coffe in the afternoon even if you was provided with dinner in some other place. all accounts however agree that the City is clear from infection. I Sincerely hope it is, but I do not know what cause need be given to so many, as must suffer through anxiety and apprehension for their Friends, when Sitting a few weeks out of the city might remove it.

Cousin Lucy cranch came from Town last Evening and brought your Letter dated Hartford I also received one from Thomas of the 17th· I suppose you will find him in the city upon your arrival there. he writes that dr Rush assures him that he may come with safety.

our people here at home have been engaged some days in getting wood—one at the high ways one in getting sea weed. by the way savil continues every day in bringing two & sometimes 3 Load I do not know how much you agreed with him for, so I have not Stopd him, as I knew you was desirious of getting a quantity I expect he will cart till he has a pretty high Bill

last Night accounts were received of a Bloody Battle between General Wayne and the Indians tis said Wayne kept the Feild tho with the loss of 500 men and that the Indians left as many dead upon the Field tis a great point gaind to keep the Feild against them I hope they will now be convinced that we have men enough to fight them—

Mrs Brisler was well yesterday she has been here two days, and went home last evening

Let me hear from you every week it will be the only thing to keep me in spirits.

I am glad the virginians had some sense & some cunning as both united produced a proper measure. the Tone in Boston is much changd of mr Consul. he begins to make his Feasts and to coax & whine like a Hyena, as if having made use of big threatning language he had terrified the puny Americans and now was willing to kiss & make Friends—

present me to all those Friends who have Survived the general calimity, and as ever I am most affectionatly yours

A Adams

CITIZEN GENET

To John Adams

my dearest Friend   Quincy dec^br 28 1793.

The weather is so extreemly cold that my Ink almost freezes whilst I write, yet I would not let a week pass without writing to you, tho I have few occurrences to entertain you with; I received last saturday your two Letters one of the 12 and one of the 13th, december; I have not yet had a Philadelphia paper. when the pamphlets are out containing the correspondence between the ministers I hope you will send me one. in Edds paper of the last week appeard a low abusive peice against the British minister for the conduct of his court towards America but it was really too low for notice. the Chronical exults, without reason however at Dallas'es Reportt, it has become as much of a party paper as Freaneus. there is a great & general Allarm arising from the depredations which it is reported & feard the Algerians have made upon American vessels. All imported articles particuliarly west India produce has risen in concequence of it; congress will indeed have their Hands full of Buisness—and will have no time I hope, and very little disposition to quarrel. I am solisitious to know what Genets conduct will be at Philadelphia. I presume he does not shew his Head at the Levee, nor will he venture a visit to you in his publick Character; I think he is much like Cain after he had murderd Abel. Columbus closed last Saturday. I hope you have seen all the Numbers we have had in the course of the last week a very suden Death dr Rhoads was taken sick with a nervious fever and dyed the 3 day leaving a most distrest family 5 children 2 of them quite Babies, and mrs Rhoads hourly expecting to get to Bed, and in want of every necessary of Life. I never was witness to a more distresst Scene. I attended the funeral, and found her in fits, the children and people in the Room all terifye'd not knowing what to do with, or for her. dr Phips had run home for some medicine; and every person seem'd to be thrown into the utmost distress. the dr was a kind Husband and an innofensive man, dejected & disspirited tis Said by his prospect, her situation is pityable indeed. she has since got to bed and happily I may say lost her Baby which no doubt sufferd from her distress of Body and mind

our Friends here are all well. I do not learn that any persons have been endangerd by going into the city of Philadelphia, so that my fears and apprehensions are much quieted. this very cold weather if it reaches you will tend to preserve the Health of the inhabitants, but I fear it will pinch you severely. it gives me the Rhumatism

I am with every sentiment of affection and Regard most tenderly your   A Adams

"I NEVER CAN BE AN UNINTERESTED SPECTATOR"

To John Adams

my dearest Friend   Quincy Dec'br 31 1793
    Your two kind Letters of the 19 & 20th reachd me on the 28th
they are my saturday evenings repast. you know my mind is
much occupied with the affairs of our Country. if as a Female I
may be calld an Idle, I never can be an uninterested Spectator
of what is transacting upon the great Theater, when the welfare
and happiness of my Children & the rising generation is involved in the present counsels and conduct of the principal
Actors who are now exhibiting upon the stage. That the Hal-
cion days of America are past I fully believe, but I cannot agree
with you in sentiment respecting the office you hold; altho it is
so limited as to prevent your being so actively usefull as you
have been accustomed to, yet those former exertions and Services give a weight of Character which like the Heavenly orbs
silently diffuse a benign influence. Suppose for Instance as
things are often exemplified by their contraries, a Man, in that
office, of unbridled Ambition, Subtile intriguing, warpd and
biased by interested views, joining at this critical crisis, his secret influence against the Measures of the President, how very
soon would this country be involved in all the Horrours of a
civil War. I am happy to learn that the only fault in your political Character, and one which has always given me uneasiness,
is wearing away, I mean a certain irritability which has some
times thrown you of your Gaurd and shewn as is reported of
Louis 14'th that a Man is not always a Hero— Partizans are so
high, respecting English and French politicks, and argue so
falsly and Reason so stupidly that one would suppose they
could do no injury, but there are so many who read and hear
without reflecting and judging for themselves and there is such
a propensity in humane Nature to believe the worst, especially
when their interest is like to be affected, that if we are preserved from the Calamities of War it will be more oweing to
the superintending Providence of God than the virtue and
wisdom of Man. How we are to avoid it with France supposing
Genet should not be recall'd I know not. must we Submit to

such insults? judging from the manner in which France has carried on the present War, I should not wonder if they feard a Partition of their Kingdom. A Frenchman reminding an English man of the Time when in the Reign of Henry the sixth, the English were almost absolute Masters of France Said sneerlingly to him "When do you think you will again become Lords of our Kingdom?" to which the Englishman replied, "When your iniquities shall be greater than ours." how can any Nation expect to prosper who War against Heaven?

By this time you will have seen all the Numbers of Columbus. I should like to know the Presidents opinion of them, as well as some other Gentlemen who are judges. they assuredly are ably written, and do honour both to the Head and Heart of the writer, who deserves well of his fellow citizens for the information he has thrown upon a subject of so much importance at so critical a period—but their is a "barberous Noise of asses Apes and dogs" raisd by it in the Chronical. nevertheless sound reason and cool Argument will prevail in the end.

Having spun my thread out with respect to politicks I will think a little of our own private affairs. dr Tufts has paid two hundred pounds and become responsible himself for the remainder. I wrote to you his further intention, the 17 of Janry he proposes to discharge two hundreds pounds more. I have closed my account this day I have kept an exact account of my expenditures & payments since you left me, which I inclose to you. mr Cary offerd to bring me an other load of Hay at the same price. what he brought is agreed to be of the first quality, and it was all weighd, but I did not feel myself in a capacity to engage it absolutely. we have heitherto had so little snow that Buisness is dull mr Belcher has cleard of all the sea weed untill some high Tide brings more. he is now getting home the pine wood.

our Friends desire to be rememberd to you. mrs Brisler and family are well. you will present me affectionately to mrs washington who I respect and Love

My Love to Thomas. I hear he is for fighting the Algerines, but I am not sure that would be the best oconomy, tho it might give us a good pretence for Building a Navy that we need not be twichd by the Nose by every sausy Jack a Nips— he had better find Law for his countrymen and prevail upon them to take it.

I am as ever most affectionatly yours   A Adams

CRITIQUING JOHN QUINCY'S BARNEVELD

To John Adams

my Dearest Friend   Quincy Jan'ry 18th 1794

I received two day ago yours of Jan'ry 6th with the Pamphlet, and last Evening our Son brought me yours of the 9th. When he comes, his first request is, to read all the Letters which I have received since his last visit. I usually grant him this indulgence. the compliment of "Learning force of Reasoning Style" &c barely compensated for the censure which follow'd. he felt it a little hard to have it upon both sides, for I had given him the week before, a similar hint respecting Barnevelt. I reminded him of Swift (I believe it was), who read all his peices to his Housekeeper, and if they passd with her, he ventured to offer them to the publick. in his last Number he corrected himself, but as for Columbus, I own it was not two high seasond for me, considering the intemperance, and contemptable Arrogance of the Man; whose conduct he Reprobated; in Rank of Life he was more than his equal; in Age no great difference, in Learning in Talants, in Wisdom, in Integrity: no man of common judgment would dispute the palm;

This post will bring you the speach of the Lieut Govenour "they call it an old woman's speach" but I would deny my sex, if any old woman in the Country would have made a speach so little to the purpose. not one word Relating to the Buisness of the Common Wealth or the affairs of the State but a long Farago, to prove what every child knows, that all men have equal Natural Rights. his Head seems to be turnd with some vague Ideas about Liberty and equality. whether he had an Idea that his want of Property might be an objection in the minds of some against voting him into the Chair—and this was addrest to his fellow citizens to remove that obstical. I am perfectly at a loss to fathom his views. then he must lug in France to shew his attachment to that part of the Nation who have so wisely leveld all distinction. the Speach has tincture of the Jacobine Spirit, and is a convinceing proof that he is wholy unfit for the chair. The Attorney General has withdrawn his Name from the Jacobine Society, having met once with them; and dissaproveing; as he says their views. he desires that all his Friends would publickly anounce this. our General court it is said, dissaprove this new Erected Tribunal. mr S. might think his popularity endangerd. Such is the Hypocricy of the Man, that I could believe him influenced by any motive, rather than a disgust from proper principals. Americanus and Barnevelt met the other Evening at a wedding visit, to a Brother Lawyer. the company was numerous. A. enterd and in the most cordial manner caught B——s hand. how do you Brother, said he shaking it. B. Bowd and replied very well. Well Brother, When do you open the Theater? to which B. answerd, by saying what do you propose to do with the Law mr Attorney General? Why I mean to go when it opens, & take with me the L. Govenour Deacon Newal Parson Eackly and some other good folks; and as you are state Attorney you must take care of that, to which B. in good humour replied that he hoped the Attorney General would not oblige the state Attorney to prosecute him. one of the company whisperingly say'd is not this curious to see Americanus & Barnevelt, so perfectly good humourd? it seems that mr Attorney General excused himself from attending the court of sessions, and requested the court to appoint some person in his Room, & they appointed their former one.

Mr Jeffersons designd resignation tho long talkd of, was not fully credited untill it took place. the reason given for it by the French partizans, is that the Nature of his office obliged him to lend his Name to measures which militated against his well known principals; and give a sanction to Sentiments which his Heart disapproved. if this is true he did wisely to withdraw. they say that he will now appear as the supporter of Genet, and they consider him as all their own, but I have always reluctantly believed ill of him, and do not credit these reports. yet I know mr Jefferson to be Deficient in the only Sure and certain security, which binds man to Man & renders him responsible to his Maker.

As I am not in the Secrets of the Cabinet, I can only judge from what comes to light, and there is sufficient visible to make me very anxious for my Country. it was certainly the intention of the National convention to embroil us with all their Enemies, and they chose a fit instrument for the purpose. I think from Genets instructions that they were quite ignorant of our Government and constitution. The President has a most difficult and Arduous Task. May he have that wisdom which is from above, which is profitable both for to direct and Counsel.

I pray in return for the many kind inquiries Mrs Washington is pleasd to honour me with, that you would present her my affectionate Regard and best wishes for her Health and happiness— Miss Louissa present her Respectfull Duty to Mrs Washington & her Love to miss Custos. Remember me, to mrs otis & miss Harriet, tell mrs otis she must write to me and tell me all she knows about our old Friends and acquaintance. I hope You have calld to see mrs Powel in her affliction. to mrs Dalton and Family remember me affectionatly. tell miss Polly I saw mr Cranch from Haverhill a few days since, that mr White was well, and I sent him word that I approved his taste, and thought him quite right not to permit Philadelphia to Rob us of so amiable a young Lady. my Love to son Thomas. we are in our Family well tho a slow Nervous fever prevails in some instances here & in Several other places— the weather changes so suddenly from one extreem to an other that it will generate sickness. it is a very poor winter for Buisness. we have not had snow enough to use a Sled at all & the Ground frequently so Rough as to render wheals impractacable.—

I presume you must have received the acknowledgment you mention before this time.

Let Brisler know that his wife was well yesterday.—

Yours most affectionatly   A Adams

To Abigail Adams Smith

My Dear Mrs. Smith,   Quincy, 10 March, 1794.
    Although the scenes in which I have been engaged for six weeks past, have been very different from those which you describe, I have been amused and entertained by your account. Though I cannot say that I am charmed with your hero's personal accomplishments, as you describe them, yet you find

> "A man of wealth is dubbed a man of worth;
> Venus can give him form, and Anstis birth."

I think our ladies ought to be cautious of foreigners. I am almost led to suspect a spy in every strange character. It is much too easy a matter for a man, if he has property, to get introduced into company, in this country, of the best kind, and that without recommendations. The entertainment you describe was really very curious.

> "Men overloaded with a large estate,
> May spill their treasure in a queer conceit;"

and I am sure this was of that kind.
    You may mix in these scenes, and sometimes join in the society; but neither your habits, your inclination, nor your natural disposition are formed for them. By nature you have a grave and thoughtful cast of temper, by habit you have been trained to more rational and durable pleasures, and by inclination you delight more in them. The frivolity of the present day has been much increased by our foreign connexions. I pray Heaven to preserve us from that dissoluteness of manners, which is the bane of society, and the destroyer of domestic happiness. I think, with the poet,

> "If individual good engage our hope,
> Domestic virtues give the largest scope;
> If plans of public eminence we trace,
> Domestic virtues are its surest base."

You complain that there is, in the rising generation, a want of principle. This is a melancholy truth. I am no friend of bigotry; yet I think the freedom of inquiry, and the general toleration of religious sentiments, have been, like all other good things, perverted, and, under that shelter, deism, and even atheism, have found refuge. Let us for one moment reflect, as rational creatures, upon our "being, end, and aim," and we shall feel our dependence, we shall be convinced of our frailty, and satisfied that we must look beyond this transitory scene for a happiness large as our wishes, and boundless as our desires. True, genuine religion is calm in its inquiries, deliberate in its resolves, and steady in its conduct; is open to light and conviction, and labors for improvement. It studies to promote love and union in civil and in religious society. It approves virtue, and the truths which promote it, and, as the Scripture expresses it, "is peaceable, gentle, easy to be entreated." It is the anchor of our hope, the ornament of youth, the comfort of age; our support in affliction and adversity, and the solace of that solemn hour, which we must all experience. Train up, my dear daughter, your children, to a sober and serious sense of the duty which they owe to the Supreme Being. Impress their infant minds with a respect for the Sabbath. This is too much neglected by the rising generation. Accustom them to a constant attendance upon public worship, and enforce it by your own example and precept, as often as you can with any convenience attend. It is a duty, for which we are accountable to the Supreme Being.

My pen has again taken a serious turn. I shall not apologize for it. Your own letter led to these reflections; and I am sure they flow from a heart anxiously solicitous for the happiness of you and yours. That they may make a due impression, is the ardent and affectionate wish of Your mother,   A. Adams.

"MY BUISNESS IS MUCH IMPEEDED"

To John Adams

My dearest Friend   Quincy March 26ᵗʰ 1794.
    our two Tenants are come, and I have occupation enough. I have set them to clear the manure out of the Barn and to digg

the Garden put all the wall up and look to the fences. when that is done, I shall send them to clear up the Bushes in Curtis's pasture. I hope you will not be detaind longer than the Month of April. you will be weary of hearing of my wants, and of supplying them, but I find we want for the Two Farms a Wheelbarrow for each place 2 spades 2 forks 2 shovels 2 axes 2 hoes. I shall order two more Sythes immediatly—each place must be supplied for it will *not be working it right* to carry from this place those articles as at present, we are obliged to, and still worse to Borrow— I shall Buy 50 weight of clover and a few quarts of Herds Grass seed. I wish you to inform me whether for the corn land which is broken up here, the manure is to be spread as the last year. Belcher is of opinion that as the land is cold it would be better to manure in hills— I am waiting for a Remittance to proceed with courage. mrs Brisler, too want me to let her have some money, or you had better let Brisler have it for her, but I shall let her have 5 dollors as I promisd it her— for myself I have spent only 2 dollors & half through the winter & that was for shoes— the whole of the Family expences are upon my Books. Arnold seemd so desirious of continuing with us, that I think to hire him for 8 Months, or by the Year if you think best.

we continue our daly Labour of tarring how long it is to hold I know not, but it will be necessary to get an other Barrel of Tar, as the animals are so thick as to oblige them to lay on plentifully every day.

Mother continues much in the same state as when I last wrote you. she is a mere shadow but the wonder is that she lives. she has been led out of the Room twice—

Trade languishes. we are full of wrath but Patient, whilst

"A Passenger the voilated Merchant comes along
    That far sought wealth, for which the noxious gale
    He drew, and sweat beneath equator suns,
    By lawless force detained"

"When ruffian force
    Awakes the fury of an injurd, state
    Even the good Patient Man, whom reason Rules
    Rouz'd by bold insult, and injurious rage
    with sharp, and sudden check th' astonishd sons
    of voilence confounds;"

Yet I see no more reason for going to war with England than with France, nor indeed so much for England does not pretend to give us the Fraternal kiss, & judas like betray us, tho I own want of power only to resent their injuries would restrain me, if negotiation should prove unsuccessfull—

the civic feast vanishd in smoke. none but the democratic club would unite in it. I have not seen our son for a long time, so that I cannot tell you so much about it as I wish.

I am my dearest Friend most affectionatly and tenderly yours.   Abigail Adams—

I have learnt this afternoon that the L. Govenour assured the Jacobines who waited upon him requesting his attendance to the civic Feast, and that he would order out the Militia, that their request should be complied with. when the real merchants and principal people found that the Government was to be drawn in; they had a meeting, & sent a committee to remonstrate to the Governour, assuring him that it was in direct voilation of their Solemn engagement to remain Neuter; and that if any such thing was attempted more than a thousand of the inhabitants would remonstrate against it; he was much allarmed and said he would use his endeavours to prevent it the Chronical asscribes it to the distress of the Town and the deplorable Situation of the Trade! misirably reduced indeed that not even one solatary Dollor pr head could be furnishd. poor spirited wretches. what shifts to support an abhored system.

I must request you to hasten me some money. my Buisness is much impeeded at this time through want of it. I know the reason has been the delay of the Appropriation Bill—

WAR WITH BRITAIN

To John Adams

my dearest Friend   Quincy April 18th 1794
Your Letter of April 5th an 7th reachd me last Evening, and they fill me with more apprehensions of a War than any thing I have before hear'd. the body of the people are decidedly

against War, and if a War is madly or foolishly precipitated upon us, without the union of the people, we shall neither find Men or Money to prosecute it, and the Government will be Cursed and abused for all the concequences which must follow I have many disputes with your Brother upon this Subject, whose passions are up, upon the insults, and abuses offerd us by Britain, and who is for fighting them instantly with out Seeing one difficulty in our way. in order to put a stop to too rash measures, Congress must rise. the people without are willing to wait the result of Negotiation as far as I can learn, and in the mean time we ought to prepare for the worst. Several vessels arrived here last Week from Jamaca, where they were only carried for examination of their Papers—and immediatly dismist.

I most devoutly pray that we may be preserved from the horrours of War, and the Machinations of Man.

You judg'd right of your Countrymen. the vote for mr Adams, notwithstanding all the Electionering was much more unanimous than I expected. in Quincy they were nearly divided between mr Cushing & him. in Braintree & Randolph they were nearly all for him.— I am glad that we shall have a Govenour Elected by the people—and you will see by a Letter received from me before this time, how nearly we agree in sentiment upon this Subject, and I may adopt the words of mr Blount in a Letter to Pope, "that I have a good opinion of my politics, since they agree with a Man who always thinks so justly" I wish it were in our power to persuade all the Nations into a calm and steady disposition of mind, while seeking particularly the quiet of our own Country and wishing for a total end of all the unhappy divisions of Mankind by party-spirit, which at best, is but the Madness of many for the Gain of a few— I shall with pleasure upon this day particularly set Apart by our Rulers, as a day of Humiliation and prayer, unite with them in wishing the temporal and eternal welfare of all mankind. how much more affectionatly then shall I do it for You to whom I am bound by the Strongest bonds of duty and affection ever yours   A Adams—

To John Adams

Quincy 27 May 1794

Thanks to the Father of the Rain, and the Bountifull dispencer of the dews of Heaven, who has plentifully waterd the dry and thirsty Earth. the Fields recover their verdure, and the little Hills rejoice. the drooping vine rears its head and the witherd flower Blooms anew.

"join every living soul,
Beneath the spacious temple of the sky,
In adoration join; and, ardent raise
one general song! To Him ye vocal gales
Breathe soft, whose spirit in your freshness
    Breathes:
Soft rool your insense, herbs, and fruits and flowers
In mingled clouds to Him; whose sun exalts
whose Breath perfumes you, and whose pencil paints"

Indeed my dearest Friend it would rejoice your Heart to behold the change made in the appearene of all Nature, after one of our old fashiond Election storms as we used to term them. I hope we may be further blessd by repeated showers.

I this day received yours of the 19th of May. I know not what became of the letter you mention. such a one there was, nor do I recollect a Syllable of its contents, excepting asking your advise about the land which was the peice owned formerly by Margeret vesey. I had 72 pounds bid for it, but it sold at 60 dollers pr acre and was purchased by dr Phips— I also mentiond that the Name of Adams might be supposed in high estimation, since by the returns received we had reason to suppose that our Govenour & Leiut Govenour were of that Name, but one & the same Man. your Brother too had that day been chosen Rep've for this Town of which I informd you, but do not recollect any thing further. I might write a string of Blessings upon the Democrats their clubs—&c but as nothing I could say of them is more than they merit, they are welcome to make the most of it, and Chronical it, if they get it.

"You caution our son to be reservd prudent cautious and silent" he is I believe all this. you bid him curb—his vanity. I know not whose praise would so soon tend to excite it, as one for whom he has so great respect and veneration, and whose judgment he so much relies upon— I will not say that all my Geese are swan I hope however that I have no occasion to Blush for the conduct of any of my Children. perhaps I build more expectation upon the rising Fame and Reputation of one of them, than of an other, but where much is given, much shall be required. I know their virtues and I am not blind to their failings—let him who is without cast the first stone.

The Jacobines are very Angry that Congress leaves them at their Liberty, and permits them with their Eyes open to rush on to destruction. that they want Gaurdians is true enough, but no one obliges them to risk their property to French British or Spanish pirates

others I believe wishd the Embargo continued from real Patriotic motives.

Speculation, has been going on rapidly.

I understand the Term *impatiently yours* but I had a good mind to be a little Roguish and ask a Question, but I think I will only say that I am most Patiently Your ever constant and affectionate   A Adams

"WHAT I THINK OF FRANCE"

To John Adams

my Dearest Friend   Quincy December 6th 1794

Your kind favours of the 19th 23 & 26 of Nov'br came safe to Hand, together with the pamphlet. the writer appears to have ransakd Pandimonium, & collected into a small compass the iniquity and abuses of Several generations, "sitting down all in Malice & Naught extermating." If the representations of our Democratic Societies both of Men and measures, for these two years past, were to be collected into one pamphlet, and could obtain belief, some future Jefferson, might cry out, that it containd "an astonishing concentration of abuses." in a Government like that of Great Britain, we know that many abuses exist, both in the Governors & Governed, but Still in no Country, America excepted, has there ever existed so great a share of personal Liberty & Security of property.

You ask what I think of France I ruminate upon them as I lye awake many hours before light. my present thought is, that their victorious Army will give them a Government in Time, in spight of all their conventions, but of what nature it will be, it is hard to say. Men Warlike and innured to Arms and conquest, are not very apt to become the most quiet Submissive Subjects.— are we, as reported, to have a new Minister from thence? I presume Munroe is to their taste. it will be well if he does not take a larger latitude than his credentials will warrent.

I am anxious for our Dear Sons. There prospects are not very pleasent, even tho the french should not get possession of Holland. This Whirligig of a World, tis difficult to keep steady in it.

It gives me pain to find you so lonesome in the midst of so many amusements. I know you do not take pleasure in them, but you would feel more cheerfull if you went more into Society. the knitting work & Needle are a great relief in these long winter Evenings which you, poor Gentleman cannot use. like mr Solus in the play, "you want a wife to hover about you, to bind up your temples to mix your Bark & to pour out your Coffe," but dont you know, that you will prize her the more for feeling the want of her for a time?

"How blessings Brighten as they take their flight"

The buisness of the Farm goes on, the plowing is all finishd & the Manure all out, the yard full of sea weed, and a little wood.

The News of the day is that mrs Hancock is going to take Captain Scot into her Employ, in plain words that she is going to marry him—an able bodied Rough sea Captain.

"Frailty thy Name is woman
 we cannot call it Love; for at her age
 the hey-day in the Blood is tame, its humble
 And waits upon the Judgment, and what Judgment
 would step so low"?

alas dorethy I never thought the very wise, but I thought the proud and ambitious.— do you say I am censorious. it may be so, but I cannot but wonder.

adieu pray write in good Spirits. you know I never could bear to hear you groan and at this distance it gives me the vapours—

I am most affectionatly Yours   A Adams—

To John Adams

my Dearest Friend   Quincy Jan^ry 4th 1795—
    I received by our Thursday Post, yours of Decbr 18 & 23 together with the Bennets Strictures. you may be sure Bennet is a favorite writer with me for two reasons. the first is; that he is ingenious enough, to acknowledg & point out the more than Egyptian Bondage, to which the Female Sex, have been subjugated, from the earliest ages; and in the Second place; that he has added his Mite, to the cultivation, and improvement of the Female Mind. much yet remains to be done. there is however more attention paid to the Education of Females in America, within these last 15 years than for a whole centry before, and the rising Generation will be benifitted by it. Conjugal fidelity holds the first place in the Rank of Female virtues, and whilst that Source is uncorrupted, we may hope to See the united efforts of Parents exerted towards the improvement & cultivation of the minds & morals of their ospring regardless of the Sex, affording to each an Education to qualify them to move with honour & dignity in their proper Sphere.

you promised me an account of the Female Commencment. was you dissapointed? either in your expectations or in your attendance?

I wrote you not long since a request that you would Subscribe for Fennos paper for mr Cranch as Post Master Since that I have not received a paper from Fenno, nor has mr Cranch received one as Post Master. I do not know how the act Stands, or whether you are subject to postage for a News paper. as post Master mr Cranch is entitled to the News paper post free: it would come regularly to him. he would have the reading of it, and I too. I lose the greater part of the debates by not seeing Fennos paper— a small proportion only is retailed to us in our Boston papers—

How insolent and impudent are the Jacobines of Pensilvana? they have adopted the very stile and language of the French Jacobines, and they breath the Sentiments of the Southern incendaries in Congress— Judge Lowel askd mr Bowdoin, how in his conscience he could vote for Jarvis? why he replied I do not like his politicks, and I despise the Man, but I have been neglected and slighted by the other Party—! such is the Patriotism of the World. how little Sterling integrity! how hard the lesson to divest one of self interest. the world however see through the veil, and it is oweing to this same Self Love, that the Man has been neglected. neither his Fathers Patronage, nor his own ample fortune have been able to raise him higher than state Senator—and there with such principals may he remain—

Winter has sit in with Rigor a flight of Snow Succeeded by cold, an inclement week we have not much to relate in the way of Buisness— getting wood, and some attentions at home, have occupied our people this week we want Snow. to day we have a heavy Rain mixt with sleight & snow— the Broad wheels are under water. the Scow—is laid up for the winter; the cable brought home; not so much Sea weed, in Joys Yard as I could wish—nor Shaws. the reason is that Quincy Meddow is coverd & 8 load upon a small spot next mr Bass—and the Scarcity of the article. our Teams have been as far as Horse neck after it. if the weather permits every opportunity will still be embraced. the persons you hired carted as long as they could find their account in it, and I have paid them 40 Dollors wanting a few shillings—40 odd for the cart wheels—& repairing the others— the pew I have a deed of, and have paid 46 pounds— I have paid to my Men & Women Tennants their 3ᵈ quarter, and, a number of Small matters; I have paid up Copland. the Time for which I engaged him expires on Monday. he tells me that his Family must want if he cannot get employ through the winter that he has 5 children, but one of which is old enough to put out and She so weakly as to be unfit. there are only two Months before we must necessarily have an additional Hand on account of the canker worm & other things. I have offerd to hire him for the Year from the first of Jan^{ry}. I believe he will stay. I tell them they must bring a great deal of work to pass— Sea weed they Say makes but little show—and wood burns up—

Shaw is a very excellent hand he has hurt himself and for a fortnight has been unable to do much Stooping under the cart to do something to an Axeltree. the cart tipd up upon the small of his back, brought him to the Ground & set him to Spitting Blood—

"o be thou blest with all that Heaven can send" is the New Years benidiction of your ever affectionate   A Adams

WEDDINGS AND ROMANCES

To Thomas Boylston Adams

Quincy Jan^{ry} 10th 1795.

Should a vessel cross the Atlantick, and my dear Thomas not find a few lines from his Mother, I know he would feel sadly dissapointed, yet not a Solitary Scrip, has reachd her yet, to assure her, of his, or his Brothers Safety. The arrival of the vessel has been confirmd by a Letter, received in Boston, in replie to one which went in the Alfred, so that my anxiety respecting the Ship was alleviated

I am now impatient to hear from you the sight of your Brothers, or your Hand writing would make my Heart leap for Joy. I wrote to you by Captain Scott who saild in December— and who when he returns is to Marry Mrs Hancock!! Liberty and Equality are her Mottos

I received a Letter from your Brother last week. he is in much affliction for the loss of his Friend and Benefactor the Baron Stuben. you know how strongly he was attached to him, and how highly he esteemed him. he made the Baron a visit in october when he went to Albany and in a few days after his return, received the News of sudden Death by a parylitick stroke.

I learn from Mrs Smith that the former connextion between Charles and Sally is renewed, as I always supposed it would be.

Heaven Bless them. I will never say anything to prevent it, only that he should see his way clear & be able to support a Family. Your cousin William Cranch would have lost his Heart at Philadelphia if it had not been engaged: he writes to his Nancy warm encomiums upon your Flame, Miss Wescot. he is perfectly in Raptures with her— you may return Nancys handkerchief —she is going to Marry mr Porter. what do you think of the English Ladies? every thing is enchantment upon that ground beware however of their Snares—does Mrs Sydons act yet upon the stage? the Royal Girls, have you seen them? Mary I used to think the Beauty of the Family. I ramble with you in imagination it is indeed & very truth a delightfull Country. I always think of it with pleasure— should you see mr Johnson the American Consul, tell him I saw his son last week and that he was well & appeard to be pleased with his situation.

for politicks I refer you to your Brother, and am my dear son affectionatly Your Mother   A Adams—

The Girls all send their Love to you.

NATURALIZATION ACT

To John Adams

my Dearest Friend   Quincy Jan'ry 16th 1795

I yesterday received yours of Jan'ry 1st 4th and 5th. I See by the papers the *judicious* Notion of Giles as it is an other Bone to pick; and brought forward with no other view or design, but to render himself popular with the Sans Culotts I cannot help despiseing and abhoring a Man, who is governd by Such base and Sordid motives. Giles' face was allways my aversion and his Heart I detest, for I believe it desperately wicked. I think however that every precaution should be taken to prevent Foreigners from gaining too great an assendency in our Country, or taking any share in our Government. a Long period of time they ought to be upon probation & after all the precautions we can devise they will be too numerous and powerfull for us if the troubles abroad continue, and increase. I hope Amsterdam will not be obliged to Surrender to the Arms of France, for altho I do not feel towards them, as I did whilst that worse than Borgia, Governd, yet I am far from thinking they have returnd sufficiently to their Reason to Govern themselves, or dictate anything good to others

Mr osgoods Sermon is going through a third Edition. there is adertiz'd an answer to it by de Novien' a misirable performance tis said, and it is asscribed to Sullivan. it is neither sense or Grammer. I have heard two Characteristic marks of Sullivans performance's, but I rather think him too cunning to wage war against So popular a performance, especially for a Man, who I am informd drinks daily the Health of the President & vice President at his table, and who has never dared openly to meet with, or give his Sanction to the Jacobines. there is much conjecture who the writer of the Jacobiniad is. he is certainly a Man of Letters, and a poet.

Master Cleverly is in great distress that the President being a Church Man, should appoint a Thanksgiving during Lent he shakes his Head, and says tis a very Arbitary thing. I Suppose he cannot help connecting plumb pudding Roast Turkey and minced Pye. he cannot give thanks upon Eggs and fish.

It will always be thanksgiving day to me, come at what time you will. it would be doubly so could I hear from our Sons— when you return I believe you must Spend a day or two with mrs Smith. she seems to be hurt that you pass on so rapidly— and do not afford her a little more Time. she feels as if it was a want of affection in her Parents, or of a proper respect & duty towarrd them from her and that the world will thus construe it. I know your anxiety to get home, and I know all your Reasons, but at the Same time I know you would not hurt or wound a derserving and affectionate child.

I have received a Bill of Laiding from mr Brisler which I shall inclose to mr Smith who has been very sick, with an inflamitory Rehumatism

You will have received my Letter respecting flower, and some other things which I wrote to mr Brisler about. he may get me a couple of hundred of Rye flower if you please. I give 8 shillings for Rye here, and I cannot get Hay, as yet at a less price than 5 & 9 pence pr hundred— Grain is so high— the

Democrats have no need to exclaim against the Salleries. I am sure they are pretty effectually lower'd Grain is twice as high as it was when they were Granted; so are all the necessaries of Life, but there is no end of their mad and absurd plots.

I had it in mind whether the canker worm would not go up, but I supposed instinct would teach them that they could not find nourishment. the weather is now quite winter, cold tho the Ground is not coverd yet being Icy & a little Snow. one Team has been employd in Sleding the manure across the Meddow from Joys. I presume they will compleat it to day. the other in getting the Stones from the common and this at a time when they *could go in* the woods to good purpose, but I would not neglect the only opportunity we have had this Winter for this Buisness.

Present me most dutifully to the President and Mrs Washington. they are both too good to be percecuted, Yet blessed are they says a high Authority when Men Revile & Speak evil falsly, of them—

Louiss desires me to present her duty to you and many thanks for your kind Present; I am very anxious for her. her Health declines and she is pale as death yet makes no complaint, but weakness. I know you will Say it is want of excercise which has brought her to it. I should think So more, if each of her sisters had not past through a Similar Weakness and debility. hers has been increasd by returns of the Ague— I am my Dearest Friend most affectionatly Yours   A Adams

THOMAS AND JOHN QUINCY IN HOLLAND

To Thomas Boylston Adams

my Dear Son Thomas   Quincy Feb^ry th 11 1795
When you address me again, let it be by the endearing Epithet of Mother, instead of the formal one Madam; I Should have thought your partiality for your Friends the Quakers would have prevented your substituting any other Epithet. and now having in a few words setled a point respecting titles, a subject which has occupied a great Legislature for many days,

and occasiond much warmth and Heat, the Mad—sonian party, insisting that previous to Naturalization, all foreigners should renounce their titles, the other Party contending, that it was the priviledges annexed to Titles which renderd them of concequence, that by the American Constitution no Man could hold a title, that Naturalization excluded him from titles as an American and that it was childish for that House to cavil at the Name of Baron Duke or Lord or Bishop which could have no effect here, and that obliging a Man to renounce them, might affect his interest in other Countries where estates were frequently annexd to titles. upon this the Yeas and Nays were call'd for. this occasiond much warmth, as it was then considerd as an Art to fix a stigma upon those who considerd the Subject too trifling in itself to occupy the House, but knowing the aversion in the Americans to the Bug Bear, it was supposed to be done to create a new allarm, and raise a cry of Aristocracy against all who opposed the motion. the vote was however insisted upon and taken and, Northern & Southern pitted against each other 58 Ayes 32 Nays—

I have my Dear Son to acknowledg the Receipt of a two Letters from you, one written immidiately after your arrival in London, and the other from the Hague the 12 December one which your Brother mentions haveing written from London I have not received. I have a letter from mrs Copley 15 Nov^br infoming me that She had procured and sent the silk for Mrs Welch. I thank you for your attention to this and my other commission, but there was one of more importance to me, of which I fear both Your Brother and you were unmindfull, and I have no fancy for a stiff Dutchman. I mean the Minatures for Braclets which I wish to have taken an Executed in England. the expence of them I should request the Willinks to reimburse. the Setting of them in gold with the Hair in cypher I would have executed by an old acquaintance of mine in cheepside Savory by Name, a Quaker a very honest and honorable silver smith and Jeweler from whom I used to procure all articles which I had occasion for in that way.

I feel your embarrassment in a foreign Country the Language of which You cannot speak. I know by experience how unpleasent it is, but that is a difficulty which will daily diminish. I rejoice that you are with your Brother. I am sure either of you alone must have been triste. England you know is the Country of my greatest partiality. Holland appeard to me Such a place of still Life, Amsterdam & Roterdam excepted, that I thought I could not be reconciled to become an inhabitant of it, and I perfectly assented to Sir William Temples Character of it, that it was a Country where the Earth is better than the Air, and profit more in request than honour, where there is more sense than Wit, and more Wealth than pleasure, more good Nature than good humour, where a Man would chuse rather to travel than to Live, where he would find more things to observe than to desire, & more persons to esteem than to Love. altho tis near a century since this Character was drawn, you will soon perceive that it, need not Sit for a New Likeness you will find many things in the Country well worthy your attention Some of those which I particularly remember, and which I would recommend to your notice. the statue of Erasmus, upon the great Bridge in the Grand market place at Rotterdam is one of them, and indeed Rotterdam itself is a curiosity. the Spaciousness of the streets and the Elegance of the Houses surpass those at Amsterdam. the Sight of Houses Masts of Ships—and the tops of Trees promiscuously huddeld together is at once Novel and Romantic. if you had any opportunity whilst in England to visit any of the celebrated Gardens and pleasure grounds, were it only those within a few miles of the city, Such as osterley place Sion House, or Tilney House, they would give you a through disgust to the stile of gardening in Holland where

> "Grove Nods to Grove, each alley has a Brother
> And half the platform, just reflects the other"

and yet you will find much expence. their walks are all a soft sand instead of the hard gravel of England. an object which struck me with the true sublime, was my ride from the Hague to scheveling. the strait Road and fine Trees are pleasing, but at the end, the Broad ocean opens Suddenly upon you when you have no suspicion of it, and creates a most pleasing sensation. in The Prines of oranges Cabinet at the Hague I thought there was the neatest, tho not the largest collection of curiosities Which I had met with, and according to the custom of the Country preserved in the nicest manner. in the little room call'd the Study are a fine collection of paintings by Dutch and Flemish Masters

There was one by Potter which You may have heard me mention. it is a Rural Scene, cattle drinking and their shade reflected in the Water, the flies upon the Cows seem alive, and a Toad Sitting upon the Grass is equally excellent.

Leyden utrecht, Harlem, all have monuments of Art worthy a strangers notice & the painted Glass in windows in a Church at Gorcum are a great curiosity. all these and many others which I visited I can traverse again with you, and it renews the pleasure to recite it to one who is going to enjoy the same gratifications

If the French get possession of Holland I hope they will not continue to war with the fine Arts as they have done

as you will see your Brothers Letter you will learn Domestic occurrences from that. present my respects to old mr Dumas to the Willinks Families—and to all others who recollect Your ever affectionate Mother   Abigail Adams

"SEPARATED FROM MY CHILDREN"

To Abigail Adams Smith

My dear Mrs Smith   Quincy August 14. 1795.

I quitted you with a heavy heart with many reflections upon my mind known only to myself. You ask me why I choose to be separated from my children? To see my children happy around me would be a felicity to me which Providence does not see fit to grant me— Some are called to act their part in a foreign land— Others are destined to live at a distance where our intercourse must be chiefly by letters— A family harmony would make so essential a part of my happiness that I could never enjoy myself without it— A mere cold civility towards each other would be far from gratifying my ideas of fraternal regard and affection— My own family are few in number but though so much separated the ties of consanguinity are not weakened. I have every reason to believe they are affection-

ately dear to each other and God grant they may ever continue
so; that neither prosperity nor adversity may lead them to neglect or forsake each other but I could have no enjoyment
with my family without a thorough harmony. I am sure I had
better be where I am, dear as my children and grandchildren
are to me than be where I am satisfied I could be of no service to either of them— I find myself advancing in years and
the early sentiments and habits which I imbibed are daily
more strongly impressed upon me— They are so old fash-
ioned that though they make a part of my enjoyment, they are
illsuited to modern style and fashion— Like other old people
I am very apt to fancy they are the best and I long for nothing
more than to have two very likely boys to educate in the same
manner in which I brought up my own sons. One great mistake in the education of youth is gratifying every wish of their
hearts. Children should know how to suffer want. They are
little capable of knowing how to abound— Their enjoyments
are much lessened by it.

A powerful motive for me to remain here during the absence
of your Father is the necessity there is that such care and attention should be paid to our affairs at home as will enable us to
live in an humble state of independence whenever your father
quits public life which he daily becomes more and more anxious to do. You, my dear daughter, must know that nearly
thirty years of the most active part of your father's life have
been devoted to the service of his Country— the pecuniary
emoluments of which have never permitted him to live equal
to the stations in which he has been placed nor by any means
equal to what as a private gentleman with his professional
abilities he would have attained if he had not been called into
public life. He has lived to see his Country rise to a state of
freedom and prosperity and is conscious that the faithful discharge of the part allotted to him has contributed largely to
her glory and independence. He has ever sustained the character of the independent freeman of America. Unseduced by
the intrigues of France on the one hand neither duped by the
Politics of Britain on the other he sought the best interests of
America with an undeviating progress through all her dangers
and perils. To an honest heart and an upright mind what must

be the feelings to behold faction Intrigue and the worst of foreign politicks with the violence of a whirlwind threatning to lay waste with the pestilence of its breath our Laws, government & Religion, and to involve in all the horrors of war, and in calamities which neither we or our children will ever see an end of, and this for the sake of gratifying the most malicious, and basest, of passions. Revenge. Stirring up hatred and animosities. Family against Family. Parents against Children, & Children against Parents? Destroying the Character of the most honest Fair and independent of men, attributing to them views and motives of which their souls were incapable, men whose consciences hold themselves accountable to a superior Tribunal than an earthly one. Who can refrain from sickning at the prospect, or when we turn our eyes towards our Allies, agonizing for their fate, and whilst we pray for their restoration to peace and order, suplicate Heaven to defend us from like calamities, for from them arises our danger, and to draw us into war with Britain a war which shall appear to be our own act is the whole system of that nation, how much so ever we pretend to be unbelievers, the people who are now running mad are *Mesmerized* most of them without knowing the secret springs which set them in motion, and this from Charlestown to New Hampshire.

THE JAY TREATY

To John Quincy Adams

My Dear Son   Quincy Sep'br 15 1795—
     I am ashamed to say how long it is Since I last wrote to You. I have received Your Letters to No 6. I believe only one, viz that from England has been lost. So valuable are Your Letters that I regreet the loss of a Line.
     Freeman as you fear, will not be heard of again, untill the Sea gives up its Dead. to his Parents he is a loss that never can be made up. they are disconsolate and almost refuse to be comforted. to his Friends and acquaintance he had greatly endeard himself, by his amiable manners and his engageing

Deportment. The House of vance & Freeman have been peculiarly unfortunate. since his absence, a valuable vessel & cargo
have been captured, belonging to them, and it is Said here that
mr Freemans affairs were much embarrassd

I have felt a reluctance at taking my pen to write you ever
since the meeting of the Senate in June, to relate the dishonour
and the disgrace of any portion of our Countrymen is a painfull task. no event Since the commencment of the Government, has excited so much undue heat, so much bitter
Acrimony, so much base invective, as has been pourd forth
against mr. Jay and the Treaty. one of the most mortifying
circumstances, is to see Some worthy and respectable Characters Drawn in to the vortex and made the Dupes of Jacobine
leaders & F——h Emisaries Your Letter to your Father No 9 is
a clue to the whole buisness. it Devolops the dark and secreet
designs of those agents of mischief. the contents of that Letter
were so important at the period, when it arrived that your Father immediatly inclosed it to the President, who returnd it
with the following Passage,

"Mr J Q Adams Your Son must not think of retireing from
the walk he is now in. his prospects if he continues in it are fair
and I shall be much mistaken if in as short a period as can be
expected, he is not found at the head of the Diplomatique
Corps—let the Government be administerd by whom so ever
the people may chuse his Letter No 9 discloses much important information and political foresight for this proof of your
kindness & confidence I pray You to accept my most cordial
thanks"

Many have been the voilent publications against the Treaty. the
Train was so concerted that a mutilated part of the Treaty, said
to be taken from memory, appeard in the Boston papers. this
was sufficient to exasperate candid & good men. no sooner
was this accomplishd, than Benny was Sent on to Boston with
Masons coppy, so that the first remonstrance was drawn up in
Boston, and as Peter Porcupine observes, in Such haste were
the Citizens of that Town, to get the start of other places that
the first copy of the Treaty had not been arrived in Town 24
hours—before a Town meeting was convened to condemn it.
at this meeting a motion was made to read the Treaty, at least
before they remonstrated against it, but this motion was not

even Seconded. Jarvis was the Demagogue, and orator. they had an unanimous vote. few persons of Character chusing to remain at a meeting where hissing and Noise and clamour excluded reason and argument. N York was not much behind Boston in point of Time, and in other respects far outstriped them, as Stones and Brick Bats were Substituded in the room of Hisses— Smith was their Chairman. a proposition was made for adjourning to a more convenient place for a fair and full discussion, but this was opposed with much clamour. there were a great majority of the Merchants Traders and people of property both in Boston & N York in favour of the Treaty, as soon as time was given them to examine & judge for themselves. this will appear by the Names of the Protestors, but the Flame was lighted up, and it spread from capital to capital, Damning cursing the Treaty, mr Jay Senators & even President. the President by a wise and cool and judicious reply to the Boston committe, appeard to allay the Ferment for a Time. several Learned and able pens have been engaged to vindicate the Treaty & enlighten the people. Camillus said to be col H   n Curtius said to be mr K   g in N York have satisfied every reasonable Man, and a writer in Boston under the Signature of a Feaderilist has written very Sensibly & cooley. Some pamphlets have appeard one written in carolina by mr smith, but none which I have read pleases me more than Peter Porcupine, written by the Author of a Bone for the Democrats. These pamphlets as well as news papers I will collect and forward to you by the first direct conveyance to England, for there do I expect to hear of you soon it is of importance that you should receive all the intelligence possible upon the subject. my Letter must swell to a volm to contain all that has been written for & against the Treaty. I should however observe to you that no commotion or meeting has taken place in any of our Country Towns in N England, Dracut the famous Dracut excepted, & that the state of Connecticut has been as usual, wise steady and discreat. their Wits have however been active and the Echo will repeat to you many Solid truths—

You are call'd upon to take a part in this important Buisness — You have put your hand to the plough, and I know you too well to believe or even wish you to look Back; or shrink from your Duty however Arduous or Dangerous the task assignd you. You will prove Yourself the Genuine Scion of the stock from whence You sprang. "Yet with Milton You may say, you are thrown on perilious Times."

My petition to Heaven for you is, that in the Hands of an over Ruling Providence you may be instrumental of much good to your country and that your Life and Health may be preserved a blessing to your Parents and a comfort to their declining Years— this and no other is the ambition of your ever affectionate Mother   A Adams

JOHN QUINCY IN LOVE

To John Quincy Adams

my Dear son   Quincy May 20th 1796

I have to acknowledge the receipt of Several Letters from You Since Your arrival in London, the first Nov^br 24th Jan^ry 6th Feb^ry 23, and Yesterday I received Yours of March 20th, for all of which, accept my Thanks, and believe that they are to me a most Valuable Deposit. The desire You express, that no warmer encomium may be bestowed upon You; than a bare approbation, may restrain my pen, but cannot suppress my feelings.

Mr Gardner arrived after a short passage, and very kindly came the next Day after, and deliverd all the Letters papers and Books, which were committed to him. I was as much rejoiced to see him, as the woman was, who saw the Man, who had seen the King. I felt an interest in him, because I knew him to be your particular Friend, and acquaintance.

The Cloaks came safe to Hand. mr Gardner paid particular attention to them. I am much pleasd with mine, and so is Louissa with hers, for which she requests You to accept her Thanks: the Young Lady who undertook the commission, shews that she inherits the taste of Elegance which her Mamma is conspicuous for. present my compliments to Both, and thank them for me, and tell them that mr T B Johnson was very well last week, when I received a very polite card from him, in reply to an invitation which I had sent him, to dine with me on a particular Day.

The Cloak which You sent to Louissa as a present I shall not object to her receiving as a present, but I must request You to Charge the one you sent to me, to the account I directed. at the same time the intention of the Donor, is gratefully received. I will thank You for any Books particularly interesting. Those which You sent me of citizenes's Roland contain many curious annecdotes. there is through the whole a display of vanity, perfectly Characteristick of her Nation. no other, but a French woman, could have written so. poor Roland stands in the back ground, however brilliant a woman tallents may be, she ought never to shine at the expence of her Husband. Government of States and Kingdoms, tho God knows badly enough managed, I am willing Should be solely administerd by the Lords of the Creation, nor would I object, that a salique Law should universally prevail. I shall only contend for Domestick Government, and think that best administerd by the Female.

I have not written to You since Feb'ry I have had such a surfeit of politicks, so contrary to My mind that it was painfull to detail them. the Majority in Congress assaild the Treaty with all the malice and Rancour of Party Spirit, and with a determined inveteracy strove to destroy it. 8 or 9 weeks were spent in this poor buisness untill the people took the allarm, and in the course of a few weeks the table of Congress was coverd with petitions from all parts of the union requesting them to make the necessary appropriations, to carry the Treaty into effect, that the Faith, and honour of the United States might be preserved. even those who did not like the Treaty, united in this wish considering the Faith of the Nation pledged. The triumph of the Friends of Government in Boston, was such as to astonish the Anarchists for a Town meeting was call'd by them, to oppose a memorial from the Merchants in favour of the Treaty, when behold, they were outvoted by an hundred to one, altho with their utmost exertions, During the ferment last summer, they could get only a few Towns in the country to join them in opposition. now the people have with one voice call'd upon the Representives to fullfill the Treaty. on no occasion since the commencment of the Government has there been such an allarm. the voice was, we will support the Government, we will not have war. even the little village of Quincy presented more than an hundred petitioners.

Mr. Ames, tho in so low and weak a state, as not to have been able to speak once through the Session, was determined to devote his Life to the cause, and 2 Days before the vote was taken in Congress, rose and made, as is universally agreed, one of the ablest and most eloquent speaches ever deliverd in that House, to the most crouded Audience. scarcly able to support himself he interested all hearts in his favour, and left an impression waterd with the Tears of his audience, tho not washed out, for it sunk too Deep. Scarcly were they restraind by the Rules of the House, from bursting forth what their full Hearts felt. yet during the Time he was speaking near two Hours, Your Father who was present, and from whom I received the account, says that the most perfect Silence reignd the Buz of a fly, might have been heard, such was the attention given.

Dr Preistly too was present, and declared that tho he had heard a Chatham, and the first orators in G B, he never heard a speach which exceeded this or a superiour Orator. perhaps the Speach may not read with So much interest. the feelings of the people were wrought up to a crisiss, and eloquence then is irresistable. even Giles said, he forgot on which Side of the Question he was, and the Genevian, pronounced him the only Orator in the House. I will send You the speach it is to be printed in a pamphlet as soon as I can obtain it.

From the close of Your Letter March 20th, I suspect that you were not so profound a proficient, in the Maxim of Horace and Pope, as you flatterd Yourself. Some Fair one has shewn You its sophistry, and taught you to admire! Youth and Beauty have penetrated through your fancied apathy, and You find yourself warmed by one and invigorated by the other; as you tell me that the enthusiasm of Youth has subsided, I will presume that reason and judgment have taken its place. I would hope for the Love I bear My Country, that the Syren, is at least *half Blood*. let me see, I think if I remember right, she has classick Locks as Virgill stiles them, Heavenly blew Eyes and plays Musick delightfully—

is Maria? has she no claims?

our Friends here are well. Your aged Grandmother is very infirm, but always sensible to warm and strong family attachments. she enters with me into the Joy and pleasure of hearing from her Grandsons. she bids me send you her blessing. Your

Sister I had a Letter from last week. she was well. her little Amelia just getting well of the Small pox. Charles was well, and like soon to be a Father. I have not heard directly from Thomas Since December I regreet your leaving London on that account, that I shall so seldom hear from You. an other Year will make Changes in America, some perhaps the concequences of which are not foreseen. I allways hope they may not be unauspicious to the best interests of our Country they fill My Mind with much anxiety. You may not be at a loss to Devine the reason.

I am My Dear Son most tenderly Your ever affectionate Mother   Abigail Adams.

ON DELAYING MARRIAGE

To John Quincy Adams

My Dear son   Quincy August 10th 1796
Since the date of my last July 11th I have received an Authentic account of Your appointment as Minister Plenipo. to the Court of Portugal. it was the last nomination which the President made, before the rising of Congress, and took place after your Father came home, without its ever being hinted to him. the appointment was agreed to as mr otis informs me, unanimously by the Senate. this is an additional proof of the confidence which Your Country reposes in You; and of the approbation of the President, who has thus honourd, and promoted You.

You will feel it a new incentive to discharge with fidelity the important trusts committed to You and to continue to deserve well of Your Country. I suppose mr King carried out Your commission and instructions.

The engagements You made in London will lead You no Doubt to go theither, on your Way to Portugal this new appointment my Dear Son has filld my Mind with a thousand anxieties on Your account. Will the Parents of the Young Lady think it adviseable for their Daughter, at so early an Age, without any knowledge or experience of the World, to be introduced into the Manners Luxeries dissapations and amusements of a foreign Court,? placed in an elevated Station, with examples before her Eyes of a Stile of living altogether incompatable with her future views and prospects in America? She has no Doubt been reard and Fosterd under the Eyes of kind and indulgent Parents, who have given her a Virtuous Education, taught her to Love the Domestic virtues, and at the Same time accomplishd her in Musick Dancing French &c I conceive the Young Lady to be accomplishd both in Mind and person not unfit to grace a Court, but the Question is thus accomplishd: is there not great Danger of her contracting such inclinations, and habits as to endanger her Youth and inexperience, as to unfit her for the discharge of those Domestic Duties, which cement the union of Hearts, and give it its Sweetest pleasures.

You know upon what an unstable foundation all the honours and promotion, in our Country rests. You know how inaddequate the allowence to an American Minister is, when compared with those of other Countries, of the same Rank, and You know, what Your prospects are when you return to America. if you were to bring Me Home a Daughter, she would be comeing to the Land of her Fathers Nativity, and would probably form no higher expectations than you might find the means of gratifying. She would assimilate herself to our Manners to our customs and our habits, which she would find so similar to those in which it is probable she has been Educated, that the Change might not be painfull to her. but who can answer for her after having been introduced into the dissipations of a foreign Court?

You have seen sufficient of the world to think soberly of these things, and to say with Ulysses

> In pomps or Joys, the palace or the Grot
> My Countrys Image never was forgot

and o may you add

> "My absent Parents rose before my sight
> And distant lay Contentment and delight"

What the Changes may be in this Country at the approaching Election is more than I am able to say one thing I can say with certainty, that you can neither hope or expect to find at the Head of the Government any Man who will do so much to promote you, as the President of the United States has Done. I sometimes think that your early promotion is in Some measure oweing to that Idea, as well as a desire to reward those abilities which have distinguishd Your late Mission—

our Country appears all tranquility. Providence is loading the Earth with Bounties a more plentifull Season was never known. may our Hearts be filled with Gratitude. we have Health in our borders, and peace in our dwellings.

I inclose You a scrip of the last weeks Paper that you may see, the Treaty is like to be complied with by the British so far as respects the Evacuation of the Forts.

I heard from N York a fortnight Since. they were all well. Charles expected Dayly to be a Father

Not a line of a later Date from my Dear Thomas than 1 of last December. my Heart sinks like a stone when I think of him, poor Dear soul, so sick, so far from Home. your last letter of May 12 informd me that you heard from him 28 April. this was a consolation to your anxious and ever affectionate Mother

A Adams

"HOLD YOURSELF FREE, FOR AN AMERICAN WIFE"

To Thomas Boylston Adams

my Dear Thomas   Quincy August 16 1796

There has been an interval of Eight Months Since I received a line from Your Hand. this Suspension of intercourse grows Daily more and more painfull to me as I learnt from your Brother that you had been sick first with a severe attack of the Rhumatism, and after ward with a Billious Remitting fever; I fear that the Climate of Holland is peculirly unfavourable to you, as your constitution is Heriditaryly disposed to those complaints. I have sufferd so severely from them myself, that beside a parentall solisitude for you, I have a sympathetic Suffering with You. at this distance I can render You no other aid than to pray for your restoration to Health, and to add my wishes that you would return to your Native Country

Your Brother has informd me that he has enterd into a connexion which he designs shall be permanant as soon as circumstances will admit.

I have supposed that he will go to England, & probably Marry before he goes to Portugal; if he should, there will not be that occasion for your continuance abroad, which there was whilst he was alone, without any one to tenderly care for him. a Young Man must have a companion, or Do worse. I hope all my Sons will avoid those snares which lead to destruction, and that you my Dear Thomas will hold Yourself free, for an American wife. I am not informd of your prospects, or designs. if you and your Brother should judge it most adviseable for You to go to Portugal, I will acquiese, tho I hope your Stay will not be long. I think You will have a better prospect of rising in your own Country, and becomeing more usefull, to it, here than abroad.

Your Friends here are all well. William Cranch is setled in the city of Washington, has a fine Boy of Eight Months old. Your sister and Family were well when I last heard from them; the col. had sufferd in his affairs by the villany of a st Hillair who married Peggy. it has however had a happy effect, so far, that he has come to a settlement with all with whom he was concernd: and tho it has obliged him to dispose of some of his Lands to less advantage, than he would otherways and stoped him in perhaps too rapid a career; he has a handsome property remaining, as I am assured. he has stoped building a Much too large Country House; and I hope will curtail all unnecessary expence, and live a more quiet and retired Life which I am sure will be more for his happiness, and the benifit of his Family. it is the wish of your sister, who you know has ever been averse to all kinds of extravagence and dissipation

Charles goes on gradually, and I hope Successfully in Buisness. he has two Clerks, he lives moderately and will do well I hope. Sally makes him a prudent discreet wife I suppose my next letters will anounce the birth of a Grandson or Daughter. poor Woman, She was Sick with the Ague & fever when I heard from her a fortnight since, which makes me anxious for her.

Your Aunt Shaw, that was, is Married to mr Peabody of Atkinson, and is very comfortably situated. William is getting on through his Education by the assistance of his Friends.

Dr Welch and Family are well Your Aged Grandmother is still living, and send you her Blessing William and Isaac Smith are setled in Buisness in North Carolina Mary is going to Washington to live with Your Cousin Cranch Eliza has been with me chiefly since Your Aunt left Haverhill Louissa is as a Daughter to me. she desires to be rememberd to you.

Your Father wrote you last week. he is as buisy as usual in attending to his Farm, which Seems his only recreation, & keeps his spirits in action, and gives him Health for his Winters confinement; indeed I belive he could not endure the one if he was not relieved by the other.

as to Politicks, it is a perfect Calm what mischief may be brewing in the Jacobinical Cawldron, time will discover. it will be composed of as venomous ingredients as Mackbeths Hell broth, but Heaven has yet graceously provided us with Antidotes for all their poison. if any Material alteration should take place at the approaching Election, there will be a new trial of their Skill.

adieu my Dear Son. Heaven Send you Health, and with it every other Blessing is the fervent prayer of Your ever affectionate Mother   Abigail Adams

WASHINGTON'S FAREWELL

To Thomas Boylston Adams

my Dear Thomas   Sep'br 25th 1796 Quincy

Your Letter of June the 29th was as refreshing to me as cold water to a thirsty Soul. the very superscription gave a flow to my spirits which I had not experienced for many Months before. be assured not one unkind thought ever enterd my mind at not hearing from you. it was anxious Solisitude for Your Health, painfull suspence at what might be the cause of Your long silence. Your Brother had informd me from England, that you had been sick, and the Nature of your Complaints. Maternal affection felt the pains, heightned by the Idea of Distance, a foreign Land, destitute of Fraternal aid, and those alleviations which Soothe the Heart, and mitigate the Sufferings. Not a

Bosom as Sterns Says to Uncle Toby, to rest Your Head upon, nor a Heart to repose Your Sorrows to. poor Fellow, if after commisiration and pity, could assuage even the pain of recollection, be assured You would find an ample fund, sufficient to allay them all, in the sympathetic Heart of Your Mother, who has herself experienced much ill Health through the Summer. I would recommend to You to try the Waters of Bath. they are said to be Soverign in those complaints to which you are Subject. Your Brothers New appointment will determine You to return Home next spring I presume. I should however recommend to you to visit France before that period. See for yourself a very extradonary People, whose future Destiny no Eye can penetrate, nor am I sufficently versd in the Prophesys, with Pater West, to rejoice in this Revolution which has consignd so many Innocent Victims to the World of Spirits, immolated so many fellow Creatures, to Mad ambition, and a thirst of Domination and conquest which now mark every step of their progress. Heaven grant that we may not be Scorched by their Flames. even at this Distance we feel the Heat of them.

The die is cast! All America is or ought to be in mourning The President of the united states refuses again to be considerd as a canditate for that office. He has addrest the people of the united states. read and Judge for yourself. is it not repleat with profound wisdom? how enlarged and comprehensive his views? How wise and judicious his advise? and, his warnings? with a modesty, I could almost say, peculiar to himself, with a Heart and mind Duly imprest with Religious Sentiments and an affectionate attachment to his Countrymen, he resigns the important trusts Committed to him, coverd with Glory and Crownd with Laurels, which will place him in the Archives of Time with the first of Heroes and the greatest of Benefactors to Mankind.

The present period is to the people of America a solemn pause! an Epoch in their Annals Big with the Fate of America.

Heaven Guide and direct them.

Before your Letter of June reachd me I felt so anxious for you, that I requested your Father to write to the Secretary of state, and inquire of him if any Letter has reachd him of a later Date. he was kind enough to reply and make some extracts from them, and at the close of his Letter, he says "the intelligence

with which the Letters of your Youngest Son have been written, shew that the affairs of the united States in the Netherlands
might very well be intrusted to his direction," but he adds, I
do not know what are the Presidents intentions.

I quote this passage to shew you that your Letters have
given satisfaction. the President has not left to a successor the
promotion of Your Brother. I find by the Secretary of States
Letter, that he was to remain in Holland untill further orders.
when he receives them, I presume he will go to England and
take his companion, who I hope will prove to him all he wants,
and all he wishes, who will Do him good and not evil all the
Days of her Life. I have felt a little anxious least I should have
hurt his feelings in some sentiments exprest to him in a Letter,
soon after I heard of his appointment, but he must asscribe
them to the real cause an anxious Solicitude for his welfare—

adieu my Dear son. may you be safely returnd to Your Native land, and to the Arms of your affectionate Mother

Abigail Adams

THIRD PRESIDENTIAL ELECTION

To John Adams

Quincy December 7th 1796

"The Morning lours, the Dawns oer cast
And heavily in clouds brings on the Day
Big with the fate of Liberty, and Man"

on the desicions of this Day, hangs perhaps the Destiny of
America, and May those into whose hands the Sacred Deposit
is committed be guided and directed by that Wisdom which is
from above, and the result prove the prosperity Peace and
happiness of our Country. this is My most fervent Wish & petition to Heaven, totally divested of every personal feeling and
sentiment.

I have twice written to you previous to this Day Which
compleats a fortnight since You left me, and in all which Time

I have not heard a word from You. I hope tomorrows post will bring me a Letter. We have had one continued turn of cold and dry weather, untill last Evening when the wind blew a Gale from the Southard & brought on rain. to Day it is very Stormy with snow hail & rain.

I Sent on our sons Letters in My first Letter. I want to know who is meant by the Pennsilvana Speculator the Intimate Friend of Munroe.? Who was Secretary to the abolition Society in Philadelphia? be so good as to send me the Secretary answer to Adet as Soon as publishd, and every Pamphlet You meet with, worth communicating to your ever affectionate

A Adams—

"MIX COMMISSIRATION WITH YOUR CONGRATULATIONS"

To Elbridge Gerry

DEAR SIR of Dec^{br} 28

Your obliging favour I received by the Hand of dr Welch. I thank you Sir for your congratulations which receive their value from the Sincerity with which I believe them fraught, the elevated Station encompassd as it is with Dangers and difficulties looks in my estimations like a Slipery precipice Surrounded With Rocks Shoals and quick Sands. No Man can have Such a concurrence of fortunate circumstances united in him as the president of the United States had to combine all Hearts in his favour & to receive twice the unanimous Suffrages of all America, if he with a full tide of favour has tasted the bitter cup of calumny & abuse what must a Successor expect who has near half the Country opposed to his Election. all the Friends of the Rival Candidates mortified at their defeat

You Sir have been too long conversant in publick Life and full well know "the pangs and Heart acks" to which it is subject not personally to mix commissiration with your congratulations, at my Time of Life, the desire or wish to Shine in publick Life is wholy extinguishd, Retirement to (Peace Feild,

the Name which mr A. has given his Farm) is much more eligible to me particularly as my Health has Severely Sufferd by
my residence at Philadelphia, personally I Shall consider myself
as the Small dust of the balance when compard to the Interest
of a Nation, to preserve peace, to support order and continue
to the Country that System of Government under which they
have become prosperous and happy. the sacrifice of an individual Life ought not to be taken into consideration

I fully agree with you in Sentiment as it respects the Election
of mr Jefferson I have long known him, and entertain for him
a personal Friendship, and tho I cannot assent to his System of
politicks, I do not believe him culpable in the manner he has
been represented. placed at the Head of the Senate, I presume
he would conduct with wisdom and prudence, and the Jarring
parties become harmonized the union Strengthend & cemented more firmly than if mr Pinckney Should be Elected
whose pretentions as a publick Man certainly will not balance
those of mr Jeffersons The Gentleman you alluded to as an
active Agent in the Elections, has no doubt his views and designs. there are Some Characters more Supple than others,
more easily wrought upon, more accommodating, more complying, Such a person might be considerd as the ostensible
Engine, which a Master Hand could wake, To what other
motive can be asscribed the Machivilean policy of placeing at
the Head of the Government. a Gentleman not heard of beyond the State which gave him Birth untill sent upon a publick
embassy, and certainly not particularly distinguishd by any Series of Services to his Country,

I feel Sir writing to a confidential Friend when addressing
you, an apology for the freedom of communication is unnecessary, The Arts and Manoevers which have been practised
during the period of this Election opens to us a gloomy prospect in future and fully proves to us that their is no Special
Providience for Americans and that their natures are the Same
with others, as it has become fashionable to quote a work
much talkd of, but little read, I will transcribe a passage from it
as it appears applicable to the occasion

"There is a natural and unchangeable inconvenience in all
popular Elections, there are always competitions and the candidates have often merits nearly equal, the virtuous & inde-

pendant Electors are often divided, this naturally causes too much attention to the most proffligate & unprincipled, who will Sell or give away their votes, for other considerations than wisdom & virtue So that he who has the deepest purse, or the fewest Scruples about useing it, will generally prevail

FIRST LADY
1797–1801

A DREAM

To John Adams

Quincy Jan.ʸ 1 1797

"O Blindness to the future kindly given
     That each may fill the circle mark'd by Heaven"

The new year opens upon us with new Scenes of Life before
us. what are to be the trials the troubles and vexations of it, are
wisely with held from our view.

> The universal cause
> Acts not by partial, but by Gen'ral laws
> who sees and follows that great Scheme the best
> Best knows the blessing, and will most be blest

To him who sits Supreem let us commit the hour the Day
the Year, and fearless view the whole. there needs but thinking
right, and meaning well, and may this ensure to you, the Souls
calm sun shine, and the Heart felt Joy.

I seldom think twice of a Dreem but last Night I had one of
so singular a nature that it has amused My mind to Day with
various conjectures. I was riding in my Coach, where I know
not, but all at once, I perceived flying in the Air a Number of
large black Balls of the Size of a 24 pounder. they appeard to
be all directed at me. all of them however burst and fell before
they reach'd me, tho I continued going immediatly towards
them. I saw them crumble all to Attoms, but During this
Scene, two Guns were dischargd at My left Ear the flash of
which I saw and heard the report. I still remaind unhurt, but
proceeded undaunted upon My course

How would the Sooth sayers interpret this Dream?

whom do you think has undertaken to read the Defence!
but Deacon Webb, and declares himself well pleasd with the
first vol.ᵐ as cousin Boylstone informs me.

I fear the Deleware is frozen up So that Brisler will not be
able to send me any flower—

Billings is just recovering from a visit to Stoughten which
has lasted him a week, the Second he has made since you went

away. from the first, as he went without the Root of all Evil, he returnd steady. the occasion of his going was the Sickness & Death of the Man who lived upon his place. I have been obliged at his request to purchase for him shirts & other Cloathing.

Your Mother desires to be rememberd affectionatly to you. one Day last week she walkt here, and spent the Day.

I am my Dearest Friend most affectionatly Yours

A Adams.

"MR JEFFERSONS HEART"

To John Adams

my Dearest Friend   Quincy Jan^{ry} 15 1796

The Cold has been more severe than I can ever before recollect. it has frozen the ink in My pen, and chilld the Blood in my veins, but not the Warmth of My affection for Him for whom my Heart Beats with unabated ardor through all the Changes and visisitudes of Life, in the still Calm of Peace Feild, and the Turbelent Scenes in which he is about to engage, the prospect of which excite, neither vanity, or Pride, but a mixture of anxiety and solisitude, which soften, but do not Swell the Heart.

By the last Post I receivd Yours of December 27th & 30. Jan^{ry} 1 & 3^d The extract from mr Madisons Letter I believe to be the genuine sentiments of Mr Jeffersons Heart. tho wrong in Politicks, tho formerly an advocate for Tom Pains Rights of Man, and tho frequently mistaken in Men & Measures, I do not think him an insincere or a corruptable Man. My Friendship for him has ever been unshaken. I have not a Doubt but all the Discords may be tuned to harmony, by the Hand of a skillfull Artist. I See by the paper of to Day that the extract is publishd in the Centinel, not through Eve, I assure you, for I have not disclosd it. it has gaind as Most storys Do, that mr J. declares he would not have taken the Vice Pressidency under any other Man. the writer adds not unaptly, from shakspear,

"the Event we hope will
  Unite the Roses Red and White together
  That on one kind and Friendly Stalk, they both may
    flourish"

My Authority for the Author of Aurelias, was William Shaw
who going one Day into Nancreeds Book store saw a young
Gentleman correctting the press. Nancreed introduced him to
William as the Writer of Aurelias and gave him one of the
Books; notwithstanding this, he may only, as he has on former
occasions for our son be the Channel only, to convey & foster
the ospring of an other.

You ask me what I think of comeing on in Feb'ry? I answer
that I had rather not if I may be excused. I have not for Many
Years enjoyd so good Health as this Winter. I feel loth to put it
to risk by passing a spring in Philadelphia. I know not what is
to be Done. I think an inventory ought to be taken of what
belongs to the United States a House ought to be provided
and furnishd in such a Manner as they chuse, or a Committe
appointed to Do it, if a sum Should be granted for the purpose.
I desire to have nothing to Do with it. there are persons who
know what is both necessary & proper. if this is Done I should
not be against going to assist in the arrangement of the
Household.

I will make the necessary inquiry respecting a Carriage and
write you word as soon as I can obtain information. my old
Chariot, I have purchased Runners and put it on. Dr Tufts
Says it must never be hung again. it has long been too shaby
for use. I was beholden to My Neighbours for a conveyance
before I got them. it answers very well for that purpose. the
Sleighing is remarkable fine and has been so for more than a
Month. I have had one Succession of visiters & company,
more than for any two years past. every Body who ever knew
one comes to pay compliments & visit who would not have
been so forward perhaps. . . . a little prematurely too, but it
shews their good wishes.

I see no prospect of the fall of any article. Grain is as high as
ever and all West India articles risen beyond bounds. Such
Sugars as were purchased last Winter at 12 Dollors pr hundred
are now 18. Loaf sugar 2/6 pr pd. Tea Coffe Chocolat risen in

proportion. at this rate we must be Starved if the House of Reps have not a sense of Justice before their Eyes.

What is to be Done with our places? I have not advertized, nor have I seen Vinton or French since you went away. Burrel I believe will stay on if we find him a yoke oxen & cart. he has not had a Drop of water since last july. Billings is getting steady. he had but a Small flight this last time, but he wants his Money as fast as he earns it

I have been so much hindred by company that I have not been able to write for these ten Days only one short Letter to you.

I took up the Note and Destroyd it.

I inclose You a Letter from an old Friend it contains some just sentiments. I need not say to you how necessary it is to lay ones finger upon their Lips—and to be upon our gaurd with *all* foreign Characters, and most domestick ones— I want to acquire an habit of silence, or of saying unimportant things.

We have had a Wedding in our Family too in the last week which has occupied some part of my Time. Nancy Adams was married on thursday last, and to Day the New married pair dinned with me. Mr and Mrs Shaw are here upon a visit to keep Sabbeth with me, and desire their Respects to you— I am Sitting up after all are a bed to write you that tomorrows post may not go without a Letter. you will write me and inform me what I must Do, or what you wish— Cabot says I must go on or all the Wheels will Stand Still, but I know better.—

Yours most affect^{ly}   Abigail Adams

return the Letter when read

January 15, 1797

COLONEL SMITH'S FINANCIAL SPECULATION

To John Adams

my Dearest Friend   Quincy Jan^{ry} 28th 1797

I received by the post on thursday the whole Mail contain-ing your Letters of the 5th 9th 11th 14 & 16th I began to be very

impatient at rude Boreas for laying an Embargo upon that intercourse which alone mitigated the pain and anxiety of
Seperation.

Gen.ᴵᴵ Lincoln had call'd upon me the beginning of the week
and informd me that you was well. the steady cold weather has
been more favourable to my Health than any Winter we have
had for Years past, and since I have been equiped with Runners
I have not faild to take the Air almost every Day. in one of My
late Letters I inclosed You Frothinghams estimate of a carriage
but as you have orderd one it will not do to apply to him and
you will want one sooner than he could make one I have been
thinking that we shall want a light travelling Carriage for me to
go to and from Philadelphia, as you can not be left without
one, and would it not be best for to sit Frothingham to make
one something upon the same plan with that which we formerly Had.? "You say your Farm appears very differently to
you now from what it did, and that it seems to you as if you
ought not to think of it."

The greater reason there is for me to turn my attention to it.
I consider it as our *Dernier* resort, as our Ark of safety. I think
it ought not to be sufferd to fall into Decay, and I shall not
regreet any pains which I can bestow upon it to render it a retirement Eligible to us when we are four Years older if we
should live to see the Day. we have been Doing, & undoing all
our Days. I would aim at making such arrangements as would
tend to make it better rather than worse even tho I expended
twice its annuall income. Billings has returnd to his senses and
conducts very well. he is going to sled stones next week, but it
is impossible to dig them we have had a covering of snow and
Ice impenetrable to every tool, the finest Sleighing I ever
knew. the snow very level so that there has been no difficulty in
turning out of the road, but for six weeks no rain & So cold as
not to Thaw at all. The price of flower which is good superfine
has been in Boston from 11/2 to 12 I have inquired divers
times, and I gave 12 about a Month ago. it is to be had now for
11/2 which capt Beal has just told me he gave last week, but it is
not of concequence whether any is Sent. I can purchase it here

in one of Your Letters you Mention having seen enough at
East Chester. in an other you exclaim alass poor Nabby, and
say you have written to the col. but get no answer; I received a

Letter from Mrs Smith in December, in which She expresses
a state of anxious suspence, and a willingness to Submit to
her Lot with resignation if she could but know that all just
demands were satisfied. Speaks of a col Walker as a Man very
Rigirous and disposed to take ungenerous advantages. Mrs
Shaw came here on a visit & spent the last week with me. she
told me of many things which I did not before know of, and
which I must give credit to. Some of them you had heard
before from Charles. the col is a Man wholy devoid of judgment & has deceived himself with visionary Schemes, and
run risks which he ought not to have Done, and led his
Family into a stile of living which I fear his means would not
bear him out in.

You have I Suppose before this Time received a Letter from
me which inclosed an other proof of your old stuanch Friends
confidence and attachment

> "The Friend thou hast, and their adoption tried
> Grapple them to thy Soul with hooks of Steel"

Mr Black told me the other Day on his return from Boston,
that col H—— was loosing ground with his Friends in Boston.
on what account I inquired. Why for the part he is Said to have
acted in the late Election. aya what was that? Why they say that
he tried to keep out both mr A——s and J——n, and that he
behaved with great Duplicity. he wanted to bring in Pinckney
that he himself might be the Dictator— So you See according
to the old adage, Murder will out. I despise a Janus tho I do
not feel a disposition to rail at or condemn the conduct of
those who did not vote for you, because it is my firm belief
that if the people had not been imposed upon by false reports
and misrepresentations, the vote would have been nearly
unanimous— H   n dared not risk his popularity to come
out openly in opposition, but he went Secretly cunningly as
he thought to work, and as his influence is very great in the
N England States, he imposed upon them. Ames you know
has been his firm Friend. I do not believe he suspected him,
nor Cabot neither whom I believe he play'd upon— Smith of
S C was Duped by him I suspect.

Beware of that Spair Cassius, has always occured to me when
I have seen that cock Sparrow. O I have read his Heart in his

Wicked Eyes many a time the very Devil is in them. they are laciviousness it self, or I have no Skill in Phisiognomy.

Pray burn this Letter. Dead Men tell no tales. it is really too bad to Survive the Flames. I shall not dare to write so freely to you again unless you assure that you have complied with my request. I am as ever most affectionately Your   A Adams

THE NEW VICE PRESIDENT

To Charles Adams

My Dear Son   Quincy Feb^ry 5 1797
    I received Your kind congratulatory Letter upon the new year. accept My thank for the filial regard and affection with which they are expresst. it is the will of Providence to place me in a very conspicious station. it shall be my endeavour so to conduct in it, as to excite neither envy ill will or Jealousy. as shakspear expresses it, I would bear my Honours meekly fully sensible that

> "High Stations tumult, but not Bliss creat
> None think the Great unhappy but the Great"

I can say with the Royall Singer

> "Still has My Life New wonders Seen
> Repeated every Year
> Behold my Days that yet remain,
> I trust them to thy care"

However wise able and discreet the Government may be conducted, the present pilot must not expect to have all Hands and Hearts united in his Support, as his predecessor has had I hope however he will be ably supported, and if he does not receive so large a portion of praise, that he will escape its attendent Envy calumny and abuse, in an equal Ratio.

    I consider the vice Pressidency as a concilitary union of the States, and on that account a fortunate event. I have always entertaind a Friendship for Mr Jefferson from a personal knowledge & long acquaintance with him. tho I cannot altogether accord with him in Politicks I believe him to be a Man of strickt honour, and of real integrity of Heart, in his judgment not so Mature as some Men, but incapable of Doing a real injury to his Country, knowing it to be so, nor will he sacrifice its interests from any pecuniary Motive. When placed at the Head of the Senate, I will venture to say he will verify the opinion I have always formd of him, for I have never sufferd calumny and abuse to hide those good qualities from my view. the most reprehensible part of his conduct, was countanancing that Freaneu when he was continually libelling the Government. there is a Character in your state who with all his pretentions to Friendship, took a very ungenerous part in the late Election. tho he thought to conceal himself under that Mask, the covering has been Seen through, and his real views and Motives discoverd. he may have superiour talents to Jefferson, but he has not half his disinterested Friendship— the Gentleman I mean was not a Canditate for either office. he is one however upon whom I placed my Eye very early, nor do I mean to withdraw it whilst I am an observer. "beware of that Spair Cassius" this is between ourselves.—

That we are in a very critical State with France every one must be sensible. their insults to our Government & their depredations upon our commerce ought not to be endured but upon the Principle that it is better to bear wrong than Do wrong. Their late victories in Italy will give a new Spur to insolence. by their own account it was so dear a purchase that I question whether ultimately it will contribute to their prosperity. every new desolation ought to excite our Vigilence & put us upon prepareing for defence, whilst we cautiously avoid every cause of offence

I have not yet made any arrangments for going to Philadelphia. I waited untill the Declaration is made and untill Something is Done by the House of Reps. the united states ought to have a House for their chief Majestrate furnished. I know not what will be Done.—

To John Adams

Quincy Feb^ry 8 1797

"The Sun is drest in Brighest Beams
To Give thy Honours to the Day"

And may it prove an auspicious prelude to each ensuing
Season. You have this Day to declare Yourself Head of A Nation. And now O Lord my God thou hast made thy servant
Ruler over the people. give unto him an understanding Heart,
that he may know how to go out, and come in before this
great people, that he may descern between good and bad, for
who is able to judge this, thy so great People? were the Words
of a Royal Soverign, and not less applicable to him who is invested with the Chief Majestracy of a Nation, tho he wear not
a Crown, or the Robes of Royalty.

My Thoughts, and My Meditations are with you, tho personally absent, and My petitions to Heaven are that the things
which make for Peace, may not be hiden from your Eyes. My
feelings are not those of Pride, or ostentation upon the occasion they are solemnized by a sense of the obligations, the important Trusts and Numerous Duties connected with it. that
you may be enabled to Discharge them with Honour to yourself, with justice and impartiality to Your Country, and with
satisfaction to this Great People Shall be The Daily prayer of
your   A Adams

"BECAUSE HIS FACE IS BLACK"

To John Adams

my Dearest Friend   Quincy Feb'ry 13. 1797
It is now the Middle of Feb'ry it will be the 20 by the Time
this reaches you. the whole Months has been a Thaw So that
to present appearences we shall have an early Spring. Billings

has been Several Day at work upon the Wall. he tells me he shall want help to cart & Digg. Veseys time is just expiring, and as he is a bird of passage, he does not incline to tarry longer, So that I have to Seek a Hand, and to hire occasionally, for I think this wall which Billings computes at 30 Days, ought to be compleated as soon as possible. the Hill must however be ploughd, in a week or ten Days. unless the Weather changes, it may be Done. write if you are like to Send Seed. French was with me a Day or two Since, to know if I had received an answer from You respecting his remaining upon the place. I told him that there was no Doubt he might have it. he proposed breaking up 3 or 4 acres upon Belchers Side adjoining to Dr Phips. he Says that will be Sufficient, and that the manure will be required upon the Ground which is to be Sown So that much corn will not be profitable. I conversd with the Dr upon the Subject. he proposed letting French take the place for two years as an inducement to him to carry on Manure, but this is as you please.

I wish you to make provision in March for the payment of Haydens Note. his Brother call'd a few Days Since and ask'd me if I would take it up. I told him I was not prepaird then, but if he wanted the Money I would procure it for him in a few Days. he replied that he would not give me the trouble to Do that. if his Brother was really in want he would let me know. I then told him I would take it up by the middle of March, but still I would get the Money immediatly if he would Send me word. I have not heard Since So presume he will wait till March. my Rates were sent the first of this Month. they amount to 178 Dollors and half the Farm tax upon which French & Vinton are to 24 Dollors, 16 Burrels. they have taken it upon them to Rate Your personal estate at 90 Dollors. I know of no one article of living which does not exceed in price this Year the last; during 8 weeks of as good travelling as ever was known in the Winter, there was a plenty, but no glut of the Market or fall of prices. I am disposed with you to curtail every expence which the Parsimony of our Rep's require, and I would calculate for a surpluss of Revenue too. it will be there Disgrace, not ours, but they will bring their Government into contempt by it. they cry out, the high prices are but temporary, but they will starve out their officers whilst that temporary continues, which has been annually proving worse for these Six Years.

I have been much diverted with a little occurence which took place a few Days since and which serve to Shew how little founded in nature, the so much boasted principle of Liberty and equality is. Master Heath has opend an Evening School to instruct a Number of Apprentices Lads cyphering, at a shilling a week, finding their own wood and candles.

James desired that he might go. I told him to go with my compliments to Master Heath and ask him if he would take him. he did & Master Heath returnd for answer that he would. accordingly James went after about a week, Neighbour Faxon came in one Evening and requested to Speak to me. his errant was to inform me that if James went to School, it would break up the School for the other Lads refused to go. pray mr Faxon has the Boy misbehaved? if he has let the Master turn him out of School. O no, there was no complaint of that kind, but they did not chuse to go to School with a Black Boy. and why not object to going to Meeting because he does mr Faxon? is there not room enough in the School for him to take his Seperate forme. Yes. did these Lads ever object to James playing for them when at a Dance. how can they bear to have a Black in the Room with them then? O it is not I that Object, or my Boys, it is some others. pray who are they? why did not they come themselves?. this mr Faxon is attacking the Principle of Liberty and equality upon the only Ground upon which it ought to be supported, an equality of Rights the Boy is a Freeman as much as any of the young Men, and merely because his Face is Black, is he to be denied instruction. how is he to be qualified to procure a livelihood? is this the Christian Principle of doing to others, as we would have others do to us? O Mam, You are quite right. I hope You wont take any offence. none at all mr Faxon, only be so good as to send the Young Men to me. I think I can convince them that they are wrong. I have not thought it any disgrace to My self to take him into my parlour and teach him both to read & write— tell them mr Faxon that I hope we shall all go to Heaven together— upon which Faxon laugh'd, and thus ended the conversation I have not heard any more upon the Subject—. I have sent Prince Constantly to the Town School for some time, and have heard no objection—

I think You will excuse My attendance at Philadelphia till October. I hope however You will be able to come on in june. I talkd with Dr Tufts on the subject of building a Barn. he says he should advise to Building only a coach House for the present and appropriate the whole of this Building for the Hay. he thinks Some alteration may take place in the course of an other year which perhaps may render it less expensive inclosed is a line which I received from mr Bracket a Day or two since. I fear your more serious occupations will put out of your mind all personal concerns. adieu my Dear Friend do not let any thing put out of Your Mind Your ever affectionate

A Adams—

"OFFENCES WILL COME"

To Mercy Otis Warren

MY DEAR MADAM　　　　　　　QUINCY March 4th 1797

I received yesterday your obliging favour of Febry 27th. I have been so little a favorite of fortune, that I never once examined my Numbers by the News papers or otherways, concluding that those who were equally interested would take proper care for me. as I had formd no expectations, I meet with no dissapointment, and am quite pleased that my adventure should be appropriated to the promotion of Science and Literature.

The few Shillings in your hands be so kind as to lay out, in the purchase of some little Books, and present them for me, to the Lovely Marcia as a token of approbation for the sweet engageing simplicity of manners, which were so conspicuous in her.

For your Congratulations upon a late important event, accept my acknowledgments, considering it as the voluntary and unsolicited Gift of a Free and enlightned people, it is a precious and valuable Deposit, and calls for every exertion of the Head, and every virtue of the Heart, to do justice to so Sacred a Trust, yet however pure the intentions, or upright the conduct, offences will come.

"High Stations, Tumult, but not bliss create"

As to a Crown my dear Madam I will not deny, that there is one which I asspire after, and in a Country where envy can never enter to plant Thorns beneath it. the fashion of this world passeth away, I would hope that I have not lived in vain, but have learned how to estimate, and what value to place upon the fleeting and transitory enjoyments of it.

I Shall esteem myself peculiarly fortunate, if at the close of my publick Life, I can retire, esteemed beloved and equally respected with my predecessor.

Old Friends can never be forgotten by me. in that number I have long been accustomed to consider the Gen^ll. and mrs Warren. it will always give me pleasure to see them at peace Field, or where ever else they may meet, their Friend and Humble Servant,   ABIGAIL ADAMS

ON THE INAUGURAL ADDRESS

To John Adams

My Dearest Friend   Quincy March 12th 1797
    After a week of anxious expectation, I received by last Thursdays post, a packet containing three News papers, a pamphlet, two excellent Letters from our dear Sons, and fourteen lines from a hand, from which I was desirious of receiving, fourteen times as much. Unreasonable do you exclaim! Publick Buisness, publick cares, allow'd, but there is a kind of communication and intercourse which is a relieaf to the burdend mind, at least I conceive so.

I have read the address, the answer, and the reply. Upon reading the first period in the address, it struck me as obscure oweing to the length of the period. I read it a second time. The Sense was clear but some how, it did not Seem what I wanted to have it; I attempted to, throw the Ideas into an other form, but could not Succeed, without weakening the force of expression or greatly lengthing the address. I therefore

concluded that you had labour'd yourself under the same difficulty. I made no remark upon it, but in my own mind, Three
persons have since mentiond to me, the same thing, and one of
them told me that he had himself been trying to place the
Ideas of the first period in shorter Sentances, but met with the
very obstical which I had myself before experienced. The address brought into view a Number of home Truths. Evident to
Some, unseen by others. As the Sentiments of the writer are
known to me, I trace their meaning, end and aim, and pronounce them all wise, just, and Good. The answer of the Senate is Manly, dignified, affectionate and cordial. The Reply will
tend to strengthen the bond of union. The whole is calculated
to remove the film from the Eyes of those who are disposed to
see. I have heard but one remark, and that was from Jarvis. He
was glad to see you come out so fully and declare that the
Senate were equal to the defence and preservation of the constitution, and that it needed not a more permanent counsel.
With mischievious men, no honest man would hold communion: but with Men who have been mislead, and who possess
integrity of Heart, every good Man would be desirious of
standing fair. To the latter the conduct of H   n has been
misterious, and they are ready to think that the *President* is a
more impartial Man than they were taught to believe, and that
the opposition and Secret machinations and intrigues of a
certain Character arose altogether from knowing that the Man
whom a majority of the people wishd to succeed the President
was too independent in his Sentiments to receive controul.
They conclude that they have been mistaken in him.

I see by the paper received last Evening that the Senate are
notified to convene, by which I judge there are Subjects of
concequence to be imparted. Are there any official accounts of
the reception of Pinckny by the Directory? Such reports are in
circulation. I am pleas'd to find Mr. Murray appointed as the
successor of our Son. I do not know where a properer person
could have been found. Russel the printer is an abominable
Blunderer; he is not fit to publish State papers. No less than
three blunders has he made in publishing the address to the
Senate and in the Reply to their answer as you will see by
reading it. My mind has ever been interested in publick affairs.
I now find, that my Heart and Soul are, for all that I hold

dearest on Earth is embarked on the wide ocean, and in a hazardous voyage. May the experience, wisdom and prudence of the helmsman conduct the vessel in Safety. I am as ever a fellow passenger.   Abigail Adams

JOINING JOHN IN PHILADELPHIA

To John Adams

My Dearest Friend   Quincy April 17th. 1797
   Tho I have not heard from you since I wrote you last, and have nothing new to say, unless it be a resital of my own perplexities, out of which I must get by myself, Yet a few lines will assure you that I am getting forward as fast as possible with my affairs, and prepairing to sit out on my journey. The weather has been as uncommonly cold and Stormy for the week just past as it was Hot for two days the week before. We have a snow storm, of some inches depth, which has lain for three days. It has retarded our Buisness on the farm and chilld our exertions. The sudden changes have confind Your mother and brought on one of her old Lung complaints. The good old Lady is sure she shall dye now her physician and Nurse is about to leave her, but she judges with me, that all ought to be forsaken for the Husband. It is an additional care and anxiety for me. I shall provide for her comfort every thing necessary before I leave her. Mary Smith is yet living. Of how uncertain a duration are all our worldly possessions and Earthly comforts? If we could not look for brighter Scenes and fairer prospects, who could wish to remain the victims of pain and sorrow? Mr. Otis has lost his son George with a dropsy in his Head.
   I have just been reading Chief Justice Elsworths Charge to the Grand jury at New York! Did the good gentleman never write before? Can it be genuine? The language is stiffer than his person. I find it difficult to pick out his meaning in many sentences. I am sorry it was ever publishd. How I run on. The Federilist say there is but one blot in your Character. The Chronical has undertaken to praise and the Jacobins to speak

well. The Snare will not hold. Action will soon break it. Critical are the Times. May you get valiently through them.

Yours for ever,   A Adams

DEATHS OF MOTHER-IN-LAW AND NIECE

To John Adams

My Dearest Friend   Quincy, April 23, 1797
  I think through all the most trying conflicts of my life, I have been called to pass through them separated from the personal condolence and support of my bosom friend, I have been taught to look for support and aid from superior power than man: there is a state of mind, when affliction dries up the source of tears, and almost bids the swollen heart burst. I have left one of those distressing scenes, and come from the house of sorrow, and bitterness, and wo, to the house of silent mourning. The venerable remains of our parent, yet lie uninterred, and the distressing pangs of dissolution of an agonizing nature, are separating the soul from the body of my dear niece, whilst her senses are perfect, and alive to every attention, willing to go, praying to be released, yet requesting her friends and sisters not to leave her dying bed; but to remain by her until she breathes her last. O it is too much to bear! my heart is too big for my bosom; it rends my frame, and you will find me, when I reach you, more emaciated than with a fit of sickness. To-morrow I have the last duties to pay to our venerable parent. I have taken upon me the care and charge of the funeral; and to-morrow she will, for the last time, enter our doors. I have requested Mr. Whitney to attend. It is not for me to say when I will leave here; the will of heaven has detained me; I must not complain.

  By the mistake or misarrangement of the mails, you will not receive my letters as I wish, but the detention will only spare you pain. I am, my dearest friend.

  Your very afflicted,   A. Adams

JOINING THE PRESIDENT

To Mary Smith Cranch

MY DEAR SISTER: Philadelphia, May 16, 1797

Most cordially welcome to me was your kind Letter of May the 4th, yet I have not found time since my arrival to thank you for it, or even to write a Line to any Friend. My Journey was as pleasent as my thoughts upon what was past, and my anticipations of what was to come would permit it to be. We reachd East Chester on thursday noon and found Mrs. Smith and Children well. My reflections upon prospects there, took from me all appetite to food, and depresst my spirits, before too low. The Col gone a journey, I knew not where, I could not converse with her. I saw her Heart too full. Such is the folly and madness of speculation and extravagance. To her no blame is due. Educated in different Habits, she never enjoyd a life of dissipation. The Boys are fine Lads. I wish they were at Hingham under your care. I tarried one day & a half, and then went into N York. Charles lives prettily but frugally. He has a Lovely Babe and a discreet woman I think for his wife, quite different from many of the Family. A Number of Ladies and Gentlemen visited me there. On Monday, the 8 of May, we left N York to persue our journey. On Wednesday morning about 25 miles from Town, I was met by my Friend who clameing his own, I quitted my own carriage, and took my seat by his side. We rode on to Bristol, where I had previously engaged a dinner, and there upon the Banks of the Deleware, we spent the day, getting into the city at sun set. I found my Family of domesticks had arrived on Saturday without meeting any accident, which was very fortunate, for 40 miles through the Jersies was the worst Roads I ever travelld. The soil is all clay. The heavey rains & the constant run of six stages daily, had so cut them up, that the whole was like a ploughd feild, in furroughs of 2 feet in deepth, and was very dangerous. To me you may well suppose such roads were more peculiarly distressing. They were so much so, as to confine me to my Room & Bed the greater part of Two days. By some applications I have in a great Measure recoverd, tho I am still a sufferer.

Yesterday being Monday, from 12 to half past two I received visits, 32 Ladies and near as many Gentlemen. I shall have the same ceremony to pass through to day, and the rest part of the week. As I am not prepaird with furniture for a Regular drawing Room, I shall not commence one I believe, as the Summer is to near at hand, and my Health very precarious. At the Winter Sessions I shall begin. Mrs. Tufts once stiled my situation, splendid misery. She was not far from Truth. To day the President meets both Houses at 12 to deliver His speech. I will inclose it to you. I should like to learn the comments upon it, with a veiw to discover the Temper and Sentiments of the publick mind. We are indeed as Milton expresses it, "Thrown on perilious Times."

We have Letters from the Minister at the Hague as late as 23 Feb'ry. I will send you in my next some extracts from them. They are in the same strain of information and intelligence with the former. The decission as it respected the Election here, was well assertaind in France & England & Holland, and it had its influence upon all those powers.

I pray you to Remember me affectionatly to all my Friends & Neighbours. I rejoice in your unanimity as it respect Mr. Whitney, who you know is the Man of my choice, without any prejudice or dissafection to Mr. Flint. The union was however unexpected but not the less agreable. The hour approaches to dress for the morning. My Love to Cousin Betsy. I wish she could run in as formerly. I do not however dispair of seeing her Here some future day.

I can say nothing to you of future prospects of returning to my own dear Home. That must be governd by circumstances. My pens are so bad I know not whether you can read. I am most affec'ly

Your Sister   A. ADAMS

Evening 8 oclock
The day is past, and a fatiguing one it has been. The Ladies of Foreign Ministers and the Ministers, with our own Secretaries & Ladies have visited me to day, and add to them, the whole Levee to day of senate & house. Strangers &c making near one Hundred asked permission to visit me, so that from half past 12 till near 4, I was rising up & sitting down. Mr. A will never be too big to have his Friends.

"THE UNBECOMEING . . . CONDUCT OF FRANCE"

To Mary Smith Cranch

MY DEAR SISTER: Philadelphia, May 24, 1797
I keep up my old Habit of rising at an early hour. If I did not
I should have little command of my Time. At 5 I rise. From
that time till 8 I have a few leisure hours. At 8 I breakfast, after
which untill Eleven I attend to my Family arrangements. At
that hour I dress for the day. From 12 until two I receive company, sometimes untill 3. We dine at that hour unless on company days which are tuesdays & thursdays. After dinner I
usually ride out untill seven. I begin to feel a little more at
Home, and less anxiety about the ceremonious part of my
duty, tho by not having a drawing Room for the summer I am
obliged every day, to devote two Hours for the purpose of
seeing company. Tomorrow we are to dine the Secretaries of
State &c with the whole Senate. The Male domesticks I leave
wholy to Brisler to hire and to dismiss; the Female I have none
but those I brought with me, except a Negro woman who is
wholy with the Cook in the kitchin, and I am happy in not
having any occasion for any others, for a very sad set of creatures they are. I believe this city is become as vile and debauched as the city of London, nay more so, for in the lower
classes, much more respect is had to Character there. Speculation in Property, in politicks and in Religion have gone very far
in depraving the morals of the higher classes of the people of
our Country.
You will see by the Chronical, I presume, that the Tone of
the Jacobins is turnd, and that the president has committed
with them the unpardonable sin "by saying, that he was convinced that the conduct of the Government had been just and
impartial to foreign Nations." Bache opend his batterys of
abuse and scurility the very next day, and has in every paper
continued them, extracts of which I dout not the Faithfull Chronical will detail. The answer of the Senate you will
find equally firm and decided as the Speech. I call it a supporting answer. The House cannot yet get theres through. The
Antis. want to qualify. They dare not openly countanance the

conduct of France, but they want to court and coax her. With Barra's insolent speech before their Eyes and Pincknys dispatches, which fully prove the unbecomeing and indignant conduct of France toward the United States, these degraded Beings would still have their Countrymen "lick the Hand just raisd to shed their Blood." Amongst that number is Freeman of our state, who yesterday appeard a full blood Jacobin in his speech in the House. Landgon in the Senate is more bitter than even Mason or any Virginian. Mr. Otis I am told appeard to great advantage, and was much admired in a speech of considerable Length.

I want to hear from you again. You must write to me once a week. How does Mr. & Mrs. Porter succeed? I will thank you to get from the table draw in the parlour some Annetts and give it to Mrs. Burrel, and tell her to make her cheese a little salter this year. I sent some of her cheese to N York to Mrs. Smith and to Mr. Adams which was greatly admired and I design to have her Cheese brought here. When she has used up that other pray Dr. Tufts to supply her with some more, and I wish Mrs. French to do the same to part of her cheese, as I had some very good cheese of hers last year. In my best chamber closset I left a white Bonnet. Be so kind as to take it and give it for me to Mrs. Norton. In a small wooden Box is a new crape cap which I designd to have sent here, but omitted it untill my other things were gone. Will you get it & fasten it down to the Box by making a small hole or two and then putting a thread through the cap & Box. In my Bathing machine you will find a peice of canvass which will cover the Box. You will have it addrest & give it into Mr. Smiths care, who will send it to me. I have Bacon in Boston which I should be glad to have sent. Mr. Belcher knows about it. Dr. Tufts will pay the expence when requested.

My Respects to Brother Cranch & to Mrs. Welch. Love to Cousin Betsy from your

Ever affectionate Sister   A. ADAMS

"I EXPECTED TO BE VILIFIED AND ABUSED"

To Mary Smith Cranch

MY DEAR SISTER: Philadelphia, June 6, 1797

I received your Letter by this days post. I began to be anxious to hear from my Friends at Quincy. I cannot but say that I was astonishd at some of its contents. I could not believe that any Gentleman would have had so little delicacy or so small a sense of propriety as to have written a mere vague opinion, and that of a Lady too, to be read in a publick assembly as an authority. The Man must have lost his senses. I cannot say that I did not utter the expression, because it has always been my opinion that the people would not be willing to support two ministers, but little did I think of having my Name quoted on any occasion in Town meeting. If he had respected my publick Character only, he would have had some scruples upon that Head, I should have supposed. I shall always consider it as a want of delicacy in him, and a real breach of confidence to make use of my Name on the occasion. I am mortified to find a Gentleman of whom I had formed so favourable an opinion guilty of such a want of decorum. It will however serve as a lesson to me, to be upon my guard, & to be very close mouthed. I have not any remembrance of saying so, tho I think it very probable that I did. By your account of the whole transaction, he has not behaved like a Gentleman. I hope however we shall not be loosers in the end.

I rejoice to hear our Farm looks well. The President is very desirious of seeing it. A journey some where will be absolutely necessary for him. Such close application for so long a period without any relaxation but a ride of a few miles, is too much for him & I see daily by a langour of his countanance that he wants rest. I fear he will not sustain himself unless congress rise so that we may quit this city during the Hot season.

I long for my rose Bush, my clover Field, and the retirement of Quincy, and the conversation of my dear Sister and Friends.

June 8th

To day is post day to Quincy, and yesterday we had the

Chronical. I think impudent as Bache is the Chronical has more of the true spirit of Satan, for he not only collects the Billingsgate of all the Jacobin papers but he adds to it the Lies, falshoods, calimny and bitterness of his own. For what other purpose could he design that paragraph, that the President was to receive one hundred & 14 thousand dollors for four years? The sallery every one knows is the same Nominal sum granted to President Washington without half its value. The 14 thousand dollors is no more the Presidents than the money voted to Rigg one of the Frigates building. Every dollor of it, is laid out for the use of the United States, and accurate Book accounts kept & vouchers taken, all of which will be regularly renderd in at our quitting the House. The son too, of 23 years old receiving this sallery of ten thousand dollors pr year. These salleries are all setled by Law. A Minister Resident has 4 thousand 500 dollors pr year, a Minister plenipotentiary Nine thousand. He is not pickd out to receive more than any other, but his fault is being the son of the President. This wretched party are sinking very fast; but the mischief of these publications arises from their circulating amongst persons and in places where no inquiry is made into facts. Bache will publich on both sides. I wish Mr. Cranch would make a true statement and see if the wretch would publish it. We give for this very House a thousand pounds a year. President Washington never gave more than 500. And every thing else in the same proportion, nay more than double—. But enough of this. I expected to be vilified and abused, with my whole Family when I came into this situation. Strickly to addhere to our duty, and keep ourselves unprejuced, is the path before us and the curse causeless shall not come. I feel most sincerely for Mrs. Greenleaf and her situation. I know it will do no good to look back but you well know how anxious I was when it might have been of use to her. Mr. James Greenleaf it is said, is absconded. Mr. Morris is confind to his House. Each Party criminate the other, as you have no doubt seen by the Washington paper. I regret that there should exist any occasion for it, but know not the state of Facts, to judge between the parties. As soon as it is in my power I will endeavour to render Cousin William some assistance to enable him to purchase some Books. Say nothing about it. I will not forget him.

The time for the post to go out prevents my adding more. Tell Mrs. Howard that I think Betsy is getting better. She begins to look more like flesh and Blood. Nabby has been sick from some imprudence of her own, but is about again, Becky well, but I have a Lad who has been sick a week, and that from eating Ice creeme when he was making it & hot. He brought on such a cramp in His stomack that his Life has been in danger ever since.

Remember me affectionatly to all Friends particuliarly to Dr. Tufts to whom I mean soon to write. My conscience accuses me that I have not.

Your affectionate sister,   ABIGAIL ADAMS

JOHN QUINCY APPOINTED MINISTER TO BERLIN

To John Quincy Adams

MY DEAR SON.   PHILADELPHIA June 15 1797

I have not written a line to you for a long time; yet scarcly an hour of the day passes in which you are not present to my mind; I fear my last Letters were captured the Ships Captain Scott, was taken by the French, you will think me more tardy than I have really been.

by the date of this you will see where I am, it was not my intention to have come here untill the Fall of the Year; I expected your Father would have been able to have returnd to me, and to have relieved himself from the weight of Buisness and care which has oppressed him; by a month or twos relaxation in the rural occupations of his Farm, which are so necessary for his Health of Body and vigor of mind.

But the critical State of our Country as it respects France, the daily and increasing depredations made upon our commerce, and refusal to receive our Minister, were Subjects of so allarming a Nature, as to induce the Executive to convene Congress. This measure left me no alternative. I thought it my duty to risk my Health, and Life in a climate which has heretofore proved injurious to the one; and hazardous to the other, for I could not permit your Father to be left Solitary, wanting my care or aid, after he had commenced Housekeeping.

on the week I was to have sit out on my journey, I was suddenly calld to pay the last sad office of respect to the remains of
your venerable Grandmother. she died on the 21 of April, after
a short illness. her wish was fulfilld which was to be removed
before I left her: She had lived to an advanced Age having enterd her 89th year.

But seldom comes a solitary woe two days after her death, I
was again arrested in my journey by the death of Mary Smith.
She had been in a decline for three months. She had resided at
your Uncle Cranchs for several years. and was a fine girl, with
a very improved mind, her death at the Age of 21, was severely
felt by us all, patient resignd and Submissive, she evinced to all
the justice of the poets sentiment That,

> "Whatever farce the Boastfull Hero plays,
> Virtue alone has Majesty in Death"

These melancholy harbingers following, so closely each other
cast a gloom over every object, and saddend the otherways
Cheerfull Scenes of Nature, which were just waking into Life.
and putting on new verdure after a long and severe winter.

I cannot Name to you the date of your last Letter to me,
having undesignedly left it at Quincy. I know the month was
March. I find here a double pleasure and advantage having
the priviledge of reading *all* your Letters. Your last publick
Letter was March 27th those which I have seen to your Father since I came here, were dated Febry. 3^d 7th & 16th March
4th and 18th. the originals and duplicats have all safely arrived, tho not always in the order of Time, but they never
come too late to communicate authentick information, and
have not been a little instrumental in disolving the facination
which had bewilderd too many of the well disposed of our
Country men.

There are so many occurences of a publick nature which
daily arise that I cannot undertake to detail them to you, that
which more particularly affects you is the Change of your
mission from the Court of Lisbon to Berlin. the reason which
opperated in effecting this Change will be obvious to you, that
of being more usefull to your Country at the present time,
than you could be in Lisbon it was necessary that the Nomination should take place early in the Session, that you might be
prevented an unnecessary voyage. the Senate concured in the

appointment 119 to 9: those who were opposed, Said it was not to the person, but to the mission; it was contended that the constitution gave them no Right to judge of that, that the power lay wholy with the Executive. The Jacobins endeavourd to make use of it, as tho it was an advancement from the Presidentship at the Hague, to a Plenipotentiaryship and being the first nomination, was held up by communications in Baches papers, as a proof of the asspiring views of the President, but this could only impose on a few. the Subject was clearly Stated, but Envy is always malignant. the Faction are not All but their views are perfectly understood.

The next nomination was of Envoys Extrordinary to France. Judge Dana, and Genll Marshal of Virginna are joind with mr Pinckny, these Gentlemen were also opposed by some in Senate, tho a very small Number, 4 against 22. 2 were absent. the reason given was that they were voilently opposed to the French; they would not have been chosen by the Executive if that had been the case. they are true Americans, and as such, will be desirious of setling all differences amicably upon just and equitable Terms, which is the Sincere desire of every real Friend of both Countries. War we deprecate with any power, and peace will be cultivated by every means consistant with our National honour and Independance.

I presume you may have seen a Letter which has been the Subject of much conversation here, and was publishd just before the meeting of Congress, the writer may Say with the poet

> "What Sin to me unknown
> dipd me in Ink"

Mazzei committed a Brach upon a private correspondence when he publishd it, from the Stile of it, and the Sentiments it contains. I presume it was written, about the period when the writer was anxious to connect all political Heriticks to French Faith. I believe it has been republishd in every News paper throughout the united States and is thought, to be genuine, as the writer has never denied it, tho publickly calld upon to do it; you may be sure it has not escaped censure, and will never be forgotten by the Characters traduced. my paper remind me that it will not contain more than the affectionate Regard of your Mother   A ADAMS

COMMISSION TO FRANCE

To John Quincy Adams

MY DEAR   PHILADELPHIA June 23. 1797
     The packet being detaind I write you a few Lines further to inform you that mr Marshal accepts his appointment, but Judge Dana declines on account of his Health The President accordingly has Nominated mr Gerry. the Senate have not yet agreed to it, the N Englanders do not like this Nomination. you are so well acquainted with mr Gerry and with his Sentiments principles and conduct and Services, that I need make no observation to you; you will at first sight conceive the reason why he is opposed by Essex men. they all allow that he is an honest honorable man, but too stiff and inflexable. for myself I believe mr Gerry will have the interest of *his Country* at Heart, and *only that*. we all know that he has on some occasions mantaind his own opinions against the majority, tho he has peaceably and quietly submitted to the Government, and firmly supported it. When it was adopted this Subject of appointments is one of the most difficult and delicat parts of the Executive department. Lewis the 14, it was I believe who used to say, that when he made an appointment, he made 99 Enemies, and one ungratefull man, I hope however he represented Humane Nature worse than it really is, but it is extreemly difficult to give satisfaction. I presume the Senate will not negative Mr. Gerry. it is not a very desirable embassy under present circumstances and pains will be taken to defeat it, and from this Country I have not a doubt, Congress have been in Session ever since the 15 May, and only two Acts have yet been past, and those originated in the Senate.
     In March last I received a very polite Letter from mrs Copley, desiring leave to introduce to me a Friend of ours, one only expression led me to suppose it was a portrait, I Sent to the Captain of the vessel, he knew not of any thing for me, mr Smith went to the custom House, and found a case with D D M upon it, he inquired of mr Rogers if any thing had been sent him for me, he had not received any advice of any thing, mr Smith orderd the case to his House, upon opening

it, we were not any of us at a moments hessitation, I recognized the striking resemblance of my dear absent Son. it is allowd to be as fine a portrait as ever was taken, and what renders it peculiarly valuable to me is the expression the animation the true Character which gives it so pleasing a likeness, and I have been not a little flatterd by strangers saying, they can trace the resemblance of my features in it, I cannot do that myself; but I have those of Thomases, who I never before thought, looked like you. mrs Copleys Letter was designdedly enigmatical, and I know not to this Hour Whether the picture was Sent me by your direction, or whether it comes unknown to you, as a present from her. it is most elegantly Framed, and is painted in a masterly manner. no present could have been more acceptable.

24

The Senate have advised and consented to Mr Gerry 21 yeas to 6. Nays I am sorry to say amongst the six were our two Senators. the other also are all good Men indeed I must regret that they did not give him their vote as all of them allowd him to be a Man, of abilities and integrity. there apprehension was, that by a too rigid opinion upon trivial matters he might obstruct the negotiation; I hope he will not fall into this Error, as he will be carefully guarded against it, he is certainly a man as impartial with respect to the two Nations France & England, as could have been pointed out, and will be as much disposed to conciliate our differences. but the successes of that Nation and their dominering power give them such a weight that all Nations appear to be sinking under their weight

no further Letters from you than those which I mentiond in my last Letter to the 27 March

I believe there is more diversity of Sentiment in Congress than is to be found in any portion of the union—more party Spirit,

I must close however and putt a check upon my pen. if I could write freely I should say many more things to you—I am as ever your & &c &.

EXPECTATION OF WAR WITH FRANCE

To Cotton Tufts

MY DEAR SIR   PHILADELPHIA July 12 1797

Your kind Letter of June 8th gave great pleasure to the President, as well as to your Friend. We were happy to learn so good an arrangement of our domestick concerns, I then hoped to have come to Quincy for a Month or two, Some difficulties arise from the [   ] of that plan, tho it is the place of all others which the President seems most desirious of visiting

We could not be accommodated at [   ] home for want of sufficient stable room we want more Chamber room. an other thing I thought we Should quite put out Porter & Family, as I did not suppose the room which I proposed having done could be finishd in time; I think it will be best to go on and compleat it, and put up a wood House in some other place. the Stables must be got in readiness for an other season, & the more which can be done about them this; the better, as I hope if it please God to spair our Lives to come on early next Spring, it will be best to get the stone for underpinning in the common pasture which is let to Field & Curtis;

All these obsticales would not have been sufficient to have prevented our return if our publick affairs had wore a less dissagreeable Face, but we are critically Situated, that the very next vessel which arrives may bring us a Formal declaration of War. Our Commerce is all sacrificing. if we had been without any intelligence from abroad during the whole Session of Congress, it would have been much shorter and much more decicive. the Mutiny on Board the English Fleet, the fall of English Credit, the troubles in Ireland the peace of the Emperor with France, but above all the victories of Buonaparte, all these Events had their influence and their opperation in various ways, and retarded those measures which in the opinion of the Executive were necessary for the preservation Security and honour of the Nation.

We must wait the event, Mr Marshall will sail from hence in a few days and Mr Gerry who has accepted the appointment with many Family difficultis to encounter; will not delay his departure.

My kind Regards to Mrs Tufts and Miss Suky. I have had an ill turn similar to that which I had at Quincy, but got much sooner over it, and I sustain the Heat much better than I expected, but we came very near losing little John Brisler last night, he was taken with a Cholera Morbus which followd him with such voilence that he fainted and was as if dead for half an hour, he appears some what better now and the disorder has abated—

inclosed is a Post Note for 100 [   ] dollors 30 cents which you will be kind enough to lay out in a certificate. it is a little balance which was found due to the President on a Settlement as Vice President.

I am dear Sir Your affectionate   A ADAMS

"YOUR KIND INVITATION"

To Mercy Otis Warren

MY DEAR MADAM   QUINCY October I^{st:} 1797

I acknowledg myself indebted to you for two kind Letters, both of which found me in circumstances of distress; the first which came to me before I went to Philadelphia, I fully intended to have replied to at the Time, but the many cares and avocations which at that time occupied my mind, preparitory to my going, And the peculiar melancholy circumstance of the death of my Mother and Neice within a day or two of each other, not only arrested me in my journey, but added to the cares with which I had before felt myself opprest. to you therefore, who have so frequently been summoned on like solemn occasions I need make no further appology.

Your Last kind Letter, which I had no right to expect, and was therefore received as a pledge of a Friendship which bears the Stamp of Time, and which I hope will endure with our Lives, however we may discent upon some Subjects, upon that of Mutual good will esteem, and real affection I trust we shall be ever united, and your Letter expressive of it should have met a ready reply, but I was dissabled both with my Eyes and Hands, having met an accident in a carriage which like to have cost me my Life.

I have however recoverd so as to leave only a small scar behind.

Your kind invitation to visit you in the only stile which can ever be agreable to me, that of Hospitality and freedom, would have given both mr Adams and myself great pleasure, a promise which he made to the Secretaries, of not being absent from Quincy more than one day at a Time. that their communications might always find him, has confined him to this place ever since his return, one only visit have I made. and that to my sister in New Hampshire. I fulfilld two duties, that of visiting a very dear Sister, which I had not done before, since her residence & Marriage in that State, and placing my two Grandsons at an accademy there, and in her Family and under her inspection, that they may receive a Genuine New England education which I am Yanky enough to prefer to any other I have yet seen.

We leave this place in a few days, without knowing where we are to Stop, the distrest State of a city which seems devoted to Calamity, and the pestilence which still [   ] there, renders it dangerous to enter it at this Time. and the certain clamour which will be raised if Congress are convened at any other place, renders it difficult for the President to know what is best and most for the Good of the Country, & the safety of its Members, without being much nearer, where a more accurate Statement of Facts can be assertaind.—The Philadelphians will complain & say there is no danger, tho at present their city is deserted of two thirds of its inhabitants

I received a Letter from Mrs Otis a few days since. She with her Family are at Bristol about 18 miles from the city, and were all well.

When I was at providence I took Tea at the late Govenour Bowens, they inquired kindly and particularly after you & your Family, and desired a particular remembrance to you.

The president joins me in an affectionate remembrance to his old Friend the Gen^ll and to mrs Warren both of whom it would have given him pleasure to have seen at Quincy.

I am dear Madam with Sentiments of Regard and esteem Your affectionate Friend ABIGAIL ADAMS

JOHN QUINCY'S MARRIAGE

To Mary Smith Cranch

MY DEAR SISTER: East Chester, October 31, 1797

I have received but one Letter from you since I left Quincy now near a Month. I have been here three weeks, except 3 days which I past at my sons in N York. Next Monday I leave here for Philadelphia, where it is thought we may now go with safety.

I was in hopes to have taken Mrs. Smith with me, but her situation is difficult, not having received any advise what to do, and she is loth to go for the present. I cannot say so much as is in my mind, the subject being a very delicate one, and wishing to have her do no one thing but what may prove beneficial to the whole. Sister Peabody has not yet written to Mrs. Smith, which she regrets. I know how much she has been engaged, and fear the concequences upon her Health. She feels most keenly, and you know by experience what it is to pass through such a Heart rending trial. I wish these repeated summonses to the surviving Brothers might have a serious influence. The sisters are not unmindfull, but William has to me, the air of a too free thinker.

Since I wrote you last I have Letters from my sons abroad, Thomas's late as 17 August. He has consented to go to Berlin with his Brother, who writes that he cannot by any means part with him, especially upon being sent into the center of Germany where "I shall scarcly meet a Countryman twice a year," he says. and Thomas writes me, I intreet you to negotiate a successor to me, for I plainly see untill some such arrangement is made, I shall not be released. He says since I wrote you last, my Brother has been married and given me an amiable and accomplished sister. He is very happy and I doubt not will remain so, for the Young Lady has much sweetness of Temper and seems to Love *as she ought*. Thomas speaks highly of the Family and of their kindness and attention to him, says they are about to embark for America & settle in the city of Washington, where Mr. Johnson has property. They will be an agreable acquisition to the city at which I rejoice for the sake of my Nephew and Neice.

I have nothing of concequence to communicate. This place is as retired as you can imagine. We however keep up a communication with N York and Philadelphia. I had a Letter from Brisler, who was well with the rest of the Family yesterday.

I write merely to keep up our communication, and to tell you that we are all well. I will thank you to go to our House and see that particular attention is paid to the Carpets. I fear they will suffer. Adieu.

Yours affectionatly   A. ADAMS

"I SINCERELY CONGRATULATE YOU"

To John Quincy Adams

EAST CHESTER 20 MILES FROM N YORK Novbr 3^d 1797.
MY DEAR SON

Since my residence at this place, now a month, occasiond by the prevalence of the yellow fever in Philadelphia, I have had the pleasure to receive two Letters from you; one from the Hague June 26th, the other from London July 29th, The joint Letter you mention as having written, is not yet come to Hand.

The News papers before I left Quincy, which was on the 2d of the last Month, had informd us of the Marriage of mr J Q Adams to miss Louissa Johnson upon which the Chronical made as usual, an ill Natured reflection. This induced some friendly Correspondent to place the Subject in its true Light in the Centinal; from whence it made its way into the Albany Gazette, and from that into Porcupines paper from which, as it become a subject of so much importance, I culled it and inclose it to you. For myself I sincerely congratulate you upon the Event, and I hope I may add, my dear Louissa too. I want not the Authority of Milton to pronounce the state, a perpetual fountain of domestic Bliss, to those who like yourself, seek for happiness and pleasure in the Bosom of virtuous Friendship, endeard by those engageing ties, of delicate Sensibility, and Sweetness of disposition, beauty will forever remain attractive, and knowledge delightfull.

It has given me real pain to find that the Change in your Embassy does not meet your ready assent; or that it should be personally so inconvenient to you, as you represent.

I cannot but flatter myself you will find it more agreable than you anticipate; Your Father has written you so fully upon the Subject, and in my mind, obviated every objection, that I think you will feel more satisfied. That you would not have been sent to Berlin at this Time: if mr Washington had continued in office, I fully believe, but I can tell you where you would have been employ'd, as one of the Envoys to France. this was the desire and opinion of all the Ministers, and nothing but your near connexion with the Chief Majestrate prevented your being nominated. he had a delicacy upon the Subject, and declined it. I have one criterion to judge of the utility of the present mission. It is the allarm the Jacobins took at it, but this did not lessen the confidence of the people who value and esteem you for what they know you are, and here I may mention an honour paid you by our Academy of Arts, who at their last meeting unanimously voted you a member. You was nominated at a previous meeting by the Rev'd Dr Belknap as I was inform'd.

The spirit of union and Federalism pervades every part of New England, with very few exceptions I have been assured from all quarters, that there is but one mind and that mind, is in support of our constitution and Government. they know no distinction between the people and the Government, on every occasion and opportunity they have shewn their attachment to the Government, by personal respect to the Chief Majestrate, both by civil and military exhibitions, which however contrary to the taste and inclination, of one, who through Life, has avoided every kind of show and parade; is now obliged to Submit to the *Will of the people.* Some specimins are inclosed. N york has endeavour'd to Rival Boston, In my journey from Philadelphia in the summer I was a feeling witness to some of these scenes, where the sincerity of the Actors renderd it peculiarly interesting, and proved to me that the people will Love & respect their Chief Majestrate, if his administration is that of Wisdom and justice.

The injustice and piratical plunder upon our unarmed Commerce, has wrought conviction upon the minds of many of the former Idolaters of our Gallic Allies, even in the Southern States. That Nation will find itself [   ] deceived if they consider the nearly equal divission of votes at the Election of Chief Majestrate. as a criterion of the voice of the people the people wish for peace. they wish the happiness of all Nations and if no undue Methods had been practised, they would have generally given their Suffrages to that person whom they supposed best qualified to promote and ensure the honour and dignity of the Government, without any respect to English or French partizens. *The Letter writer* is now more generally known and the hollowness of his principles better understood. There is an other tale of a more recent date, yet to be unfolded. You can witness for me, how loth I have been to give him up. It is with much reluctance that I am obliged to look upon him as a Man whose Mind is so warped by prejudice, and so Blinded by Ignorance as to be unfit for the office he holds, however wise and Scientific as a Phylosopher as a politician, he is a Child, and the Dupe of party.

On the 13 of this Month Congress are to meet, but I have not any expectation that they will make a Congress untill December. The yellow fever has been again raviging that poor Devoted City. the mortality has not been so great as in the year 1793, but the city has been deserted 30 thousand inhabitants fled from it very soon after it appear'd. 5 Physicians have fallen Sacrifices to it. It has so far abated as to be thought safe to return to it. I hope it is, as next week we go on.

You will see I date from hence, a Farm purchased by Col S. h. Prudence requires me to be silent. You will however understand me, when I tell you that I took William and John when I went on to Quincy in july, that I have placed them at an Academy in Atkinson and in the Family of your Worthy Aunt Peabody, whose kindness and benevolence are well known to you. your sister is going with her little daughter to pass the Winter with us.—

In one of my Letters I acknowledgd the receipt of the Watch, but unaccompanied by any Bill of the cost. I requested some Sattin, and mentiond sending Bills, but I found you had given orders to your Brother to draw for some money to be laid out for your use. I therefore thought it might be more Eligible to pay the sum to him as your Agent, or to any other person so employd I now request you to send me the amount, as your Brother writes me you have orderd the Silk. I accepted formerly a Cloak as a testimony of your filial regard, but I have no design to tax you with my commissions, nor can I send any more untill you comply with my request. Without any disparagement to your Brother whom I doubt not will do the best he can with your property I would advise you to employ our old tried and Faithfull Friend Dr Tufts whose experience and judgment, will not permit him to run any risks, as I know what money you have must be saved by a rigid œconomy, I wish you might have it placed in safe and productive funds. I have only room left to say to you & yours accept my maternal Blessing.

A A

COLONEL SMITH'S ABSENCE

To Mary Smith Cranch

MY DEAR SISTER: Philadelphia, Novbr. 15, 1797

I yesterday about 11 oclock went into the Presidents Room to see if John had returned from the post office. My good Gentleman was soberly standing at the fire with your Letter open and very gravely reading it. I scolded and very soon carried it of. I thank you for all your communications. The P says one of Sister Cranchs Letters is worth half a dozen others. She allways tells us so much about home. And if he does not get them clandestinely he does not often see them. I wrote you a few lines the day before I left East Chester. On that day Mrs. Smith got Letters from her Brother Justice by a private hand, informing her that both he and the Col had written frequently by the post, and were astonished that she had not received any Letters, that by a private hand he had written and sent her some money in October. The Col was not then at Shenang, the Name of the place which Justice owns, but was expected in a few days. These Letters communicated some comfort. She came to N York with me in search of the Man by whom the money and Letter was sent. Since I have been here, I have had a Letter from her informing me that he had been sought where he formerly lived, but had removed from thence. I have contemplated the plan you mention. It may be put into effect if future circumstances require it. At present, it would be expensive and lonely, and not less subject to unpleasent feelings than being here on a visit, which is all that at present is expected, nor will she be obliged to appear on my publick Evenings, unless it is her choice.

I found Mr. and Mrs. Brisler and the Children very well and much the better for their country excursion. The Girls Becky and Nabby were very well, and both Mr. and Mrs. Brisler say, behaved with great prudence and discretion, quite to their satisfaction. I found every thing in the House in perfect good order, and all my old Hands escaped through the Pestilence. One only of them had the fever. The others returnd as soon as Brisler got home, those whom he had dismisst when he went out, and those he retaind in pay, so that at present I could not wish to be better off than I am with respect to domesticks, which greatly enhances the comfort of Life.

I regret that there should be an opposition to Mr. Whitman, and that it should principly arise from Mr. & Mrs. Black, whom I very sincerely regard, tho I cannot say I respect their judgment in this case. I have not a doubt but Mr. and Mrs. Black will be reconciled in time. Reasoning and not railing will have the effect. Mr. Flint was opposed by the latter. Present my compliments to Mr. Whitman, & tell him if our State constitution had been equally liberal with that of New Jersey and admitted the females to a vote, I should certainly have exercised it in his behalf. As it is, he may be sure both of the Presidents and my good wishes for him, with a sincere desire for his settlement.

I have received one Letter from Sister Peabody written just after the death of Charles, but Mrs. Smith has not had a line from her since her Children have been with her. Sister Peabody has so many cares that she has not much time to write, but I wish she would to Mrs. Smith. In her lonely hours she thinks much of her Children, and wishes to have from her Aunts hand some account of them. I have written her twice since I came from home, beside, one or two Letters just before I left home. I know not if she has received them. I am sorry to learn that Mrs. Cranch is unwell. I have just been writing to him, and I have recommended to her to keep good spirits, and that it is a long lane which has no turn. Ask Cousin Betsy when I am to speak for the weding cap? No Congress yet. A House but no Senate. Ben Bache is as usual abusing the President for *forceing* the respect from the people, degradeing this city by representing the military parade here as all forced. That it is a corrupt mass of Jacobinism, Quakerism and *abominationism*, I will most readily admit, but at the same time there are many worthy and respectable people here. Inclosd is a specimin of Bache Gall. But all will not do. I can see where the respect and attention is sincere. Many affecting proofs I have witnessed in this tour, one in particular of a private nature, at Brunswick. A white headed venerable Man desired to be admitted to the President. When he came in, he bowd respectfully and said he was happy to see him, inquired if that was his Lady? I came, said he, many miles this morning on purpose. I told my wife this morning that I would come, and she said why aint you affraid. No said I. Why do you think I should be affraid to go and see my Father? This was said with so much hearty sincerity, that to me it was of more value than the whole Military calvalcade of Pensilvannia.

Write me often, and remember me affectionatly to all Friends. Yours as ever   ABIGAIL ADAMS

A NEW DAUGHTER-IN-LAW

To Louisa Catherine Adams

MY DEAR DAUGHTER   PHILADELPHIA November 24 1797
    Thus has my Son given me a legal right to address you, I feel also, that I have an affectionate right devolved to me from

him, to stile you thus. it would have given me great pleasure to have embraced you as Such in America, but as it has been otherways ordered, I must Submit to that destiny which has through the greater part of my Life Seperated me from my dearest connections.

I feel a tender Sympathy for you that at this early period of your days, you are seperated from all your Natural connections, and introduced into a new and untried Scene of Life. I should feel still more solisitude, if I had not been assured of your attachment to domestic Life, and of your possessing those mental accomplishments, which need not Seek abroad for entertainment, and those qualities of the Heart which assimulate you by the strongest bonds of affection, to the well Chosen partner of your Heart. long may you live, mutual blessings to each other ameliorating the Rugged path of Life

> with "Every Matron grace combin'd
> Chast deportment, artless Mien
> Converse Sweet, and Heart Serene"

Strengthen the bond of union between us my dear Louissa by a frequent communication by Letters your observations and remarks upon the new Scenes before you and the Manners and customs of Foreign Nations, will both amuse and entertain me, always however keeping in mind, your own public Character, and the Critical Times in which we Live. I recommend to your Sisterly kindness my dear Thomas. I have received from under his Hand a gratefull acknowledgment of the Hospitality of your whole Family towards him—I hope e'er long to welcome them all to America.

Your Father directs me to say for him, that he is already prepared to Love you, from the amiable Character he has received of you from all who know you.

accept my dear Daughter the Sincere Regard of your affectionate Mother   ABIGAIL ADAMS

LETTERS FROM COLONEL SMITH

To Mary Smith Cranch

MY DEAR SISTER: Philadelphia, Novbr. 28th, 1797
   I received your kind Letter of Nov'br. 19th by this days post. I had previously received two others both of which I had replied to, but I do not know how to pass a week without hearing from you. At the same time I received your Letter, I also had one from Mrs. Smith informing me that she had received Letters from the Col of 2d of Nov'br and that he had written her word that he should be home soon. She accordingly gave up the thoughts of comeing to Philadelphia, which is a very great dissapointment to me. I fear she will be waiting & expecting, expecting & waiting, the rest of the winter, but I cannot advise her not to stay a reasonable time. She writes me in anxiety at not hearing a word from her Aunt. Sister Peabody did not use to be inattentive to her Friends. She knows the Boys are well and happy, but she should know that there Mother is not so, and for that reason is the more anxious for her Children, and wishes to have it to say that she hears often from them; for she may be blamed for placing them at such a distance from her, without considering the utility it is of to the Children. I have written repeatedly, so has Mrs. Smith, both to Sister and the Children. Before I left home I wrote & inclosed in one Letter a ten Dollor Bill. I never received any acknowledgment of it. Betsy should write if her Mamma cannot. Pray do you represent the matter to her. I have requested that all Letters may be sent on under cover to the President at Philadelphia, and I will see them forwarded.
   The city of Philadelphia is very Healthy at this time. I have had my Health much better than for several years past. I have not had a single days confinement since I left Quincy. The President took a bad cold by riding with the carriage windows down a very raw day in complasance to the Military, and was confined ten days after we came here, but good Nursing got the better of it. The Senate and House have dispatchd their answers already to the speech. I believe they were asshamd of their delay the last session. What, said the Duke de Liancourt to the President, soon after the

late constitution was adopted in France, do you think of our Constitution? I think, replied the President, who was then Vice President, I think that the Directory are Daniel in the Lions Den. The Directory however, saw their Fate, and having an Army at their beck, banishd the Lions, before they devoured them. But still the Den yawns for them and will sooner or later have them.

The measure of their iniquity is not yet full. They are instruments in the hands of Providence to scourge the nations of the Earth.

29th: Mr. Bartlet from Haverhill attended the Levee. I requested the President to ask him to take a Family dinner with us, which he did, and I was happy to learn by him that he brought Letters to Mrs. Smith, so that I hope her mind is more at ease. I did now however get any, but that, as I hear they are well, I do not so much care for. I will thank you to make my Bacon for me, and when it is fit to smoak let Mr. Belcher carry it to the same place he got the other smoakd at. But I do not want it here. God Willing I will eat it at Home, & stay not an hour here longer than duty requires. I should like to have a Barrel of cheese sent if it can come immediatly. Otherways I fear we shall be frozen up. As to Butter I do not know as I am not there to make it myself I fear it will not be put up so as to keep. I hope Mrs. Pope will not forget me. Pork I should like to have a plenty of that.

I inclose you a 5 dollor Bill. I forgot amongst my pensioners old Mrs. Hayden. Pray send her two, and get some salt peter & molasses with the other to do my Bacon. Will you be so good as to see that Pheby does not suffer for wood or any necessary.

I this moment have received a Letter from your son of 21 Nov'br, a very excellent Letter. He writes me that Mrs. Cranch was better, that Richard had been sick with the Quincy but was better. William had a bad cold. He is doing well I hope. He writes in pretty good spirits. No News of Mr. Johnsons Family tho they saild the 10 of Sepbr. I am under great fears for them.

I think Baxters resolution a good one. The next News I expect the parson will be courting. I am sorry to hear Mrs. Greenleaf has been so unwell. My Love to her and Mrs. Norton. A kind remembrance to all Friends.

Affectionatly your Sister　　　　　　　　　A. ADAMS

COLONEL SMITH RETURNS

To Mary Smith Cranch

MY DEAR SISTER: Philadelphia, Feb'ry 6th, 1798

I was very anxious to receive a Letter from you this morning, and Betsy was wishing yet dreading to hear from her sister. That she yet lives, is some hope for to build upon. Mr. Brisler has just brought your Letter from the office dated 29th Jan'ry. I believe I have written you every week, but fancy the Ice may have prevented the post from arriving. I wish Polly was where you could often see her. I have a great opinion of cabbage leaves. I would apply them to her feet, to her neck & to her Head. You know how opprest she always was at her Lungs if any thing ailed her. I want to be doing something for her. Tell her I am very anxious for her and hope she may yet recover. But great care and tenderness is necessary or she will be lost. Pray take care. But why should I ask what I am sure is always done. Pray tell Mr. Cranch to take great care of himself, and, my dear Sister, my cellar is always open to you. Do not let so good a man want wine to make his Heart glad, when you know where it can be had with a hearty welcome. I have written to Dr. Tufts to get my Room & chamber new painted and that as soon as it can be done in March the closset floor & the entrys and stairs. They will have time then to dry sufficiently. I had a letter on Saturday from Mrs. Smith. The Col returnd last week and has notified his Credittors to meet him in order to adjust with them his affairs. I cannot suppose that he has it in his power to satisfy the demands they have, but if he can settle so as to be able to do any buisness in future it will be a great relief to my mind as well as to hers. But I am affraid of vissions, of Ideal Schemes &c. At any rate I am glad he has returnd. It really seemd to me at times, as if Mrs. Smith would lose herself. She has sometimes written me that existance was a burden to her; and that she was little short of distraction. I have been more distresst for her than I have been ready to own. You know she always kept every thing to herself that she could, but she writes in better spirits, and is at least relieved from that worst of States, I think, a constant anxious expectation, and anticipation.

I have had Letters from my sons abroad to October. They were then well, but none since they left London. I hope they are safe at Berlin long before this time. You saw a Letter or rather an extract of a Letter in the Centinal from [   ] dated as if written at Paris about a fortnight since in order the better to disguise the source. It is probable you may see publishd from Fennos paper some observations upon the operation of the French constitution as exemplified in the transactions of the 4 Sep'br by the same hand.

You complain of always having a share of Rhumatism. That is just my case. I have it floting about, sometimes in my head, Breast, Stomack &c, but if I can keep of fever I can Parry it so as not to be confined. Dr. Rush is for calling it Gout, but I will not believe a word of all that, for Rhumatism I have had ever since I was a Child. When I feel any thing like fever, nitre in powder of about 6 Grains with a 6 part of a Grain of tarter Emetic & a 6 part of a Grain of Calomil in each taking 3 powders in a day, generally relieves me.

Inclosed is a ten dollor Bill out of which be so good as to give two to the widow Green, Mr. Pratts Mother, and to pay Sister Smith for the stockings knit, and supply her with Cotton. Buy Pheby a load of wood if necessary. I know you Love to be my almoner. I wish it was in my power to do more abundantly. If there is any thing in the way of oranges, Milk, Bisquit &c, which will be for Pollys comfort do be so kind as to procure it for her and send to her for me.

I hope captain & Mrs. Beal are recoverd and that Mr. & Mrs. Black are well. I pray you to remember me to Brother Adams & Family when you see them. My Love to Mrs. Norton, to Mrs. Greenleaf, & respects to Mrs. Welch. From your ever

Affectionate Sister   ABIGAIL ADAMS

When you see Mrs. Pope, ask her about the Butter, the quantity & price. I should wish to pay for it, as well as two or three of her Cheses.

PRESIDENTIAL APPOINTMENTS

To William Smith

Dear Sir   Philadelphia 6th. Febry. 1798

I received your Letter of Janry. and observed your communication, somewhat alterd to better suit the Times. I thought the alteration not amiss. The paper you inclosed to me I put into the Hands of the President. He could not apply the Character as he did not recollect that any such person had applied. I had an opportunity of shewing it to the Secretary at War. He was at no loss, and mentiond a circumstance of one Gentleman who had put his Name to a paper in recommendation of that same person, who had written a private Letter giving his reasons for so doing, but at the same time recommending an other person as much more suitable for the place. Gentlemen who recommend to office, should consider that as far as their recommendation has an influence, they are answerable to their Country for the proper discharge of the trust, and that in very many instances recommendations are the only grounds upon which the Executive can act, for it is impossible to have a personal knowledge, in a Country so extensive, as this, and tho it may be the wish and desire of the Executive to appoint to office only such persons as will faithfully discharge the trust reposed in them he may frequently, by the facility with which respectable people are led to recommend those who apply to them for office, give to those from whom he would withold, if he had a personal knowledge of them, and after all the bluster and racket which has been made by those who would readily expose all power to themselves, concerning Executive patronage, it is attended with much trouble and great anxiety. Louis the 14 once observed, that when he appointed a man to office, he made 99 Enemies and one ungratefull person, for every person who applies considers his own claims at the best, and his own pretensions the strongest. Since I have been here, I have known a member of Congress quit his seat and go home, vowing he would not return again, merely for being dissapointed in a recommendation which he gave. The Jacobins think they have little Chance, and are therefore for taking from the President the power vested in him by the constitution. The Question has not yet been determined respecting the foreign intercourse Bill as it is termd, that gives place to a very dirty Buisness which has already occupied the house 3 days, and is like to continue 3 days longer for ought I see. Yet it is a subject which as Gentlemen I should suppose might have been setled in one day. The papers will give you a statement of the Buisness. Mr. Griswold is a very respectable Member from the State of Conneticut, a Gentleman of strong sensibility and high spirit, but very fortunately on this occasion so far respected the House and the decorum due to it whilst sitting that he restraind his uplifted Hand, and with held the blow he was just going to lay upon Lyon. Party, party Spirit enters into this degrading buisness, and it is thought that 2 thirds of the House will not vote for the expulsion of this unclean Beast; you will find on the Nay side citizen Nickolas and citizen Jacobins from our own state I doubt not.

Not a word yet from our Envoys. Either they are held in durance vile, or their dispatches are intercepted. Knowing how great the anxiety of our Country must be, I am certain they would take early and constant measures to inform their Government. Mr. Murrey writes in one of his dispatches, that he learnt that no communication was permitted them with any citizen of France, that they were not allowd even to speak to them. This being the case, no communicatioons can be made but such as our good Allies chuse.

You will see in Fennos paper of the 5 and 6th. of Febry. "observations upon the operation of the French Constitution &c. written by the same Hand as those which I sent you before. You will judge of the propriety of having them published in Boston. The people of N England generally read more, and judge better than they do here, where so many discordent particles are jumbled together as in this city. As you take the papers I do not think it worth while to inclose them to you.

Mr. Otis got in this morning and will add one to the respectable Number of Federilist, but it is a sad thing to have such a— worse than dead weight attachd to them, benumbing every active measure, and opposing every dignified proposition.

My kind regards to Mrs. Smith and Children, to the Doctor and Mrs. Welch and to all other inquiring Friends. The

President request me to ask you for what you can purchase a genuine pipe of old Maderia wine. You will not forget a hundred Bushels oats for us, even tho you give 2/6 pr Bushel. The P.t will send you an order upon Genll. Lincoln for any sum of money you may lay out for him.

When any vessel is about to sail for Hamburgh or Bremin, will you be so good as to send Mr. Adams the latest papers addrest to the care of the different consuls. He complains much for want of intelligence from his Country. I fear he will get less now than ever.

Let Dr. Welch know that the Gentleman mentiond by him is placed upon the List of applicants.

There are Letters from Mr. King as late as October and from Mr. Murrey to the 10 Novbr. They are as much in the dark with respect to our Envoys as we are here. If the French are seriously bent upon a decent upon England, no doubt an Embargo has taken place. There will nothing be done in Congress I fear untill we receive dispatches, and whether then any measures for defence can be carried is by some doubted. The Spirit must come from the East and from the North. Pray my dear sir, do all in your power to promote the choice of true federilist from our state at the next Election. Do not send Men who would bear to have their faces spit in, or countanance it in others. This constant uphill work is enough to discourage every Man who has not the strength of Hercules and might be set down for an Eigth Labour. My paper admonishes me to subscribe Yours &c., A A

INVESTMENTS

To Cotton Tufts

My dear Sir   Philadelphia Febry. 6th. 1798
I have not had the pleasure of receiving a Line from you for some time. I laughd at my Friend not long since when he sent a Letter to you the contents of which he appeard to be very private about. I told him I knew it was the Farm he had written about, and that he would not tell me because he knew I was

averse to encumbering ourselves as we grew older with more cares. It is not my wish to add to our landed property without we were sure of a fund to improve it, and if my inclination was followd it would be to put all our [　] into deferd Stock. But you must follow your directions. I shall however when I can lay by any thing do it, and tho it may be but a triffel, I shall apply it to that fund which if I should live will prove usefull to me. If I do not, it will not be lost to the Family. I inclose to you two Hundred dollors. One hundred you will apply to my Stock. The other, you will use to compleat the out house as soon as work can be done. Let the Building upon the back designd for a dairy Room be large enough to take of a part as a closset or store Room. Might it not be so constructed as to have a half cellar for milk and a cheese Room over it? The small House at the end of the out house I proposed to Mr. Porter to dig a vault for and stone it, and remove it upon it. A wood house might then extend from the out house to the end of the Garden fence leaving a passage to the small House through the wood House. I do not see any prospect of accomplishing my views in a Building in addition to our House untill I return and consult further about it, but I must have the out house so that our families may not interfere and I should be glad to have our dinning parlour painted as soon as it can be done together with the closset, stairs and entrys. I could wish an experienced person to do it, that particular attention may be paid to the wainscoat over the Chimny by white washing or otherways making it fit for to receive the paint that it may dry. If March should be a pleasent Month, the sooner it is done the better for drying, and my Chamber I would have new painted at the same time.

I believe as this is wholy upon Buisness of a private nature, I must omit politicks particuliarly as the most important matter now under discussion is occasiond by the Brutal conduct of that wild Irishman Lyon, who as you will see stated in the papers, spit in the face of a man whose shoes he was not worthy to clean, but notwithstanding the insult, one of the greatest that could be offerd a Gentleman. Mr. Griswold so far respected the House as to restrain his anger. Yet will there not be found impartial men enough in the House to expell the wretch, it requiring two thirds. O tis a pityfull buisness.

My kind regards to Mrs. Tufts and to Miss Warner as well as to your son and daughter from dear Sir your ever affectionate
Abigail Adams

You will note to me that the Letter and contents come safe to Hand. Can you secure us a hundred Bushels of oats? We shall want that quantity and more. I do not often give currency to Baches papers, but it is the most accurate account of the proceedings of yesterday. I send you a report of the proceedings of the college of Physicians. As they will not allow that the pestilence which lays waste so many of the inhabitants is of domestic origion, so will they annually be exposed to its ravages. I shall hope for an early escape from the city, but I fear these French men will keep us in fire one way or other.

CELEBRATION OF WASHINGTON'S BIRTHDAY

To Mary Smith Cranch

MY DEAR SISTER: Philadelphia, Feb'ry 15, 1798
    I have not received a Line from you since the last of Jan'ry. Betsy is much distresst to hear from her sister and I am not a little anxious. I hoped the twesday post as usual would have given me some information. I must attribute it to the weather. For, my dear Sister, write me a line every post if only to tell me how you all are. You will see much to your mortification, that Congress have been fitting, not the French, but the Lyon, not the Noble British Lyon, but the beastly transported Lyon. I am of the Quakers mind whom Peter Porcupine quotes. Speaking of the Irish, he says, "There is no mediocrity, or medium of Character in these people: they are either the most noble, brave, generous and best Bred: or the most ruffian like dirty and blackgaurd of all the creation." What a picture will these 14teen days make upon our Journals?! Yet are the supporters of Lyon alone to blame: *the Gentlemen* the real federilist would have expeld him instantly, and if it were possible a federilist could be found thus to have degraded himself, he would not have cost the Country 14 days debate, besides the

infamy and disgrace of sitting again there. I inclose you a paper containing a speach or two upon the subject. The Brute has not been in the house for several days, but he is unfealing enough to go again, and if he does, I have my apprehensions of something still more unpleasent.

These Philadelphians are a strange set of people, making pretentions to give Laws of politeness and propriety to the union. They have the least feeling of real genuine politeness of any people with whom I am acquainted. As an instance of it, they are about to celebrate, not the Birth day of the first Majestrate of the union as such, but of General Washingtons Birth day, and have had the politeness to send invitations to the President, Lady and family to attend it. The President of the United States to attend the celebration of the birth day in his publick Character of a private Citizen! For in no other light can General Washington be now considerd, how ever Good, how ever great his Character, which no person more respects than his Successor. But how could the President appear at their Ball and assembly, but in a secondary Character, when invited there, to be held up in that light by all foreign Nations. But these people look not beyond their own important selves. I do not know when my feelings of contempt have been more calld forth, in answer to the invitation. The President returnd for answer, "that he had received the card of invitation, and took the earliest opportunity to inform them, that he declined accepting it."—That the Virginians should celebrate the day is natural & proper if they please, and so may any others who chuse. But the propriety of doing it in the Capital in the *Metropolis* of America as these Proud Phylidelphians have publickly named it, and inviting the Head of the Nation to come and do it too, in my view is ludicrious beyond compare. I however bite my Lips, and say nothing, but I wanted to vent my indignation upon paper. You must not however expose it, nor me. It will be call'd pride, it will be calld mortification. I despise them both, as it respects myself, but as it respects the Character I hold—I will not knowingly degrade it—

Let me know whether a Letter coverd to Mr. Cranch for Dr. Tufts has reachd you safely. We are all as well as usual. The Baby was here on Sunday and is very well. Remember me kindly to all Friends.

Your ever affectionate Sister   A. ADAMS

To Mary Smith Cranch

MY DEAR SISTER: Philadelphia, March 5th, 1798

I received on Saturday Evening the 3d March your kind Letter of 25 Feb'ry. You estimate much too highly the little services I am able to render to my Friends, and you depreciate the value of your own, the benifit of which I have too often experienced to sit lightly by them, for whilst you visit the widow, the orphan, the sick, and console them by your presence, enliven them by your conversation & prescribe for their necessities, you prove that it is possible to be very benevolent and Charitable tho with small pecuniary means. When you do all the good in your power, you enjoy all the happiness the practise of virtue can bestow, and long may you receive the Reward.

Your son has been with us near a fortnight. I feel very loth to part with him. He must leave us, he says, tomorrow. I believe he has just received Letters from Mrs. Cranch. I will stop and ask him how she is.

I have read Nancys Letter. She and the Children are both well. It is dated the 27 Feb'ry. She is very anxious for her Brother, which is very natural. I know not how she could be otherways, for tho unfortunate benevolence has been a striking trait in his Character—Mr. and Mrs. Law have been three weeks in this city. You know he married Miss Custos, who seems to inherit all the benevolence of her Grandmother. She is a charming woman. The more I see of her the more amiable she appears. She is to spend the day with me tomorrow, in the family way, for which she seems to be found. I loved her the more for the friendly manner in which she expresses her Regard for your son and for Mrs. Cranch and Betsy Eliot who she says, she misses very much. Mrs. Law is so easy, so tranquil, so unaffected, that her first appearence preposseses you in her favour, so different from most of the formal Ladies of this city. Yet there is sociality enough here amongst some of them. I always however sit it down when I meet with it, that N. England comes in for some share of it. I have visited sometimes & sit half an hour in company in some families with whose reception and manners I have been particuliarly gratified. Upon making inquiries of my intellingenser, Dr. Rush, who knows everybody and their connections, I discover that Grandfather or Mother or some relative originated from N. England. Two Nations are not more different than the N. Englanders and many Natives of this city. I must not however be too local. Which has the preference I have not said—

You will learn that at length dispatches have arrived from our commissoners, but with them, no prospect of success. We have letters to the 9 Janry. I inclose you the paper which contains the message from the President with the Letter to both Houses of Congress. We shall now see how the American pulse beat. I fear we shall be driven to War, but to *defend* ourselves is our duty. War the French have made upon us a long time.

I cannot learn what is become of Mr. Beal. Is he not yet got to Quincy?

Let Mrs. Black know that the Nurse and Baby were with me yesterday. It had had a bad cold but was better. We put on the cap and it lookd very pretty. I gave the Nurse the 5 dollors sent by Mrs. Black for which she was very thankfull, and says Mrs. Black may assure herself that she shall take the best care of the child. She told our people Mrs. Brisler and Betsy, that Mr. Black complaind a good deal of the expence, but she could not keep it for less. She had to give at the rate of 15 dollors pr cord for wood, which I know to be true, and that she could not do any other buisness than look after the two Children. She seems to think that carrying the Children by water when the weather becomes pleasent will be less fatigue to them than by land, but this for a future days consideration. Louisa desires the letter to her sister may be sent to her if she is gone to Atkinson. Thank Mr. Cranch for his kind Letter. I would have the floor painted in the kitchin & the stairs a plain yellow unless the floor is too thin. I believe it is much worn, the closset too. The best time for painting is when there can be time enough for it to dry without any persons treading upon it, and that makes me earnest to have it done quite early, and with boild oil. I should be glad if Mr. Billings would new lay the wall against the Garden as soon as the frost is out the Ground. Be so good as to desire

Mr. Porter to lay in a load of Charcoal. Dr. Tufts will give him money to pay for it. We cannot do without it when we are there. I hope too he will get wood enough home. I must get you to have an Eye to the painting or I fear it will not be done to my mind. As soon as the season will permit I would have persons enough employd to compleat what is to be done. And my strawberry bed Stutson must attend to very soon in the Spring. I should not like any other person should touch it. As to the rest of the Garden, I must look to Tirril to do it, I suppose. But more of this an other time. I had rather prepare to come Home than to go from it. Adieu, my dear Sister,

Most affectionately yours   A. ADAMS

Foreign intercourse the Question upon Nicolas motion was taken to day & regected by the 52 Gentlemen. 44 in favour of it. 3 federilist absent.

FASHION TRENDS

To Mary Smith Cranch

MY DEAR SISTER: Philadelphia, March 14th, 1798

Yesterday dispatches were received from Mr. King up to the 9th Jan'ry. In a post scrip he says, I have just learnt that Mr. Adams has been received by the new King notwithstanding his commission was to his Father. This is civil and will enable him to proceed with buisness. I received a Letter from Dr. Tufts yesterday that allarmd me. I thought I inclosed him some Bills. I might, as I wrote you the same time have put them into yours, for the Dr. in a post scrip says that you had written him that you had them. When the Dr. writes to me inclose his Letters in yours, for as those are *held sacred* now by a promise not to open them, I shall receive them, in a way I wish. The Dr. and I have some buisness transaction which are between ourselves.

Nothing new transpires but what your Boston papers have; warm words in congress must be apprehended, whilst some are for going shares with France submitting intirely to her will and quietly disposed to receive every lash she pleases to inflict. Northern Blood boils, and I do not know what will take place. I hope they will be cooler to day, but Giles has just opend his batteries.

Pray, is Betsy going to steal a wedding upon us? She inquires the fashions. They are as various as the Changes of the moon. The young Ladies generally have their Hair all in Curls over their heads, and then put a Ribbon, Beads, Bugles or a Band of some kind through the fore part of the Hair to which they attach feathers. The Band is put upon Ribbon, sometimes on wire. Frequently two are worn which cross each other. They tye behind over the hind Hair & then a small Bunch of Hair turns up behind in which a small comb is fixd and the ends of the hind Hair fall Back again in curls. The Gounds are made to have only one side come forward and that is confind with a belt round the waist. The waist made plain. Some sleaves are drawn in diamonds, some Robins drawn up & down with bobbin in 5 or 6 rows. In short a drawing room frequently exhibits a specimin of Grecian, Turkish, French and English fashion at the same time, with ease, Beauty and Elegance equal to any court—What a medley are my Letters. I had yesterday to visit me after the Presidents Levee, the Kings of 3 Indian Nations. One of them after sitting a little while rose and addrest me. He said he had been to visit his Father, and he thought his duty but in part fulfilld, untill he had visited allso his Mother, and he prayd the great spirit to keep and preserve them. They all came and shook me by the Hand, and then took some cake and wine with me. There were nine of them. One of them spoke English well. They then made their bow and withdrew, much more civil than the Beast of Vermont. Adieu, my dear Sister.

I am most affectionatly yours   A. ADAMS

PUBLISHING DISPATCHES FROM FRANCE

To Mary Smith Cranch

MY DEAR SISTER: March 20th, 1798

I write you a few Lines this mor'g just to inclose to you the Newspaper of yesterday which contains an important Message from the President. It is a very painfull thing to him that he cannot communicate to the publick dispatches in which they are so much interested, but we have not any assurance that the Envoys have left Paris and who can say that in this critical state of things their dispatches ought to be publick? Our foreign Ministers can never be safe, or they will cease to be usefull to us abroad, if their communications are all to be communicated. This was not the case during our revolution. Under the old Congress, dispatches were never made publick. I expect the President will be represented as declaring War, by taking off the restriction which prevented Merchantmen from Arming. It was always doubtfull in his mind, whether he had a Right to prevent them, but the former President had issued such a prohibition, and he thought it best at that time to continue it. You see by the papers that Bache has begun his old bilingsgate again, because Mr. J. Q. Adams is directed to renew the treaty with Sweeden which is now just expiring, and for which not a single sixpence will be allowd him as the King of Sweeden will empower his Minister at Berlin to renew it there. Dr. Franklin made the treaty in Paris with the Sweedish minister, and the President made the Treaty with Prussia in Holland, yet this lying wretch of a Bache reports that no treaties were ever made without going to the courts to negotiate them, unless the power where they were made, were concernd in them, and says it is all a job in order to give Mr. Adams a new outfit & additional sallery at every Court. But there is no end to their audaciousness, and you will see that French emissaries are in every corner of the union sowing and spreading their Sedition. We have *renewed information* that their System is, to calumniate the President, his family, his administration, untill they oblige him to resign, and then they will Reign triumphant, *headed by the Man of the People.* It behoves every pen and press to counteract them, but our Countrymen in general are not awake to their danger. We are come now to a crissis too important to be languid, too dangerous to slumber— unless we are determind to submit to the fraternal embrace, which is sure and certain destruction as the poisoned shirt of Danarius. Adieu my dear Sister. I intended only a line but I have run to a great length. We have had snow and rain for three days. What has been your Weather? Love and a kind remembrance to all Friends from

Your ever affectionate Sister   ABIGAIL ADAMS

"RENEWED INSULTS"

To Mary Smith Cranch

MY DEAR SISTER: Philadelphia, March 27, 1798

I received yesterday your kind Letter of March 19th, I expect a Letter every week if you have nothing else to say, but as Sterne observes, "how the Shadows Lengthen, as the Sun declines." And this may be applied to the Moral as well as the Natural System. As we descend the Hill of Life, our gay and vissonary prospect vanish, and what gilded our Meridian days, our Zenith of Life, as the Shadows lengthen, we see through a different medium and may justly estimate many of our persuits, as vanity and vexation of spirit.

"But theres a Brighter world on high" which opens to us prospects more permanant, and pleasures more durable. To that let us aspire in the sure and certain hope, that by a patient Continuence in the path of Religion and Virtue, we shall assuredly reap, if we faint not, the happy fruits of a glorious immortality.

When I took my pen this morning, with the rising Sun, I did not think of moralizing thus, but the visions of the Night had left an impression upon my mind, and those visions were occasiond by reflections upon the dangerous and Hazardous situation into which our Country is brought, by that demoralizing, wicked and abandoned Nation, or Government of France. When no sacrifice on their part was required, when justice and Equity is all we wanted, when two repeated offers of accommodation have been generously offerd to them, they turn a Deaf Ear and refuse to listen either to the voice of Reason, or the call of Honor; but answer only by renewed insults and more audacious plunder. In this situation our Country is calld upon to put themselves in a *state of defence*, and to take measures to protect themselves by Sea. This is calld a declaration of war on the part of the President, by those who would gladly see their Government prostrate, Religion banishd and I do not know if I should judge too hardly if I said our Country Shared by France. That war will not be the concequence of the conduct of France towards us is more than I can say; it certainly leads to it, as the most probable Event. But the President did not make our difficulties, nor has the Government. No Nation has more strictly adhered to nutrality, none sufferd so much, none bourn with more patience the spoiling of their Property.

Union is what we want, but that will not be easily obtaind. It is difficult to make the people see their danger, untill it is at their doors, or rouse untill their country is invaded. The Senate are strong. They are much more united in their measures than the House. There is an attempt in this city to get a petition signed to congress declaring their determination not to go to war with France, and they hope to sit this measure in opperation through the different States. Is it possible that any person can suppose this Country wish for war by which nothing is to be obtaind, much to be expended and hazarded, in preference to Peace? *But in self defence* we may be involved in war; and for that we ought to be prepared, and that is what the President means. What benifit can war be to him? He has no ambition for military Glory. He cannot add by war, to his peace, comfort or happiness. It must accumulate upon him an additional load of care, toil, trouble, malice, hatred, and I dare say Revenge. But for all this he will not sacrifice the honor and independance of his Country to any Nation, and if in support of that, we are involved in war, we must & we ought to meet it, with firmness, with Resolution & with union of Sentiment.

I shall sigh for my retirement at Peace Feild, before I shall reach it. If I can leave here in May, I shall be content, but I cannot say positively. The Roads will not be tolerable untill then; I should like to have what I proposed done as soon in the season as it can be with advantage.

The President says you may keep a Cow at the Farm through the season.

I had a Letter from your son two days after he got home. He found little William had been dangerously sick with a fever, but he was on the recovery. And he mournd the loss of a very valuable Friend a Mr. Deakins who dyed in his absence, a Man possessd of a most estimable Character in whom he says he had found an other Father. Mr. and Mrs. Law returnd last week. I really think she is a truly worthy woman.

I inclose to you a News paper because it contains a speech of Mr. Reads upon the foreign intercourse Bill. It contains as much good sense and is more to the point than the three & four hours Harangues of some others. Mr. Read very seldom speaks.

What, have I got so near the End of my paper before I was aware. I have more to say yet, but Louisa warns me to Breakfast, and I bid you adieu for the Present.

Affectionatly yours   A. ADAMS

"WE HEAR NOTHING OF OUR ENVOYS"

To John Quincy Adams

My dear Son   Philadelphia March 29th. 1798

I embrace every opportunity to write to you which I know of. The present I heard of but yesterday. I hope some of my Letters will reach you if others fail. I know you must be very anxious for the situation of our Country, and for the state of politicks. I can only be general, and say to you, that the people are daily becomeing more firmly decided, and united, more disposed to repel insult with due energy, and having failed in attemps to negotiate, I think they will unite to defend our Country and protect our commerce, and if we are driven to the last resort, you will not find your Countrymen more disposed to submit to the domination and usurpation of France, than they formerly were to the unjust demands of Great Britain. War with any power they deprecate, but they deprecate more dishonour, submission and abject slavery. There is more of party spirit, and Jacobinism in the Anti federal members of Congress, than you will find in the Country at large. The Senate are firm and strong. An attempt for an Embargo was tried there this week, and rejected by 22 to 4.

Congress I think will agree to put our Country in a state of defence and to protect our commerce and that speedily.

I send you two pamphlets and some papers. I shall write you again by the April packet. We hear nothing of our Envoys having left France.!!! We are impatient for their return.!!! There last accounts were in Janry. in which they say, they had not been received, and had not any hopes that they should be. It is now the last of March, and they are not returnd!!!

We have not received any dispatches of a publick or private Nature from Berlin, except those which I noticed in a former Letter of Novbr. 10 and 17th. to the Secretary of State. We are anxious to hear from you.

We are in Health and I think in pretty good spirits. We trust our Cause and our Country to the Great Arbiter of Nations and Kingdoms.

Your Father presents you his blessing and his affectionate remembrance to you and yours. Your Brother is not omitted in the benidiction. I cannot now write to him. I hope my dear Louisa hears from her parents and sisters. I had a Letter last week from T. B. Johnson at George Town. The family are anxious to hear from you. All that I learn I communicate to them.

The Spanish minister de Yrujo is this week to be married to Miss McKean daughter to the Chief Justice of this State.

I had Letters from your sister this week. She was well. So was your Brother Charles and family, and our Quincy Friends.

Mr. Harper continues making good speaches. I shall have them in a few days in a pamphlet. I will send them.

I am my dear son most affectionatly your Mother,

A Adams

SINGLE WOMEN

To Thomas Boylston Adams

My dear Son   Philadelphia April 4th. 1798

To know that one Cannot freely say that Black, is Black; even tho it be "darkness visible," or that white is white, tho the new fallen snow is not purer, is fettering ones faculties, as well as restraining ones pen. Yet in such perilious Times as the present, freely to discuss motives which lead to measures, or to Characterize the Actors "who fret and strut their hour upon the stage" would not be prudent in me Considering where I stand. In writing to your Brother, and to you, I am constantly considering what I may not write. Accordingly my Letters can afford you but little information or entertainment. Our publick affairs grow too serious to be speculated upon; Of one thing however you may rest assured, that the present Helms Man will quit his Station Sooner than sacrifice the honour, interests, and independance of our Country to any Foreign Nation or power, and He who is resolved to hazard his existance, rather than abandon those objects, must have a superiour advantage over those who are resolved to yeald rather than carry their resistance beyond a certain point. If we do not oppose even by force the Fraternal embraces of our Allies, they will prove as fatal to us as the poisoned Shirt of Dejanire. Happy for us that old ocean rolls between us.

You cannot wonder that I wait with impatience to hear from you. I chide the tardy vessels, and abhor the piratical search.

I wrote to you a week since by a Mr. Millar from this city who has saild for Hamburgh and who gave us some reason to hope that he would visit Berlin before his return; he is the son of a Mr. Magnus Millar of this place Merchant.

Some of your old acquaintance here remember you with affection; and kindly inquire after you. Miss Wescot is yet unmarried and very lovely still. Miss Wilson is in ill Health, and much dejected with the embarrassments of her Fathers affairs which wholy prevent him from residing here. She is an amiable Girl. Many of those whom you knew as Children, have in the course of three years, come forward into society since you left this city, and in the drawing Room is frequently to bee seen an assemblage of as much Beauty and elegance, as is to be met with in any foreign Court.

My Son keep thy Heart with all diligence, not doubting but there is in reserve for you a Crown! a Crown! Doth not the Scripture say, a virtuous woman is a Crown to her Husband!

With the tenderest solisitude For your happiness I am most affectionatly your Mother,   A Adams

Louissa and other Friends desire to be rememberd. Your Brother and Sister were well.

"SOLD TO THE FRENCH"

To Mary Smith Cranch

MY DEAR SISTER: Philadelphia, April 13, 1798
    I inclose a Letter to Cousin Betsy, who has been very frank with me upon the subject of her approaching connection. I hope they will live to enjoy mutual happiness.

    I believe I have been deficient in not mentioning to you that Mr. Greenleaf was liberated from Prison on Saturday week. I have not seen him. Mr. Malcomb was present at Court and heard the examination. He returnd quite charmed with Mr. Greenleafs manners and deportment, tho not so with the counsel against him, who he said used Mr. Greenleaf in a very ungenteel manner but still Mr. Greenleaf did not forget what belongd to himself, by which means he obtaind many advocates.

    I know my dear Sister you will rejoice that I can hear from my Children publickly, that is officially, tho I have not received any Private Letters. Mr. King writes that he has put on board a vessel bound to Liverpool Letters from Mr. Adams to his Family. That vessel I presume waits to sail under the convoy granted. The Secretary of State has received by the British packet duplicates of Letters from Mr. Adams at Berlin dated 6 December in which he writes that he was received by the New King of Prussia on the 5th of December, that the King had waved the common ussage with respect to him, considering the distance of the United States, and received him. Upon presenting his Credentials, he assured the King that he had no doubt that new ones would be sent him, and that he doubted not he should be warranted by his Government in assureing him of the interest the United States take in his welfare and prosperity, and that he should but fulfill their wishes by reiterating to him the sentiments of Friendship and good will which he had in Charge to express to his Royal Father and Predecessor. To which his Majesty answerd, that he was much gratified by the mark of attention which the United States had shown to the Government, and wished to assure him of his recipriocal good will, and good wishes for their happiness and prosperity, that the similarity of the commercial interests of the two

Countries renderd the connection between them important, and might be productive of mutual benifit. On the same Evening Mr. Adams had an Audience of the Queen Mother.

This is rather different from the treatment which our Envoys meet with from the 5 Kings in France. The publick opinion is changeing here very fast, and the people begin to see who have been their firm unshaken Friends, steady to their interests and defenders of their Rights and Liberties. The Merchants of this city have had a meeting to prepare an address of thanks to the President for his firm and steady conduct as it respects their interests. I am told that the French Cockade so frequent in the streets here, is not now to be seen, and the Common People say if Jefferson had been our President, and Madison & Burr our Negotiators, we should all have been sold to the French—It is evident that the whole dependance of the French is the devision amongst ourselves. Their making such a Noise & pretending to be very wroth at the Presidents speech, is designd only to effect a Change in the chief Majestracy. They dare not openly avow it, but the declaration that all vessels should be subject to capture which had passports on board signd with the Presidents signature is one amongst the many personal insults offerd, but they have sprung a mine now which will blow them up. They have discoverd a greedy appetite to swallow us all up, to make us like the Hollanders, to cut us up like a capon, and deal us out like true Gamesters.

I sent and bought Kings Pantheon as soon as I found myself foild in my recollection.

I shall write to your son tomorrow. I have not heard lately from him.

I don't care whether Mrs. Pope puts me down any butter, if she will only let me have fresh when I come home. I could never find any body who would take the pains which she does, and make so good Butter in the heat of summer.

My Love to Mrs. Norton & Greenleaf. To each I have sent a cimplicity cap. Respects to Mr. Cranch & Mrs. Welch, from

Your truly affectionate Sister   ABIGAIL ADAMS

CARING FOR AN ORPHAN

To Esther Black

My Dear Madam   Philadelphia Sunday mor'g April 15 1798
   The sooner Mr. Black comes to Philadelphia, the better it
will be for the Child. As I was yesterday dressing for dinner the
Nurse desired to see me. She came up, but not as usual with
the Baby which allarmd me. I instantly inquired how it was to
which she replied very well and burst into Tears. I inquired
what had happend? She replied that Mr. Black had been the
Evening before and taken the child from her. She said she expostulated with him, and begd him not to take it, untill he had
informd me; "it was of no avail; let then stay till the morning.
No it should go directly, but why? Have I not taken good care
of it? Have I not watchd it night and day through the small
Pox, and now it is just recovering its strength, you take it from
me, to kill it. She says she was Angry." No persuasion would
prevail. She says, Mr. Black told her, he was determined to take
it away out of spight, for that the doctor had brought in his
Bill the day before of 30 dollors for innoculating the Baby, her
child, and one in the house belonging to a woman whose child
would have been exposed by the others, and which child I had
told the doctor I would myself be answerable for and that he
had payd the Bill. I was sure it could not be so. I supposed,
what was really the case, that the doctor might have sent his
Bill in, for his attendance upon Mr. Hall during his sickness as
Dr. Cox and he were jointly concernd. I immediatly wrote to
the Dr. I inclose you his answer. I then wrote to Mr. Black, and
told him I was sorry he should think it necessary to take the
child away as it appeard to me to be very well taken care of,
and I hoped he would be so kind as to restore the child to the
Nurse again, that if any Bill had been presented him for the
innoculation of the Children it was through mistake as no
charge was ever intended to be made to him. I thought I
would let him know, that I knew he had given this as a Reason.
I added that if any misfortune of sickness or death should
happen in concequence of his depriving the child of its nurse

just as it was recovering its strength, I thought he could not answer it either to Mr. Black or to you.

With this Billet I sent Mrs. Brisler and Betsy in the carriage with orders to take the child if they could obtain his consent, and carry it back to the Nurse, and to tell her that I would be answerable to her for its Nursing untill Mr. Black should come for it. They accordingly went, and were told by his House-keeper, that he was not at home. However Mrs. Brisler was not content. She went to the store where she found him, and de-liverd my Note, and requested his permission to take the child to the Nurse. He said it was so expensive keeping it at Nurse that he thought to have it weand and then he had such a Bill to pay for innoculating the children. Mrs. Brisler replied it could not be for *that*, as I had just received it, from under the doctors Hand that no Bill had been offerd him on that ac-count. He said no more on that subject, but went into the House and consented to let it go for a fortnight longer. The woman who ever she is, appeard very Angry and said she would carry it herself the next day. Mrs. Brisler said she had come in the carriage on purpose to take it, and she should be glad to report to me that she had deliverd it to the Nurse. The House keeper tried to get an opportunity to speak to Mr. Black but Mrs. Brisler followd him so close that she would not let her. After some delay to find the Bonnet and Cloak she deliverd the child to them and they carried the Baby to the Nurse, to the great joy of the dear little orphan who stretchd out its Arms and cryd as bad as the Nurse.

Mr. Black told Mrs. Brisler that he did not know whether he should let it go if his Brother came for it. She replied, that was a subject which she had nothing to do with, that I certainly could have no interest in the Matter but what I felt for an or-phan child whose Mother I knew, and whose Friends had re-quested my attention to it. Both Betsy and Mrs. Brisler think Mr. Black was governd in this matter by the Housekeeper as he appeard to be affraid of her resentment.

I received the Bundle you sent for it, and had sent it to the Nurse. They were exactly the things she told me last Sunday that she wanted for it, only that you had been more liberal than her request. This was an other source of Resentment to Mr. Black, that so much attention should be paid to the child, and so little to him.

I think the sooner Mr. Black can sit out the better. If this Letter reaches you by Saturday next, it will be a fortnight or 20 days before Mr. Black can get here from this time, That will bring it into May when the roads will be well setled, and if he should take the child away again it will not be in my power to do any thing more.

My kind Regards to Mrs. Beal who I am sorry to learn is unwell again. I cannot say when I shall see you but hope it may be in June. When you see Mrs. Lamb my compliments to her.

Be assured my dear Friend of the Regard of

Abigail Adams

BUILDING A LIBRARY AT PEACEFIELD

To Cotton Tufts

My dear Sir   Philadelphia April 16 1798

I received your Letter of the 30 of March on the 14th. of this Month, but the one you mention as having enclosed the plan of the out House is not come to Hand. I do not regreet it, because I suppose I should not wish any alteration. Your Idea of throwing two Chambers into one for the Librairy I approve. That will take in the Books and will give the President a Room in which he can do buisness for which he sufferd last Summer. You will open the Chimny into it so as to give a fire place in it, and in the other Chamber too upon the opposite Side. Let access be made to the Book Room from without doors by Stairs that it may not interfear with the other part of the House. Then what is now the Book Room may be used for a Bed Room by Mrs. Bates, and I think the Building will be very compleat for the use we want it.

I wish you would make an estimate of the cost of the whole, as it is my intention to oconomise and save it out of our Sallery here, and to remit it to you as I find I can, so that I wish a seperate account of it, unless inconvenient to you. As to Mr. Bass, the old man is usefull and I believe it will be quite as well to give up Billings at the close of his term. We give him larger wages than he ought to have considering his frequent frolicks. As to Mr. and Mrs. Porter, let them have every indulgence you think proper. A maid she must certainly have for the Summer.

Would it not be best to paint the outside of our House and fence again? A smaller quantity will answer now than if it goes longer and the fence was only primed.

I would leave it wholy to you with respect to Mr. Bass. You will be governd in the Wages by those given to others, certainly not more than we gave him last Year if he is hired for 8 or 9 Months. Eight dollers a month I presume will be sufficient.

The President desires me to ask you to pay to Mrs. Murrys printer His subscription for two sets of her works which he has received, or whoever is to receive the money.

I inclose you an other Bill of an Hundred dollors towards the building.

My kind Love to Suky if living, to Mrs. Tufts and to you Sir all the consolation which Religion can afford in so trying and distressing circumstances.

Affectionately yours,   A Adams

"THE HYDRA MONSTER OF JACOBINISM"

To John Quincy Adams

My dear Son   Philadelphia April 21 1798

It was with a mixture of pleasure and pain that I read your Letter of December 25th from Berlin No. 32. It gave me pleasure to see your Hand writing addrest to me after a painfull interval of three months. Some of your communications were attended with circumstances which gave me pain, and anxiety, for my dear Louissa whose Situation under the circumstances you describe, must have been peculiarly distressing to both her, and you. Nurterd as she ever was, under the tender care and Fostering wing of the tenderest of parents; unaccustomed to fatigue, and inconveniencies of travelling, either by Land or Sea, she has had them all to encounter in a Situation less able to bear them than usual. Happy for you both that they did not prove fatal to her. You must have had your Share of Sufferings, new terrors, and allarms, for new and dear Connections, "even where you had garnerd up your Heart," all your Sensibility must have been awakend by a Species of anxiety and distress before unknown to you, and as woes are seldom solitary, The dangerous sickness of your Brother must have enhanced your affliction; I have enterd fully into your domestic distresses, and gratefully acknowledge the kind Providence which has carried you safely through them.

I wrote you largly by Mr. Thornton who saild from hence, in the British packet, or rather from N York; the Letters were addrest to the care of Mr. King. I have not omitted a month since October last, and have frequently written more than once. By this opportunity to Bremin, I send you a duplicate of the dispatches from our Envoys and instructions to them, together with some News papers. By the latter you will see that our Countrymen are seriously allarm'd and are vigorously exerting themselves to put our Country in a proper State of defence. The effects of the communication which have been made in compliance with the request of the House of Rep's has made the blind to see and the deaf to hear; it has been like an Electrical Shock, as far as it has yet extended. The instructions which were communicated at the same time, were so candid, so liberal, so fully up to any thing which the *party themselves* had venturd to a vow, that the words of Milton might justly be applied.

> Abash'd the devil stood,
> And saw virtue in her own shape, how lovely?

It would be difficult for you at the distance you are, to conceive the change which has taken place in this City; the center of foreign influence and Jacobinism. The *Real French* Men, the *unprincipled Jacobin*, the *Emissaries of France remain unchanged*, but real Americans who have been deceived, and betray'd by falshood, and deception, are the mass of the lower class of the people. They are uniting and united, and I would fain hope that the Hydra Monster of Jacobinism is crushd never to rise with such mischevious effects again. Those in Congress who dare not *now act*, fearing the voice of the people will cry out against them, whom they have deceived, are falling off, and going home. Giles, Nicholas, Clayton, Clopton from Virgina are gone and going. *Old Findly* has written a Letter to his Friends in the western County, which has by some means got into Peters paper; it is one contin'ed tissue of Lies from begining to end. The Journals of Congress and Senate are proofs that it is so and the old wretch could not but know it. He will get enough of it before Congress rises. The subtle Jesuit Gallatin will turn, and twist, twist and turn, but the Indignation of the House rises against him so strongly that he is quite placed in the back ground, and must quit the feild or take a less conspicuous station. After the arrival of the dispatches the President sent to both Houses of Congress the Letter of Jan'ry 8th (in which the envoys say, that they have not been received neither do they expect to be,) accompanied with a message to them. A day or two after arrived the whole Bugget which being in cypher took some days to decypher. After reading and considering them, the President sent an other Message which you will find in the pamphlet I send you; that Message contains the result drawn from a view of the dispatches, but which at that time the President thought might risk the safety of our Envoys if made publick. He therefore withheld them. This Message was openly and publickly call'd *a War Speech* and the Jacobin party did not fail to make the allarm general. They attempted first to stir up the Quakers in this city, but a timely address to them the morning of their meeting by Peter, who is held in much estimation by them prevented them from petitioning against war. Having faild here, there next step was to excite meetings in more remote parts of the union: and to procure them in the *Presidents own state*. Accordingly through the influence of Genll. Heath a meeting was held in Roxbury, then in Milton, Dochester, Cambridge and Abington, but before any were received here except those from Roxbury, the House calld for the dispatches, and instructions which being communicated, produced the effect I have described and now addresses are comeing in from all quarters expressive of the intire satisfaction of the addressors in the conduct of the executive and of their determination to support him and to adhere to their Government. Some you will find in the papers I send you. Others are not yet made publick. N York and Baltimore are following this city and state. York Town presented one yesterday and the one inclosed was presented to day. I send it you to prove the change wrought.

"They seem already to have quench'd seditions Brand
And Zeal that burnt it, only warms the land
The jealous Sect's that durst not trust their cause
So far from their own Will, as to the laws.
Him for their umpire and their Synod take
And their appeal alone to Ceasar make."

I heard last week from Mr. Johnston's and Family. They were well. I mournd with you, and with all good people the loss of Your much esteemed Friend Dr. Clark of Boston of whose sudden death I gave you an account in my last Letter.

To my dear Thomas I will write by the May packet. I am sorry he is so great a sufferer by his mother but the Rheumatism is an heriditary Gift I fear.

I wrote to Mrs. Adams in answer to her kind and joint Letter. I hope she has received it. I wrote to you and to Thomas whilst I was at East Chester, about the 6 or 7th of November. Your sister also wrote to you at the same time. That your Father does not write you often, you can easily devine the cause.

With Love to Mrs. Adams and Thomas, I am my dear Son affectionatly your Mother,   A Adams

HAIL, COLUMBIA

To Mary Smith Cranch

MY DEAR SISTER: April 26, 1798

I inclose to you a National Song composed by this same Mr. Hopkinson. French Tunes have for a long time usurped an uncontrould sway. Since the Change in the publick opinion respecting France, the people began to lose the relish for them, and what had been harmony, now becomes discord. Accordingly their had been for several Evenings at the Theatre something like disorder, one party crying out for the Presidents March and Yankee Doodle, whilst Ciera was vociferated from the other. It was hisst off repeatedly. The Managers were blamed. Their excuse was that they had not any words to the Presidents March —Mr. Hopkinson accordingly composed these to the tune. Last

Eve'ng they were sung for the first time. I had a Great curiosity to see for myself the Effect. I got Mr. Otis to take a Box, and silently went off with Mr. and Mrs. Otis, Mr. & Mrs. Buck to the play, where I had only once been this winter. I meant now to be perfectly in cogg, so did not sit in what is calld the Presidents Box. After the Principle Peice was performd, Mr. Fox came upon the stage, to sing the song. He was welcomed by applause. The House was very full, and at every Choruss, the most unbounded applause ensued. In short it was enough to stund one. They had the song repeated—After this Rossina was acted. When Fox came upon the stage after the Curtain dropt, to announce the Peice for fryday, they calld again for the song, and made him repeat it to the fourth time. And the last time, the whole Audience broke forth in the Chorus whilst the thunder from their Hands was incessant, and at the close they rose, gave 3 Huzzas, that you might have heard a mile—My Head aches in concequence of it. The Managers have requested the President to attend the Theater, and twesday next he goes. A number of the inhabitants have made the same request, and now is the proper time to gratify them. Their have been six differents addresses presented from this city alone; all expressive of the Approbation of the measures of the Executive. Yet dairingly do the vile incendaries keep up in Baches paper the most wicked and base, voilent & caluminiating abuse—It was formerly considerd as leveld against the Government, but now it is contrary to their declared sentiments daily manifested, so that it insults the Majesty of the Sovereign People. But nothing will have an Effect untill congress pass a Sedition Bill, which I presume they will do before they rise—Not a paper from Bache press issues nor from Adams Chronical, but what might have been prossecuted as libels upon the President and Congress. For a long time they seem as if they were now desperate—The wrath of the public ought to fall upon their devoted Heads.

I shall send a paper or two because your Boston papers cannot take in one half of what these contain. Mr. Otis's Letter is a very judicious, sensible, patriotic composition, and does him great honour.

You may rely upon it from me, that not a single line from our Envoys have been received but what has been communicated, and nothing has been received from them since the last communication.

I received your Letter of the 20 this day. I am very sorry the closet should be omitted because it wanted painting very much and does not easily dry. I wrote to the Dr. and proposed having the outside of the house new painted, and the Garden fence also which never was more than primed, but I would not put too many Irons at once in the fire.

If you have got Cousin Betsys Box or she has, as I see the vessel is arrived, you will then find what a drapery dress is, and the Young Lady will teach how it is to be put on. A Cap for you should be made as you usually wear yours, and as I wear mine, of handsome muslin with a pleated border or a lace—I wear no other but upon publick Evenings when I wear a Crape dress cap.

I do not wear the drapery dress myself as I consider it too youthfull for me. I have both sides alike, but they both come forward upon the top & then fall away and are worn with a coat or the Apron lose.

Will you desire Mr. Porter to get some slips of the Quince Tree and sit out in the lower garden.

Adieu my dear Sister. My pen, I think, is scarcly ever dry.

Yours in Love, affection ABIGAIL ADAMS

P.S. Since writing the above the song is printed. Bache says this morning among other impudence that the excellent Lady of the Excellent President, was present, and shed Tears of sensibility upon the occasion. That was a lie. However I should not have been asshamed if it had been so. I laughed at one scene which was playd, to be sure, untill the tears ran down, I believe. But the song by the manner in which it is received, is death to their Party. The House was really crowded, and by the most respectable people in the city.

"AN INCENDARY LETTER"

To Mary Smith Cranch

MY DEAR SISTER: Philadelphia, May 10th, 1798

Rumour at a distance magnifies and seldom reports truth. I have not written you a word upon a subject which I know would have made you at least very uneasy. About three weeks ago, a Letter was sent, or rather brought here of a Sunday Evening by two young women of the City, one of whom said passing the House a few days before She took up a paper in a small alley which runs between our house & our Neighbours. It was wet by lying at the Edge of a gutter which passes through the passage. The Girl, finding it in this way opend the Letter, and read it, but being allarmd at the contents, knew not what to do. Her mother, who was absent at the Time, returning & finding what she had done, directed the Girl to bring it herself, & relate the circumstances. The purport of the Letters was to inform the President that the French people who were in this city had formed a conspiracy with some unsuspected Americans, on the Evening of the day appointed for the fast to sit fire to the City in various parts, and to Massacre the inhabitants, intreating the President not to neglect the information & the warning given, tho by an annonimous Hand, signd a Real tho heretofore a misguided American. The President conceived it to be an incendary Letter written to allarm & distress the inhabitants. An other Letter of the same purport was sent ten days after, thrust under the door of Mr. Otis's office. These with some Rumours of combinations got abroad, and the Mayor, Aldermen &c kept some persons upon the watch through all parts of the city, & the Governour gave orders privately to have a troop of Horse in case of need. The Young Men of the city as I wrote you on Monday to the amount of near Eleven Hundred came at 12 oclock in procession two and two. There were assembled upon the occasion it is said ten thousand Persons. This street as wide or wider than State Street in Boston, was full as far as we could see up & down. One might have walkd upon their Heads, besides the houses window & even tops of Houses. In great order & decorum the Young Men with each a black cockade marchd through the Multitude and all of them enterd the House preceeded by their committe. When a Young Gentleman by the Name of Hare, a Nephew of Mrs. Binghams, read the address, the President received them in his Levee Room drest in his uniform, and as usual upon such occasions, read his answer to them, after which they all retired. The Multitude gave three Cheers, & followd them to the State House Yard, where the answer to the address was again read by the Chairman of the committe, with acclamations. They then closed the scene by singing the new song, which at 12 oclock at night was sung by them under our windows, they having dinned together or rather a part of them. This scene burnt in the Hearts of some Jacobins and they determined eitheir, to terrify, or Bully the young men out of their Patriotism. Baches publishd some saussy peices, the young men resented and he would have felt the effects of their resentment if some cooler Heads had not interposed. Yesterday was observed with much solemnity. The meeting Houses & churches were fill'd. About four oclock as is usual the State House Yard, which is used for a walk, was very full of the inhabitants, when about 30 fellows, some with snow Balls in their Hats, & some with tri-coulourd cockades enterd and attempted to seize upon the Hats of the Young Men to tear out their cockades. A scuffel ensued when the Young Men became conquerors, and some of these tri coulourd cockades were trampled in the dust. One fellow was taken, and committed to Jail, but this was sufficient to allarm the inhabitants, and there were every where large collections of people. The light Horse were calld out & patrold the streets all Night. A gaurd was placed before this House, tho through the whole of the Proceedings, and amidst all the collection, the Presidents name was not once mentiond, nor any one grievance complaind of, but a foreign attempt to try their strength & to Awe the inhabitants if possible was no doubt at the bottom. Congress are upon an Allien Bill. This Bache is cursing & abusing daily. If that fellow & his Agents Chronical, and all is not surpressd, we shall come to a civil war. I hope the Gen'll Court of our State, will take the Subject up & if they have not a strong Sedition Bill, make one—Before I close this I shall send to the post office.

Quincy address and a Letter from Brother Cranch, News papers but not a line from my sister. Well, I trust the next post will bring me some.

I must now close my Letter or the post will be gone. The Nurse & childern and Nabby Hunt are all going on Board this morning. Nabby holds me to my word that I would let her go home this spring, no difficulty or uneasiness on either part. She is wrong for herself. I have given her a dollor pr week ever since she has been with me, paid her doctor, and she is now going to ——. She will find the difference. I suppose she thinks she may get a Husband at home. Here there is no chance.

Your ever affectionate   A. ADAMS

Mr. Black was here & well to day.

"THE PRESIDENT IS MOST WORN DOWN"

To Mary Smith Cranch

MY DEAR SISTER: Philadelphia, May 13, 1798
    I write you a few lines by Mr. Black altho I know the post will go quicker. I hope to get Letters to day from Quincy. Now a week since I heard. We are thank God all well. The President is most worn down. I tell the Gentlemen if they do not give him a respit soon, it will be too much for him. The Numerous addresses which pour in daily in abundance give him much additional writing. They are however a gratefull and pleasing testimony of the satisfaction of the publick mind, assurances to support the Government, notwithstanding the pains which has been taken to poison it.
    I send you my dear Sister a peice of Muslin for two Crowns of caps. It must be done up with great care. It is calld Deca Muslin. It does not look well to tell the price of any thing which is for a present, but that you may know its real value, I will tell you that it was six dollors pr yd. It is accompanied by a peice for a Border which to get the blew out you must put in vinigar & water. I have also sent you a narrow lace for to put on them. If you put a double Border there will be enough for only one. Let me know, because when I find a pretty Edging I will send you enough for the other. You will want to run the lace upon a narrow peice of Muslin. Ladies of your age wear such fine Muslin, with white Ribbons made like the dress close caps, with a little Hair seen at the Ears. I have not time to add more, than

    Yours,   A. A

CONGRESS'S SUMMER RECESS

To Cotton Tufts

I wish he did not Love Land so well, because I know we have enough to torment us—when we come to look to that for support, we shall find it difficult enough to procure it, and very much swallowd up by taxes & Labour. I am for having as little trouble as possible as we pass down the vale of years we shall want repose if we live. I have no objection to mr Clarks having the House an other year.

My kind regards to mrs Tufts, and to mr & mrs Norten as well as your Son and daughter. I hope, but know not when to say Congress will rise. It depends much upon Events which may turn up. they talk of the middle of June. I fear it will be later. when ever it is, I am determined to bring on the President if we can only Stay a fortnight, for he stands in great need of a journey. I order the carriage every afternoon & take him out, but tis only a few miles, and he does not these long days get a walk once a week. he is thin & pale but in good Spirits. Indeed he has not time to groan. he however smoaks more Segars than I wish he did.

On the 11 of May the President nominated Samll Snow of the Eastern Stats to be consul at Canton.

I am dear sir with Sentiments of Sincere esteem & affection your   A Adams

May 25, 1798

"A SYSTEM OF DEMORALIZING THE WORLD"

To John Quincy Adams

My Dear Son   Philadelphia May 26 1798
I am loth a vessel should sail without a few lines from me, and the Secretary of State is very good to inform me of every opportunity, and tho I have not received any Letter since I wrote you last, which was on the 4th or 5th of this month, I

will acknowledge one for your Father, dated 17 Febry. the duplicate of which the original is not yet come, No 53. A Letter for
your Brother accompanied it which I sent on to him. The Secretary of State also got a Letter from you in Cypher. He will look
after that. The consul you recommended is appointed.

You will see by the papers I send you some of the numerous
addresses which are pouring in from all quarters like a flood
from North Carolina to the province of Main. They Breathe
one Spirit. They speak one Language, that of Independant
Freemen, approving the measures of Government, and expressive of a full confidence in the wisdom virtue and integrity of
the Chief Majestrate, and a fixed determination to defend and
support their Government, and to repell every attempt against
it, spurning with indignation the bass servile terms of conciliation with France, as tenderd to our Envoys. The youth of all
the Great Cities have come forward, from 18 to 23, and tendered their personal Services. The Colleges, and Seminaries of
Learning join in the general voice. The Students of Harvard
College say in their address.

"We solemnly offer the unwasted ardour, and unimpaired
energies of our youth to the services of our Country, our Lives
are our only property, and we were not the Sons of those who
sealed our Liberties with their blood, if we woud not defend
with these lives that Soil, which now affords a peaceful grave to
the mouldering bones of our Forefathers."

The people are much higher toned than their Representatives in the National Legislature, The opposition with Gallitin
at their Head go on striving to obstruct every energitic measure, and there will be some timid pidling Genius's who fear
every thing, in Senate the Majority is large and respectable.
Much will depend upon the issue of the projected invasion of
England, if the French attempt it, I do not hesitate to say, that
I hope the fate of Pharaoh and his Host will be there's what
remaining Barrier of Freedom is there beside old England?

In the Letter of Yours of Feb'ry 17th, you mention, a Society
by the Name of Theo-Philanthropic, which the French were
about to establish in Hamburgh with a view to dessiminate
their principles. I presume, you had not at that time read a
Book, lately publishd, calld proofs of a conspiracy against all
the Religion & Governments of Europe, collected from good

Authorities By John Robison A M, professor of Natural philosophy, and Secretary to the Royal Society of Edinburgh. It has been reprinted here, and has gone through three Editions. This work discloses such a System of demoralizing the World, as is scarcly to be credited if we did not see it, in actual opperation, if you have not met with the Book, you would do well to write to some Friend in England to procure it for you.

I have sent by this opportunity an other Set of the dispatches and a few pamphlets together with a few News papers.

Our Friends are well. tell Mrs. Adams that her Mother sent me a Letter to read written by her Godmother after she left England. the Letter is full of praises, both of her and her Husband, All tongues unite in speaking highly of my dear daughter, for whom I sincerely feel a mothers anxiety. I hope she will never again be so dissagreably situated as when she first went to Berlin—Her Mother is distresst at not getting any Letters from her, and I have been obliged to send yours to me, to quiet her. She returnd them with the warmest expression of gratitude. tell my dear Thomas that I do not love him the less because I do not write to him often. I always rejoice at hearing from him. Peter got a sweet morsel from his last Letter, and *Bene* a Taiter.

Your Father sends his Love to you, but has more writing than he knows how to get through with answering addresses

We have just had the committe from the youn Men of N York to present there's

adieu my dear Son I am your ever affectionate

Mother Abigail Adams

"PROOFS OF A CONSPIRACY"

To Mary Smith Cranch

MY DEAR SISTER: Philadelphia, May 26, 1798

Yours of the 18 I received on thursday 23, and I rejoice to hear Mr. Black got home so soon, as I think he could dissipate your anxiety on our account. I may be too confident, but I do not feel as if any body wanted to hurt or injure us. Bearing neither

malice or ill will towards any one, not even the most deluded, I
cannot be particuliarly apprehensive. I wish the Laws of our
Country were competant to punish the stirer up of sedition, the
writer and Printer of base and unfounded calumny. This would
contribute as much to the Peace and harmony of our Country
as any measure, and in times like the present, a more carefull and
attentive watch ought to be kept over foreigners. This will be
done in future if the Alien Bill passes, without being curtaild &
clipt untill it is made nearly useless. The Volunteer Corps which
are forming not only of young Men, but others will keep in
check these people, I trust. Amongst the many addresses have
you particuliarly noticed one from the state of N Jersey with the
Govr. at their head, as commander in chief? It is from all the
officers, and they are not vain and empty tenders, for a deputa-
tion from their Body is comeing to Present the address on
Monday next, and to tender their services as a volunteer Corps.
I wish with you that I could see as great a Change for the better
in Morals as in politicks, but it is a part of Religion as well as
morality, to do justly and to love mercy and a man can not be an
honest & Zealous promoter of the Principles of a True Government, without possessing that Good will towards man which
leads to the Love of God, and respect for the Deity; so that a
proper appreciation of our Rights & Duties as Citizens, it is a
prelude to a respect for Religion, and its institutions. To destroy
and undermine Religion has been the cheif engine in the accomplishment of this mighty Revolution throughout Europe.
We have felt no small share of the balefull influence of the Age
of Reason, but to have a thorough Idea of the deep laid system,
you must read a work lately publishd calld proofs of a conspiracy
against all the Religions and Governments of Europe, by John
Robison, Professor of Natural Philosophy in the university of
Edinburgh. This Book I have sent to Dr. Belknap with a request
that if he possesst a Copy, that he would send it to Mr. Cranch.
If he has not, he will lend it to him. You will read the Book with
astonishment. What led me to send the Book at this Time, was
from a Letter from my son at Berlin, who I know from his
manner of writing had not seen the Book. It was first publishd
last Sep'br in Edinburgh. In his Letter he mentions a society
calld a *Theo Philanthropick*, and describes it as a Theological
& political mixture of deism, morality and Anti-Christianity

—that to propagate these doctrines, persons had been sent lately to Hamburgh; and that *Dupont de Nemours* was talkd of as comeing out to America to establish such societies here.

I have made the extract from his Letter at length, and sent it to Dr. Belknap together with Robisons work, which fully unfolds the whole scheme, and displays the effects of the Principles in the Revolutions in Europe to their full extent. I thought I could not do a better service than to put our Countrymen upon their Gaurd. The son of this Dupont has just arrived in this city from Charlstown S C, where he was Consul. He is now sent here in order to superceed Le Tomb, as consul-general. He told a Gentleman who mentiond it at the drawing Room last Evening that his Father was gone to Hamburgh in order to embark for America, which corresponds with the account given by Mr. A.—and he added that he found the spirit of the times such, that he should be very sorry to have his Father come out. The intention was that he should have come out to accompany the Marquiss La Fayett & Family. By this means you see, he would naturally have been cordially & kindly received, and have crept unsuspected into the Bosoms of Americans, untill he had bit like a Serpent and stung like an Adder. Was there ever a more basely designing and insidious people? Burk was right, when he described the French republick to be founded upon Regicide, Jacobinism and Atheism, and that it had joind to those Principles: a body of systamatick manners, which secured their opperation.

Robisons Book will shew you how much the corruption of manners has aided in the destruction of all Religious and moral Principles. All the new institutions strike at the root of our social nature. Mr. Burk goes on to observe in his Letters upon the Regicide Directory, "that other Legislators knowing that marriage is the origin of all Relations, and concequently the first Element of all duties, have endeavourd by every Art to make it sacred." The following observation ought to be indelbly written upon every mind. "The Christian Religion by confining it to pairs and by rendering that Relation indissoluable, has by these two things, done more towards the peace, happiness, settlement and civilization of the world, than by any other part in this whole scheme of divine wisdom."

I objected to the answer to the Boston address upon the same Principle you mention. I did get an alteration in it, but between ourselves, I think the address itself as indifferent as most any one which has been sent. But this is confidential.

Inclosed is a Letter for Mr. Black, which I return as he requested. I hear nothing yet of the Box sent for Cousin Betsy. I hope it is not lost.

We have had some delightfull rains these two days past. I want to escape the cage & fly to Quincy but know not when to say it will be. I am, my dear Sister,

Affectionatly yours   A. ADAMS

P.S. Louisa desires me to inquire when you expect her sister back. My Letters to you are first thoughts, without correction.

A SECRETARY FOR JOHN QUINCY

To Thomas Welsh Jr.

Dear Sir

I yesterday received a Letter from my Son Thomas in which he repeats his Brothers request that I would look out for some person as a sutable Successor to supply to his Brother his place The young Gentleman whom mr Adams desired me to make inquiry about, the Son of Judge Dana, his former patron is engaged in the persuit of merchandize, and I presume would not wish to quit that Buisness, as it was his choice in preference to the Law which his Father was desirious of having him Bred to, I have not therefore thought it expedient to apply to him on the Subject.

Both the President and I have concured in one opinion which is to propose to you to become Thomas's Successor.

Thomas writes me thus, Let me intreat you to negotiate a Successor to me in my present office. Some good temperd confidential person who will be willing to undertake a voyage across the Atlantic and pass a few years in the capacity in which I have served, To such an one you may say, that the Service is not difficult or laborious, tho unremitting, and that with prudence and oeconomy the appointment annexed to the Service, will enable him to live decently and independantly, the opportunity which it gives of seeing Europe in its various parts is valuable."

In july next I have a Nephew who will come out of colledgde and who will then be ready to take your place with the President.

My Reason for applying thus early, is that I may inform my Sons, that such a Gentleman as they describe & wish for will be ready to go to them, and this I shall do with the more confidence from a personal knowledge of his disposition and abilities.

If you have any inclination to travel I think this opening cannot but be a pleasing one if you consent, some time next fall you can Embark for Europe.

You will be so good as to give an answer as soon as you have sufficiently weigh'd the Subject to your Friend

Abigail Adams

c. June 4, 1798

MEETINGS WITH TALLEYRAND

To Mary Smith Cranch

my dear sister   Philadelphia June 5th 1798
    I write you this morning just to say that there are dispatches from our Envoys up to April by which it appears that they have had Several conferences with Tallyrand, the Subject of which was obtaining Money—They are just decypherd and will be communicated. no Reception from the Directory, no like to be any. I can not but Say to you, what will Strike every one, that every hour they remain in France degrades their Country, and embarrasses our counsells beyond conception—
    yours &c   A Adams

JOHN QUINCY'S INVESTMENTS FAIL

To John Quincy Adams

My dear Son   Philadelphia June 12th 1798
    The June packet is to sail tomorrow, As I know you must be anxious for constant intelligence at this critical & important

period I will not let her sail without writing to you, tho it is a hazard whether she will go safe, for our very coasts are infested with French privateers, who insult us in our own Waters.

Every exertion is making to get our Frigates to Sea. We have some 20 Gun vessels out, Newburryport has sit an example, by voteing & raising money to Build a 20 Gun Ship and loaning it to Government. Newyork have voted 2 & this City 2; the Sea ports will all follow the example and we shall have a Navy Spring up like the Gourd of Jonah; I hope however that it will not wither, as soon. The eagerness with which the Youth of Family fortune & Education enter the Navy, and Army, is a Surety for our Country, that the Spirit of the Fathers, live in their Son's.

I cannot send you a hundred part of the addresses which have been, and still, are pouring in from every State Town and village. no sovereign, ever had more voluntary Lives, and fortunes tendered to him, in proportion to his dominions, than have been offerd to the Chief Majestrate of *United America*, in defence of the Liberty and Independance of the Country.

This City, which was formerly torpid with indolence, and fettered with Quakerism; has become *one* Military School, and every morning, the Sound of the drum and fife, lead forth "A Band of Brothers joind" The Martial Spirit resounds from one end of the Country, to the other.

An age of peace, would not have informd and enlightened our Countrymen, with respects to their Rights, & the just value of a free and equitable Govermment, as the unprovoked and unjust conduct of France towards us.

I inclose to you a Boston paper, in which you will read, a wise & judicious speach of Gov'r Sumner a song written by Mr. T. pain, and the last Dispatch. Heaven Grant that it may be *the last*, dispatch from our *Lamb like envoys*.! There pulse beats, not like my dear Thomases, who tho absent near four Years, has not forgotten that he is An American. By his last Letter to his Father of March the 4th, he judges better of the feelings of his Countrymen, than to belive them capable of crouching to the terms of the haughty Gauls. Let them know; "that united we stand, and defy the foul Friends."

I have just recived a Letter from Mrs. Johnson dated the 4th of June, in which she informs me, that she had at length received Letters from you & her dear Louisa. She meant to write by the packet, but will be too late. the Family were all well. Mrs. Johnson is frequently troubled with Billious complaints. She must have a seasoning. She appears better contented by her last Letters than she was. we write often to each other, and keep up a friendly intercourse. Tell Mrs. Adams that she must keep a Journal. It will become pleasent to her by habit, and greatly facilitate her writing, which is only urksome by disuse. She will find it a Source of amusement to her, and her Friends hereafter.

Your Brother Charles and Family and sister Smith were well last week. Whilst I am writing, I have lade down my pen, to read a Letter brought me from your Aunt peabody. her Letters were always a treasure, and she knows as well as ever Shakspear did, every avenue to the Heart. I can never get through a Letter of hers, without wetting it with my tears. She is very anxious now for her daughter Betsy who had a fever in the winter which has left her with many allarming Symptoms of a consumptive nature, and tho in her person she is not her Mother, she is otherways every way Lovely and Desirable, and to lose her would be a Stroke, which her mother would not know how to support. She writes me pleasing accounts of my Grandsons. it will be the making of them, The Fathers misfortunes will prove the Salvation of the Children. has their Grandfather some times observed to me, your Aunt desires to be rememberd in the most affectionate terms to you & to your Brother, whom next to her own Children she loves. She participates in your pleasure; and she has sympathized in the suffering of your dear Louisa, whom she says you must instruct to Love her. I know it will give you pleasure to learn, that Mr Cranch has removed to George Town, at the request of Mr Johnson, who has patronized him, and put his buisness into his Hands

I have to communicate to you the painfull event of Dr. Welchs failure in property, The inclosed Billet will state the particulars. I fear you are a sufferer, I have written to Charles to stop his making any remittance to him on your account, even tho you had orderd it, and requested to be informd by him of the State of your property in his Hands. Tho a week has elapsed. I have not an answer. I wish I knew *of a certainty that it was safe.* Indeed my dear Son, I am not with out my fears, that you will lose all you have been so prudently and carefully saving.—I will do for your security what I can. The 25 Guineys are still in my hands which I owe you and which I will pay into Mr Smiths or Dr Tufts Hands when I know which of them you will commit your interest to.—

I am distrest for the Dr. and Family and do not know but that I shall send Thomas Welch to you to take Your Brothers place—

God Bless and preserve you and Yours, and all who are dear to your truly affectionate   Mother A Adams

Your Father send you his Blessing. You know he cannot write—any thing but answers to the addresses—

ENCLOSURE

I am sorry to announce, an event that must afflict you, as it has, every friend & connection of the family. Dr. W. for some-time past has been much embarrassd. The last Week he clos'd his Doors. judge what Mrs. W. situation must be, not to have the least suspicion 'till the moment it took place. she is in the greatest destress. What has become of his property is a mystery to all his Friends. The demands against him are more than double to all his property he ever possest. all his nearest Friends will suffer severely by him. I have secur'd all the property that I know of & yet it will not be sufficient for my demand. The Dr. holds flowers from Mr. J. Q. A. to take charge of his business. If you think proper you may recommend his assigning it to me.

"A LETTER FROM TALLEYRAND"

To Mary Smith Cranch

MY DEAR SISTER: Quincy, 19 June, 1798
I expected to have heard from you on Saturday, but no Letter came and on Wednesday but still no Letter. I was

dissapointed, but knowing your many avocations I concluded it must arise from thence, I hope not from sickness, tho you wrote me you was not well. I who have more leisure, and no care of Family affairs but my orders can, and do devote almost every morning in writing to some Friend or other. You will hear before this reaches you of the arrival of Mr. Marshall at N York. Mr. Pinckney is gone to the South of France with a persuit for the Health of a daughter suposed in a consumption. Mr. Gerry stays untill he hears from our Government, which as appears to me, is a very wrong step. The Government you will be informd received last week an other dispatch of a Letter from Talleyrand, and a very lengthy reply by our Envoys, which being in a press copy & part cypher, two copies being to be prepared of it, could not be got ready in one or two days. In the meantime Talleyrand had sent out to Bache his Letter for to be publishd here, & without the replie of our Envoys. This he exultingly gave to the publick on Saturday. It really appears a very fortunate circumstance that, our government, should have received tho by an other conveyance the dispatches about the same time, and so soon be able to counteract the villany intended by Talleyrand. It has an other good effect, that of convinceing the most unbelieving of the close connection between the Infernals of France & those in our own Bosoms. And in any other Country Bache & all his papers would have been seazd and ought to be here, but congress are dilly dallying about passing a Bill enabling the President to seize suspisious persons, and their papers. We shall be favour'd soon I suppose with the pamphlet written by the Clerk in Talleyrands office—All this however works for good, and will tend to work out our salvation I hope. I will send the papers as soon as publishd. In the mean time I send you some pamphlets to be distributed for the publick Benifit, and send one in my Name to Mrs. Webb with my compliments.

We are all well but a servant who has been voilently attackd with an inflamitory Soar Throat, & very dangerously sick for several days. We hope he has past the worst. The season has not yet been uncommonly Hot, I am weary of conjectures, so shall say nothing of when it is probable Congress will rise. I believe they will decarle war against the French first.

Mr. Marshalls arrival will hasten the buisness—O Mr. Gerry!

Mr. Gerry, that you had but been wise enough & resolute enough to have come too.

Mrs. Malony got home yesterday morning, in six days. I have not seen her. I have only heard that she is come.

With a kind remembrance to all Friends

Yours   A. A

"MR. GERRYS REMAINING IN FRANCE"

To Elizabeth Smith Shaw Peabody

My Dear Sister   Philadelphia June 22 1798

I received last week your very excellent Letter. Whatever you write is always precious to me. No one better knows how to touch every feeling of the humane Heart. I can allow for your long Silence, tho I wish it were not imposed upon you, by your numerous cares, and unavoidable avocations. the anxiety which you feel for the Health of a Beloved child, whom I pray God to restore to Health, and preserve to you, is I well know more exhausting to the Spirits, and wearisome to the Body than labour. My Heart sympathizes with you. Whatever Scenes you may be call'd to pass through, may you be sustain'd and supported by that Being in whom we trust. satisfied that however greivious his dispensations, they are wise and just, and we will strive to adore the Hand that "Strikes our comforts dead."

I am anxious to hear frequently tho it be only by a few lines. Cousin Betsy must write to her Sister.

Our Country my dear Sister is in Jeopardy [   ] no prospect of remaining at peace, I hope if the Sword must be drawn, that we Shall have union amongst ourselves. Mr. Gerrys remaining in France embarresses our Government. I believe he acts from the purest motives, and have not the Least fear that his integrity will be brought into Question, but his judgment in staying was wrong, very wrong.

Mr. Marshal whose arival you will have learnt, Says that the Directory have been deceived with respect to the people of this Country. not from any regard to our Rights and Liberties would they have restraind their Hands but from Interest. Interest, as they want our trade, they would have acted a different part, but swoln with pride at their victories, imperious, haughty, and vindictive, they hold us in too much contempt to retract from a single demand which they have made, or receed a single Step, the pomp, expence and parade which the Directory assume and exact, is much greater than that, of any crownd Head and more oppressive to the people ten fold than the Court of Verssails ever was. This is there Republick, this there Liberty and equality! a military despotism. the New Members are all of the party call'd Terrorist. What has America to expect, but to weild her own Arms and prepare to defend herself.

The President you may easily Suppose has a very arduous task, nor is it probable that it will be lighter. he has had an accumulation of Buisness in replying to the numerous addresses which have kept him at his pen three Hours in a day, upon an average for 5 or 6 weeks past. He has more than 30 at this moment unanswerd. Tho a gratefull and pleasing employment as it assures him of the approbation, confidence and Satisfaction of the people in his conduct and administration, it has been a weight of Buisness added to 6 hours more which is every day devoted to other investigations and attentions which the publick calls for [   ] is really worn down. I never saw him so thin. Yet his Spirits are good and his fortitude unshaken. He frequently breaths out a Sigh for the purer air of Braintree, and the tranquil Shades of Quincy It has become oppressively Hot, and this Evening is to be my last drawing Room for the Season. You were misinformd. The President was not insulted on the Fast day. it was in the State House Gardens the Nobility met, and there they had their contest which terminated by sending half a dozen to prison. there had been some incendary Letters, and some threats, which allarmd the Citizens and put them on their gaurd. The light Horse were held in readiness and turnd out. They placed a gaurd before our door where some hundreds of citizens assembled, but not for assault, but protection. I was not allarmd but at Eleven went to Bed and Slept quite easy, when the whole City appeard quiet, tho I believe few went into their Beds.

I know not my dear Sister when I shall be at Quincy. My

Boys will suffer for want of Summer cloathing. I inclose to you
20 dollors, relying upon you to have what is necessary made
for them. I See no charge for washing in your Bill. I insist that
you receive pay for it

I hear mrs Allen is in a decline. It may only be a change of
Life. She should be bled—Alass what Changes since I left
Quincy not quite Nine Months? I number with the dead, the
Aged, the Friends and companions of my own Standing [   ]
as well as Youth and childhood, the Change of circumstances
[   ], which has involved those I loved, and esteemed most
tenderly [   ] distress and difficultys is not the least painfull
reflection [   ] upon the vissitudes of human Life.

How often do those words occur to me, "this Lifes a Dream,
an empty Show." tell Cousin Betsy I will write to her soon.
You can Scarcly believe how much writing I have to do—

I hope mr Blodget deliverd my Letter to you and the Books
for the Children. I had a Letter from mrs Smith this week. She
was well. Caroline better. she longs to see her children. I have
this moment received a Letter from william your son. May he
as he promisses, live to be a comfort to you. My kind Love to
my dear B Q S—Tell her to keep up her Spirits. To cousin
Betsy, my abbe William & John the affection of their and your

A Adams

MEDICAL ADVICE

To Elizabeth Smith Shaw Peabody

My Dear Sister　　　　　　　　Philadelphia July 7th. 1798

I received your Letter of June 21. on the 29th. The extreem
heat of the last week so totally unfitted me for every exertion
that I could neither Eat, Sleep Read write or do any thing but
labour to Breathe. I took the earliest opportunity to consult
Dr Rush upon my dear Neices case, What is past, cannot be
remidied, His opinion, as to her case is that Bleading would
have been the first application necessary. He even thinks now
that it might be salutary to take as much as 3 or 4 oz from her.
If releaved by it, it might be repeated as she could bear it. a

Blister to her Side and that repeated as soon as one drys up he conceives might be of use— he apprehends an abscess forming in her Side from the Statement made by you. he advises to vegetable diet, to the use of whey or Butter milk if her Stomack will bear it. and if she can take animal food, it should be of the Salt kind, such as a little Bit of Tongue or ham—Moderate Excercise. As to pukes, he is altogether averse to the use & habit of them. They procure a temporary determination to the Surface of the Body, and so far lessen pain & cough as to enable patients to use proper exercise, but he conceives Blood letting to remove the Symptoms of Inflammatory Diathesis of much greater utility & riding on Horseback of great use if the patient can bear it these remidies must however be conformd to the Strength & ability of the patient. There is a Lady in this city whom I well know who has been thought to be in a consumption for these 10 Months. Nothing which has been used could conquer the fever. She has a voracious appetite. She is not a patient of Dr. Rush's but her physicians have confind her altogether, for two Months past to Bread & whey. I have not learnt what effect it has had She has not a cough her disorder was produced by a miscarriage—She Sometimes Rides out

we had a case of a Man in Quincy, Anthony Baxter, I believe Cousin Betsy Remembers him who for a long time was thought to be in a consumption an Abessess formd in his Side & dischargd it self by the application of Blisters he is now recoverd. he had every complaint in his Limbs of a Rhumatick kind & did not walk for many Months. His appetite was Ravinious at times, and his Bowels frequently affected—I hope still that my dear Neices case is not past recovery. The Numbness which you say she complains of is an other indication of the Abesess in the Side. Keep her Spirits Cheerfull, and her mind easy. and you my dear Sister will endeavour to bring your mind to that State of Submission and resignation, "which shall say thy will be done." He Gave, and blessed be his Name, he takes but what he Gave." You have a Friend and comforter in your worthy partner whose tenderness upon this trying occasion must endear him, more & more to you. I could say much more to you, and of my dear Neice whose amiable qualities I loved, whose mild & complying temper was a continual feast but I forbear. The fitter she for the abode which may be prepared for her.

I have written to you once Since the Letter by Judge Blodget, and inclosed some money I hope you have received it—

I flatter myself with the hopes of passing a little time at Quincy, but many of my pleasures have fled since I left it the losses I have sustaind by the death of some of my most valuable acquaintance & Friends cast a Gloom over the Scene. Mrs Gill, Mrs Quincy, Dr Clark and Belknap, "grow not on every tree," as Young expresses it. nor can I expect at my Age to have their loss supplied. For those I have left God be praised. May they be continued as Blessing to me.

The worldly circumstances of others is an other Source of affliction to me. To see Families reduced from competance to necessity, and that without even Suspecting their Situation is at one a Stroke unkind and I almost Said, treacherous. I could not forgive such deception—our worthy Friend Mr. Smith is a much injured Man. By the benevolence of his Heart, and the readiness of his Hand, I wish such Men possessd Mines. who upon this Stage of existance can say he is without trouble? the Scripture assures us that Man is born to it, and Religion alone teaches us to bear it like Christians.

It will be scarcly possible to detail these which fall to the Lot of Him who precidies over a Nation in a Season of Such Danger and at a period so critical as the present, they cannot be enumerated. I hope they may be Surmounted, and that as the day is so may the Strength and Support be proportioned,

I wish I could send my dear Boys some of my 4th. of July plumb cake. out of two Hundred & 20 weight I have a Slice remaining for them and that which I think is very good. it would have been a Glorious Sight to them to have seen 400 young Men all in uniform and 60 Grenadeers none of whom exceed 22 years, marching in Review as volunters whose services had been tenderd to their Country in a free will offering to the Chief Majestrate of united America. I feel when I see any of them as tho I had a more than common interest in them. many of them are the Sons and Brothers of my particular Friends and acquaintance and of the first Families in the city. To the committe of young Men from N york I presented a cockade in the middle of which is a small silver Eagle, being the Arms of the United States. They have been polite enough to Name them after me, & the whole volunteer Corps have adopted them,

Louisa is writing to her Sister her Health is very delicate. She has no flesh, yet I know not the reason. I think she suffers for want of proper exercise, to which she is the most [   ] averse of any Young person I ever saw. kiss my little Abbe for me. God preserve her to you To my dear Neice I pray for those comforts & consolations which are neither few nor small. with respectfull Regard to Mr. Peabody & Love to all others I am my ever dear Sister Your truly affectionate

Abigail Adams

GENERAL WASHINGTON CALLED UPON

To Cotton Tufts

Dear Sir   Philadelphia July 10 1798
Congress have agreed to rise on Monday the 16. I doubt however whether they will be able to accomplish it so soon, I sincerely wish they could. You will learn that Capt. Decauter has brought in one, out of the Many privateers which afflict and distress our trade. The Captain of the privateers commission was from the Infamous Hedonvile & to capture all the Enemies of the French Republic, tho the Consul Le Tomb assures us that France has no Idea of a Rupture with us. Congress are getting on with buisness, which be sure might have been compleated three Months ago, much more to their honour & reputation. The Secretary of War went off to Mount Vernon yesterday morning with Letters & Commission for the old Hero & General, not however without some fears and apprehensions for the Success of the Mission—Yet when the Genll takes into view the State of the Country, the desire the President has that he should aid in raising an Army advise in officering and organizing of it, the confidence which the publick have in his wisdom, Virtue and integrity and the weight his Name, fame & Character will give both at Home and abroad I do not See how the Remnant of Life can be more usefully employd, and that I trust is what he will respect. An other consideration will weigh with him, Whom is it safe to commit so important a trust to? That decission is of much more

concequence and importance now, than it was in our Revolution. Many passions have Since grown up to which our Country was then a Stranger. the State of the world has changed much for the worse, and the Spirit of innovation, Revolution and change is become the order of the day. I think no appointment could have been made which would have stifled the Envy and Ambition, the thirst of power and command which was rising in a Mass throughout the United States. those who expected to have filld this place, dare not publickly avow their dissapointment.

We are waiting with the utmost anxiety to hear from abroad, No News of the arrival of any dispatches which went from hence, nor can we learn a word from our Ministers of a later date than the begining of April.

Soper has been here for more than a week. He disclosd all our Secret buisness about the Building, and I gave as good a Statement as it was in my power to do. I had no repremand, but a wish that the Building had been extended the whole Length, and a fear least it was done upon too narrow a Scale, so you see Sir that I was aware the thing would give pleasure when done, provided no care or concern was calld for in consultation. Mrs. Porter must have tables proper for her, and half a dozen chairs if she wants as I suppose she will—

It was the Presidents desire that Dr. Welch Should give into your Hands, all mr Adams concerns with which he was intrusted together with the power, if transferable. I have written thus to the Doctor—and I now inclose a Letter of mr Adams's to the Dr, which when you have read you will return to the doctor. The Dr writes me that he had not drawn for the money in Holland which mr Adams requested him to, as he had not seen a prospect of disposing of it to advantage. This I think a very fortunate circumstance. The House in Boston & some share in the cannals is I believe all the property, or real estate mr Adams owns. I have written to mr Adams but the uncertainety of receiving an answer for a long time make me wish that you might have the care of his little affairs untill I know his mind

I know not what can be done for the Dr. The office which he requested the President could not consistant with the duty he owed the publick give him—In his profession I should suppose he might support his Family. It is Strange, very Strange to what lengths honest Men will go deceiving themselves—

The Weather the beginning of July was insufferably Hot. Since which, it is quite cool—and more like our Northern weather. The Season for second crops very promising—I hope we shall have the pleasure of meeting in August. I fear not before. With my kind Regards to Mrs. Tufts, and all other Friends, I am dear Sir Your obliged Friend,   Abigail Adams

In order to read Mr. Adams's Letter you must hold it singly to the light

PREPARING FOR WAR

To Thomas Boylston Adams

my dear Thomas   Philadelphia July 1798
   As there is some probability that Thomas Welch will Embark before I shall return to Quincy, I write from hence; I shall esteem myself peculiarly fortunate to see you again in your Native Country, a longer residence abroad in your Situation, would be wholy incompatable both with your interest and future establishment in Life, as you will have to commence again in your profession—you may also find it necessary to take an active part in defence of your Country, I should like to see you enrolld in the Grenadeer Company of this city. I send you by this opportunity what I presume he will not himself neglect too, your Friend Quincys oration deliverd upon the fourth of July, it is a very handsome performance, and does honour to him. I hope it will bring him forward in political Life. I wrote you the loss he sustaind in the winter past, by the Death of his Mother. Never was parent and Child more cordially united. His marriage previous to her death to an accomplishd and amiable woman, is in some measure a compensation to him. you will learn from the papers I send, and have forwarded allready, in the week past by way of Hamburgh, the temper and disposition of our Country, that She is approaching to very

serious times, when every citizen will find it necessary to exert all his Energies to preserve, and secure the Liberty and independance of the Country. Congress have risen this week after a session of Eight Months, the first part of which was neither employd to their honour or the benifit of the Country. their last deeds may be ranked amongst their best, an Alien Bill, a Sedition Bill and a Bill declaring void, all our Treaties & conventions with France, are of the Number.

You who were here at the Time of the insurrection and was witness to the apathy which for a long time possessd this City, would now be gratified to see the Martial Spirit which exists here; all the young Men of the City are training to Arms. they have at their own expence put themselves in uniform, and are about four hundred in Number, beside a Grenadeer Company and a company of Cavilery. Genll Mackpherson commands them. a Company of Artilliry is forming. Mackpherson expects soon to have a regular Legion. for a time, they excercised every morning, now twice a week some young Quaker have joind them, as they say *to prevent War*. many more would, if they could obtain the consent of their parents. The Quakers are more united in opposition to France than they ever were in any former war. Whilst this State have come forward and retreaved their Character by active exertion, and a firm spirit, the City of N York manifests a coldness and an apathy, quite astonishing, as they have all at hazard, and are in a very exposed and defenceless situation. the Levingstone Aristocracy, their corruption & venality, is a millstone upon the federal part. there is as much of Jacobinism there, as in any other state in the union, and I would hope more. even Virginna is assumeing a more cordial & candid asspect. the Members lately Elected to Congress, are said to be Six out of ten, antifederal from N york.

N England behaves well, with few exceptions they have done themselves great honour at the late Session of the Legislature mr Dexter is Chosen Senator to Congress in lieu of mr Sedwick resignd. it is the exchange of one good Man, for an other, but that is not always the case Freeman will not be reelected, I wish I was as certain that Varnum would fail. I inclose to you the list of Nomination for the Staff of our Army you will naturally ask where is the Col.? Gen'll Washington who was consulted, Named him for Adjutent General. he was nominated to the Senate but decidedly negatived, for prejudices which as an officer I think ought not to have influenced them. it was done in a hurry, without proper inquiry, and upon the last day of the Session, thus is one of the best officers we have, rejected for reasons which would have equally applied to Lee of Virgina and I shall be glad if at the winding up, it will not be found to apply to many others a Military Life I have ever considerd him as peculiarly calculated to shine in, he has fought and bled in the Service of his Country, and I believe would have cordially done so again, if call'd to the trial—I expect it will compleatly depress him, and tho it was done by Friends as well as foes I cannot but think better information would have exculpated him from "charges which would have been proved unfounded." You know and the world know that in pecuniary affairs he never conducted with the approbation of his nearest relatives, but the School of adversity is a usefull one, and tho not pleasant, her paths are strewed with instruction.

I hunger for Letters from you. we have not any intelligence to be relied upon since the month of April, from any quarter. Rumours only that mr Gerry had left Paris: Mrs Johnson desires me to present her Love to you. She says that She was mortified that you did not mention her in Mrs Adams Letter, that you was much of a favorite with her. Mrs Johnson is not fixd in the most agreeable part of America. Mr Cranch has removed to George Town, and is very intimate with the Family. Our Friend are all well, who survive, but we have lost many valuable ones in the year past. Dr Clark and Belknap are of the Number who will long be rememberd and regreted.

I am my dear Son with the tenderest affection your Mother
Abigail Adams

July 20, 1798

RECOVERED FROM ILLNESS

To John Quincy Adams

My dear Son   1798 Quincy November the 15th
Once more my dear Son it is permitted me to address you by Letter, thanks to the great Giver of every blessing.

I wrote to you previous to my leaving Philadelphia by Thomas Welch the 20 of July. Since which I have not been able to write a single Letter. I left Philadelphia on the 25th of July; on the 8th of August, I reachd my own Habitation at Quincy; went into my Chamber, and for eleven weeks did not leave it; great part of the time, I hourly expected my dissolution—

I took leave of all my Children, and left with your Father my Blessing for them; your Sister was with me the whole time, which was a very great Satisfaction to me; her filial affection & constant attention afforded me much comfort and relief amidst the distressing disorder which threatned my Life. The Season of my journey was the hottest I ever knew; the fatigue proved too great for my constitution, and brought on a Billious dierea which accompanied with an intermitting fever baffeld the skill of my Physicians. I am releived from the former of my complaints, but the fever I cannot get rid of. It hangs upon me, depressing my Spirits and depriving me of my Sleep in a manner which I never before experienced. I have hopes that it will wear away as the cold weather approaches.

This dangerous Sickness my dear Son has prevented my acknowledging the receit of your many kind Letters which I have received during my sickness as well as wholy interupted my communication with you. The Letters which I have received and are yet unacknowledged are No 36 May the 4th., 37 May 30th, No 35 June 11th, 39 June 22, No 40 June 27th and this day I have received your excellent Letter of july 25 No 41. I cannot sufficiently thank you for your punctuality. If Life is spaired me, I shall be constant in my returns, but my opportunities for obtaining intelligence will not be so good as at Phyladelphia. I am obliged tho most reluctantly to relinquish my journey this winter, and submit to your Fathers going without me. As the Session will I trust be short, I am supported with that hope. the thought of being seperated at so great a distance in my low State of Health, has contributed to keep me low Spirited, but when duty calls my own happiness has always been with me; but a secondary consideration.

Since I left Philadelphia it has again experienced that desolating pestilence, the yellow fever, which has raged with greater malignity than at any former period. Brisler and Family fled as I directed when I left them, but four of my domesticks who belonged to the City fell a sacrifice to it.

Many of my acquaintance have been the unhappy victims, amongst the Number the amiable Miss Lucy Breck & the Lovely Miss Wescot, tho both out of the city. Mr Anthony the Elder, a greater loss Philadelphia could not have sustaind of a private Citizen. Death who is no distinguisher of persons or Characters leveld with the dust, the disorganizer Bache, & the true Friend of his Country, the honest upright Fenno. His Son still carries on the paper, treading in the Steps of his Father. N York has been severely dealt by, with this same fever, which made the city nearly desolate for several Months, by the fleeing of the inhabitants and the destruction of those which remain in the city. Nor has Boston been exempt from this deadly foe, tho it proved less mortal there; thousands of the inhabitants removed into the Country. they are now returning to it.

Our Country with few exceptions, continues to increase in vigor, and to be ready in spirit to meet the Great Nation; despising both their arts and their Charms. from the most remote and distant parts of the union addresses flow in, speaking the same decided language and approbating the measures persued by our Government. Powder and Ball are the only tribute talkd of for Tallerand. I cannot omit the pleasure of inclosing to you a Character of him drawn by T Paine at the opening of the new Theatre. You know his talent for Satire. I wish it could be translated into French without loosing any of its point. The compliment to the president is inimitable, but read and judge for yourself—

In several of your late Letters you have mentiond a subject which has been a source of distress to me for a long time. It is hard, upon you to have your prudence and oceonomy thus trifled away, by one and an other—

I have written again upon the subject and expostulated in such terms as must procure an explanation, and replie. I will write you what ever I can collect, but the poor child is unhappy I am sure. He is not at peace with himself: and his conduct does not meet my wishes. he has an amiable wife, prudent and discreet, who has every wish and disposition to render *Home* the most delightfull Spot. Two lovely Children—I hope my Letters will in time have their effect. I have discharged my duty, I hope faithfully but my dying Bed was embitterd (as I then thought it) with distress for the only Child whose conduct ever gave me pain.

I hoped you would e'er this have sent a power to Dr Tufts to have taken your property into his Hands—Dr W-h has never said a word respecting it tho I once wrote him upon it, and my sickness prevented my doing any thing further for you—

My Love to Mrs Adams to whom I will write. poor Thomas Johnson was very dangerously sick at the same time I was. I think from the nature of his complaints, a Spitting of Blood, that he can never be well. Nancy is married. I suppose however you get Letters frequently from the Family which give you a circumstantial account of all that concerns them. My Sickness has interupted my intercourse by Letters as formerly—We have had one weding in our Family and it was at this House. Betsy Smith was married to Mr Foster, whom I dare say you knew, a worthy young Man in Boston an upholsterer. My paper only allows me room to say I am Your affectionate   M—

THANKSGIVING LETTER

To John Adams

My dearest Friend   Quincy Nov'br 29 1798

This is our Thanksgiving day, when I look Back upon the year past. I perceive many, very many causes for thanksgiving, both of a publick and private nature. I hope my Heart is not ungratefull, tho sad; it is usually a day of festivity when the Social Family circle meet together tho seperated the rest of the year. No Husband *dignifies my Board*, no Children add gladness to it, no Smiling Grandchildren Eyes to Sparkle for the plumb pudding, or feast upon the mincd Pye. Solitary and alone I behold the day after a sleepless night, without a joyous feeling. Am I ungratefull? I hope not. Brother Cranchs illness prevented Him and my sister from joining me, and Boylston Adams's sickness confineing him to his House debared me from inviting your Brother and Family. I had but one resource and that was to invite mr and mrs Porter to dine with me: and the two Families to unite in the Kitchin with Pheby the only surviving Parent I have, and thus we shared in the Bounties of providence.

I was not well enough to venture to meeting and by that means lost an excellent discourse deliverd by mr Whitman, upon the numerous causes of thankfullness and gratitude which we all have to the Great Giver of every perfect Gift; nor was the late Glorious victory gained by Admiral Nelson over the French omitted by him, as in its concequences of Great importance in checking the mad arrogance of that devouring Nation.

And here let me congratulate you upon the event, as now made certain. I hope it will prove of great advantage to us, as well as to all the powers Whom France has abused debased and insulted.

I cannot speak of them in the stile of Gov. Henry, tho I like his Speech, and belive he made it without the aid of Laudanum, the address from thence I like, make a good answer to it.

I presume you reachd Philadelphia on saturday. I wrote to you twice to N york to the care of Charles and twice I have written to you addrest to Philadelphia. I hope you received the Letters.

I am as ever your truly affectionate   A Adams

JOHN QUINCY'S INVESTMENTS

To John Quincy Adams

My dear Son—   Quincy december 2d 1798

Last Evening I received your Letter of Sepbr—4th No 42— Accept my thanks. it grieved me to think how anxious you must feel before an other Letter from my hand would reach you. I was rejoiced to Learn that Thomas Welch was safely arrived at Hamburgh. I hope you will find in him a true American, but as you observe your Brothers place cannot be supplied to you. I am anxious least he should make a winters voyage here. our coast is dreadfull and every Storm will distress me, but He who careth for the fowls of heaven and the Small Sparrow of the Field will be his Guardian & protector, and I pray Him to return this dear amiable Son to his parents and country in Safety—

You judge and think so accurately respecting the affairs of your Country, the conduct it ought to take, preserve and mantain, that every Syllable you write, ought to be made publick. I hope and trust that you will not be dissapointed in the final result. I am sure you will not, if the advice and counsel of the Head of the Nation is sufficiently attended to; but intrigue art and wickedness work in darkness, envy and ambition stand ready to seize the Reigns, and push the possessor from His hold—but I trust this cannot be effected even by the aid and power of the Great Nation. The Authentick account of Admiral Nelsons Glorious victory over the French fleet in Rosetta Bay has fortunately arrived before the meeting of Congress and will I trust have its influence in Silencing the advocates for the Great Nation. Logan has returnd but neither he or those who sent him will reap any lawrels from his mission. he is much despised by all fiderilist. We shall see what figure mr Gerrys correspondence with Tallerand will make when publishd. He will not sink I trust more than he has already. Genll Pinckney appears much the boldest firmest and most decided Character. mr Marshall has sunk his Character very much with all his real Friends by His answers to certain questions proposed to him by an Elector previous to his voting for him as a Representitive to Congress. I own I was astonishd that a Man of his knowledge should condemn the Alien and Sedition Bill, past the last Session of Congress, Tho they were shaved and pared, to almost nothing. they have had a salutary effect, weak as they are. Can any Good thing come out of Nor can a Virginnian have a clear Head?

I received a Letter from your Father on Saturday, informing me of his safe arrival on the 25 of November at Philadelphia. I wrote you on the 15 of the last Month in which Letter I accounted to you for my long Silence oweing to a dangerous Sickness of three months, and that my infirm State of Health prevented My accompanying your Father this winter. During my Sickness your Father wrote to you—

Since I wrote to you I have received a Letter from N York— in answer to one I wrote upon receiving yours of July 25. I transcribe it. "my Brother's money was secured upon Mortgage. the first years interest I payd out of my own pocket. I was prevaild upon to transfer that Security for a Note to save colonel S——h from immediate confinement. Mr. Justice Smith is the drawer of the Note, which is certainly Good in the event, but oweing to the fall of the price of Land he has not been able to advance the interest in time how could I write this to my Brother who would have charged me with imprudence in the appropriation of his money, when had he been upon the Spot, as much as I have done would have been Sanctiond by him. I have not enjoyd one moments comfort for upwards of two years on this account, my Sleep has been disturbed, and my waking hours embitterd."

I believe the account true because I learnt as much from Sally last Novbr twelve month upon which I cautiond you. Justice Smith lives upon his Lands and has a large tract in possession. but what he owes I know not Charles you know never had the power of resistance, I dare say his own property has gone the same way. I have written Charles and blamed him for not writing you and laying facts before you in which case you would not have thought so hardly of him as from his total Silence you had reason to, I have also written Dr. Welch a second time desiring him to transfer to Dr. Tufts his power and to commit your affairs to his Hands. Charles says you have directed him to pay the interest now due to me which he will do by the first of Jan'ry. I have not received any direction from you what to do with it, but I shall deliver it to dr Tufts to be laid out in publick Securitys, if you had purchased with your Money the deferrd Stock you would have done better than you could any other way. our Stocks rise, very little at Market but in case of a war they would undoubtedly fall. I think however I should risk them;

your Aunt Cranch desires me to tell mrs Adams that her Son is a near Neighbour to her Father, that both he and mrs Cranch have found parental attention towards them mr Cranch removed to George Town, and took mr Cooks office at the request of Mr Johnson & has taken mr Johnsons buisness into his Hands Both Families live in the greatest Harmony, and are mutually a comfort to each other. I regret that mrs Adams has got into a Habit which I fear will injure her constitution. I Love her for the Good qualities she possesses, and rejoice that your Heart trusteth in her. may she continue to do you good all the days of Your Life.

The Seperation from your Father this Winter is a trial to me more severe I think than formerly. the danger I was a long time in of a final Seperation, has only more closely bound us to each other, and having during our connection been so often Seperated, we wish the few years remaining to us might be Spent together, but I early learnt the lesson of sacrificing to the publick. I do not write to my dear Thomas I hope to embrace him e'er long in his Native Land. With the Sincerest and Warmest affection I am   Your Mother

"LIVING WITHOUT FEMALS"

To John Adams

my dearest Friend   Quincy December 15 1798
   I last Evening received yours of Novbr 28th. If oceans do not rool between us, mountains have arrisen. The late sevear snow storm has shut me in, as close as a mouse in a trap, and that so early in the Season, that no probability appears, of any comfortable travelling this winter. The Banks are so high, so hardly compacted together that they will not be removed untill Spring; I am well persuaded, so that I must sigh at Quincy, and you at Philadelphia, without being able to afford each other any personal comfort, or Genial warmth; you say you are fractious; you will have causes enough for vexation I doubt not. The Military arrangment is an ample Feild if you had no other; I see by the paper of to day, that Genll Brooks has resignd. It reminds me of a story of a certain Irishman who observing that his outer rows of corn were not so good as his others, determined that in future he would have no outer Row. It is very difficult so to place the outer row as to satisfy those which succeed, but nothing tends so much to render a Man Fractious as living without Femals about him. Even tho Sometimes they may be glad to lie low and let the sand fly over, they know how to temper the wind to the shorne Lamb and to Sooth into good humour, the jaring Elements. You see I am willing to keep up my self concequence, as well as the honour and dignity of the Sex. I have on Authority in

point, our minister at Berlin in his last Letter Speaking of his wife says, "her Lovely disposition and affectionate heart, afford me constant consolation amidst all the distresses, cares and vexations which the publick concerns, as well as my private affairs so thickly strew in my way." I hope you can sleep a nights. I find it such a comfort to have my rest returning to me, that I know not how to prize it sufficiently. It restores the little indispositions of the day but I find tranquility of mind so necessary to my rest, that a little matter agitating me is sufficient still, to rob me for the night of that slumber which is indispensable for my Health.

Brother Cranch is getting better. He sees a fullfillment of the Prophecies in the report of the Russians being permitted to pass through the Dardenells an Event he has been long looking for, that once obtain the door will never be closed untill the Turks are driven out and their citys destroyed, according to holy writ.

I shall write to mrs otis from whom I received a kind Letter last Evening, next week, but I rememberd you warnd me against writing much yet it is all my amusement. I want to know how the world passes, tho I cannot gain admittance now into the Cabinet.

Remember me to all my old Friends and acquaintance who inquire after me, and tell them that I very much regreet, that I have it not in my power to shew them those attentions which I should take pleasure in manifesting, if my Health had permitted me to have accompanied you to Philadelphia. A Good repose to you. I hope I shall enjoy the Same. Ever yours

A Adams

WELCOME HOME

To Thomas Boylston Adams

My dear Thomas   Quincy Janry. 20th 1799

I Congratulate you my dear Son, upon your safe arrival in your Native Country; and myself that I have the prospect of seeing you again, a prospect which for many Months I had no hopes of realizing. as your Father can inform you, and to the very low State of my Health, it is oweing that I cannot so soon as I wish enjoy the pleasure of welcomeing you Home; and meeting you at Philadelphia, where I should have been, if my Health would have permitted. I am however much recoverd since your Father left me. I have been in an anxious State of mind for your Safety ever since I learnt that you would have a winters voyage, and it was no small releif to me when the paper announced the Arrival of the Alexander Hamilton, and "mr T B Adams, the third Son of our Beloved President" the printer was so obliging as to add. I hope in the course of the week to receive a confirmation from your own Hand. your duty and your inclination must carry you first to Philadelphia, and if I can be assured of your safety and of your Health, I shall wait patiently for your return here, as will best correspond with your views, and your convenience requiring however as early intelligence from you; and from your Brother & Sister, as you can transmit to me. your Friends here all rejoice with me, and congratulate me upon your arrival.

I am my dear Son your ever affectionate Mother,

A Adams.

"THE INTEGRITY OF MR. GERRYS HEART"

To John Adams

My dearest Friend   Fryday Quincy Janry. 25 1799

I Received yours of the 15th on wedensday, and participated in the Joy and pleasure you must have experienced in meeting a dear and amiable Son after a four years Seperation. How happy should I have been to have folded him at the same time to my Bosom, and felt a pleasure which the Childless can never experience,

I have already written both to you, and to him, respecting his comeing to Quincy. I know so well your lonely Situation, and your need of Some Solace, from the weight and cares of your office, that I can restrain my impatience to see him; whilst I know he is affording comfort to you;

I hope you all had an agreable Evening on wednesday. I should have ventured a sleepless night I believe if I had been with You. They have managed the matter better this Year; than the last;

On Wednesday I received a visit from president Willard, and Mr. Gerry. They were so polite as come on purpose; they both requested me to make their respects to you. The president appears to be quite recoverd tho paller and thinner than formerly; in the course of the conversation Mr. Gerry asked me if the paper's had yet been laid before Congress? I replied that I had not seen any account of them. It is a subject of daily inquiry and some observe that, tho they presume there cannot be any thing very important, Yet as the Message denoted some communications, it is rather extrodanary that they have not yet appeard,—

If they are detaind for comments: I should suppose they had been long enough in the Hands of [   ] to write annotations upon them. The S—y will not acquire any popularity by this conduct. The public are quite competant to judge upon them without any aid. I own I have felt angry with [   ] ever since I read a Letter. Marshall has done more mischief than Mr Gerry, as his own State demonstrates. Who ever questions the integrity of Mr. Gerrys Heart, does him an injury, tho I thought yesterday from his Slowness of Speech and his round about & about, manner of conveying his Ideas, I would as soon vote for a voluable old women to an Embassy, as for him.

The weather is now very fine. I hope you have as good in Philadelphia.

Mr. Porter wishes me to ask you weather you meant the Barn Manure or the Yard Manure carried upon the Hull? or Both.

With the tenderest affection I am Yours,   A Adams

Tell Thomas he must prepare to see his mother ten years older than when he left her; time and Sickness have greatly altered her.

"A STATEMENT OF THIS BUISNESS"

To John Quincy Adams

My dear Son   Quincy Febry 1 1799

It is with pleasure insepressible, I inform you of the safe arrival of your Brother Thomas at N york after a passage of 46 days. My Mind was relieved from a load of anxiety by this agreable intelligence from his own Hand, the danger from comeing upon our Coast in the Winter Season, and the severe and frequent Snow Storms we have experienced this winter kept me in a constant allarm for his Safety, but thanks to a kind and overruling providence which has preserved his Life, and restored him to his Country and friends again, often have I had cause of Gratitude that my dear connections have been protected in their various voyages; some of them made in very inclemnant Seasons and amidst the dangers of War; your Brother went on to Philadelphia immediatly where he was most joyfully and kindly received by an affectionate Father; I relinquish the prospect of speedily folding him to my Bosom, in the hope of his being able to solace and entertain his Father, deprived as he is, of every other branch of his Family, he will experience a double pleasure from his Society, he wants that comfort, and relief encompassed as he is with public cares and perplexities as well as a share of private anxiety for the Health of your Mother, which is still feeble.

I received by your Brother your kind and affectionate Letter, the regret you express at parting with him, is a pleasing proof of his merrit, and your affection, I wish it was thought consistant with the publick Service to call you home, a foreign Embassy is but an honorable Excile, yet it qualifies for future usefullness; when rightly improved.

You will learn from the public papers I send you, the politicks of the day; William Shaw has been very attentive in sending them to me since he has been in Philadelphia. The Govenour Senate and House of this State, are truly Federal there are but 4 Jacobins in the House, Hill of Cambridge the only one of *any* abilities, they make no Head with 90 or 100 Majority against them. Virgina alass poor Virgina and her bantling Kentucky there conduct is despised and rejected; But your Brother will now detail all these Subjects to you with more accuracy and precission than I can, and to him I shall consign the task, and proceed to give you some account of your own private affairs.

If you have received two Letters which I have written you, since my Sickness, you will learn from them what was then in my power to communicate respecting your affairs. It became indispensable to obtain your papers from dr W. a Friend was so kind as to inform me, that two Hundred dollors were due upon your Canal Shares, that the dr. had been repeatedly calld upon for payment; always promised, but had not performed, and that the Shares must be sold, unless the Money was immediatly paid. I wrote to the dr. W., with as much delicacy as possible, requesting him to transfer his power to dr Tufts; I hinted to him that money might be necessary upon the Shares of the Canals, and that he would oblige me by sending the papers. I heard not a word for a fort night. I then wrote to Mr Smith, (who is a very great sufferer by the dr) and stated to him the Situation in which I was, he went to the dr and prevaild upon him to go with him to a Notiary public, and transfer, the power, & send me the papers: I deliverd them to dr Tufts, and paid into his Hands the 200 dollors which were required, 25 Guineys of it, together with a Year and half interest upon that Sum. I took the dr receit for being the money due to you from me; and which I retaind that it might not be lost, as too much of your property already has been. I have written your Brother a Statement of this buisness; you have I find by your Letter to me, committed all your concerns to his care, but unless he resides here, I should think those in this State, had best remain with the dr. I forgot to take a list of the papers deliverd: but will get it and send you tho I have not a doubt, but they are all you left, the Rent of the House had been all paid up, the last quarter a few days previous to the delivery of the papers. No account or Receit accompanied them, but a few lines informing me, that an account had been sent you. When a Man gets embarrassed in his circumstances it seems to stiffel all moral feelings, and he permits himself to do things, which he would have started at, if he had been thought capable of them, the Society of Arts to which the dr was Secretary lose 500 dollors—Mr Smith by indorcments for him, thousands—

I am Grieved for him and for his Family the Stroke was so unexpected to mrs W—h that it threw her into a fever. She has however recoverd in some measure tho both he & she are much depressed—Your Friends here desire to be kindly rememberd to you—I hear from your Father two or three times a week, he is well

William Shaws account, of his reception of Thomas was really affecting. Thomas says in a Letter to me, "I received the cordial welcome of a Father, who approved of the conduct and behaviour of the Son who had been absent."—

William Shaw performs the part of private Secretary to Satisfaction, he is attentive and obliging and will improve, it is a fortunate Situation for him.

Your Aunt Peabody Sustaind such a Shock from the loss of her dear daughter, as her feeble Frame can scarcly sustain. Religion alone bears her Spirits up—and to the Brighter world above she looks with a pleasing hope, of meeting the departed Spirit of her amiable daughter, who exhibited through a painfull Sickness, the Cheerfull hope, and the full assurance of a blessed immortality.

My Love to your dear Louisa may you mutually supply to each other, every Relative and Friend from whom you are seperated. I am grieved to learn that my Friend Mrs Johnson does not enjoy good health She suffers from depression of Spirits, and from the pecuniary embarressments of mr J—s affairs. Mr Cranch writes me that a decision will soon take place, which he hopes will relieve them. I have not received but one Letter from her for a long time. From your Sister I heard not long since she was well. She has a lovely Girl, soft in her manners, mild and affectionate as a Lamb, yet sprightly and active as a Bird, Sensible and intelligent beyond her Years. She was with me with her Mamma during all my Sickness, the Boys are at Atkinson academy in mr Peabodys Family, are studious governable and promise fair. My paper is exhausted leaving me only Room to add Your ever affectionate Mother

"I BLUSH FOR MY COUNTRY!"

To John Quincy Adams

my dear Son   Quincy Febry 10th 1799
   I will not let a vessel Sail for Hamburgh that I know of,
without taking a few Lines from me, if it be only to inform you
of the State of my Health, which I know you are affectionately
interested in. It is not what I wish it was, tho by no means So
low as in the Summer past.
   your Brother is on his way to Quincy. I hope to see him in
the course of the Week, and to disswade him from his present
intention of settling in philadelphia. The plague, for I know
not by what other Name to call it, must drive him annually
from it, or what is more to be dreaded, he will fall a Sacrifice to
it, unless some measures are Speedily discoverd to Stop its
progress. it becomes every year more destructive and horible.
there is no doubt of its Still being in the City, tho the winter
checks its banefull influence. N York and Boston both Sufferd
the last Season. much pains is taking to investigate the causes.
I hope the Reserches may prove successfull, and God grant a
Remedy may be found. it has proved a Soar judgment; and
Calamity to the Country.
   I send you by this opportunity the latest papers, and mr
Gerrys correspondence with Talleyrand as communicated to
Congress, and the Secretary of States Report upon it.
   Whilst our Countrymen in General repell with, Indignation
every attempt upon their Independance, there are to be found
degenerate wretches, who Strive to create divissions and fo-
ment animosities. The Alien and Sedition Bills are made their
Agents, by grosely misrepresenting them, and the views and
designs of Goverment.
   You will see the poison working in Virgina & Kentucky. foreign influence is united with domestic intrigue. Blount the Impeached Blount is Elected president of the Kentucky assembly
   I Blush for my Country! Yet their honesty and federilism is
prevelant, for the Mad Resolutions of Virgina & Kentucky will
be rejected by every Legislature in the union. four have already
done it.

I inclose a Letter received last week from Mrs Johnson. it may arrive when no one of so late a date may come to hand. I wish the contents were more consoling to her daughter. tell her She must write frequently to her Mother and keep up her Spirits. my kindest love to her

adieu my dear Son. God Bless and preserve you and yours prays your ever affectionate Mother,   Abigail Adams

I wrote you by way of Hamburgh the latter end of Janry. Your Father was well on the 1st of this month. I had Letters from him

"THEY WISHT THE OLD WOMAN HAD BEEN THERE"

To John Adams

My dearest Friend   Febry. 27th 1799. Quincy

Yesterday afternoon Mr. Greenleaf returnd from Boston, and as he, as well as my others Neighbours; are particularly attentive and kind, in bringing Letters and papers to me as well; as of communicating all News. He came full fraught, with the appointment of Mr. Murrey minister Plenipo to France, a measure which had astonishd all the Federilist; and was a Subject of great Speculation in Boston. Soon after Thomas returnd from Boston, thinking to bring me great News but found himself forestall'd. He however got a Good Story in Boston. Some of the Feds who did not like being taken so by Surprize, said they wisht the old woman had been there; they did not believe it would have taken place. This was pretty sausy, but the old woman can tell them they are mistaken, for she considers the measure as a master Stroke of policy; knowing as she did that the pulse had been feeling through that minister for a long time. Besides the appointment shows that the disposition of the Government is still pacific, and puts to the test the Sincerity of the directory, who if they are really inclined to accommodate have the door held open to them; and upon them rests in the Eyes of all the World, the responsibility. It is a measure which strikes in the

Head Jacobinism. It came as unexpected to them, as to the Federilists. It will also prevent the Directory sending a French minister here which was not desirable, knowing the Nature of the animal. It cannot be considerd as a degradation restricted as I lean the appointment is, that no negotiation shall commence. But with a minister of equal Rank specially appointed to treat; I have not heard an opinion upon it, but revolving the Subject upon my pillow, I call it a master Stroke of polocy, Even tho it should terminate in a buble it brings the directory, to the touch Stone.

I was vext however to see our House of Rep's stop in the midst of a wise measure, and take for granted, what they had no buisness to consider; not a [   ] should be released in concequence of the appointment. To ensure any kind of Success to the negotiation, they should be prepared at all points for War, if it fails.

Pray am I a good politician?

We have had for the last ten days winter as severe as any before. It has frozen the Rivers and bay more than any time before, and it is now snowing with voilence. As to my own Health, it has its up's and down's. As soon as I feel any thing tolerable, I get out, and will not lose the air. Then I get housed a day or two; but I endeavour to keep up my Spirits, and take what comfort I can; as I go along comforting myself that it will be better by and by.

In my last I mentiond to you leaving Clinker for Thomas but I did not calculate that he was the only Saddle Horse you had, untill afterwards, when I recollected the loss of one and that I had two here;

You mention that Dr. Tufts might draw upon you for any Sum within Reason. The Sum which he will draw for will be 500 dollors, unless you should give orders that any further Sum should be laid out in public securities; I know not the reason, but the funds are allways a shilling in a pound higher here than at Philadelphia. They are now 6 per cents, at 16 & 4 pence, fallen a shilling in a pound since the new loan. As to defered Stock, there is not any to be had. The 6 per cents are the most advantages, only that two per cent is [   ] annually paid off.

I wrote you that French would give with Belchers place, 52 pound ten shilling.

It looks so like the depdth of winter that Spring appears far off. I hope you will be at home before much is wanted to be done.

I am my dear Friend affectionatly Your　　　　　A Adams

28th

I forgot to mention to you that the Lot of Mrs. Veseys sold at Auction for 4 hundred and 90 dollors. Prat has bought it as he did the pew I suppose.

"OUR NATIONAL AFFAIRS PROSPER"

To John Quincy Adams

My dear Son　　　　　Quincy June 12th 1799

It was with inexpresible pleasure that I yesterday read a Letter to your Father from you dated the 18th of Feb'ry, This is the first line which has reachd us from you; since the return of your Brother; I have not any from you of a later date than Sep'br. By the last No. 7 or Eight of your Letters must be missing, one public Letter of december was received from you, by the Secretary of State; he writes your Father that he has not had any since; the Severity of the Winter will in some measure account for the difficulty of intercourse—You can easily imagine how solicitious I am to hear of your Health, and that of my much esteemed Daughter, whose repeated misfortunes makes me anxiously concernd for her.

I have not written to you so frequently as formerly for two reasons, I knew your Brothers information would be more correct, and his intelligence better communicated than mine, and other, and more powerfull reason with me, has been oweing to my low State of Health, which has made writing hurtfull and burdensome to me. my constitution sufferd so severe a shock the last Summer, that I have never recoverd it, and at my Age, have little reason to expect it. I am so well as to be able to attend to the necessary affairs of my Family, but all large and mixt Societys I am obliged to avoid, or I should have this day accompanied your Father to the funeral of our much regreted

Govr. Sumner. Whilst I am writing I hear the constant discharge of minut Guns. The military tribute whilst honour, affection and gratitude flow from the hearts of his fellow Citizens, the inclosed papers will shew you that no Man could be more beloved nor his death more sincerely lamented;

Beloved honourd and Respected, in the meridian of his Reputation, and midst of his usefullness, he is by a short and painfull disease, which from the first attack, was pronounced by his physicians Mortal, he is taken from his Country Family and Friends, just as the suffrages of 24 thousand of his fellow citizens had again called him to the Chief Majestray of the State. He was a firm undaunted steady, uniform patriot, all Hearts acknowledge his worth, every tongue laments his death.

Our National affairs prosper our Navy is rising most rapidly, and our Commerce is amply protected, our Revenue abundantly productive, in spight of all the Gallic wickedness plunder and Robbery—National honour and Respectability is increasing, the Spirit of Jacobinism is sinking, Virginia and N York have shewn by their late Elections that those who have heretofore Represented them have not deserved their confidence, they have made very great changes and I hope the Government will be benifited by a more respectable union of counsel's.

The News from abroad, as it respects the Great Nation affords us much satisfaction, we cannot but rejoice when we see any check to the progress of that desolating gigantic power which has proved the Besom of destruction to every Nation, whether cloathed in the Hostile Garb of an Enemy, or the specious Mantle of Friendship.

Your Brother Thomas left Quincy in April, with a resolution of setling in Philadelphia where he has taken lodgings and an office. I hope he will not be driven away by the yellow fever, nor fall a sacrifice to it. I have many anxieties upon account of his Health; I question whether it will ever permit him, to practise at the Bar.

Your Brother Charles is, what shall I say that will not pain us both? Would to God that I might kill the fatted calf, and put upon him the Robe of rejoicing. he has formed some good resolutions Could he keep them how would it rejoice us all, but the Heart, the principles must co-opperate. "How sharper than a Serpent tooth," it is to have a graceless child, may you my dear Son never experience.

Blessed be God, I have those in whom I can rejoice. May their Lives and usefullness be continued.

I congratulate you upon the safe arrival of your Books from Lisbon. We shall get them to Quincy next week, where every necessary attention shall be paid to them. They shall be opend aired and repacked and safely lodgd untill you call for them, which I hope will not be a very distant day.

Our Friends here are all well, but one breach has been made, since I last wrote you, our venerable Aunt Thaxter at the Age of 80 dyed a month since.

A son of dr Warrens will be the bearer of this Letter to Mr. Thring who I hope will convey it safe to you from your ever affectionate Mother   A A

I have this moment received a Letter from Thomas at Philadelphia in which he says he has got one from you dated Jan'ry. I opend a Letter in your Hand writing which comes by way of Salem addrest to the President, but how was I mortified to find the inclosure for George Town and not a line for me; I shall directly forward it. Thomas says mr & mrs Johnson are well, and accompanied him upon a visit to mount Vernon, where he was cordially & heartily welcomed, that he has twice written you since he has been upon the excursion

CLOTHING HER GRANDSONS

To Elizabeth Smith Shaw Peabody

My dear Sister   Quincy July 19 1799

I had the pleasure of seeing mr Peabody here, yesterday mor'g he got here the night before, but it was late, and I was gone to Bed, tho' I had exceeded my usual Hour before the President arrived. he brought William with him. I think I do not feel my last Summers Sickness in any way, so sensible, as by being languid, and wanting my rest at a particular Hour. If I vary much, I lose my Sleep—

I have intended every day since my return to have written you, but every day has produced some cares which have retarded me; and the heat oppresses me very much. I had a pleasent Journey, & have found myself better ever since. I was so sick last Summer, that I could not see company to dinner, and therefore we made no great dinners, so that I have a double share of that buisness to do. We had one last week, and I got through better than I expected. We have an other next week—I am happy to learn the little present to Mr. Peabody proved acceptable. I lookd when I was at Boston at linnen, but I could not see any under a dollor fit to make up, and that not better than we used to get for 3 & 6, or 4 Shillings—William chose to suit himself as in the purchase of a coat & Gown. the Coat I like much but could not fancy his choice for a Gown. we made it up and it does very well. I think he will do better as to linnen at Philadelphia and as you have been so good as to send him two, he will not want, till then, and if I go, I will endeavour to persuade him to wear cotton in winter.—I think it will be for his Health—His cough has left him, and I think he is better. I would have you try upon abbe the worm wafers. they have been used with great effect, and I believe She has still some remaining I want you to come here in Sep'br. Do not defer your visit to a longer day. the days grow short and the weather cold—If I keep well enough to go to Philadelphia, I design to go the beginning of october.

I know you will rejoice to hear that I have received Letters from Berlin to the middle of May. My Children were then well, but mrs A continues to meet with one misfortune after an other. She was just recovering from the third—I heard from Thomas at Philadelphia this week; he is going into the Country about six miles from the city, The fever has not got to any Head yet, but I fear it will when the Season arrives in which it used to Ravage—In Boston and new york it is Healthy—

I will procure some Stockings for the Boys. I could have been almost angry with William, tho so handsomely supplied with Cloaths, do you think he put them on, but went to commencment in those he wore down which be sure, were proper enough for common use but when he had others & with him, to go into so much company and so drest it mortified me—But children want consideration—I send my little Neice a Book. I did not Read it untill I bought it, there is no harm in it, many useful lessons, but some which I do not assent to or approve of—I will never consent to have our sex considered in an inferiour point of light. Let each planet shine in their own orbit. God and nature designd it so—If man is Lord, woman is *Lordess.* That is what I contend [   ] for, and if a woman does not hold the Reigns of Government, I see no reason for her not judging how they are conducted—

When you read the Book you will easily know the part alluded to—

I am my dear Sister with Love and affection ever yours

A Adams

To Miss Palmer a kind remembrance, and to John whose commencment will be next Year—

FEARS FOR LOUISA CATHERINE

To Mary Smith Cranch

MY DEAR SISTER: East Chester, October 31, 1799

I received your Letter on Saturday the 26th by Brisler, who with his family arrived here in safety. John was taken with the Mumps the day before. He was not so sick, as to prevent their proceeding to cross the Ferry—I have not heard of him since, but expect to, this day. Louissa has had the Mumps, so as to be swelld up to her Eyes. They have been a week upon her, and are not yet gone. Caroline was seizd last week with the worst inflamation in her Eyes that I have ever seen a child have. It threw her into a fever. She has been blisterd for it, and kept without light, which she could not bear a Ray of. It seems to be going of, but is still bad. Mrs. Smith had designd to go on to Philadelphia with me, and remain untill the Col. got into his winter quarters in the Jersies, and then go to him and pass the winter with him. It was my intention to have gone from hence on Monday the 4th of November, but I fear Caroline will detain me longer. The President is still at Trenton. We keep up a communication by the post at Rochell, which is three miles from hence; and there I requested you to direct a Letter for me, but after this week I think you may address them to

Philadelphia. Mr. & Mrs. Atkinson calld with Nancy Storer to see us this morning on their way to N York, all well, and yesterday I met Col. & Mrs. Morton, Mrs. Quincys Brother, returning. Mrs. Adams and Nancy Smith went in on Tuesday. I expect they will return on Saturday to take in the children. Tell Mrs. Norton I should like to present my Granddaughters to her sons; They are sprightly lively children. Susan is very forward and intelligent for three years, and would stand all day to hear you read stories, which she will catch at a few times repeating, and has got all goody Goose stories by Heart as her uncle J. Q. Adams did Giles Ginger Bread. She tells me all her Letters and would read in a month if she had a good school. Abbe went alone at nine months, and is very pretty, more so than Susan, having the advantage of sprightly Eyes. Both have fine complexions. But I cannot look upon them my dear Sister with that Joy which you do upon yours. They make my Heart ache, and what is worse, I have not any prospect of their being better off. But shall we receive Good, and not Evil? Yet it is a trial of the worst kind. Any calamity inflicted by the hand of Providence, it would become me in silence to submit to, but when I behold misiry and distress, disgrace and poverty, brought upon a Family by intemperence, my heart bleads at every pore.

When I get to Philadelphia I will write to Mr. Cranch, and enjoin it upon Thomas to do so. He will rise superiour to his troubles. He has no vices to disgrace himself and Family. His misfortunes have arrisen from trusting to the honesty of others.

I am exceedingly anxious for my dear son abroad. The last accounts from him lead us to fear, that the next will bring us an account of the death of his wife. He too, had been sick of an intermitting fever. Where is the situation in Life which exempts us from trouble? Who of us pass through the world with our path strewed with flowers, without encountering the thorns? In what ever state we are, we shall find a mixture of good and evil, and we must learn to receive these vicissitudes of life, so as not to be unduly exalted by the one, or depressed by the other. No cup so bitter, but what some cordial drops are mingled by a kind Providence, who knows how as Sterne says, to "temper the wind to the Shorn Lamb."—But I shall insensibly run into moralizing.

You mention a pr of stockings. I left a pr for you. Betsy might have put them into the black trunk in the entry. You will look there for them. With a kind remembrance to all our Friends and Neighbours, I am, my dear Sister,

Your truly affectionate   A. ADAMS

When you write let me know how Pheby does.

PICKERING OPPOSES PEACE WITH FRANCE

To Mary Smith Cranch

MY DEAR SISTER: Philadelphia, December 11, 1799
I received this week your Letters of Novbr 24th and 28th, and this morning yours of Decbr. 3d, the contents of which gave me much pleasure. It will be a real subject of rejoicing to me, if we obtain Mr. Whitney for our pastor. It will greatly add to the pleasure I anticipate upon my return to Quincy to find that we are in possession of a Gentleman of Mr. Whitneys known and acknowledged talents, so well adapted to the profession he has chosen. I hope that no root of bitterness will spring up, to injure his usefullness, or to impeed his settlement.

The season continues remarkable mild, but the late rains have prevented my riding more than through the city to return visits, of which I have a more than ordinary share, many persons visiting me now who never did before. They think, I suppose, that as it is the last season Congress will sit in this city, they will not be wanting in attention—I sometimes walk for exercise and make some visits in that way. I yesterday made one in this way to Mrs. Morris, which to both of us was painfull. I had not seen her since the very great reverse of her circumstances. She received me with all that dignity of manners for which she more than any Lady I ever saw, is distinguished. I calld rather at an improper hour, (having been detain from going sooner by visitors). She was in a small neat Room and at dinner with her daughter & youngest son, who is with a merchant, and on whose account she said, she always dinned at one oclock, but instead of refusing herself, she rose and met me at the door. Her feelings were evidently strongly excited. She endeavourd to smile away the Melancholy which was evident upon her whole countanance, and enterd into conversation. When I left her, I requested her to come and take Tea with me. I took her by the Hand. She said she did not visit, but she would not refuse herself the pleasure of comeing some day when I was alone. She then turnd from me, and the tears burst forth. I most sincerely felt for her.

I have sent to Mrs. Black and Suky Adams a model of the New fashiond cap. They are not such as you or I should wear. If I thought Mrs. Norton and Greenleaf would like them I would send each of them one. With the Hair drest as I have directed they look very pretty.

The politicians have before this, got the speech which Duane says, in his paper, was as anxiously expected, and sought for, as a speech is, from the tyrant of Britain. It has been received here, with more applause & approbation than any speech which the President has ever before deliverd, and what is very surprizing and remarkable, the answer to it by the House past unanimously without a motion for alterating but one sentance, which motion did not obtain. The answer was draughted by Mr. Marshall, and contains so full and unqualified an approbation of the Measures of the President in his late Mission, as not only gives him sincere pleasure, but the unanimnity with which it past the whole House, being the first instance of the kind is a proof that the Measure meets the wishes of the people at large. The documents upon which the measure was founded I inclose to you in the paper. What would the people of this Country have said, if the President had neglected to meet the advances of France, and have sufferd himself to have been governd by a spirit of personal resentment because he had been ill used, and abused by some of their Rulers. Would such conduct have become the Head of a Great Nation? Should France conduct herself dishonorably, we shall not be to blame; and the President will have the satisfaction of knowing: that he has done every thing Encumbent upon him to preserve Peace and restore harmony. The replie of the Senate cold and Languid, fully discovers in what school they have imbibed their sentiments. The committe chosen to draught the replie, were known to be some of the most opposed to the Mission. There is a man in the cabinet, whose manners are forbidding, whose temper is sour and whose resentments are implacable, who neverless would like to dictate every Measure. He has to deal with *one*, who knows full well their respective departments— and who chuses to feel quite independant, and to act so too, but for this He is abused. But I am mistaken if this dictator does not get himself ensnared in his own toil. He would not now remain in office, if the President possesst such kind of resentments as I hear from various quarters, he permits himself to utter—From this fountain have flowed all the unpopularity of the Mission to France, which some of the federilists have been so deluded as to swallow large draughts off.

Thomas keeps so constantly at his office that I see him only at meal times. He sends his Respects. As to William, we have rubd of so many of his peculiarities that he has scarcly one left for us to laugh at. He is a good creature. I heard yesterday from Mr. Cranch and Family. They were all well. Mr. Wainright has been there, and will see you as soon as he returns. Mrs. Smith sends her Love. My paper reminds me to close. I will write to Dr. Tufts by the next Mail. Love &c

Your affectionate   A. A

DEATH OF GEORGE WASHINGTON

To Mary Smith Cranch

Philadelphia, Sunday Eve'ng, Decbr. 22, 1799

MY DEAR SISTER:

I wrote to you the day after we received the account of the death of Gen'll Washington. This Event so important to our Country at this period, will be universally deplored. No Man ever lived, more deservedly beloved and Respected. The praise and I may say addulation which followed his administration for several years, never made him forget that he was a Man, subject to the weakness and frailty attached to humane Nature. He never grew giddy, but ever mantaind a modest diffidence of his own talents, and if that was an error, it was of the amiable and engageing kind, tho it might lead sometimes to a want of decisions in some great Emergencys. Possesst of power, possest of an extensive influence, he never used it but for the benifit of his Country. Witness his retirement to private Life when Peace closed the scenes of War; When call'd by the unanimous suffrages of the People to the chief Majestracy of the Nation, he acquitted himself to the satisfaction and applause of all Good Men. When assailed by faction, when reviled by Party, he sufferd with dignity, and Retired from his exalted station with a Character which malice could not wound, nor envy tarnish. If we look through the whole tennor of his Life, History will not produce to us a Parrallel. Heaven has seen fit to take him from us. Our Mourning is sincere, in the midst of which, we ought not to lose sight of the Blessings we have enjoy'd and still partake of, that he was spaired to us, untill he saw a successor filling his place, persueing the same system which he had adopted, and that in times which have been equally dangerous and Critical. It becomes not me to say more upon this Head.

I inclose to you a News paper which contains all that has yet been done in commemoration of the late dispensation. Tomorrow the Senate come in a Body with a sympathetic address, and on thursday a Eulogy is to be deliverd by Genll. Lee, in the Dutch Church in this city, to which we are all invited.

Monday, 23

Company comeing in last Evening, I was prevented finishing my Letter. This morning I received yours of December 15. It is unhappy that what is liked by one should for that very reason, be the object of aversion to an other, but when a spirit of private animosity is permitted to influence the mind, it always produces an illiberal conduct. The two B's who are now opposed to Mr. Whitney, are pretty nearly upon a footing in point of talants and capacity, taking into view the comparative advantages they have had. But their influence will not be very extensive. I am sorry you had such a cold time in looking for my Gown. I shall not have occasion now for any thing but Black, untill Spring. Then I shall put on half mourning. I shall be glad to have it, if it can be conveniently sent. Mrs. Smith wants her white, as she will after a certain period appear in white trimd with black. At Present the whole Family are in full mourning.

I hope Mrs. Black has received her Cap safe. Mr. Wainright did not go so soon as I expected, and Betsy Howard got a Mr. Whitney, with whom she was acquainted, to take it. It was to be left at Mr. Lambs.

Mrs. Smith has worked you a Crown of a Cap & Band, which I request you to accept of. I will send a Border the next time I write.

We all desire to be kindly rememberd to all Friends.

Your affectionate Sister   A. ADAMS

I send a paper containing the speech of Mr. Hopkinson upon the trial of Peter Porcupine for defamation. The Jury brought in five thousand dollors damages and the court confirmed the verdict.

"THE PROPRIETY OF SENDING THE ENVOYS"

To Mary Smith Cranch

MY DEAR SISTER: Philadelphia, December 30th, 1799

I received your Letter of the 23d this morning. I should be glad you would inform me from time to time the state Mrs. Mears is in. I have told Mrs. Brisler that she was ill, but as it can not be of any service to Mrs. Mears, I think best not to let her know of her relapse tho I fear it will finally be fatal to Mrs. Mears—Mrs. Brisler would so distress herself as very probably to bring on her fits and render her wholy useless in the Family.

I think every days experience must convince the people of the propriety of sending the Envoys at the time they went. After the President had received the Letter from Tallyrand containing the assureances from the Directory which he re-quir'd, he would not allow it, to be made a question whether they should proceed tho he knew certain persons set their faces against it as far as they dared. Gen'll. Hamilton made no secret of his opinion. He made the Pt a visit at Trenton, and was perfectly sanguine in the opinion that the Stateholder would be reinstated before Christmass and Louis the 18th upon the

Throne of France. I should as soon expect, replied the P, that the sun, moon & stars will fall from their orbits, as events of that kind take place in any such period, but suppose such an event possible, can it be any injury to our Country to have envoys there? It will be only necessary for them to wait for new commissions. And if France is disposed to accomodate our differences, will she be less so under a Royall than a Directorial Government? Have not the Directory Humbled themselves to us more than to any Nation or Power in contest with her? If she proves faithless, if she will not receive our Envoys, does the disgrace fall upon her, or upon us? We shall not be worse off than at Present. The people of our own Country will be satisfyed that every honorable method has been try'd to accommodate our differences. At the period the envoys went, France was loosing ground. She was defeated, and the combined powers appeard to be carrying victory with them. If they had been detained untill now, how mean and despicable should we have appeard? Reports have been circulated that the British Minister remonstrated: However dissagreable the measure might be to him, he is too old a minister, and understands the nature of his Mission too well, to have ventured upon any such step. As an independant Nation, no other has a Right to complain, or dictate to us, with whom we shall form connections, provided those connections are not contrary to treaties already made.

Last frydays drawing Room was the most crowded of any I ever had. Upwards of a hundred Ladies, and near as many Gentlemen attended, all in mourning. The Ladies Grief did not deprive them of taste in ornamenting their white dresses: 2 yds of Black mode in length, of the narrow kind pleated upon one shoulder, crossd the Back in the form of a Military sash tyed at the side, crosd the peticoat & hung to the bottom of it, were worn by many. Others wore black Epulets of Black silk trimd with fringe upon each shoulder, black Ribbon in points upon the Gown & coat some plain Ribbon, some black Snail &c. Their caps were crape with black plumes or black flowers. Black Gloves & fans. The Gentlemen all in Black. The Ladies many of them wanted me to fix the time for wearing mourning, but I declined, and left them to Govern themselves by the periods prescribed by the Gentlemen. The assembly

Room is burnt down, and they have not any place to display their gay attire but the drawing Room and private parties, and as they expect it will be the last winter they will have the opportunity, they intended shining.

Mr. Shaw is gone to Mount Vernon the Bearer of Letters from the President & the Resolutions of congress, to Mrs. Washington. It was thought most respectfull to send a special Messenger. He sit out last Saturday. I wrote to your son by him, and he will be able on his return to give a particuliar account of their health and welfare. I expect he will be absent 10 days.

Tuesday, 31

We have a report here that the plague is in Boston, brought by a ship from the Levant. I hope it is without foundation, but let me know the Truth. The weather here has been so mild, foggy, and thawey that colds universally prevail. Dr. Rush says there is a procession fever. I do not wonder at it, for the processions was an hour and quarter from congress Hall to the churrch & an hour & half in church. The Gentlemen say they walkd over shoes in Mud. I went at Eleven & did not get home till 20 minuts before four oclock. I then had to dress and sit down to dinner with 30 Gentlemen & Ladies. I went to Bed the moment the company left me, which was not till nine oclock. I felt sick enough & expected to pay for my exertions, but the next morning I was quite smart, and went through the drawing Room ceremonies in the Evening. You may be assured that my Health is much firmer than the last winter. I was at the Theater last night to hear the Monody performd—I think sufficient has been done to express the gratefull feelings of a people towards the Character of even a Washington. The danger is, least the enthusiastic disposition of some should proceed too far. Some things are requested of the P which really appear improper, and may tend to turn what is designd as respect, into Ridicule. He will withstand it if he can without giving umbrage to the Representatives *of the People*. If the thing is done, you will know what it is.

I inclose the Border I promised, and am
Your affectionate Sister   A. ADAMS

PRESIDENTIAL APPOINTMENTS

To Catherine Nuth Johnson

My dear Madam   Philadelphia Jan'ry 19 1800

I have the Satisfaction of inclosing to you a Letter from our dear Daughter at Berlin, received yesterday by my Son Thomas, and the additional pleasure of assureing you of her confirmed State of Health. I have not any Letter myself, but mr T B Adams has one from his Brother of october 17th, which contains this agreable information, as well, as that of his own recovery.

our pleasure upon this occasion is mutual as Water to a thirsty Soul; so is good News from a far Country. I hope mr Johnson and you will receive a fresh Supply of Spirits and Health. I Sensibly feel that the Health of the Body depends very much upon the tranquility of the mind.

I have to acknowledge the receipt of [   ] Letters from you; and I have mentiond to the president your communications. It would give him pleasure to aid or assist your family by any means in his power, consistant with the public trust which he holds. The late president laid it down as a rule that during his administration he would not appoint any person to office connected with him by the ties of Blood, from this rule I believe he never departed. I could not however think it one of his best rules—very great delicacy ought undoubtedly to be preserved by every person holding a public trust; and it scarcly ever fails to excite jealousy and envy When the power of Appointments with which a Chief Majestrate is vested, is used in promoting either particuliar Friends or connections, tho they are well qualified for the trust reposed in them. It cannot have escaped you, that a torrent of abuse was poured forth against the president, for only barely removeing his son from one court to an other, without the least additional Sallery or emolument, but to his personal disadvantage. the newspapers for Months teemed with reproach lies and falshood. One Member of Congress wrote a circular Letter to his constituents, that one of the first acts of the president, was to appoint his own Son Minister abroad, and that he had received three outfits to three different courts, and a sallery for each; this Letter I Saw in the time it was written. it was by a Member belonging to this State; a man of considerable talents who coud not but know, that he was deceiving those to whom his Letter was addrest, by the basest falshoods; I mention this to Show, how eagerly The Jacobins Seize upon every Shadow, untill they make it a Giant: and the people believe in the Conjurer.

The president would recommend to mr Johnson to write to the Secretaries upon the Subject of any office he wishes to obtain; the Letters will then come regularly before him; and receive weight from the proper Channel. The president has not forgotten a negative upon a nomination of an officer, tho that officer was named and recommended by Gen'll Washington, and that officer allowd by all Military Men, to be peculiarly qualified for the office to Which he was named. It was alledged that he was a Bankrupt at the Same time. others past, without objection, whose pecuniary affairs were not less embarrassed. I mention this to you in confidence, and to Shew you how very Jealous the people are, least the president Should excercise What they call *Executive patronage* in favour of any person. how ever distantly connected, I have no scruple in telling you that in the List of officers named by Genll Washington, Coll. Smith was nominated by him for Adjutent Generall—the Senate negatived him—and gave for a reason the one I mentiond—I Shall not dispute their Right: however I will arraign their judgment—all appointments must have their Sanction, Which your Friend the Secretary of the Navy declares a defect in the constitution, for they have a power to which no responsibility is annexed.

My kind Regards to every Member of your Family. I shall have an exelent private opportunity of sending Letters to our Children, soon, and I will with pleasure convey any you may please to forward to your assured Friend   A Adams

FEARS FOR HER GRANDCHILDREN

To Elizabeth Smith Shaw Peabody

My dear Sister   Philadelphia Febry 4 1800

I cannot but lament that the cares and avocations of your

Family should so fully occupy your Time, as to deprive your Friends of the pleasure of Your Epistolarly communications, —A very excellent Letter to your Son, did but add to my Regreets, that talents so usefull should be encumbered by the daily Cares; and obstructed by the numerous calls of your Family. That the fire of imagination should be checkd, that the effusions of genious should be Stifled, through want of leisure to display them, is sometimes the lot of those who seem born to Shine in higher Spheres of Life, the mind which is necessarily imprisoned in its own little tenement; and fully occupied by keeping it in repair; has no time to rove abroad for improvement, and the Book of knowledge is closely clasped against those who must fullifil there daily task of manual labour.

> "full many a flower is born to blush unseen
> and waste its Sweetness on the Midnight air."

In early Life you treasured up a stock of usefull knowledge which time has matured. Wrap not up the talents the returns of which are tenfold when ever you bring them into action.—I am disposed to make an other apology for my sister, she has of late so little accustomed herself to the use of the pen that the thought of reassuming it, becomes a task to her—This I know from the experience of many months during my late sickness, when I was so debilatated as to find every exertion painfull, particuliarly those of the mind, and I lost all love for my pen. When obliged to use it, I found it a burden—and I have not yet brought myself to the Old Standard which must be some apology for my not having written to my much loved Sister, who has not however, been less in my thoughts. I see her daily occupied in the laudible task of instruction, watchfull over the Morals and Manners of those intrusted to her care, loping the luxurient Shoots, prueneing the tender branches, Straitning the Crooked, and leading on the flourishing plants to vigor; and maturity. I feel many anxieties for my Grandsons, I wish them so to cultivate their Genious, and improve their understandings, that there may be a prospect of their future usefullness. On the one hand, I see their aged Support, fast descending the vale of Time, encompassed with innumerable public Care's. His domestick troubles such as become not a parent to relate, but Such as bring the Grey Hairs with Sorrow to the Grave; an amiable woman with two Children, probably soon to be dependant for their daily Support. To this add an only daughter calculated to adorn the first situation in Life, with three Children, who have no other prospect before them, but that of Humility; and brought to this by wild Speculations, in which they had no lot, or voice, but reflections will not alter the Situation. The tear which I see suffusing the Eye, and the Sigh which sometimes burst forth in Silence, too well informs me of the reflections within, and wound me to the Heart. You cannot wonder my dear sister that in the midst of Laughter, as to the world it seem's the Heart is Sad. Everyone knows their own bitterness—Should our Lives be continued a few more Years, still it may not be in a situation which will enable us to render the assistance we have heitherto done. This makes me reflect the more seriously upon the Education proper for the Children—. Writing, Arithematick and Mathematicks appear to me to be the most essential branches of their present persuit. I fear that there is not so much attention paid to these, as to the languages in the academy. I have heretofore mentiond this Subject to Mr. Vose. As the Boys have time before them, I would wish that none of it may be misapplied. I want to have them, not Smatterers intoxicated with Superficial knowledge but hard Students, and deep thinkers. impress them with the Idea that they have not any dependence but upon their own exertions, that they are born Heirs to what they must obtain for themselves. Their Education I am desirious of having continued, knowing that it may prove their best Legacy.

Your Son has his Health better than the last winter. he is daily loping of his peculiaritys and having been trained up in virtuous principles, will not depart from them—his conduct is satisfactory, his manners affable, and pleasing; his knowledge increasing. Yet with You: I cast an anxious thought about the future. his present situation can be but of short duration, and then he must have to buffet the world. he will however go into it, with an increased knowledge of Men and Manners; with a fair and honarable Character, and a thirst for knowledge which I hope will render him usefull through Life as well as a comfort and consolation to your declining Years—for he has no vice.

There is not any part of the united States, where the knowledge of the death of Washington has been heard but with

Sorrow lamentation and mourning. The virtues which embalm his memory, add Dignity to the Character of the Hero and Statesman, and the gratitude of his Country, has been upon this occasion, commensurate with his past Services—In some instances, the Orator and Eulogists have forgotten that he was a Man! and therefore subject to err, that it is only now when Mortality has put on immortality, that he is incapable of human frailty—Washingtons fame stood not in need of any such exageration. Truth is the brightest diadem with which his memory can be crowned, and the only Eulogy which will render his fame immortal—

> "In praise so just let ev'ry voice be join'd
> And fill the gen'ral Chorus of Mankind"

Mrs Smith desires to be kindly remembered to you, and to her sons. The good humourd and sportive Caroline wants to see her Brothers—She is such a Cheerful Girl that she keeps us all in Spirits and I know not how I shall part with her. Thomas presents you his Respects. Louisa allso presents her duty. how is my Neice this winter? my Love to her and to miss Palmer as well as to my Grandsons, the account of whose improvements contribute much to their Grandfathers and my satisfaction—I shall for safety get mr Bartlet to inclose for mr Peabody a Letter in which will be 50 dollars for Board &c of my Grandsons—

I hope to hear soon from you, and am your affectionate Sister   Abigail Adams

SEDITION INDICTMENTS

To John Quincy Adams

my dear Son   Philadelphia April 27th 1800

By a vessel going to Liverpool I write you a few line's with the hope that the communication may be now open, for no Letters have been received from you of a later date than Nov'br. I have written to You several times Since I came to this City, and your Brother oftner—I have the pleasure to acquaint you that we have all enjoyd our Healths this Winter. my own is better than for several years past. our Friends in Boston Quincy, and Weymouth, thank God have not had any breach made upon them. they were all well when I last heard from them, as was your sister, who with her little daughter Spent the Winter with me. Tell your Louisa, I have had the pleasure of her Mothers and Brothers company for these last three weeks, that her Mamma looks quite Youthfull, for a grandmamma, her Spirits are sometimes lively: We sit together and talk of our Children with all the delight of fond parents—we anticipate the pleasure of meeting them some day in this our dear Country; and your Father some times breaks out into this exclamation, "I must call him home. It is not right that he should be thus shut up. He will do more good here than he can where he is"

Congress are still in Session; they have gone on with more harmony than at some former period's. Mr Levingston of N York as the Head of a party, brought forward a String of Resolutions, with a design to criminate the conduct of the President, for delivering up to the British Government, Jonathan Robbins, alias Thomas Nash, for Murder and piracy on Board the British frigate the Hermionie, tho in conformity with an article in the Treaty; the resolutions were couched in very artfull language tending to mislead the people: the Subject was amply discussd, and very ably by the friends of Government, and very artfully by its opponents. I wish I could send you all the debates. They took up 14 or 15 days—The resolutions were then rejected by a Majority of 65 to 32—Mr Marshals Speech I venture to Send you by this conveyance.

The Supreem Court of the united States is now sitting in this city before which Cooper, the Friend of Dr Preistly, and the Hot headed Democrat of Norththumberland County Was indited for publishing a false scandelous and malicious libel against the President of the united States. After a fair trial, Cooper being his own counsel, and as the judge Chase observed, being no Lawyer; much to Coopers mortification; he should permit and allow him, to read News papers, and to cite authorityes which would not have been allowd to Counsel; the judge treated him with so much candour so much lenity; and so much of the dignified Majestrate, that Cooper shrunk into nothing before him; one of his allegations was that the President had borrow'd money at 8 pr cent, that he was desirious of establishing a standing Army. this he attempted to prove by an answer to an address from the Young Men of Boston, in which he said To Arms my young Friends, to Arms—that he had said in replie to an other address, "that a Republican Goverment might be made to mean any thing" therefore he was an enemy to a Republican Government, that he had given up to the British Government to be murderd by them, *Jonathan Robbins*, an *American Citizen* with a dozen more such like lies and falshoods—the Jury however not agreeing with Mr. Cooper, after ten minuts absence, found him Guilty. His circumstances being inquired into, he was fined four hundred dollers & Six Months imprisonment—Duane the Editor of the Aurora, has a warrent against him for publishing a libel against the Senate of the united States, he therefore hides himself & sculks—The trial of Fries for Treason has been this last week before the Court; he is found Guilty. tis his Second trial, in both of which he has recived the Same Verdict.

There has been in our native State a close run for the Election of Govenour between mr Strong & mr Gerry. The last returns were for mr Strong 17165. for mr Gerry 15892, more votes than were ever given at any former Election, and tho mr Strong will undoubtedly be elected; yet we are not a little surprized that mr Gerry should run so high. We know that mr Gerry is a fast friend to him Country, that he is a Man of a fair Character, no Jacobin Certainly, tho as we think, not correct in his politicks—The Mission to France obtain him all the antifederal votes. united to those were many very many good federalists. The Jacobins despaired of carrying any of their party, and as they love mischief, they were determined to divide the federal interest; and they have Succeeded yet no abuse or Servility has been adopted by either party. All had proceeded amicably—Much use would have been made of mr Gerrys Election, both in Virgina & this State, to strengthen the antiparty—in our own State I did not apprehend the Same danger.

The Leiut Govenour is very Sick in a decline. It is not expected that he will ever go abroad again—

Mr. Gore arrived here from England last week, when he returns which will be in a few weeks I will send you papers and pamphlets as many as I can collect—

The Prussian Consul carried out Letters for you in abundance mr Sitgreaves also—

When Congress meet again it will be at the City of Washington.

My Love to my daughter whose Health is much restored as I hope. I would write to her, for tho I Love her, and know that I shall more and more when I personally become acquainted, there is something very much like affectation in expressing warm regard and affection towards a person Whom we know but by reputation. I will Love her by proxy, and depute you as my representitive:

I inclose a Letter from her Brother and an other from her Mother, and am my dear Son Your truly affectionate

A A—

HOME IMPROVEMENTS

To Cotton Tufts

Dear Sir   April 30 1800 Philadelphia

I received yours of the 22d yesterday. I have already written you that the president and I are both well satisfied with what you have done respecting help. I forwarded to you the *ways*, and *means* in a Letter of April 17th the receit of which I wish to learn as soon as possible. I have never lost any thing by post, and hope that what I then inclosed went safe—a vessel is now here going to Boston it is too late to send Grass seed, or we might have done it to advantage. the president has authorised me to have a number of Lombardy poplars sit out opposite the House near the wall which was new sit two years ago. he says he will have them extended from the gate agains Beals to the corner against mr Black. I am first for making an experiment of about 50 as far as they will extend in front—and that those should be of same size. if Hay is to be purchased at 4/6 pence the president would have three or 4 Ton bought, but thinks we are pretty well for Hay in our stables, but it is not like it can be lower.

by this vessel we propose to send the marble for the herths

and the sides and front of the chimny which I request may be made to conform to them. mr Bates is to make a mantle peice in both the Rooms & the chimnys to be both alike for bigness —the sides of the Jams will also send which will be of cast Iron. the back you will provide I propose that there should be a portico over the back door the same as the front. I believe we had better not purchase any stock for fatning you mention a cow & there is one yoke of the oxen must either be sold or fatned. we have so many Horses that they devour all before them. Shall we not want a supply of corn? will it not be best to get 50 or 60 Bushel & Rye. the price will rise as there is such a scarcity in England that they are obliged to go to their Enemies to feed them. 20 dollars pr Barrel is offerd for flower untill Sep'br next, which will cause a great exportation of it from hence.

I shall write to you immediatly upon the sailing of this vessel. She is expected to go on Saturday the 3d of May tho I wish the buisness expidited. I do not wish to have it so hurried as not to be well done—

I hope to leave here the week after next the President will soon follow—I am most concernd about Garden stuff enough—

We are all well mrs Smith and cousin Betsy surprized us with a visit we were very glad to see them affectionatly yours

A Adams

LEAVING PHILADELPHIA

To Mary Smith Cranch

MY DEAR SISTER: Philadelphia,

I think you have been exercised in deeds of Charity to that poor, forlorn Man who would once have said, is thy Servant a dog, that he should become a living prey to worms, or what is worse? He is a most striking instance of Indolence, and having no stimulous to action? none of those tender endearing ties of wife, child, sister, or Brother, Indolence Created first an apathy, and apathy Crept on untill all that was estimable and praise worthy in Man, was sunk into torpor, like waters that stagnate when they cease to flow. It ought to be a warning to every man not to contract habits of sloth, and inaction, to consider that no Man liveth for himself. Mr. Wibird is punished in this Life, not for sins of commission but of omission. Talents have been committed to him, which from the same source of indolence, have not been improved to the best use and advantage. For the Good he has done, may the Lord reward him, and for what he has neglected to do, pardon him. We all have much to be forgiven, and as we hope for mercy, so may we extend it to others.

But to quit moralizing—Last Eveng was my Last Drawing Room. Both Rooms were so crowded as to render the Air very oppressive. It was judged that about 200 Gentlemen & Ladies were present: We got through, some what fatigued you may easily suppose, but I got sleep, which I did not expect, and to day feel bright enough to dine between 20 & thirty persons. On thursday next will be the last dinner of a formal nature. Mrs. Johnson & son leave me on Monday. Mr. Cranch and family were well this week. I heard from him.—Yesterday I sent some Trunks on Board a vessel with my Hearths and Jams. When they arrive and are to be put up, I will thank Mr. Cranch to be present with his advice. I would have the chimneys made to conform to them. I am much affraid of having the Chimneys contracted too small, which in a Room so large would look bad. I have mentiond to the Doctor the method in which I am told the Hearths & fronts must be put up. I will thank you when the Rooms new painted, are quite dry to have the furniture replaced. I expect to leave here the week after next. It will bring it near the last of May before I can get home, so that I hope there will be time enough for the paint to dry.

I will thankfully accept Mr. Blacks offer for Mr. Adams's Books.

Congress persist in saying they shall rise the week after next. The weather is fine indeed, as growing and Luxurient a season as I ever knew. With Love regards &c

Affectionatly your Sister   A. ADAMS

Love to Mrs. Norton & thanks for her Letter.

May 3, 1800

HAMILTON'S "SCHEEMS"

To Abigail Adams Smith

My dear Mrs Smith May 4th. 1800
I have not written you for several days, you will easily suppose
my time much occupied by having Mrs Johnson, & now our
Boston friends here and making preparation to go away. Mrs
Johnson will go tomorrow or Tuesday. Mrs Smith on Friday.
Thursday will be my last public dinner. Mr. and Mrs. Stevens can
tell you what a crowd we had on friday evening. The rooms and
entry were full, and so hot as to give me a great cold. Some of the
company appeared really sorrowful others said they were so.

Antifederalism is like to bear sway in New York; if it does the
federalists must thank themselves, the conduct of the little General has done more injury to that cause than he has ever done
service to this country in any station in which he has ever acted,
the Antis think there is no possibility of crushing him, but by a
total change in the administration, and it is said here, with what
truth I know not, that he has quarrld with all his old federal
friends, they insisting upon supporting the present executive and
he upon setting up some other, in opposition to both P. and vice
P. The fact is that the Antifederal party carry the election, and
upon that tis said the pivot turns. He will draw upon his own
head a total annihilation of all his own scheems, for Jefferson will
in spite of all his efforts be President. I do not think in that case,
that if he could set himself he would overturn the constitution,
but the party which brings him in, will rule and govern him, and
he has not firmness enough to resist the current. I do not believe
that Mr. Jefferson has a malignant heart, or that he would act the
tyrant, but his party have views very different from him. Of one
thing, I am certain we do not escape a war four years more. However I do not croak, We see but little before us.

Monday morning
I left my letter unfinished that I might add to it this morning, if I should receive one from you which I have. Major
Tousard said it was sickly he heard in camp. I feared it, I inquired last evening of the Secretary of War, he said it was very

much so at Harpers ferry, but that he had not learnt that it was so in the Indies. If the small pox is got into camp the sooner innoculation takes place, the better. I presume Col. Smith will take measures to obtain proper directions. Since you left me Richard has had it, and very lightly, he was not so sick a single day so as to be laid by. The cooks children have both had it. Genrl Brooks has been nominated to the Senate in the room of General Buoy, resigned; the nomination has not been Passed upon, the Jacos. have been fabricating a Bill to prevent the President from appointing any new officers. It will not pass in their form, the President is by law obliged to fill vacancies, it will pass it is supposed leaving a discretionary power with the President. I heard from Tousard, and from others that the troops were to be removed but where I cannot say. I question whether it is yet determined. General Hamilton I suppose has the direction. As the purveyor of supplies is dead possibly something may as well be provided in other places, as the City of Philadelphia. More than a dozen applications are already made for the office. Who will have it is more than I can say.

The President has nominated Mr Johnson Stamp master. some of the Senate gaped, some scouted, some wanted *more light*, some more *information*. The tenth Mr Johnson's daughter married to the son of the President, this was too bare faced to declare, but I know their hearts. Some hoped and solicited the office for their friends were disappointed. It has been already a week upon the table, the fate of it is dubious.

I sometimes feel sick of human nature, so much intrigue, so much management, necessary to carry through any object. I believe power in one hand better than in many, at least, they should be responsible where it is placed which is not the case in Senate, they have a voice without responsibility.

Adieu Yours &c

CHANGES TO THE CABINET

To Abigail Adams Smith

My dear Mrs Smith   May 12th. 1800
    Mr Smith called upon me a few moments this forenoon &

brought me your letter of May 9th. I received the favour in due order. General Marshall is nominated Secretary of State, Mr Dexter Secretary of War in lieu of General Marshall promoted, further I say not, sensations of various Kinds will undoubtedly be felt and many reflections no doubt be cast, yet so it is. You Know the resolution has not been sudden but, mum, you must not Know a word, but what you see in public papers. The removals have made me feel sad. I Know that honesty, integrity and industry have marked the Secretary of States office, and that his removal is not from any doubts upon those heads. Honesty and Integrity are equally believed to be unblemished qualities in the Secretary of War, for both the gentlemen I know the President has a personal regard, and that it hurt every tender feeling of his soul to do what he thought the public service demanded. If you hear any surmizes or insinuations to the disadvantage of the gentlemen, then speak for them. I expect it will be attributed to other causes, That some will say the President has done it to obtain popularity and to secure his election, to such let it be said that the gentlemen taken from the house and Senate would have personally been more influential where they were, than in the Stations assigned them. But the President is incapable of acting from personal motives merely. I believe I mentioned to you this morning, that he is going to Washington as soon as he can get away. Adieu you had best consign this to the flames.

Yours   A A.

To John Quincy Adams

                                                                    May 15 1800

We are still without Letters from you. The Secretary of State received one dated in December; but no private Letter has reached any of your Family of a later date than early in Nov'br, now six months. I have noticed by the last English papers that many mails were due from Hamburgh. I fear that Letters from you have been intercepted, or stoped.

I have written to you a Number of times since I came to this

City. My next will probably be from your own native Town, whither I go the next week, taking a final adieu of this place as a residence. The P——t. will go to the City of Washington immediatly upon the rising of Congress. The Changes which have taken place in the public offices require that he should see the newly appointed Secretaries fixed in the federal city. In future your Letters must be addresst, to John Marshall Esqr Secretary of State, Aron Dexter, Secretary of War. I could were it prudent, say many things to you which would satisfy you of the why, and the wherefore. Your own mind will suggest to you some. A Critical period is approaching in which it is not improbable there will be a Change in the Chief Majestracy. Should it be so the concequences may prove of a very serious nature to our Country for tho I am far from considering the candidate as a person inimical to the established Government and constitution of the Country, he would not be permitted to act his own judgement but would be born down with the opinions of others who are as wild and mad as the democrats of France have been; it will require cool dispassionate Heads, as well as honest Hearts (the latter has never been doubted to be fully possesst by the late Secretaries) to conduct the affairs of the Nation. You will be surprized to find how nearly equaly divided the votes of your native State have been between Mr Strong, and Gerry. 40 thousand votes have been returnd for Govenour at this Election, which is Seven thousand more than were ever before given at any former Election. Mr Strong is elected by a small majority. The Antis new very well that one of their own Stamp could not be carried. They therefore put up Mr Gerry to divide the federal interest which they have pretty effectually done. Many causes contributed towards Mr Gerrys Success. He lives in the Neighbourhood of Boston. Mr Strong will reside there only during the Sitting of the Legislature, Mr Strong was not so generally known. The former services of Mr Gerry, and the confidence reposed in him by the President in sending him upon the embassy to France all conspired to gain him votes, added to the general wish for peace upon honorable terms. The antis intended to answer an other purpose by it, namely that it should be considered by this State and Virgina as approving of their measures. The use made of Mr Gerrys Election, if it had succeeded, would have been much more pernicious out of the State than in it. There has been a great effort made in Newyork to get in antifederal Men for their assembly and Senate, with the double purpose of turning out Gov'r Jay by their influence, and for choosing such Electors as would determine the vote for Mr Jefferson at the approaching Election. These people at the Head of whom was Burr, laid their plan with much more skill than their opponents. They placed upon their list Govr Clinton, the Hero of Saratogo osgood and Brooks Livingstone. The first of these, having been very many Years Gov'r must be supposed to retain much influence still; the 2d they considerd as an old soldier who had been used ill, the other as a man who had filld several offices with reputation. The name of the latter had weight and influence. The federalists had taken a list whom they might have easily carried, but truly they would not serve; this greatly disconcerted them, and they were obliged to have recourse to the Mechanicks for candidates, Men of no note, Men wholy unfit for the purpose, only two Names of any respectability graced their list, and those were quite young men. The Election of the antifeds was as might be supposed carried. The wonder is, that it was not by a more powerfull Majority. The returns however of the State at large is said to be federal.

We shall become sick of our popular Elections, after a few years more experience. We find that it is impossible to keep them free from cabal, intrigue, and bribery. It has been said, with how much truth I know not, that fifty thousand dollors were expended upon this very Nyork Election. Their Leader declared that he had done no other buisness for Six weeks, than arrange his troops.

He is now here in this city upon a similar buisness. Mr King has written the Secretary of State that our Envoys arrived in Paris the 4th of March and that the Brother of Buonaparty was nominated with an other minister, to treat with them. There is not any dispatches from them.

Tell Louisa that her Father is appointed Supervisor of the Stamp office, the Sallery 2000 dollors pr an. Her Mamma & Brother past a Month with me. I was much gratified by the visit. Heretofore our acquaintance had been only of a transient kind—it was now recommenced with very different feelings upon my part. I have conjectured that your Louisa is like her

Mother. I hope she is, for I found her Mamma sensible, discreet, prudent, lively, sedate, judicious, impressive, elegant, all that can constitute a fine woman, and I feel my Heart drawn with stronger ties towards my daughter ever since I became familiar with her Mother.

Your Brother left us this week to make a circuit. He will not return untill I am gone. Your Father is so occupied at this time that he can only by me send his Love to you. Your Sister was well this week.

By Mr Treat of Boston I send you a Number of papers and pamphlets and am Your truly affectionate &c &c

Mr Welchs family were all well last week.

"I MUST RECOMMEND THE WARM BATH"

To John Adams

My dearest Friend   Bristol May 19 1800

We reachd this place at half after six. We found the old inhabitants gone, the new inn keepers name Tombes, the people civil and obligeing, every thing very neat. Jackson drove very well, Farmer and Favorite lazy Traveller and Ceasar brisk. I am fully of the mind that a middle Size Horse travels with more ease to himself, and pleasure to the driver. We shall get on slowly. I had rather have the Horses want driving than be kicking and flowncing.

I hope you will be very carefull in your journey not to take cold. I must recommend the Warm Bath to you once or twice before you sit out on your journey. Not hot that will drive the Blood to the Head; but it clears the Skin and renders the perspiration free. I wish you a pleasent journey, and a speedy return to Your   A Adams

"COL. SMITHS SITUATION"
To Mary Smith Cranch

Norwalk, State of Conneticut,
MY DEAR SISTER: Monday, 26 May, 1800
   Detained here by a cold North east rain, I write to inform
you I am thus far on my journey to Quincy 100 44 miles from
Philadelphia, which I left this day week in the afternoon; I
tarried one day in N York and have taken Little Susan on with
me. I went to the incampment upon Scotch Plains and lodged
one night in the Col's Log House, which I found quite a comfortable habitation. Mrs. Smith was there, tho she soon must
quit it, as the Army is disbanded. I should have taken her with
me, but she was not quite ready. I brought Caroline on to her
Grandmamma Smiths. She has taken a House at Newark in the
Jersies. The Col. talks of going up with his Brother to the Miami.
In that case Mrs. Smith and Caroline will spend the summer
with me, I was present at the Review of the Troops by Genll
Hamilton, who had come on for the purpose. They did great
honor to their officers and to themselves. The Col. has been
the Principle hand in forming and disciplining them. They
need not be ashamed of appearing before regular troops. The
officers & men Respect and Love him, and it is with much pain
that they seperate. There is a very general feeling exprest for
Col. Smiths situation, and a wish that he might receive some
appointment. This is a very delicate subject. I hope however
that he will get into some buisness. You may be sure that I
have my feelings on this subject, and that they are not of the
most consolatary kind. Every soul knows its own bitterness. I
wish I had no other source of sorrow than that which I have
just named—My mind is not in the most cheerfull state. Trials
of various kinds seem to be reserved for our gray Hairs, for our
declining years. Shall I receive good and not evil? I will not
forget the blessings which sweeten Life. One of those is the
prospect I have before me of meeting my dear sister soon, I
hope in health and spirits. A strong immagination is said to be
a refuge from sorrow, and a kindly solace for a feeling Heart.

Upon this principle it was that Pope founded his observation, that "hope springs eternal in the human breast."

My intention was to reach Home on fryday next, but the Election Storm as we term it with us, may continue and prevent my making the progress I hope to. I will request you to have the House open and aired, the Beds shook up. If there was time and a fine day, I should like to have them sun'd, as they have not been slept in for a long time. I have not heard from Philadelphia but once since I left it. I do not yet know whether the President has left it. I have heard of so many lies and falshoods propagated to answer electioneering purposes since I left Philadelphia and for the last three weeks that I was there, that I am disgusted with the world, and the chief of its inhabitants do not appear worth the trouble and pains they cost to save them from destruction—You see I am in an ill humour. When the rain subsides and the sun shines, it will dispell some of the gloom which hangs heavey at my heart. I heard a sermon yesterday upon the subject of Humility. I believe I do not yet possess enough of that negative quality to make me believe that I deserve all that can be inflicted upon me by the tongues of falshood—I must share in what is said reproachfull or malicious of my better half—yet I know his measures are all meant to promote the best interest of his Country—Sure I have enough of public and Private anxiety to humble a prouder Heart than mine. Adieu, my dear Sister, and believe me ever

Your affectionate Sister

FURNISHING THE PRESIDENT'S HOUSE

To Catherine Nuth Johnson

My dear Madam   Quincy August 20th 1800—
I have been determined for several weeks to write to you, but one avocation after an other, has calld of my attention and prevented me. I was seizd with a voilent fever soon after my return, and confined to my bed during the absence of the President. he found me upon his return confined to my Chamber, and unable to leave it for some time. Since my recovery I

have enjoy'd better Health, and past through the Hot season beyond my expectations.

The President returnd, tho somewhat fatigued with his journey highly gratified with his Tour, and the friendly and polite reception he met with. He speaks in such flattering terms of the Federal City—that I should be tempted to accompany him this winter, if there was any certainty of my remaining there beyond the fourth of March—the Same uncertainty make me feel very delicate upon saying any thing respecting the furniture which is to be purchased for the House. if I should have any voice in the buisness, I should certainly recommend the knowledge, taste and experience of mrs. Johnson; before my own, or any Ladys of my acquaintance; the Ladies of the Heads of departments for reasons obvious to you; I think ought to be consulted—Mr. Stodart has written to mr. Shaw, requesting a list of the furniture, belonging to the House—this is not in our power to furnish him with here. mr. Brisler my Steward says mr Whelen, the purveyor has it—The furniture which is sent, will furnish Several of the smaller Room's. the principle Rooms will require new. There are 5 Carpets which may be made to fit 5 Rooms of 18 by 20 foot, the Stairs and entry carpets having been made, only of Wilton are worn out. there are three dozen of crimson damask Chairs & Settees and 12 window curtains, all of which were in a good situation when I left them. The window curtains will not Suit, as the windows at Washington are so much larger and higher— much of the old furniture, some of which was purchased by the President from Genll. Washington, was so worn, and defaced as not to be worth the freight the Gentlemen however thought best to send it. If my opinion may be taken it is, to take time for furnishing the House: and to send abroad for such furniture as cannot be procured Here, as there will not be any Lady there the ensueing winter; the furniture which is there, will suffice for the present; with the addition of some new carpets, window curtains and looking Glasses. If it should be my lot, to go to the House. I would then mention the propriety of a Superior Sett of Tea, & table China; and an additional quantity of table and Bed Linnen will be wanted. it will be thought proper also to furnish one Bed Chamber elegantly —As you will probably see some of the Gentlemen, you will be kind enough to mention to them what I have hinted to you. there is an other Subject upon which I must trouble You, I mean help. My Steward requests me to apply to you to find some trusty woman of middle age, for a Housekeeper, who can assist him in the oversight of the House and domesticks. Blacks may be had I presume for the Subordinate Stations, and possibly as Cooks. My Cook who served me in Philadelphia did not incline to go to Washington—My Stewards wife has been sick previous to her return, & ever Since she is threatned with a decline, and would not be fit to undertake the Charge of a Family—I cannot make any arrangements, to extend beyond the fourth of March which throws many obsticals in my way. Brisler will be at Washington in Sep'br. and the President early in October—

And now my dear Madam in reply to your inquiries respecting our Children, Mr Adams has not yet written for to be recall'd, tho I daily expect such Letters from him, I have just written to him upon the Subject, and have advised him to the measure, from a thorough conviction that it will be best for him; it is my opinion that he might render more essential service to his Country at home, than he can abroad, but if his Country should not see fit to avail itself of his tallents, it is high time for him to think, of making some steady and permanant establishments for himself. The longer this is deffered, the more difficult and urksome it will be to him, the more mortifying to find himself forgotten and neglected—Our Countrymen are very apt to suspect, and not without reason that a Man cannot be long absent, from the place of his nativity, without contracting foreign Manners, tastes and habits, which are ill calculated to assimilate with theirs, and the first inquiry, upon his return is, is he altered? Beside a foreign embassy is but an honorable banishment, and unless upon a special occasion, or any important Service, it is held up as an useless expence, an envidious station by one part of Society, and a mere out of Sight lucrative post by others; I am therefore for calling him Home and that immediatly. Here he cannot be hidden, for his light will Shine before men—I will not temporize to you for speaking thus proudly of him; if I have pride, I have also Humiliation—Would to God it arose not from a source "sharper than a Serpents Tooth." An other reason for wishing the return of his dear and valuable son, is that my declining years and those of his Father may be sweetned by his company and conversation. I feel that retirement, and domestic pleasures, are those only which I expect to receive pleasure from. My other children are scatterd, and settled from their native state. he only can I expect to become a resident in it— An other argument for his return is Mrs. Adams's ill Health. I despair of its becoming firmer, unless a voyage and change of climate should make it so—The accident alluded to by you, was a singular one. Mrs Adams was at one of the assemblies of some of the Royall Family, and happend to stand next to the Lady of the Spanish Minister, who having a very long train, in dancing caught her foot in it, fell and broke her Leg—Mrs Adams over exerted herself to assist her, and was so shocked by the accident, that she fainted, and was carried home, when the misfortune similar to those she had formerly experienced took place, and again brought her Life into Jeapordy. She cannot get the better of these repeated shocks. Some way must be found to Strengthen her constitution. I received a Letter last week of May 25 Mr Adams writes that she had been sick of an influenzy but was recovering, that she had not for several months heard from her Friends, which gave her some uneasiness. Mr Paleske was arrived in England, the Prussian Consul by whom I sent Letters from you. She must have received them soon after—

You will be so good as to let mrs Cranch know that her Friends in Quincy are all well. Mrs Norten we hope is upon the recovery from a very dangerous illness—Mrs Dexter will go on to Washington in October. You will I think be much pleased with her, and find her a very valuable acquisition to your Society—

I say nothing about politicks—I have lived to witness changes, such as I could never have imagined, and having seen them, I have good reason to believe, that they may change again. But for the honour of humane nature, I could wish they had not taken place— Brittania & Gallia, are the two Rivals which have severed very Friends—One party is making Love to one, and an other party to an other—and they are ready to sacrifice some of their friends, and their chief into the Bargain because he insists upon it, that he will not quarrel with either, if they are willing to be Friends—But say they, if you accept the profferd hand of one, the other will certainly pick your Eyes out—Besides if you will not quarrel, you shall not rule us—We will bring in a military man, but you are so intollerably heavey, than we fear we shall not be able to shove you off by all our devices of coalitions &c; and then we can not come forward so openly, as we wish to. Certain long public services at very important crisises, and in very dangerous times, stand in our way. Curse upon the old heads, who will not forget them. The Man is superannuated now, our ambition is to ride over him—are not dogs more gratefull than Man?

"I NOW ADVISE YOU TO RETURN"

To John Quincy Adams

Quincy Sep br 1st 1800—
I have not written you a line my dear son since I return'd to this place, now three months; I felt almost discouraged from writing, by not having received a line from you, for a very long period of time. Yours of Febry 19th at last reachd me in the month of july, and two days Since I received your favour of May 25th, for which accept my fervent thanks. the 17 of the present Month will compleat six years since you left your native Country. As I then advised you to go, I now advise you to return Six years is a period full long enough for a Man at your age to remain seperated from all those with whom he is hereafter to take a part, whether in private, or public Life, It is too long to be parted from those who have but a short leise of Life remaining to them, and to whom you are very dear. Services renderd to a Country in a diplomatic line can be known only to a few; if they are important and become conspicious they rather excite envy than gratitude, but at present it is my opinion that you may Serve your country to more advantage at home than abroad. You have tallents which cannot fail of being brought into action let who will hold the Helm; I have no great allurements to hold up to you. if you serve your Country, you must do it from motives as disinterested, as your Father

has done before you; and very like, meet with as much abuse and calumny. You must endure envy, Jealousy and Mortifications of various kind's. You will find those who have grown rich and prosperous under a wise and just administration of Government, rising up to over throw that System of political wisdom which has raised them to their present oppulence I still request you to return to the Bosom of your parents and make some establishment for yourself. it is high time that you were setled, and in some regular course of buisness, tho a return to the Bar may be urksome to you after a Lapse of years, I certainly would adopt the resolution; and come back to my profession with resolutions of moderation and oeconomy so gratefull to your Countrymen, tho very little practised by them—To think of again seeing you, a wise and virtuous Man is a cordial to my Heart and mitigates in some measure the pressure of Sorrow which weighs it down from an other Source, by one from which I have not a hope of change, habits are so rooted. the temper so soured, the whole Man so changed that ruin and destruction have swallowd him up, and his affairs are become desperate. Sally and her Infant daughter are gone to her Mother, Susan I brought home with me—All is lost— poor poor unhappy wretched Man. All remonstrances have been lost upon him—God knows what is to become of him. His Father has renounced him. but I will not my dear Child afflict you. I bless God that I have Dear and Worthy Children, who serve to comfort and support me under so trying a calamity. Your Sister and her little Girl have past the Summer with me; the two Boys are at Atkinson in an accadamy where they behave well. the Col. has been appointed Supervisor and inspector of the Port of N York, Since the Disbandment of the Army, as he has sufferd in the School of adversity, I hope he will consider; and make a proper estimate of Life. Your Sister will return to NYork this Winter.

Thomas is Still in Philadelphia. the City has as yet escaped the fever, and as the Season is so far advanced I hope it will not be again visited with it—he will write to you as he frequently does. he is getting into buisness, and if his Life and Health Should be continued, I trust he will be successfull. he possesses honor, Virtue and integrity upon principles which are well founded

Your Father made a visit to the city of Washington before he returnd to Quincy. he was received with politeness and respectfull attention throughout his journey, he returnd the begining of July: much pleasd With his Tour.

The approaching Election occasions some fermentation; it is very difficult for me to give you a clue to the present political agitation, without bringing before your view Characters which we have considered as the most respectable in this State, so changed in their Sentiments, and in their conduct as to create astonishment; the Mission to France has never met with there approbation. the late Secretary of State took, whilst in office every possible occasion to excite the public Sentiment against it the removal of him became absolutely necessary; the disbandment of the Army tho an act of Congress, and really a popular measure, destroyed the hopes of a certain Little General possessd of as much ambition, as talents. No hopes of becomeing commander in chief, but by intrigueing and bringing in at the approaching Election a person who Should hold the Reins whilst he conducted the vehicle. to effect this purpose certain federilists in every State must be trained to the purpose, and deciplined. the removal of the late Secretary, who tho naturally sour could not be Supposed to be Sweetned by So decisive a disapprobation of him, gave a good opportunity to Seize upon him, to excite a clamour against the administration. the Essex junto were proper persons to carry into effect their measures and being much devoted to H   n he came on early in the Spring to concert his measures with them—previous to the rising of Congress a caucus was held by some influential Members who agreed to put up Gen'll Pinckny as Vice President, Hamiltons language, here was, that the President had made himself so unpopular, by the mission to France, that there was no chance of his being reelected, and therefore tho he ought to be voted for, mr Pinckny was the Man who ought to be Elected. Jefferson must be sacrificed at all events—to Some the Party have represented the President as Superanuated; true he was to be respected for former Services, but now he was grown old, and incapable of conducting the Government: lies and falshoods of all kinds have been raised and circulated, one that a coalition had taken place between the President and Vice President— and they had mutually engaged to support each other—Writers in the public papers have arrayed, against each other. a series of papers under the Signature of Dicius call'd the Jeffersoniad to prove him an Atheist, and every thing bad, have been publishd in Boston republishd in Philadelphia: Young Lowell said to be the writer—Character of Hamilton in three numbers, in which he is extolled to the Utmost pitch, as the first Character now upon the Stage, ascribed to George Cabbot. Signd no jealous Rival—the Characters leagued together are Cabbot, Ames, Lowell, Higginson and the Chief Justice, your old Master is also said to be in the Same Box, tho he does not go all lengths with them. the animosity of the judge, may be traced to the nomination of Gerry, and the mortification of finding Gerry Stand So high as a candidate for Govenour of the State—every method and art is practised to bring the other—NEngland States over to their System, but many are aware of their views. they see that these people are driving the Country into an unhappy division, and that confusion and Anarchy must ensue—In what it will terminate time alone will disclose. the Jacobins are so gratified to see the federilist Split to peices—that they enjoy in Silence the game, in this quarter whilst in the Southern States, they combine to bring mr Jefferson in as President—So much for Elective Governments—If we pass the ordeal this time, I am satisfied from what I have seen and heard, that it is the last.

God save the United States of America—I do not know: by what conveyance this Letter Will go. I do not send you any papers now, but Should you get B Russel's Centinal I would notify you that, that paper is devoted to *the party*, & Russels is the only paper of repute in Boston—I mean it is less of a party paper—and has never given into any abuse upon the Government. the English party have quite overuled the French party—but true Americans will not be duped by either—I hope you will Send us the poem you have been engaged in translating; your observations upon the Letters of the Northumberland philosopher have been considerd as very accurate and just, a Wrestless Spirit: Cooper is still in prison writing Jacobinism for Duane' paper—

The late Successes of Buonaparte in Italy give him a reputation as a Warriour, and his usurpation as a Sovereign—I believe other powers will be led to treat, beside America that our differences will be so speedily and so readily accommodated as Some Imagined. I am far from believing, yet tho we fail we certainly have not lost any thing—and we have gained time— We have not any official communications from our Envoys since May. Rumour Says that the negotiation is broken of—if it is not, I believe it will be protracted from the hope that a new President may grant them greater favours—

I shall endeavour to be more punctual in my correspondence, and give you our State of parties from time to time. I however see but little difference between French Jacobins and federal Jacobins as they are call'd one are for democracy and the other would be for Monarchy if they dare openly avow it.

Your Father enjoys good Health and bears all this bustle with that calm Philosophy which conscious integrity imparts; he will not voluntaryly quit his Station at this critical time. if he is releasd the concequences to the public will not lie at his door—

Adieu.

CHARLES'S ALCOHOLISM

To William Stephens Smith

dear Sir   Quincy Sep'br 6. 1800

Your Letter by Mr Rogers did not reach me untill the last week. The Crisis which I have long apprehended is arrived and brought with it the misiry I foresaw, but could not avert. All that intreaties, and pursuation could affect, I have attempted. I have conjured the unhappy Man by all that is dear; Honour, reputation, and Fame, his Family and Friends, to desist, and to strive to regain what he was daily loosing in the estimation of the World. I have painted before him the misiry he was bringing upon himself, his amiable wife and lovely innocent Children, but all has been lost upon him. He has already brought down a load of disgrace upon himself, Family and connections, which even the bitterest repentance can never wash out: but of Repentance & reformation, & despair, his constitution is nearly destroyd and still he persists in practises which must soon terminate in death tho in the Eyes of the world he can never restore himself to that fair reputation which he has lost, yet with joy would his parents draw a veil over all which is past; could they have the joy of seeing a returning penitant, could they say, "this my son was lost, but is found."—He well knows that his Father always told his Children, that he would assist them to the extent of his ability, in their education; and that he would do for them as far as he was able provided they exerted themselves & behaved well, but that he would never pay a debt that any of them should contract by vicious conduct or profligacy; if any of them made so bad a use of their talents, they must abide the concequences. When his Father apprehended that he was conducting wrong, he wrote to him and repeated the same thing to him. He also wrote to mr Sands and to Mr. Malcom more than a year ago to put them upon their guard—to advance any thing for him, would be only to give him a new credit, and to pay his debts would be to uphold a profligate child, to the injury of the virtuous; His wife and Children we are willing to assist. Susan I have taken with the expectation of bringing up, provided my Life is prolonged. They are the innocent victims of a misirable man, whom I can no longer consider as my Son. Yet am I wounded to the Soul by the consideration of what is to become of him—What will be his fate embitters every moment of my life.

I can say no more—but that I am your affectionate Mother
A Adams

LAST VISIT TO CHARLES

To Mary Smith Cranch

MY DEAR SISTER: Philadelphia, Novbr. 10, 1800
I arrived in this City last Evening & came to the old House now occupied by Francis as a Hotel. Tho the furniture and arrangment of the House is changed I feel more at home here than I should any where else in the city, and when sitting with my son & other friends who call to see me, I can scarcly persuade myself, that tomorrow I must quit it, for an unknown & an unseen abode. My Journey has hetherto been as propitious

as I could have expected at this season. Hearing by Louissa & from my worthy Brother Cranch that you & yours were regaining your strength & gradually advancing I hope to Health, has given a new spring to my spirits, and I shall go on my way rejoicing. Mercy & judgment are the mingled cup allotted me. Shall I receive good and not evil? At N York I found my poor unhappy son, for so I must still call him, laid upon a Bed of sickness, destitute of a home. The kindness of a friend afforded him an assylum. A distressing cough, an affection of the liver and a dropsy will soon terminate a Life, which might have been made valuable to himself and others. You will easily suppose that this scene was too powerfull and distressing to me. Sally was with him, but his Physician says, he is past recovery— I shall carry a melancholy report to the President, who, passing through New York without stoping, knew not his situation.

I shall not say any thing to you upon political subjects, no not upon the little Gen'll's Letter but reserve it for a future Letter when I arrive at Washington and you have more health to laugh at the folly, and pitty the weakness, vanity and ambitious views of, as very a sparrow as Sterne commented upon, in his Sentimental Journey, or More describes in his fables.

With my best wishes for your perfect restoration to Health and that of your Family, I am, my ever Dear Sister,
Your affectionate   A. ADAMS

Thank Mr. Cranch for his kind Letters & Mrs. Black for her sisterly attention. Heaven reward her. May she never know the want of a Friend.

JOURNEY TO WASHINGTON, D.C.

To Mary Smith Cranch

MY DEAR SISTER: Washington, Nov'br 21, 1800
I arrived in this city on Sunday the 16th ult. Having lost my way in the woods on Saturday in going from Baltimore, we took the road to Frederick and got nine miles out of our road.

You find nothing but a Forest & woods on the way, for 16 and 18 miles not a village. Here and there a thatchd cottage without a single pane of glass, inhabited by Blacks. My intention was to have reachd Washington on Saturday. Last winter there was a Gentleman and Lady in Philadelphia by the Name of Snowden whose hospitality I heard much of. They visited me and were invited to dine with us, but did not, as they left the city before the day for dinner. They belong to Maryland, and live on the road to this place 21 miles distant. I was advised at Baltimore to make their House my stage for the night, the only Inn at which I could put up being 36 miles ride from Baltimore. Judge Chase who visited me, at Baltimore, gave Mr. T Adams a Letter to Major Snowden, but I who have never been accustomed to quarter myself and servants upon private houses, could not think of it, particuliarly as I expected the chariot & 5 more Horses with two servants to meet me. I sit out early, intending to make my 36 miles if possible: no travelling however but by day light; We took a direction as we supposed right, but in the first turn, went wrong, and were wandering more than two hours in the woods in different paths, holding down & breaking bows of trees which we could not pass, untill we met a solitary black fellow with a horse and cart. We inquired of him our way, and he kindly offerd to conduct us, which he did two miles, and then gave us such a clue as led us out to the post road and the Inn, where we got some dinner. Soon after we left it, we met the chariot then 30 miles from Washington, and 20 from our destination. We road as fast as the roads would allow of, but the sun was near set when we came in sight of the Majors. I halted but could not get courage to go to his House with ten Horses and nine persons. I therefore orderd the coach man to proceed, and we drove rapidly on. We had got about a mile when we were stoped by the Major in full speed, who had learnt that I was comeing on; & had kept watch for me, with his Horse at the door; as he was at a distance from the road. In the kindest, and politest manner he urged my return to his House, represented the danger of the road, and the impossibility of my being accomodated at any Inn I could reach: A mere hovel was all I should find. I plead my numbers. That was no objection. He could

accomodate double the number. There was no saying nay and
I returnd to a large, Handsome, Elegant House, where I was
received with my Family, with what we might term true English Hospitality, Friendship without ostentation, and kindness
without painfull ceremony. Mrs. Snowden is a charming woman
of about 45. She has a lovely daughter of 16 & one of 6, a son
whom I had seen often in Philadelphia and who had several
times dinned with us. I need not add that they are all true
federal Characters. Every attention possible was shown me and
the next morning I took my departure, having shared in the
common bounty of Major Snowdens hospitality, for which he
is universally celebrated—I arrived about one oclock at this
place known by the *name* of *the city*, and the Name is all that
you can call so. As I expected to find it a new country, with
Houses scatterd over a space of ten miles, and trees & stumps
in plenty with, a castle of a House—so I found it—The Presidents House is in a beautifull situation in front of which is the
Potomac with a view of Alexandria. The country around is
romantic but a wild, a wilderness at present.

I have been to George Town and felt all that Mrs. Cranch
described when she was a resident there. It is the very dirtyest
Hole I ever saw for a place of any trade, or respectability of
inhabitants. It is only one mile from me but a quagmire after
every rain. Here we are obliged to send daily for marketting;
The capital is near two miles from us. As to roads we shall
make them by the frequent passing before winter, but I am
determined to be satisfied and content, to say nothing of inconvenience &c. That must be a worse place than even George
Town, that I would not reside in for three Months.

I found your dear son here at the House to receive me. He
is well and grows much like his Father. He dinned with us on
Sunday & yesterday, and yesterday I went to see Nancy and
your dear little modest Boys. Richard is a fine Boy. William is
more bashfull, and Nancy is a fat little doe. They are all pretty
children, and Mrs. Cranch tho thin is handsomer than she was
as a Girl.

When I arrived here I found a Boston News paper, which
contain the celebration of the Birthday at Quincy. It was truly
gratifying to find in a world of calumny and falshood, that a
Prophet could meet with honour in his own native soil. I hope

the benidiction prounounced upon those who are reviled and persecuted falsly, may be his, who conscious of his own pure views and intentions; walks steadfastly on, tho the shafts and arrows of dissapointed ambition are hurled at him from every quarter. The Letter of Hamilton, which you have no doubt seen, can never be answerd properly but by the person to whom it is addrest, because no one else knows all the circumstances, or can deny what he has published for facts; many of which are as grose lies as Duane has told in the Aurora—Such a replie may one day appear, when the Man may appear still more odious than he now does. I have heard from every quarter, but one voice. It is Hamilton has done his own buisness. Pray can you inform me by whom those passages were selected from Shakespeare which composed the Quincy toasts? The President says if his Friends intended to flatter him, they have succeeded, for he would not exchange the Quincy celebration for any other that he has heard off.

My dear Sister the few lines in your own hand writing were a cordial to my spirits. I pray most sincerely for your perfect restoration to health and my dear Mrs. Norton. I have received all the kind Letters of my Brother Cranch and thank him for them. If my future peace & tranquility were all that I considered, a release from public life would be the most desirable event of it—I feel perfectly tranquil upon the subject, hoping and trusting that, the Being in whose Hands are the Hearts of all Men, will guide and direct our national counsels for the peace & prosperity of this great people.

Remember me affectionatly to all my Friends, never omitting Mrs. Black.

I have the pleasure to say we are all at present well, tho the news papers very kindly gave the President the Ague and fever. I am rejoiced that it was only in the paper that he had it.

This day the President meets the two Houses to deliver the speech. There has not been a House untill yesterday—We have had some very cold weather and we feel it keenly. This House is twice as large as our meeting House. I believe the great Hall is as Bigg. I am sure tis twice as long. Cut your coat according to your Cloth. But this House is built for ages to come. The establishment necessary is a tax which cannot be born by the present sallery: No body can form an Idea of it but those who come into it. I had much rather live in the house at Philadelphia. Not one room or chamber is finished of the whole. It is habitable by fires in every part, thirteen of which we are obliged to keep daily, or sleep in wet & damp places.

Yours as ever   A. A

THE NEW CAPITAL

To Abigail Adams Smith

MY DEAR CHILD,   Washington, 21 November, 1800.

I ARRIVED here on Sunday last, and without meeting with any accident worth noticing, except losing ourselves when we left Baltimore, and going eight or nine miles on the Frederick road, by which means we were obliged to go the other eight through woods, where we wandered two hours without finding a guide, or the path. Fortunately, a straggling black came up with us, and we engaged him as a guide, to extricate us out of our difficulty; but woods are all you see, from Baltimore until you reach *the city*, which is only so in name. Here and there is a small cot, without a glass window, interspersed amongst the forests, through which you travel miles without seeing any human being. In the city there are buildings enough, if they were compact and finished, to accommodate Congress and those attached to it; but as they are, and scattered as they are, I see no great comfort for them. The river, which runs up to Alexandria, is in full view of my window, and I see the vessels as they pass and repass. The house is upon a grand and superb scale, requiring about thirty servants to attend and keep the apartments in proper order, and perform the ordinary business of the house and stables; an establishment very well proportioned to the President's salary. The lighting the apartments, from the kitchen to parlours and chambers, is a tax indeed; and the fires we are obliged to keep to secure us from daily agues is another very cheering comfort. To assist us in this great castle, and render less attendance necessary, bells are wholly wanting, not one single one being hung through the whole house, and promises are all you can obtain. This is so great an inconvenience, that I know not what to do, or how to do. The ladies from Georgetown and in the city have many of them visited me. Yesterday I returned fifteen visits,—but such a place as Georgetown appears,—why, our Milton is beautiful. But no comparisons;—if they will put me up some bells, and let me have wood enough to keep fires, I design to be pleased. I could content myself almost anywhere three months; but, surrounded with forests, can you believe that wood is not to be had, because people cannot be found to cut and cart it! Briesler entered into a contract with a man to supply him with wood. A small part, a few cords only, has he been able to get. Most of that was expended to dry the walls of the house before we came in, and yesterday the man told him it was impossible for him to procure it to be cut and carted. He has had recourse to coals; but we cannot get grates made and set. We have, indeed, come into *a new country.*

You must keep all this to yourself, and, when asked how I like it, say that I write you the situation is beautiful, which is true. The house is made habitable, but there is not a single apartment finished, and all withinside, except the plastering, has been done since Briesler came. We have not the least fence, yard, or other convenience, without, and the great unfinished audience-room I make a drying-room of, to hang up the clothes in. The principal stairs are not up, and will not be this winter. Six chambers are made comfortable; two are occupied by the President and Mr. Shaw; two lower rooms, one for a common parlour, and one for a levee-room. Up stairs there is the oval room, which is designed for the drawingroom, and has the crimson furniture in it. It is a very handsome room now; but, when completed, it will be beautiful. If the twelve years, in which this place has been considered as the future seat of government, had been improved, as they would have been if in New England, very many of the present inconveniences would have been removed. It is a beautiful spot, capable of every improvement, and, the more I view it, the more I am delighted with it.

Since I sat down to write, I have been called down to a servant from Mount Vernon, with a billet from Major Custis, and a haunch of venison, and a kind, congratulatory letter from Mrs. Lewis, upon my arrival in the city, with Mrs. Washington's love, inviting me to Mount Vernon, where, health permitting, I will go, before I leave this place.

The Senate is much behind-hand. No Congress has yet been made. 'T is said —— is on his way, but travels with so many delicacies in his rear, that he cannot get on fast, lest some of them should suffer.

Thomas comes in and says a House is made; so to-morrow, though Saturday, the President will meet them. Adieu, my dear. Give my love to your brother, and tell him he is ever present upon my mind.

Affectionately your mother,   A. ADAMS.

DEATH OF CHARLES ADAMS

To Sarah Smith Adams

My Dear Daughter   Washington December 8th 1800

Whilst I feel as a parent, I sympathize with you as a wife, hopeing that all the frailties and offences of my dear departed son may be forgiven and buried with his mortal part.

I besought the throne of grace that he might find mercy from his God, to the great judge of us all we must leave him, resigning our wills to the Sovereign of the universe.

From my own thoughts and reflections I trace the sorrow of your Soul and feel every pang which peines your Heart, would to God that I could administer to you that comfort which stand in need of myself.

Upon your part, you have the consolation of having performed your duty, no remembrance of any unkindness has detered your fulfilling it. Even to the last distressing scene, may you be rewarded by a self approving conscience; untill fatal propensities took intire possession of this poor deluded man. He was kind, and affectionate, beloved by all his acquaintance, an Enemy to no one but a favorite where ever he went, in early Life no child was more tender and amiable; but neither his mind, or constitution could survive the habits he but too fatally persued, in the midst of his days his course is stoped and his years numberd. May I be enabled in silence to bow myself in submission to my maker whose attributes are Mercy, as well as judgments. The Children will be ever dear to me, may they be trained up in the way in which they should go. I will supply to them as far as in my power the parent they have lost.

The president sends his Love to you and mourns with, as he has a long time, for you. I am with a respectfull remembrance to your Mother and Love to Nancy and Abbe, my dear daughter, your affectionate Mother,   Abigail Adams

Susan is well accept a cold, sends her duty.

"AFFLICTIONS OF THIS KIND"

To Mary Smith Cranch

MY DEAR SISTER: Washington, 8 December, 1800

I know, my much loved Sister, that you will mingle in my sorrow, and weep with me over the Grave of a poor unhappy child who cannot now add an other pang to those which have peirced my Heart for several years past; Cut off in the midst of his days, his years are numberd and finished; I hope my supplications to heaven for him, that he might find mercy from his maker, may not have been in vain: His constitution was so shaken, that his disease was rapid, and through the last period of his Life dreadfully painfull and distressing; He bore with patience & submission his sufferings and heard the prayers for him with composure; His mind at times was much deranged thro his sufferings, and through a total want of rest; He finally expired without a groan on Sunday week. Mrs. Smith & Sally have had a distressing scene to pass through, yet I cannot be thankful enough that Mrs. Smith got home when she did, and that she took him into her care. She has a satisfaction in knowing that she spared no pains to render his last moments less distressing to his Parents and relatives than they could have been else where. I was satisfied I had seen him for the last time when I left him. Three weeks only has he been really confined, but his constitution was broken down. Food has not been his sustanance, yet he did not look like an intemperate Man—He was bloted, but not red—He was no mans Enemy but his own—He was beloved, in spight of his Errors, and all spoke with grief and sorrow for his habits.

Afflictions of this kind are a two Edged sword. The Scripture expresses it as a mitigation of sorrow when we do not sorrow as those who have no hope—The Mercy of the almighty is not limited; To his sovereign will I desire humbly to submit.

Mr. Cranch in the cover of his Letter refered me to one written to his son for the state of your Health. Mr. Cranch did not get the Letter, so I have not heard, but I know I should see your own hand writeing if you were able. I have not been well myself for the week past. I have been afflicted with a loss of voice & a sad cough—It is not worse—I hope it is going off. The President is well and has been so ever since we have been here. Your son dinned with us yesterday. He and family were well—Pray remember me kindly to all our Friends and let me hear of or from you as often as possible. I am, my dear Sister,

Your truly affectionate but afflicted Sister   A. ADAMS

"WE RETIRE FROM PUBLIC LIFE"

To Thomas Boylston Adams

Washington Novbr 13. 1800

Well my dear son S. Carolina has behaved as your Father always said she would. The consequence to us personally, is that we retire from public Life: for myself and family I have few regreets; at my age and with my bodily infirmities I shall be happier at Quincy. Neither my habits nor my Education or inclinations, have led me to an expensive Stile of living; so on that score I have little to mourn over; if I did not rise with dignity, I can at least fall with ease; which is the more difficult task. I wish your Fathers circumstances were not so limited, and circumscribed as they must be, because he cannot indulge himself in those improvements upon his Farm which his inclination leads him too, and which would serve to amuse him, and contribute to his Health; I feel not any resentment against those who are comeing into power, and only wish the future administration of the Government may be as productive of the peace, happiness and prosperity of the Nation as the two former ones have made it. I leave to time the unfolding of a drama. I leave to posterity to reflect upon the times past, and I leave them Characters to contemplate upon. My own intention is to return to Quincy as soon as I conveniently can, I presume in the Month of January. The peice of linnen I orderd, need not be sent here. The other articles I wish to get, and you will oblige me by making an inquiry of Bringhurst or any other trusty coachmaker whether they have any well made new Coaches by then, or could get one ready in a few weeks. It must be strong and well built, such a one as I have now, only they shape them different. Bringhurst once made me an excellent one, that was close all round with a coachmans Box, but this I should not require. I would chuse to have it open as the one I have with Glass windows. Let me also know the price with Brass harness for a pr Horses. You must write me immediatly upon this Subject. You wrote to William Shaw inclosing me some cotton. You may obtain what you want much nearer than N. England, by giving the Sample to Mrs. Kirkham. She can get it at a shop very near to her own, where I have often bought it. Three threaded which is the strongest and best will be about 2 dollars pr pound.

Gov'r. Davie arrived yesterday with the treaty. Judge Elsworth was landed in England for the benifit of his Health. The public curiosity will be soon satisfied. Peace with France, a Revenue increased beyond any former years, our prospects brightning upon every Side. What must be the thoughts, and the reflections of those who calling themselves federalists, have placed their country in a situation full of dangers and perils, who have wantonly thrown away the blessing heaven seemd to have in reserve for them? The defection of N. York has been the source. That defection was produced by the intrigues of two Men. One of them sowed the seeds of discontent and division amongst the federilists, and the other seazd [   ] lucky moment of mounting into power upon the Shoulders of Jefferson. The triumphs of the Jacobins is immoderate, and the federilists deserve it. It is an old and a just proverb, never hallo untill you are out of the woods. So compleatly have they gulled one an other by their Southern promisses, which have no more faith, when made to Nothern Men, than Lovers vows.

I have not heard from N. York since I wrote you last.

I am my dear Thomas Your ever affectionate Mother

A. Adams

December 13, 1800

To Mary Smith Cranch

My dear Sister   Washington Dec'br 21 1800

On fryday the 19th I returnd from mount vernon where at the pressing invitation of Mrs. Washington I had been to pass a couple of day's. The shades of that solitude corresponded more with my present feelings than the company which I am obliged to see in the city of Washington. The Sight of an old Friend and the cordial reception I met with from every branch of the family, served to sooth my Heart, wounded by a recent Grief, and penetrated with a Sorrow which time may soften, but cannot heal; I had been ill a week or ten days, confined to my Room, before the event which I had daily reason to look for, was made certain to me; tho I had strove for firmness and submission, nature yealded, and bowed beneath the stroke.

I wished my dear sister to be able in all respects to fullfill every duty; and the expectation of soon taking a final adieu of this City, prevaild with me to comply with the repeated requests of a much respected Friend, and visit her whilst I had it in my power. I took Louissa, and young Mr. Johnson (Mr. Shaw upon account of public buisness could not attend me,) and crosst the ferry to Alexandra where I past one night, and the next day reachd Mount Vernon. In the summer it would only be a pleasent ride, but at this Season the Roads are so bad as to render it tedious. Mount Vernon is a retired spot, beautifull as a summer residence, but not calculated for any intercourse in winter, there not being a single house or Neighbour nearer than Alexandra which is nine miles distant. The House has an ancient appearance and is really so. The Rooms are small and low, as well as the Chambers. The greatest Ornament about it, is a long piazza from which you have a fine view of the River Potomac at the bottom of the Lawn. The grounds are disposed in some taste, but they evidently show that the owner was seldom an inhabitant of them, and that possessing judgement, he lacked Guineys instead of acres. It required the ready money of large funds to beautify and cultivate the grounds so as to make them highly ornamental. It is now going to decay. Mrs. Washington with all her fortune finds it difficult to support her family, which consists of three Hundred souls. One hundred and fifty of them, are now to be liberated. Men with wives and young children who have never seen an acre beyond the farm, are now about to quit it, and go adrift into the world without house, Home or Friend. Mrs. Washington is distrest for them. At her own expence, she has cloathd them all, and very many of them are already misirable at the thought of their Lot. The aged she retains at their request; but she is distrest for the fate of others. She feels as a parent and a wife. Many of those who are liberated, have married with what are call'd the dower Negroes, so that they quit all their connections, yet what could she do. In the State in which they were left by the General, to be free at her death, she did not feel as tho her Life was safe in their Hands, many of whom would be told that it was there interest to get rid of her. She therefore was advised to sit them all free at the close of the year. If any person wishes to see the banefull effects of Slavery, as it creates a torpor and an indolence and a spirit of domination, let them come and take a view of the cultivation of this part of the United States. I shall have reason to say, that my Lot hath fallen to me in a pleasant place, and that verily I have a goodly Heritage. Tho limited and curtaild in future I know

> "that Man wants but little here below
> Nor wants that little long."

I can truly and from my heart say, that the most mortifying circumstance attendant upon my retirement from public Life is, that my power of doing good to my fellow creatures is curtaild and diminished, but tho the means is wanting, the will and the wish will remain. For myself, I hope I have not neglected the lesson of the apostle; but that I may know how to be abased and that without repining, for my Country. What is before that, God only knows. That they were a happy and a prosperous people under a mild and equitable Government is a truth they have experienced, but may they not be made to experience a sad reverse by tumults and convulsions, by party Spirit and bitter animosity, by a total change of all those wise and benificial establishments which have given us a Name and a fame amongst the Nations of the Earth. The democratic party are already divideing the loaves and fishes amongst themselves, but it would require a miraculous multiplication of offices to gratify all the hungry Cravers.

For myself I can most sincerely join in the petition of Popes prayer

> This day be Bread, and peace my Lot
> All Else beneath the Sun,
> Thou know'st if best bestowed or Not
> And let thy Will be done.

My Letter has lain unfinishd untill this day the 27th. I have received your Letter my dear sister, and bless God that you have been enabled to write to me again. May he in whose hands our days are mercifully be pleased to spair us to each other, mutual blessings to each other, sweeting our declining years with the remembrance of the harmony which have ever reignd between all the members of our families. This year it has pleased our heavenly Father to visit us with various sorrows and afflictions, yet he hath rememberd Mercy in the midst of judgement, and tho a Breach hath been made in my family, my dear Sister has been spared to me, and she has not to mourn the death of a daughter who tho brought to extremity, hath been raised up.

I have a long tedious winter journey to encounter. I dread it, but it must be encounterd. To repine would be weak. To regreet it, would be folly.

My spirits you see are low. I am not very well. Pray give my Love to Mrs. Black, and thank her in my Name for all her sisterly kindness to you.

I will write you again soon. I saw Mr. Cranch yesterday. He was well and so was his family. Mr. Mason lodges with him and Major Pinckny. He is to dine with me to day.

My best Love to Mr. Cranch. I rejoice that he has been car-
ried through the fatigue and trouble he has had to encounter.
Adieu my dear Sister.
Your truly affectionate   A. A.

APPOINTMENTS UNDER THE NEW PRESIDENCY

To Thomas Boylston Adams

My dear Thomas   Washington december 25 1800
    We have public worship every Sunday in the Representitive's
Chamber in the Capitol; I have just returnd from hearing
Bishop Clagget deliver a discourse from those words in the
Gospel of St Luke, Glory to God in the highest Peace on
Earth, and Good Will to Men," This is a doctrine full of Mercy
and benevolence, which the present generation appear little
disposed to cultivate and cherish;—Should I put down one
half my thoughts and reflections upon the present prospect of
our Country I should be considerd as gloomy and dissapointed
but I see not where we are to land; the Government will un-
dergo a compleat revolution. every office and departments is
already parceled out. The misfortune is that there are as many
hungry antis, as there have been meritorious candidates for the
federal side; and therefore many must be dissapointed Baltimore Smith is cut out for Secritary of Navy, Maddison Secretary of State Dearbourn Secretary of War; Mercer Gallitin and
Tench Cox Secretary of the Treasury, Munroe Minister to
France, and who should you think of to England? Can you
believe that JQA, is named by the party for that embassy; for
(all the present Ministers are to be recall'd), I do not believe
that any of this distribution is Jeffersons, but the party are very
buisy for him, in concequence of this intimation the President
has determined to recall Your Brother directly, that he cannot
and will not accept an appointment under the change of administration I am very sure of. You know he wrote me that he
was making arrangements to be ready to return in the Spring,
if the Change which I predicted should take place; the probability is, that mr Jefferson and Burr stand upon an equal

footing, the federal party will therefore be in a Strait betwixt two, a choice of difficulties, if they had the nerve and firmness of the Pensilvanna Senators—they would take neither—To be obliged to give their voice and vote where they declare they have not any confidence, and the Government resting upon the pillars of public confidence, if they are broken down, upon what can it Stand? the difference is, the Democrats, rely upon Jefferson, but neither Party upon the other—It would be raising a man to the Government uncontemplated by the people—the federalist suppose they might bargain with Burr, and receive him upon certain conditions—but if he has his price, how is he to be trusted?—

Gov'r Davie said to me, that he was surprized at the federilists; they had lost all, by aming at two ralling points; he said that he had not conversed with any person here who appeard to have any adequate Idea of the effects the Change would produce abroad; from a State of the highest respectability, which the wisdom and energy of the Government had created in the minds of foreign Nations; we Should now be considerd, as unstable fluctuating and Revolutionary—our Credit would diminish, and our funds sink or rather depreciate—that no one could calculate upon the injury we should experience—there is not any buisness done by either House. they meet and adjourn. Harper who has been absent most of the Session came last week to assist in making a Speech to raise the Mausoleam, and the House have voted one, & two Hundred thousand dollars to build it—I think fully with you upon the Subject. I was Shocked at Lees virginna delicacy; but it is like the Man, not to feel and to reflect upon the conduct of our Legislators, a person must be as insensible as the Stones with which this Egyptian pyramid is to be raised—washington was a virginian. to him temples shall be built and alters raised—be sure he monopolized in his own person a large proportion of the virtue and talents of the State from whence he originated, and he deserved all the gratitude and affection which a gratefull people can bestow, but at the very period when they are voting to raise trophies to his memory, they are placeing those very Men in the Seat, which he occupied with so much dignity to himself, and benifit to his Country who they know, will pull down the Edifice which he and his Successor, have laboured to preserve, beautify Strengthen and adorn they are for Spreading Such a Glory around him, as to cast into a Shade Services as disinterested, as meritorious as arduous as he ever acchived the World, & posterity will Show a more impartial judgment.—

I went last week to Mount Vernon and past a couple of days with my old Friend Mrs washington who gave me a most cordial reception; I was much dissapointed in the House, and in the richness of the Soil, the prospect of the River is fine, but tho mr Duane thinks the magnificence of the Washington Palace less suited to the President of the united States than his Farm House at Quincy I would not exchange it, for the Mount Vernon House—nor the grounds around it—my House in its present State, presents a handsomer front, has larger Rooms, and is better finished. Preistly you know was angry with Cobbet for depreciating his House—tho my Quincy House was not made for the President of the United States, it has more comforts and conveniences, in and about it than this Huge Castle and all I want or wish for, would be about 5000 dollars a Year to spend in it, and about it——

my Spirits are Sometimes ready to sink under my private troubles, and public ingratitude. I endeavour to rally them again, least I should become unfit for the discharge of those duties which are still incumbent upon me, one of which is to encounter a tedious winter journey; I own I have a dread of it—and have not yet fixed my plan: I have thought as the Season will be like to prevent my travelling in my own carriage that it would be best to leave to the public all which we have here and get a new Coachee made, handsome and good as it will be the only carriage we can afford to keep, for this purpose I made the inquiry, I do not know whether what are calld Quarter lights were included in the calculation made; you know the one I have is Stuft and not made to rool up—beside it has long Steps of three turns which come near the ground which are necessary for me—Bringhurst is most acquainted with the manner in which I want one made—

I am not Satisfied but that I Should do better to have one made in Boston by Frothingham—the only difficulty will be the time it requires to do it—

I received the articles Sent by mr. Thornton Safe. the Silk Stockings you inquire after we have not nor have I seen any

Since you left us last winter. The woolen I took—they were put in the trunk which went by water, and were forgotten by me untill I found them in putting up my things to come away. I then Sent them with Some worsted to be done; so by an other Season you may look for them—

The President has appointed mr Jay chief Justice. If he refuses as I fear he will, mr. Cushing will be offered it, but if he declines, then mr Patterson will be appointed. I know it to be the intention of the President to appoint mr Ingersell a Judge if a vacancy offers—this is in confidence, Your opinion is So correct and judicious upon all those Subjects upon which you offer it, that I have great confidence in it, and so has the President, I send the Letter requested—and am your truly affectionate Mother   A A

"OF PUBLIC LIFE HE TAKES A FINAL FAREWELL"

To Mary Smith Cranch

MY DEAR SISTER: Washington, Janry 15, 1801
    I received from you two kind Letters which I have not yet acknowledged; I am surprized to find that the frost & cold have not yet put a stop to the fever. I hope it will not be permitted to make a renewed visit, at the approach of the summer with a severity never before experienced in our healthy and delightfull village. I cannot say that I have enjoy'd so much health this winter as the last. I am very frequently shut up, tho but for a few days at a time; I fancy we have too much damp here for Rhumatick Constitutions, but my constitution appears to have sufferd severely from the Ague and fever, and to be much broken by repeated attacks of an intermitting kind. I patch up, but it is hard work. Heretofore I have had spirits which would surmount & rise above bodily infirmity; whether they will be continued to me, I know not; I hope they may, for a groaning, whineing, complaining temper I deprecate.

    I have no disposition to seclude myself from society, because I have met with unkind or ungratefull returns from some; I would strive to act my part well and Retire with that dignity which is unconscious of doing or wishing ill to any, with a temper disposed to forgive injuries, as I would myself hope to be forgiven, if any I have committed. I wish for the preservation of the Government, and a wise administration of it. In the best situation, with the wisest head and firmest Heart, it will be surrounded with perplexities, dangers and troubles, that are little conceived of by those into whose Hands it is like to fall. The President had frequently contemplated resigning: I thought it would be best for him to leave to the people to act for themselves, and take no responsibility upon himself. I do not regreet that he has done so. He has had the pleasure of appointing your son to the office of commisoner for the city, in the place of Mr. Scott, who dyed a few weeks since, and tho this will be sit down by the Antis, as a promotion on account of Relationship, we care not now what they say. The Senate had nothing to do with this appointment, and therefore could not quibble as they have done upon some former occasions. The principle proprieters in the city came forward in a recommendation of Mr. Cranch to the President, and I trust the appointment will give general satisfaction—I think Mr. Cranch is rising fast and will be one of the first Men in the city in a short time—The duties of his office will be arduous, and delicate to give satisfaction to the contending interests, but I hope he will act impartially, tho it may sometimes be difficult to persuade interested people to believe that he is so. The sallery I think is sixteen hundred dollors a year.

I hope I shall return to Quincy sometime in Feb'ry but I own it is a mountain before me, so many horrid Rivers to cross and such Roads to traverse—my health very delicate.

I feel most sensibly for our dear Respected and venerable uncle. I know not, nor do I think it possible to supply to him the loss he has sustaind. Tho Mrs. Pope's temper was not pleasent, she was attentive towards him, knew all his wants and wishes. She was prudent and saveing of his interest, and had many excellent qualities. To a person of his years it is peculiarly urksome to have new faces, new habits, new fancies to conform to—It will probably shorten the period of his existance—but it would seem as if there remained but little desirable in this world to him—Yet we must live all the days of our appointed time, and when our change commeth, may it be happy to us.

I thank you, my dear Sister. I have not any thing yet to ask for. I rejoice you are in such health as to be able to assist your Friends, and I rejoice that our dear Mrs. Norton is spaired to her family and Friends. Surely we may sing of mercy as well as judgment.

We all send Love. The President has enjoyed very good health ever since he has been here, and hopes to be a good Farmer yet. He some times says he would go to the Bar again if he had the powers of speech, but of public Life he takes a final farewell.

Betsy Howard and her Lover have chosen to signilize their marriage by having it performed whilst in the Family of the President. I did not much oppose it, tho I thought they had better have waited untill they returnd, as I supposed it would subject them to reports wholy groundless & unfounded, but they, conscious of their innocence, disregarded such rumours and last Sunday Evening were married. Richard and Becky have not yet proposed a similar subject to me. I trust they think themselves young enough yet.

Adieu my dear Sister. It is my large dinner party to day and I must dress to sit at table as I have Ladies, tho I have not been below for three days. I make an exertion as it is the last time I expect the pleasure of dinning them.

Affectionatly your Sister   ABIGAIL ADAMS

MARSHALL APPOINTED CHIEF JUSTICE

To John Quincy Adams

My dear Son   Washington Jan'ry 29 1801

Your Brother Thomas has performed the painfull office of announcing to you the death of your Brother Charles. with what a weight of sorrow is my bosom opprest, when I reflect, that he was cutt down in the bloom of Life, in the midst of his days. he is numberd with the dead; it becomes me in Silence to mourn; mourn over him living, I have for a long time, and now he is gone.—the tender remembrance of what he once was rises before me, and I wish to forget. I wish to draw a veil

over all those propencities, which have rung my Heart, with
unutterable pang's. I would hope, that from that Throne of
Sovereign Mercy, where I have often besought it for him, he
may have obtain forgiveness—think of him my Son with the
compassion of a Brother, and if you are permitted to return to
your native Country, be a Father to the little Girl who bears
my Name—the other I have taken, and if my Life is Spared, I
mean to bring her up,—the Mother has no means of Support
but that which She derives from her Friend's She is amiable
and worthy; I can lay no blame to her Charge. She attended
with constant and unwearied Solisititude, to the last Scene, his
Sickness was short; his constitution was undermined; his Sufferings were Severe, his patience under them was great, a
dropsey in his Chest was the cause of his Dissolution; I knew
not that he was Sick: indeed he had not been more than a
week confined, when I arrived in November at Newyork, on
my way to this City, I went to see him but you may judge of
my feelings, when I Saw that his case was desperate, tho he
entertaind no Idea himself that it was so, but he Survived only
a fortnight. he was at Lodgings. your sister Smith who had
Spent the Summer with me, returnd to Nyork when I did. She
removed him immediatly, and every kind care and Sisterly attention was Shewn him, both from the Col. & herself. the removal of him, was all the releaf, all the consolation I could
derive; I came to this city with a heavey Heart; in daily expectation of his death, which took place on the first of december;
my Residence in this City, has not Served to endear the World
to me, to private and domestick Sorrow, is added a prospect of
publick Calamity for our Country. the Spirit of party has over-
powerd the Spirit of Patriotism. the Intrigue of one Man, and
the dissapointed ambition of an other has divided the Strength
of the Country, and thrown into the antifediral Scale the
weight of Numbers; this Change has been produced by the
practise of all those low arts of calumny, and falshood, which
are the weapons of unprincipled Men, and the power of faction, the corrupt and infatuated members of it, have acted without any regard to right, or wrong, and the question with them
has been who shall govern, not how they shall be governed; If
as is expected a total Change of Men, and measures follow,
universal confusion will be the concequence. The Election is not

yet determined, for two candidates being equal, the House of Representitives must decide; if they stear from Scylla, they must wrecked upon Charibdis—what is before us Heaven only know's time only can unfold—that ingratitude was considerd by the Athenians as a Sin; we are told could Athens produce stronger instances, than are to be found in our Country? you can trace the train of my thoughts, when you consider the wise and judicious administration of our Government for the last 12 years—when you view it rising in power at home, and respectability abroad, acquiring wealth, and oppulence daily; who but must lament, that this fair prospect is vanishing like the baseless fabrick of a vision—it would require a vol'm instead of a single Letter; to unfold to you, all the Machinations which have combined to produce this Change in the Administration; honest Men have been cheated, and duped, ambitious Men have Seen themselves, and their plots discoverd, and counteracted by a watchfullness which they could not elude; and were therefore determined to get rid off, at any hazard; If you received a Letter I wrote you, just before I left Quincy it will Serve you, in Some measure as a clue to the *objects* of a certain Party call'd the Essex Junto, but a pamphlet written by Hamilton concerning the public conduct & Character of John Adams President of the united States, and which I presume has been sent you, will more fully display the falshood and malignity of the Anglo Federalist. from this pamphlet however the Author has not acquired more fame, or reputation than he did from the precious confession of an other; to Burr is the merrit due, with the antifederal party for turning the Election of Nyork in their favour. to Burr then will that party owe their President, provided mr Jefferson is chosen—and this was a bargain and Sale buisness!! Is it not sufficent to give every considerate, and reflecting person a surfeit of Elective Governments, when in this young Country and thus early such proffs appear of corruption and want of principle?—

I turn from this disgusting object to one nearer my Heart. I mean the return of my dear Son to his family and Friends my last letter was full upon this Subject; tho it will be urksome to you to return with Such prospects opening before you; I presume you will not feel as tho you could remain abroad;

I expect to take a final leave of this City next week, and return to Quincy; could I be assured that the remainder of my

days might be passed in Peace and quietness, I should have
reason to rejoice in a liberation from public Life; The President
retains his Health, and his Spirits beyond what you could
imagine; he has the conscienciouss of having served his Country with pure intentions; with upright views and from the most
disinterested motives, as his own pecuniary affairs manifest.
tho free from debts, or embarassments of that nature; his income will oblige us to a strickt oeconomy, in order to preserve
that independance upon which Our future tranquility rests. I
repine not, at any of the allotments, or dispensations of providence; we have been a scatterd family if some of my Children
could now be collected round the parent Hive it appears to
me, that it would add much to the happiness of our declining
Years; Thomas has determined to remain in Pennsilvana he is
the joy of our Hearts. his conduct in all respects, is prudent
and judicious I think it not unlike that the State he has chosen
for his residence may become under the new administration
Such a hot bed of turbulence and Sedition as to induce him to
change his Quarters; Some recent Changes have taken place in
the public offices. mr Wolcot has resignd, and mr dexter is appointed in his place; Mr Marshall is appointed Chief Justice of
the united States in the Room of mr Elsworth, resignd. mr
Griswold is this day nominated in the place of mr Dexter; Secritary of War. no Secretary of State is yet nominated and I
cannot say that any will be; it is difficult to get Such Gentlemen
as are esteemed proper, to accept offices from which they may
be removed in the course of a few weeks—Yet in the present
critical State of the Country when it is undetermined, and altogether uncertain which of the candidates will be our future
President, or whether there will be any Election at all, the
President has thought it best to fill up the offices with Such
men as are fit, and capable of discharging the duties of them in
any Event; if they are to be removed; let the world See how
they will again be filled.

I have not any Letter from you of a later date than July
11th, I have seen Letters from Louisa to her Father in August
and to the 5 of Sep'tr. Your Brother has Letters of as late a
date from you which have been a source of much entertainment to me; I have very little cause to accuse you of not
writing to me. I have myself been very deficient. tell Louisa
that her Family are all well Situated about one mile from the

Presidents house, but Such a quagmire between, that our intercourse is much impeeded. Caroline has had a long fit of Sickness, a Nervious fever from which she has so far recoverd as to have Spent one Day with me. I expect the Family all to dine with me on Saturday for the last time. Col. Smith is now in an office which affords him and his Family a handsome Support. my mind is easier upon their account. mr W. Cranch will do very well here. he is appointed one of the city Commissoners—my paper obliges me to conclude. Your truly affectionate &c &c.

"HE IS NOT A BELIEVER IN THE CHRISTIAN SYSTEM"

To Mary Smith Cranch

MY DEAR SISTER: Washington, Febry. 7th, 1801

I suppose the reason why I have not had a Letter from you for a long time, arises from your expectation that I am upon my Journey; The Roads have been represented to me as so intolerable bad, and I know them to be so, that I have been prevaild upon to remain longer than I designd. I now think I shall stay untill after the 13th of Febry, the great important day, which may in its concequences deside the fate of our Country. I feel as it is so near at hand, as tho I could not quit the city untill I know what, or rather who is to be our future Ruler. Never were a people placed in more difficult circumstances than the virtuous part of our Countrymen are at the present Crisis. I have turnd, & turnd, and overturned in my mind at various times the merits & demerits of the two candidates. Long acquaintance, private friendship and the full belief that the private Character of one is much purer than the other, inclines me to him who has certainly from Age, succession and public employments the prior Right. Yet when I reflect upon the visonary system of Government which will undoubtedly be adopted, the Evils which must result from it to the Country, I am sometimes inclined to believe that, the more bold, daring and decisive Character would succeed in supporting the Government for a longer time.

A Sceptre, snatch'd with an unruly hand
Must be as boistrously mantain'd as gain'd;
And he that stands upon a slipp'ry place
Makes nice of no vile hold to stay him up.

What a lesson upon Elective Governments have we in our young Republic of 12 years old? What is the difference of Character between a Prince of Wales, & a Burr? Have we any claim to the favour or protection of Providence, when we have against warning admonition and advise Chosen as our chief Majestrate a man who makes no pretentions to the belief of an all wise and suprem Governour of the World, ordering or directing or overruling the events which take place in it? I do not mean that he is an Atheist, for I do not think that he is—but he believes Religion only usefull as it may be made a political Engine, and that the outward forms are only, as I once heard him express himself—mere Mummery. In short, he is not a believer in the Christian system—The other if he is more of a believer, has more to answer for, because he has grosely offended against those doctrines by his practise.

Such are the Men whom we are like to have as our Rulers. Whether they are given us in wrath to punish us for our sins and transgressions, the Events will disclose—But if ever we saw a day of darkness, I fear this is one which will be visible untill kindled into flame's.

My Health is better than it was the first part of the winter: I hope I shall be able to encounter this dreadfull journey, but it is very formidable to me, not only upon account of the Roads, but the Runs of water which have not any Bridges over them, and must be forded—Mr. and Mrs. Cranch are very well and dinned with me last Sunday, as did William and Richard. To day the Judges and many others with the heads of departments & Ladies dine with me for the last time—My best Regards to all my Friends and acquiantance. With the hope of seeing them e'er long, I am,

Your truly affectionate Sister   A. ADAMS

Susan sends her duty. She has had the hooping cough, but is getting better.

CONVENTION OF 1800

To John Adams

My Dear Sir

I write you once more from this city. The Trenton River is impassable, and has prevented my sitting out. We hope however that the Rain may clear it. I sent Townsend of to day; I have heard Some of the democratic rejoicing Such as Ringing Bells and fireing cannon; what an inconsistancy Said a Lady to me to day, the Bells of Christ Church ringing peals of rejoicing for an Infidel President! The People of this city have evidently been in terror, least their Swineish Herd should rise in rebellion and seize upon their Property and share the plunder amongst them; they have permitted them really to overawe them; I foresee some day or other that N England will be obliged to march their militia to preserve this very state from destruction.

There is great uneasiness with the Merchants. They say the senate by rejecting the article in the convention to which they have excepted, have plunged them into great difficultys, that they know not what to do, that a better convention as it respects Commerce could not have been made and why it should be hazarded by the Senate they cannot conceive. The difference mr Breck told me it would make to this Country in one Year, would be nine Millions of dollors. The Chamber of Commerce meet this Evening, and send off an express tomorrow to the Senators of this state, hoping that something may yet be done; that the President may be requested to return the convention to the Senate with his reasons, and by means give the Senate an other opportunity of accepting it. Mr Breck says that he wrote the Sentiments of the merchants of this city to Secretary otis requesting him to communicate them to mr Bingham and others. Whilst the convention was before the Senate; they regreet that they did not exert themselves more.

I could not help smiling when mr Breck told me he had conversed with mr Wolcott, but could get no satisfaction. Only mr Wolcott Said that there was no faith to be placed in French promisses treaties or conventions.

I shall leave this city tomorrow. I believe there is scarcly a Lady who ever came to the drawing Room but has visited me, either old or young, and very many Gentlemen; as to a return of their visits, they cannot expect it; I believe they have made a point of it; who publishd my arrival in the papers I know not, but the next morning by ten oclock rainy as it was, they began to come and have continued it by throngs ever since. I thank them for their attention and politeness, tho I shall never see them again.

Adieu my dear Friend. I wish you well through the remainder of your political journey. I want to see the list of judges.

With Love to William. Yours affectionatly   A A

February 21, 1801

RETIREMENT
1801–1818

To Thomas Boylston Adams

My dear Thomas   Quincy monday morg 22 March 1801
     I have not written you a line since my return to Quincy. I have found full employ to get my House in order, and my Family arranged, against your Fathers return which was on Wednesday last; we have all once more assembled at the old Habitation in Safety, without any accident, except to myself. I unfortunatly, got my foot in a hole in one of the carriages as I was getting out, and fell through, by which misfortune one of my Legs was terribly bruized; and I renderd incapable of walking. Some Straw was laid over the bottom of the carriage so that the hole was hiden; and I broke through, wounding me sadly; it was the day before I reachd home, so that I have been enabled to Nurse, and take care of it; it was a fortunate circumstance that I did not break my Leg, and came off, with only bruizing me to pumice.

     I am now in 12 days able to walk about without much inconvenience. I paid the money you sent by me to dr Tufts, and inclose his receit, as the Equinox is now past, and a terrible one it has been; raining and blewing, for ten days, so that I have seen but one Sun Shine day, since my return to Quincy, now 12 day's—I would have you get Fowler to Send the Carriage on board the first good Vessel bound to Boston. I must request your care also to take a Bill of lading and agree for the freight, any expence attending, you shall be paid upon notice—

     as to news—We have not any. all seem to be luled to quiet rest, by the Song of the Syren—B Russel puffing up the Composition as a model of *correct* writing and eloquence I however conceive it to have, more of duplicity than sincerity. Since I read a coppy of a Letter, which W Shaw is possessd of, I believe the writer to have given countanance to the most unfounded assertions respecting his predecessor. if he believed what he wrote; it is but one proof, amongst many others, that he knew not the Character, he thus abused, and that his knowledge of Men, is Superficial as I believe his administration will show.

     Your Father was as much moved as I was, respecting the

franking; the Jacobins overshot their mark by publishing the nature of the Bill; the same Error was committed respecting Gen'll Washington. mr. Otis coppied the resolution as it stood, but did not attend to its being afterwards alterd. When your Father saw the comment in the paper, he told mr Secretary Otis, that he would never sign the Bill. this led to an examination, and to an alteration. the thing was not designd—so that my Children may in the course of a Year, be benifited by means of their Fathers having been *President* of *the United States* to the prodigious sum, and amount of Ten or twelve dollars—!!! —Tell it not in Gath—whilst they have been the loosers, I doubt not of thousands.

give us, my dear Thomas the pleasure of hearing from you often as you can. Striped of all of you and William must soon leave us; I know not how your Father or I shall feel; We will go to Farming and Gardning.

What a Jewel of a Letter has your Brother written to your Father; how accurately, yet how candidly has he judged of Men and Measures? What comforting argument does he use to reconcile us to the ingratitude of the world—

God preserve his Life and health and continue him a blessing to his Family and an honour to his Country; which however is unworthy of him—

My dear Thomas adieu—I must go below and make my pudding—

most affectionatly Your Mother   A A

"A SPIRIT OF PARTY"

To John Quincy Adams

my dear Son   Quincy May 30. 1801—

Your Letter of march the 10th is before me; your Brother informs me that he has one of April. It is true my dear Son, that I have read with much interest, and Sincere pleasure, your Letters to your Brother Thomas, and with many others, have been highly entertaind with your journey into Silicia. Whilst those letters convey usefull information, to the Merchant, the

Mechanic, and the Farmer, they are calculated to delight the Man of taste, and Science. the lover of Literature; the Patriot, the Phylosopher, and the divine. The Sentiments contained in them, are so congenial to my heart; that I feel them as my own, tho they wear a dress Superior to my talents to have given them. Your Newburry Friends who remember you I think with more attachment than any others, are reprinting them from Dennies paper. To that they have given a greater celebrity, and a more extensive circulation, than all his other publications.

I have not been so remiss, as from the failure of my Letters, I may appear to have been, tho I confess I have not written so frequently as formerly; before I left Quincy in October last, I wrote you a very lengthey Letter (at the same time I wrote to Louisa). In mine to you, I stated the divisions which had taken place amongst the Federilists, the causes which had produced it, the blind infatuation which had possesst them, and the concequences which I expected would follow; Hamilton found that he was not consulted as an oracle. Pickuring that, he could not communicate the resentments of his own Breast to that of the President; McHenry and Wolcott were drawn in by those men to adopt Sentiments, and to pursue a conduct, which I have every reason to believe the latter repented of most sincerely, but Hamilton was the active, the envious, the secreet, and the unblushing contriver of all the mischief. He had in all the N England States warm partizens, and great admirers of his talents, devoted to him; and to him as the principle may be attributed the division of the federilists. He could not however bring N England to revolt against her old faithfull and long tried Friend, but he forced an other into their list, against the opinion, against the judgement, of the most judicious, and firm Friends of the Government; The other party exulted to find that a division existed, they fomented it; and exerted all the powers of darkness to triumph over them.

> "A Sceptre, snatch'd with an unruly hand,
>   Must be as boist'rously mantain'd as gain'd;
>   And he that stands upon a slippery place
>   Makes nice of no vile hold to stay him up."

Accordingly Callender the infamous, is pardoned and released from confinement. Duane has been patronized by a remission of all Suits against him insstituded by the Attorney General, Lyon has been call'd in as an adviser and counsellor with Stephen Thomson Mason; and Gallatin is appointed to the important trust of Secretary of the treasury—a Man, who beside his being a Foreigner: was implicated in the insurgency, and took Shelter in the general amnesty, who has uniformly been in opposition to every measure of the Government, and whose every effort has been to pull it down, who cannot articulate a word of our language. Such is the Man exalted to one of the highest trusts of confidence. I say nothing of Lincoln and Madison. Upon the principles of the party, they are wisely placed. Dearbone will show how competent he is to his department. I presume he is not less so, than McHenry was. Many men have been removed from office merely for their opinions, and those against whom any charge of Toryism ever existed, however unimpeachable their conduct in office have been, Sure to feel the full effect of the new powers—Marshalls are universally removed where the power of chusing Jurymen lay with them,

"Alas poor Country, Thou are affraid to know thyself."

If I did not apprehend a prospect of confusion, and had not a dread of anarchy, If I had a soul capable of rejoicing at the terpitude of Man; I Should be amply revenged to see the junto and their sattilites so foild, so mortified, so compleatly put to route; and that by their own folly and desertion.

"But the rarer virtue is in mildness, than in vengance
And I hold the world, but as the world."
An Habitation Giddy and unsure
Hath he that buildeth on the vulgar Heart."

To say that your Father and I have not felt for our Country, and for ourselves, would be to deny the best of sentiments, the consciousness of having merited more gratefull returns from those who are daily reaping the fruits of a Life devoted to the Service, and best Interest of the Country; I See not in him, nor do I feel in my own Breast, any animosity, or resentment against the World, or even those individuals who have maligned and abused us; we know what allowence to make for a Spirit of party which has unhappily taken full possession of our

Countrymen. It is of all others the blindest, and most absurd. It refuses to do justly, to excercise mercy or demean itself Humbly. It blinds the understanding and perverts the judgment. This State has had its vibrations, and in some measure partook of the contagion which has spread from the Head, to the remotest Limbs. When the whole Head is sick, the Body partakes largely of the disease. The State at large is sound; but the Weight added to the light particles from the change produced in the National Counsels, have produced a various coulourd Fabrick; the Town of Boston Represented exclusively by the most voilent democrats, Jarvis, Austin, Fellows &c (of the Senate, a Majority are Federal;) opposed to this medly, is a Federal Gov'r, chosen by a majority of 5000 votes—N York. All in the wrong, Clinton and Birds of the same feather compose their legislature.

Your prospects my dear son are not very bright. You must summons resolution and return to the druggery of the Bar. Be not disgusted with the prospect; I know how reluctant you feel at the Idea; at the same time I know how zealously you will Seek after that independance without which no man can feel himself happy.

Your Father and I were both much affected with the Fillial and affectionate tender of what, thank God we have not any occasion for; you know our Habits; and tho we feel many curtailments necessary, and have made them; we have many comforts and enjoyments; and we can adopt the words of Shakespear

> Hath not old custom made this Life more Sweet
> Than that of painted pomp?

Are not these Fields more free from peril? than those Scenes so envied by others, but which will yeald thorns instead of Roses.

I have had domestick calamity to encounter and a portion of sorrow which has weighd heavier at my Heart, than any change I have experienced from the ingratitude or fickleness of the world. I wrote to you from Washington soon, after the death of your Brother which from the circumstances which produced a premature dissolution, the State of Health in which I found him, the Situation of his Family, the prospect for them, and for me if he had lived; were of a most distressing Nature, and I could not but consider the Event, afflicting as it was, as a dispensation of Heaven in Mercy to his near connection's. Such was the infatuation which had taken possession of him, that he was lost living, and renderd every one misirable, who possesd a regard and affection for him—Of his restoration to Reason and temperance, all hopes and expectations faild. In his last sickness, which was rapid, he appeard most tender and affectionate. He suffered, much, endured much. His mind was constantly running upon doing justice, and making reperation; early principles tho stiffled, now discoverd themselves; and Mercy I hope was extended to him; but it rends my Heart to think upon the Subject—In silence I must submit.

All that is left of him we have, His wife and two children, they are fine promising Children. Susan I have had for more than a year. Your Father is very fond of them; and they amuse us in our retirement. Your Father is quite the Farmer, so far as the Rural Scenes delight and amuse him.

I hope to see you return before the expiration of the Seventh Year. I have had it hinted me that Louisa is like to become a Mother. I shall feel anxious for her, untill I learn the event. She has been so unfortunate that I scarcly know how to believe the report, especially when I know what a Tour she made through the Summer. My Love to her. She will feel I hope an additional motive to return to America—

I was very sorry to learn that through the mere wanteness of a printer, you was made unhappy upon your Fathers reputed Sickness. Both he and I feel the advances of old Age; Seven Years has added to our furrows but thank God, we are in the enjoyment of a great portion of health than for many years past. Your Sister and Brother were both well the last week. Hopeing that this Letter may have a more fortunate passage to you than my two last, I am my dear Son Your ever affectionate   Mother—

JOHN QUINCY IN AMERICA

To John Quincy Adams

Quincy Sepbr 13 1801

Welcome, welcome, my dear Son to your native Land after a seven years absence from it. God be praised that you and Louissa, and my dear John George &c have arrived in Safety, but I have trembled for you, least the extreem Heat you must have experienced Since your arrival should be too much for you all. The Sudden change we have experienced of no less than 30 degrees, is equally trying to weak constitutions. I hope it is not Sickly at Washington, but last october Agues and fevers were very prevelant; I can have no objection to the visit first to washington, but Say to you as I did in my last Letter, that it Should not exceed the middle of october. It is a long and tedious journey, but both you and mrs Adams are well ennured to travelling. at Quincy you can be accomodated with your Family untill you can do better. we ardently long to See you all.

mrs Adams is going to a place different from all she has ever yet visited, and amongst a people, where it will be impossible for her to be too gaurded; every Syllable She utters will be scaned not with loss of candour, but carping malice; Such is the spirit of party. think not that I veiw the aspect of public affairs through the medium of dissapointment. unhappily for our Country, you will find it all too true. I doubt not She will be prudent; but her Family have been very basely traduced. there are persons no doubt hungrying after mr Johnson's office. I hope however he will retain it, as it was the casting vote of the new president, which gave it to him.

You too my Son must look for your Share of calumny, and arm yourself [   ] against it by patience temperance and moderation, and by applying yourself Solely to your own private affairs. I hope you will be here Soon. I have a thousand things to Say to you, but none with more Sincerity than that I am your ever affectionate Mother   A Adams

JUDICIARY ACT OF 1802

To Hannah Phillips Cushing

my dear Madam   Quincy Febry 3d 1802

I received your kind Letter, began at Washington, and finished at philadelphia. I received much pleasure from the perusal. the communications were of a nature to excite sober reflections: I find your sentiments in perfect unison with my own: we have both of us been for a series of years so intimately connected with political affairs that we must have been very inattentive observers not to have seen the motives which led to a Change in the administration, and the chance some were determined to run, to effect that change. this we know could not have been produced, if the Federal part of the community had been united. if they had not sacrificed the interest of their Country to gratify their resentment, and ambition I have you well know; reason to say this of some of the Federal Leaders; to them, more than their opponents, is to be ascribed all that we have feard, all that we shall be made to feel. the ax is already laid to the Root of the Tree; if it destroyd only those which brought forth bad fruit, we ought to rejoice, but when we see a spirit of party, deaf to all reasoning, all argument, determined with noted malignity to destroy all that is good wise and just, merely to glut their resentment; what a hopefull prospect for the future? If *we* have nearly finishd our cause, still we cannot be unmindfull of the lot, and portion of those who are to succeed us. Must not the patriot say, verily we have labourd in vain, and spent our strength for nought. the repeal of the late judiciary Law, (I take it for granted, it is decreed,) is a measure so full of banefull concequences that like a Comet it will end I fear in the conflagration of the constitution touch not mine anointed, and do my judges no harm; ought to have sounded terror to the evil doers.

The golden Age is past—god grant that it may not be succeeded by an age of terror, of disorder and confusion. peace and tranquility, are desirable objects in my eyes [   ] the few remaining days allotted me; tho I should live to three score years and ten, which from my frequent infirmities, I have little reason to expect; I have not a wish, not a desire the most distant, to be any other, than I now am; and tho some may suppose that I am like the fox in the fable who cryd out that the grapes were sour; they must judge from their own Hearts; not from mine; I frequently felicitate myself, and my partner that we are released from the cares and responsibility of a situation, too cumberous, for to be sustained with ease or tranquility; and which the inconstancy of the people, and the Ambition of demagogues renderd every day more Burdensome.

I have written more freely to you than I should to many others. I have avoided writing a single Letter to Washington, except to Mrs Johnson in a domestic Line, and last week, I wrote one to mrs otis—

If the outside frank should induce anyone to scrutinize the within, thinking to collect the sentiments of a statesman they shall be welcome to the Female benidictions they find. when I see you, we will more cordially exchange our thoughts.

with my best respects to the judge, I subscribe your Friend
A Adams

"MY PIN MONEY"

To Thomas Boylston Adams

My dear Son   Quincy Febry 28th 1802
Your Father received a Letter from you last Evening; full of political information, and judicious reflections; there is a darkness visible upon all our national prospects, which cast a Gloom upon my declining days. What of Life remains to me, I should rejoice to pass in tranquility; but danger takes rapid strides, and faction and party Rage will soon involve us in a civil war: or a Lethargy and Stupor render us fit subjects for Southern despotism; the rising Generation will have more dangers to encounter than there Fathers have surmounted; such are your prospects my Son but be not dismayed at this, or the little success you have met with hitherto in your profession; I know it must require a large portion of patience, and perseverence to preserve an equal mind through so many strugles.

The reflection will obtrude, why was I educated to this profession? why am I placed in a situation where I cannot with all my assiduity, frugality and oeconomy provide me an independance? has my Family made no sacrifices for the benifit of their Country? have they lived for themselves only? You have the consolation of knowing that no mean, or disgracefull action has tarnishd the public conduct of either Father or Brother; that there Reputation and your own are built upon solid and durable Material. Honor, virtue and integrity, they will out live the popular Clamour of the present age, and shine brighter from the Shades with which future Historians must contrast them.

My own reflection upon what has been, and now is, are frequently tinged with a melancholy hue, not on my own account, so much, as for those who are to succeed me. With frugality we have enough for all our wants, because we can circumscribe them within narrow bounds. I once wrote you that I had a small matter saved from expences which I curtaild, and which I have been many years collecting, expecting a time when I might have occasion for it, as I could. I have placed it in the Hands of our good Friend Dr. Tufts who has managed it for me in such a manner as to yeald me an interest of 200 dollers per annum. This I call my pin money, As I have not had occasion for any of it, I have yearly added the interest to the principle. I have now happily by me half yearly interest which I calld for a few days since, and as I have not an immediate use for it, and can receive more in April, I inclose it to you, requesting you to accept it as a small token of the Love and affection I bear you, wishing at the same time, that it was ten times the value. I have but one injunction to make you. It is that you make no mention of it; further than to say you received my Letter safe of the 28th of Feb'ry.

We have had winter enough since the 22d of Feb'y, snow in abundance, and cold. We are confined to our house by Banks of snow, Ice and blocked roads. Your Father has been employd in reading a work of 14 volms of Le Harps which your Brother has furnishd him with. He has lately read the Studies of nature by [   ] I am happy to inform you that your uncle Cranch has surmounted his late illness so far as to give us hopes he may be spaired to us a little longer. Your Brother and sister have not been here for three weeks. They have had the measles in their Family, and my domesticks have been sick. Remember me to all those who inquire after your affectionate Mother

Abigail Adams

RUMORS OF THOMAS MARRYING

To Thomas Boylston Adams

Dear Thomas   Quincy Dec'br 13th 1802

I was in Boston at your Brothers when mr Shaw received your Letters. according to the direction given him, he deliverd them. your Letter of Novbr 24th in some measure discloses the motives which have opperated to fasten you to the spot where you now reside.

Rumour has been buisy in reports of your design to change your situation, but as I could not learn who the object was, I gave not any heed to the report. I knew too well your Love for independance and the honour you had of involveing yourself, or others in embarresments and difficulties to credit it

I have read you Letter over and over, several times, altho you have so far communicated your thoughts, as to convince me that you have some entanglement, which has long perplexd and embarressed you; you have not given me a clue sufficiently clear, by which I can unravel the whole—As I am at a loss how to follow, I will lead and be explicit. I was asked this Summer if mr T B Adams corresponded with miss Nancy Harod of Haverhill? I replied, not to my knowledge—Yet I recollected that some three or four years ago, a Letter fell into my hands addrest to her. Since I received your Letter, some other circumstances have occured to my recollection, which have past merely as accident before, yet still I am in a puzzel, and am left in the wide field of conjecture, either to suppose that you have formed an attachment in Philadelphia, which weds you to that place, and is the reason why you are still desirious of combatting every difficulty there; rather than hazard the loss of the object by a removal, or your attachment is in New England and you cannot think of returning here, untill you can do it, "in the Spirit and feeling of independance" which will entitle you to make an open and avowed declaration of your attachment —altho you should arrive at this desirable point; beleive me my son, you judge wrong in thinking that any thing can exclusively affect you, which does not Relatively concern those so nearly allied to you as your parents. more particuliarly so important an event as a connextion for Life; which introduces into a family a near relative with all those claims which bind society together—a connection in which are involved Honour reputation peace of mind, domestic comfort and happiness—I have not in any Instance opposed my will to the inclination of my children. I have only advised them not to hazard their happiness or that of others, by connecting themselves before they saw the path plain before them. if their union by marriage has not altogether met with my wishes, they have never experienced from me, any other than Maternal tenderness. none of them have disgraced themselves or family by dissolute or unprincipled connections, nor have any of them advanced themselves in the world by their marriages, or confered any honor, or brought any Emolument into their Family by them. you therefore stand upon a ground of equality with them. if your attachment is of so early so constant so persevereing a nature as to be fixed upon Miss Harod, against whom personally, I have not the smallest objection, nay more I think her, so far as my acquaintance extends—a very amiable Girl, and as well calculated to make what I call a good wife, as any one with whom I am acquainted, nor should I be asshamed to place her beside either of my daughters—nor have I a belief that your Father would oppose himself to your wishes—tho they might not meet his own—neither he or I can expect in the order of Nature, but a short period here, to see our Children happily situated is the object now nearest our Hearts—If however my conjectures are wrong, and you have fixed your affections upon some Lady, who is wholy unknown to me, I can only say that I hope, and trust she is an object worthy of your affections, and your attachment, and that your happiness may be promoted by a union with her. If you think proper to be more communicative you may rely upon the trust as a sacred deposit, and your Letters may be conveyd as the former—

Inclosed, is a small matter from my fund—my demands

upon it have been rather larger than I intended, as I support Susan at School from it. it may serve to purchase you a suit of Cloathing.

I am my dear Son your truly affectionate Mother

Abigail Adams—

"PRIVATE CONFIDENCE HAS BEEN BETRAYED"

To Mercy Otis Warren

My dear Madam   Quincy Jan'ry 16th 1803

It was with much pleasure I recognized the Hand writing of an old Friend, tho only in the signature of her name. It recalled to mind those days of pleasureable intercourse, "when thought met thought," and a happy union of sentiment endeard our Friendship, which neither time, or distance has effaced from my Bosom. I have sympathized with you, in sickness and in sorrow, much oftner than my pen has detailed it to you. I too have tasted of the bitter cup of affliction—and one is not, cut off in the Meridian of Life.

I was happy that my son had an opportunity of paying his respects to the ancient Friends of his parents. We should be equally glad to see your sons when ever they pass this way. his visit to Plimouth was necessarily short, or he would have spent more time with you.

You observe that you have not seen any effect of my pen for a long time. Indeed my dear Madam, I have avoided writing for these two years past a single Letter, except to my Sister, and Children. the sacred deposit of private confidence has been betrayed, and the bonds of Friendly intercourse snapt assunder to serve the most malicious purposes; even a jocular expression has been made to wear the garb of sober reality: the most in-nocent expressions have been twisted, mangled & tortured into meanings wholy foreign to the sentiments of the writer. I have been ready to exclaim with the poet, "What sin unknown dipt you in Ink?"

There now lies before me an Ægis of the present year; in which is draged to light, the intercepted Letter, said to have been written to your worthy Husband, in the year 1775, and publishd in an English Magazine. The design of the publisher appears from the introduction of the Letter, to make it believed, that the person alluded to as a pidling Genius, was Gen'll Washington, and that the supposed writer was engaged in a plot to get him removed from the command of the Army, that he possesst a Sanguinary revengefull temper, and was desirious of punishment without mercy: without adverting to the period when the Letter was written the state of the country at that time, before the declaration of Independance had sit it free from the Shackles and Chains which were prepared for it, and when we were hazarding an attempt to form a Government for ourselves, it was natural for the Letter writer to inquire: will your judges be Bold? will they feel firm? will they dare to Execute the Laws under their present circumstances? with their Capitol in the possession of a powerfull Enemy, and many of their near and dear Friends shut up within it, prisoners to them. The old Actors are gone off the Stage. few remain who remember the perils and dangers to which we were then exposed, and fewer still who are willing to do Justice to those who hazarded their lives and fortunes, for to secure to them the blessings which they now possess, and upon which they Riot, and Scoff. little regard is paid to that prohibition, thou shalt not bear false witness, or to that system of Benevolence which teaches us to Love one another, and which I trust, we my dear Madam shall never lose sight of, however reviled and despightfully used.

Your friends tho not exempt from the infirmities of age, are in the enjoyment of many blessings, amongst which is a comfortable portion of Health, and rural felicity. We enjoy the present with gratitude, and look forward to brighter prospects, and more durable happiness in a future state of existance, where we hope to meet, and rejoice with those whom we have loved, and revered upon Earth.

As to the little pecuniary matter between us, which but for your reminding me of, would never have been recollected by me, I know not where the papers are. I have not seen them or thought of them for many years. I have not any thing upon Book and the amount can be but a triffel, and I beg you not to give yourself any further concern about it, as I have not any demand upon you, but a continuence of that Friendship and regard, commenced in early Life, and never designedly forfeited by Your Friends   Abigail Adams

Both Mr Adams and your Friend unite our best wishes for the Health and happiness of Genll Warren and yourself and Family.

FINANCIAL RUIN

To Thomas Boylston Adams

My dear Son   Quincy April 26th 1803.
   A very bad whitloe upon the finger of my right Hand has prevented my holding a pen; or useing my hand for a long time, or I should not have been so long silent. altho my communications will give you more pain than pleasure. it may releive your mind respecting the loss your Brother has sustaind; but it will be only shifting the Burden upon older Shoulders; you know your Father had some Money in Holland, which since your Brothers return, he concluded to draw out, and vest in the Farm which belonged to your Great Grandfather Quincy Mr Tufts after keeping his part a year, made an offer of it to your Father and he concluded to take it; relying upon the property he had abroad to pay for it, your Brother undertook the management of the buisness abroad and as the exchange was more in favour of England than Holand, the money was drawn from thence, and placed in the Hands of the House which has lately faild, Bird Savage & Bird; a Catastrophe so unexpected to us, and at a time when we had become responsible for so large a sum; has indeed distrest us, at no other—time of our lives could we have been equally affected by it. the cloud is not however so black as it first appeard; the Bill which past through your Hands, and upon which such heavey damages would arise if returnd. the House inform your Brother that Mr King kindly agreed to take up, upon honour: if this should be true as I sincerely hope it may, it will save us from such sacrifice of property as at first appeard necessary to

us—your Brother tho no way to blame in the Buisness; having conducted it with as much circumspection as possible, still insists upon selling some property which he has in Boston; a House which he lately purchased in order, to aid in raising the money necessary upon this occasion: we shall endeavour to make him secure so that he shall not finally be a looser any further than in common with the rest of the family. At first my phylosophy was put to a trial, different from any I had ever before experienced I have in the various stages of Life, been call'd to endure afflictions, & dangers of many kinds, but this was something so new, so unexpected, that I could scarcely realize it. your Father bears it as well & better, than I could have expected—but as yet we hardly knew what we may call our own there is the Farm, that has not vanished, and will fetch as much as we agreed to give for it—but what the damages will finally amount to, upon the Bills we cannot yet determine: let it not depress your—Spirits—it is one of the unfortunate incidents in human affairs to which no remedy but patience & Submission applies. It was not dissipation; extravagance or lack of Judgement which on our part produced the event—I hope we may yet be able to obtain some part of the property in time—in the mean time; the sacrifices we must make shall on my part be cheerfully borne. if I cannot keep a carriage, I will ride in a chaise. if we cannot pay our labourers upon our Farms, we will let them to the halves, and live upon a part to know how to abund, & to suffer want is a new lesson, but I will bring my mind to my circumstances—I do not dread want, but I dread debt, and for that reason I would contract no debt which I do not see a way clear to pay—

I shall upon the next arrivals from England be able to let you know further respecting the State of this Buisness—

I have not had a letter from you for a long time—Adieu my dear Son, my anxiety is chiefly upon my childrens account— neither your Father or I can have a much longer lease—we should have been rejoiced to have left our children with better prospects—your affectionate Mother   AA

"YOUR BROTHER IS TO BE THE PURCHASER"

To Thomas Boylston Adams

My dear Son   Quincy May 8th 1803

Your Letter of April 30th put me into good Spirits. I had felt more upon your account, I can truly say, than upon my own, in the late misfortunes which have assailed us. I had pland a future scene of domestic comfort for you; I had anticipated Seeing a worthy woman rewarded for her steady attachment, and all that happiness given & received which so unstable a state of existance allows frail Mortals; I had pleased myself with having Some Share in effecting the object. but my plans are in a measure marred. Some real estate must be parted with; Shall it be the Quincy Farm or that upon which Brisler lives? the determination is in favour of the latter and your Brother is to Be the purchaser: he has sold a House in Town and raised Seven thousand dollers: Land will be sold him as an Equivelent. The Whole at that end of the Town is to be apprized, and the Farm upon which Burrel lives. The Quincy estate is a noble one, and in the course of a few years should we be so fortunate as to recover a part of the property now in Jeopardy your Father will have that place a very productive one. Situated so advantageously as it is for obtaining manure, I do not know whether I wrote you that just previous to the failure of the House, mr. Tufts had sold out his part of the Farm to your Father for Seven thousand dollors, so that he was Lord of Mount W—n

The Severity of enormus Charges and damages upon protested Bills, has been kindly mitigated, by the union of Mr. King, Gore and Williams who took up the Bills, and paid them upon honour, which will be a saving of Some thousand of dollors to us; We shall see in the course of the year how matters will terminate. In the mean time any success of yours will give us great pleasure, and I will not, I cannot relinquish the pleasing Idea of having you near to us: your Brother will let his House in Boston & remove here in August & remain with us untill the begining of October, when he will sit out for washington with his family. he proposes to reside in Quincy whenever he returns from thence.— I think you ought to come here upon a visit this Summer. Tho there may be occasion for delay, there can be none for secrecy. If the Subject is ever mentiond to me, I shall not hesitate to avow it, and vindicate it—

I read the Port Folio with much interest, who has been the Reviewer of Camillus? I have read them without having seen the Letters tho mr Shaw promissed them to me.

We have as cold a spring as we had mild winter; this 8th of may, we have had quite a snow storm. It melted as it fell, but was quite picturesque to see the Blosoms and flowers drest in white ground.

Adieu my dear Thomas, let me hear often from you.

Your affectionate   Mother A Adams

DEATH OF POLLY JEFFERSON

To Thomas Jefferson

SIR   Quincy May 20th 1804

Had you been no other than the private inhabitant of Monticello, I should e'er this time have addrest you, with that sympathy, which a recent event has awakend in my Bosom. But reasons of various kinds withheld my pen, untill the powerfull feelings of my heart, have burst through the restraint, and called upon me to shed the tear of sorrow over the departed remains, of your beloved and deserving daughter, an event which I most sincerely mourn.

The attachment which I formed for her, when you committed her to my care: upon her arrival in a foreign Land: has remained with me to this hour, and the recent account of her death, which I read in a late paper, brought fresh to my remembrance the strong sensibility she discoverd, tho but a child of nine years of age at having been seperated from her Friends, and country, and brought, as she expressed it, "to a strange land amongst strangers." The tender scene of her seperation from me, rose to my recollection, when she clung around my neck and wet my Bosom with her tears, saying, "O! now I have learnt to Love you, why will they tear me from you"

It has been some time since that I conceived of any event in this Life, which could call forth, feelings of mutual sympathy. But I know how closely entwined around a parents heart, are those chords which bind the filial to the parental Bosom, and when snaped assunder, how agonizing the pangs of seperation.

I have tasted the bitter cup, and bow with reverence, and humility before the great dispenser of it, without whose permission, and over ruling providence, not a sparrow falls to the ground. That you may derive comfort and consolation in this day of your sorrow and affliction, from that only source calculated to heal the wounded heart—a firm belief in the Being: perfections and attributes of God, is the sincere and ardent wish of her, who once took pleasure in subscribing Herself your Friend   ABIGAIL ADAMS

JAMES CALLENDER

To Thomas Jefferson

SIR   Quincy July 1st 1804

Your Letter of June 13th came duly to hand; if it had contained no other sentiments and opinions than those which my Letter of condolence could have excited, and which are expressed in the first page of your reply, our correspondence would have terminated here: but you have been pleased to enter upon some subjects which call for a reply: and as you observe that you have wished for an opportunity to express your sentiments, I have given to them every weight they claim.

"One act of Mr. Adams's Life, and *one* only, you repeat, ever gave me a moments personal displeasure. I did think his last appointments to office personally unkind. They were from among my most ardent political enemies."

As this act I am certain was not intended to give any personal pain or offence, I think it a duty to explain it so far as I then knew his views and designs. The constitution empowers the president to fill up offices as they become vacant. It was in the exercise of this power that appointments were made, and Characters selected whom Mr. Adams considerd, as men faithfull to the constitution and where he personally knew them, such as were capable of fullfilling their duty to their country. This was done by president Washington equally, in the last days of his administration so that not an office remaind vacant for his successor to fill upon his comeing into the office. No offence was given by it, and no personal unkindness thought of. But the different political opinions which have so unhappily divided our Country, must have given rise to the Idea, that personal unkindness was intended. You will please to recollect Sir, that at the time these appointments were made, there was not any certainty that the presidency would devolve upon you, which is an other circumstance to prove that personal unkindness was not meant. No person was ever selected by him from such a motive—and so far was Mr. Adams from indulging such a sentiment, that he had no Idea of the intollerance of party spirit at that time, and I know it was his opinion that if the presidency devolved upon you, except in the appointment of Secretaries, no material Changes would be made. I perfectly agree with you in opinion that those should be Gentlemen in whom the president can repose confidence, possessing opinions, and sentiments corresponding with his own, or if differing from him, that they ought rather to resign their office, than cabal against measures which he may think essential to the honour safety and peace of the Country. Much less should they unite, with any bold, and dareingly ambitious Character, to over rule the Cabinet, or betray the Secrets of it to Friends or foes. The two Gentlemen who held the offices of secretaries, when you became president were not of this Character. They were appointed by your predecessor nearly two years previous to his retirement. They were Gentlemen who had cordially co-opperated with him, and enjoyed the public confidence. Possessing however different political sentiments from those which you were known to have embraced, it was expected that they would, as they did, resign.

I have never felt any enmity towards you Sir for being elected president of the United States. But the instruments made use of, and the means which were practised to effect a change, have my utter abhorrence and detestation, for they were the blackest calumny, and foulest falshoods. I had witnessed enough of the anxiety, and solicitude, the envy jealousy and reproach attendant upon the office as well as the high responsibility of the Station, to be perfectly willing to see a transfer of it. And I can truly say, that at the time of Election, I considerd your pretentions much superior to his, to whom an equal vote was given. Your experience I venture to affirm has convinced you that it is not a station to be envy'd. If you feel yourself a free man, and can act in all cases, according to your own sentiments, opinions and judgment, you can do more than either of your predecessors could, and are awfully responsible to God and your Country for the measures of your Administration. I rely upon the Friendship you still profess for me, and (I am conscious I have done nothing to forfeit it), to excuse the freedom of this discussion to which you have led with an unreserve, which has taken off the Shackles I should otherways have found myself embarrassed with.—And now Sir I will freely disclose to you what has severed the bonds of former Friendship, and placed you in a light very different from what I once viewd you in.

One of the first acts of your administration was to liberate a wretch who was suffering the just punishment of the Law due to his crimes for writing and publishing the basest libel, the lowest and vilest Slander, which malice could invent, or calumny exhibit against the Character and reputation of your predecessor, of him for whom you profest the highest esteem and Friendship, and whom you certainly knew incapable of such complicated baseness. The remission of Callenders fine was a public approbation of his conduct. Is not the last restraint of vice, a sense of shame, renderd abortive, if abandoned Characters do not excite abhorrence. If the chief Majestrate of a Nation, whose elevated Station places him in a conspicuous light, and renders his every action a concern of general importance, permits his public conduct to be influenced by private resentment, and so far forgets what is due to his Character as to give countanance to a base Calumniater, is he not answerable for the influence which his example has upon the manners and morals of the community?

Untill I read Callenders seventh Letter containing your compliment to him as a writer and your reward of 50 dollars, I could not be made to believe, that such measures could have been resorted to: to stab the fair fame and upright intentions of one, who to use your own Language "was acting from an honest conviction in his own mind that he was right." This Sir I considerd as a personal injury. This was the Sword that cut assunder the Gordian knot, which could not be untied by all the efforts of party Spirit, by rivalship by Jealousy or any other malignant fiend.

The serpent you cherished and warmed, bit the hand that nourished him, and gave you sufficient Specimens of his talents, his gratitude his justice, and his truth. When such vipers are let lose upon Society, all distinction between virtue and vice are levelled, all respect for Character is lost in the overwhelming deluge of calumny—that respect which is a necessary bond in the social union, which gives efficacy to laws, and teaches the subject to obey the Majestrate, and the child to submit to the parent.

There is one other act of your administration which I considerd as personally unkind, and which your own mind will readily suggest to you, but as it neither affected character, or reputation, I forbear to state it.

This Letter is written in confidence—no eye but my own has seen what has passed. Faithfull are the wounds of a Friend. Often have I wished to have seen a different course pursued by you. I bear no malice I cherish no enmity. I would not retaliate if I could—nay more in the true spirit of christian Charity, I would forgive, as I hope to be forgiven. And with that disposition of mind and heart, I subscribe the Name of

ABIGAIL ADAMS

RESCINDING JOHN QUINCY'S APPOINTMENT

To Thomas Jefferson

SIR   Quincy August 18th 1804

Your Letter of July 22d was by some mistake in the post office at Boston sent back as far as New York, so that it did not reach me untill the eleventh of this Month. Candour requires of me a reply. Your statement respecting Callender, (who was the wretch referd to) and your motives for liberating him, wear a different aspect as explaind by you, from the impression which they had made, not only upon my mind, but upon the minds of all those, whom I ever heard speak upon the subject. With regard to the act under which he was punished, different persons entertain different opinions respecting it. It lies not with me to decide upon its validity. That I presume devolved upon the supreem Judges of the Nation: but I have understood that the power which makes a Law, is alone competent to the repeal. If a Chief Majestrate can by his will annul a Law, where is the difference between a republican, and a despotic Government? That some restraint should be laid upon the asassin, who stabs reputation, all civilized Nations have assented to. In no Country has calumny falshood, and revileing stalked abroad more licentiously, than in this. No political Character has been secure from its attacks, no reputation so fair, as not to be wounded by it, untill truth and falshood lie in one undistinguished heap. If there are no checks to be resorted to in the Laws of the Land, and no reperation to be made to the injured, will not Man become the judge and avenger of his own wrongs, and as in a late instance, the sword and pistol decide the contest? All the Christian and social virtues will be banished the Land. All that makes Life desirable, and softens the ferocious passions of Man will assume a savage deportment, and like Cain of old, every Mans hand will be against his Neighbour. Party spirit is blind malevolent uncandid, ungenerous, unjust and unforgiving. It is equally so under federal as under democratic Banners, yet upon both sides are Characters, who possess honest views, and act from honorable motives, who disdain to be led blindfold, and who tho entertaining different opinions, have for their object the public welfare and happiness. These are the Characters, who abhor calumny and evil speaking, and who will never descend to News paper revileing. And you have done Mr. Adams justice in believing him, incapable of such conduct. He has never written a line in any News paper to which his Name has not been affixed, since he was first elected president of the united States. The writers in the public papers, and their employers are alltogether unknown to him.

I have seen and known that much of the conduct of a public ruler, is liable to be misunderstood, and misrepresented. Party hatred by its deadly poison blinds the Eyes and envenoms the heart. It is fatal to the integrity of the moral Character. It sees not that wisdom dwells with moderation, and that firmness of conduct is seldom united with outrageous voilence of sentiment. Thus blame is too often liberally bestowed upon actions, which if fully understood, and candidly judged would merit praise instead of censure. It is only by the general issue of measures producing banefull or benificial effects that they ought to be tested.

You exculpate yourself from any intentional act of unkindness towards any one. I will freely state that which I referd to in my former Letter, and which I could not avoid considering as personal resentment. Soon after my eldest son's return from Europe, he was appointed by the district Judge to an office into which no political concerns enterd, personally known to you, and possessing all the qualifications, you yourself being Judge, which you had designated for office. As soon as congress gave the appointments to the president you removed him. This looked so particularly pointed, that some of your best Friends in Boston, at that time exprest their regret that you had done so. I must do him the Justice to say, that I never heard an expression from him of censure or disrespect towards you in concequence of it. With pleasure I say that he is not a blind follower of any party.

I have written to you with the freedom and unreserve of former Friendship to which I would gladly return could all causes but mere difference of opinion be removed. I wish to lead a tranquil and retired Life under the administration of the Government, disposed to heal the wounds of contention, to cool the rageing fury of party animosity: to soften the Rugged Spirit of resentment, and desirious of seeing my Children and Grand Children, Heirs to that freedom and independance which you and your predesessor, united your efforts to obtain. With these sentiments I reciprocate my sincere wishes for your Health and happiness.   ABIGAIL ADAMS

CLOSING A CORRESPONDENCE

To Thomas Jefferson

SIR   Quincy October 25 1804

Sickness for three weeks past, has prevented my acknowledging the receipt of your Letter of Sepbr the 11th. When I
first addrest you, I little thought of entering into a correspondence with you upon political topics. I will not however regret it, since it has led to some elucidations and brought on
some explanations, which place in a more favourable light occurrences which had wounded me.

Having once entertained for you a respect and esteem,
founded upon the Character of an affectionate parent, a kind
Master, a candid and benevolent Friend, I could not suffer
different political opinions to obliterate them from my mind,
and I felt the truth of the observation, that the Heart is long,
very long in receiving the conviction that is forced upon it by
reason. Affection still lingers in the Bosom, even after esteem
has taken its flight. It was not untill after circumstances concured to place you in the light of a rewarder and encourager of
a Libeller whom you could not but detest and despise, that I
withdrew the esteem I had long entertaind for you. Nor can
you wonder Sir that I should consider as personal unkindnesses
the instances I have mentiond. I am pleased to find that, which
respected my son, all together unfounded. He was as you
conjecture appointed a commissioner of Bankruptcy together
with Judge Daws, and continued to serve in it, with perfect
satisfaction to all parties. At least I never heard the contrary,
untill superseded by a new appointment. The Idea sugested, that
no one was in office, merely because it was not perminent, and
concequently no removal could take place, I cannot consider
in any other light, than what the Gentlemen of the Law would
term a quible—as such I pass it. Judge Daws was continued, or
reappointed which placed Mr. Adams, in a more conspicuous
light, as the object of personal resentment. Nor could I upon
this occasion refrain calling to mind the last visit you made me
at Washington, when in the course of conversation you assured
me, that if it should lay in your power to serve me or my family,

nothing would give you more pleasure. I will do you the justice to say at this hour: that I believe what you then said, you then meant. With respect to the office it was a small object but the disposition of the remover was considerd by me as the barbed arrow. This however by your declaration, is withdrawn from my mind. With the public it will remain, and here Sir may I be permitted to pause, and ask you whether in your ardent zeal, and desire to rectify the mistakes and abuses as you may consider them, of the former administrations, you are not led into measures still more fatal to the constitution, and more derogatory to your honour, and independence of Character? Pardon me Sir if I say, that I fear you are.

I know from the observations which I have made that there is not a more difficult part devolves upon a chief Majestrate, nor one which subjects him to more reproach, and censure than the appointments to office, and all the patronage which this enviable power gives him, is but a poor compensation for the responsibility to which it subjects him. It would be well however to weigh and consider Characters as it respects their Moral worth and integrity. He who is not true to himself, nor just to others, seeks an office for the benifit of himself, unmindfull of that of his Country.

I cannot agree, in opinion, that the constitution ever meant to withhold from the National Government the power of self defence, or that it could be considerd an infringment of the Liberty of the press, to punish the licentiousness of it.

Time Sir must determine, and posterity will judge with more candour, and impartiality, I hope than the conflicting parties of our day, what measures have best promoted the happiness of the people: what raised them from a state of depression and degradation to wealth, honor, and reputation; what has made them affluent at home, and respected abroad, and to whom ever the tribute is due to them may it be given.

I will not Sir any further intrude upon your time, but close this correspondence, by my sincere wishes, that you may be directed to that path which may terminate in the prosperity and happiness of the people over whom you are placed, by administring the Government with a just and impartial hand. Be assured Sir that no one will more rejoice in your success than   ABIGAIL ADAMS

Quincy Nov. 19. 1804.

The whole of this Correspondence was begun and conducted without my Knowledge or Suspicion. Last Evening and this Morning at the desire of Mrs. Adams I read the whole. I have no remarks to make upon it at this time and in this place.

J. ADAMS

JOHN QUINCY'S HEALTH AND APPEARANCE

To Louisa Catherine Adams

My dear Mrs Adams   Quincy December 8th 1804

I received yesterday your Letter of Novbr 27th. and was rejoiced to learn that you and the Children were well. I was just contemplating writing a Letter to my son to chide him for not writing to inform me, how George was grown, and improved, what he said when he saw his pappa again, and how mister John came on, whether he is as grave as his Brother George was how Master Georges socks fitted him, and whether Mamma let him wear them. Sundry of these domestic matters interesting only to those who are Mammas, and Grandmamas—also whether Capt Brackets Vessel had arrived safe with the cloaths cheese &c and a small Box containing some current jelly. I am glad to learn from you that George goes to School. Mrs Judge Cushing when she arrives has two pr more Socks which I could not get finishd soon enough to send by mr. Adams.

I regret to hear that my dear Sons health is not good. he lost his flesh so the last winter that he did not recover it through the Summer I do not think that he took sufficient excercise. his pen and Books engrossed almost his whole time I wish you would not let him go to Congress without a craker in his pocket the space between Breakfast and dinner is so long, that his Stomack gets filld with flatulencies, and his food when he takes it neither dijests or nourishes him. this and too great an anxiety of mind wears upon his constitution, and impairs his health. the first may be remedied by taking a dry bisquit and a Glass of wine—the latter I fear is constitutional and habitual—he must strive however to get the better of that, which he can neither prevent, by his anxiety or remove by his assiduity. all who know him, know him for a man of strickt honour and integrity, candid and liberal towards those who differ from him in opinion, where their views are honest. I can readily assent to your well drawn portrait, but there is one thing in which we must also unite, that of prevailing upon him to pay more attention to his personal appearance upon this Subject I have labourd to convince him of its necessity even as it conduces to his usefullness in Society, and as the writer in the port folio calling himself a British Spy, observes with respect to mr. Parsons, "that whilst the sublimity of his genius intitles him to admiration, the cut of his coat, the strangeness of his wig, or the coulour of his neckcloth; are the subjects of reprehension." It is in vain to talk of being above these little decorums—if we Live in the world and mean to serve ourselves and it, we must conform to its customs, its habits and in some measure to its fashions.

My health I thank God is much mended. I have regained my appetite, and in some measure my Strength. my flesh, it will be long before I remit if ever. it went of like the snow under a hot sun. My decline was so rapid that I had very little expectation of living more than a few months—the day before my son left Quincy, my spirits were so deprest with the Idea that I should never see him again, I sufferd an anguish which I kept to myself, and strove to appear cheerfull, that I might not embitter his journey with painfull reflections—the next day after he left me I was confind to my Chamber; & for six weeks growing daily weaker, & more feeble. Since then, the complaint I labourd under has gradually subsided, and I have gained strength, and spirits—I hope my Health may be confirmd, and that I may yet be permitted to welcome you both with your little ones at Quincy the next Spring. How is your good Mother and your Sisters? tender them my regards. let me hear frequently from you & yours. Louissa requests me to present her regards, and thanks for your kind remembrance of her. Thomas must answer for himself, he has not been well the last fortnight.

Affectionatly yours,   Abigail Adams

"YOU HAD AN APPARENT STIFFNESS OF TEMPER"

To John Quincy Adams

My dear son   Quincy december 18th 1804
    I last week received your Letter of december 3d in replie to
mine of Novbr 11th, not having made any mention of it before
I thought it had miscarried. I am very sorry to learn by it, that
you have been unwell. you must not let the mind wear so
much upon the Body. Your disposition to a Sedentary Life
prevents you from taking that regular excercise which the
Body requires to keep it in a healthy State. I used frequently to
remind you of it during your stay here. You eat too little; and
studied too much.
    You observe in a Letter to your Father, that you had an ap-
parent Stiffness of temper. Now that I smiled at, if you had said
that you had contracted a reserve and a coldness of address
upon entering company which was not natural to you, I would
have assented to it, and rejoiced that you had made the discovery as a means towards a Remedy. I have accounted for it from
Several causes one your having resided abroad during such
critical periods as you witnessd both in Holland and England.
you were obliged in your public capacity to be constantly upon
your gaurd, that nothing improper escaped you either in words
or looks. The constant State of anxiety for your Family served
to fix a weight of care upon your Brow incompatible with that
ease and freedom for which you was once noted. Your constant
application to your pen & your Books has had as great an influence as either of the other causes; for frequently after having
been a short time absent from them, your pleasentness & ease
would revive, the Brow contracted with care would unbend,
and the whole countenance be lightned up into Social good
humour. Could not the Student be left in the Study, and a
smile illumine the face when an old acquaintance appeard, a
smile which is so cheering that I think I could not feel myself,
happy not thus to meet my Friends, or be received by them,
possessing all the most valuable requisites of virtue, knowledge, honour and integrity. I am anxious that you should have
what Lord Chatham calls, Benevolence in trifles. I know it to

be in the Heart; to the outward Man only it is wanting. I have the more free in my remarks and observations because, tho others may make the same, they will not so readily account for the causes which produce the effects, or view them perhaps with so much candour.

I thank you my dear Son for the solicitude you express for my Life and Health. Without the latter in a tollerable degree, the former would soon be a burden to myself and others—Whilst I can be usefull, I hope they may be continued to me. I have recoverd my Strength beyond what I thought 5 weeks ago I ever should again. My Spirits have also returnd—My flesh is not of so much concequence. Your Father I think is as well as he was through the summer except that he has a weakness & swelling in one of his knees which prevents him from walking so much as he likes. I believe it to be Rheumatick. For your cough if it is not much better try the cough drops which cured mrs Cranch after the Physicians had in vain exerted their Skill—I beg you would not go such a length of time as you did last year without some refreshment—I know your stomack fills with wind, and then your food will not nourish you—

You must take the advise you gave your Father, and feel less for the State of public measures. They are tending to consequences which few if any of the actors see through. I feel much for Judge Chase. I believe him to be an honest and upright judge. So do most of his percecutors, and upon their heads may the ignominy rest. Thou shall not bear false witness.

Your Uncle Cranch is confined to his chamber, never I fear to leave it. He suffers inexpressible agony from the itching of his Legs.

Thomas will write you himself.

My Love to Mrs Adams. Do not let George forget Quincy, and his Grandparents—

Your most affectionate Mother

Present my Regards to mr Tracy & Bayard. assure them that I entertain a high esteem for them   A Adams

GEORGE WASHINGTON ADAMS

To John Quincy Adams

My Dear Son   Quincy December 30th 1804
   Your affectionate Letter of December 19th reach'd me a few days since, and found me and the rest of the family in good Health, and Spirits, blessing for which we ought to be truly thankfull. as all the Gifts of providence are enhanced and enjoyed with tenfold pleasure when attended by them, we can never so justly appreciate the blessing we enjoy, as when we are deprived of them.
   I was glad to hear so good an account of Master George. You must not look for an old head upon young Shoulders: a Grave Sedate Boy will make a very mopish dull old Man to my Grandmother I often refer for wise and just observations upon Humane nature, and as a consolation for my own volatile giddy disposition, she used to quote the old adage, wild colts make the best Horses. I used to be more afflicted by Georges grave deportment before he was two years old, than you can be now by his volitility and am really rejoiced to hear that he is a wild Boy. George has that within him which will show itself in time to his honour & your pleasure, or I have no skill in physiognomy. as to the other little Gentleman whom you, and mrs Adams describe as very fractious time may cure that tendency to irritability, but it requires much care and attention to rear such a child or his temper may be spoiled for Life.
   I shall attend to your request respecting help. I have a woman in my Eye to whom I will speak as soon as I can see her She has lived with me; and last year lived with mrs T. Greenleaf I think she would answer for you. She is an old Maid concequently has her oddities, but she is used to house keeping, and is prudent. as to a Man; you know how difficult it is to procure help of that sort for the Country, and Boys are much trouble and little Service—I can tell mr Shaw to make inquiries respecting the House & place of mrs Shaws of Robert Shaw in Boston. I presume yours would let for 80 or 90 dollers with the Garden and peice of ground which mr Whitny occupied I think I have a Tennant in my Eye who would give you that for it.

I have found Stuarts receipt and now inclose it to you. I have thoughts of writing him a few lines when you call upon him for the portrait. I wish he could be prevaild upon to Execute the one of your Father, which was designd for the State House in Boston. Genius is always eccentrick I think. Superiour talents give no security for propriety of conduct; there is no knowing how to take hold of this Man, nor by what means to prevail upon him to fullfill his engagements.

I have a request to make to you. it is to immortalize my Juno. You know many of her virtues, her affectionate attachment, her good humour, her watchfullness, and her sportive graces together with her personal Beauties, then she is as chaste as Diana—Homer has immortalized the dog of Ulyssus, Johnson had his favorite and Cowper his Spanil Beau, all celebrated in verse and why not my favorite Juno?

we have had an uncommon cold & snowe December, the weather very fluctuating, not more than one fair day at a time—a day or two sleighing, then a rain succeeded by cold and Ice, yet it very healthy. I have been much benifitted by the cold weather. I am anxious for your Health my dear Son. the Straitness upon your Breast, and your cough are undoubtedly a Rheumatic affection, but not the less to be attended to on that account. for many years I was sadly afflicted in that way, not a winter past that I did not experience more or less of it. many times I could not lie down in my Bed without two or three pillars. I pray you to take some advise and not to neglect yourself untill you and your Friends have cause to regret it—I shall send mrs Adams a recipe for a mixture which I have found very benificial, have both taken and given with good effect.

Your uncle Cranch remains much as he was your Father is very well; Thomas cannot be otherways whilst his darling is with me, tho he has kinks of the Rheumatism entaild upon all of you—Your Father has read two Romances this winter, tempted by the Eaves and I think he enjoyed them as highly as a Girl in her teens

Company comeing in obliges me to close my Letter, but not untill I have Subscribed your affectionate Mother,

Abigail Adams

GRANDSONS GEORGE AND JOHN

To John Quincy and Louisa Catherine Adams

my dear son and daughter   Quincy Novbr 29 1805
     The reason that you did not receive a Letter from me when
you arrived at Philadelphia, was oweing to my being so sick
that I could not write. I got your Brother to write, but not so
soon as I should, if I had been able. as soon as I could hold my
pen I wrote you a few lines, since which I have received your
Letter from Newyork; I have rejoiced in the fine weather
which has followed you ever since you left us. with the excep-
tion of a rainy day or two, we have had it uncommonly mild
and pleasant, much more so than for a fortnight before you sit
out. I presume you have by this time arrived in Washington
where I hope you have found your Friends in health. your
children are both in better Health than when you left them.
George breaths quite easy & is hearty, & lively goes to school
every day to Mrs Turner, who keeps in a Room in Gays House,
where she takes Major Barrets, two of Capt Brackets & those
at your uncles—John is very well & has lost his cough intirely;
he is rather too early a riser even for me, but the nights are
now so long that it is not to be expected that children will
sleep till it is fully light. He goes to bed about six—seldom
cries, goes by himself into bed, and asks neither for light or any
one to stay by him. he is a very pleasent child, and easily managed, with a steady hand. we take care of him ourselves. both
Louissa and his Aunt Adams are very fond of him, and he of
them—In fine weather I let him walk out I told him I was
writing to you and askd him what I should say—shall I say
John is good. No shall I say John is Naughty. No. he stood a
moment and his little Eyes glistned—say John has got a Beauty
new Hat—
     yesterday being Thanksgiving Brother and Sister Cranch
dinned with me and George with a Group of mr Nortens
Children. mr Shaw was up, and brought up mr Quincys Children to mr Terrys at the Bridge. tell mr Quincy they were very

well, as was miss Sophia who made me a visit yesterday and grows finely. Son having a fellow feeling for your Friend, you must not forget to tell all this to him, however trivial it may appear to those who are not parents.

Now all family matters are arranged. I shall turn my mind to those which are National; and begin to look out for the *Message*. Miranda is one of Tallyrands agents I have not a doubt and as such every movement should be carefully watchd. we shall hear more of that man. he is capable of troubling the waters, and fishing in them too.

your Brother & sister are gone to Haverhill present me kindly to all Friends and let me hear from you as often as you can

your affectionate Mother   Abigail Adams

"SEPERATIONS OF ALL KINDS FROM CHILDREN"

To Louisa Catherine Adams

Dear mrs Adams   Quincy Jan'ry 19th 1806

Your Letter of Jan'ry 6 I received last Evening. your Children are very well, and very well taken care of. so do not give yourself any anxious solisitude about them. I believe they are much better off than they could have been at any boarding House in washington, where they must have been confined in some degree; or have mixd with improper persons; with respect to John, the Child enjoys perfect Health, as I see to him myself, and he is always with me, never left to the care of any domestick unless when I go to meeting. I know that he has every thing which is proper for him, and nothing which can prove injurious; I never knew him either ask for pork, or eat a mouthfull, except one day, which was previous to your going from here. I agree with you that it is too grose food for a child inclined to be so fleshy as John—With regard to George if you will write to Mrs. Cranch She will give you all the information respecting him which you can desire. I can only say that every person who has a young Child for which they are particularly anxious think themselves peculiarly fortunate if they can place it under her care—ask Mrs. Quincy if she does not consider herself So? That you should wish to hear often from them, is natural and highly proper. I have seldom mist a week in writing unless mr Adams has written to his Brother when I know he has mentiond the Children. There cannot be any thing more dissagreable than transporting young Children twice a year, either by water, or in crowded Stages at such a distance, and however reluctant you might feel, at being seperated from them, I should suppose that your own judgement, experience and good sense would have convinced you of the propriety of the measure without compulsion——I have experienced Seperations of all kinds from Children equally dear to me; and know how great the Sacrifice & how painfull the task—but I considerd it the duty of a parent to consult the interest and benifit of their Children.

When you see Mrs. Quincy present my Love to her and tell her her little Sophia is very well, grows finely and is very lively and sprightly.

I do not know but you are Still Blooming at Washington, but here we have winter in good earnest—not much Snow; but intensly cold and that for six days successively. again it is Snowing:

I am glad to learn that your family are all well and hope Eliza has got rid of her cough. I hope she will be more attentive to her person, and not be guilty of self Murder. the Savages cover their persons with oil and Brick dust which is a great Security against the cold. Nay frown not Eliza if your sister reads this to you

> And still to make you more my friend
> I strive your Errors to amend.

My Love to mr Adams when he is at leisure to take a lesson I have one for him—Remember me to your Mother, Let me hear frequently from you, and I shall not be defficient in writing to you or to my Son. George and John both Send duty to their Parents, tho John never like to see me write—

affectionatly yours   Abigail Adams

DEATH OF A FRIEND'S CHILD

To Louisa Catherine Adams

To the Same
my Dear Mrs Adams　　　　　　　Quincy Feb'ry 15th 1806

I shall begin my Letter by putting your mind at ease respecting your children, who are both very well. George I saw yesterday quite in Raptures; his uncle Cranch had made him a little Sled with a small box upon the top; similar to one which Dexter had made John; and which employs half his time. Sometimes to draw about miss Juno, who seems to like the ride very well, and sits in it as grave and demure, as tho she could never skip, and play. he has his Hammer, and his Shovel, sometimes mimicks Jobe in Shoveling the Snow and at other times Hammers Stoutly enough; at other times uses his needle, and sews away with Susan. he is also a great rider, but it must be in a Sleigh or carriage—I devote my chamber where I sit to him, and it is pretty well litterd from morning to night—Whilst as a Mother you must be anxious to hear frequently from your Children; you will still bear in mind that they are mortal: and that no Solisitude or care can at all times sheild them from the common lot of Mortals. poor Mrs. Smith is now mourning over the remains of her dear Mary, who is this day to be committed to the silent Tombe—12 weeks she has languished in a decline, a slow fever, which has been fatal to many children the last Season, was her first complaint, no medicine could remove it. it fixed upon her Lungs. She fell into a consumption which in 12 weeks terminated her Life, during which time Mrs Smith has held her in her Arms. She would not be prevaild upon to lie upon the Bed in the day time. Mrs Smith has been nearly worn out, and the anguish of her mind has prey'd upon her health and Spirits.

I am not a little concernd for the Health of my dear son. the cold weather used to brace him up—but I learn from his Friends at Washington that he looks pale, thin, and slender.—I know his anxiety upon the State of our public affairs will wear him, and harrass his mind I wish he had less reason for it

we have had some severe cold weather and plenty of snow. I

presume you must have had some taste of it at Washington. how is your Mother this winter; has Eliza got rid of her cough! Is Caroline well have you heard from your Brother—Does he like Norfolk and his own situation?—

we all send our Regards to all our inquiring Friends, what shall I Say to Mamma John I am writing to her? Say little Johns good Boy. what shall I say to Pappa. that little John is roleing upon the Carpet, playing with Juno:

Affectionatly yours,   A Adams

FRANCISCO DE MIRANDA

To John Quincy Adams

My dear Son   Quincy March 5th 1806
    I fear your Father may have given you unnecessary anxiety; I told him at the time it was not best to mention an indisposition so slight as John's was, but he said if he wrote; he must tell all. I had observed for several days about noon a high coulour in his cheeks, and at that time, he was unusually irritable, Some other Symptoms indicated a redundancy of Bile, which proved to be the case. for the first time, Since he has been with me, I gave him a little medicine and it relieved him. he was quite well the next day, and I took him with me to Boston, where he both gave, and received much delight; he is very fond of his Aunt Adams, and the meeting between them is always a very joyous Scene after a little absence. I told him to day that I should write to you. he is never willing to see me take my pen: it requires a little more Silence from him than he likes—but when I tell him I am going to write to you, or his Mamma, he is more reconciled to it. to day he requested me to say that he was a good Boy, and added of himself, ask Pappa to come home. George Spent March meeting day with him and is very well. I thought I perceived upon his face a few of the old pimples returning, and advised his Aunt to give him some of the black powders, which She will do. It is about the Season when he was so afflicted the last year—

    I rejoice to learn, as we have by a Letter from mrs Quincy

that mr Cranch is appointed Chief Justice of the district of Columbia—the appointment will do honour to mr Jefferson, a thing very necessary to him, nor can I believe as some persons do, that he did it reluctantly—I have more pitty for him than many others, more compassion for his errors and Some of his frallties—ill treated as some of my Friends have been—I never could, or did receive any Satisfaction from the oblique cast upon his Character.

What a Strange Buisness is this in which Miranda has engaged? When I saw the first account in a Newyork paper, it Struck me as something in which the administration must have some concern, and knowing the enterprizing Character of Miranda I thought it probable that he might be engaged in some Secret progect, particularly so as so much secrecy had been preserved in Congress, and so much buisness done with closed doors—but the Sensation which has been, since his sailing excited and the Queries which have been made to mr Madison have given me not a little uneasiness, least an innocent and amiable youth may fall a Sacrifice. the first intimation I ever had respecting him—was in a Letter which I received last week—in which it was Said, you know his mind has been long intent upon the Sea. an opportunity offering which was considerd advantages, he has gone a voyage. I no Sooner read it, than I drew the conclusion, and tho not an other Syllable has been written upon the Subject, I conclude the Query in the paper to be true. I this day received a Letter, from the same quarter, but the Subject is not even mentiond. I dare not say all I fear or half I apprehend; you know in what light it will be considerd here by his . . . and how execrated—

a strange coalition is taking place in Newyork—What a medly!

I hope the buisness of congress will be well matured dijested, sifted, purified, refined—If you can accomplish a shield for the president, you will Shew the World, that you can requite evil with good, the most honorable and glorious victory in my estimation which can be obtain over our Enemies—bless them who curse you. do good to those who despightfully use you—

With my Love to Mrs A I Subscribe affectionatly Your Mother   Abigail Adams—

To John Quincy Adams

My dear Son   Quincy March 24th 1806
   I was much pleased at receiving your Letter of March 14th.
It was a longer interval than had occured before, without receiving a line from you. but Mrs Quincys kindness in always
mentioning you to my sister had relieved me from the fears
that you might be sick. it is with Sincere Satisfaction that I
learn from your own hand that your Health is much mended.
When a Man enjoys good Health, good Spirits are a natural
attendant, and he is more disposed to attend to his personal
appearance—now this is a subject that I have not hinted at this
Winter. Indeed I found so much real cause for it last Summer,
that I was fearfull you would get callous to my admonitions.
   "A good Coat is tantamount to a good Character; and if the
world be a stage it's as necessary to dress as to act your part
well," says Tangore, in the play—"Why Man when I landed
from the packet in my old blew coat, shabby waistcoat, and
decayed kerseymeres—I was pushd and smok'd by every ap-
prentice and shopkeeper I met: oh in this age of false appearences, there's nothing like a shewy outside—" I recollect a
Story in the Spectator, mr Bickerstaff remarks that his servant
always bowed lower to him, and was more attentive whenever
he had his full bottomd wig on, than when he wore his night
Cap. Now I hope you never appear in Senate with a Beard two
days old, or otherways make, what is calld a shabby appearance.
Seriously I think a mans usefullness in Society depends much
upon his personal appearance—I do not wish a Senator to
dress like a Beau, but I want him to conform so far to the
fashion, as not to incur the Character of Singularity, nor give
occasion to the world to ask what kind of Mother he had? or
to Charge upon a wife neglegence and inattention when she is
guiltless
   The greatest Man observed a Lady the other day, wants his
wife to pull up his coller, and mind that his coat is brush'd.
   We have received very little intelligence from congress this
Session. So much of the time the doors have been closed, that

the open debates have but just commenced. Mr Randolph appears to become driver of the Whole Body, and he uses the whip and scourge freely, tho we have only mutilated Scraps of his Speech. The Ninth Congress will make a most Misirible figure in History.

We are totally in the dark respecting the Electioneering Campaign, or who the candidates held up by the Ancient dominion are. We Suppose mr Madison, Munroe, perhaps Giles. the little Musketo himself cannot think of rising to that height surely.

Our April Election approaches. how it will terminate is uncertain; if Govr. Strong is reelected, this year the democs will drop him as a future candidate, it is said

The death of mr Pitt, and the change which has taken place in the British Cabinet may be favorable to America If a judicious negotiator could be sent, will not mr Jefferson adopt such a measure?

I suppose Mr. Shaw has written to you respecting a House, but you will be here soon enough to determine Whether it will be proper to take one this Summer George dinned with us yesterday and is well. John is better and sits by, singing four and twenty black Birds; and O my kitten my deary.

I wish Congress may rise at the time you mention, but I doubt it—

I am most affectionatly, your Mother,   Abigail Adams

"WHAT DOES MR ADAMS THINK OF NAPOLEAN?"

To Mercy Otis Warren

my Dear Mrs Warren   Quincy March 9th 1807

To your kind and friendly Letter I fully designd an immediate replie, but a Severe attack of a rheumatick complaint in my Head has confined me to my Chamber for Several weeks and renderd me unable to hold a pen. tho recovering from it, my head Still feels crakd: Shatterd I am Sure it is—you will therefore pardon any inaccuracy I may commit. my Health which you so kindly inquire after, has been better for two years past, than for many of those which preceeded them. I am frequently reminded that here I have no abiding place. I bend to the blast. it passes over for the present and I rise again.

your Letter my dear Madam written So much in the Stile of Mrs Warrens ancient Friendship, renewed all those Sensations which formerly gave me pleasure, and from which I have derived sincere and durable gratification, and I anticipate a Still closer and more cordial union in the World of Spirits to which we are hastning, when these earthly tabernacles Shall be moulderd into Dust.

If we were to count our years by the revolutions we have witnessed, we might number them with the Antediluvians, so rapid have been the changes; that the mind tho fleet in its progress, has been outstriped by them—and we are left like Statues gazing at what we can neither fathom, or comprehend.

you inquire what does mr Adams think of Napolean? If you had asked Mrs Adams, She would have replied to you in the words of Pope.

> If plagues and Earthquakes, break not heavens design
> why then a Borgia or a Napoline?

I am Authorized to replie to your question, What does mr Adams think Napoleon was made for? "My answer Shall be as prompt and frank as her question. Napoleons Maker alone can tell all he was made for. in general Napoleon was, I will not Say made, but permitted for a catonine tails, to inflict ten thousand lasshes upon the back of Europe as divine vengeance for the Atheism Infidelity Fornications, Adulteries Incests and Sodomies, as well as Briberies Mobberies Murders Thefts Intrigues and fraudelent Speculations of her inhabitants—and if we are far enough advanced in the career—and certainly we have progressd very rapidly—to whip us for the Same crime's—and after he has answerd the end he was made, or permitted for, to be thrown into the fire—now I think I have meritted the answer from Mrs Warren which She has promised me to the Question, What was Napoleon made for?"

May I ask mrs Warren in my turn—what was col Burr made for? and what can you make of him or his projects? enveloped in as many Mystery as Mrs Ratcliffs castle of udolphus? how he mounted to power we know, and a faithfull historic page ought to record, and after he had answerd the end for which he was permitted, we know how he fell. what is yet left for him to perform, time must unveil.

I thank you my dear Madam for your inquiries after my Daughter—She was well a few days Since—She had Letters from her Son dated in Nov'br he was then at Trinidad where he expected to pass the winter, a don Quixot expedition which could never have met with his Grandfathers or my assent or consent, if it had been known to us before he had Saild. it has been a source of much anxiety to us, and to his Mother.

I cannot close this Letter without droping a Sympathizing tear with you over the remains of your beloved Neice, and my valued Friend. She was from her Youth all that was amiable Lovely and good, the youthfull companion of my daughter. I always saw her with pleasure, and parted from her with regreet. She was endeard to me by the misfortunes of her youth which from her Strong Sensibility, and dutifull affection, I was frequently made the depositary of her Sorrow and tears. She always exprest for me a Sincere Regard—when I learnt her new engagement, knowing the Delicate State of her Health, I feard She might find it too arduous for her, but her companion She had long known, esteemd and valued as his many virtues deserved

Heaven Spared her to act well the Mothers part towards her Sons, to whom She devoted herself and having reared them to Manhood, for wise ends which we cannot comprehend—took her out of Life—what can we Say, but that the ways of Heaven are dark and intricate—

I pray you to present mr Adams and my regards to Gen'll Warren—we both of us rejoice to hear that he enjoys So much health at his advanced period of Life. we Shall always be happy to hear of the welfare of Friends whom we have loved from our early years and with Whom we have past many, very many Social hours of pleasing converse, in unity of Bond and Spirit.

with Sincere Regard I Subscribe Your Friend

Abigail Adams

FAMILY NEWS

To Elizabeth Smith Shaw Peabody

My dear sister   Quincy June 10th. 1807.

If I had written to you my dear sister half as often as I have thought of you and contemplated writing, you would have had a Letter by every Mail for these two months: I have to acknowledge the receipt of two kind Letters from you since I have made you any return the last bearing date May 29th, which came last week to hand, and to which I should have replied yesterday by a young Man who lives with us who was going home for a week, and had promised me to call and tell you how we do: and bring me word of your welfare; I attempted writing to you yesterday, but the weather had become so suddenly so intencely hot, that my feeble frame sank under it, and renderd me wholy unfit for any exertion of body or mind; To day an easterly wind has given me new Life and spirits, and I determined, no longer to delay returning you thanks for your kind favours which always do my Heart good; tho they are so sparingly bestowed that I have frequently to regret, that Talents so brilliant and powers so harmonious and touching, should not more frequently be displayed for the improvement, and edification of those who know how to appreciate their value.

I know you can plead a thousand cares and avocations which necessarily devolve upon you; Surrounded as you are by your numerous family, in which you are continually doing good, and communicating it to others, knowing so well as you do, that we live not to ourselves.

My own Family when collected together consists of 21 persons. Mrs Smith, John & Caroline have been these three weeks in Boston upon a visit to my Son J. Q. Adams, who with his family are residents in Boston. I say residents, because they mean to take their flight in the fall like the Birds of passage to the southward. I shall inform mrs Smith of your kind invitation to her and her children—She is a woman of great firmness of mind you know, from her youth up—She has had ample Scope for the exercise of it, in the visissitudes of fortune which have attended her. To herself are confined her troubles. She never makes them a subject of complaint to her most intimate Friends—but they evidently wear upon her spirits, and produce many a silent tear—her present Situation is painfull to her, her future prospects . . . we see but a little way into futurity —"or who could suffer Being here below"?

This world we are told is our School may we all of us improve aright, the usefull Lessons we are taught.

I hope Lydia has recoverd, and that you will make us a visit soon. We are now, all in pretty good health. I have recoverd from the disorders which confined me, from the first week in Febry untill the middle of April, I was threatned with a Lung fever for many days, which finally terminated in an Eruption upon the skin, which with its dissagreeble qualities gave me one pleasure—that of scratching.

Mrs T B Adams hopes you will come before she makes her visit to Haverhill, or not untill her return. She will go there the first week in July. My little name sake is a sweet child—pretty enough I think. I have little John with me too. Susan is grown to the stature of a woman before she is in her teens—a great misfortune to have the Body out grow the mind—I never saw two children more different in their turn of mind behaviour and tempers than Caroline Smith and Susan—I sometimes think of what Mr. Joseph Dyar, used often to say to me when I was young and very wild, Nabby you will either make a very bad, or a very good woman. Caroline is soft in her manners compliant in her temper and disposition, yealding to the opinions of those whom she considers her superiours—and every way engageing—A thread would govern one, a cable would be necessary for the other—yet time is doing much for her, and reason and argument begin to take hold, and make impression which give hopes that a very good woman may be made from seeds Sown. If you had been near me, I should have sent her to you long ago; but the distance has been an obstacle—She has a strong mind and a generous temper. She is not proud, haughty or envious—but an ardent temper, and a Spirit of contradiction odious in youth—You have had a variety of tempers and dispositions to deal with. How would you manage one, upon whom you could not impress any subordination— any true defference to age, or relation or Rank in Life?

how hard it is to rule the Spirit and govern the tongue—

Brother and Sister Cranch are well. Mrs Norten looks very thin—She is indeed multiplied in children—I hope she will live to see them a comfort to her, and reward her for all her toil and trouble.

Your son is well-envoloped in Science a promoter of literature with all his Heart and Soul and Strength—no man engages more zealously, or is more persevering. There is Some talk of his sacrificeing to the graces—he will not however acknowledge it Yet I belive he has his favorite—and in time will make it appear so, if other circumstances are favorable. I have at length prevaild upon him to get him a peice of linnen, and mrs. Smith with Susan & Caroline have made it up: and a very good peice it was—but he wants a care which neither you or I can help him to, a stich in time—and a care of his own things, and indeed a knowledge of them—a man whose mind is so engrosed with great objects—cannot descend to the minutiea of an odd sock—a raggid ristband &c &c.

My Love to my dear amiable Neice I hope she will accompany you. My best respects to mr Peabody in which we all join. I shall tell John Smith what you have written respecting him. He is the same in mind and manners that he early presaged.

Pray my dear Sister do not let it be long e'er you make us all happy by seeing and embraceing you with that sincere and tender affection which has ever Subsisted between us—and which still burns with undiminished fervour in the bosom of your Sister   Abigail Adams.

GRANDSONS SENT TO SCHOOL

To John Quincy and Louisa Catherine Adams

Dear Children   Quincy october 25th. 1807

I address you jointly and congratulate you upon the fine weather we have had since you commenced your journey I hope e'er this day, you have reached washington, with your dear little Boy; for whose Safety, I was not a little anxious through so long and fatigueing a journey. We had the pleasure to receive a Letter from you, informing us of your arrival at New york—

The week after you left us your Father and I undertook a visit to Atkinson to carry George—it really appeard as formidable as a journey to Philadelphia used to, when we were accustomed to make it Annually. we found our Friends all well, and desirious of making master George happy. it was vacancy and mr & mrs Vose were gone a journey. there are two lads from Baltimore one of them near George's age with whom he will be very companionable, and what you will consider more fortunate, there is a very geenteel young French Gentleman of about 17 who attends mr vose to learn the english Language: who was quite pleasd, to find George Speaking French. I requested that he would Speak always French to George: by which means I hope he will not lose what he has already acquired—I could not but admire to see how readily George enterd into all the rules, & regulations, of the Family, appeard quite at home, and attachd himself to mr Peabody as if he had always lived with him. when we left him, he did not express any desire to return, only desired that I would write to you that he determined to be very good, one of the best Boys in School.

John I sent to his Aunt Cranch's he goes to school everyday, but is not quite so well weaned from Grandmamma as George. to day being Sunday I brought him home to dine but he could not consent to go to meeting, without I would promise to take him home with me to night; so here he lies upon the cushing in my chamber eating an apple very happy. when he does not See me he is quite content—I told him I was writing to you, and he desires I should Say that he is a very good Boy.—

our Family are all getting over their great colds. News we have not any, to communicate, but are waiting to hear what the great counsels will do & say when they assemble. Let us hear frequently From you—and remember me affectionaly to your Mother and other connextions—

your affectionate Mother   Abigail Adams

"YOUR DEPARTURE WAS SO SUDDEN"

To Abigail Adams Smith

my dear daughter   Quincy Janry. 14th 1808
   your departure was so sudden that I had scarcly time to
think of it, or realize that you could be about to leave me and
when you was really gone I felt the full force of your absence
and sat down without a wish to move from my chair the whole
day or to see any one; I had fully believed that you would pass
the winter with me, yet when the col came for you, I could not
but approve of your determination; knowing as I do your fixed
resolution to make every situation in which you are placed as
agreable to your self and Friends as you can, by a cheerfull
compliance and a ready acquiescence in all circumstances,
times and places: I shall try to reconcile myself to what was
deemed best, and think it most prudent, weighing all things in
their proper balance that you should have acted as you have
done. I hope you will be prospered in your Basket and store,
and if you have not the elegancies you will have the comforts
of Life.
   I rose the morning after you left us, fearfull that rain was
suddenly comeing and would retard your journey but the
clouds dispersed and we had a fine day, rather too warm but not
enough so to greatly injure the travelling. yesterday was much
colder, and I traveld on with you very successfully. but this day,
thursday, by ten oclock a snowstorm commenced and has
continued through the day, damp, threatning to end in rain.
you cannot get on—yet I know not where to place you. your
road is out of my track. that beyond Northhampton I am a
stranger to—
   you must write me all your adventures, and how you and
caroline employ youself, how your House is and you must be
sure to plant out some trees and call them after your names— I
am rejoiced that you are to have mrs St Hillier with you I know
how cheerfull she used to be, and I have always considerd her
as a heroine her Life and history a Romance her attachment,
her patience her fortitude her affection through trials and

sufferings unabated— I really look at her History so far as I
have known it with supprize and astonishment

I shall write to you as soon as I hear from you. Love to my
dear Caroline whom I miss not a little. my Love also to the col
whose good spirits served to enliven mine, and made us all regret that his stay with us was so short. I have got the Cambrick
for Williams shirts and Louisa is putting it on

most tenderly you affectionate Mother

Abigail Adams

GRANDSON WILLIAM SMITH'S PROSPECTS

To Louisa Catherine Adams

my dear daughter   Quincy April 4th. 1808

It is a long time since I wrote you, or rather since I sent a
Letter, for an unfinished one has lain by so long that like an
old Almanack it is out of date. The writing Spirit is not always
present, and it is shy and coy. If you do not frequently solisit it,
neglect is sure to be followed by indifference, and indifference
by disgust; I need not any other prompter at present than the
desire I have to write of your children from whom you have
not heard for some time. By a Letter from Atkinson I hear that
George is very well, and a very Good Boy. Abbe Shaw has
been very sick, even to an allarming degree, seizd with a puking which could not be checked for several days untill She was
reduced almost to the grave. I have my fears that it will terminate in a decline which will be to my poor Sister a heart rending stroke, and will break it I fear. She has never recoverd the
loss of Betsy, altho like a good Christian, she has bowd with
Submission, and devoted her time, and all the powers of her
mind to the improvement of those young persons committed
to her care; by which, as she has some times Said she has alle-
viated her affliction. John is very well now, but he was sadly
troubled with fits of the cholick for some time, so as to wake
from his Sleep and cry. Some medicine which he took gave
proof of the cause and he has been relieved by the discharge of
several living creatures and I am now pretty well convinced

that the gasping for breath which at times has been so allarm-ing, arose from some knot of those vile reptiles.—We are all in pretty good Health. I cannot add Spirits. The aspect of public affairs throughs a gloom over the approaching Spring. The Husbandman can neither till or sow with a prospect of gain; as his handmaid commerce has both her hands lop'd of and her feet tied. She is laid prostrate, and her Lovers go about the Streets mourning. We may truly add we are beset on every Side—who is wise enough to say what ought to be done?

I have thought the administration more blamed by the Federal party than they merrited, during these critical times. They have too closely imitated their opponents during the former administration—I cannot defend very many of the measures of the Government; I think they have brought us to the present crisis of our affairs. Yet those who see but, in part, and know but in part are not the most competent judges.

how can congress be permitted to rise. The Country is so critically and so dangerously situated, that every man should be at his post. Every wind may waft as tidings of vast importance—

Mrs Allcut mentiond to me when She was here, that She thought the Rooms of your House ought to be open'd and aird and the furniture looked too, if you did not return early in the Spring would you have her do it, if she should be at leisure? You will write me what you would have done;

William Smith left us last week, and is gone to his Father. His attention and punctuality to his School gave great Satisfac-tion, and after it closed he could not bear to remain idle, and there were not any prospects for him here. His inclination leads him to the Army, and he is desirious of obtaining a com-mission there. His Grand Father told him he would write for him, both to the President and mr Madison and the Secretary of War—I should like to know his Uncle's opinion, and if consistant with his judgement, whether he would mention him to Mr. Madison as a young man of regular habits, modest, discreet & I believe brave. I should hope that his engagement with Miranda would be no bar to his employment in the Army. He was under age, and was placed with him by those in whom he naturally confided, and knew not Mirandas views—

I should have written to mr Adams myself upon the Subject,

but shall wait to hear further from William and I only mention it now, merely to know if any Scruple lies in his own mind against recommending him.

Mrs. Adams is well and her little ones, with me desires to be remember'd to your Sister Buchanna.

Louissa has been in Boston this Month—or She would request a Remembrance also—to you and your Friends a kiss for my Boy Charles. I suppose when I know him, he will claim an equal Share of the Love and affection of his Grandmother with his Brothers—He must be very good to get as large a portion as John—I shall write next to my Son.

Your affectionate Mother   Abigail Adams

"A NOVEL CALLED THE WILD IRISH GIRL"

To Caroline Amelia Smith

MY DEAR CAROLINE: Quincy, May 28th, 1808.

Your letter of May the 8th, your grandpapa brought home with him from church, on Sunday the 20th; owing to sickness I was not able to go, and am yet confined to my chamber. My fever and cough are both leaving me, and I hope a few days more will give me health sufficient to enjoy the fine season.

I have been reading a novel called the Wild Irish Girl. Why the term wild is given, I know not, unless as a ridicule upon those who imbibe national prejudices, merely from vague report. She is represented as living in an ancient barony with her father, who in the wars had been despoiled of his property, and had retired with his daughter, her old nurse, and Father John, a learned, polite, and liberal minded priest, from whom she received her education. Here she lived, a recluse from the world, but with a lively imagination, a sportive fancy, a devotion to music, which she practised upon her harp, the favourite instrument of her country. She studied, and was perfectly versed in the historic knowledge of her native land; as a resource, she became a botanist, and on a thousand occasions, displayed such a love of nature and its productions, which she describes so artlessly, with such a vivid display of superior powers, that she charms and enchants the reader. She had gathered the first rosebud of the spring, which she had watched with much care, and presented to a young stranger, whom chance had led to the barony, and who had for some months been an inmate there, and who at the request of her father had been her preceptor in drawing. In return she repeated to him a little ode from the French. "Oh beautiful! beautiful!" exclaimed Glorvina, "I thank you for this beautiful ode; the rose was always my idol flower in all its different stages of existence; it speaks a language my heart understands, from its young bud's first crimson glow, to the last sickly blush of its faded bloom; it is the flower of sentiment in all its sweet transitions; it breathes a moral, and seems to preserve an undecaying soul in that fragrant essence which still survives the bloom and symmetry of the fragile form which every beam too ardent, every gale too chill, injures and destroys."

Your little darling A. has been sick, and looks like the flower or the bud in its faded form, which I have just been describing; more interesting in decay than bloom—one exciting all the pleasing sensations, the other a softer and tenderer sentiment.

Our friends here are all well. To-morrow will be our general election day; the embargo should not be complained of by the federalists, for it has increased their number ten fold, and will be like to give them such a weight in the councils of the nation, as no other measure of a peaceable kind could have effected.

With the love and affection of the whole family, jointly and severally, I close my letter to my dear Caroline, and am her truly affectionate grandmother,   A. A.

JOHN QUINCY LOSES HIS SENATE SEAT

To Abigail Adams Smith

my dear daughter   Quincy June 19th 1808
    Here we are Sitting by a good fire in the parlour, and wearing, our winter coats to meeting, whilst our windows are coverd with a profusion of roses, our Wall's decorated with flowers expanding their Beauties to the cold Northern blast, which rudely lacerates their delicate texture, unmindfull of their Beauty; and headless of their fragrance.

I rose the other morning delighted with the visit I had made you; and the pleasing interview I had with you, and the Coll. William your Brother Mrs. St. Hillair, all but my dear Caroline not least beloved, whom I did not see. Your Father accompanied me, and we came rather unexpectedly upon you, but were not the less joyfully received. I was quite delighted with your situation, and found you so cheerfull and happy, that it augmented the pleasure of my visit which was only interrupted by the strikeing of the clock at the morning hour when I usually rise. Altho only a dream it left upon my mind so pleasing an impression, that I could not refrain communicating it at the Breakfast table, and calling upon the family to participate the pleasure.

It is some time since I received a Letter from you. Susan received one from Caroline of May 25th a few days since, full of her lovely lively spirits which delighted us all. I have been much confined at home from indisposition, for three weeks to my chamber with a bad cough and some fever: it has now left me, altho a change of weather produces a hoarsness. I have not been in Boston since your Brothers return there. He comes to Quincy almost every Saturday, and passes Sunday with us, but yesterday the rain and storm prevented him. Miss Kitty Johnson has been with us the week past, Altho she has not so many personal Charms as Eliza, her manners are more correct, and pleasing to me. I think she resembles her Mother in person and manners more than any other of her daughters. Our little Abbe is gone with her Aunt Mary to Haverhill. You may easily immagine how much we miss her. Mrs. James Foster has an other son—thus for domestick occurrences.

You have no doubt seen that our state Legislature and senate have a federal majority, and that they have elected Mr. Loyed a Senator to congress in the room of your Brother. Mr. Loyed is the only son of Dr Loyed, a Merchant, a gentleman of tallents & Education, of a fair and honorable Character, whom I presume will not discredit the State—How much of an Essex Man he is, Time will disclose. During the present session of the House, a number of Resolutions were brought forward, and adopted, with instruction to the Representitives and Senators, to use their influence in congress to carry them into effect. Those of them which recommend a Navy for the defence of our harbours and commerce, and fortifications for our security, not only your Brother, but every Man who is sensible of our exposed Situation, and the allarming State of our Country with respect to Foreign powers, would most readily assent to, but these resolutions were connected with others which calld for a decided opposition to the National Government, and in the view of your Brother, relinquished our Neutral Rights, and deserted our Seamen Subjects which he had ardently mantaind, and strenuously asserted against British orders, and French Edicts, and which he considerd as essential to our independence. Consistant therefore with his principles, he could not any longer hold his seat in the Senate. He resignd it, by a Letter to the two Houses, like an honest Man and true American.

The Federal Party have acted towards him a most ungenerous part—one which no honest Man can justify. They have vilified, abused and calumniated him because he could not adopt their principles, and become a party man, because he would have an opinion of his own. Every federal printer in Boston, refused to publish any thing which was written by way of justification, or explanation of his conduct. Let us pull him down, by any means, and any falshood, was the language of their conduct: the Republicans saw this, and eagerly caught the occasion to place him upon their side, and support him by their votes. This exasperated the federalist—and they rejected a man whose conduct and principles will reflect honour upon his country in Spight of all their mean jealousy, and narrow views. The Republicans have acted towards him, with more candour and liberality than they usually practise. They have not resorted to flattery but represent him as he really is, a man of a candid liberal mind, free from party views, of a pure heart, and unblemished Character, of distinguished tallents and integrity.—

I cannot say that he has not felt, being wounded in the House of his Friends, yet his elevation of mind will enable him to bear with mildness and patience the jealousy of his equals, Which upon this occasion has been very conspicuous, the ill treatment of his fellow citizens, and the calumnies of his Enemies, being fully sensible that true greatness of Soul consists in Suffering these Trials without complaining, or abating any thing of zeal for the public good. Plutarch observes that the ill usage of our Country, like that of our Parents, should be borne with Submission.

I must close this Letter with my best Love and regards to the Coll, who has Shared largely in these *Bounties* of his Country and who knows how to estimate good report, and evil report.

Verily there is a Reward for the Righteous. Let us act consciencously and leave the event.

With Love to every Branch of your Family from every twig of ours—I am my dear daughter Most affectionately Your Mother,   Abigail Adams—

"FOR HAVING CHOSEN AN INFIDEL PRESIDENT"

To Abigail Adams Smith

My dear Daughter   Quincy December 8th. 1808
    I am indebted to you for two Letters one of [   ] the last bearing date Novbr 20th. & 24th. I am always rejoiced to see your handwriting, altho the contents of your Letters some times give me pain, and none more so than those which contain an Idea that your Relatives, and Friends have not exerted themselves for you as they might have done. With respect to william. Your Father himself went to Town: and advised with some of his commercial acquaintance, who oweing to the total supression of Commerce did not like to take any young Gentleman into their stores—most of those who had any Number were obliged to dissmiss them. Dr Welchs youngest Son John returnd home, and he sent him to an accademy to keep him out of Idleness. Mr Greenleafs son Price is returnd home. Capt. Beals two son, are here intirely out of Buisness. The Shop keepers have buisness for a time, but that is like to come soon to a close by the nonintercourse Bill which has recently past in congress—So that the youth of our country have not any other resourse, but to till the land for Bread to Eat. This state of things cannot last long. We are wrought up to a crissis which must break forth in vengence some where or other. Heaven preserve our Country underserving as it is of the favour and protection of Providence. Parson E[   ] told his congregation that we were suffering the judgments of Heaven

for having chosen an infidel president to rule over us. We as a people have crying sins enough beside to draw down the punishments we feel. Let each individual look into his own breast, and root out every evil and Corrupt propencity. Then may we expect to be a people Saved of the Lord.

I am much grieved at the misfortune of your Brother. a more generous benevolent Heart exists not in Man. the Season of the year is in his favour, and I hope he will be spaired to his family and Friends. in the midst of Life we are in Death. We have had a recent instance of this in the late Death of Mrs. Price, the Mother of Mrs Greenleaf—invited to a tea party, well and vigorus as age can be, She declined only on account of the late hours of Return, rose from her chair was seizd with an oppression upon her lungs, went to her Bed, and expired the next day, to the inexpressible Grief of her distresst and afflicted daughter. by painfull experience I know how afflictive the Death of Parents is—at a period when their Lives are usefull instructive and pleasant, the Source of our own Life seems dried up, our best Friends and counselors removed. Yet this is the order of Nature, and we who are yet living must soon expect to follow our Aged Friend.— Our old Friend Genll. Warren is also numberd with the great congregation. he was very infirm, and Aged—84 I think. I felt as tho former Friendship demanded from me a Sympathizing Letter, and requested that the bitterness of party Spirit had severd us, but after the injustice she had done your Fathers Character in her History, and the opportunity he had given her of making some acknowledgment for it, which she wholy omitted to do. I thought a Letter of the kind would appear insincere, and altho I feel for her berevement, and know how keenly she must feel it, I have declined writing to her.

We are all in pretty good Health at present. Mrs. S Adams is much better. My dear sister Cranch is recoverd in some measure, but I can see that her whole frame is Shaken, and that she is failing—Your Brothers family in Boston are well except John who I think in a very critical state of Health. he has many Hetick Symptoms. They all kept thanksgiving with us, your uncle and Aunt Cranch & Sister Smith—all of whom desired to be affectionatly rememberd to you. we calld you all to mind, and found our party incompleat. Last year you were with us.

Susan desires me to present her Duty to you, and to say to you, that she was at Atkinson when her Mother arrived here; and did not know it for a week, when be sure she was anxious enough to return, but was obliged to wait an other week for her Aunt Peabody—T B A and his Mil desire to be kindly rememberd to you. All our domesticks remember you and yours with Love and affection—I was yesterday at Weymouth —our Friends there were well—We tallk of you—I expect Aunt Edwards tomorrow to make her Annual visit—She fell and broke her Arm in October, when she intended to come —I expected she would give up the Idea of her visit, but she sent me word her Arm was well, and she must come and kiss the President—

Yours affecly,   A Adams

JOHN ABUSED IN THE PRESS

To Abigail Adams Smith

MY DEAR DAUGHTER: Quincy, April 10th, 1809.

Your two last letters of March 10th and 23d, came safe to hand. They gave me great pleasure, not only from learning by them that you enjoyed good health, but your spirits were more animated from your little excursions from home, and from your prospects with respect to your family. I most sincerely rejoice in any event which looks like prosperity. Your trials have been many and various. You have hitherto been supported through them with dignity and firmness, with Christian patience I trust, and due submission to the allotments of Providence. It will greatly tend to improve our wisdom, to promote our piety, and increase our pleasure, to take frequent and particular views of our lives, and to observe the changes which have taken place in our circumstances, from time to time, in connection with the means and instruments which have been employed, and through which we have succeeded or failed in our enterprises, that by experience we may learn wisdom; and put our trust and confidence in that Being who holds the lives and fortunes of individuals in his hands, as well as the fate of kingdoms and nations. Let us say with Pope,—

> "What blessings thy free bounty gives,
> Let us not cast away."

If we have not all we may wish, we have all that is best for us. When I look back upon my past days, I can see many faults, many errors, both of omission and commission, for which I have need of pardon and forgiveness. Many are the blessings which I have received, and am still in the enjoyment of. One of the first I consider the life and health of your father; who, thank God, is still vigorous, and in the full possession of his mental faculties, although the tremour upon his nerves I think increases. His books and his pen are his constant amusement. The effusions of his pen, though only a private letter, written in reply to two gentlemen, strangers to him, have drawn down upon him the abuse of the federal party. These gentlemen wrote him, by direction of a number who had met together for the purpose of consulting upon public affairs, a very respectful and handsome letter, addressing him as their venerable father, to whom they applied for counsel and advice; whose age, experience, long and faithful services, and sacrifices in the cause and service of his country, entitled him to its confidence and its gratitude. To this letter, which was a very long one, he returned the enclosed reply without any idea of its being published. I recollect our visit to the Baron de Stael; but think we did not dine with him; that, however, is not a matter of consequence. I enclose to you the letter. You see they made the most of it for electioneering purposes. I have lived to see the day, when those who were the most clamorous against your father and his administration, now speak what I believe was then their true sentiments, though the spirit of party led many to deny the truth; and the desire of power and influence stimulated them to pull down an administration under which they saw little hope of obtaining it. For it is very true, that the federal party were as hungry and rapacious after office, as ever their opponents have been, and of a spirit quite as selfish and intolerant. I once said, or rather wrote to Mr. Jefferson, "if you are a freeman, and can act yourself, you can do more than either of your predecessors could." Such was the bitterness of the federal party, or rather the leaders of it, and   was one of them, that they would not hear a word of any nomination to office, of even the cool and moderate republicans. There will never be any harmony between parties, until public offices can be shared; and this your father used to tell them. The leaders in our State have gone great lengths, assumed powers which belong only to the national government; and are meditating schemes which they dare not openly avow; and which your father and mother think destructive to the Union, and independence of the country, and which will subjugate us to the power and domination of Great Britain. It was for lifting this veil, and declaring his private opinion and judgment, that writers in the federal papers have come out with as barefaced falsehoods, and as scurrilous language, as was ever used by the jocobins.

The times are perilous, and the country must not be forsaken by its friends, although men revile and persecute for righteousness' sake. May the blessing pronounced upon such, descend upon those who have hazarded life, health, fame, and fortune, to save their country.

Adieu, my dear daughter. Remember me kindly to the Colonel, Mrs. S. &c., and be assured of the tenderest love of

Your affectionate mother,   ABIGAIL ADAMS.

EDUCATION FOR WOMEN

To Elizabeth Smith Shaw Peabody

Quincy June 5th 1809

I was unable to replie to my dear Sisters Letter of May 19th when I received it, being visited by St Anthony, who scourged me most cruelly. I am sure I wished well to the Spanish patriots in their late Struggle for Liberty, and I bore no ill will to those whose tutular saint thus unprovoked beset me. I wish he had been preaching to the fishes who according to tradition have been his hearers, for so ill did he use me, that I came very near loosing my senses—I think he must be a very bigoted Saint, a favourer of the inquisition, and a tyrant, if Such are the pennances of Saints, I hope to hold no further intercourse with them—For four days and Nights my face was so Swelld and inflamed that I was almost blind, it Seemd as tho my Blood boild, untill the third day when I sent for the Doctor, I knew not what the matter was. it confined me for ten days; my face is yet Red but I have rode out to day, and feel much better. I think a little journey would be of service to me, but I find as years and infirmities increase my courage and enterprize diminish. "ossian says Age is dark and unlovely" when I look in my glass, I do not much wonder at the story related of a very celebrated painter Zerweis who it is said died of laughing at a comical picture he had made of an *old* woman. if our glass flatters as in youth, it tells us Truths in Age. The cold hand of Death has frozen up some of the streams of our early friendships; the congelation is gaining upon our vital powers, and marking us for the Tomb. May we so number our days as to apply our hearts unto wisdom.

"The man is yet unborn, who duly weighs an hour"

When my family were young around me. I used to find more leisure. and think I could leave it with less anxiety than I can now, there is not any occasion for detailing the whys and the wherefores, it is said, if Riches increase, those increase that Eat them, but what shall we say, when the eaters increase without the wealth?

you know my dear sister, if there be Bread enough and to spair, unless a prudent attention manage that sufficiency: the fruits of diligence will be scatterd by the hand of dissipation, no man ever prospered in the world; without the consent and cooperation of his wife. it behoves us, who are parents, or grandparents. to give our Daughters & Granddaughters. when their education devolves upon us, Such an education as shall qualify them for the usefull and domestic duties of Life, that they should learn the proper use, and improvement of Time. Since "Time was given for use, not waste." The finer accomplishments such as musick, dancing and painting, Serve to sit off and embellish the picture; but the ground work must be formed of more durable coulours,

I consider it as an indispensable requisite; that every American wife, should herself know, how to order, and regulate her family, how to Govern her domesticks, and train up her

Children. for this purpose, the all wise creator made woman an help meet for Man and she who fails in these Duties; does not answer the end of her creation.

> "Life's cares are comforts; such by Heaven design'd
> they that have none, must make them, or be wretched
> cares are employments; and without employ,
> The soul is on a rack, The rack of rest;"

I have frequently said to my friends when they have thought me overburdend with cares; I had rather have too much, than too little, Life stagnates without action—I could never bear to merely vegetate, "waters Stagnate, when they cease to flow"

has your Son sent you, or his sister the Letters from the mountains? I think them the finest selection of Letters, which I have ever read. you may with safely recommend them to all your young female Friend's. I cannot find in them any principle, either of morals manners or Religion. to which I cannot most heartily subscribe, read them and give me your opinion of them.

Mrs T B Adams desires me to say to you, that her regret at not seeing you was mutual, She had a hired Horse and was confined to a weeks stay. She has left behind her one of our dear Sprigs. we miss her much, altho another is comeing forward to supply her place; as lively and as lovely, how they twine around our hearts, and steal our affections, of such said our great teacher, is the kingdom of heaven. our dear valued Friend dr Tufts is raised up to bless us yet a little longer. not yet having done all the good assigned him—may he yet be spared to us.

I want to recommend to your perusal and mr Peabodys a News paper under the tittle of the Boston Patriot; I know my dear Friends are of no party, but that of Truth and Justice. upon the 19 of April a series of Letters and publications were commenced in that paper and are continued to this day. which will serve to inform the unprejudiced mind: and to erase those false coulourings which all our Federal papers have thrown over our public affairs for the last 12 months— there is also a review of the late mr Ames writings which have lately been exhibited to the world under the Tittle of the dangers of American Liberty. I inclose one of the papers, If there is not any Body who takes the paper with you, I will endeavour to send you a cause of them, as they have been publishd, by some privat conveyance to mr Harods's at Haverhill. our Friends here are well, as usual and all desire to be rememberd to you. So does your truly affectionate Sister   Abigail Adams.

AGAINST PRESERVING HER LETTERS

To Abigail Adams Smith

MY DEAR DAUGHTER: Quincy, June 19th, 1809.

I yesterday received your letter of June 1st. I think letters are longer upon their passage than they used to be, when you were at Quincy. Since I wrote to you in May, I have been visited by St. Anthony, and most severely scourged by him: he first attacked one of my ears, but as I was wholly ignorant of the holy visiter, I paid little attention to him, except endeavouring to quiet him by bread and milk; but when he seized my face, eyes, and head, I was obliged to bow to him, and acknowledge his power—even send for a physician and exorcise him. I swelled to such a degree, that I could see my cheeks project beyond my nose; the fever was violent, and the pain in my head excruciating. It kept continually flashing up, and reminded me of poor Mr. Bishop, who called it the northern lights: it lasted me ten days, before it entirely left me; but I have been comforted by Dr. Dexter, who sent me word, that an attack of it, like that which mine was described to be, was as good as a fit of the gout, to mend the constitution. It is certain I have felt much better since than I did before.

You alarm me when you tell me that you have preserved my letters, and collected them together, in order to transmit them to Caroline. Your affection and your partiality to your mother, stamp a value upon them which can never be felt by those less interested in them; they are letters written without regard to style; and scarcely ever copying a letter, they must be very incorrect productions, and quite unworthy preservation or perpetuity: do not let them out-live you; you may select a few, perhaps, worth transmitting, but in general, I fear, they are

trash. Can you inform me who is the editor of the Albany
Register? he is republishing your father's letters, with high encomiums upon them. I presume he is a republican, because no
praise comes now from any other quarter, except when you
find a genuine American, of which there are a small number
who can judge impartially. I mean by this, that the spirit of
party so warps the judgment, and blinds the understanding, as
to lead good and honest men blindfold. I enclose to you, your
father's letter upon the King of England's proclamation, which
was first published in the Boston Patriot, the demand of which
became so great, as to induce the printer to publish them in a
pamphlet. His text, as he calls it, is a quotation from Col.
Pickering's letter, to which your brother replied, and which
cost him his seat in the Senate; but which I consider one,
amongst many others, of his disinterested actions and true love
of his country, and which will thus be considered by an impartial historian.

No one can accuse Mr. Madison for want of a frank and
honourable spirit of accommodation with Great Britain. When
she held out her hand with a spirit of conciliation, he received
it with true magnanimity; and I rejoiced sincerely that our
causes of animosity were to be removed. I own I am not satisfied with the subsequent conduct of the British Ministry: what
powers the new minister may be clothed with, time must disclose. I feel at present safe in the hands of Mr. Madison. I
presume he will not permit himself to be cajoled into any relinquishment of our national rights, or infringement of our independence. Whatever predilection Mr. Jefferson had in favour
of France, or has against Great Britain, I believe, in his public
transactions, he strove to act with impartial justice towards
both. I read all the despatches with care and attention, expecting to find what had so often been declared, a blind partiality
towards France, and hatred towards England; but justice requires me to say, that I could discover no such thing: and when
party spirit yields to reason and sober sense, this will be the
equitable decision. I wish I could justify all Mr. Jefferson's
measures with the same candour; but to his own Master, he
must stand or fall.

The federalists are courting Mr. Madison—let them do him
no wrong, and I am one who at present believe that he will do

no wrong to his country. With respect to Mrs. Madison's influence, it ought to be such as Solomon describes his virtuous woman to be—one who should do him good and not evil all the days of her life, so that the heart of her husband may safely trust in her. I believe I may say with safety, that her predecessors left her no evil example.

Our friends are all well. That health is a blessing, which may be enjoyed by all of us, is the sincere wish of
Your affectionate mother,   A. ADAMS.

JOHN QUINCY APPOINTED MINISTER TO RUSSIA

To Elizabeth Smith Shaw Peabody

my dear sister   Quincy July 18th 1809
    It looks like a want of those gratefull feelings which I am sure are inmates of my Heart, that three weeks have elapsed since I left my dear sister, and her Hospitable Mansion, and I have not written her a line to tell her that I was highly gratified with my ride and visit; that my Health and that of Louisas was much benifited by it, and that I have wanted to hear directly from my dear Neice, whom I left rather indisposed. tho I have not had any direct communication, I have heard twice from her and you, since I left you, through mrs Foster, and sister Cranch—I have been so constantly occupied since my return both head hands, and I may say Heart full, that I have only written one Letter, and that to mrs Smith—in the first place I have had a succession of company, which added to the numerous family I have during Hay time. and the addition of aiding my sons family in prepareing for their voyage all these circumstances will account to you for my silence this embassy to Russia sits heavey at my Heart. altho I know it to be a very important one at this eventfull period, to our country. yet the season is so far advanced, and the voyage so long together with so many other painfull circumstances which occur to me, that I find it very difficult to reconcile my mind in any measure to it. at the advanced years both of his Father and myself, we can

have very little expectation of meeting again upon this mortal theater—both his father and I, have looked to him as the prop and support of our advanced and declining years. his judgment his prudence his integrity, his filial tenderness and affection, his social converse and information, have renderd his society peculiarly dear to us. and as the world receeded from us, with its pleasures and amusements, these qualities became daily more and more, our solace and delight. like sterling coin, the alloy alass is in our being deprived of them. indeed my dear sister, a Man of his worth ought not to be permitted to leave the Country—a country which wants such supports, I say this to you, the world would call it vain glory but how much has one Man frequently in the History of Nations been able to accomplish? "envy will merit, as its shade pursue"

such is humane Nature, in all ages and countries. It has been the intolerant spirit of party, which has induced him to accept this mission—and the hope of yet being serviceable to his Country, altho traduced and vilified by the same intollerent faction

you must not suppose by what I have written "respecting" my son J Q A, that I depreciate the good and amiable qualities of my other son, who has ever been towards me a Dutifull and affectionate Child. but being so much younger, and not having been placed in such conspicious stations, cannot be supposed to have the knowledge and experience of his Brother—he will now have a Double task to perform, to fullfill the Duties which belong to himself and supply those of his Brother—mr Adamss takes with him as private secretary William S Smith his Nephew—this I know will be a great gratification to his sister, as it is to me—he proposes to leave George & John under my care to be placed at their uncle Cranch—I think I could not consent to part with them all—of the few Children I have had, how they have been divided, brought together again & then scatterd—God knows what is best. his will be done

my dear sister your bountifull hand has supplied the President with many a supper for which he tenders you his thanks. you could not have sent him a more acceptable present. he is so much delighted with it, that he asks the favour of you to see if you could procure one of mr. Little, an old one he wants; if the stage could take it to Haverhill to mr Harrods we could get it on to Boston—and he wishes to speak for one Hundred & 50 wt of the same kind of cheese for the present year when it is sufficiently dry—we have a very cold storm & voilent wind—unusual at this season—mrs T B A still keeps up cousin B Smith is upon a visit to sister Cranch—Eliza Smith is going to be married to mr Cruffts—Aunt Edwards with mr Smiths family made me a visit last week and dinned with me Aunt is 95 years old. She depends much upon her semi Annual visits She is indeed a very extradanary woman—

Adieu my dear sister with Respects to mr Peabody and Love to Abbe. I am your truly affectionate sister   Abigail Adams

JOHN QUINCY SAILS FOR RUSSIA

To John Quincy and Louisa Catherine Adams

my dear Children   Quincy August 5th 1809
I would not come to Town to day because I knew I should only add to yours, and my own agony, my Heart is with you, my prayers and blessing attend you, the dear Children you have left, will be dearer to me for the absence of their parents, and my care whilst, Providence continues to me my faculties, and my Life. If your Father and I Should be removed, they cannot fail of finding Friends and protectors in Your Brother and Sister, who will feel for them the solisitude of parents—God bless preserve and prosper you.

most tenderly and affectionatly your Mother
                                        Abigail Adams

To my dear William who shares my Love give my blessing also—I forgot to ask by what means I could convey Letters to you. mr grey will no doubt know from this quarter—

To Mercy Otis Warren

Dear Madam　　　　　　　　Quincy December 31st 1809

Standing as we do upon the confines of the other world, you at the age of four-score, and I at three score and near a half, no other sentiment ought to posses our Bosoms but those of benevolence and good will towards each other. A Friendship upon my part was instilled into my mind by one who knew you earlier in life and who estimated your virtues, and talents as they justly deserved—

And from a judgement which I respected, and qualities, which I found upon acquaintance so worthy to be cultivated and cherished, my regard was matured into a Friendship and intimacy which I fondly hoped, would end, but with our Lives.

A difference in opinion upon the great political questions, which have divided, and still agitate the Nation, might have subsisted between us, without imparing our Friendship. If in a History to be transmitted to posterity you had not misrepresented and mis-construed, not merely facts, but principles, views, and designs, all together foreign to the Character you have delineated, and whom from a long and intimate acquaintance and a frequent correspondence with him, I should have supposed it, impossible you could have thus mistaken.

But what I have still thought more unkind, is, that when those Errors were pointed out, and means furnished you for rectifying them, not a Solitary line ever acknowledged the receipt of a Letter or any disposition to retract. It was this which dried up the fountain of my ink, and withheld my hand, when my Heart most tenderly Sympathized with you, on the bereavement you sustained of the companion of your Life endeared to you by every tender tie which a long course of years, and the fondest and tenderist affection could bind.

I most Sensibly feel your loss and longed to pour the balm of consolation into a Bosom whose wound time may heal but never can close—and which religion alone can mitigate—

A letter received last evening from a Friend who lately visited you and who was too unwell to stop with us, upon his return to Cambridge mentions his visit to you, and did in writing deliver your verbal messag viz to give your love to your former Friend, and say to him, there was no man living you more respected." I feel myself much affected by this message and presumed you could not have said this without a conviction that you had misrepresented him—I can assure you my dear Madam there has not been any change in his political Sentiments, as they respect our National honour and the independence of our Country, from the period of your early acquaintane to this day

I determined once more to address you, and with a disposition to forgive, as I hope to be forgiven—and to assure you that there Still exist the [   ] ancient Friendship in the Bosom of   Abigail Adams

"SOME OF THE FLYING REPORTS OF THE DAY"

To Louisa Catherine Adams

my dear daughter   Quincy Janry 12 1810
I congratulate you upon your safe arrival in the cold Regions of the North: to which I hope your constitution will get enured: you must borrow the ermin from the inhabitants of the forests, and wrap yourself in the furs which Nature has amply provided in those cold climates. How does my dear Boy Charles? I have learnt by way of young Mr Grey, that he was quite an amusement to them upon the voyage. I hope you will write very particularly. I followed you through all the Seas, and was very fortunate to hear of and from you 5 times during your voyage

I mix so little with the gay world that I have little by way of amusement to write you. Yet in a distant land, far seperated from our Friends and connexions trivial circumstances of a domestick kind become interesting—I will not however place under this head, the marriage which is to take place in your family in the Month of March or April between Mr Pope and Eliza—She has got absolution, without doing pennance, which she must have done, if the former connection had taken place.

The circumstances of the gentleman who is setled upon seven hundred dollars pr An, must have made her Miserable—in the next place I congratulate you upon the appointment of your Brother as post Master in New Orleans, worth about three thousand dollars pr An. The expence of living there is very great. I am told Board is at 18 dollars pr week—I give you these two peices of News from your Mother, with whom I have commenced, or rather renewed a correspondence. Mr Senator Loyed has married Miss Hannah Breck, and carried her to Washington this winter—tell Kitty Mr Nehimiah Parsons is paying his devours to Miss Ann Thaxter, and will succeed it is said. "It is best repenting in a Coach and six."—Eliza Otis is engaged to Mr Lyman. Mr Wells gave a very splendid Ball at the exchange Hall this winter. Five hundred person were invited. It cost him twelve hundred dollars, two hundred dollars in artificial flowers—Ladies *borrowed* most of them—! William S Shaw, Sole manager, says the Ladies never looked more divine!

Now I have given you some of the flying reports of the day. I shall tell you that your dear Boys are well, behave very well. George as steady as a man. John reads and spells very well clasps me round the neck and says, often I do Love you Grandmamma Mr and Mrs Cranch desire to be rememberd to you. I ought to have mentiond to you that Mrs Buckhanna lost her Baby—to save her own Life she was recoverd, and returnd to Baltimore—your Mamma and family were well last week—I have been thus particular with respect to them least you might not have heard from them—pray write to me as often as opportunities occur. My Love to William S Smith. I have not time to write to him myself, but I forward him some Letters from his Mother and Brother. Susan had a Letter from Caroline this week they were all well. Mrs Sally Adams, Louissa Susan & Abbe all present you an affectionate remembrance. Tell Kitty I will write to her soon for the pleasure of having a Letter from her lively pen—

Mrs T B A is writing—

I subscribe your affectionate Mother   Abigail Adams

"DIFFICULTIES YOU WILL NO DOUBT ENCOUNTER"

To Louisa Catherine Adams

my dear daughter   Quincy March 6 1810
   your Letter from St petersburgh of october 28th I received
the last week, four Months after the date; it was quite as soon
as I expected to hear considering the season of the year. I rejoiced to learn that you were safe from the dangers of the Sea,
and had reached the City of your residence in health, after the
fatigues, and dangers of so long a voyage.
   difficulties you will no doubt encounter in a Country like
Russia, a stranger to every human Being, without any knowledge of the language of the Natives, at the approach of winter
when you require better accommodations than are readily obtaind. I judge so from Porters Schetches of his travels in Russia,
which I have lately been much interested in reading. French I
presume is spoken by all persons of Education, and you are fortunate in being so ready and conversant with that Languge here,
I cannot but laugh whilst I relate to you, an annecdote which I
heard a day or two since. I have not yet seen it in the paper altho
I do not think it improbable it will appear in it, the Emperor
Napoleons dissolution of his marriage with the Empress
Josophina, has been published in the papers, and it has been
asserted, upon what Authority I know not, that he is to marry
a sister of the Emperor of Russia, and mr Adams's mission to
that Court is to assist as *Bride man* upon that occasion in
behalf of the united States! Laugh here we must. the *junto*
have several times told us what his instruction were, but it
seems the whole has not transpired untill this new, and wonderfull discovery.
   I have always understood that a mission to Russia was one of
the most expensive Embassys—but our wise Legislators make
no difference, whether little or much is required. the sum is
too small at any court, even for a single gentleman, for a family
quite inadequate, as I know by experience—
   The articles you have written for I shall endeavour to procure with the assistance of Mrs TBA, and forward them by a
mr Harrod, a cousin of hers, who is going out in a Ship, and

will take particular care of them—you will undoubtedly hear of
Elizas marriage with mr Pope from her own hand, but I also
communicate the pleasing intelligence, as Letters are so liable
to miscarry. I congratulate you and Catharine upon the event
so much to all appearene preferable to a former engagement;
without any reflection upon the gentleman who personally, I
believe was every way worthy of her, but we cannot live by
Bread alone.

My dear son I have written to him three times, and twice
to you. I am anxious for his Eyes, least the glare of the snow
should blind him. heaven preserve and bless him. his dear
Boys, are dearer to me for the absence of their parents they
are good Children, very orderly and correct. I inclose a Letter
from George. John who is with me (there being no school
this day or two,) desires me to give his duty to his Father
& Mother and Aunt Catharine. he has written before. our
Little Groupe are all well. Thomas is a fine Boy. I shall not
have time to write to my Son now. Let him know that I
received his Letter from Cronstradt—If I have time I will add
a few more lines after I have procucured the articles you
requested.

The blessing of your Father accompanies this Letter to you
and my son as well as that of your truly affectionate Mother

Abigail Adams

Kiss dear Charles for me do not let him forget his Country

REQUEST TO RECALL JOHN QUINCY

To James Madison

SIR   QUINCY August 1st 1810

I take the Liberty of addressing you in behalf of my son,
now at st petersburgh, and to ask of you, permission for his
return to his native Country. I hope you may have already received, through the Secretary of State, his own request to this
effect.

From Several Letters which I have received from Mrs Adams,

I have been led to think their Situation very unpleasent, as it respected their domestic Establishment, and I am now confirmed in the fact; by a Letter recently received from him.

The outfit and sallery allowed by Congress, for a public Minister; is altogether so inadequate to the Stile, and Manner of living, required, as indispensable at the Court of st petersburgh, that inevitable ruin must be the concequence to himself and family.

To quote his own words—"you can judge how congenial it is to my habits, and disposition to find extravagance and dissipation become a public duty. You will readily conceive the embarrassment in which I find myself and of the desire which I feel to get out of a situation irksome beyond expression."

I will allow sir that there are Situations and circumstances in which a Country may be placed, when it becomes the duty of a good citizen to hazard, not only property, but even his Life, to Serve and save it.

In that School I was trained, but those days I hope have passed. I have too much confidence in your wisdom and justice to imagine that you would require a sacrifice not only of the most valuable Season of Life for active pursuits, but Subject a gentleman whom you have honourd with your confidence to pecuniary embarrassments which would prevent his future usefullness.

In making this request, I am not insensible to the honor done mr Adams, by your repeated nomination of him to this Embassy. Whatever confidence you have been pleased to repose in him, I trust will never be forfeited by him.

The expence attendent upon this Mission, was I presume as unknown to you, as to him, however readily you might be disposed to consider his Situation, I presume their is no way to extricate him, but by allowing him as speedily as possible to return to America.

I Should not so earnestly make this request if the circumstances of his Father would enable him, to aid in Supporting him there, but after near fifty years devoted to public Service, a rigid œconomy is necessary for us, to preserve that independence; which asks no favours; and Solicits no recompence.

As this is the only opportunity I have ever had of addressing you sir, permit me to Say that I entertain a high respect for your person, and Character, and to add my best wishes for the Success, and prosperity of your administration. I am Sir your Humble Servant   ABIGAIL ADAMS

RECEPTION AT THE RUSSIAN COURT

To Catherine Nuth Johnson

my dear Madam   Quincy Septr 19th 1810
    The Horace arrived last week after a passage of 85 days—I hope she brought Letters for you. as I learn the captain was charged with dispatches for the President. I inquired if there was any thing for you; but could not find that there was, as vessels Saild at the same time for Baltimore. perhaps mrs Adams made use of that conveyance I have a Letter from her of 2d June, and one from him of the 6th—She says they had a Snow Storm the day before. the latter part of the winter was uncommonly Severe. it has brought upon mrs Adams a deafness —She writes in tolerable Spirits, and says they were just going to Housekeeping—She & Kitty had been at the Ball, given by the French Ambassador in honour of Napoleans late Marriage. the Emperor honourd them with his hand, and danced with them. Charles has been presented to the Emperor & Empress who caressed him, and Showed him some prints which she had. She is pasionately fond of children having lost one near Charles Age—Mr Adams's thinks very highly of the Emperor—he has every reason to be pleased and gratified with his reception at Court, where he has even been shown, a *marked respect* and attention. he lives upon terms of cordiality with all the foreign Ministers. he has nothing to complain of but the Serverity of the climate and the expensive living, they mention other Letters which we have not received. the Danes Capture every thing so that we have little chance of getting even Letters—
    it is some time since I have received a Letter from you. I hope indisposition has not been the cause—how is mr Hellens health? I am not a little anxious for him.

My old Friend judge Cushing is dead. he is happily released from infirmities which were increasing upon him, and which had deprived him of his public usefulness and personal comfort. he leaves behind him a fair and honorable Character—as an upright Man, a candid just and impartial judge unbiased by party animosity—always Steadfast to the interest and honour of his Country. those who knew him best, respected him most—so much, so intirely was mrs. Cushing devoted to him, that his death will be most sensibly felt by her—

I hope the President may find a successor equally worthy—I am sure it must be his wish mr Parsons and Dexter are both Spoken of here, as well as mr Story the two first being federal, some suppose will be objected to—the qualifications of the candidates will weigh more with the President, I presume, than political opinions—

your Grandsons are well and desire me to present their Duty to you—with a cordial remembrance to every branch of your family I am dear Madam your Friend   Abigail Adams

"YOUR GRANDFATHER MISSES YOUR SINGING"

To Susanna Boylston Adams

Dear Susan   Quincy October 25th. 1810
Your Letter of Monday 22d reachd me today as I presume mine of the same date did you yesterday with its inclosure.

You appear to have laid out the week, and put home at a distance, I am pleased that you are gratified, and not unwilling that you should spend a few more days, as your Friends desire it. but I would have your return with Miss Hannah and not exceed *some day* in the nextweek. You have had fine weather, altho cold for the season, November will soon be here and that you know is not a very pleasant month. your Grandfather misses your singing, and your Guitar. You must thank all the Ladies who have been so polite to you and tell Miss Coombs that she must come to Quincy, and pass some time with me and your Aunt. Elizabeth has got quite well. Mrs Harrod is with your Aunt now. and will dine with me tomorrow, Harriot Welch is here, and Charlot got here last week

Ann Beal was here on Sunday Evening. I told her if she would write, I would Send her Letter. but She has not done it, nor can I persuade Abbe to write to you—she has had a bad cold and sour Throat with her broken Nose She has been pretty Sober. She ran her head against a door in the Dark or rather her Nose—Miss Glide is gone to Boston to stay—Miss Quincy and family have removed into Boston—Lucy Tufts is at Cambridge, We drank Tea with her Mother yesterday at Weymouth, your Cambrick gown was sent last Saturday to Mr Smiths to be Sent to you. Your blew was sent home—You had better get somethings washed, if I attempt to send; they will not reach you untill you are ready to return. which you remember is to be some day of the next week—I suppose you have got your cloth, and as soon as you get home I believe you will find it cold enough to have it made—you must not expose yourself too much; you know you are subject to a sad cough when you get cold. how is your face. you have not told me? I have not had any Letters from Lebanon since you went away—I have written you all the occurrences of any *note*—you must make my Regards or Compliments which you chuse to Miss Tracy and my Love to Hellen

Your Mother and Sister send their Love to you; and your Grandfather is very zealous to send your Letters—your Grandfather will dine in Boston on Saturday he will then learn what day in the week Mrs Smith expects Hannah to return. I Send this to the Port for Tomorrow and presume you will get It on Saturday from your affectionate   Grandmother
                                                                Abigail Adams.

DEATH OF LOUISA CATHERINE'S SISTER

To John Quincy Adams

No 2—
My dear Son   Quincy Jan'ry 26 1811
I have already written to you twice by this opportunity. I had not intended to have taken my pen the third time, but

having received intelligence from Washington which I wish'd might be communicated to mrs Adams, and her Sister with that prudence and tenderness which so distressing an event calls for I thought it best to communicate to you the Sudden death of Mrs Hellen, who was at Church on Christmas day; and burried on the New year. She *died* in Child bed. I have not yet any Letters from the family. I wrote immediatly to mrs Johnson, who I know must be overwhelmed with Grief as well as the whole Family, with whom as well, as with my dear daughter & her sister I do most tenderly Sympathize. "My dyeing Friend's come o'er me like a cloud" for these three Months past, the Aged, the Middle Aged, and youth & Infancy have followed in quick succession—I had scarcly wiped the tears from my Eyes, feeling as I have done the distress of my Friends in Washington, when a stroke nearer home cloaths me in mourning

The death of Mrs Norten is almost as sudden as that of Mrs Hellen, not 48 hours from the time she was first attackd, before her blessed spirit winged its way to Realms of Bliss; then why Should I mourn for her? here she had little health much care, anxiety, and more labour, than her poor Frame could Sustain. To her family she is indeed a loss; her prudence her Eoconomy, sustain them in credit. her counsel & example trained them up in the way in which they should go.

> "what tho' short her date,
>   virtue, not rolling Sun's the mind matures.
>   That life is long, which answers life's great end"

your uncle and Aunt, feel keenly this distressing event, but as Christians, they say the will of the Lord be done.

Say to your wife, that I enter into her grief, and most tenderly sympathize with her, and Kitty;

However we may live there is not any Religion by which we can die, but the Christian which gives us the glorious prospect of Life eternal. If Says the Apostle "in this Life only, we have hope; we are of all men the most misirable.

> Religion! Providence! an after-State!
> "Here is firm footing; here is solid Rock
>   This can support us;

His hand the good man fastens on the Skies,
And bids Earth, roll, nor feels her idle whirl"

I have no hope of hearing again from you for many Months. what other changes await us in that period is known only to that Being, "whom from all Creatures hides the Book of fate" Whilst we are directed so to number our days, as to apply our hearts into Wisdom and may this Salutary admonition, be duly impress'd upon the mind and heart of your affectionate Mother

Abigail Adams

FREQUENT ELECTIONS

To John Quincy Adams

N 6

my Dear Son   Quincy Febry 22d 1811

The Schooner Washington owned by mr Gray is ready to Sail for St Petersburgh. I have already sent some Letters on Board of her, but the great bulk mr Erving is charged with, and when he will Sail, I know not. he has been ready, and waiting this Month for his Dispatches. concequently our Letters are already a Month old. There is a Charm in a Letter of recent date, Consisting in its very figures, if it has not any thing more to recommend it, than the latest intelligence of the health of your Friends. my late Letters have borne you such melancholy intelligence, both from home; and washington, that I am rejoiced to have it to say, that at present we are all in comfortable health. my arm I believe is the most infirm; I have however been riding out, amidts Snow banks through which passages have been dug of 10 & 12 feet height.

I Stated to you in my last, that I had received all your Letters to No 8; except No 4, and from mrs Adams I have received as many as Eight. She has not however numberd hers, and one from Kitty, to all of which I have replied.

The news papers will be Sint you by mr Gray. you will find from them, that Electionering has commenced, and that the

Fed's have coupled the Honble William Philips, with mr Gore.

Mr Gerry and mr Gray, have been the very Men, who have conducted the affairs of the Government, with that moderation and justice, which you recommend, and which certainly has had the benificial effect of Softning the asperity of Party animosity; and harmonizing the discordent String's. by it, they have themselves, enjoyed their Short lived honours: in more tranquility: than any of our chief Majestrates; for a long period before—you will be comfirmd in this opinion; when you read the Gov'r Speech, and the Replie of the Senate—but no Sooner has the Waves Subsided, and a trancient calm Succeeded, than a new Election comes to foment and agitate them again, and to blow up all the turbulent passions into a Storm—

I am full in opinion with the British Statesman in the house of Lords, when a Motion was made to repeal the Septennial Act, "he observed that Frequency of Election, had uniformly proved the curse of every State in which it was indulged; it renders the counsels of a Nation as fluctuating as the popular will, and as flagitious as the popular will disposition's it, substitutes in legislation, for the energy of wisdom, and the coolness of discretion. the voilence of folly, and the rashness of that party intemperence which it enkindles; it keeps a Nation perpetually heated by the ferment it necessarily excites, and lets loose to prey upon Society the worst of human passions. it vitiates publick Morals, and poisons individual Comfort"

are we not in the daily experience of these Solid truths? could it be that eagerness for publick employ, and that hunger for office, for which our countrymen are more notorious than any other, that could lead the Framers of our Constitution to leave so wide a Feild, so open a common for the unbridled herd to range in, not only to display their wanton tricks of triping up each others heels; but Gladiators like, to worry and tear each other to peices;?

If they had foreseen the rapid increase and population of the Country and the wealth which has kept pace with it, not only new States Springing up, but Foreign States purchased, and incorporated with our own? would they have lift such a field open for corruption and intrigue as annual Elections for the

Chief Majestrates? I mean the Framers of our Massachusetts Constitutions?

you will See in Some of the papers an extract of a Letter from you to me. I thought justice to You required it.

Mr James Foster was here, and read the Letter, and Said, he would get it into the paladium—I told him, as they had been partly free with publications respecting the purport of your mission to Russia he might take it, to them: but if they declined to give it, to the patriot, they publishd it, immediately, and the Patriot & Chronical both republishd it—Since it has been found necessary to Send a Minister to denmark, all is Silence with respect to the Russian embassy. only a report is still kept up, that you were comeing home. Lincoln when appointed judge, was to keep the Seat for you. Lincoln declined; and now Alexander Wolcot is appointed. I do not know what they will find to say next. only that much fault is found with the nomination.

I do not know but you may have received a Letter from the Secretary of State, which you may not be able to account for, for which reason I inclose to you coppies of two Letters. you will See by their dates, that they were written near a year ago, If I errd, you must attribute it to an over anxious zeal for you, and a fear that you would find yourself So embarressed as not to be able to extricate yourself.

In your Letter of Sep'br 17th you mention having been Sick through the Months of March & April. what were your complaints. I hope not the Rheumatism, which so many of our Family are afflicted with. I have felt anxious for that weak Eye of yours least the constant Snow and ice Should injure it by its brightness, but it seems that you have not much Sun to dazzel you.

you sent me two peices of Sheeting but you have not Sent me any Bill, and I am unable to pay the amount into the hands of your Brother through want of it. I have to request you to Send me by any of mr Grays vessels, Sheeting or table Linnen to the amount of one hundred Dollors, 50 by one vessel & 50 by an other. I wish the Sheeting to be of a finer texture than the last; that is one part of it, and let it be accompanied by the cost, as it must be enterd at the custom House

you will See by the number of this, that I have not been deficient in writing to you Since this year commenced.—

I met with an observation in one of your Letters. Speecking of your Lectures, "you observe, that correctness is always cold" now that is Such a charming mantle for me, that I cannot but be rejoiced at the observation and wrap myself and all my incorrectnesses under its cover. what I write is from the heart, and that always dictates a Warmth of Love, and affection, which Age cannot chill, or time diminish in the Bosom of your affectionate Mother   Abigail Adams

"JUNO YET LIVES"

To Caroline Amelia Smith

Quincy, 26 February, 1811.

YOUR Letter, my dear Caroline, gave me pleasure. As all yours are calculated to enliven the spirits, I taken them as a cordial, which during the residence of the bald-pated winter and a close confinement to my chamber for several weeks, I have been much in want of. And now what return can I make you? What can you expect from age, debility and weakness?

Why, you shall have the return of a grateful heart, which amidst infirmities is not insensible to the many blessings which encompass it. Food, raiment and fuel, dear and kind friends and relatives, mental food and entertainment sufficient to satisfy the most craving appetite, and the hopes and prospect of another and better country, even an heavenly.

> "Eternal power! from whom these blessings flow,
> Teach me still more to wonder—more to know,
> Here round my home still lift my soul to thee,
>
> And let me ever midst thy bounties raise
> An humble note of thankfulness and praise."

Although my memory is not so tenacious as in youth, nor my eye-sight so clear, my hearing is unimpaired, my heart warm and my affections are as fervent to those in whom "my days renew" as formerly to those from "whom my days I drew." I have some troubles in the loss of friends by death, and no small solicitude for the motherless offspring, but my trust and confidence are in that being who "hears the young ravens when they cry." I do not know my dear Caroline, that I ever gave you encouragement to expect me at the valley, although I should rejoice to be able to visit you—but I now look forward with the hope of seeing you here as an attendant upon your mother as soon as the spring opens and the roads will permit.

We have snow by the cargo this winter. Not a bird flits but a hungry crow now and then, in quest of prey. The fruit trees exhibit a mournful picture, broken down by the weight of the snow; whilst the running of sleighs and the jingle of bells assure us that all nature does not slumber.

As if you love me, proverbially, you must love my dog, you will be glad to learn that Juno yet lives, although like her mistress she is gray with age. She appears to enjoy life and to be grateful for the attention paid her. She wags her tail and announces a visiter whenever one appears.

Adieu, my dear child—remember me with affection to your brother and with kind affection to your honored father and also to your uncle whose benevolent qualities I respect and whose cheerful spirits have made "the wilderness to smile and blossom as the rose."

Most affectionately,
Your Grandmother,   ABIGAIL ADAMS.

ON HER OWN EDUCATION

To Elizabeth Smith Shaw Peabody

my dear Sister   Quincy Feb'ry 28th 1811
I received your Letters by the Mail of yesterday, and by the return of it to day I write to give you all the information I have been able to collect, respecting your Son

Mr George Black has lodgings near him and is frequently at Quincy. I got him to call and bring me word respecting him. my last account was on Monday, 2 days since. he was then getting better; tho not able to go out. the weather has been much against him, and the travelling so bad that not one of our Family have been able to go in to see him. since I wrote you last, his uncle wrote to him last week and repeated the invitation to him, of comeing out, which I hope he will embrace as soon as he get out.

your Letter of the 16th came to me last week. your Apology for not writing before, and the Source from whence it Sprang. I should not have suspected my Sister of! Pride do you say?

you remind me of an observation of mrs Chapones in a Letter to her Friend Mrs Carter (the Lady who translated Epictetus,) "what says She is the meaning I wonder that imperfections are so attractive? and that our hearts recoil against gigantic and unnatural excelence? it must be because the Sweetest charm and most endearing ties of Society, arise from mutual indulgence to each other's failings."

Altho I willingly grant the palm of excellence to the pen of my Sister, I cannot permit the acknowledgment, to influence her, or persuade her from writing tho not as correctly as her Pride demands. I have the Authority of my Son, for Saying, Studied correctness is always cold" I had rather have one line warm from the heart than twenty correctly cold, from the Head. I need not add, for it is too apparent, that I never Studied Stile.

> "The little knowledge I have gaind
> Is all from simple Nature draind"

you well know what our early Education was. neither Grammer or orthography were taught us. it was not then the fashion for Females, to know more than writing, and Arithmatic. no Books upon Female Education were then in vogue. no Accademies for Female instruction were then established—

To our dear and venerable Brother Cranch do I owe my early taste for Letters, and to the nurture and cultivation of those habits, which have since afforded me rational pleasure and Satisfaction; he it was who taught me to Love the poets, and put into my hands, Milton, Pope, and Thompson, and Shakespear, he it was who taught me to realish, and distinguish their merits, and to him I was indebted for the Works of Richardson; then just published, and in high estimation, whatever I possesst of delicacy of Sentiment, or refinement, taste, in my early and juvenile days, I ascribe to the perusal of those Books; and to them I feel my obligation, for restraints of which I now know the full value. Mrs More in her [   ], has given an opinion which perfectly corresponds with mine respecting the writings of Richardson altho they have past away with the fashion of the times, and are borne down by a Redundence of new publications. I give it as the Sober opinion of 67 years, that not any work of the kind, before, or since, has equalled those of Richardson, for purity of Morals, refinement of taste, or delicacy of Sentiment, for a knowledge of the human heart; who that is not abandoned can read him, without rising better from the Tenet? Yet there must be some corresponding Sentiments, and feelings, to realish, and taste his excellence. Mrs Chapone Says, he never wrote any thing which did not Show an excellent Heart, and a very uncommon understanding She was only affraid that the Character of Sir Charles would occasion the Kingdom to be over run with old Maids. it is true, it is a model but nothing beyond what human nature is capable of attaining—his Character was not faultless. Mrs Chapone held a correspondence with Richardson upon filial obedience; and parential Authority, in which She differd from him. I have been much entertaind in reading her Letter which with her Life, have been lately publishd—

I know my dear Sister you will rejoice to learn that I have had Letters from my Son in St Petersburgh as late as the 16 Nov'br, at which time they were all well. the rivers were all frozen over, bridges taken up, and winter with all its privations making rapid strides; one of its most painfull privations was that of cutting of all communication with their Friends for six months.

our dear Brother and Sister Cranch are much perplexed to know what to advise mr Norten to. it does not appear as tho he could keep house. he has no faculty as it respects the domestic charge of it. his Sister finds herself unequal to the charge and the little all will soon be run out. who can he get who would be Spent for his family to the last spack of existance, like the departed and reliesed Sufferer? in vain will it be for him to Seek anew. he may find a companion, but who that is capable would be a mother, who would take him embarassed in circumstances, with no Earthly care upon his mind, if they knew what they were about? I pitty him, and his Children, and may he who hears the young Ravens when they cry, have compassion upon them. My Love to my Neice. I do hope for a visit from you both when the Spring opens. I have not ventured to leave my chamber yet. the weather has been so cold and Snowe Remember me to mr Peabody, not forgetting good Lydia of whose Life I prophesied—and whose usefullness will be commensurate with it. I have only room to add the name of your affectionate Sister   A Adams

APPOINTMENT TO THE SUPREME COURT

To John Quincy Adams

No 7

my dear Son   Quincy March 4th 1811

You will no doubt receive from the President of the United States permission to return home, as he has been pleased to appoint you to an important office in the judiciary of the United States. the unanimous approbation of the Senate, and the Satisfaction which all parties unite in expressing must weigh in your mind powerfully. From What ever motives this general consent arrises, it proves, that you are by your Country considerd qualified for it—for it was not an appointment Solicited by your Friends for you, nor was it necessary to encumber the Presidents table with Letters of recommendation with which he was already overburdend by numerous applications from various quarters as I have been informd, after, having made one appointment, and one nomination, he broke his fetters, and acted from his own judgement.

Your Father has written you his opinion which I know you will give due respect to. Shall I Say forsake not the Law of thy Mother. I will not impose my judgement as a Law upon you, but I will Say I consider it as a call of Providence, to you. I hold it in higher estimation than the Place of First Majestrate, because the duties of it are not So arduous, the Responsibility of a different kind, tho both grounded upon the Same principles of immutable justice and integrity. "The Rule of the judges Duty is uniform, and invariable; having nothing to consult but the Law"

The permanancy of the office must be one inducement to you; not So much, for its durability, as that it will in a Great measure set you free from that Spirit of party which has divided very Friends, and renderd your residence in your Native Country unpleasent to you.

I believe you can be more extensively usefull to your Country in this than in any other employment. certainly you can be of more benifit to your Children by being able to Superinted their Education and Should the lives of your Parents be prolonged a few more years, your presence will prolong and heighten the few remaining pleasures & comforts which remain to advanced Age—I will take it for granted that after mature reflection you will resign yourself to the call of your Country, and hold the Scales of Justice with an honest heart, and a Steady hand.

Mr Erving is to Sail in a few days for Denmark in the US Corvette John Adams. I think it probable that She will be orderd to Peters burgh for you. I have in a former Letter requested you to Send me out by any vessel of mr Grays Sheeting and table Linnen to the amount of one hundred Dollors. I do not want fine table Linnen, but Such as is usually made in Russia—If it will not be inconvenient to you to Spair the money; I Should wish to have you take it and it Shall be repaid you upon your arrival here.

I would advise to your bringing home your Beds, and linnen, both Sheeting and table Linnen, and any other furniture you have Suitable for this Country.

we are now in health. all the members of our Families. Mr Gore lies very dangerously Sick. Lethargic. I think it doubtfull if he recovers. the United States bank received its dissolution by the casting vote of the vice President. we are in a very Sorry Situation, between the two great, contending powers—the British King distracted, and the French Emperor delirious—and America is like the Bed of Procrustus, too Short for one and too long for the other.

with the tenderest Solicitude for your happiness I am my dear Son most affectionatly your Mother

Abigail Adams

"HONORABLY BACK TO HIS NATIVE COUNTRY"

To Louisa Catherine Adams

My dear daughter—   Quincy March 4th 1811
   When I wrote last to you, I was at a loss What to say to you,
to console, and reconcile you to your situation. the thought
struck me to say, that some light might spring up, where we
did not foresee it, and extricate you from your difficulties.
   Such a light appears to me to have arrisen in the midst of
surrounding darkness, by the appointment of mr Adams an
associate judge of the Supreem judicial Court of the united
States: An appointment so honorably made, so unanimously
concured in, and so universally approved, cannot fail to excite
in his Breast the most pleasing Sensations
   An extract of a Letter from Washington, is thus published in
the patriot of yesterday

                                    Washington Feb'ry 21 1811
   "The Hon'ble John Quincy Adams, our minister at the
Russian Court, has been nominated as associate judge of the
Supreme Court of the US, and will no doubt be approved,
when the Bench of Justice shall be irradiated by worth, and
tallents so Transendently Great, as those of mr Adams, when
Virtue and Patriotism so rare, and so distinguished shall be-
come the expounder, and the Administrator of our Laws the
Nation will indeed be blessed. If his influence may have the
weight which will be due to it, in the Supreem Court of his
Country.

                                                   22—
   Since the above was written mr Adams has been unanimously confirmd by the Senate—"

   early in the Session I was informd by a Friend from Washington, that if mr Adams had been at home, no other person
would have been thought of by the President. considering that
as an insurmountable objection I replied, that I presumed the
President would consider it his duty to fill the place, that there
were many persons no doubt qualified to fill the office, and

many more, who thought themselves so, who would feel hurt, to have the place given to an absent person. Mr Lincoln was appointed but upon account of his Eye sight, declined, pressing solicitations from various quarters in favour of Friends: Weigh'd down the President desk, and by the solicitations of Joel Barlow, Alexander Wolcot was nominated, a general murmur of discontent arose, and he was negatived by the Senate.

The President then determined to break through the obstacle of absence, and nominated mr Adams—I have already related how it has been received, parties have united in a general approbation—I scan not the motives of any person, those of the President, I believe to be worthy of his Wisdom, knowledge, and judgement, and personal Friendship.

I know not what mr Adams's Sentiments may be upon this occasion, but judging from his usual conduct, and knowing how ably he has discussed and painted out the duties of the Station in one of his Lectures, I am led to believe, he will accept the appointment which calls him so honorably back to his Native Country. The permanancy of the office will extinguish that party animosity, which annual Elections always excite, between Rival competitors, and their partizens. he is not call'd home to bury his tallents in a Napkin, or to hide them under a Bushel, but to irridiate and shine as the brightness of the firmament in the Seat of Justice

I would apply to him the advice of wolsey to Cromwell,

> "Be just and fear not;
> Let all the ends, then aim'st at, be thy Countrys
> Thy Gods, and truths"

I do my dear daughter most Sincerely congratulate you upon the prospect you now have of returning to America. it has given me a new gleam of hope that I may live to see the day, and invigorated my Spirits—Your children are delighted with the expectation of your return and that their Father, Will have it in his power to direct their studies, and improve their minds, is amongst one of the blessings I anticipate—

My Love and Regards Where ever due From your Truly affectionate Mother   Abigail Adams

"A GREAT BLESSING TO THIS NATION"

To Abigail Adams Smith

my dear Daughter   1811.
    It is so long Since I received a Letter from you or any of the
Family that I am not a little anxious to hear. I have attributed
it to the great fall of Snow which has prevented the Southern
post getting in Regular Succession—and we have learnt that
the Northern Roads are still more obstructed—yet I have Sent
every Post to the office in hopes to hear. I have written You
Several Letters to which I have not any return it is now the 10
of March & the Snow is ten foot high in banks between here
and the meeting house—
    I have been out only three times since Jan'ry and then no
farther than your Brothers—
    You have learnt by the publick papers I trust that your Brother
is honorably recalld to his Native Country—unexpectedly to
us, because we thought his absence would have been an objection which could not be overcome—I knew from early information from Mrs Johnson that it was the wish of the President
to place him in that office, but I presume he was so harassed
and beset by Recommendations and urgent Supplications, that
he was led to the Nomination of a man Whom it appears was
not esteemed qualified for the place and after one Resignation and one negative, the President was determined to
Nomminate from his own judgement and personal knowledge, the unanimous concurrence of the Senate, and the universal approbation it meets with from *all parties*, is very
gratifying to me, upon many accounts It is peculiarly So, I
am Sensible the duties of the Station are arduous and highly
responsible. of his qualification, there is no question. the
permaancy of the office will releave him from a great portion
of envy and jealousy which a Rivalship for other offices might
excite in the minds of candidates, and which with other circumstances renderd his Residence here unpleasent to him—he
will be able to be at home Some part of the year and by that
means can Superintend the Education of his Children. he can
reside where he pleases. I hope during the lives of his parents it

will be at Quincy—he can live within his income, and tho he cannot grow rich, he can live independent—

I am making calculations for him as tho upon the Spot, and as tho no ocean divided us—I have a confidence, and a firm belief that his Life will be protected and Spaird, and that he is designd to be in the hands of Providence a great Blessing to this Nation—call it vanity or by what name they please Such is my Faith, and may it be unto me all or to it—you will naturally feel anxious for William. I hope he will have an inclination for merchandise, but with its present prospects, it is truly deplorable, but this State of things cannot last long, and William residence in Russia may give him Some opportunities and acquaintance which may assist in future enterprises. mr Gray proposed his engaging in Some thing of the kind—and if he returns I do not doubt but Some thing may be found out benificial for him—he can barely live in Russia I am sure upon what is allowed him—I have forwarded Several Letters from him Since I received any acknowledgment that they had been received. I am very anxious respecting what in your last Letter dated Janry you mentiond to me. I have sent you Dr Welchs opinion. dr Hollbrook concurrd in the application of the medicine, but both agreed you had better be present, that they could judge better & advise to more effect. let me know particularly concerning the State of it. and let me hear from you as Soon as possible

Your affectionate Mother   A Adams
                                              March 10, 1811

SECRETARY OF STATE ROBERT SMITH

To Catherine Nuth Johnson

my dear Madam   Quincy March 30 1811
    The Letters you forwarded to me, for Saint Petersburgh, I had an opportunity of Sending immediatly through the Russian Consul. mr Gray has a vessel which will Sail Soon, for the North, by which I can Send Letters, if you please to forward any.

would their be any impropriety in inquiring, either of the Secretary of State, or Navy; if any vessel is orderd to peters-burgh to bring home mr Adams? It has been reported that the Frigate which carried out mr Erving, was to go to Russia, but I know nothing but the Report. will you be so good as make the inquiry of the proper Authority.

I hope mrs Adams's Situation will not be Such, as to prevent her comeing home this fall. If they Should be compelled to stay an other year, it will be with great regret. Mr Adams will not get his recall untill June—and it will necessarily take him Some time to make his arrangements—all these Matters, and his Safe return, we must leave to higher powers.

you no doubt have Seen in the public papers the dispassion-ate, *Lamb like* complaining of the discarded Secretary, who has not any Gall. all resentment long ago Subsided. no point to carry by comeing forward at this period, when the Country is greatly agitated by the Conduct of the two unrelenting Na-tions, who So injuriously treat us: and at the time of our Elec-tion for Govenour, whilst his own Election as Senator of the US is Suspended, the Senate chuseing him: and the House Noncurring their vote and Sending up an other Man; So that no choice has taken place, and the Govr must appoint, in this case. If the Republicans prevail, he knows he has not the Smallest chance.

When a Man So mistakes his own temper, and motives, he ought not to be so forward, to arraign others, and bring for-ward Charges which are absolutely false. his attack upon mr Jeffersons personal Character, is mean, bitter, and base, altho there were Some acts of mr Jeffersons Administration, which either, through want of judgment, and experience were in the estimation of candid Men: injurious to the National Character, and some others, which were too Strong Marks of Seeking popularity, to the Sacrifice of nobler motives. yet he never de-served the Character, which this Portrait Champion has drawn of him: Mr Jefferson never designd by any of his measures, to injure his Country. you know my lenity towards him has been arraigned—I care not—I will not join in bearing false witness.

His next attack is upon his old Friend, whom he cannot forgive, for dismissing him his Service—and that without giv-ing his reasons for so doing, but leaving him, and his Friends all this time to puzzel and distract their brains to discover the cause.

It Surely could not be for obstructing, and perplexing the Presidents embassy to France, for making a Clamour against the Nomination of mr Murry, nor for consulting certain juglars behind the Scene, who were "more wise and more Righteous" than he was, who wished for a war with France, and this negotiation might prevent it. but if it could not be prevented, a delay might frustrate the plan. instructions which were directed to be made out, were delayed, month after month ("The President being at Quincy, the Secretary at Trenton, oweing to the yellow fever) and finally a Letter Signed by three of the Secretaries giving their decided opinion against the Embassy. the president must be censured the embassy would give offence to Great Britain, yet all this, and much more which may one day be told, was no cause for removal of this Secretary, but different motives have just been discoverd—mr Adams courted the Democrats, and made a corrupt bargain with them, to dismiss mr Pickering from office to obtain their votes for his next Election! for this purpose he represents him as courting the mr Smiths, one of whom; the Secretary, he never to his knowledge Saw in his Life 'mr Smith and other Democrats were known to dine with the President, at his private dinners' and were Seen visiting at his House." that mr S Smith did dine once, with us at what he calls private dinners, is true. but it was with a number of Federal Members, not one of the description he names ever was invited to a private dinner at the house. The mr Smiths I hope will have the justice and candour, to repell the unfounded assertion.

If mr Adams had Sought the favour of mr Smith, he would have appointed his Brother a judge when he was recommended, and that by Some of the Secretaries. ask mr Pickering who opposed him and to whom was to be attributed the appointment of an other person?

If mr Adams had Sought popularity instead of the interest of his Country, he might have continued mr Pickering in office. it was no way Surely to ensure his Reelection, to dismiss a Man of So *much concequence*, with Such a numerous *host of Friends*, as to be able to turn the Election against him—. The poor Mans Story will not hang together any way.

Mr Pickering has very much mistaken his ground Mr Adams was never in his whole Life, known to ask any Mans vote, or influence to obtain any of all the various, and important offices which have voluntarily, been bestowed upon him by his Country, and his Character is out of the reach of mr Pickerings Libels. who will not be noticed by him at present. he will be permitted to go the Length of his Tether—

I hope the country will be preserved from intestine commotions, during the perplexity of our foreign relations and that we may Still preserve, our Peace, independence and happiness for happy and prosperous we are beyond all other countries, in defiance of Timothy and all his coadjutors. I am dear Madam yours   A Adams

FAMILY HISTORY

To Caroline Amelia Smith

My dear Caroline.   Quincy April 18. 1811.
    I write you a few lines just to say that I send your mother a century Sermon, preached in this town when your Grandfather was about four years old. He says he recollects the day—as his mother carried him to meeting and pointed out to him the old lady Penniman mentioned in the Sermon said to be near an hundred years old—The Sermon had got out of print—A number of persons who wished to preserve it more as an ancient Record than for any particular merit there is in it, had it reprinted—and as many of my ancestors as well as those of your grandfather are named in it I thought your mother would like to have one to preserve. You will see by these records that this town was originally a part of Boston—that it was not separated until the year 1634. The only part of the town which retains the name of Mount Wollaston was owned by my Grandfather Col. John Quincy and after the death of my Uncle Norton Quincy the Farm was purchased by your Grandfather and is now in his possession.

    The reverend Moses Fisk who was ordained here in 1672 married my Grandfather Quincy's Mother and Madam Marsh the Mother of Mrs Josiah Quincey formerly Ann Marsh was a daughter of the Reverend Mr Fisk. The first Deacon of the Church Mr Samuel Bass married an Alden—A daughter of their's married an Adams the great grandfather of your Grandfather now living. Madam Mary Norton mentioned as having presented a velvet cushion to the church was my Great-Grandmother by the Mother's side. Hon. Edmund Quincy who went as Agent to Great Britain and died there with the small pox was Uncle to my grandfather Quincy.

I have written this to you because it is a subject which young people scarcely ever think of but as they advance in years they become more inquisitive about their ancestors. As this country was settled by a religious and learned people although somewhat bigotted we can trace our Ancestors much easier than those people who are settled by conquest—and we can trace them to pure unadulterated English blood.

With my love to you father and Mother I am, my dear child, Your affectionate Grandmother   Abigail Adams.

"A CANCER IN HER BREAST"

To Louisa Catherine Adams

my Dear Daughter   Quincy April 28th 1811
Scarcly a week has past, for these two Months in which I have not written either to my Son, or to you, but our Letters are not only committed to the Chance, of winds and waves, which may Scatter them like the leaves of the Sibyls, but they have many other hazards to run, through the Dens of Cyclopes, and the fangs of the Harpies.

I write this to Send you by the Ship Hugh Johnston, Captain William Johnston Master, belonging to the House of Loring & Curtis American Merchants, belonging to Boston, and with whom Price Greenleaf, the Son of mr Thomas Greenleaf of Quincy, and Brother of Thomas Greenleaf junr, well known to you, Served his time.

They have requested to take Letters to the American Minister at Petersburgh, knowing that in case of Capture, they might be considerd as Some Evidence of their perfect Neutrality

other Merchants have made Similar applications having been informd, that Letters from the Family, had been the means of the clearing of more than one vessel. I wish the fair and honest Merchant to be Secure; and every imposture detected, and punished.

I received a Letter from your good Mother this week, dated April 16th from Baltimore, where She had been to visit Mrs Buchanna whom She writes me, has a fine Son, as mrs Boyed had, before she left washington.

Mrs Pope continues at washington through the Summer as a Session of Congress is not improbable. Adelade is better in health. mr Hellen, very feeble, and infirm

Your Brother left them last week for new orleans

all this you might learn from your own Family but the chances are So much against the Security of vessels, that it will be no injury to repeat the Same thing

your dear Sons, are well, and good Boys. George grows fast. John has not yet taken a start. Mrs Cranch has a great charge having taken the three Daughters left by mrs Norten and one Son, which with a Son of mrs Greenleafs and your two Boys, make up a Group of young ones the eldest of the whole, is but 12 years old, yet she gets on with great care method and regularity.

Mrs T B A—expects to be confined in June. her Little ones are now, all Sick at once, with what the dr calls a Catarrhous fever, and to add to our anxiety, her Husband was necessitated to leave them having been appointed one of three commissoners to go to the Eastern Country to adjust claims of Lands. he has been much out of health, ever Since last Spring I had hoped a journey might be of Service to him, if he could have left home with a mind at ease. I Still hope he may be benifited, but he has many very dissagreable complaints.

My anxiety is great also for my dear and only daughter I have not mentiond it before, I know that It would distress william—She is apprehensive of a cancer in her Breast. I have besought her to come on to Boston and take advise, and I have consulted dr Welch, and Holbrook. they have advised as well as they could without Seeing her, but wish her to come here I cannot yet prevail upon her. She thinks that She cannot leave home without the Col. and that he cannot come, but the real Truth is, I believe, She thinks the Physicians would urge the knife, which she says, the very thoughts of would be Death to her

Heaven knows what is proper for our trials in this Life. I pray that I may be resignd, and Submissive, what ever I may be calld to endure. heitherto, I may Say; Goodness and mercy have followed me.

Tomorrow Your Father has the Melancholy office of pall holder to the Remains of his much esteemed Friend and companion through many trials, Judge Dana. he was Seizd Suddenly with a paralitick Stroke about a week Since, which in a few days terminated his Life

I know my dear Son will mourn the Death of his Friend and Preceptor with whom he first trod the Russian territory, near thirty years ago, and with whom he was intimatly connected, and for whose memory he will always preserve a high respect and Esteem. alass I fear I Shall Soon have to add to the Melancholy List, his Worthy Pastor, Mr Emerson—whose case is thought incureable—your Father and I are both well at present. at our Age, we cannot promise ourselves length of years. that it may please heaven to prolong them, in vigor, untill we may hail your return to America, is the wish nearest the heart, of your truly affectionate Mother   Abigail Adams

My best Love to my Son to whom I wrote last week. to your Sister, to william and Charles a kind remembrance—our last Letters were dated in December which we have received from you. your Mother mentions that She has received Letters of the same date. I coverd two Letters for William from his Father and Mother last week, which were committed to the Leiut Govenour—

ABIGAIL 2ND CONSULTS DOCTORS

To Elizabeth Smith Shaw Peabody

My Dear Sister   Quincy July 10th 1811
   Not having Wholy dissolved by the intense heat of the last week, I am enabled from a change of the weather to take my pen, in lieu of my fan, and to ask you how much of you is left? when I Saw how much you sufferd the Saturday I left you in Boston from the heat, I was not a little anxious for you the last week: when it was 20 degrees hotter. I know not whether for four days together, I ever endured more from heat, and poor Juno labourd so hard for existance as any of us.
   our dear Sister Sustaind it to astonishment, altho She was weakend with it. She is frail feble and panting, recovers very slowly, is Short breathd, and cannot walk or move without loosing her Breath. her Mouth is better, her appetite was good as we could expect, and as fancyfull as sick people usually are, but what a wreck does age and Sickness make of the human Frame? Such a Struggle for existance, which appears Scarce worth holding when obtaind. how justly does the Scripture describe it, Labour and Toil and pain, but what a Glorious prospect opens to our view. this Corruptable, shall put on incorruption, and this Mortal shall put on immortality. Let us look through this vale and trust the Ruler of the Skies.
   Why my dear Sister your Letter was as fancifull as romantic as mrs Ratcliff—I Should say it was the ospring of one Score, rather than three, yet you left us in the dark as to the name of the Modest Swain "whose air was dignified where expression was literary and classical" but whom Morpheus placed upon your Shoulder
   Susan was very earnest for a further history respecting him—
   Last Sunday morning arrived here through all the dust and heat of the week, my dear daughter Smith, with John and Caroline they came in an open carriage, a Light waggon upon springs Such as they use in their part of the State, and in 6-days from their own door. I need not Say how much rejoiced we were to meet after a Seperation of three years, and a half. Mrs Smith is gone to Town to day to consult dr

Welch respecting her complaint which has not yet appeard to injure her health, altho the appearance is Allarming. I pray heaven it may not terminate in one of the most to be dreaded of all complaints.

I have Spent part of yesterday, and of this day with our dear Sister. She Says I must write for her, and thank you for your Letter. She is not able to hold a pen, but the disposition for talking is as great as ever, and the care about her Family predominant in her mind She exhausts her Spirits and Strength, by talking. She cannot bear to be left alone, and we are some or other of us with her almost every day. our dear Brother has revived with the hopes of her recovery upon whom, under heaven, his own existance depends. I do not think our Sister can possibly be able to attend to her Family for many Months to come, if ever. the Springs of Life are languid and worn down

and now I must ask my dear Grandaughter how She is? She must not think Quincy cooler than Atkinson. we Slept with all our windows wide open. I hope She is content. I will attend to her wants as soon as my Tennant will attend to mine

we have to day some rain. I hope the life blessing is extended to you. Many persons fell sacrifices to the heat of the last week, both in our own State, and others. I have not heard of any in this Town. pray my dear Sister Send Abbe on as Soon as you can Spair her. She will be an acquisition to us, and much comfort to our Sister who she can be occasionally with; we will all take our turns. John returns tomorrow with regret, that he cannot visit Atkinson first. he desires to be affectionatly rememberd to Mr Peabody to you and the Abbe's Mrs Smith also presents her duty and hopes to see you, and yours before She returns—

company and many avocations oblige me to bid you adieu. Respects and Love were due From your Sister

A Adams

July 11th

"NECESSARY . . . TO PROCURE YOU A LIVING"

To Abigail Louisa Adams

dear Abbe   Quincy July 23d 1811
    your Mother has been So constant in writing that I have
been the more remiss. I am glad to find that you are content,
and happy I hope. I was in Boston on Saturday, and bought for
you a Box of paints, and Bennets Letters. I Sent them to mr
Phineas Fosters with a request that he would take them to
Haverhill for you. Charles Welch who understands paints pronounced them very good, and in the one Row Box, all the
coulours you have occasion for; I also bought four Brushes for
you. if anything more is wanting, you must let me know, with
respect to your Studies. I would have your hand writing and
Arithmatic and Grammer particularly attended to. make yourself Mistress of each Branch. you may find them necessary to
you to procure you a living. we know not what we may be
called to pass through in this world, if you are not thus obliged
to improve them. no Lady is qualified to pass through Life
with credit to herself and usefulness to others without Some
knowledge of them all, and why when you undertake a thing
should you not excell in it? it requires only Steady habits, and
application to obtain the prize Set before you.
    your Aunt Smith, and Caroline are here and well your Aunt
Cranch gets along but Slowly. She is very weak, and has a bad
cough which troubles her very much. She has rode out a little
ways Several times, but is obliged to crawl up Stairs upon her
Hands when She returns—Riding Suits her. She thinks She could
ride Several miles, but her Spirits are much beyond her Strength
    your Aunt Adams is quite well She dined here last Friday,
and on Sunday carried the Baby out which She named Francis
Foster. She looks much like Elizabeth. Thomas grows pretty
daily—
    Give my Love to your Aunt, and tell her that I think mr
Shaw walks much better. he was here on Sunday, and Says he is
better. he talks of taking a journey, to be absent Several weeks
as Soon as the Court rises. I think it will Serve his Health
    when are we to See Cousin Abbe? we have been looking for

her Some time. I got your Aunts Letter about the Same time She got mine—I Shall write to her Soon—

I was amused with your politicks. you must tell the young Ladies that I have heard it observed that a Ladies politicks Should be always those of their Husbands now if they fix theirs, they must be Sure they are Right, and chuse accordingly, or they may chance to Spar, and that would be very unpleasant. I fix it as a principle that every Lady Should Love her own Country in preference to any other, and that whatever tends to promote its prosperity its happiness and welfare Should be regarded by her, next to her near Relatives—for in the Fredom and Independence of her country, is contain her own happiness, and that of her connections. I ask them to Name a Country equally Blest with our own, not withstanding all the Clamours against our Rulers, and all the injuries we have Sustaind from forign powers? neither war, Pestilence or Famine waste and destroy our Land. we dwell in peace and Safety. our Country produces us every necessary, and many of the Luxuries of Life. no hard task Master gripes them from us. no Children of want Starve for Bread. there is one thing we want. we want gratefull Hearts and deserve not the abundant mercies we receive—

My pen grows So bad that I must close my Letter with the hope of hearing from you, and that in better hand writing than what is written by your affectionate Grandmother

Abigail Adams—

PS—your Aunt and cousin desire to be rememberd to your uncle and Aunt Peabody and to your cousin & you

OPINION OF THE DOCTOR

To William Stephens Smith

Dear Sir   Quincy July 23 1811

I hope you will not impute my not writing to you by your son to want of attention to you, or a proper Sensibility to your request contain in your Letter to me. The extreem Heat of the weather, and my joy at the arrival of a dear and only Daughter after an absence of three years and a half, realley disqualified me for my pen, and Johns Stay was so limited that I could not Say by him What I wished, as I had not then Seen the Doctor myself. since then I have conversed upon the Subject. his opinion is, that no outward application Should be made, and that mrs Smiths general State of health is so good as not to threaten any present danger. he does not pronounce it to be of the nature we feared, tho he cannot say but what it may terminate in one and he further say that it may remain in its present state many years unless improper applications should be made. he advises to the use of the Hemlock pills.

Mrs Smith and Caroline Sustaind the heat of the weather and the fatigue of the journey with much vigor. The Idea of Distance has greatly diminished since I find that one week can bring us together. by Johns Letter to his Mother he has made a more rapid retrogade—a Rogue—he frightned us all, by his list of untoward accidents, which he never experienced

I began to think before his Mother got through his Letter, that the whole sum of the Misiries of human Life had befallen him at once—when behold it was a vision of the Night.

I consider it a very fortunate circumstance that your good Mother & sister are with you, to supply the place, and in some measure compensate for the absence of your Best Friend, and Dear Daughter, who I find no way alterd but in her more womanly appearence, and deportment, her lively disposition, So sweetly chastned with that first of Female virtues, Modesty, and her tender attentive and affectionate behaviour endears her to every one.

I hope you will not be impatient for their Return, but spair them to us as long as you can, you may live many Years to rejoice in them, neither the Father or Mother can expect to Remain much longer, infirmities increase with years, but I will enjoy the present. nor damp the joy, by anticipations of the future

Your domestic Naration amused us much, I could see the Zeal of your Mother, and the anxiety of Nancy to make every thing correspond with ancient establishments. present my kind and affectionate Remembrance to them

we wish you may make it convenient to visit us, when ever

mrs Smith returns—a journey and the Sea air may benefit your Health—The president desires to be Rememberd to you & yours—we all unite in Love and affection to the whole Family of whom we talk Daily—

I am dear Sir yours in Love and Friendship

Abigail Adams

LOUISA CATHERINE'S PREGNANCY

To Catherine Nuth Johnson

My dear Madam   Quincy July 31 1811

yours of July 21, I received by the last Mail I was just going to ask the cause of your long Silence, when your Letter arrived and fully explaind it to me. I regrret that it arose from so many painfull causes, but our Lot is a Checkerd one. I have had a Share of late my dear Sister, whose Life I despared when I wrote last to you, Still Survives, for some little time We flatterd ourselves that She would recover, but a most distressing Cough and loss of appetite, with a very Soar Mouth, have Succeeded her other complains untill exhausted Nature appears Sinking under the accumulated Burden.

I am with her as often and constant as I am able and feel, but little inclination to attend to the wordy warfare of contending parties.

Mr Smith like his Brother pamphlet writers "will fret, and Strut his Hour upon the Stages" and then I hope be heard no more. he will not bear away any Laurels—altho he has furnished fuel for the disorganizers. The great Body of the people are with the government, and will Support it, "peacebly if they can, forcibly if they must" I wish however the Nonintercourse removed and permission given to the Merchants to arm their vessels and defend them. Frigates instead of Gun Boats, would have given us protection and Secured, us from many insults which we have borne too tamely.

With respect to the person you Name as the only one, of whom it is Said mr Madison thinks formidable against him, he may rely upon it, he will never suffer himself to be a rival

Candidate—No. No my dear Madam, the Lader of Ambition mounts not so high. That mr has in his own State, many persons who think highly of his tallents, and respect his abilities, I will know, and believe mr Hamiltons information correct, but one Swallow makes no Summer. I also know that he is held in high estimation by many respectable Characters throughout the Union, but neither Father or Mother Would give a Single vote to place him in the Station you allude to, if they certainly knew that their vote would accomplish the object. I Love him too well to See him tortured, and I despair of Seeing the Wisest Head and the purest Heart, protected from insult & injury whilst our presses are Suffer'd to groan under the licentious libelings of British hirelings, and American Tories. Foreign Emissaries are employed by both France and England to divide and Set us at variance, and we are fools enough to be danced upon their wins—and to Echo their Slanders—dissapointed ambitions and vicious American join in the Chorus—

I never See the Man in the Almanack. Stuck all over with darts, but what I think he is an emblem of a president of the united States, and no Man has more of my compassion and commisiration, than he who Stands upon the giddy height of the pinnacle.

I rejoice in the Success of mr Pope. I think him an able and an honest Man—and Such we want—

Poor mr Hellen. I am grieved for him—he held Life by a Slender thread indeed. My kind regards to him to Mrs Buchanan, Mrs Boyed and Mrs Pope. I hope her dear little Girl is quite recoverd. I am rejoiced to learn that Adelade has regaind her Health. Miss Smith is with me and thanks you for remembring her desires to be presented to all the Ladies. My Daughter Smith and Caroline are both here upon a visit—they have been absent three years and a half—Mrs Smith desires to be kindly rememberd to you—

I last Night received Letters from Russia. o my dear Madam. I must fear we Shall not see them this year. I believe Mrs Adams is not in a Situation to go to Sea Mr Adams Says, "I have at present no expectation of returning home the next Summer—indeed it is doubtfull whether in any event, I should find it possible. I Say this because you may perhaps expect us." there is not any other circumstance which would have induced him to have written thus positively. this Letter is of 28 of Febry before he heard or rather before his appointment took place— but if that is the case, as I have always feared it might be, I do not see how he can undertake such a voyage—

if you have any Letters containing any intelligence of the kind, pray let me know it, as this has cast a great damp upon my Spirits. I Shall continue to write by every opportunity untill I hear from them, after the receit of Letters from us. I do not think it best to Say any thing upon the Subject abroad. you may hint it to Mrs Madison when you see her, as I am certain he would not thus Strongly have exprest himself if an impediment of this kind had not been in the way—

Pray do not refrain from communicating your intelligence, altho I express Some infidelity with respect to it

I do not build upon the New Mission—I wish well to the Nation, but I know their pride & their injustice We have felt, and their wisdom is not from above. it is neither gentle or peaceabl. Let us be just, and we shall not be miserable

My paper draws to a close, and my thread is Spun quite long enough for me to add only my Love and affection

A Adams

CONSULTING WITH MORE DOCTORS

To William Stephens Smith

My Dear Sir   Quincy August 28th 1811

your Letter of August 12th I received in the absence of Mrs Smith, who was upon a visit to mrs Guild, and therefore I could not communicate it to her; she past Several days, in Boston at Dr welch's, and as I had requested Dr warren was consulted in conjunction with Dr Welch upon her complaint, and their opinion was Similar to Dr Holbrook's who is a Skilfull physician, and practises in our Family. Dr Tufts alone varies in some measure from them, he is at a loss as to its natures; but the result is by no means to do any thing to worry or irritate the part, by no means to [   ] it. would it not be best having advised with Surgeons and Physicians, to follow their advice?

She is not taking even the hemlock pills—a Lady of my acquaintance labourd under a similar Tumour and was advised to have it removed, but upon a consultation with a Gentleman of the profession, he prevaild upon her to defer it for a time. She did so and lived to the Age of 82 without any further trouble from it—I know it will be a Source of anxiety to herself, and Friends. I pray that it may never be more So—

your preposition to remove near to me would of all things be most agreable to me. but I would not require such a Sacrifice as you must make to gratify my desire of having my dear Daughter near to me. it would give me more pain, than it could possibly add to my pleasure, to know that you must sacrifice your present prospects and comforts—and however gratefull I feel for the offer, and the more generous I consider it in you, the more loth I am to acceed to it.

No like Ruth of old, whither thou goest, she will go and where thou abidest she will abide—

your State has become in population in commerce and Manufactories one of the first, if not the first in oppulance in the Union—it enrools in the Militia, according to a late account one Hundred thousand Men. this State only 80 thousand—we have become a great, and we might be a powerfull Nation. we shall require Strong cords to keep us together. we have prospered beyond calculation for the last 20 years. considering the many difficulties we have encounted, and the injustice we have met with foreign Nations—we wax fat—and we forget the hand which has raised us up. whilst war and desolation has spread carnage through Cities, and Kingdoms, and laid them waste, we have sit under our own vines in Peace and Security. —if we have too tamely endured insults, and oppression from others, we are [   ] that we have done less injury. the war which has desolated Europe, [   ] been of a singular Kind, and if we can yet mantain our honour, an Secure our Rights; I hope our Rulers will not be driven from their Neutral Ground. you will perceive that I do not think them Guilty of the Charges of partiality, or disposed to favour one Nation more than an other—

at present we are in a Critical Situation, but as we have been deliverd in times past—I hope we Shall be So again. Union amongst ourselves, could it be obtaind would be one of the

Strongest Bulworks against our Enemies. but those who were denominated Federalists under the two first Administrations, have now taken the ground of their opponents, and rise up in opposition to Government & the Laws and still those Apostates, who will not join with them.

I presume mrs Smith has written to you that we have Letters to the 18th of May from Mr Adams, when they were all well, but he had not then received any Letters from America for Six Months. the Baltick was not clear of Ice So that vessels could get up. Several had arrived in the out ports—

please to make my best Regards to Your Worthy Mother and Sister. I am sorry to say that Mrs S Adams is in very misirable Health, her complaints are Such as if not soon removed will end in a decline

I am dear Sir with Sentiments of Love and affection, your Mother   A Adams

JOHN QUINCY TO REMAIN IN RUSSIA

To Catherine Nuth Johnson

my dear Madam   Quincy Sep'br 22d 1811

At last it is decided—it is as I conjectured in my last Letter to you, the Situation of Mrs Adams prevents their return to America this Season, and obliges mr Adams to decline his Appointment as Judge.

I have received from him Several Letters of an old date Since I last wrote to you, but it was not untill yesterday that I received a Letter from my Grandson William Smith, of June 25th in which he Says, "you have no doubt learnt by Letters from my uncle, the Circumstances which will prevent his return to America this year." Those Letters have not yet come to hand, one only excepted, which is to his Brother and mentions the Receipt of Letters from us by mr Erving, and by the Brig Washington which belonged to mr Gray, and Saild from Boston in Febry. by that vessel the melancholy news of the Death of Mrs Hellen reachd them; and the Death of Mrs Norten

Mr Adams Says, it was at a most unfortunate period for his wife, and came very near producing an Event She has so often experienced. She had in Some measure Recoverd from the first Shock, but was then much deprest, and he still was full of fears for her Safety. by his Letter this Month She expects to be confined. After october, if they could find a conveyance, it would be presumptious in them to attempt to Embark. they could not do it without the greatest hazard of their Lives—I have always Supposed that his Return was left to his own choice. the Reasons he will have to offer for his declineing the Seat upon the Bench, will I trust be Satisfactory to the President. where ever he is, there he will Serve his Country.

Altho I most Sensibly feel my dissapointment, I have never permitted myself to be so sanguine as some of his Friends, who never calculated Family circumstances or thought that he could not as easily Embark from Russia; as from England or France.

As the Event which detains him there is not under the controul, Either of the present, or absent, it must be Submitted to, and I Shall Sit myself down quiet, presumeing that it is orderd for the Best.

I fear you will think, I have been remiss in not replying to your Letter of August 11th. it really gave me a Fit of Melancholy, and the more So, because I know not what to offer you by way of consolation, or how to releive you from your trouble.

Is there any office vacant in Washington to which your Son could be appointed which would give him a Living? and I might ask, for which there are not more Candidates, than dollors?

I do not wonder that you feel reluctant at the thought of going to new orleans, so distant from your other Children, and to a climate at particular Seasons unhealthy. your Son has had the good fortune to escape, and is Seasoned to the Climate.

My own Family my dear Madam is distresst with Sickness. Mrs Charles Adams has been Seven weeks confined to her Chamber—a vomiting of Blood, reduced her much, and have produced Symptoms which tend to a Hectic, and the Physicians give me but little hope, that it can be averted. add to this my dear Sister Cranch is so low, that She cannot long Survive. the powers of action have almost ceased. She has a most distressing cough, but no Severe pain. her decline is gradual, but no hope remains that She can recover—her spirits have been unusually vigorus through the whole of her Sickness, and her care and Solicitude for her Family Strong even in Death. alass, what a loss will that Sustain!

Why Should I trouble you further, but that Sympathy is a Solace which Friendship can bestow.

My Friends in Boston are mourning the Recent death of a dear and beloved Son, William Smith, the Eldest Son of mr W Smith, aged 23 was last week committed to the Tomb; a rapid consumption Since july carried him off—

I had a visit last week from Dr Ewell and his wife, the Daughter of my old Friends, Mr & Mrs Stodard

It really gave me great pleasure to recognize their Likeness in their Daughter, whom I knew only as a child when I resided at Washington, and it added to my Satisfaction, to find the Respect and Esteem of the Parents transmitted to their Children. through her I learnt much respecting my Friends and acquaintance at washington whom I inquired after, and of your Family in particular, to every Branch of which, be kind enough to Remember your Friend   A Adams

Written by candle Light, "with Eyes by reading almost blind" as dean Swift Said—George has a Letter from his Mother dated in June—both G & J are well

SICKNESSES AND DEATHS

To John Quincy Adams

My Dear Son   Quincy Sep'br 24 1811
    your Brother returnd this Evening from Boston and gave me notice that a vessel would Sail for Sweeden tomorrow the notice is So Short, that I can only write you a Short Letter. I Shall in future follow your advice, have a Letter ready for the occasion and not wait for the opportunity. it was not however,

untill last Saturday that I received a Letter from William Smith, that I was informed of the necessity you were under of passing an other Season in Petersburgh. I had conjectured it from what you wrote in Your Letter of May 19th, which is the latest date I have yet received from you; your Brother received one last Saturday from you dated in June; and George one from his Mother of the Same date. by your Brothers Letter, I found you had received those written to you by mr Erving, as well as those by the Washington—I have written many Since, but not So frequent as I Should, if I had not flatterd myself that you would return.

your Children are well, but they as well as I, are in danger of loosing one of their dearest and best Friends. In the Month of May, my dear Sister Cranch was Seizd with a fever, of the plurisy kind. it was So voilent, as to require Severe Remedies. for Several weeks She was So ill, that we expected every day would be her last. the fever however Subsided, but Nature is exhausted. it is near four Months that She has lain Sick in a consumption. her feet have Swelld, and a voilent Cough daily waste her. She is taken up in a chair and put into a carriage and carried out to ride, and thinks She Shall recover. during the height of her disorder, your uncle was so opprest and borne down with affliction, that we all thought one grave would Soon receive them both. through the whole of this most distressing Sickness, She has had an uncommon flow of Spirits, a care and Solicitude for her Family, which only death can diminish. when She was first taken for several Weeks, I had as many of the Children with me, as I could, George and John & one of mrs Nortens. but as Soon as her fever Subsided, She would have them all back. it really has appeard to me, and to all her Friends, that as her Body weakend, her mental powers brightend. what is very Singular; She Will think that She Shall yet be restored, altho all her Friends, and her Physicians would not be Surprized at her departure at any hour. Hard indeed have I found the trial,. my heart recoils when I endeavour to realize the Seperation. To her Family, her death will be—a loss not to be estimated—To the Children committed to her care—She has been more than a Mother—Gaurdian, Friend companion—The will of heaven be done If we part, we Shall Soon meet again.

In my own Family I have a Sever Sickness. mrs C Adams has been Seven weeks confined to her Chamber by complaints which tend to a Hectic. She was Seazd with a puking of Blood to a very allarming degree. when that Subsided, it left her in Danger of an affection upon her Lungs She remains yet very Sick—

William Smith dyed last week in a Consumption, of the most rapid kind, to the great distress of his parents and Friends;

My Chapter of Melancholys is closed

with a gratefull heart, I thank heaven For the health of Body and vigor of mind which your Father enjoys, altho he met with an accident a fortnight Since which has lamed him ever Since —he went out in the dark to view the Comet, and Struck his Leg against a Sharp Stick & cut it, So much as to lay him by—I hope it is now in a good way to recover.

I have got this far through the Season without any Severe Sickness, altho it has been the hottest Summer we have had for many years—

your Sister and Caroline have made me a charming visit this Summer. they have been a comfort to me under my trouble, tho I could not but regret that they were call'd to so painfull a duty— they will leave me next Month. Caroline is all that is Lovely in a woman— She has all the virtues, and graces united, not so much in a Regular Set of features or complexion, "but an animated form which Speaks a mind within."

I Shall not touch upon politicks. my Letters I hear are Sometimes opened. they cannot be any great booty to any one, and this I am Sure will have no charms to attract attention—

The dissapointment your Friends all experience at the necessity you have been under to decline your appointment is a proof that they believe you well calculated for it.

I had flatterd myself that I Should See you again. I will Still Cherish the Idea.

My Love to your dear companion whom I hope I may congratulate on the Birth of a daughter—If a Son, I Shall not repine. your Brothers last is a daughter—one judge is perhaps as much as falls to the Share of one Family. Your Brother is Chief Judge of the County of Norfolk, under the New Regulation the Countys of plimouth, Barnstable & Bristol will be included I Suppose you will learn all this from himself—as well as that he is one of the Govenours Counsel—

Mr Smiths pamphlet will no doubt be Sent you—you can make your own comments—Mr Pickerings Letters too will appear in a pamphlet—the Mountains labour—

If the Country [   ] disgraced by such publications it would be of little concequence—"as it is they fret their hour upon the Stage"

I had a Letter form Washington not long Since The Families were all well. mr Hellen had given up his House to the British Minister—

I hope we shall Soon receive Letters of a Recent date from you and from Mrs A—Remember me to Caroline To my Grandsons, and to every Member of your American Family

George and John Shall both write Soon

you will hear a long Story about the Frigate President, and little Belt, Captain Bingham—the result of the Court of inquiry attach no blame to Comodore Rogers.

I have no time to coppy or correct.

most tenderly and affectionably Yours   A—

"SUBMIT TO AN OPERATION"

To Benjamin Rush

With a gratefull heart I address you to thank you for the earnest and decision with which you gave you opinion respecting the case of My Dear Daughter, Smith.

She had consulted several physicians here all of whom agreed on saying, that if the Tumor became discolored or inflamed, she must apply for surgical aid, with this opinion she was preparing to return home, when you letter arrived, which instantly determined me to prevail with her, if possible to submit to an operation.

October 15, 1811

DEATH OF RICHARD CRANCH

To William Cranch

MY DEAR NEPHEW,   Quincy, 17 October, 1811.

YOUR dear father has joined the spirits of the blessed made perfect. On Saturday last he was taken sick, appeared as he frequently has upon former days, was wandering in his mind,— but a general prostration of strength took place. He was sensible only for a few moments at a time; exhausted nature sunk to rest, without pain or struggle, and Heaven has been pleased to save him the anguish of following your dear mother to the tomb. She supports herself with the resignation of a true christian; saying "the Lord's will be done, we are parted only for a few hours or days. I shall soon meet him in the realms of bliss."

She can have but a few days longer upon earth. Emaciation, so that her bones are almost bare, together with swelling of her feet, hands, and face, show us daily that her passage to the grave is speedily hastening; and, my dear nephew, we have every reason to believe that your dear and blessed parents are gone and going to their God, and our God, whom they have faithfully served upon earth—and if we trust in him, as I hope we do, we shall be supported through life and through death.

I am, my dear nephew,

Your sympathizing and afflicted aunt,

ABIGAIL ADAMS.

DEATH OF MARY SMITH CRANCH

To Elizabeth Smith Shaw Peabody

my Dear Sister   Quincy October 22d 1811

I wrote to you upon fryday, but I do not now recollect what I have written. I know that my heart was full and my mind wrought up, to a pitch, beyond what it would bear.

The Solemn Scene which presented to me, two Dear Relatives Sleeping in Death at the same moment, can never be effaced from my mind. upon Saturday I followed their remains to our own Tombs and Saw them dposited Side by Side, never more to be Seperated. 50 years had they lived together in the greatest harmony Love and Friendship, united in their Religious principles and Sentiments as well as in their worldly pursuits. together they have I trust assended to their God and our God. they have joined the Spirits of the just made perfect and are Singing Hallelujah to the most high. these reflections my dear Sister rob Death of his Sting, and assuage the too Selfish grief of my heart. why do I ask myself—Should I wish their longer Stay upon Earth? they had fulfilld the Age allotted to Man. they lived to every usefull purpose whilst upon Earth, and were not permitted to become burdensome and helpless, to themselves, or others. I really feel a releaf from [   ] when I reflect, that neither is left to mourn for the Death of the other.

"The thought of death indulge" I will give it its wholesome Empire, and may it Still the tumult of my ruffled breast"

Mr Whitney deliverd a most excellent discourse from the hundred and 12 Psalm, 6 verse, the righteous Shall be held in everlasting remembrance, in which he drew the Character of our dearly beloved, and Respected Brother. while he was writing this Sermon intelligence was carried to him, that our dear Sister had expired. affected as he was, he added a handsome Sketch of her Character to his Sermon. Truth was his Guide. there was not any flattery, nor any part of the Character over charged, as a large and crouded Audience testified by their attention, their tears and their Silence. the Relatives and Friends will apply for a coppy for the press—The week before her death, I was with her when mr Whitney visited her, and prayed with her. She calld him to her Bedside, and thanked him, conversed with him upon her faith and hopes Said, that She frequently thought, that She was not an inhabitant of this world if She could be write down her thoughts, we should find that She held converse with Superiour Beings—

Mr Cranch came in. mr Whitney asked him how he did? he replied, well only in trouble. trouble Says She with the most Cheering voice, what troubles you? Your Sickness my dear he replied. O Says She, be like me. there is not any thing troubles me. She preserved that Cheerfullness to the last moment. I never saw her Shed a tear through her whole Sickness. when she was told that he was gone—She replied we Shall soon meet again. he has left me only for a few moments. I Shall know where to find him. the day before her death She sufferd much, was lost and wandering at times—Said once to me—Seems to me, never any body faild So fast as I have, yet even then exprest hopes of Recovery. I did not live to Say Sister we think you cannot get well. how could I damp the ardour of her Spirits, which Strove to keep alive the wish of living for the poor Motherless Children of her departed Daughter?

She Said in the conversation which I think in my last Letter, I mentiond her having with Susan about an hour before her Death, that She was both ready and willing to depart if it was the will of heaven. an hour before I was there, mrs Quincy calld to See her. She was going to Boston for the Season. She took a most tender and affectionate leave of her, told her She Should never see her again—thanked her for all her kindness to her, and to her Family. Seeing Mrs Quincy much affected, She desired her to retire, and overcame [   ]—

She had received Letters from mrs Clark and mrs Foster from abroad She call'd for them, and gave them me to read, desired me to write answers to them—directed me with the utmost Calmness to the draw where mr Cranchs will was deposited, gave directions respecting the post office, and in all respects appeard collected and more like her former self than I had Seen her. I had not any Idea when I left her but that She might continue Several days. She spoke to the President when he went in, with as much cheerfullness and Spirit as usual, desired me to direct Some Rice boild for her. her exit was as Sudden when it took place as possible. a Suffocation as I Suppose from the water which I heard the Evening before rolling within her.

I thank heaven that her Suffering was not prolonged and much greater. She never complaind or [   ], every body was kind, and good—every thing She ate or drank was pleasent.

Mr Cranch was Lethargic from the first. he had Some lucid intervals, but could not express himself in a connected Sentence. this I regret, as I know we Should have all been Edified by his conversation. he did not Suffer any pain, but a distress for Breath—thus my dear Sister has the Scene closed upon our dear Friends. may we be prepared to follow them, our lives as blameless and our death as happy and Peacefull as theirs that we may be of that happy number who shall be held in Everlasting Remembrance—Mrs Greenleaf has conducted herself with the calm temper of a Christian, and a worthy descendent of Such pious parents.

My dear Neice has behaved with propriety as She always does. every thing proper and necessary was done for her. She is gone to day to Boston to get her a coat, which I Shall have made for her when She returns.

Col Smith arrived here upon Sunday morning, and was [   ] releived to find mrs Smith had gone through the dreaded opperation and to find her also so well She walks from one chamber to an other, and Sits up the chief of the day. the wound has closed and healed. her arm She is forbidden to use, keeps it in a Sling, and is not allowd to lift it up—She is weak but not more so than might be expected. Abbe Adams is getter better Slowly—

Since I began this Letter I have received yours of october 29th—I beg mr Peabody to take great care of his Leg a wound in the Leg, is a serious matter. Six week has the president Sufferd from his. it is [   ] just so that his [   ] upon it now [   ] in vinigar, and wash the bruised places. it will remove the [   ] Blood, and restore the circulation. Let me hear from you, and know how he does—

we all desire to be kindly rememberd to you and I doubt not, we have your prayers for us—as we are mindfull of you in our petitions to heaven— I am my dear Sister your Sympathizing and afflicted Sister   Abigail Adams

ABIGAIL 2ND'S RECOVERY

To Elizabeth Smith Shaw Peabody

my dear Sister   Quincy Nov'br 8 1811
    I recieved your Letter by the last Mail inclosing one for your daughter, who left me last week, to our great regreet. I

expostulate with her for making her visit So short She Said She had been five weeks with us. I could Scarcly credit it, untill I looked back, and then So many events had during that period rapidly Succeeded each other, that I had not calculated how the time had passed

It was a visit fraught with Such impressive Scenes, as will not I trust be Soon, or can eradicated from her mind.

> "Tis a prime part of happiness, to know
> How much unhappiness must prove our Lot"

I Sent the Letter in to my Neice the Same day I received it. She is well, and proposed to remain in Boston three weeks. She was very fortunate going into Town while I had a Tailoress with me, getting her Coat and a Bempant Gown which She had made immediatly and is quite Equiped for the winter. I have not been able to write you the week past. you know what a large and encumberd family is added to a constant Succession of trancient company. The calls upon me are numerous. Col Smith has been here nearly 4 weeks. Mrs Smith will not be able to return with him this winter. She cannot use her Arm at all. She has rode out three times but being a little presumptious and riding one day rather too far—She has not been so well Since, and is now Satisfied that She must not attempt the journey this winter. the Col will return, and Mrs Adams and Abbe will go with him. it is an excellent opportunity for her visit her Mother, and I hope it will benifit her health—and it will lessen the cares of my Family which have been numerous this Summer. but I desire to be gratefull for the Health I have enjoyed, and for the blessings which have been mingled with my afflictions. it is a gratification to me to have the Habitation which I have So long been accustomd to visit, as the dear abode of our venerable Brother and beloved Sister, occupied by her worthy Daughter and her descendents

Mr & Mrs Greenleaf have removed into it, and She will keep her Sisters daughters with her through the winter. Brother Cranch left a will, written many years ago, in which after ordering his debts and funeral Charges to be paid, he gave the whole of his Property to his wife, to be used by her for the Benifit of her Children and Grandchildren—His will must be proved, and an administrator appointed, and altho She died without a will, Still as the Estate could not be [   ] untill the condition of the will was fullfilld, and as She had property in trust for her, now Bonds and Administration must be taken upon her estate. this will be attended with more expence & trouble. there were not I believe any heavey debts, a hundred dollors which he borrowd during her Sickness & the drs Bills and funeral Charges will be the principle—I hope there will be Something left for mrs Greenleaf—as well as for the others; mr c Norten I presume has had nearly all his Share—Nine Hundred dollers are due from him which ought to go to the Children.

My last accounts from washington were that mrs Boyed and Pope were upon the recovery, but a Letter which came yesterday from Baltimore, written at the request of Caroline informs us of the Death of her Husband—and at the Same time what I feared was the case, that he dyed leaving no property. She has one child by him & he left four by his first wife—they have Some property which came to them by their Mother, and in which their Father had his Life but not a farthing of which She can claim—I do most Sincerely compassionate her. it was a marriage, not of choice, but persuasion of Friends and who can paint the feelings of a delicate mind. Subjected to dependence and Seeing no prospect of releif, but in a marriage which might intittle you to a home—but that very home depending upon the Brittle thread of Life—The Death of Mrs Johnson, which I [   ] for the Sake [   ] respected worldly affairs a release to [   ]

George and John I must commit to your Care. they have not been kept So regular this Summer, as they ought to have been: oweing to the Sickness of their Aunt, and of their being Some times in one place & sometimes in an other. here they would find too much time for play and my Family is not calculated to keep Such Children in. various work people with whom they will occasionally mix, and learn what is improper, cannot be avoided. I hope they will not give you any unnecessary trouble George is a good temper Child, and may be managed by reasoning but I discover in John a quickness of passion, and a Stiffness which requires Subduing. I wish their hand writing may be particularly attended to, English Grammer for John, before he commences Lattin George will pursue his Studies in Lattin and Greek—

Mr Adams will be so much absent this winter, that it appeard to me out of the question for them to go there. I have therefore engaged to take upon my own Shoulders the responsibility of placeing them at Atkinson. there entrance money will be Sent with them, and we Shall expect to pay the Same as others. Mr T B Adams will always answer their quarter Bills or any other expences you may necessarily be at for them—

I must close or the mail will leave me—we have Letters from Russia dated in Sep'br All well there

Let me know how mr Peabodys leg is the President found great benifit from the use of Ledwater, and putting it into poltice—I am dear and only Sister

DEATH OF CATHERINE NUTH JOHNSON

To John Quincy Adams

my dear son   Quincy Novbr 17th 1811

The intercourse between us is daily more and more obstructed, it may prolong your tranquility that it is so: I know not how to take up my pen, yet painfull as the Duty is, I must perform it, untill the task may devolve upon some other, to tell you that your Parents are also numberd with the dead. I wrote you in Sep'br, an account of my dear Sister Cranchs Sickness, and of the little prospect I had of her Recovery. This Letter if you received, may have prepared you to expect the painfull intellegence of her death. She Sickened the beginning of June, with a plurisy fever, and from that, fell into a consumption. While the frail tennament decayed and sank under the weight of years; and disease, her mind became more active, more vigoras, and

"The Souls dark Cottage, batterd and decayed,
  Let in New light, through chinks which time had made"

I have past through Scenes, my dear Son in this last year; most Solemn, and impressive. God grant that it may be good for me that I have been afflicted; I have consignd to the Tomb in one day, my dear and venerable Brother Cranch, and my beloved Sister, after a sickness of four months, She expired upon the 17 day of october. Mr Cranch had flatterd himself with the hopes of her Recovery, untill the last week of her Life. It was always his wish, and prayer that he might not survive her, & his prayer was answerd, upon the Saturday previous to her death, he was Seized with a lethargy which deprived him of his Speech, and with a few lucid intervals only, he continued untill tuesday morning, when he expired She Survived him only untill the next day at Noon, willing and ready as she exprest herself to depart, having no earthly tie to hold her longer—when told that he was gone, She replied in an extacy —O he has only Stept behind the Scene, I shall know where to find him—

Amiable, virtuous, and good through Life, united in the strongest Bonds of harmony Love and affection, they were united, also in death, and their deaths, were such as is desirable. they did not out live their usefullness, nor exhibit a Second Childhood so humiliating in Age. their minds were vigoras to the last period of existance, and together their spirits have joind the Angelic Choir, and will I trust receive the Sentance of well done good and faithfull servants, enter into the joy of thy Lord.

Mr Whitney deliverd a discourse upon the day of their interment to a numerous and crowded Audience from Psalms— "The Righteous Shall be in Everlasting Remembrance" I wish for your pen to do justice to the Life and Character of one of the best of Men. Mr Whitney gave a Short and handsome Scetch of him, and of your Aunt, but he did not know him as you did.

"String, after String is Sever'd from the Heart" the three fold cord is broken—as Sisters we never knew contention, our only Struggle was who Should Serve the other most.

Your Children have lost most valuable Friends, and gaurdians of their minds and Morals—So indeed have all the youths committed to her care. I have had the Children with me for some time, and think the next best place for them is Atkinson —I Shall give you my reasons in a future Letter.

Would to heaven my tale of Sorrow was closed a more distressing one remains to be told. Reluctantly with the written request of Adelaid to me, do I comply—Most sincerely do I

wish not to be the first to communicate to my dear daughter
and Catharine, the loss they have Sustained in the death of
their Mother. a Malignant Billious fever has prevaild in Washington the two last months, and Swept, the young, the middle
aged & the Aged from the Stage. upon the 11 of Sepbr I received a Letter from Mrs Johnson in which she wrote, that she
had not been well, upon the 29th of the Month she died, the
10th day of her fever; Mrs Boyd and Mrs Pope were dangerously Sick at the same time, Mr Pope and mr Boyd were both
in Kentucky, which renderd their Situation more distressing.
Mr Buchana, was Seizd with the Same fever in Baltimore;
and died the Wednesday after Mrs Johnson—I have Letters
from mrs Hellen, from Adelaid, and from mrs Buchana, to
all of whom I wrote upon the first notice of their distress and
affliction—Mrs Johnson was taken Sick at mr Boyds She went to
Stay with her daughters during the absence of their Husbands
—Mr Hellen had given up his House to the British Minister,
and taken one upon the pensylvania avenue, Mrs Boyd and
Pope they were obliged to remove to mr Helens, and they are
upon the recovery, when my last letters from Washington
arrived.

My own Bosom has been so lacerated with repeated Strokes
of woe, that I can mingle, tear for tear, with the afflicted
daughters of my esteemed Friend and correspondent, Whose
death I most Sensibly feel and whose loss will be long regreted
by me.

Tell them my dear Son that I pray for them, that they may
be comforted, and that they may find consolation in that Religion which teaches us Submission, and Resignation under
every dispensation of Providence. Mrs Buchana has a much
harder trial then they are call'd to endure; deprived both of
Husband and Mother at the same time, with an Infant Babe,
and I fear, without any means of Support

They must excuse my writing to them untill time has healed
the wounds now bleeding. What could I say to them but that
which would increase their greif—?

Many Letters have lately arrived from you to Your Sons,
Your Father & Your Brother, I do most sincerely rejoice with
you in the Birth of a daughter. May She live a blessing to her
Parents— The last date to me was the 11th of June No 20 and

compleats my list to that time, one inclosed from mrs Adams of the 6th of June. Your Father received one dated in Sepbr and your Brother also.

Shall I fill my paper with dirges? let me sing of Mercies as well as judgment, altho

> "The winter is as needfull as the Spring
> The thunder as the Sun"

In the midst of the troubles which encompassed me through this Season I had one trial more to endure—

This was an opperation upon your Sister, who came here with Caroline in july to consult the Physicians upon a tumour in her Breast, and which was pronounced a cancer—after taking the opinion of Drs Warren Welch & Hoolbrook, she wrote her case to dr Rush—who gave a decisive opinion, that there was no chance for her Life, but by an immediate opperation, to this with the persuasion of her Friends She finally consented and five weeks since was performed by dr. Warren and his son attended by Dr Welch and Hoolbrook—She supported herself through it with calmenss & fortitude, & bears with much patience, all the concequences of weakness and confinement, and loss of the use of the Arm, as any Heroine—She is doing well, and recovering as fast as could be expected after an opperation in which the whole Breast was taken off—the wound is intirely healed, and every affected part was removed, So that we have every prospect of her perfect recovery to Health and Usefullness again. but She remains with us this winter not being able to ride, only a short distance, at a time. Tell William this and that his Father left us this last week, having past a Month with us—that he was well, and that he came upon my writing to him, that his Mother has consented to an opperation, but she would not wait his arrival. She chose to save him the pain, and past through it ten days before he reach'd Quincy.

And now my dear Son, let me say to you that your Father and I are quite Satisfied with your declineing the Seat upon the Bench as you could not return in Season, and as the public Service certainly requires its being immediatly fill'd—but I am not Satisfied with your other Arguments I think your Samples not well founded, but you must think and judge for yourself

I know not how, or when this Letter will reach you. Should

the address of it, prompt the prying Eye of a British officer to Creak the seal, as in former instances, he will not find any thing to gratify his curiosity, but the Solemn Events to which human Nature is Subject, and to which the Sovereign as well as the Subject, is equally liable—I feel for and commisirate the unhappy State of mind to which his own Sovereign is now reduced to teach the world, that neither Rank or power wisdom or virtue can Secure from the Lot of humanity Kings or Princes—

at present we are all well. Your sons went to Atkinson the last week, with Thomas Norten & two of Judge Cranchs Sons whom he has sent on for their Education. they are fine Boys older by Several years than George—Most tenderly and affectionatly I tender my Love to my daughter & Infant Grandaughter & to Charles and to William and Kitty—and to yourself my Blessing—   A A

"YOUR SISTER WAS BAPTIZED"

To John Adams 2nd

my dear John   Quincy december 8th 1811

I have not written you a Letter yet, but I promised you one, and I now have the pleasure of inclosing a Letter from your Brother Charles to you. I had a Letter from your Father dated in Sepbr th 11: the day after your Sister was Baptized. she was call'd Louisa Catharine, the Rev'd Dr Pitt, Chaplain to the English Church in St Petersburgh performed the Service, and mr Harris our Consul there was Godfather, and the Lady of the Portuguese Minister and Madam Kreham an English Lady, were the two Godmothers. The Flag of the united States was extended from a pier in the garden from the House in which your Father Resides. upon this occasion The Saxon minister & the Minister from westphalia attended the service, and Many American who were at st petersburgh, So that the young Ladies Christning will be rememberd by many Nations—George and his sister have something uncommon to remember, with respect to their Birthplace; one Born in Berlin, the Capital of the King of Prussia, and the other in St Petersburgh the

Capital of the Emperor Alexander. they must never forget, that they are Americans, for tho born in foreign Countries, where ever a Minister resides that spot is considerd, as the Territory of the Nation to which he belongs. I hope they will both be good Citizens.

I miss you and your Brother not a little, especially upon the Sunday, as you seldom faild of being with me upon that day ever since your Father & Mother left us—but I consider you are for yourself much better situated. when you grow older, you will be convinced that it is so—

it will always give me pleasure to hear that you are obedient and Studious, that you are kind, and obligeing to your school mates, and that you love your uncle and Aunt and always believe that they know better than you do what is best for you. never be possitive [   ]. Remember the broken jug the day you went away.

I beleived it too heavey for you to carry. O No Grandmamma it is not. you will break it child. o No I Shall not. I gave it up, contrary to my own judgment. what became of the jug, John?

Poor fellow you looked so mortified that I had not the Heart to find fault with you; I only chid myself for yealding to importunity against my better knowledge. now I do not mention this, only to remind you that those who have lived longer in the world than you have; and have more experience ought to be minded, and their judgment submitted to without murmuring. attend my dear Boy to your hand writing. Your Father expects to find you improved—and you must write him a Letter Your Aunt or cousin, Abbe will assist you.

I inclose to you, your Fathers Letter which you left with me. get your Aunt to take care of it for you, that it may be preserved

The printer of that vile Paper which gave you so much offence, calld the Scourge, has been indited for four different Libels, and sentenced to pay a fine & be imprisoned Six Months. So you see that the wicked will not go unpunished—but private Revenge is not lawfull.—

give my Love to your Brother and tell him his Father is very anxious about his Education; but more so that his Morals shoud be pure; that he should pay a sacred regard to truth and upon no account ever deviate from it—

Remember to the Young Cranch's & to Thomas Norten—to your Cousin Abbe to whom I charge you always to be oblige-ing, and Good Lydia allways respect & love

I am dear John most affectionatly your Grandmother

Abigail Adams

"AFTER SUCH AN OPERATION"

To Mercy Otis Warren

my dear Madam   Quincy December 14th 1811

I thank you for your kind inquiries after my Daughter Smith. She is, and has been as well, the Physicians Say, as any one could expect, after Such an Operation, as She has endured—to me it was agonizing—She Sustaind it with firmness, and fortitude

The wound has been intirely healed for this month, but the mussels from the Arm, which communicate with the part af-fected, were necessarily laid So bare, and Sufferd So much, that it will be a long time before the use of the Arm can be restored. it is a misfortune to her, that She cannot bear the motion of a carriage nor write a line herself, but we are encouraged to hope, for a perfect restoration from time.

My dear Madam, I know you have often thought of me, and your feeling heart has Sympathized with me under the various, and uncommon trials, I have been call'd to pass through the year past, but mercies have been blended with my afflictions.

Knowing the regard you ever entertaind for my dear de-parted Brother & Sister, I had determined to write to you, previous to the receipt of your Letter, and to offer to your ac-ceptance the tribute of Respect, paid to their memory by our Benevolent Pastor which I now do—

If we live untill the Spring of the year, and my Daughter so far recovers, as to be able to ride, She will not return home untill She has paid her Respects to one of her most ancient Friends—and if health permits, I will once more embrace in this world, the Friend I hope to meet in that world, where all Sorrow is to be wiped from all Eyes.—

I am Dear Madam as Ever your   A Adams

BATTLE OF TIPPECANOE

To John Quincy Adams

No 1

My dear son   Quincy Janry 5 1812

I rejoice that I can begin the new year without a Repetition of any mournfull, or afflictive Family dispensation, and that I can congratulate you upon the Life of your Father, and his continued Health, upon that also of your Sons, your Brother, and upon the restoration of your Sister, and last of all that I am still enabled to hold a pen & can write to you, altho frequently assaild by sickness, yet I have great reason for thankfullness that I was supported through the trying scenes of the last Summer. My Letters of Sepbr, october and November, were of such a nature as to excite the most painfull and distressing sensations both to you, and my dear daughter. Some of them I think must have reachd you, and I would not again repeat the tale of woe.

I fear instead of a pleasurable sensation excited at the reception of a Letter, you will feel, a dread of opening them—yet so many of your near and dearest connexions are by age, just droping into the Tomb, that your mind must be prepared for the Stroke—

I have not any letter from you of a later date than Sepbr No 24, and not any from Mrs Adams of a later date than June. Little miss must not engrose so much of her time, as to make her relinquish her correspondents here—My last accounts from Washington were late in Nov,br. Mrs Boyed was very low. Mrs Pope quite recoverd. Mrs Buchana I fear in very low circumstances. I hope she will find friends where she is. She is a very deserving woman—her dear Babe she says is all that is left her of past happiness.

Congress have been in Session since Novbr never since the first commencement of the government have they been so unanimous, one Hundred and 17 teen to 11. to 15 and never more than 20 Minority—both Parties unite in the great object of defence, and that with a spirit and decision which animates the Nation. war with England appears inevitable, unless that Nation receeds from her unjust pretentions and her injurious conduct. we have had an Indian War, in the Indiana territory. our Troops fought valiently. it was a battle on the Wabash, commanded by govr Harrison. the Indians fought and were under the control of the shawanoe Prophet, who has been for many Months stiring up different tribes of Indians to engage with him, which he finally effected we lost one hundred and 38 officers and Men—the Indians were routed & their Towns burnt, many kill'd so that they have sent debutations to sue for Peace.

I can only give you a scetch of any thing. Col P Boyd 4 Reg. of the united states Infantry obtain great credit and proved how much more Superiour Regular troops are for action, than Militia

with Respect to the politickes of our own State, The Boston Assemblage have nôt yet cooled down and they will exert all their power and talents to remove Govr Gerry at the next Election, unless appall'd at the uninimity of Congress, and the prospect of a war with England. beside they cannot agree in a candidate. some propose trying Govenour Strong again, but they will not succeed. Govr Gerry has conducted with great firmness and inflexable Integrity. he marked out his path, and has not deviated from it, tho assaild by an trust—calumny has vomited forth all her venom. abuse of the lowest kind has been wealded by hands, who would blush at detection, threats, and menaces in abundance, in private Letters, and publick papers untill a federal grand jury thought it necessary to present one Printer. Bill were found against him. he pleaded guilty, and a federal judge condemnd him to fine and six Months imprisonment—

I confide in the good sense and intelligence of our people to support the National Government, in a particular manner at this juncture, when union is necessary for our existance—and those who prefer the government of great Britain should have liberty to retire to it, with this proviso, that they never return to us again—their banishment should be for Life—If the spirit rises a little higher, *Our Writers* must not be tolerated, nor he who dares assume the Name of Rebel—

your Brother has written to you by this conveyance, and I presume has given you more correct veiws of the Nation and its affairs than I have. Mr. Storey is appointed Judge in your stead—I have said to you in a former Letter, circumstanced as you were I approved your decision—you observe in one of your Letters, "that you must come home to your parents, and to your Children." to your Parents your return would give great joy: and would tend to render their descent to the Grave, less solitary to them, but that is a consideration of far less moment in my Estimation than the duties you owe to your Children. they are comeing into Life and it is of great and important concern to them to be trained up under the Eye, care and admonition of their Father, to imbibe his sentiments, to catch the fire of his Patriotism, and to drink from the fountain of knowledge which he has acquired in the various and important occupations in which he has been engaged. George is at the very age when your presence and instruction, would be of the utmost concequence to him.

we have done for them the best we could by placeing them under the care of their uncle and Aunt Peabody and at the Academy in Atkinson, but I consider it only as a temporary residence for them—what are the views of the President for you, I am wholy Ignorant of—

The Horace has not yet arrived. I wish I could send you the vol,m of dispatches, but it is so large that I cannot unless a vessel is going direct to Cronstrad—I inclose you the report of a Committee upon the Navey. I am sure it will meet your approbation. I also inclose two Letters, from your children I am ashamed of Georges handwriting. he is so himself, and I hope will mend in concequence of his resolution—

My Love to Mrs Adams to Miss Johnson and to William. tell him his Mother recovers fast that she and Caroline remain with us through the winter.—

I am my dear son your truly affectionate Mother   A A

"PHEBY IS TOO INFIRM"

To Elizabeth Smith Shaw Peabody

my dear sister   Quincy july 17th 1812
    I received your Letter written upon the Birth-day of my
only daughter, and memorable to me for that occasion, as well
as the Eleventh of the Same Month upon which was Born J Q
Adams, and a Sister whom I lost, and whom no doubt you
recollect from the circumstances attending it, for you were
with me.
    so much for Egotism. now I will replie to your queries. in
the first place, I have the pleasure to Say we are all well at this
House, but my poor Son and daughter have a double share of
sickness in their Family. the Children are but just recovering
from the hooping cough. when Abigail is taken down with the
Scarlet fever—She is a very sick child. I have brought Elizabeth
away hoping she may escape it. it is the third day and it will
run to 5th or 7th

Quincy 2d
    Col Smith has not yet arrived altho we have been looking
every hour for more than a week. he gave us notice that he
should leave home upon the 6th. upon the 4th he was detained. we begin to fear, that either mrs Adams or her sister
Nancy who was to accompany her, is taken Sick upon the
journey. we will however hope the best,

Quincy 3d
    dr Tufts rode here yesterday for the first time, much ex-
hausted, but better than I ever expected to see him again—

Quincy 4th
    Pheby is better than she was a fortnight ago. She does not
want for any necessary or comfort, except Sometimes a constant attendence with nourishment, which the girl who lives
with her is too neglectfull of, and being young and heedless,
and knowing that Pheby is too infirm to compel her, she
sometimes wants her food before She can get it,— Mrs Adams

& mrs Greenleaf are very kind and attentive to her. It is very difficult to get any proper person to Stay with her—we have not any Blacks in town, & white people who are good for any thing, do not like to live in a negro house—but if as I fear, She Should be quite helpless, we must find some person who will do it—

She is gratefull for kindness, the high affusion Blood runs in her veins, and she has much of the sovereign yet—

I love and respect and venerate her and would not See her want, while I had Bread to divide with her.

I am sorry Mr Peabodys mouth continues bad yet. it has been a disease many families have—

I do not yet despair of making you a visit some time before winter. I want to See you and my Boys to whom I send my Love—and as the President is waiting to take my Letter to the post office I must close it and Subscribe your affectionate Sister

Abigail Adams

THE WAR OF 1812

To John Quincy Adams

my dear son   Quincy July 29th 1812.

Mr Benjamin Beal jun'r Who has long resided in France, returnd last Winter upon a visit to his Family here as he connected himself in France, his stay here has been Short, and he is now going back in a [   ] to Liverpool, and from thence to France

I request him to take this Letter for you, which I shall place under-cover to Mr Barlow our Minister in France that he may forward it to you by the first conveyance

The declaration of War by the United States against Great Britain, the necessity for which is deplored, renders the communication between us so hazardous, that I despair of hearing from you or conveying intelligence to you

In this Situation of the Country, you will not expect that my Letter should contain any other intelligence than that which is of a domestic Nature.

your Father and myself are in as good health as our Age will permit, your Sons are also well—I have been dissapointed in a visit which I expected to have made to them, before your Sister left me. I hope however to see them soon—We have not any Letters from you of a later date than the 4th March, and we wait in anxious expectation of hearing. I have written to you by various opportunities—and I could now fill many pages with subjects which ought to come to your knowledge of a political nature, if I did not feel myself restrained by the desire I have, that this Letter may reach you, as it contains no Subject, to gratify the curiosity of any one and can be only interesting to yourself as a testimony of the health of your Friends—

Col Smith came last week, accompanied by mrs Adams his Sister Nancy and Abbe—in return, he will take back your Sister & Caroline and his sister Nancy, whose health has been much impared by greif for the loss of her Mother—I cannot but regret that necessity, which places them at such a Distance from me. Caroline, without being Handsome, is all in manners disposition habits and principles that a Lovely woman ought to be, united with personal care and elegance of manners. It is something, than Beauty dearer

yet is this Lovely flower destined to Bloom in the wilderness, and Shed her Sweetness in Seclusion from the world—and that without repineing, or a single expression that she wishd it otherways—

your sister returns in good health—and without any further apprehensions from the cause, which gave so just allarm to her Friends—

your Brothers Eldest Daughter is just recovering from a severe and dangerous attack of the Scarlet fever, she cannot yet stand upon her feet or sit up.

From Washington I heard last week—Mrs Pyre had recovered from her late indisposition—Similar to those which have so frequently brought mrs Adams low.

mr Hellens eldest son had been sick of a fever, but was recovering Adelaide not yet married—but soon to be so

I heard also from Mr Johnson at N'orleans he was well and doing well

all our Family request to be rememberd to you in which they are joined By your Ever affectionate Mother   A A

"WE GLORY IN OUR INFANT NAVY"

To John Quincy Adams

My Dear Son   December 30th 1812
  Despairing almost of conveying a Letter to you amidst the
war of Empires and Kingdoms, I have had but little encouragement to write, yet knowing how anxious you must be Relative to your Family, your Children your Friends and Country
I Shall make the attempt, and trust this Letter on Board a
Cartel now going from Nyork to England, hopeing that it will
be treated with the Same lenity, with which we treat our Enemies. Send them to the place of their destination.
  The intelligence which personally concerns you to know, is
that, which is nearest Your Heart, the Health and welfare of
your sons. I have the pleasure to assure you that they are both
in fine Health, and making good progress in their Studies.
Your Father and Brother were both of opinion, that it would
be best to remove them from Atkinson to Hingham academy.
My object in removeing them was to get George under the
care and tuition of the Revd Mr Coleman but his Number was
already compleat, and he could not be admitted untill the
Spring. there is an excellent Preceptor in the Academy, and not
crowded with Scholars. there they have been Since, the beginning of Nov'br they came home to our anual festival of
Thanksgiving much pleased with their Situation. they Board in
the Family of the preceptor Mr Kimble, who has a fine woman
for his wife, of whom the Boys appear fond—they are now so
near to us, the road being much Shortned by the new Bridge
over the point call'd *Bents*, that it is but a short walk of 3 miles
for them, and we can attend to their Progress in their Studies
much easier than when they were so distant as Atkinson
George has not forgotten his French, but reads it daily.
  Your Parents enjoy as much health, as at their advanced years
as they have reason to expect, and enjoy as much tranquility, as
the interest they take in the welfare of the Country now Seriously engaged in War, will admit. Sincerely wishing & praying
for a restoration of Peace, upon Safe and honorable Terms.
  We have had our misfortunes and our Disasters to contend

with; oweing to want of skill, discipline and proper arrangement, but we Shall learn wisdom by Chastisement, and Skill by
experience. in the mean time we shall have our sufferings to
contend with the defeats we have met with upon the land, in
our imperfect attacks upon Canady have been mortifying to
us—because we have reason to believe they might have been
successful. our Country have been so nobly remunerated upon
the ocean, by our Hull, Jones and Decater, that we glory in
our Infant Navy, and hope to add a new line to the Song, "of
Rule Britania Rule the waves," and to convince the Self Stiled
Queen of the ocean, that there is a power rising up, not to
usurp the title, but to contend for their own Rights and to
oblige others to yeald them—to this and the Bill which is now
past in Congress, to build with all possible dispatch four Seventy four Gun ships & Six 44 Gun frigates, making ten with
those already agreed upon, these with those we already have in
Commission, will be Sufficient to protect our commerce, and
teach other Nations to respect it also; our Navy has already
instructed Great Britain in Some wholesome truths, and it
would be much for her interest to listen to them. She may rest
assured that this increase of our Naval establishment, will be
the binding chain of the Union and She will hear very little
more of the cry of N England for peace, if She persists in her
injustice—the Reellection of mr Madison, now certain by a
Majority of 36 already returned, and of Mr Gerry who has Still
more votes—plainly Show, that altho a great Clamour has
been excited, and British Partizens have been active in fomenting it, yet the great Body of the people are united. She need no
other proof of this, than the universal applause with which our
Naval victories have been hailed, and celebrated, and the honours bestowed upon the conqueres throughout the United
States.

We look with Sorrow, and with heartfelt anguish upon the
desolation of the "Cloud capt Towers and Gorgeous palaces"
of that ancient, wealthy, and magnificent city of Moscow.
Charles the 12 of Sweden was as brave as Napolean. May the
Emperor Alexander be as fortunate and as Successful as the
Great Peter.

What havock and destruction of the Human Species! can
Man be born then, only to be destroyed by his fellow Man. Yet

plagues and Earthquakes break not heavens designs" are we rational creatures?

I am not a little anxious for your Situation it must be unpleasant to you, and to your Family, deprived by the Wars of all the Diplomatic Society you have been accustomed to associate with and few or none of your Countrymen arriveing to give you information respecting your own Country—feeling for the distress brought you upon that in which you reside—at a loss which way you can leave it—

I am equally at a loss what to advise you to, cannot you be permitted to go to England and return to America in a Cartel.? I wrote to you the last month, and acknowledgd your Letters No 35 july 12th No 36 August 10th No 34 missing—one from my dear Daughter of June 13th and one from Catharine of June 9th and one from William of the 13th of the same Month. I have Letters from the Valley of a recent date that they were all well, and Col S Smith elected a Member of the next Congress by the district where he resides.—

You will not expect my dear son to receive from me a confidential Letter, nor one free from the impression that it may be Scrutinized as formerly in a British court of admirality, or in a police office in Paris—as it is a Ladies Letter, into what ever hands it may fall, my request is that it may be forwarded to a long absent Son. Who is anxious to hear from parents, "whose days are dwindled to the Shortest Span" and from the two dear Sons left in their care—may the benevolent feelings of Nature triumph over National resentment, and give to this Letter a safe conduct to the place of its destination

from an affectionate Mother to her long Absent Son—

Abigail Adams

a long Letter which I wrote to you last May, to go by a private hand was returnd to me a few days since, the gentleman changeing his mind, it has lain six months in mr Shaws office, and mist many opportunities of conveyance—now like an old Almanack out of date—

DEATH OF BABY GRANDDAUGHTER

To Louisa Catherine Adams

my dear Daughter   Quincy Janry 30 1813—
How shall I address a Letter to you, how share and participate in your Grief without opening affresh the wound which
time may in some measure have healed? distance excluded me
from knowing Your distress, or shareing your Sorrows, at the
time when you most needed consolation but neither time, or
distance has banishd from my Bosom, that Sympathy which
alltho, Billows rise; and oceans Roll between us; like mercy is
not confined to time or space, but crosses the atlantic and
mingles tears with you over the grave of your Dear departed
Babe, whom with an Eye of faith, I behold with other Inno-
cents, surrounding the Throne of their Maker, and singing
Halelujahs to the most high; or who knows but they may be
call'd "to act as Seconds to Some Sphere unknown"
    For ourselves only we can mourn, and how Selfish is that
Sound? early in Life I was call'd to taste the bitter cup. forty
years has not obliterated from my mind the anguish of my
Soul upon the occasion. I have since that day Sustaind more
weighty afflictions, but it has pleased Heaven to Support me
through them, and to permit me to live to advanced Age. let
us with gratitude bless our preserver that we have Yet so many
blessings left us—such I hope will prove to you, and to their
Father Your surviveing Children, who most earnestly long for
your return to your Native Country, that they may embrace,
you and their Brother of whom all the Americans who have
seen him speak highly, but none So warmly, So tenderly affectionate as mr Ingraham—
    The war which took place between America and England,
before your Letters reach'd us, put a decisive bar to yours, and
their Fathers request to send them to you. I knew not how I
could have parted with them, altho I should have thought it
my Duty to have complied—while they remain with us, I feel
as if I had not lost all that pertains to you. they are the Branches
which entwine around me, altho the parent Stock is far removed from me, and they are the more closely linked as they

feel their dependence upon us,—as they look with joy for a vacation when they can come to their Home. I have much pleasure in their Society, and now see their advancement and improvement in their studies daily increasing

All the Members of my Family desire to be affectionatly rememberd to you. Louissa in particular to yourself and Sister to whom I am indebted for a Letter, and to whom I Shall Soon write

From washington I had Letters not long since. Adelaid remans Still Single. the ill Health of mr Hellen is alledged as the cause. Mrs Pope did not come to washington this winter, as mr Popes period of service expires, and he was a man who acted from his own judgment which did not suit his constituents, who chose others perhaps more pliable

Mrs Buchanan returns with mr Pope to Kentucky—

I had Letters from the valley this Day; mrs Smith has had but poor health Since her return there. she has been sadly afflicted with the Rhumatism. col Smith is chosen a Member of Congress by a large Majority of votes—our Naval officers win laurels and wear them—of our Campaigns by land as yet—I boast not. peace is my dear delight when it can be mantaind with honour—

I Love the Land of my fore fathers, and Respect and venerate many Characters—but should we meanly bow our Necks and take the Yoke, we Should be unworthy of our Ancestors. the real American will not do it—

I pray you to write by every way you can devise. nothing else can alleviate this long banishment from your family and your affectionate Mother   Abigail Adams

WAR NEWS

To John Quincy Adams

No 2.
my dear son   Quincy Febry 25 1813.
    upon looking over my list, I find that I have written to you a Letter every month, since october. my last Letter was in Janry

21st, written immediatly after receiving yours of Sepbr 21, informing me of the loss of your Dear Babe. I wrote to Mrs Adams at the Same time. the Letters went in a cartel to Liverpool, through the kindness of a Friend. Since that period I have not received a line from you, nor have any public dispatches been received from you by the Government, as the Secretary of State informd your Father this Day. he adds that the president was looking for them with anxious solicitude.

I inclose to you the result of the Election for president and vice president. I could fill a dozens pages with the political affairs of our Country, with the Disasters of our *irregular* Army, the causes which produced them, and the effects which have followd them. much of this you will get from the English News papers, with as much of truth and accuracy, as a French Bulleten. I lament that much of what you ought to know cannot be communicated to you. the channel through which this Letter must pass wholy forbids it. but one thing I will tell you, and let the lord Clarion of Fame proclaim to the world the laurels wars and the victories acchieved by our Naval commanders. first in the triumph was Captain Hull in the frigate Constitution, who engaged and Captured the British frigate Guerriere, making her a wreck, was obliged to blow her up. Capt Jones in the Wasp Sloop of war fought dismasted and took the British sloop of War the Frolick afterward both were taken by a 74. Commodore Decatur in the frigate us. Captured the British frigate Macedonian and brought her safely in to N york, altho at a vast distance from home. Commodore Bainbridge who took the command of the Constitution, to enable Captain Hull to secure, and make his own, a *prize*—called the, *Hart*, and for other private reasons; he sufferd not the laurels won by Hull to fall upon his brow. he engaged fought, and conquerd the British frigate Java, but was necessitated to blow her up, landed her officers and crew at St Salvador, the Captain soon died of the wounds he received. I have been concise, for time would fail me to detail to you, how these conquerers have been recived, and the honours which have been conferd upon them by Legislatures and public Bodies—in the various States. in Spight of all British partialities, American Blood exalts us in the trophies won. alass! alass! our 74s are yet in Embrio, were they as they ought to have been, upon the ocean the Chesapeak would not now be in a State of Blockade by a British squadron. for with equal force we have proved; that our Countries wrongs can and will be avenged. our loss have been comparatively small.

Tell it in Britain, proclaim it to the world, that the trident of Neptune has bowed to the valour and Genius of Columbia, unless a speedy peace ensue, of which I see not any prospect. She is raising up a power, and a force which will humble her pride and Share the ocean with her,

unto that Being who Governs the destiny of Nations, let us asscribe the Glory, and ask for his Support, and guidence in the war in which we have engaged

I could tell you a tale which would raise your Blood, would raise your passions; would grieve your heart; and make you exclaim O my Native State, how art thou fallen?

degenerate Sons, return, return or sink in Oblivion! may the waters of Lethe pass over you.

I have the pleasure to Say that in our domestic circle, we are all well. that your son's are so and doing well

From your Family Friends at washington I hear by Adelaide that they are all well, that mrs Buchanan is going to Kentucky with mr pope whose term of service in the Senate expires.

From your Sister I had Letters to day She has had a very sick winter with the Rheumatism, her mind is much agitated least—expences have been unnecessarily incured—I would hope not, but a mother will feel, and the more So from their inability to meet the demand.

My Love to my dear Daughter, would, it were in my power to heal the wounded Bosoms of my Children; I could Soothe and Soften them if I could but again embrace them. God Almighty Bless and preserve you—prays daily Your affectionate

A—

JOHN QUINCY TO NEGOTIATE PEACE

To John Quincy Adams

No 5

My Dear Son   Quincy—April 23d 1813—

For three weeks past there have been many & various reports in circulation respecting the Mediation to Russia & there has been much Said and written respecting the persons to be appointed. It was not untill yesterday that your Father & I was officially notified that mr Gallatin and Bayard were associated with you in a commission to Negotiate a Peace between Great Britain and the united States, and that they would be ready to Sail in a few days.

I embrace the opportunity of writing by them, and have already Sent Some Letters, upon the faith of the rumour

The gentlemen so well known to you; will carry with them all the information necessary for you to know, respecting the State of our public affairs—and our prospects—it is therefore unnecessary for me to Say any thing further than to express my ardent wishes, that you may all unite and become instruments in the hands of Providence to restore Peace to our Bleading Country upon just and honorable terms—the Negotiation is all importent to our Country, and alltho encompassed with difficulties—honest hearts, and upright minds upon both Sides may effect it—

It has been my constant and daily petition to heaven for you: that you might be made an instrument in the hand of Providence of much good to your native Land. Should my petition be answerd by accomplishing an honorable peace for your Country, I Should Say with Simeon, "mine Eyes have seen they Salvation."

To God and my Country I resign you—Relinquishing all personal considerations, with the anticipated pleasure of Seeing you and Your Family the ensueing Season.

Your Brother has been absent a fortnight attending Court, and will be an other week, So that I fear he will miss this, I hope, Safe conveyance. I have written you every month, but fear my Letters will never reach you—I have also written to my Daughter after her heavey affliction—to Kitty & to William—

I will note here, least you Should not have received my Letters, that your Letter of 26 Sepbr. 8th and 25 october all have reachd us, and that the 25 is the last we have received also your Letters to your sons by mr Jackson.

The vacation commenced yesterday at Hingham. it will be a fort night. I attended the Lecture yesterday, and mr Tremble the Preceptor assures me John will make a fine Scholar—

George I hope will attend to the advise given him, in your

excellent Letter. he is, as formerly, much attached to Books and grows most rapidly—when at home, every attention and instruction will be given them in my power—but we cannot any of us supply the fathers Place. should you come *nearer to us*—and peace be restored—I Should not object to their being sent to you.

I shall not be able to give them timely notice at the Valley, so as to get Letters in Season. but I had a Letter today from your sister. she has been confined all winter with the Rhumatism, from which she has endured great and Severe pain. She recoverd so far as to walk about her Room, but was again attackd and is Still Suffering. I wish'd her to have come when the col. went to Congress and have past the time with me. at present she is not able—

The Glory which our Navy has acquired, and the Fame of our Gallant Commanders, must surely have been wafted to you upon the wings of the wind. five such important conquests over the British flag, have never before been achieved by any Nation With equal force—Truly it is the Lords Doings and it is Marvelous in our Eyes—undaunted in Battle, generous in conquest, modest in victory. these are the Characteristic traits of our Naval commanders. they have redeemed the honour of our Country and coverd themselves with Glory, altho they may experience a reverse, and be compeld to yeald to Superiour force. Hull, Jones, Decature, Bainbridge and Lawrence will never be forgotten by Britain or America

you may easily Suppose the pleasure your Father experiences in the Laurels they have won. they were most if not all, officers of his appointment, when the power rested with him—and they hail him as the Father of the Navy.—

My Love to my dear daughter I hope more prosperous days are in reserve for her—and her Children I never was of a desponding make—what ever may be the allotments of Providence for me or mine, my confidence in the Supreme ruler will remain unshaken—and my beleif that all partial Evil will terminate in universal good is firm—altho we cannot perceive how or when—the History of Joseph and Brethrun is lesson full of instruction.

adieu my dear Son. heaven bless you and yours prays your ever affectionate Mother   Abigail Adams.

To Mercy Otis Warren

my dear Madam   Quincy June 20th 1813

your Letter this morning received So kindly inquiring after my Dear Daughter, demands from me, not only my thanks, but an immediate reply.

Mrs Smith, through her whole Life has enjoyd good health, untill the painfull opperation She endured the last Summer, after which her nerves were much affected.

Soon after her return to the valley She wrote me word, that She had been Severely attacked with the Rheumatism in her Back. it left her Back and Seizd upon her left hip, from which She Sufferd great pain. She was easiest in Bed in this way it continued through the winter. She obtaind Some releif from Blisters. as the Spring approachd it put on an inflamitory form and attackd her Side like a plurisy—She was then Bled, and Blisterd again, in consequence of which she is much Weakned and debilitated. about three weeks Since, She was voilently at-tackd in her Stomack which greatly allarmd Caroline, and the rest of her Friends—the more So for the cols being absent in Congress.

it was at this time that both Caroline and her Aunt Nancy Smith were So anxious, and wrote to us in Such a manner as excited our poignant distress—

it appeard impossible for me to undertake, a journey of Such a distance, Sick as I have been for more than a Month, con-fined to my chamber with a fever—

Mrs Smith knew this, and did not Send for me, but Still hopes that She may So recover, as to make herself a journey here when the col. returns—it was my desire that She Should have been with us, when the Coll, first went on to Congress, but She was too Sick to undertake it—I still flatter myself that She will be able to, if no Severe attack again prevents it, but I fear She will never again enjoy health—

My Dear Madam I have not written to you in replie to your last Letter.

Such is the warlike State of Nations and their various

Destinies, that we cannot calculate what is to be the end of these things, who are to be the Conquerers, or why they thus destroy each other, but thus it has been from Age to Age, and will continue So, as long as time endures—

whether Bonaparte is again to become the conquerer, time must decide—

The conduct of our own State Government cannot Surely meet the approbation of any real American I Should much rather chuse, that the Name of my Family Should be blotted from the page of History, than appear upon Record as the proposer of Such a Resolution as past the Senate in their late Session—I do not view this War, as waged for conquest, or ambition, but for our injured Rights, for our freedom, and the Security of our Independence—and therefore Shall rejoice When any Naval victory, or Milatary Success attend upon our Arms; which may give us any hope or prospect of Peace, which always ought to be the object aimd at, and I Sincerely beleive is So by our Government. most Sincerely do I wish that war could have been avoided—

I inclose to you for your perusal Several Letters from my Son. they will perhaps give you a better Idea of the contending powers there I am able to. You will be So good as to return them when read—

I am dear Madam with Sentiments of Love veneration and esteem your Friend   Abigail Adams

my Family join in Regards to yours—

OPINIONS OF THE WAR

To John Quincy Adams

My dear Son   Quincy july 1st 1813
I wrote to you upon the 14 of June, I knew that my Letter is gone upon a doubtfull journey; it had first to make its way through British Ships of the line & cruizers, to France, and then through a Country at war with Russia. it is almost a forlorn hope that it should ever reach you, unless if capturd; it

Should meet with a Sir John Sherbrook, who politely Sent us
by a cartel from Halifax, a packet of Letters from you, containing two to your Father, two to me, and two to your
Brother, one to your Sons, they were ocbr. and Novbr. Letters 1812—So that if you turn to your Book you will See what
was read at the Admiralty office, and by the Commander in
cheif—it was very civil and polite in Sir John to Send them to
us—saying it might give pleasure to his Friends to receive
them.

Mr Gorden who is ever attentive to us, has now notified to
us, that a Sweedish Ship is about to Sail, and that mr Storer,
Brother to the judge, is going to Gotenburgh in her, and will
take Letters for us.

In a few days, altho I cannot calculate, that they have yet
arrived. I hope you will See your Colleagues mr Gallatin and
Bayard, and from them derive Such information respecting
our Country as you can rely upon—by them I wrote you. I
again acknowleg your Letters received, and any numbers compleat, up to Febry 15th—that containd, and the one dated 30
Janry. News altogether unexpected, there is an old proverb,
the least Said, is Soonest mended, So I take the hint—

Domestic occurrences are those in which as individuals we
are most interested, I Shall therefore begin by Saying, that
your Sons are both well, and closely following their Studies. I
visited them with their Grandfather last week. John has the
promise of keeping his Birth day at home. George's growth is
very rapid. he is nearly as tall as you are, and he is Slender.
John grows, but not so fast. they are both trying to acquire a
good hand and Say they will write as Soon as they can. George
promised me a Letter—they are both healthy—our respective
Families are well your Brother will write to you, and tell you,
that he has a Son, whom he has named Isaac Hull.

of your dear and only Sister, I can only Say that She has
been, and Still is a patient Sufferer under Severe and afflicting
pain, So much reduced that She cannot either write, or walk.
my last account to the 21 of June, was that She was gaining
Strength. She was Seizd early in the winter, with a voilent fit of
Rheumatism from which She has never recoverd—I fear her
constitution was essentially injurd by the opperation She past
through, and which to my inexpressible grief has not freed her

from a Similar complaint upon the other Side. Heaven only knows to what Sufferings She may yet be reserved. my Heart bleads—I cannot get to her, nor She to me I am too infirm myself to undertake Such a journey—

unto the will and disposal of our heavenly Father, I commit her

> "Safe in the hand of one disposing power
> or in the Natal, or the Mortal honor"

my only Source of Satisfaction says dr Preistly, "and it is a never failing one, is my firm persuasion that every thing—and our oversights, and mistakes among the rest are parts of the great plan, in which every thing will in time appear to have been orderd and conducted in the best manner—"

> "who finds not providence all good and wise
> Alike in what it gives, and what it denies."

Altho I Sometimes feel my own insignificance in the creation, especially when contemplating, "the first good first perfect, and first fair" I derive pleasure and assurance from the word of inspiration, that not a Swallow falleth without notice.

From domestic occurences, Shall I turn to those of a public nature? and here I am lost in a Labyrinth almost without a clue, partaking in calamities, from which the advice of Hercules might releive us, but which appears lost upon our Native State not a Shoulder will they voluntarily put to the wheel, but leave it to Stick fast; or be drawn out by others, whom they try, by every method to dishearten and discourage: even to passing a Resolution in the Senate of this State, brought forward by a Friend of ours—who beclouded by party prejudice, discernd not the disgrace which History will attach to it: take it in the following words.

"Resolved as the Sense of the Senate of Massachusetts that in a war like the present, *waged* without *justifiable cause*, and proscuted in a Manner which indicates that *conquest* and *ambition* are its real motives, it is not becomeing a moral and religious people to express any approbation of Milatary or Naval exploits, which are not immediately connected with our defence of our Sea Coast and Soil"!

I know not how to express my contempt of Such a mean

dasterdly, mercinary Resolution; so falce in principle, so degrading in its Concequences. I blush for my Native State, as much as I once prided myself in it, when its counsels were directed by Heroes, patriots, and Statesmen.

Can it be that the Love of gain like the god of Aron, has Swallowd up all public Spirit, and Love of Country? I would rather that the Names of my whole Family Should be blotted from the page of History, and the conspicuous Stations they have fill'd in their Country, wholy forgotten than Such a Resolution Should be recorded upon the Archives of the State as Sanctiond by any of the Name, and I almost regret that a [   ] Should be annexed to any of the family.

I the more regreet this political Mania, because in private Life, I esteem the Man, as a Friend a Neighbour benevolent and kind, a model of conjugal and parental affection. I Love and highly value his wife, and his amiable Children, and I mourn over the victum, Sacrificed to the Junto, and the vindictive party Spirit, which rages more in this State, than in any other of the Union—

Placed as you are, at a great distance from the passing events, your Eyes have discerned, and your judgment portrayd what would take place—"true it is, The Spirit of our people is equal to any exigency," but they must be led with Skill, and feel a confidence in their Leader, their must be wisdom to plan as well as a disposition to execute, and we must purchase at a dear rate, that experience which years of peace and prosperity have not called into action—and which time has nearly deprived us of, few, very few of our Revolutionary officers remain, with powers of Body capable of fatigue & enterprize.

you will learn the fate of the Chesepeake of the Brave, but too daring Lawrence—of the fall of almost every officer, of the capture of the Ship—the causes of the Capture were undoubtedly oweing to the, too near approach to each other, by the wearing of the Chesepeake. She was entangled with the Shannon, and gave her the opportunity of making the Chesepeake and instantly Boarding her. Such are the chances of war—let not him who putteth on the harness Boast.

My paper warns me to close—yet I feel as if I had much more to Say. it Shall be upon an other Sheet—my Blessing be with you, and yours—　　　　　　　　　　　　　　A Adams.

"GREAT CALLS UPON YOUR FORTITUDE"

To Louisa Catherine Adams

my dear Daughter   Quincy July 24th 1813.
    I received yesterday your Letter of the 4th April. I was grieved to find by it, that your spirits are so deprest, and your health so infirm.

    you have had great calls upon your fortitude, and the trial of your virtues, since your seperation from your Friends—

    we know upon what terms we hold our existance here. the Christian looks beyond this State of trial for the reward promised to those who endure unto the end, altho when in trouble the dark Shade of the picture only is seen. we find the light is the more powerfull, for it dispell's the Darkness. few of us but have greater cause to Sing of mercies than of Judgment, when we can bring our minds to think that all

"Partial Evil, is universal good"

and that what ever troubles assail us in this Life, are but parts of the great plan, in which every thing will in time appear to have been orderd and conducted in the best manner. we are in the hand of a mercifull Being who does not willingly afflict, and who will heal the wounded heart which trusts in him.

    Despond not my dear daughter. bee cheerfull Submissive and resignd. God loves a Cheerfull Christian, and he will not call us to harder trials than he will give us Strength to endure

    I have only time to write you a few lines by this vessel. she has been waiting for a wind for several days—a Gentleman on Board—a mr Storey has Letters from me to my son.

    your two Dear sons are well. I shall Go & See them and carry their Fathers Letters & your Blessing to them

    I inclose a Letter from George to his Father, to whom give my Love and tell him his Mother intreats him to take care of his health.

    I hope you will remove to a more temperate climate the onsueing winter. I shall rejoice to hear of you at Prague. our Minister I feel confident have arrived before now and I hope they will give you all spirits—their Mission is for peace and

God grant that it may be crowned with success—and a stop put to the horrid carnage which is laying waste Nations, and kingdoms

we are partaking of the same cup—the Southern States are all Blockaded and kept in constant allarm

a Letter from col smith yesterday from washington states that an Express had just arrived, Stateing that the Enemy had enterd the mouth of the Potomac—with five ships and one leading armed Brigg and that an attack was hourly expected. women and Children flying in all directions in great confusion—

Congress sitting with closed doors—

My Love to Charles of whose improvements I hear with pleasure

we are all in usual health. Age and infirmities will come—but we have had our day—and as yet are neither Blind or deaf, which I consider amongst many other blessings, not the least.

I have not yet had any Letter from my son by this vessel which brought yours; I shall still look for them. his punctuality is habitual.

If my Grandson and daughter are still with you give my Love to them. I wish I could write them some favorable account of their Mother, but alass I cannot. I hope however they will succeed in getting her here. they are now attempting it—at much hazard—you see my dear daughter I have my sorrows and my trials—May I be equal to them, and while I feel them, may they prepare me for a better world, where I hope we shall all meet and rejoice together

Adelaid is not yet married. I know not the cause of the delay—I heard a few days since that they were all well—

Your Sister Boyed has an other Son

The President has been very dangerously sick with a fever, but is now thought out of danger, and upon the Recovery

I am my dear Daughter your truly affectionate Mother
Abigail Adams

"SHE IS INDEED A VERY SICK WOMAN"

To Lucy Cranch Greenleaf

Mrs Smith reachd here yesterday at about ten oclock was like your dear Mother taken out of the carriage in a chair and carried to her chamber—She is indeed a very sick woman, spasms draw her up, cannot take food. every thing oppresses her—any Indian meal and water—her stomack seems to have lost its tone. how she got here is a marvel to me, a constant worry upon her nerves, so that at times she cannot be in Bed, riding saved her when she rode that stages—I thank you for your kind offer. I shall have occasion for all the kindness and attention of my Friends I fear, as well as their support— come and see her in a day or two—at present quiet is best

yours affec'ly   A Adams

c. July 1813

"A SCHIRROUS CANCER SEATED IN THE BREAST"

To Mercy Otis Warren

my Dear Madam   Quincy August 8 1813
    I cannot let my Son visit Plimouth without bearing a few lines to my old Friend who has always taken a kind interest in the welfare of my dear Daughter Smith, who reached here a fortnight Since with her Sister Son and daughter, but So helpless in her Limbs as not to be able to walk across the Room, obliged to be carried in a chair from the Chamber to the Carriage—If this was all the melancholy circumstance attending her case, hope might be left to comfort and flatter her Friends—I had flatterd myself that her disorder was a Rheumatic affection—but that hope is extinct. all the Physicians who have been consulted agree in opinion that it proceeds from a Schirrous Cancer Seated in the Breast and extending itself over the Stomack contracting the mussels both of that, and the Bowels so as frequently to create Spasms over the

whole Surface, like being as She expresses it cased up in Armour. it has not yet burst out, but there are appearnces which indicate it—

She is perfectly Sensible of her Situation and resignd to it—as She expresses herself—She gets a temporary relief from the use of opiates. how in her helpless debilitated State, She had the courage to attempt a journey of three hundred miles, I can Scarcly realize

I Should think it a hazard to take her for the great desire She had to reach the Habitation of her parents and to be with them, gave her courage and Strength—to have her with me was my most earnest desire. to mitigate Sooth and releive her distress as much as human aid can, will be a Solace to me amidst the anguish I am call'd to Sustain in my advanced Age—it is the will of Heaven and I desire to Submit without a murmur—however dark the ways of Heaven appear, to us in the dispensations of Providence, they are undoubtedly designd for our moral improvement

My daughter request me to present her Duty to you, and to Say Love and Respect for You will continue as long as her Life.

During the last ten days my affliction has been doubled. my daughter in Law mrs Charles Adams has lain dangerously Sick in the next Chamber to mrs Smith, with one of the most painfull obstinate and dangerous of diseases—an inflammation of the Intestines. it baffeld medicine for Several days, but has we hope at last has yealded So that the Physician considers her out of Danger—altho much reduced and weakend in the midst of my troubles—I have my Blessings kind and Sympathizing Friends and Neighbours—and my own health altho feeble, yet I am able to attend the Sick; and look to my Family—

I hope to hear that you Still preserv your health and that cheerfull Spirit, which is yet willing to live and not affraid to die—looking to the unseen world for brighter prospects and clearer views of its almighty Framer. there may we meet, and renew that Friendship which Death only can disolve for a Short period

I hope your Son has recoverd from the late unhappy voilenc offerd him, without So great injury as was apprehended

I am Dear Madam Your affectionate Friend

Abigail Adams

DEATH OF ABIGAIL 2ND

To George Washington Adams and John Adams 2nd

My dear Children   Quincy August 15th 1813
It is better to go to the House of mourning than to the House of Feasting, or dancing, for the living lay it to heart.

you my dear Children are now calld to the House of mourning and Sorrow, by the death of your dear Aunt Smith and the only daughter of your Grandparents, the only Sister of your Father.

your Aunt died last night, to the deep affliction of the whole Family—her pure Spirit I trust assended to her Maker. She was all in Life that was Lovely amiable and virtuous. She exhibited a firmness and fortitude through Life rarely to be found. She was patient uncomplaining and resignd, under the presure of a disorder hopeless and helpless. She was permitted and enabled to encounter a most hazardous journey in her weak State, and allowd to see her Parents, & Friends again and to live untill your uncle returnd from Congress, when as tho all her wishes were fullfilld—She cheerfully resignd her Life into the hands of her Maker.

you will be Sent for on Tuesday morning the funeral will be on that day at 3 oclock—

you will acquaint our Friends and Relations in Hingham, with whom I sincerely sympathize under the heavey affliction they have recently experienced.

I am your affectionate and afflicted Grandmother
Abigail Adams

OBITUARY FOR ABIGAIL 2ND

To John Quincy Adams

my dear Son   Quincy August 30th 1813—
your Sons are well. your Parents are still living. your Brother is well—

O my full Heart, shall I wish for Life for her who is releived from pain and Sufferings, which wring my heart with anguish, and was daily increased by the anticipation of Still greater Sufferings? No, I will bless the Being who had compassion for her: and who was pleased to take to the Arms of mercy as I fully beleive, the Dear departed Child, whose loss I weep, but whose death, I consider a blessing to herself—

I have in Several Letters to you by various ways; given some account of her previous illness, which I had considerd Rheumatic, and therefore was not greatly allarmed at it, hoping the warm weather would restore her. In the month of May I received a Letter from Nancy Smith, informing me of a circumstance of which I was before ignorant—your Sister not willing to give pain to her Friends, had kept the Source of all her complaints to herself. having endured one opperation, She found the other breast deeply affected. when the Physician examined it, he gave it as his opinion to her Friends; that the disease was without remedy, having contaminated the whole mass of Blood, and that all her complaints and Sufferings loss of use of Limbs; and pains had arissen from thence. her Life might be protracted, but with an increase of suffering

you will more easily conceive, than I describe the affliction this occasiond us. I had been pleasing myself with the expectation of her passing the time when the col. was in Congress with us—to see her ever again, I now despared of—Yet Such was her earnest desire to be with us—to see again her Parents, and other relatives that She had courage and resolution given her, to be taken from her Bed, and placed in a carriage where after a Journey of 15 days and three hundred miles, She reached her Fathers House upon the 26 day of July attended by her dutifull Children, and her affectionate Sister in Law—

Emaciated, worn down with pain, still she appeard delighted to again embrace her Parents, and feel herself Surrounded with all that Love, respect, and affection could afford.

Immediatly the best medical aid and advice was obtaind, but alass the decree was gone forth—and the Same opinion was confirmd by the Physicians here, and opium was the only paliative, the only releif She could obtain, to releive the spasms which as She described it, cased her up in armour. She told her Physician, that She was perfectly Sensible of her Situation, and reconciled to it, that She was both ready and willing to die.

when she had a temporary ease she was cheerfull, conversing of her Friends abroad, and wishing that She might have Seen them again—altho she was bolsterd up in her Bed & could neither walk or Stand. She was always calm collected, patient, and Submissive—

Her Sufferings were terminated upon Sunday morning the 15 of this Month, just three weeks after her arrival here

Heaven be praised, your Father and I have been Supported through all this Solemn afflicting Scene with fortitude, and I hope christian resignation, but to heal the wound which nature has received, time is necessary, and religion only can give consolation. a day or two previous to her death, She calld for a Hymn Book, and read the 1093 Hymn & turnd the leaf, it is so expressive of her Life, and the turn of her thoughts, that I transcribe it for you, and a Character which appeard in the paper, drawn as I have Since learnd; by a Friend who knew her well—and was not unacquainted with her various changes in Life—

Her Remains were deposited in the family vault from the house of worship, attended by a numerous concourse of Relatives & Friends, as well as others. Mr Whitney in his prayer, did ample Justice to her Life Death and character, and his address to the throne of grace for her absent Son, and Brother was most pathetic—

She was permitted to live untill all her wishes were accomplishd, save that of Seeing her Son again. the week before her death, the col returnd from Congress, where he reluctantly went but she had insisted upon his going—we did not, any of us think that She was so near her end, untill two days previous to it—

I cannot but consider it as the Benignant hand of Providence which Supported her through a journey of Such length, and gave us an opportunity of witnessing her calm resignation, her patient sufferings and her peacefull death.

whilst my full heart bleads, and the recollection deepens my sorrow, I bow Submissive to the heavenly mandate, and ask for you my Son, that consolation which you need, under this additional Stroke of Providence

The amiable Caroline we have adopted to Supply the place of her Mother—whom She nursd through a long and tedious winter, with all the affection and assiduity of fillial piety—and who behaves with all the propriety of more mature years, watchfull of every look of her Father, attentive to every want and care to lessen his loss—John too, when he heard how ill his Mother was quitted his office and buisness in Nyork, and went with all Speed to the Valley, exerted himself to procure every end to assist her upon her journey—and attended her here. having paid the last rights to her Remains, he has returnd again to Nyork. the Col will remain with us, untill congress meet again—

there was one circumstance which added to our Family distress during your Sisters Sickness. Mrs Charles Adams two days after your Sister arrived was seazd with a dangerous disease which for near a fortnight threatned to terminate in a mortification but it happily terminated and she has since gone to the valley with her Sister—

I have written to william So has his Brother his Mother never heard of his marriage, in which we all wish him happiness; we have just heard of the arrival of our Peace Makers at Gottenburgh. No Letters have been received from you of a later date than May.

you will easily Suppose that we are anxious for intelligence—the President of the united States has had a Severe illness, a fever which has brought him low—God grant that he may recover—

I know of no conveyance, but through mr Michell at Halifax by a cartel—and from him to mr Beasley American Agent in England—my Letters will I Suppose be Subject to inspection but as they relate only to Family affliction, I presume they will be permitted to reach you—

My kind Love to my daughter to whom I wrote Some time Since, and gave my Letters to mr Wire, lately appointed Consul to Riga

I am my dear Son with every sentiment of the tenderest Love and affection your afflicted Mother

Abigail Adams

ENCLOSURE

Died in Quincy on Sunday morning August 15th. 1813 Mrs Abigail Smith, consort of the Hon' William S, Smith, of New-york, and only Daughter of his Excellency John Adams, aged

48. Funeral will be this afternoon at 3 oclock, from her Fathers House, when the connections and Friends of the United Families, are respectfully requested to attend the solemnity.

Mrs Smith possessed a mind firm, cultivated and delicate; a temper gentle and sweet; a spirit composed, in difficulty patient, in suffering; humble, in prosperity; cheerful, in adversity; a demeanor chastened and regulated by clear perceptions of duty and high standards of propriety. As a Child, exemplary of filial reverence; as a Wife, for conjugal tenderness: As a Mother, for parental affection.—Forgetful of herself and studious only of the happiness of others, it was the effort of her being to please and support; comfort and to bless.—Her death in unison with such a life, was full of resignation and hope. she departed expressing her strong confidence of a Blessed immortality through the merits of her Lord and Saviour Jesus Christ, and her gratitude that she had been permitted to close her days in the mansion of her Father surrounded by her Venerable parents, her Husband, Children, and dearest relatives.

There are no consolations for the death of such a person, but those which religion proffers. And religion forbids us to lament except on account of the bereavement of friends, the transition of a Spirit so elevated and pure to the places, prepared for its eternal felicity and reward.

> Heaven lifts its everlasting
> Portals high,
> And bids the pure in heart
> Behold their God.—

"A MELANCHOLY LETTER"

To John Quincy Adams

my dear Son   Quincy Sepbr 1813

I have just closed one Letter to you which is to go to Lisbon from thence to the care of mr Beasley. this is to go to France. upon the 30 of August I wrote you a melancholy Letter nor will this be less So. it is allotted to me to be the maven who is to convey to you all the Calamities which afflict our family and they have rooled in wave after wave, the Death of your Dear and only Sister who departed this Life three weeks after she reachd this House; I have detaild to you in various ways by various Letters, and to her Son, more particularly than I think it necessary to repeat. Suffice it to Say that She died as She had lived calm tranquil and resignd, leaving mourning Parents weeping Husband and children to deplore their loss—

To me the loss is irreparable. I contemplate her virtuous Life filld with usefullness—tried by afflictions, which She Sustaind with Silence, borne down by dissapointments which She endured without a murmur, Suffering with firmness and Submitting to a most painfull operation; but alas to little purpose, as the Same calamity again assaild her with accumulating voilence destroyd her Constitution, and Subdued her. I view her in the last Scene with admiration, and prasine up her Patience Resignation and submission as a solace for my woes—

If William has not received Letters, you will communicate tenderly to him this most afflictive event—there have not any Letters been received from you of a later date than May— which I have repeatedly acknowledged

Your Sons are well. they had a fortnights vacation, and enjoyd themselves with a Friend and Schoolmate, whom they invited to pass part of it with them, a son of the mr Bradford who was formerly your Tennant, a very fine Boy—There Grandfather was yesterday to visit them and found them well.

I was much delighted the other day with a visit from mr Woodard who was a Year or two in Russia and whom you noticed. as I enterd the Room, he said this Lady is the Mother of mr J Q Adams. I bowed assent. your Son Madam is very fond of you. he talkd much of you indeed he is very fond of you—I replied that the attachment was reciprical this he said not in a cold formal manner, but with a warmth and ardour as tho he enjoyd what he described—and you may be sure it was a cordial Balm to the Heart of an affectionate Parent

September 13, 1813

"YOU CALLED UPON ME TO TALK OF MYSELF"

To Thomas Jefferson

DEAR SIR   Quincy Sepbr 20th 1813

Your kind and Friendly Letter found me in great affliction for the loss of my dear and only daughter, Mrs. Smith.

She had been with me only three weeks having undertaken a journey from the State of N. York, desirious once more to see her parents, and to close her days under the paternal roof.

She was accompanied by her son and daughter, who made every exertion to get her here, and gratify which seemed the only remaining wish she had, so helpless and feeble a state as she was in. It is wonderfull how they accomplished it. Two years since, she had an opperation performed for a cancer in her breast. This she supported, with wonderfull fortitude, and we flatterd ourselves that the cure was effectual, but it proved otherways. It soon communicated itself through the whole mass of the Blood, and after severe sufferings, terminated her existance.

You sir, who have been called to seperations of a similar kind, can sympathize with your bereaved Friend. I have the consolation of knowing that the Life of my dear daughter was pure, her conduct in prosperity and adversity, exemplary, her patience and resignation becomeing her religion. You will pardon my being so minute, the full Heart loves to pour out its sorrows, into the Bosom of sympathizing Friendship.

A lively only daughter of her Mother, lives to console me.

> "who in her youth, has all that Age required
> And with her prudence, all that youth admired"

You called upon me to talk of myself, and I have obeyed the summons from the assurrance you gave me, that you took an interest in what ever affected my happiness.

> "Greif has changed me since you saw me last,
> And carefull hours, with times deformed hand
> hath written strange defections o'er my face"

But altho, time has changed the outward form, and political

"Back wounding calumny" for a period interrupted the Friendly
intercourse and harmony which subsisted, it is again renewed,
purified from the dross.

With this assurrance I beg leave to subscribe myself your
Friend   ABIGAIL ADAMS

"YOUR PORTRAIT OF FEMALE EXCELLENCE"

To François Adriaan Van der Kemp

DEAR SIR,   Quincy, 3 February, 1814.

EVER since your letter to the President, of December last, I
have had a great inclination to address a letter to Mr. Vanderkemp; and, being now confined to my chamber, by an attack
of the rheumatism, I find a leisure hour to address my friend in
his solitude.

And in the first place, to put him perfectly at his ease, I assure him that I make not any pretensions to the character of a
learned lady, and therefore, according to his creed, I am entitled to his benevolence. I can say, with Gay's hermit,

> "The little knowledge I have gained,
> Is all from simple nature drained."

I agree with Mr. Vanderkemp, that, in declaring his opinion,
he has expressed that of most gentlemen, the true cause of
which I shall trace no farther that that they consider a companion more desirable than a rival. In reading the life of Madame de
Staël, I learn that it was her superior talents and learning, perhaps too ostentatiously displayed, which produced that coldness,
estrangement, and unhappiness, which marred all her pleasure
with the Baron de Staël, soured every domestic enjoyment, and
was the occasion of that sarcastic question to her by the Emperor Bonaparte. Upon some occasion, she had solicited an interview with him, and recommended to him some measure for
him to pursue. He heard her, but made her no other reply than
this; "Madam, who educates your children?"

I like your portrait of female excellence. Solomon has also
drawn one in the character of a virtuous woman; but, if a

sound understanding had not been united with virtuous habits and principles, is it probable that he would have represented the heart of her husband as safely trusting in her? or that he would have derived so much lustre from her character, as to be known in the gates, when he sat with the elders of the land? It is very certain, that a well-informed woman, conscious of her nature and dignity, is more capable of performing the relative duties of life, and of engaging and retaining the affections of a man of understanding, than one whose intellectual endowments rise not above the common level.

There are so few women who may be really called learned, that I do not wonder they are considered as black swans. It requires such talents and such devotion of time and study, as to exclude the performance of most of the domestic cares and duties which exclusively fall to the lot of most females in this country. I believe nature has assigned to each sex its particular duties and sphere of action, and to act well your part, "there all the honor lies."

Have you seen John Randolph's letter, and Mr. Lloyd's reply?

Present me in friendly terms to Mrs. Vanderkemp. Tell her, I wish we were neighbours. I should then have a pleasure which our residence in the country deprives us of, that of the society and converse of a gentleman of taste, science, and extensive information; and, although much of his learning might be above my comprehension, his benevolence, politeness, and urbanity would render it grateful, and be in unison with the good-will and friendship entertained for him by

ABIGAIL ADAMS.

THE BURNING OF WASHINGTON

To John Quincy Adams

My dear Son   Sepbr 7th 1814

I wrote to you on the 26 of August, and sent my Letter to N york to go in a dispatch vessel. I did not at the time know of the Humiliating and disgracefull Catastrophy which had befallen the city of Washington!! nor have I language to describe my feelings at the Torpor which blinded the Government to a sense of their danger, and their defenceless situation

The Capitol is destroyed, but America is not conquerd, and I trust in God that it will not be. when private afflictions assail me by the immediate Hand of heaven I bow with submission to the sovereign will.

But when calimities are brought upon us through want of foresight and energy to repell them—through incapacity of those, who Govern and direct the counsels of the Nation, we have reason to complain. The whole force of Great Britain liberated by the General pacification of Europe, is now leveld against America—and assails us upon every quarter where we are most vulnerable—upon our sea coast, to destroy our cities, and lay waste our Borders appears to be the object of the hostile fleets—to guard them all, so extensive as they are is impossible —and we shall suffer calamities similar to other Nations. you will no doubt receive the British account of the destruction of the Capitol of America and high exultation, yet you who know this City, know that it is but a city in Name in embrio—a wilderness city, thinly inhabited, without a back country to supply a militia and inhabited by slaves, who were as much feard by the inhabitants, as the Enemy who attacked them—

We at this distance have not yet a regular and Authentic narative of the transaction. private property we have heard was Respected—but a general destruction of the public—I cannot enumerate—to the sons of the Fathers who fought & Bled to obtain independence it belongs to inquire. have they fought & Bled in vain? will their ospring renounce their parentage? forbid it Heaven—

I will turn from these painfull scenes to acknowledge with an overflowing heart, the pleasure I received two days since by the receipt of your Letter of the 30th of June from Ghent to receive a Letter only two Months from its date was joy to me, who had not before one of a later date than 1 Feby; to learn that you were well, and left your Family in health, gave a new spring to my spirits—deprest by the calamities of my country and by Bodily Sickness. I will now state to you the Letters received, since I wrote you, No 45 April 7th No 46 May 1st June Letter missing No 48 July 19th August 23d No 49, Sepbr & October missing from the numbers I presume more than one was written in each Month, for the next number received is of Novbr 19th No 53. December 30th No 54 press coppy—Janry 17th No 55 Febry 1st No 56—from thence to No 60, dated June at Ghent all are missing, every line you write is so precious to me that I can ill afford to lose any of your Letters and I do not despair that some of them will yet find there way to me, and now you are so much nearer to me, that I feel the influence in the warmth of the Atmosphere which surrounds me, and in the pulsation of my Heart.—nor can I endure the thought that you should ever again return to the cold Regions of the north. as much as I esteem and respect the Character of its sovereign—I could wish that you was releaved from that mission—that you could send for your Family, and return to your Native Country that I might once again behold you. I shall ask no questions of you respecting your mission—I know with what eagerness every syllable is watchd for and multiplyd—& missaplied, that you should be surrounded with curiosity from various motives is to be expected—it is indeed a time of anxious expectation for our Country—and every Breize that blows comes fraught with tydings which makes us all anxious that peace may again be restord to us—

Newyork is all alive and taking every measure for Defence. Boston is waking from its Lethargy and like the Sleeping Lyon, when chased will manifest its strength. I well know from my own feelings what yours must be, at a distance from your country when surrounded by dangers so thick and sanguinary Yet will they not submit to an Ignominious peace

"I SEE NOT ANY CHANCE FOR PEACE"

To John Quincy Adams

My dear Son   Quincy october 18th 1814
The john Adams arrived last week at Nyork, with mr dallas and brought me your Letters, which have been missing, viz No 57. March 30th No 58 April 28th; No 59 May 12th and August 15th. No 62—I have before acknowledged No 60, June 30th, and upon the 21 of Sepbr 1814 I received your No 50,

just the day year, upon which it was written. My numbers are now nearly compleat, your Letters are all carefully preserved, to be left by me as a Legacy to your Children, and may form in some future day interesting pages in History:

Before you can receive this Letter you will have learnt, the Capture of Washington by Genll. Moss and Cockburn, Moss has since paid the forfeit of his Life, in the attack upon Baltimore

The defeats of the British fleet upon Lake Champlain, and of Genll prove's at Plattsburgh, is marvelous in our Eyes literally it may be said, one Man put a thousand to flight. I inclose you the official Letters of Macdonough & Macomb. Macdonough is from the State of delaware, and mr Bayard may feel proud, that the Same State, gave birth to both of them. Macomb is the Son of mr Macomb of Nyork, who lives in Broad way, and whose second wife, is mrs Rutger, who was in Paris and England when we were there. and whom you no doubt recollect, a young Man of 30. thus has providence raised up to us: Heroes, and champions, to Supply the place of the revolutionary patriots, who fought and bled to obtain that independence, which their ospring must now defend, with their Blood, and treasure. Heaven grant that the Sons, pray prove worthy of their sire's.

From the dispatches received from you and your colleigues, I See not any chance for peace—perhaps it was best that Great Britain Should Show herself, thus haughty, overbearing and Insolent, to unite all parties, in execrating her government, and holding her in as much abhorence as the Exiled Tyrant at Elba, that she has it in her power greatly to distress us; we see, and we feel most heavily, but she must Conquer us before we can submit to such humiliating terms, and by gods blessing. She shall not conquer us: She is sewing the Seeds of hatred and vengance, where harmony, and Friendly intercourse might dwell. we engage at great odds—our best citizens; against her mercenary Troops

Boston is strongly fortified—and the Labour, has been, the free will offering of the Citizens of our Country, of every class, and description; as the Song I inclose, which is literal truth, will show you, not for its poetic Merit, but its truth.

we have had for a month past, about ten thousand Troops

under arms, training and dissiplined, in Boston, and near it, a Company of young men light Infantry to the number of 40 all in uniform from this Small Town are of the number; and about 20 more drafted Militia.

I take it for granted, that you have returnd to St Petersburgh—I shall therefore put my Letters under cover to mr russel, and I must send them off immediatly to go by the mail to the Secretary of State.

I have not time to write to my daughter nor to charles from whom I have recived two pretty Letters. I will do it Soon, tho I fear with little prospect of sending them—

our dear Caroline was married on Sunday Evening the Eleventh of Sepbr and on Monday the 12th. I left me for Newyork. She arrived at mr de wints Seat, calld ceadar grove fishkill the Saturday following, and was affectionately recived by his Mother and Friends.

I have received Letters from her every week, Since. She expresses her intire satisfaction with her situation.

John A Smith, is the orderly Sergant of a company call'd the Iron Greys, formed of the best Blood and families in Nyork. they take their Name from their uniforms.

If William is still with you, remember me affectionatly to him, and to Mrs Smith, I hope they may have the Life of their daughter, and that they will name it for his dear mother, whose last words were, "I shall never see my dear William more."

Mrs James Foster had a daughter born the week before the death of your sister. She named the child Abigail Smith it had the hooping Cough this Summer, and fell a sacrifice to it. the last month it is gone to join its kindred spirit, a Brother whom they named for you, who died about the same Age.

we have been, not a little anxious for your Brothers youngest child, about seventeen months old. who has the hooping Cough is teething, and attacked with the full complaint. We hope however that he is better.

I know Mrs Adams must be anxious to learn something respecting her connexions in washington. I hope they will so inform her. I have written, but have not received any answer to my inquiries. Congress are sitting there, not very easy however.

Your sons went from here this morning, they come home on Saturdays, and remain untill Monday. they are very buisy prepareing for an examination, which is to take place on wednesday

I have so much to say, that I know not when to stop—the fear that I shall not get this ready for the mail obliges me to close

But not without the renewal of my tenderest affection Yours as ever   AA—

DEATH OF MERCY OTIS WARREN

To Caroline Smith De Windt

MY EVER DEAR CAROLINE: Quincy, Oct. 23d, 1814.

If you find as many joyful faces to receive you, as you have left sorrowful hearts behind you, you will have no reason to complain. When upon former occasions you have been separated from me, it was always with the expectation of having you again with me; since I have considered you as mine, you have been to me one of the chief props and supports of my declining years. By your watchful attention, and cheerful readiness to prevent even my wants, you have rendered yourself so necessary to me, as to be the solace of my days. It is natural to feel a privation in proportion to our enjoyments; what then, think you, is the void left in my breast? True, I have other comforts in the faithful and constant attention of Louisa, and the sprightly vivacity of Susan.

Your letter to my venerable friend, Mrs. Warren, was received by me and forwarded to her. "Tell my dear Mrs. Adams to write to me, or to see me very soon, else we only meet in Heaven," was one of the last expressions of your departed friend, my ever to be respected mother. Thus writes her son to me upon the 19th: "Upon the 18th the imprisoned spirit ascended from the decayed and ancient fabric. She had but a few days of suffering."

I may with truth say, that take her all in all, we shall not look upon her like again. String after string is severed from the heart; the lamp of life burnt bright to the last. Dr. Freeman told me she wrote him a letter upon the 6th of the present month, when she entered her 87th year. I rejoice that you visited her; your remembrance of her will always be pleasant. Seldom does old age wear so pleasing, so instructive an aspect. To me she was a friend of more than fifty summers ripening.

Yesterday completed half a century since I entered the married state, then just your age. I have great cause of thankfulness that I have lived so long, and enjoyed so large a portion of happiness as has been my lot. The greatest source of unhappiness I have known in that period, has arisen from the long and cruel separations which I was called in a time of war, and with a young family around me, to submit to.

My pen runs on, "but," as the gallant Adam said to Eve, "with thee conversing I forget all time."

That you and the rest of my posterity may enjoy as large a share of felicity as has fallen to me, is the sincere wish and prayer of your affectionate grandmother,   A. A.

BATTLE OF NEW ORLEANS

To Elizabeth Smith Shaw Peabody

My dear Sister   Quincy Feb'ry 26th 1815
    your Letter of Feb'ry 15th, lies yet unacknowledged

My Spirits have been in a whirl, the intelligence from new orleans, of the total defeat of the British forces, with the circumstance of Such Slaughter amongst the assailants, and Such unheard of protection of our Troops, ought Surely, by every *Moral* and *Religious* people, to be asscribed unto that Being, unto whom we pray, to "teach our hands to war, and our fingers to fight," and unto whom if there is any gratitude, in our Hearths, we ought to asscribe praise, and thanks giving

The temple of Janus is closed, with our green laurels around the Brows of genll. Jackson, who with consumate Skill planed and led on his Brave Army, to defend, in concert with the inhabitants, the Territory of New orleans, a Name immortalized in History. May the vanquished Brittons, learn humanity from their conqueror and respect for their Enemies.

While the joy occasiond by this Signal Smile of providence

upon our Arms, was Still vibrating in our Ears, and thrilling in our hearts, the Still more gratefull, and pleasing intelligence reachd us, that we might beat our Swords into plough Shares, and our Spears into pruning hooks, for that peace was restored to our Land! This news so unnexpected as to Time, "flew upon the wings of the Wind" and in the words of Shakspeare we might Say

> "Now is the Winter of our discontent
> Made glorious Summer by the Men of Ghent"

Joy beamed from every countenance and every tongue, resounded with, peace, peace, May we use it, as we are directed to use the world, without abusing it—

of all the States in the union New England has the least reason to complain. if any of her rights are brought into question or abridged, to her want of National feeling to her various contracted policy, to her misconduct in the war, to her turbulent factious party Spirit, and her open and avowed hostility to the National Government, She may asscribe it.

If Says my A. She had been true to herself, Great Britain would not have dared to hang the issue of peace or war, upon two points which he names, but which I am not at liberty to state, and which if they had not finally agreed to leave to future negotiation, he would have persisted, in refusing his Signature to the Treaty.

Great Harmony subsisted between him and his Colleigues, and upon most points they were unanimous. May the Blessing of the Peace Makers be theirs, but I know it will not, and there will be found discontented partizens to find fault & condemn, every measure however wise just and upright, while they have not the supreem command. for this "is a lust in Man, no charm can tame"

Mr Adams writes me, that he Should go to Paris in about ten days and Send to mrs Adams to join him there, that he Should wait there for further orders from the President.

I know pretty well what his destination was to be, if peace took place—Alass! Alass Shall I never See him again

It is a Singular circumstance in our Family History, that both Father & Son Should make peace with the Same nation at the distance of 30 years.

Your query upon buisness I have not replied to; I think you had better empower your Son to purchase Some Stock for you as your agent. I hope he will secure to himself some real estate. I will converse with him upon the Subject. pray write to me for your Letters always do good to Your affectionate Sister

Abigail Adams

All my Family request a kind remembrance to yours—

To Thomas Baker Johnson

Dear Sir   Quincy March 3d 1815
I congratulate you sir, from my Heart I congratulate my Country, upon the blaize of Glory, achieved by the valient General Jackson, and the copatriots, and troops, under his command in the defence of New orleans.

I have not been indifferent, or insensible to the Great, and most importent transactions which have given to New orleans the first Rank in our hemisphere, and made her a blazing Star upon our Shield. It requires the pen of a Homer to do justice to her deed's In the language of ossian I ask

"Can we forget thee, our valient warriors,
  or thy path of fire in the field?
 upon the Soul of the Fair come the deeds of the mighty
    in Arms
 Be the warrior rememberd in peace when
 Echoing shields are heard no more"

Altho the Youngest Sister, of the union, she has surpasst her Elder sisters in Arms, in vigor and activity, and some of them in patriotism. altho a Native of one of the Eldest, I bear testimony against her stuborn opposition to a just, and necessary War.

I would feign draw a veil, over conduct which I must con-demn; and which when recorded by the faithfull Historian will shade her former Lustre. would, that I had, a Leteran fountain to wash out her Shame.

The transports of Joy, with which the defeat of our Enemy; and the victory of New orleans was received had not ceased to vibrate upon our Ears, before the news of peace came with healing upon her Wings, and hushed the cannons Roar and Sheathed the warriors Sword, directing us to train our weapons of war, into implements of Husbandry.

The news of Peace exhilirated all hearts, and every countanance beamed with joy, and while Humanity mournd over the Enemy Slain, justice considerd them as victims, sacrificed upon the Alter of Ambition.

The temple of Janus is once more closed and long may it remain so.

Some of our Friends and connections will now return to their Native Land

Mr Adams has written me that he should go to Paris, and there send for your sister from St Petersburgh to meet him. it lies with the president to direct his Return—

your Brother and Sister Smith have been at Ghent, waiting since Sep'br for a passage home

I expect them in the Neptune with their Infant, a fine baby as mr A Says.

When ever you visit your Friends at Washington, it will give me pleasure if you would extend your visit to Quincy, where you may be assured of a sincere and friendly welcome from Sir Your Friend   Abigail Adams.

MINISTER TO GREAT BRITAIN

To John Quincy Adams

My Dear Son   Quincy March 8th 1815

yesterdays Mail brought us the Nominations to foreign Courts, yours of course, was to England. altho no event could have been so agreable to me, as your return to America. I feel a relief that you have left the cold region of the North; and come so much nearer to me, where I can hope, with the return of peace, a freer intercourse with you, the only solace left me, to compensate for your absence, which I hope will not exceed an other year.

According to your request; I shall prepare your sons to go to you, as soon as the Season will give us a prospect of a favorable passage. I feel as old Jacob did, When he said "and will you take Benjamin also?"

George has grown to Mans Nature, and like all overgrown Boys—he does not know, how to use his Limbs—he is quite a companion, with a very amiable disposition I think, ready to listen to reason, and advise. his Grandfather will miss him very much

I consider it an opportunity which may be of great utility, to him: John is ardent, active zealous full of fire and spirit, which requires a steady hand to direct, but he has not that eager desire for Literature, which is Georges meat and drink; he is too volatile for it, George feels some qualms at the thought of leaving us, and John thinks it will be very hard. they cannot however feel as I do, when I think that I shall see their faces no more.

I have written to you once since the News of peace, by a mr. Wright, Son of Deacon Wright of Boston who sails for Liverpool. this is to go by Captain Glover of this Town—The Favorite was the vessel which bore the olive Branch to us—and never was peace haild with greater Enthusiasm, and demonstrations of Joy—in every State from which I have heard—no one Stoped to inquire, What Were the terms of the Treaty? The dispatches which had been previously published had convinced them, that it could not be a dishonorable one to America. Such was their confidence in the Negotiaters—and in their Hearts in the Administration, although they will not allow it; The junto say—mr Madison has given up all that he declared War for, Sailors Rights, paper—Blockade and some say, our Rights to fish, as by the peace of 1783. this last is however questiond. I have seen most of the federal papers, and altho they will not praise, they do not censure; the unanimous vote of the Senate, and its speedy ratification; is proof enough; that it is consider'd an honorable peace—

If the success of our Arms at New orleans had been previously known, at the time the peace was made, we might perhaps have obtain more advantageous terms, the News of peace following immediately after the glorious Victory obtain at New Orleans, exalted mr Madison, and placed him upon high ground, while the destruction of the Capital, is almost forgotten, in the Union, and stimulous which it gave to our Armies; and the Success, which has ever since followed them—

I presume the British Will not call the loss of four or five thousand Men, and their retreat to their Shiping with the dead Bodies of their commander in chief, and other Gen'lls a Victory. While we cannot count, one Man to a hundred, in all that were wounded or Slain; upon our side—it was a defence, and a Victory with all the circumstances attending it, which has not its like!

The Transit arrived last week. by it I received your Letter of 24th december: mr Huges was much surprizd when he came; to find that he was not the first to bring the Treaty, but that it had not only arrived: but was ratified, and returnd, and all the public exhibitions of rejoicing Balls illuminations &c were over—

I shall be anxious to learn that mrs Adams and Charles have arrived—your Brother has been writing to you, and your Father says he will—he has written by mr Wright. we are all in comfortable Health.

Your affectionate Mother   A Adams—

DEATH OF ELIZABETH SMITH SHAW PEABODY

To Stephen Peabody

My dear afflicted Friends   Quincy April 11th 1815

By the Agony of your own Bosoms you can judge of the affliction of mine, at the Sudden, and unexpected Stroke, which has deprived you, my Brother of the best of wives, and her dear Children of the most tender and affectionate of Parents. Her only Sister, of the last bond of union, of the ancient Stock; the last ligament which bound her to Earth. her Sex are deprived of one of the purest examples, of Conjugal Maternal, and Sisterly affection, united with universal Benevolence, and a conscientious discharge of every christian virtue.

My full heart could pour forth an ever ending Strain, while

my Selfish Sorrow would have wished, to have detained her longer upon Earth.

unto that Being, in whom She trusted as her consolation and Support, under all the trials of Life, I commend you my dear Friends, and Relatives, praying that we may each of us find that consolation which is never refused to those who ask in Sincerity

My own feeble State of health, and weakness of Lungs, has prevented me from attending the Remains of the dear departed Saint to the Tomb.

The President Louissa and Susan were prepared to Set out this morning, when the Rain, and excessive bad roads discouraged them—

altho not personally present, our Hearts are with you

affectionatly your Sympathizing and afflicted Sister and Aunt,   Abigail Adams—

"I AM LEFT ALONE"

To Louisa Catherine Adams

My dear Daughter   Quincy April 14th 1815

I address you, altho I know not where to find you, which is, and has been a source of much anxiety to me, four months have elapsed since the signature of the Treaty of Peace; when mr Adams wrote from Ghent, that in ten day's, he should go to Paris, and from thence, send on to St petersburgh, to request you to join him there, and if he should, (as was expected,) be sent to England, that your Sons might be Sent to join their parents there. Altho Since the 27th of december, no letter has reached us from him. We have in compliance with his request, prepared the Children to meet you.

I need not Say, how painfull there seperation from me will be. Age, infirmities, and many recent afflictions, which I have met, in the Death of many near and dear Friends, and relatives, have broken me down, and give me little reason, to boast myself of tomorrow, as I know not, what a day may bring forth, So that when they go from me it is with the painfull Idea; that

I shall see their faces no more, may we all finally meet in a better world.

The Sudden death, of my dear and only Sister the last week; has opened every wound affresh, and caused my tears to flow anew—George and Susan, are now gone to Atkinson, to pay the last tribute of Respect, to her remains.

She went to Bed on Saturday night well except a Slight Soar throat, which she complaind of, having read two sermons in the evening's about 12 oclock she awoke, complaind that She was chill'd and oppresst upon her lungs. Mr Peabody rose, call'd up a Maid Servant. Abbe also got up, sent for the doctor, Who soon came, but found the spirit had taken Wing, Without the knowledge or least suspicion of her attendents.

So tranquil was her exit; so few her sufferings, a translation from this earthly abode, to the mansions of glorified Spirits, her whole Life was one continued Series of usefull Services. and her circle was rendered extensive by the many youths, of both Sexes, committed to her care, She always considerd her charge, to extend beyond, food, and raiment, to their minds, to their manners, and to their Morals. Many, very Many Youths, have cause to embalm her memory in their hearts, and to hold her in gratefull remembrance. To her Family—I cannot estimate her loss. her Husbands Heart Safely trusted in her, for she had done him good, all the days of her Life. she was his pride, his glory, and his crown.

To me, She was most dear, and now I am left alone; the Sole Surviving branch from the parent Stock.

I had flatterd myself, with the hope that my Son, with his Family, are convened together in his Native Country, would have once more blessed my Eyes. I now despair of it, and the only consolation remaining to me, for his continuence abroad, is his having changed climates, and comeing so much nearer to me, that I may hear frequently from him, and from you, who I hope will feel yourself invigorated by the Air of your Native soil. and meeting with your sons, So long absent from you, in a period of their Lives, When they have almost grown out of your knowledge—George's growth has been so rapid, that it has given him a Rusticity; which he feels—he Scarcly knows what to do with himself. but his mind is a Casket, which contains jewels, that only want culling, refine-ing, and burnishing, in his Fathers Crucible to render them bright—John is quick at comprehension, ardent in pursuit: may be drawn to what you please, but liable to be cast away, without watchfull attention. I trust they have not imbibed any bad habits—

I have not been profuse with their cloathing, Broadcloth has been so very high in price, up to 15 dollars pr yd, that I have had only one suit a peice for them, tho the peace reduced the price to 9 or 10 dollars pr yd, it is still out of reason. they have ordinary cloth for their Sea trip. I had them made a day new shirts, flannels & draws &c every thing which I conceived would be wanting, untill they Should reach you, and mr Perkins has promised to supply any wants they may have, untill they can meet their Father.

Mr Everett the Brother of Alexander is a passenger with them, and a mr Ticknor, a Young Gentleman held in high estimation by our literary Gentleman—

I have Sent to your Friends at Washington, and they have forwarded Letters for you, which I commit to the care of the Children. I did not know when mr Boyd went, or I Should not have omitted So good an opportunity of writing.

Louisa & Susan desire to be affectionatly remembered to you, write to me my dear Daughter, and tell me all your adventures. I long to hear of your safe arrival with that of our dear Charles, either in Paris or England—which would cheer the Heart of your affectionate and afflicted Mother

Abigail Adams.

GEORGE AND JOHN JOIN THEIR PARENTS

To Louisa Catherine Adams

My Dear Daughter   Quincy May 9th 1815
    It was with great pleasure, that I received your Letter from St. Petersburgh, bearing date july the 10th 1814 forwarded by mr Smith and your Sister, who from a combination of circumstances were detaind abroad: untill the 2d of May 1815 when they happily arrived in N york—bringing with them the

pleasing, intelligence that you had reach'd Paris—the day after
they left it—

I cannot describe to you—the releif which this circumstance
has given me, from the anxiety I experienced upon your account, from the Time, when I learnt, that mr Adams, could
not return to you through the winter. I thank Heaven you
have escaped from that cold Northern Region with your
Lives,—and that you are placed in a Situation more conjenial,
to your personal feelings and happiness. you will I hope be
blest with the Sight of your Dear Sons, before this reaches
you—I anticipate the pleasure, you will mutually experience in
your interview with them. may they prove to you all your
fondest wishes hope, and expect. as School Boys, they want,
the polish of the world. they have a diffidence, natural and becomeing in youth.

I fully agree with you, in opinion respecting, propriety of
behaviour, and the weight which true politeness caries with it.
I rank it amongst the virtues. its influence upon the manners is
constant and uniform. how many fine tallents have been lost to
the world, merely through a deficiency of good Breeding, a
proper Respect and deference for the opinions of others, and a
modest distrust of their own. a mere Singularity of speaking, or
walking, constructed in youth, is injurious to a Man, through
his whole Life. a Student is Seldom free from some peculiarity,
unless he mixes much in the World, and associates with polite
company. nor can "Good Sense" which Pope tells us "only is
the Gift of Heaven"

"And tho no Science, fairly worth the Seven," compensate
for the want of good Breeding, Dear George can tell you, how
many lessons, and admonitions, he has received upon Subjects
of a Similar kind, untill his impatience would Some times break
out; yet they had their influence in time, and he was convinced
they were all lessons of Love.

Since your Letter was written Great Changes have taken
place in the Civilized World, and for a Short time we welcomed
Halcyon Days, of peace, restored to the warring Nations.

Peace in America; was received with unfeigned, and universal joy—altho She was at that time, triumphing with victory,
conquering both by Sea, and Land, exhalting our National
Character and humbling her Enemy. the war is happily termi-

nated, leaving to us Commanders both by Land, and Sea, whose Bravery Courage, intrepidity & Skill, have been, only exceeded, by their Benevolence, and Humanity to the conquerd. they have coverd themselves with Glory, effaced former Stains and crowned their Country with honour, quietly returnd to their Homes and reassumed the impliments of Husbandry, for the weapons of war—

The tumult has ceased—but the waves have not wholy Subsided—whilst you are deputed in the Character of a Frindly power. you must as Christians forgive, tho you are not enjoind to forget the injuries, which have been so wantonly inflicted upon an unoffending Nation. O Britain! how art thou fallen, from a warlike to a petty plundering Nation—The desolated Infant Capitol of America will rise from its ashes against thee! Science and literature will point the finger of Scorn at thy Gothick deeds, and Modesty veil her face, and curse the voilater!

My Son has a difficult part assignd him. on the one hand, he cannot but feel what his Country has endured, and Britain must feel that She has been foild a Second time; and that as it were by Hereditary descent. She must receive as an Ambassador of Peace, the Son of the Father who was instrumental in Severing the two Countries, and afterward in Representing the Sovereignty of that Same Country to the Kingdom of great Britain. it is a Singular Instance. I know not however any man, beter Calculated to fullfill the Duties assignd him, with Credit to himself and honour to his Country—

now the intercourse between the two Countries is free, write to me often, and keep me informd, not only what is passing of a public Nature, but of your domestic arrangements, in which I Shall feel, more than ever interested, now you have all your children with you.

My Letter from mr Adams of Janry and Febry are missing, or I Should have had Some information respecting both his and your movements, but from 24 december, untill 19th of March we heard not a word, and sufferd much anxiety for you—

My Letters by George to you, and to his Father together with his own account, will inform you of the affliction I have recently experienced, and which I do not wish to renew by a fresh recital.

you have been an Eye witness to transactions which put all human calculation at defience. we may truly Say we know not what a day will bring forth. I most devoutly pray, that we may not be again entangled in the webb, or bitten, by the Tarantula.

Louisa and Susan desire to be kindly rememberd to you, and to the Children for whom they cherish a Sincere regard.

Shall I ever See you all again? is a question too painfull for me to reflect upon, without watering my paper with my tears, yet half the blessing is granted me, by having you So much nearer— To Your affectionate Mother

Abigail Adams

REQUESTED APPOINTMENT FOR GRANDSON

To Dolley Madison

Dear Madam   Quincy May 14th 1815

My Grandson William Stuben Smith, having returnd from abroad, declines the honour which I have been informd, was intended him by the President, as secretary of Legation, to the Mission to England. His Brother, John Adams Smith, has written to me; to request of the President, the appointment, if he Should deem it proper to grant it to him.

As Congress do not allow a private Secretary to their Foreign Ministers, they are placed in rather a dissagreable Situation, if a Secretary of Legation is appointed, who is a Stranger to them, and in whom they may not be able to place a confidence.

Mr Smith who will have the honour to deliver you this Letter, has been Educated to the Bar, is a young Gentleman of correct principles, and by no means addicted to dissipation.

unaccustomed to ask favours of this Nature for Friends or connections—I have the matter addrest you Madam, than the President, altho I have never had the pleasure of a personal accquaintance with you, that I may thus introduce myself to you, and embrace the opportunity of expressing my esteem for

your Character, and respect for the President, and with these
Sentiments I Subscribe myself your Humble Servant

Abigail Adams

"THIS LITTLE HISTORY OF THEIR CHARACTERS"

To John Quincy Adams

my dear Son   Quincy May 20th 1815
   This day compleats five weeks since my dear Boys embarked
for Liverpool, and now I anticipate their arrival and your, and
their Mothers joy at the prospect of meeting them. if it is equal
to the pain I felt at parting with them, I can wish you no
greater enjoyment. My Reason and judgment, both approved
of their going to you, for they were approaching an Age, when
more vigilance was necesary, to gaurd their Morals, and protect their innocences, than was, or could be in the power, of
advanced Age, to afford. Caution, advice, even precept and
example, are but weak barriers, against the ardour of youth,
the warmth of passion, and the allurements of pleasure.
   George had set his mind upon entering colledge this year.—I
thought him too young, too premature in his growth for his
Age, and that his unripened judgment, would Subject him to
become the prey, of every artfull designer, and Such you know
there are in all Societies—a mind like Georges, ever active requires no common Share of vigilance, and attention to direct it
Right
   It is an observation of a judicious writer, that if we expect
Boys, Should make valuable Men, they must continue, Some
time, in the State of Boys; or they will never make men worth
forming," it is further Said, that against learning, against talents of any kind, nothing can Steady the Head, unless the
heart is fortified with real Christianity. in raising the Moral
edifice, we must Sink deep in proportion as we build high—
Great thoughts make great minds.
   in our New England States, Rank is less thought of and
practised than in any other part of the union. No Native white

American will permit himself to be call'd a Servant, or acknowledge a Master. being the yeomanary of the Country, they consider their Rulers as the work of their own hands and as they really are; dependent upon them, for the power they possess—from hence arrises that familiarity in Society, between the rich and the poor; which levels distinction. Not so in Europe—upon this head, you will find it necessary to put the Children upon their gaurd, and to watch over them, as it respects any familiarity with Domesticks—

George has by *hereditary descent* an unrivalled passion for Books. I Should have Supposed that his Grandfathers and your Library would have Satisfied him—but Sometimes he would contract a debt upon that Score.

John, not having lived with you, and being younger, Reads and learns, and plays, as other School Boys do—in Some of his habits, he is more correct, than his Brother. I never knew him contract, even a Small debt, without knowing that he had the means to discharge it. he has a little too much, confidence in himself, and independence, where experience is necessary. I am not a convert to Rousseau plan of Education. in the very Warmth, and impetuosity, of his character I perceive the germ of the most excellent qualities—under your watchfull care, and Study of their different tallents: I have no doubt they will prosper—God grant: they may prove worthy of their Ancestors—

In this little history of their Characters, you will perceive my anxiety for them, not any distrust of Your ability to guide and direct them. George has a profound respect for You. John very tender feelings.

I fear, *now you* are so *near to me* I shall tax you too heavily—with my Letters—

you are so punctual and regular in your Correspondence, and abroad at So eventfull a period of the civilized world, and upon the very Theatre of action, that I am loth to relinquish a Single Letter from you. that from Paris of the 21st of Febry was peculiarly interesting, and personally So. it brought to recollection Scenes of "olden Times" The Family interview, between, the Marquis Le Fayette, at Count de Tracy's with all the Groupe you describe assembled to See the man, who had interested himself, and obtain a partial liberation of one of the Family, held as a prisoner in a Foreign Country; together with recollections, of former kindness renderd the Same Family, when Prisoners, which no doubt was felt by the Marquiss, altho in your Letter you do not even allude to it—

> "Mercy is twice blest. it blesseth him that Gives and him that takes"

How much more gratefull are the feelings, which Spring from benevolence and kindness to our fellow Creatures, than all the triumphs of conquerors

I have been much interested in your visit to Madam de Stael. I have been reading her Germany and think it the best of all her Works; which I have read. it is in high reputation here: and much read.—The original of the Letter which you wrote from St Petersburgh in March 1812, giving an account of your interview with her there; never came to hand and the press coppy was So faint, as to render it almost impossible to decypher it. it was laid by for Several months, hopeing to receive the original: when we found it did not come. Susan who has much perseverance, as well as curiosity; assisted by Caroline, and the help of a looking Glass—picked out most of it, and I took it down a few paragraphs are wholy lost. viz your replie to her question "whether you thought it right that America Should declare war against England?" if you have leisure, I Should like an accurate coppy of that Letter. your Letter of Jan'ry from Brussells has not arrived—the packet in which I presume it was Sent, was lost at Sea—

I have also to request coppies of the 3d and Seventh of these Letters Addrest to George upon the Bible, they never arrived.

I have already written to you acknowledging your Letter of 19 & 20th March, Since which date we have not received any further accounts. I can only observe that the wrath, and bitterness, So lavishly bestowed upon the Emperor of France, has Subsided in a great degree. astonishment, Awe, and even a Respect for his tallents, his courage, his dareing enterprize has paralized all Parties. the Clergy know not how to pray about him. for him, few orisons are offerd. alass, allass, most of our N England Clergy have been, Ignorant Guides, leading the Blind, taking their opinions from party Newspapers, party Pamphlets, and English Partizens amongst us—to their dishonour, and disgrace, they have published against the President the administration and the Government as Many Bulls as the Popes against Heriticks. Cobbets Sausy letter addrest to them, contains too much truth, and in grose language, but it is even Surpast by that of Some of our Clergy. to my great Regreet, that teachers of Religion should so far forget the Precepts of their divine master, to Respect Rulers—and to live Peacably with all Men

My Paper leaves me only room to Say that I am your affectionate mother   A Adams

"BY WAY OF AMUSEMENT"

To François Adriaan Van der Kemp

Dear Sir   Quincy 26 May 1815
In the absence of your good Lady and daughter, whom I congratulate upon their excursion, I thought it a debt of Friendship to address a few lines to you by way of amusement, and in the first place I must exhort you to cultivate a cheerfullness of mind, which doeth good like a medicine. surely You are too much of a Phylosopher and a christian, to let the "Rubs and Stings of outrageous fortune" deprive you of that Serenity of mind which retrospect of a Life pure and unblameable before God and Man affords you—was it not for the enjoyment of civil and Religious Liberty that you resignd your establishments and quitted your Native Land, to become an inhabitent of this Still freer Country? and are you not daily doing good as you have opportunity. If a field is not opend to you for the improvement of your ten talents; more will not be required of you than is given, why then my good Sir do you So often Suffer the glooms of imagination to take Such fast hold of you? the facitious Pindar upon some occasion wrote thus

> Care to our Coffin adds a nail, no doubt
> And every grin So merry draws one out
> I own I like to laugh and hate to Sigh
> and think that visibility was given
> For human happiness; by gracious heaven
> And that we came not into Life to Cry;

"enjoy, be lively, innocent adore
And know that hea'n hath not one Angle more,
In concequence of groaning nuns and friars"

This is agreable to that admonition in the Scriptures which bids us rejoice always again I say rejoice—yet there are Seasons in human Life when we are calld upon to mourn as well as rejoice. such has been my portion, and my call—over the grave of my dear and only Sister, the Mother of mr Shaw whom you well know. Suddenly taken out of Life, tho always of a delicate constitution and feeble Frame. no sickness had recently assaild her, but wakeing from Sleep—a Sudden oppression upon her lungs Seizd upon her, with the Chill of death, and her pure Spirit without a Struggle assended to her Maker,—to me dear sir the Shock was great indeed, but her Life and character were Such as will be held in durable remembrance and upon her Tomb Stone might be engraved the Epitaph which Pope rote upon a Ladys—

under neath this stone doth lie
as much virtue as could die
which when alive did vigor give
To as much virtue occurred live

in the words of her disconsolate husband, I have known her many Years, and under many trying circumstances. I think She was as near perfection as human nature could attain to. this Dear Sister it has pleased heaven to take from me, and tho her death is most keenly felt by me, and She was Several years younger, I consider her as more worthy the inheritance She possesses, a fitter being for the Society of the blessed—and that I am permitted a longer Sojourn to fullfill Some duty, to repent of Some omission or commission, to releive Some wants to correct Some errors to Sooth Some anguish; and happy Should I be if in this effort of Friendship I could dispell Some of that Gloom which appears to overshaddow the mind and distress the heart of mr vanderkemp

Thus may all those dear Friends who have gone before us and we who are Soon to follow rise to a happy life of immortality in the day of final retribution, thus prays your Friend

A Adams

GILBERT STUART

To Abigail Adams Shaw

My dear Neice   Quincy June 6th. 1815
    Your Letter of May 28th, I received and Should Sooner have replied to it, but was in hopes to have seen your Brother, and have consulted with him. he did not come up on Sunday as I expected.

    I have Seen mrs Foster, and paid the three dollars and half, which was all that was due to her from you, She having past the Nyork [   ] which you gave her. There remains 34 dollars [   ] to your order, which if you have not occasion for, I should advise you, to ask your Brother to vest in Treasury Notes. these Notes bear an Interest of 2½ per cent, and may be had under par, So that Should you want to Sell them in future you will be no looser. I believe they will give to their full value on time. I shall however wait, untill I hear again from you.

    I have had a melancholy, and yet delightfull pleasure, in viewing at Stuarts the admirable likeness of your beloved Mother, and my dear Sister. he has finished it, and it is so like; so her, very character. And you will contemplate it, with reverence, respect and veneration, [   ] with all those tender emotions, which so correct, a view of her features must inspire. I was temped to apply to Stuart the lines addrest to the memory of the Great painter Mr [   ].

> "Stuart by Heaven, and not a master taught
> Whose Art was nature, and whose pictures thought"

    I rejoice that She was prevaild upon to Sit for her portrait. it will be more precious to her Friends who Survive her, than if it had been taken in the prime and vigor of youth. That which was twenty years past, taken for me, Serves only to remind me of the ravages of time, and the decays of Nature, the Image of time past, my grandchildren will never know it, nor the present question.

    Mr JQA has Several times written to request his Father to Sit to Stuart for his likeness by the persuasion of your Brother, who is getting a copy of one formerly taken by him he has consented, and I have accompanied him three days for the [   ], I think Stuart will be happy in his likeness, altho nine years dear than I am, he retains his continuance with better than I do.

I have not received any Letters from abroad by the late arrivals from England. mr Adams went, from Ghent to paris, to remain there, untill he should receive dispatches from his own Government, and these vessels saild from England before he could have received his Commission as Minister to that Court.

Beleiving that you would like to read his Letters, two of which, contain some particulars of an event So wonderfull in its Nature, so unprecedented in History, as to astonish the world, to which he was an Eye witness. I inclose them to you, with a request, that you would carefully return them to me, by the next Mail.

I hear very frequently from Caroline whom, I expect to make me a visit, this month. from Abbe, I hear but Seldom, nor from her Mother often. Susan writes very frequently and Some times gets a [   ].

I am forgetfull, but I beleive I wrote you that William, his wife and child, went with Caroline to the Seat of mr De wints Mother, call'd cedar Grove, and that They are Still there.

Remember me to your worthy parent could you not prevail upon him to make us a visit with you? we Should be rejoiced to see him, pray tell him so. but if he cannot come why not you? Remember me to miss Foster. I respect her, not only for her own worth, but for her kindness to you in your affliction—

Mr and Mrs Foster with all their children came out last week; they left Charles and James to keep Election with us. they will return this week; Susan went yesterday to Boston. your cousin Louisa desires to be remembered to miss Foster, and to you.

I am my dear Neice yours affectionate Aunt

Abigail Adams

ENGLISH SOCIETY

To Louisa Catherine Adams

My Dear daughter   Quincy Sepbr 2d 1815—
Your Letter of July 9th was joyfully received by me, it was not untill your Letter arrived, that I had any certain knowledge where you were, altho I had presumed from mr Adams Letter of 19 March from Paris, that you might have reachd there, the day after your Sister Smith left it.

It grieves me to Say to you, that she has, had a Severe trial and affliction since she arrived in America, in the loss of her dear Infant, Born under your patronage, and a daughter, you must have had for it, a strong attachment, and will sympathize with her, under this berevement, I do not know whether I ought to regret, not having seen it, as it would have been an agravation to my son an for its loss.

Caroline dewint, was here upon a visit at the time, which she regreted, as your Sister had not any female friend with her as a relation, but she found kind friend's in those who were not so by kindred

If you remain abroad, I hope the government will allow an outfit, I do not see how you can decently appear without, but they cannot form any Idea of its necesity, or how much the honor and dignity of the Country requires it.

The society You describe, is very similar to what it always has been. I found it so, when under similar circumstances I resided there; distant haughty and unpolite.

We must allow Something for their feelings, humbled as they really are, in the Eyes of all Europe, at the triumphs and victories obtain over them, by land, and by sea. It is only Americans who forgive their Enemies, and Hug them too!

there is very little Friendship, or cordiality in the polite circles, you find much more of it, in the country, in the middle walks of Life.

By the King I was always treated politely, I cannot say so much in favour of her Majesty. I despised, and looked down upon her, and as seldom as decency, and the duty I owed to my country requird gave her an opportunity of displaying her Airs.

I have a curiosity of knowing something of the said princess of Salm whom the Duke of Cumberland has married,—as so much freedom has been used in the House of commons, with both their Characters, it will not be any slander, to relate what has given so much disgust to the Royall Family. can it be any thing worse then his hopefull Brothers have pratised?

Alas Alas! poor France, how will order spring out of confusion, how many more humane victims must be offerd up before tranquility will succeed?

what will England; or the Allies dare to do with Napolean. must not his person be held sacred by the Laws to which as a prisoner of war he has Surrenderd?

I should not have feard him, if he had come to America, but it was fortunate that he did not. it would have caused a good deal of warmth, and excited much party Spirit.

at present we are tranquil Electioneering for the presidency has not yet commenced—mr Madison is so popular that he might be reelected if he chose to retain the Station. I think mr Munroe will be the candidate who will carry the vote. I wish mr Dexter might be chosen for Vice President.

I hope you will continue to write to me frequently, the Letter before me disproves your assertion, "that you are not a good correspondent," and you must permit me to be a judge in this case by adding my testimony to that of the letter, which does great honor to the writer

need I add my assurance of the affection and attachment with which I am your Mother   Abigail Adams

"MR MUNROE WILL BE OUR NEXT PRESIDENT"

To John Quincy Adams

My dear Son   Quincy December 2d 1815
This Letter will derive some merit from its being the latest date, and I hope will reach you soon. it comes to inform you that mr Tarbel has Letters for you—your Father has given you his opinion respecting the publication of the extract of his Letter to dr price by mr Morgan. I send you the copy from the

original and am ready to ask mr Morgan, in the words of the play. "who was the dupe?" with respect to George, I think with you if you go to London; You will find it necesary to place him where he can receive the systematic instruction of a School.

Our Fisheries have been more productive this year, than they ever were before; most plentifull fares made, and I have not heard of any molestation of any of them, except one or two Smuglers.

our university at Cambridge is growing very rich, the donations to it, the last year, are said to amount to more than and hundred thousand dollars—20 thousand for the Greek professorship 20 thousand given by mr parkman, Count Rumford Donation, and mr Abial Smiths 25 thousand, make a handsome sum.

You will mourn with Dr Waterhouse in the loss he has sustaind, by the death of mrs Waterhouse. She had been in a decline, a consumption for more than a year. She was a very valuable woman, and has left an amiable Family—

Mr Hall sent your Letter to him, to your Father to read. I find by your observations and remarks in it, that you See most of our Newspapers, and pamphlets—and you have not spaired the wise Men of the East, who are pretty well ashamed I should think of their conduct, the peace came at a fortunate moment, to save them from further disgrace. and perhaps the Nation from civil war. Boston most assuredly would have been laid in ashes. God be praised that it did not come to such an extremity

I think mr Munroe will be our next president, who will be vice P. is more problematical—

We are in our usual health, but four score years, are not to be relied upon, more than three score and ten. the depredations of time are daily visible, and not less more seen than felt.

With gratitude I would acknowledge the Blessings which remain, both of hearing and Seeing. I pray that I may never be a cumberor of the Ground.

While I live in possesion of my faculties my heart will beat, with Love and affection for you and yours,   A Adams

My Love to mrs Adams, mrs Tarbel has Letters for her.

DEATH OF COTTON TUFTS

To John Quincy Adams

My Dear Son   Quincy December 24 1815
By mr. Tarbel, who left here the last of Nov'br I wrote to
you, and to mrs Adams, introducing him to you, as the Grandson of our Ancient, and beloved Friend, dr. Tufts, who then
enjoyed his faculties and was active in buisness—but upon the
8th of this month, closed a Life of virtuous usefullness. having
finishd the works assignd him, he fell asleep—for his death was
not preeceeded by any Sickness or allarming Symptoms. he
was not confined to his Room, or Bed a Single day. hearing
that he was unwell, your Father, and I went to visit him, as we
had more frequently practised, for the year past. we found him
in his parlour, Social and cheerfull, altho I perceived that he
conversed with more difficulty than usual. he had taken a bad
cold, and coughd much. when I took leave of him, he gave me
a pressure of the hand, and an earnest expression in his countanance which Sunk deep to my heart, and I Said to your Father, He is going. altho I did not consider the event So near at
hand, he Survived only one day.
    untill you arrive at old Age, you can not realize the Sensation
caused, by the removal of a Friend, of many years growth,—so
ripened by our Side, So endeard to us by every virtue
    The death of Such a man, who through Life has sustaind, in
every Relation, and character a pure and unspotted Reputation, and who filled every hour with Some active Service to his
fellow creatures—causes a universal Shock, and Electric Stroke
    who of us would not wish thus to live, and thus to die? his
death has imprest upon my mind, with increasing force, the little
Time, which in the course of Nature, is alloted to your Parents,
the Suddeness with which we may drop into the Grave, and it
has determined me to write to you, and Say, that which ever of
us may be first taken, the other will Survive but a Short period,
and Should Such an event take place in your absence, the Survi-
vour will need all your filial consolation, and Support. I therefore request you would immediatly return or as Soon as you
could obtain permission, to your Native Country.

your Fathers bodily health is much firmir than mine, yet he bends under the weight of years, and decays fast. my health is crumbling under frequent attacks of Sickness, and age. while my Reason is Sound; and my mind tranquil I have Some things to impart to you. you know that Louisa Smith, has been to me at all times, as a daughter, always faithfull to my interest, and constant and affectionate in her attendance in Sickness, as well as health that She is peculiarly Situated, not having a relative, or any kindred, nor Sister excepted, upon her Mothers Side. I am desirious of doing what I can for her if I Should be taken away. I have therefore retaind a Note of yours; part of which is already paid, and which your Brother would have paid the whole, but for my request to the contrary.

There remains about twelve hundred dollars. this Note I shall inclose in a Letter addrest to you, and seald up, which I Shall give to her, for you, relying upon you, to discharge it agreable to my request. Dr Tufts has always been my Trustee. there was some property, left me, by my Fathers will, which dr Tufts who was Executor, after I went abroad converted into public Stock. the interest of this, and Some other Small Sums, which was purchased by him, I have found convenient for Family use, during the late war, when our income was much diminished—of this I have your Fathers consent to dispose of as I please—I Shall leave directions to you for this purpose—

I have written you more than once requesting the price of the cloth Sent your Father & the knives and forks Sent me. the Seal and Books your Father has written you about. they will all be deducted from the Small remains of your Note to your Father, nearly the whole of which has been paid. The Boys have Sent for their watches—I have only waited for your, or their mothers direction to comply.

I am my dear Son most affectionatly your Mother

Abigail Adams

Will of Abigail Adams

Copy   Quincy 18th: January 1816.

I Abigail Adams wife to the Honble: John Adams of Quincy

in the County of Norfolk, by and with his consent, do dispose of the following property. First, that injustice may not be supposed to be done to my Sons, I have conveyed to John Quincy Adams by Deed, all my right and title in the farm given me by my Unckle Norton Quincy valued at $2200, and to my Son Thomas Boylston Adams, all my part, being one half of the Medford farm given to me, by my Honoured Father William Smith of Weymouth, which I consider of equal value with what I have given to his brother.

Having in the hands of James H Foster, as Trustee to me, Bank Stock to the amount of Four thousand dollars, perhaps more, as it was estimated by my late Trustee the Honble. Cotton Tufts Esq, lately deceased, whether more or less, I direct that it be disposed of and divided as follows.

1st: My Will is, that my Grand daughter Caroline Amelia DeWint shall have Seven hundred and fifty Dollars, exclusive of a Note of One hundred, which I gave her at her marriage, and of my clothing, a white Sattin gown and coat trimm'd with black velvet.

2d I give to my Neice Louisa Catharine Smith, a Note of hand given me by my Son John Quincy Adams, part of which is paid; the remainder, being over Twelve hundred dollars, I give to her and leave in her possession, and have written to him concerning it. I also give her the Bed Matress and Curtains, 1 pair Blankets, Counterpane Looking-Glass, belonging to her chamber, and twenty-Dollars to buy Chairs. Also 2 pair good-sheets and pillow-cases. Also a purple Sattin, spotted gown, and a Green Irish Tabinet gown and coat; Also a flesh-coloured-Sattin, my black lace cloak and my white lace Shawl, which she worked for me, and any of my common cloaths, which she may wish to take.

3. I give to my Grand daughter, Susanna B Adams, Seven-hundred and fifty dollars and my gold watch, and the upper part of my pearl ear rings; my white Sattin gown and coat trim'd with silver, a blue lutestring gown, and half of a gown trim'd with gold trimming, being a Lace Muslin; also a Scarlet Sattin.

4: I give to Abigail Louisa Smith Johnson, Five hundred dollars and a clay-coloured silk gown, and ten dollars for a Ring, and the other half of the lace Muslin.

5 I give to my grand daughter Abigail Smith Adams and

Elizabeth Coombs Adams, Four hundred dollars each; and each a share in the Weymouth Bridge, and to each the drop of my Pearl Ear-ring, and my gold necklace between them.

6th: I give to my Son John Quincy Adams a ring with my Unckle Quincy's hair and name, and I give to Catharine Louisa Adams, his wife, one hundred and fifty dollars and ten dollars for a Ring.

7. I give to Sarah Adams, Widow of my Son Charles, one hundred and fifty dollars; in lieu of clothing I give the fifty dollars and ten dollars for a ring.

8 I give to Ann Adams wife of my son Thomas B Adams, One hundred dollars. A black silk gown and coat-red spots; A garnet Sattin gown and a white lutestring gown and coat, and one share in the Weymouth Bridge.

9. I give to my Sister in Law Catharine Louisa Smith, Fifty dollars for mourning, and a changeable silk gown and coat. Also my black silk Cloak.

Item. I give to my Neice Mary Turner, Widow of Elisha Turner, Seventy five dollars and a black-silk gown.

Item. I give to Lucy Greenleaf wife of John Greenleaf, a Ring given me by Abby Shaw with my Sister Peabody's hair, and a Ring with my Aunt Smith's hair, given me by Mrs: Hall, and my black-silk-gown twill'd and garnet striped Sattin.

Item. I give to Charlotte Bailey and to Harriet Welsh a piece of Sattin to be divided between them; it being a piece which I bought of their Mother.

Item.* I give to Abigail *Smith* Shaw a brown Sattin gown and return to her the pin she gave me with her Unckle & Aunt Cranch's hair.

Item I give to Elizabeth Foster my Neice, wife of James H Foster a light brown lutestring gown and a ring.

Item. I give to Rebecca Dexter wife of Richard Dexter, Thirty dollars in token of her faithful Nursing me in various sicknesses. I also give her a brown silk gown, like one I divided with Louisa. Item, I give to Esther Briesler, Twenty Dollars and a led-coloured silk lutestring gown

Item. I further give to my Neice Louisa C. Smith, one share

---

* NB. The name of Abigail Smith Shaw, is intended for Abigail Adams Shaw, now Mrs: Felt. Note by T.B Adams.

in Haverhill Bridge, and to Susanna B Adams, one share in Haverhill bridge. I also give one share in Weymouth bridge to my Son John Q Adams and one to my son Thomas B Adams.

To any of the girls who may live with me at my decease, I give each a Calico-gown to be chosen out of mine which I leave and ten dollars in money.

My will is that all my clothing—body linen &ca not already named shall be equally divided between my five Grand daughters and Louisa C Smith, Caroline Amelia DeWint, Susanna B Adams, Abigail Louisa Smith Johnson, Abigail Smith Adams, & Elizabeth Coombs Adams, and the same, if any Surplus of money remain.

I request my Son Thomas B Adams to take upon himself the payment of these Legacies, from the   now in the hands of Mr James Hiller Foster of Boston Trustee to Abigail Adams; and Louisa Catherine Smith will deliver the clothing agreeable to my request.

I hope that no unkind or hard thoughts will be entertained that I have given to Louisa more than the rest. Her case is peculiar, having no relative upon her Mother's side but a Sister. I commend her to the kindness of my children.

Abigail Adams

It is my request to my dear Husband, that the old Silver Tankard given me by my Father as a piece of family plate, may be given to our Son Thomas B Adams. The Quincy Tankard, I hope, will go with its name to our Son JQ Adams.

PORTRAITS BY STUART AND MORSE

To John Quincy Adams

my Dear Son   Quincy Feb'ry 10th 1816
    your Letter of Nov'br 7th allarmd me when I opend it, and Saw that it was in the hand writing of mrs Adams, and I read with trembling—while I rejoice that you have So able a Substitute, I cannot but regret the occasion for it—your hand may be restored to its use again, but your Eyes have reason to

complain that you have used them too hardly. in this instance only—have you been a hard master to members which have afforded you knowledge and entertainment, your Friends much pleasure, your Country more benifit, than I fear it will ever acknowledge, or Reward.

I beg you to be more choice & Spairing of your Eyes in future—and to use glasses to Save them—

I shall be anxious untill I hear again from you. your october Letter I have received, and acknowledgd and one from George of the Same month.

I rejoice that Georges emulation has taken a proper turn—My dear John, it pains me to hear he has been unwell. he used at times, to have a shortness of Breath which I attributed to woorms. he always had a feverish habit at those times, about the Same time last year, that you mention his Sickness—he was Sadly afflicted with Boils.

are there any low lands near you or does he pass any in going to School?

I have been confined a month to my chamber, and must think it is oweing to weakness and debility of Age—my constitution is giving way—and you must prepare your to hear that I am numberd with the dead. I could have wished to have lived to See your return to your native Country, but if heaven orders it otherways, its will be done—you have my Blessing, and my prayers for you, your partner, and all your dear Children—

your Father performd a great feat the other day. he went to Stuarts the other day and brought home his portrait and mine. his own is a most admirable likeness, a Speaking likeness. but mine—alass will be known only to those who knew me 20 years ago. my Grandchildren will not know it. there is a likeness to be Seen in the features of that which mr Copley took of you.

Stuart took one of your Father this last Summer for mr Shaw; to be placed in the Athenæum, equally good

Mr Morse has been taking a likeness of your Father, at the request of a Gentleman in Philadelphia, a mr de La Plain, who is collecting the likeness of all our great revolutionary Heroes. mr Morse is a fine young Man. their is Genius in his Eyes. He came here to take the portrait, and past near a week with us. I hope he may be Sucessfull in introducing a taste for the fine Arts amongst us—but in the portrait he has taken of your Father, he has failed. it is a Stern unpleasing likeness. Age has Softned his features, and Shed a mild lusture over them, which Stuart has happily Seazd—I regret that mr Morse is So bad a likeness as it was taken to be engraved. your Brother claims your Fathers portrait for you. mine must not be Seperated from it. I beleive I gave you mine Some years Since. I owe it you in return for yours—

I Shall Send you the Books you request when ever any vessel Sails direct for London. I read enough in mr Tuckers Light of Nature, to find him a pleasing visionary, who could only be follow'd as an Ignis Fatuus—Life and immortality are brought to light only by the gospel. Good people cannot think alike, even upon important Subjects fear god and keep his commandments, is the whole Duty of Man, and his faith cannot be essentiallialy wrong, whose Life is in the Right.

I am warn'd and forbiden to write, yet I cannot refrain while my hand can hold a pen, of Subscribing your ever affectionate Mother   Abigail Adams

I am taking the Bark in large quantities if it gives me Strength, I Shall try to write to my daughter

"HOW INADEQUATE THE SALLERY WAS"

To Richard Rush

Dear Sir   Quincy Febry 26 1816
It is a long time since we have received a Line from you at Quincy. I have been so very sick myself, as not to be able to write for several weeks; I am still confined to my chamber very feeble. during this period, I have been, more than once informed that you had been Named for a mission to Russia. While on the one hand, it would give me pleasure to learn that my son was succeeded by so respectable a successor, on the other, I should regret, that any one, whom I so highly respect

should risk his Life, his health, and fortune, in so cold so dark and Dismal a climate, upon an Embassy so expensive—the narrow Sallery alluded by Congress to their foreign ministers, renders their situation abroad very unpleasent to them, and subjects them to the contempt of all classes, who judge of the importance of a Nation by the figure their Representatives make abroad.

Mr Adams is now subjected to the mortification of being obliged to take a small house in a Country Village, near the City, having no outfit provided for him since his mission to England, and having had it intimated to him, that there would not be any, he cannot take a house in the city, nor furnish one on his Sallery. he cannot receive, nor notice his own Country Men, who carry introductory Letters to him from all parts of the United States, with that hospitality which a public Minister ought to Sustain and be able to offer.

In a time of war, or in any great calamity which may threaten a country, I consider it the Duty of a good citizen, to Sacrifice property, and even Life, to save it upon this principle I have always acted. When called upon for a Seperation from those most Dear to me, which wrung my heart with anguish and placed me, a Solitary Being in the world—for Sixteen years of my Life, and that at a period, when it may be supposed, Life is best enjoyed—I was deprived of the Support, the Comfort, and Society of Him whom I most Loved, and esteemed, in the World.

ask mrs Rush if she could be reconciled to such a Sacrifice? With the Tower of London before her Eyes?

But these are scenes, which have long since past, and live only in the memory of a few ancient individuals. they will soon sink into oblivion, while the rising generation reap the reward.

There is a Spanish proverb, if you are well Stand Still. but Ambition and enterprize forbid it—I see not any reason in a time of peace, for Sacrificing Time and tallents abroad which might be as usefully employed at home; and I have advised mr Adams to ask leave to return in the Spring, unless an outfit should be allowd him, he has three Sons to Educate, and it cannot certainly be his Duty, to expend upon his small private property as he already has done, to support his family with decency.

I have heard that when mr Adams expected a successor in mr Bayard, he wrote a Letter to the president stateing to him, how inadequate the Sallery was, for a mission to Russia, and how unable an American Minister was, to Support the Honour, and Dignity, of the Nation he represented.

This Letter was captured, and carried to Barmuda and there made a Subject of ridicule, of the Country and Government which would not support their foreign Ministers in Character, at a table of British officers. the gentleman who heard it, and from whose mouth I heard it, was an American, but not known to be so by the officers. Being acquainted with the Family he obtaind the Letter, with some others for us, and after the peace, he Brought them here: that for the president was forwarded to him.

my trembling hand, & feeble Frame will only allow me to add, my best Regards to mrs Rush—and an assurance of the continued of them and Friendship of   Abigail Adams

"WE JOINTLY ADVISED HER"

To Louisa Catherine Adams

My Dear Daughter   Quincy March 20th 1816.
I attempted to write to you, by Captain Bronson in Jan'ry but my strength failed me, and I have been ever since, in so low, and debilitated a state of Health, as to despair of ever recovering strength again, but for the last ten days, I have gained some, and my physician, encourages me, that I shall be benefitted by the returning Spring.

I have not had any disease, such as fever, cough, or pain, except in my Head occasionally. it seems to, me to be an universal debility, and dissolution of my constitution.

with the Blessing of heaven, and the kind assidious attention of my Friends, who hope to build me up, again upon Bark and wine, I have gained for the last ten days, and

"kind Natures sweet restorer, Balmy Sleep"

has again visited me.

I had been deprived of this blessing, for near two months, save what was obtaind by the use of anodynes, and my Nerves have been dreadfully agitated. I am much fallen away, and am but the Specter of what I once was; but enough of this poor Frame, scarcly worth retaining—

Since I wrote to you last, I have received your two kind favours, of Nov'br 7th and dec'br 23d for which I thank you, and also for copying my sons.

I rejoice that your health, appears to have mended, so as to be able to aid your best Friend, under the affliction which seazd upon his Eyes. If he could go to Bath, and take of the waters, and Baths—I think he would find much releif, from that Hereditary Scourge the Rheumatism—which proteus like puts on all forms; from pains in the Limbs, to disorders in the Eyes. this I know by painfull experience—as I presume he has not any Right to the Gout—he must try to rid himself, of its near Relative.

In one of your Letters your mention mrs Hellen—early in the winter, and not long after the death of mr Hellen, she wrote to me in confidence, inclosing to me a copy of the will, and requesting my advice, whether she ought to accept it? at the same time stateing, that mr Hellens property was estimated from 50 to 60 Thousand dollars, part of which, was daily increasing in value.

By the will, she could only receive four hundred dollars pr year, and living in the House; with the use of the furniture, so long as she remaind his widow—

It is not my buisness to remark upon this will. with respect to her I soon made up my mind, and gave her the same advise; which I should have given to my own child.—I thought there was one near me, whose judgment I could better rely upon than my own; I communicated the will; and your sisters request. the result, was the Same; and we jointly advised her, to reject the will, and claim her dower; which she has done: and she has since written me, that the property left by mr Hellen, was found to be much larger than She had stated; so that with her dower, she will be in comfortable circumstances. She wrote me, that if she received her dower, she should not charge Board for the children—I think however she ought to make a charge of it.—it is a maxim with me; that children should go to their parents, not parents to their children—and that she should hold it, in her power to remit it to them or not as circumstances might hereafter arise. they have a double claim upon her, both as Aunt, and Mother—I took the Liberty to say to her that if she should marry again, she ought previously to secure to the Children, the property which belonged to their Father, after her discease

I hope if she has ability, she will render kindness to those of her Family who need it, one of which, is a widow sister of mr Hellens, to whom, he left only 50 dollars—

I had a Letter from your Brother dated 23 Janry he writes in good Spirits, altho he says, he is a Banishd man—and longs for the intercourse of consanguinity—

I am rejoiced to find George so fond of writing, and *really do think*, that he improves in his hand writing altho his superscriptions look a little as if the Spiders had dipt their Legs in the Ink; and crawld over the paper.

I had hoped, to have written you that your sister Smith, was Safe a Bed, with a son, or daughter, but I must wait for News from N york, which I daily expect, as they have promissed me John I perceive is the same gay Lad, full of fire and enterprize. strong and powerfull are his feelings, which promise a goodly harvest, if properly restraind, and directed—but we must bear in mind,

> "That what composes man can man destroy"

of my dear Charles Character, I know but little, that little has been in his praise—Shall I ever behold them again?

your Martha Godfrey is married, and I hear very well married to a mr John Osburn, a musical instrument maker—I rejoiced when I learnt it, for Martha was too handsome to keep a milinars shop. her behaviour however has been perfectly correct, for any thing to the contrary which I have ever heard—

Louisa desires to be affectionatly rememberd to you, and to George and John—Susan is writing to George and will express her own Regards.

we have been in danger of loosing our little John Quincy, with a Lung fever. he is now out of danger—

Let me my dear daughter hear from you as often as possible. Letters from abroad refresh my drooping Spirits, and Light up the Lamp of Life affresh—

Beleive me with sincere Love and affection your Mother
                                            Abigail Adams

To Charles Francis Adams

My Dear Charles   Quincy March 28th 1816
  I must write you a short Letter, least you Should think
yourself neglected, as I have written to both your Brothers,
and your Grandfather is so much engaged with his Books that
he cannot write to any of his Grandsons now.
  your Mother writes me word, that you have forgotten your
Russian & German Languages. you should not forget, what
you learn that is valuable. that is the misfortune of old Age,
which I too often find to my own mortification—
  By this time, I suppose your daisys and cowslips begin to
Bloom in your garden; while all here is like winter, the ground
this week coverd with snow; I rode, out two days, last week in
a close Sleigh.
  tell your Brother George that his school mate Coffin is gone
to Carolina. I was mistaken in his being yet at Hingham. ask
your Father if he will send me by some private hand half a
pound of such fine sealing wax, as he uses I cannot get any fit
to use in Boston—
  when you come home you will find a little generation of
cousins; growing up. your uncle Adams has 5—and then come,
an other generation of Sons, and Daughters, Great Grandchildren. I have three already—whom I never saw, and one whom
you know, is gone to heaven—
  You write a very handsome hand my dear child; and your
Brothers have improved very much. this makes glad the heart
of your affectionate Grandmother,   A Adams

THEOLOGY

To John Quincy Adams

My Dear Son   Quincy May 5th 1816
  It was not untill this morning that I received your Letter of

December 5th No 79, just five months from the date. where it has been ever since, I know not. it came to me from Nyork, and had just arrived there. The subject of it, you will Remember by turning to your coppy. There is not any reasoning which can convince me, contrary to my Senses, that Three, is one, and one three. Is it possible for the Humane mind to form an Idea of the Supreme Being, without some visible qualities, such as wisdom, power, and goodness. The creator, preserver and Govenour of the World, the first commandment forbids the worship of but one God.—That Jesus Christ was sent into the world by the Father to take upon him Humane Nature, to exalt redeem and purify the world, to sit an example to all his followers of sinless obedience, and holiness of Life, and conversation, and to bring Life and immortality to Light, The Scriptures fully testify, and that a conformity to his precepts and example, as far as humane Nature is capable of it, will be rewarded by future happiness in the world to come, is my firm beleif.

Is there not a subordination to the Father manifested in the whole Life and character of Jesus Christ? why said he, call ye me Good. there is none good but one that is God. again, I do nothing of myself, but the Father in me and when Jesus Christ, applies to the Father. If it be possible let this Cup pass from me, and again, in his agony upon the Cross, my God, my God why hast thou forsaken me? from these and many other passages of Scripture, I am led to beleive, in the unity of the Supreme Being, and that Jesus Christ was divinely inspired, and specially delegated to communicate the will of God to man; and that after having fullfild his Mission upon Earth, he assended into heaven, from whence we are assured he Shall come to Judge the world in Righteousness, all power being given him, *by the Father*. we are assured that those who fear God and work righteousness Shall be accepted of him, and that I presume of what ever sect, or persuasion, after all our inquires, we are permitted to see but through a Glass darkly.

And must say with the poet

> "Thou great first cause, least understood,
> whom all my Thoughts combine
> To know but this; that thou art good
> And that myself am blind"

May 9th

I had written thus far, and put by my paper, when your Letter of March 4th arrived—the Sentiments of affection which you so powerfully express, and which are so dear to my Heart, have always been manifested by you, towards your parents, through your whole Life, and will I hope be rewarded by similar, Love duty, and affection, towards you by your own offspring.—my Health has mended since the spring commenced, much more than I had Reason to expect, from the great debility to which I was reduced, but my constitution has past through so many trials, that I have little reason to expect my continuance for any long period—your Father fails in his Limbs, and can encounter but little care, wants frequent Rest, and repose, yet he enjoys his Book, his pen, and society, when he can meet with those who can enter into his literary amusements—of this Sort Quincy has few to Boast. what pleasure do the delightfull scene's of Nature afford to those, who have no one, to whom they can say How pleasent it is? participation is the Root of pleasure. in reading a fine passage, how greatly is the enjoyment heightned by communicating it to one who can equally share in it? it is Sterns who say's he would have a companion, if it was only to say how the shadows lengthen as the sun declines—all the reasoning and Eloquence of Zimerman, could never reconcile me to solitude. it is a cold unsocial feeling,

> "for where are the charms
>   which Sages have seen in thy face?
>   Eden was tasteless till an Eve was there"

I have to thank you my dear son for your very entertaining Letter of the 4th March, and rejoice that your visit to Paris was so well timed, and that you received so much gratification from the works of Art, which were there collected. one cannot help feeling a regret; that after being so well arranged, they should be again dispersed, without inquiring, by what means they were obtaind. the Bourbones in exile, were more respected, than upon the Throne, holding it as they do; by the power and courtesy of foreign Nations—

I see by the papers, that you was a Guest, at the Lord Majors feast. the Toast you gave, is very popular here and considerd, judicious, conciliary, and honorable to both countries

I send you a new paper, containing a speech of mr Calhouns during the debate upon the direct Tax. I should often send you News papers, but most of our vessels go to Liverpool, and from thence, the postage would be heavy. the English papers which we receive some times contain interesting debates, but the most of them, make me Shrink with horror, at the catalogue of crimes which they detail we have in this country crimes sufficient, to call for humiliation & Repentance, but I may venture to assert, that the criminal callender of the whole united States for one year, will not exhibit as black a Catalogue of enormus crimes, as the annals of one Session of old Bailey of these which excite my greatest Regret, is the prostration of the Female character, and the frequent infidelity, of those who hold in their hands, the honour and dignity of the Nation, and posterity all conjugal principles, appear to have lost their weight, and the seduced, and seducer compromise their iniquity by a fine, by a payment of a fine for damages.—Reputation, Reputation, oh She who has lost her Reputation, has lost the immortal part of herself,—lost that, which not enriches the spoiler, and makes her poor indeed

> "Beauty like the fair Hesperian Tree
> Laden with blooming gold, hath need the gaurd
> of dragon watch, with uninchanted Eye
> To save her Blossoms, and defend her fruit
> From the rash hand of Bold incontinence"

My pen has ran away with me I must close or my paper will fail me. ever your affectionate Mother   A Adams—

MARRIAGE OF SUSANNA BOYLSTON ADAMS

To John Adams 2nd

my Dear John   Quincy May 21 1816
    I always feel gay, when I take my pen to write to you. it is the recollection of your ardour, your intrepidity and your Sparkling Eyes, and rosy cheeks which appeard to me the other Night, heightned by your return to your Native State & country which animated your whole frame, when you ran eagerly

into the Arms of your Grandmother, which so gratified me, that I regreted when I awoke, and found it was but a dream—

Can you keep a Secret John? can you beleive that your cousin Susan, whom you know always favour'd the Navy; had enterd on Board the United States Ship Independence, as mate to a Leiut.?! In Sober truth, an officer from that Ship, was So Smitten with her, upon Seeing her at a Hingham Ball as to Surrender at discretion. it appears that a certain Sly urchin in revenge for his having escaped powder and Ball from the cannons Mouth, undertook to try the fire of an arrow, and Shot him to the Heart. The wound is not like to prove mortal, but may be healed, if he can obtain a certain Balsam, called Success—of which he has some flattering hopes

The Gentleman, whose Name is Clarke is a Native of Maryland, has been Six years in the Service, appears a very modest, Solid, Sensible Gentleman, and Stands high with his Commander Commodore Bainbridge. He is an orphan, has one Brother and one Sister only—who reside in Maryland, has received a Liberal Education, and commenced reading Law, his Father having been of that profession, but fell into bad health, was obliged to quit it, and entered the Navy. he is not quite 24, tall well made, a good face, not handsome however. I cannot yet Say, how the matter will terminate.

I have expected mrs De wint, and my great Grandaughter Caroline Elizabeth, for some time. they have not yet arrived the weather has been uncommonly cold—and the Spring very Backward—

I was pleased to find you forming Some intimacy and Friendship with your school mates. in many Respects English Men and Americans, are of the Same Family, Speak the Same language venerate the Same principles of Liberty, and Independence, and the Ashes of our Ancesters repose in that Island, and their descendents can never be wholy alienated from them. I wish to See a mutual Spirit of Love & good will, so honorable to human Nature—substituted for that Spirit of bitterness, which is too much encouraged, upon both Sides of the Atlantic and which is so contrary to the precepts, and example of him, who exhorted his followers, to prove themselves his deciples by Loveing one an other—

Since you left me, I have received from you Six Letters,

seven I Should Say, of the following dates. May 2d 1815 21 May
—June 25th july 18th & 26th Sepbr 11th 1815 and March 10th
1816 your Last Letter Shows great improvement in your hand
writing—

You think you have arrived on an Age when a Boy ought to
behave as a man, but Nature made you a Boy first, and while
you are a child, you wilt think as a child, and act as a child—I
do not wish you to be prematurely a Man—but a discreet
Boy—of manly Sentiments honorable principles, and hold
yourself accountable to your Maker for your conduct, and you
will then learn to bear the troubles of Life, when they assail
you, with firmness—

I am dear John your affectionate GM—

Abigail Adams

DEATH OF WILLIAM STEPHENS SMITH

To John Quincy Adams

My Dear Son   Quincy June 29th 1816

If I write you ten Letters, to one from you, Still I Should be
your debtor, for one of yours is worth ten of mine, and one
over—

yet in Love, and affection, the account Shall be balanced—I
Shall always recollect with a pleasure, which I cannot describe,
the Sensation I felt, when mr Woodard returnd from Russia
and came to see me. I know well his Father, and Family, but
him I had never Seen before. is this mr Adams Mother Said he?
to which I bowed assent. O Madam Said he, with a warmth
and ardour, your Son Loves you much—Yes he does Love you
most tenderly.—of this I never doubted, but Some how, at
that time, thus exprest by a Stranger, it found the tender place
in my Heart, where it has remained, and will depart but with
the Life Blood

your Father in his Letter to you; has been So jocose respecting me, that I am at a loss how to return the compliment but
he represents me, as of more consequence, & more business,
than I really perform—it is true, that I have large demands

upon my pen, from my Children, & Grandchildren—and other occasional correspondents—I hope I may Some times do good in this way.

your Father retains his faculties, and his hearing wonderfully —his Spirits are generally good—but his Limbs fail him—he is less fond of exercise—tho he walkd to your Brothers yesterday, & back, which is three miles—Yet our decayed Tenements must Soon Crumble to dust, but I hope we have an other and a better Country to repair to, whose builder and Maker is the most high—and where I trust we Shall meet those Dear to us, who have gone before us—the last of whom is Col Smith he died upon the tenth of the Month—after a confinement of two Months following two Brothers in rapid Succession—I have written to you before his dangerous Situation, so that the event will not meet you unprepared, or my Grandson to whom I have also written—much of this Sympathy. I have in the course of the few last years of my Life been calld to partake of, and I have fre- quently been assured, that I have mitigated the pangs I could not wholy assuage and healed the wounds I could not cure.

This Letter will be deliverd to you by the Rev'd E Tucker- man of Chelsea, who like many others of his Cloth, have had recourse to a Voyage for the restoration of their Health. I hope he may be more Successfull than those, who have gone before him—

I thank you for Pauls Letters, which I have not yet read through; having received them only a few days Since Walter Scott is a character in which we in America, have taken much interest from his Poems—as well, as in those, of that Strange half mad Man, and poet—Lord Byron—we look in vain for any fixed [   ]

As to politicks, we have left off wrangling about politicks— even our approaching Presidential Election, scarcly moves the waves—

I Shall expect to have some account of the Royall Marriage —the news paper be sure which contains it, and I Should like your opinion of the Allied pair? I have a fancy that the Lady, has a Character, which will, if circumstances call it out; make no ordinary figure upon the Page of History—I will however ask nothing improper. If I do I know you will have prudence enough to withhold it.

I pray you to be very carefull of Georges health. do not let him blow the flute. he must use gentle regular exercise and take nourishing food—no danger of Such a *Stocky, Stuffy Chap* as John unless of a little Roguery—how he would be delighted with a Book which I dare not Send him. I mean the journal of a young Man of Massachusetts who was captured by the British, first carried to Melville Island Halifax & afterward on Board the Prison Ships & then in dartmore Prison—it is a wonderful Book of 3 or 4 hundred Pages—I can Say with the Lady in the Patriot "that I have never read a Novel, that arrested my attention more than this Singular production." I must Still further quote the Lady in her dialogue for She has exprest my Sentiments of the Work—"the work is Strictly moral and even Religious—It is patriotic, humane and gallant, with all the Spirit of ancient chivalry; and I am curious to know if it can be all true—for it Strikes me, that there are more traits of extensive reading and accurate knowledge of character than can be Supposed to have fallen to the Share of a young Surgeon of a privateer"

I will add that the real American Character is wonderfully preserved through the whole narative and your Father and I have laughd more in reading it, than ever we did, over Hudibrass or don Quixot.—four thousand Copies have already been Sold and a new Edition call'd for—I wish the Same hand which Sent one to us would Send you one,—I dare not. Such a Book found in the House of the Peace Maker, would not do—but I beleive the whole narative to be true—I know from accurate information, that much of it is so—

It is Said that Alexander Selkirk who resided Several Years on a desert Island, put his manuscript journal into the hands of daniel de Foe, who made out of it the renouned history of Robinson Crusoe—I fancy the Young Surgeon, has found Some *de Foe* here—

your last Letter was very Short the 18 April

I hope you will find more leisure Soon—but I should be ungenerous to complain, knowing Some of your avocations, and how fully Your time must be occupied—I am my dear Son most tenderly and affectionatly your—Mother

A Adams

JOHN QUINCY APPOINTED SECRETARY OF STATE

To John Quincy Adams

My dear Son   Quincy december 5th 1816
"Oh that I too, could make a visit to my Father," was your
exclamation in your last Letter. more than a visit You may
make, my dear Son, If the Newspapers may be credited, for
they announce from South to North, that you are to be recall'd
and to fill the department of State. this is repeated over and
again, & appears to give universal satisfaction. this I learn from
all quarters—I rejoice in any circumstance honorable to you,
which may recall you here again.

You have been absent much longer than You contemplated
when You went from us. The Lives of your parents have been
lengthend out, to a date, beyond expectation, and I now flatter
myself with the hope, that we may be spaired to See you again—

our Season is now become very cold and the failure of the
crops of Hay, and Indian Corn, gives us serious allarm for the
support of the poor. We should not want, if the price abroad
did not induce the Speculator to monopolize, and to Ship for
foreign markets, what we need at Home. Sixteen thousand
Barrels of flower were enterd in one week at the custom house
in Boston, yet it keeps up the price, from 12—to 13 dollars pr
Barrel.

The Electors met this day in Boston for the choice of president. two Electors declined, one was sick, and the vote in
consequense, was not taken to day—It is universally believed
Mr Munroe will be Elected, altho this State Should refuse to
vote for him—as I Suppose they will.

I see by the paper that mr T B Johnson is chosen one of the
Bank Directors of the National Branch in New Orleans—He is
much respected there—

we are all at present in good Health, but the weather So
cold that my fingers are stiff as I write. no Snow yet—Your
Father reads continually, in the morning by candle Light, frequently at five oclock; I cannot rise untill day Light, and try to
keep him in Bed, but he cannot Sleep, and rise he must. the
Evening too, he reads, unless company prevents, or I read to

him. I am now writing by candle Light. So neither of us will Say much about our poor Eyes—

George I hope is better. I inclose a Letter from Claudius for him. I look for the promised journal—

I have written myself quite out, and Sent last week by the Galen—no war no politicks what shall I say?

Why that I am as ever your affectionate Mother   A—

ANTOINE DESTUTT DE TRACY

To Thomas Jefferson

DEAR SIR   Quincy December 15th 1816

My good Husband has called upon me for some Letters, written to me by my son, when he was last in paris, in 1815 in which he gives me a particular account of the Family of Count deTracy and of the circumstances which introduced him to their acquaintance.

Beleiving that it will give you pleasure to become aquainted with this happy domestic circle, I readily embrace this opportunity of transmitting them to you, with two or three other Letters which follow in succession, and are interesting, as they describe the novel and important events, to which Mr. Adams was an Eye witness.

I rely upon your known care and punctuality to return them to me. I need not add, how valuable they are to me. They may also afford some entertainment to your Grandaughter Miss Ellen Randolph, whose praises are in the mouths, of all our northern Travellers, who have been so happy as to become acquainted with her. They bring us also: such delightfull accounts of Monticello and its inhabitants that I am tempted to wish myself twenty years younger, that I might visit them, but I am so far down Hill, that I must only think of those pleasures which are past. Amongst which, and not the least is my early acquaintance with, and the continued Friendship of the phylosopher of Monticello, to whom are offerd the respectfull attachment of Dear Sir your Friend

ABIGAIL ADAMS

To Richard Rush

Dear Sir   Quincy March 24 1817

I was rejoiced when I found the *justice* of Congress had made some necessary Provision for the office you now hold, altho they withheld a Clerk. I Should have been more gratified if their Liberality had extended to that, and an increase of the Sallery. the Duties of your office, must I am Sure, occupy the greater part of your time; but nothing is harder than to convince the purse holders that to command the first talents, it is necessary to place them in a Situation Suitable to the Station assigned them

I have had the pleasure of hearing of your health, and that of mrs Rushs, as well as of your friendly attentions through Mr Clark, who has really been dissapointed in all his plans—not through any fault of his own, but providentially, by sickness, and the season.

The prospect of Seeing my Son return with his family, is Cheering to our hearts, and gives a new Spring to our Spirits.

There is a rumour Circulating here which gives us some uneasiness, it is that mr Clay is openly unfriendly to mr Adams, and that he refused to make one of the Cabinet in concequence of mr Adams's Nomination. I know there was a difference of opinion respecting the importence of the Fisheries, and the Navigation of the Misissippi, at the Treaty of Ghent. can it be from that source that this animosity has arisen? if it is So, I thought mr Clay a more liberal minded Man.

You will consider this Letter confidential From Your Friend
Abigail Adams

Since I finishd this Letter I have Seen the correspondence between mr Barbour and mr Clay, and the debate in Senate!!

I have no further observation to make. it is before the public. they must judge

SEEKING AN APPOINTMENT FOR A GRANDSON

To William Cranch

Dear Sir   Quincy March 26th 1817
   Mr W S Smith with Mrs Smith are upon a visit to her Relations in Washington. he is desirious of paying his Respects to
you, as a Relation, and as a desendent of the Venerable Characters, whom he remembers with Respect and veneration—
   He is desirious of obtaining employment under the Government. in what Capacity I do not know. His being So nearly
Related to me, deprives him of all the advantage he might
otherways derive, from application to the higher Powers.
   It is, and has been an invariable Rule with his Grandfather,
not to ask any favours, or even to give a recommendation to
office, for any of his Relatives, and very rarely for any one
Else In mr Madisons administration, he did recommend two
young Men for the Army, and one as a midshipman for the
Navy.
   any advise, or information you can give to mr Smith, who is
a Stranger in Washington will be thankfully received by him
and gratefully acknowledged by your affectionate Aunt
                                        Abigail Adams

"ONE OF YOUR TORMENTORS?"

To Thomas Jefferson

DEAR SIR   Quincy, April 29th 1817
   What right have I to be one of your tormentors? And
amongst the numerous applicants for introductory letters?
   Why I will plead, old acquaintance, old Friendship and
your well known benevolence. But to the subject of my present address. Mr. Theodore Lyman, who possesses an ardent
thirst for Literature, and whose Father, is one of our most
respectable Characters for probity, honour, and wealth, this

young Gentleman has been much out of health, occasioned by too close application to his studies. He is now going abroad with the hopes of regaining it. He is desirious of getting an introduction to some Gentlemen of Letters in France—my good Husband has furnished him, with one to the Marquis La Fayette, one to Mr. Marbois, and one to Mr. Gallatin. But as your acquaintance with men of Letters in France is of a more recent date, I thought it probable that you might give him a Letter or two, which might be of much service to him, from the weight and respectability of your Character. He understands the French language, and is a young Gentleman of most estimable Character, and acquirements, whom I am not ashamed to recommend. He is a nephew of Mr. Williams, late consul of the U S in England. He has been once in England and in France before, and knows full well that to Men of Letters he cannot be easily admitted, without honorable introduction. He has been so attentive in supplying us with such rare and valuable Books that I feel indebted to him for his kindness. And as I am not able myself to repay his civility, like other debtors, I am drawing upon my Friend's. Any Letter you may think proper to forward, you will please to send under cover to my Husband, and they will be gratifully acknowledged by your old and steady Friend   ABIGAIL ADAMS

JOHN QUINCY IN AMERICA

To John Quincy Adams

My Dear Son   Quincy August 10th 1817 Sunday morg
   Through the kind of attention of mr Crafts we learnt yesterday morning of the arrival of the Washington, and in the Evening, through our watchfull centinal Harriet, I received the gratefull intelligence under your own hand, that you were Landed and all well for which joyfull News to your parents; God be thanked—we now wait, in pleasing expectation of welcoming You; one and all, to the old Habitations alterd only by the depredations of Time; like its ancient inhabitants. Come

then all of you; we will make you as comfortable as a cup of cold water, tempered with Love and warm affection can render you—Fill the Children, I am Sorry they were not here a week sooner, to have been present at the wedding of their Cousin Susan, who is now gone with her Husband, to Visit her Mother at utica—I am anxious to know how mrs Adams Sustaind the Voyage, as her last Letter, gave me concern for her Health—I remember what a voyage was of 57 days, from the Same place;—so you were seven day more fortunate than Your affectionate Mother   A Adams.

your brother and sister Louisa & all Friends Send Love and greetings—Your Father will write himself.

JOHN QUINCY ARRIVES HOME

To Harriet Welsh

Dear Harriet   Quincy August 18th 1817
    Before I go into Bed, I must write you a few lines, after the agitation of the day—about Ten this morning Louisa announced a carriage & four comeing down the Hill. I ran to the door, it arrived in a few moments, the first who sprang out was John, who with his former ardour was round my neck in a moment. George followd half crazy calling out o Grandmother—o Grandmother. Charles half frightned, and not feeling the same remembrance of person and things, or the affection which bound his Brothers to us approachd with respect & Reverence—by this Time Father and Mother, well both out, and mutually rejoicing with us
    Mr Adams really larger than his Brother mrs Adams looking better than I ever saw her, and younger I think—all of them seen burnt & Brown
    George is going to mr Coleman to be examined tomorrow. mrs Adams gives a pleasing account of Caroline—and mr Adams an excellent one of John Smith, which really delights me—tho his retired Life has injured his Health for want of

excercise—I have a Letter from him. mrs Adams says you must go as with them to see Caroline.

Mr Marston promises to deliver you this Letter tomorrow morning your affectionate   A Adams—

DEATH OF THOMAS GREENLEAF JR.

To Harriet Welsh

Dear Harriet   Quincy October 1st 1817

while I congratulate dear Caroline upon the Birth of a daughter, I am calld to mourn with her Brother, upon the loss of a son. mr Adams writes me, that he found them in great affliction He is with mr & mrs Fry—expecting to get to Housekeeping by the first of this month. He is entering upon the Duties of his office, with fear and trembling. His Eyes and his right Hand threaten to fail him, and all are requisite in his office. mr Rush has agreed to remain with him untill he gets initiated into it. Mrs Rush is just confined, So that the Frankling could not go out at Present, if as is reported, She is to take mr Rush to England.

we have all been thrown into great Distress by an awefull Catastrophe in our Neighbourhood—Thomas Greenleaf Junr put a period to his Life by a pistol, at his office about 8 oclock on Monday Evening. he put it into his mouth and blowed his Head to attoms—Mrs Thayer heard the report, went into his Room, and found the Deed done. they Sent for his Father, who upon entering the Room, fell Senseless upon the floor—was carried out, and it was a long time before he recoverd his faculties—I went yesterday as I thought it my Duty, to see the afflicted Family—but what comfort could I offer them? Sympathy alone. the poor Mother in an agony, not able to lie down, fearfull of loosing her Reason—the Sisters struggling to suppress their feelings least they should add to their Mothers, the Father walking the Room Speachless—pale, sick & his stomack heaving—none of them had either Sleep or food. I prevaild upon mrs Greenleaf to take a cup of Tea, and to consent to have the Body conveyd to the Family Tomb in Boston, without a funeral here; to look upon him, was out of the question—and to have a funeral would only Still more Distress the Family—She heard to the reasons, and last Evening he was burried—I Shall go again to day to see them. Thomas had been melancholy at times, for Several months, deprest in his Spirits—his Father had Strove to remove it, but he would frequently wish himself Dead—He left a paper addrest to his Father, thanking him for all he had done for him, and a farewell to his Mother Brother and Sisters—Saying that he took this method to save them farther affliction

His having read Law with mr Adams & liveing in Such habits of intimacy with the Family, makes us feel the Shock most Sensibly—

on Monday while writing to washington—I was three times calld of to company—and Some of them Staid So unconscionable* long that I mist the Mail. I finishd one for the Grove—near one oclock I Saw Stop at the gate a Jersey Waggon with a Gentleman & two Ladies—I imediatly thought they must be Carolines Friends—they proved So—I gave them as cordial a welcome as I could; mortified a little, that I had not a better dinner to give them, and notice of the day—they were proceeding on their journey—and brought with them the best Sense for travellers—a good appetite—Your Grandfather was much pleased with mr Verplank as I was with the Ladies—they will tell Caroline that we were not Stiff with them, but endeavourd to make them feel at their ease

poor Louisa being So confined, and requiring constant attention, makes it more difficult for me to entertain company as a good Second is always wanting—on Sunday last I had 21 persons who Dinned with us, and I knew not of more than my own Family

Give my Love to Caroline & read her as much of the Letter as you think proper—I do not coppy I have not time, nor would what I write be worth it—I thought I should not have any Letters to write to washington but to mrs A upon family Subjects, but mr A Says I hope you and my Father will write frequently and keep me in Spirits—do not let me thirst in vain—and instead of praises, let me have your prayers for the

* Spelt wrong

discharge of my duties—Love to all—I write Slow to what I used to—

Yours most affectionaly   A A

To Julia Stockton Rush

Dear Madam   Quincy October 15th 1817

I am indebted to you, for two very kind Letters The first, was written after my Grandaughter miss de Wint, had made you a visit. I ought to have inform'd you, how much She regreted, that it was not in her power to repeat it, and writing to me upon her return, that She was gratified in having visited a Lady, whom She knew; was much esteemd by her Grand Parents: as well as by her own Father, and Mother, and who was the beloved Companion of one of the Best of Men—my Grandaughter left the City the day after She call'd upon you last; but will avail herself of your kindness Should She visit the City, an other season—

My Son and daughter most certainly considerd it one of their first duties, to visit you. They had every motive of Respect, affection, and Reverence to do so—the connexion in the Family has not been disolved, tho one of its first Members, has been removed to a higher Station.

The Branches remain, and the union between them is marked by peculiar Circumstances of Succession in office. it is no Small personal gratification to me, that mr Rush, is the Successor of mr Adams, at the court of St. James He will Support the honour and dignity of his Country, and his pure moral Character is a Gem of inestimable value, respected even by those who have not any Regard for their own—

I can Sympathize with you most feelingly in the deprivations you are frequently called to endure by the Seperation and dispersion of your Family, but we must, Remember that no man liveth for himself

"waters Stagnate, when they cease to flow"

I have indeed enjoyd a Blessing I had little reason, at my

Age to expect, after Eight years absence, to See my Son and Family all returnd in Health and safety—ought I then to complain that they are so Soon Seperated from me? tho the Distance is much diminishd, yet it is Seperation—I regret my dear Friend that You should feel any restraint in—I know full well, that if the pen is not kept in constant practise; writing becomes urksome.

If any opportunity Should occur to bring your Julia this way, it would give us Sincere pleasure to welcome her to Quincy or other member of your Family.—We had an unexpected pleasure a few days Since in receiving a visit, from a Son, and two daughters of our highly respected Friend Govr. Jay—who I may Say, has been dead to the world these Seven years—refuseing to take any part in the political concerns of it

"The world forgetting, by the World forgot" altho one of its Brightest ornaments—Such is the Lot of Man—as Goldsmith Says a New Generation "come tittering on, and push us off the Stage"

It is now our turn to Step asside as others have done for us—

My Good Friend, desires a kind Remembrance to you, in which he is joined by your affectionate Friend

Abigail Adams

"I AM AGED WRINKLED & DECAYED"

To Harriet Welsh

dear Harriet   Quincy December 1st 1817

The moon shone so bright this morning that I rose, as it seems while it was yet Night, and allotted a portion to my Maidens, & set my whole house hold in motion, for you must know that we have Six Men at this day, three ladies, who love us so dearly that they must stay. a cold winter comeing & no Home, and wish the old Gentleman was but 25—I had a specimin of a compliment this morning from one of them, & said it was earlier when I call'd them than I was aware of, thinking Six when it was only four, but having had much sickness in my Life time, I could not sleep in the morning. o Madam one would not suppose you had ever had much sickness—that you perceive was a compliment to my *youthfull* appearence & activity. now my Glass will neither flatter or lie—and that tells me I am Aged wrinkled & decayed. thanks to a kind Providence that I can hear & see so well, and enjoy so large a share of health.—when I wrote you last, I forgot to mention to you that mrs Q Adams desired me to say She wrote you a Letter which you had not noticed, and she was half affronted that you had not. She says She addressed it to fish Kill possibly you had not received it—I have got mrs Sampson to make Johns pantaloons, and his waistcoat or rather Jacket is ready to try on. She wishes him to come out as early on Wednesday as he can. being at work in the Neighbourhood She can try it on—but She cannot come here agin untill a fortnight from monday—I see at Lane & Lampsons merino cloths for Ladies dresses—I wish when you walk out you would get me some patterns of the pearl & Barry coulours the width & price

I cannot find that the Franklin has yet Saild—poor Clark has a mournfull time of it on Board—mr Rush and Family have been on Board more than a week ten days now—Let me hear from you to night.—

Yours affecly   A A

I want a peice of Narrow white Ribbon like that you got for Louissa. Susan got a peice 18 yd for five shillings

FAMILY NEWS

To Louisa Catherine Adams

my dear daughter   Quincy december 12th 1817

I have been haunted with the Deamon of omission, and a hundred Sprights in the garb of excuses, Such as Company, family avocations Noisy Boys &c &c This morning, being very Stormy, I determined to expel them all, and commence writing a Letter to you. I beleive I had promised to write to my Son. I know that he must be so enveloped in publick Buisness, that he can ill afford time to attend to domestic affairs—and as those of State, are out of my department, I Shall address this to you.

please to inform me where you are Situated? and how you are accommodated? &c &c when your good Mother was living She kept me always informed of passing Events. Her Letters are a History of the period in which they were written.—be Sure those were times of danger and Strife. now all is Smooth water—tho I perceive a disposition in mr Speaker to trouble them.

There is one part of your Letter which gives me much concern —and the more, because I do not See any possible way for re- leif If there is a Bankrupt Law in the State of N york, mr S had better declare himself So, and give up to his Fathers creditors, all that by his Fathers will, was given to him—I fear he is as deficient in judgment as his Father was, who by all accounts was indebted much more than it was in the power of any of his con- nections to releive him from, and vastly beyond any Sums which I had any Idea of—I never knew any thing of his affairs nor did Mrs Smith during her Life. enough was however con- jectured to make her Life a Scene of anxiety, patience Submis- sion, and Resignation for I never heard a complaint, or murmur from her Lips. I know not but that I ought to rejoice that She was taken from Life at the period She was, for greatly indeed would her affliction been increased—at the events which have since taken place.—Labour with my hands, I have never declined, and altho I was reduced to earn my Bread, I could Submit to it, but to Beg—I am ashamed

we had a pleasent Thanksgiving Day a vacation took place upon Wednesday and lasted untill Monday—George John and Charles made three of the Nine Grandchildren present—we wished for their Parents to have compleated the festival—with nine Boys, and Girls we made a full chorus—you know what a vacation means—

I have had miss Sampson to Repair Johns cloathing, and make him a new Jacket and pantaloons, his others being quite worn out at Elbows, & knees—our common Friend Harriet procured the materials—His Broad cloth Cloaths which are nearly as good as new, he has So out grown that he can scarcly get them on—and must go to Charles—I hope he will make them do untill Spring, but he has not an outside coat. the coat he wore at Sea, is not proper for him, either the fashion, or the Texture of the cloth it is very dirty & wholy unfit for him. He pronounced it so, but I did not give into the belief untill I examind it myself—He wants only a spencer which as he is pretty hardy; may answer for him—neither his Father or you would have him drest, but as becomes his Standing and Station. I Shall have a Spencer made for him—He has not got his Boots which he is in great want of. but when he does get them, I think it very probable—he will have out grown them—as Charles has his, but he has two pr and he can wear his Russia great coat, tho short for him—and he has an other which he uses—as is well enough—

I am sorry that John should have given cause of complaint. He is apt to think himself too independent, and loves to be his own Master—He must be accountable & Submit to the regulations of the Family—He is a fine Boy, but such an active Spirit, requires a Rein—Charles is by himself, a quiet Solid Boy easily directed—not being well, I kept him a few days. he had a Soar Throat and bad cold—he was as grave and Steady—as an old man, reading his Book

I hope mrs Fry has recoverd her Health, and mrs Hellen to whom please present my Love—we are in daily expectation of an addition to our Number of grandchildren. Mrs T B A. look daily to be confined, and in time, I find I may have a Great Grandchild—thus the world goes on—

Louisa thanks you for your kind remembrance of her. her health is very poor. mrs Clark also presents her duty to her uncle and to you, and regreets that mr Clark had not the pleasure of Seeing you, before he went a broad—

I forgot to inform you that we had a pr of Twins born in our Neighbourhood. mrs Beal got to Bed a week Since, one only was born alive—two Girls. there was 12 hours between them & the first died when the second was born dead—they were two very pretty Children—my Love to William & his wife—my Heart feels heavey when I think of them—

I beleive I must write a line or two to my Son

His and your affectionate Mother   Abigail Adams

STUART'S PORTRAIT OF ABIGAIL 2ND

To John Quincy Adams

my dear son   Quincy december 14th 1817
    As you accused me last Evening, or rather Night with pre-
venting the Ladies from writing to you; I apologized by saying
that I had a Letter written to you at home, which was really
the case. I made a Fairy visit to Washington last night, in which
time I visited mrs Munroe, mrs Madison &c, and meeting you
and mrs Adams in the street, in fine Health and Spirits, you
accosted me as above—I was too late for the last mail, and by
that means was prevented from thanking you, for the Liveing
likeness of your Dear Sister—for such I esteem it. Stuart never
has, or could make such a painting—altho the drapery is unfinishd, the portrait is admirable—Some future day, I shall wish
to pay for it, as I have promised Caroline, that it shall be Hers
when I can see it no more. with respect to your Fathers full
Length picture taken by Copeley, I may say in the word of the
song—"our roof is too low, for so Lofty a Head" and I am in
the same predicament with the vicar of wakefeild, not having a
Room in which it can stand upright, Hanging it up is out of
the question I had it brought here, because you desired it, it is
no doubt a fine painting—but the Likeness by Stuart, is much
to be prefered—I have preserved the case that it may be enclosed again should you wish to give any further directions
about it. it seems only fit for a public Building.
    I have written to mrs Adams respecting the children—and as
you have left to my Judgment to provide such things as are
necessary for them, I shall not trouble you further than to give
to your Brother the accounts, which he will transmit to you
    I received a Note last Evening from Harriet, in which she
writes me that John has got his lessons in their parlour by 8
oclock and, the remainder of the Evening they found amusement for them, and that John and Charles had both received
commendation for their application to their studies—the only
difficulty with John was his opinion that he was his own Master
—and not accountable to the Family in which he lived when he
went or how he spent his time He is a fine Boy, if his Spirits do

not run away with his Judgment. Charles is a thinking Boy, much slower, but not less sure in the end. the week has been so rainy & the roads so muddy that I recommended to them to stay in Town, over Sunday, as they had just had 5 days vacation—

I presume you are crowded with Business. I hope you have able assistants, the Presidents speech is much approved; the only objection to any part of it, which I have seen, is that, in which he recommends the repeal of Taxes— we are all well— what can be done for William? How could I recommend him, or to whom? his own exertions & fidelity in his trusts must do it for himself—I feel for him & for his wife—and there are others also, for whom I have to feel more than I express, surrounded with a numerous Family—and still increasing—

But I will not add to your anxieties, enough of which you must experience, both public & domestic—"what Blessings thy free Bounty gives"

"Let me not cast away"—or bewail or complain when I have so many comforts to be thankfull for—and one of the greatest is, I have found in the Duty and affection of a beloved son To his Mother   A Adams

Mrs Clark wishes me to ask the favour of you to give her timely Notice when any vessel is going to the Mediterranean with public dispatches as she is desirious of writing by them, we forgot not the day, 14 december but drank a Glass of wine to the Treaty of ghent

"A RECORD OF PRESIDENTIAL CEREMONY"

To Harriet Welsh

Dear Harriet   Quincy December 31 1817.
    I received last Evening the Calico & your Bill, in which I find Several mistakes which I Shall point out as I proceed. when you purchased me the Bombazet, I enclosed ten dollars. You bought me 7 yd 2 Skeins of Silk Some linen, one pound Tea 6 pd currents & 3 pd of coffe, the last of which I took tho I did not Send for it. all these articles of Groceries you have

omitted in Your Bill—I then Sent for 12 yd of cotton cloth enclosed a 5 dollar Bill. the cotton you Sent and have charged— you then informd me that the Editor of the Christian deciple Said, there was an arrears of three years—I then enclosed 5 dollars and requested You to Settle with him and declined renewing my Subscription. on Saturday fortnight I Sent by mr E Adams enclosed in a Letter Eleven dollars with a request that you would get me one yd black twild Silk 3 quarters yd of Black velvet, 1 yd of Shalloon & twist, all of which you procured. one Bandano hankerchief which you Sent afterward, but which is not upon your account. on Sunday Evening I enclosed by the Children a ten dollar Bill requesting you to get me 16 yds calico which I thank you for procuring—I also enclose your Nov'br Bill by which you will find that 75 cents only was due to my credit

If you have any of my Scraps left you will See that I am accurate, by enumerating the articles I thought to refresh your memory. Mrs Adams's Letter I beleive I must not trust out of the hand which it is now in; She has a delicate and difficult part to Steer, and will require much prudence & circumspection, more So than in any Situation She has yet been placed in. Mrs Munroe will find that She must have her drawing Rooms, or She will have no popularity She may hold them only once a fortnight, but if She means to See Ladies only at morning calls She will very Soon get rid of them. if She had Succeded to mr Jefferson, She might have establishd a rule for herself, but comeing after Mrs Madison, who by her long acquaintance of 16 years in public knew every Body, and made herself acceptable to all. She must have a task to get along without comforming to her predecessors—Mrs Adams will if She pleases be very popular, and envy and Jealousy will be the consequence at least I fear So—there never was any improper company introduced while I had the Honour of preciding at Philadelphia. indeed it was more Select than mrs Washingtons drawing Rooms, because in her day, it was a Novel establishment

I think mrs Munroe ought to be allowed without censure to take her own time; Mrs Washington held her drawing Rooms every week—I only once a fortnight, yet no one found fault with me for the alteration, but to be every day in the week Subject to continual visits, was not my wish—I received visits from 12 untill 2 oclock all days but Sunday—and then I always denied myself—I returnd the first visit made me; but no more, never took Tea, but with the Ladies of Home & Foreign Ministers—never dined abroad except one or twice with mrs otis—So now you have a record of presidential ceremony—

George has not Sent his Coat nor John his Jacket

Yours affec'ly   A Adams

"LETTERS OF MINE TO PUBLISH?"

To François Adriaan Van der Kemp

Dear Sir   1818

When President Munroe was upon his Tour Surrounded by the Military, encompassed by Citizens, harased by invitations to parties—and applications innumerable for office—Some Gentleman asked him if he was not compleatly worn out—to which he replied—o No—a little flattery will Support a man through great fatigue—I may apply the observation to myself and Say that the flattery in your Letter leads me to break through the aversion which is daily increasing upon me to writing, and my correspondence is now confined to my children & Grandchildren. my Son JQA, whose Letters used always to be my delight when abroad, is now So prest and occupied with the Duties of his New department, that I Seldom get a Letter from him Mrs Adams however kindly Supplies his place and gives me the Daily occurences of the beaumond—tinctured Sometimes with a little political Suet.

You terify me my Dear Sir when you ask for Letters of mine to publish? It is true that dr Disney to whom the late mr Hollis bequeathed his Property found amongst his papers Some Letters from the President and from me, which he asked permission to publish. we had both forgotten the contents of them, but left it to his judgment to do with them as he pleased—and accordingly he publishd Some of them—one other addrest to my Son when he first went to France in the year 17. by Some means got into an English Magazine, and those I beleive are all the mighty Works which ever have or will by my consent appear before the public—Still I never Studied, my language is warm from the Heart & faithfull to its fires the Spontaneous effusions of Friendship—as Such I tender them to mr Vanderkemp —Sure of his returning Kindness and indulgence since I have no pretentions to the Character which he professes to fear that of a learned Lady—I have been So much flatterd with her. attention to the writings of my Son that as a mark of my perfect confidence in mr vanderkemp I venture to Send him for his perusal alone including his Lady and daughter, an Epistle written to me in the year [   ] which I think a good History of the events of that period and which [   ] to preserve as Such—you will See the political Sentiments at this day might keep alive animositys which it will be best to burry for the present. as the time has past by when the transactions took place—I have never ventured to communicate them but to a few chosen Friends—must therefore request you to return it to me with particular Care—as it is the original & only Copy I have—The Life which you Sent to my Friend was read by me with no Small interest and I could not keep communicating it to my Friend miss Welsh—She was So much pleased that She beged to take it with her to N york where She was going upon a visit to my Granddaughter mrs de wint. this must account for the delay in transmitting it to your Son in Philadelphia who I hope has received it long over this time present me kindly to your Lady and Daughter and beleive me with Sincere esteem and ardent Friendship Your Humble Servant   A Adams

January 24, 1818

"I HAVE NOT ANY AMBITION TO APPEAR IN PRINT"

To Harriet Welsh

The President has a letter from Vanderkemp, in which he proposes to have him send a collection of my letters to publish! A pretty figure I should make. No. No. I have not any ambition to appear in print. Heedless and inaccurate as I am, I have too much vanity to risk my reputation before the public.

January 24, 1818

To Louisa Catherine Adams

my dear Daughter   Quincy Feb'ry 1818
   Your Journal No 7. to Janry 30th, Harriet brought me to day,
just as we had sat down to dinner; It being thursday, John and
Charles thought they would treat themselves, and miss Harriet
with a Sleigh ride to Quincy—our Friends and acquaintance do
not fail to improve the Season, and sometimes come upon us a
little unwarily, for one day last week, I had nine at once to dine,
when I knew only of my own Family.—However a cordial welcome, and a cup of cold water with it; is more gratifying; than a
Royal Feast, into which the Heart does not enter.
   I designd to have written to you the day after I received your
Letter, but was again prevented by company—Indisposition
followd—and as this is a month most trying to my constitution, I have been obliged to Nurse a day or two—I was the
more desirious of writing to you immediatly, as some parts of
your Letter gave me anxiety—I perceive by what you have
written, that the point of Ettiquette is not settled to satisfaction, between the Ladies of Senators; and the Ladies of the
Secretaries. I beleive it was determined that the Secretaries
should Rank with the Senators, but that the first visit should
be made to the Senators—as I presume you would not willingly give offence, and if the Secretaries make the first visit: I
think their Ladies should follow the example—I do not know
what new principles may have been adopted since I was at
Philadelphia, or what the practice of those Ladies was. not
more than one MacHenry kept a carriage. your situation in
some respects, is different from those who have gone before
you. you have resided so long abroad, and at different Courts,
that you will be considerd as taking the lead. there will be a
jealousy of you, that you are sitting up pretensions, which our
"proud Republicans," as Madam de Neuvile aptly calls them,
will not Swallow—I would inquire of Mrs Munroe what had
been her practice—and call a council of the Ladies of the other
Secretaries, and act in concert. I know there was an attempt to
bring this subject to a decision, while General Washington was

President, but the Gentlemen always appeard to shrink from it—and to be so fearfull of the Hideous cry of monarchy, that they dared not exert their own dignity; about this period French democracy was, in its full vigor, and all distinction, was swallowd up in the cry, of Liberty and equality

I know the delicacy of your situation, and the circumspection necessary for you—while on the one hand, you would not wish to be considerd as seeking popularity. on the other, you would not exact homage from equals—I consider mr Adams and you, as a city sit upon a hill, where every Bird of prey will allight upon you—I would propose to have a new office created—a Master of Ceremonies—! Similar to a Garter-King at Arms, for with all our boasted Simplicity, there is not upon the Globe; a prouder people; or one more tenacious of Rank, and tittles, from the Subaltern, to the President of the united States, without the honesty to acknowledge it—

The obnoxious word "well Born" which has rung as many changes in America; as Burks Swineish multitude has in England is founded in the principles of Human Nature—

> "In pride, in Reasoning Pride the Error lies
> All quit their sphere, and rush into the skies"

I hope mrs Smith has a son, or daughter by this time—I expect one of the same grade in my own Family in due time—there is not any necessity in America, of adopting the Dey of Algiers Bastinado to promote Matrimony. I have heard of flagellation as a cure for madness, but never before to excite the tender passion—my Love to my son who I hope will not expose his health. excercise is better than bleeding if he can take it—but I fear he is obliged to too close application to business—If you was here to day I beleive you would feel the cold as much as you did in Russia; tho the weather is clear. I cannot keep warm before a large walnut fire—with the sun shineing into four windows—

Gen'll Forest whom you mention I was well acquainted with. He was one of Col Smiths Brides men when he was married—the Col. served in the Army with him, and Loved him as a Brother—I went once to visit him at his seat while I resided at Washington, accompanied by your Mother—I am glad to learn that a daughter of his, is so respectably married—

As the Boys were here on thursday, they have contented themselves to stay in Town over Sunday.—the Bird and dog are both in fine health and spirits. we tollerate them for the Love we bear to John. the Bird is under no controul, and sings so loud, especially if we are reading as to be quite a Nuisance— he is a true worshiper of the riseing sun, and mr Booth is such a church going animal, that we are obliged to shut him up to prevent his disturbing the congregation.

we all send Love, but the Severe Cold, is too much for us old people

affectionately your Mother   Abigail Adams
                                                     February 27, 1818

To Caroline Smith De Windt

MY DEAR CAROLINE: Quincy, March 22d, 1818.

"Delightful praise, like summer rose,
   That brighter in the dew-drop glows."

They were sweet drops which flowed from the heart to the eyes both of your grandfather and grandmother, when I read to him the two letters you had transcribed to your uncle and to your father, in commendation of your brother. You could not have offered a sweeter incense to your grandfather; and flow-ing from the pen of an old friend of your father's, it carried the marks of sincerity, without the alloy of adulation, and merits a grateful return. "A good name is better than precious oint-ment; it is the immediate jewel of the soul."

The freshet which carried away the bridges, and made such havoc with the roads, together with the robbery of the mail, has prevented our regular communication, and I suspect I have lost a journal; I enclose you the only one you have not seen.

I hear that Duane has got hold of my letter to Niles, and spits forth vulgar abuse at me and the Secretary of State, who had not any more to do with the subject than the Emperor of

China. He has revealed who the person was, who sent the ungentlemanly refusal to dine; how he knew, I cannot divine—he abuses him also; but the low sarcasms of these people affect me no more at this day than the idle wind.

I have not seen, only heard of the laudable efforts of those foreigners, who will foment a party spirit if they can. They wish to engage us in a war with Spain; and finding our growth rapid, and our national strength increasing in proportion, more than one European power would rejoice to find us embroiled with any power which could retard our progress; they know the administration is averse to war, they think to abuse it with impunity.

I was much gratified to see the overpowering vote of the house to reject the Spanish petition; an unprecedented attempt in any country, to appeal from the sovereign to the Parliament. Genet appealed to the people at large, which he found abortive.

The Boston subscription for the bust soon filled, although no person was allowed to subscribe more than two dollars; a very respectable committee was sent, with a short and handsome address upon the occasion, and on Thursday the artist came. He takes the bust first in clay; he has been a part of three days engaged upon it; he does not require any formal sitting; he works with much ease; his name Binon, a Frenchman by birth, with all the vivacity of his nation; quite a gentleman, and well acquainted with books; he has passed twelve years in Italy; he will have an admirable likeness.

I have never before heard of Cox's Female Biography; I should like to read it. Many of the female characters in Scripture, both of the Old and New Testament, do great honour to the sex. It is a pleasing and grateful circumstance, to read in the life and character of our Saviour, the affection and tenderness which he manifests to women—to Mary, to Martha, to the widow of Samaria, and many others.

It grows too dark to see or write; so with love to you and yours, I am your affectionate   A. A.

To John Quincy Adams

Dear Son   Quincy June 23d 1818
  enclosed is a Letter which you will see contains a request to
me; and through me to you. the ploughing with the Hiffer is
not yet out of date. were the object an office, I should refuse to
medle with it, but as it is only a simple renewal of a midshipman from one ship & station to an other, I would hope no
great interest necessary; particularly as his Health has sufferd
severely in this Southern expidition. Mr John Marston has
been with Captain Finch to Amelia Island, to Savanah & I
think Charlstown. he took a fever in which his Life for some
time was despaird of, and his Father and Family are very anxious about him. If you will speak to the Secretary of the Navy
for him, perhaps he may obtain his wishes—Your Father empowers me to add that he joins in the same request. we have
on former occasions experienced the Friendly and obligeing
disposition of the Secretary; in applications of a similar kind,
in favour of mr Clark who is now daily looked for in the
Washington—
  Yours Sons were all well, the last week: George & Josiah
Quincy past last Wednesday with us. Being ordination day in
Boston, & holiday in Cambridge—
  with the hope of seeing you e'er long if only for a short
time—I am consoled with the prospect, and am your affectionate Mother   Abigail Adams—

To Louisa Catherine Adams

dear daughter   Quincy August 21st 1818
  Since the 18th July, I have not received a Line from you or
my Son, altho I have been in daily expectation of hearing that
you were sitting your faces this way. I have learnt from mr

Cruft that mr Adams contemplated being here, as I understood him by the last of this Month, or sooner if he could. The intercourse between us, is not so frequent as I could wish. Even tho it consisted of "How do you?" only for at this Season of the Year, Sickness is more frequent—since I wrote you, we have burried Mrs Bass, the rest of the Family have, & are recovering from the fever. it is generally Healthy here. The vacation of the Childrens School began yesterday; and they are now here—I wish you to come, that I may consult you, about Winter cloathing for them—of which they will want considerable—

Mr Marston wished me to say to you that his son Henry would do himself the honour of calling upon you, and mr Adams, on his return from N Orleans, where he has seen your Brother, and may have a Letter for you from him; if he should call; you will see him, he has travelled by land from N Orleans for the sake of visiting the Western States—

We are burnt up here, with the Severest drought that I ever knew at this Season.

I have just been reading the Life of Genll Jackson—and I admire the Man; as his character is represented—I esteem him, much more highly than I did before, I read it. He appears to have been raised up for the Command he had, and for the defence he made He is as Brave as Buonaparte, without his embridled Ambition—I wonder if my Son has read it?—tho Jackson has lately given him Specimins of his Character—which have some what embarrassed the President, I fancy—

With a Kind Remembrance to all Friends and a hope of seeing you e'er long I am Your affectionate Mother

A Adams

John is not well. he grows too fast, is very thin, mere Skin & Bone. his food hurts him—

CHRONOLOGY

LIST OF CORRESPONDENTS

NOTE ON THE TEXTS

NOTES

INDEX

Chronology

1744   Born Abigail Smith on November 22 (November 11, Old Style) in Weymouth, Massachusetts, the second child of the Reverend William Smith and Elizabeth Quincy Smith. (Parents, married on October 16, 1740, represent several respectable lines of descent in colonial Massachusetts, with many of the colony's Puritan founders among their ancestors. Mother, born 1721, is the daughter of Colonel John Quincy, Harvard 1708, speaker of the Massachusetts House of Representatives from 1729 to 1741 and a military and political leader in Suffolk County. Father, born 1707, Harvard 1725, comes from a merchant family, and has been minister of Weymouth's First Congregational Church since 1734. Sister Mary born December 9, 1741.) The Smith family lives in a modest parsonage that dates to 1680 (now known as the Abigail Adams Birthplace).

1746   Brother William born December 1.

1750   Sister Elizabeth born in late April or early May (baptized May 8).

1751   An epidemic of diphtheria ("throat distemper") decimates Weymouth, claiming more than a hundred lives, roughly a tenth of the small community. The village's church building is destroyed by fire caused by an explosion of gunpowder stored in the loft, and rebuilt two years later.

1752–58 Abigail suffers bouts of rheumatic fever, which continues to plague her periodically for the rest of her life. Throughout her childhood she makes frequent visits to Mount Wollaston and her genteel Quincy grandparents. She receives no formal education, but is tutored at home by her parents, especially her mother. The typical curriculum for young girls includes religious instruction, domestic skills, reading, writing, some arithmetic, and, in Abigail's case, rudimentary French. Abigail reads freely from her father's large library, which includes religious tracts and secular works of history and literature, as well as periodicals such as *The Spectator*. She later credits Richard Cranch, a watchmaker courting her sister Mary, with introducing her to

Shakespeare and other literary classics. Abigail recalls late in life that a neighbor "used often to say to me when I was young and very wild, Nabby you will either make a very bad, or a very good woman."

1759 Meets John Adams (born October 30, 1735), who accompanies his friend, Richard Cranch, to the Weymouth parsonage. Son of John Adams Sr., farmer, shoemaker, and deacon of nearby Braintree, Massachusetts, and his wife Susanna Boylston Adams, John attended Harvard (class of 1755) and taught school in Worcester, Massachusetts, before studying law and being admitted to the Suffolk County bar. At the time of his visit he is courting Hannah Quincy, Abigail's cousin, and he confesses in his diary that he finds the Smith sisters "not fond, not frank, not candid," though he acknowledges them to be "Wits."

1760 The Weymouth parsonage is enlarged with an addition, more than doubling its size.

1762 John Adams, who has become a freeholder by virtue of inheriting half of his father's Braintree property the previous year, begins serving on town committees. He is also admitted as a barrister in the colony's superior court, and commences traveling the court circuits, which he will continue to do for the next fourteen years. Now well established, he begins courting Abigail. In October he addresses her in a letter as "Miss Adorable." Mary Smith marries Richard Cranch, November 25.

1763 Abigail sends first extant letter to John, dated August 11. She signs with the pen name "Diana," an epistolary convention among young people, to his "Lysander," admitting she is bound to him by a "threefold cord" of humanity, friendship, and caring. John begins to publish anonymous newspaper essays in the *Boston Evening Post* touching on political disputes between the colony's ruling clique and its popular opposition, siding firmly with the latter, among whose leaders is his cousin, Samuel Adams. This marks the beginning of an engagement with provincial and eventually imperial politics that will come to dominate more and more of his time.

1764 In April and May John is quarantined in Boston while undergoing inoculation for smallpox. The couple weds on October 25 in the living room at the Weymouth parsonage. Abigail's father presides at the ceremony; according to tradition, the text he preaches on is Luke 7:33: "For John came neither eating bread nor drinking wine, and Ye say 'He hath a Devil.'" The couple moves to Braintree into the house John inherited from his father (known today as the John Quincy Adams Birthplace), adjacent to the home of John's widowed mother (the John Adams Birthplace).

1765   In a bid to raise revenue from the colonies, the British House of Commons passes the Stamp Act on February 27, imposing a tax, effective November 1, on the paper used in the colonies for newspapers, almanacs, pamphlets, broadsides, and legal and commercial documents. Protests against the Stamp Act occur throughout the colonies during the summer, including two especially violent episodes in Boston in August, and the law is effectively nullified before it can go into effect. Daughter Abigail "Nabby" born July 14 and baptized the same day by her grandfather. Abigail writes to her friend Hannah Green, "Your Diana become a Mamma—can you credit it?" John writes the instructions for the Braintree representatives to the Massachusetts General Court (legislature) denouncing the Stamp Act, which are adopted by the town meeting on September 24; the Braintree instructions are printed in the *Massachusetts Gazette* on October 10 and adopted by some forty other towns in the colony, raising his profile considerably (he observes in his diary, "the Year 1765 has been the most remarkable Year of my Life").

1766   The House of Commons repeals the Stamp Act on February 24 but at the same time sows the seeds of future conflict when it issues a Declaratory Act announcing Parliament's authority to legislate for the colonies "in all cases whatsoever." In August, Abigail and John sit for portraits by Benjamin Blythe.

1767   Tensions with Great Britain resurface when Parliament imposes new duties on lead, glass, paper, tea, and other goods imported into America. Passed by the House of Commons on July 2, the Townshend duties, as they are called, are to be enforced by a newly established board of customs commissioners headquartered in Boston. John is frequently absent from home, traveling the court circuit, including lengthy trips to the Eastern circuit, in what is today southern Maine. "Sunday seems a more Lonesome

Day to me than any other when you are absent," Abigail writes. Son John Quincy born July 11; he is baptized on July 12 and named for his ailing great-grandfather, who dies the next day.

1768   In April, John declines re-election as a Braintree selectman and moves the family to a rented house on Brattle Square in Boston to accommodate his increased legal practice and political activities. The colony's attorney general, Jonathan Sewall, a longtime friend of the Adamses, offers John the post of advocate general in the admiralty court, a lucrative position that would make him a crown official. John declines, citing his "political Principles." The first of five British regiments lands at Boston on October 1 after regular troops are requested by the increasingly harassed customs commissioners. Daughter Susanna, named for John's mother, is born December 28 and baptized by the Reverend Dr. Samuel Cooper, minister of the liberal Brattle Street Church, which the Adamses attend. Fellow congregants include patriot leaders John Hancock, Samuel Adams, and Joseph Warren, who is also the family's physician.

1769   In the spring the Adamses move to Cole (or Cold) Lane in Boston. John takes on two clerks to help with his expanding legal practice, which is conducted out of the family home.

1770   Baby Susanna dies on February 4, just thirteen months old. British soldiers under the command of Captain Thomas Preston open fire on an angry, taunting crowd on March 5, killing five Boston residents. Preston and eight soldiers are indicted for murder, March 13. Parliament repeals most of the Townshend duties in April, retaining only the duty on tea. John agrees to lead the defense of Preston and the soldiers charged in the "Boston Massacre." Son Charles born May 29. Abigail writes to her young cousin Isaac Smith Jr., encouraging him to take advantage of the opportunity he has to travel to Charleston, South Carolina, quoting at length from Polonius's speech to his son in *Hamlet*. John successfully defends Captain Preston, October 24–30, and the eight soldiers, November 27–December 5; two are convicted of manslaughter, while the remaining six are acquitted. By year's end the family has moved again, this time to "another House in Brattle Square."

1771 John falls ill, complaining of "great anxiety and distress," and the family returns to Braintree in April for his health. Abigail writes to cousin Isaac, now in London, that she is pleased to be away from "the Noisy Busy Town" of Boston. In the same letter she gives vent for the first time in her correspondence to resentment about social constraints on women, noting with respect to travel that while women "inherit an Eaqual share of curiousity with the other Sex," they confront obstacles that "prevent their Roving." Without such fetters, John leaves the family and travels to take the mineral springs at Stafford, Connecticut, in late spring in an effort to restore his health. He receives a letter, dated July 19, from the English Whig historian Catherine Sawbridge Macaulay praising one of his political tracts, which has been reprinted in London.

1772 Son Thomas Boylston born September 15; he is named for John's maternal grandfather. With John recovered, the family returns in November to Boston, to a house on Queen Street, where he will maintain a law office until the outbreak of hostilities.

1773 John begins to publish political essays in the *Boston Gazette* under his own name and, though not a member, he writes speeches on behalf of the Massachusetts House of Representatives in its dispute with royal governor Thomas Hutchinson over Parliament's claim to legislate for the colonies. In May the House elects John to seat on the Governor's Council, the upper house of the legislature, but Hutchinson vetoes the appointment. That same month Parliament passes the Tea Act, giving the East India Company a monopoly over the colonial tea trade. In July, Abigail visits Mercy Otis Warren and her husband James (whom John met the year before) in Plymouth, Massachusetts, inaugurating a complicated forty-year friendship with a woman who becomes a profound influence on her. Thanking Mercy for her invitation to correspond, Abigail writes: "Thus imbolden'd I venture to stretch my pionions, and tho like the timerous Bird I fail in the attempt and tumble to the ground yet sure the Effort is laudable." The first of three ships carrying East India Company tea arrives in Boston on November 28. Duty is payable upon off-loading, which must by law be accomplished within twenty days of docking, but which Boston mobs prevent. On December 5, in her first extended political commentary, Abigail writes to Mercy, "The Tea that bainfull weed is arrived. Great and I hope Effectual opposition has been made to the landing of it." Governor Hutchinson refuses entreaties to allow the ships to depart with their cargo in order to defuse the situation, as happens in several other colonial ports. As the deadline approaches, on December 16, a large crowd boards the ships and dumps 342 chests of tea, worth an estimated £10,000, into the harbor.

1774   In February John purchases his father's homestead from his brother Peter (now known as the John Adams Birthplace) and family again moves to Braintree. Parliament responds to the "Boston Tea Party" by passing four punitive Coercive Acts that close the Boston port, abrogate the 1691 royal charter that gives Massachusetts a measure of self-government, change judicial jurisdiction in cases of capital crime, and order the housing of British soldiers in private homes. At the same time Hutchinson is replaced as governor of Massachusetts by General Thomas Gage, commander of the British army in North America. A Continental Congress is called among the colonies in response to these acts. John is elected as a delegate from Massachusetts and departs for Philadelphia on August 10. Nine days later, Abigail writes: "The great distance between us, makes the time appear very long to me. It seems already a month since you left me." She also writes that she has "taken a very great fondness for reading Rollin's ancient History since you left me," finding the "Misfortunes of Sparta" instructive for the current crisis. She adds that she has "perswaided Johnny to read me a page or two every day, and hope he will from his desire to oblige me entertain a fondness for it." Widespread mob action and disobedience in Massachusetts prevent Gage from enforcing laws outside of Boston, and on September 5 he begins to fortify the town. Congress (later known as First Continental Congress) opens in Philadelphia on September 5. Consumed by his first experience as a public figure outside of Massachusetts, John fails to write to Abigail. She begins the litany of loneliness that will mark her letters to him over the next decade and more. "Five Weeks have past and not one line," she writes. Another time she complains that while Samuel Adams, also a delegate, has written to his wife more than once, John has yet to send a single letter.

Abigail also writes to Catharine Sawbridge Macaulay in England: "Should I attempt to discribe to you the complicated misiries and distresses brought upon us by the late inhumane acts of the British parliament," she writes, "my pen would faill me." Congress calls for a boycott of British imports after December 1 and for the election of delegates to a second Congress in May 1775. In early November, John returns home. He is reelected as a delegate from Massachusetts to the Second Continental Congress.

1775 Abigail writes to Mercy, "the Friends of Liberty . . . will rather chuse no doubt to die the last British freemen, than bear to live the first of British Slaves." Parliament declares Massachusetts to be in a state of rebellion on February 9. An attempt by Gage on April 19 to destroy military supplies stored at Concord leads to fighting at Lexington, Concord, and along the road to Boston in which seventy-three British soldiers and forty-nine Americans are killed. Massachusetts militia begin siege of Boston, and on April 23 the Provincial Congress votes to raise an army of 13,600 men. John returns to Philadelphia, where Second Continental Congress meets on May 10. "If we look back we are amazed at what is past, if we look forward we must shudder at the view," Abigail declares to Mercy. The crisis is increasingly evident in Braintree, as refugees from Boston fan out into the rest of Suffolk County, and local militia recruits engage in increasingly urgent drilling. The pattern for living apart that will define so much of their marriage begins to take shape, with Abigail assuming many of John's roles in the family, in addition to her own. She adopts the pen name "Portia," first proposed by Mercy, a reference to the wife of the Roman statesman, Brutus. As "Portia," her epistolary exchanges proliferate; she writes to John, to Mercy, to Edward Dilly (an English bookseller whom John patronizes), and to other friends. Responding to a plea from her husband ("Pray write to me, and get all my Friends to write and let me be informed of every Thing that occurs") she also serves as his informant on local developments in Massachusetts, now the center of action in the dispute with Great Britain. By the end of May, threats of invasion are rife, and she writes: "Our House has been upon this alarm in the same Scene of confusion that it was upon the first—Soldiers comeing in for lodging, for Breakfast, for Supper, for Drink &c. &c. Sometimes refugees

from Boston tierd and fatigued, seek an assilum for a Day
or Night, a week—you can hardly imagine." Congress
votes on June 14 to form a Continental army and names
Virginia delegate George Washington, whom John has
nominated, as commander-in-chief. Abigail meets Washington soon after he arrives in Cambridge in July to assume command of the militia forces laying siege to Boston;
favorably impressed, she writes to John that while "you
had prepaired me to entertain a favorable opinion of him,
. . . I thought one half was not told me." On June 17
Abigail and John Quincy climb Penn's Hill in Braintree
from which they observe the battle of Bunker Hill. John's
friend Dr. Joseph Warren is killed in the fighting while
serving with the Massachusetts militia. John Quincy will
later reminisce: "The year 1775 was the eighth year of my
age . . . I saw with my own eyes those fires, and heard
Britannia's thunders in the Battle of Bunker's hill and witnessed the tears of my mother and mingled with them my
own, at the fall of Warren a dear friend of my father, and a
beloved Physician to me." John's younger brother, Elihu,
serving as an officer in the colonial militia, dies of dysentery on August 11. George III proclaims colonies in rebellion on August 23. By September the dysentery epidemic
spreads to Braintree and Abigail's entire household is afflicted. Her mother dies, October 1; Abigail writes to John,
"Have pitty upon me, have pitty upon me o! thou my beloved for the Hand of God presseth me soar." Congress
adjourns December 9 and John returns to Braintree.

1776   *Common Sense*, a pamphlet by Thomas Paine denouncing
monarchical rule and advocating an independent American republic, is published anonymously in Philadelphia on
January 10, and sells tens of thousands of copies throughout the colonies, galvanizing popular opinion. After John
leaves for Philadelphia at the end of January, Abigail writes
to Mercy: "Our Country is as it were a Secondary God. . . .
It is to be preferred to parents, to wives, children, Friends
and all things the Gods only excepted. These are the considerations which prevail with me to consent to a most
painfull Seperation." John sends Abigail a copy of *Common Sense* on February 18, noting that "it has been very
generally propagated through the Continent that I wrote
this Pamphlet." While conceding it has "so manly and
striking a style," he suggests that its author "seems to have

very inadequate Ideas of what is proper and necessary to be done." She informs him of the local bombardment that deprives her of sleep for over a week, "a most Terible and incessant Cannonade." British garrison evacuates Boston on March 17 and sails to Nova Scotia. On March 31, with independence looming, Abigail writes her now famous letter that includes a bold call for more equal treatment of women in the new government taking shape: "In the new Code of Laws which I suppose it will be necessary for you to make I desire you would Remember the Ladies." (As this letter became widely known in the twentieth century, Abigail's call to "Remember the Ladies" became not just her signature historical comment, but a petition that has resonated for centuries as women's claim for more equal treatment by men.) John is named to a committee to draft a declaration of independence in June, and he plays a leading role in the final debate (Thomas Jefferson later describes him as "our Colossus on the floor"). The Declaration of Independence is adopted on July 4 and John sends a copy to Abigail. On July 12, with children, servants, and several relatives, Abigail travels to Boston to be inoculated against smallpox. She returns to Braintree in September after a successful, if protracted and painful, process. The Continental Army suffers major defeat at the battle of Long Island, August 27, and shortly after Abigail learns that John, along with Benjamin Franklin and Edward Rutledge, has been sent on a futile mission to negotiate with Admiral Lord Richard Howe on Staten Island. She writes John with accounts of family and friends who have joined the army (or not) and shortages of items at home and requests that he send items in short supply in Braintree, like pins and paper, tea and salt, and handkerchiefs. Later she discovers that the articles he sends in response can be sold locally for profit, and so inaugurates her small merchandising enterprises that continue for almost a decade and bring her a small income. John obtains leave of absence from Congress in October and returns to Braintree in early November.

1777   John leaves Braintree in early January for Baltimore, where Congress had temporarily relocated in December 1776. Though she is pregnant, Abigail does not try to prevent his departure, justifying his absence by her now resolved conviction that without his presence at Congress, the entire enterprise would fail. Daughter Elizabeth is stillborn on July 11. Abigail writes a letter to John between contractions, giving voice to her fear and pain in a rare historic record of the birthing process: "I pray Heaven that it may be soon or it seems to me I shall be worn out. I must lay my pen down this moment, to bear what I cannot fly from—and now I have endured it I reassume my pen." Once recovered, her mood shifts to acceptance of their separation, and her letters reveal her improved health and mood; in them she describes her extensive reading of poetry, novels, and history (citing Pope, Goldsmith, and Moore, among many others), and her expanded role as head of household. Congress leaves Philadelphia and reconvenes in York, Pennsylvania, as British army under General William Howe, brother of Admiral Howe, occupies the city on September 26. Abigail's sister Elizabeth marries the Reverend John Shaw, October 16. After a series of defeats, General John Burgoyne surrenders army of 5,000 men to Americans at Saratoga, New York, on October 17; this first major victory of the war for the Americans is crucial to gaining the confidence of the French, whose financial support is needed to sustain the war effort. John obtains leave from Congress on November 7 and returns to Braintree on November 27, intending to resume his law practice. Instead he is chosen by Congress to replace Silas Deane as commissioner to France, where he will join fellow envoys Benjamin Franklin and Arthur Lee. To Abigail's dismay, he accepts the commission on December 23.

1778 France and the United States sign treaties of alliance and commerce in Paris on February 6; under their terms, France recognizes the independence of the United States and pledges to fight until American independence is won if the treaties lead to war between Britain and France. On February 15, John departs for France onboard the American frigate *Boston*, taking with him John Quincy, age ten. Abigail will hear nothing of them for months. They land in Bordeaux on April 1, after an eventful passage that includes a March 10 encounter with a hostile letter of marque vessel. In May, having settled with Franklin at Passy, outside Paris, John has his first audience with Louis XVI at Versailles. War begins between Britain and France on June 14. The relationship between Adams and Franklin becomes increasingly tense as they take sides in a controversy between Arthur Lee and departed commissioner Silas Deane; Adams supports Lee, who has accused Deane of financial improprieties, charges that Franklin rejects. Abigail initiates a correspondence with James Lovell, Massachusetts delegate to the Continental Congress, whom she presses for information about John and about the war's progress. Lovell addresses her flirtatiously, and their correspondence, by turns lighthearted and serious, continues for several years. In September, Congress votes to disband the commission in France, and names Franklin as sole minister plenipotentiary to France. On October 21, Abigail informs John that the French admiral, the comte d'Estaing, whose fleet has entered Boston Harbor as the first tangible sign of the new Franco-American alliance, had recently visited her and invited her and any of her friends to dine with him and his officers aboard his ship. She later reports that the evening was "An entertainment fit for a princess." In December, Abigail 2nd makes an extended visit to the Warrens in Plymouth, where she will remain until May of the next year.

1779   In January, Abigail writes to Lovell criticizing Deane's controversial address in support of his conduct in France. John learns of the loss of his commission on February 12 and writes to Abigail on February 20 to inform her of his intention to return home and resume his law practice: "I will draw Writs and Deeds, and harrangue Jurys and be happy." He leaves Passy with John Quincy on March 8 and travels to Nantes and Lorient. At Nantes they make the acquaintance of Joshua Johnson, whose daughter, Louisa Catherine, John Quincy will marry in 1797. They sail from Lorient on June 17 onboard the French frigate *La Sensible* and arrive in Boston on August 3. On September 27, Congress appoints John as the sole minister to negotiate peace with Britain. Abigail is determined to accompany him, but he resists, citing the dangers of sea travel in winter and during wartime. John sails for France on November 15 on *La Sensible*, taking with him sons John Quincy, age twelve, and Charles, nine; their difficult journey lasts three months and involves an overland trek through Spain. From Bilbao, he sends Abigail the first of many consignments of European goods for resale in America. Abigail settles into a now familiar if still lonely pattern of living, describing herself as "a nun." She rids herself of farming responsibilities by taking on two tenants ("brothers newly married"), but expands her commercial enterprises by purchasing land and securities, and selling items that she now imports directly from European suppliers. Throughout she is much engaged with family (Mary and Richard Cranch as well as her father and John's mother live nearby), friends (an ongoing correspondence and sometimes visits from Mercy Otis Warren and others), occasional visits to Boston, and always the care of her remaining children, Abigail 2nd and Thomas Boylston. Correspondence with John during next few years is irregular, dependent upon the passage of ships and availability of trusted messengers.

1780   On May 12, reflecting on his important mission, John writes to Abigail that "I must study Politicks and War that my sons may have liberty to study Mathematicks and Philosophy. My sons ought to study Mathematicks and Philosophy, Geography, natural History, Naval Architecture, navigation, Commerce and Agriculture, in order to give their Children a right to study Painting, Poetry, Musick, Architecture, Statuary, Tapestry and Porcelaine." In June, he is commissioned by Congress to raise a loan in Holland, where, frustrated by the state of affairs in Paris, he has already decided to venture on his own initiative. John and the boys leave Paris on July 27 and arrive in Amsterdam on August 10. In letters to her sons Abigail continues to exhort them about their behavior: she hopes that the "neatness and Cleanliness" of the Dutch will cure John Quincy of his "slovenly tricks." On December 29, Congress empowers Adams to seek a treaty of amity and commerce with the Netherlands in place of Henry Laurens, who was captured by the British crossing the Atlantic.

1781   In January, John arranges for John Quincy and Charles to attend lectures at the University of Leyden in addition to their tutorial lessons. In the spring, Abigail investigates the purchase of land in Vermont. At the same time, James and Mercy Otis Warren and their family move to Milton, where they occupy the home formerly belonging to Thomas Hutchinson; they are now much closer to Abigail in Braintree. In July, Abigail writes to Lovell and to Elbridge Gerry, another congressman and family friend, defending John against aspersions originating in letters from Franklin. On July 7, John Quincy leaves for St. Petersburg with Francis Dana, the American envoy to Russia, where he will serve as Dana's secretary and French interpreter from August 1781 to October 1782. Ten-year-old Charles, dreadfully homesick, leaves the Netherlands for the United States on August 12, arriving in Braintree in late January of the following year. John falls seriously ill with a fever, possibly malarial, in Amsterdam from August to October. Meanwhile, on October 19, French and American troops force the surrender of a large British army at Yorktown, Virginia, in the last major military engagement of the Revolutionary War. When she does not hear from him for an entire year, due in part to the vagaries of sea traffic and in part to his fever, Abigail writes to John at the end of 1781: "Two years my dearest Friend have past away since you left your Native land. Will you not return e'er the close of an other year?" She confesses that she has no desire for fame or glory, which, she suspects, keeps him at his foreign post. "I feel no ambition for a share of it. I know the voice of Fame to be a mere weathercock, unstable as Water and fleeting as a Shadow."

1782   John achieves what he later considers to be one of his greatest accomplishments when the States General of the Netherlands recognizes American independence on April 19; on June 11, he crowns this success when he negotiates a loan of five million guilders to the United States. Abigail continues to plead for John's return. In December, she writes to apprise him that Abigail 2nd, at age seventeen, has a suitor. "We have in the little circle an other gentleman," she reports, informing him that a young lawyer, Royall Tyler, has set up shop in town and is boarding with the Cranches. John responds: "I dont like the Subject at all. My Child is too young for such Thoughts."

1783   John attends signing of preliminary Anglo-French and Anglo-Spanish peace treaties at Versailles on January 20. Signs Definitive Treaty of Peace with Franklin, Jay, and British negotiator David Hartley in Paris on September 3. Falls ill with fever, September–October, and recovers in Auteuil outside of Paris. Abigail's father, William Smith, dies on September 17. His will frees Phoebe, the Smiths' slave, whom Abigail calls "the only surviving Parent I have." In November, Abigail receives her first letter from John Quincy in two years. In response to John's "pressing invitation," she decides to join John in Europe, where he expects Congress to appoint him as the first American minister to the Court of St. James's. Phoebe lives in Braintree house during Abigail's absence.

1784   Despite her many reservations—"mere American that I am"
        —Abigail sets sail for Europe on June 20, avowing that
        nothing but the prospect of meeting her "good husband"
        could induce a "Lady upon the ocean." Abigail 2nd accompanies her, having promised her hand to Tyler upon
        her return. Charles and Thomas Boylston remain in Massachusetts with Abigail's sister Elizabeth. In letters to her
        family, Abigail records the details of seasickness and wretched
        accommodations on six-week voyage that ends in London,
        July 21. John Quincy joins them there, July 30, and John
        on August 7. The reunited family travels together to Paris
        and settles in Auteuil, in a forty-room mansion with seven
        servants, where they reside for the next nine months. In
        order to learn French, Abigail sets herself the goal of reading one French play a day. She forms a close friendship
        with Thomas Jefferson, who with John and Benjamin
        Franklin has been appointed to negotiate treaties of amity
        and commerce with states in Europe and North Africa.

1785   John is officially named by Congress on February 24 as
        the first American minister to Great Britain. John Quincy
        leaves France to return to the United States, May 12, in
        order to attend Harvard (which his parents judge will be
        superior to the "decadent" environment of European
        universities). With Abigail 2nd and John, Abigail moves to
        London, arriving May 26. John has an audience with
        George III, June 1, and Abigail and Abigail 2nd are presented to the King and Queen, June 23 (Charlotte "is not
        well shaped or handsome"). The family moves into house
        on Grosvenor Square that becomes the first American legation in London, July 2. Amid a hostile reception from
        the British press, the family visits museums and views art,
        hears *The Messiah* at Westminster Abbey ("Only conceive
        six hundred voices and instruments . . . I could scarcly
        believe myself an inhabitant of Earth"), tours the countryside, spending weekends at country homes, attends Anglican
        church services in the absence of their own denomination,
        and takes in the social season at Bath. Charles admitted to
        Harvard College, August 17.

1786   John Quincy admitted to Harvard College as a junior,
        March 15. Family members inform the Adamses of Royall

Tyler's dubious behavior. John's new secretary, Colonel William Stephens Smith, a former aide to General Washington, begins courting Abigail 2nd. Abigail narrates the unfolding drama to her sisters and to John Quincy, including her strange premonitory dream on the eve of her daughter's marriage. Abigail 2nd marries William Stephens Smith on June 12. Abigail visits Braintree in Essex with John, Abigail 2nd, and Colonel Smith in August, then travels to the Netherlands with John where he exchanges ratifications of a treaty with Prussia. Thomas Boylston admitted to Harvard College, August 30.

1787   Grandson William Steuben Smith born in London, April 2. John Quincy graduates from Harvard College. In June, Jefferson's daughter Mary (Polly), age nine, and his slave, Sally Hemings, age fourteen, arrive in London and stay with the Adamses for several weeks, en route to live with Jefferson in Paris. Abigail arranges with her uncle, Cotton Tufts, for the purchase of the Vassall-Borland house in Braintree, Massachusetts, which John will call "Peacefield" and which will later be known as the "Old House," in preparation for the family's return from Europe. Brother William Smith dies, September 3. In October Congress approves John's request that he be recalled from his diplomatic missions.

1788   Sails from Portsmouth with John in late April and arrives in Boston on June 17 to a celebrity welcome in Boston. The couple leave quickly for their new home in Braintree to discover it in great disrepair, a "wren's house," Abigail calls it. After eleven of the thirteen states ratify the new federal Constitution, Congress passes an election ordinance on September 13 setting dates for choosing presidential electors and electing a president and vice president. John's political future is ambiguous, but in the interim he happily farms his lands. Abigail travels to New York, where Abigail 2nd is now settled, to be present for the birth of her second grandchild, John Adams Smith, on November 9. John is elected to the House of Representatives in the First Federal Congress, but never serves.

1789   Presidential electors meet in their states on February 4 and vote for two candidates in balloting for president. George Washington receives the votes of all sixty-nine electors and is elected president, while John receives thirty-four votes and is elected vice president (John Jay receives nine votes, and twenty-six votes are divided among nine other candidates). John travels to New York City, the federal capital, rents a country estate called Richmond Hill overlooking the Hudson River in lower Manhattan (located near what is now Varick and Charlton Streets), and presides over the Senate for the first time on April 21. Abigail arrives in New York on June 24. She writes to her sister Mary that if ever Mary or other "intimate Friend's" notice her changed behavior due to her elevated status, she requests that they would "with the utmost freedom acquaint me with it." Charles graduates from Harvard College and begins studying law in the New York offices of Alexander Hamilton (he later moves to the office of John Laurance). The first session of the First Federal Congress adjourns on September 29.

1790   John presides over the Senate in the second session of Congress, January–August. Thomas Boylston graduates from Harvard College. Grandson Thomas Hollis Smith born August 7 in New York. Abigail moves with John to Philadelphia, where the federal capital has been relocated until 1800, and takes up residence at Bush Hill, an estate along the Schuylkill west of the city. John presides over third session of the Senate, December 1790–March 1791.

1791   John Quincy moves to Boston to begin his law practice. An American edition of Thomas Paine's *Rights of Man* is published in May with an endorsement by Jefferson alluding to "the political heresies which have sprung up among us," a remark widely understood to be a reference to John's "Discourses of Davila." Assuming the name "Publicola," John Quincy responds by criticizing Paine and Jefferson in series of essays published in the Boston *Columbian Centinel*, while other newspapers accuse John of supporting monarchy and aristocracy. Grandson Thomas Hollis Smith dies July 8. John presides over the Senate during the first session of the Second Congress, October 1791–May 1792. Abigail moves with John from Bush Hill to a smaller house at Fourth and Arch Streets in Philadelphia.

1792   The North Precinct of Braintree is incorporated as the town of Quincy in February, in honor of Abigail's grandfather. In August, Charles gains his certificate to practice law. John returns to Philadelphia in the fall while Abigail remains in Quincy for health reasons (she will stay in Massachusetts for the remainder of John's vice presidency). John presides over the Senate in the second session of the Second Congress, November 1792–March 1793. During their separations Abigail writes, as she always has, of the local news, but also often shares her opinions on the increasingly fractured state of national politics, as controversial issues like Hamilton's economic policies, Jay's Treaty, and the French Revolution encourage the coalescence of political factions that will in time become known as Federalists and Republicans. Abigail remarks that "I firmly believe if I live Ten years longer, I shall see a devision of the Southern & Northern states, unless more candour & less intrigue, of which I have no hopes, should prevail." In the electoral balloting on December 5, Washington is reelected with the votes of all 132 electors, and John is reelected as vice president with seventy-seven votes, while George Clinton receives fifty electoral votes, Jefferson four, and Aaron Burr one.

1793   John presides over the Senate during the first session of the Third Congress, December 1793–June 1794. Thomas Boylston is admitted to the Philadelphia bar.

1794   Washington appoints John Quincy minister resident to the Netherlands, May 30. He sails for Europe in September with Thomas Boylston as his secretary. Abigail's brother-in-law John Shaw dies September 29. John presides over the Senate during the second session of the Third Congress, November 1794–March 1795.

1795   Granddaughter Caroline Amelia Smith born in New York, January 28. Adams presides over a special session of the Senate called on June 8 to consider Jay's Treaty. The Senate votes 20–10 on June 24 to ratify the treaty after a secret debate. Published on July 1, the treaty is widely attacked for failing to secure American rights with Great Britain, and the controversy further divides Republicans and Federalists. Charles marries Sarah Smith, sister of William Stephens Smith, in New York on August 29. John presides over the Senate during the first session of the Fourth Congress, December 1795–May 1796. Abigail's sister Elizabeth marries the Reverend Stephen Peabody, December 8.

1796   Granddaughter Susanna Boylston Adams, first child of Charles and Sarah, is born August 8 in New York. George

Washington announces that he will not run for a third term and delivers his farewell address on September 19. In the presidential election, Federalists support John while Republicans support Jefferson; neither candidate makes any public statements. The friendship between the Adamses and Jefferson is one of the many casualties of partisan strife in the new republic. John is particularly embittered by the support for Jefferson shown by longtime friends and associates, including James and Mercy Otis Warren, Benjamin Rush, and Samuel Adams. John returns to Philadelphia for the second session of the Fourth Congress, which begins on December 5. On December 7, the presidential electors meet and select John Adams as president with seventy-one votes; Thomas Jefferson, with sixty-nine votes, becomes vice president. Writing to John Quincy shortly after the election, Abigail (quoting the English poet Edward Young) confesses: "It is the will of Providence to place me in a very conspicuous station. . . . I would bear my Honours meekly fully sensible that 'High Stations tumult, but not Bliss creat / None think the Great unhappy but the Great.'" But she concludes on a note of optimism: "Still has My Life New wonders seen / Repeated every Year."

1797   John is inaugurated as president on March 4 and elects to retain Washington's cabinet. Abigail remains in Quincy, running the farm as well as caring for John's ailing mother, aged eighty-eight. At first determined to function without her, John soon discovers the loneliness and isolation of the presidency and in a series of letters begs Abigail to come to him. The French Directory orders Charles Cotesworth Pinckney, who had been appointed as minister to France by Washington in 1796, to leave the country, and the French navy increases its seizures of American ships trading with Britain. John moves into the President's House at Sixth and Market Streets. Abigail's mother-in-law Susanna Boylston Adams dies in Quincy, April 17. Abigail joins John in Philadelphia on May 10. In her role as the second First Lady she follows closely in the footsteps of Martha Washington, whom she admires, but the Adamses never acquire the privileged cachet of the Washingtons. John addresses a special session of Congress on May 16, calling for the strengthening of the navy while announcing that a new diplomatic mission will be sent to France. He nominates Charles Cotesworth Pinckney, John Marshall, and Elbridge Gerry to serve as commissioners to France and appoints John Quincy minister plenipotentiary to Prussia. The press accuses the president of nepotism. "The appointments of Envoys extraordinary, like every other measure of Government will be censured by those who make a point of abusing every thing," Abigail writes to her sister Mary. Abigail leaves Philadelphia with John for Quincy on July 19. John Quincy marries Louisa Catherine Johnson in London, July 26; they move to Berlin in October with Thomas Boylston. Abigail and John leave Quincy in early October, staying in East Chester, New York, where Congress meets until the yellow fever epidemic in Philadelphia ends in early November. American envoys to France have a brief informal meeting with Talleyrand, the French foreign minister, on October 8, and are then approached by three of Talleyrand's agents, who solicit a $240,000 bribe as precondition for further negotiations; the agents also demand that the Americans agree to loan France $12 million and repudiate critical remarks about French policy made by John in his address to Congress on May 16. The American commissioners refuse to pay, and describe their reception in dispatches sent to Pickering on October 22 and November 8. John delivers his first annual message to Congress on November 22.

1798   Pickering receives coded dispatches from the envoys on March 4, along with an uncoded letter reporting that the Directory has closed French ports to neutral shipping and made all ships carrying British products subject to capture. John sends message to Congress on March 19 announcing failure of the peace mission and requesting the adoption of defensive measures. In response to request from the House of Representatives, John submits the dispatches to Congress on April 3, and they are quickly published, with Talleyrand's agents referred to as X, Y, and Z. Revelation of the "XYZ" Affair causes popular furor against France. John signs into law the Alien and Sedition Acts, which extend the period required for naturalization from five to fourteen years; give the president the power to expel or, in time of declared war, to imprison dangerous aliens (no one is expelled under the law, though many French leave voluntarily); and make the publication of "false, scandalous, and malicious writing" attacking the federal government, the president, or the Congress a crime punishable by up to two years in prison. (Ten Republican editors and printers are convicted under the Sedition Act during the Adams administration.) Abigail cheers the acts—"Let the vipers cease to hiss. they will be destroyd with their own poison" —even as they catalyze opposition among Republicans, Jefferson foremost among them, for whom the acts are a transparent Federalist attempt to quash legitimate opposition. By summertime relations between the United States and France have descended into a state of quasi-war, with American shipping increasingly subject to French depredations. Abigail leaves Philadelphia with John for Quincy, July 25, where she becomes seriously ill. Writing to George Washington in early October, John despairs that "her Destiny is Still very precarious, and mine in consequence of it." Granddaughter Abigail Louisa Smith Adams, second child of Charles and Sarah, is born September 8. Thomas Boylston departs Berlin, September 30, arriving in Quincy on February 12. On November 12, John returns to Philadelphia without Abigail. That Thanksgiving, she laments: "No Husband *dignifies my Board*, no Children add gladness to it." She invites her neighbors and Phoebe to dine with her. John delivers his second annual message to Congress December 8, in which he suggests the possibility of appointing a new peace mission to France.

1799   Contrary to the opinion of his cabinet, which favors war with France, John nominates William Vans Murray, a seasoned envoy and minister to the Hague, as special envoy to France, February 18, and declares that Murray will be sent only after Talleyrand gives assurances that he will be properly received; he later names Chief Justice Oliver Ellsworth and William Davie as additional negotiators. Abigail describes the reaction in Boston: "the whole community were like a flock of frightned pigions." John returns to Quincy in mid-March, where he remains until September 30. There Abigail and John learn that Charles, who has been drinking heavily for years, has deserted his family and is bankrupt. In early October, John travels to Trenton where the government has relocated during the yellow fever epidemic in Philadelphia. In November he returns to Philadelphia where Abigail joins him. George Washington dies, December 14. "No man ever lived, more deservedly beloved and Respected," Abigail writes. "History will not produce to us a parrallel."

1800   Aware that these will be their last months of living in Philadelphia, Abigail once more expresses "melancholy in the Idea of leaving a place for the last time. It is like burying a Friend." The members of the cabinet either resign or, in the case of Pickering, are fired as the president refuses to withdraw his peace overture to France. Abigail is infuriated with the dithering in Congress, in part because a presidential election is imminent. "One or two more Elections will be quite sufficient I believe to convince this people that no engine can be more fatally employd than frequent popular Elections, to corrupt and destroy the morals of the people," she writes to Mary. There are the usual social obligations to be attended to ("My last drawing Room is notified for the 2d of May") and arrangements made for their arrival at Quincy. The Federalist caucus again endorses John's reelection. Abigail leaves for home in June, while John travels to survey the new capital city, Washington, D.C., before returning to Quincy. The summer months are tranquil except for the subversive aura of campaigning that prevails; former treasury secretary Alexander Hamilton, who has been orchestrating the cabinet's resistance to the president's policies, meets with leading New England Federalists in June and urges them to support Charles Cotesworth Pinckney, the Federalist vice presidential candidate, for the presidency over Adams. American envoys in France sign the Convention of 1800 on September 30, ending the undeclared naval war between the two countries and suspending the 1778 treaty of alliance. John will regard the aversion of full-scale war with France to be among his greatest achievements. Hamilton publishes a derogatory pamphlet on October 24 describing Adams as unfit for the presidency. John arrives in Washington on November 1. Abigail travels separately, stopping first to visit Abigail 2nd and then Charles who is dying of alcoholism. "Shall I receive good and not evil," she writes to Mary. "You will easily suppose that this Scene was too powerfull and distressing to me." John and Abigail become the first occupants of the still-unfinished President's House (now called the White House) in the new federal city, which is inconveniently situated in a malarial swamp. "This House is built for ages to come," Abigail writes to her sister about the presidential mansion. "Not one room or Chamber is finished of the whole. It is habitable by fires in every part, thirteen of which we are obliged to keep daily or sleep in wet or damp places." Nor is firewood available, except in Georgetown, "the dirtyest Hole I ever saw for a place." Charles dies of liver failure in East Chester, New York, November 30. Presidential electors meet on December 3. Thomas Jefferson and Aaron Burr tie for the presidency with seventy-three votes each to Adams's sixty-five. "The consequence to us personally, is that we retire from public Life," Abigail writes to Thomas Boylston. "For myself and family I have few regrets," she insists, but she worries about John. He claims that he will retire with ease to farming.

1801   The House of Representatives elects Jefferson president on February 17 after thirty-six ballots; Burr becomes vice president. Abigail presides over her last formal dinner parties. Adams nominates, and the Federalist Senate confirms, Federalist circuit court judges. (These "midnight appointments" anger Jefferson and the Republicans, and in 1802 a Republican Congress repeals the Judiciary Act of 1801 and abolishes the new circuit court judgeships.) John recalls John Quincy from his position in Prussia. Abigail leaves Washington for Quincy on February 13; John follows early on the morning of Jefferson's inauguration, March 4. Grandson George Washington Adams, the first child of John Quincy and Louisa Catherine, is born April 12 in Berlin. John Quincy and family leave Berlin for Boston in July.

1802   John Quincy is elected to Massachusetts Senate in February, and in November, defeated in a close election as a Federalist candidate for Congress.

1803   In February, John Quincy is elected U.S. senator from Massachusetts (serves until 1808). Because of the failure of British bank Bird, Savage, & Bird, in which they had invested, Abigail and John lose $13,000. In a long-term arrangement to compensate for these losses and support his parents, John Quincy purchases Peacefield and the surrounding property. John Adams 2nd, second son of John Quincy and Louisa Catherine, born on July 4.

1804   Following the death of Mary (Polly) Jefferson Eppes, whom Abigail had cared for in London, a brief correspondence takes place between Abigail and Jefferson in which they rehearse their former friendship and the causes of its collapse, including the Sedition Act and the "midnight appointments."

1805   Thomas Boylston marries Ann Harrod of Haverhill, Massachusetts, May 16. In August, John Quincy becomes first Boylston Professor of Rhetoric and Oratory at Harvard.

1806   Granddaughter Abigail Smith Adams is born on July 29, the first child of Thomas Boylston and Ann.

1807   After reading Mercy Otis Warren's three-volume *History of the Rise, Progress and Termination of the American Revolution,* which he feels considerably understates the significance of his contributions, John engages in an angry correspondence with Mercy between July 28 and August 19 in which he attacks her both as a historian and as a friend. Abigail does not correspond with Mercy for several years (in 1809, she will write: "what I have still thought more unkind, is, that when those Errors were pointed out, and means furnished you for rectifying them, not a Solitary line ever acknowledged the receipt of a Letter or any disposition to retract. It was this which dried up the fountain of my ink"). Grandson Charles Francis Adams, third son of John Quincy and Louisa Catherine, is born August 18.

1808   John Quincy resigns his Senate seat on June 8, a move that signals his break with the Federalist Party. Granddaughter Elizabeth Coombs Adams, second child of Thomas Boylston and Ann, is born June 9.

1809   John Quincy is appointed minister plenipotentiary to Russia by President James Madison, June 27, and leaves for St. Petersburg with Louisa Catherine and their youngest child, Charles Francis, in August, accompanied by the Adamses' grandson William Steuben Smith, age twenty-two, who serves as John Quincy's secretary. Their older two sons, George, age eight, and John, age six, are left under the supervision of Abigail and John, who send them for schooling first to her sister Mary and later to Elizabeth, who with her husband Stephen Peabody runs a school in

Atkinson, New Hampshire. The children spend weekends and vacations at Peacefield. Grandson Thomas Jr. is born to Thomas and Ann on August 4. Abigail observes to granddaughter Caroline Smith that "old age with its infirmities assail me, I have reason to be thankful, that my senses are so much in action, that my hearing is not at all impaired, but memory, and recollection are not what they once were." Yet she continues: "My heart is still warm, and my affections fervent towards my dear children and friends."

1811   Eager for John Quincy to return home, Abigail writes to President Madison urging him to recall the diplomat, which he does, appointing him to the Supreme Court on February 22. John Quincy declines. In March Abigail learns that Abigail 2nd is ill. Abigail 2nd travels from New York to Quincy for further diagnosis. In June, Thomas Boylston is appointed chief justice of the Massachusetts Circuit Court of Common Pleas for the Southern Circuit. Granddaughter Frances Foster Adams, fourth child of Thomas Boylston and Ann, is born June 22. Granddaughter Louisa Catherine Adams, fourth child of John Quincy and Louisa Catherine, is born in St. Petersburg, Russia, August 12. On October 8, Abigail 2nd undergoes a mastectomy without anesthesia in her parents' home. She remains in Quincy with her daughter Caroline through the winter to recuperate. Brother-in-law Richard Cranch dies of a stroke, October 16, and Abigail's sister Mary Cranch of consumption, October 17. "I have past through Scenes, my dear Son in this last year, most Solemn, and impressive," Abigail writes to John Quincy. "God grant that it may be good for me that I have been afflicted."

1812   On January 1, John resumes a correspondence with Thomas Jefferson, ending a rift that has divided the two founders for more than a dozen years. John will write more than twice as many letters as Jefferson over fourteen years, while Abigail will write to Jefferson three times. Frances, infant daughter of Thomas and Ann, dies March 4. Congress declares war on Great Britain, June 17. The Adamses support President Madison and the war. Louisa, one-year-old daughter of John Quincy and Louisa Catherine, dies in Russia, September 15. Phoebe dies in the fall or winter. Abigail writes: "I love and respect and venerate her."

1813   Grandson William Steuben Smith marries Catherine Maria

Frances Johnson, sister of Louisa Catherine Adams, in St. Petersburg, February 17. Grandson Isaac Hull Adams, the fifth child of Thomas Boylston and Ann, is born May 26. Abigail 2nd's breast cancer recurs, this time metastasized throughout her body. In July she endures a three-week journey from upstate New York, accompanied by her son and daughter, to her parents' home, where she dies on August 15. "To me the loss is irreparable," Abigail writes to John Quincy. Devastated, she still counts her blessings, foremost being her family and "the Life, health, and cheerfullness of your Father. bowed down as he has been by our late affliction, he has not sunk under it."

1814   In January, John Quincy is appointed to a five-member commission to negotiate a peace treaty with Great Britain. The Treaty of Ghent is signed on December 24. Granddaughter Caroline Amelia Smith marries John Peter de Windt, September 11. Granddaughter Abigail Louisa Adams marries Alexander Bryan Johnson, October 23. Abigail and John celebrate their fiftieth wedding anniversary, October 25. Abigail reflects to her sister Elizabeth, "after half a century, I can Say my first choice would be the same if I again had youth, and opportunity to make it." Mercy Otis Warren dies, October 18: "take her all and all, we shall not look upon her like again."

1815   Like his father before him, John Quincy is appointed minister plenipotentiary to Great Britain, February 28. Abigail writes to Louisa Catherine: "My Son has a difficult part assignd him. on the one hand, he cannot but feel what his Country has endured, and Britain must feel that She has been foild a Second time; and that as it were by Hereditary descent. She must receive as an Ambassador of Peace, the Son of the Father who was instrumental in Severing the two Countries, and afterward in Representing the Sovereignty of that Same Country to the Kingdom of great Britain. it is a Singular Instance." Louisa Catherine travels with six-year-old Charles from St. Petersburg to Paris, arriving March 23. Abigail and John send grandsons George and John to meet their parents in London. Abigail's sister, Elizabeth Smith Shaw Peabody, dies suddenly on April 10. Grandson John Quincy Adams, sixth child of Thomas Boylston and Ann, is born December 16.

1816   Son-in-law William Stephens Smith dies, June 10.

1817   John Quincy is appointed secretary of state by President Monroe, March 5; he and his family return from London, arriving in Quincy in August before moving to Washington, D.C., in September. Granddaughter Susanna Boylston Adams marries Charles Thomas Clark, August 3. Grandson George Washington Adams enrolls at Harvard, August 28. Grandson Joseph Harrod Adams, seventh child of Thomas Boylston and Ann, is born December 16.

1818   John Quincy and Louisa Catherine visit from Washington in August. Writing to Jefferson on October 20, John reports that "the dear Partner of my Life for fifty four Years as a Wife and for many Years more as a Lover, now lyes, in extremis, forbidden to Speak or be Spoken to." Abigail does not survive this final bout of typhoid fever and dies on October 28. Thomas Jefferson commiserates with John, writing on November 13 that "the same trials have taught me that, for ills so immeasurable, time and silence are the only medecines."

List of Correspondents

Abigail Louisa Smith Adams, granddaughter (September 8, 1798–July 4, 1836). Born in New York, younger daughter of Charles and Sarah Smith Adams. Married Alexander Bryan Johnson (1786–1867) a philosopher, author, and banker, on October 14, 1814; they had nine children. Died of uterine cancer in Utica.

Charles Adams, son (May 29, 1770–November 30, 1800) Born in Boston, Massachusetts, the second son of Abigail and John Adams. Traveled to Europe in 1779 with his father and older brother, John Quincy, and studied briefly in Passy, Amsterdam, and the University of Leyden. Homesick, returned to the U.S. in 1781. Entered Harvard in 1785, where he began to drink frequently and became embroiled in a scandal in which several boys were caught running naked across Harvard Yard. Graduated in 1789. Studied law, briefly under Alexander Hamilton, and established practice in Hanover Square in New York, 1792, upon passing the bar. Married Sarah "Sally" Smith, sister of brother-in-law William Stephens Smith, on August 29, 1795, and had two daughters, Susanna Boylston Adams Clark Treadway and Abigail Louisa Smith Adams Johnson. In 1798, lost $4,000 of John Quincy's savings in land speculation. His alcoholism escalated, and he died in East Chester, New York, from liver failure.

Charles Francis Adams, grandson (August 18, 1807–November 21, 1886) Born in Boston, Massachusetts, third son of John Quincy Adams and Louisa Catherine Johnson Adams. Raised in St. Petersburg, 1809–15, and London, 1815–17, due to father's diplomatic appointments. Graduated from Harvard, 1825. Studied law with Daniel Webster. Admitted to the bar, 1829. Married Abigail Brown Brooks (1808–1889) the same year, with whom he had seven children. Served as a Whig in the Massachusetts House of Representatives, 1841–43, and in the state senate, 1844–45. Vice presidential candidate of the Free Soil Party, 1848. Edited *The Works of John Adams* (1850–56). Served in Congress as a Republican, 1859–61. As U.S. minister to Great Britain, 1861–68, helped maintain British neutrality in the Civil War. Edited the *Memoirs of John Quincy Adams* (1874–77). Died in Boston.

John Adams 2nd, grandson (July 4, 1803–October 23, 1834) Born in Boston, Massachusetts, the second son of John Quincy Adams and Louisa Catherine Johnson Adams. Spent most of his childhood in Quincy with his grandparents while his parents were on diplomatic appointments abroad, before boarding with Richard and Mary Cranch in Quincy and later with the Reverend Stephen and Elizabeth Peabody in Atkinson, New Hampshire. Studied at Derby Academy in Hingham, Massachusetts. Reunited with parents in 1815 and attended boarding school in Ealing, England. Returned to U.S. in 1817 and attended Boston Public Latin School. Entered Harvard in 1819. Participated in student rebellions and was expelled in 1823, just shy of graduation (was graduated posthumously in 1873). Studied law with father. In 1825, when John Quincy became president, was appointed his father's private secretary. In 1827, became manager of Columbian Mills, a flour mill in Washington, D.C., owned by his father since 1823. Married cousin Mary Catherine Hellen (1806–1870) at the White House on February 25, 1828. Daughters Mary Louisa born in 1828 and Georgeanna Frances in 1830. Died in Washington, D.C., from complications of alcoholism.

John Quincy Adams, son (July 11, 1767–February 23, 1848) Born in Braintree, Massachusetts, second child of Abigail and John Adams. In 1778 he accompanied his father on a one-year diplomatic mission to France and attended school in Paris. Served as private secretary to Francis Dana, American minister to Russia, 1781–82, before joining father in the Netherlands after the signing of the Treaty of Paris in September 1783. Graduated from Harvard College in 1787, and began to practice law in Boston in 1790. In May 1794, appointed minister to the Netherlands by George Washington. In 1797 married Louisa Catherine Johnson in London; they had four children. Following his father's election as president, he was appointed minister to Prussia, serving until 1801, when his father lost his bid for reelection to Jefferson. Elected to the Senate in 1803, he resigned in 1808 after being repudiated by fellow Massachusetts Federalists for supporting Jefferson's Embargo Act of 1807. Named the first Boylston Professor of Rhetoric and Oratory at Harvard in 1805, he published his *Lectures on Rhetoric and Oratory* in 1810. Appointed minister to Russia by James Madison in 1809. As leader of the American peace commissioners, helped negotiate the Treaty of Ghent (signed December 24, 1814), which brought an end to the War of 1812; he subsequently served as minister to Great Britain, 1815–16. As secretary of state under James Monroe, 1817–25, he supported Andrew Jackson's invasion of Florida, negotiated Spain's cession of Florida and the abandonment of its claims in the Pacific Northwest, secured an agreement with Great Britain on the U.S.-Canadian border, and played a major role in the formulation of the Monroe Doctrine. In the four-way presidential contest of 1824, which was decided by the House of Representatives, he was elected sixth president of the United States. Defeated for reelection in 1828. Elected to Congress as an independent in 1830 and served until his death. As a congressman, opposed the extension of slavery and the annexation of Texas and waged a long, ultimately successful campaign (1836–44) to overturn the "gag rule" that prevented congressional debate of antislavery petitions. In 1841 he successfully defended African mutineers of the slave ship *Amistad* before the Supreme Court. He suffered a stroke during a session of Congress and was carried to the Speaker's Room, where he died two days later.

George Washington Adams, grandson (April 12, 1801–June 9, 1829) Born in Berlin, then the capital of Prussia, first child of John Quincy and Louisa Catherine Johnson Adams. Named after the first U.S. president, disappointing the second, grandfather John Adams. When father was appointed minister plenipotentiary to Russia, he and brother John Adams 2nd were separated from their parents for six years, staying with assorted relatives until entering Derby Academy in Hingham, Massachusetts. In 1815, reunited with his parents in London. Enrolled at Harvard, 1817, graduating in 1821. Studied law with his father and with Daniel Webster. Elected to the Massachusetts House of Representatives in 1826 and served for one year. Served on the Boston Common Council in 1828. Mistress Eliza Dolph, a chambermaid, allegedly gave birth to his child in 1829. Struggled with alcoholism, depression, and paranoia, and while journeying from Boston to Washington, D.C., to assist in his parents' move to Quincy after father's defeat for reelection to the presidency, disappeared while on the steamboat *Benjamin Franklin* in Long Island Sound. Body washed ashore four days later. Believed to have committed suicide.

Louisa Catherine Adams, daughter-in-law (February 12, 1775–May 15, 1852) Born Louisa Catherine Johnson in London, the second of eight children, to Catherine Nuth Johnson, an Englishwoman, and Joshua Johnson, a merchant from Maryland. Father moved the family to Nantes, France, 1778–83, because of the American Revolution. Developed a fluency in the French language. Met John Quincy Adams, who was serving as minister to the Netherlands, at a party in 1795; they married on July 26, 1797, at All Hallows by the Tower church in London. Suffered from frequent miscarriages; three children survived to adulthood. Moved to Prussia after the wedding for John Quincy's appointment as minister plenipotentiary to Berlin. Moved to U.S. in 1801. Moved to St. Petersburg in 1809, when husband was appointed minister to Russia; separated from her two eldest sons for six years. Bore a fourth child in 1811, Louisa Catherine Adams, the first American citizen born in Russia, who died a year later. In 1815, made six-week journey through Russia, Poland, and Germany with her sister, Kitty, and son Charles while the Napoleonic

Wars raged to rejoin husband in France. Became the only First Lady born outside of the U.S. when her husband was elected president, 1825. Believed Abigail Adams's letters should be published as an inspiration to all American women, and was a strong proponent of women's rights. Suffered from migraines, fainting spells, and a deep depression with the premature deaths of her two eldest sons. Authored several autobiographical writings: "Adventures of a Nobody," "Record of a Life, or My Story," and "Narrative of a Journey from Russia to France, 1815." Died from a stroke in her home in Washington, D.C.

Sarah Smith Adams, daughter-in-law (November 6, 1769–August 3, 1828) Born in New York, one of ten children of John Smith, a New York merchant, and Margaret Stephens Smith. Nicknamed "Sally." Married Charles Adams at First Presbyterian Church in Manhattan, New York, on August 29, 1795, in a double wedding ceremony with her sister Margaret Smith and Felix Leblond de St. Hilaire. Bore two daughters, Susanna Boylston and Abigail Louisa Smith. Upon her husband's death from alcoholism in 1800, lived with John and Abigail Adams until 1814, when she moved to Utica, New York, to live with her younger daughter and son-in-law. Died in Utica.

Susanna Boylston Adams, granddaughter (August 9, 1796–January 21, 1846) Born in New York, older daughter of Charles and Sarah Smith Adams. Married Charles Thomas Clark (b. 1793) in 1817. Bore Susanna Maria Clark in 1818 and widowed a short time later. Married William Reed Holmes Treadway (b. 1795) in 1833. Widowed three years later. Died in Baltimore.

Thomas Boylston Adams, son (September 15, 1772–March 13, 1832) Born in Braintree, Massachusetts, third son of Abigail and John Adams. Lived with aunt Elizabeth Peabody when mother and sister moved to Europe, 1784. Admitted to Harvard in 1786, graduating in 1790. Studied law in Philadelphia; admitted to the bar in 1793. As secretary to his brother John Quincy, accompanied him to the Netherlands and Prussia from 1794 to 1798. Recorded his experiences abroad, published in 1915 as *Berlin and the Prussian Court in 1798: Journal of Thomas Boylston Adams, Secretary to the United States Legation at Berlin.* Practiced law in Philadelphia and then Quincy. Secretly pursued a literary career, editing the national magazine *Port Folio.* Married Ann "Nancy" Harrod (1774–1845) of Haverhill, Massachusetts, on May 16, 1805, with whom he had four sons and three daughters. Represented Quincy in the Massachusetts legislature, 1805–6. In 1811, appointed chief justice of the Circuit Court of Common Pleas for southern Massachusetts. Struggled with alcoholism and frequent illness and moved with his family back into his parents' house. Died in Quincy.

Esther Black (September 25, 1762–?) Born Esther Duncan in Londonderry, New Hampshire, one of seven children of George Duncan and Mary Bell Duncan. Married Irish-born Moses Black (d. 1810) in Boston on November 17, 1785. Husband later served as Quincy's town moderator and represented it in the Massachusetts legislature. Purchased and settled in the "Dorothy Q." House (named for the previous tenant, Dorothy Quincy Hancock) in Quincy. Became guardian to Nancy Hall, whose parents died in Philadelphia during the yellow fever epidemic of October 1797 (mother was Anna Hall, husband's orphaned niece and a distant relative of John Adams).

Elizabeth Cranch, niece (November 20, 1763–January 25, 1811) Born in Braintree, Massachusetts, the first child of Richard Cranch and Mary Smith Cranch. Nicknamed "Betsy." Married Reverend Jacob Norton (1764–1858) of Weymouth, Massachusetts, on February 11, 1789, and had eight children. Died of pleurisy in Weymouth.

Mary Smith Cranch, sister (December 9, 1741–October 17, 1811) Born in Weymouth, Massachusetts, eldest child of Reverend William Smith and Elizabeth Quincy Smith. Married Richard Cranch (1726–1811), a watchmaker, legislator, and jurist originally from Devon, England, on November 25, 1762, with whom she had three children. Died of consumption two days after her husband's death from a stroke, in Quincy.

William Cranch, nephew (July 17, 1769–September 1, 1855) Born in Weymouth, Massachusetts, youngest child of Richard Cranch and Mary Smith Cranch. Graduated from Harvard with honors in 1787. Admitted to the Massachusetts bar in 1790. Moved to Washington, D.C., the following year to become a legal agent for a real estate firm that made speculative investments in the city, which soon failed. Married Anna "Nancy" Greenleaf (1772–1843) on April 6, 1795, in Boston, and had thirteen children. Appointed by President John Adams in 1800 as the commissioner of public buildings for the Federal district, and in 1801, served as an assistant judge of the D.C. Circuit Court. At the same time, served as the second reporter of the Supreme Court, 1801–15. Promoted to chief judge of the circuit court in 1806 and led the court for fifty years. In 1817, delivered a series of lectures about John Adams, which were later published as *Memoir of the Life, Character, and Writings of John Adams* (1827). Elected in 1826 as the first law professor at Columbian College (now George Washington University). Collected and published in 1852–53 six volumes of the decisions from his own court. Died in Washington, D.C. Great-grandfather of poet T. S. Eliot.

Hannah Phillips Cushing (July 31, 1754–May 12, 1834) Born in Middletown, Connecticut, daughter of George and Esther Phillips. Married on October 11, 1774, distant cousin William Cushing (1732–1810), a judge of the Massachusetts Superior Court, and moved to Scituate, Massachusetts. Moved to New York when husband was appointed to the Supreme Court in 1789, and then as the capital moved, to Philadelphia in 1791 and Washington, D.C., in 1800. Died in Scituate.

Elbridge Gerry (July 17, 1744–November 23, 1814) Born in Marblehead, Massachusetts, one of eleven children of Thomas Gerry, a wealthy merchant, and Elizabeth Greenleaf Gerry. Entered Harvard at thirteen, graduated in 1762, and received a master's degree in 1765. Won election to the Massachusetts General Court in 1772. Delegate with John Adams to Second Continental Congress in 1776. Signed the Declaration of Independence. Left Congress in 1785, and a year later, retired from business, took a seat in the Massachusetts state legislature, and married Ann Thompson (1763–1849) on January 12, 1786, at Trinity Church in New York; they had ten children. Delegate from Massachusetts to Constitutional Convention in Philadelphia in 1787, where he refused to sign the Constitution, which he thought gave too much power to the federal government. Elected to the U.S. House of Representatives in the first and second Congresses and served 1789–93. Appointed by President John Adams to be a member of diplomatic commission sent to France in 1797; involved in the XYZ Affair, in which French agents demanded substantial bribes from the commissioners before negotiations could continue with Foreign Minister Talleyrand. Joined the Democratic-Republican Party in 1800 and became the ninth Massachusetts governor in 1810, a position he held for two years. Signed controversial legislation allowing electoral redistricting to favor the party in power, leading to the term "gerrymandering." Elected vice president under James Madison in 1812, and served until his death in Washington, D.C.

Hannah Storer Green (May 22, 1739–September 2, 1811) Born in Boston, daughter of Ebenezer Storer, a merchant, and Mary Edwards Storer, she was a childhood friend of Abigail Adams. Married Joshua Green (1731–1806) on October 7, 1762, in Bristol, Massachusetts. Son Joshua Green, born October 5, 1764, later became a judge and politician. Settled and died in Wendell, Massachusetts.

Lucy Cranch Greenleaf, niece (September 17, 1767–February 18, 1846) Born in Braintree, Massachusetts, second daughter of Richard and Mary Smith Cranch. Married John Greenleaf (1763–1848) on April 4, 1795, and had seven children. Resided in Quincy.

Thomas Jefferson (April 13, 1743–July 4, 1826) Born in Goochland (now Albemarle) County, Virginia, son of Peter Jefferson, a landowner and surveyor, and Jane Randolph Jefferson. Educated at the College of William and Mary and admitted to the Virginia bar in 1767, he served in the Virginia House of Burgesses, 1769–74. Married Martha Wayles Skelton in 1772; they had six children before Martha died in 1782, only two surviving infancy. (Evidence suggests that he later had at least five children with his slave Sally Hemings, half sister of his deceased wife.) Active in the patriot cause, he published *A Summary View of the Rights of British America* in 1774 and was a delegate to the Continental Congress, 1775–76, where he drafted the Declaration of Independence. During the Revolutionary War he served in the Virginia Assembly, 1776–79; as governor of Virginia, 1779–81; and as a delegate to the Continental Congress, 1783–84. He replaced Benjamin Franklin as American minister to France, 1785–89, establishing his residence in Paris, and there had printed a private edition of *Notes on the State of Virginia* in 1785. Appointed secretary of state by George Washington, 1790–1793. The "Republican" candidate for president in 1796, he finished second in the electoral voting to John Adams and served as vice president, 1797–1801. In the electoral ballot of 1800 he tied with fellow Republican Aaron Burr and was elected president by the House of Representatives, and served as the third president of the United States, 1801–9. In 1814, in the wake of the British sack of Washington, and in the face of mounting personal debts, he sold his library to the federal government; it became the foundation of a revived Library of Congress. In 1817, he completed plans for the University of Virginia, which was formally chartered by the Virginia Assembly two years later; he served as the university's first rector. Died at Monticello, his estate near Charlottesville.

Catherine Nuth Johnson (1757–October 29, 1811) Born Catherine Young Nuth or Newth in London. Beginning in 1773, had eight children with Joshua Johnson (1742–1802), a merchant from Maryland who served as first U.S. consul at Nantes, France, during the American Revolution. Secretly and belatedly married Johnson on August 22, 1785. Husband's business failed and family moved to Washington, D.C., 1797. Widowed in 1802. Died in Washington, D.C.

Thomas Baker Johnson (1779–October 14, 1843) Only son of Joshua and Catherine Nuth Johnson. Attended Harvard in 1799. Appointed postmaster of New Orleans, 1811, serving until 1824. Died in Washington, D.C.

James Lovell (October 31, 1737–July 14, 1814) Born in Boston, son of John and Abigail Lovell. Graduated from Harvard in 1756 and received a Master of Arts there in 1759. Taught at Boston Latin School along with his father, who was headmaster. Married Mary Middleton on November 24, 1760; they had several children. An ardent patriot, he was chosen to deliver the oration to mark the first anniversary of the Boston Massacre in 1771. Following the battle of Bunker Hill, June 17, 1775, he was arrested by British authorities and was transported to Halifax, Nova Scotia, as a prisoner when the British evacuated Boston on March 17, 1776. Released as part of a prisoner exchange, and returned to Boston in the autumn of 1776. Elected to the Continental Congress in 1777 and served until 1782. During his years in Congress he exchanged nearly one hundred letters with Abigail Adams, becoming her closest correspondent outside her family. A member of the Committee for Foreign Affairs, he was an invaluable source for information from and about her husband. Served as tax collector in Massachusetts from 1784–88 and as customs officer of Boston and Charlestown in 1788–89. Appointed naval officer for Boston and Charlestown and served from 1789 until his death while visiting family in Windham, Massachusetts (now Maine).

John Lowell (June 17, 1743–May 6, 1802) Born in Newburyport, Massachusetts, the only surviving child of Sarah Champney Lowell and Reverend John Lowell. Graduated from Harvard in 1760. Admitted to the bar in 1763. Established a law practice in Newburyport and became active in the patriot cause. Married Sarah Higginson on January 8, 1767; they had three children. Widowed in 1772. Married Susanna Cabot on May 31, 1774; they had two children including the future industrialist Francis Cabot Lowell. Widowed again in 1777 and moved to Boston where he served several terms in the state House of Representatives. Married third wife Rebecca Russell Tyng on Christmas of 1778; they had four children. Delegate to the Massachusetts Constitutional Convention in 1779. Served in the Continental Congress in 1782 and in the Massachusetts state senate in 1784–85. Appointed as judge to the Massachusetts Court of Appeals in 1784 before being appointed by President George Washington to sit on the U.S. District Court for the District of Massachusetts in 1789. Appointed by President John Adams in 1801 as the first chief judge on the U.S. Circuit Court for the First Circuit. Died in Roxbury, Massachusetts. Descendants include poets James Russell Lowell and Robert Lowell.

Catharine Sawbridge Macaulay (April 2, 1731–June 22, 1791) Born in Kent, England, the daughter of Elizabeth Wanley Sawbridge and John Sawbridge, a land-owner. Married George Macaulay, a physician from Scotland, on June 18, 1760, and lived in London; they had one child, Catherine Sophia Macaulay. Widowed in 1766. Published eight-volume *History of England from the Accession of James I to that of the Brunswick Line*, 1763–83, and is sometimes called the first English woman historian. Scandalously married in 1778 to William Graham, a ship surgeon's mate who was twenty-six years her junior, which damaged her reputation. Published *Treatise on the Immutability of Moral Truth* (1783) and *Letters on Education with Observations on Religious and Metaphysical Subjects* (1790). Died in Binfield, England.

Dolley Madison (May 20, 1768–July 12, 1849) Born Dolley Payne in Guilford County, North Carolina, to Quaker parents who moved in 1769 to Virginia and in 1783 to Philadelphia, where her father, John Payne, operated a small business supplying laundry starch. In 1790, she married John Todd, a lawyer; they had two children before Todd and the younger child died in the Philadelphia yellow fever epidemic of 1793. In 1794, she married James Madison, then a congressman from Virginia; they had no children. The Madisons lived in Philadelphia until her husband retired in 1797, when they moved to the Madison family plantation, Montpelier, in Orange County, Virginia. She moved to Washington, D.C., in 1801, where her husband served as secretary of state in the Jefferson administrations (1801–9); during this time she often acted as hostess in the White House of the widower Jefferson. She was First Lady of the United States, 1809–17, and was famously said to have refused to leave the Executive Mansion before Gilbert Stuart's portrait of George Washington was removed to safety during the British assault on the capital in August 1814. (Her slave, Paul Jennings, recalled that she was more concerned with rescuing the White House silver.) She retired with her husband to Montpelier in 1817. After her husband's death in 1836, confronted by considerable personal debt as well as obligations stemming from the dissolute lifestyle of her surviving son, John Payne Todd, she decided to sell Montpelier and many of the estate's slaves (without their consent, in contravention of her husband's last wishes). In 1844 she moved permanently to Washington, where, in increasing financial distress, she died.

James Madison (March 16, 1751–June 28, 1836) Born in King George County, Virginia, son of James Madison, a planter, and Nelly Conway Madison, and raised at Montpelier, the family's plantation in Orange County, Virginia. Graduated from the College of New Jersey (now Princeton) in 1771. Delegate to the Continental Congress, 1779–83, and the Constitutional Convention in Philadelphia in 1787, where he drafted the Virginia plan. He wrote the *Federalist* papers (with Alexander Hamilton and John Jay) to promote the Constitution's ratification and was a member of the Virginia ratifying convention of June 1788. After ratification, he served in the U.S. House of Representatives,

1789–97. Married Dolley Payne Todd in 1794; they had no children together, though she had a son from her first marriage. In collaboration with Vice President Thomas Jefferson, drafted the Virginia Resolutions opposing the Alien and Sedition Acts in 1798. He was appointed secretary of state by Jefferson in 1801 and held office until 1809. Won the electoral vote to become the fourth president of the United States, 1809–17. Confronted by the economic fallout from Jeffersonian trade restrictions, rising tensions over the refusal of European belligerents to recognize U.S. neutral rights, and pressure from Western interests who held the British responsible for fomenting Indian resistance to U.S. expansion, he led the nation into the War of 1812, which Federalist critics derided as "Mr. Madison's War." In retirement, succeeded Jefferson as rector of the University of Virginia, 1826, and attended the Virginia Constitutional Convention in Richmond, 1829–30. Died at Montpelier.

Elizabeth Smith Shaw Peabody, sister (April or May 1750–April 10, 1815) Born in Weymouth, Massachusetts, youngest child of Reverend William Smith and Elizabeth Quincy Smith. Nicknamed "Betsy." Married Reverend John Shaw (b. 1748), minister at Haverhill, Massachusetts, on October 16, 1777, and had three children. Widowed in 1794. Married on December 8, 1795, to Reverend Stephen Peabody in Atkinson, New Hampshire. Died suddenly in her sleep in Atkinson.

Stephen Peabody, brother-in-law (November 11, 1741–May 23, 1819) Born in Andover, Massachusetts. Graduated from Harvard in 1769. An orthodox Calvinist, became the first minister of the First Congregational Church of Atkinson, New Hampshire, in 1772. Married Mary "Polly" Haseltine (b. 1741) in 1773, and had two children. Founded Atkinson Academy in 1787, the oldest co-educational school in the U.S. Widowed in 1793. Married Elizabeth Smith Shaw on December 8, 1795. Died in Atkinson.

Benjamin Rush (January 4, 1746–April 19, 1813) Born in Byberry Township, outside of Philadelphia, son of Susanna Hall Harvey and her second husband, John Rush (gunsmith and farmer who died in 1751). Graduated from the College of New Jersey (now Princeton) in 1760. Studied medicine with John Redman, the leading physician in Philadelphia, from February 1761 to July 1766. Attended Edinburgh University and received M.D. degree in 1768. Opened medical practice in Philadelphia in 1769. Became the first professor of chemistry at the College of Philadelphia. Elected to the American Philosophical Association and in 1774 helped found the Pennsylvania Society for Promoting the Abolition of Slavery. Married Julia Stockton, daughter of Richard Stockton, trustee of College of New Jersey and a signer of the Declaration of Independence; they had thirteen children. Delegate from Pennsylvania to the Continental Congress in 1776, where he signed the Declaration of Independence. Served as surgeon general in the Continental Army in 1777, but resigned after his complaints to Washington about conditions and medical treatment were not heeded. Joined staff of the Pennsylvania Hospital in 1783. Supported various reform movements, including temperance, women's education, and improved treatment for the indigent sick. In 1787, he helped found the Philadelphia College of Physicians. Delegate to Pennsylvania ratifying convention of 1787, where he strongly supported ratification. Resigned from Philadelphia College of Physicians after dispute over treatment of yellow fever in 1794. Pioneered studies of insanity and wrote *Medical Inquiries and Observations Upon the Diseases of the Mind* (1812). Supported Jefferson for president in 1796. Appointed treasurer of the U.S. mint by John Adams in November 1797 and retained that position until his death. Helped bring about reconciliation between Jefferson and Adams in 1812. Died in Philadelphia.

Julia Stockton Rush (March 2, 1759–July 7, 1848) Born on the family estate of Morven in Princeton, New Jersey, the eldest daughter of Annis Boudinot Stockton, a poet, and Richard Stockton, a signer of the Declaration of Independence. Married her father's good friend, Benjamin Rush, on January 11, 1776, and had thirteen children. Helped raise money for the Continental Army. Died in Philadelphia.

Richard Rush (August 29, 1780–July 30, 1859) Born in Philadelphia, the third child of Benjamin Rush and Julia Stockton Rush. Graduated in 1797 from the College of New Jersey (now Princeton) at the age of seventeen, the youngest member of his class. Studied law and admitted to the bar in 1800. Married Catherine Eliza Murray (1780–1862) on August 29, 1809, and had ten children. Appointed attorney general of Pennsylvania in 1811, and that same year, was named comptroller of the Treasury by President James Madison. Advised Madison throughout the War of 1812. Attorney General of the U.S., 1814–7. Succeeded John Quincy Adams to become the minister to Britain, 1817–25. Under President John Quincy Adams, served as Secretary of Treasury, 1825–29, leaving his successor with a surplus, and was selected as a candidate for vice president with Adams in 1828. Secured funds from England to establish the Smithsonian Institution, of which he became one of the first regents. Became the minister to France under President James K. Polk, 1846–49. Died in Philadelphia.

Abigail Adams Shaw, niece (March 3, 1790–July 5, 1859) Born in Haverhill, Massachusetts, to Reverend John Shaw and Elizabeth

Smith Shaw Peabody. Married Joseph Barlow Felt (1789–1869) of Salem, Massachusetts, a prominent historian, antiquarian, and minister, on September 18, 1816. Died in Boston.

Abigail Adams Smith, daughter (July 14, 1765–August 15, 1813) Born in Braintree, Massachusetts, the first child of Abigail and John Adams. Nicknamed "Nabby." Briefly engaged to Royall Tyler, 1783. Traveled to Paris with her mother, 1784. Moved to London when father became U.S. minister to Great Britain in 1785. Her correspondence and journal of European life and customs during this time were published by her daughter in 1841. Married Colonel William Stephens Smith, her father's secretary, on June 12, 1786, in London, with whom she had four children. Moved to New York in 1788. Diagnosed with breast cancer in 1810, and on October 8, 1811, underwent a mastectomy without anesthesia. Malignant tumors reappeared in 1813. Returned to her parents' house in Quincy, Massachusetts, where she died.

Isaac Smith Jr., cousin (May 7, 1749–September 30, 1829) Born in Boston to one of Boston's wealthiest families, a son of Isaac Smith Sr. and Elizabeth Storer Smith. Graduated from Harvard in 1767. Traveled to England in 1775, where he associated with American Loyalists in exile. Ordained as minister at the Sidmouth Presbyterian chapel. Returned in 1784 to Massachusetts and obtained a reinstatement of citizenship. Served as Harvard College librarian for a three-year term in 1788, and during that time, helped compile a catalog of the library, *Catalogus Bibliothecae Harvardianae Cantabrigiae Nov-Anglorum* (1790). Preceptor at the Dummer Academy in Byfield, Massachusetts, 1791–1809. Died in Boston.

Isaac Smith Sr., uncle (July 24, 1719–October 16, 1787) Born in Charlestown, Massachusetts, son of Captain William Smith and Abigail Fowle Smith. One of the wealthiest merchant-shipowners in Boston, he sold wine and other imported goods and became involved in the cod fishery. Married Elizabeth Storer (1726–1786) on October 9, 1746, and had four children, including Isaac Smith Jr. Both husband and wife were subjects of portraits by John Singleton Copley. Died in Boston.

William Stephens Smith, son-in-law (November 8, 1755–June 10, 1816) Born in New York City, son of John Smith, a merchant, and Margaret Stephens Smith. Graduated from the College of New Jersey (now Princeton), 1774. Joined the Continental Army in 1776. Promoted to lieutenant colonel for his actions at the battle of Trenton, and served on the staff of General George Washington. Became the secretary of the American legation in England on March 1, 1784, arriving in London in May, just before the Adamses. Married Abigail

"Nabby" Adams in London on June 12, 1786; they had four children. Appointed by President George Washington first U.S. marshal for New York in 1789. Served as the president of the Society of the Cincinnati, 1795–7. In 1800, chosen by President John Adams as surveyor of the Port of New York. Recruited soldiers of fortune to fight for Venezuelan independance. Stood trial and found not guilty of violating the Neutrality Act of 1794. Moved family to upstate New York, 1808. Widowed in 1813. Served in Congress, 1813–15. Died impoverished in Lebanon, New York.

Hannah Quincy Lincoln Storer, second cousin (September 11, 1736–August 25, 1826) Born in Boston to prominent and wealthy Quincy family of Braintree, daughter of Colonel Josiah Quincy and Hannah Sturgis Quincy. John Adams almost proposed to her in 1759. Married Bela Lincoln (b. 1734), a physician from Hingham, on May 1, 1760. Widowed in 1773. Married Boston philanthropist Ebenezer Storer (1730–1807) on November 5, 1777, becoming stepmother to his six children, and had one child of her own. In 1820, as an elderly widow, visited John Adams, whose face lit up "and he said impishly: 'What Madam, shall we not go walk in Cupid's grove together.'"

John Thaxter Jr., cousin (July 5, 1755–July 6, 1791) Born in Hingham, Massachusetts, the son of Reverend John Thaxter and Anna Quincy Thaxter. Graduated from Harvard in 1774. Clerked in John Adams's law office. Tutored Adams's sons while boarding with the family. Held clerkship in the office of the secretary to Congress in 1778. As John Adams's private secretary, accompanied him on diplomatic missions to England, France, and the Netherlands, 1779–83. Established a law practice in Haverhill, Massachusetts, in 1784. Married Elizabeth Duncan in 1787. Less than a year after the death of his infant son and just ten days after the birth of his daughter, Anna Quincy Thaxter, he died in Haverhill.

Cotton Tufts, uncle and cousin (May 30, 1732–December 8, 1815) Born in Medford, Massachusetts, son of Dr. Simon Tufts and Abigail Smith Tufts. Studied medicine at Harvard and graduated in 1749. Settled in Weymouth, Massachusetts, where he developed a large medical practice. Married Lucy Quincy (b. 1727) on December 2, 1755, with whom he had one son. Became a financial advisor to the Adamses during and after the Revolutionary War. Member of both the Massachusetts ratifying convention and the state senate. Served as president (1787–95) and original member of the Massachusetts Medical Society. Helped found the Academy of Arts and Sciences in 1780. Widowed in 1785. Married Susannah Warner (1744–1832) of Gloucester on October 22, 1789. Died in Weymouth.

Lucy Quincy Tufts, aunt (c. December 7, 1729–October 30, 1785) Born in Braintree, Massachusetts, the youngest child of Colonel John Quincy and Elizabeth Norton Quincy. Married Cotton Tufts on December 2, 1755, and gave birth to Cotton Tufts Jr. in 1757. Died in Weymouth.

Royall Tyler (July 18, 1757–August 16, 1826) Born William Clark Tyler in Boston, son of Mary Steele Tyler and Royall Tyler, a wealthy merchant. Upon his father's death, changed name to Royall Tyler. Graduated from Harvard as valedictorian in 1776. Served as a major in the Massachusetts militia in an unsuccessful attempt to supplant the British at Newport in 1778, then returned to Harvard and law studies, earning an MA. Admitted to the bar in 1780, and practiced in Falmouth, Maine, before moving to Braintree, Massachusetts. Briefly engaged to Abigail "Nabby" Adams, but the relationship ended when she and her mother joined her father in London and the Adamses heard rumors of Tyler's dissipation and profligacy. Became a literary celebrity when his play *The Contrast* premiered on April 16, 1787, at the John Street Theatre in New York, the first American comedy to be professionally produced and commercially successful. Married Mary Palmer (1775–1866) in 1794, and settled in Brattleboro, Vermont; they had eleven children. Allegedly conducted an affair with his mother-in-law, Elizabeth Hunt Palmer, resulting in one or two daughters. Published *The Algerine Captive* (1797), a novel, and *The Yankey in London* (1809), a collection of essays, among other works. Appointed a justice of the Vermont Supreme Court, 1801, serving as chief justice, 1807–12. Taught law at the University of Vermont, 1811–14. Died in Brattleboro after suffering from facial cancer for over a decade. Believed to have inspired the character of Jaffrey Pyncheon in Nathaniel Hawthorne's *The House of the Seven Gables* (1851).

François Adriaan van der Kemp (May 4, 1752–September 7, 1829) Born in Kampen, the Netherlands, son of John van der Kamp, an army officer, and Anna Leydekker van der Kamp. Studied Oriental languages and botany at the University of Groningen, where he developed heterodox religious ideas and an affinity for radical politics; he left the university in 1773 and was ordained a Mennonite minister at Leyden in 1776. In 1781, befriended John Adams, who was in the Netherlands trying to garner support for America. Married Reinira Engelbartha Johanna Vos, a daughter of the burgomaster of Nijmegen, on May 20, 1782; they had three children. Became active in anti-Orangeist Patriot Party and was imprisoned. After his release, emigrated with his family to New York, settling first in Ulster County and later in Oneida County. Founded the Agricultural Society for the Western District of New York in 1795. Undertook numerous scholarly projects, including the translation of documents related to the early history of the New Netherlands colony. Elected a Fellow of the American Academy of Arts and Sciences in 1807. Received an honorary degree from Harvard in 1820. Died of cholera in Barneveld, New York (now Trenton).

Mercy Otis Warren (September 14, 1728–October 19, 1814) Born in Barnstable, Massachusetts, the third of thirteen children of Mary Allyne Otis and Colonel James Otis, a prominent lawyer and politician. Her brother, James Otis Jr., was an early and outspoken leader of opposition to British imperial reforms in the 1760s. Married James Warren (1726–1808), a sheriff and distinguished politician, on November 14, 1754, settled in Plymouth; they had five sons. Because of her husband's political associations, hosted meetings with leading patriots in her home; husband eventually became president of the Massachusetts Provincial Congress. Corresponded with notable leaders such as John Adams, Samuel Adams, and John Hancock, among others. Despite no formal education, wrote several satiric, polemical plays, published anonymously: *The Adulateur* (1772), *The Defeat* (1773), *The Group* (1775), *The Blockheads* (1776), and *The Motley Assembly* (1779). Published *Pomes, Dramatic, and Miscellaneous* (1790), her first work bearing her name. Completed the three-volume *History of the Rise, Progress, and Termination of the American Revolution* in 1805; critical of John Adams, the book caused a public rift between the Adamses and Warren. Died in Plymouth.

Martha Washington (June 2, 1731–May 22, 1802) Born Martha Dandridge in New Kent County, Virginia, on a plantation near Williamsburg. Married wealthy planter Daniel Parke Custis (b. 1711) in 1749 and moved to estate on the Pumunkey River in New Kent County. Widowed in July 1757. Married George Washington (1732–1799) on January 6, 1759, and moved with her two children to Washington's Mount Vernon estate. Spent winters with Continental Army at Cambridge, Morristown, Valley Forge, and Newburgh. Lived in New York and then Philadelphia during Washington's presidency. Died at Mount Vernon.

Harriet Welsh (d. 1857) Born in Boston to Thomas Welsh, a doctor, and his first wife. Her stepmother, Abigail Kent Welsh, was a first cousin of Abigail Adams. Helped watch over Abigail Adams in her dying days.

Thomas Welsh Jr. (January 8, 1779–July 11, 1831) Born in Boston, Massachusetts, to Dr. Thomas and Abigail Kent Welsh, Abigail Adams's first cousin. Graduated from Harvard in 1798. Replaced Thomas

Boylston Adams as John Quincy Adams's secretary in Berlin, 1798–99. Returned to Boston and practiced law. Imprisoned for debt in 1829. Died in Boston.

Caroline Amelia Smith De Windt, granddaughter (January 27, 1795–July 28, 1852) Born in New York, the youngest child and only daughter of William Stephens Smith and Abigail Adams Smith. Married John Peter De Windt (1787–1870) of Fishkill, New York, on September 11, 1814, with whom she had eight children. Edited and published her mother's journals and correspondence, *Journal and Correspondence of Miss Adams* (1841). Published a book of poetry, *Melzinga: A Souvenir* (1842). Died in the burning of the steamboat *Henry Clay* on the Hudson River, New York.

Note on the Texts

This volume prints the texts of 430 letters written by Abigail Adams between the beginning of her courtship with John Adams in 1763 and her death in 1818, a period encompassing the American Revolution, the presidencies of Washington, Adams, Jefferson, and Madison, and the War of 1812, all of which she witnessed. It is the largest one-volume collection ever published of Adams's letters, more than 2,300 of which have been preserved. It also includes the diary of her return voyage to America in 1788, after living for several years in France and England, as well as her will.

Abigail Adams was modest about her letter writing, often requesting that her letters be destroyed. "You will burn all these letters," she wrote to John Adams in 1774, "least they should fall from your pocket and thus expose your affectionate friend." Though frequently pressed by her husband to keep letter-book copies of her letters, she rarely did. Toward the end of Adams's life, her daughter Abigail Adams Smith mentioned that she was preserving her mother's letters to give to her own daughter, Caroline. Adams replied:

> You alarm me when you tell me that you have preserved my letters, and collected them together, in order to transmit them to Caroline. Your affection and your partiality to your mother, stamp a value upon them which can never be felt by those less interested in them; they are letters written without regard to style; and scarcely ever copying a letter, they must be very incorrect productions, and quite unworthy preservation or perpetuity: do not let them out-live you; you may select a few, perhaps, worth transmitting, but in general, I fear, they are trash.

Nevertheless many of her letters were preserved by family members, some in the family's papers that passed to John Quincy Adams, some in the papers of her daughter, Abigail Adams Smith, and some in the papers of her sister, Mary Smith Cranch.

Abigail Adams Smith passed her mother's letters on to her daughter, Caroline Amelia Smith De Windt, who published a collection of her mother's and grandmother's letters as *Journal and Correspondence of Miss Adams, Daughter of John Adams*, 2 vols. (1841–42). Most of the originals of these letters were destroyed during a fire in the De Windt home in upstate New York in 1862. Mary Smith Cranch passed her letters to her daughter Lucy Cranch Greenleaf. In 1942 the American Antiquarian Society purchased the letters from the estate of Greenleaf's great-granddaughter Mary Greenleaf Dawes, and a majority of them were published in 1947 as *New Letters of Abigail Adams 1788–1801*, ed. Stewart Mitchell (Boston: Houghton Mifflin).

John Quincy Adams entrusted his family's papers to his son, Charles Francis Adams, who edited and published a collection of correspondence, *Letters of Mrs. Adams, the Wife of John Adams* (1840). Charles Francis Adams later had a separate fireproof building, the Stone Library, built on the grounds of the family estate in Quincy, Massachusetts, to house the family archive. On his death in 1886 he left his papers, and those of John Adams and Abigail Adams, and of John Quincy Adams and his wife, Louisa Catherine Adams, to his four sons, one of whom, Charles Francis Adams Jr., later became president of the Massachusetts Historical Society. In 1902 Charles Francis Adams Jr. had the family papers moved from the Stone Library to the Massachusetts Historical Society building in Boston, and in 1905 he created the Adams Manuscript Trust to ensure continued family ownership and control of the papers for the next fifty years. In 1954 the Adams Manuscript Trust entered into an agreement with the Massachusetts Historical Society and Harvard University Press to publish the papers of John Adams, John Quincy Adams, Charles Francis Adams Sr., and their families through the year 1889. The Adams Manuscript Trust was dissolved in 1956 after it transferred ownership of its papers to the Massachusetts Historical Society, which began to identify and photocopy Adams documents in repositories outside of the family archive, including those from the De Windt and Cranch–Greenleaf collections. Publication of the Adams Family Papers began in 1961 and has proceeded in three series, of which *Adams Family Correspondence* (11 volumes to date; Cambridge: The Belknap Press of Harvard University Press, 1963–2013) contains Abigail's letters. Documents are transcribed and printed without alteration in their spelling and paragraphing, and with minimal alterations in their capitalization and punctuation, mostly in the substitution of periods for dashes used to end sentences and the omission of dashes in instances where a dash appears following another punctuation mark. In volumes 8–11 of *Adams Family Correspondence* the previous textual policy of the series has been revised, so that documents are now transcribed and printed without alteration in their capitalization and punctuation; in addition, superscript letters used in abbreviations and contractions are no longer brought down to the line.

This volume prints 221 letters from *Adams Family Correspondence*, volumes I–11 (1963–2013), its preferred source of texts. Another 50 letters not so far included in *Adams Family Correspondence* are taken from a variety of printed sources, including the collections edited by

Charles Francis Adams, Caroline Smith De Windt, and the American Antiquarian Society. Adams's will, along with an additional 139 letters for which there are at present no printed sources, is taken from a digital source, the Adams Papers at Founders Online, a project of the National Historical Publications and Records Commission of the National Archives. The texts of the remaining 20 letters are printed from transcriptions prepared by the Adams Papers Editorial Project at the Massachusetts Historical Society.

The present volume prints texts as they appeared in these sources, but with a few alterations in editorial procedure. Bracketed editorial conjectural readings in the source texts, in cases where the original manuscript was damaged or difficult to read, are accepted without brackets in this volume when that reading seems to be the only possible one; but when it does not, or when the editor made no conjecture, the missing word or words are indicated by a bracketed two-em space, i.e., [   ]. In cases where the editor supplied in brackets punctuation, letters, or words that were omitted from the source text by an obvious slip of the pen, this volume removes the brackets and accepts the editorial emendation. Bracketed editorial insertions used in sources to expand abbreviations and contractions, identify persons, or clarify meaning have been deleted in this volume.

When printing the complimentary closing at the end of a letter, the editors of volumes 8–11 of *Adams Family Correspondence* run the closing together in paragraph style and use virgules to indicate line breaks within the closing; the present volume omits the virgules and prints the closing in paragraph style. In some cases where the writer made changes in a document, the canceled text, if decipherable, is printed in *Adams Family Correspondence* with a single line through it and in *New Letters of Abigail Adams* in square brackets; this volume omits the canceled material.

The following is a list of the documents included in this volume, in the order of their appearance, giving the source of each text. The most common sources are indicated by these abbreviations:

AFC *Adams Family Correspondence*, volumes 1–2 (1963), ed. L. H. Butterfield; volumes 3–4 (1973), eds. L. H. Butterfield and Marc Friedlaender; volume 5–6 (1993), eds. Richard Alan Ryerson, Joanna M. Revelas, Celeste Walker, Gregg L. Lint, and Humphrey J. Costello; volume 7 (2005), eds. Margaret A. Hogan, C. James Taylor, Celeste Walker, Anne Decker Cecere, Gregg L. Lint, Hobson Woodward, and Mary T. Claffey; volume 8 (2007), eds. Margaret A. Hogan, C. James Taylor, Hobson Woodward, Jessie May Rodrique, Gregg

L. Lint, and Mary T. Claffey; volume 9 (2009), eds. Margaret A. Hogan, C. James Taylor, Karen N. Barzilay, Hobson Woodward, Mary T. Claffey, Robert F. Karachuk, Sara B. Sikes, and Gregg L. Lint; volume 10 (2011), eds. Margaret A. Hogan, C. James Taylor, Sara Martin, Hobson Woodward, Sara B. Sikes, Gregg L. Lint, and Sara Georgini; volume 11 (2013), eds. Margaret A. Hogan, C. James Taylor, Sara Martin, Neal E. Millikan, Hobson Woodward, Sara B. Sikes, and Gregg L. Lint. Copyright © 1993, 2005, 2007, 2009, 2011, 2013 by the Massachusetts Historical Society.

Cappon *The Adams-Jefferson Letters: The Complete Correspondence Between Thomas Jefferson and Abigail and John Adams*, ed. Lester J. Cappon (Chapel Hill: The University of North Carolina Press, 1959, 1988).

CFA *Letters of Mrs. Adams, Wife of John Adams. With an Introductory Memoir by her Grandson, Charles Francis Adams*, 2nd ed. (Boston: Charles C. Little and James Brown, 1840) and 4th ed. (Boston: Wilkins, Carter, and Company, 1848). Originally published in 1840, Charles Francis Adams immediately published a corrected and enlarged second edition in two volumes. He added further additional letters in the fourth edition (one volume) of 1848. This volume publishes letters that were included for the first time in the enlarged second and fourth editions.

De Windt *Journal and Correspondence of Miss Adams, Daughter of John Adams*, 2 volumes, ed. Caroline Smith De Windt (1841–42).

Founders Founders Online, National Archive (http://founders.archives.gov/). Accessed October 2015.

Friend *My Dearest Friend: Letters of Abigail and John Adams*, eds. Margaret A. Hogan and C. James Taylor (Cambridge: The Belknap Press of Harvard University Press, 2007). Copyright © 2007 by the Massachusetts Historical Society.

MHS Manuscript transcribed by the Adams Papers Editorial Project, Massachusetts Historical Society.

New Letters *New Letters of Abigail Adams 1788–1801*, ed. Stewart Mitchell (Boston: Houghton Mifflin, 1947).

COURTSHIP AND MARRIAGE, 1763–1773

To Isaac Smith Jr., March 16, 1763, *AFC*, 1: 3–4.
To John Adams, August 11, 1763, *AFC*, 1: 6–7.

To John Adams, September 12, 1763, *AFC*, I: 8–9.
To Cotton Tufts, April 2, 1764, *AFC*, I: 12–14.
To John Adams, April 7, 1764, *AFC*, I: 15.
To John Adams, April 16, 1764, *AFC*, I: 32.
To John Adams, April 19–20, 1764, *AFC*, I: 36–38.
To John Adams, May 9, 1764, *AFC*, I: 46–47.
To John Adams, October 4, 1764, *AFC*, I: 50–51.
To Hannah Storer Green, post July 14, 1765, *AFC*, I: 51.
To Mary Smith Cranch, January 31, 1767, *AFC*, I: 60–62.
To John Adams, September 13, 1767, *AFC*, I: 62.
To Isaac Smith Jr., April 20, 1771, *AFC*, I: 76–77.
To Mercy Otis Warren, July 16, 1773, *AFC*, I: 84–85.

REVOLUTION, 1773–1777

To Mercy Otis Warren, December 5–11, 1773, *AFC*, I: 88–89.
To John Adams, December 30, 1773, *AFC*, I: 90.
To Mercy Otis Warren, ante February 27, 1774, *AFC*, I: 97–99.
To John Adams, August 19, 1774, *AFC*, I: 142–43.
To John Adams, September 14–16, 1774, *AFC*, I: 151–54.
To John Adams, October 16, 1774, *AFC*, I: 172–74.
To Catharine Sawbridge Macaulay, October–November 1774, *AFC*,
   I: 177–79.
To Mercy Otis Warren, c. February 3, 1775, *AFC*, I: 183–86.
To Mercy Otis Warren, May 2, 1775, *AFC*, I: 190.
To John Adams, May 24, 1775, *AFC*, I: 204–6.
To John Adams, June 18–20, 1775, *AFC*, I: 222–23.
To John Adams, June 25, 1775, *AFC*, I: 230–33.
To John Adams, July 5, 1775, *AFC*, I: 239–40.
To John Adams, July 12, 1775, *AFC*, I: 243–45.
To John Adams, July 16, 1775, *AFC*, I: 245–50.
To John Adams, August 10–11, 1775, *AFC*, I: 272.
To John Adams, September 8–10, 1775, *AFC*, I: 276–78.
To John Adams, September 17, 1775, *AFC*, I: 278–80.
To John Adams, September 25, 1775, *AFC*, I: 284–85.
To John Adams, October 1, 1775, *AFC*, I: 288–89.
To John Adams, October 9, 1775, *AFC*, I: 296–98.
To John Adams, October 21, 1775, *AFC*, I: 305–8.
To John Adams, November 5, 1775, *AFC*, I: 320–22.
To John Adams, November 27, 1775, *AFC*, I: 328–30.
To Mercy Otis Warren, January 1776, *AFC*, I: 422–24.
To John Adams, March 2–10, 1776, *AFC*, I: 352–55.
To John Adams, March 16–18, 1776, *AFC*, I: 357–60.
To John Adams, March 31–April 5, 1776, *AFC*, I: 369–71.
To Mercy Otis Warren, April 27, 1776, *AFC*, I: 396–98.

To John Adams, October 8, 1780, *AFC*, 4: 1–4.
To John Adams, November 13–24, 1780, *AFC*, 4: 12–17.
To John Adams, January 15, 1781, *AFC*, 4: 63–65.
To John Quincy Adams, January 21, 1781, *AFC*, 4: 67–68.
To John Quincy Adams and Charles Adams, February 8, 1781, *AFC*, 4: 77–78.
To John Adams, April 23, 1781, *AFC*, 4: 103–6.
To James Lovell, May 10, 1781, *AFC*, 4: 111–12.
To Charles Adams, May 26, 1781, *AFC*, 4: 135–36.
To John Quincy Adams, May 26, 1781, *AFC*, 4: 136–37.
To John Adams, May 27, 1781, *AFC*, 4: 137–38.
To James Lovell, July 14, 1781, *AFC*, 4: 176–78.
To Elbridge Gerry, July 20, 1781, *AFC*, 4: 182–84.
To John Adams, August 1, 1781, *AFC*, 4: 190–91.
To James Lovell, c. September 26, 1781, *AFC*, 4: 215–16.
To John Adams, September 29, 1781, *AFC*, 4: 220–22.
To John Adams, December 9, 1781, *AFC*, 4: 255–58.
To James Lovell, January 8, 1782, *AFC*, 4: 273–75.
To Elizabeth Smith Shaw, February–March 1782, *AFC*, 4: 284–86.
To John Adams, April 10, 1782, *AFC*, 4: 305–8.
To John Adams, July 17–18, 1782, *AFC*, 4: 343–47.
To John Adams, September 5, 1782, *AFC*, 4: 376–77.
To John Adams, October 8, 1782, *AFC*, 5: 4–7.
To John Adams, October 25, 1782, *AFC*, 5: 21–24.
To John Quincy Adams, November 13, 1782, *AFC*, 5: 37–39.
To John Adams, December 23, 1782, *AFC*, 5: 54–58.
To John Adams, April 7, 1783, *AFC*, 5: 116–19.
To Royall Tyler, June 14, 1783, *AFC*, 5: 173–75.
To John Adams, June 20, 1783, *AFC*, 5: 179–83.
To John Adams, September 20, 1783, *AFC*, 5: 253–55.
To John Adams, October 19, 1783, *AFC*, 5: 258–60.
To John Quincy Adams, November 20, 1783, *AFC*, 5: 272–75.
To John Adams, December 15, 1783, *AFC*, 5: 278–81.
To John Quincy Adams, December 26, 1783, *AFC*, 5: 282–84.
To John Adams, January 3, 1784, *AFC*, 5: 290–93.
To John Adams, February 11, 1784, *AFC*, 5: 302–5.
To John Adams, May 25, 1784, *AFC*, 5: 330–32.
To Mary Smith Cranch, July 6–30, 1784, *AFC*, 5: 358–83.
To John Adams, July 23, 1784, *AFC*, 5: 397–99.
To Elizabeth Smith Shaw, July 28–30, 1784, *AFC*, 5: 402–7.
To John Adams, July 30, 1784, *AFC*, 5: 408–9.
To Elizabeth Cranch, September 5, 1784, *AFC*, 5: 433–35.
To Lucy Cranch, September 5, 1784, *AFC*, 5: 436–38.
To Mary Smith Cranch, September 5, 1784, *AFC*, 5: 439–44.

To Elizabeth Cranch, December 3–13, 1784, *AFC*, 6: 3–9.
To Elizabeth Smith Shaw, December 14, 1784, *AFC*, 6: 28–31.
To Royall Tyler, January 4, 1785, *AFC*, 6: 45–50.
To Elizabeth Smith Shaw, January 11, 1785, *AFC*, 6: 55–59.
To Cotton Tufts, April 26–May 10, 1785, *AFC*, 6: 103–8.
To Mary Smith Cranch, c. May 5–10, 1785, *AFC*, 6: 118–20.
To Mercy Otis Warren, May 10, 1785, *AFC*, 6: 138–40.
To Thomas Jefferson, June 6, 1785, *AFC*, 6: 169–72.
To Mary Smith Cranch, June 24–28, 1785, *AFC*, 6: 186–93.
To Elizabeth Smith Shaw, c. August 15, 1785, *AFC*, 6: 280–82.
To Lucy Cranch, August 27, 1785, *AFC*, 6: 312–14.
To Elizabeth Cranch, September 2, 1785, *AFC*, 6: 327–30.
To Lucy Quincy Tufts, September 3, 1785, *AFC*, 6: 331–32.
To John Quincy Adams, September 6, 1785, *AFC*, 6: 342–45.
To Thomas Jefferson, October 7, 1785, *AFC*, 6: 414–15.
To Charles Adams, c. February 16, 1786, *AFC*, 7: 60–61.
To John Quincy Adams, February 16, 1786, *AFC*, 7: 62–70.
To Mary Smith Cranch, March 21, 1786, *AFC*, 7: 101–2.
To Elizabeth Cranch, April 2, 1786, *AFC*, 7: 122–25.
To Isaac Smith Sr., April 8, 1786, *AFC*, 7: 135–37.
To Mary Smith Cranch, June 13, 1786, *AFC*, 7: 217–21.
To Thomas Jefferson, July 23, 1786, *AFC*, 7: 287–88.
To Mary Smith Cranch, September 12, 1786, *AFC*, 7: 333–39.
To John Quincy Adams, November 28–December 3, 1786, *AFC*, 7: 405–6.
To John Adams, December 23, 1786, *AFC*, 7: 410–11.
To John Quincy Adams, January 17, 1787, *AFC*, 7: 442–43.
To Mary Smith Cranch, January 20, 1787, *AFC*, 7: 445–51.
To Thomas Jefferson, January 29, 1787, *AFC*, 7: 455–57.
To Thomas Boylston Adams, March 15, 1787, *AFC*, 8: 10–11.
To Lucy Cranch, April 26–May 6, 1787, *AFC*, 8: 24–26.
To Elizabeth Smith Shaw, May 2–6, 1787, *AFC*, 8: 37–39.
To Thomas Jefferson, June 26, 1787, *AFC*, 8: 92–93.
To Thomas Jefferson, June 27, 1787, *AFC*, 8: 93–94.
To Cotton Tufts, July 4, 1787, *MHS*.
To Thomas Jefferson, July 6, 1787, *AFC*, 8: 107–8.
To Mary Smith Cranch, July 16, 1787, *AFC*, 8: 116–21.
To Thomas Jefferson, September 10, 1787, *AFC*, 8: 151–52.
To Mary Smith Cranch, September 15, 1787, *AFC*, 8: 153–61.
To Cotton Tufts, November 6, 1787, *AFC*, 8: 201–3.
To Thomas Jefferson, December 5, 1787, *AFC*, 8: 208.
To Mary Smith Cranch, February 10, 1788, *AFC*, 8: 224–27.
To Thomas Jefferson, February 21, 1788, *AFC*, 8: 236.
To John Adams, March 23, 1788, *AFC*, 8: 247–48.

Diary of Her Return Voyage to America, March 30–May 1, 1788, *Diary and Autobiography of John Adams*, Vol. 3, ed. L. H. Butterfield (Cambridge: The Belknap Press of Harvard University Press, 1962).

VICE PRESIDENT'S LADY, 1788–1796

To Abigail Adams Smith, July 7, 1788, *AFC*, 8: 277–78.
To John Adams, December 3, 1788, *AFC*, 8: 313–14.
To John Adams, December 15, 1788, *AFC*, 8: 318–20.
To John Adams, May 1, 1789, *AFC*, 8: 338–40.
To John Adams, May 31, 1789, *AFC*, 8: 364–66.
To Mary Smith Cranch, June 28, 1789, *AFC*, 8: 377–79.
To Mary Smith Cranch, July 12, 1789, *AFC*, 8: 388–91.
To Mary Smith Cranch, August 9, 1789, *AFC*, 8: 397–401.
To Mary Smith Cranch, January 5–10, 1790, *AFC*, 9: 1–3.
To Cotton Tufts, May 30, 1790, *AFC*, 9: 63–64.
To John Quincy Adams, July 11, 1790, *AFC*, 9: 77.
To Mary Smith Cranch, August 8, 1790, *AFC*, 9: 84–85.
To John Quincy Adams, August 20, 1790, *AFC*, 9: 92–93.
To Mary Smith Cranch, August 29, 1790, *AFC*, 9: 94–95.
To Cotton Tufts, September 6, 1790, *AFC*, 9: 103–4.
To John Quincy Adams, November 7, 1790, *AFC*, 9: 141–43.
To Mary Smith Cranch, December 12–14, 1790, *AFC*, 9: 155–56.
To Abigail Adams Smith, January 25, 1791, *AFC*, 9: 181–82.
To Cotton Tufts, March 11, 1791, *AFC*, 9: 196–99.
To William Stephens Smith, March 16, 1791, *AFC*, 9: 203–5.
To Martha Washington, June 25, 1791, *AFC*, 9: 218–19.
To Mary Smith Cranch, October 30, 1791, *AFC*, 9: 237–38.
To John Quincy Adams, February 5, 1792, *AFC*, 9: 258–60.
To Mary Smith Cranch, April 20, 1792, *AFC*, 9: 277–79.
To John Adams, December 4, 1792, *AFC*, 9: 333–34.
To Abigail Adams Smith, February 28, 1793, *AFC*, 9: 414–15.
To John Adams, November 28, 1793, *AFC*, 9: 457–58.
To John Adams, December 28, 1793, *AFC*, 9: 486–87.
To John Adams, December 31, 1793, *AFC*, 9: 494–95.
To John Adams, January 18, 1794, *AFC*, 10: 43–45.
To Abigail Adams Smith, March 10, 1794, *AFC*, 10: 106–8.
To John Adams, March 26, 1794, *AFC*, 10: 127–28.
To John Adams, April 18, 1794, *AFC*, 10: 144–45.
To John Adams, May 27, 1794, *AFC*, 10: 195–97.
To John Adams, December 6, 1794, *AFC*, 10: 288–89.
To John Adams, January 4, 1795, *AFC*, 10: 333–35.
To Thomas Boylston Adams, January 10, 1795, *AFC*, 10: 345–46.
To John Adams, January 16, 1795, *AFC*, 10: 347–49.
To Thomas Boylston Adams, February 11, 1795, *AFC*, 10: 376–79.

To Abigail Adams Smith, August 14, 1795, *AFC*, 11: 16–18.
To John Quincy Adams, September 15, 1795, *AFC*, 11: 22–24.
To John Quincy Adams, May 20, 1796, *AFC*, 11: 295–98.
To John Quincy Adams, August 10, 1796, *AFC*, 11: 356–58.
To Thomas Boylston Adams, August 16, 1796, *AFC*, 11: 360–61.
To Thomas Boylston Adams, September 25, 1796, *AFC*, 11: 381–83.
To John Adams, December 7, 1796, *AFC*, 11: 437.
To Elbridge Gerry, December 28, 1796, *Founders*.

FIRST LADY, 1797–1801

To John Adams, January 1, 1797, *AFC*, 11: 478–79.
To John Adams, January 15, 1797, *AFC*, 11: 499–501.
To John Adams, January 28, 1797, *AFC*, 11: 520–22.
To Charles Adams, February 5, 1797, *AFC*, 11: 538–40.
To John Adams, February 8, 1797, *AFC*, 11: 545–46.
To John Adams, February 13, 1797, *AFC*, 11: 560–62.
To Mercy Otis Warren, March 4, 1797, *Founders*.
To John Adams, March 12, 1797, *MHS*.
To John Adams, April 17, 1797, *MHS*.
To John Adams, April 23, 1797, *Friend*, 446.
To Mary Smith Cranch, May 16, 1797, *New Letters*, 89–91.
To Mary Smith Cranch, May 24, 1797, *New Letters*, 91–93.
To Mary Smith Cranch, June 6–8, 1797, *New Letters*, 96–98.
To John Quincy Adams, June 15, 1797, *Founders*.
To John Quincy Adams, June 23–24, 1797, *Founders*.
To Cotton Tufts, July 12, 1797, *Founders*.
To Mercy Otis Warren, October 1, 1797, *Founders*.
To Mary Smith Cranch, October 31, 1797, *New Letters*, 109–10.
To John Quincy Adams, November 3, 1797, *Founders*.
To Mary Smith Cranch, November 15, 1797, *New Letters*, 110–13.
To Louisa Catherine Adams, November 24, 1797, *Founders*.
To Mary Smith Cranch, November 28, 1797, *New Letters*, 113–15.
To Mary Smith Cranch, February 6, 1798, *New Letters*, 130–32.
To William Smith, February 6, 1798, *MHS*.
To Cotton Tufts, February 6, 1798, *MHS*.
To Mary Smith Cranch, February 15, 1798, *New Letters*, 132–33.
To Mary Smith Cranch, March 5, 1798, *New Letters*, 139–42.
To Mary Smith Cranch, March 14, 1798, *New Letters*, 144–46.
To Mary Smith Cranch, March 20, 1798, *New Letters*, 146–47.
To Mary Smith Cranch, March 27, 1798, *New Letters*, 147–49.
To John Quincy Adams, March 29, 1798, *MHS*.
To Thomas Boylston Adams, April 4, 1798, *MHS*.
To Mary Smith Cranch, April 13, 1798, *New Letters*, 155–57.

To Esther Black, April 15, 1798, *MHS.*
To Cotton Tufts, April 16, 1798, *MHS.*
To John Quincy Adams, April 21, 1798, *MHS.*
To Mary Smith Cranch, April 26, 1798, *New Letters,* 164–66.
To Mary Smith Cranch, May 10, 1798, *New Letters,* 170–72.
To Mary Smith Cranch, May 13, 1798, *New Letters,* 172–73.
To Cotton Tufts, May 25, 1798, *Founders.*
To John Quincy Adams, May 26, 1798, *Founders.*
To Mary Smith Cranch, May 26, 1798, *New Letters,* 179–82.
To Thomas Welsh, c. June 4, 1798, *Founders.*
To Mary Smith Cranch, June 5, 1798, *Founders.*
To John Quincy Adams, June 12, 1798, *Founders.*
To Mary Smith Cranch, June 19, 1798, *New Letters,* 193–94.
To Elizabeth Smith Shaw Peabody, June 22, 1798, *Founders.*
To Elizabeth Smith Shaw Peabody, July 7, 1798, *Founders.*
To Cotton Tufts, July 10, 1798, *Founders.*
To Thomas Boylston Adams, July 20, 1798, *Founders.*
To John Quincy Adams, November 15, 1798, *Founders.*
To John Adams, November 29, 1798, *Friend,* 451–52.
To John Quincy Adams, December 2, 1798, *Founders.*
To John Adams, December 15, 1798, *Friend,* 452–53.
To Thomas Boylston Adams, January 20, 1799, *Founders.*
To John Adams, January 25, 1799, *Founders.*
To John Quincy Adams, February 1, 1799, *Founders.*
To John Quincy Adams, February 10, 1799, *Founders.*
To John Adams, February 27–28, 1799, *MHS.*
To John Quincy Adams, June 12, 1799, *Founders.*
To Elizabeth Smith Shaw Peabody, July 19, 1799, *Founders.*
To Mary Smith Cranch, October 31, 1799, *New Letters,* 210–12.
To Mary Smith Cranch, December 11, 1799, *New Letters,* 219–22.
To Mary Smith Cranch, December 22–23, 1799, *New Letters,* 222–23.
To Mary Smith Cranch, December 30–31, 1799, *New Letters,* 224–26.
To Catherine Nuth Johnson, January 19, 1800, *Founders.*
To Elizabeth Smith Shaw Peabody, February 4, 1800, *Founders.*
To John Quincy Adams, April 27, 1800, *Founders.*
To Cotton Tufts, April 30, 1800, *Founders.*
To Mary Smith Cranch, May 3, 1800, *New Letters,* 249–50.
To Abigail Adams Smith, May 4–5, 1800, *Founders.*
To Abigail Adams Smith, May 12, 1800, *Founders.*
To John Quincy Adams, May 15, 1800, *Founders.*
To John Adams, May 19, 1800, *MHS.*
To Mary Smith Cranch, May 26, 1800, *New Letters,* 252–53.
To Catherine Nuth Johnson, August 20, 1800, *Founders.*

To John Quincy Adams, September 1, 1800, *Founders*.
To William Stephens Smith, September 6, 1800, *Founders*.
To Mary Smith Cranch, November 10, 1800, *New Letters*, 254–56.
To Mary Smith Cranch, November 21, 1800, *New Letters*, 256–60.
To Abigail Adams Smith, November 21, 1800, *CFA*, 2nd ed.,
    II:239–42.
To Sarah Smith Adams, December 8, 1800, *MHS*.
To Mary Smith Cranch, December 8, 1800, *New Letters*, 261–62.
To Thomas Boylston Adams, December 13, 1800, *MHS*.
To Mary Smith Cranch, December 21–27, 1800, *MHS*.
To Thomas Boylston Adams, December 25, 1800, *Founders*.
To Mary Smith Cranch, January 15, 1801, *New Letters*, 262–64.
To John Quincy Adams, January 29, 1801, *Founders*.
To Mary Smith Cranch, February 7, 1801, *New Letters*, 264–66.
To John Adams, February 21, 1801, *Friend*, 475–76.

RETIREMENT, 1801–1818

To Thomas Boylston Adams, March 22, 1801, *Founders*.
To John Quincy Adams, May 30, 1801, *Founders*.
To John Quincy Adams, September 13, 1801, *Founders*.
To Hannah Phillips Cushing, February 3, 1802, *MHS*.
To Thomas Boylston Adams, February 28, 1802, *Founders*.
To Thomas Boylston Adams, December 13, 1802, *Founders*.
To Mercy Otis Warren, January 16, 1803, *Founders*.
To Thomas Boylston Adams, April 26, 1803, *Founders*.
To Thomas Boylston Adams, May 8, 1803, *Founders*.
To Thomas Jefferson, May 20, 1804, *Cappon*, 268–69.
To Thomas Jefferson, July 1, 1804, *Cappon*, 271–74.
To Thomas Jefferson, August 18, 1804, *Cappon*, 276–78.
To Thomas Jefferson, October 25, 1804, *Cappon*, 280–82.
To Louisa Catherine Adams, December 8, 1804, *Founders*.
To John Quincy Adams, December 18, 1804, *Founders*.
To John Quincy Adams, December 30, 1804, *Founders*.
To John Quincy Adams and Louisa Catherine Adams, November
    29, 1805, *Founders*.
To Louisa Catherine Adams, January 19, 1806, *Founders*.
To Louisa Catherine Adams, February 15, 1806, *Founders*.
To John Quincy Adams, March 5, 1806, *Founders*.
To John Quincy Adams, March 24, 1806, *Founders*.
To Mercy Otis Warren, March 9, 1807, *Founders*.
To Elizabeth Smith Shaw Peabody, June 10, 1807, *Founders*.
To John Quincy Adams and Louisa Catherine Adams, October 25,
    1807, *Founders*.

To Abigail Adams Smith, January 14, 1808, *MHS.*
To Louisa Catherine Adams, April 4, 1808, *Founders.*
To Caroline Smith De Windt, May 28, 1808, *De Windt,* I:211–13.
To Abigail Adams Smith, June 19, 1808, *Founders.*
To Abigail Adams Smith, December 8, 1808, *Founders.*
To Abigail Adams Smith, April 10, 1809, *De Windt,* II:188–91.
To Elizabeth Smith Shaw Peabody, June 5, 1809, *Founders.*
To Abigail Adams Smith, June 19, 1809, *De Windt,* II:201–4.
To Elizabeth Smith Shaw Peabody, July 18, 1809, *Founders.*
To John Quincy Adams and Louisa Catherine Adams, August 5, 1809, *Founders.*
To Mercy Otis Warren, December 31, 1809, *Founders.*
To Louisa Catherine Adams, January 12, 1810, *Founders.*
To Louisa Catherine Adams, March 6, 1810, *Founders.*
To James Madison, August 1, 1810, *Founders.*
To Catherine Nuth Johnson, September 19, 1810, *Founders.*
To Susanna Boylston Adams Clark Treadway, October 25, 1810, *MHS.*
To John Quincy Adams, January 26, 1811, *Founders.*
To John Quincy Adams, February 22, 1811, *Founders.*
To Caroline Amelia Smith, February 26, 1811, *CFA,* 4th ed., 403–4.
To Elizabeth Smith Shaw Peabody, February 28, 1811, *Founders.*
To John Quincy Adams, March 4, 1811, *Founders.*
To Louisa Catherine Adams, March 4, 1811, *Founders.*
To Abigail Adams Smith, March 10, 1811, *Founders.*
To Catherine Nuth Johnson, March 30, 1811, *Founders.*
To Caroline Smith De Windt, April 18, 1811, *Founders.*
To Louisa Catherine Adams, April 28, 1811, *Founders.*
To Elizabeth Smith Shaw Peabody, July 10–11, 1811, *Founders.*
To Abigail Louisa Adams, July 23, 1811, *Founders.*
To William Stephens Smith, July 23, 1811, *Founders.*
To Catherine Nuth Johnson, July 31, 1811, *Founders.*
To William Stephens Smith, August 28, 1811, *Founders.*
To Catherine Nuth Johnson, September 22, 1811, *Founders.*
To John Quincy Adams, September 24, 1811, *Founders.*
To Benjamin Rush, October 15, 1811, *MHS.*
To William Cranch, October 17, 1811, *CFA,* 4th ed., 406.
To Elizabeth Smith Shaw Peabody, October 22, 1811, *Founders.*
To Elizabeth Smith Shaw Peabody, November 8, 1811, *Founders.*
To John Quincy Adams, November 17, 1811, *Founders.*
To John Adams 2nd, December 8, 1811, *Founders.*
To Mercy Otis Warren, December 14, 1811, *Founders.*
To John Quincy Adams, January 5, 1812, *Founders.*

To Elizabeth Smith Shaw Peabody, July 17–August 4, 1812, *Founders.*
To John Quincy Adams, July 29, 1812, *Founders.*
To John Quincy Adams, December 30, 1812, *Founders.*
To Louisa Catherine Adams, January 30, 1813, *Founders.*
To John Quincy Adams, February 25, 1813, *Founders.*
To John Quincy Adams, April 23, 1813, *Founders.*
To Mercy Otis Warren, June 20, 1813, *Founders.*
To John Quincy Adams, July 1, 1813, *Founders.*
To Louisa Catherine Adams, July 24, 1813, *Founders.*
To Lucy Cranch Greenleaf, c. July 1813, *Founders.*
To Mercy Otis Warren, August 8, 1813, *Founders.*
To George Washington Adams and John Adams 2nd, August 15, 1813, *Founders.*
To John Quincy Adams, August 30, 1813, *Founders.*
To John Quincy Adams, September 13, 1813, *Founders.*
To Thomas Jefferson, September 20, 1813, *Cappon,* 377–78.
To François Adriaan van der Kemp, February 3, 1814, *CFA,* 4th ed., 415–16.
To John Quincy Adams, September 7, 1814, *Founders.*
To John Quincy Adams, October 18, 1814, *Founders.*
To Caroline Smith De Windt, October 23, 1814, *De Windt,* I:228–30.
To Elizabeth Smith Shaw Peabody, February 26, 1815, *Founders.*
To Thomas Baker Johnson, March 3, 1815, *Founders.*
To John Quincy Adams, March 8, 1815, *Founders.*
To Stephen Peabody Family, April 11, 1815, *Founders.*
To Louisa Catherine Adams, April 14, 1815, *Founders.*
To Louisa Catherine Adams, May 9, 1815, *Founders.*
To Dolley Madison, May 14, 1815, *Founders.*
To John Quincy Adams, May 20, 1815, *Founders.*
To François Adriaan van der Kemp, May 26, 1815, *Founders.*
To Abigail Adams Shaw Felt, June 6, 1815, *MHS.*
To Louisa Catherine Adams, September 2, 1815, *Founders.*
To John Quincy Adams, December 2, 1815, *Founders.*
To John Quincy Adams, December 24, 1815, *Founders.*
Will of Abigail Adams, January 18, 1816, *Founders.*
To John Quincy Adams, February 10, 1816, *Founders.*
To Richard Rush, February 26, 1816, *Founders.*
To Louisa Catherine Adams, March 20, 1816, *Founders.*
To Charles Francis Adams, March 28, 1816, *Founders.*
To John Quincy Adams, May 5–9, 1816, *Founders.*
To John Adams 2nd, May 21, 1816, *Founders.*
To John Quincy Adams, June 29, 1816, *Founders.*
To John Quincy Adams, December 5, 1816, *Founders.*

To Thomas Jefferson, December 15, 1816, *Cappon*, 500.
To Richard Rush, March 24, 1817, *Founders*.
To William Cranch, March 26, 1817, *Founders*.
To Thomas Jefferson, April 29, 1817, *Cappon*, 511.
To John Quincy Adams, August 10, 1817, *Founders*.
To Harriet Welsh, August 18, 1817, *Founders*.
To Harriet Welsh, October 1, 1817, *Founders*.
To Julia Stockton Rush, October 15, 1817, *Founders*.
To Harriet Welsh, December 1, 1817, *Founders*.
To Louisa Catherine Adams, December 12, 1817, *Founders*.
To John Quincy Adams, December 14, 1817, *Founders*.
To Harriet Welsh, December 31, 1817, *Founders*.
To François Adriaan van der Kemp, January 24, 1818, *Founders*.
To Harriet Welsh, January 24, 1818, *CFA*, 2nd ed., I:lxxxi–lxxxii.
To Louisa Catherine Adams, February 27, 1818, *Founders*.
To Caroline Smith De Windt, March 22, 1818, *De Windt*, I:236–39.
To John Quincy Adams, June 23, 1818, *Founders*.
To Louisa Catherine Adams, August 21, 1818, *Founders*.

This volume presents the texts of the editions chosen as sources
here but does not attempt to reproduce features of their typographic
design. The texts are printed without alteration except for the changes
previously discussed, some changes in headings, and the correction
of typographical errors. Spelling, punctuation, and capitalization are
often expressive features, and they are not altered, even when inconsistent or irregular. The following is a list of typographical errors corrected, cited by page and line number: 38.28, thy [   ] Days; 73.19,
live ~~with~~; 86.19, have Reinforcements; 91.5, Cranch; 139.16, for acquiring; 266.10, me to seriously; 410.3, Mr; 413.8, at; 427.2–3; QuincYs;
428.31, m up; 439.2, all all; 447.27, make and; 467.4, see the; 482.28,
it a; 498.7, Mr. Bush's; 504.7–8, well I; 541.39, able say; 562.14,
Gound; 564.15, 4^(th)th; 583.28, where I shall; 583.28–29, year," he says.";
599.24, but but; 601.23, belevolence; 606.27, eitheir; 613.13, me; it;
616.17, ditressing; 628.39, as a a; 633.6, Mr.; 650.7, wack in; 663.38, co-
opperate. How; 681.16, t is his; 682.2, abundancemr; 709.1 as well as
well; 710.20, affiicted; 718.6, Is; 724.4, Say; 733.18, Pichuring; 736.16,
reitrement.; 745.3, Adam; 770.25, Adams:; 774.40, Rark; 782.25, any
of her other; 796.28, dired; 800.28, 18010; 804.9, rmoved; 811.12,
hears; 813.2, Mavens; 813.6, eabody,; 820.11, (,"The; 821.25, if your;
829.30, not impatient; 865.15, Letters; 865.26, in were; 870.1, John &
Sherbrook,; 870.2, s by; 892.17, a avowed; 892.19, It; 892.21, pints;
893.13, copariots,; 901.18, past; 908.29, that if; 912.2, dupe? with;
912.4, School"; 912.12, Mumford; 932.29, J B; 941.8, you;.

Notes

In the notes below, the reference numbers denote page and line of this volume (the line count includes headings, but not rule lines). No note is made for material included in the eleventh edition of *Merriam-Webster's Collegiate Dictionary*, except for certain cases where common words and terms have specific historical meanings or inflections. Biblical quotations and allusions are keyed to the King James Version; references to Shakespeare to *The Riverside Shakespeare*, ed. G. Blackmore Evans (Boston: Houghton Mifflin, 1974). For further biographical background, references to other studies, and more detailed notes, see *Adams Family Correspondence*, edited by L. H. Butterfield et al. (12 vols. to date, Cambridge: Harvard University Press, 1963–2015); Lester J. Cappon, ed., *The Adams-Jefferson Letters: The Complete Correspondence Between Thomas Jefferson and Abigail and John Adams* (Chapel Hill: The University of North Carolina Press, 1959, 1988); Edith Gelles, *Portia: The World of Abigail Adams* (Bloomington: Indiana University Press, 1992); Gelles, *"First Thoughts": Life and Letters of Abigail Adams* (New York: Twayne Publishers, 1998); and Gelles, *Abigail & John: Portrait of a Marriage* (New York: HarperLuxe, 2009).

COURTSHIP AND MARRIAGE, 1763–1773

3.12 Mrs. Wheelwrights Letter] Esther Wheelwright (1696–1780) was captured by Indians in Wells, Maine, in 1703 at the age of seven and taken to New France (Canada). She was baptized as Catholic, later became a nun, and by 1760 was Mother Superior of the Ursuline Convent in Quebec. This "Letter, to her Nephew," probably written in French to her sister's son, was widely circulated.

4.20 your Diana] Abigail's pen name. Diana was the Roman goddess of the moon and hunting and the patron of virgins. Classical pen names were commonly used by letter writers in the eighteenth century, suggesting a character the writer might identify with.

4.22 Seneca, for the sake of his Paulina] Pompeia Paulina, the wife of Seneca the Younger (c. 4 B.C.E.–65 C.E.).

4.25 Lysander] John Adams's pen name, after a Spartan statesman.

5.25 a Cousin of yours.] Zabdiel Adams (1739–1801), Harvard 1759, who would become minister at Lunenburg, Massachusetts, in 1764, was a double first cousin of John.

5.32 your fellow traveler] John followed the local court circuit to try cases.

Abigail accompanied him on this journey, as a November 23, 1763, letter from her married friend Hannah Storer Green (see List of Correspondents) suggestively comments:

> Now I shall proceed upon your former Letter, wherein you give an account of your journey. I could not help laughing at the gaiety of your fancy, in supposing that there was any resemblance between that and Matrimony; I'm sure it would have been very distastfull to me to have been jumbled into Married Life—aye and to you too for there *it ought to be* a smooth road, if no where else.

6.18–19   too infectious . . . to wish for any Communication] Tufts had recently been inoculated with smallpox in Boston. Smallpox was one of the most deadly diseases of the premodern world, with estimates of as many as 30 percent of those contracting the disease dying and those surviving often being badly disfigured. Inoculation had been a controversial issue in Boston since it was first introduced in 1721 by Cotton Mather, especially when outbreaks occurred in 1730 and 1752. There was public concern for two primary reasons: First, the danger to the individual—the disease was voluntarily induced in a milder form—as well as fear of contagion. Second, it was beyond the means of ordinary people to partake of it. Nevertheless, by 1760, there was evidence of the effectiveness of the process, and two public inoculating hospitals had been established in Boston. An epidemic in 1764 raised the issue again, and Boston voted on March 13 to allow anyone to be inoculated during the next five weeks. By March 30 there had been 699 cases of natural smallpox with 124 deaths, and 4,977 cases of inoculated smallpox with only 46 deaths.

6.21   dieted too low] An extreme diet of milk and vegetables as well as purgatives constituted the prescribed preparatory treatment for the inoculation. It was popularized by Dr. Adam Thomson of Philadelphia, in his *Discourse on the Preparation of the Body for the Small-Pox* (Philadelphia, 1750).

7.4   Dr. Perkins] Nathaniel Perkins (1715–1799), Harvard 1734, a Boston physician, later a Loyalist.

7.5   Tom] Tom was the Smiths' servant, possibly a slave. Reverend Smith's diary records baptizing "my Negro man Thomas" on March 22, 1741. He died in 1766.

7.26   Pope—("Not to go . . . advance")] Cf. Alexander Pope, *Satires, Epistles, and Odes of Horace, Imitated* (1733–38) bk. 1, Epistle 1, "To Lord Bolingbroke," l. 54.

9.8   Rattle] A person who talks incessantly.

10.32   the Alborack of Mahomet] In Islamic tradition, the Al-Burāq is a cross between a mule and a donkey that carried the prophet Muhammad from Mecca to Jerusalem and back in one night.

10.36–37   a precipice . . . Edgar describes to Lear] Cf. *King Lear*, IV.vi.

10.38–39 light as the Gosemore . . . shiver into atoms] Cf. *King Lear*, IV.vi.49–51: "Hadst thou been aught but goss'mer, feathers, air / (So many fathom down precipitating), / Thou'dst shiver'd like an egg." The 1608 first quarto spells "gossamer" as "gosmore."

11.1 the witches Broth in Macbeth] Cf. *Macbeth*, IV.i.

11.26 Thou canst not prove a villan] Cf. *Richard III*, I.i.28–30.

12.1–2 Gold and Silver . . . unto thee] Acts 3:6.

12.29 The Capotal fault] On May 7, 1764, John sent Abigail a list of "your Faults, Imperfections, Defects, or whatever you please to call them." Abigail jokingly promised to rectify the "Capotal," or head, fault: John wrote, "In the Fourth Place you very often hang your Head like a Bulrush. You do not sit, erected as you ought, by which Means, it happens that you appear too short for a Beauty, and the Company looses the sweet smiles of that Countenance and the bright sparkles of those Eyes."

12.33 The 5th fault] John wrote, "Another fault, which seems to have been obstinately persisted in, after frequent Remonstrances, Advices and Admonitions of your Friends, is that of sitting with the Leggs across. This ruins the figure and the Air, this injures the Health. And springs I fear from the former source vizt. too much Thinking."

13.4 The sixth and last] John wrote, "A sixth Imperfection is that of Walking, with the Toes bending inward."

13.25–27 the phylosopher who laught . . . weept at them] Fifth-century B.C.E. Greek philosophers Democritus and Heraclitus, respectively.

14.13 Caliope?] Green's pen name, for the muse of heroic poetry.

15.24–25 the Doctor and Mr. Wibird] Abigail's uncle Cotton Tufts (see List of Correspondents) and the Reverend Anthony Wibird (1720–1800), minister in Braintree.

15.31 Camblet] A garment made of a mixture of wool and either silk or cotton.

15.32 Unkle Smiths] Isaac Smith Sr. See List of Correspondents.

16.1–2 Sermons to young women] *Sermons for Young Women* (1766), a popular advice book that went through many editions, by James Fordyce (1720–1796), a Scottish Presbyterian minister.

16.6–7 Cards . . . Mr. Cranch would send me a pair] For combing wool. Richard Cranch, Abigail's brother-in-law, was a watchmaker and cardmaker.

16.20 The Doctor] Cotton Tufts; see List of Correspondents.

16.20–21 New Braintree] In the western part of Worcester County.

16.27 when you are absent] John was in Worcester, Massachusetts, for a legal case at the superior court.

17.3   Mr. Gridly] Jeremiah Gridley (1702–1767), Harvard 1725, John's mentor who had been a leading lawyer in Boston, died on September 10.

17.12–13   "Where Contemplation . . . pitty Kings."] Pope, *Satires of Dr. John Donne, Dean of St. Paul's, Versified* (1735), Satire IV, ll. 313–14.

18.33   Mr. Whitefield] George Whitefield (1714–1770), English Anglican evangelist who made sensational tours throughout the colonies, preaching to enormous crowds, and who figured prominently in the Great Awakening. He had died at Newburyport, Massachusetts, the previous September.

18.38–39   Dr. Sherbear in his remarks upon the english Nation] *Letters on the English Nation* (1755, 2 vols.) by John Shebbeare (1709–1788), a British political satirist.

19.10   Mrs. Maccaulays] Catharine Sawbridge Macaulay. See List of Correspondents.

19.22   the West Indian] Smith had sent Abigail *The West Indian* (1771), a comedy by Richard Cumberland then being performed in London at the Drury Lane Theatre.

20.19   Mrs. Seymore upon Education] *On the Management and Education of Children: A Series of Letters Written to a Niece* (1754) by John Hill, an English author and botanist, writing under the pseudonym Juliana Seymour.

20.31–32   "rearing the tender thought, . . . the Mind."] Cf. "Spring" from *The Seasons* (1726–30) by Scottish poet James Thomson (1700–1748), who also composed the lyrics to "Rule, Britannia!"

21.1–16   "Parent who vast pleasure . . . her chair."] From a poem prefixed to the 1772 edition of English dramatist John Gay's collected plays, possibly by Gay himself.

REVOLUTION, 1773–1777

25.26–27   Develloped the Dark designs of a Rapatio's Soul] Mercy Otis Warren had anonymously written a blank verse play based on the Boston Massacre, *The Adulateur. A Tragedy, as It Is Now Acted in Upper Servia* (1772), in which Rapatio, "Governor of Servia," represented Governor Thomas Hutchinson.

25.29   The Tea that bainfull weed is arrived] The first of three ships carrying East India Company tea had arrived on November 28. For an account of the Tea Party, see Chronology for 1773.

26.4–5   the Speach of Cato . . . save our Country."] Cf. Joseph Addison, *Cato* (1712), IV.iv.80–81.

26.6–8   "Tender plants must bend . . . sullen State."] John Dryden, *Don Sebastian*, II.i.50–54.

26.30   His Cit. turnd Gentleman] Cf. *The Bourgeois Gentleman* (1670) by Molière.

27.31–32   the progress of Dulness] *The Progress of Dulness*, a collection of three poems published in 1772 by John Trumbull (1750–1831), Yale 1767, was a satirical attack on the prevailing educational methods. Trumbull worked in John's law office and later became a judge in Connecticut.

28.16–18   a dethroned chief Justice . . . the bench] Peter Oliver, chief justice of the Massachusetts Superior Court, was impeached by the colony's House of Representatives on February 24 for accepting a crown salary in lieu of a salary paid by the assembly. Lieutenant Governor Hutchinson blocked the proceedings, but afterward jurors refused to serve while Oliver was on the bench, and by August he was forced to step down.

28.20–25   What tho . . . Extort from me] Cf. *Paradise Lost*, bk. I, ll. 105–11.

28.30–33   Alaxander to weep . . . second in Rome] For the story about Alexander the Great, see Plutarch, "On Tranquility of Mind," in *Moralia* (c. 100 C.E.). The story about Caesar comes from Plutarch's "Life of Julius Caesar" in his *Lives of the Noble Greeks and Romans.*

28.33–34   the arch Fiend Himself . . . serve in Heaven.] Cf. *Paradise Lost*, bk. I, l. 263.

29.22–24   Zeal for a publick cause . . . betrayed them.—] Joseph Addison, *The Spectator* No. 125 (July 24, 1711).

29.30–31   "and barter Liberty for gold."] John Brown (1715–1766), English divine, essayist, and poet, "An Essay on Satire, Occasioned by the Death of Mr. Pope" (1745), Part II, l. 302. Brown's poem was printed in front of *The Works of Alexander Pope Esq. Volume III Containing His Moral Essays* (1770).

29.33–34   the very worthy bearer of this Letter] Mercy's husband, James Warren (1726–1808), a member of the lower house of the Massachusetts General Court.

29.39   3 part of the progress of Dulness] See note 27.31–32.

30.18–26   the Misfortunes of Sparta . . . liberty.] Cf. Charles Rollin's *Ancient History*, vol. 4, bk. XII, ch. I, sec. IV.i. See also note 31.1–2.

30.31–34   Locrians . . . American Amphyctions] In 339 B.C.E. the Amphyctionic Council, a religious body made up of representatives from the various Greek tribes, was attacked at Delphi by members of the Locrian tribe. The action triggered the Fourth Sacred War among the Greek states, and became a pretext for the council's decision to appeal to Phillip II of Macedon to intervene against the Locrians, which in turn opened the door to his eventual conquest of southern Greece. This episode is treated at length in Rollin's *Ancient History.*

31.1–2   Rollin's ancient History] Charles Rollin (1661–1741), rector of the University of Paris, wrote narrative histories of classical Greece and Rome widely read in America.

31.22 a dollar for a letter] The cost of postage. John and Abigail had been primarily sending letters by acquaintances traveling between Boston and Pennsylvania in order to prevent strangers from opening them.

32.25 Cleverlys and Etters] Braintree had one small Anglican church and among its parishioners were the Cleverly, Etter, and Miller families, who were inclined to Toryism.

33.2 The church parson] Edward Winslow (1722–1780), Harvard 1741, who had settled at Braintree in 1763, was forced to leave early in 1777 as a person "Inimical to the United States."

33.7 Coll. Quincys] Colonel Josiah Quincy (1710–1784), a distant cousin.

33.10–11 Mr. Samll. Quincys wife] Hannah (Hill) Quincy (1734–1782) disagreed with her husband's politics and did not flee with him into exile the next year.

33.11 Mr. Sumner] Increase Sumner (1746–1799) of Roxbury read law in Samuel Quincy's office. He became a justice of the Supreme Judicial Court, and from 1797 to 1799 governor of Massachusetts. Sumner's mother was a first cousin of John's mother.

33.11 Mr. Josiah and Wife] Abigail (Phillips) Quincy (1745–1798), wife of Josiah "the Patriot" Quincy (1744–1775), the son of Colonel Josiah Quincy. Josiah "the Patriot" had been John's co-counsel during the trials of the soldiers involved in the Boston Massacre, and died in 1775 of tuberculosis.

33.15–16 Speach of the Bishop of St. Asaph] *A Speech Intended to Have Been Spoken on the Bill for Altering the Charters of the Colony of Massachusett's Bay* by Jonathan Shipley (1714–1788), Bishop of St. Asaph, in which he said that he looked "upon North-America as the only great nursery of freemen now left upon the face of the earth." Shipley was an early advocate of the American cause who voted in the House of Lords against the Coercive Acts.

33.17 Mr. Thaxter] John Thaxter Jr., Abigail's cousin. See also List of Correspondents.

33.28 my two Neighbours] Thaxter and Nathan Rice (1754–1834), Harvard 1773, both of whom had entered John's law office as clerks in June or July 1774, and were living above John's office in the house in Braintree.

34.17 wisdom will flow . . . cities of our God.] Cf. Amos 5:24 and Psalm 46:4.

34.22–23 the peoples preventing the court from setting] The Massachusetts Government Act, one of the four Coercive Acts, gave the crown the authority to appoint and remove judges in all Massachusetts courts. The colonists responded by preventing any courts with royally appointed judges from opening.

34.24 Anger] Oakes Angier (1745–1786), a former law clerk of John who was admitted to the bar in 1771.

34.26   Miss Eunice] Eunice Paine, sister of Robert Treat Paine (for whom see note 82.2–3).

34.34   Dr. Tufts] Cotton Tufts; see List of Correspondents and Family Tree.

35.20   every day dispensing to you] Every day being dispensed to you. In eighteenth-century construction, a present participle was often used instead of a passive verb.

36.30–31   Mr. Williams . . . Mr. Hills] Jonathan Williams (d. 1780) and Edward Hill (1755–1775), two of John's law clerks.

37.2–3   Mr. Quincy's so secret departure] Josiah Quincy II, "the Patriot" (1744–1775), had sailed for England on September 28. Only John and a few of Quincy's closest friends knew of his mission to appeal for American patriots to both the British administration and the friends of America in England. He died of tuberculosis on his return voyage, late in April 1775, never communicating the result.

37.10   the Bearer] William Tudor (1750–1819), one of John's former law clerks.

37.36   the Lady before introduced] Mercy Otis Warren, who also became a correspondent of Macaulay.

38.8–10   "Tender plants . . . sullen state.] See note 26.6–8.

38.12–13   inhumane acts of the British parliment] The four Coercive Acts. See Chronology for 1774.

38.26–29   Are these thy deeds . . . early fame] From John Trumbull, "An Elegy on the Times," composed in August 1774 in response to the closing of the Boston port due to the Coercive Acts.

39.3–4   "bare their bold . . . generous Blood."] Cf. "The Choice of Hercules," 1743 poem by grammarian and Church of English bishop Robert Lowth, which was turned into the libretto for George Frideric Handel's oratorio *The Choice of Hercules* (1750) by English librettist Thomas Morell.

39.6   that which is right in his own Eyes] Cf. Judges 17:6.

39.24   the association which accompanied them] The first Continental Congress had passed an agreement ("association") on October 20 that recommended nonimportation, nonconsumption, and nonexportation of British goods.

39.36–39   the words of the revered . . . with her.] From the speech of William Pitt the elder (1708–1778) on the Stamp Act, January 14, 1766.

40.12–13   such a Speach from the Throne] George III's speech at the opening of Parliament, November 30, 1774, which was published in the *Massachusetts Spy* on February 2, 1775. Abigail paraphrases the speech in lines 19–21.

40.23–41.2   the envy of nations . . . first of British Slaves] Paraphrasing "A

Dissertation on Parties," Letter XVII, by Henry St John, 1st Viscount Boling-broke (1678–1751), who had been a leader of the Country Party movement opposing Robert Walpole's government of the 1730s. His works became a ma-jor influence on John Adams, Thomas Jefferson, James Madison, and other American patriots.

41.8–10 Tho an hoste . . . be confident] Psalm 27:3.

41.31 the admired Farmer] In a series of twelve letters, published in news-papers in 1767–68 and then as *Letters from a Farmer in Pennsylvania*, John Dickinson argued that the colonies were sovereign in internal affairs and British taxes were unconstitutional. Dickinson was widely celebrated in the colonies.

42.2–3 Lord North . . . Neroisim.] By the end of 1774, the British prime minister, Lord North, had begun to have reservations about the use of force in America and considered dispatching peace commissioners to the colonies to resolve the dispute. But the Coercive Acts had sealed his character as a latter-day Nero for many Americans, and when word of such overtures reached America, they were viewed with caution and suspicion. North's formal Concil-iatory Proposal, issued by Parliament a few weeks after this letter was written, afforded individual colonies an exemption from taxes if they provided regular contributions to the crown on their own initiative. Critics saw the offer as a disingenuous attempt to sow disunion in America, and it was dismissed by the colonies because it failed to recognize the legitimacy of the Continental Congress.

42.22–24 comply with my request . . . conditions] Mercy wrote to Abigail on January 28: "Yours of Jan. the third begins with an instance of Curios-ity which I am willing to Cherish. Nay Even to Gratify provided I may be indulged in Return with the sight of Mr. and Mrs. Adams's Correspondence with the Lady Refered to," i.e., Catharine Sawbridge Macaulay.

42.28–30 a certain Group . . . female character] Mercy had sent her satiri-cal play *The Group* to John for his opinion and assistance with its publication. John arranged for the first two acts to be printed in the *Boston Gazette* on January 23, 1775, and for the entire play to be published as a pamphlet, both anonymously.

42.30–31 "Tho an Eagles talon asks an Eagles Eye"] John Brown, "An Essay on Satire, Occasioned by the Death of Mr. Pope" (1745), Part I, l. 192.

42.37 hideing a talent . . . napkin.] Cf. Luke 19:12–27.

42.38 "Who combats virtues foe is virtue's friend"] Brown, "An Essay on Satire," Part I, l. 147.

43.5–12 "Well may they Dread . . . toad."] Ibid, Part I, ll. 133–40.

43.17–28 "When Virtue sinks . . . head."] Ibid, Part I, ll. 87–98.

44.20–21 Colln. Quincys family . . . flee] Colonel Josiah Quincy's house in Quincy, built in 1770, overlooked Boston Harbor.

45.8 Mr. Welds was then ringing] The church bells, rung by the Reverend Ezra Weld.

45.15 the Drs.] Cotton Tufts; see List of Correspondents.

45.35–36 the Arival of Doctor Franklin] Benjamin Franklin (1706–1790) had been in London acting as an agent for several American colonies. He returned to Philadelphia on May 5, 1775, and was immediately elected to the Second Continental Congress.

46.14–15 The bad conduct of General Gage] Charles Francis Adams, in his edition of his grandmother's letters, noted that Gage "had taken the engines under guard, in consequence of a report that the liberty party intended to fire the town."

46.19 Isaac] Isaac Copeland, hired farmhand.

46.20 Mr. Rice] See note 33.28.

46.31–34 "Yet to the Houseless . . . good will."] Cf. Oliver Goldsmith, "Edwin and Angelina," ll. 13–16, in *The Vicar of Wakefield* (1766).

47.1 wrote to Mr. Dilly] Edward Dilly, a London bookseller.

47.20 Portia] Abigail adopted the pen name of "Portia," from the wife of the Roman republican politician Brutus, the most famous of the assassins of Julius Caesar, in place of "Diana."

47.21–22 Sister Betsy . . . to you.] In Elizabeth Smith's hand.

47.28–29 Dr. Warren is no more] Dr. Joseph Warren (1741–1775), Harvard 1759, a close friend of John's, was killed in the battle of Bunker Hill while serving in the Massachusetts militia.

48.3 The race is not . . . strong] Ecclesiastes 9:11.

48.4–5 the God of Israel . . . his people.] Psalm 68:35.

48.5–6 Trust in him . . . refuge for us.—] Psalm 62:8.

48.17 a retreat at your Brothers] John's brother Elihu's farm was located further inland, in what is now Randolph, Massachusetts.

48.35–49.8 How sleep . . . Hermit there.] William Collins, "Ode Written in the Beginning of the Year 1746" (1747).

49.31 Welch fuzelers] The Royal Welch Fusiliers, an infantry regiment of the British army. Only five men were left alive and unwounded after the battle of Bunker Hill.

49.34 14 and 15 hundred slain and wounded] The colonists lost 450 men killed, wounded, and captured at the battle of Bunker Hill, and the British 1,054 men killed and wounded.

50.4–9 "Extremity . . . *Shakespear.*] *Coriolanus,* IV.i.4–9.

50.10–11   Battle upon the plains of Abram] A pivotal battle in the Seven Years' War, fought for control of the fortress city of Quebec on September 13, 1759, in which Howe, then a colonel, took part.

50.27–32   Good Nehemiah . . . houses.] Cf. Nehemiah 4:13–14.

50.39   Mr. Taft] Reverend Moses Taft (1722–1791), Harvard 1751, minister of the South Church in Braintree, in what is now Randolph, Massachusetts.

51.4   a *Cooper* and an *Elliot*.] Reverend Samuel Cooper (1725–1783), Harvard 1743, minister of the Brattle Street Church in Boston, which the Adamses had attended when they lived there; and Andrew Eliot, Harvard 1737, minister of the New North Church in Boston.

51.6–7   "And in his Duty . . . for all."] Oliver Goldsmith, "The Deserted Village" (1770).

51.8   General Heaths regiment] Brigadier General William Heath (1737–1814), from nearby Roxbury, Massachusetts.

51.16–17   Mr. Boylstone and Mr. Gill the printer] Thomas Boylston (1721–1798), a cousin of John's mother, and John Gill (1732–1785), printer of the *Boston Gazette*.

51.18   the black list] A list drawn up by British officials of men involved in the Tea Party who were not allowed to leave Boston during the siege.

51.19   your Brother Swift] Samuel Swift, Harvard 1735, a lawyer and close friend of John's.

51.20   Mr. Mather] Reverend Samuel Mather (1706–1785), Harvard 1723, minister of the Tenth Congregational Society in Boston, and son of Cotton Mather.

52.1   Mr. Bowdoin] James Bowdoin Sr. (1726–1790), a local political leader and later second governor of Massachusetts (1785–87).

52.8–9   Mr. Winslows family] Edward Winslow. See note 33.2.

52.21   Bracket] A farmhand.

52.25   Bass] Joseph Bass, a shoemaker from Braintree, accompanied John to Philadelphia as a servant.

53.12   Our prisoners] The thirty men captured during the battle of Bunker Hill, most of whom were seriously injured. Twenty of the prisoners died before release.

53.20   the Admiral] Admiral Samuel Graves (1713–1787) of the British Royal Navy.

53.27   Master Lovel] James Lovell. See List of Correspondents.

53.27–28   a Son of Mr. Edes] Peter Edes, son of Benjamin Edes (1732–1803), printer of the *Boston Gazette*.

53.36–37   death of Warren] See note 47.28–29.

54.7   your Judas.] Joseph Galloway (1731–1803), a Pennsylvania delegate in the First Continental Congress who had proposed a Plan of Union to avoid a break with Britain. He declined to serve in the Second Congress and later became a Loyalist.

54.26   Col. Palmer] Brigadier General Joseph Palmer (1716–1788), who was married to Richard Cranch's sister Mary Cranch.

55.2–3   your Friend Gorge Trott] George Trott (1741–1810), a Boston jeweler and an active Son of Liberty who married John's cousin Ann Boylston Cunningham.

55.15   your Brothers house] Peter Boylston Adams.

55.20–21   Mr. Hayden] The Haydens were a prolific Braintree family, and it is not clear which Haydens were tenants in the John Adams Birthplace at this time.

56.4–5   Sister Adams got to bed] Mary Crosby Adams delivered a daughter, Susannah, who was baptized on July 16 and died in April 1776.

57.5   Mr. Collins and Kaign] Stephen Collins, a Whig Quaker who lived near Philadelphia, and John Cain, another Quaker.

57.23–24   The appointment of the Generals Washington and Lee] George Washington was appointed commander in chief of the newly formed Continental Army on June 15, 1775, and Charles Lee a major general on June 17.

57.31   Major Miflin] Major General Thomas Mifflin (1744–1800), a member of the Continental Congress from Pennsylvania, who had left the Congress to serve in the Continental Army.

57.34   Mr. Read] Brigadier General Joseph Reed, another member of the Continental Congress from Pennsylvania who served with the Continental Army.

58.7–10   "Mark his Majestick . . . God."] John Dryden, *Don Sebastian*, II.i.385–88.

58.12–13   his namesake Charls the 12] In Voltaire's *History of Charles XII, King of Sweden* (1731), the king was described as "a tall handsome gentleman, but immoderately dirty and slovenly; his behaviour and carriage more rustic than you can imagine in so young a man should be."

58.23–24   a Lady . . . you should value] Mercy Otis Warren. See List of Correspondents.

58.36–37   not been more accurately informd] John had written, "We are constantly obliged to go to the Delegates from Connecticutt and Rhode Island for Intelligence of what is passing at Boston."

59.14   L M] Lawful money, the official Massachusetts currency.

59.32   Capt. Tupper] Major Benjamin Tupper (1738–1792).

59.35   Simple Sapling] In *The Group*, Mercy used this satirical name for Nathaniel Ray Thomas (1731–1787), Harvard 1751, a well-to-do and prominent Loyalist. After the action at Concord, Thomas fled to Boston and then to Nova Scotia, where he died impoverished.

60.23   This Town . . . Representative] The election for the Massachusetts House of Representatives was held on July 10.

60.36   General Thomas] Major General John Thomas (1724–1776), who would die of smallpox the next year after the unsuccessful invasion of Canada.

61.1   Every article . . . West india way] Coffee, tea, sugar, etc.

61.4   caliminco] Wool fabric with a shiny surface.

61.12   tantulus like] Tantalus, a Greek mythological figure subjected to the eternal punishment of standing in a pool of water under a fruit tree with low-hanging branches, but never being able to reach either the fruit or the water to eat or drink.

61.28–31   Be not afraid, . . . increase.] Joel 2:22.

61.35–38   "This Day be Bread . . . done."] Pope, "The Universal Prayer" (1738).

62.1–6   But is the Almighty . . . more.] "The Choice: A Poem" (1752) by Dr. Benjamin Church, written while he was a student at Harvard. See also note 72.20–21.

63.19–20   The return of thee . . . absence] After a four-month absence, John had returned home, stopping first in Watertown, seventeen miles to the northwest, before reaching Braintree. For the remainder of August John spent weekends at home and weekdays attending the Massachusetts Provincial Council in Watertown, the upper chamber of the Provincial Congress established the previous year as the de facto government of Massachusetts.

63.22   the looss of your Brother] In his autobiography, John wrote: "My brother died greatly lamented by all who knew him and by none more than me."

64.18–21   Susy . . . Patty] Servants.

64.29–30   Deacon Adams . . . Mr. Wibird] Deacon Ebenezer Adams (1737–1791) was a double first cousin of John's. For the Reverend Anthony Wibird, see note 15.24–25.

65.17   Mr. Trot] George Trott. See note 55.2–3.

65.26   Indian root] Aralia racemosa, or American spikenard, a member of the ginseng family.

65.31   small pox in the natural way] I.e., contracted in an epidemic and not through inoculation.

66.27 Mr. Mason] A law clerk of John's, Jonathan Mason (1756–1831), of Boston, College of New Jersey 1774. He was admitted to the bar in 1779 and later served in both the Massachusetts houses and in the U.S. Congress.

66.34–35 Mr. Tudor . . . Mr. Wibird] For William Tudor, see note 37.10. For Reverend Anthony Wibird, see note 15.24–25.

67.1–3 directeth the arrow . . . Darkness.] Cf. Psalm 91:5–6.

67.12 him who mounts . . . Storm] Cf. Pope, *The Dunciad*, bk. 3, ll. 264–68.

67.22 the intercepted Letters] Two letters by John dated July 24, 1775, were seized by the British when Benjamin Hitchborn of Boston, who was carrying the letters, was captured near Newport, Rhode Island. One letter was to Abigail, which said, "When 50 or 60 Men have a Constitution to form for a great Empire, at the same Time that they have a Country of fifteen hundred Miles extent to fortify, Millions to arm and train, a Naval Power to begin, an extensive Commerce to regulate, numerous Tribes of Indians to negotiate with, a standing Army of Twenty seven Thousand Men to raise, pay, victual and officer, I really shall pity those 50 or 60 Men." The other was to James Warren, which alluded to James Dickinson, a fellow delegate to the Continental Congress, as "A certain great Fortune and piddling Genius" who had "given a silly Cast to our whole Doings." The letters were published in the *Massachusetts Gazette* in August and later in London, leading to an ongoing quarrel between John and Dickinson, and gaining John notoriety as the leading advocate of military resistance to Britain.

67.24 infamous versification of them] Abigail elsewhere identifies it as "A pharaphrase upon the Second Epistle of John the round Head to James the prolocutor of the Rump parliment." No copy has been found.

67.29 remonstrance, address and petition] "An Address, Petition, and Remonstrance in favor of the Americans presented by the City of London to the King on 5 July," printed in the *Massachusetts Spy* on September 13, 1775.

67.31 God helps them that help themselves as King Richard said] Proverbial phrase that originated in ancient Greece. Benjamin Franklin used it in *Poor Richard's Almanack* in 1736.

68.30 Sister Elihu Adams lost her youngest child] Thankful White Adams lost an unnamed infant daughter.

69.4–5 Have pitty . . . me soar.] Cf. Job 19:21 and Psalm 38:2.

69.15–16 his Ear . . . Trouble.] Cf. Isaiah 59:1 and Psalm 50:15.

69.31–32 the pestilence . . . noon day] Cf. Psalm 91:6.

70.8–9 "Rare are solitary . . . others heal."] Edward Young, *Night Thoughts* (1742–45), Night III, ll. 63–64.

70.32 Breach upon Breach] Cf. Job 16:14.

70.34 Your Aunt Simpson died] Mary Boylston Simpson (1714–1775), the sister of John's mother.

71.8 time alone . . . Edg of Sorrow.] From *The History of Lady Julia Mandeville* (1763) by English novelist Frances Brooke (1724–1789).

71.9 He who deignd to weep . . . Friend] Cf. John 11.

71.13–14 tho he slay . . . holy Job.] Cf. Job 13:15.

71.36–37 "The sweet . . . sleep in Dust."] Cf. Isaac Watts's Psalm 112, ll. 15 and 18, in his 1719 metrical psalter, *The Psalms of David*, rendering the psalms into "the language of the New Testament." Abigail seems to have found the quote in *The Works of the Reverend George Whitefield*, Volume II (1771), Letter 544 (December 31, 1743).

72.1–3 "Give Sorrow words. . . . Break."] *Macbeth*, IV.iii.209–10.

72.20–21 the viliny of . . . a patriot] A suspicious letter in cipher written by Dr. Benjamin Church to his brother-in-law, a Loyalist in Boston, was discovered late in September. Church, who was highly regarded as a patriot, never admitted his guilt, and it wasn't until the twentieth century that documents were published showing that Church had been furnishing information to the British command since early 1775.

72.26 the Day . . . to be loosed?] Cf. Revelation 20:7–8.

72.28 Gage . . . How in his place] Sir William Howe (1729–1814) replaced General Gage as commander of British forces on October 10.

72.30 Burgoine is gone to Philadelphia.] British Major General John Burgoyne (1722–1792) remained in Boston until December 5, when he sailed to England seeking a command post, and was sent to Canada in early 1776.

74.16–18 the fate of Dr. Church . . . Lovel] See note 72.20–21. Church was court-martialed and then imprisoned by the Continental Congress until 1778, when he was named in the Massachusetts Banishment Act and sailed for Martinique. The ship he was on disappeared. For James Lovell, see List of Correspondents.

74.34 a kingdom a kingdom for a horse] *Richard III*, V.iv.7.

75.5–7 There's not a day, . . . seeing more.] Young, *Night Thoughts* (1742–45), Night VIII, ll. 80–82.

75.11–12 "A foe to God . . . does."] Young, *Night Thoughts*, Night VIII, ll. 704–5.

75.21 the Gentlemen . . . committe] Benjamin Franklin, Thomas Lynch, and Benjamin Harrison were sent from the Continental Congress to meet with General Washington to discuss how Congress could better support the Continental Army.

75.31–32   "Each Friend snatchd . . . vanity."] Young, *Night Thoughts*, Night III, ll. 285–86.

75.33   Mrs. Hancoke] Dorothy Quincy, daughter of Justice Edmund Quincy, married John Hancock on August 28.

76.21   Carolina pink root] *Spigelia marilandica.*

77.31   A late appointment] As chief justice of the Massachusetts Superior Court. John was appointed but never served.

77.36   The Dedication of Dr. Zublys] John Joachim Zubly, *The Law of Liberty. A Sermon on American Affairs, Preached at the Opening of the Provincial Congress of Georgia* (1775).

78.4   the paper you sent for.] The Massachusetts Committee of Safety's "Relation" of the battle of Bunker Hill, July 25, 1775, signed by Joseph Palmer.

79.13–14   the Court . . . an other month.] On November 11 the Massachusetts House of Representatives extended the commissions of the current delegates from the end of December to the end of January because of a struggle then going on between radicals and moderates in the House over who should represent Massachusetts in the Continental Congress in 1776. The radicals succeeded. In January, Thomas Cushing was displaced by Elbridge Gerry (see List of Correspondents). Robert Treat Paine, who was nearly replaced, in the end was retained. Hancock as well as John and Samuel Adams was reelected.

79.25   like the grave cries give, give.] Cf. Proverbs 30:15–16.

80.20   the only Daughter of your Brother;] Susanna (1766–1826), daughter of Elihu and Thankful White Adams.

81.3   Marcia] Mercy's pen name, after a Roman woman with strong republican views, who was either the wife or the daughter of Cato.

81.25–26   "will often sigh . . . Mankind."] Pope, "To Augustus," *Satires, Epistles, and Odes of Horace, Imitated*, ll. 13–14.

82.2–3   a canting hypocrate] Robert Treat Paine (1731–1814). James Warren had included some sarcastic remarks about Paine in a letter to John on December 3, 1775. John forwarded the letter to Samuel Adams, but it miscarried and was shown to Paine, who in early January wrote angrily to Warren, accusing John of "machinations" that had lost Paine an appointment as chief justice to the Massachusetts Superior Court (the appointment went instead to John). John had long been on uneasy terms with Paine, a rival at the Massachusetts bar.

82.15   a request, I dare not comply with.] Mercy had requested to see some of John's diary volumes.

83.2   your President] John Hancock, president of the Second Continental Congress.

83.17   Common Sense] Thomas Paine's pamphlet was published anonymously in Philadelphia on January 10. John sent Abigail a copy on February
18, and in his response on March 19 to this letter, he wrote:

> You ask, what is thought of Common sense. Sensible Men think
> there are some Whims, some Sophisms, some artfull Addresses to
> superstitious Notions, some keen attempts upon the Passions, in this
> Pamphlet. But all agree there is a great deal of good sense, delivered in
> a clear, simple, concise and nervous Style.
>
> His Sentiments of the Abilities of America, and of the Difficulty of a
> Reconciliation with G.B. are generally approved. But his Notions, and
> Plans of Continental Government are not much applauded. Indeed this
> Writer has a better Hand at pulling down than building.
>
> It has been very generally propagated through the Continent that I
> wrote this Pamphlet. But altho I could not have written any Thing in
> so manly and striking a style, I flatter myself I should have made a more
> respectable Figure as an Architect, if I had undertaken such a Work.
> This Writer seems to have very inadequate Ideas of what is proper and
> necessary to be done, in order to form Constitutions for single Colo-
> nies, as well as a great Model of Union for the whole.

83.26–27   to morrow and to morrow] Cf. *Macbeth*, V.v.19.

83.30–31   orders I find . . . monday night] General Washington placed the cannons captured at Fort Ticonderoga the previous year at Lechmere's Point and
Cobble Hill above Boston as a diversion (see note 84.26–27) and opened fire
on the night of March 2. Militia were called in expectation of a British response.

84.10–11   Palmer . . . Bass . . . Soper . . . Hall] For Colonel Joseph
Palmer, see note 54.26; Jonathan Bass; Edmund Soper; and John Hall Jr., a
stepson of John's mother by her second marriage.

84.17–18   dear country men must fall?] Washington reported to Congress
that the purpose of this bombardment was "to harrass the Enemy and divert their attention" preparatory to assaulting and fortifying the heights on
Dorchester Neck, an operation begun on Monday night, March 4.

84.26–27   we got possession of Dorchester Hill] General John Thomas
and 2,000 troops spent the night of March 4 quietly marching to the top
of Dorchester Heights and hauling the cannons up to the new fortifications.
Howe originally planned to try to take the hill, but a snowstorm the night of
March 5, the sixth anniversary of the Boston Massacre, delayed the battle, and
Howe reconsidered. British forces evacuated Boston on March 17.

85.7–8   a committe for Canada.] Benjamin Franklin, Samuel Chase (1741–
1811), a delegate from Maryland, and Charles Carroll (1737–1832), another
delegate from Maryland who was fluent in French, were sent by Congress on
a diplomatic mission to Canada to persuade the French Canadians to join the
colonies in the Revolution. John Carroll (1735–1815), Charles Carroll's cousin

and a Roman Catholic priest, accompanied the committee in an effort to promote goodwill among Catholics there. The mission was unsuccessful.

85.10   General Lee has left us] John had reported in his February 18 letter that Lee was to command the invasion of Canada. Instead he went to Virginia as commander of the Southern Department.

85.21   our Cousin] Isaac Smith Jr. See List of Correspondents.

85.23–24   certain intercepted Letters] Isaac Smith Jr. wrote to his father on September 26, 1775, "Very unluckily for us, two intercepted letters, wrote by Mr. John Adams, and one from another member of the Congress have been republished here, and (especially the former,) have furnished a topic for general conversation the week past. They are supposed to contain proof that the Congress, some of them at least, have very different views from what they profess in their publications." For the intercepted letters, see note 67.22.

85.28–35   "There is a tide . . . Shakespear] *Julius Caesar*, IV.iii.218–24.

86.3–4   Blood . . . so familiar] *Julius Caesar*, III.i.265–66.

86.11   Nook Hill] Nook or Nook's Hill at Dorchester Point, overlooking the harbor and the British lines on Boston Neck. After seeing movement on the hill, the British fired on it all night. Four men were killed.

86.22–23   Man wants but Little . . . long.] Goldsmith, "Edwin and Angelina," ll. 31–32.

86.27   Tooks Grammer] On February 18, writing of the diplomatic mission to French Canada, John had written, "Pray write me in your next the Name of the Author of your thin French Grammar, which gives you the Pronunciation of the French Words in English Letters." Abigail was mistaken in her answer and corrected herself in her letter of March 16–18, pages 86–90 in this volume. It was J. E. Tandon, *A New French Grammar Teaching a Person . . . to Read, Speak, and Write That Tongue*, 3rd edition (1736).

87.33–34   I'll meet you at Philippi . . . Brutus.] Cf. *Julius Caesar*, IV.iii.283.

87.35   Sunday Noon] Boston still celebrates March 17 as Evacuation Day.

88.7   Great Hill] On Hough's Neck in Braintree (now Quincy).

88.13–14   tis generally Thought to New york.] The fleet actually sailed to the British stronghold at Halifax, Nova Scotia.

89.4   the Expectation of commisioners] In an October 26, 1775, speech to Parliament the king promised to commission "certain Persons on the Spot" to grant pardons and to receive the "Submission of any Province or Colony" that wished "to return to its Allegiance." The crown empowered General William Howe and his brother Admiral Lord Richard Howe, newly appointed commanders of British land and naval forces in North America, to act as peace commissioners as well as military leaders—contradictory roles that proved difficult to reconcile. On September 11, 1776, after a huge British expeditionary force successfully occupied New York and its environs, Admiral Lord Howe would meet a congressional peace delegation that included John Adams, Benjamin Franklin, and Edward Rutledge at Billup Manor on Staten Island, but negotiations stalled as Howe refused to recognize American independence.

89.10   Cleverly] See note 32.25.

89.17   John and Jonathan] John Quincy and a farmhand.

89.19   Bass] Joseph Bass, who had been John's servant in Philadelphia.

89.25–26   tis Tandons, instead of Took.] See note 86.27.

89.26–27   Lord Chesterfields Letters] Philip Stanhope, 4th Earl of Chesterfield, *Letters to His Son on the Art of Becoming a Man of the World and a Gentleman* (1774). John replied on April 12: "Chesterfields Letters are a chequered sett. You would not choose to have them in your Library, they are like Congreeves Plays, stained with libertine Morals and base Principles."

89.28   your couplet of Lattin] From Virgil, *The Aeneid*, bk. 2, ll. 521–22: "Non tali Auxilio nec Defensoribus istis Tempus eget." Not such aid nor such defenses does the time require. Quoted in his letter of February 13, 1776, in which he wrote that "I longed more ardently to be a Soldier than I ever did to be a Lawyer."

89.32   Lord Sterlings character] William Alexander (1726–1783), a major general in the Continental Army, claimed the title of Earl of Stirling.

89.33   harmony with ——] Robert Treat Paine. See note 82.2–3.

89.35   the Speach from the Rostrum] The funeral oration for General Richard Montgomery delivered by the Reverend William Smith of Philadelphia on February 19, 1776.

90.9–10   it is the Lords . . . Eyes.] Psalm 118:23.

90.27   Dunmore] John Murray, 4th Earl of Dunmore (1730–1809), governor of the colony of Virginia, issued Lord Dunmore's Proclamation in November 1775 offering freedom to slaves who joined the British side.

91.1   Mr. Crane] Her agent in Boston.

91.18   your President] John Hancock, president of the Second Continental Congress.

91.19   the Solister General] Samuel Quincy (1735–1789).

92.2   I desire you would Remember the Ladies] On April 14, 1776, John replied:

> As to your extraordinary Code of Laws, I cannot but laugh. We have
> been told that our Struggle has loosened the bands of Government

every where. That Children and Apprentices were disobedient—that schools and Colledges were grown turbulent—that Indians slighted their Guardians and Negroes grew insolent to their Masters. But your Letter was the first Intimation that another Tribe more numerous and powerfull than all the rest were grown discontented.—This is rather too coarse a Compliment but you are so saucy, I wont blot it out.

Depend upon it, We know better than to repeal our Masculine systems. Altho they are in full Force, you know they are little more than Theory. We dare not exert our Power in its full Latitude. We are obliged to go fair, and softly, and in Practice you know We are the subjects. We have only the Name of Masters, and rather than give up this, which would completely subject Us to the Despotism of the Peticoat, I hope General Washington, and all our brave Heroes would fight.

92.23   Neighbour Trot] George Trott. See note 55.2–3.

92.37   Salt peter] Potassium nitrate, a major component in gunpowder, could be produced by a compost mixture of manure and ash.

93.12   Your Brothers youngest child] Susanna; see note 56.4–5.

94.9   He is very sausy to me] For John's reply, see note 92.2.

95.4   And charm . . . sway.] Pope, "Epistle to a Lady," l. 263 (1743).

95.11–14   "Though certain . . . his heart."] Lady Mary Wortley Montagu, "An Epistle to Lord Bathurst," ll. 27–30.

95.16   our worthy Friend Mrs. W————e] Hannah Tollman Winthrop (d. 1790), the wife of John Winthrop, one of John's professors at Harvard. The draft of this letter reads: "I congratulate my Friend upon her Honorable apointment; I was told a few days ago, that a committee of 3 Ladies was chosen to Examine the Tory Ladies, your Ladyship, our Friend Mrs. W————e and your correspondent were the persons."

96.24   Dr. Lorthropes] Nathaniel Lothrop (1737–1828), Harvard 1756, a physician from Plymouth.

96.34–35   The Captain . . . Harden] Seth Harding (1734–1814).

96.38–39   lieutenant . . . Smelden] Samuel Smedley.

97.15   General Thomas.] Major General John Thomas died of smallpox on June 2, 1776. See note 60.36.

97.18   Dr. Bulfinch] Thomas Bulfinch (1728–1802), Harvard 1746; M.D., Edinburgh 1757. Bulfinch inoculated Abigail and her children the following month.

97.35   Capt. Burk] Captain William Burke of the Continental schooner *Warren*.

98.12–13   cloaths the lilies . . . Ravens] Cf. Matthew 6:26, 28.

98.24   Our Friend has Refused his appointment.] James Warren declined appointment as associate justice of the Superior Court. This would become a sore point between the Adamses and Warrens as John continued to serve, despite the hardships to his family.

99.8–9   innoculated for the small pox.] See note 6.18–19.

99.11   her Little Neice] Louisa Catherine Smith (1773–1857), whose family was impoverished. She lived in the Adams household for much of her life and served as amanuensis to John in his old age.

99.22   Dr. Bulfinch] Thomas Bulfinch. See note 97.18.

99.26   Mrs. Quincy, Mrs. Lincoln, Miss Betsy and Nancy] Ann Marsh Quincy (1723–1805), third wife of Colonel Josiah Quincy, and his daughters: by his first wife Hanna Sturgis, Hannah (1736–1826), married to Dr. Bela Lincoln (1734–1773), whom John had almost proposed to in their youth (see List of Correspondents); by his second wife Elizabeth Waldron, Elizabeth "Betsy" (1757–1825), who later married Benjamin Guild; and with Ann Marsh, Ann "Nancy" (1763–1844), who later married Asa Packard.

100.5   Lord Hows comeing with unlimited powers.] See note 89.4.

100.13   I received two Letters] On July 3, John wrote to Abigail:

> The Second Day of July 1776, will be the most memorable Epocha, in the History of America.—I am apt to believe that it will be celebrated, by succeeding Generations, as the great anniversary Festival. It ought to be commemorated, as the Day of Deliverance by solemn Acts of Devotion to God Almighty. It ought to be solemnized with Pomp and Parade, with Shews, Games, Sports, Guns, Bells, Bonfires and Illuminations from one End of this Continent to the other from this Time forward forever more.
>
> You will think me transported with Enthusiasm but I am not.—I am well aware of the Toil and Blood and Treasure, that it will cost Us to maintain this Declaration, and support and defend these States.—Yet through all the Gloom I can see the Rays of ravishing Light and Glory. I can see that the End is more than worth all the Means. And that Posterity will tryumph in that Days Transaction, even altho We should rue it, which I trust in God We shall not.

100.25–26   Expunged from the printed coppy.] John may have sent a copy of the Dunlop broadside in one of the packets of printed matter that he frequently forwarded to Abigail. Or Abigail may have received John's autograph copy of Jefferson's draft of the Declaration and compared it with a text of Dunlap's broadside. (Jefferson's draft mentioned the evils of the slave trade.) It appears that John had said nothing to Abigail about the authorship of the Declaration, and she might have inferred that he was the author and objected to changes by Congress in her husband's document.

100.27   Poor Canady] The smallpox outbreak had infected about three thousand Continental Army soldiers in the north.

100.37   Our Friends from Plymouth] Mercy Otis and James Warren.

102.7   India herb] Tea.

102.27–28   the new method as tis call'd, the Suttonian] After Daniel Sutton (1735–1819), a London practitioner, whose method used only a small puncture to infect the patient.

103.18   Col. Crafts] Colonel Thomas Crafts (1740–1799), a decorative painter who had participated in the Boston Tea Party and who commanded the artillery unit during the Revolutionary War in which Paul Revere served.

103.19   Belcona] Balcony.

103.25   Mr. Bowdoin] James Bowdoin Sr. See note 52.1.

103.32   conspiricy at New York] Thomas Hickey, a private in the Commander-in-Chief's Guard, which protected General Washington, was arrested in March 1776 for counterfeiting money. While in jail, he confessed to another prisoner that he had been part of a conspiracy of Continental Army soldiers planning to defect to the British. He was court-martialed, found guilty on June 26 of mutiny and sedition, and executed on June 28. Rumors surrounding Hickey's conspiracy alleged that it included plans to assassinate Washington.

103.37   Gorge] George III.

103.38   a Borgia and a Catiline] The Borgias, a prominent Renaissance family known for using crimes, including theft, bribery, and murder, to gain political and ecclesiastical power. Catiline, a first-century B.C.E. Roman senator involved in a conspiracy to overthrow the Roman Republic.

104.17   Mr. Smith] Benjamin Smith of South Carolina (1757–1826), a distant cousin of Abigail and an aide-de-camp to Washington.

104.34   The Dr.] Samuel Cooper. See note 51.4.

105.2   Dr. Chancys] Charles Chauncy (1705–1787), minister of First Church, Boston, and leader of the "Old Lights" who had been opposed to the Great Awakening.

106.9   Mr. A] Samuel Adams.

106.26   you had never Received . . . expences] There is no clear information available for John's salary during 1776; in 1777 he was paid 24 shillings a day besides expenses.

107.5–6   the Mayor . . . at large.] David Mathews, mayor of New York City, was accused of supporting the plot to assassinate Washington (see note 103.32). He was arrested on June 22 and held under house arrest in Connecticut.

107.18   your going to N.Y.] Congress sent John with Benjamin Franklin and Edward Rutledge to meet Admiral Lord Richard Howe at Staten Island to determine whether Howe was authorized to negotiate peace. They met on September 11, and Howe refused to recognize American independence, so they were unable to negotiate. John wrote to Abigail on September 6 about the proposed conference; as of September 20 she had only received his letters up to September 5.

107.27–28   Mr. Gerry] Elbridge Gerry. See List of Correspondents.

108.20–21   R. T. Paine . . . Greenleafe] Robert Treat Paine wrote to Joseph Greenleaf about the Staten Island delegation.

108.28   Regulus'es steward] Marcus Atilius Regulus, third-century B.C.E. Roman consul who, according to Cicero, petitioned the Senate for recall from war in Africa because his hereditary farm was in ruin and his family in want. The Senate reimbursed Regulus for his losses so that he could continue to prosecute the war.

110.2–4   a field Battle . . . defeated.] On August 27, the Continental Army under Washington was routed from Brooklyn by British troops commanded by General William Howe. General Mifflin commanded the Pennsylvania troops during the retreat to Manhattan.

110.16–17   War is our Buisness, . . . Heav'n!] *The Iliad*, bk. XXII, ll. 171–72.

110.28   Barrel] William Barrel of Boston, who was John's neighbor in Philadelphia.

111.6   Mr. Winslow] Winslow Warren (1759–1791), the second son of James and Mercy Otis Warren.

111.28–29   loss at forts Washington and Lee] The British captured Fort Washington, taking 2,800 prisoners, on November 16, and then forced the evacuation of Fort Lee on November 20.

111.29–30   the loss . . . General.] General Charles Lee was captured by a British patrol on December 12. He was exchanged in 1778.

111.33–34   "affliction . . . shining time."] Proverbial.

111.38–39   the report . . . the Farmer.] As the British neared Philadelphia in December 1776, John Dickinson resigned his commission as a brigadier general in the Pennsylvania militia and retreated to his estate in Delaware, giving rise to rumors that he had turned Loyalist. While the rumor was unfounded, it was true that Dickinson, who had grown disaffected with the Pennsylvania government, had advised family members not to accept Continental money. Washington may have had Dickinson in mind when he wrote to Robert Morris on December 25, 1776, that "the late Treachery and defection of those, who stood foremost in the Opposition, while Fortune smiled upon us, make me fearful that many more will follow their Example."

112.1   Lord what is Man?] Cf. Psalm 144:3.

112.21   Hazard] Ebenezer Hazard (1744–1817), surveyor general of the Continental post office.

112.29–113.1   "But tis a day . . . bondage of ages?"] Thomas Paine, *The American Crisis, No. II*, January 13, 1777.

113.8–13   What is said . . . own expence.] David Hume, *The History of England, from The Invasion of Julius Cæsar to The Revolution in 1688*, Volume III (1759).

113.16   not being frank'd cost me a Dollor.] For postage. John, as a member of the Continental Congress, could send letters postage free if he signed, or franked, the outside of the letter.

114.7   your namesake.] Samuel Adams.

114.14–16   a situation . . . expressd.] An allusion to her pregnancy.

114.20   your Message to Betsy] On February 10, John wrote, "Tell Betcy I hope She is married."

114.23   The ordination is the 12th] The ordination of John Shaw, Elizabeth Smith's fiancé. Abigail disapproved of Shaw and made her opinions known to her younger sister.

115.4   Spado is lost.] General Charles Lee's dog Spada, with whom Abigail had become acquainted at a social event, when Lee insisted that she shake hands with his pet. "You must love his dogs if you love him," John wrote of Lee. For General Lee's imprisonment, see note 111.29–30.

116.3   Mrs. Howard] Elizabeth (Clarke) Mayhew Howard of Boston had died on the 13th, presumably as a result of childbirth.

117.31   Daunbury] On April 25, a British force under Major General William Tryon marched to Danbury, Connecticut, and destroyed Continental Army supplies there. Major General David Wooster led militia to harass Tryon's force on April 27 and was mortally wounded. Twenty men from Wooster's force were killed and between 40 and 80 wounded; the British suffered between 104 and 154 men killed and wounded and 40 captured.

118.9–10   loss of General Wocester.] Wooster died on May 2.

118.23   my Brothers going with MacNeal.] William Smith joined the *American Tartar*, a 24-gun privateer commanded by Captain John Grimes, as a captain of marines.

118.30–31   salt rhume] Perhaps either a skin rash or a head cold.

119.10   Col. Holland . . . excape.] Colonel Stephen Holland of Londonderry, New Hampshire, was later caught in Boston.

119.15   Hhds.] Hogsheads, large casks holding about sixty-three gallons each.

119.17   Tierces] A cask holding about forty-two gallons.

119.29–30   the Regulating act] An "Act to prevent Monopoly and oppression" passed in Massachusetts on May 10 to prevent economic exploitation during the war.

120.15–21   The House . . . forbid them.] As mandated by the Continental Congress, each of the newly independent states was writing a new constitution.

121.10–11   the Hampshire money] See pages 117–19 in this volume.

121.22–29   A certain Gentleman . . . where he is.] Robert Treat Paine was reelected as a Massachusetts delegate on December 10, 1776, but never returned to Philadelphia. He instead was elected attorney general in 1777.

123.4–5   to bear what I cannot fly from—] A labor contraction.

123.9   Manly] Captain John Manley (c. 1733–1793), of the Continental Navy.

123.19   Tyconderoga] American forces evacuated Fort Ticonderoga on July 5 after British troops placed cannons on a hill overlooking the fort.

123.30   It cannot go till monday] The post for this letter.

124.9–10   the Spleen or the Vapours] Melancholy feelings.

125.7–8   This day 12 years the Stamp office was distroyd.] A Boston mob pillaged the stamp office and later the residence of stamp officer Andrew Oliver, who was also hung in effigy from Boston's Liberty Tree, in 1765 in response to the Stamp Act.

125.25–26   "those dogs . . . cry Havock] *Julius Caesar*, III.i.273.

126.2   Mr. Lees Letter] Arthur Lee (1740–1792), currently American minister to Spain.

126.20   Russel] A corded fabric made of cotton and wool often used for academic and clerical gowns.

126.22   Garlick thread] A kind of linen that came from Gorlitz, Germany.

127.4   News of the Surrender] See Chronology for 1777.

127.25–27   Burgoine . . . Blocade of Saratago.] General Burgoyne had previously written a play, *The Blockade of Boston*, which was acted in Boston by British army officers in 1776.

127.28–29   the old South] The Old South Meeting House, which British officers had used as a riding school during the occupation of Boston.

127.31–32   king Richard . . . themselves"] See note 67.31.

128.1–2   May future . . . Blessed] Cf. Proverbs 31:28.

128.7   William Smith] Abigail's cousin William Smith (see Family Tree). During this visit to Boston, Abigail stayed at her uncle Isaac Smith's home.

128.15–16   your plot against him.] In November 1777, John obtained leave from the Continental Congress and returned home. Intending to resume his law practice, he had traveled in December to the circuit court in Portsmouth, New Hampshire, when a letter arrived from James Lovell (see List of Correspondents) announcing John's appointment as a commissioner to France.

128.19   Mr. Geary] Elbridge Gerry, who proposed the nomination in Congress. See List of Correspondents.

128.31–32   restored . . . painfull absence] Lovell was arrested after the battle of Bunker Hill in June 1775 and spent nine months in the Boston Stone Jail before being taken to Halifax, Nova Scotia, and spending a further nine months imprisoned there. He was exchanged in November 1776 and was immediately elected to be a delegate to the Continental Congress.

THE YEARS ABROAD, 1778–1788

133.8–9   last Mondays paper gave me a Shock] On Monday, February 23, 1778, the *Boston Gazette* published an erroneous report that Benjamin Franklin had been assassinated: "the illustrious Patriot Dr. Benjamin Franklin has been assassinated in his Bed-Chamber, at the Instance of Lord Stormont. The Villain left him for dead; but one of the Doctor's Ribs prevented the Stab from being instantly fatal, and he lay in a languishing Condition when the Vessel sail'd that brings this Account."

134.2   Ravelick] François Ravaillac (1578–1610), who murdered Henry IV of France in 1610.

134.10–11   she has . . . a worthy Man] Hannah Quincy Lincoln, a widow since 1773, married Ebenezer Storer on November 5, 1777. See List of Correspondents.

134.34   the weapon . . . Franklin] See note 133.8–9.

135.1–4   "For Nought avails . . . guard."] John Trumbull, "An Elegy on the Times" (1774).

135.13   not a Sparrow . . . Notice.] Cf. Matthew 10:29.

136.14–15   Rove like the Son of Ulissis] In the first four books of *The Odyssey*, Telemachus, the son of Odysseus (or Ulysses), travels to Pylos and Sparta in search of his father.

136.20–22   cloathes the lilies . . . Sparrows] Cf. Matthew 6:28–30, Psalm 147:9, and Matthew 10:31.

137.9–15   O Would'st thou . . . Blood.] Cf. *The Choice of Hercules* (1743), as translated by Robert Lowth, ll. 125–30. See also note 39.3–4.

137.28   conciliatry plan] On February 17, 1778, Lord North, the prime minister, proposed to Parliament a conciliation plan that would include repealing the Tea Tax and the Coercive Acts, and sending a new peace commission to the colonies.

137.30–31   treasure . . . exalteth a Nation] Cf. Proverbs 14:34.

137.33–34   the Duke of Richmonds Speech.] Charles Lennox, 3rd Duke of Richmond (1735–1806), gave a speech in the House of Lords on February 11 that was critical of the North ministry's stance toward America. It was reprinted in the Boston *Independent Chronicle* on May 14.

137.36–38   "and the Laws, . . . forefathers"] Addison, *Cato*, III.v.72–74.

138.8–9   Mr. MacCrery] William McCreery, a merchant from Baltimore with whom John and John Quincy had stayed in April 1778 when they passed through Bordeaux.

139.5–8   talents put . . . your numbers.] Cf. Matthew 25:14–30.

140.3–4   a Monster . . . to be seen.] Pope, *An Essay on Man*, Epistle II, ll. 17–18.

140.9   Nero, Caligula or Ceasar Borgia.] Nero (37–68 C.E.) and Caligula (12–41 C.E.), Roman emperors known for cruelty, sadism, and tyranny. Cesare Borgia (1475–1507), an Italian nobleman and cardinal who was an inspiration for Machiavelli's *The Prince*. For the Borgia family, see also note 103.38.

140.22–23   a New York paper . . . Plimouth.] On April 30, the *Newport Gazette*, a loyalist paper, reported that the *Boston* had been taken and destroyed by the British. Abigail did not learn of John and John Quincy's safe arrival until June 18.

140.33   Stevens] Joseph Stevens, a former soldier and seaman who was John's servant in Europe from 1778 to 1783.

141.29–30   Virtues which shun . . . life] Addison, *Cato*, II.iv.56–57.

143.9–10   Sir James Jay and Mr. Diggs.] Sir James Jay (1732–1815), a doctor from New York who had been knighted by George III in 1763, and George Digges (1747–1792), who had been in England during the outbreak of the Revolution and traveled to Maryland via Boston at this time to take an oath of loyalty. They carried at least one letter from John to Abigail.

143.14   modes and customs of ——] Probably "France" or "Paris."

143.16–17   fondness of the . . . . . .] Probably "ladies."

144.14   Haverhill] Abigail had written to John on June 18 about sending Charles to board with the Shaws in Haverhill because there was "a very good School" there. See also note 114.23.

144.37–38   the French fleet . . . Chesepeak.] A French fleet and expeditionary force of 4,000 men under Charles Hector, comte d'Estaing (1729–1794), arrived off Delaware Bay on July 8.

144.38   The Enemy have left Philadelphia] General Sir Henry Clinton had evacuated British troops from Philadelphia on June 18 under the orders of Lord North.

145.27   Failure in the Rhode Island expedition] A combined American and French attack on Newport, Rhode Island, August 5–31, failed, in part due to poor coordination between Comte d'Estaing and General John Sullivan, the American commander.

145.29–30   The Terible Storm] On August 10, as d'Estaing prepared to engage Lord Howe's fleet, a major storm broke, lasting for two days and scattering both fleets. The French flagship was severely damaged and a number of ships required repairs in Boston.

145.33–34   A pretty smart engagement ensued] The battle of Rhode Island, on August 29, in which the Americans lost 211 men killed, wounded, and missing, and the British 260.

146.9   the Count] Comte d'Estaing; see note 144.37–38.

146.29   I ought to come to the Continent.] To petition the Continental Congress for financial support.

146.36   captivated] I.e., captured.

147.17–18   á vous dire . . . l'inquietude.] French: To tell you the truth, such a long silence was already beginning to give me anxiety.

147.19   We have here . . . French Navy.] See note 145.29–30.

148.14–15   do not gather . . . Thistles] Cf. Matthew 7:16.

149.11–12   intelligence that . . . removed.] Congress revoked John's commission and appointed Benjamin Franklin sole minister plenipotentiary to France on September 14, 1778. News reached John in Paris on February 12.

149.29   the late indiscreet appeal to the publick] The Silas Deane affair, in which Deane, one of three commissioners to France with Franklin and Arthur Lee, had been accused of corruption and was recalled in 1778 by Congress (John became his replacement). In 1779, Deane sent letters to the press attacking Lee and the Congress.

149.36–150.4   Virtue! . . . ruin rush.] James Thomson, *Liberty* (1735–1736), Part V, ll. 109–12, 95–98. See also note 20.31–32.

150.6–8   the News paper altercation . . . assemblies] On January 12, 1779, a bill for "suppressing theatrical Entertainments, Horse-Racing, Gaming, and such other Diversions as are productive of Idleness, Dissipation, and a general Depravity of Manners," was introduced into the Massachusetts House of Representatives; later the House voted to add "a Clause in the Bill to prevent public Assemblies for Dancing." It proved controversial and did not pass.

150.11–12   the same necessity . . . a *Man.*] Abigail has mistaken Timon of Athens for Diogenes (c. 412–323 B.C.E.), a Greek philosopher and one of the founders of Cynicism. He reputedly conducted a search for an honest man in broad daylight with a lantern.

150.12–13   Monkies, Maccoronies and pate Ma'ters] Monkeys, macaronis, and *petits-maîtres*—slang terms for dandies or fops.

150.16   "that Manly Soul of Toil,"] Thomson, "Britannia. A Poem" (1729).

151.2   To Abigail Adams 2nd] Abigail 2nd was staying with Mercy Otis Warren in Plymouth.

151.24–25   threats of Prussians] John wrote "Russians" in his letter of November 6, 1778. The error in transcription may have been made by Abigail or by a copyist or a printer when Abigail 2nd's letters were published in 1842.

151.33   the unfortunate event at Rhode Island] See notes 145.27 and 145.29–30.

152.5   Madam la Grand] Marie Silvestre Grand (1721–1793), whom John had met at a dinner party, requested a correspondence with Abigail. (Her husband, Rodolphe-Ferdinand Grand, acted as America's banker in France during the Revolution.) Both her letter and Abigail's response, written in French, have been lost.

153.11   all that a Man hath . . . life.] Job 2:4.

153.25   Bohea Tea] Black tea.

153.27   Rates] Taxes.

154.14   rest under . . . the Almighty] Cf. Psalm 91:1.

154.18   Dr. Winthrope] Professor John Winthrop (1714–1779), John's former teacher at Harvard and lately a fellow patriot, died on May 3, 1779.

154.20–28   Let no weak . . . compeers.] Cf. Thomson, "A Poem Sacred To the Memory of Sir Isaac Newton," ll. 176–84.

154.33   Brother Cranch . . . Buisness] Cranch was a member of a committee conducting the sale of confiscated loyalist estates in Suffolk County as well as a Braintree representative to the Massachusetts House.

156.15   "baseless fabrick of a vision."] Cf. *The Tempest*, IV.i.151.

156.32   Your dissertation upon Letter peaping] In his letter of June 5, 1779, Lovell wrote: "In those Cases where Improprieties of Stile or Sentiment or Secrets intended only for the Eyes of the Correspondent are supposed to be penned, it is criminal to venture. But where there is undoubted Right to expect only the Product of a Pen directed by the Fingers of a virtuous elegant discrete Writer, I hold it lawful, comparatively, to peep; if a man is quite at Leisure, and in danger moreover of running into notorious mischief unless he so employs himself, Curiosity also having at the same Time its stimulating Goads at work upon him."

156.38–39 Antient Sage . . . faults.] Cf. 1 Peter 4:8.

156.39 The Manuscript] Lovell had forwarded to Abigail John's letter book and book of accounts.

157.3–4 retaining both . . . Stockings] Lovell had kept several items from a shipment from Europe that he had forwarded to Abigail.

157.17–18 a Letter . . . Dr. Winship] Amos Windship (1745–1813) was a Boston physician and apothecary who at this time served as surgeon aboard the *Alliance*. Since he had met John at Brest and Lorient, he had recent information.

157.30–31 This state . . . supply the places] A perennial problem for the Massachusetts General Court was to find representatives to the Continental Congress who would serve. For instance, in October 1778, seven delegates had been elected (or reelected) to serve for the year 1779: Samuel Adams, Francis Dana, Timothy Edwards, Elbridge Gerry, John Hancock, Samuel Holten, and James Lovell. But three—Dana, Edwards, and Hancock—did not attend at all in 1779.

157.34 says my absent Friend on a similar occasion] In John's letter to Abigail of December 2, 1778.

157.37–38 Fabricus . . . Aristedes] Gaius Fabricius Luscinus Monocularis, third-century B.C.E. Roman consul depicted in Canto XX of Dante's *Divine Comedy*, in which a voice says, "O Good Fabricus, you who chose to live with virtue in your poverty, rather than live in luxury with vice." Aristides the Just (530–468 B.C.E.), an Athenian statesman whom Herodotus called "the best and most honourable man in Athens."

158.22 the cruel torture of Seperation.] John and John Quincy arrived home on August 3, 1779. On August 9, John was elected Braintree representative to the state constitutional convention. He drafted the constitution, which was adopted after revisions. It remains today the oldest functioning constitution in the world. He was soon appointed by the Continental Congress to return to France to negotiate a peace treaty with Britain. Again Abigail wanted to accompany him and again John rejected this idea because of the arduous and dangerous travel in wartime for a woman. He took with him John Quincy and Charles as well as Francis Dana (1743–1811) as secretary to the legation, leaving November 15. A series of leaks caused the ship to land at El Ferrol in northwest Spain from which the Adams party traveled overland to Paris, a grueling journey of almost two months. See Chronology for 1779.

159.7–8 "Portia did not write to him."] James Lovell to John Adams, November 1–2, 1779: "I see my Correspondence with Portia is all over. She cannot write because I should see the mark of the Tear on the Paper."

159.16–17 "Give sorrow vent. . . . Break."] *Macbeth*, IV.iii.209–10.

159.27 Fame, wealth . . . Love?] Pope, "Eloisa to Abelard," l. 80.

160.6–7 I return . . . the journals.] Lovell had been sending Abigail the Congress's journals that John, when he was at the Continental Congress, had sent her.

160.9 pages 78] Pages of Congress's journals for 1778.

160.25–27 congress are Drawing Bills . . . 100,000 Sterling.] On November 23, 1779, Congress voted to draw bills of exchange on Henry Laurens, commissioner, to seek loans in Holland, and John Jay, minister to Spain, and sell them in order to raise money for the war.

161.11 John Paul Jones] Scottish-American sailor (1747–1792) who successively commanded several ships for the Continental Navy during the Revolutionary War. Jones became an acquaintance if not friend to both Adamses over the years. Abigail refers here to his published letter of May 8, 1778, to the Countess of Selkirk, explaining why, in his raid the month before on St. Mary's Isle, he had taken her household silver, and declaring his intention to return it.

161.16–17 Penobscot expedition.] The unsuccessful naval operation against the British in Penobscot Bay during the summer of 1779.

162.8–9 "Having learnt . . . Heart."] Pope, "The Second Satire of the Second Book of Horace," *Satires, Epistles, and Odes of Horace, Imitated* (1733–38).

163.3–6 Some Author . . . along.] Quoted from William Melmoth, *The Letters of Sir Thomas Fitzosborne* (1750).

163.15–17 Would Cicero . . . Millo] Cicero, first-century B.C.E. Roman philosopher, was a friend, not an adversary, of Milo. As consul in 63 B.C.E., Cicero stopped a conspiracy led by Catiline to overthrow the republic; early in his political career he helped to prosecute Gaius Verres, governor of Sicily, for misgovernment; and after Julius Caesar's assassination in 44 B.C.E., he became an enemy of Mark Antony.

165.28 in Eighteen days] Abigail miscounted by five days. The *Sensible* had sailed from Boston on November 15 and reached El Ferrol on December 8.

166.2–8 "The Counsel . . . private Interests."] Arthur Lee to John Adams, September 24, 1779.

166.13–22 "After your . . . Malignity."] Nicholas Maurice Gellée, secretary to the American commission at Passy, to John Adams, October 11, 1779.

166.34–35 wisdom of a more subtle animal] A snake. Cf. Matthew 10:16.

167.6–7 a Letter . . . Chesterfields Letters.] Mercy Otis Warren to her son, December 24, 1779. Early in 1776 Abigail had requested that John buy her a copy of *Lord Chesterfield's Letters* in Philadelphia, but he declined to do so; see note 89.26–27. Eventually Abigail arranged for Mercy's strictures on Chesterfield to be published in a Boston newspaper.

167.13 a mere Lovelace] Richard Lovelace, a misogynistic character in Samuel Richardson's *Clarissa* (1748) who seduces Clarissa.

168.16–17   the Philosophical Society] The American Philosophical Society, a scholarly association, was founded in 1743 by Benjamin Franklin, William Alexander, Francis Hopkinson, John Bartram, and others in Philadelphia as an offshoot of an earlier club, the Junto, whose purpose was the promotion of science and the humanities.

169.31   not the *famous* Adams.] When John arrived in France in 1779, he was continually mistaken for his cousin, Samuel Adams, whose reputation was already established. John had continually to make the distinction until finally, it became painfully clear: he was a man "of no Consequence—a cipher."

169.37   A prophet is not . . . country.] Mark 6:4.

170.10–14   "In vain . . . swallow any thing."] Nicholas Maurice Gellée to John Adams, October 11, 1779.

170.34   a more subtle animal] See note 166.34–35.

170.37–39   a subject . . . confidential Friend] In the eighteenth century, the full and correct usage of titles had great significance. For example, on May 25, 1780, John wrote to John Bondfield, a merchant from whom he had ordered some wine: "There is not a Being upon Earth who has a greater Contempt for all kind of Titles than I have in themselves, but when I find them in this Country not only absolutely necessary to make a mans Character and Office respected, but to the transaction of the most ordinary Affairs of Life, to get a glass of Wine to drink a pamphlet to read or a shirt to put on, I am convinced of their Importance and necessity here. . . . I therefore request that for the future, you would address every Letter, Packet, Bundle Case and Cask, for me A Son Excellence, Monsieur Monsieur John Adams Ministre Plenipotentiaire des Etats Unis De L'Amerique, Hotel de Valois, Ruë de Richelieu a Paris."

171.20   Dangers which threatned you.] See note 158.22.

172.9–10   Cloathing . . . cry] Cf. Matthew 6:26, 28.

172.16–17   "Thou shalt . . . as thyself"] Matthew 22:39.

172.19–24   "Remember, Man, . . . kind."] Pope, *An Essay on Man*, Epistle IV, ll. 35–40.

172.30   "Eden was tasteless till an Eve was there."] Dr. Benjamin Church, "The Choice: A Poem" (1752). See also note 62.1–6.

173.17   "Passions are the Elements of life"] Pope, *Essay on Man*, Epistle I, l. 170.

173.37–39   an inspired writer . . . city.] Proverbs 16:32.

174.8   "Virtue alone is happiness below,"] Pope, *Essay on Man*, Epistle IV, l. 308.

174.14 "What composes Man, can Man destroy."] Pope, *Essay on Man*, Epistle II, l. 114.

175.13 Mr. Guile] Benjamin Guild (1749–1792), Harvard 1769, a tutor at Harvard College since 1776.

176.6 Mr. Guardoqui] Gardoqui & Son was the mercantile firm in Bilbao with whom John set up commissions for Abigail; see Chronology for 1779.

176.19 purchaseing an article which you directed] A "genteel Chaise," being made by Thomas Bumstead of Boston.

176.27–28 the House . . . Natell. Belcher] The Belchers owned several farms near John's. Since at least 1771, John had his eye on acquiring Belcher properties. It is not certain whether Abigail succeeded in this purchase.

177.7 Ells] A measurement for cloth of forty-five inches.

177.7 Lutestring] Glossy silk commonly used for dresses.

177.8 changeable] I.e., changing-colored lutestring silk.

177.9 peice of Narrow] Narrow cloth, or a piece of cloth under fifty-two inches wide.

177.9 sols] French coin equal to one-twentieth of a livre.

177.18–19 his wife is far gone in a consumption.] Mary Crosby Adams, wife of John's only surviving brother, Peter, died on June 1, leaving several children, including an infant, Elizabeth, who lived only a few months.

177.21–22 The old gentleman is almost helpless.] John Hall, John's stepfather, died on September 27, 1780.

178.1 the death of a Sister in Law] See note 177.18–19.

178.8 the fate of Charlestown] On May 12, General Benjamin Lincoln surrendered the garrison at Charleston, South Carolina, with 2,500 Continental soldiers and 3,000 militia to General Sir Henry Clinton after a siege of over a month.

178.10–11 we shall have a constitution . . . soon.] The new Massachusetts constitution that John had drafted was promulgated on June 16. See note 158.22.

178.30 my agreable correspondent.] John Thaxter Jr. See List of Correspondents.

179.6–7 General Gates misfortune] General Horatio Gates's army of 4,000 men was defeated by Lord Charles Cornwallis with a force of 2,000 men at Camden, South Carolina, on August 16. The Continental Army suffered 900 killed and wounded and 1,000 captured, while the British Army lost 324 killed, wounded, and missing.

179.8–9 the treachery of Arnold] General Benedict Arnold fled to the British on September 25 after his plan to turn West Point over to the enemy was discovered.

179.25–26 all the force of Graves and Rodny] Vice Admiral Samuel Graves and Admiral George Brydges Rodney, 1st Baron Rodney, of the Royal Navy.

180.5–6 account of the death . . . poor Babe] See note 177.18–19.

180.18 chints] Chintz, painted or stained calico fabric from India.

180.40 Dr. Lee] Arthur Lee, who had been recalled from his post as American commissioner in Paris.

181.22 Stevens] Joseph Stevens, John's servant. See note 140.33.

181.22–23 a strange story about the Alliance] Captain Pierre Landais had been relieved of the command of the *Alliance* the previous year by fleet commander John Paul Jones, but in June Arthur Lee persuaded Landais that Jones had not had the authority to do so. Landais seized control of the *Alliance*, which soon set sail for America with Lee onboard. During the voyage, Landais began abusing officers, sailors, and passengers, and came close to stabbing Lee. On August 11, the other officers forcibly relieved Landais of command and sailed to Boston, arriving August 19. Captain John Barry (1745–1803) was then appointed to take command of the ship.

181.33–182.4 that sentiment . . . thing to lose."] Jean-Jacques Rousseau, *Julie, or the New Heloise* (1761), Letter 81.

182.12 "Its pomp, . . . nonesence all?"] Thomson, "Spring," from *The Seasons* (1726–30).

183.5–6 the poet says, . . . renewal of Love."] Terence, *Andria* (166 B.C.E.), III.iii, translated by Samuel Patrick (1767).

183.7–8 Be to my faults . . . ever kind] Cf. English poet Matthew Prior (1664–1721), "An English Padlock," ll. 75–76.

183.21–22 "Here Love . . . purple wings."] Milton, *Paradise Lost*, IV.i.763–64.

183.35 Mr. de Neufville] Jean de Neufville (1729–1796), head of an Amsterdam mercantile firm that supported the American cause.

184.5 Capture of Mr. Lawrence.] Henry Laurens, of South Carolina, appointed by the Continental Congress to negotiate a loan from the Netherlands, had sailed in August 1780 and was captured by the British off Newfoundland in September. Taken to England, he was charged and imprisoned for high treason. His release from the Tower was negotiated in late 1781 in exchange for General Cornwallis. He later joined the American commissioners for the signing of the Treaty of Paris.

184.16–17 your story to Madam Le Texel] An incident at a dinner party in Bordeaux in April 1778, where a Frenchwoman asked John a pointed question about sex. He later related it in his *Autobiography* as an illustration of women's greater freedoms in France.

184.21 Dr. Winship] Dr. Amos Windship. See note 157.17–18.

184.25–26 The cabals on Board the Ship] See note 181.22–23.

185.28–29 exacting it by Martial Law.] At a convention held at Hartford, Connecticut, in November, New Hampshire, Massachusetts, Rhode Island, Connecticut, and New York proposed resolutions (later struck down by the Continental Congress) to use "Coertion" if necessary to fill up state quotas of "Men Money Provisions or other Supplies."

186.2–3 Two good Men . . . Leiut. Governour.] John Hancock was elected governor over James Bowdoin, who declined to serve as lieutenant governor. James Warren next declined that office. Finally, Thomas Cushing, a supporter of Hancock and Suffolk judge of probate, was chosen and accepted.

186.4–5 Last week . . . very Grand Ball] The *Continental Journal* reported on November 30 that "Thursday evening last a ball and entertainment was given by His Excellency the Governor to the officers of the army and navy, and principal ladies and gentlemen of this city."

186.7–9 It was a maxim . . . Good.] Quoted from *Political Dispositions*, Volume III (1775), by British Whig politician James Burgh.

186.12–16 A writer observes . . . services.] From Burgh's *Political Dispositions*.

186.36–37 Tamies, Durants or caliminco] Tamis or tammy, worsted cloth made for straining, sifting, or needlework; durant, woolen fabric, a type of tamis; calamanco, a Flemish woolen cloth with a glossy surface.

186.40–187.1 Your Brother has lost his youngest daughter.] See note 177.18–19.

187.6 bed tick] Fabric to make bedticks, rectangular cases that would be stuffed with feathers or straw to make a bed.

187.7 tippets] Either a small cape made of fur or a long piece of cloth attached to sleeves.

187.12 Ells] See note 177.7.

187.13 Scotch carpet] A two-ply carpet originally manufactured in Scotland, such as a Kidderminster carpet.

188.22 I enclose to you a Letter and resolve] The letter was from James Lovell, and contained Congress's resolution of December 12, 1780, expressing "the Satisfaction which Congress receives from [John's] Industrious Attentions to the Interest and honor of these United States, abroad."

188.30–31 The Letter . . . Germains Speach] John Adams to Samuel Huntington, June 2, 1780.

188.34 Arnold is gone . . . to Virginia] After defecting, Benedict Arnold was commissioned as a brigadier general in the British Army and led 1,600 troops into Virginia, where he captured Richmond on January 5.

188.37–38 Andry . . . Generous Enemy] Major John André (1750–1780), a British Army officer hanged as a spy for his part in Benedict Arnold's plot. George Washington wrote of him that "he was more unfortunate than criminal" and called him "an accomplished man and gallant officer."

189.22 Erasmus, Grotius and Boerhaave] Desiderius Erasmus Roterodamus, known as Erasmus (1466–1536), Dutch humanist and theologian. Hugo Grotius (1583–1645), Dutch jurist who laid the foundations for international law. Herman Boerhaave (1668–1738), Dutch botanist and physician regarded as the founder of physiology.

189.26–29 Tis said of Socrates, . . . Thoughts.] Quoted from *The Spectator*, June 18, 1712.

190.4–5 "an Honest Man is the Noblest work of God."] Pope, *Essay on Man*, Epistle IV, l. 248.

191.2–4 General Warren . . . Governor Hutcinshon] Former governor Thomas Hutchinson owned a house on Milton Hill, overlooking Boston Harbor. As Tory property, it was seized and sold at auction in 1779. In January 1781 this estate was purchased by James Warren for £3,000. The Warrens lived there from May 1781 until 1788, when they returned to Plymouth.

191.8 Master Samll's Pappa] Gabriel Johonnot (d. 1820), father of John Quincy's companion and schoolmate in France, Samuel Cooper Johonnot.

191.28 Union of Mars with Belona] Roman god and goddess of war.

192.4–5 Your predictions . . . Provinces] Without waiting to be formally received as an envoy, John had drafted and submitted a memorial to the States General, urging Dutch recognition of American independence. He further arranged for its publication in English, Dutch, and French.

192.16–24 cruel Alva . . . Philip and a Gorge] Fernando Álvarez de Toledo, 3rd Duke of Alba, called the Iron Duke in the Netherlands, an advisor of Philip II of Spain who defeated the troops of Prince William of Orange during the Dutch War of Independence from Spain and who was known for the brutalities he allowed during the capture of several Dutch cities. Philip is Philip II of Spain and George is George III of Britain.

192.29 a 14tenth State] Vermont became an independent republic in 1777–78 but was not admitted to the Union as a fourteenth state until 1791.

193.11–12 The Capture of Eustatia . . . england] The Dutch-controlled island of St. Eustatius was the first foreign power to recognize American independence, and was one of the few places where the colonies could obtain military supplies, with about half of all stores coming through the island. This became a main incitement for the Fourth Anglo-Dutch War, with Britain declaring war on Holland on December 20, 1780. The island was invaded on February 3, 1781.

193.17   Bohea tea] See note 153.25.

193.23   Suchong] Tea made from the lower, coarser leaves of the tea plant instead of the bud, or pekoe.

194.15   Mr. Moylan] James Moylan, a merchant in Lorient.

194.32   Book Muslin] Fine muslin folded like a book when sold by the piece.

194.33   caliminco] See note 186.36–37.

194.34   cambrick] Fine white linen made at Cambray in Flanders.

195.1–2   The Town was divided into classes] Massachusetts divided inhabitants into tiered tax classes in order to pay for enlistees in towns that had not met their troop quotas.

195.10–11   a desire . . . State of Vermont.] Abigail had for several years contemplated purchasing a "retreat" in Vermont, which she eventually did in 1782. John's preferences were different; he wrote to James Warren in June 1782: "God willing, I wont go to Vermont. I must be within the Scent of the sea." They never visited the land; John Quincy sold his portion in 1825, and Thomas Boylston still owned his at his death.

195.26–32   Upon opening . . . accompanied it.] A letter that Lovell had written to Elbridge Gerry on November 20, 1780, was published in a Halifax paper and in James Rivington's New York *Royal Gazette*. It caused a scandal in which Abigail feared she might be named; she worried that a letter she had sent him might become public as well. It was falsely rumored that in the captured letter Lovell had demeaned his wife, Mary Middleton Lovell. Lovell explained himself and the letter in several subsequent letters.

195.34–35   some Stricktures . . . Friend.] Lovell.

196.15   harrow up my Soul] Cf. *Hamlet*, I.v.16.

199.16   Mr. Dexter] Aaron Dexter (1750–1829), Harvard 1776. His partner was Dr. Thomas Welsh Sr. of Boston; see List of Correspondents.

199.29   Your favour by General Ward] Lovell's letter of June 16, 1781, in which he responds to her reprimand of May 10, 1781 (see pages 195–96 in this volume), as well as the censure of the rumormongers who had accused him of staying away too long from his family: "Do those who condemn my absence mean to take me into their Stores as a clerk," he writes, inferring that others stayed home and earned fortunes while he labored for a pittance at the Continental Congress.

200.10–11   strain at a knat . . . camel] Cf. Matthew 23:24.

200.16–17   regard you profess for a Lady] Lovell's wife, Mary Middleton Lovell.

200.29 "Dutch Idea"] On March 17, in the letter she feared had been published (see note 195.26–32), Abigail objected to Lovell's writing to her as "lovely" or "charming," saying, "What right has she who is appropriated to appear Lovely or charming in any Eyes but his whose property she is?" Lovell replied on June 16: "Property! oh the dutch Idea!"

200.32 Johnson] Dr. Samuel Johnson's *Dictionary of the English Language*.

201.8 Mr. ——.] Samuel Adams.

201.10–11 False insinuating disembling wretch] Benjamin Franklin. A diplomatic dispute arose between John and French foreign minister the Comte de Vergennes, and Vergennes asked Franklin to forward to Congress letters John had written criticizing French policy. Abigail's "preparitive" was a text of Franklin's letter to Congress of August 9, 1780, which criticized John and asserted that he had "given extreme offense to the court here." Lovell had characterized the Franklin missives as "most unkind and stabbing" toward John.

201.17–18 the same Game . . . Dr. Lee] In the controversy between Arthur Lee and Silas Deane (see note 149.29), John had supported Lee, who accused Deane of financial improprieties, charges that Franklin rejected.

203.2–4 a Righteous few . . . Gomorrah.] Cf. Genesis 19.

203.22 Mr. L——ll and Mr. A——s] James Lovell and Samuel Adams.

203.23–24 malicious aspersions . . . character] See note 201.10–11.

204.18–20 "What can Cato . . . Bondage."] Addison, *Cato*, I.i.35–37.

204.23–24 "that we . . . Sink with it."] James Burgh, *Political Dispositions*, Volume III (1775).

205.19–20 A Specimin . . . Mr. Cranch] Franklin's letter of August 9, 1780. See note 201.10–11.

205.23–24 Falsehood and fraud . . . Ceasar.] Addison, *Cato*, IV.iv.44–45.

205.29 True consious Honour is to know no Sin—] Pope, "The First Epistle of the First Book of Horace," *Satires, Epistles, and Odes of Horace, Imitated* (1733–38).

205.34–206.2 that self . . . loud Huzzas.] Pope, *Essay on Man*, Epistle IV, l. 255.

207.5 Hogarths] Cf. William Hogarth (1697–1764), English painter and engraver.

207.12–13 my harp was . . . willows] Cf. Psalm 137:2.

207.25 Possibly Rivington may give it to me.] In fact, the missing letter was published by James Rivington's New York *Royal Gazette* on September 8, 1781.

208.5 Maria] Lovell's wife, Mary Middleton Lovell.

208.15 Mynheres] That is, mijnheers, the Dutch. On May 22, 1781, John had written in frustration from Amsterdam that "I know not what this People will do. I believe they will awake, after some time. Amsterdam, Harlem and Dort have represented the Necessity of an Alliance with America but when the rest will be of their Mind, I know not. If they neglect it, they and their Posterity will repent of it."

208.31 There realy existed the Dialogue I related] Cf. her letter to Lovell of June 23, 1781.

209.24 the Indian] A frigate under the command of Commodore Alexander Gillon.

209.36–37 the Fate of Burgoine] British general John Burgoyne surrendered his entire army to American general Horatio Gates at Saratoga in October 1777.

210.13 Your Memorial] *A Memorial . . . to the States General*, April 19, 1781.

210.18 Mr. DeNeufvilla] Jean de Neufville, an Amsterdam merchant. See note 183.35.

211.19–20 Marquis Fayett and the Count de Noiales.] Gilbert du Motier, marquis de Lafayette (1757–1834), French military officer who fought for the United States in the Revolution. Louis Marie, vicomte de Noailles, Lafayette's brother-in-law.

212.9 Gillon has acted a base part] Alexander Gillon commanded the ship on which Charles sailed from the Texel in August 1781. Gillon departed secretly in order to escape his creditors, and proceeded to take a highly circuitous route. Charles and his companion, William Jackson, finally left the ship at La Coruña, Spain, traveled overland to Bilbao, and sailed to Boston on the *Cicero*, arriving in late January.

213.26–27 render them some assistance] John had long assisted prisoners, often privately since he had no public funds to support them.

214.5–8 "an elegant Sufficency, . . . Heaven."] Thomson, "Spring," from *The Seasons* (1728), ll. 1158–61.

214.25–26 Ingraham Bromfild, . . . de Neufvilla.] Ingraham & Bromfield, American merchants in Amsterdam; for de Neufville, see note 183.35.

214.37–38 bengalls, Nankeens, . . . hankerchiefs] Bengals, small goods exported from Bengal; Nankeens, pale yellow cotton cloth made at Nanking, or possibly unbleached silk; bandanna handkerchiefs, richly colored silk handkerchiefs with white or yellow spots.

215.20 the passengers all left the ship] See note 212.9.

216.5 Slander impeach and abuse] Lovell had been the subject of previous charges of immorality, stemming from his undergraduate days. This latest charge stemmed from the intercepted letters (see note 195.26–32) and the fact that he had served for five years at Congress without returning home. As a result, he did make a visit to his wife and family in Boston.

216.37–38 your late honorable appointment] Lovell returned home that month and was appointed to the post of "continental Receiver of taxes" in Massachusetts.

218.7 a most severe sickness.] See Chronology for 1781.

218.18–19 the increasing way] I.e., pregnant.

218.22–23 cousin B——y] Not identified.

218.24 Mrs. Gray] Abigail's cousin Mary Smith Gray, widowed in 1779, married the widower Samuel Allyne Otis on March 28, 1782. See Family Tree.

219.28–30 the cruel . . . Mr. Laurences] See note 184.5.

220.20–21 the philosopher . . . a Woman.] A traditional Jewish prayer includes thanksgivings for not having been made a gentile, a slave, or a woman.

220.36–39 "Oh! haste to me! . . . age."] English poet Elizabeth Rowe, "Penelope to Ulysses," from *Letters Moral and Entertaining*, Part III (1732), ll. 126–29.

221.17–18 "While pride, . . . Catos presence."] Addison, *Cato*, IV.iv.24–25.

221.29 Cincinnatus and Regulus] After being chosen by the Roman Senate as dictator to fight a war against the Aequi, Cincinnatus (519–430 B.C.E.) was summoned to Rome by a group of senators who found him at his plow. He resigned his dictatorship at the end of the war and returned to his farm. For Regulus, see note 108.28.

222.35 Mr. Rogers and Lady] Daniel Denison Rogers, a Boston merchant, and his wife, Abigail Bromfield Rogers. Later, when the Adamses resided in England, they became good friends.

223.16 The Count de Grasse misfortune] The battle of Saint Kitts, a naval battle on January 25–26, 1782, between a French fleet under the Comte de Grasse and a British fleet under Rear-Admiral Sir Samuel Hood. The French fleet suffered severe damage.

223.26–27 "Man wants . . . little long."] Goldsmith, "Edwin and Angelina," ll. 31–32.

223.33 a publick Commencement] The Boston *Continental Journal* reported that on July 17 Harvard held "a public Commencement . . . for the second time since the year 1773 . . . with its ancient splendor."

223.36 Mr. Thomas of Bridgwater] Thomas Perkins, Harvard 1779. He soon moved to Kentucky to practice law.

224.12 She proposes it.] Abigail 2nd's letter, probably written at the same time as Abigail's, has not been found. In it, she proposed her coming to Europe to keep house for her father. John's reply on September 26 discouraged the idea on the ground that he hoped to return home in the spring.

226.5–6 Ingraham and Bromfield] See note 214.25–26.

226.19 the Braintree prisoners] See note 213.26–27.

226.24 a Jo] A Portuguese gold coin.

227.10 calaminco . . . tamies] See note 186.36–37.

227.14–15 you can give her better advice.] See note 224.12.

227.20 Hyson tea] Chinese green tea.

228.22 Mr. Smith is the person I mean] Abigail's cousin William Smith (see Family Tree). It would be nearly two years before Abigail and Abigail 2nd finally joined John abroad in June 1784.

228.29–30 Mr. Jackson and Mr. Osgood] Lovell had been the longest-serving delegate in the Continental Congress. Jonathan Jackson and Samuel Osgood succeeded him.

228.34–35 The acknowledgment . . . provinces] The States General of the Netherlands recognized American independence on April 19, 1782.

229.7–16 Bolingbrook in his political . . . dirt."] English politician and political philosopher Henry St. John, 1st Viscount Bolingbroke, "The Occasional Writer," in *A Collection of Political Tracts* (1769).

230.11 Mr. Guile] Benjamin Guild. See note 175.13.

231.8–9 a News paper . . . your patience] Prepared by Richard Cranch and published in the Boston *Independent Chronicles* on September 19, 1782.

232.20 stiver] A small coin used in the Netherlands, worth about as much as an English penny.

232.30–31 P. M——n, B——n H——n] Probably Boston lawyers Perez Morton and Benjamin Hichborn.

232.32–33 Hogarth . . . topsa turva.] William Hogarth; see note 207.5.

233.18 Book Muslin] See note 194.32.

234.22 No Man liveth . . . authority] Romans 14:7.

235.2 "But will you come and see me"] Quoting John's April 1, 1781, letter.

235.10 you have a better likeness] On July 24, 1780, Abigail had requested a miniature. Neither it nor the "better" one has been found. Only two engravings, by Flemish painter Reinier Vinkeles, survive from this period.

235.13 fall of Gibralter] As a condition of entering the war as an ally of

France, Spain stipulated that a condition of the eventual peace treaty should be the surrender to Spain of British-controlled Gibraltar. French and Spanish fleets blockaded Gibraltar for four years in an ultimately unsuccessful siege, and it was not mentioned in the Treaty of Paris.

235.15–16 The appointment of Dr. F. . . . Instance.] On June 25, Benjamin Franklin, responding to a request from the Swedish ambassador, asked Congress to grant him power to negotiate a treaty with Sweden. John, learning of this, wrote that Francis Dana, not Franklin, had been empowered to treat with Sweden, and, further, that "the feelings, if not the rights of every American Minister in Europe have been wantonly sacrificed to Dr. F.'s vanity."

235.23–24 The prisoners have all arrived] See pages 211–15 in this volume.

235.38–39 a cousin in England] Isaac Smith Jr. See List of Correspondents.

236.35–237.1 your Friend and patron] Francis Dana.

237.22–23 your own reflections . . . Voltair] John Quincy frequently copied descriptions from travel literature into his diary of this period as well as his correspondence. Much of his brief letter of October 23, 1781, was a description of St. Petersburg copied from Voltaire's *Histoire de l'empire de Russie sous Pierre le grand*.

237.24 precisian of a Robinson] Scottish historian William Robertson, author of *The History of the Reign of the Emperor Charles V* (1769), which John Quincy had read while in St. Petersburg in March–April 1782.

237.35 Mr. Robins] Chandler Robbins Jr., Harvard 1782, of Plymouth, Massachusetts.

239.37 His Name is Tyler] Royall Tyler; see List of Correspondents.

239.40 Mr. Anger] See note 34.24.

242.24 The Fate of Gibralter] See note 235.13.

242.38 The judge] Edmund Trowbridge (1709–1793), uncle of Francis Dana.

243.17–18 our spears . . . hooks] Micah 4:3.

243.24–25 Yours of December 4th] On December 4, 1782, John wrote, "upon the whole, I think it will be most *for the Happiness of my Family, and most for the Honour of our Country that I should come home.* I have therefore this Day written to Congress a Resignation of all my Employments, and as soon as I shall receive their Acceptance of it, I will embark for America." Congress did not accept John's resignation, instead appointing him in May 1784 to negotiate treaties with European and North African states.

243.26–27 "And shall I . . . speak"] "There's nae Luck about the House," an eighteenth-century Scottish song.

244.5   Feast of reason . . . soul.] Pope, "The First Satire of the Second Book," *Satires, Epistles, and Odes of Horace, Imitated*, l. 128.

244.7   "Your "Image . . . Emelia] Paraphrasing John's greeting to Abigail 2nd in his January 29, 1783, letter to Abigail.

244.11   Selim] Royall Tyler, who had a reputation for dancing, singing, and card playing as a student at Harvard.

244.26–27   Mr. Guile] Benjamin Guild. See note 175.13.

244.32   Mr. Shaw] The Reverend John Shaw, husband of Abigail's sister Elizabeth, ran a school at Hingham. See also note 144.14.

244.35–37   Mr. Shutes . . . Andover] The Reverend Daniel Shute, pastor at Hingham, and friend of the Adamses from the 1760s. Phillips Academy at Andover, founded in 1778.

244.39   my little Neice] Louisa Catherine Smith, who lived with the Adamses for much of her life.

245.3   an absent Man] John Adams. John Hancock was elected governor.

245.11   Mr. Smith] Abigail's cousin William Smith; see Family Tree.

245.26   a passage from my Last Letter.] From John to Abigail, March 28, 1783.

246.28–32   Doubling the Talant . . . deemed?] Cf. Matthew 25:14–30.

246.36   a Friend of mine] John.

248.1–2   the joint commission . . . Britain.] Congress's resolution of John's appointment to negotiate a commercial treaty with Britain was more complicated than Abigail realized and would not be settled until May 1784.

248.21–25   an other Theseus . . . domination.] I.e., a modern Theseus, a military hero (perhaps a George Washington or other military man), will arise to unite the army and destroy the free confederacy of the states (alluded to here as the Amphictonic League of city-states during Greece's classical period). Abigail and John were particularly distrustful of the army, as reflected in their letters after 1784 and especially in their criticism of the newly formed Society of the Cincinnati.

248.29–30   lost their Seats, . . . Mr. Brattle] Abigail associated the turnover in the last election, which she clearly did not approve of, with the case of Thomas Brattle, who had left Massachusetts in 1775 and now wished to return. Because it was assumed that he had been a loyalist Tory, his citizenship application was denied, despite a letter of endorsement by John, until sometime after 1783, when he won it through court action.

249.23–24   "And wish . . . purling rill?"] Pope, *Essay on Man*, Epistle I.

251.3   The family in which he boards] Richard and Mary Cranch.

251.22 Russia sheeting] A plain-weave hemp linen.

251.24–25 Marsels cotton and silk quilts] Marseilles or Provençal quilts, known for their intricate sewn designs.

251.30 a son of Capt. Newcombs] Bryant Newcomb was one of the men whose release from Mill Prison in Plymouth, England, John had arranged. See pages 211–15 in this volume.

252.7–8 an inhabitant . . . returns.] *Hamlet*, III.i.79–80.

252.21 the strangery] Strangury, disease of the urinary organs causing a blockage.

252.30–33 "Here real . . . virtue peace."] Young, *Night Thoughts*, Night II.

253.14–15 "The Sweet remembrance . . . dust."] Cf. Isaac Watts, Psalm 112 in his 1719 metrical psalter; see also note 71.36–37.

253.20–24 "The Chamber . . . death."] Young, "The Complaint," Night II.

253.31 his Children . . . blessed] Cf. Proverbs 31:28.

253.33–34 Like good old Jacob . . . ofspring] Cf. Genesis 48 and 49.

253.36 "We gaze'd . . . joy."] Young, "The Complaint," Night II.

254.8–10 "His God sustain . . . her own."] Ibid.

255.30 the Great Dr. Price] Richard Price (1723–1791), pro-American dissenting minister and political writer, was a longtime British correspondent of John. When they resided in England, the Adamses regularly attended his services at Hackney. Abigail quotes from *A Sermon, Delivered to a Congregation of Protestant Dissenters, at Hackney* (1779).

255.39–40 a subject . . . embarrasses me] In his letter of July 13, John had requested that she write more about Royall Tyler's courtship of Abigail 2nd: "Pray let me know the History of the Affair you mentioned formerly. I hope there is an End of it."

256.23 Perkings] Thomas Perkins. See note 223.36.

257.12 my Neighbour Feild] Perhaps Job Field, who would accompany her to England in 1784; several other Fields also lived in Braintree.

259.4–5 a treasure . . . devour.] Cf. Matthew 6:19–20.

259.11 He has made me a request] On September 10, 1783, John wrote, "If this Letter arrives in Season, that you can come to me this Fall with Miss Nabby, I shall be Supreamly happy to see you."

259.24–25 "little Learning . . . divind."] Cf. John Gay, "The Shepherd and the Philosopher," ll. 33–34, in *Fables* (1727).

259.33–34 a similar vow, . . . Hanible] In 237 B.C.E., Hannibal was made to swear eternal enmity to Rome, with whom Carthage had been at war for three decades.

260.5–6   our Anual festival.] The annual commemoration of the Boston Tea Party.

260.6–7   Cooper . . . Clark . . . Chauncey] For Cooper, see note 51.4; John Clarke, Harvard 1774, assistant to the Reverend Charles Chauncy (see note 105.2). Clarke succeeded Chauncy in 1787.

260.30–31   the memorable 17th. of April] The battles of Lexington and Concord had taken place on April 19, 1775, a week before John departed for Philadelphia as a delegate to the Second Continental Congress.

262.19–21   the chaste Lucretia . . . distruction.] In Roman legend, immortalized in Ovid and Shakespeare, Lucretia was remembered for her virtue. While other military wives danced and reveled, she and her handmaidens were weaving. She was raped by Sextus, son of Tarquin, king of Rome, and before killing herself, vowed revenge by her relatives which, in turn, led to an uprising that established the Roman Republic.

262.33–35   I therefore surpresst the extract; . . . alluded to] On September 18, 1783, Elbridge Gerry sent Abigail an extract from Benjamin Franklin's letter of July 22 to Robert R. Livingston, which read in part, "I write this to you to put you on your Guard (beleiving it to be my Duty, tho I know that I hazzard by it a mortal Enmity) and to caution You respecting the Insinuations of this Gentleman against the Court, and the Instances he supposes of their Ill Will to us, which I take to be as imaginary as I know his Fancies to be that the Count de Vergennes and myself are continually plotting against him . . . he means well for his Country, is always an honest Man, often a Wise one, but sometimes and in somethings absolutely out of his Senses." James Warren wrote to John on October 27: "the Old Man . . . is, as You might expect Your determin'd Enemy,—You will before this reaches You get a Paragraph of one of his Letters, which if You should by an Interval be in possession of Your right Mind will put the Matter out of Doubt." John probably did not know about this letter prior to receiving Warren's and then Abigail's letter.

263.32–33   "with her orange Groves, . . . Musick"] British Whig politician James Burgh, "Of Travel," *The Dignity of Human Nature* (1754).

264.1–3   setting down . . . affraid.] Micah 4:4.

264.8–9   "A day, an hour . . . Bondage."] Addison, *Cato*, II.i.98–99.

264.31–33   Cyrus . . . Alexander] Cyrus the Great of Persia (c. 600–530 B.C.E.) and Alexander the Great of Macedon (356–323 B.C.E.).

265.1–2   "O city, ready for Sale, . . . found!"] Sallust, *Jugurthine War*, 35. Abigail likely came across the quotation in James Burgh's *Political Disquisitions* (1775), in a passage about Jugurtha, a prince of Numidia who assassinated one of his brothers and then bribed Roman army commanders to help him gain the throne.

265.8 the loss of her Andry.] Major John André. See note 188.37–38.

267.7–8 he purchased Mrs. Borelands Farm] Royall Tyler purchased this farm in 1784, intending to settle there after his marriage to Abigail 2nd. After their relationship dissolved, he abandoned Braintree and the farm reverted to the Borland family, who sold it to John in September 1787.

267.22 State Notes] Massachusetts had passed legislation that consolidated outstanding state debts from the war and redeemed old paper money and debt certificates with the issuance of state, or consolidated, notes. A further act had exempted the income from consolidated notes from taxation.

267.29 L M] Lawful money, the official Massachusetts currency.

267.40 the trust of the Medford estate] Property left to Abigail and her sister Elizabeth by their father.

268.10–11 Your account Books . . . Mr. Tyler] Abigail entrusted Royall Tyler to keep these accounts of John's legal practice from 1783 to 1786. Upon the dissolution of his relationship with Abigail 2nd, he turned them over to Cotton Tufts.

268.27 My Neice] Louisa Catherine Smith. See note 244.39.

269.9 baseless . . . vision."] *The Tempest*, IV.i.151.

269.28 Pheby] Phoebe had been a slave or servant in the Smith home, sometimes referred to by Abigail as her "nursemaid." By his will, Reverend Smith freed Phoebe, left her a legacy of £100, and entrusted her lifetime care to his daughters. During her absence in France and England, Abigail left Phoebe and her husband, Abde, in charge of her house and much of the farm.

270.3 our old tennant] Matthew Pratt.

270.7–11 John Brisler . . . a Sister of his] John Briesler did accompany Abigail to England, though not his sister. As her maid, Abigail took Esther Field, another Braintree neighbor. John Briesler and Esther Field married in London, and Esther gave birth on shipboard during their return on May 28, 1788. The Brieslers served the Adamses well into the 1790s. John Briesler, especially, became an indispensable member of their household.

270.13–14 an old servant who had lived 7 years with me] Jane Glover, for whose marriage to Bryant Newcomb see pages 247–51 in this volume, and note 251.30.

270.35 Col. Quincy lies very dangerously ill] Colonel Josiah Quincy died on March 3, 1784.

271.22–23 The Cincinati makes a Bustle] The Society of the Cincinnati (founded in May 1783). The controversial Society of the Cincinnati, an association of officers of the Continental Army, was formed at the suggestion of General Henry Knox in June 1783, and George Washington was its first president. Named for the Roman hero Cincinnatus, its stated purpose was to raise funds to protect officers and their families from hardship and to promote closer ties among the states. Membership would be inherited through the eldest son, but when there was no direct descendant, other relatives were eligible. John and Abigail were by no means alone in expressing concern about the Society, and in response to such criticism Washington, at the Society's May 1784 general meeting, urged the abolition of hereditary membership and the institution of other changes designed to alleviate public apprehension. These were accepted; however, hereditary membership was quietly reinstated several years later.

272.6–7 Mr. Jay . . . add Mr. Jefferson] John Jay had, in fact, already departed. Jefferson had been appointed to replace Benjamin Franklin as minister to France.

272.35 finding] Supplying.

273.15 two excellent servants.] Esther Field and John Briesler. See note 270.7–11.

273.28 Tis said of Cato the Roman censor] In Plutarch's life of Cato the Elder (234–149 B.C.E.). His other two regrets were entrusting a woman with a secret, and remaining intestate for an entire day.

274.17 for Jobe] Job Field was an acquaintance from Braintree who was one of the ship's crew. During the war, he had been taken prisoner and held in Plymouth, England. He was one of several prisoners to whom John had sent money out of his own pocket; see pages 211–15 in this volume.

274.34 Swift, or Smollet] Satirical novelists Jonathan Swift (1667–1745), author of *Gulliver's Travels* (1726); and Tobias Smollett (1721–1771), author of *The Adventures of Peregrine Pickle* (1751).

275.4 our Captain] Nathaniel Byfield Lyde of Boston.

275.12 Col. Norten] Beriah Norton, colonel in a Massachusetts militia regiment and a state senator.

275.15 Mr. Green] A secretary to British admiral Mariot Arbuthnot.

275.23 Dr. Clark] Dr. John Clarke (1754–1788), Harvard 1772, a physician from Boston.

276.4 Mr. Foster] Joseph Foster from Boston, who was co-owner of the ship.

276.13 My Name sake] Love Lawrence Adams. Her husband Joseph Adams, a physician, was a loyalist refugee.

276.32 my Cabbin] Abigail sometimes used "cabbin" to mean "berth" and in other places to mean a room.

277.9   Mrs. Adams'es Brother] Probably thirteen-year-old Abel Lawrence.

277.18   Yankee Bundlers] Bundling was a widespread courtship custom in New England whereby persons of the opposite sex lay, at least partly clothed, in the same bed.

277.28–29   "Thou makest . . . Billows sleep."] Psalm 89, *A New Version of the Psalms of David* by Nathaniel Brady and Nahum Tate (1696).

277.31–32   who maketh . . . wind] Psalm 104:3.

278.3–5   We are so formed, . . . trivial] From William Buchan, *Domestic Medicine; or, the Family Physician* (1769).

278.6–7   Pleasures, . . . hands or Eyes.] *Essay on Man*, Epistle II, l. 123.

278.14–15   Tompsons Seasons . . . Ansons Voyages] Scottish poet James Thomson's *The Seasons* (1728) and George Anson, 1st Baron Anson's memoir *Voyage Round the World in the Years MDCCXL, I, II, III, IV* (1748).

278.29–35   some lines of Miss Mores . . . weep."] From "Sir Eldred of the Bower" (1776), by English religious writer Hannah More, friend of David Garrick and Samuel Johnson.

279.13   the western Islands.] The Azores.

279.25   Buchans domestick Medicine.] Buchan, *Domestic Medicine; or, the Family Physician* (1769).

280.11   a blaizing ocean.] Phosphorescence, or bioluminescence, caused by the oxidation of a pigment found in certain marine organisms.

280.16–18   "Great and Marvellous . . . all."] Psalm 104:24.

280.27   *hickel tapickelta*] Higgledy-piggledy.

281.18–20   "Ye too ye winds, . . . Calm?"] Thomson, "Winter," from *The Seasons* (1728), ll. 111–12 and 116–17.

282.13–14   exactly Such a Character as Mr. Anger] Abigail 2nd compares Mr. Green to John's former law clerk Oakes Angier, whom Abigail disliked. See also note 34.24.

284.1   an Equinoctial] An equinoctial gale. Storms were believed to be stronger around the time of the autumn equinox in September.

285.21   Naiades] River nymphs in Greek mythology.

286.27–29   Canterburry to Rochester . . . Chatam] Rochester is twenty-seven miles from Canterbury, close to Chatham. The town she stopped at in between Chatham and Canterbury was probably Sittingbourne.

287.30–31   the Hotel . . . here.] John and John Quincy stayed at Osbourne's Hotel, in the Adelphi Buildings in the Strand, in the fall of 1783, to which Abigail moved on July 22, not David Low's hotel on the west side of Covent Garden, which was her first too expensive lodging.

287.32   Mr. Smith] Abigail's cousin William Smith; see Family Tree.

287.36   Mr. Storer] Charles Storer (1761–1829), Harvard 1779, a relative of Abigail's who had served as John's private secretary since 1782.

288.28–29   Mr. Jackson . . . Mrs. Atkingson] Jonathan Jackson (1743–1810), a Massachusetts merchant who had been a delegate to the Continental Congress in 1782. Winslow Warren; see note 111.6. For Daniel Denison Rogers and his wife Abigail Bromfield Rogers, see note 222.35. Ward Nicholas Boylston (1747–1828), a relative of John and a well-to-do merchant. Elizabeth Storer Atkinson was Charles Storer's sister.

288.35–36   *Parson Walter* and Mrs. Hollowell.] Reverend William Walter, Loyalist minister of Trinity Church in Boston until 1776. Mary Boylston Hallowell, a Loyalist first cousin of John's mother, was the mother of Ward Nicholas Boylston.

289.9   Lutestrings] See note 177.7.

289.14   a draw back] An import duty on silk that was partly refunded on goods that were reexported to America.

289.22–23   Mrs. Hay Mr. Appleton] Katherine Farnham Hay, the wife of Captain John Hay, from Newburyport, Massachusetts. John Appleton was a merchant who had met John and John Quincy in France and Holland.

289.27   Mr. Bromfeild, a Mr. Murray] Henry Bromfield Jr., a Boston merchant, had known John and John Quincy in the Netherlands. William Vans Murray (1760–1803), a law student from Maryland.

289.31   Prentice Cushing] The son (1758–1786) of Reverend Jacob and Anna Williams Cushing of Waltham, Massachusetts, who had formerly boarded with Mary and Richard Cranch.

289.33   Mr. Copeleys pictures.] John Singleton Copley (1738–1815), American painter who painted a life-size portrait of John in December 1783.

289.35–36   removed Mr. Dumas and family] For many years, Charles William Frederic Dumas had supported the American efforts in the Netherlands and had become a good friend of John's. He had been living at the American legation building in The Hague with his wife and daughter.

290.11   Mrs. Haley] Probably Mary Wilkes Hayley, sister of radical English politician John Wilkes. She had visited Boston toward the end of the Revolution.

290.30   Mr. Ellworthy] Husband of one of Richard Cranch's nieces.

291.2   the whole Bugget] I.e., a pouch or wallet, or its contents.

291.4   my dear and aged parent] Susanna Boylston Adams Hall.

291.20   Sunday morg july 25] Learning on this day that a ship was departing for America, Abigail wrote a brief version of this letter to Mary Cranch, adding a few details about her life in London. After referring to tours of various London sites, she added: "I have refused going to any place of publick Amusement untill Mr. Adams comes, or Master John." And she recorded the furnishings of her room at Osborne's Hotel: "My drawing room and chamber are very Elegant. A light Green borderd with Gold a Soffa and red Morocco chairs with arms to them 2 card tables and a dining table with 2 Elegant Glasses make up the furniture of the room, in short nothing but the dust is wanting to have every thing Heart can wish." Abigail sent this journal letter to Boston with William Smith at the end of the month.

291.22   to Mr. Copelys to see Mr. Adams picture.] John had already purchased the picture, though it remained in Copley's possession for a time. Abigail's description is not wholly accurate: John is pointing to, rather than holding, a map of Europe and North America, and only one female figure, representing peace, is in the background.

291.29–30   death of Lord Chatham in the House of Commons] *The Death of the Earl of Chatham* (1781). Upon its presentation in May 1781, this painting caused a sensation in London, establishing Copley's reputation. It depicts the final collapse of William Pitt the elder, Earl of Chatham, during a debate on the war in America in the House of Lords (not Commons, as Abigail related). In it the artist painted portraits from life of over fifty individuals.

291.39   the death of Major Peirson] Copley, *The Death of Major Peirson, 6 January 1781* (1783).

292.13   Mrs. Wright] Patience Wright (1725–1786), a wax sculptor and Quaker from New Jersey, had moved to London in 1772, where she was patronized by George III and also worked as an American spy during the Revolution.

292.35–37   Nelly Penniman . . . Unity Badlams.] The Penniman family lived in Braintree. The Bedlams lived in Weymouth.

293.14   the foundling Hospital] An orphanage founded in 1739. After 1760 the hospital accepted only the illegitimate children of identified mothers.

294.31   the Magdeline Hospital] Magdalen Hospital, founded in 1758 on Blackfriars Road, was a refuge and reform institution for prostitutes. It housed about eighty women, who sang for visitors from behind a screen.

295.18   Col. Trumble] John Trumbull; see note 27.31–32.

295.20   Mr. Joy] Son of a loyalist Boston house builder, Michael Joy left Massachusetts with his parents after the British abandoned Boston in 1776. Joy also became a house builder and later engaged in commerce.

296.36   the tastety folks] I.e., having good taste.

298.14–15   Mr. Duchee who officiates at the Assylum] Reverend Jacob

Duché, formerly chaplain to the Continental Congress, became a Loyalist in 1777 and moved to England. The Asylum, founded in Lambeth in 1758, was an orphanage for girls.

298.27 Drapers Hall] In 1667, the Draper's Guild Hall replaced Thomas Cromwell's great house on Throgmorton Street near the Stock Exchange. It was destroyed later by fires.

299.24–25 not feeling 20 years younger, . . . he does] John replied to Abigail's letter announcing her arrival in London, "Your Letter of the 23d. has made me the happiest Man upon Earth. I am twenty Years younger than I was yesterday."

300.30 Dr. Loyd] Dr. James Lloyd of Boston, whose son James was later at Harvard with John Quincy.

301.8–9 Mr. Smith] Abigail's cousin William Smith; see Family Tree.

301.34 He urged me to wait] Jefferson offered to accompany Abigail to Paris, but arrived too late to book passage on the *Active*; nor did Abigail wish to travel to New York where Jefferson took the packet for France on July 15.

302.16–17 you must not expect to see me pined] Wasted away or diminished in weight.

302.27 when I finishd the last page] This letter is a continuation of an earlier letter to Elizabeth Smith Shaw that Abigail had written onboard ship.

302.32–33 Molieres fine Gentleman] Molière, *Le Bourgeois Gentilhomme*.

303.1–2 sister Cranches Letter] See pages 273–300 in this volume.

303.17–18 He had removed . . . House] See note 289.35–36.

303.28–29 a Mr. Joy . . . knowledge.] Michael Joy, who had possibly been a suitor of Elizabeth prior to her marriage to John Shaw in 1777. See also note 295.20.

303.37 Mr. and Mrs. Hollowell] Mary Boylston Hallowell was first cousin to John's mother. She and her husband were Loyalists.

304.4–5 Mrs. Atkinson . . . Mrs. Hay] Elizabeth Storer Atkinson, the daughter of Ebenezer Storer, the treasurer of Harvard College. Katherine Farmham Hay; see note 289.22–23.

304.8 Parson Walter] William Walter; see note 288.35–36.

304.11–12 Dr. Clark . . . Col. Trumble] For John Clark, see note 275.23. For John Trumble, see note 27.31–32.

304.15–16 Mr. Appleton, . . . Smith] John Appleton, a merchant from Boston; Michael Joy, see note 303.28–29; Prentice Cushing; William Vans Murray, see note 289.27; Charles Storer, see note 287.36; and Abigail's cousin, William Smith, see Family Tree.

304.34   Mr. Wests paintings.] Benjamin West (1738–1820), American-born painter who later became president of the Royal Academy.

304.35   picture of Mr. Adams . . . Mr. Copely] See note 289.33.

305.3–4   the death of Lord Chatham in the house of Lords] Copley, *The Death of the Earl of Chatham* (1781).

305.6–7   Major Peirson . . . Island of Jersey.] Copley, *The Death of Major Peirson, 6 January 1781* (1783).

305.10–11   "Copely! by heavn . . . pictures thought;"] Cf. Pope, "On Sir Godfrey Kneller," ll. 1–2.

307.3   Mr. Duchee] See note 298.14–15.

307.9   the Magdelin] See note 294.31.

307.20   Mr. Leanard of Taunton] Daniel Leonard had written the anonymous "Massachusettensis" letters, to which John responded in his "Novanglus" letters of 1775. John, however, did not know that Leonard was the author until the 1820s.

307.21–23   Col. Norton Mr. Foster . . . Mr. Parker] Colonel Beriah Norton, see note 275.12; Joseph Foster, see note 276.4; perhaps Jonathan Mason Jr. of Boston, one of John's former law clerks; John Parker Jr. of South Carolina.

307.27   Bugget] See note 291.2.

308.9–10   representations . . . through Glasses] Painted glass slides inserted into a magic lantern, an early image projector.

308.34–35   Mr. Whites . . . Mrs. Marsh] Friends from Haverhill, where Elizabeth Smith Shaw lived: John and Sarah White, Nathaniel Peaslee Sargeant, and Mary Marsh.

309.22   a Lutestring] See note 177.7.

310.8   Mr. Tracy] Nathaniel Tracy, a merchant from Massachusetts.

310.25   a rich India patch] A fashionable *indienne* textile.

312.26–27   your uncle is engaged at Passy] John, Franklin, and Jefferson met daily at Franklin's house in Passy, where they prepared to negotiate commercial treaties between the United States and several European powers.

312.32–33   a M. le Comte de Rouhaut.] The Comte de Rouault purchased the house, which dated from early in the century, in 1767.

314.21   one French Lady] Anne Catherine, comtesse de Ligniville D'Autricourt, Madame Helvétius, a friend of Franklin and near neighbor of the Adamses, whom Franklin called "Notre Dame D'Auteuile" and apparently proposed to sometime between 1778 and 1780.

314.29   tiffanny] A thin transparent silk.

316.22   General Warrens Hall] Joseph Warren; see note 47.28–29.

316.39   a merry Andrew] A clown.

317.13   Abbe Mabble has lately published a Book] French philosopher Abbé Gabriel Bonnot de Mably (1709–1785), *Observations sur le gouvernement et les lois des États-Unis d'Amérique* (1784).

317.15   Abbe Charnon 75 and Arnou] Abbé Arnoux and Abbé Chalut, his superior.

317.18   Mr. Barcleys our Consuls] Thomas Barclay (1728–1793), the first American consul in France.

317.21–22   Monsieur Grands] Ferdinand Grand, a Parisian banker.

317.25   opera . . . very near us.] Probably the Comédie du Bois de Boulogne.

318.9   congress have Cut of 500 Guineys] On May 7, 1784, Congress reduced the annual salaries of its ministers from $11,111 to $9,000.

320.10   mourning, for a prince] Charles August Frederick (c. 1776–1784), only child of Charles II, Duke of Zweibrücken.

321.14   son of Dr. Mather and Mrs. Hay] Samuel Mather, a Loyalist, the son of Reverend Samuel Mather, grandson of Cotton Mather, and nephew of the late Governor Thomas Hutchinson. Before the Revolution he had been chief clerk of the Boston customs office. Katherine Farmham Hay; see note 289.22–23.

321.16–17   Mr. Tracy Mr. Williams Mr. Jefferson and Humphries] Nathaniel Tracy and Jonathan Williams, who had served as American commercial agent at Nantes. Lieutenant Colonel David Humphreys had been an aide-de-camp to General Washington during the Revolution and was named by Congress as secretary to the commissioners in 1784. In the 1790s he served as a secret agent in London, Lisbon, and Madrid, then as commissioner to Algiers, and finally as minister to Spain.

322.23   Monsieur D'Ambassodor de Sweed] Erik Magnus, baron de Staël Holstein (1749–1802), who was the Swedish minister in Paris from 1783 to the mid-1790s and previously to the Netherlands, 1775–79.

322.24–25   Mr. d'Asp . . . Baron de Walterstorff] Per Olof von Asp (1745–1808), the secretary of the Swedish ministry in Paris; Baron von Geer, Sweden's former envoy to the Netherlands, 1775–79; Ernest Frederik, Count von Waltersdorff (1755–1820), a Danish diplomat.

322.30   Mr. Short] William Short (1759–1848), a founding member of Phi Beta Kappa, was Jefferson's close friend from 1781. He later became American minister to the Netherlands and a commissioner to Spain.

322.31   Mr. Jackson and Mr. Tracy Mr. and Mrs. Bingham] For Jonathan Jackson, see note 288.28–29. For Nathaniel Tracy, see note 321.16–17. Anne Willing Bingham (1764–1801) was an American socialite from Philadelphia, regarded as one of the most beautiful women of her day. She was the eldest daughter of Thomas Willing, president of the First Bank of the United States, and the wife of the wealthy William Bingham (1752–1804), later a Pennsylvania delegate to the Continental Congress.

322.32   Dr. Bancroft] Edward Bancroft (1744–1821), from Massachusetts, was a physician, novelist, and a double agent for Britain. John had disliked Bancroft since they met in France in April 1778, but he did not suspect him of treason, which only became known in 1890.

322.32   Chevalier Jones] John Paul Jones. See note 161.11.

323.4   the Author of Charles Wentworth.] Dr. Bancroft published his three-volume novel, *The History of Charles Wentworth*, anonymously in London in 1770.

323.25   *Abigail*] Cf. 1 Samuel 25.

323.40   Mr. and Mrs. Church] Englishman John Barker Church had gone to America under the name John Carter during the Revolution, where he had sent supplies to the French army. His wife, Angelica Schuyler Church, was the daughter of a distinguished New York family and the sister-in-law of Alexander Hamilton.

325.25–27   Madam vous alléz . . . viens] French: Madam, will you have your hair curled today? It is noon. Yes. I am coming.

325.36–37   Racine, Voltaire, Corneille and Cribillons plays] French dramatists Jean Racine (1639–1699), François-Marie Arouet, known as Voltaire (1694–1778), Pierre Corneille (1606–1684), and Prosper Jolyot de Crébillon (1674–1762).

326.5–6   in the office] John's study in Braintree.

326.23   Who is [   ] at Weymouth?] I.e., living at the Weymouth parsonage. The town had not yet found a new minister to replace Abigail's father.

326.24–25   Mr. and Mrs. Weld] The minister of Braintree and his wife.

326.25   Mrs. Hay] See note 289.22–23.

327.29–35   Buckhan . . . voyage at sea] Quoted from *Domestic Medicine* (1769) by William Buchan (1729–1805), a Scottish physician.

328.17–18   Boileau, Mollire, d'Aguesseau and Helvitius.] Nicolas Boileau-Despréaux (1636–1711), French poet and critic; Jean-Baptiste Poquelin, known as Molière (1622–1673), French dramatist; Henri François d'Aguesseau (1668–1751), chancellor of France; and Claude Adrien Helvétius (1715–1771), French philosopher and writer.

330.19–20 Swifts High Dutch Bride . . . pride.] Cf. "Artemisia," published in the *Works of Jonathan Swift* but probably written by Pope.

331.13–16 D'ailleurs, j'ai . . . incompatible] From Philippe Poisson, *Le Procureur arbitre* (1728), ii.54–57.

332.20 Telemack] Perhaps *Les aventures de Télémaque* (1699) by François Fénelon, an attack on the French monarchy.

333.7–9 du palais du bon . . . parvenu."] *Le palais du bon goût*, first produced in 1785, *Le mensonge excusable* (1783), and *Le nouveau parvenue* (1782) by Charles Jacob Guillemain; and *L'intendant comédien malgré lui* (1784) by Louis Dorvigny.

333.32–33 as a pestilence . . . noon day.] Cf. Psalm 91:6.

334.7 The Phythagorian doctrine . . . thyself] From *The Golden Verses of Pythagoras* (c. fifth–third century B.C.E.).

334.24 Hesperian fruit] In Greek mythology, the golden apples that grew in the Garden of the Hesperides were guarded by a hundred-headed dragon.

334.28–31 Be to her faults . . . mind.] Cf. Matthew Prior, "An English Padlock," ll. 79–82.

335.2–10 The Count D Artois . . . wounded.] This occurred on Mardi Gras, March 3, 1778, and involved the Duc de Bourbon's wife rather than his sister. Charles Philippe, the comte d'Artois, later became Charles X of France.

335.13 the Hydra headed Cincinnati] See note 271.22–23.

337.1–2 "a parents thoughts flew quick."] In an earlier letter, Elizabeth Shaw speculated about Abigail's concern that Charles might take an interest in Nancy Hazen, a sixteen-year-old who had come to live with the Shaws.

337.9–12 "so shall discretion . . . understanding."] Proverbs 2:11 and 2:2.

337.19–20 an Omphalia to bring him to the distaff] In Greek mythology, Omphale, a Lydian queen, bought Hercules's labor for a year and set him to performing domestic chores.

337.34 Enfans trouvés] The Hôpital des Enfants-Trouvés, a foundling hospital in Paris created in 1670 and part of the General Hospital of Paris.

339.6–7 "Where can they hope . . . Breast."] English dramatist Aaron Hill, "Verses made for Mr. Savage, and sent to Lady Macclesfield, His Mother" (c. 1740).

339.30 has Mr. Allen carried home his Lady yet?!] Her cousin Elizabeth Kent married Reverend Jonathan Allen on December 11, 1785. See Family Tree.

341.25–27 I know that your Family . . . vacancies.] During school vacations. Lucy Quincy Tufts (see List of Correspondents) was not in good health.

342.4   Army certificates] Salary certificates given to troops in lieu of cash, which were bought and sold like bonds.

343.6–7   "look . . . deeds of Men,"] *Julius Caesar*, I.ii.202–3.

343.17   obtaining the Frontier Posts] The Treaty of Paris stipulated that Britain should relinquish control of its forts in the Great Lakes "with all convenient speed," but British troops remained stationed at numerous forts for over a decade.

343.21–22   Mr. Hales at dinner at Count Sarsfields] Daniel Hailes, the secretary of the British embassy, and Guy Claude, comte de Sarsfield.

344.4   Settled with Ireland] The Pitt ministry had proposed new Anglo-Irish commercial legislation that met with resistance from merchants in northern England. In the end the proposal was rejected by the Irish Parliament, and no further reforms were attempted for several years.

344.8   His Grace the Duke of Dorset] John Frederick Sackville, 3rd Duke of Dorset (1745–1799), the British ambassador to France.

345.3   Mr. Pratt] A tenant of one of the Adams farms in Braintree. Pratt had requested that the Adamses pay part of the taxes on the farm.

345.22   a Young Friend of hers] Royall Tyler.

346.2–3   Mr. Smith the Secretary of Legation] William Stephens Smith. See List of Correspondents.

346.21   A Lady who is my Neighbour being very sick] Madame Helvétius. See note 314.21.

346.32   the Dove of Noah] Cf. Genesis 8:8–12.

347.4–5   "Kind . . . flower"] Pope, *Essay on Man*, Epistle I.

347.26–27   We must first go to Holland] Originally, John planned to travel first to The Hague to take formal leave of the Dutch court, from which Congress had not recalled him. He decided, however, not to visit The Hague until he received a formal recall.

349.32–33   the completion of an ancient prophecy] Sometime after his departure from home as a public servant, John had proposed to apprise Mercy of "the character of every new personage I have an opportunity of knowing" and requested she do the same. She responded that she had the better end of the bargain, for he would meet "not only some of the Most Distinguished Characters in America, but of the Nobility of Britain. And perhaps before the Conflict is Ended, with some of those Dignifyed personages who have held the Regalia of Crowns and Scepters."

350.18   Madam da la Fayette] Marie Adrienne Françoise de Noailles, marquise de Lafayette (1759–1807), the wife of Gilbert du Motier, marquis de Lafayette.

351.1 forfeit him the right of citizenship.] Two states—Maryland and Massachusetts—had conferred citizenship on Lafayette. It is unlikely that, had he accepted a position as French minister in America, he would have forfeited that honor.

351.3 Knights of Cincinnatus] See note 271.22–23. Lafayette was the head of the French chapter.

351.11–16 Col. Humphries . . . Col. Smith] For David Humphreys, see note 321.16–17. For William Stephens Smith, see List of Correspondents.

351.19–20 Hancok has resignd the Chair!!!] John Hancock unexpectedly resigned as governor of Massachusetts on January 29, 1785.

351.23 Mrs. Macauly] Catharine Sawbridge Macaulay toured America with her second husband, William Graham, in 1784, and visited George Washington at Mount Vernon in 1785. See also List of Correspondents.

352.24 the Adelphia] The same hotel where Abigail and Abigail 2nd stayed—Osbourne's Hotel in the Adelphi Buildings in the Strand—when they arrived in London in July 1784. See also note 291.21.

352.31–32 the celebration of Handles Musick] A "Commemoration" of George Frideric Handel's music took place in Westminster Abbey in May–June 1784, the twenty-fifth anniversary of his death. It was such a large success that similar festivals were held in 1785, 1786, 1787, and 1791.

353.6–7 I found one in Grovenor Square] This late eighteenth-century structure, at the northeast corner of Grosvenor Square, still stands, with a heritage marker that denotes it as the first American legation in Britain.

353.8–9 his reception at Court] John wrote to John Jay on June 2, 1785, about his meeting with George III: "The King listened to every Word I Said: with dignity, it is true, but with an apparent Emotion. Whether it was the Nature of the Interview, or whether it was my visible Agitation for I felt more than I did or could express, that touch'd him, I cannot Say, but he was much affected, and answered me with more tremor, than I had Spoken with."

353.21 Asbestos] A mythical stone that, when kindled, was unquenchable.

353.37–38 Sub Iove, . . . Barbato] Latin: "Under Jove, but Jove not yet barbaric."

354.1–3 "Mr. Adams . . . Americans ever had."] From the anti-American *Morning Post and Daily Advertiser*, June 7, 1785.

354.12 powers of Musick could still.] The draft adds: "for she had such a general acquaintance throughout the whole abbe that not a person enterd but what she knew and had some observation to make upon their dress or person which she utterd so loud as to disturb every person who sat near her."

355.24–25 the famous Celebration . . . Handle] See note 352.31–32.

357.18–19   The News Liars . . . purpose.] John regarded his meeting with
King George III as a diplomatic success. The press was less generous: the *Daily
Universal Register* of June 10 included a squib describing the "cool reception
of the American Ambassador." *The Morning Post and Daily Advertiser* of June
13 asserted that John was so embarrassed at his first audience with George III
that he could not "pronounce the compliment prescribed by etiquette."

357.25   the Countess of Effingham.] Catherine Howard, Countess of Effingham (1746–1791).

357.33   The Earl of Effingham . . . America] Thomas Howard, 3rd Earl of
Effingham, had been an outspoken supporter of America in the House of
Lords both before and during the Revolution.

358.22   lappets] Streamers attached to a cap, hanging down over the ears.

359.16–17   Lord Carmathan . . . Cotterel Dormer] Francis Godolphin Osborne, marquis of Carmarthen (1751–1799), served as secretary of state for
foreign affairs from 1783 to 1791. Sir Clement Cottrell-Dormer (d. 1808) was
master of ceremonies at St. James's Palace. He wrote to John on June 22 to
explain the protocol for Abigail's presentation to the Queen.

359.18–19   The sweedish and polish ministers] Gustaf Adam, baron von Nol-
cken (1733–1813), from Sweden; and Franciszek Bukaty (1747–1797), from Poland.

359.22   the Marquiss of Lothan] William Kerr, 5th Marquess of Lothian
(1737–1815).

359.39   Lord Onslow] George Onslow, 4th Baron Onslow (1731–1814), a
politician and lord of the royal bedchamber.

360.12   princess Royal] Charlotte Augusta Matilda (1766–1828), eldest
daughter of George III and Queen Charlotte.

360.15   princess Augusta] Augusta Sophia (1768–1840).

360.32   Ranaleigh] Ranelagh Gardens in Chelsea were public entertainment
rooms for the British upper classes. They closed in 1803.

360.34   Lady Salsbury and Lady Talbot] Mary Amelia, Lady Salisbury (1750–
1835), and her sister Charlotte, Lady Talbot (1754–1804).

361.6–7   It bites . . . like an adder.] Proverbs 23:32.

361.22   furniture . . . landed tomorrow.] John's furniture from the American legation at The Hague was sent to London.

361.22–23   the sweet meats] A gift of preserves and cayenne pepper sent to
Abigail in Massachusetts from Mary Fitch, wife of one of John's Boylston relatives.

362.12   Mrs. Temple] Lady Elizabeth Bowdoin Temple, wife of the British consul-general to the United States, Sir John Temple (1731–1798), and daughter of James Bowdoin (see note 52.1).

362.15 Mrs. Rogers] Abigail Bromfield Rogers; see note 222.35.

362.16–17 A sister of hers . . . near you] Sarah, who married Eliphalet Pearson, the principal of the Phillips Academy. They lived in Andover, near Haverhill.

362.22 Mrs. Hay] Katherine Farnham Hay; see note 289.22–23.

362.26 Swift's journal of a modern fine Lady] "Journal of a Modern Lady" (1729) by Jonathan Swift.

364.34 kickshaws] Tidbits or delicacies, such as an appetizer or hors d'oeuvre.

364.35 syllabub] A sweet drink or dish made from milk or cream, often flavored.

365.11 "There's na luck about the house,"] First published in 1776 as "The Mariner's Wife" by Scottish poet Jean Adam (1704–1765) as a lament for a husband at sea.

366.7–13 "which, if it does not lead . . . virtue."] Sir Joshua Reynolds (1723–1792), *Discourses* (1769–90), IX.

366.17–18 scripture, . . . glory] Cf. 1 Corinthians 15:41.

366.30–31 a gentleman . . . daughter of Richardson.] Edward Bridgen, who had married Martha Richardson in 1762.

368.20–21 Otway expresses it "Variety of Wretchedness,"] Restoration poet and dramatist Thomas Otway (1652–1685), *The Orphan; or, the Unhappy Marriage* (1680), II.i.

369.18–19 the celebration of Handles] See note 352.31–32.

369.22 the Messiah] See pages 351–55 in this volume.

370.26 Ton] Fashion or vogue.

370.35 Sadlers Wells] Theater in Clerkenwell in London, recently rebuilt in 1765. Not being a patented "theatre royal," like the Covent Garden and Drury Lane theaters, it was unable to perform drama, and instead showed pantomime, comedy, and melodrama.

372.28 Foundling Church] The chapel of London's Foundling Hospital, famous for its children's choir. See also note 293.14.

372.28 Dr. Price] See note 255.30.

372.34–35 Mr. Brown the painter] Mather Brown, an American painter of portraits and historical scenes (1761–1831). See also note 399.3.

373.1 Barrow] Isaac Barrow, master of Trinity College, Cambridge, and a teacher of Isaac Newton, was both an eminent seventeenth-century mathematician and a divine; his sermons were popular in the eighteenth century.

373.40–374.6 "Col. Smith . . . taste."] John Adams to Richard Henry Lee, August 26, 1785.

374.33–36 "The Marquiss . . . Minister."] Paraphrasing the Marquis de Lafayette's letter to John, July 13, 1785.

374.38–39 The Marquis of Carmathan] See note 359.16–17.

375.1–2 ought to be payd for] Slaves taken by the British Army during the Revolutionary War.

375.38–39 the extrodanary affair . . . Cardinal Rohan.] Cardinal Louis René Édouard de Rohan (1734–1803), who had been out of favor with Queen Marie Antoinette, was tricked by his mistress, Jeanne de Saint-Rémy de Valois, into believing that the Queen was in love with him and needed his help to purchase an expensive diamond necklace. In fact, Valois was working with the jewelers, who had been trying to sell the necklace for thirteen years. Rohan purchased the necklace, which Valois smuggled to London, where it was broken up and sold as individual stones. In August 1785 the whole affair came to light and Rohan and Valois were both arrested. The scandal contributed to the French people's disillusionment with the monarchy in the years before the French Revolution.

376.11 Col. Franks] David Salisbury Franks (1740–1793), former aide-decamp to Washington, now vice-consul to the American mission at Marseilles.

376.25 The Marquis of Carmarthan] See note 359.16–17.

377.5 Irish linen] Shirt linen.

377.16 the insurance of Mr. Hudons Life] French sculptor Jean-Antoine Houdon (1741–1828) was to depart for Virginia to sculpt a bust of George Washington. Jefferson requested that John arrange for a life insurance policy for him.

378.27–29 Hubbards history . . . Hutchinsons] William Hubbard, *A General History of New England* (1680); Daniel Neal, *The History of New-England* (1720); and Thomas Hutchinson, *The History of the Colony of Massachusets-Bay* (1764–67).

379.28–29 Grove Butler Smith. Dr Watts] Henry Grove, *A System of Moral Philosophy* (1749); Joseph Butler, *The Analogy of Religion, Natural and Revealed, to the Constitution and Course of Nature* (1785); Adam Smith, *The Theory of Moral Sentiments* (1759); and Isaac Watts, *The Improvement of the Mind; or, A Supplement to the Art of Logick* (1741).

380.26 mr and mrs Blake] William (1739–1803) and Anne Izard Blake (1740–?).

380.30 he owns 15 hundred Negroes] According to the 1790 federal census, Blake held 695 slaves. Abigail 2nd, in a letter to John Quincy of February 9, 1786, put the Blakes' annual income at £15,000 per year.

381.8 mr Bridgen] Edward Bridgen, a London artisan who was a close friend of the Adamses and had been a colonial sympathizer during the war.

381.22 Daphne] In Greek mythology, a naiad who is chased by the god Apollo.

382.2–3 col Humphries] David Humphreys; see note 321.16–17.

382.5–7 "His Eyes . . . Spirit aw'd."] John Home, *Douglas, A Tragedy* (1756), IV.208–10.

382.18 a wreck is left behind—] Cf. *The Tempest*, IV.i.148–56.

382.20–22 Rouchfoucault says . . . new one.] Cf. Maxim No. 10 from François, duc de La Rochefoucauld, *Moral Reflections and Maxims* (1746), and *The Two Gentlemen of Verona*, II.iv.192–95.

382.35 The final dismission] Abigail 2nd terminated her relationship with Tyler by a brief letter on August 11, 1785, in which she returned his letters.

384.27–28 He has publishd an other Poem] *The Happiness of America* (1786). Humphreys's first poem was *A Poem, Addressed to the Armies of the United States of America* (1785).

384.35–36 the Death of poor Williamos.] Charles Williamos, suspected after July 1785 of being a British spy, had become a friend of Jefferson and the Adamses in Paris in 1784. He died in early November 1785. Jefferson assisted Williamos financially during his illness.

385.6 Mr and Mrs Bingham] See note 322.31.

385.9 Lord Landsdown and my Lady Lucans] William Petty-Fitzmaurice, 1st Marquess of Lansdowne (1737–1805), who had been prime minister, 1782–83, and Lady Margaret Bingham (1740–1814), wife of Charles Bingham (1735–1799), Baron Lucan of Castlebar.

385.24 "She Shone . . . a Queen."] Cf. Pope, *The Iliad of Homer*, Book III, l. 208.

385.33 Emperers Ambassador] Friedrich Graf von Kageneck, minister from the Holy Roman (Austrian) Empire to Great Britain, 1782–86.

385.35–36 mr Chew] Benjamin Chew Jr. (1758–1844), a lawyer.

385.38 Miss Hamilton] Ann Hamilton from Philadelphia. Her uncle, William Hamilton (1745–1813), owned Bush Hill, the house where the Adamses would live during part of John's vice presidency.

386.14 Benidict the married Man.] Cf. *Much Ado about Nothing*, I.i.267–68.

386.17 a widow Lady] Maria Anne Fitzherbert (1756–1837), who had been twice widowed before her secret marriage to the Prince of Wales in December 1785.

386.37 Friend Murry] William Vans Murray; see note 289.27.

387.4 C—ss Blush . . . degrade] See note 318.9.

387.9–11 Like the Swine . . . Beam.] Cf. Proverbs 11:22.

387.40 mr Anstey] John Anstey, appointed by the Loyalist Claims Commission, which was established in 1783 by Parliament to conduct inquiries into claims by loyalists of persecution and loss of property in America.

388.7–8 cross the River] Reverend Jonathan and Elizabeth Kent Allen lived across the Merrimac River from Elizabeth Shaw and her family.

388.16 mr and Mrs Rogers] See note 222.35.

391.7–12 "Nor can . . . we Sup."] Jonathan Swift, "Journal of a Modern Lady" (1729), ll. 211–12, 219–22.

391.19 orgee] Orgeat, a drink made from barley, almonds, or orange-flower water.

391.22–23 Madam de Pintos the Portegeeze Ministers.] Luiz Pinto de Balsamão had been the minister from Portugal to Britain since 1774.

391.33–34 "Heaven forbid . . . rise"] Pope, *Essay on Man*, Epistle I, l. 14.

391.37 mr Paridices] John Paradise (1743–1795), an Englishman whose wife was a Virginian heiress, Lucy Ludwell (1751–1814).

392.23 a large Pharo table] A card game in which players bet on the order in which certain cards will be dealt.

392.36 Mrs Fitzherbet] See note 386.17.

393.12 a vandike ribbon] A ribbon with a deeply cut edge, imitative of the collars depicted in the paintings of Flemish artist Sir Anthony Van Dyck (1599–1641).

393.14 a Poem of col Humphriess.] See note 384.27–28.

394.16–17 project of a Treaty] John and Jefferson had been trying to negotiate a treaty of commerce with Great Britain before their commissions to make treaties would expire on May 12.

394.19–20 mr Pitt's Surpluss] British prime minister William Pitt the Younger (1759–1806), whose report on the budget purported a surplus for the year. Some members of Parliament suggested that the proposed budget contained irresponsible and profligate spending.

394.23–25 Mr Randle . . . mr Barclay] Paul Randall, a New York lawyer, traveled with John Lamb, the American envoy in Algiers, and Thomas Barclay (1728–1793), the envoy to Morocco, to attempt to negotiate a treaty of friendship with the Barbary States (Morocco, Algiers, Tunis, and Tripoli) in order to protect American ships from Barbary pirates.

394.35 Tropoline minister] Sidi Haggi Abdurrahman Aga.

396.25–27   performd the ceremony . . . Friends of col Smiths.] Abigail 2nd and William Stephens Smith were married on Sunday, June 11, 1786, in a ceremony officiated by Jonathan Shipley, the bishop of St. Asaph; Uriah Forrest, Daniel Parker, John Singleton Copley, and John Adams were witnesses.

397.11   Dr Bartletts] A character in Samuel Richardson's *The History of Sir Charles Grandison* (1753) who is "learned, prudent, humble. You'll read his heart in his countenance, the moment he smiles upon you."

398.16–17   take a journey . . . Housekeeping] The Adamses toured Portsmouth a week later, viewing the Painshill estate near Cobham in Surrey, and Windsor. Abigail 2nd and William Stephens Smith moved to their own house on Wimpole Street on June 30.

398.19   keep a table by themselves.] In her draft, Abigail wrote that Wimpole Street was "not far from Grosvenor Square," and that "I know it is most for the happiness of families to live by themselves. I have not therefore opposed their remove."

399.3   Portrait] Mather Brown (see note 372.34–35) painted two portraits of Jefferson during his spring 1786 visit to London. One was purchased by the Adamses and was bequeathed to the National Portrait Gallery in 1999. The second was sent to Jefferson in the fall of 1788, but has since been lost. Brown also painted two portraits of John, one for Jefferson that was ultimately bequeathed to the Boston Athenaeum, and one that has been lost, as well as portraits of Abigail and Abigail 2nd. Abigail 2nd's portrait is in the possession of the Adams National Historic Site in Quincy. There is disagreement whether Abigail's portrait has survived.

399.9   benevolence of their minds.] Instead of the preceding two paragraphs, the draft opens: "As it appears to be doubly as long since I had the honour of a line from you, as the time you have stated to have received one from me, I am at a loss to know whether we shall understand the language of each other, nothing but the space being wholly lost to me, could justify my omitting to inform mr Jefferson how much we regreeted the loss of his company. But we reflect upon it with that consideration which tends to molify our grief for the loss of departed Friends, that they are gone to a better Country, and to a society more congenial to the benevolence of their minds."

399.17–19   Captain Stanhopes ship . . . Bowdoin.] In August 1785, Captain Henry Stanhope of HMS *Mercury* escorted a merchant vessel to Boston to collect a shipment of cattle. While there, two American seamen formerly impressed into service under his command during the Revolutionary War, Jesse Dunbar and Isaac Lorthrope, confronted Stanhope. Stanhope then complained to James Bowdoin, governor of Massachusetts, writing that "if any further insult was offered to the King's flag or his officers, he would lay part of [Boston] about [Bowdoin's] ears."

399.28   but one Daughter.] Abigail's draft concludes at this point with the following: "Now suppose Sir you should give me Miss Jefferson, at least till I return to America. Some future day, perhaps I might tender you a son in exchange for her. I am lonely in concequence of this, Theft I had almost said. I should think myself very happy to have miss Jefferson come and Spend the Summer and winter with me. Next Spring I hope to return to America."

400.14–15   one lately published . . . mr Andrews.] John Andrews, *History of the War with America, France, Spain, and Holland, Commencing in 1775 and Ending in 1783*, 4 vols. (1785–86).

401.4   Nick Frog] John Arbuthnot created the caricature of Holland as Nicholas Frog in *Law Is a Bottomless Pit; or, the History of John Bull* (1712), which has sometimes been attributed to Jonathan Swift.

401.19   mr van Staphorst] Either Nicolaas or Jacob van Staphorst, bankers who were among the first to negotiate loans with John after American independence was recognized by the Dutch in 1782.

401.32   Scaven] Scheveningen, from which Charles II left exile in 1660 after the death of Oliver Cromwell.

401.35–37   the same doctrines . . . earth.] On February 7, 1777, John wrote to Abigail about his visit to the Moravian settlement in Bethlehem, Pennsylvania, that "they have a Custom, peculiar, respecting Courtship and Marriage. The Elders pick out Pairs to be coupled together, who have no Opportunity of Conversing together, more than once or twice, before the Knot is tied. The Youth of the two sexes have very little Conversation with one another, before Marriage."

402.8   Czar Peter whose ship Carpenter shop] During his Grand Embassy in 1697–98, Peter the Great of Russia spent a week studying shipbuilding in Zaandam.

402.14   his retreat to Loo] The palace of Het Loo in Apeldoorn to which William V had withdrawn during a dispute with the States General, the governing body.

402.16–18   Sir James Harris's . . . Lady Harris] James Harris, later the 1st Earl of Malmesbury (1746–1820), and his wife, Harriet Maria Amyand (1761–1830).

402.24   the Marquiss de Verac] Charles Olivier de Saint Georges, marquis de Vérac (1743–1828).

403.11   tammy Aprons, . . . russel Skirts] For tammy, see note 186.36–37; for russell, see note 126.20.

403.21   our forefathers] The English Separatists, or Pilgrim.

404.20   Cut of in early Life] Lucy Thaxter Cushing died in childbirth. See Family Tree.

404.26–27 family distresses of a Gentleman] On July 2, 1786, Mary Cranch wrote to Abigail about Royall Tyler: "His Sister is dead and bury'd and I am told he neither visited her in her sickness nor attended her Funeral, altho he was Sent for to do both. The poor woman dy'd of a broken heart. Her Husband has spent her fortune at the Tavern and Gameing Table, and is become quite a Sot I hear. Her poor Mother will now have two more little ones to take care off. She has Johns three and himself into the bargain. How unhappy that poor woman is, not to have one child in whome she can take much comfort. How much of the comforts of our Lives may be distroy'd by the ill conduct of our near connections."

404.40 tabinet] Irish silk and wool fabric, similar to poplin.

406.5–6 breaking a constitution . . . broken before?] The Adamses had just learned about Shays' Rebellion, which began in western Massachusetts on August 29, 1786, when a mob protesting the state's tax and finance policies prevented the Court of Common Pleas from convening. The court was going to impose notices of seizure against area farmers for nonpayment of taxes.

406.15–16 Honestus to attack the order of the Lawyers] In a debate in Boston newspapers during 1786 that grew to include about 150 letters, Boston Republican leader Benjamin Austin Jr., writing under the name "Honestus," accused the "order of lawyers" of having an evil and divisive influence over the community and called for their "annihilation."

407.15 fryday afternoon] Abigail, accompanied by Abigail 2nd and William Stephens Smith, journeyed to Bath in December while John remained in London.

407.32 you traveld this road formerly] John visited Bath with John Quincy in December 1783.

407.34 the Book] John had begun to write *A Defence of the Constitutions of Government of the United States of America*.

408.3 mr   abbe Green] Blank in letter.

409.10 Mr and Mrs Rucker] John Rucker, a partner in Robert Morris's New York shipping and banking firm.

409.15 seditions in Massachusetts] Shays' Rebellion.

409.27–28 the two American Bishops . . . Dr Rees] Reverend William White (1748–1836) of Philadelphia and Reverend Samuel Provoost (1742–1815) of New York were consecrated as bishops of the American Episcopal church on February 4, 1787. Richard Price (1723–1791), Andrew Kippis (1725–1795), and Abraham Rees (1743–1825), English dissenting ministers; and Reverend John Disney (1746–1816), English Unitarian minister.

409.30–31 "for peace . . . thy own."] Pope, *Essay on Man*, Epistle IV, l. 82.

409.32–35 written at the Hyde . . . little coin] The Hyde, the home of Thomas Brand Hollis (1719–1804), a political radical, dissenter, and antiquarian who befriended the Adams family. Abigail and John visited Hollis's home in July 1786, and the coin may have come from him.

410.8–9 Some accounts . . . Shocked me.] Mary Cranch had written to Abigail on September 24, 1786, that "We live in an age of discovery. One of our acquaintance has discover'd that a full grown, fine child may be produced in less than five months." She referred to the rumor that the newborn daughter of Elizabeth Hunt Palmer, wife of Joseph Pearse Palmer of Boston, at whose home Royall Tyler was boarding, was fathered by Tyler.

410.27–29 Mrs Guile . . . Mrs Rogers] Elizabeth Quincy Guild (1757–1825), who had married Benjamin Guild in 1784, and Abigail Bromfield Rogers (see note 222.35).

410.31 The Letter you mention] In her letter of October 9, 1786, Mary Cranch quotes a letter from Elizabeth Palmer to Royall Tyler: "I am distress'd, distress'd by many causes, what can we do. I know you would help me if you could. Come to me immediately."

411.6–9 Eastern Monarch . . . vexation of spirit] Cf. Ecclesiastes 1:14, 2:11.

411.13–15 mr and Mrs Rucker . . . Count Zenobia] For John Rucker, see note 409.10; Thomas Lee Shippen, the son of Dr. William Shippen Jr. of Philadelphia; Richard Harrison, a friend of William Stephens Smith; William Vans Murray, see note 289.27; John Paradise, see note 391.37; Edward Bridgen, see note 381.8; Alvise Zenobio, a Venetian nobleman living in England.

411.21–24 mr Fairfax and Lady . . . Mr John Boylstone] George William Fairfax (1724–1787) and his wife Sarah Cary, originally from Virginia, had lived in England since the early 1770s. Mary Hartley (1736–1803), half sister of member of Parliament David Hartley. John Boylston (1709–1795), a cousin of John's mother, who lived in Bath.

411.40 A Certain King Bladud . . .] Her description of the city quotes from a popular guidebook, *The New Bath Guide; or, Useful Pocket Companion for All Persons Residing at or Resorting to This Ancient City* (c. 1762).

412.2 Leporissa] Leprosy.

413.5 Beau Nash] For fifty-five years, Richard "Beau" Nash (1674–1761) was instrumental in developing Bath into a popular resort town, promoting the construction of some of its buildings and instituting codes of conduct for dancing, bathing, and gambling.

413.22 What is the Chief end of Man?] The first question in the Westminster Catechism, with the answer "Man's chief end is to glorify God, and to enjoy him forever."

413.32   the Birth day] Queen Charlotte, though her birthday was May 19, traditionally celebrated it on January 18.

414.39   Speach of the Chief justice] Chief Justice William Cushing denounced the Shays rebels and argued for the importance of the rule of law at the opening of the Massachusetts Supreme Judicial Court at Cambridge on October 31, 1786.

415.4   the dangerous concequences of unbalanced power.] See John's *Defence of the Constitutions.*

415.17   Tuscorora Rice] So called for the Tuscarora people.

415.22   The old granddame] Possibly Sybilla Masters (d. August 23, 1720), the first person to be given an English patent in America, and possibly the first female inventor in America. She was given a patent for a corn mill in 1715 in her husband Thomas's name, as women were not allowed to hold patents.

416.13   British oil] Liquid petroleum.

416.17   Tumults in my Native state] Shays' Rebellion; see note 406.5–6.

417.23–24   Jackson and Higgonson] Lieutenant Colonel Jonathan Jackson (1743–1810) and Lieutenant Colonel Stephen Higginson (1743–1828), both former congressmen from Massachusetts.

417.26   Shattucks Parker and Page.] Job Shattuck (1736–1819), Oliver Parker, and Benjamin Page, leaders with Daniel Shays of Shays' Rebellion.

417.29   Your request . . . your daughter] Jefferson had written Abigail on December 21, 1786, that his eight-year-old daughter Mary (Polly) would sail from America in May, accompanied by a nurse, and was expected to land first in England and then travel to Paris. The intended nurse could not make the trip and instead Polly was accompanied by Sally Hemings (see also note 424.30).

417.32–33   Miss Jefferson . . . Marquiss and his Lady.] Jefferson's daughter Martha (Patsy), who was already in Paris and enrolled in a convent school, and the Lafayettes.

418.5   *To Thomas Boylston Adams*] This is the earliest extant letter from Abigail to Thomas Boylston.

419.29   last Thursday by dr Price] William Steuben Smith was christened on April 19, 1787, by Richard Price, a dissenting minister (see note 255.30).

420.16   Routes] Card parties. See pages 390–93 in this volume.

420.20   Seven Lectures out of 12 to which I Subsribed] Abigail had enrolled in a lecture series taught by Robert Young, discussing "the Mechanism and Motions of the Universe," what would now be considered a physics course.

420.31–32   dr Moyes] Dr. Henry Moyes (c. 1750–1807), a Scottish lecturer on natural history, had lectured in Boston in the fall of 1785.

420.33–34   The Study of Household Good, as milton terms it] Cf. Milton, *Paradise Lost*, Book IX, l. 233.

421.2   wisdom . . . face to shine.] Cf. Psalm 104:15 and Ecclesiastes 8:1.

421.4–5   the virtuous wife . . . Tongue] Proverbs 31:26.

421.13–15   the price . . . safely rest—] Proverbs 31:10–11.

421.32   Flora & Virtumnus] Flora, the Roman goddess of flowers and spring, and Vertumnus, the god of seasons and gardens.

421.37–38   Louissa a novel] *Louisa; or, The Cottage on the Moor* (1787) by English writer Elizabeth Helme (d. c. 1814).

422.4   mr Blodget] Nathan Blodget, the purser of the USS *Alliance*.

423.2–3   Honestus] See note 406.15–16.

423.4–5   do they want to make him a man of straw?] On March 10, 1787, the General Court of Massachusetts voted to reduce the governor's salary from £1,100 to £800. Governor James Bowdoin vetoed the bill, which contributed to John Hancock's victory in the spring elections.

423.18   Mrs Allen] Their first cousin, Elizabeth Kent Allen. See Family Tree.

424.3   broken Breast] An abscess on the mammary gland.

424.11–12   safe arrival of your Little daughter] Jefferson's youngest daughter, Mary (Maria) Jefferson (1778–1804), called "Polly," had remained with relatives in Virginia. Jefferson had sent for her, and she sailed aboard the ship *Arundel* under the care of Captain Andrew Ramsay. Abigail hosted her for the several weeks that she was in London.

424.18–19   I did not see her sister cry once.] Mary's sister Martha, called Patsy, arrived in Paris in 1784 during the Adamses' stay in Auteuil.

424.20–21   I Shew her your picture.] The Mather Brown portrait of Jefferson; see note 399.3.

424.28–30   the old Nurse . . . unable to come] Jefferson had asked that Isabel, "A careful negro woman," accompany Mary, but Isabel had given birth in April and could not travel.

424.30   a Girl of about 15 or 16] Sally Hemings, a fourteen-year-old slave. Her brother James had come with Jefferson to Paris in 1784, where he was trained as his cook. See also note 752.7–8.

424.32   your late excursion] Jefferson had just returned to Paris from a fifteen-week tour of southern France and northern Italy.

425.1   sadlers wells] See note 370.35.

425.6   mr Short] William Short. See note 322.30.

426.19   purchase Mr. Borlands place] The Adamses decided to purchase a larger residence (later called "Peacefield") for their return to Quincy, and Tufts became their agent for this transaction. Royall Tyler had once purchased this property with the expectation of marrying Abigail 2nd, so the exchange was complex in many dimensions; see note 267.7–8. While Abigail often negotiated real estate deals, as a woman she could not own the property in her own name.

427.35   her Aunt Epps.] Polly had lived with her aunt, Elizabeth Wayles Eppes (b. 1752), half sister to her deceased mother Martha Wayles Jefferson, for four years.

428.3   petit] Jefferson's French servant.

428.9–10   I expostulated with her] In her draft, Abigail added, "my little girl for so She chuses I Should call her."

428.33–34   the particulars I will send by petit.] Abigail's draft continues: "I should have done something more for the maid with regard to the article of Linnen which She wants, to have Saved you trouble, but we hear that English goods are cheeper in Paris than here, so that for her I have only purchased cloth for 2 Aprons & calico for 2 Jackets & coats which my maid made up for her and amounted to one pound forteen & four pence I have still to add Some stockings & a few articles more."

429.1–2   I know will be the case] The draft continues, "indeed I have not the Heart to do it, & her Girl has no more influence over her than a straw."

429.3–4   I can hear again from you.] In her draft Abigail continued, "unless she is willing to go with him before. I Shall write again by miss Jefferson and answer some queries which you put in your Letter."

429.9–10   as fine a Boy as any in the Kingdom—] The draft adds: "duty to my pappa miss adds, & kindest Love to sister Patsey but do pray write him how I want to stay here."

429.15   expectation makes the blessing sweet] Sir John Suckling, "Against Fruition," l. 23.

430.34–35   a certain Gentleman] James Warren.

431.7   The comedy writer . . . Character] Royall Tyler's play, *The Contrast* (1787), had recently received laudatory reviews for its premiere in New York City. It is considered the first play by an American citizen to have been performed on the stage.

431.12   "unstable . . . not excell"] Genesis 49:4.

431.17   The House at Braintree] See note 426.19.

431.31–32   the disorder] A diphtheria epidemic in Haverhill.

433.18–19   Sir George Stanton] Sir George Leonard Staunton (1737–1801), a botanist who worked for the East India Company.

433.25   Lady Effingham] See note 357.25.

434.17   Dr Bulfinch] Thomas Bulfinch; see note 97.18.

435.11–14   mr Tessier . . . mr Grand] Louis Tessier was the Adamses' London banker, and Ferdinand Grand was their Paris banker.

435.16–18   your Harpsicord . . . mr Kirkmans] Jacob Kirckman (1710–1792) and his nephew Abraham Kirckman (1737–1794) were among London's leading harpsichord makers. Jefferson purchased a Kirckman harpsichord in 1786.

435.19   [   ]] Several words missing.

435.20   [   ]] Several words missing.

435.36   mr Littlepage] Lewis Littlepage (1762–1802) from Virginia was appointed chamberlain by King Stanislaus II of Poland on March 2, 1786, with the power to negotiate treaties with Russia and Spain.

435.39   any thing from mr Jay] John Jay wrote on July 4, 1787, that he had not been able to present John's resignation as minister to Britain to Congress because the proceedings of the Constitutional Convention had stalled Congress's activities. He further wrote that if the convention were unsuccessful, "the Duration of the Union will become problematical."

436.17   Saar de Quincy] Saer de Quincy (c. 1170–1219), 1st Earl of Winchester, was one of the council of rebellious barons who agreed on the provisions of the Magna Carta in 1215 with King John. None of the barons signed the charter; Abigail may have seen a list of the barons in the British Museum.

436.29   a Geneological Table] A twentieth-century study disproved the Quincy family claim of descent from Saer de Quincy, instead tracing the American line to William Quincy of Aldwynkle, Northampton (c. 1485–1550).

437.8–10   those who voted . . . Grandfather] Abigail's grandfather, John Quincy (1689–1767), was among thirty-two members of the Massachusetts House of Representatives who voted against the Explanatory Charter of 1725/26, which replaced the previous colonial charter of Massachusetts and reduced local governmental power.

437.18   partly built in the year 1079.] Construction began on Winchester Cathedral around 1079, and it was dedicated in 1093.

437.24   two or three, . . . together] Cf. Matthew 18:20.

437.27–28   a Bathing place] Sea bathing resorts became popular in mid-eighteenth-century England. Bathing was segregated by gender, and resorts used bathing machines, walled carts in which bathers would change that would then be rolled into the sea.

439.17   mr J Cranch] John Cranch, William Cranch's nephew.

439.33–34   mr Bowering] John Bowring, a relative by marriage of William Cranch's brother Andrew.

444.23–24   whatever they may assert] Abigail's draft identifies "they" as "democrats or Arostocrats."

444.24   his principals] The draft has "monarchacal principals."

444.29   partizan of any Country] In her draft she specifies "France England or Holland."

446.1–2   better to go . . . Feasting.] Cf. Ecclesiastes 7:2.

446.5   "my dyeing . . . cloud"] Young, *Night Thoughts*, Night III, l. 278.

446.6   our Second parents House is become desolate] Isaac Smith Sr. died in October 1787.

446.18–22   mr Smith . . . mrs otis] William Smith, who had recently married. The "orphan Daughter" is Abigail's unmarried cousin Betsy, who went to live with her brother, and Mrs. Otis is their sister, Mary Smith Gray Otis. See Family Tree.

446.24–25   "God suits . . . yorick"] From Laurence Sterne, *A Sentimental Journey through France and Italy.*

446.29–30   "Why should we grieve, . . . share"] From Henry St. John, 1st Viscount Bolingbroke, "Reflections upon Exile" (1753).

446.31   the Death of an other Relative] Abigail's brother, William Smith Jr., died of jaundice on September 10, 1787. William had served in the militia at Lexington and Concord, and had been long estranged from his three sisters. He had repeatedly deserted his wife and children (his daughter, Louisa, had been taken in by Abigail and lived with the Adamses for much of her life), and was plagued by intemperance and indebtedness.

447.9–10   a natural tendency . . . Disorder] Abigail, Thomas Boylston Adams, Norton Quincy, and Mary Smith Cranch, among others in their family, suffered from rheumatism.

447.20–21   like the *Animal* . . . Hay] Buridan's ass: a hypothetical situation in which a starving ass is placed precisely midway between two identical stacks of hay and, unable to choose, dies of hunger.

447.30–31   a marri'd woman & perhaps a Mother] Esther Field and John Briesler had been married on February 15, 1788, at St. Mary le Bone church in London. Their daughter Elizabeth was born at sea in May.

448.10–11   an Elderly woman] Abigail later refers to this woman as "old nurse Comis."

450.5   mr Duer] William Duer (1743–1799), a lawyer, represented New York in the Continental Congress alongside John.

450.21   *Diary of Her Return Voyage to America*] This is the third and final fragmentary diary that Abigail kept. In the early years of the Revolution, John had urged Abigail to keep a "letter book" to record what she wrote, but she rarely did. Nor did she keep diaries, except for her journey to England in 1784, her tour from London to Plymouth in 1787, and this brief record of her return voyage from England.

451.26   Charles the first was kept a prisoner] During the English Civil War, Charles I was imprisoned for fourteen months in Carisbrooke Castle on the Isle of Wight before his execution on January 30, 1649.

452.26   the ship Lucretia Captain Callihan] Captain John Callahan (1745–1806) of Boston had named his ship for his wife, Lucretia Greene (1748–?). The Adamses had paid £200 for their passage and for transportation of their furniture.

452.27   Mr. Murry a Clergyman] John Murray (1741–1815) founded the Universalist denomination in the United States. Born in England, he was minister of the Church of Christ in Gloucester, Massachusetts. He wrote an account of this voyage in his autobiography, *The Life of Rev. John Murray* (1870).

452.35   now 8 days] Actually seven days.

453.4   Trust in the Lord, and do good.] Psalm 37:3.

453.12   This day 3 weeks Mr. and Mrs. Smith saild] The Smiths likely landed at New York on May 13.

453.23–25   "Thou shalt not . . . Name in vain."] Exodus 20:7; the third of the Ten Commandments.

453.32–33   loss . . . Prices Sermons] See note 255.30.

454.2   we past Sylla] The Isles of Scilly, off the southwestern tip of Cornwall in England.

454.13–14   attached me to America.] The remainder of the voyage, as Abigail later wrote her daughter, was lengthy, stormy, and eventful. The *Lucretia* aided an American vessel bound for Baltimore that had been dismasted, and Esther gave birth to a daughter on May 28. They arrived in Boston Harbor on June 17. See also pages 457–58 in this volume.

VICE PRESIDENT'S LADY, 1788–1796

457.11   Mr. Knox] William Knox, a clerk in the War Department and the younger brother of Secretary of War Henry Knox.

457.19–20   our gracious reception] When the Adamses arrived in Boston on June 17, "the Pier was crowded—and his Excellency welcomed on shore by three huzzas from several thousand persons." On the following day, the General Court formally congratulated John with a statement of his "many successful labours in the service of your country."

458.18–19 not heard a word from thence.] Abigail had travelled to the home of her daughter at Jamaica on Long Island after the birth of John Adams Smith.

460.8 George Storer] Brother of Charles Storer; see note 287.36.

461.4 Clinton] George Clinton (1739–1812), governor of New York.

461.7 Col Wadsworth] Jeremiah Wadsworth (1743–1804), a Connecticut delegate to the Continental Congress in 1788.

461.25–27 the peice called a Tribute . . . papers—] This article celebrated John's career to date, including his work negotiating treaties with the European powers and securing a loan from the Netherlands, as well as the *Defence of the Constitutions.*

461.30–31 they mean both to unite in mr A.] John was being considered for governor of Massachusetts.

462.20 the address to the Senate] John had been nervous about the reception of his first speech to the Senate on April 21. Most memorably, he stated: "Not wholly without experience in public assemblies, I have been more accustomed to take a share in their debates, than to preside in their deliberations. It shall be my constant endeavor to behave towards every member of this MOST HONORABLE body with all that consideration, delicacy, and decorum which becomes the dignity of his station and character: But, if from inexperience, or inadvertency, any thing should ever escape me, inconsistent with propriety, I must entreat you, by imputing it to its true cause, and not to any want of respect, to pardon and excuse it."

462.26 a dr Johnson for the Editor] Samuel Johnson (1709–1784) re-created debates in Parliament for *The Gentleman's Magazine* in 1741–44 under the slightly fictional guise of "Debates in the Senate of Lilliput."

463.5–7 Johnson . . . domestick Greatness] Samuel Johnson wrote in *The Idler*, No. 51, "It has been commonly remarked, that eminent men are least eminent at home."

463.30 mr Bourn] Sylvanus Bourne (1761–1817), Harvard 1779, whom the Senate had appointed to notify John of the election results.

464.16–17 the House you have taken] Richmond Hill, located on a promontory over the North (Hudson) River, near the present-day intersection of Varick and Charlton Streets in lower Manhattan. The building was razed in 1849.

465.15 The President & Lady] The president of Harvard, Joseph Willard (1738–1804), and his wife, Mary.

466.11　kian] Cayenne pepper, used medicinally.

466.25　mr Brown & Lady] John Brown (1736–1803), a wealthy Providence merchant, and his wife Sarah Smith (1738–1825).

466.28–29　Antifederal state.] The state of Rhode Island did not ratify the Constitution until May 1790. It was the only state to withhold sending delegates to the 1787 Convention or electors to choose a president and vice president.

467.11–12　mr & Mrs Francis] Abby Brown Francis (1766–1821), the daughter of John and Sarah Brown, married John Francis, a merchant from Philadelphia (1763–1796).

467.15–16　the Lady & two sisters of Governour Bowen.] Jabez Bowen (1739–1815), Yale 1757, was deputy governor of Rhode Island. His wife was Sarah Brown (1742–1800) and his sisters were Nancy (1762–1801), Betsey (b. 1765), and Frances (b. 1768).

467.20–25　mr Merchant . . . his Lady & daughters.] Henry Marchant (1741–1796) had known John in the Continental Congress, where he served from 1777 to 1779. He became a staunch advocate of ratification. He was married to Rebecca Cooke, with whom he had two daughters, Sarah and Elizabeth, and a son, William.

467.23　my Neice] Louisa Catherine Smith. See note 244.39.

467.27　Captain Brown . . . his wife] Captain James Brown was married to Free-love Brown (c. 1765–1819).

468.3　mr MacCormick] Daniel McCormick (d. 1834), a friend of William Stephens Smith, and one of the directors of the Bank of New York.

468.6　mr otis the secretary] Samuel Allyne Otis (1740–1814), the first secretary of the United States Senate, and younger brother of Mercy Otis Warren. He was married to Abigail's cousin Mary Smith Gray Otis. See Family Tree.

468.25　*his majesty* was ill] George Washington suffered from an infection caused by a tumor in his leg that was removed on June 17, 1789. By early July, he was able to conduct government business though he remained weak for some time. Abigail referred to the president as "his majesty"; the issue of titles was not yet settled and would later cause John trouble with Congress.

468.27　col Humphries] David Humphreys; see note 321.16–17.

468.29–30　mr Lear the Private Secretary] New Hampshire native Tobias Lear (1762–1816), Harvard 1783, was Washington's private secretary from 1786 to 1793.

468.32–33　the Lady & daughter . . . Mrs Knox] Sarah Cornelia Tappen Clinton (1741–1804), wife of New York's governor, George Clinton. The Clintons had five daughters. For Lady Elizabeth Bowdoin Temple, see note 362.12. Anne Flore Millet, marquise de Bréhan (1749–1826), the sister-in-law of the French ambassador to the United States, Elénor-François-Élie, marquis de Moustier (1751–1817), was a painter who had completed several portraits of George Washington. Lucy Flucker Knox (1756–1824), wife of General Henry Knox, the secretary of war (1750–1806).

470.25–26 the judiciary, and the Collecting Bills.] The "Act to Establish the Judicial Courts of the United States" was signed into law on September 24, 1789, providing for six Supreme Court justices and establishing a circuit court structure. The Collecting bill, authorizing import duties, was passed by both houses and signed into law on July 31, 1789.

470.31 mr. G——y] Elbridge Gerry. See List of Correspondents.

471.20–31 a certain Lady . . . you cannot mistake] Mercy Otis Warren wrote to John on May 7 requesting patronage for her family. She and her family had become strong anti-Federalists in opposition to the adoption of the Constitution and the new federal government. John refused; Abigail quotes his reply of May 29.

471.35 mr W——n & mr G——y] James Warren and Elbridge Gerry.

472.25 North River] The Hudson River.

472.25 Pauls hook] Paulus Hook, later Jersey City.

473.7 mr Guile & dr Craigy] Benjamin Guild; see note 175.13. Boston native Andrew Craigie (1743–1819), apothecary general of the Continental Army during the Revolution.

473.10 mrs Palmer] Mary Cranch Palmer, Richard Cranch's sister.

474.6 the form of Reception is this] For a later depiction of Martha Washington's levees, see "The Republican Court (Lady Washington's Reception Day)," 1861–65, by the artist Daniel Huntington (1816–1906). Painted during the Civil War, this grand historical group portrait was meant to celebrate an earlier period of American unity.

474.6–7 col Humphries or mr Lear] For David Humphreys, see note 321.16–17. For Tobias Lear, see note 468.29–30.

475.22–23 the Board of Treasury say.] A congressional committee had recommended "that it would be proper to allow the President 20,000 dollars per annum, exclusive of the expences of secretaries, clerks, furniture, carriages and horses. To the Vice President 5,000 dollars per annum." The debate regarding the vice president's salary focused on whether he should receive a salary or merely a per diem, with no consideration of an additional sum for his expenses. Ultimately, the presidential salary was set at $25,000, which George Washington declined to accept, and the vice presidential salary at $5,000.

476.4 he shrunk not] John cast the tie-breaking vote as president of the

Senate to allow free presidential removal of officers from the Department of Foreign Affairs.

476.12 Mr Bond] William Bond, who married Hannah Cranch, one of Richard Cranch's nieces.

476.16 dr Price] Richard Price; see note 255.30.

476.19 Charles studies with mr Hamilton] Charles studied law with Alexander Hamilton until Hamilton was appointed secretary of the treasury in September. He then studied with John Laurance.

476.34–35 Let us rejoice & be glad] Cf. Psalm 118:24.

477.25–26 a Birth Night at St James] One of the birthday celebrations of the British royal family.

478.25–27 my Neice mrs Norten . . . a mother] Elizabeth Cranch Norton gave birth to her first child, Richard Cranch Norton, on March 12, 1790. See also List of Correspondents.

479.20 great anxiety for the President.] To avoid causing alarm, Washington's family and advisors tried unsuccessfully to prevent news of his illness from becoming public.

479.32–33 James powders had been administerd] James' powders were used to treat fevers. The medication, containing oxide of antimony and phosphate of lime, was patented by Dr. Robert James (1703–1776) of London in 1746. Habitual use of James' powder has been suggested as a cause of Oliver Goldsmith's death.

480.5–6 the age of the two gentlemen being so near alike] Washington was three years older than John.

480.22–23 Speech of Father Sherman . . . Mr Ames's.] Speeches by Roger Sherman and Fisher Ames supporting federal assumption of state debts, a highly controversial part of Hamilton's financial reforms.

480.32 mr Parsons] John Quincy studied law under Theophilus Parsons (1750–1813) of Newburyport, Massachusetts. On August 2, 1790, the Adamses paid Parsons a fee of £100 for John Quincy's clerkship.

481.5 such a Numerous Family.] Matthew and Chloe Pratt with their eight children had lived in John's childhood home (the John Adams Birthplace) since 1778. They vacated the property by 1792.

481.26–27 anxious for your welfare] In the draft, Abigail finished this sentence, "and hope as you advance in Life that your prospects will brighten upon you."

481.31 "that . . . affairs of Men"] *Julius Caesar*, IV.iii.218.

482.1–2 "envy . . . shade persue"] Pope, *An Essay on Criticism* (1711), l. 468.

482.3–4 "make not haste to be rich"] Cf. Proverbs 28:20.

482.15–16 we are destined to Philadelphia] The Residence Act of 1790 was part of a compromise in which the northern states that favored federal assumption of states' debts, and southern states that did not, agreed to Hamilton's plan in exchange for locating the nation's permanent capital on the Potomac. The temporary capital would be located for ten years in Philadelphia.

483.9–10 Lucy when is she to be married] Mary Smith Cranch replied on October 4 that "there never was the least probability" of a marriage taking place.

483.15–18 Creeck Savages . . . Treaty] The Treaty of New York was passed by the Senate on August 7, 1790. It specified that the United States would replace Spain as the Creeks' main ally, and in return, the U.S. promised to protect a large area of Creek land from encroachment by white settlers. Within two years, the treaty was abandoned as the U.S. government was unable to halt white settlement in Creek territory. The Creek chief signed a new treaty with Spain in July 1792.

483.28 MacGillvery] Creek chief Alexander McGillivray (1750–1793), the son of a Scottish trader and a woman of Creek and French ancestry, was educated in Charleston and Savannah and rejoined the Creek nation after his loyalist father returned to Scotland during the Revolution. McGillivray became a principal chief of the Upper Creeks in 1783.

484.23–24 Lady Temple & mrs Atkinson] See notes 468.32–33 and 304.4–5.

484.31 no prospect of any other at present.] Washington named and the Senate approved William Stephens Smith's nomination as marshal for the district of New York on September 25, 1789. He would be appointed supervisor of revenue for the same district in March 1791.

484.35 "Marriage is chargeable"] Thomas Otway, *Venice Preserv'd; or, A Plot Discovered* (1682), II.ii.42.

485.6 sordid souls of earthy mould.] Isaac Watts, "Few Happy Matches," l. 13.

485.7–9 Nancy Quincy . . . ralying you about it.] Ann (Nancy) Quincy (1763–1844), daughter of Josiah Quincy Sr. and Ann Marsh Quincy, had married the Reverend Asa Packard (1758–1843) in July 1790. On August 14, 1790, John Quincy wrote to Abigail, "Miss Nancy Quincy is married, to Mr Packard, and thus you will perceive your *darling* project for the advancement of your Son blasted even before the bud.—"

485.11–12 Websters New) plan.] Noah Webster's (1758–1843) spelling book, later known as *The American Spelling Book*, was introduced in 1782 for American schoolchildren in order to standardize spelling and pronunciation, and became widely popular.

487.6–7   the remaining part . . . ten years] The Funding Act, which absorbed the debts of the individual states into the federal government, passed on August 4. Under the act's provisions, the owners of state bonds could exchange their certificates for three types of federal securities: some paying 6 percent interest immediately, some 3 percent immediately, and some 6 percent in 1801.

487.14–15   they will . . . present act.] On September 22, 1789, Congress temporarily established the Post Office under the Constitution, allowing postal privileges for most high officers of the government. On February 20, 1792, an act reorganizing the postal service became law; it specifically authorized franking privileges for the president and vice president.

488.26–27   I most sincerely hope he will be reelected.] Elbridge Gerry was reelected to the House of Representatives; he served until March 1793.

488.29–30   we are like to lose Governour Bowdoin] John Quincy wrote to John on August 9 that Governor James Bowdoin was "dangerously ill." He died on November 6.

488.35–489.3   tell mr Codman . . . communicate] John requested that Richard Codman of Massachusetts be considered for the position of consul at Cadiz and Codman's name was included on a list of candidates in February 1791, but was passed over.

490.9–10   attachd to a young Lady.] John Quincy had fallen in love with Mary Frazier (1774–1804), of Newburyport, Massachusetts. Their relationship ended a few months later.

491.38   dr Rush] Benjamin Rush. See List of Correspondents.

492.6–7   col smith . . . England] William Stephens Smith traveled to Europe on an unsuccessful speculative venture.

492.16–17   she was in her Fathers House.] During Smith's extended trip to the Continent in 1787, when he served as John's secretary in London, and before his marriage to Abigail 2nd. For many months the Adamses were concerned about his whereabouts until he finally showed up in Paris, where he met with Thomas Jefferson.

493.7   minister is in nomination from England] George Hammond (1763–1853) became the first British ambassador to the United States in autumn 1791.

493.7–8   Mrs. C—— . . . Mrs. P——] Susanna Farnham Clarke Copley (1745–1836), wife of the American painter John Singleton Copley, and Lucy Ludwell Paradise, an American living in London, both wrote to Abigail about diplomatic affairs in Britain.

493.9–11   Mr Friere . . . successor] Cipriano Ribeiro Freire was the first Portuguese ambassador to the United States, 1794–99. He had previously been minister to Great Britain, and was replaced by João Caballero de Almeida Mello e Castro.

493.27–29 Mrs. Powell . . . Mrs. Allen] Elizabeth Willing Powel (1742–1830), whose husband Samuel Powel (1738–1793) was the mayor of Philadelphia. Elizabeth Lawrence Allen (1750–1800) of Philadelphia, and her daughters Anne Penn (1769–1851), Margaret Elizabeth (1772–1798), and Mary Masters (1776–1855).

493.32–33 Mrs. C——] William Stephens Smith's sister, Belinda Clarkson (b. 1765), who had married Matthew Clarkson on December 18, 1790.

494.22 my son Set of on his return] John Quincy, after visiting his parents in Philadelphia for nearly two months, departed on March 3 with Massachusetts congressmen Elbridge Gerry, Fisher Ames, and several others. After a short visit with his sister in New York, he arrived in Boston on March 16.

495.4 Argus Eyes] In Greek mythology, Argus was a giant with one hundred eyes.

495.6–11 the Accession of the state . . . not yet organizd.] Virginia's District of Kentucky, under the terms of the Kentucky Statehood Act of February 4, would become a state on June 1, 1792. The Vermont Act of March 2, 1791, granted Vermont status as the fourteenth state.

495.13–14 this state feel . . . three Branches] Pennsylvania adopted a new constitution on September 3, 1790, that replaced its unicameral government with a tricameral system consisting of a strengthened executive, senate, and house of representatives.

495.34 suchong Tea] See note 193.23.

495.35 Grain Rye & Indian] Indian grain is maize.

496.17 the Name of G——m instead of Jackson] To oversee the collection of taxes under the Duty on Distilled Spirits Act, Washington appointed Nathaniel Gorham supervisor of revenue for Massachusetts on March 4. Jonathan Jackson was appointed under Gorham as inspector of revenue.

496.23–24 the President has Appointed . . . Nyork] Washington appointed William Stephens Smith supervisor of revenue for the District of New York, with a salary of $800 and 0.5 percent of revenues collected.

498.7 Mr. Burke's letter] Edmund Burke's *Reflections on the Revolution in France*, presented as a letter to a young Frenchman, appeared in November 1790. Burke condemned the recent political and social upheaval in France and particularly attacked the theory of natural rights that justified the political revolution.

498.11–13 my worthy and venerable divine . . . censure.] Richard Price, whose support of the Revolution, Burke claimed, led to antimonarchical violence.

498.15–16 Mr. Hollis] Thomas Brand Hollis; see note 409.32–35.

498.21–22 Mr. Lewis . . . Mr. Jackson] Robert Lewis (1769–1829) and Major William Jackson (1759–1828), personal secretaries to President Washington.

498.27 your safe arrival.] The draft adds the following paragraph: "Your little Boy runs into the Room and says by the direction of Polly— please Mamma to give my duty to dear Pappa and pray him to bring Johnny Some pretty things. my Eldst son is just returnd to Boston having made us a visit of near two Months Charles is returnd to Nyork & Thomas is with us but not in good Health, the severe sickness he had through the winter he has not yet recoverd—."

499.16 the death of Dr Jones.] John Jones (1729–1791) had attended Benjamin Franklin during his final illness in April 1790 and George Washington during his nearly fatal bout with influenza that May.

499.37 master Washington & miss Custos] Bushrod Washington (1762–1829), the son of George Washington's younger brother John Augustine, and Martha Parke Custis (1756–1773), Martha Washington's daughter from her first marriage.

499.37–38 mr and mrs Lear] Tobias Lear (1762–1816), personal secretary to Washington, and his wife Mary Long Lear (1770–1793). Their son, Benjamin Lincoln Lear, was born in March 1791.

500.24 the Bustle of Removal] Rather than return to the Bush Hill house, the Adamses moved into a house at the corner of Fourth and Arch Streets. John had requested that Tench Coxe (1755–1824), a Philadelphia businessman, find them a residence, as "any house and any rent is better than what We Suffered last year."

502.2–3 The col & Family embark for England] Abigail 2nd and her family sailed for England on March 29, 1792, arriving in England in early May. William Stephens Smith's business was probably an extension of his speculative ventures during his 1790–91 trip to England. He was displeased that Washington and Jefferson failed to provide him with what he considered an adequate governmental appointment.

502.21 Post office Bill Representation & Indian War] For the Postal Service Act, see note 487.14–15. On April 5, Washington would veto a bill to apportion representatives among U.S. states. The Northwest Indian War (1785–95); on November 4, 1791, General Arthur St. Clair was defeated in a surprise attack by Little Turtle and other Miami and Shawnee leaders in the Battle of the Wabash with 832 deaths and 264 wounded.

502.25 Cheeseman] John Cheesman, a Braintree Loyalist.

503.1 Espinasse] Isaac Espinasse, *A Digest of the Law of Actions at Nisi Prius* (London, 1789; Philadelphia, 1792).

503.16 mrs dalton] Ruth Hopper Dalton (1739–1826), the wife of Massachusetts senator Tristram Dalton (1738–1817).

503.32–33 I am grieved . . . shaw] Billy Shaw was ill.

505.24–26 a little deserved Burlisque . . . such umbrage.] Massachusetts governor John Hancock objected to the use of the word "shall" in a directive from Congress on the basis that it represented coercive language from the federal government against the state. Therefore, he stated, "when an Act of Congress uses compulsory words with regard to any Act to be done by the Supreme Executive of this Commonwealth, I shall not feel myself obliged to obey them."

505.32–33 Fenno . . . his paper] John Fenno (1751–1798) of Boston published the *Gazette of the United States* out of Philadelphia.

506.34 a Lucius & a Marcus] In two articles in the Philadelphia *American Daily Advertiser*, November 14 and 24, 1792, Lucius, probably the pseudonym of Melancton Smith (1744–1798), an anti-Federalist member of Congress from New York, argued that Adams's *Defence of the Constitutions* demonstrated that the vice president was opposed to "the republican system."

507.15 The five thousand dollars] The vice president's annual salary.

509.10–11 a Bloody Battle between General Wayne and the Indians] The report that Abigail read of an October 17 attack by the Miami on a supply train of General Anthony Wayne's forces near Fort St. Clair was greatly exaggerated. In fact, fifteen soldiers were killed and seventy horses lost.

509.22 mr Consul] Edmond Charles Genet (1763–1834), the French ambassador to the United States known as "Citizen Genet," who had been trying to build American support for France's wars with Spain and Britain, to the embarrassment of U.S. attempts at neutrality.

510.4–5 a low abusive peice against the British minister] The *Boston Gazette* published an article on December 23 denouncing the British (and the British ambassador, George Hammond) for seizing U.S. provisions that were shipped to France and for their part in the Indian Wars.

510.7–8 Dallas'es Reportt, . . . Freaneus.] Alexander James Dallas described Genet in the Philadelphia *American Daily Advertiser* on December 9 as "intemperate" in his appeal to the people. Washington asked the French to recall Genet but ultimately granted him asylum after the Jacobins came to power during the French Revolution and issued an arrest notice for Genet.

510.14–15 Genets conduct . . . Philadelphia.] John noted in his December 13 letter that Genet had arrived in Philadelphia.

510.20 very suden Death dr Rhoads] Dr. Joseph Wanton Rhodes (b. c. 1752) of Boston died on December 19. His wife was Catherine Greenleaf Rhodes (b. 1760).

510.26–27 dr Phips] Dr. Thomas Phipps (1738–1817), Harvard 1757, a Braintree physician.

511.12–13 I cannot agree . . . office] On December 19, John had written, "my Country has in its Wisdom contrived for me, the most insignificant Office that ever the Invention of Man contrived or his Imagination conceived: and as I can do neither good nor Evil, I must be born away by Others and meet the common Fate."

512.3–8   A Frenchman . . . greater than ours."] Quoting from Benito Jerónimo Fiejóo y Montenegro, "The Most Refined Policy," in *Essays, or Discourses, Selected from the Works of Feyjoo*, translated by John Brett (1780).

512.10–11   all the Numbers of Columbus.] John Quincy published a series of letters in the Boston *Independent Chronicle* under the name Columbus defending the constitution and expressing "my opinion upon the pretensions of Citizen Genet," whom he called "the most implacable and dangerous enemy to the peace and happiness of my country."

512.16–17   "barberous Noise of asses Apes and dogs"] Milton, Sonnet XII, ll. 3–4. The Boston *Independent Chronicle* published an attack of Columbus's essays on December 18 by "Americanus," the pseudonym of Massachusetts attorney general James Sullivan (1744–1808).

512.36   the Algerines] The Barbary pirates.

513.14   Barnevelt] Under the pseudonym "Barnevelt" (probably a reference to the Dutch statesman Johan van Oldenbarnevelt, 1547–1619), John Quincy had written a series of letters answering those of "Columbus" (who was also John Quincy; see note 512.10–11) and "Americanus" (James Sullivan; see note 512.16–17) and debating Secretary of State Jefferson's removal of the French vice-consul Duplain in Boston for intrigue. The issue ultimately had to do with the executive power under the Constitution to remove officers. Both Abigail and John critiqued their son's prose style rather than the content.

513.20–21   the Man; . . . no great difference] Edmond Charles Genet, who was four years older than John Quincy; see note 509.22.

513.24   Lieu^t Governor.] Samuel Adams.

514.5   Attorney General] James Sullivan resigned from the Massachusetts Constitutional Society, called the Jacobin Club, claiming that membership in a "secret society" would be in conflict with his office.

514.29   Mr Jeffersons designd resignation] In conflict with Hamilton's policies and concerned about the president's proclamation of neutrality in the French Revolution, Jefferson resigned from the position of secretary of state on December 31, 1793.

515.4   National convention] The governing assembly of France during its revolution, from September 21, 1792, to October 26, 1795, which dispatched Genet to America as French consul.

515.8–9   wisdom . . . to direct] Cf. Ecclesiastes 10:10.

515.16   mrs otis] Abigail's cousin Mary Smith Gray Otis. See Family Tree.

515.18 mrs Powel] Elizabeth Willing Powel, wife of Samuel Powel, had died in the yellow fever epidemic in Philadelphia on September 29, 1793.

515.18–19 mrs Dalton] See note 503.16.

515.20 mr White] Leonard White of Haverhill married Mary Dalton on August 21, 1794.

516.9–10 "A man of wealth . . . Anstis birth."] Pope, "The Sixth Epistle of the First Book of Horace," ll. 81–82.

516.17–18 "Men . . . queer conceit;"] Young, *Love of Fame, the Universal Passion*, Satire 1, ll. 185–86.

516.30–33 "If individual . . . surest base."] Reverend Samuel Bishop, "The Family Fireside," ll. 51–54.

517.6 "being, end, and aim,"] Cf. Pope, *Essay on Man*, Epistle IV, l. 1.

517.14–15 "is peaceable, . . . entreated."] James 3:17.

518.11 Herds Grass] A perennial grass grown for hay.

518.30–39 "A Passenger . . . voilence confounds;"] Thomson, "Britannia," ll. 46–50, 154–60.

519.6 the civic feast vanishd in Smoke.] Some citizens of Boston had planned a civic feast to celebrate French victories in Europe, but it was canceled after being challenged in the press.

519.28 the Appropriation Bill—] "An Act Making Appropriations for the Support of Government," providing compensation for government office-holders, including John.

520.11–14 Several vessels arrived . . . dismist.] Two American ships had been carried to British-ruled Jamaica to ascertain that they had no French property onboard. On April 15, the House of Representatives passed a resolution "That, until the Government of Great Britain shall cause compensation for all losses and damages sustained by the citizens of the United States . . . in violation of the rights of neutrality; . . . all commercial intercourse . . . shall be prohibited." The Senate did not vote on the resolution.

520.17–18 vote for mr Adams] For governor of Massachusetts.

520.24–27 the words of mr Blount . . . justly"] Edward Blount to Pope, in *The Works of Alexander Pope*, Volume 4 (1778).

520.32–33 this day particularly set Apart . . . prayer] Massachusetts customarily celebrated "A Day of Public Fasting, Humiliation and Prayer" each spring.

521.9–17 "join every . . . paints"] Thomson, "A Hymn on the Seasons," ll. 37–41, 56–58.

521.34   Democrats their clubs—] Democratic societies in support of the French Revolution.

522.1–2   "You caution our son . . . curb—his vanity.] On May 19, 1794, John wrote, "M⟨r⟩ John, I hear rises in his Reputation at the Bar as well as in the Esteem of his fellow Citizens. His Writings have given him a greater Consideration in this Place than he is aware of.— I am Sometimes told that I ought to be proud of him; and truly I dont *want* to be told this. He will be made a Politician too soon. But he is a Man of great Experience, and I hope sound Philosophy. He was a greater statesman at Eighteen, than some senators I have known at fifty.— But he must learn Silence and Reserve, Prudence, Caution— above all to curb his Vanity and collect himself. faculties or Virtues that his Father has often much wanted.— I have often thought he has more Prudence at 27. than his Father at 58.—"

522.30–31   "sitting . . . extermating."] *Othello*, V.ii.342–43.

522.35   "an astonishing concentration of abuses."] Jefferson's comment on Scottish political pamphleteer James Callender's *The Political Progress of Britain* (1792), as reported in the advertisement for the 1794 American first edition.

523.11   a new Minister from thence?] Jean Antoine Joseph Fauchet (1763– 1834) was appointed French ambassador to the United States in 1794, with orders to arrest Edmond Charles Genet.

523.12   Munroe is to their taste.] James Monroe (1758–1831), a supporter of the French Revolution, was appointed as United States ambassador to France on May 28, 1794, replacing Gouverneur Morris (1752–1816), who had been critical of the Revolution and sympathetic to Marie Antoinette.

523.21–24   "like mr Solus in the play, . . . your Coffe,"] Elizabeth Inchbald, *Every One Has His Fault*, III.ii.

523.26   "How blessings . . . flight"] Young, *Night Thoughts*, Night II, l. 602.

523.30–31   mrs Hancock . . . Captain Scot] On July 28, 1796, Dorothy Quincy Hancock married Captain James Scott, former advisor to her husband, who had died on October 8, 1793.

523.33–37   "Frailty thy Name . . . low"?] *Hamlet*, I.ii.146 and III.iv.68–71.

524.11   Bennets Strictures] The Reverend John Bennett, *Strictures on Female Education* (London, 1787).

524.27   the Female Commencement] John had written on December 18 that he planned to attend a "female commencement ceremony." On January 16, he replied that he had been unable to attend due to a debate in the Senate.

524.31   Fennos paper] John Fenno's *Gazette of the United States*.

525.8–9   Judge Lowel askd mr Bowdoin . . . Jarvis?] John Lowell Sr. (see List of Correspondents); James Bowdoin Jr. (1752–1811), a former Massachusetts state congressman and son of James Bowdoin Sr. (see note 52.1); Dr. Charles Jarvis of Boston (1748–1807), Harvard 1766, a political follower of Jefferson, had been reelected to the Massachusetts House of Representatives; in his *Autobiography*, John wrote of Jarvis's "virulence against me."

526.9   "o be thou blest . . . send"] Pope, "To Mrs. M.B. on Her Birthday," l. 1.

526.28   Baron Stuben] Friedrich Wilhelm von Steuben (1730–1794), a major general of the Continental Army during the American Revolution who served as Washington's chief of staff, died on November 28, 1794.

527.5   Miss Wescot] Elizabeth Wescott (1772–1798) of Philadelphia.

527.9   Mrs Sydons] Sarah Siddons (1755–1831), a famous Shakespearean actor in London.

527.10–11   Mary . . . Beauty of the Family.] Princess Mary (1776–1857), the fourth daughter and eleventh child of King George III and Queen Charlotte.

527.13–14   mr Johnson the American Consul] Joshua Johnson. His daughter, Louisa Catherine, would marry John Quincy in 1797. His son Thomas Baker Johnson was living in Boston, preparing to enter Harvard. See Family Tree.

527.23   the *judicious* Notion of Giles] Congress hotly debated the use of titles. William Branch Giles (1762–1830), member of the House of Representatives from Virginia, 1790–98, introduced an amendment to the naturalization bill that would require aliens to renounce hereditary titles. The naturalization bill with Giles's amendment was passed in both houses and signed by the president on January 29, 1795.

527.25   Sans Culotts] A term used in the French Revolution for the common people; literally "without culottes," silk knee-breeches worn by the nobility.

528.7   Mr osgoods Sermon] The Reverend Daniel Osgood (1748–1822), Harvard 1771, *The Wonderful Works of God Are to Be Remembered: A Sermon, Delivered on the Day of Annual Thanksgiving, November 20, 1794.*

528.8–9   an answer . . . asscribed to Sullivan.] James Sullivan, the Massachusetts attorney general, had written a strong justification of the French Revolution, *The Altar of Baal Thrown Down; or, The French Nation Defended.* See also note 512.16–17.

528.16   the writer of the Jacobiniad] "Remarks on the Jacobiniad," a series of satirical articles about Democratic societies in Boston (see note 521.34) published in the Boston *Federal Orrery* in December 1794 and January 1795. It was later attributed to John Sylvester John Gardiner (1765–1830), an Episcopal priest in Boston.

528.18   Master Cleverly] Joseph Cleverly, Quincy schoolmaster and a lay leader in the Episcopal Christ Church, objected to Washington's choice of February 19 as a day of Thanksgiving, because it fell during Lent.

529.16–18   blessed . . . falsly, of them—] Matthew 5:11.

529.34–35   titles . . . great Legislature] See note 527.23.

530.24–26   mrs Copley . . . Mrs Welch.] Susanna Clarke Copley, see note 493.7–8; and Abigail's cousin Abigail Kent Welsh, see Family Tree.

531.5–11   Sir William Temples . . . esteem than to Love.] Sir William Temple, *Observations upon the United Provinces of the Netherlands* (1673).

531.16–17   the statue of Erasmus] In bronze, by Dutch sculptor Hendrick de Keyser (1565–1621).

531.25   osterley place Sion House, or Tilney House] Mansions with extended parks in the suburbs of London: Osterley Park, Syon House, and Wanstead House, which had been built for Richard Child, 1st Earl Tylney.

531.28–29   "Grove Nods to Grove, . . . other"] Pope, *Moral Essays*, Epistle IV, ll. 117–18.

531.33   scheveling] Schevingen, the port of The Hague.

532.3   one by Potter] Abigail conflates two paintings by Paulus Potter (1625–1654): "The Dutch Bull" and "Cows Reflected in the Water." Prince William of Orange, stadtholder of the Netherlands, owned both and had opened his gallery to the public.

534.31   Freeman] Jonathan Freeman Jr., partner with William Vans, the American consul in Paris, in Freeman & Vans, a commercial partnership that experienced several shipwrecks and captures in 1794–95. Freeman died on February 20, 1795, in a shipwreck. His parents lived in Boston.

535.11   Mr. Jay and the Treaty.] Washington had dispatched John Jay to negotiate with Britain over several issues that had remained unsettled since the Treaty of Paris in 1783. He returned home with a treaty that, while it favored Britain in many respects, succeeded in the long run to maintain peace. Still, it exacerbated the political divisions between emerging factions of Republicans and Federalists. It would be ratified by Congress in late spring 1796, by which time the debate surrounding it had confirmed the existence of a two-party system.

535.33   Benny] Benjamin Franklin Bache (1769–1798), grandson of Benjamin Franklin and editor of the opposition newspaper the *Philadelphia Aurora*.

535.34   Masons coppy] Washington had hoped to keep the terms of Jay's Treaty secret. Senator Stevens Thomson Mason of Virginia disclosed a pirated copy of the treaty to Benjamin Bache, who published it.

535.35   Peter Porcupine] William Cobbett (1763–1835), a pro-British pamphleteer, who had first published John's *Defence of the Constitutions* and who lived in the United States as a political refugee from 1792 to 1800 and 1817 to 1819.

536.1   Jarvis] Dr. Charles Jarvis; see note 525.8–9.

536.7   Smith was their Chairman.] William Stephens Smith.

536.16   the President . . . judicious reply] Washington responded to the Boston town meeting with a letter to the selectmen of Boston dated July 28, 1795, in which he wrote, "the Constitution is the guide which I never can abandon.—it has assigned to the President the power of making Treaties with the advice and consent of the Senate."

536.23   mr smith] William Loughton Smith (1758–1812), a congressman from South Carolina.

536.33   Dracut the famous Dracut] Dracut, Massachusetts, which passed resolutions in opposition to the treaty.

536.35   the Echo] *The Echo; or a Satirical Poem on the Virtuous Ten, and Other Celebrated Characters* (Hartford, Connecticut, 1795). The "virtuous ten" were the ten senators who voted against Jay's Treaty.

536.38–39   hand to the plough, . . . Back;] Cf. Luke 9:62.

537.29   The Young Lady who undertook the commission] Probably Louisa Catherine Johnson, who would become John Quincy's wife. When in London, John Quincy and Thomas visited the home of the American consul, Joshua Johnson, and his wife Catherine Nuth Johnson, as had his parents during their years in London. At first John Quincy was attracted to her older sister Ann, but soon his affections focused on Louisa Catherine. See also List of Correspondents and Family Tree.

538.6   citizenes's Roland] Marie Jeanne Roland (1754–1793), wife of the former leader of the Girondist faction of the French Revolution, was executed for "antirevolutionary" ideas. During three months in prison prior to her death, she composed a memoir that was published in 1795 and became a classic.

538.14   salique Law] Salic law, governing inheritance exclusively by male heirs.

539.1   Mr. Ames] Fisher Ames (1758–1808), a congressman from Massachusetts.

539.15–16   Dr Preistly . . . Chatham] Joseph Priestley (1733–1804), a British dissenting theologian who is credited with the discovery of oxygen. William Pitt, 1st Earl of Chatham (1708–1778), famous for his oratory.

539.20   Giles] William Branch Giles; see note 527.23.

539.25–26   Maxim of Horace and Pope] John Quincy vowed in a November 11, 1795, letter "not to admire" (to resist falling in love).

539.33 *half Blood.*] Louisa Catherine Johnson was American on her father's side; her mother was British.

539.34 classick Locks as Virgill stiles them] Cf. *Aeneid*, Book I, ll. 402–3.

539.36 is Maria? has she no claims?] John Quincy had previously courted Mary Frazier; see note 490.9–10.

540.17–18 Your appointment . . . Court of Portugal.] Prior to leaving office, Washington appointed John Quincy minister to Portugal, a post he would never assume.

540.30 The engagements You made in London] John Quincy and Louisa Catherine had become engaged in April.

541.31–35 In pomps . . . and delight"] Homer, *The Odyssey*, translated by Pope, Book IX, ll. 35–38.

542.12 Evacuation of the Forts.] One of the terms of Jay's Treaty called for the British to vacate western forts. Fort Oswego in New York was evacuated on July 14, 1795.

543.20–21 the villany of a st Hillair who married Peggy.] Margaret Smith, Williams Stephens Smith's sister, married Felix Leblond de St. Hilaire, a French merchant and art and dance instructor, on August 29, 1795. On April 10, 1796, Abigail had written to John that St. Hilaire "came possessd of a Note indorsed by the Col, of five thousand Dollors, this Note in order to raise ready Money, he gave to a Banker and orderd him to Sell it for a thousand Dollers less than the face of the Note, it was offerd to a Friend of the Col's who immediatly informd him, but the Note had been handed about to others, and given such a general allarm, as to occasion the Col to put a Stop to his buisness, & come to a Settlement with his Creditors, prehaps, this in the end may be no disservice to him. I wish it might serve as a check upon that too great propensity to extravagance in living, which has given so much cause of apprehension to the Col's best Friends."

544.1 Dr. Welch and Family] See note 530.24–26.

544.14–15 Mackbeths Hell broth] Cf. *Macbeth*, IV.i.10–19, 35–38.

544.35–545.2 Not a Bosom . . . Your Sorrows to.] Laurence Stern, *The Life and Opinions of Tristram Shandy* (1759–67).

545.11 visit France] Thomas visited France in April–May 1797.

545.13–14 Prophesys, with Pater West] Reverend Samuel West, Harvard 1754, of New Bedford, Massachusetts, was known for his belief in biblical prophecies.

545.37–38 Secretary of state] Timothy Pickering.

546.11–12 Do him good . . . her Life.] Cf. Proverbs 31:12.

546.22–24 "The Morning . . . Man"] Addison, *Cato*, I.i.1–4.

547.7–8 the Pennsilvana Speculator . . . Munroe] Dr. Enoch Edwards (1751–1802), a Pennsylvanian and friend to James Monroe who speculated in French Revolutionary funds.

547.8–9 Secretary . . . Society in Philadelphia?] Benjamin Kite, a Quaker schoolteacher.

548.10–15 mr Jefferson . . . union Strengthend] Gerry responded on January 7, 1797, "he is a gentleman of abilities, integrity & although not entirely free from a disposition to intrigue, yet in general a person of candor, & moderation."

548.38–549.5 "There is a natural . . . generally prevail] From John's *Defence of the Constitutions.*

FIRST LADY, 1797–1801

553.4–5 "O Blindness . . . mark'd by Heaven"] Pope, *Essay on Man*, Epistle I, ll. 85–86.

553.9–12 The universal cause . . . blest] Ibid, Epistle VI, ll. 35–36, 95–96.

553.30 Deacon Webb] Jonathan Webb Jr. of Braintree.

554.23 extract from mr Madisons Letter] John had sent Abigail an extract from Jefferson's December 17, 1796, letter to Madison (published in several newspapers, including the Boston *Columbian Centinel*, on January 14), claiming that Jefferson had no ambition or desire to become president and that between John and himself, "Mr. Adams may be preferred. He has always been my Senior from the commencement of our public life, and . . . this circumstance ought to give him the preference."

555.1–4 "the Event . . . flourish"] *Richard III*, V.v.19–22.

555.5 the Author of Aurelias] *A Brief Consideration of the Important Services . . . Which Recommend Mr. Adams for the Presidency*, published under the name "Aurelius" in the Boston *Columbian Centinel* in October–November 1796, and later collected into a pamphlet. Abigail had correctly identified Aurelius as John Gardner of Boston, a friend of John Quincy's, in her December 23, 1796, letter to John.

555.27 never be hung again.] I.e., on wheels rather than runners.

556.13 a Letter from an old Friend] Elbridge Gerry wrote to Abigail on January 7, 1797, reflecting on Washington's presidency, that "it is said nevertheless & if true, to be lamented, that by the wiles of insidious & unprincipled men, he has nominated to offices foreign as well as domestic, some characters which would not bear the public test & are a reproach to religion, morality, good government & even to decency."

556.19 Nancy Adams] John's niece, Ann Adams, married Josiah Bass on January 12.

556.21 Mr and Mrs Shaw] Benjamin and Charity Smith Shaw. Charity was the sister of William Stephens Smith.

557.1 Boreas] Greek god of the north wind.

557.4 Gen^ll Lincoln] General Benjamin Lincoln (1733–1810), a major general in the Continental Army during the Revolution and former lieutenant governor of Massachusetts.

557.9 Frothinghams] Nathaniel Frothingham (1746–1815), a Boston coachmaker.

557.16–18 "You say your Farm . . . think of it."] Quoting from John's January 11 letter, in which he wrote, "The most unpleasant Part of the Prospect before me, is that of remaining [in Philadelphia] till June or July—"

558.4 col Walker] Colonel Benjamin Walker, who had served with William Stephens Smith on Washington's staff during the Revolution.

558.5–6 Mrs Shaw] William Stephens Smith's sister, Charity. See note 556.21.

558.15 your old stuanch Friends] Elbridge Gerry.

558.17–18 "The Friend . . . Steel"] *Hamlet*, I.iii.62–63.

558.20 col H——] Alexander Hamilton.

558.26 a Janus] Roman god with two faces.

558.34–37 Cabot . . . Smith of S C] George Cabot (1752–1823), senator from Massachusetts; William Loughton Smith (see note 536.23).

559.17–18 "High Stations . . . the Great."] Young, *Love of Fame, the Universal Passion*, Satire I, ll. 237–38.

559.20–23 "Still has My Life . . . thy care"] Psalm 71, part 1, in Isaac Watts's metrical psalter *The Psalms of David Imitated in the Language of the New Testament* (1719).

560.10 Freaneu . . . libelling the Government.] Jefferson and Madison had helped found Phillip Freneau's Philadelphia *National Gazette* as an anti-Federalist organ.

560.11 a Character in your state] Alexander Hamilton.

561.4–5 "The Sun . . . the Day"] Cf. James Hervey, "Ode from Casimire," ll. 9–10.

561.7–8 declare Yourself Head of A Nation.] As president of the Senate, John presided over the counting of the electoral votes and announced his own election as president. Washington was in attendance as were many diplomats and "gentlemen and ladies" who were inhabitants of the city.

561.8–13 And now O Lord . . . Soverign] 1 Kings 3:7–9.

563.9–12 James . . . Master Heath . . . Faxon] James, a black servant whom Abigail had brought home to Quincy from Philadelphia. Samuel W. Heath, the schoolmaster. James Faxon, a tenant of the Adamses who had seven school-age sons.

563.39 Prince] Another servant.

564.18 my Numbers] Mercy had purchased Abigail a ticket in the Harvard College Lottery, which raised money to build a new dormitory, and wrote to Abigail on February 27 to inform her that she had won $8.

565.1 "High Stations, . . . create"] Young, *Love of Fame, the Universal Passion*, Satire 1, l. 237.

565.27 I have read the address] John responded to her criticism of his farewell speech to the Senate on March 22: "I am highly pleased with your Criticisms and Observations on my Adieus to the Senate, their Answer and my Reply. Before [you?] now you have a long Speech, which I hope you will descant on as learnedly and ingeniously."

566.14 Jarvis] Dr. Charles Jarvis; see note 525.8–9.

566.21 H⸺n] Alexander Hamilton.

566.32 Pinckny] Prior to leaving office, Washington had appointed Charles Cotesworth Pinckney of South Carolina (1746–1825) as minister to France. The Directory, having been angered by Jay's Treaty, refused to accept his diplomatic credentials and ordered him to leave the country.

566.33 Mr. Murray] William Vans Murray (see note 289.27) served as minister to Netherlands, 1797–1801.

567.23 Mary Smith] Abigail's niece, who died on April 22 from tuberculosis.

567.29 Chief Justice Elsworths] Oliver Ellsworth (1745–1807), the third Chief Justice of the United States Supreme Court.

568.27 Mr. Whitney] Reverend Peter Whitney, who would become minister of the First Church of Quincy under Reverend Anthony Wibird in early 1800.

570.9 His speech.] His first message on relations with France.

570.13 the Minister at the Hague] John Quincy.

570.20–22 Mr. Whitney, . . . Mr. Flint.] Quincy was searching for a new minister to assist Reverend Anthony Wibird, whose ill health prevented him from preaching regularly. For Reverend Peter Whitney, see note 568.27. Reverend Jacob Flint was minister in Reading, Massachusetts. In Mary Smith Cranch's May 4 letter to Abigail, she reported the search committee's unanimous vote in favor of Whitney.

571.31 Bache] Benjamin Franklin Bache; see note 535.33.

572.2   Barra's insolent speech] The speech that Paul François Jean Nicolas, vicomte de Barras (1755–1829), president of the French Directory, made to departing minister James Monroe on December 30, 1796, was published in the Philadelphia *Aurora* on March 24, 1797. It reads, in part: "France, rich in her liberty, encompassed by her train of victories, strong in the esteem of her allies, will not abuse herself by calculating the consequences of the commission of the American government to the suggestions of her ancient masters. The French Republic hopes, that at least the successors of Columbus and of Penn always jealous of their liberty, will never forget what they owe France, Assure, Sir, the good American people, that, like them, we adore liberty; that they shall always have our esteem; and that they will find in the French people, that republican generosity which knows how to grant peace as it knows how to make its sovereignty respected."

572.5–6   "lick the Hand just raisd to shed their Blood."] Pope, *Essay on Man*, Epistle I, l. 84.

572.6–7   Freeman of our state] Nathaniel Freeman Jr. (1766–1800), representative from Massachusetts.

572.8   Langdon] John Langdon (1741–1819), senator from New Hampshire (1789–1801).

572.9   Mason] Stevens Thomson Mason (1760–1803), senator from Virginia, 1794–1803.

572.9   Mr. Otis] Harrison Gray Otis (1765–1848), elected to succeed Fisher Ames of Massachusetts in the House of Representatives, was the son of Samuel Allyne Otis (see note 468.6).

572.14   Annetts] Dill.

573.14   Town meeting.] Over the position of assistant to Reverend Anthony Wibird; see note 570.20–22. Peter Whitney (see note 568.27) sent a letter to the Town Meeting refusing an appointment and quoting Abigail about the selection process.

574.13–14   The son too, of 23 years old] John Quincy was almost thirty years old.

574.33   Mr. James Greenleaf] In the Panic of 1797, a series of downturns in credit markets in the United States and Great Britain started when a land speculation bubble burst in the U.S. In 1796, James Greenleaf's North American Land Co. failed, and he was confined in the debtors' prison in Prune Street, Philadelphia. He was discharged in 1798 in one of the earliest bankruptcy cases in U.S. law.

574.33–34   Mr. Morris] Robert Morris Jr. (1734–1806) a Philadelphia merchant who earned the sobriquet "Financier of the Revolution" through his financial assistance to the Continental Congress and his later service as a financial manager in the Washington administration. After his bankruptcy in 1798 during the economic downturn, he served a few years in debtors' prison until his release in 1801.

574.38 Cousin William] Abigail's nephew William Cranch (see List of Correspondents) was another loser in the Panic of 1797; he was legal counsel in Greenleaf's North American Land Co.

576.8 the death of Mary Smith.] See note 567.23.

576.14–15 "Whatever farce . . . Majesty in Death"] Young, *Night Thoughts* (1742–45), Night II.

576.34–35 Change of your mission . . . to Berlin.] Washington had appointed John Quincy as minister to Portugal, but upon taking office, John decided to change that appointment to Prussia in order to renegotiate a lapsed treaty. John Quincy was displeased because he believed, correctly, that the press would seize on this issue to accuse the president of nepotism and himself as profiting from his father's position.

577.12 Envoys Extrordinary to France.] After receiving information from both William Vans Murray and John Quincy that the French Directory might be receptive to renewed overtures, John appointed three commissioners to France—Charles Cotesworth Pinckney, the recently snubbed minister; John Marshall (1755–1835), a Virginia lawyer who had been a delegate to the Virginia convention that ratified the Constitution; and Francis Dana (who declined and was replaced by Elbridge Gerry)—to negotiate the outstanding disputes, especially seizure of American ships trading with Britain.

577.24–25 a Letter . . . much conversation] On April 24, 1796, Jefferson wrote a letter to his friend Philip Mazzei (1730–1816), an Italian physician who had helped purchase arms for Virginia during the Revolution, in which he wrote:

> The aspect of our politics has wonderfully changed since you left us. In place of that noble love of liberty and republican government which carried us triumphantly thro' the war, an Anglican, monarchical and aristocratical party has sprung up, whose avowed object is to draw over us the substance as they have already done the forms of the British government. . . . Against us are the Executive, the Judiciary, two out of three branches of the legislature, all of the officers of the government, all who want to be officers, all timid men who prefer the calm of despotism to the boisterous sea of liberty, British merchants and Americans trading on British capitals, speculators and holders in the banks and public funds a contrivance invented for the purposes of corruption and for assimilating us in all things, to the rotten as well as the sound parts of the British model. It would give you a fever were I to name to you the apostates who have gone over to these heresies, men who were Samsons in the field and Solomons in the council, but who have had their heads shorn by the harlot England.

The letter was published in the Paris *Gazette Nationale ou Le Moniteur Universel* on January 25, 1797, and then translated into English and published by Noah Webster in the New York *Minerva* on May 2, 1797. The publication of the letter made Jefferson the target of partisan attacks and soured his relationships with Washington and others.

577.28–29   "What Sin . . . dipd me in Ink"] Pope, "An Epistle from Mr. Pope to Dr. Arbuthnot" (1735), ll. 125–26.

578.7   Nominated mr Gerry.] See note 577.12.

578.32   it was a portrait] This 1796 portrait of John Quincy by John Singleton Copley hangs in the Museum of Fine Arts, Boston. Copley painted it at the request of his wife, Susanna Copley, as a gift for Abigail.

580.29   the Mutiny on Board the English fleet] The Spithead and Nore mutinies of Royal Navy sailors in April–June 1797 over living conditions and salaries, while Britain was at war with Revolutionary France, sparked fears of another revolution.

580.29–30   the fall of English Credit] English credit was hurt by the Panic of 1797; see note 574.33.

580.30   the troubles in Ireland] In the winter of 1796–97 the French Directory attempted to help an Irish republican group rebel against British rule by landing an expeditionary force in Ireland. A force of 15,000 soldiers set sail from Brest, France, in December 1796 but was scattered by severe storms.

580.30–31   the peace of the Emperor with France] On April 18, the Treaty of Leoben was signed between the French Directory (represented by General Napoléon Bonaparte) and Emperor Francis II, the Holy Roman Emperor, ending the War of the First Coalition (1792–97).

580.31   the victories of Buonaparte] Napoléon Bonaparte (1769–1821) was appointed commander-in-chief of the French Army of Italy in March 1796, and in the following year, forced the surrender of both Austria and Sardinia in a series of French victories.

580.36   Mr. Marshall] See note 577.12.

581.3   Miss Suky] Tuft's granddaughter Susanna Tufts.

581.6   John Brisler] Son of John and Esther Briesler.

581.7   Cholera Morbus] Gastroenteritis, a stomach virus.

582.22   the pestilence] Yellow fever.

582.31   Mrs Otis] Abigail's cousin Mary Smith Gray Otis; see Family Tree.

582.34–35   Govenour Bowens] Jabez Bowen (1739–1815), deputy governor of Rhode Island, 1778–80 and 1781–86.

583.11–12   her situation is difficult] William Stephens Smith had disappeared on a business venture without communicating his whereabouts to his family.

584.3–4   Washington, where Mr. Johnson has property] Having suffered a financial setback in Britain, Joshua Johnson (see note 527.13–14), his wife Catherine Nuth Johnson (see List of Correspondents), and their children moved to the new capital city of Washington, hoping to reestablish themselves.

585.1–2   Milton . . . Bliss] Cf. *Paradise Lost*, bk. 4, l. 760.

585.24   Academy of Arts] The American Academy of Arts and Sciences, of which John was a founding member.

585.26   Rev'd Dr Belknap] Reverend Jeremy Belknap (1744–1798) of Dover, New Hampshire.

586.16   *The Letter writer*] Thomas Jefferson. See note 577.24–25.

587.32   Brother Justice] Justus Bosch Smith (b. 1761), brother of William Stephens Smith.

588.8   the plan you mention.] On November 2, Mary Smith Cranch had proposed that Abigail 2nd live in Quincy in the Adamses' house while William Stephens Smith was away, where "she would . . . be among those Friends who know that she had no hand in producing the difficulties she suffers."

588.25   Mr. Whitman] In the ongoing search for an assistant to Reverend Wibird (see note 570.20–22), the Reverend Kilborn Whitman (1765–1835) was offered the position on October 23, but he declined.

588.26   Mr. and Mrs. Black] Moses and Esther Duncan Black (see List of Correspondents), who owned a mansion in Quincy.

588.32   equally liberal . . . New Jersey] The constitution and laws of New Jersey specifically endorsed female suffrage after 1790. This was the first historical example of women being allowed to vote. This privilege was revoked in 1807 in an effort to narrow the vote, when the possibility arose that slaves and aliens might also exercise the franchise.

589.12   Ben Bache] Benjamin Franklin Bache; see note 535.33.

590.16–18   "Every Matron grace . . . Heart Serene"] William Melmoth, *The Letters of Sir Thomas Fitzosborne* (1750), Letter XXXV, Air III.

591.37   Duke de Liancourt] François Alexandre Frédéric, duc de la Rochefoucauld (1747–1827), known as the duc de Liancourt until September 1792, was president of the National Assembly, which created the first written constitution in France in 1791.

592.10   Mr. Bartlet] Bailey Bartlett (1750–1830), U.S. representative from Massachusetts.

592.31–32   Richard . . . William] Sons of William Cranch and Anna Greenleaf Cranch.

593.9   Polly] Mary Carter Smith, the daughter of Abigail's cousin William Smith; she died on April 28 at the age of seven.

594.4   a Letter in the Centinal from [   ]] John Quincy wrote a "Copy of a Letter," dated September 21, 1797, from Paris, which was published in the *Columbian Centinel* on January 27, 1798. He stated that he had no hope for the success of the three commissioners to France, because the new revolution in Paris had driven moderate men from power.

594.8–9   the transactions of the 4 Sep'br] On September 4, 1797, the three Republican members of the French Directory seized power from their royalist colleagues in the Coup of 18 Fructidor.

594.15   nitre] Saltpeter.

596.12–13   the blow . . . upon Lyon.] On January 30, 1798, congressman Roger Griswold of Connecticut (1762–1812) disparaged the military record of Irish-born Matthew Lyon of Vermont (1749–1822), who spat in his face on the floor of the House. Then on February 15, Griswold responded by beating his fellow congressman with a hickory stick, and Lyon fought back with a pair of fire tongs. The two were cheered on by supporters on both sides before being separated.

596.15   the expulsion of this unclean Beast] The House voted on Lyon's expulsion on February 12, 1798; it received a majority but not the two-thirds necessary to expel him.

596.28–29   "observations . . . the same Hand] John Quincy.

599.25–29   Peter Porcupine . . . all the creation."] From William Cobbett's *Gazette of the United States*, February 13, 1798.

601.20   Nancys] Anna Greenleaf Cranch, wife of Abigail's nephew William Cranch. Her brother was James Greenleaf (see note 574.33).

601.24   Mr. and Mrs. Law] Elizabeth Parke Custis Law (1776–1831), granddaughter of Martha and George Washington, had married Thomas Law (1756–1834) in 1796 and resided in the federal city, where they were friends of William and Nancy Cranch.

602.9–10   dispatches . . . no prospect of success.] For the "XYZ Affair," see Chronology for 1797 and 1798.

602.19–20   Nurse and Baby were with me yesterday.] The orphaned niece of Moses Black of Quincy, Anna Hall, and her husband had died in the yellow fever epidemic, leaving behind an infant. Abigail took charge of the child's well-being and eventually arranged for her to be taken to the Blacks.

603.13   Nicolas motion] The Nicholas Amendment, introduced by Virginia member of the House John Nicholas (1764–1819), would have reduced the salaries of foreign ministers.

603.19   Mr. King] Rufus King (1755–1827), Harvard 1777, minister to the Court of St. James's, 1796–1803. Born in Maine (then part of Massachusetts), he practiced law in Massachusetts where he served as a representative, before moving to New York where he was elected to the U.S. Senate.

603.28   *held sacred* now] See pages 587–89 in this volume.

604.3   Giles] William Branch Giles; see note 527.23.

604.17   Robins] Robing, bands or stripes of trimming on a gown.

604.30   Beast of Vermont.] Matthew Lyon; see note 596.12–13.

605.31   *the Man of the People.*] Thomas Jefferson.

606.6–7   Stern observes, . . . Sun declines."] Cf. Young, *Night Thoughts*, Night V.

606.13   "But theres . . . on high"] Psalm 24, l. 5, in Isaac Watts, *The Psalms of David Imitated in the Language of the New Testament* (1719).

607.40   Mr. Reads] John Reed (1751–1831), Federalist member of the House, 1795–1801, from Massachusetts.

608.26   An attempt for an Embargo] On March 26, 1798, the Senate voted on a motion to lay an embargo on ships owned by U.S. citizens in order to maintain a state of neutrality.

609.15   Spanish minister de Yrujo . . . Miss McKean] Carlos Martínez de Irujo (1763–1824), Spanish minister to the United States, 1796–1807, and later the secretary of state of Spain, married Sarah McKean (1777–1841) in April 1798.

609.19   Mr. Harper] Robert Goodloe Harper (1765–1825), member of the House from South Carolina, 1795–1801, gave a speech about the XYZ Affair, declaring "Millions for defense, but not one cent for tribute."

609.27   "darkness visible,"] Milton, *Paradise Lost*, bk. 1, l. 63.

609.31–32   the Actors "who fret . . . stage"] *Macbeth*, V.v.25.

610.10   poisoned shirt of Dejanire.] Deianira, in Greek mythology the wife of Hercules who unwittingly poisoned the shirt that killed him.

610.19   Miss Wescot] Elizabeth Wescot (1772–1798), whom Abigail described in a January 10, 1795, letter as "your Flame." She died in a yellow fever epidemic later that year.

610.30   a virtuous woman . . . Husband!] Proverbs 12:4.

611.9   Mr. Greenleaf was liberated] See note 574.33.

611.22–23   New King of Prussia] Frederick William III (1770–1840), who became king on November 16, 1797, after John Quincy had received diplomatic credentials as ambassador to his father, Frederick William II.

612.4   the Queen Mother] Frederika Louisa of Hesse-Darmstadt (1751–1805), the second wife of Frederick William II, and the mother of Frederick William III.

612.5   5 Kings in France.] The French Directory.

612.26   Kings Pantheon] *Description of the allegory painted for the curtain of the King's theatre, Pantheon* (1791) or *An Alphabetical List of the Subscribers to the King's Theatre, Pantheon* (1791).

612.35   cimplicity cap] A small flat cap worn informally indoors or under a hat.

613.5   for the Child.] See note 602.19–20.

613.9–10   Mr. Black had . . . taken the child] William Black, the brother of Moses Black; see note 588.26.

615.36   Mr. and Mrs. Porter] David and Lydia Harmon Porter of Abington, Massachusetts, who had been hired as caretakers of Peacefield.

616.27–28   Louissa whose Situation . . . distressing] Louisa Catherine had suffered a miscarriage in November 1797.

616.35–617.1   "even where you had garnerd up your Heart,"] Cf. *Othello*, IV.ii.57.

617.25–26   Abash'd . . . how lovely?] Milton, *Paradise Lost*, bk. IV, ll. 846–49.

617.38–39   Giles, Nicholas, Clayton, Clopton . . . going.] Members of the U.S. House of Representatives from Virginia: William Branch Giles, see note 527.23; John Nicholas, see note 603.13; and John Clopton (1756–1816). Dr. Joshua Clayton (1744–1798) was a senator from Delaware.

617.39   *Old Findly*] William Findley (c. 1741–1821), a member of the House from Pennsylvania.

618.2   Peters paper] William Cobbett's *Gazette of the United States*, published under the pseudonym Peter Porcupine. See note 535.35.

618.5–6   Jesuit Gallatin] Albert Gallatin (1761–1849), Pennsylvania member of the House. Gallatin was an ardent anti-Federalist and opponent of Hamilton's financial policies. He later served as secretary of the treasury under Jefferson and Madison.

618.28   Genll. Heath] General William Heath (1737–1814) of Roxbury, Massachusetts.

619.1–6   "They seem . . . alone to Ceasar make."] John Dryden, "To His Sacred Majesty. A Panegyrick on His Coronation" (1661), ll. 79–84.

619.9   Dr. Clark of Boston] Reverend John Clarke (1755–1798), minister of First Church, Boston, had died suddenly on April 2.

619.24–25   a National Song . . . Mr. Hopkinson.] "Hail Columbia," lyrics by Joseph Hopkinson (1770–1842), set to "The President's March," tune composed by Philip Phile (c. 1734–1793) in 1789 for Washington's inauguration.

619.31   Ciera] "Ca ira," the first popular song of the French Revolution, was sung by the insurgents as they marched to Versailles.

620.3   Mr. and Mrs. Otis, Mr. & Mrs. Buck] Abigail's cousin Mary Smith Gray Otis and her husband Samuel Allyne Otis; see Family Tree. Daniel Buck (1753–1816), a former member of the House from Virginia, 1795–97.

620.6   Mr. Fox] Gilbert Fox (1776–1807), a singer, actor, and engraver. He had encouraged Hopkinson to write "Hail Columbia."

620.10   Rossina] *Rosina* (1771–72), a comic opera by English composer William Shield (1748–1829) with libretto by English novelist and playwright Frances Brooke (1724–1789).

620.28   a Sedition Bill] See Chronology for 1798.

620.30   Adams Chronical] The *Independent Chronicle*, published by Adams & Rhoades in Boston.

622.21–22   Mr. Otis's office.] Samuel Allyne Otis was secretary of the Senate.

622.36   Hare, a Nephew of Mrs. Binghams] Robert Hare (1781–1858), a chemist; Anne Willing Bingham (see note 322.31).

623.10   Yesterday . . . much solemnity.] May 9, 1798, was declared a national day of public fasting and prayer.

623.27   Allien Bill.] See Chronology for 1798.

624.20–21   Deca Muslin] Dacca muslin, a filmy fabric made in Dhaka (formerly Dacca), Bangladesh.

625.8   mr Clarks] Their tenant.

625.21–22   Samll Snow . . . consul at Canton.] Samuel Snow (1758–1838), a merchant from Providence, Rhode Island, in the firm of Munro, Snow, & Munro, was appointed United States consul at Canton (now Guangzhou, China). He later served as chief justice and then deputy governor of Rhode Island.

626.7   addresses which are pouring in] In the wake of the XYZ Affair (see Chronology for 1798), John received hundreds of complimentary addresses from state legislatures, town meetings, college students, grand juries, Masonic lodges, military companies, and other organizations, congratulating him on his stand against the French. Giddy with unaccustomed popularity, John replied to them all; indeed, he worked so hard on his responses that Abigail feared for his health.

626.27   Gallitin] Albert Gallatin, see note 618.5–6.

626.31–32   projected invasion of England] A French Armée d'Angleterre under Napoleon gathered on the Channel in 1798, but the campaign was delayed
and finally cancelled in favor of campaigns in Egypt and Austria.

626.36   Theo-Philanthropic] Theophilanthropy was a system of deism based
on a belief in the immortality of the soul that appeared in France during its
revolution.

627.1   John Robison] John Robison (1739–1805), a famous Scottish physicist,
mathematician, and author of *Proofs of a Conspiracy against all the Religions
and Governments of Europe, carried on in the secret meetings of Freemasons, Il-
luminati, and Reading Societies* (1797).

627.21–22   Peter . . . *Bene* a Taiter.] Newspaper editors Peter Porcupine
(see note 535.35) and Benjamin Franklin Bache (see note 535.33). Taiter: a tater,
or potato.

628.8   Alien Bill] See Chronology for 1798.

628.11   the many addresses] See note 626.7.

628.30–31   John Robison] See note 627.1.

628.32   Dr. Belknap] See note 585.26.

629.2   *Dupont de Nemours*] Pierre Samuel du pont de Nemours (1739–1817),
a French political economist and politician and a friend of Jefferson's who im-
migrated to Delaware in 1799, hoping to found a model community of French
exiles.

629.9   The son of this Dupont] Victor Marie du Pont de Nemours (1767–
1827) was French consul at Charleston, South Carolina, until being appointed
French consul-general at Philadelphia in 1797. John refused to recognize his
appointment, and he returned to France.

629.11   Le Tomb] Philippe André Joseph de Létombe (b. 1733), a friend of
John's who had been French consul in Boston from 1781 to 1795 and thereafter
consul-general at Philadelphia until July 1798, when John revoked recognition
of all French consular agents.

629.22–25   Burk was right, . . . opperation.] From Edmund Burke, *Two letters to Gentlemen of Bristol on the Bills relative to the Trade of Ireland* (1796).

629.39–40   I objected to the answer . . . you mention.] In her letter of
May 18, Mary Cranch reported that John's answer to the Boston address was
misunderstood as censuring the writers; she wrote, "the complement was too
delicate for their uneducated minds—Tis dificult for a man of Science to form
an Idea how hard it is for those unus'd to Letters to discover those delicate
Strokes in composition which charm a cultivated understanding."

631.20   conferences with Tallyrand] See Chronology for 1797.

632.9   the Gourd of Jonah] Cf. Jonah 4:5–11.

632.22–23   "A Band of Brothers joind"] A line from "Hail Columbia"; see note 619.24–25.

632.30   Gov'r Sumner] Increase Sumner (1746–1799) succeeded Samuel Adams as governor of Massachusetts (1797–99), the first Federalist in that office.

632.32   our *Lamb like envoys.*!] Marshall, Gerry, and Pinckney.

633.4   have a seasoning.] I.e., adapt to the climate of the South.

633.34–35   Dr. Welchs failure in property] Dr. Thomas Welsh Sr. had served as financial agent to John Quincy and lost a fortune, including funds of John Quincy's, in a 1798 business failure. See List of Correspondents.

635.15–16   Talleyrand had sent out to Bache his Letter] On June 16, 1798, Bache's *Aurora* published a letter from Talleyrand to the American envoys dated March 18, without their lengthy reply. The official copy of the correspondence did not reach Philadelphia until after Bache's publication, leading to a suspicion that Bache was a French agent. Bache never revealed his source for the letter.

635.29–30   work out our salvation] Cf. Philippians 2:12.

636.22–23   "Strikes our comforts dead."] Isaac Watts, Hymn 5, "Naked as from the earth we came."

637.29   You were misinformd. . . . insulted] Cf. pages 621–24 in this volume.

638.13–14   "this Lifes . . . Show."] Isaac Watts, Hymn 638, "What sinners value, I resign."

638.31   my dear Neices case.] Betsy Shaw was dying of tuberculosis.

639.34   He Gave, and . . . he Gave."] Isaac Watts, Hymn 5, "Naked as from the earth we came."

640.7–8   "grow not . . . expresses it.] Young, *Night Thoughts*, Night II.

640.15–16   Mr. Smith] William Stephens Smith.

641.15   Capt. Decauter] Stephen Decatur Sr. (1751–1808), naval captain during the Revolutionary War and the Quasi-War with France, and father of Stephen Decatur Jr. (1779–1820), naval hero of the War of 1812.

641.18   the Infamous Hedonvile] General Gabriel Marie Joseph, comte d'Hédouville (1755–1825), a general in the French army.

641.19   Consul Le Tomb] See note 629.11.

641.23   The Secretary of War] James McHenry (1753–1816).

642.8–9   those who expected to have filld this place] Alexander Hamilton covertly campaigned for the appointment as commander-in-chief of the newly formed army.

642.16   our Secreet buisness about the Building] The renovations of Peace-field in Quincy, which Abigail had secretly been overseeing as a surprise for John.

643.25   your Friend Quincys oration] Josiah Quincy III (1772–1864) was appointed town orator in 1798 and later served as president of Harvard (1829–45). He married Eliza Susan Morton of New York in 1797.

644.15   Genll. Mackpherson] General William Macpherson (1756–1813), who served in the Revolutionary War under Washington, was the inspector of revenue for Philadelphia and the naval officer of the Port of Philadelphia.

644.26   the Levingstone Aristocracy] The Livingston family of New York, which included many politicians, had held the title of "Lord of Livingston Manor" before the Revolution.

644.34   mr Dexter] Samuel Dexter (1761–1816), senator from Massachusetts. In 1800, John appointed him secretary of war and in 1801, secretary of the treasury.

644.34–35   mr Sedwick] Theodore Sedgwick (1746–1813) resigned his Senate seat to become a member of the House of Representatives.

644.36–37   Freeman . . . Varnum] Jonathan Freeman (1745–1808), Federalist U.S. representative from New Hampshire, was reelected and served until 1801. Joseph Bradley Varnum (1751–1821), U.S. representative from Massachusetts, was also reelected.

646.31–32   your Fathers going without me.] John had remained with Abigail during her illness until November 12, when he left for Philadelphia in time to attend the opening of Congress. Their nephew William Shaw accompanied him as his secretary.

647.6   Bache] Benjamin Franklin Bache (see note 535.33), died of yellow fever at age twenty-nine.

647.7   Fenno] John Fenno (see note 505.32–33) also died of yellow fever.

647.22   T Paine] Thomas Paine was fiercely opposed to Jay's Treaty and attempted to influence Talleyrand in his reception of the American commissioners.

647.33–34   the poor child is unhappy I am sure.] Charles, who had invested with Thomas Welsh Sr. on behalf of John Quincy.

648.2   Dr W-h] Dr. Thomas Welsh Sr. See List of Correspondents.

648.29–30   Boylston Adams's] Boylston was the son of Peter Boylston Adams, John's brother, and his wife, Mary.

648.32 mr and mrs Porter] Abigail's tenants.

648.33 Pheby] See note 269.28.

649.2 mr Whitman] Reverend Kilborn Whitman; see note 588.25.

649.5 Admiral Nelson] Admiral Horatio Nelson (1758–1805) won a decisive British victory over Bonaparte's navy in the battle of the Nile in August 1798.

649.13 Gov. Henry] Patrick Henry (1736–1799), suffering from stomach cancer, gave a stirring speech challenging the Kentucky and Virginia Resolutions that opposed the Alien and Sedition Acts.

650.14 Logan] George Logan of Pennsylvania (1753–1821), who was alleged to have gone to France as a private citizen to try to negotiate peace during the Quasi-War.

650.36 a Letter from N York—] From Charles.

651.1–2 Mr. Justice Smith] Brother of William Stephens Smith.

651.36–37 mrs Adams has got into a Habit] Louisa Catherine had suffered another miscarriage.

652.24–25 Genll Brooks has resignd.] General John Brooks (1752–1825), later governor of Massachusetts, 1816–23.

652.32 temper the wind to the shorne Lamb] English proverb.

653.1 our minister at Berlin] John Quincy.

655.5 president Willard] Joseph Willard (1738–1804), president of Harvard from 1781 to his death in 1804.

655.18 The S—y] Secretary of State Timothy Pickering.

656.37 Virgina alass . . . Kentucky] The Virginia and Kentucky Resolutions, written secretly by Jefferson and Madison, took the position that the Alien and Sedition Acts were unconstitutional.

658.14–15 the loss of her dear daughter] Betsy Shaw died of tuberculosis.

659.31 poison . . . Virgina & Kentucky.] See note 656.37.

659.32 Blount] William Blount (1749–1800), senator from Tennessee, was impeached after a scandal involving land speculation in the western territories. On December 3, 1798, he was named speaker of the Tennessee Senate.

660.18 Mr. Murrey] John nominated William Vans Murray (see note 289.27) as a special envoy to France on February 18.

663.1 Govr. Sumner] Increase Sumner (see note 632.30) died while in office on June 7 from angina pectoris.

663.26 Besom] A broom made of a bundle of twigs tied around a pole.

663.35–36 kill the fatted . . . rejoicing.] Cf. Luke 15:22–24.

663.38–39 "How sharper . . . graceless child] Cf. *King Lear*, I.iv.298–99.

665.27 recovering from the third] Miscarriage.

667.1 Mr. & Mrs. Atkinson] John Atkinson, a British merchant, and Elizabeth Storer Atkinson (see note 304.4–5). Nancy Storer was Elizabeth's niece, the daughter of Charles Storer (see note 287.36).

667.10–11 goody Goose stories . . . Giles Ginger Bread.] Goody Goose, a series of children's stories. John Newbury and Giles Jones, *The Renowned History of Giles Gingerbread: A Little Boy who Lived upon Learning* (c. 1765).

667.38–39 "temper the wind . . . Lamb."] English proverb.

668.13 Mr. Whitney] The Reverend Peter Whitney; see note 568.27. For the search for a new pastor in Quincy, see note 570.20–22.

668.17 no root of bitterness] Whitney had previously refused the appointment; see note 573.14.

668.26 Mrs. Morris] Mary White Morris, wife of Robert Morris (see note 574.33–34).

669.9 Mrs. Black and Suky Adams] Esther Duncan Black (see List of Correspondents); and Susanna Adams (1777–1816), daughter of John's brother Peter Boylston Adams.

669.14 Duane] William Duane (1780–1865), publisher of the *Aurora*.

669.16–18 It has been received here, . . . deliverd] John delivered his third annual message to Congress on December 3, which adopted a pacific tone in relation to France.

670.1 a man in the cabinet] Timothy Pickering (1745–1829), the secretary of state, opposed John's pursuit of peace with France. John dismissed him from office on May 8, 1800.

670.17 Mr. Wainright] Peter Wainwright, a tobacconist from Boston.

671.21 Genll. Lee] Henry "Light-Horse Harry" Lee (1756–1818) of Virginia, cavalry officer in the Revolution, served as governor of Virginia, 1792–95, and was the father of Robert E. Lee. He drafted the memorial resolutions offered by John Marshall in Congress that referred to Washington as "first in war, first in peace, and first in the hearts of his countrymen."

671.29 The two B's] Moses and Esther Duncan Black of Quincy (see List of Correspondents) opposed the appointment of the Reverend Whitney as a minister to their parish.

672.11 the trial of Peter Porcupine] William Cobbett (see note 535.35) was sued for libel by Dr. Benjamin Rush (see List of Correspondents) for attacking his medical procedures of violent purges and copious bleeding during the yellow fever epidemic of 1797. Joseph Hopkinson, author of "Hail Columbia," successfully represented Rush in court.

672.18–19 Mrs. Mears] Mrs. Mears was sister of Esther Mears Briesler, Abigail's servant.

673.36 Snail &c.] Chenille.

674.28 Monody] Musical lament.

677.14–15 "full many . . . Midnight air."] Thomas Gray, "Elegy Written in a Country Churchyard" (1750), ll. 55–56.

678.20 Mr. Vose] John Vose (1767–1840), educator in Atkinson, New Hampshire.

679.12–13 "In praise so . . . Mankind"] Pope, *An Essay on Criticism* (1711), ll. 187–88.

679.19 miss Palmer] Richard Cranch's niece.

680.15–16 Mr Levingston of N York] Edward Livingston (1764–1836), Democratic statesman, member of the House of Representatives from New York (1795–1801), mayor of New York City (1801–3), and later secretary of state under Andrew Jackson (1831–33).

680.18–19 Jonathan Robbins, alias Thomas Nash] Jonathan Robbins led a mutiny aboard *HMS Hermione* in 1799 and then fled to South Carolina, where he changed his name. He was found, and Britain demanded extradition. At this early stage of nationhood, President John Adams, his cabinet, and Congress had no experience with political extradition. When it was discovered that Robbins was not an American citizen as he claimed, he was delivered up to Britain and hanged. Marshall's speech to the House of March 7 was in defense of John's action in extraditing Robbins.

680.29 Cooper, the Friend of Dr Priestly] Thomas Cooper (1759–1839), an anti-Federalist philosopher and educator, was tried under the Alien and Sedition Acts. He attempted to subpoena John, but Justice Samuel Chase dismissed the request. For Joseph Priestley, see note 539.15–16.

681.12 Duane the Editor of the Aurora] See note 669.14.

681.15 trial of Fries for Treason] The trial of John Fries at Philadelphia for treason began on April 11, 1799. He and two others were sentenced to death for inciting rebellion. John pardoned all three in 1800.

681.19 mr Strong & mr Gerry] Caleb Strong (1745–1819), Federalist lawyer and politician, served as the sixth and tenth governor of Massachusetts, 1800–1807 and 1812–16. For Elbridge Gerry, see List of Correspondents.

681.36 The Leiut. Govenour] Moses Gill (1734–1800), lieutenant governor since 1794. After the death of Increase Sumner (see note 663.1), Gill served briefly as acting governor.

681.38   Mr. Gore] Christopher Gore (1758–1827), commissioner to Britain under Jay's Treaty, later governor of Massachusetts, 1809–10, and a U.S. senator, 1813–16.

683.30–31   is thy Servant a dog] Cf. 2 Kings 8:13.

684.4   Mr. Wibird is punished] The local clergyman, an eccentric bachelor, the Reverend Anthony Wibird (1720–1800), had refused to relinquish his position and made his replacement difficult; see notes 570.20–22, 573.14, and 588.25.

685.13–14   the little General] Alexander Hamilton.

685.34–35   Major Tousard] Louis de Tousard (1749–1817), a French-born soldier who had served in the Continental Army and was in 1800 an inspector of artillery.

686.7   Genrl Brooks] John Brooks (1752–1825), later governor of Massachusetts, 1816–23.

687.3   Mr Dexter] Samuel Dexter (1761–1816) served as senator from Massachusetts (1799–1800), as secretary of war (1800–1801) and as secretary of the treasury (1801).

687.8   The removals have made me feel sad.] Exasperated after much intrigue and concluding that his cabinet members had been colluding with Hamilton against his administration, John had asked for resignations from Secretary of War McHenry and Secretary of State Pickering. Pickering alone refused to resign, so John fired him.

688.23–24   Mr Strong, and Gerry] See note 681.19.

689.4   Gov'r Jay] John Jay (1745–1829), first Chief Justice of the U.S. Supreme Court, 1789–95, and second governor of New York, 1795–1801. In 1801 he declined reelection.

689.7   Burr] Aaron Burr (1756–1836), previously a senator from New York, who was elected vice president under Thomas Jefferson in 1801.

689.8   Govr Clinton, The Hero of Saratogo osgood and Brooks Livingstone] George Clinton (1739–1812), first governor of New York, 1777–95, and vice president under Jefferson and Madison, 1805–12. Horatio Gates (1727–1806), to whom General Burgoyne surrendered at Saratoga, was in 1800 a member of the New York state legislature. Samuel Osgood (1747–1813), postmaster general of the United States, 1789–91. For John Brooks, see note 652.24–25. For Edward Livingstone, see note 680.15–16.

689.30   Mr King] Rufus King (1755–1827), minister to Great Britain, 1796–1803.

691.8 Little Susan] Abigail's granddaughter Susanna, whom she brought to live in Quincy after Charles's death.

691.32 Shall I receive good and not evil?] Cf. Job 2:10.

692.2 "hope springs eternal in the human breast."] Pope, *An Essay on Man* (1734), l. 95.

693.22 Wilton] A type of carpet with velvet pile.

694.40 "sharper than a Serpents Tooth."] Cf. *King Lear*, I.iv.298–99.

695.28 Mrs Dexter] Catherine Gordon Dexter of Boston, the wife of Samuel Dexter, the new secretary of war.

698.11 late Secretary of State] Timothy Pickering.

698.15–16 Little General] Alexander Hamilton.

698.25 the Essex junto] A group of New England Federalist lawyers, merchants, and politicians, many of whom were from Essex County, Massachusetts. They offered first Hamilton and then Burr a place in their plot to break off New England from the Union.

698.29 Gen'll. Pinckny] Charles Cotesworth Pinckney; see note 566.32.

699.9–10 Cabbot, Ames, Lowell, Higginson and the Chief Justice, your old Master] Members of the Essex Junto: George Cabot (1752–1823), senator from Massachusetts; Fisher Ames (1758–1808), member of the House from Massachusetts; John Lowell Jr. (1769–1840), a Federalist lawyer from Boston; Stephen Higginson (1743–1828), delegate to the Continental Congress, 1783, from Boston; and Francis Dana, then Chief Justice of the Massachusetts Supreme Court.

699.27 B Russel's Centinal] Benjamin Russell (1761–1845), publisher of the *Columbian Centinel*, a semiweekly Boston newspaper with Federalist affiliations.

699.36 Cooper] See note 680.29.

701.4 "this my son was lost, but is found."] Cf. Luke 15:24.

701.13–14 mr Sands and to Mr. Malcom] Men to whom Charles might have applied for credit in his father's name: Joshua Sands (1757–1835), a merchant and collector of the port of New York; and Samuel Bayard Malcom (1777–1817), an attorney who served as John's private secretary for several years during his presidency.

701.29–30 the old House now . . . a Hotel.] The President's House in Philadelphia, occupied first by the Washingtons and then by the Adamses.

702.6 Shall I receive good and not evil?] Cf. Job 2:10.

702.17 the little Gen'll's Letter] See note 705.5.

702.20–21   a sparrow as Sterne . . . fables.] Cf. Laurence Sterne, *A Senti-mental Journey Through France and Italy* (1768), in which a sparrow interrupts a learned philosopher; and Edward Moore's *Fables for the Female Sex* (1744).

703.6   Snowden] Major Thomas Snowden, whose family settled in Maryland before 1675, and who had built a magnificent colonial manor house, named "Montpelier" by his wife, Ann Ridgely Snowden.

703.12   Judge Chase] Samuel Chase (1741–1811), appointed to the Supreme Court by Washington.

704.38   celebration of the Birthday at Quincy.] The public celebration of John's birthday on October 19.

705.5   The Letter of Hamilton] Hamilton's "letter" was, in fact, a fifty-four-page pamphlet entitled *The Public Conduct and Character of John Adams Esq., President of the United States*, a savage attack not only on the policies but on the temperament of the President, excerpts of which were published in the *Aurora*. John had considered responding immediately to this calumny of the charges, but delayed until 1809 in a series of letters in the Boston *Patriot*.

705.13–14   passages . . . from Shakespeare] Cardinal Wolsey's words from *Henry VIII*, III.ii.194–99.

707.38–40   Major Custis . . . Mrs. Lewis] George Washington Parke Custis (1781–1857) and Eleanor Parke Custis Lewis (1779–1852), two of Martha Washington's grandchildren.

708.4   —— is on his way] Thomas Jefferson.

709.3   trained up . . . should go.] Cf. Proverbs 22:6.

709.8   Love to Nancy] The sister of Sarah Smith Adams.

710.5–7   The Scripture . . . hope—] Cf. 1 Thessalonians 4:13.

710.24–25   S. Carolina has behaved . . . would.] Each state chose its own election day for its electors, so that voting in the 1800 presidential election lasted from April to October. South Carolina was the last state to vote, and broke the 65–65 tie in the Electoral College—between the Federalist ticket of Adams and Charles Cotesworth Pinckney and the Republican ticket of Jefferson and Aaron Burr—by choosing eight Democratic-Republicans, thereby electing Jefferson and Burr.

711.26–27   Gov'r. Davie . . . treaty. Judge Elsworth] William Richardson Davie (1756–1820), Federalist and tenth governor of North Carolina, 1798–99, who had resigned the governorship to help negotiate the Convention of 1800, ending the Quasi-War with France. Oliver Ellsworth (1745–1807), senator from Connecticut, 1789–96, and third Chief Justice of the Supreme Court, 1796–1800, was one of his fellow commissioners, along with William Vans Murray.

711.35–36   That defection . . . two Men.] Hamilton and Burr.

712.27   young Mr. Johnson] Louisa Catherine's brother Thomas Baker Johnson (see List of Correspondents).

713.21   the dower Negroes] Martha Washington received at least 85 slaves as part of her "dower share" after the death of her first husband, Daniel Parke Custis, in 1757, which she owned during the course of her life but could not sell or set free, as they were part of the estate that would pass to her children upon her death. By 1799, these slaves and their children numbered 153. George Washington also owned 124 slaves, whom his will stipulated should be freed upon his death so that the intermarried families would not be broken up if sold. His wife freed them in January 1801.

713.30–32   my Lot hath . . . goodly Heritage.] Psalm 16:6.

713.33–34   "that Man . . . little long."] Oliver Goldsmith, "The Hermit" (1765), ll. 31–32.

714.1–2   the lesson . . . abased] Cf. Philippians 4:12.

714.13–18   Popes prayer . . . Will be done.] Pope, "The Universal Prayer" (1738), ll. 45–48.

715.10   Bishop Clagget] Thomas John Clagett (1743–1816), first bishop of the newly formed Protestant Episcopal Church in the United States, which, after the Revolution, separated from the Anglican Church of England. The Adamses often attended Episcopal services in the capital.

715.11–12   St Luke, Glory . . . Men,"] Luke 2:14.

715.21–25   Baltimore Smith . . . to France] A partial list of Jefferson's appointments: Robert Smith (1757–1842), secretary of the navy; James Madison (1751–1836), secretary of state; Henry Dearborn (1751–1829), secretary of war; Albert Gallatin (see note 618.5–6), secretary of the treasury; Tench Coxe (see note 500.24) was in 1803 appointed by Jefferson purveyor of public supplies; James Monroe (see note 523.12) was appointed to negotiate the Louisiana Purchase.

715.35–716.1   Jefferson and Burr . . . footing] Jefferson and Burr each received 73 electoral votes; the tie was resolved in the House of Representatives, where in February 1801, Jefferson received a majority vote of 10 states after 36 ballots and was elected president.

716.13   Gov'r Davie] William Richardson Davie; see note 711.26–27.

716.25   a Speech to raise the Mausoleam] A proposal was debated in Congress to build a mausoleum for George Washington in the Capitol building, but in the end, the Washington family refused to move his remains from Mount Vernon.

717.14–15   Priestly . . . angry with Cobbet] For Joseph Priestley, see note

539.15–16; he had built a large house in Pennsylvania in order to found a utopian community. For William Cobbett, see note 535.35.

718.6   Mr. Jay chief Justice.] John Jay declined his nomination to resume the office of Chief Justice of the United States, which he had resigned in 1795 to become governor of New York. Rather than promote Associate Justice William Cushing (1732–1810) or William Paterson (1745–1806), John appointed Secretary of State John Marshall (1755–1835). Marshall served until 1835, the longest tenure of any Chief Justice, and is credited with giving the Court its equal stature as the third branch through several landmark decisions.

718.9   mr Ingersell] Jared Ingersoll (1749–1822), lawyer from Philadelphia and attorney general of Pennsylvania, 1791–1800.

719.12–13   appointing your son . . . commissioner] William Cranch (see List of Correspondents), son of Mary and Richard Cranch, was one of John's "midnight judges," appointed to the District of Columbia Circuit Court, where he served until his death.

719.30–31   venerable uncle.] Sarah Whiting Pope (1734–1800), Norton Quincy's housekeeper, had just died. See Family Tree.

720.11   Betsy Howard] A servant from Quincy brought by Abigail to Washington.

722.1   two candidates being equal] See note 715.35–716.1.

722.11–12   baseless fabrick of a vision] Cf. *The Tempest*, IV.i.151.

722.21   the Essex Junto] See note 698.25.

722.21   a pamphlet written by Hamilton] See note 705.5.

723.20–23   mr Wolcot . . . mr Dexter] Oliver Wolcott Jr., the outgoing secretary of the treasury. For Samuel Dexter, see note 687.3.

723.22–23   mr Griswold] Roger Griswold (1762–1812), a Federalist lawyer and member of the House of Representatives from Connecticut, 1795–1805, declined John's request to serve as secretary of war. Instead, Jefferson appointed Henry Dearborn (1751–1829), a colonel on Washington's staff during the Revolution and a former member of the House from Massachusetts.

724.22   our future Ruler] See note 715.35–716.1.

725.1–4   A Sceptre, . . . up.] *King John* III.iv.135–38.

726.18   the convention] See note 711.26–27.

726.23   mr Breck] Samuel Breck (1771–1862), a Philadelphia merchant and later member of the House of Representatives from Pennsylvania, 1823–25.

726.31   Secretary otis] Samuel Allyne Otis; see note 468.6.

726.31–32   mr Bingham] William Bingham (1752–1804), senator from Pennsylvania.

726.35   mr Wolcott] Oliver Wolcott Jr. See note 723.20.

727.11   the list of judges.] The "midnight judges"; see Chronology for 1801.

RETIREMENT, 1801–1818

731.28–29   B Russel puffing up the Composition] The March 21 edition of the Boston *Columbian Centinel*, Benjamin Russell's Federalist newspaper, included a column praising Jefferson's inaugural address for its moderation and "for inculcating all those admirable principles and maxims which we have endeavoured to uphold and enforce."

731.30–31   I read a coppy of a Letter] Probably referring to a September 4, 1800, letter from Jefferson to John Vanmeter of Virginia, which was subsequently published in newspapers throughout the country. In the letter Jefferson professed his usual passive disinterest in the coming election and argued that "a preponderance of the executive over the legislative branch cannot be maintained but by immense patronage, by multiplying offices, making them very lucrative, by armies, navies, &c which may enlist on the side of the patron all those whom he can interest, & all their families & connections. but these expences must be paid by the laboring citizen. he cannot long continue therefore the advocate of opinions, which, to say only the least of them, doom the labouring citizen to toil & sweat for useless pageants."

732.1   franking] The debate over franking privileges for former presidents.

732.11   Tell it not in Gath—] 2 Samuel 1:20.

732.34   your journey into Silicia.] In 1800 John Quincy and Louisa Catherine took a two-month tour of Silesia that he described in a series of letters to Thomas Boylston. Impressed by the depth of description as well as the literary value of the letters, Thomas arranged for their publication in the Philadelphia *Port Folio*, a literary magazine published by Joseph Dennie and Asbury Dickens.

733.34–37   "A Sceptre, . . . up."] *King John*, III.iv.135–38.

733.38   Callender the infamous] James T. Callender (1758–1803), journalist prosecuted in 1800 by the Adams administration under the Sedition Act for his pamphlet *The Prospect Before Us*, which alleged political corruption among the Federalists.

734.2   Lyon] Matthew Lyon; see note 596.12–13. Lyon was jailed in 1798 for four months under the Sedition Act for criticizing the Quasi-War with France.

734.3   Stephen Thomson Mason] See note 535.34.

734.3   Gallatin is appointed] See note 618.5–6.

734.10   Lincoln] Levi Lincoln Sr. (1749–1820), the new attorney general.

734.20 "Alas poor . . . thyself."] *Macbeth*, IV.iii.166–67.

734.26 "But the rarer . . . vengance] *The Tempest*, V.i.28–29.

734.27 And I hold . . . world."] *The Merchant of Venice*, I.i.79.

734.28–29 An Habitation . . . vulgur Heart."] *2 Henry IV*, I.iii.696–97.

735.2–3 do justly, . . . Humbly.] Cf. Micah 6:8.

735.11 Jarvis, Austin] For Charles Jarvis, see note 525.8–9. Benjamin Austin (1752–1820), a Boston merchant who served in the Massachusetts senate and wrote newspaper articles critical of John during the Adams presidency; see also note 406.15–16.

735.14 Clinton] George Clinton; see note 689.8.

735.27–28 Hath not . . . pomp?] *As You Like It*, II.i.2–3.

738.26–27 verily we . . . for nought.] Cf. Isaiah 49:4.

738.30–31 touch not . . . no harm] Cf. Psalm 105:15.

739.3–4 like the fox in the fable . . . grapes were sour] One of Aesop's fables; the fox tries to eat grapes but cannot reach them, so rather than accept defeat, it declares that they must be sour.

739.13 mrs otis—] Abigail's cousin Mary Smith Gray Otis. See Family Tree.

740.36 14 volms of Le Harps] Jean-François de La Harpe, *Lycée; ou, Cours de littérature ancienne et moderne* (1799), a series of lectures on literature.

740.37 the Studies of nature by [   ]] Jacques-Henri Bernardin de Saint-Pierre, *Études de la nature* (1784).

743.32–33 "What sin unknown dipt you in Ink?"] Pope, "Epistle to Dr. Arbuthnot," ll. 125–26.

743.35 the intercepted Letter] See note 67.22.

745.25 the House . . . lately faild] See Chronology for 1803.

746.25–26 to know . . . suffer want] Cf. Philippians 4:12.

747.28–29 Mr. King, Gore] Rufus King; see note 603.19. Christopher Gore; see note 681.38.

748.5–6 the Reviewer of Camillus?] William Duane's 1803 pamphlet *The Mississippi Question Fairly Stated*, consisting of seven letters about the Louisiana Purchase and navigation of the Mississippi, published under the name Camillus, was reviewed in *The Port Folio* by Thomas Boylston in April.

748.22–23 the departed remains, of your . . . daughter] Mary "Polly" Jefferson Eppes, who had stayed with the Adamses in London as a child, died on April 17, 1804.

750.10–12 at the time these appointments . . . upon you] Abigail is mistaken; Jefferson was elected president on February 17, 1801, and John made these appointments in the beginning of March.

750.27–28 The two Gentlemen . . . secretaries] Benjamin Stoddart, secretary of the navy, was appointed in 1798, and Samuel Dexter, secretary of war, was appointed in 1800. Dexter was appointed secretary of the treasury in 1801.

751.19–20 first acts . . . liberate a wretch] James Thomson Callender; see note 733.38. Jefferson pardoned him in 1801 after Callender had served his sentence.

751.38 your reward of 50 dollars] After his pardon, Callender sought an appointment as postmaster of Richmond, which Jefferson denied. Callender in turn threatened to blackmail Jefferson, and Jefferson sent him $50 through an intermediary.

752.7–8 The serpent . . . nourished him] Making good on his blackmail threats, Callender publicly exposed for the first time Jefferson's long-term sexual relationship with his slave Sally Hemings in a series of articles published in Richmond in the fall of 1802.

752.21 Faithfull are the wounds of a Friend.] Proverbs 27:6.

752.35–753.1 your motives . . . explaind by you] In his letter to Abigail of July 22, 1804, Jefferson wrote: "My charities to Callendar are considered as rewards for his calumnies. . . . I was told in Philadelphia that Callendar, the author of the Political progress of Britain, was in that city, a fugitive from persecution for having written that book, and in distress. I had read and approved the book: I considered him as a man of genius, unjustly persecuted. I knew nothing of his private character. . . . My charities to him were no more meant as encouragements to his scurrilities than those I give to the beggar at my door are meant as rewards for the vices of his life."

753.9 If a Chief Majestrate can by his will annul a Law] Jefferson had written, "I discharged every person under punishment or prosecution under the Sedition law, because I considered and now consider that law to be a nullity as absolute and as palpable as if Congress had ordered us to fall down and worship a golden image."

753.20 as in a late instance] Hamilton and Burr's duel on July 11, 1804, in which Hamilton was killed.

754.18–19 you removed him.] Shortly after Jefferson took office his allies in Congress had repealed the Judiciary Act of 1801, reducing the size of some federal courts and giving the president power to dismiss judges. John Quincy, recently appointed district judge in Massachusetts, lost his position.

755.23–24 that, which respected my son . . . unfounded] In his letter of September 11, Jefferson wrote: "The act of personal unkindness . . . is said in your last to have been the removal of your eldest son from some office . . .

he must have been a Commissioner of bankruptcy, but I declare to you on my honor that this is the first knolege I have ever had that he was so."

755.26 Judge Daws] Thomas Dawes (1731–1809), associate justice of the Massachusetts Supreme Court.

757.1–6 Quincy Nov. 19. . . . J. ADAMS] This note in John's hand appears at the end of the Adamses' letter book copy.

758.10–11 mr. Parsons] Theophilus Parsons (1750–1813), a lawyer and member of the Essex Junto (see note 698.25) who was later the chief justice of the Massachusetts Supreme Court. John Quincy had read law under Parsons; see note 480.32.

759.37 what Lord Chatham calls, Benevolence in trifles.] I.e., politeness. William Pitt the Elder, Earl of Chatham, *Letters Written by the Late Earl of Chatham* (1804).

760.24 Judge Chase] Samuel Chase; see note 703.12. In May 1803, Chase had denounced the repeal of the Judiciary Act of 1801, by which many Federalist judges had lost their appointments (including John Quincy; see note 754.18–19). Jefferson wrote to Congressman Joseph Hopper Nicholson, asking, "Ought the seditious and official attack . . . to go unpunished?" The House of Representatives served Chase with eight articles of impeachment in late 1804 focusing on his conduct on the trials of John Fries (see note 681.15) and James Callender (see note 733.38), charging him with political bias. Chase was acquitted of all charges by the Senate on March 1, 1805.

762.8 fullfill his engagements.] American portraitist Gilbert Stuart's (1755–1828) dilatory habits were notorious. In 1798, the Massachusetts legislature commissioned John's portrait to be hung in the House of Representatives in Boston, and in 1800, Abigail paid $100 for her own portrait. Despite frequent prodding from Adams family members, neither portrait was completed and delivered to John until 1816. Both portraits remained for several generations in the hands of Adams descendants until 1954, when they were presented to the National Gallery of Art in Washington, D.C.

762.9–10 my Juno.] Her dog.

764.7 Miranda] Francisco Miranda (1750–1816), a Spanish revolutionary whose attempt to liberate Venezuela involved Abigail's grandson William Steuben Smith, who was captured and imprisoned. Infuriated with William Stephens Smith, who had gotten his son involved, John refused to intercede to rescue William.

765.28–29 And still to make . . . amend.] Thomas Moore, "Fable II: The Panther, the Horse, and Other Beasts" (1787), ll. 11–12.

768.2 the appointment will do honour to mr Jefferson] Jefferson had appointed Abigail's nephew William Cranch chief justice of the D.C. Circuit

Court. Cranch had been one of John's last appointments as district judge in Washington, D.C.

768.9–10   Buisness . . . Miranda has engaged?] See note 764.7.

768.33–34   If you can accomplish a shield for the president] Jefferson's party split in March 1806 over resolutions to limit or ban British imports in retaliation for British plunder of American merchant ships.

769.15–21   "A good Coat . . . shewy outside—"] British dramatist Frederic Reynolds, *Speculation* (1795), III.i.

770.1   Mr Randolph] John Randolph of Roanoke (1773–1833), member of the House from Virginia, who broke with Jefferson in 1803 and led the "Tertium quid" faction, which advocated for restricting the federal government.

770.8   We Suppose mr Madison, Munroe, perhaps Giles.] Madison and Monroe were indeed presidential candidates for the Democratic-Republican Party in the 1808 election; William Branch Giles (see note 527.23) was not.

770.11   if Govr. Strong is reelected] Caleb Strong; see note 681.19. He was not reelected in 1807, but came out of retirement in 1812 and served as governor until 1816.

770.13–14   The death of mr Pitt, . . . British Cabinet] William Pitt the Younger, prime minister of Great Britain, died in office in January 1806. The new prime minister was William Grenville, 1st Baron Grenville, who inaugurated the short-lived "Ministry of All the Talents," which failed to bring peace with France, but did accomplish the abolition of the slave trade.

771.19–20   If plagues and Earthquakes, . . . Napoline?] Cf. Pope, *An Essay on Man*, Epistle I, ll. 155–56.

771.38   Mrs Ratcliffs castle of udolphus?] *The Mysteries of Udolpho*, by Ann Radcliffe, published in 1794, is often cited as the archetypal Gothic novel.

772.7   her Son] William Steuben Smith, who had followed Miranda to South America. See note 764.7.

774.6   "or who could suffer Being here below"?] Pope, *An Essay on Man*, Epistle I, l. 80.

776.10   mr & mrs Vose] For John Vose, see note 678.20.

777.33   mrs St Hillier] Margaret Smith St. Hilaire, William Stephens Smith's sister; see note 543.20–21.

779.26   William Smith] Her grandson, William Steuben Smith.

780.21   the Wild Irish Girl.] *The Wild Irish Girl; a National Tale* (1806) by Irish novelist Sydney Owenson (c. 1781–1859), who became Lady Morgan in 1812 upon her marriage to Sir Thomas Charles Morgan.

782.30–31   elected Mr. Loyed a Senator . . . your Brother.] John Quincy had served in the U.S. Senate as a Federalist since March 1803. However, when he broke ranks to vote with Republicans on several issues, including support for the Louisiana Purchase and the Embargo Act, he was publicly repudiated by Massachusetts Federalists in the state legislature and resigned his office. He was replaced by James Lloyd (1769–1831), who had been a Massachusetts state senator.

782.34   an Essex Man] See note 698.25.

783.39–40   Plutarch observes . . . Submission.] Plutarch's *Life of Coriolanus*.

785.1   an infidel president] Jefferson.

785.21–22   Genll. Warren] James Warren, husband of Mercy Otis Warren, died on November 28, 1808.

785.25–26   the injustice she had done] Mercy Otis Warren had published in 1805 a three-volume *History of the Rise, Progress and Termination of the American Revolution*. In the work she accused John of having been corrupted by his residence in England and of having forgotten the principles of the Revolution. Adams was infuriated, and in a month's time he fired off ten long, angry, and bitter letters to his former friend, after which their relationship was terminated.

786.5   Mil] Possibly short for "milady."

787.3–4   "What blessings . . . cast away."] Pope, "The Universal Prayer" (1738), ll. 17–18.

787.16   the abuse of the federal party.] John published two different series in the Boston *Patriot* in 1809. The first series was a continuation of his memoir, what is now considered Part II of his *Autobiography*. He also published a series on the impressment of American seamen, later collected in a pamphlet: *The Inadmissable Principles, of the King of England's Proclamation of October 16, 1807—Considered* (1809).

787.25–26   we did not dine with him] Abigail is mistaken that she did not dine at the home of the Baron de Staël. In a letter written from Auteuil to her niece, Elizabeth Cranch, on May 12, 1785, she described dining at his grand palace on "furnishings" that were "burnished and shone with Royal Splendor."

788.16–17   revile . . . sake.] Cf. Matthew 5:11.

788.27   St Anthony] St. Anthony's (Fire) is an obsolete name for what was either *Herpes zoster*, also known as shingles, a viral disease characterized by a painful skin rash, or erysipelas, an acute infection and skin rash.

788.30   tutular saint] Saint Anthony of Padua (1195–1231).

789.8   "ossian says Age is dark and unlovely"] Cf. "Carthon" (1762) by Scottish poet James Macpherson, which he claimed was a translation from an ancient Gaelic poet called Ossian.

789.10   painter Zerweis] Zeuxis, a fifth-century B.C.E. Greek painter, is supposed to have died laughing at a portrait he painted of Aphrodite, for which the old woman who commissioned it insisting on modeling.

789.17   "The man . . . an hour"] Young, *Night Thoughts*, Night II, ll. 96–97.

789.21–22   it is said, . . . Eat them] Cf. Ecclesiastes 5:11.

789.33   "Time was given for use, not waste."] Young, *Night Thoughts*, Night II, l. 153.

790.4–7   "Life's cares . . . rack of rest;"] Ibid, Night II, ll. 160–63.

790.12–13   Letters from the mountains?] *Letters from the Mountains; Being the Real Correspondence of a Lady, Between the Years 1773 and 1807* (1809) by Scottish author and poet Anne Grant, about her travels through the highlands of Scotland.

790.24–25   of such . . . heaven.] Cf. Matthew 19:14.

790.30   the Boston Patriot] Semiweekly newspaper founded in 1809 and published until 1812 that supported the Democratic-Republican Party.

790.32   a series of Letters] By John. His series of autobiographical letters continued until May 1812.

790.37–39   mr Ames . . . the dangers of American Liberty.] *The Dangers of American Liberty* (1809) by Fisher Ames (1758–1808), a former Federalist U.S. representative from Massachusetts. It was reviewed critically in the *Boston Patriot* by John Quincy.

791.12   St. Anthony] See note 788.27.

791.28–29   transmit them to Caroline.] Caroline did inherit both her mother's and her grandmother's letters, and published a number of them as *The Journal and Correspondence of Miss Adams, Daughter of John Adams* (1841). Most of the manuscripts were lost in a fire at her home in upstate New York in 1862.

792.1–2   the editor of the Albany Register?] Solomon Southwick (1773–1839). The Republican newspaper was founded in 1788 to oppose the ratification of the Constitution.

792.8–9   your father's letter . . . proclamation] *The Inadmissable Principles of the King of England's Proclamation, considered* (April 1809). On October 16, 1807, George III issued a royal proclamation that recalled all British seamen from foreign service and ordered naval officers to impress any British subjects they found aboard neutral merchant ships. John's essay asserted that the proclamation "furnished a sufficient ground for a *declaration of war.*"

792.12–13   Col. Pickering's letter, . . . replied] Jefferson's Embargo Act, signed into law on December 22, 1807, made illegal all American outbound traffic, in an attempt to force Great Britain and France to end seizure of

American ships and impressment of American seamen. It was opposed by
Timothy Pickering, one of the senators from Massachusetts, in a public letter
addressed to Governor James Sullivan in 1808. John Quincy, the other senator
from Massachusetts, answered Pickering's letter in a public letter to Harrison
Gray Otis in defense of the Embargo Act. The Massachusetts legislature responded by electing his successor six months early, and John Quincy resigned
his Senate seat; see also note 782.30–31.

792.18   No one can accuse Mr. Madison] Madison replaced Jefferson as president on March 4, 1809, and in April attempted to get Britain to withdraw the
Orders in Council of 1807, wartime regulations restricting the trade of neutral
nations with France and its allies; his efforts, however, were rejected by British
foreign secretary George Canning (1770–1827).

792.24   the new minister] The British minister to the United States, David
Erskine, 2nd Baron Erskine (1776–1855), had offered the withdrawal of the
Orders in Council, and was therefore recalled by Foreign Secretary Canning.
He was replaced by Francis James Jackson (1770–1814), who was known to be
less willing to negotiate peace.

793.3–5   do him good . . . her.] Cf. Proverbs 31:11–12.

793.28–29   this embassy to Russia] Madison appointed John Quincy to be minister plenipotentiary to Russia. He departed in August with Louisa Catherine and
their youngest son, Charles Francis. The two older boys remained in Quincy.

794.14   "envy will merit, as its shade pursue"] Pope, *An Essay on Criticism*
(1711), l. 466.

796.17–21   a History . . . Character you have delineated] Mercy Otis Warren's three-volume *History of the Rise, Progress and Termination of the American Revolution* (1805); see note 785.25–26.

796.24–25   when those Errors were pointed out] See Chronology for 1807
and note 785.25–26.

798.9   Senator Loyed has married Miss Hannah Breck] James Lloyd, who
had replaced John Quincy in the Senate. John Quincy was a friend of Hannah
Breck's brother, Samuel Breck Jr. (1771–1862).

798.12   "It is best repenting in a Coach and six."] Epilogue to Addison's
Cato, l. 18, by Sir Samuel Garth (1661–1719), an English physician and poet.

799.14   Porters Schetches] Robert Ker Porter (1777–1842), an English artist,
author, diplomat, and traveler known for his account of traveling in Russia and
Sweden, *Travelling sketches in Russia and Sweden during the years 1805, 1806,
1807, 1808* (1809).

801.9–13   "you can judge . . . expression."] John Quincy's salary as American minister to the court of Russia proved inadequate to support his diplomatic and social functions as well as providing for his family's needs. Most

diplomats came with private fortunes that allowed them to live lavishly and entertain extravagantly.

803.1 My old Friend judge Cushing] See note 718.6.

803.8 mrs. Cushing] Hannah Phillips Cushing. See List of Correspondents.

803.10 a successor] To Cushing's seat on the Supreme Court.

803.11 mr parsons and Dexter] Theophilus Parsons, see note 758.10–11; and Samuel Dexter, see note 644.34.

803.12 mr Story] Joseph Story (1779–1845), a lawyer from Massachusetts, was nominated by Madison to succeed Cushing in November 1811 and was confirmed a few days later.

804.1–2 Harriot Welch] Harriet Welsh. See List of Correspondents.

805.10–11 "My dyeing . . . cloud"] Cf. Young, *Night Thoughts*, Night III, l. 277.

805.17 The death of Mrs Norten] Elizabeth Cranch Norton, Abigail's niece, died, leaving eight children. See also List of Correspondents.

805.24 trained them . . . should go.] Cf. Proverbs 22:6.

805.25–27 "what tho' short . . . great end"] Young, *Night Thoughts*, Night V, ll. 771–73.

805.34–35 Apostle . . . misirable.] Cf. 1 Corinthians 15:19.

805.36–806.2 Religion! Providence! . . . idle whirl"] Young, *Night Thoughts*, Night IV, ll. 557–62.

806.5 "whom from all . . . fate"] Cf. Pope, *Essay on Man*, Epistle I, l. 77.

807.1–2 William Philips, with mr Gore.] William Phillips Jr. (1750–1827) was elected as lieutenant governor of Massachusetts in 1812 and served until 1823. For Christopher Gore, see note 681.38.

807.3 Mr Gerry and mr Gray] Elbridge Gerry (see List of Correspondents) and William Gray (1750–1825) were the outgoing governor and lieutenant governor of Massachusetts, respectively.

807.16–17 the Septennial Act] The Septennial Act 1716 increased the maximum length of a parliament from three to seven years.

807.17–26 "he observed that . . . individual Comfort"] Sir William Wyndham's speech in the House of Commons, March 13, 1734.

808.13–14 Lincoln when appointed . . . for you.] Levi Lincoln Sr. (see note 734.10) declined the position of associate justice on the Supreme Court because of his poor eyesight.

808.14–15 Alexander Wolcot] Alexander Wolcott (1758–1828), a customs inspector nominated by Madison in February 1811 to fill Cushing's seat on the Supreme Court but not confirmed, partly because as customs inspector he had enforced the unpopular Embargo Act, and partly for his lack of judicial experience.

808.17–18 a Letter . . . account] See pages 800–802 in this volume.

809.24–28 "Eternal power! . . . praise."] From English poet Robert Bloomfield, "Winter," in *The Farmer's Boy* (1800).

809.31–33 "my days renew" . . . I drew."] Cf. Henry Brooke, "The Sparrow and the Dove," ll. 311–12.

810.2–3 "hears . . . cry."] Cf. Job 38:41.

810.22–23 "the wilderness . . . as the rose."] From British theologian Adam Clarke's commentary on the Bible (1811), in his notes to Numbers 11.

811.9 mrs Chapones] Hester Mulso Chapone, author of *Letters on the Improvement of the Mind, addressed to a Young Lady* (1773). The quotation comes from Letter XXII in *The Posthumous Works of Mrs. Chapone* (1807), edited by Samuel Richardson and Elizabeth Carter.

811.10 Mrs Carter] Elizabeth Carter (1717–1806), an English poet, translator, and member of the Blue Stockings Society.

811.24–25 "The little knowledge . . . draind"] John Gay, "The Shepherd and the Philosopher," ll. 33–34.

811.35 Thompson] Scottish poet James Thomson; see note 20.31–32.

812.3 Mrs More] Hannah More; see note 278.29–35.

812.16 the Character of Sir Charles] In Richardson's *The History of Sir Charles Grandison* (1753), the title character is portrayed as an ideal man, both masculine and virtuous.

813.2 he who hears . . . cry] Cf. Job 38:41.

813.35–814.2 "The Rule . . . Law"] From Lecture XIII, "Judicial Oratory," in John Quincy's *Lectures on Rhetoric and Oratory* (1810).

814.30–31 Mr Gore] See note 681.38.

814.36 the Bed of Procrustus] In Greek mythology, Procrustes had an iron bed and invited every passerby to spend the night. If they did not fit, he used his smith's hammer to either stretch or amputate them to fit.

815.10 associate judge . . . Court] After recalling John Quincy, Madison appointed him to the U.S. Supreme Court, an office that John Quincy declined as he and Louisa Catherine, who was pregnant, had decided to remain in Russia.

816.2–6 Mr Lincoln . . . Alexander Wolcot] See notes 808.13–14 and 808.14–15.

816.6 Joel Barlow] Poet, author of the *Columbiad* (1807), and in 1811 minister plenipotentiary to France, charged with negotiating a commercial treaty with Napoleon.

816.22–23 bury his tallents . . . Bushel] Cf. Luke 19:20 and Matthew 5:15.

816.26–28 "Be just . . . truths"] *Henry VIII,* III.ii.19–20.

818.19–20 what . . . you mentiond to me.] This is the first mention of Abigail 2nd's illness, later diagnosed as breast cancer.

818.20–21 Dr Welchs . . . dr Hollbrook] For Dr. Thomas Welsh Sr., see List of Correspondents. Dr. Amos Holbrook (1762–1842), a pioneer in smallpox innoculations.

819.14 discarded Secretary] Thomas Pickering; see note 687.8. He lost his Senate seat in 1811 to Joseph Bradley Varnum (see note 644.36–37).

819.27 Charges which are absolutely false.] In spring 1811, Pickering published a series of angry and slanderous "Letters to the People of the United States" in the *Boston Centinel.*

820.5 mr Murry] William Vans Murray; see note 660.18.

820.6–7 "more wise and more Righteous"] Quoting from Pickering's fifth *Letter to the People of the United States,* which attacked John.

820.21 one of whom; the Secretary] Robert Smith (1757–1842), secretary of the navy, 1801–9 and secretary of state, 1809–11.

820.24–25 mr S Smith] Samuel Smith (1752–1839), brother of Robert Smith, and a member of the House from Maryland, 1793–1803, and senator, 1803–15 and 1822–33.

821.18 century Sermon] Celebrating the one hundredth anniversary of the incorporation town of Braintree in 1740.

822.25 leaves of the Sibyls] The priestess of Apollo's oracle at Cumae, called a sibyl, from the ancient Greek word for prophetess, would prophesy by writing on oak leaves and arranging them at the entrance to her cave. If the leaves were scattered by the wind, she would not help to reassemble the prophecy.

823.15 Your Brother] Thomas Baker Johnson; see List of Correspondents.

823.21 three Daughters left by mrs Norten] See note 805.17.

823.27–28 a Catarrhous fever] Inflammation of mucous membranes in the head.

823.39 dr Welch, and Holbrook] Dr. Thomas Welsh Sr.; see List of Correspondents. For Dr. Amos Holbrook, see note 818.20–21.

824.9–10 Goodness . . . followed me.] Cf. Psalm 23:6.

824.13 Judge Dana] Francis Dana, whom fourteen-year-old John Quincy had accompanied to Russia in 1803, died on April 25, 1811.

824.21   Mr Emerson] Reverend William Emerson (1769–1811), pastor of Boston's First Church and father of Ralph Waldo Emerson, died on May 12.

825.25   mrs Ratcliff] Anne Radcliffe, English author of Gothic novels.

827.7   Bennets Letters] See note 524.11.

829.12   Hemlock pills] Hemlock, a poison, was believed to help cure cancerous ulcers.

830.23   Mr Smith] Robert Smith; see note 820.21. Madison had just forced Smith to resign as secretary of state, citing a long list of issues including disloyalty, indiscretion, and opposing the administration's negotiations with Britain and France. Smith responded by publishing *Robert Smith's Address to the People of the United States* (1811), an attack on Madison's foreign policy.

830.23–24   "will fret, . . . Stages"] Cf. *Macbeth*, V.v.25.

830.27–28   "peacebly . . . if they must"] Abigail quotes Henry Clay (1777–1852), senator from Kentucky, who himself was misquoting Josiah Quincy III's threat of secession of some of the states ("it will be the duty of some, to prepare definitely for a separation, amicably if they can, violently if they must") if Louisiana was admitted to the Union as a state in 1811.

830.28   Nonintercourse] In the last days of Jefferson's presidency, Congress replaced the Embargo Act of 1807 with the Non-Intercourse Act of 1809, which reinstated shipping except to ships bound for British or French ports.

830.35–831.1   rival Candidate] John Quincy.

831.23   the Success of mr Pope.] Senator John Pope (1770–1845), who was married to Louisa Catherine's sister Eliza, became president pro tempore of the Senate on February 23, 1811.

832.15   the New Mission—] By the summer of 1811 President Madison and Secretary of State Monroe had come to believe that war would prove necessary in the absence of substantial concessions from Great Britain by year's end. The new British minister, Augustus John Foster (who replaced Francis James Jackson; see note 792.24), arrived in Washington on July 2, and he and Monroe entered into a series of discussions in which the secretary of state demanded the repeal of the Orders in Council (see note 792.18) and an end to impressment, while the British envoy called for repeal of the Non-Importation Act, which he held was discriminatory because it applied only to trade with Britain and not France. Ultimately Abigail's pessimism would prove warranted: though the talks continued throughout the autumn, they were unsuccessful and by the time the British government finally decided to repeal the Orders in Council in June 1812, the United States had already declared war.

832.26   mrs Guild] Elizabeth Quincy Guild (1757–1825), married to Benjamin Guild (see note 175.13). See also note 99.26.

833.1   hemlock pills] See note 829.12.

833.8   your preposition to remove near to me] The Adamses' motives for turning down William Stephens Smith's offer to move near them are obscure. Abigail mentions that New York prospers while Massachusetts declines. Another possibility is that John was exasperated with Smith's improvidence.

833.16–17   wither thou goest, . . . abide—] Cf. Ruth 1:16.

834.12   Mrs S Adams] Sally Adams.

835.2–3   an Event She has so often experienced.] I.e., a miscarriage.

835.39   Hectic] The eighteenth- and nineteenth-century term for a fever that is accompanied by sweating and chills.

836.11   William Smith] Abigail's nephew; see Family Tree.

836.14   Dr Ewell and his wife] Dr. Thomas Ewell, a surgeon for the U.S. Navy, and his wife Elizabeth Stoddert Ewell, daughter of Benjamin Stoddert, the first U.S. secretary of the navy, and his wife Rebecca Lowndes Stoddert.

836.24   "with Eyes by reading almost blind"] From Jonathan Swift, "Cadenus and Vanessa" (1712).

838.23–24   "but an animated form . . . within."] English poet Mark Akenside (1721–1770), "A Song" (1763).

839.5–6   they fret . . . Stage"] Cf. *Macbeth*, V.v.25.

839.28–29   submit to an operation.] Abigail 2nd wrote to Benjamin Rush on September 12, 1811, describing her condition and asking, "if in the course of your researches you should have discovered any thing that you find of use in this state of it, you would confer a great obligation upon me by communicating it." Rush's response was written to John and recommended immediate surgery: "From her account of the *Moving* state of the tumor it is now in a proper Situation for the Operation. Should She wait 'till it suppurates, or even inflames much, it may be too late."

841.7   the Spirits . . . made perfect] Cf. Hebrews 12:23.

841.17–18   "The thought of death . . . ruffled breast"] Young, *Night Thoughts*, Night III, ll. 303–4, 307.

843.13–14   the dreaded opperation] On October 8, a radical mastectomy without anesthesia was performed on Abigail 2nd in the Adams home. Although neither Abigail 2nd nor her mother described the operation in their letters, Fanny Burney, the English novelist, had a similar operation on September 30, 1811. She was given a wine cordial and laid on a bed. The knife was inserted, "describing a curve—cutting against the grain, if I may say so, while the flesh resisted . . . against the breast bone—scraping it!" Burney describes screaming through the whole operation, which lasted twenty minutes, and losing consciousness several times. Both Burney and Abigail 2nd lost the use of their right arms after the operation.

844.8–9   "Tis a prime part . . . our Lot"] Young, *Night Thoughts*, Night IX, ll. 414–15.

846.1   Mr Adams] Thomas Boylston.

846.11   Ledwater] Leadwater, a solution of water and lead acetate.

846.29–30   "The Souls dark . . . made"] English poet Edmund Waller, "Of the Last Verses in the Book" (1686), ll. 13–14.

847.25   "The Righteous . . . Remembrance"] Psalm 112:6.

847.30   "String, after String is Sever'd from the Heart"] Thomson, "Elegy on the Death of Mr. Aikman the Painter," l. 2.

849.6–7   "The winter . . . the Sun"] Young, *Night Thoughts*, Night IX, ll. 484–85.

850.25   mr Harris] Levett Harris (c. 1780–1839), a Quaker from Philadelphia, had been appointed American consul at St. Petersburg by Jefferson in 1803.

850.29–30   Saxon . . . westphalia] Constituents of the Holy Roman Empire until 1806 and 1807, respectively, when Napoleon defeated Holy Roman Emperor Francis II and then Frederick William III of Prussia and made Saxony and Westphalia French vassal states.

851.33   the Scourge] *The Scourge: or, Monthly expositor of imposture and folly*, an English satirical journal printed from 1811 to 1816.

854.10   govr Harrison.] On November 7, 1811, William Henry Harrison (1773–1841), governor of the Indiana Territory, having marched a small army into Shawnee country as a show of force, sustained heavy casualties in the battle of Tippecanoe but drove off the attacking Indians. The next day he burned Prophet's Town, the center of an emerging Indian confederacy, and the food supplies there. This marked the beginning of an Indian war in the Old Northwest that would blend into the War of 1812.

854.11   shawanoe Prophet] Tenskwatawa (1771–1836), called "the Prophet," who established Prophet's Town with his brother Tecumseh (1768–1813), the leader of the Shawnee.

854.22   remove Govr Gerry] Elbridge Gerry was defeated for reelection due to the buildup to the War of 1812 as well as a redistricting controversy that is the origin of the word "gerrymandering." See also List of Correspondents.

854.25   Govenour Strong] See notes 681.19 and 770.12.

855.6   Mr. Storey is appointed Judge] See note 803.12.

856.29   Pheby] See note 269.28.

857.26   Mr Barlow] Joel Barlow; see note 816.6.

858.15 the loss of her Mother—] Margaret Stephens Smith (1739–1812), mother of William Stephens Smith, Nancy Smith, and Sally Smith Adams.

859.9 Cartel.] A safe ship, used for humanitarian purposes.

859.17 Hingham academy] Probably the Derby Academy, founded in 1784, which is still in operation.

860.33–35 the desolation of . . . Moscow.] Napoleon had reached Moscow on September 14, 1812, in his bloody invasion of Russia, finding the city mostly deserted and many buildings destroyed by the departing Russians.

860.36–38 Charles the 12 of Sweden . . . the Great Peter.] In the early eighteenth century, Charles XII of Sweden was turned back in his effort to invade Russia, lastly under the leadership of Peter the Great.

861.1 plagues . . . heavens designs"] Cf. Pope, *Essay on Man*, Epistle I, l. 155.

861.24–25 "whose days . . . Shortest Span"] Anonymous, "The Beggar" (1769), l. 3.

862.18–20 forty years . . . upon the occasion.] A rare reference to the death of Abigail's one-year-old daughter, Susanna, on February 4, 1770.

863.18–19 col Smith is chosen a Member of Congress] William Stephens Smith was elected as a member of the House of Representatives from New York and served until 1815.

864.20–21 Captain Hull . . . Guerriere] On August 19, 1812, as a continuation of an earlier exchange between the USS *Spitfire* and HMS *Little Belt* that ended in the capture of *Little Belt* with heavy casualties, HMS *Guerriere* (49 guns) opened fire on the USS *Constitution* (55), commanded by Commodore Isaac Hull (1773–1843). After the *Guerriere*'s mizzenmast was damaged, the battle ended with a British surrender.

864.22–24 Capt Jones . . . a 74.] Master Commandant Jacob Jones (1768–1850) commanded the USS *Wasp* (18 guns) and on October 18, 1812, captured HMS *Frolic* (22), despite having lost a jib boom in a storm two days earlier. Both ships were heavily damaged and immediately captured by HMS *Poictiers* (74 guns).

864.24–26 Commodore Decatur . . . Macedonian] Captain Stephen Decatur (1779–1820) and the USS *United States* (56 guns) captured HMS *Macedonian* (49) on October 25, 1812.

864.27–33 Commodore Bainbridge . . . wounds he received.] Commodore William Bainbridge (1774–1833) succeeded Captain Hull in commanding the USS *Constitution* (now 54 guns). On December 29, 1812, he encountered HMS *Java* (49) off the coast of Brazil and quickly sank the ship, which had a very inexperienced crew. Captain Henry Lambert of the *Java* died of his wounds on January 4, 1813.

865.11   I could tell you a tale] The War of 1812 had been a partisan affair from the start, and throughout its course Federalists in Congress had maintained an extraordinary level of cohesion born of the shared conviction that the war had been launched for cynical political purposes by the Democratic-Republicans. "I regard the war, as a war of party, & not of the Country," one leading party member had said in 1812. Though Federalists everywhere were opposed to the war, only in New England were they able to use the machinery of state and local government to obstruct the war effort, by refusing to raise funds and by resisting demands to mobilize militia. Massachusetts governor Caleb Strong was especially defiant in this regard. Madison decried this "seditious opposition," which has "so clogged the wheels of war, that I fear the campaign will not accomplish the object of it."

865.15   waters of Lethe] One of the five rivers of Hades, associated with oblivion.

866.3–4   mr Gallatin and Bayard . . . Peace] The appointment of a peace commission had been under consideration for many months. In January 1813, Madison named his negotiators: John Quincy would head the mission, and also appointed were Albert Gallatin (see note 618.5–6); James A. Bayard (see note 921.2); Henry Clay (see note 830.27–28); and Jonathan Russell (1771–1832), the chargé d'affaires in Paris. They and the British negotiators settled on the neutral city of Ghent in Belgium to meet.

866.23–24   Simeon, . . . Salvation."] Cf. Luke 2:25–35.

867.11–12   the col. went to Congress] See note 863.18–19.

867.24   Hull, Jones, Decature, Bainbridge, and Lawrence] See notes 864.20–21, 864.22–24, 864.24–26, and 864.27–33. Captain James Lawrence (1781–1813) commanded the USS *Chesapeake*, which was captured by HMS *Shannon* on June 1, 1813. Lawrence, who was fatally wounded in the attack, was immortalized for his last command: "Don't give up the ship!"

869.5   whether Bonaparte . . . conqueror] After the disastrous defeat of his armies in Russia in 1812, Napoleon once more attempted to break the coalition of enemies in a German campaign during the spring of 1813.

869.7   conduct . . . State Government] See note 865.11.

869.11   proposer of Such a Resolution] See note 871.31–37.

870.1   Sir John Sherbrook] Sir John Coape Sherbrooke (1764–1830), commander of British forces in the Atlantic provinces and lieutenant governor of Nova Scotia.

870.15–16   mr Gallatin and Bayard] See note 866.3–4.

871.7–8   "Safe in the hand . . . Mortal honor"] Pope, *Essay on Man*, Epistle I, ll. 211–12.

871.9–13   says dr Preistly, . . . best manner—"] British theologian Joseph Priestley (see note 539.15–16), letter to Theophilus Lindsey, November 4, 1803.

871.14–15 "who finds not . . . denies."] Pope, *Essay on Man*, Epistle I, ll. 129–30.

871.17–18 "the first good . . . first fair"] Ibid, Epistle II, l. 24.

871.22–24 advice of Hercules . . . wheel] Cf. Aesop's fable "Hercules and the Wagoner," the origin of the proverb "God helps those that help themselves."

871.31–37 "Resolved as the Sense . . . Coast and Soil"!] A report written by Massachusetts senator Josiah Quincy III (see note 643.25), in response to a naval battle in which the USS *Hornet*, Captain James Lawrence (see note 867.24), sunk HMS *Peacock* on February 24, 1813.

872.30 the fate of the Chesepeake] See note 867.24.

873.16 "Partial Evil, is universal good"] Pope, *Essay on Man*, Epistle I, l. 216.

874.7–8 the Enemy had enterd the mouth of the Potomac—] Part of a British naval blockade of the Atlantic coast.

875.7 Indian meal] Cornmeal.

876.37 your Son . . . late unhappy voilenc] Mercy had written to Abigail describing "party violence" affecting her son Henry's appointment as tax collector in Plymouth.

879.13 1093 Hymn] Isaac Watts, hymn 1093: "While sinners, who presume to bear."

879.20 Mr Whitney] Reverend Peter Whitney. See note 568.27.

881.24–27 Heaven lifts . . . God.—] From "Epitaph on Mrs Mason" (1767) by English poet Thomas Gray, ll. 3–4.

883.4 Your kind and Friendly Letter] On August 22, 1813, Jefferson wrote to Abigail: "A kind note at the foot of Mr. Adams's letter of July 15. reminds me of the duty of saluting you with friendship and respect; a duty long suspended by the unremitting labors of public engagement, and which ought to have been sooner revived . . . I will now take time to ask you how you do, how you have done? and to express the interest I take in whatever affects your happiness."

883.27–28 "who in her youth, . . . admired"] George Crabbe, "Arabella," from *Tales* (1812), ll. 11–12.

883.32–34 "Greif has changed me . . . face"] *The Comedy of Errors*, V.i.299–301.

884.1 "Back wounding calumny"] *Measure for Measure*, III.ii.186.

884.18–19 "The little knowledge . . . drained."] John Gay, "The Shepherd and the Philosopher," ll. 33–34.

884.20 his opinion] On December 28, 1813, Van der Kemp wrote to John a

letter reminiscing about a visit he had made to the Adamses, in which he highly
praised Abigail's wit: "I hear with delight the chat of your female companions—
and listen to mrs Adams—as often She pleases to amuse or instruct her Society
— . . . your valuable librarÿ did fall Short to the conversation of mr. & mrs
Adams—How I regret, that I could not Stay—only a few weeks—What Subjects
would have been canvassed—in Politics in Theology and Philosophÿ—What
whims and paradoxes protruded—and defended with zeal: and what bickerings
might have ensued—and been maintained with warmth—till a Significant look
of your Ladÿ—or a well directed raillerÿ would have placed us both Hors de
combat . . . recommend me to Mrs Adams—assure Her of mÿ high and affectionate regard—and tell—that I ardently wished—that two young Ladies—now
my correspondents—could form herselves in her School—and Letter writting
would be celebrated as an exquisite ornament of a Ladÿ."

884.23–24   Madame de Staël]   Anne-Louise-Germaine de Staël-Holstein
(1766–1817), born Anne-Louise-Germaine Necker, daughter of Louis XVI's
minister of finance, Jacques Necker, married to Baron Erik Magnus Staël von
Holstein (1749–1802), the Swedish ambassador to France. She was famous as
a literary figure, political commentator, and for decades as host of a distinguished salon that attracted political and literary elite. Her arranged marriage
was unhappy and she eventually separated from her husband. An opponent of
Napoléon, he banned her from Paris in 1803.

884.33–34   Solomon . . . virtuous woman] Proverbs 31.

885.17–18   "there all the honor lies."] Pope, *Essay on Man*, Epistle IV, l. 194.

885.19   John Randolph's letter, and Mr. Lloyd's reply?] John Randolph of
Roanoke; see note 770.1. His letter to James Lloyd, a former state senator in
Massachusetts (see note 782.30–31), responded to radical Federalist cries for
secession, arguing that though a separation of states might someday occur, it
was not the right time.

885.34–35   Catastrophy . . . the City of Washington!!] On August 24, 1814,
British forces occupied Washington and set fire to many public buildings, including the Executive Mansion.

888.6   Genll. Moss and Cockburn] Major General Robert Ross (1766–1814)
led the destruction of Washington, D.C. as retaliation for American raids into
Canada. Admiral of the Fleet George Cockburn (1772–1853) served as Ross's
advisor.

888.7–8   forfeit of his Life, . . . Baltimore] Ross lost his life in the assault on
Baltimore in which the Americans repelled the British; his death led to a delay
that allowed the Americans to better prepare for the defense of the city.

888.9–10   Lake Champlain . . . Plattsburgh] The battle of Plattsburgh, September 6–11, 1814, also known as the battle of Lake Champlain, ended the invasion of the northern states by the British under the command of General Sir
George Prévost (1767–1816). The New York and Vermont militias, commanded

by Brigadier General Alexander Macomb (1782–1841), and ships commanded by Commandant Thomas Macdonough (1783–1825) halted the British assault.

888.16 mrs Rutger] Janet Marshall Rucker.

888.38 the Song I inclose] Possibly "The Star-Spangled Banner," composed by Francis Scott Key on September 14, 1814, during the assault on Baltimore and published as a broadside on September 17.

889.5–6 returnd to St Petersburgh—] John Quincy did not return to St. Petersburg but rather sent for his wife to join him in Paris. Louisa Catherine made a harrowing forty-day journey, accompanied by six-year-old Charles Francis, by coach across Europe.

890.34 Dr. Freeman] Nathaniel Freeman (1741–1827), a medical doctor from Massachusetts who was also a brigadier general in the Revolutionary War.

891.13 "with thee . . . time."] *Paradise Lost*, bk. IV, l. 639.

891.21–22 new orleans, of the total defeat of the British] The battle of New Orleans on January 8, 1815, was the final major battle of the War of 1812, in which the American forces were commanded by Major General Andrew Jackson (1767–1845). British forces sustained 2,000 casualties; the Americans 70. The Treaty of Ghent, ending the war, had been signed on December 24, but was not ratified until February 1815.

891.26–27 "teach . . . to fight,"] Cf. Psalm 144:1.

891.29 The temple of Janus is closed] In ancient Rome, the doors of the Temple of Janus were open during war and closed during peace.

892.3–4 beat our Swords . . . hooks] Cf. Isaiah 2:4.

892.5–6 "flew upon the wings of the Wind"] Psalm 18:10.

892.8–9 "Now . . . Men of Ghent"] Cf. *Richard III*, I.i.1–4.

892.30–31 "is a lust in Man, no charm can tame"] William Harvey's translation of Juvenal's *Satire IX*.

893.20–25 "Can we forget . . . no more"] From James Macpherson, *Temora*, Book VII (1763). See also note 789.8.

893.26 the Youngest Sister, of the union] Louisiana became the eighteenth state on April 30, 1812.

893.32 a Leteran fountain] I.e., Lethe; see note 865.15.

894.11 The temple of Janus] See note 891.29.

895.5–6 will you take Benjamin also?"] Cf. Genesis 42:36.

897.20 I know not where to find you] Louisa Catherine reached Paris on March 23, 1815, after a forty-day journey from St. Petersburg; see note 889.5–6.

898.23–24   her Husbands . . . Life.] Cf. Proverbs 31:11–12.

900.26–27   "Good Sense . . . worth the Seven,"] Pope, *Moral Essays*, Epistle IV (1731), ll. 43–44.

903.25–28   if we expect Boys, . . . forming,"] Joseph Priestly, *Discourses on the Evidence of Divine Revelation* (1794), Discourse I, "The Importance of Religion to enlarge the Mind of Man."

903.28–32   against learning, . . . great minds.] Hannah More, *Coelebs in Search of a Wife* (1809), chapter XXXIX.

904.20   Rousseau plan of Education] *Émile, or On Education* (1762), by Jean-Jacques Rousseau, which attempts to set forth a plan of holistic education for citizenship.

904.38   the Marquis Le Fayette, at Count de Tracy's] For Lafayette, see note 211.19–20. Antoine Destutt, comte de Tracy (1754–1836), French Enlightenment philosopher.

905.5–6   "Mercy is twice blest. . . . that takes"] *The Merchant of Venice*, IV.i.186–87.

905.10   Madam de Stael.] See note 884.23–24.

905.11   her Germany] *De l'Allemagne* (1810), translated to English in 1813.

905.32–34   the Emperor of France, . . . tallents] On February 26, 1815, Napoleon escaped from his exile on Elba and began the period of rule known as the Hundred Days.

906.18–19   "Rubs . . . fortune"] Cf. *Hamlet*, III.i.57.

906.31–907.3   Care to our Coffin . . . friars"] Peter Pindar (pseud. John Wolcot), Ode XV, *Expostulatory Odes* (1789), ll. 5–10, 18–20.

907.18–21   "under neath . . . occurred live] Ben Johnson, "Epitaph on Elizabeth, L.H." (1616), ll. 3–6.

908.19–20   the admirable likeness . . . Sister.] Gilbert Stuart, who lived in Boston after 1805, painted a portrait of Elizabeth Peabody in 1809. It resides currently in the collections of the Arizona State University Art Museum.

908.26–27   "Stuart by Heaven, . . . thought"] Pope, "On Sir Godfrey Kneller" (1723), ll. 1–2.

909.3   Stuart will be happy in his likeness] See note 762.8.

909.12–13   an event . . . so unprecedented] John Quincy was in Paris during Napoleon's arrival there during the Hundred Days. On March 19, 1815, he wrote: "I am afraid you will think I am sporting with credulity when I assure you that now, at the moment when I am writing, the impression almost universal throughout Paris, is that within six days he will enter this city as a conqueror, without having spent an ounce of gunpowder on his march."

911.1–2   the said princess of Salm . . . Cumberland has married] Ernest Augustus, Duke of Cumberland (1771–1851), later King of Hanover, married Princess Frederica of Mecklenburg-Strelitz in 1815, who was Princess of Solms-Braunfels by a previous marriage. Frederika had already asked the Prussian king for permission to divorce her husband and marry Ernest Augustus when the Prince suddenly died.

911.34–35   the extract of his letter . . . Morgan.] John Adams to Richard Price in 1789, paraphrased in *Memoirs of the life of the Rev. Richard Price* (1815), edited by his nephew, William Morgan. The letter regarded the French Revolution, of which "he spoke with contempt . . . at its commencement, and foretold the destruction of a million of human beings, as its probable consequence."

912.9   our university at Cambridge] Harvard.

912.12   mr parkman] The Parkmans were Boston Brahmins and one of Boston's richest families.

912.23–24   peace came . . . further disgrace.] The Hartford Convention met from December 15 to January 5 to protest the war and a decade of Republican policies, even as the Treaty of Ghent was signed on December 24. News of the Convention, the battle of New Orleans, and the signing of the Treaty of Ghent reached Washington more or less simultaneously, making the Federalists appear defeatist, if not disloyal.

915.28   Tabinet gown] See note 404.40.

916.13   lutestring gown] See note 177.7.

916.16   changeable silk gown] See note 177.8.

918.26   great feat] See note 762.8.

918.31   that which mr Copley took] See note 578.32.

918.35   Mr Morse . . . likeness of your Father] Samuel F. B. Morse painted a portrait of John in 1816 for a planned collection by Philadelphia book publisher Joseph Delaplane. The portrait is now in the Brooklyn Museum.

919.11–12   mr Tuckers Light of Nature] English philosopher Abraham Tucker, *The Light of Nature Pursued* (1768–78).

919.21   taking the Bark] Tree barks were used for various medicinal purposes, like contemporary aspirin (originally derived from willow bark) or quinine.

921.2   mr Bayard] James A. Bayard (1767–1815) of Delaware had been a peace commissioner with John Quincy, negotiating the Treaty of Ghent. He declined the offer to succeed John Quincy in Russia.

921.33   "kind Natures . . . Sleep"] Young, *Night Thoughts*, Night I, l. 1.

922.2   anodynes] Painkillers.

922.33   claim her dower] American statutes, modeled upon British common law, provided that a man had to leave his wife at minimum life interest in one-third of his real estate plus a set proportion of his personal property. Failing that, she had the right to challenge his will in court.

923.10 he says, he is a Banishd man—] Thomas Baker Johnson was postmaster in New Orleans.

923.23 "That what composes man can man destroy"] Pope, *Essay on Man*, Epistle II, l. 114.

925.3 The subject of it] On December 5, 1815, John Quincy wrote to Abigail about the Athanasian Creed, the first historical creed of the Christian church in which the equality of the persons of the Trinity is stated explicitly.

925.36–39 "Thou great first . . . blind"] Pope, "The Universal Prayer" (1738), ll. 5–8.

926.23–24 Zimerman . . . solitude.] Cf. Johann Georg Ritter von Zimmermann, "Of solitude" (1756).

926.25–26 "for where are . . . thy face?] William Cowper, "The Solitude of Alexander Selkirk," ll. 5–6.

926.27 Eden was tasteless till an Eve was there"] Dr. Benjamin Church, "The Choice: A Poem" (1752). See also note 62.1–6.

927.1 mr Calhouns] John C. Calhoun (1782–1850), congressman from South Carolina who would later be vice president during the presidency of John Quincy.

927.21–25 "Beauty like the fair . . . incontinence"] Milton, *Comus* (1634), ll. 93–97.

929.32–33 your Father in his Letter . . . respecting me] On June 25, 1816, John wrote to John Quincy: "Your Mother who was Sick, all Winter, is recovered and restored to her characteristic Vivacity, Activity Witt Sense and benevolence. Of Consequence She must take upon herself the Duties of her Granddaughter Neice, Maids Husband and all. She must be always writing to You and all her Grandchildren which is as dangerous to her health as her domestic Exertions. I say She must because She Will."

930.25 Pauls Letters] Walter Scott, *Paul's Letters to his Kinsfolk* (1816), a collection of letters about Waterloo and Napoléon's last campaign.

930.34 the Royall Marriage] Princess Charlotte Augusta (1796–1817), the only child of the Prince Regent and second in line to the throne, married Prince Leopold of Saxe-Coburg-Saalfeld on May 2, 1816. She died in childbirth the following year.

931.5–6 the journal of a young Man of Massachusetts] Benjamin Waterhouse, *A Journal, of a young man of Massachusetts, . . . confined first, at Melville island, Halifax, then at Chatham, in England, and last at Dartmoor prison* (1816).

931.22–23 Hudibrass] A satire by Samuel Butler (1663–78) in the style of Cervantes's *Don Quixote*.

931.29 Alexander Selkirk] Selkirk (1676–1721) was a Scottish sailor whose four years living as a castaway inspired Daniel Defoe's *Robinson Crusoe* (1719).

933.13–14 Count deTracy] See note 904.38.

933.20–21 Mr. Adams . . . witness.] See note 909.12–13.

934.5 the office you now hold] Richard Rush (see List of Correspondents) served as acting secretary of state until John Quincy took office. He then succeeded him as minister to Britain.

934.21 mr Clay is openly unfriendly to mr Adams] Henry Clay Sr. (see note 830.27–28) had been one of John Quincy's fellow negotiators at Ghent. Clay had hoped to be appointed secretary of state by Monroe.

935.29 Mr. Theodore Lyman] Theodore Lyman II (1792–1849), Harvard 1810, visited Europe from 1817 to 1819 and was later the mayor of Boston, 1834–36.

936.5–6 the Marquis La Fayette . . . Marbois . . . Gallatin.] For Lafayette, see note 211.19–20; François Barbé-Marbois (1745–1837), a French politician and honorary member of the American Academy of Arts and Sciences, of which John was a founder; for Gallatin, see note 618.5–6.

938.17–18 She is to take mr Rush to England.] See note 934.5.

938.20 Thomas Greenleaf Junr] Thomas Greenleaf Jr. (c. 1788–1817), Harvard 1806, a lawyer and son of Thomas Greenleaf, Harvard 1784, a state representative from Quincy.

940.24–25 mr Rush, is the Successor] See note 938.17–18.

941.12 Govr. Jay] See note 689.4.

941.15 "The world forgetting, by the World forgot"] Pope, "Eloisa to Abelard," l. 208.

941.26–28 I rose, . . . my Maidens] Cf. Proverbs 31:15.

943.8 mr Speaker] Henry Clay was the current speaker of the House (see notes 830.27–28 and 934.21).

943.12 mr S] William Steuben Smith.

944.4 spencer] A "spencer" was a waist-length, double-breasted man's jacket, adapted in the 1790s from a woolen tailcoat with the tails removed.

945.7 a Fairy visit] I.e., in a dream.

945.18 "our roof is too low, for so Lofty a Head"] From a song traditionally performed during Act IV of Shakespeare's *The Winter's Tale*, with words by David Garrick.

945.19   the vicar of wakefeild] In Goldsmith's *The Vicar of Wakefield* (1766), the vicar's family commission a portrait of themselves as great historical figures, but the painting is too large for their home and must be propped up against a wall.

946.6   the Presidents speech] Monroe's first annual message to Congress, December 12, 1817.

946.9   William?] William Steuben Smith.

946.15–17   "what Blessings . . . cast away"] Pope, "The Universal Prayer" (1738), ll. 17–18.

946.31   Bombazet] A thin woolen cloth.

948.27   dr Disney . . . mr Hollis] John Disney (1746–1816), an English Unitarian minister who inherited the estate of Thomas Brand Hollis (see note 409.32–35).

950.33   Madam de Neuvile] Ann Marguerite, baroness Hyde de Neuville (1771–1849), a French watercolorist and wife of a French diplomat, Jean-Guillaume, baron Hyde de Neuville (1776–1857), who was exiled by Napoléon in 1806 and lived in New Jersey from then until his return to France in 1814. In 1816 he was appointed French ambassador to the United States.

951.10   a city sit upon a hill] Cf. Matthew 5:14.

951.20–21   "In pride, . . . into the skies"] Pope, *Essay on Man*, Epistle I, ll. 123–24.

951.24–25   the Dey of Algiers Bastinado] Bastinado was a form of punishment involving whipping the soles of the feet. "Dey" was the title given to the rulers of Algiers from 1671 to 1830. *The Analetic Magazine* for January to June 1818 reported, "The plague having horribly depopulated Algiers, the new dey has commanded, that all the unmarried men above twenty years of age should be conducted to the public square, and amply *gratified* with the bastinado, to give them a desire for wedlock."

951.34   Gen'll Forest] Uriah Forrest (1746–1805), who served in the Revolutionary War and was later a U.S. congressman.

952.16–17   "Delightful praise, . . . glows."] Sir Walter Scott, "The Lady of the Lake," Canto Two (1810).

952.25–26   "A good name . . . soul."] Cf. Ecclesiastes 7:1 and *Othello*, III. iii.161.

952.32   Duane] William Duane; see note 669.14. Abigail had written to Hezekiah Niles, the editor of *Niles' Register*: "Your correspondent must have been misinformed when he states, that there was any distinction of party made at the drawing room while I had the honor to preside there; any gentleman or lady, of either party, who chose to visit there, were received with equal civility. . . . and but one of the whole number ever so far forgot the character of a gentleman, as to send an uncivil refusal." Niles printed her letter on January 31.

953.14   the Spanish petition] Spain's New World empire was in precipitous decline. In recent years Argentina (1810), Paraguay (1811), and Uruguay (1815), the states of the former Viceroyalty of Río de la Plata, had declared independence, and in the early months of 1817 an insurgent army led by General José de San Martín gained control over Chile with a speed that startled Spanish authorities. Faced with this crisis, Spain sought the collective intervention of the allied powers, particularly Britain, to assist in the pacification of its colonies. John Quincy tried to gratify the American popular will to support the revolutions without falling into open conflict with Spain. On March 14, 1818, Congress refused to receive a petition from Vicente Pazos Kanki (1779–c. 1852), an agent of the Spanish American republics, who was residing in Washington but who had not been officially recognized. The petition had called for the U.S. government to reverse its suppression of "patriot" movements in Florida and Texas, settlements at Amelia and Galveston Islands, which really amounted to nothing more than unauthorized American filibusters. The same day, President Monroe presented to Congress John Quincy's correspondence with Don Onis, the Spanish minister, about the boundaries of Florida and Louisiana. These letters made clear that the administration had refused a Spanish offer to submit the points in dispute to British arbitration.

953.18   the bust] By French sculptor John B. Binon, originally made for Faneuil Hall in Boston. Other casts were made; one resides in the Boston Atheneum and several at the "Old House." One was sent to Thomas Jefferson; it has disappeared.

953.28   Cox's Female Biography] Francis Augustus Cox (1783–1853), *Female Scripture Biography* (1817).

954.10   Mr John Marston] John Marston (1785–1885), a U.S. Navy officer. John's influence had gained him his original appointment as midshipman in 1813.

955.20   the Life of Genll Jackson] Probably *Memoirs of Andrew Jackson* (1818) by Samuel Putnam Waldo.

Index

THE LIBRARY OF AMERICA SERIES

The Library of America fosters appreciation and pride in America's literary heritage by publishing, and keeping permanently in print, authoritative editions of America's best and most significant writing. An independent nonprofit organization, it was founded in 1979 with seed funding from the National Endowment for the Humanities and the Ford Foundation.

To subscribe to the series or to order individual copies, please visit www.loa.org or call (800) 964–5778.

*This book is set in 10 point ITC Galliard, a face
designed for digital composition by Matthew Carter and based
on the sixteenth-century face Granjon. The paper is acid-free
lightweight opaque that will not turn yellow or brittle with age.
The binding is sewn, which allows the book to open easily and lie flat.
The binding board is covered in Brillianta, a woven rayon cloth
made by Van Heek–Scholco Textielfabrieken, Holland.
Composition by Dedicated Book Services.
Printing and binding by Edwards Brothers Malloy, Ann Arbor.
Designed by Bruce Campbell.*

Quincy Family

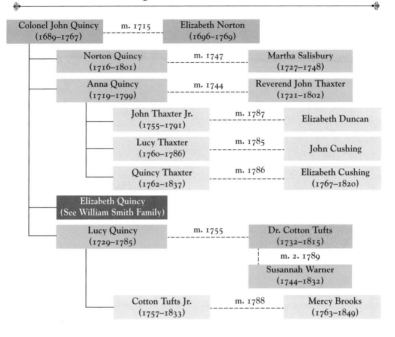

Colonel John Quincy (1689–1767) — m. 1715 — Elizabeth Norton (1696–1769)

Norton Quincy (1716–1801) — m. 1747 — Martha Salisbury (1727–1748)

Anna Quincy (1719–1799) — m. 1744 — Reverend John Thaxter (1721–1802)

John Thaxter Jr. (1755–1791) — m. 1787 — Elizabeth Duncan

Lucy Thaxter (1760–1786) — m. 1785 — John Cushing

Quincy Thaxter (1762–1837) — m. 1786 — Elizabeth Cushing (1767–1820)

Elizabeth Quincy (See William Smith Family)

Lucy Quincy (1729–1785) — m. 1755 — Dr. Cotton Tufts (1732–1815)

m. 2. 1789 — Susannah Warner (1744–1832)

Cotton Tufts Jr. (1757–1833) — m. 1788 — Mercy Brooks (1763–1849)

Johnson Family

Joshua Johnson (1742–1811) — m. 1785 — Catherine Nuth (1757–1811)

Ann (Nancy) Johnson (1773–1810) — m. 1798 — Walter Hellen (1766–1815)

Louisa Catherine Johnson (See Adams Family)

Carolina Virginia Marylanda Johnson (1777–1862) — m. 1. 1807 — Andrew Buchanan (1766–1811)

m. 2. 1817 — Nathaniel Frye

Thomas Baker Johnson (1779–1843)

Harriet Johnson (1781–1850) — m. 1805 — George Boyd (1781–1846)

Catherine "Kitty" Maria Frances Johnson (See Adams Family)

Eliza Johnson (d. 1818) — m. 1810 — John Pope (1770–1845)

Adelaide Johnson (1789–1877) — m. 1813 — Walter Hellen (See above)

CAPTAIN

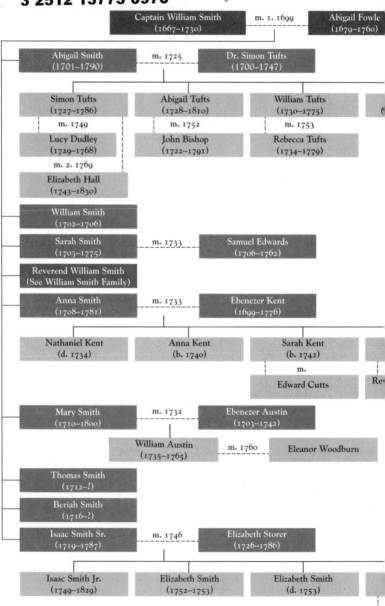

Captain William Smith (1667–1730)	m. 1. 1699	**Abigail Fowle** (1679–1760)

Abigail Smith (1701–1790) — m. 1725 — **Dr. Simon Tufts** (1700–1747)

Simon Tufts (1727–1786)
m. 1749
Lucy Dudley (1729–1768)
m. 2. 1769
Elizabeth Hall (1743–1830)

Abigail Tufts (1728–1810)
m. 1752
John Bishop (1722–1791)

William Tufts (1730–1775)
m. 1753
Rebecca Tufts (1734–1779)

William Smith (1702–1706)

Sarah Smith (1703–1775) — m. 1733 — **Samuel Edwards** (1706–1762)

Reverend William Smith (See William Smith Family)

Anna Smith (1708–1781) — m. 1733 — **Ebenezer Kent** (1699–1776)

Nathaniel Kent (d. 1734)

Anna Kent (b. 1740)

Sarah Kent (b. 1742)
m.
Edward Cutts

Rev

Mary Smith (1710–1800) — m. 1732 — **Ebenezer Austin** (1703–1742)

William Austin (1735–1765) — m. 1760 — **Eleanor Woodburn**

Thomas Smith (1712–?)

Beriah Smith (1716–?)

Isaac Smith Sr. (1719–1787) — m. 1746 — **Elizabeth Storer** (1726–1786)

Isaac Smith Jr. (1749–1829)

Elizabeth Smith (1752–1753)

Elizabeth Smith (d. 1753)